ADVANCED STRUCTURED COBOL

BATCH, ON-LINE, AND DATA-BASE CONCEPTS

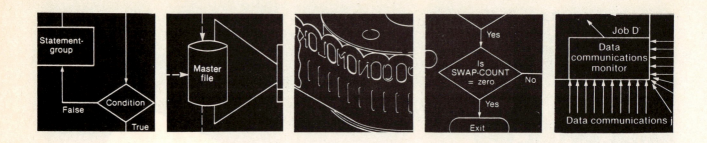

ADVANCED STRUCTURED COBOL
BATCH, ON-LINE, AND DATA-BASE CONCEPTS

TYLER WELBURN

MAYFIELD PUBLISHING COMPANY

MITCHELL PUBLISHING, INC.

To Karen Richardson,
the **K R** of **s**, for her *c*, *w*, and *v*.

COBOL Is an industry language and is not the property of any company
or group of organizations. No warranty, expressed or implied, is made
by any contributor or by the CODASYL Programming Language Committee as to the accuracy and functioning of the programming system
and language. Moreover, no responsibility is assumed by any contributor, or by the committee, in connection therewith.

The authors and copyright holders of the copyrighted material used
herein—FLOW-MATIC (trademark of Sperry Rand Corporation), Programming for the UNIVAC® I and II, Data Automation Systems, copyrighted 1958, 1959, by Sperry Rand Corporation; IBM Commercial
Translator Form No. F 28-8013, copyrighted 1959 by IBM; FACT, DSI
27A5260-2760, copyrighted 1960 by Minneapolis-Honeywell—have
specifically authorized the use of this material in whole or in part, in
the COBOL specifications. Such authorization extends to the reproduction and use of COBOL specifications in programming manuals or
similar publications.

Library of Congress Catalog Card Number: 82-073737
International Standard Book Number: 0-87484-558-0

Manufactured in the United States of America
Mayfield Publishing Company
285 Hamilton Avenue
Palo Alto, California 94301
(415) 326-1640

Sponsoring editors: Chuck Murphy and Steve Mitchell
Technical editor: Sondra Wallace
Manuscript editor: Claire Comiskey
Managing editor: Pat Herbst
Text designer: Nancy Sears
Cover designer: Barbara Ravizza
Art director and project coordinator: Lawrence Peterson
Technical artist: Pat Rogondino
Production manager: Cathy Willkie
Compositors: Acme Type Company and Frank's Type
Printer and binder: George Banta Company

CONTENTS

PREFACE

This text presents current COBOL program design and coding techniques together with contemporary business computer system concepts. It offers an abundance of resource material appropriate for both advanced COBOL students and professional COBOL programmers.

Although this work has been designed as a coordinated companion volume to my beginning text, *Structured COBOL: Fundamentals and Style*, it could be used as a "follow-on" volume to any good-quality beginning COBOL book.

Features of the Text

Advanced Structured COBOL: Batch, On-Line, and Data-Base Concepts is designed for teaching and learning; it offers abundant features to aid both the advanced COBOL student and the instructor.

Coordination of Beginning and Advanced Classes

One of the difficulties I have encountered when embarking upon the teaching of an advanced COBOL course is the varied level of knowledge typically present in the class. Because computer programming is a dynamic and evolving discipline, many students who completed their beginning course only a couple of years ago did not receive contemporary structured COBOL training. Student proficiency also ranges widely because of the specific content covered and computer equipment used in the beginning class. For many reasons, course content and equipment usage often vary not only from one institution to another but also from one instructor to another within an institution.

In an attempt to smooth such course transition problems, I have designed the first five appendixes of *Advanced Structured COBOL: Batch, On-Line, and Data-Base Concepts* to be review and reference summaries. Using the content of the companion beginning volume as a foundation, these appendixes present review material as follows:

- Appendix A: COBOL Language Elements
- Appendix B: COBOL Syntax and Style Reference
- Appendix C: Table-Processing Reference
- Appendix D: SORT/MERGE Program Reference
- Appendix E: Data-Validation Checklist

Students can use those five appendixes for review or to fulfill remedial assignments that instructors may sometimes choose to make.

The appendixes were written with another important benefit in mind: to limit the student's need to refer to the beginning COBOL text for reference material. Thus the student is spared the inconvenience of lugging the beginning COBOL book around and trying to find adequate working space in cramped library or data-processing laboratory facilities.

Hardware/Software Concepts Chapters

Five chapters (labeled *A, B, C, D,* and *E*) are included to teach general hardware and software concepts in tandem with the program design and coding. They contain little or no specific coverage of the COBOL language but instead discuss related background information on (A) disk and tape hardware, (B) printers and report design, (C) common routine logic, (D) video display terminal hardware, and (E) data-base management systems. Some of this material is covered in introductory or other data-processing/computer science courses. However, this is another area in which transition problems commonly occur because either the student took the introductory course some time ago or the introductory course did not adequately cover the subject matter.

In any event, the coverage provided in the hardware/software concepts chapters emphasizes information with which the advanced COBOL student should be familiar. For most students, a certain portion will be new material; some will be review.

Chapter/Topic Organization

Each numbered chapter contains a preliminary overview discussion, following which the chapter material is organized into topics. Such topic organization clearly identifies the subject of each text segment and permits easy identification of material that the instructor might choose to skip.

Structured Design and Coding

Up-to-date structured design and coding principles are fully developed and are an integral part of the text. Structure charts are provided for each of the file-maintenance programs presented. The structure charts are supplemented by in-depth discussion of pertinent program modules.

The logic presented in Chapter C has intentionally been specified by various methods—pseudocode, traditional flowcharts, tables, and the like. This allows the background information presented in Chapter C to be used as a reference for certain programming assignments in later chapters while still affording the student the opportunity to independently design and code the structured solutions. Also, detailed design documentation preferences (pseudocode, structured flowcharts, Warnier-Orr diagrams, and so forth) have been left open so that instructors who wish to emphasize such assignments can exercise their preference.

American National Standard Orientation

This text is designed for use with COBOL compilers that adhere to the 1974 American National Standard (ANS). It can also be used with 1968 ANS compilers. Important 1968 differences are covered in Topic F of Chapter 4 and in Appendix B.

In Chapters 4, 5, and 6, the file-status data-item is discussed and used in the programming standards. The file-status data-item was introduced in the 1974 standard. However, because IBM chose to implement the file-status data-item together with its proprietary Virtual Storage Access Method (VSAM), many programmers have the mistaken impression that the file-status data-item is a special VSAM feature rather than a standard COBOL one.

Because this text is not oriented to a specific hardware or compiler vendor, VSAM is not mentioned in Chapters 4, 5, and 6. However, the program design and coding within these chapters are not only compatible with VSAM but have been developed as examples of high-quality VSAM code. They are of course similarly appropriate for and compatible with non-VSAM 1974 compilers.

For use with 1968 compilers, Topic F of Chapter 4 presents a model program approach that enables the student to simulate the file-status data-item. Further information regarding VSAM and file-status simulation is presented in the Instructor's Guide.

Uniformity of Program Code

Consistently numbered modules with a uniform organization are used throughout the programs of both the beginning text and this volume. This permits use of a building-block approach to the presentation of coding concepts, which facilitates the student's grasp of new coding techniques as they are presented.

Combination Tutorial/Reference Approach

Students very often react to COBOL textbooks in one of two ways. Typically, either they feel that the text is a good reference manual but doesn't really explain how to write certain types of programs, or they claim that a book explains things well but is hard to use as a reference. *Advanced Structured COBOL: Batch, On-Line, and Data-Base Concepts* blends tutorial and reference features. Whenever a subject is presented, it is covered fully in one place. However, to guard against information overload, topics are covered on a step-by-step basis and are integrated with programming examples.

Illustrations, Examples, and Appendixes

Over 450 figures illuminate the text. Twelve appendixes provide a wealth of review, reference, and auxiliary material.

Inside Cover Material

A mock-up of the IDENTIFICATION and ENVIRONMENT divisions is presented on the inside front cover together with a checklist of other items that vary with the computer system being used. This page can be filled in at the beginning of the course and then used as a reminder for coding the first two divisions and as a reference whenever installation-dependent coding is encountered.

For easy reference, the COBOL reserved word list and the format notation legend appear on the inside back cover.

Chapter Summaries

At the conclusion of each numbered chapter, a chapter summary is presented.

Programming Assignments

Twenty-three challenging, well-documented programming assignments are provided in the text. At the conclusion of most chapters, three assignments are presented. These programming assignments relate directly to the material covered in the chapter. They are arranged in order of increasing complexity. Assignment 1 is the easiest and quickest to code; assignment 3 is the most difficult.

Additional Materials for Instructors

An Instructor's Guide is available for use with this text. Also available to adopters are test data sets and worked solutions for the programming assignments.

To maintain continuity within subject areas and/or to provide transitional material for students not using the companion beginning COBOL volume, certain material covered in *Structured COBOL: Fundamentals and Style* has been repeated or expanded upon in this book at the following locations: Chapter 1, Topic A; Chapter 2, Topic C; Chapter B.

Course Organization

Advanced Structured COBOL: Batch, On-Line, and Data-Base Concepts is designed to support the requirements of advanced COBOL courses that differ in duration (quarter versus semester terms), content requirements, and instructor preference. I expect that most instructors will use the book in ordinary sequence, beginning with Chapter 1 and proceeding to the final chapter. The accompanying table, however, presents an alternative grouping of the material.

The table shows the chapters organized into the five general subject categories covered in the text. Instructors may begin study with any category and may use the categories in any sequence. I recommend, though, that, within

Topical organization of chapters

Miscellaneous concepts	File maintenance and retrieval	Report features	Miscellaneous data handling	Subprograms
1: Structured programming	A: Disk and tape hardware	B: Printers and reports	C: Application logic	10: Subprograms
D: Video display terminals	2: Files	7: Report logic	8: Variable-length records	
11: On-line processing	3: Sequential file maintenance		9: Character manipulation	
E: Data-base management	4: Indexed file maintenance			
	5: Relative file maintenance			
	6: Retrievals			

a category, study commence with the chapter listed at the top of the column in the table. I also suggest that, in classes where the companion *Structured COBOL* text was not used, Chapter 1 of the advanced book be covered first, followed by study of either the file-maintenance and -retrieval category or the report-features category. This ordering of topics will ensure that the student understands the general coding methods followed uniformly throughout the two volumes.

Acknowledgments

I want to thank and express my appreciation to all those who helped make this book a reality. The original project plan was improved by the help and advice received from Howard V. Carson, Wright State University; Michael Bilbrey, University of Wisconsin at Eau Claire; Neil A. Blum, County College of Morris; Al Johnson, Worcester State College; Chadwick H. Nestman, Virginia Commonwealth University; Charles Port, Bergen Community College; O. Poupart, Schoolcraft College; Lloyd A. Robblin, DeAnza College; Stuart J. Travis, Ferris State College; and Susan P. White, Catonsville Community College. Special thanks go to Anne M. McBride of California State University at Chico and George Vlahakis of Evergreen Valley College, who have kindly provided helpful comments with regard to both this and the beginning volume.

Jan Mathis of Cameron University and Susan Hinrichs of Missouri Western State College class-tested portions of the manuscript. All the good ideas, comments, and corrections they gave me are sincerely appreciated. The majority of the manuscript was also presented to the Advanced COBOL seminar at the Ninth Annual National Computer Educator's Institute in 1982. I received excellent suggestions and comments from every single participant, for which I am most grateful. Particular thanks are due Mel Simmons of San Joaquin Delta College for "debugging" practically every word of the manuscript and each byte of the program code.

Sondra Wallace of Hewlett-Packard Corporation offered many good ideas and sound advice, as she always does. I sincerely appreciate her suggestions and only wish I could follow all her advice. My thanks also go to Donald F. Nelson of Tandem Computers, Chairman of the CODASYL COBOL Committee. He provided insightful information about the status of the next COBOL standard, which is presented in the Instructor's Guide.

As with the beginning text, those associated with Mayfield Publishing Company went way beyond the call of duty to put this book together. Chuck Murphy served as editor and became a good friend. Pat Herbst managed editorial production; and I marvel at her ability to (1) be patient with me, (2) work long and hard on the project, and (3) maintain her composure. Nancy Sears, text designer, once again made sure that reams of computerese, endless sheets of computer printouts, a dose of squiggly line drawings, and a few snapshots all fit together attractively. Claire Comiskey, manuscript editor, amazed me by catching obscure COBOL programming inconsistencies along with my blatant English errors. During production of the earlier text, Michelle Hogan taught me a fundamental publishing principle, and during production of the advanced text, she personally contributed to its execution once again. Her special assistance and photo research are truly appreciated. I enjoyed working again with Lawrence Peterson, art director and project coordinator, and am sincerely grateful for his extraordinary efforts and fine work. My thanks also go out to all the others who worked behind the scenes to contribute to the quality of this book.

Tyler Welburn

CHAPTER 1

STRUCTURED PROGRAMMING

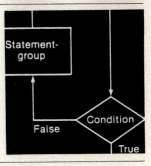

1 STRUCTURED PROGRAMMING

During the first 25 years of computer programming (1950 to 1975, or thereabouts), most programmers designed and wrote programs on a linear basis. That is, the instructions that the program would execute first were placed at the front of the program. The instructions that the program would execute last were placed at the end of the program. A program that is designed and written on this linear basis can be called an **unstructured program**.

Unstructured programs can become exceedingly difficult to design, test, make operational, comprehend, and maintain. Many deficiencies that are associated with unstructured programs are caused by two characteristics: (1) an unstructured program does not have a concise mainline module to direct the overall program flow, and (2) an unstructured program contains GO TO statements to direct the flow of program control.

Consider an unstructured program with thousands of instructions and hundreds of GO TO statements. The control flow of such a program often winds through the PROCEDURE DIVISION like a strand of vermicelli in a plate of spaghetti. Indeed, programs of this type are often (not too fondly) referred to as "bowl-of-spaghetti" or "rat's nest" programs.

As practicing programmers and managers struggled with the problems that unstructured programs presented, certain computer scientists, educators, and practitioners were involved in research that contributed to a method of programming that has come to be called **structured programming**. In Topic 1-A of this chapter, the structured COBOL-coding principles and conventions that are used in this book and most data-processing installations will be discussed. Structured-module design considerations are discussed in Topic 1-B.

■ TOPIC 1-A: **Structured COBOL-Coding Principles and Conventions**

The Development of Structured Programming
    The Theoretical Basis for Structured Programming
        Sequence structure
        Selection structure
        Iteration structure
    Harmful Effects of the GO TO Statement
    A Commercial Application of Structured-Programming Theory
    What "Structured Programming" Means Today

Structured COBOL-Coding Principles
    Control Structures
    Single-Entry Point and Single-Exit Point for Each Module

Structured COBOL-Coding Conventions
Module-Forming Conventions
Single-paragraph modules
Multiple-paragraph modules
SECTION modules
Independent Module Conventions
Module-Naming Conventions
Module-Numbering Conventions

The Development of Structured Programming

The development of structured programming can be traced by these four important milestones: (1) laying of the theoretical foundation, (2) identification of the harmful effects of the GO TO statement, (3) the application of structured-programming theory to a commercial data-processing application, and (4) the adoption of structured-programming concepts by the commercial data-processing community. Structured-programming development milestones are shown in Figure 1A.1.

The Theoretical Basis for Structured Programming

Two mathematicians, Corrado Bohm and Guiseppe Jacopini, presented a paper at the International Colloquium on Algebraic Linguistics and Automata Theory in Israel in 1964. Bohm and Jacopini presented proof that any program logic—regardless of complexity—can be expressed by sequential processes and two other control structures.

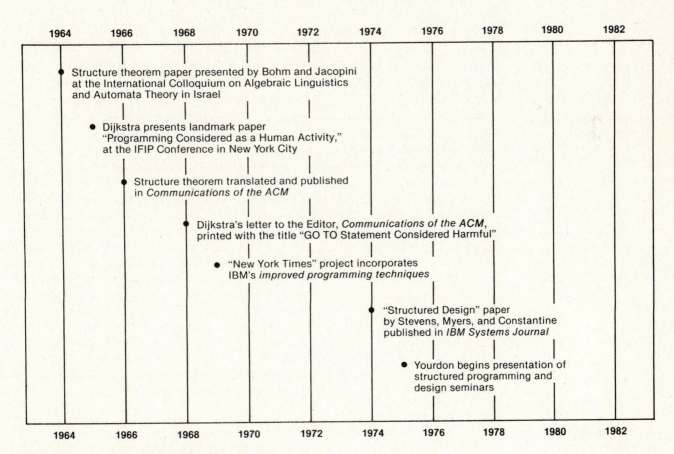

Figure 1A.1. Structured-programming milestones.

The concepts originally presented by Bohm and Jacopini have been developed and can be termed the **structure theorem**. According to the structure theorem, it is possible to write any computer program by using one or more of the three basic control structures: sequence, selection, and iteration. Figure 1A.2 illustrates these structures and provides a COBOL-coding example.

Sequence structure

The **sequence structure** is the most basic of the three control structures. It simply means that statements are executed in sequence, one after another, as they are coded.

Selection structure

The **selection structure** is sometimes termed the **if-then-else structure**. It presents a condition and two choices of actions depending upon whether the condition is true or false. In COBOL, the selection structure is achieved by use of the IF statement.

Iteration structure

Do-while is a name often given to the **iteration structure** because certain programming languages use those words to provide this structure. The iteration structure causes a set of instructions to be executed repeatedly as long as a given condition exists. COBOL does not have a statement that provides true do-while processing. However, the PERFORM/UNTIL statement is similar.

There are two minor differences between the strict do-while interpretation of the iteration structure and the action of PERFORM/UNTIL. First, the PERFORM/UNTIL statement causes a set of instructions to be repeatedly executed *until*—rather than *while*—a given condition exists. Second, the COBOL PERFORM/UNTIL statement tests the condition *before* instead of *after* the set of instructions is executed.

Harmful Effects of the GO TO Statement

Bohm and Jacopini's original paper was published in Italian. In 1966, an English translation was published in the United States. Because of its theoretical nature and complexity, the paper did not receive a great deal of attention.

However, in 1968, a letter was printed that *did* attract a good deal of attention. This letter, entitled "GO TO Statement Considered Harmful," was written to the editor of *Communications of the ACM* (a publication of the Association for Computing Machinery) by Professor Edsger W. Dijkstra of the Technological University at Eindhoven, Netherlands. Professor Dijkstra wrote: "For a number of years I have been familiar with the observation that the quality of programmers is a decreasing function of the density of GO TO statements in the programs they produce." He further suggested in this letter that "... the GO TO statement should be abolished from all higher level programming languages ... it is an invitation to make a mess of one's program."

At the time that this letter was written, programmers felt no disdain for the GO TO statement. Most could not even conceive of a program written without it. Of course, the work of Bohm and Jacopini proved that it could be done. Thus, by 1968, the theoretical basis for structured programming was established and a spark of interest was ignited in the programming community.

A Commercial Application of Structured-Programming Theory

The IBM Corporation used structured-programming concepts, together with certain other methods—often termed **improved programming techniques**—on the "New York Times Project" from 1969 to 1971. This project is generally con-

Sequence structure

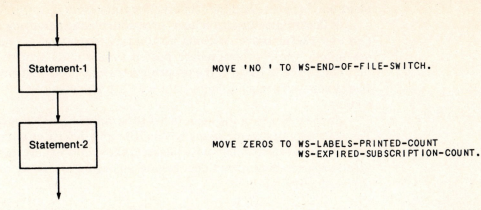

```
MOVE 'NO ' TO WS-END-OF-FILE-SWITCH.



MOVE ZEROS TO WS-LABELS-PRINTED-COUNT
             WS-EXPIRED-SUBSCRIPTION-COUNT.
```

Selection structure

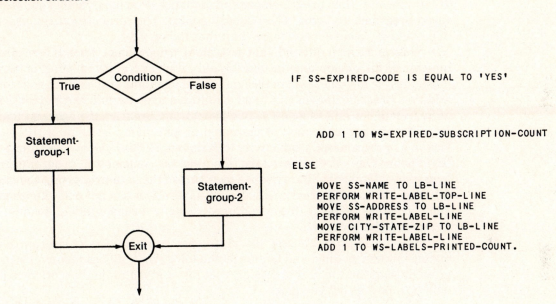

```
IF SS-EXPIRED-CODE IS EQUAL TO 'YES'


    ADD 1 TO WS-EXPIRED-SUBSCRIPTION-COUNT

ELSE

    MOVE SS-NAME TO LB-LINE
    PERFORM WRITE-LABEL-TOP-LINE
    MOVE SS-ADDRESS TO LB-LINE
    PERFORM WRITE-LABEL-LINE
    MOVE CITY-STATE-ZIP TO LB-LINE
    PERFORM WRITE-LABEL-LINE
    ADD 1 TO WS-LABELS-PRINTED-COUNT.
```

Iteration structure

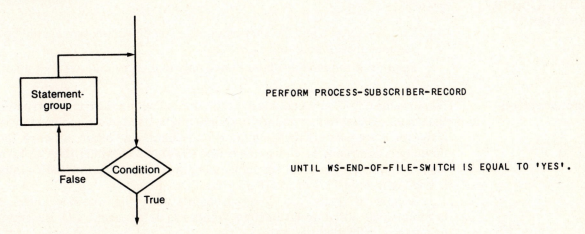

```
PERFORM PROCESS-SUBSCRIBER-RECORD



UNTIL WS-END-OF-FILE-SWITCH IS EQUAL TO 'YES'.
```

Figure 1A.2. Structure theorem control structures and COBOL examples.

sidered to be the first one in which structured-programming concepts were applied to a large-scale data-processing application.

In this project, programmers' productivity and accuracy were measured so that the usefulness of various structured-programming techniques could be evaluated. These programmers posted productivity figures from four to six times higher than those of the programmers who used unstructured techniques. The error—or program bug—rate was a phenomenally low .0004 per line of coding.

As the success of the structured-programming techniques in the New York Times Project began surfacing within IBM and in written accounts, members of the data-processing community began to show interest. By the mid-1970s, structured-programming practices began emerging at many commercial data-processing installations.

What "Structured Programming" Means Today

One of the most controversial and immediately identifiable aspects of the structure theorem is the concept that programs can be written without the use of GO TO statements. Thus programmers and students often incorrectly equate structured programming with "GO-TO-less" coding. The term *structured programming* actually means much more than that today.

Studies have indicated that a typical programmer spends less than a quarter of his or her time on the job actually programming—that is, writing code. Most of the time is spent designing, documenting, and testing programs. In addition, programmers must attend meetings and do certain clerical tasks such as searching for and filing away documentation, program listings, and the like.

Therefore, a collection of improved programming techniques (IPT)—also known as **programmer productivity techniques (PPT)**—have evolved along with the application of the structure theorem to commercial programming in business and industry. Today, when members of the data-processing community talk about stuctured programming, they generally mean not only the programming aspects, but also the structured design, documentation, testing, and organizational precepts.

Structured programming, therefore, may be defined as a program design, documentation, coding, and testing methodology that utilizes techniques in program development to create proper, reliable, and maintainable software products on a cost-effective basis.

Structured COBOL-Coding Principles

There are two basic principles to be followed in the coding of structured programs:

1. Only the three control structures of the structure theorem should be used: sequence, selection, and iteration.
2. Each program module should have only one entry and one exit point.

Control Structures

Because the GO TO statement is not represented within the control structures of the structure theorem, it generally should not be used in a structured program. However, because of COBOL syntax requirements and other software "guest" language requirements, there are a few situations in which the GO TO statement is required. The most common example occurs when the SORT statement is used with an INPUT or OUTPUT PROCEDURE.

Because of such GO TO requirements and other considerations, some organizations adopt programming standards that permit GO TO statement usage in restricted situations.

Single-Entry Point and Single-Exit Point for Each Module

If GO TO statements are not used and PERFORM statements that name only one procedure-name are used, a program will be in compliance with this single-entry and single-exit point principle. That is, each module will be entered before the first statement and exited after the last statement of the module. When a GO TO statement is used, this single-entry and single-exit point rule must be relaxed.

Structured COBOL-Coding Conventions

In addition to the two structured-programming principles, a number of other COBOL-coding conventions are commonly adhered to. Although some are not strictly related to structured programming, these coding conventions contribute to the same general goal of producing correct, readable, and maintainable COBOL programs.

Module-Forming Conventions

A program **module** can be defined as a contiguous group of statements that can be referred to as a unit. COBOL provides four ways to create and perform a module: as a single paragraph, as two or more contiguous paragraphs, as a single section, or as two or more contiguous sections. (Subprograms, which are discussed in Chapter 10, can also be considered program modules.)

Depending upon installation standards, any one of these four methods except the last one may be encountered in a structured COBOL program (use of multiple sections is rarely recommended or practiced). Examples, together with common variations, are shown in Figure 1A.3. Each one will be discussed.

Single-paragraph modules

The formation of program modules as single paragraphs provides the best results. When single paragraphs are used, use of the GO TO statement is not necessary; thus it can be prohibited. Therefore, use of single paragraphs provides total compliance with the structured-programming principles in which (1) only the three control structures of the structure theorem are used, and (2) each module contains only one entry point and one exit point. A related advantage is that the physical relationship of one paragraph to another in the PROCEDURE DIVISION is not significant (except, of course, for the mainline procedure). This means that when a new paragraph is to be added to the program, it cannot be inserted at an incorrect location because this would cause a program malfunction.

The only disadvantage to the single-paragraph approach is that four COBOL features *require* the use of sections: SORT (when an INPUT or OUTPUT PROCEDURE is used), MERGE (when an OUTPUT procedure is used), segmentation, and declaratives. Hence the single-paragraph method must be slightly altered and the restricted use of GO TO statements must be permitted within certain sections. However, of these four features, SORT is the only one that is commonly used.

Because of its compliance with the structure theorem, single-paragraph modules are used within the programs of this text (except where sections are required).

Multiple-paragraph modules

A multiple-paragraph module is enlisted with a PERFORM/THRU statement. Multiple-paragraph use has two variations. We will refer to these as the **exit-GO TO** and the **forward-GO TO** approaches.

Single-paragraph module

```
PERFORM PRINT-LABEL.
    .
    .
    .

PRINT-LABEL.
    IF SUBSCRIPTION-EXPIRED
        NEXT SENTENCE
    ELSE
        MOVE SS-NAME TO LB-LINE
        PERFORM PRINT-LABEL-TOP-LINE
        MOVE SS-ADS-LINE-1 TO LB-LINE
        PERFORM PRINT-LABEL-LINE
        IF SS-ADS-LINE-2 IS NOT EQUAL TO SPACES
            MOVE SS-ADS-LINE-2 TO LB-LINE
            PERFORM PRINT-LABEL-LINE
            MOVE SS-CITY-STATE-ZIP TO LB-LINE
            PERFORM PRINT-LABEL-LINE
        ELSE
            MOVE SS-CITY-STATE-ZIP TO LB-LINE
            PERFORM PRINT-LABEL-LINE.
```

Multiple-paragraph modules

Exit-GO TO

```
PERFORM PRINT-LABEL THRU PRINT-LABEL-EXIT.
    .
    .
    .

PRINT-LABEL.
    IF SUBSCRIPTION-EXPIRED
        GO TO PRINT-LABEL-EXIT.
    MOVE SS-NAME TO LB-LINE.
    PERFORM PRINT-LABEL-TOP-LINE.
    MOVE SS-ADS-LINE-1 TO LB-LINE.
    PERFORM PRINT-LABEL-LINE.
    IF SS-ADS-LINE-2 IS NOT EQUAL TO SPACES
        MOVE SS-ADS-LINE-2 TO LB-LINE
        PERFORM PRINT-LABEL-LINE.
    MOVE SS-CITY-STATE-ZIP TO LB-LINE.
    PERFORM PRINT-LABEL-LINE.

PRINT-LABEL-EXIT.
    EXIT.
```

Forward-GO TO

```
PERFORM PRINT-LABEL THRU PRINT-LABEL-EXIT.
    .
    .
    .

PRINT-LABEL.
    IF SUBSCRIPTION-EXPIRED
        GO TO PRINT-LABEL-EXIT.
    MOVE SS-NAME TO LB-LINE.
    PERFORM PRINT-LABEL-TOP-LINE.
    MOVE SS-ADS-LINE-1 TO LB-LINE.
    PERFORM PRINT-LABEL-LINE.
    IF SS-ADS-LINE-2 IS EQUAL TO SPACES
        GO TO PRINT-LABEL-CITY.
    MOVE SS-ADS-LINE-2 TO LB-LINE.
    PERFORM PRINT-LABEL-LINE.

PRINT-LABEL-CITY
    MOVE SS-CITY-STATE-ZIP TO LB-LINE.
    PERFORM PRINT-LABEL-LINE.

PRINT-LABEL-EXIT.
    EXIT.
```

SECTION modules

Exit-GO TO

```
PERFORM PRINT-LABEL.
    .
    .
    .

PRINT-LABEL SECTION.

PRINT-LABEL-NAME-ADS.
    IF SUBSCRIPTION-EXPIRED
        GO TO PRINT-LABEL-EXIT.
    MOVE SS-NAME TO LB-LINE.
    PERFORM PRINT-LABEL-TOP-LINE.
    MOVE SS-ADS-LINE-1 TO LB-LINE.
    PERFORM PRINT-LABEL-LINE.
    IF SS-ADS-LINE-2 IS NOT EQUAL TO SPACES
        MOVE SS-ADS-LINE-2 TO LB-LINE
        PERFORM PRINT-LABEL-LINE.
    MOVE SS-CITY-STATE-ZIP TO LB-LINE.
    PERFORM PRINT-LABEL-LINE.

PRINT-LABEL-EXIT.
    EXIT.
```

Forward-GO TO

```
PERFORM PRINT-LABEL.
    .
    .
    .

PRINT-LABEL SECTION.

PRINT-LABEL-NAME-ADS.
    IF SUBSCRIPTION-EXPIRED
        GO TO PRINT-LABEL-EXIT.
    MOVE SS-NAME TO LB-LINE.
    PERFORM PRINT-LABEL-TOP-LINE.
    MOVE SS-ADS-LINE-1 TO LB-LINE.
    PERFORM PRINT-LABEL-LINE.
    IF SS-ADS-LINE-2 IS EQUAL TO SPACES
        GO TO PRINT-LABEL-CITY.
    MOVE SS-ADS-LINE-2 TO LB-LINE.
    PERFORM PRINT-LABEL-LINE.

PRINT-LABEL-CITY
    MOVE SS-CITY-STATE-ZIP TO LB-LINE.
    PERFORM PRINT-LABEL-LINE.

PRINT-LABEL-EXIT.
    EXIT.
```

Figure 1A.3. Module-forming conventions.

Exit-GO TO

This method is similar to the single-paragraph approach. The logic of each module is likewise expressed in a single paragraph. However, immediately following each logic paragraph, a dummy paragraph that consists of only an EXIT statement is coded. The dummy paragraph is usually named the same as the initial paragraph except that it is suffixed by the word -EXIT, -END, or the like. When the module is referenced by the PERFORM/THRU statement, the initial paragraph is coded after the PERFORM verb and the dummy-exit paragraph is specified as the object of the THRU phrase.

Limited use of the GO TO statement is sometimes permitted within the module. Given this convention, a GO TO statement can be used within the logic paragraph with the restriction that it must reference only its counterpart exit paragraph.

The reason for using the exit-GO TO approach is that it provides a common exit point for a performed module. This means that GO TO statements can be used within a module to minimize the need for nested IF statements.

Forward-GO TO

As with the exit-GO TO method, this approach uses a dummy-exit paragraph at the end of the module. The difference is that the logic for each module is not limited to one paragraph; it may be subdivided into any number of paragraphs.

Use of the GO TO statement is less restricted. The typical convention is that a GO TO statement can be directed to any paragraph-name within the module provided that the paragraph is in a forward direction in relation to the GO TO statement location. This forward-GO TO method allows even more flexibility in regard to conditional processing within a module than does the exit-GO TO approach.

Both multiple-paragraph module methods are in violation of the two structured-programming principles because GO TO statements are used and multiple-entry and -exit points are introduced. However, even though additional entry and exit points are in fact coded, only one entry and one exit point should actually be used to maintain conformance with structured-programming conventions. That is, each PERFORM/THRU statement should reference only the first and exit paragraphs of each module.

Errors can creep into multiple-paragraph module programs if (1) a new paragraph or module is inadvertently inserted at the wrong location, (2) the THRU phrase is inadvertently omitted from the PERFORM statement, or (3) a GO TO statement is directed to a paragraph-name outside the module.

SECTION modules

SECTION modules are similar to multiple-paragraph modules. With the SECTION approach, each module is formed as a SECTION. A SECTION can contain any number of paragraphs. The convention is to terminate each SECTION by a dummy EXIT paragraph so that a common exit point for the module is established. GO TO statement usage conventions can be established to conform to either the exit-GO TO or forward-GO TO approach. The **case structure**, as shown in Figure 1A.4, is a SECTION-module form that uses both forward- and exit-GO TO statements.

The use of SECTION modules is probably somewhat preferable to that of multiple-paragraph modules because of the uniformity that it affords; use of sections is required for the SORT, MERGE, segmentation, and declarative features.

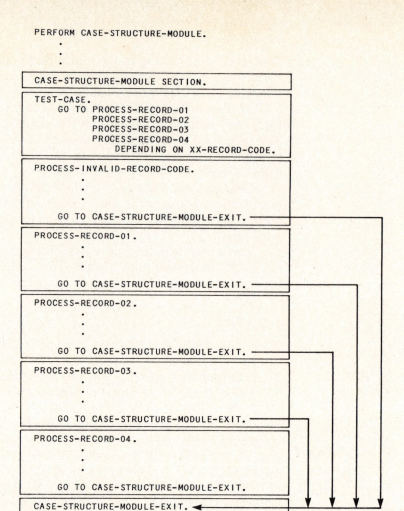

```
          PERFORM CASE-STRUCTURE-MODULE.
                       .
                       .
                       .
          ┌─────────────────────────────────────────────────┐
          │ CASE-STRUCTURE-MODULE SECTION.                    │
          ├─────────────────────────────────────────────────┤
          │ TEST-CASE.                                        │
          │     GO TO PROCESS-RECORD-01                        │
          │           PROCESS-RECORD-02                        │
          │           PROCESS-RECORD-03                        │
          │           PROCESS-RECORD-04                        │
          │              DEPENDING ON XX-RECORD-CODE.          │
          ├─────────────────────────────────────────────────┤
          │ PROCESS-INVALID-RECORD-CODE.                      │
          │      .                                            │
          │      .                                            │
          │      .                                            │
          │      GO TO CASE-STRUCTURE-MODULE-EXIT.             │
          ├─────────────────────────────────────────────────┤
          │ PROCESS-RECORD-01.                                │
          │      .                                            │
          │      .                                            │
          │      .                                            │
          │      GO TO CASE-STRUCTURE-MODULE-EXIT.             │
          ├─────────────────────────────────────────────────┤
          │ PROCESS-RECORD-02.                                │
          │      .                                            │
          │      .                                            │
          │      .                                            │
          │      GO TO CASE-STRUCTURE-MODULE-EXIT.             │
          ├─────────────────────────────────────────────────┤
          │ PROCESS-RECORD-03.                                │
          │      .                                            │
          │      .                                            │
          │      .                                            │
          │      GO TO CASE-STRUCTURE-MODULE-EXIT.             │
          ├─────────────────────────────────────────────────┤
          │ PROCESS-RECORD-04.                                │
          │      .                                            │
          │      .                                            │
          │      .                                            │
          │      GO TO CASE-STRUCTURE-MODULE-EXIT.             │
          ├─────────────────────────────────────────────────┤
          │ CASE-STRUCTURE-MODULE-EXIT.                       │
          │      EXIT.                                         │
          └─────────────────────────────────────────────────┘
```

Figure 1A.4. Case-structure example.

Independent Module Conventions

It is a good idea to establish a separate, independent module for each READ, WRITE, or other input-output (I-O) statement that is used in a program. Program logic and debugging are simplified when a common input or output operation for a file is handled at a single location. When records are read or written, certain related functions must frequently be provided for: counting records, counting lines, testing for end-of-file, and so forth. Rather than writing separate READ or WRITE statements in-line, coding is more efficient and easier to debug when separate modules are established and performed whenever that particular I-O operation is required.

In certain cases, more than one write-module must be provided for a file. For example, two write-modules are needed when a report file requires one WRITE statement to skip to the top of the next page to print report headings and requires another WRITE statement for normal line spacing in the body of the report. The WRITE statement that skips to the top of the page must use either the PAGE or the **mnemonic-name** option, whereas the line-spacing statement will use either the **ADVANCING integer** or **identifier** form. Thus, for report files, two WRITE statements are normally required. If page skipping to additional locations on the report form is required, additional write-modules should be established.

```
READ-INVENTORY-RECORD
PRINT-REPORT-HEADINGS
VALIDATE-PRICE-FIELD
PROCESS-SALES-RECORD
WRITE-REPORT-LINE
```

      Verb   Adjective   Object

Figure 1A.5. Module-naming conventions.

Another situation in which more than one write-module may be required occurs when variable-length records are written. Such processing is discussed in Chapter 8.

Table lookup and subprogram call logic are other examples of routines that should be established as independent modules. Just as I-O modules, they are often required at multiple locations within a program.

Module-Naming Conventions

Each program module should handle a specific function. The name that is chosen for a module should describe the module function. As shown in Figure 1A.5, module names that contain a single verb followed by an adjective and an object tend to describe functional modules. So that the module name can be accommodated within the COBOL 30-character user-defined word maximum, it is recommended that module names be composed of a one-word verb followed by a two-word object. By naming modules in this manner, the programmer is forced to consider the true function of the module. The module-naming process can thus be an aid to functional module design. If the coding for a module is made to conform to its description, module cohesion is enhanced. Module cohesion and other module-naming considerations are covered in Topic B of this chapter.

Module-Numbering Conventions

Module numbers are helpful aids to the reading, writing, and debugging of COBOL programs. Trying to locate a particular unnumbered module of a long program can pose difficulties, such as those that are encountered when trying to find a certain topic in a book that has no index. Module numbers can be used as reference numbers to aid speedy location. For example, a 3-digit sequence number can be assigned to each module-name and then the modules can be arranged in the program in ascending order according to the number.

A bevy of module-numbering systems have been proposed. Some utilize 3-digit numbers, others use 4-digit numbers. Often a letter code is placed before the numbers to indicate the structure chart level (A = level-0, B = level-1, C = level-2, and so forth). Sometimes decimal numbers are used. With this method, number 1.3.2 represents the second module subordinate to module 1.3, which, in turn, is the third module below block 1.0. (When the decimal-numbering system is used, decimal points are usually expressed as hyphens in the COBOL program procedure-names; decimal points cannot be used in the formation of user-defined words.) Some module-numbering plans use significant numbers in which certain types of modules are assigned specific number ranges; others use insignificant numbers. The module-numbering system that is used in this text is shown in Figure 1A.6.

Generally, the use of numbers that reflect specific structure chart levels is cumbersome because structure chart placement for a module will sometimes

Module number	Module function
000	Mainline
100–199	Initialization of variable fields
200–699	General processing
700–799	End-of-run totals, statistics, etc.
800–849	Input (READ, ACCEPT)
850–869	General nonreport output (WRITE, REWRITE, DELETE, DISPLAY)
870–879	Report headings
880–889	Report top-line output (page skipping)
890–899	Report-line output (line spacing)
900–999	Subprogram communication (CALL) and abnormal program termination

Figure 1A.6. Module-numbering system example.

change during a program's development or maintenance. Flexibility is increased, therefore, by not tying module numbers to structure chart levels so that the number need not be changed when chart location changes.

Although specific number ranges for certain modules can also limit flexibility, they tend to provide program organizational commonality from one program to another. Use of consistent module numbers within a programming group helps programmers to comprehend programs written by other group members more quickly. Perhaps more important, consistent module numbering permits one program to be used as a model, or skeleton, for another program with a similar function. When modules are numbered consistently according to function and modern text-editing utilities are used, source program-coding time can be significantly reduced.

■ TOPIC 1-B: **Structured-Module Design Considerations**

Cohesion
    Coincidental Cohesion
    Logical Cohesion
    Temporal Cohesion
    Procedural Cohesion
    Communicational Cohesion
    Sequential Cohesion
    Functional Cohesion
    Recap of Cohesion Levels

Coupling
    Content Coupling
    Common Coupling
    External Coupling
    Control Coupling
    Stamp Coupling
    Data Coupling

Consider the telephone for a moment. In Alexander Graham Bell's original design, the transmitter, receiver, and inner workings were all contained within one physical unit. Later models separated the receiver and connected this earpiece by cord to the remainder of the set. Today the transmitter and receiver are typically packaged together as a handset with the dial and electronics in a separate case. Telephone sets were once hard-wired into a wall receptacle; modular plug-in connections are now pre-wired into buildings.

The design of the telephone evolved for functional, economic, and maintenance reasons. Most telephone users understand or care little about how the device actually works. Rather, they want to be able to dial a number and get a connection. Design engineers call a system such as this one, with known inputs, known outputs, and a known transform—*but with unknown or irrelevant contents*—a **"black box."** That is, the case in which its mechanism is enclosed can be considered opaque; one can use the device fully without a detailed knowledge of its inner workings. It is almost imperative that complex products be designed as black boxes. In today's world, a person would have little time to use such devices if it were necessary that he or she first understand all of the scientific principles that contribute to their operation.

Many of these design and "black-box" aspects of telephones and other electronic devices apply also to computer programs. Programs must fulfill their functional requirements, make effective use of computer resources, and be easy to maintain. The program module should be a black box; the input is the data that is provided to the module, the logic of the module is the transform, and the output is the data that the module generates. Modules should be designed so that they may be understood by their function, thus minimizing the need to delve inside and examine their contents.

Such design considerations for modules will be discussed in this topic. Credit for much of the original study and research of structured-module design is to be given to Larry Constantine, who conceptualized and began work on the subject in the mid-1960s. His later work and contributions by Glenford J. Myers, Wayne G. Stevens, Edward Yourdon, and others have expanded the body of knowledge.

Cohesion

The formation of individual program steps into modules is a prime factor in structured-program design. Appropriate module design contributes to the development of proper programs. The objective is to build modules whose internal elements are closely related to one another so that each performs a single, specific task. This intramodular functional relatedness is called **cohesion**—a term that is used for similar concepts in sociology, engineering, and certain other disciplines.

Cohesion is the measure of a module's internal strength; how closely associated, or tightly bound, its internal elements are to one another. As cohesion is increased, module independence, clarity, maintainability, and portability are increased.

Figure 1B.1 shows levels of cohesion in accordance with the scale advanced by Constantine and Yourdon.* Each level will be discussed, from weakest to strongest.

Coincidental Cohesion

Let us say that our hero, Titus T. Code, as a programmer, decides to make a list of activities to be done on his day off from work. However, he finds that he has only small scraps of paper to write on—only two items will fit on each page.

*Edward Yourdon and Larry Constantine, *Structured Design: Fundamentals of a Discipline of Computer Program and Systems Design* (Englewood Cliffs, NJ: Prentice-Hall, 1979), p. 108.

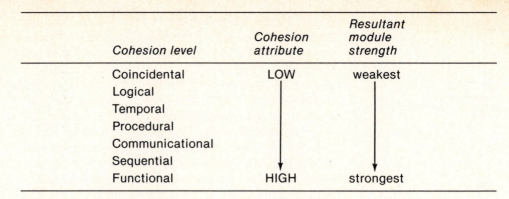

Cohesion level	Cohesion attribute	Resultant module strength
Coincidental	LOW	weakest
Logical		
Temporal		
Procedural		
Communicational		
Sequential		
Functional	HIGH	strongest

Figure 1B.1. Cohesion scale.

Coincidental cohesion exists when modules contain unrelated elements

Example for Titus

    SPEND-DAY-PAGE-1
        Launder clothes
        Pay bills

    SPEND-DAY-PAGE-2
        Watch football on TV
        Make dental appointment

    SPEND-DAY-PAGE-3
        Mow lawn
        Attend opera

    SPEND-DAY-PAGE-4
        Pick up cleaning
        Play arcade video game

COBOL example

```
PRINT-REPORT-TOTALS-1.
    MOVE SPACES TO TL-TOTAL-LINE.
    MOVE WS-RECORDS-READ TO TL-RECORD-COUNT.

PRINT-REPORT-TOTALS-2.
    MOVE 'RECORDS READ' TO TL-RECORD-COUNT-DESC.
    MOVE TL-TOTAL-LINE TO AUDIT-ERROR-LINE.

PRINT-REPORT-TOTALS-3.
    MOVE 3 TO WS-LINE-SPACING.
    PERFORM 890-WRITE-REPORT-LINE.

PRINT-REPORT-TOTALS-4.
    MOVE WS-VALID-RECORDS TO TL-RECORD-COUNT
    MOVE 'VALID RECORDS' TO TL-RECORD-COUNT-DESC.

PRINT-REPORT-TOTALS-5.
    MOVE TL-TOTAL-LINE TO AUDIT-ERROR-LINE.
    MOVE 1 TO WS-LINE-SPACING.

PRINT-REPORT-TOTALS-6.
    PERFORM 890-WRITE-REPORT-LINE.
    MOVE SPACES TO AUDIT-ERROR-LINE.
```

Figure 1B.2. Examples of coincidental cohesion.

Thus he comes up with a list as shown in Figure 1B.2, with different activities randomly recorded on various pieces of paper.

This result can be equated to **coincidental cohesion**, which exists when there is no meaningful relationship between the elements of a module. One characteristic of a coincidentally cohesive module is that it is difficult to concisely define its function. Notice in the COBOL example (Figure 1B.2) that the module names do not describe the processing; instead, a numeric suffix is used to differentiate the modules.

Because coincidentally cohesive modules are lowest in module strength, it is fortunate that they are rare. They typically occur only as the result of one of the following conditions:

1. An existing program was arbitrarily segmented into smaller modules to accommodate the restrictions of operational hardware, such as size of page storage and size of storage partition.

2. Existing modules were arbitrarily subdivided to conform to an ill-advised programming standard, which mandates that each module shall contain no more than some number, say 50, of program statements.

Logical cohesion exists when modules contain a group of related elements

Example for Titus

    DO-CHORES
        Launder clothes
        Pay bills
        Make dental appointment
        Mow lawn
        Pick up cleaning

    BE-ENTERTAINED
        Watch football game on TV
        Attend opera
        Play arcade video game

COBOL example

```
DO-ALL-IO-OPERATIONS.
    IF IO-CODE IS EQUAL TO '1'
        READ TRANS-FILE INTO TRANS-WORK-AREA
    ELSE IF IO-CODE IS EQUAL TO '2'
        READ MASTER-FILE-IN INTO MSTR-WORK-AREA
    ELSE IF IO-CODE IS EQUAL TO '3'
        WRITE MASTER-FILE-OUT FROM MSTR-WORK-AREA
        MOVE MSTR-PENDING TO MSTR-WORK-AREA
    ELSE IF IO-CODE IS EQUAL TO '4'
        WRITE ERROR-RECORD FROM TRANS-WORK-AREA
    ELSE IF IO-CODE IS EQUAL TO '5'
        WRITE MASTER-FILE-OUT FROM MSTR-WORK-AREA
        READ MASTER-FILE-IN INTO MSTR-WORK-AREA.
```

Figure 1B.3. Examples of logical cohesion.

3. A number of existing modules were combined into one module to either reduce the number of modules or to increase the number of statements within a module to a certain minimum.
4. A new module was created to consolidate multiple occurrences of a random sequence of statements.

All of these actions are usually initiated as a result of the limitations of computer storage or the requirements of programming standards. With continually increasing storage sizes and virtual storage features, such severe storage restrictions seldom occur in today's environment. Although occasionally suggested or espoused, programming standards that enforce artificial statement or module limits contribute few, if any, benefits and hence are generally either revoked or ignored.

In item 4 of the above list, consolidation of statements into nonfunctional modules is an action that "hot-shot" programmers, who want to conserve bits, sometimes take. It is a practice that was inspired when storage was dear and compilers were more primitive. Today the programmer should relinquish this function to an optimizing compiler. The coincidental cohesion that is generated when optimization is done at the source level introduces severe maintenance problems. On the other hand, optimizing compilers can handle it perspicaciously and without risk of error by using the object code.

Logical Cohesion

Titus now has his day's activities recorded on a few scraps of paper strewn before him on the kitchen table. As with many programmers, although his personal habits may not be orderly, his mind is, so Titus decides to organize his activities. Spotting a paper tablet on the floor, he relists his activities—this time grouped into chores and entertainment. This list is shown in Figure 1B.3.

Such **logical cohesion** occurs when elements are grouped into a class of related functions. During each iteration of a logically cohesive program module, one or more functions are typically selected on the basis of determinants that are established from outside the module. As shown in the COBOL example (Figure 1B.3), containing a group of I-O statements, only one or a small subset of choices is typically selected at each iteration.

Thus a logically cohesive module contains a number of elements that fall into some general category. They are slightly stronger than coincidentally cohesive modules because their elements are, at least, somewhat related. However, the elements do not contribute to the performance of a single task and, although the elements have similarities in function, they also have differences. This causes logically cohesive modules to be like a simmering pot of noodles—they are a prime contributor to "bowl-of-spaghetti" programs.

Temporal cohesion exists when modules contain elements related by time

Example for Titus

RISE-AND-SHINE
Go jogging
Take shower
Get dressed
Eat breakfast
Read newspaper
Make bed

COBOL example

```
INITIALIZATION.
    OPEN INPUT CONTROL-FILE
                TRANSACTION-FILE
        OUTPUT REPORT-FILE.
    READ CONTROL-FILE
        AT END MOVE 'YES' TO CF-EOF-SW.
    MOVE CR-DATE TO H1-DATE.
    CLOSE CONTROL-FILE.
    MOVE 1 TO H1-PAGE-NBR.
    PERFORM HEADING-ROUTINE.
    MOVE ZERO TO REPORT-TOTAL.
```

Figure 1B.4. Examples of temporal cohesion.

Procedural cohesion exists when modules contain elements related by control-flow sequence

Example for Titus

SPEND-DAY
Launder clothes
Mow lawn
Make dental appointment
Pick up cleaning
Play arcade video game
Watch football on TV
Attend opera

COBOL example

```
PROCESS-LOOP.
    WRITE TRANS-RCD-OUT FROM TRANS-RCD.
    READ TRANS-FILE-IN INTO TRANS-RCD
        AT END MOVE 'YES' TO TR-EOF-SW
            GO TO PROCESS-LOOP-EXIT.
    IF TR-AMOUNT IS NOT NUMERIC
        MOVE 'AMOUNT NOT NUMERIC' TO ERR-MSG
        WRITE ERROR-RCD FROM TRANS-RCD
        MOVE ZEROS TO TR-AMOUNT.
PROCESS-LOOP-EXIT.
    EXIT.
```

Figure 1B.5. Examples of procedural cohesion.

Temporal Cohesion

Thinking back over his morning, Titus recalls prior activities that have brought him to his present position—sitting at the breakfast table. Upon rising, he donned his sweat suit and went jogging. Upon his return home, he took a shower, got dressed, ate breakfast, read the newspaper, and made the bed.

These activities are related by time—Titus goes through this routine each morning to get ready for the day. The classic example of a program module that exhibits **temporal cohesion** is also one that handles "get-ready" and "housekeeping" functions—an initialization module, as shown in the COBOL example of Figure 1B.4. A termination or "wrap-up" module is another prime example.

A temporally cohesive module could be considered a logically cohesive module in which time is the logical category. It is slightly stronger than other logically cohesive modules because time-related classification is one in which all or most—rather than just a small subset—of the elements are generally executed during each iteration. Nevertheless, temporally cohesive modules are weak because they become a repository of miscellaneous elements that are related to other functions. It is usually preferable to place such elements together with others that are associated by application function rather than time.

Procedural Cohesion

Looking back at his list of pending activities for the day, Titus spends a moment anticipating the fun and dreading the chores. He quickly recognizes that the activities had better be scheduled so that they can all be accomplished. Whipping out his trusty programming template, Titus proceeds to flowchart the day's activities. The flowchart sequence is shown in list form in Figure 1B.5.

Communicational cohesion exists when modules contain elements operating
upon the same input or output data item

Example for Titus

    FRESHEN-UP
        Shave
        Brush teeth
        Take shower
        Shampoo hair
        Clip nails

COBOL example

```
PROCESS-INVENTORY-ITEM.
    IF II-WAREHOUSE IS NOT EQUAL TO 'P' OR 'A'
        MOVE '*' TO II-WAREHOUSE.
    IF II-UNIT-OF-MEASURE IS EQUAL TO SPACES
        MOVE 'EA' TO II-UNIT-OF-MEASURE.
    IF II-PRICE IS EQUAL TO ZERO
        SET PT-INDEX TO 1
        SEARCH PRICE-TABLE
            AT END MOVE 'Y' TO II-MANUAL-PRICE-IND
            WHEN II-PART-NBR IS EQUAL TO PT-PART-NBR
                MOVE PT-PRICE TO II-PRICE.
    IF II-BALANCE-ON-HAND IS NEGATIVE
        MOVE HIGH-VALUE TO II-BACKORDER-IND.
```

Figure 1B.6. Examples of communicational cohesion.

Procedural cohesion exists when elements of a module are related by control-flow sequence. A product of flowchart thinking, such modules are comprised of activities related more to program procedure than to problem function.

Procedural cohesion is at the intermediate cohesion level. Whereas temporally cohesive modules contain various steps that are executed within a particular time span, procedurally cohesive modules contain steps that must be executed serially within a particular sequence. The weakness that procedurally cohesive modules exhibit is that they tend to cut across functional boundaries and thus contain either part of an application function, multiple functions, or fragments of various functions.

Communicational Cohesion

When Titus freshened-up for the day, he performed a number of grooming operations. He shaved, brushed his teeth, took a shower, shampooed his hair, and clipped his nails. One could say that all of these grooming operations used his body as input.

Communicational cohesion occurs when modules contain elements that operate upon the same input or output data-item. Communicationally cohesive modules are commonly encountered in business applications. The COBOL example of Figure 1B.6 presents a situation in which all validations of an input inventory record are performed. Assembling a report line prior to printing is an example for output data.

At this level on the cohesion scale, the relatedness shifts from control flow to data. This is the first point at which problem-dependent relationships are addressed. Hence communicational cohesion is stronger than procedural. However, performing a combination of processing for a particular piece of data can introduce scope, timing, and sequence interdependencies that make communicationally cohesion modules weaker than those at the two cohesion levels which remain to be discussed.

Sequential Cohesion

One of the chores that Titus has scheduled for the day is to do his laundry. To do this task, he first sorts his clothes into groups: whites, colors, and permanent-press fabrics. Then he washes each group, dries the articles, and irons those items that are not permanently pressed. When he is doing laundry, each step must be completed before the next can be started.

A program module that contains elements in which the output data from one processing element serves as input data to the next element is said to

Sequential cohesion exists when modules contain elements in which the output data from processing operations serves as input data to the next

Example for Titus

LAUNDER CLOTHES
    Sort dirty clothes
    Wash clothes
    Dry clothes
    Iron clothes

COBOL example

```
VAL-ZIP-AND-FIND-ST-AND-TAX.
    SET ZIP-INDEX TO 1.
    SEARCH-ZIP-TABLE
        AT END MOVE 'NO ' TO ZIP-ENTRY-FOUND-SW
        WHEN IN-ZIP IS EQUAL TO ZIP-ARG (ZIP-INDEX)
        MOVE ZIP-STATE-NUM (ZIP-INDEX) TO ST-SUB
        MOVE 'YES' TO ZIP-ENTRY-FOUND-SW.
    IF ZIP-ENTRY-FOUND
        MOVE ST-TAX (ST-SUB) TO TAX-RATE
        MULTIPLY SALES-AMOUNT BY TAX-RATE
            GIVING TAX-AMOUNT ROUNDED
        ADD TAX-AMOUNT TO SALES-AMOUNT GIVING TOTAL-AMOUNT.
```

Figure 1B.7. Examples of sequential cohesion.

Functional cohesion exists when modules contain elements that all contribute to the performance of a single, specific task

Example for Titus

MAKE-CUSTOMER-CHANGE
    Accept cash amount
    Subtract purchase amount
    Extract least number
      of bills and/or coins
        to equal purchase amount
    Hand to customer

COBOL example

```
CALCULATE-SOCIAL-SECURITY-TAX.
    IF EMP-YTD-TAX IS LESS THAN SS-TAX-MAX
        MULTIPLY EMP-GROSS-PAY BY SS-TAX-RATE
            GIVING EMP-THIS-PER-TAX
        ADD EMP-THIS-PER-TAX TO EMP-YTD-TAX
    ELSE
        MOVE ZERO TO EMP-THIS-PER-TAX.

    IF EMP-YTD-TAX IS GREATER THAN SS-TAX-MAX
        SUBTRACT SS-TAX-MAX FROM EMP-YTD-TAX
            GIVING EMP-OVER-TAX
        MOVE SS-TAX-MAX TO EMP-YTD-TAX
        SUBTRACT EMP-OVER-TAX FROM EMP-THIS-PER-TAX.
```

Figure 1B.8. Examples of functional cohesion.

possess **sequential cohesion**. A sequentially cohesive module is like an assembly line; the linear sequence of steps perform successive transformations of data. Figure 1B.7 shows a COBOL example.

Sequential cohesion is more of an end-product or problem-oriented module than communicational cohesion and is, therefore, stronger. Its only weakness is one found also at lower-cohesion levels: the scope of the module may span multiple functions or merely fragments of functions.

Functional Cohesion

When Titus picked up his cleaning, the bill came to $7.80. He handed the clerk a $10 bill and received the change. The process of making change is an easily definable specific task.

Modules with **functional cohesion**, the highest level on the cohesion scale, contain elements that all contribute to the performance of a single, specific task. Mathematically oriented modules are prime examples of functionally cohesive modules. In the Social Security tax routine of Figure 1B.8, there are known input fields (the employee's gross pay amount for this period, the employee's year-to-date Social Security tax withheld amount, the Social Security tax rate, and the Social Security maximum withholding amount), and known output field requirements (the employee's Social Security tax withholding amount for this period and the employee's updated year-to-date Social Security tax withheld). All elements of the module are an integral part of the calculation and are essential in producing the correct Social Security tax amount.

Cohesion level	Module qualities			
	Independence from other modules	Ease of maintenance	Portability to other programs	Ease of comprehension
Coincidental	Low	Low	Low	Low
Logical	Low	Low	Low	Low
Temporal	Low	Medium	Low	Medium
Procedural	Medium	Medium	Medium	Medium
Communicational	Medium	Medium	Medium	Medium
Sequential	High	High	High	High
Functional	Very high	Very high	Very high	High

Figure 1B.9. Cohesion attributes.

Recap of Cohesion Levels

When designing program modules, the objective is to form modules that have a single problem-related function. This functional orientation increases independence, clarity, maintenance, and portability attributes of the module, as summarized in Figure 1B.9.

In Topic 1-A of this chapter, module-naming conventions were mentioned as an aid to functional module design. It should be possible to describe a functionally cohesive module with a simple sentence that contains an imperative verb and a specific singular object. If a compound sentence, or one that contains a comma or multiple verbs, is required, the module is probably less than functional. Clues to the cohesion level are as follows:

- If the sentence is a general, umbrella description containing the word "all," either explicitly or implicitly, logical cohesion may be indicated.
- Words such as "initialization," "housekeeping," "termination," and "wrap-up" probably mean that the module is temporally cohesive.
- Temporal, procedural, or sequential cohesion may be revealed by time-oriented words such as "first," "next," "last," "before," "after," "start," "continue," or "finish."
- Use of flowchart-oriented words such as "loop" and "step" may evidence procedural cohesion.
- Need for the word "and" may indicate that the module has communicational or procedural cohesion.

Coupling

When designing modular-structured programs, it is, of course, necessary to connect the modules. The fewer and simpler the connections between modules, the easier it is to understand and maintain one module without reference to other modules. Such connections between modules are called **interfaces** or **couples**.

Coupling is a measure of the interdependence between modules. Hence, whereas cohesion is an *intra*-module quality, coupling is an *inter*-module aspect. A well-partitioned program has low, or loose, coupling. A program with highly, or tightly, coupled modules will be susceptible to **cascading** or **rippling errors** whenever the program is modified; a higher number of connections means that there will be many paths along which errors can propagate into other parts of the system.

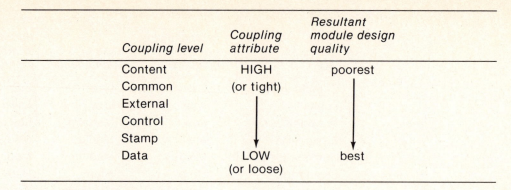

Coupling level	Coupling attribute	Resultant module design quality
Content	HIGH	poorest
Common	(or tight)	
External		
Control		
Stamp		
Data	LOW	best
	(or loose)	

Figure 1B.10. Coupling scale.

Content coupling occurs when one module directly references or modifies the insides of another

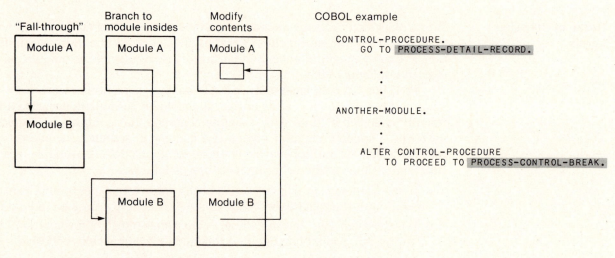

Figure 1B.11. Example of content coupling.

Perhaps you may recall the old-fashioned Christmas tree lights that were wired in a series. When one bulb burned out, the entire string went dark. This can be considered to be a highly coupled system. On the other hand, modern-day strings that are parallel-wired are loosely coupled; the status of one bulb has no effect upon the others.

Figure 1B.10 depicts the coupling scale that Myers devised.* Each type of coupling will be discussed.

Content Coupling

Two modules show **content coupling** when one *directly* references or modifies the insides of the other. Pioneer assembler language programmers often perpetrated the most flagrant example of content coupling. Instead of branching to a labeled instruction in another module, programmers would sometimes branch to a location that was a given displacement from the branch instruction. This meant that, should any instruction be added, deleted, or modified (resulting in an instruction length change) within the span of the displacement, the branch

*Glenford J. Myers, *Composite/Structured Design* (New York: Van Nostrand Reinhold, 1978), p. 41.

Common coupling occurs when two modules reference the same global data structure

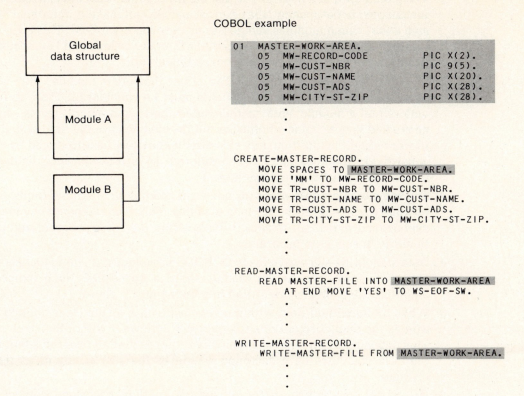

COBOL example

```
01   MASTER-WORK-AREA.
     05   MW-RECORD-CODE           PIC X(2).
     05   MW-CUST-NBR              PIC 9(5).
     05   MW-CUST-NAME             PIC X(20).
     05   MW-CUST-ADS              PIC X(28).
     05   MW-CITY-ST-ZIP           PIC X(28).
              .
              .
              .

CREATE-MASTER-RECORD.
     MOVE SPACES TO MASTER-WORK-AREA.
     MOVE 'MM' TO MW-RECORD-CODE.
     MOVE TR-CUST-NBR TO MW-CUST-NBR.
     MOVE TR-CUST-NAME TO MW-CUST-NAME.
     MOVE TR-CUST-ADS TO MW-CUST-ADS.
     MOVE TR-CITY-ST-ZIP TO MW-CITY-ST-ZIP.
              .
              .
              .

READ-MASTER-RECORD.
     READ MASTER-FILE INTO MASTER-WORK-AREA
         AT END MOVE 'YES' TO WS-EOF-SW.
              .
              .
              .

WRITE-MASTER-RECORD.
     WRITE-MASTER-FILE FROM MASTER-WORK-AREA.
              .
              .
              .
```

Figure 1B.12. Example of common coupling.

instruction had to be updated or the program would fail. This is an example of a *direct* reference to the insides of another module; one that is not resolved by the compiler, linkage editor, or another binding mechanism.

Fortunately, there are only a few ways that content coupling can be introduced within a COBOL program. A notorious example is through use of the ALTER statement, as shown in Figure 1B.11. An ALTER statement that references a paragraph within another module modifies the branch address within another. The comprehension and maintenance problems that can arise from such coding has caused the ALTER statement to be recognized as a "bug-breeder" statement.

Content coupling also occurs when structured-programming principles that use normal PERFORM and CALL statement linkage conventions are bypassed so that (1) a GO TO instruction within one module points to a procedure within another module or (2) the control flow "falls through" from one module to another.

Common Coupling   When two modules reference the same global data structure, they exhibit **common coupling. Global data** is that which is accessible to the program as a whole (the "whole world" of the program). Common coupling is named after the FORTRAN COMMON statement, which defines such global data. Figure 1B.12 provides a COBOL example. When data is common coupled, it is shared. Certain problems that occur when individuals share items arise when modules share data. When an individual is ready to use the item, it may not be in the condition that one expects, and it is difficult to determine who all the users are.

Modules with common coupling suffer from the following problems:

1. The global data is available for use by any module. This unrestricted and unmanaged access means that a programmer can make a unilateral decision about which modules should use or even modify a field. This is akin to leaving valuables out in the open rather than under lock and key. Within a program, it is a prime source of cascading errors.

2. Module readability is reduced. The effect that other modules may have upon the contents of the global fields must be considered. Thus, to fully understand a module, each module subordinate to it—at all levels—must be studied to determine whether or not the modules use the field and, if so, to what effect. In addition, any side effects that may be introduced by non-subordinate modules must be considered. (A cross-reference listing of data-names greatly aids these tasks.)

3. The same explicit data-name (or names, if redefined) for global fields must be known and shared by various modules. This name dependency makes modules more difficult to reuse—both within the same program and particularly in separate programs.

4. Data *structures*—group fields in COBOL—introduce data dependencies by exposing more data to the module than is necessary. Such exposure amplifies the problems identified in points 1 and 2 above.

5. When an individual field within a composite data structure is changed, it affects the displacement of each field that follows it within the structure. This dependency on field size typically requires that all programs that use the data structure be recompiled whenever the size of any of its fields changes.

6. For a data structure to be reused in another program, it must be duplicated. Even though not all fields within the structure are required for the additional use, the dummy structure must be artificially created—in other words, *faked*—to permit reuse. Not only does this create additional coding effort, but it also obscures data requirements.

Unfortunately, all data within the DATA DIVISION for a single COBOL program is global data. To reduce the amount of global data, subprograms with CALL statement linkage must be used. (Subprograms and the CALL statement are covered in Chapter 10 of this text.) An approach that can be used to effectively minimize global data is to establish conventions to subdivide the common DATA DIVISION into dedicated data areas. The major difficulty with this approach is that there is no enforcement or notification by the compiler to ensure that the data areas are not accessed globally.

External Coupling

External coupling occurs when two or more modules reference the same global data *element*. It is similar to common coupling; the difference is that the global data is a field rather than a record structure. An example is shown in Figure 1B.13.

Of the six problems listed above for common coupling, the first three apply whereas the latter three do not. Hence external coupling is somewhat looser on the coupling scale.

Control Coupling

Control coupling occurs when one module passes a field to the other, which is intended to control the latter's internal logic. Such control fields are typically referred to as switches, flags, or function codes. Examples are shown in Figure 1B.14. The weakness inherent in control coupling is that passing and using control fields between modules implies that one module is aware of the inner workings of another.

External coupling occurs when two modules reference the same global data element

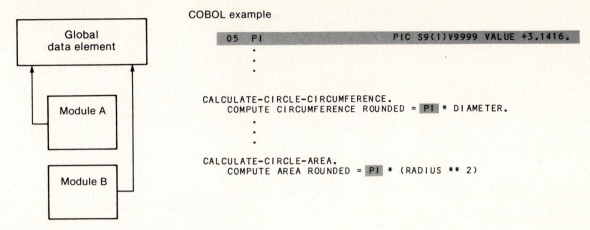

COBOL example

```
         05  PI                            PIC S9(1)V9999 VALUE +3.1416.
             .
             .
             .

         CALCULATE-CIRCLE-CIRCUMFERENCE.
             COMPUTE CIRCUMFERENCE ROUNDED =  PI  * DIAMETER.
             .
             .
             .

         CALCULATE-CIRCLE-AREA.
             COMPUTE AREA ROUNDED =  PI  * (RADIUS ** 2)
```

Figure 1B.13. Example of external coupling.

Control coupling occurs when one module passes a data element to another, which is intended to control the logic of the latter

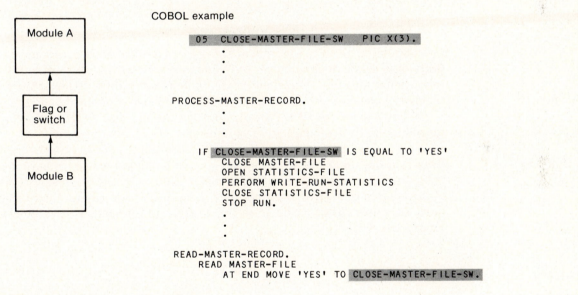

COBOL example

```
         05  CLOSE-MASTER-FILE-SW   PIC X(3).
             .
             .
             .

         PROCESS-MASTER-RECORD.
             .
             .
             .

             IF  CLOSE-MASTER-FILE-SW  IS EQUAL TO 'YES'
                 CLOSE MASTER-FILE
                 OPEN STATISTICS-FILE
                 PERFORM WRITE-RUN-STATISTICS
                 CLOSE STATISTICS-FILE
                 STOP RUN.
             .
             .
             .

         READ-MASTER-RECORD.
             READ MASTER-FILE
                 AT END MOVE 'YES' TO  CLOSE-MASTER-FILE-SW.
```

Figure 1B.14. Example of control coupling.

Passing of control fields can either be downward—from superordinate module to subordinate module—or upward. When control fields are passed downward, it generally indicates that the subordinate module is logically cohesive. Passing of control fields upward—from subordinate module to superordinate module—is termed an **inversion of authority**; it can be likened to a situation in which a worker gives orders to his or her supervisor.

Stamp Coupling   When two or more modules refer to the same nonglobal data structure, they evidence **stamp coupling**. Stamp coupling is parallel to common coupling except that nonglobal data structures are referenced. Therefore, those problems that

Stamp coupling occurs when two modules reference the same nonglobal data structure

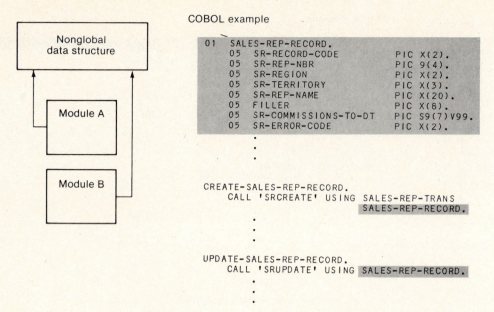

COBOL example

```
01    SALES-REP-RECORD.
      05    SR-RECORD-CODE          PIC X(2).
      05    SR-REP-NBR              PIC 9(4).
      05    SR-REGION               PIC X(2).
      05    SR-TERRITORY            PIC X(3).
      05    SR-REP-NAME             PIC X(20).
      05    FILLER                  PIC X(8).
      05    SR-COMMISSIONS-TO-DT    PIC S9(7)V99.
      05    SR-ERROR-CODE           PIC X(2).
      .
      .
      .

CREATE-SALES-REP-RECORD.
    CALL 'SRCREATE' USING SALES-REP-TRANS
                          SALES-REP-RECORD.
    .
    .
    .

UPDATE-SALES-REP-RECORD.
    CALL 'SRUPDATE' USING SALES-REP-RECORD.
    .
    .
    .
```

Figure 1B.15. Example of stamp coupling.

are associated directly with global data—unrestricted access, obscured readability, and name-dependency—are eliminated. However, the difficulties that are attributable to data structures—unnecessary data exposure, field-displacement dependency, and structure dependency—remain.

As shown in Figure 1B.15, use of subprograms and the CALL statement are required to reach this coupling level with the COBOL language.

Data Coupling

Data coupling—loosest on the scale—is exhibited when two or more modules refer to the same nonglobal fields. Hence data coupling is closely related to stamp coupling; the difference is that individual fields rather than composite data structures are passed from one module to another. This is depicted in Figure 1B.16.

Summary

Topic 1-A Structured COBOL-Coding Principles and Conventions

In 1964 Bohm and Jacopini established the theoretical basis for structured programming when they presented proof that any program logic can be expressed by using one or more of three basic control structures: sequence, selection, and iteration. This concept is referred to as the **structure theorem**. The **sequence structure** refers to statements that are executed in order, one after another. The **selection structure (if-then-else)** presents a condition and choices of action depending upon whether the condition is true or false. The **iteration structure (do-while** or **perform-until)** causes a set of instructions to be executed repeatedly as long as a given condition exists.

The publication of a letter by Dijkstra in 1968, entitled "GO TO Statement Considered Harmful," attracted considerable attention in the programming

Data coupling occurs when two modules reference the same nonglobal data element

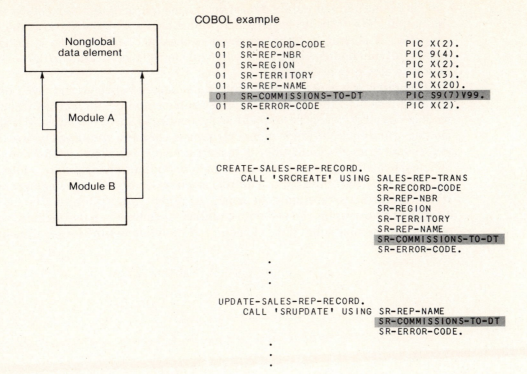

COBOL example

```
01    SR-RECORD-CODE          PIC X(2).
01    SR-REP-NBR              PIC 9(4).
01    SR-REGION               PIC X(2).
01    SR-TERRITORY            PIC X(3).
01    SR-REP-NAME             PIC X(20).
01    SR-COMMISSIONS-TO-DT    PIC S9(7)V99.
01    SR-ERROR-CODE           PIC X(2).
                    .
                    .
                    .

CREATE-SALES-REP-RECORD.
      CALL 'SRCREATE' USING SALES-REP-TRANS
                            SR-RECORD-CODE
                            SR-REP-NBR
                            SR-REGION
                            SR-TERRITORY
                            SR-REP-NAME
                            SR-COMMISSIONS-TO-DT
                            SR-ERROR-CODE.
                    .
                    .
                    .

UPDATE-SALES-REP-RECORD.
      CALL 'SRUPDATE' USING SR-REP-NAME
                            SR-COMMISSIONS-TO-DT
                            SR-ERROR-CODE.
                    .
                    .
                    .
```

Figure 1B.16. Example of data coupling.

community. This letter, together with proof of the structure theorem, led to a decline in the use of the GO TO statement.

Along with other **improved programming techniques**, structured programming concepts were applied to a commercial application—the "New York Times Project"—from 1969 to 1971. The success of this application caused the data-processing community to take note. By the mid-1970s, structured-programming practices began emerging at many commercial data-processing installations.

Today the term **structured programming** may be defined as a program design, documentation, coding, and testing methodology that utilizes techniques in program development to create proper, reliable, and maintainable software products on a cost-effective basis.

Structured COBOL-coding principles state that (1) only the three control structures of the structure theorem should be used and (2) each program module should have only one entry point and one exit point. In addition to the structured COBOL-coding principles, certain coding conventions should be followed with regard to module formation, independent modules, module naming, and module numbering.

Topic 1-B Structured-Module Design Considerations

Cohesion is the measure of a module's internal strength. Modules with **coincidental cohesion** are at the weakest level of cohesion—they contain unrelated elements. Modules with **logical cohesion** contain a group of related elements. A module whose elements are related by time is one with **temporal cohesion**. When a module contains elements that are related by control flow sequence, it is said to possess **procedural cohesion**; this is at the midpoint of the cohesion scale. A module with **communicational cohesion** contains elements that operate upon the same input or output data-item. If a module contains elements in which the output data from processing operations serve as input data to the next operation, it is said to be of **sequential cohesion**. The objective is to design modules of **functional cohesion**, in which all elements contribute to the performance of a single, specific task.

Coupling is a measure of the interdependence between modules. **Content coupling** produces the tightest, least desirable coupling and occurs when one module directly references or modifies the insides of another module. When two modules reference the same global structure, **common coupling** occurs. If the global data is an element rather than a structure, it is called **external coupling**. When one module passes one data element to another element that is intended to control the logic of the latter, **control coupling** occurs. **Stamp coupling** occurs when two modules reference the same nonglobal data structure. The loosest, most desirable coupling level—**data coupling**—occurs when two modules reference the same nonglobal data element and no other tighter forms of coupling exist.

HARDWARE/SOFTWARE CONCEPTS
CHAPTER A

DISK AND TAPE HARDWARE

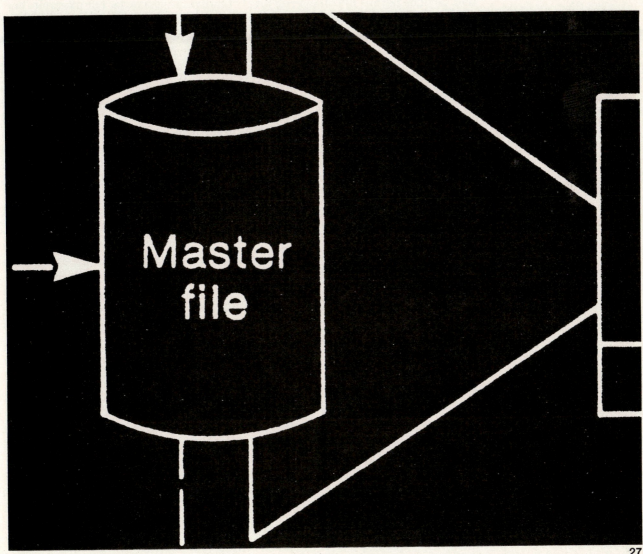

A DISK AND TAPE HARDWARE

Disk-Storage Devices

Practically all computer systems that are currently being marketed use disk storage as their primary medium for storing data files. A disk-storage device is often referred to as a **direct-access storage device**, or **DASD** (pronounced DAZ-dee).

The term **direct access** is used to distinguish disk hardware from serial-processing devices such as card readers, paper tape readers, and magnetic tape drives. Whereas serial-processing devices are limited to processing records, one after another, in accordance with the physical sequence of the file, disk devices permit the direct retrieval of individual records. For example, suppose that there are 6,000 records in a file. To obtain the last record of the file that is stored on tape, all 5,999 records that precede the last record must be processed. Disk storage (together with an appropriate file-organization method, which will be discussed in Chapter 2) allows each record to be retrieved directly, without reference to the preceding records.

When discussing disk hardware, it is necessary to distinguish between the disk drive and the disk-storage medium. The **disk drive** is the device that handles the physical operations of reading and writing on the **disk-storage medium** upon which the data is recorded. This is somewhat parallel to a stereo system in which the record player is the device that plays back the audio from the storage medium—the phonograph record—upon which the sounds are recorded.

Various types and forms of disk hardware are shown in Figure A.1 and will be described in the following discussion.

Disk-Storage Media

Just as phonograph records come in various sizes (45, LP, etc.), there are various forms of disk-storage media: pack, fixed-disk, data-module, cartridge, sealed-disk, and diskette.

Large-scale computer systems usually use disk-pack, fixed-disk, or data-module devices. Cartridge disks are commonly found on minicomputer systems; sealed disks and diskettes are usually attached to microcomputers.

Disk pack

A **disk pack** is a collection of attached platters upon which data is stored. It looks similar to a stack of phonograph records mounted on a turntable spool. Just as phonograph records are placed on the turntable to be played and removed for storage, disk packs are mounted on the disk drive for use and unmounted for storage.

The platters are 14 inches in diameter and are usually stacked either 6, 11, or 12 to a pack. Disk-pack storage capacities are measured in **megabytes** (millions of **bytes**, or storage positions, and abbreviated as **Mb**) and range from 25 to 300 Mb.

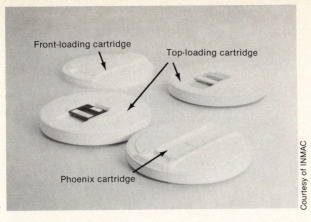

Front-loading cartridge

Top-loading cartridge

Phoenix cartridge

Disk cartridges and drive

**Fixed sealed disks
(Winchester technology)**

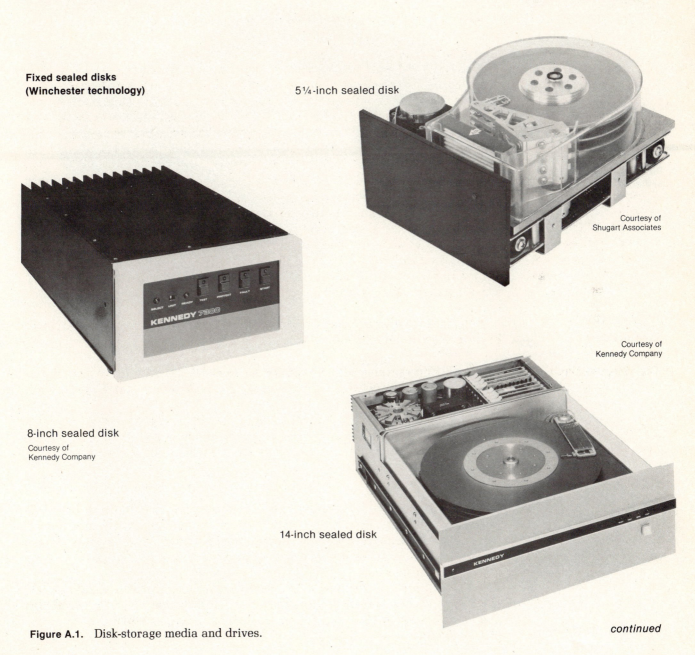

5¼-inch sealed disk

8-inch sealed disk

14-inch sealed disk

Figure A.1. Disk-storage media and drives.

continued

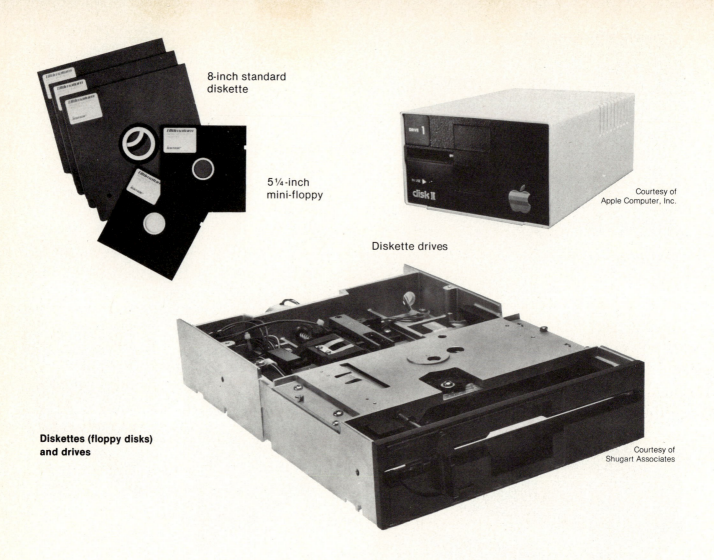

8-inch standard
diskette

5¼-inch
mini-floppy

Diskette drives

Courtesy of
Apple Computer, Inc.

**Diskettes (floppy disks)
and drives**

Courtesy of
Shugart Associates

Fixed disk drive

IBM 3370 Disk Storage Unit

Courtesy of
International Business
Machines Corporation

Figure A.1. (continued)

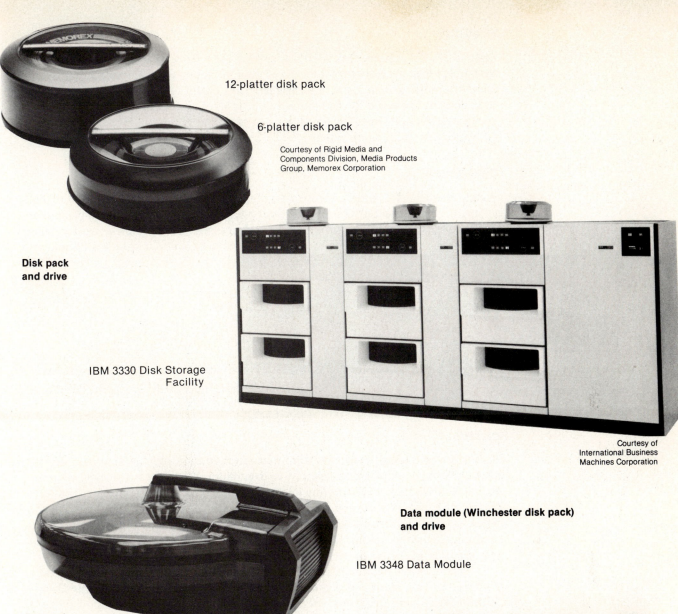

12-platter disk pack

6-platter disk pack

Courtesy of Rigid Media and
Components Division, Media Products
Group, Memorex Corporation

**Disk pack
and drive**

IBM 3330 Disk Storage
Facility

Courtesy of
International Business
Machines Corporation

**Data module (Winchester disk pack)
and drive**

IBM 3348 Data Module

Courtesy of
International Business
Machines Corporation

IBM 3340 Disk
Storage Facility

Courtesy of
International Business
Machines Corporation

Figure A.1. (continued)

Fixed disk

Instead of packs, some disk drives are designed with a nonremovable **fixed-disk** assembly. The architecture of a fixed disk is generally comparable to a disk pack; the main difference is that the fixed disk is stationary in the disk drive and thus does not provide for the mounting of interchangeable packs.

Storage capacities for fixed-disk units range from 300 megabytes to over 1.2 **gigabytes** (billions of bytes).

Data module

A **data module** is a sealed, removable disk pack that contains not only the disk-recording surfaces but also certain hardware components (the access mechanism, read-write heads, and spindle) that are part of the disk drive for traditional disk-pack devices. A data module is more commonly called a **Winchester** disk pack. (Winchester was the code name for its development project within the IBM Corporation.)

The storage capacity for 14-inch data modules is from approximately 35 to 70 Mb.

Disk cartridge

A **disk cartridge** is a one- or two-platter disk contained in a plastic cartridge enclosure. Disk cartridges can be classified as **top-loading**, **front-loading**, or **Phoenix**. Storage capacity ranges from about 2 to 20 Mb.

Diskette

A **diskette** is a small polyester film disk—approximately the size of a 45-rpm phonograph record—that is coated with a magnetic oxide substance. Because this disk is flexible, it is sometimes termed a **flexible disk** and popularly called a **floppy disk** or just a **floppy**. The diskette is enclosed by, and rotates within, a black polymer jacket. Diskettes are commonly used (1) as a data-entry storage medium, (2) as disk storage for microcomputers, and (3) to store and load system and diagnostic software on larger computers.

Diskettes are produced in two sizes: 8-inch and 5¼-inch. The former size is referred to as a **standard diskette**; the latter is commonly called a **mini-floppy**. Within each size, diskettes are recorded on one-sided or two-sided disks at either **single-density** or **double-density**. Diskette capacities range from 110 **kilobytes** (thousands of bytes; abbreviated **kb**) to 2Mb. Figure A.2 depicts the various recording configurations and their storage capacities.

Fixed-sealed disk

Nonremovable **fixed-sealed disks** with either 8- or 5¼-inch platters are now commonly being used with microcomputer systems. Although "Winchester" originally meant a removable data module with 14-inch platters, the term "Winchester technology" is now also popularly affixed to these smaller, nonremovable units.

The storage capacity for 8-inch disks is generally from 10 to 30 Mb; for 5¼-inch devices it ranges from approximately 3 to 15 Mb.

Disk-Storage Architecture

Although it was once important for the professional programmer/analyst to have a detailed knowledge of the disk hardware that was being used, recent hardware and software developments are beginning to allow the programmer

Recording configuration	8-inch Diskette		Approximate storage capacity	5¼-inch Diskette		Approximate storage capacity
Single-density single-side	256 kb		0.25 Mb	110 kb		110 kb
Double-density single-side	256 kb 256 kb		0.5 Mb	110 kb 110 kb		220 kb
Single-density two-side	256 kb / 256 kb		0.5 Mb			
Double-density two-side	256 kb 256 kb / 256 kb 256 kb		1 Mb	110 kb 110 kb / 110 kb 110 kb		440 kb
Half-track double-density two-side	256 kb 256 kb 256 kb 256 kb / 256 kb 256 kb 256 kb 256 kb		2 Mb	110 kb 110 kb 110 kb 110 kb / 110 kb 110 kb 110 kb 110 kb		880 kb

Figure A.2. Diskette-recording configurations.

to design and code programs independently from the specifications of the actual disk equipment that is being used. One significant development in this direction is the introduction of **fixed-block disk architecture** in which the details of the disk-recording elements are of no concern to the programmer.

Nevertheless, today's programmer/analyst should have at least a general awareness of disk-storage architecture. Figure A.3 depicts the elements of a commonly used disk-pack device. A brief explanation of disk-storage architectural terms follows.

Recording surfaces

Just like a phonograph record, each disk platter usually has two **recording surfaces**—top and bottom—upon which data is stored. However, with removable disk packs, top and bottom platter surfaces are reserved for protective purposes and are not used for recording. This is because they are exposed to possible damage or contamination when the pack is attached to or removed from the drive.

Each surface is coated with a magnetic oxide substance. Data is recorded as magnetized and unmagnetized spot patterns.

Track

Unlike a phonograph record, where the audio is recorded in a continuous spiral groove, data on a disk surface is stored in concentric circles, which are called **tracks**. A top view of the tracks on a recording surface is shown in Figure A.4. The number of tracks per surface ranges from 74 for a diskette to over 800 for large disks. The storage capacity of a track can likewise vary from approximately 3,500 to over 47,000 bytes.

Figure A.5 shows examples of how, with a commonly used recording format, data records are recorded on a track. Further information on the **count-data** and **count-key-data** formats is presented in Appendix F.

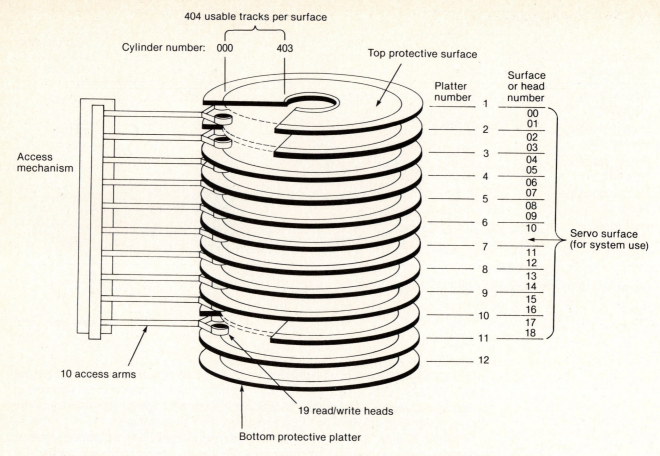

404 usable tracks per surface

Cylinder number: 000   403

Top protective surface

Platter number

Surface or head number

1
   00
   01
2
   02
   03
3
   04
   05
4
   06
   07
5
   08
   09
6
   10
7
   11
   12
8
   13
   14
9
   15
   16
10
   17
   18
11
12

Servo surface (for system use)

Access mechanism

10 access arms

19 read/write heads

Bottom protective platter

Figure A.3.   Schematic representation of IBM 3330-1 Disk Storage Drive and 3336-1 Disk Pack.

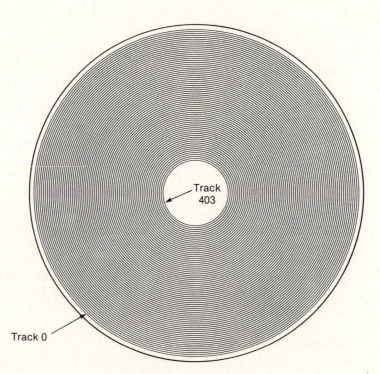

Track 403

Track 0

Figure A.4.   Top view of tracks on a disk surface.

Count-data format (formatted without keys):

Count-key-data format (formatted with keys):

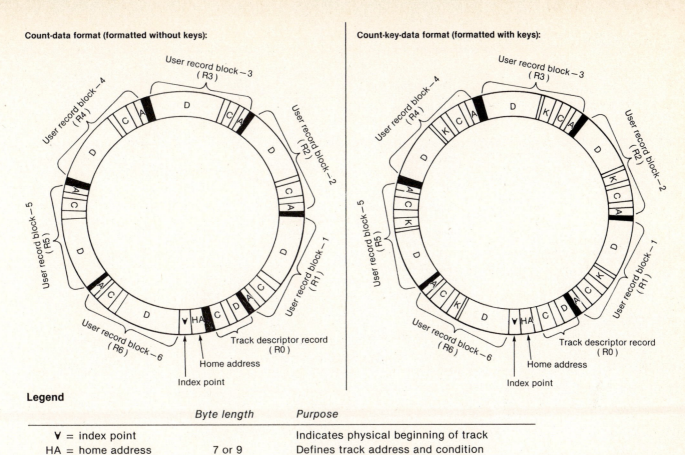

Legend

	Byte length	Purpose
V = index point		Indicates physical beginning of track
HA = home address	7 or 9	Defines track address and condition
A = address marker	2	Indicates beginning of data record
C = count area	11 or 13	Identifies record location (cylinder number, head number, record number) and format
K = key area	1 to 255	Identifies key of the following data record
D = data area	User defined	Data record

Figure A.5. Schematic representation of how data is recorded on a track.

Read/write head

Just as a phonograph needle is used to transmit vibrations from a phonograph record, **read/write heads** are used to record and retrieve data from each disk-recording surface.

There is usually one read/write head for each recording surface. Thus a disk drive for a pack with 19 recording surfaces will have 19 read/write heads. Only one head, however, can be transferring data at any given time.

Fixed disks sometimes have a few or all tracks with a dedicated read/write head fixed above them. A **fixed-head device** provides processing-speed advantages.

Access mechanism

Each nonfixed read/write head is mounted on an **access arm**. The comblike **access mechanism** contains the group of access arms and moves the read/write heads horizontally, as a group, to any track location.

Cylinder

A collection of tracks that can be accessed when the access arm is stationed at a location is called a **cylinder**. Recognize that tracks are not really contained in

Cylinder 31
is composed of:

Relative track 310
(surface 0)

Relative track 311
(surface 1)

Relative track 312
(surface 2)

Relative track 313
(surface 3)

Relative track 314
(surface 4)

Relative track 315
(surface 5)

Relative track 316
(surface 6)

Relative track 317
(surface 7)

Relative track 318
(surface 8)

Relative track 319
(surface 9)

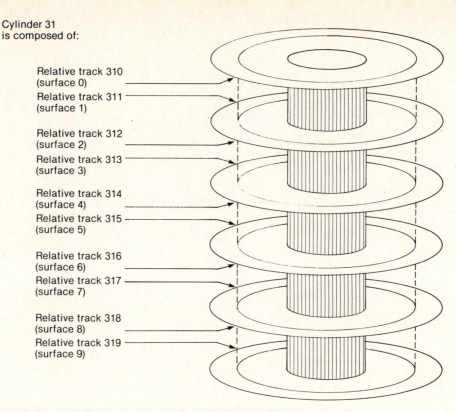

Figure A.6.   Schematic representation of cylinder concept.

a physical cylinder; rather, the cylinder is merely conceptual. Figure A.6 depicts the cylinder concept (cylinder number 31 is arbitrarily used in the example) with a 6-platter disk pack. Thus if a recording surface has 404 tracks, there will be 404 cylinder locations.

Sector

With fixed-block architecture and diskette equipment, tracks are subdivided into sectors and have a **sector** or **block** orientation rather than a cylinder one. When sectoring information is recorded magnetically, a diskette is called **soft-sectored**; when it is delineated by physical holes, it is called **hard-sectored**. Figure A.7 shows standard sectoring specifications for diskettes.

Record access

Four access stages are required to retrieve an individual record from its location on the disk. These four stages, often termed **timing** considerations because they make up the length of time required to obtain a record, are access motion time, head selection time, rotational delay time, and data transfer time.

Access motion time

This is the first stage in which the access arm is moved to the cylinder where the desired record exists. There is no access motion time with fixed-head devices. The duration of time is dependent upon the current position of the access arm. That is, if the mechanism is already at the correct cylinder, the access motion time is zero because there is no need to move it. The farther the desired cylinder is away from the current position, the longer the access motion time. Access motion time is sometimes called **seek time**.

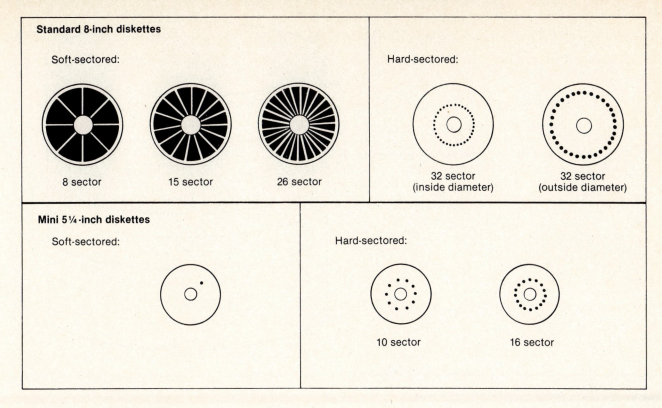

Figure A.7. Diskette sectors.

Head selection time

Very little time is required to accomplish the electronic switching to select the correct read/write head of the access mechanism. Because this second-stage time interval is negligible, it is not usually considered in disk-timing estimate calculations.

Rotational delay time

Because the disk is rotating, time is required for the desired record on the track to pass under the read/write head. This third stage, alternately termed **latency**, can range from zero to almost the time that is required for a full revolution. When making disk-timing estimates, the time that is required to make half a revolution is usually used as the average rotational delay.

Data transfer time

The last stage is the time that is required to transfer a record from the disk-storage medium to the computer-storage channel. This time period, usually nominal, is a function of the rotation speed, the density at which data is recorded on the track, and the length of the record.

Software-related concepts

Disk labels

Most operating systems require that each disk pack or **volume** be initialized with a standard **volume label**. A volume label contains the serial number that is assigned to that pack and other associated information. It also holds the disk

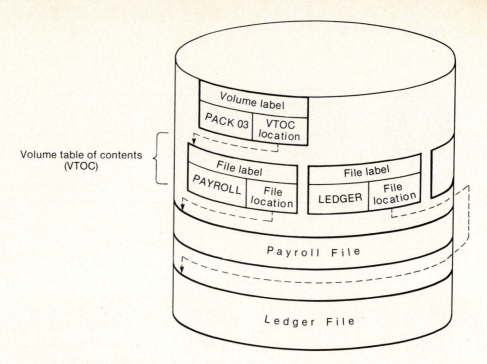

Figure A.8. Disk labels.

address of the area where the standard **file labels** reside on the volume. One or more file labels for each data file are stored on the volume. A file label identifies the file, tells its location on the volume, and contains an **expiration date** that is used to prevent premature eradication of the file. The number of file labels that are required for a file depends on the file organization method and the number of separate areas, or **extents**, that are allocated to the file.

The area that contains the collection of file labels is called the **volume table of contents**, or **VTOC** (pronounced *VEE-tock*). Figure A.8 depicts disk labels on a disk pack.

Blocked records

Data is written on magnetic-storage media in the form of physical records. A **physical record** is one or more **logical records** accessed as a group. A physical record is sometimes called a **record block**, or simply a **block**. The number of logical records that are contained in one block is called the **blocking factor**. Therefore, if there are 10 logical records in one physical record, the blocking factor is 10. Usually, each record block is designed to be contained on one track. When a block is allowed to extend from one track to another, it is termed a **spanned record**.

Generally, the larger the blocking factor that is used for a file (up to the maximum capacity of the track or sector), the more efficient the use of the disk-storage medium. This is because physical records are separated by unused gaps. With fewer physical records, there are fewer gaps, hence, less unused space.

When a disk file is processed sequentially, another advantage of high-blocking factor is faster input-output processing. A file with a blocking factor of 2 will require 50 disk accesses to read 100 records; a file with a blocking factor of 25 will require only 4 accesses.

Disk devices	Typical storage-capacity range	Typical size of computer configuration
Disk-pack	25-300 Mb	Medium/large
Fixed-disk	300-1,260 Mb	Large
Data-module	35-70 Mb	Medium
Disk cartridge	2-20 Mb	Mini/small
Fixed-sealed disks	3-70 Mb	Micro/mini/small
Diskette: 8-inch	0.25-2 Mb	Small business micro
Diskette: 5¼-inch	110-880 kb	Personal micro

Figure A.9. Recap of disk-storage devices.

However, there is a trade-off to the storage capacity and processing-speed advantages of high-blocking factors—increased program-storage requirements. With cylinder/track devices, a block length that occupies approximately a quarter-, third-, or half-track is usually chosen. For sector devices, the block size is usually as close as possible to, but not in excess of, the sector capacity.

When records are accessed randomly, blocking may degrade performance. Data-transfer requirements will increase because the entire block must be processed for each logical record. Also application program logic is sometimes required to locate the record within the block.

Disk-Storage Usage

With computer systems that are devoted to batch applications, removable disk-pack devices are popular because they allow a maximum amount of data to be stored with a minimum number of disk-drive units. However, as an installation develops more on-line systems, fixed disks become more appropriate. This is because on-line files must be accessible to the system at all times; a removable pack always mounted on a drive offers no advantage. Further, the access time and storage capacity for fixed disks can be engineered to offer speed and capacity advantages.

Fixed disks are also suitable for larger computer installations that are running a high volume of jobs in a multiprocessing mode. The use of removable packs in such an environment makes scheduling difficult, and disk-pack mounting and demounting also becomes tedious and time-consuming.

Fixed-sealed disks reduce exposure to environmental contamination, thereby reducing maintenance requirements for the access mechanism, read/write heads, disks, and spindle. In addition, reliability is improved by having dedicated read/write heads, each of which reads only data that it originally wrote.

Although flexible diskettes have traditionally been used with microcomputers, the sealed Winchester units are increasingly being employed. As microcomputer users build up larger data volumes, increasing numbers of floppies are required to store the information. This means that mounting and demounting of individual diskettes become more frequent, awkward, and wearisome. Also, the maintenance advantages coupled with increasing production volumes are making the Winchester units more competitive in price with the diskettes.

Figure A.9 presents a recap of storage capacities and the typical usages of various disk devices. Specifications for common disk devices are shown in Figure A.10.

IBM-compatible model number		DASD type	Approximate total megabyte capacity	Tracks per cyl-inder	Usable cyl-inders	Bytes per track	Average access motion time	Average rota-tional delay time	Data transfer rate per second	Year intro-duced
Drive	Pack									
2314	2316	RP	30	20	200	7,294	60 ms	12.5 ms	312 kb	1970
3330-1	3336-1	RP	100	19	404	13,030	30 ms	8.4 ms	806 kb	1971
3330-11	3336-11	RP	200	19	808	13,030	30 ms	8.4 ms	806 kb	1971
3340	3348-35	DM	35	12	348	8,368	25 ms	10.12 ms	885 kb	1973
	3348-70	DM	70	12	696	8,368	25 ms	10.12 ms	885 kb	1973
3344	na	FD	280	30	560	16,736	25 ms	10.12 ms	885 kb	1974
3350	na	FD	317.5	30	555	19,069	25 ms	8.3 ms	1198 kb	1976
3370	na	FD (fba)	571.3	12	1,500	31,744	30 ms	10.12 ms	1859 kb	1979
3375	na	FD	819.7	12	1,918	35,616	19 ms	10.12 ms	1859 kb	1980
3380	na	FD	1,260	15	1,770	47,476	16 ms	8.3 ms	3000 kb	1981

Legend: na = not applicable
RP = removable pack
DM = data module
FD = fixed disk
fba = fixed-block architecture
ms = milliseconds

Figure A.10. Specifications for common disk devices.

Magnetic Tape Equipment

Just as disk hardware can be compared to phonograph equipment, magnetic tape computer hardware resembles audio tape systems. The device that is used to read from or write on the tape is termed a **tape drive**. Audio tape systems use either reel-to-reel, cartridge, or cassette media; so do magnetic tape systems.

Figure A.11 illustrates the various magnetic tape-recording media and hardware.

Reel-to-Reel Tape

The type of tape media that is used on all except smaller computer systems is the **tape reel**. A diagram of a typical tape-drive mechanism that is used with reel media is shown in Figure A.12.

Tape specifications

Width

Magnetic tape that is used with reel equipment is a ½-inch-wide strip coated on one side with a metallic oxide substance. Just as with disks, data is recorded as magnetized and unmagnetized spot patterns.

Length

Standard tape-reel sizes are 2,400, 1,200, and 600-feet in length. They are wound on reels with diameters of 10½, 8½, and 7 inches, respectively.

Tracks

The term **track** has an entirely different meaning when it is used in conjunction with tape hardware than it does when it is used with disk equipment. Magnetic tape tracks are the rows of bits, sometimes termed **channels**, that are recorded lengthwise on the tape. Characters are coded as a pattern of magnetized bits within the group of 7- or 9-bit tracks.

With first- and second-generation computers (pre-1964 or so), 7-track recording was standard. Currently, 9-track recording is standard.

Magnetic tape reels and drive

Mini-cartridge

Standard cartridge

Tape cartridges and drive

Digital tape cassette

Tape drive

Figure A.11. Tape-storage media and drives.

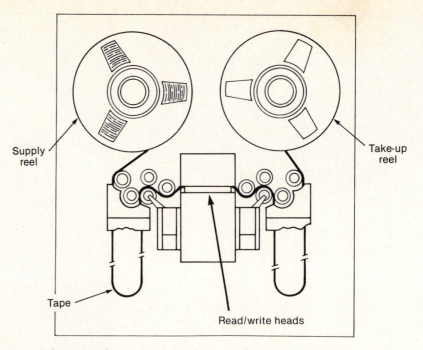

Figure A.12. Schematic of magnetic tape-drive mechanism.

Adapted from David M. Kroenke, *Business Computer Systems* (Santa Cruz, Calif.: Mitchell Publishing, 1980), p. 130.

Density

This refers to how closely the magnetic bits are recorded lengthwise on the tape. **Density** is rated in bytes per inch, abbreviated **bpi**, which corresponds to the number of characters that can be represented in a 1-inch length of tape.

Early tape equipment recorded 7 tracks at densities of either 200 bpi or 556 bpi. Such devices are no longer marketed but are still used in a few older installations. Currently marketed densities are 800, 1,600, and 6,250 bpi. Tape drives rated at 800 bpi usually record in 7-track format and are generally found only on smaller computer systems. Larger computer systems use 9-track, 6,250-bpi recording density; 9-track 1,600-bpi density drives are typically marketed with medium-scale systems.

Recording format

The bit-pattern specifications that are used to record characters on the tape are called the **recording format**. Two recording formats are commonly used: **EBCDIC** and **ASCII**. The former acronym (pronounced EB-s'dic) stands for **E**xtended **B**inary **C**oded **D**ecimal **I**nterchange **C**ode, and the latter (pronounced ASK-ee) stands for **A**merican **N**ational **S**tandard **C**ode for **I**nformation **I**nterchange.

IBM introduced the EBCDIC format with its System/360 series of third-generation computers. EBCDIC is used today in medium- and large-scale IBM and IBM-compatible systems. Most other computer vendors use the ASCII format. The EBCDIC and ASCII bit-pattern codes are itemized in Appendix I.

Figure A.13 shows the bit patterns for various characters coded in EBCDIC on 9-track tape. Notice the **parity** track. It is a track that is used to help detect any errors that occur when recording or reading data. Before the tape is recorded, a convention of either **odd** or **even parity** is established. Odd parity is shown in the figure and means that regardless of how many bits are required to

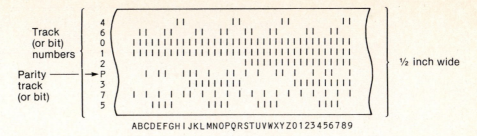

Figure A.13. Data recorded on 9-track magnetic tape.

represent the character value, an odd number of bits will always be "on" within any column of bits. This is accomplished by causing the parity bit to be "on" when the character uses an even number of bits and "off" when the character is composed of an odd number of bits.

When a tape is recorded with odd parity and an even number of bits have been read for a character column of bits, the hardware can identify an error. This ensures that when a bit is "dropped" because of defective tape media or equipment, the error will not be propagated.

Interblock gap

The unoccupied space that is used to separate records recorded on a tape is called the **interblock gap**, or **IBG**. A synonymous term sometimes used is **inter-record gap**, or **IRG**. Although the exact length of an interblock gap varies, depending upon the tape-drive specifications, each IBG is approximately ½-inch in length.

Tape markers

Reel-to-reel tapes require blank footage at the beginning of the tape in front of the usable portion so that the supply reel can be threaded onto the takeup reel. The end of this unusable portion of tape and the beginning of the usable area is signaled by a rectangular aluminum reflective spot, called a **load-point marker**, that is affixed to the tape about 15 feet from its beginning.

Similarly, about 15 feet of blank space is required at the end of the tape so that the tape does not unwind completely off the supply reel. A reflective **end-of-tape** marker is used to signal this point near the end of the reel.

Tape drives

Tape drives have traditionally operated in what can be called a **start-stop** mode, in which tape movement is started when the command to write a physical record is issued and stopped at the completion of the write operation. Figure A.14 shows a table of specifications for representative tape-drive hardware.

The increasing use of tape as a backup for disk storage has resulted in the introduction of tape drives with **streamer** transports that record and read "on the fly" without stopping or starting. Streamer drives are designed to serve specialized-disk backup and recovery functions and are not intended for normal record-processing applications.

IBM-compatible model number	Tracks		Density, in bpi			Tape speed, in./sec.
	9	7	6250	1600	800	
2401-1	S	O			S	37.5
-2	S	O			S	75
-3	S	O			S	112.5
-4	S	O		S	O	37.5
-5	S	O		S	O	75
-6	S	O		S	O	112.5
2420-5	S	O		S	O	100
-7	S	O		S	O	200
3410-1	S			S		12.5
-2	S			S	O	25
-3	S			S	O	50
3420-3	S	O		S	O	75
-4	S	O	S			75
-5	S	O		S	O	125
-6	S	O	S			125
-7	S	O		S	O	200
-8	S	O	S			200

Legend: S = standard
O = optional

Figure A.14. Specifications for common tape devices.

Software-related concepts

Tape labels

Figure A.15 contrasts external and internal tape labels.

External gummed label. The external gummed-tape label normally contains the tape-volume serial number together with other identifying information that the tape librarian and computer operations staff need for manually handling the tape. The label is usually originally affixed to the reel of tape when the tape is first initialized and then the computer operator updates it whenever new data is recorded on the tape.

Internal tape labels. The exact type and format of tape labels depends upon the computer and the operating system that are being used. A typical set will be discussed here.

The **volume label** immediately follows the load-point marker and identifies the serial number of the reel of tape together with associated information. After the volume label, each file on the reel of tape is preceded by a **file-header label** to identify the file and followed by a **file-trailer label** that contains block and record counts.

With magnetic tape, one or more files can be stored on one tape reel, or **volume**. When more than one file is recorded on a tape, it is called a **multifile volume**. Part A of Figure A.16 shows a tape volume that holds two files: a price file and a name file. A file that is so voluminous that it cannot be wholly contained on one reel is termed a **multivolume file**. Part B of Figure A.16 shows an accounts-receivable file that uses three volumes.

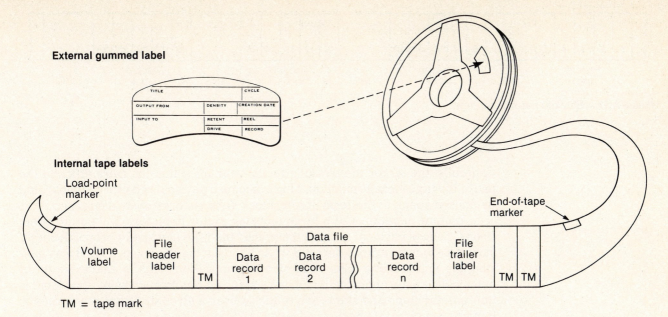

External gummed label

TITLE		CYCLE
OUTPUT FROM	DENSITY	CREATION DATE
INPUT TO	RETENT	REEL
	DRIVE	RECORD

Internal tape labels

Load-point marker

End-of-tape marker

| Volume label | File header label | TM | Data file | | ... | | File trailer label | TM | TM |

Data record 1 | Data record 2 | ... | Data record n

TM = tape mark

Figure A.15. Tape labels.

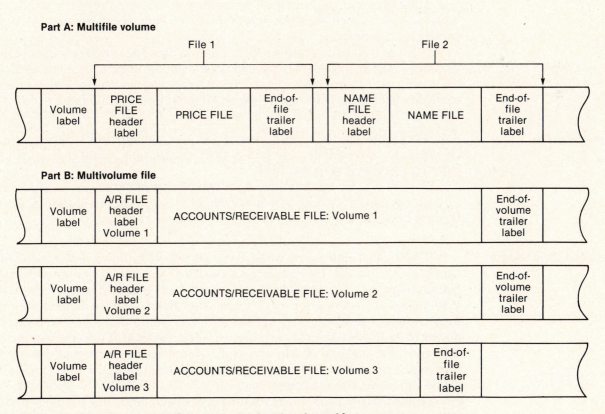

Part A: Multifile volume

File 1   File 2

| Volume label | PRICE FILE header label | PRICE FILE | End-of-file trailer label | NAME FILE header label | NAME FILE | End-of-file trailer label |

Part B: Multivolume file

| Volume label | A/R FILE header label Volume 1 | ACCOUNTS/RECEIVABLE FILE: Volume 1 | End-of-volume trailer label |

| Volume label | A/R FILE header label Volume 2 | ACCOUNTS/RECEIVABLE FILE: Volume 2 | End-of-volume trailer label |

| Volume label | A/R FILE header label Volume 3 | ACCOUNTS/RECEIVABLE FILE: Volume 3 | End-of-file trailer label |

Figure A.16. Organization of multifile volumes and multivolume files on tape.

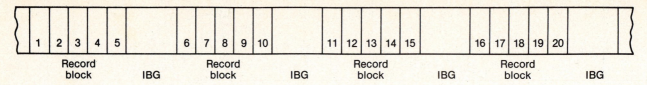

Figure A.17. Blocked records on tape.

Blocked records

Generally, the larger the blocking factor used for a file, the more efficient the use of the tape-storage medium. This is because physical records are separated by unused space in the form of interblock gaps, as previously discussed.

Another advantage of a large blocking factor is faster input-output processing. Longer physical records mean that the tape can spend proportionately more time moving across the read/write heads at maximum speed and less time stopping and starting each read or write operation. This is analogous to an automobile on the highway. It can move along optimally at cruising speed, but if intermittent stops and starts are required over a given distance, the deceleration and acceleration periods consume additional time.

Figure A.17 depicts logical records recorded on tape with a blocking factor of five.

Tape Cartridge

A **tape cartridge** contains ¼-inch-wide tape in lengths from 140 to 600 feet. The number of tracks is typically either 4 or 7, and a 16-track model has been introduced. Recording density is predominantly 6,400 bpi, but the older 1,600-bpi density is still used. Tape cartridges typically store from 23 to 35 Mb of data; the larger-capacity cartridges can store up to 67 Mb of data.

Although streamer transport technology was originally developed in conjunction with ½-inch tape transports, it is currently being applied to ¼-inch cartridge transports.

Tape cartridges are rarely used for actual data records. Their usual role is as a main-storage or disk-backup medium for small computer systems. With the increasing use of Winchester-type disks in small systems, the incidence of tape-cartridge backup devices can be expected to increase in the future.

Tape Cassette

A **tape cassette** for data looks exactly like the familiar audio tape cassette. However, to be certified as a data-grade cassette, the actual tape must pass more stringent specification tests.

The use of tape cassettes in data-processing applications is usually limited to certain data-entry and personal computing applications in which an extremely low-cost and/or compact storage device is required.

Magnetic Tape Usage

It is estimated that approximately two-thirds of all current magnetic tape usage is as a backup for disk-storage devices. Within larger data-processing installations, reel-to-reel tape drives with ½-inch tape are usually employed. With increasing sales of low-cost Winchester disk devices, a number of newer tape transport products and technologies are being developed as a backup device to match the economy and high-storage capacity of these newer sealed-disk units. For disks of 30 Mb and over, streamer transports that use ½-inch tape are being marketed. Streamer cartridge transports are in development for disks with lower-storage capacities.

Besides disk backup, the remaining uses of magnetic tape are for (1) actual data processing and (2) software and data distribution.

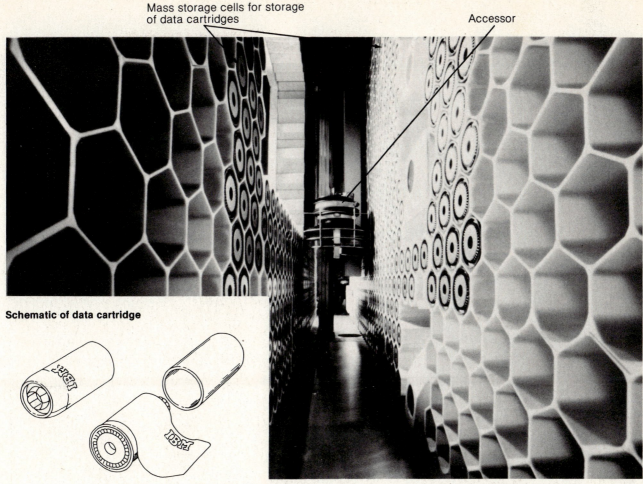

Mass storage cells for storage of data cartridges

Accessor

Schematic of data cartridge

Courtesy of International Business Machines Corporation

Figure A.18. The IBM 3850 Mass Storage System.

Mass-Storage System

A hybrid form of disk and tape storage, called a **mass-storage subsystem**, is used in some larger data-processing installations. As illustrated in Figure A.18, data cartridges that contain magnetic tape with a capacity of approximately 50 Mb each are stored in cells. The accessor retrieves the cartridges and the data is moved to a disk in an automatic process under the control of the operating system called **staging**.

The role of a mass-storage system is to provide storage capacity that is equivalent to a tape library without the sequential processing limitations, tape-mounting labor, and mounting time-delay disadvantages of magnetic tape processing. Although the staging process from tape to disk consumes more than pure disk-storage devices, the storage cost per megabyte is targeted to be close to that of traditional magnetic tape storage.

CHAPTER 2

CONCEPTS OF FILE ORGANIZATION, DESIGN, AND MAINTENANCE

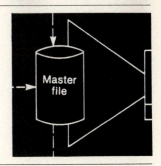

Topic 2-A: File-Organization Concepts
Topic 2-B: File and Record Design Concepts
Topic 2-C: Master File Maintenance Program Design

2 CONCEPTS OF FILE ORGANIZATION, DESIGN, AND MAINTENANCE

This chapter surveys concepts of file organization, design, and maintenance from a general perspective as preparation for the file-maintenance program design and coding techniques to be presented in Chapters 3 through 6.

General concepts of file organization are presented in Topic 2-A. As such, generic terms for the file-organization methods are used; in Chapters 3 through 6 the specific COBOL terminology is adhered to.

Aspects of file and record design are covered in Topic 2-B. Topic 2-C introduces aspects of master file maintenance program design that apply to all file-maintenance programs regardless of the file-organization method. Later, in Chapters 3 through 5, the details that apply to the specific organization method of the master file that is being maintained will be covered.

■ **TOPIC 2-A:** **File-Organization Concepts**

Sequential Organization

Direct Organization
    Record Address
        Directly addressed files
        Indirectly addressed files
    Relative Record Number
    Recap of Direct Organization

Indexed-Sequential Organization

Subjects Related to Data File Organization
    Partitioned Organization [IBM OS Only]
    Access Mode
    Virtual Storage Access Method (VSAM) [IBM OS/VS and DOS/VS Only]

There are three commonly used methods of data file organization: sequential, direct, and indexed-sequential. We will discuss each of these file-organization techniques. Following that, we will discuss the topics that are related to file organization.

Sequential Organization

Sequential organization is the most straightforward approach to organizing records within a file. With sequential organization, records are simply stored serially, one after another, in a card deck, on a tape reel, disk pack, or some other storage medium. Sequential organization is sometimes referred to as **physical sequential** or **standard sequential**.

Actually, the term sequential is a bit of a misnomer; **serial** would probably be a better name for this file-organization method. Although records of a sequential file are usually arranged sequentially according to the value of one or more key fields, a file with haphazard or no sequencing of its records is also considered to be a sequential file.

To use an analogy, consider books on a bookshelf. They could simply be stacked on the shelf at random. Or, perhaps as each new book is purchased, it is added to the shelf after the last volume. Then again, the books could be organized according to a certain attribute. For example, they could be arranged alphabetically by author's name, title, or subject. All of these approaches—haphazard, chronological, and sequenced—are considered to be a sequential organization when they are applied to data files.

A record **key** is one or more of the data fields contained within the record that is used to uniquely identify the record and relate it to the data entity that it represents. For instance, if a record contains information about an inventory part, its key field would probably be part number; an employee record key will usually be Social Security number or an employee number. When the value of the record key is used to determine the record's placement in the file, it can be termed a **key-sequenced** file.* When a file is organized haphazardly or according to the time that the record was entered into the file, it is called an **entry-sequenced** file. Most sequential files are key-sequenced, but entry-sequenced examples are commonly used for data entry, transaction history, and certain other applications.

A representation of the records of a key-sequenced sequential file that is stored on a disk is shown in Figure 2A.1. The 3-digit numbers shown within the disk identify the key value for each record. Three records are stored on each disk track. The key values range from 101 to 877. Observe that, with a disk of cylinder/track architecture, the records of a sequential file are recorded sequentially on each track. When a track is full, records are recorded on the next available track within the cylinder. After the cylinder is filled, records are recorded on the next available cylinder.

Figure 2A.1 shows an example of a **contiguous** allocation of disk space. That is, all 9 cylinders of the file have been allocated in a contiguous area—arbitrarily placed at cylinders 101 through 109—of the disk. The advantage of contiguous allocation is that movement of the disk-access mechanism is minimized for sequential processing. On the other hand, gaps of unused areas will usually occur when processing files of various sizes with a device-independent operating system; this wastes disk space. Further, if another program is concurrently using the disk in a multiprogramming environment, access mechanism movement will occur when the other program is accessing the disk. So, although contiguous allocation is appropriate in certain cases, programming standards for larger data-processing installations using device-independent operating systems usually call for the programmer to omit the specification of contiguous allocation. Specification of particular file-storage locations is generally done in the job control language of the operating system, not in the COBOL program.

Sequential organization is effective for batch processing an entire file of records. Because the records are stored serially and can be blocked, optimum utilization of tape- or disk-storage space can be obtained. In addition, serial-processing and high-blocking factors permit rapid input-output processing.

---

*IBM's Virtual Storage Access Method (VSAM) uses indexed—not sequential—organization for key-sequenced files. Although this situation may tend to cause confusion in terms, it does not affect the validity of the definition provided above. Refer to the section "Virtual Storage Access Method (VSAM)," which appears later in this chapter.

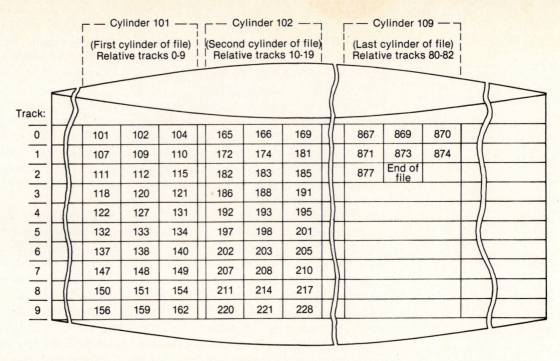

Track:	Cylinder 101 (First cylinder of file) Relative tracks 0-9			Cylinder 102 (Second cylinder of file) Relative tracks 10-19			Cylinder 109 (Last cylinder of file) Relative tracks 80-82		
0	101	102	104	165	166	169	867	869	870
1	107	109	110	172	174	181	871	873	874
2	111	112	115	182	183	185	877	End of file	
3	118	120	121	186	188	191			
4	122	127	131	192	193	195			
5	132	133	134	197	198	201			
6	137	138	140	202	203	205			
7	147	148	149	207	208	210			
8	150	151	154	211	214	217			
9	156	159	162	220	221	228			

Figure 2A.1. Sequential file-organization example. Sequential file of 247 records: recorded at 3 records per track on a disk with 10 tracks per cylinder; occupies 83 tracks; example shows cylinders 101 to 109.

Furthermore, sequential organization provides maximum file and program **portability**. That is, sequentially organized files can be moved from one computer or operating system to another with few or no changes to the data. COBOL programs that process sequential files can usually be converted from one system to another by merely changing the ASSIGN clause.

However, a major drawback to sequentially organized files is that individual records cannot be located quickly because the records are processed in accordance with their physical location in the file. For example, if a record for employee number 873 is the 245th record in an employee master file, that record cannot be processed until after the 244 previous records of the file have been read. For this reason, sequentially organized master files are limited to batch applications; another file-organization method must be used for on-line master files.

Direct Organization

Files of **direct organization** are designed to provide rapid access to individual records within the file. Quick retrieval is made possible because the location of an individual record can be determined from the value of its key field. Files of direct organization are limited to direct-access storage devices; they cannot be processed on tape devices.

To access a record directly, either the **record address** or **relative record number** must be determined. We will discuss both of these concepts.

Record Address

When a record is physically written on a disk, the physical disk address is referenced. The exact specifications for such an address depend upon the disk hardware that is being used. With COBOL, one common way to specify a symbolic record address (for conversion by the compiler or operating system to an actual record address) is to supply the relative track number of the disk device

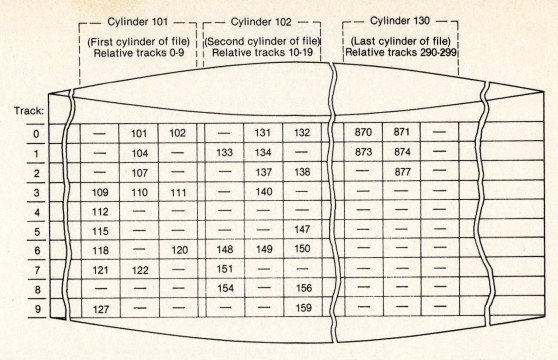

Figure 2A.2. Directly addressed direct file-organization example. Directly addressed file with permissible key values of 100 to 999: recorded at 3 records per track on a disk with 10 tracks per cylinder; occupies 300 tracks; example shows cylinders 101 to 130.

followed by the actual key of the record. Regardless of how the record address is specified in the COBOL program, the file can be considered to be either directly addressed or indirectly addressed.

Directly addressed files

When every possible record key value will convert to a unique physical record address, the file is **directly addressed**. For example, if we have 4-digit customer account numbers and have allocated DASD space for 10,000 customer master records (customer account numbers 0000 through 9999), then each record can be assigned its own unique record address.

Figure 2A.2 shows a representation of the records of a directly addressed direct file (the same file of 247 records shown in Figure 2A.1). The dashes in the record areas of the figure indicate unused record locations. Observe that, whereas the sequential file occupied 9 cylinders, this directly addressed file requires 30 cylinders to handle 3-digit keys ranging from 100 to 999. This is because a record location is allocated for every possible key value within the range regardless of whether or not a data record exists for the key.

Directly addressed files provide the fastest processing of individual records because the exact record can be obtained with one access. Another advantage of directly addressed files is that the records are also physically arranged in key sequence so that they can be processed directly for sequential report outputs.

Unfortunately, however, few actual data-processing applications lend themselves to directly addressed files. This is because key-field values usually have either unassigned-number gaps or alphanumeric characters in them. Unassigned-number gaps waste direct-access storage because a record location must be reserved for every key value within the possible range, regardless

	Computation steps	Worked example
System design steps	1. Determine the logical record length.	200 bytes
	2. Estimate the number of records to be stored in the file.	8,000 records
	3. Increase the record count figure by decreasing the packing factor to minimize synonyms and to allow for file-population expansion.	Packing factor = 80% $$.80\overline{)8,000} \quad 10,000 \text{ locations}$$
	4. Determine the number of records that can be stored on a track. (Refer to the appropriate disk reference manual or to the representative examples provided in Appendix F.)	3336 Model I pack = 33 records per track
	5. Divide the file record capacity by the number of records to be stored on each track to find the number of tracks that will be required for the file.	$$33\overline{)10,000} \quad 303 \text{ tracks}$$
	6. Find the prime number closest to, but not greater than the number of record locations. (Refer to the prime number list in Appendix H.)	9973
Program logic	7. Divide the key by the prime number.	$$9973\overline{)74829} \quad 7 \text{ remainder } 5018$$
	8. Divide the remainder by the number of records per track.	$$33\overline{)5018} \quad 152 \text{ remainder } 2$$
	9. Use the quotient as the relative track address; the remainder plus 1 as the record number on the track	Relative track address = 152 Record number (2 + 1) = 3

Figure 2A.3. Indirectly addressed direct file-randomizing computation: randomizing to record address.

of whether or not it is actually used. When there are excessively large gaps or alphanumeric values in the key, directly addressed files are not practical.

Indirectly addressed files

When the range of possible key-field values is greater than the number of record locations allocated for a direct file, the file is **indirectly addressed**. Indirect addressing can be used when the range of key-field values contains such a high percentage of unused ones that direct addressing is not feasible. For example, if we had an employee master file application with 5-digit employee numbers, 100,000 record locations (00000 through 99999) would be required for a directly addressed file. However, suppose that there were only about 8,000 to 10,000 employees on the company's payroll. An indirectly addressed file could be used to achieve the advantages of direct organization and to minimize wasted disk space. Indirect addressing can also be used when the key values contain alphanumeric values.

To determine the record location for an indirectly addressed file, a **randomizing (or hashing) algorithm** must be used to convert the actual record key value to a valid record location value. Let us say that we decided to allocate 12,000 record locations for the employee file that we previously mentioned. We would then want a randomizing technique that would convert any 5-digit employee number to a valid record location value (00000 to 11999 or 00001 to 12000).

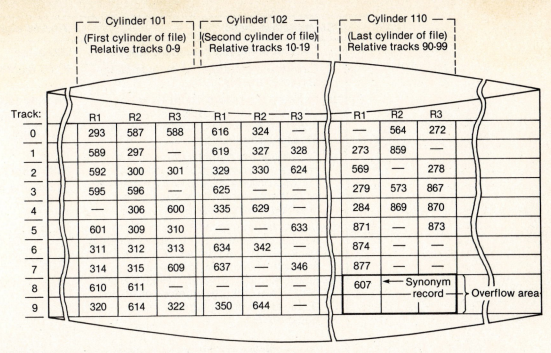

Track:	Cylinder 101 (First cylinder of file) Relative tracks 0-9			Cylinder 102 (Second cylinder of file) Relative tracks 10-19			Cylinder 110 (Last cylinder of file) Relative tracks 90-99		
	R1	R2	R3	R1	R2	R3	R1	R2	R3
0	293	587	588	616	324	—	—	564	272
1	589	297	—	619	327	328	273	859	—
2	592	300	301	329	330	624	569	—	278
3	595	596	—	625	—	—	279	573	867
4	—	306	600	335	629	—	284	869	870
5	601	309	310	—	—	633	871	—	873
6	311	312	313	634	342	—	874	—	—
7	314	315	609	637	—	346	877	—	—
8	610	611	—	—	—	—	607 ← Synonym record		Overflow area
9	320	614	322	350	644	—			

Figure 2A.4. Indirectly addressed file-organization example: randomized to record address. Indirectly addressed direct file randomized to record address with 300 record locations: recorded at 3 records per track on a disk with 10 tracks per cylinder; occupies 100 tracks (97 prime tracks; 2 overflow tracks); example shows cylinders 101 to 110.

Randomizing algorithm:
257 records to be stored with 80% packing, approximately 300 record locations are required: with 3 records stored per track, 100 tracks must be allocated; prime number closest to 300 is 293.

Record address computation given key value 873: 873/293 = quotient 2, remainder 287; 287/3 = quotient 95, remainder 2; relative track = 95; record number on the track (2 + 1) = 3.

Randomizing computations will inevitably produce what are called **synonyms**—two records whose key values convert to the same record location. A good randomizing algorithm will (1) ensure that every possible key in the file will randomize to a valid record location, and (2) minimize the number of synonyms by developing record addresses that are evenly distributed throughout the file. The former objective can be mathematically assured; the latter will depend upon the number of excess record locations that are provided and the actual key values of the records.

The randomizing technique that usually produces the best results is the **prime number division/remainder method**. A **prime number** is a number evenly divisible only by 1 and itself. An example of its computation for an indirectly addressed file randomized to record address is shown in Figure 2A.3.

Figure 2A.4 represents the same file that is shown in the sequential and directly addressed direct file-organization figures—this time as an indirectly addressed file that is randomized to record address. The first 98 tracks of the file are termed the **prime area**; with the randomizing algorithm that is being used, each key value from 101 to 999 will convert to a track address from 0 to 97 and to a record address on the track of 1, 2, or 3. Tracks 98 and 99 have been allocated as an **overflow area**; when a record already occupies the record address to which it randomizes, that record is a synonym and will be stored in the overflow area. (The size of the overflow area is limited in the example to what will conveniently fit in the figure; it would generally bear a larger ratio to the prime data-area volume.)

Computation steps	Worked example

<table>
<tr><td rowspan="6" style="writing-mode:vertical">System design steps</td><td>1. Determine the logical record length.</td><td>200 bytes</td></tr>
<tr><td>2. Estimate the number of records to be stored in the file.</td><td>8,000 records</td></tr>
<tr><td>3. Increase the record count figure by decreasing the packing factor to minimize synonyms and to allow for file-population expansion.</td><td>Packing factor = 80%
          10,000 locations
.80 ⌐ 8,000</td></tr>
<tr><td>4. Determine the number of records that can be stored on a track. (Refer to the appropriate disk reference manual or to the representative examples provided in Appendix F.)</td><td>3336 Model I pack =
33 records per track</td></tr>
<tr><td>5. Divide the file record capacity by the number of records to be stored on each track to find the number of tracks that will be required for the file.</td><td>   303 tracks
33 ⌐ 10,000</td></tr>
<tr><td>6. Find the prime number closest to, but not greater than the number of tracks. (Refer to the prime number list in Appendix H.)</td><td>293</td></tr>
</table>

<table>
<tr><td rowspan="2" style="writing-mode:vertical">Program logic</td><td>7. Divide the key by the prime number.</td><td>   255 remainder 114
293 ⌐ 74829</td></tr>
<tr><td>8. Use the remainder as the relative track address;</td><td>Relative track
    address = 114</td></tr>
</table>

Figure 2A.5. Indirectly addressed direct file-randomizing computation: randomizing to track address.

Observe the synonym record, key value 607, in the overflow area. Key value 607 randomizes to track 7, record number 1. Since that location is already occupied by record key 314, the 607 record must be stored in the overflow area.

Figure 2A.5 shows the prime number division/remainder computation for an indirectly addressed file that is randomized not to the specific record location but instead merely to the track location.

A representation of an indirectly addressed file that is randomized to track address is presented in Figure 2A.6. Each key value will convert to a prime data-area track address of 0 through 96. If a key value randomizes to a track address that is full (and not already present in the file), it is a synonym and must be stored in the overflow area.

Notice record key 681 in the overflow area. The key value of 681 randomizes to track 2. Track 2 is full, however, with records 293, 390, and 584. Thus record 681 is stored in the overflow area. Randomizing to track address generally provides better results than randomizing to record address because synonyms tend to be reduced.

Although the prime number division/remainder randomizing technique is the one that is most predominantly used, Figure 2A.7 provides a summary that describes other methods.

In normal commercial data-processing applications, indirectly addressed direct files are seldom used* because of the complexity involved with coding the routines that (1) handle the randomizing, (2) keep track of the occupied or unoccupied status of the record areas, and (3) place and locate synonyms.

*Although indirectly addressed direct files are seldom used for nondata-base applications, they are a common component of most generalized data-base management systems.

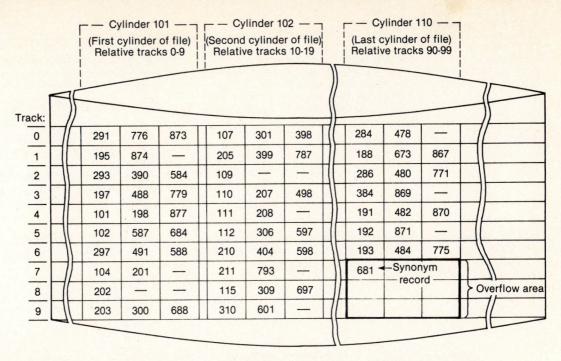

Figure 2A.6. Indirectly addressed direct file-organization example: randomized to track address. Indirectly addressed direct file randomized to track address with 300 record locations: recorded at 3 records per track on a disk with 10 tracks per cylinder; occupies 100 tracks (97 prime tracks; 3 overflow tracks); example shows cylinders 101 to 110.

Randomizing algorithm:
257 records to be stored with 80% packing, approximately 300 record locations are required: with 3 records stored per track, 100 tracks must be allocated; closest prime number is 97.

Record address computation given key value 873: 873/97 = quotient 9, remainder 0; relative track = 0.

Randomizing technique	Description	Example (with 4-digit record address ranging from 0000 through 9999)
Prime number division/remainder	The key-field value is divided by the prime number closest to, but not greater than, the number of allocated record locations (or disk tracks, sectors, etc.).	See Figures 2A.3 and 2A.5

Digit extraction	The assigned key-field values are analyzed to determine which digit positions of the key are more evenly distributed. The most evenly distributed position is chosen as the low-order record-address digit. The other more evenly distributed digit positions are assigned, from right to left, until each position of the record address field is accounted for.
	
	Then, to form a record address, the specified digit values are extracted from the key-field contents.
		Given: 9-digit key-field
		
		An analysis of the key values reveals that the four more evenly distributed digits are the 9th, 7th, 5th, and 2nd.
		
		                              position
		                            123456789
		For key value: 546032178
		The record address is: 8134

Figure 2A.7. Summary of randomizing techniques.

continued

Randomizing technique	Description	Example (with 4-digit record address ranging from 0000 through 9999)

Folding	The key-field is split in two or more parts and then summed to form the record address value. If excess digits occur, they are discarded.	Given: 8-digit key-field
		
		For key value: 25936715
		
		The record address is:
		Folding in half: 2593 + 6715 9308
		Folding in thirds: 259 + 36 + 715 1010
		Folding
		  alternate digits: 2961 + 5375 8336
		Other folding: 2 5 9 3 6 7 1 5
		                  2367 + 5915 8282

Base (or radix) conversion	The key-field value is converted to a different base (radix). Any excess high-order digits are truncated.	Given: 5-digit key-field
		       conversion to base 11
		
		For key value: 38652
		
		(3×11^4) 43923
		$+ (8 \times 11^3)$ + 10648
		$+ (6 \times 11^2)$ + 726
		$+ (5 \times 11^1)$ + 55
		$+ (2 \times 11^0)$ + 2
		                        55354
		The record address is: 5354

Square-value truncation	The key is multiplied by itself. Superfluous high-order digits of the squared value are truncated.	Given: 5-digit key-field
		
		For key value: 10395
		
		                  10395
		           × 10395
		        108056025
		The record address is: 6025

Digit transformation	This is a technique used in conjunction with one of the above methods (except it is not required with prime number division) when the decimal number of record areas allocated to the file is not a power of 10. There is no specific algorithm by which a digit is transformed. Rather, a method is devised that will yield a good distribution of records among the available record addresses.	Given: the digit-extraction example shown above except that there are 20,000 record addresses ranging from 00,000 to 19,000 The fifth most evenly distributed digit position is position 8. If position 8 is an even number, the first digit of the record address is 0; if position 8 is an odd number, the first digit of the record address is 1. For key value: 546032178 [8th position (7) is odd] The record address is: 18134

Relative Record Number

The ANS COBOL method for handling direct files is by **relative record number** within what is termed a **relative file**. A relative file consists of a serial string of areas, each capable of holding a logical record and each identified by a relative record number. Records are stored and retrieved on the basis of this number. For example, the 98th record is the one addressed by relative record number 98 and is in the 98th record area, regardless of the number of records that are actually present in the first 97 record areas.

Relative files, like those that use record addresses, are either directly or indirectly addressed files. The only difference is that relative-file record addresses are symbolically expressed in relation to the relative record number, whereas record addresses refer to disk track, cylinder, sector, or some other aspect of the disk hardware.

Recap of Direct Organization

Direct organization provides the fastest random-access capabilities, particularly for directly addressed files. Because of (1) the limited number of situations in which directly addressed files can be used, and (2) the complexities that are involved in handling indirectly addressed file applications, files of direct organization have traditionally been limited to high-usage master files within large on-line application systems in which the need for quick random access is a priority.

Assuming that there are continued hardware speed and software efficiency improvements, indirectly addressed direct files will probably be used even less frequently in the future (except within data-base management systems). Even when the programming and maintenance complexities of indirectly addressed files are provided for, the lack of efficient sequential-processing capabilities is usually a severe drawback. So, as hardware and software speed improves, the random record-retrieval speed of indexed-sequential organization—although not as quick—will more often satisfy access time requirements and also provide sequential-processing ability.

Disk-storage utilization will vary with directly addressed files. When the key usage is dense (no or few unused record locations), it is efficient; with sparse key usage, it is poor. With indirectly addressed files, disk utilization is degraded by the need for allocation of excess record locations to minimize synonyms. Of course, as disk-storage costs decline, concerns about utilization of storage space decrease.

The ANS COBOL equivalent of direct organization is termed **relative organization**. A directly addressed file can be handled on a straightforward basis with ANS COBOL, but an indirectly addressed file will require routines for randomizing and synonym processing. Certain COBOL compilers, however, have not yet or do not intend to implement relative file-processing capabilities.

Indexed-Sequential Organization

Indexed-sequential organization is designed to combine the sequential-access properties of sequential files with the rapid individual record-access capabilities of direct files. Like direct files, indexed-sequential files are limited to direct-access storage devices; they cannot be processed on tape devices. Indexed sequential is a generic name for this file-organization method; ANS COBOL names it simply **indexed**, IBM's Virtual Storage Access Method refers to it as **key-sequenced**, and it is sometimes called **keyed-sequential** or **control sequential**.

The data records of an indexed-sequential file are loaded in sequential order when the file is initially created. As the file is being built, **index records** are also established. The sequential order of the data records is used to provide sequential access to the records; the index records are used for the rapid location of individual records.

As records are added to the file, the indexes are updated. Although new data records will probably not be physically stored in sequence, the indexes provide for the proper sequential or random retrieval of records.

Locating an individual record within an indexed-sequential file is similar to finding a particular book in a library. Suppose you wanted to find the novel *East of Eden*. You would probably hunt through the card catalog index to find the *East of Eden* entry. Then you would note the catalog number PS3537.T3234 and walk down the library aisles, looking at the signs that identify the range of catalog numbers until you located the stack where PS3537 is located. After that, you would search through the volumes on the shelves until you zeroed in on the exact catalog number. Then you would pull out the book.

Just as some libraries use Library of Congress catalog numbers and some use the Dewey Decimal System, different COBOL compilers use different methods to index the records of an indexed-sequential file. With one commonly used method, the system searches a general index of key-field values to determine what disk cylinder contains records with key values that encompass the range of the record that the program is seeking. On each disk cylinder, a finer index indicates the disk track of the cylinder that should contain the record. Then the system examines the key value of each record on that track until it finds a corresponding value. At that point, the record is retrieved.

Suppose that the library has just acquired *East of Eden* and has not put it on the proper shelf yet. Since, in this case, you would not have located it at its proper place, you might continue your search by looking for it on the book cart or in the temporary area that is reserved for new and returned volumes.

This procedure for handling new and returned books is somewhat analogous to the way that new records are added to an indexed-sequential file after the file was initially created. The additions to the file are usually stored in one or more **overflow areas**. When a record cannot be located in the regular **prime area**, the overflow areas are searched.

Continuing the analogy, suppose you did not know the exact title of the book but you did know that the author was John Steinbeck. Or say you wanted to determine which of Steinbeck's books were in the library's collection. In these situations, you probably would have consulted the author catalog, which can be considered an **alternate index** (as the subject catalog also is). Some COBOL compilers allow the specification of one or more alternate indexes. Although indexing methods differ with the access methods of various operating systems, a general representation of an indexed-sequential file is shown in Figure 2A.8.

The use of indexed-sequential files has been increasing substantially within recent years together with the increase in the number of on-line systems. It is a popular file-organization method because it combines random record access and sequential-processing capabilities.

Indexed-sequential file use also has been increasing for batch systems. Factors that contributed toward retarding its earlier use were slower disk-access speeds, less efficient operating-system software, and lack of COBOL standards. (ANS COBOL did not include specifications for indexed files until the 1974 standard.)

As a "compromise" between direct and sequential organizations, indexed-sequential organization does introduce some inefficiencies. For random processing, it is slower than direct organization because the indexes must be searched. For sequential processing, it is slightly less efficient than sequential organization because the indexes must be used to obtain overflow records. Its disk-storage space utilization is degraded by the need for index and overflow areas. There is generally a trade-off between overflow-area assignment and processing speed. That is, as more disk space is assigned for overflow areas, random record-processing speed for overflow records can be improved.

In today's data-processing environment, any inefficiencies introduced by indexed-sequential organization are usually outweighed by its advantages.

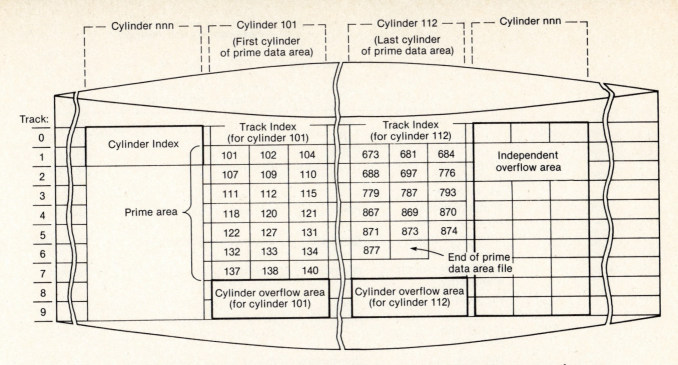

Figure 2A.8. Indexed-sequential file-organization example. Indexed-sequential file with 247 prime data-area records: recorded at 3 records per track on a disk with 10 tracks per cylinder; 1 track per cylinder used for track index, 7 tracks per cylinder used for prime data area, 2 tracks per cylinder allocated for cylinder overflow area; cylinder index assigned to a separate cylinder, 1 cylinder allocated as independent (general) overflow area.

Indexes

1 cylinder (coarse) index per file: contains 1 index entry for each cylinder in the prime area. Each entry indicates the address of the cylinder and the key of the highest record of its respective cylinder.

1 track (fine) index per prime area cylinder: 2 index entries (alternating normal and overflow) for each prime track on the cylinder. Each normal entry indicates the address of the track and the key of the highest record of its respective track.

Each overflow entry indicates the address of the next overflow record in sequence (if any) for that track and the key of the highest record assigned to that track.

Figure 2A.9 recaps the characteristics of each of the three primary file-organization methods.

Subjects Related to Data File Organization

Partitioned Organization (IBM OS Only)

IBM's Operating System (OS) provides for another method of file organization. It is termed **partitioned organization**; a file created using this method is called a **partitioned data set**, or **PDS**.

Partitioned organization is not normally used for files of application data records; its primary use is to store program libraries. A PDS contains sequentially organized subfiles called **members**. In addition, it includes a **directory** that contains each member's name and beginning address. The size of the directory is allocated when the PDS is established and contains one record for each existing or intended future member of the data set. Individual members can be modified, added to, or deleted from the PDS as required. When a member is added, the directory is updated; when a member is deleted, the directory entry

| | File-organization method | | | |
| | Sequential | Direct | | Indexed-Sequential |
		Directly addressed	Indirectly addressed	
Storage medium	Cards, Tape, Disk	Disk only	Disk only	Disk only
Sequential-processing capabilities	Excellent	Excellent	Poor	Good
Random record-retrieval speed	Poor	Excellent	Excellent-Good	Good
Storage-medium space utilization	Excellent	Excellent-Poor	Good	Good-Poor
COBOL programming complexity	Normal	Normal	Complex	Normal
Portability	High	Low	Low	Medium
Master file-processing suitability	Batch only	Batch or on-line	Batch or on-line	Batch or on-line
IBM disk-recording format	Count-data	Count-key-data or count-data	Count-key-data or count-data	Count-key-data
IBM VSAM terminology	Entry-sequenced data set (ESDS)	Relative record data set (RRDS)	Not directly supported	Key-sequenced data set (KSDS)
COBOL ORGANIZATION reserved word	SEQUENTIAL	RELATIVE	Not supported by ANS COBOL (Some compilers provide extensions to support)	INDEXED

Figure 2A.9. Recap of file-organization method characteristics.

for that member is removed. Figure 2A.10 provides a schematic representation of a PDS.

Access Mode

We have been discussing methods of file organization. **Access mode** is a related subject that refers to the way in which logical records are retrieved from or placed into a file. There are three access modes that can be specified with ANS COBOL: sequential, random, and dynamic. With **sequential access**, logical records are obtained from or placed into a file consecutively in a sequence that is determined by the physical order of the records within the file. **Random access** allows a program-specified key value to identify the logical record that is to be obtained from, deleted from, or placed into an indexed or relative file. When **dynamic access** is specified, records can be both (1) randomly obtained from or placed into an indexed or relative file, and (2) obtained from the file sequentially during the scope of the same OPEN statement.

Sequential files are restricted to sequential access. Indexed and relative files can be accessed in any of the three modes. Figure 2A.11 shows these relationships of organization method and access mode in tabular form.

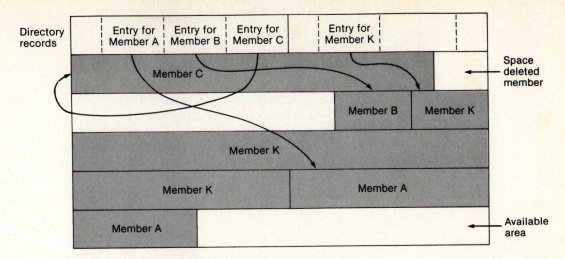

Figure 2A.10. An example of a partitioned data set.

Source: Introduction to IBM DASD and Organization Methods Student Text, IBM Publication GC20-1649. Reprinted by courtesy of IBM Corporation.

If the ORGANIZATION method is:	Then the ACCESS MODE(s) permitted are:		
	SEQUENTIAL	RANDOM	DYNAMIC
SEQUENTIAL	Yes	No	No
INDEXED	Yes	Yes	Yes
RELATIVE	Yes	Yes	Yes

Figure 2A.11. Organization/access method relationships.

Because of the interrelationship between organization method and access mode, programmers frequently use the terms erroneously. For example, you might hear a programmer say that he or she is working on a program that processes a random file. The file cannot be random; it must be either a direct file or an indexed-sequential file; it is the access mode that is random. Similarly, one often hears programmers speak of ISAM files. ISAM is an acronym for IBM's Indexed Sequential Access Method. Thus, it is not really an ISAM file; rather, it is an indexed file. ISAM is the access method that is being used to add or retrieve records from the file. The term **sequential**, however, is properly used to refer to both a file-organization method and an access mode.

Virtual Storage Access Method (VSAM) [IBM OS/VS and DOS/VS Only]

Virtual Storage Access Method (VSAM) is an access method that is supplied with IBM OS/VS and DOS/VS operating systems to provide rapid record storage and retrieval. VSAM provides three types of file organizations: entry-sequenced, key-sequenced, and relative-record. **Entry-sequenced organization** is similar to entry-sequenced sequential organization. The organizational counterpart of **key-sequenced files** is indexed-sequential. **Relative record files** can be categorized as directly addressed relative files.

It would not be uncommon to have a program that processes both a VSAM key-sequenced file and one or more standard sequential (non-VSAM) files. Today, VSAM key-sequenced file organization is almost always chosen in preference to the older Indexed Sequential Access Method (ISAM) because it provides significant processing-speed advantages. However, standard sequential (non-VSAM) organization is still commonly used for key-sequenced and entry-sequenced sequential files. Relative record files are seldom used for the reasons discussed under the section "Direct Organization."

Because key-sequenced files are commonly used with VSAM, whereas entry-sequenced and relative record files are seldom specified, it is common to hear a programmer refer to a file as a "VSAM file." What the programmer usually means is that it is a VSAM key-sequenced (indexed) file.

■ TOPIC 2-B: **File and Record Design Concepts**

Types of Files
    Master File
    Transaction File
    Summary File
    Table File
    Control File
    History File
    Journal File
    Data-Base Management Systems (DBMS)

Characteristics of Files
    Size
    Activity
    Volatility

Master Record Design Guidelines
    Logical Record Length
    Record Identification
    Field Placement
    Field Length
    Special Master File Maintenance Fields
        Date-last-activity field
        Delete-flag field

Update-Transaction Record Design Guidelines
    Update-Type Field
    Add Transaction
    Change Transaction
    Delete Transaction
    Replace Transaction

Types of Files

Files can be classified according to one or more of the following categories: master file, transaction file, summary file, table file, control file, history file, or journal file. Characteristics of each type of file are indicated in Figure 2B.1. Data-base management systems (DBMS) is a related topic.

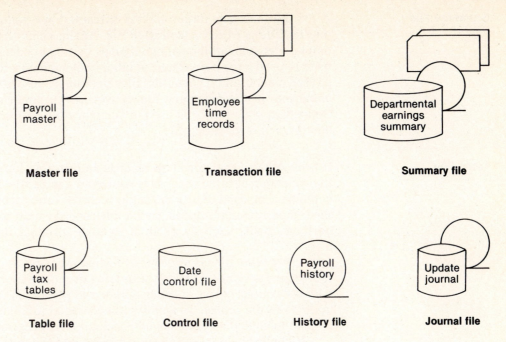

Figure 2B.1. File-type categories.

Recognize that, although file-organization method categories are explicit, file-type classifications are qualitative and used only as a "handle" to describe a file's predominant usage. Often, a given file will function in more than one classification because of multiple-processing requirements.

Master File

A **master file** contains permanent and semipermanent information about the data entities that are contained within it. It usually also contains pertinent cumulative or summary totals that reflect the current status of each entity. For example, a payroll master file contains permanent data such as each employee's Social Security number; semipermanent data like rate-of-pay, marital status, and number of exemptions claimed; plus cumulative totals such as year-to-date earnings and deductions. Design considerations for master file records will be discussed further later in this topic.

Transaction File

Master file records are not generally designed to hold all of the individual transaction data that accounts for the cumulative or summary totals contained within each master record. Collections of such activity records are usually termed **transaction files**.

In the payroll application example, a transaction file commonly contains records that reflect how many hours an employee worked, the dollar amount of sales made, or the number of pieces processed. The transaction records for employees are processed against their respective master records to generate payroll checks, labor distribution reports, and the like. At the same time, the effect of the transactions—money earned, deductions for that payroll period, and so forth—may be posted to the master file.

Another type of transaction file is one that contains records that will update a master file with add, change, and delete transactions. Update-transaction files and records are covered in greater detail at the end of this topic.

Summary File

A file that contains data which is extracted and reduced from the records of another file is called a **summary file**. Again, using the payroll application example, departmental-earnings figures can be accumulated, summarized, and used to produce a departmental labor-cost summary file. Recognize that in the payroll master and transaction files previously described, the data entity is the employee. In the summary file, however, the department is the data entity. Depending upon how it is used, a summary file may sometimes act as either a master or a transaction file.

Table File

If table entries are stored as records rather than hard-coded into a program, the collection of table records is known as a **table file**. For example, a table file could be composed of product table records—one record for each product that the company manufactures. Each table record would contain a table entry with, perhaps, fields such as product number, product description, and product price.

   Using table files is appropriate when the population of or the function of a table entry is volatile. In such situations they are superior to hard-coded tables because control clerks or other authorized personnel can process changes and updates to the tables. To modify a hard-coded table, a programmer is usually needed to code the changes and recompile the program.

   When table entries are stored in a table file, a table-load routine or subprogram is usually required for each program that uses the table. An alternative is to treat the table file as a master file and access table records as required. This approach then requires that the organization method to be used for the table file be compatible with the access method that is being used for the file that contains the search arguments. And, to process the table file, instead of a table-load routine, a table record-retrieval routine is needed.

Control File

A file that contains a limited number of records to be used for program control or accumulative run statistics is termed a **control file**. An example is a run control file that contains one or more records with fields such as the processing-cycle run number, the number of records on the run master files, the last consecutive code number that the program assigns, the date of the last run, and so forth.

   Another example would be a date control file that contains the accounting period, manufacturing workday number, day of the week, holiday status, and day of the week for each date of the previous, current, and future year. (This type of date control file could perhaps additionally be considered a table file or even a master file.)

History File

A **history file** is maintained either to facilitate reconstruction of a master file or to permit retrieval of past transaction data. Often, history files that are retained for reconstruction purposes are merely superseded master and transaction files. Those that are saved to retrieve historical data are often collecttions of previously processed transaction files.

   When disk data files are periodically copied on tape or some other medium to allow for future file recovery, the resulting history file is generally termed a **backup** or **archive** file.

Journal File

A special-purpose chronologically sequenced history or audit file for on-line systems is called a **journal file**, or just a **journal**. Journals contain the data that is needed to handle the subsequent reconstruction of events or data changes, when such actions are necessary. As an audit trail, journals usually contain "before" and "after" images of each master record updated and/or a record of each transaction that passes through the system. A journal file that contains only transaction images is alternately termed a **log file**.

Data-Base Management Systems (DBMS)

A **data base** is a collection of data that is logically organized to satisfy an organization's information and time requirements. A **data-base management system**, often referred to by its acronym **DBMS**, is a software system that is designed to manage the data base. It contains the facilities for organization, access, control, security, and recovery of the data base. Data-base management systems are discussed in Chapter E.

Characteristics of Files

There are three characteristics of files that the programmer/analyst must consider when he or she is designing file-processing systems and programs: file size, transaction activity, and volatility.

File Size

File size is determined by the number of records in combination with the length of records. The number of records, or **population** of the file is usually the more significant file-size factor. Once the programmer/analyst establishes the length of the record, then he or she must not only determine the present file size but also the anticipated growth requirements. Planning for future growth is particularly critical when the programmer/analyst designs systems that use files of direct organization.

The programmer/analyst must ensure that there is adequate file-storage hardware to accommodate the file size. This is crucial when designing on-line systems or batch systems of indexed or direct organization. When sequential files are stored on tape or removable volume disk devices, hardware requirements are impacted less by file size because, although mounting and de-mounting may be inconvenient, larger files can be processed by recording on additional tape or disk volumes.

Activity

With batch systems, **activity** refers to either the number of transaction records that are processed or the percentage of master records that are updated during a processing run. Activity for on-line systems is measured by the number of transactions that are processed during a time period, such as a minute or an hour.

One of the traditional problems with sequential files of high file size and low activity is that processing time is largely a function of the file size rather than the actual amount of updating that is to take place. For example, if there are 27 transaction records to be processed against a sequential file of 100,000 records, all 100,000 records must be read from the old master file and written to the updated master file, even though only a few of the master records are actually updated.

On the other hand, high-activity indexed and direct files for batch systems are sometimes more time-consuming to update than sequential files. This is because the processing time spent in randomly locating and retrieving records becomes more significant as activity increases.

Volatility

The frequency with which records are added to or deleted from a file is known as **volatility**. A file whose activity contains a high percentage of additions and deletions is a **volatile file**; one with a low percentage is considered to be a **static file**.

Volatility has little impact upon sequential file-processing time. High volatility can appreciably degrade the efficiency of nonsequential files, particularly for indexed-sequential organization.

The key-value distribution of volatility activity is also significant. When the key values of records that are to be added to an indexed file are clustered within a narrow range or when they result in a high percentage of synonyms for a direct file, the processing time can be lengthened significantly. An example of a common but undesirable situation for an indexed file is one in which key values are assigned to records in ascending sequential order. This results in all of the newly added transactions being clumped at the end of the file.

Master Record Design Guidelines

Records are usually designed and documented on some type of record layout worksheet. Figure 2B.2 shows examples of commonly used forms. When the programmer/analyst is designing master records, he or she must consider logical record length, record identification, field placement, and field data representation (USAGE).

Logical Record Length

The length of punched-card records is determined by the punched-card equipment and media; it is either 80 or 96 characters of data per card. For programming ease, the logical record length is usually limited to the physical size of the card. When an application requires a longer logical record length, a group of two or more cards is used to contain the logical record.

Magnetic tape, because it is a continuous medium, can accommodate records of practically any length. Although magnetic disk record length may be limited to the character capacity of the recording track or sector, such lengths are usually long enough to impose little restriction upon the size of the logical record.

The length of a logical record is generally determined by the number and length of the fields that it is to contain. To that aggregate length, the programmer/analyst should allocate an expansion area (that is, an unassigned FILLER area) to provide for the addition of new fields or an increase in the length of existing fields. If an expansion area is not provided, every field addition or length increase will lengthen the logical record itself. Modification of the logical record size should be avoided or at least minimized. This is because the file description (FD) and record-description entries of a COBOL program must be altered whenever the record length changes—even if the program does not use the field that is being added or changed.

Provision of an expansion area helps to minimize program maintenance. When an expansion area exists, only those programs that use the new or changed field need be immediately modified and recompiled upon implementation of a record change.

The amount of space that is allocated for an expansion area should be based upon an evaluation of how long the system will be used together with the plans for future development and enhancement of the system. Available tape- or disk-storage space may also be a factor in the choice. Admittedly, guesses about future system requirements are difficult to quantify. As a rule of thumb, an expansion area from 10 to 40% of allocated record length is usually appropriate. (A higher percentage of expansion area must be assigned to shorter records to ensure that the area can be used effectively.)

The placement of expansion area is normally at the trailing end of the record. That is, currently required fields are defined adjacent to one another and the expansion area is the unused portion at the end of the record. On the other hand, if certain fields can be expected to increase in length, the expansion area should be placed alongside those fields. For example, if a customer-

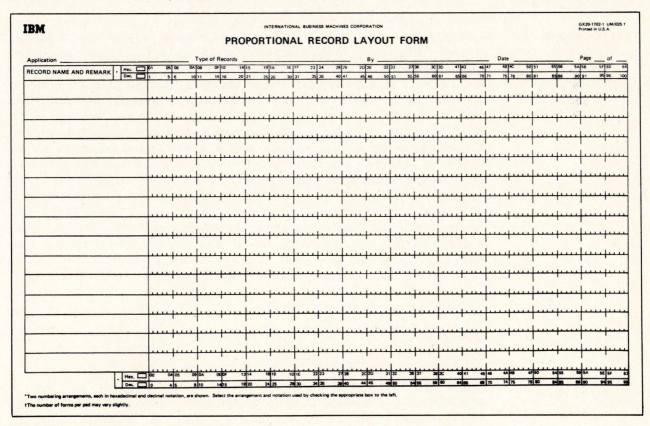

Figure 2B.2. Record layout worksheet forms.

number field is currently 4 digits in length but will require expansion to 5 digits, it would be wise to allow 1 or more digits of expansion area to the immediate left of the customer-number field. Or, if a customer-name field is currently 20 characters in length, and users feel that a 25-character field would be less restrictive, then an expansion area of 5 characters or more should be provided to the right of the customer-name field. Thus, to minimize data-field realignment at the time of expansion, adjacent expansion areas should be specified to the left of numeric fields and to the right of alphanumeric fields.

Record Identification

Just as form numbers are usually assigned to paper documents, a record code should always be assigned to the data-processing records. By providing a record code, each processing program can then ensure that it is receiving the correct type of input records. A payroll program, for example, certainly should not be reading customer accounts-receivable master records.

When a record-code field is assigned to all logical records, then each different record type can be assigned a unique number. As an example, payroll name-and-address records can be assigned record code 21, payroll transaction records can be coded 25, accounts-payable vendor master records could be code 30, and so forth.

The length of the record-code field should be two, three, or four characters, depending upon the number of record types within the data-processing installation. A small organization may find a two-position code adequate; a large corporation might allocate four places. Numeric record codes are usually easier to handle, but alphanumeric record-coding systems are often used.

It is a good practice to place the record-code field in the same relative location for all record types. The best place for the record-code field is at the beginning of each record.

Field Placement

Usually it does not matter where fields are placed in a logical record; haphazard arrangement may present no processing difficulties. But there are a couple of field-placement considerations that should be discussed.

For card records that must be keypunched, field locations are normally specified in the order by which they are read from a source document. Such field placement facilitates the keypunching process. However, with the declining use of punched cards as a data-entry medium, source document location of the data becomes less of a concern. Newer electronic data-recording devices (terminals and key-to-disk devices, for instance) can place the fields at locations other than in the sequence that is keyed.

Another field-placement consideration relates to record-sorting requirements. Fields that determine the record sequence should be located in the same relative positions for all record types that will be sorted together. Figure 2B.3 illustrates this concept. Unfortunately, at the time that a record is being designed, it is sometimes not possible to define or foretell all of the future sorting requirements. Thus, alternative sorting provisions must sometimes be made.

Probably the best general recommendation for the placement of fields within a logical record, as depicted in Figure 2B.4, is the following:

1. Place the record-code field first.
2. Follow the record code by the key fields for that record.
3. Continue with indicative fields containing permanent or semipermanent data.
4. Proceed with indicative fields containing temporary data.
5. Conclude the record with an expansion area.

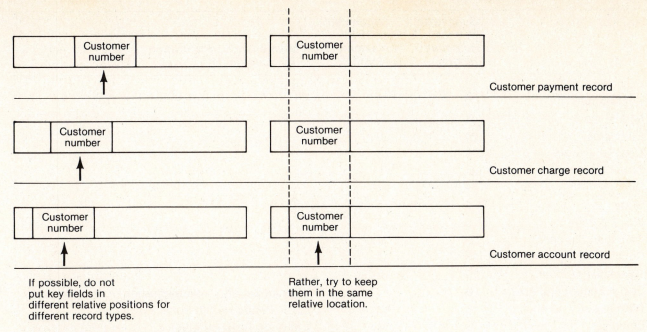

If possible, do not put key fields in different relative positions for different record types.

Rather, try to keep them in the same relative location.

Figure 2B.3. Field-placement considerations for sort-key fields.

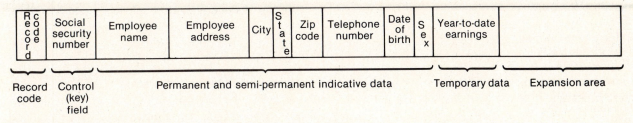

Record code | Control (key) field | Permanent and semi-permanent indicative data | Temporary data | Expansion area

Figure 2B.4. Example of field placement in a logical record.

Field Length

The length of a field is determined by application requirements and may be influenced by computer hardware data-representation considerations. Figure 2B.5 provides character-length guidelines for fields commonly used in commercial data-processing applications.

Special Master File Maintenance Fields

There are two fields that are either required or appropriate for master records involved in the process of master file maintenance: date-last-activity and delete-flag.

Date-last-activity field

This field can be optionally specified in a master record to store the date that the record was last changed by the master file maintenance program. The date of last activity can be an aid to user application decisions. For example, with a customer charge account application, the date-last-activity field can help to identify inactive accounts that should perhaps be treated with a promotional campaign to augment sales revenue for an organization.

Field	Suggested or usual minimum length	Suggested or usual maximum length	Maintenance organization (for code fields)
Last name	12	25	
First name	9	13	
Middle name	1	13	
Full name	24	30	
Company name	24	48	
Street address	24	48	
City	13	24	
State	2	14	
U.S. Zip code	5	10	
Canadian Zip code	6	6	
Country	18	40	
Telephone number	10	12	
Social Security number	9	11	Social Security Administration
Birth registry number	11	13	U.S. Public Health Service
Employer identification no.	9	10	Internal Revenue Service
D-U-N-S® number	8	9	Dun & Bradstreet, Inc.
Standard industrial classification (SIC) code	4		Department of Commerce Office of Federal Statistical Policy and Standards
Uniform commercial chart of accounts (UCCOA) code	4		
Committee on uniform security identification procedures (CUSIP) code	9	11	Standard & Poors Corporation
Universal product code (UPS)	10	11	Uniform Product Code Council, Inc.
Universal industry numbering code	9		National Assn. of Electrical Distributors
Universal numeric code for distilled spirits	21	27	Distilled Spirits Institute
Standard transportation commodity code (STCC)	7		Association of American Railroads
National health related items code (NHRIC)	10		
National drug code (NDC)	10		
RVS code	4		
International disease code (IDC)	5		
Library of congress card catalog number	8		Library of Congress
International standard book number (ISBN)	10	13	International ISBN Agency R. R. Bowker Company

Figure 2B.5. Field-length guidelines.

When specifying a date-last-activity field, it is most appropriate to specify it in **yymmdd** (**y** = year digit; **m** = month digit; **d** = day digit) format. Formatting the date with the year as the most significant digits makes it easier to use the date in any program-required comparisons for an earlier or later date. The only disadvantage to the **yymmdd** format is that most people (at least in the United States) are more accustomed to the **mmddyy** format. However, date-last-activity is a field that would usually be referenced more frequently by programs than people. Where it might be necessary to display the field on a report or video-display terminal screen, it could be program-converted to **mmddyy** format.

In addition to a date-last-activity field, a date-record-established field is sometimes included to store the date when the record is initially placed on the master file. Further, with on-line systems, a time-of-day field is frequently appended to date fields.

Delete-flag field

Some operating-system access methods do not provide for the physical deletion of records from a master file (IBM's ISAM is an example). Similarly, to guard against loss of data from erroneous deletions, some system designers are reluctant to allow users to actually delete records from a file; a fail-safe method to retain the data for a period of time is thus designed into the system.

Both of these situations call for the specification of a delete-flag field within the master file record. The delete-flag field is usually one character in length and is specified at the beginning of the master file record. When a record is active, the delete-flag normally contains SPACE or LOW-VALUE; at the time of logical deletion, it is usually set to HIGH-VALUE or to a "D" (to indicate deletion).

Delete-flag fields are commonly used with indexed-sequential and directly organized master files. They are not specified for sequential master file-maintenance programs because (1) sequential file-maintenance logic always allows actual physical deletion, and (2) sequential file records are always updated in a batch mode and thus records can be reconstructed by reprocessing prior generations of transaction and master files.

Update-Transaction Record Design Guidelines

There are three typical transaction updates: add, change, and delete. Occasionally a transaction type to replace a record is also specified. First, the update-type field will be covered and then each update type of transaction will be discussed.

Update-Type Field

When an update transaction is to be processed by a master file-maintenance program, its function is to either (1) add a record to the master file, (2) change the corresponding master file record, or (3) identify a master file record to be deleted. A field must be provided in the transaction record to identify the type of processing that is to take place. An **update-code** field is typically specified as a 1-character field. The values of "A," "C," and "D" are commonly used to denote **a**dd, **c**hange, and **d**elete, respectively. An alternate technique is to use numeric codes, such as "1," "2," and "3," to indicate the update code.

Add Transaction

An **add transaction** is used to establish a record on the master file. An add transaction record should contain the following fields:

1. record-code field
2. update-code field

3. key field

4. all fields required at the time the record is initially added to the master file

Before the record is added to the master file, the master file maintenance program should check the master file to ensure that a record with an identical key is not already in the master file. If a record with the same key is already on file, an error condition exists.

Change Transaction

A **change transaction** causes one or more master record fields to be changed in accordance with the transaction record values. A change transaction should contain, as a minimum, the following fields:

1. record-code field

2. update-code field

3. key field

4. those indicative field values that are to be changed

Before a change transaction can be applied to the master file, the master file maintenance program must locate the corresponding master record that is to be changed. If there is no master record with a corresponding key field within the master file, an error condition exists.

Delete Transaction

A **delete transaction** triggers the deletion of the corresponding master record from the master file. A delete transaction should contain, as a minimum, the following fields:

1. record-code field

2. update-code field

3. key field

Before a delete transaction can be applied to the master file, the master file maintenance program must locate the corresponding master record that is to be deleted. If there is no master record with a corresponding key field within the master file, an error condition exists.

Replace Transaction

A **replace transaction** is, in effect, a combination delete transaction of an existing master record and an add transaction of new data. Thus in situations in which replace transaction capability is provided, the replace transaction should contain the same type of fields as the add transaction.

Before a replace transaction can be applied to the master file, the master file maintenance program must locate the corresponding master record that is to be replaced. If there is no master record with a corresponding key field within the master file, an error condition exists.

■ TOPIC 2-C: **Master File Maintenance Program Design**

Transaction Data Validation

Interfile Errors
    Add Transaction with Master Record Already on File
    Change Transaction without Matching Master Record
    Delete Transaction without Matching Master Record

Audit/Error Lists
    Master Record Displays
    Consolidated Data-Validation/Update-Error Lists

Error Record Handling

Transaction File Sequence

Multiple Transactions for the Same Master Record
    Update-Type Sequence
    Date Sequence
    Date and Time Sequence

Change-Transaction Considerations
    Modifiable Fields
    Change-Record Formatting
    Changing a Field to Null Values

Change- and Delete-Transaction Correspondence Checking

When designing a master file maintenance program, certain considerations apply regardless of the file-organization method of the master file. These items will be covered in this topic.

Transaction Data Validation

Before actually applying a transaction record to the master file, the fields of the record should be validated to help assure the integrity of the data within the master file. Such data validation can be done either as a separate **front-end edit** or within the master file maintenance program (prior to the update function). Figure 2C.1 provides system flowcharts to illustrate these two approaches.

The advantage to the front-end edit approach is that both programs—data validation and master file maintenance—have a more functionally cohesive task, thus simplifying program design and future program-maintenance efforts.

On the other hand, when the data-validation function is combined into the master file maintenance program, input-output processing requirements are reduced (the need for the front-end edit program to perform a separate read and write of each record is eliminated). Also, the master file record is available for key presence validations and relationship tests. (Of course, although additional coding will be required, provisions for reference to the master file can be coded into a separate data-validation program, too.)

Interfile Errors

In addition to transaction record errors concerning the data values within fields, certain interfile errors can occur. These were briefly mentioned in Topic 2-B and are indicated in Figure 2C.2, in which a hypothetical hardware store product master file is being updated. Each interfile error type will be discussed.

Add Transaction with Master Record Already on File

As shown at point A in Figure 2C.2, the 103-HAMMER transaction record to add a hammer product record to the master file *can* be processed because the key of the hammer record (103) does not exist on the master file. Notice, however, that the 110-PLIERS, NEEDLENOSE transaction record identified at point B in the figure *cannot* be added because its key (110) already exists on the master file. That is, product code 110 is used on the master file for PLIERS, VISE GRIP, so a transaction record requesting that a product code of 110 be added to the file should *not* be processed. If it were, there would be two records on the master file with the same key value. If duplicate records were allowed to exist, erroneous processing would occur for the records with identical product-code key values.

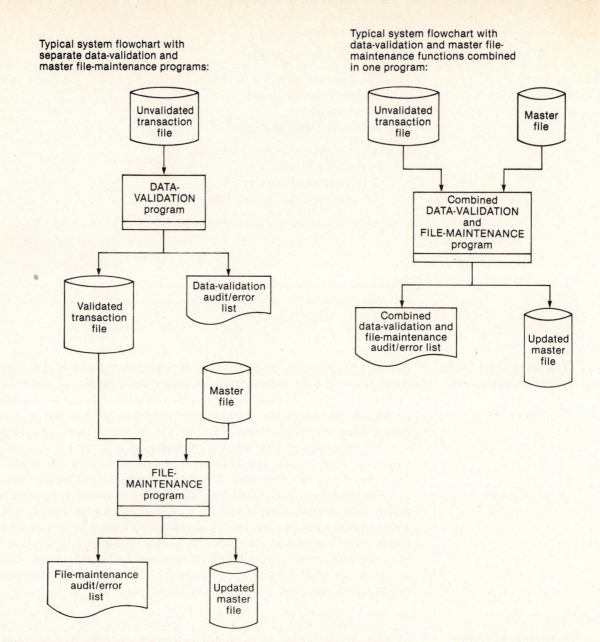

Typical system flowchart with
separate data-validation and
master file-maintenance programs:

Unvalidated
transaction
file

DATA-
VALIDATION
program

Validated
transaction
file

Data-validation
audit/error
list

Master
file

FILE-
MAINTENANCE
program

File-maintenance
audit/error
list

Updated
master
file

Typical system flowchart with
data-validation and master file-
maintenance functions combined
in one program:

Unvalidated
transaction
file

Master
file

Combined
DATA-VALIDATION
and
FILE-MAINTENANCE
program

Combined
data-validation and
file-maintenance
audit/error list

Updated
master
file

Figure 2C.1. The data-validation function within master file maintenance systems.

Change Transaction without Matching Master Record

A valid change transaction is shown at point C in Figure 2C.2. The transaction record indicates that the master file record with a key value of 107 should have its description changed. Notice that the 107 master record currently contains a description of "SCREWDRIVER." After the change transaction has been processed, the master record product-description field will contain "SCREW-DRIVER, PHILLIPS."

The change transaction at point D in the figure cannot be processed, however. The transaction record calls for the master record with a product code of 115 to have its description changed to "HAMMER, BALL PEEN." Because a master record with a key value of 115 is not on file, the change transaction cannot, of course, be processed.

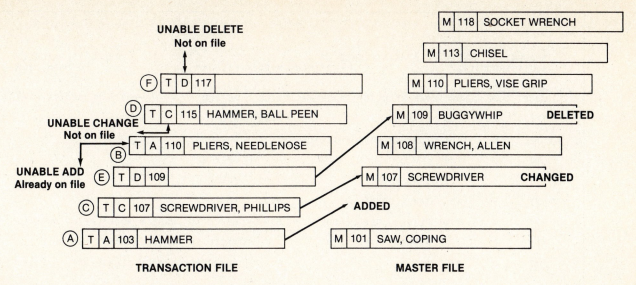

UNABLE DELETE
Not on file

UNABLE CHANGE
Not on file

UNABLE ADD
Already on file

M	118	SOCKET WRENCH	
M	113	CHISEL	
M	110	PLIERS, VISE GRIP	
M	109	BUGGYWHIP	**DELETED**
M	108	WRENCH, ALLEN	
M	107	SCREWDRIVER	**CHANGED**
M	101	SAW, COPING	

ADDED

TRANSACTION FILE   MASTER FILE

Figure 2C.2. File maintenance updating with interfile errors.

Delete Transaction without Matching Master Record

The delete transaction shown at point E in Figure 2C.2 will cause the 109-BUGGYWHIP master record to be deleted from the master file.

The delete transaction at point F, however, cannot be processed. It is requesting that the master record with a product code of 117 be deleted. Observe that a master record with a key value of 117 does not exist; hence the delete transaction cannot be processed and must be identified as an error condition.

Audit/Error Lists

Most batch file-maintenance programs produce an **audit list** and an **error list**. Often, the two lists are printed as a combined **audit/error list**. With on-line programs, the journal file usually serves the function of an audit list, whereas the error messages are typically displayed on the video-display terminal screen that originated the transaction.

An audit list prints out the contents of each record input to the system and is usually retained merely for control purposes. The audit list provides an accounting trail should it be necessary to determine when, where, or in what form the data originated. The error list, on the other hand, is an action document that reports what error discrepancy conditions have arisen. Error reports require action to correct or confirm identified discrepancies, whereas audit lists need only be retained for reference over a specified period of time. A combined audit/error list serves both functions. Voluminous audit lists are frequently stored on microfiche or some other nonprint storage medium to conserve printing time and costs.

As shown in Figure 2C.3, an audit/error list for a master file maintenance program is usually designed so that the fields of the input transaction records are displayed on the left-hand side of the report; this may be referred to as the **record image** area. To the right of the record image area, the **update action** and any applicable **error messages** for that transaction are printed. The update actions reflect the permissible update actions provided (e.g., ADDED, CHANGED, DELETED, REPLACED, and so on) and REJECTED, NOT PROCESSED, or a similar message.

Instead of error messages, error codes are sometimes printed. Identification of errors by meaningful error messages is obviously preferable to the use of more cryptic error codes. Whenever codes are used, the discrepancy clerk must

```
SEQUENTIAL MASTER FILE MAINTENANCE                                     RUN DATE MM/DD/YY
AUDIT/ERROR LIST                        ** PART MASTER FILE **              PAGE ZZZ9

RCD   UPDATE   PART                               UPDATE
CODE  CODE     NBR.   --PART DESCRIPTION---  PRICE ACTION     ------ERROR MESSAGE-------

TT      A      103    HAMMER                  7.95 ADDED

TT      C      107    SCREWDRIVER, PHILLIPS        CHANGED

TT      D      109                                 DELETED

TT      A      132    SAW, WOOD              19.95 ADDED

TT      A      135    SAW, COPING             8.95 ADDED

TT      A      110    PLIERS, NEEDLENOSE      5.98 REJECTED  UNABLE ADD-ALREADY ON FILE

TT      C      115    HAMMER, BALL PEEN            REJECTED  UNABLE CHANGE-NOT ON FILE

TT      D      117                                 REJECTED  UNABLE DELETE-NOT ON FILE


     TRANSACTIONS READ        8
        ADDS                  4
           PROCESSED          3
           REJECTED           1
        CHANGES               2
           PROCESSED          1
           REJECTED           1
        DELETES               2
           PROCESSED          1
           REJECTED           1
        ERROR UPDATE CODES    0

     MASTERS READ           578
     MASTER CHANGES           1
     MASTERS WRITTEN        580
```

Figure 2C.3. Typical master file maintenance audit/error list.

refer to a legend to comprehend the meaning. Sometimes, however, space limitations in a report may call for the use of error codes.

Master Record Displays

In addition to printing each transaction record on the audit/error list, the contents of each master record that is being changed or deleted can be displayed. This is helpful as an audit trail and to those personnel who must work with the report.

Consolidated Data-Validation/Update-Error Lists

One major disadvantage in designing a master file maintenance system with separate data validation and update programs is that two separate error lists will result—one for data-validation errors and one for interfile errors. Dual error lists can be awkward and confusing for clerical personnel to maintain and process.

This problem can be overcome by consolidating the audit/error lists from the two program steps. Probably the best way to do this is *not* to print an audit/error list during the data-validation program. Instead, each erroneous transaction can be flagged with an error code and/or message and then passed to the file-maintenance program together with the valid records. When the file-maintenance program encounters a transaction record with a flagged error, it merely writes the record and error message to the audit/error list and does not attempt to apply the erroneous transaction to the master file.

Error-rejection
master file maintenance
processing:

Error-abeyance
master file maintenance
processing:

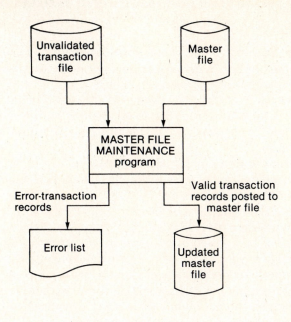

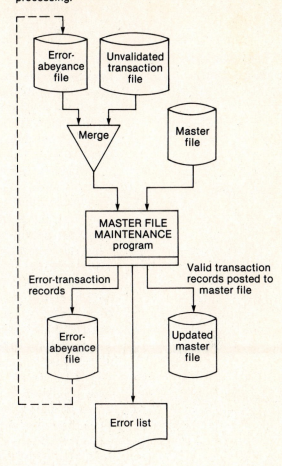

Figure 2C.4. Error record-handling approaches for file-maintenance programs.

Another approach is to write the data-validation and file-maintenance program errors to separate files and then to merge them to print an error or audit/ error list. The only disadvantage of this method is that it requires one more separate program step to merge and print the errors.

Error Record Handling

There are two general ways to handle erroneous transaction records. We can term these methods **error rejection** and **error abeyance**. Their effect is depicted in Figure 2C.4.

The error-rejection approach is commonly used in smaller, simpler, less critical system applications. With it, the "good" transaction records are appropriately processed against the master file and the erroneous transactions are rejected by simply identifying each one on an error list. The erroneous transaction records must, of course, be corrected and then reentered into the system in a later run.

With the error-abeyance method, erroneous transactions are written to an **abeyance, or suspense, file** that keeps track of all outstanding erroneous transaction records. Then when an error is corrected, the original error record is removed from the abeyance file. The obvious advantage of the error-abeyance approach is that error records are retained on a file to ensure that each discrepancy is resolved and that the correction is reentered into the system. However, it requires more programming effort than the error-rejection method.

Transaction File Sequence

For sequentially organized master files, the transaction file must be sorted into the same sequence as the master file. With master files of indexed-sequential or direct organization, sorting of the transaction file is optional.

With on-line programs, each transaction record is processed individually. Thus, although there are transaction records to be applied to the indexed-sequential or direct file, there is not really what could be considered a transaction file.

When a batch program updates indexed-sequential or direct files, the transaction file is often sorted—even though not required—into the sequence of the master file. This is done for three reasons.

First, the processing of the maintenance program can be made more efficient, especially for indexed-sequential master files. Suppose there are two transaction change records to be applied to the same master record. When the transaction records are not in sequence, two separate retrieval and two corresponding update input-output (I-O) operations must be performed to accomplish the two changes. However, as depicted in Figure 2C.5, if the transactions have been sorted into key sequence, the program logic could accommodate two or more changes with just one retrieval and one output operation.

Before an individual record can be retrieved from an indexed-sequential file, index lookups and perhaps overflow-area searches must be made. Moreover, when certain record key values are added to the file, the indexes must be updated. Thus the processing of add transactions can be relatively time-consuming. Appropriate sequencing of the transaction file can aid in minimizing the number of I-O operations and thus decrease processing time.

As additions are made to an indexed file, the overflow areas become more populated with records. When the overflow areas get crowded, processing efficiency is further degraded. To clear out the overflow areas, indexed files are periodically processed through a **reorganization** run that combines the newly added records in the overflow areas into their proper sequence in the prime data area. Sometimes this reorganization step is integrated into the maintenance run by means of a sequential update—instead of random—of the indexed-sequential file. A sequentially accessed indexed-sequential file maintenance program requires a sequenced-transaction file.

A second reason for sequencing the transaction file is that the date and time a transaction occurs is usually significant to the file's status. Suppose a year-to-date balance field of a general ledger master record is in error. Let us say that the clerk prepares a change-transaction record on October 7 to reflect what he or she believes the correct balance to be. Then, on October 9, the clerk discovers that the value entered on the seventh is not correct either, so the clerk enters a second corrected balance on October 9. If the transaction records are not sorted, it would be possible for the correction of the ninth to be applied to the master record before the correction of the seventh, thereby resulting in erroneous data. On the other hand, if the transaction file were sorted not only into master file key sequence but also into transaction date order, then the proper arrangement of transaction records for application to the master file could be assured.

Third, when the transaction file is sequenced, the audit/error list will be sequenced. Users find ordered lists much more convenient to work with than lists with random entries.

Part A: Unsequenced-transaction file

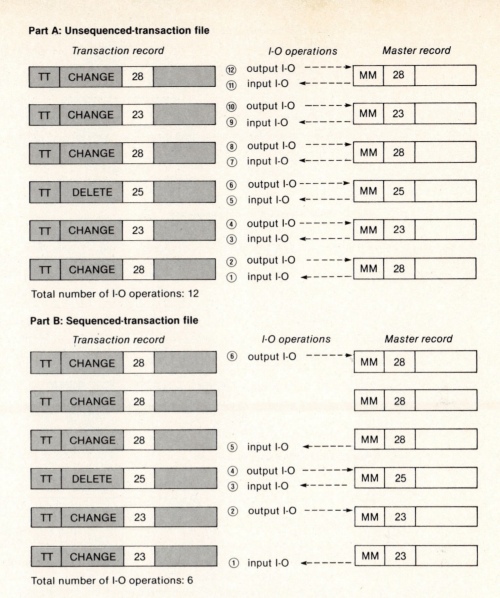

Total number of I-O operations: 12

Part B: Sequenced-transaction file

Total number of I-O operations: 6

Figure 2C.5. Effect of transaction file sequence upon I-O operations for randomly accessed master file maintenance.

Multiple Transactions for the Same Master Record

A batch master file maintenance program should always be designed to allow any number and combination of transaction records to be processed against one master record. When such processing is provided for a sorted transaction file, there are three keys by which multiple transactions for the same master record are sequenced: update type, date, and date plus time. These sequence alternatives are contrasted in Figure 2C.6.

Update-Type Sequence

The order of processing multiple-update transactions for a single master record is usually based upon the type of update. One of the three following update-type sequences is usually specified:

1. add (first), changes (next), delete (last)
2. delete (first), add (next), changes (last)
3. delete (first), changes (next), add (last)

Part A: Update-type sequence alternatives

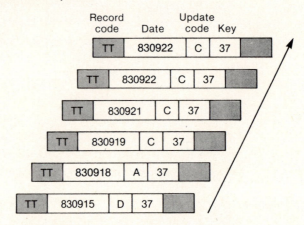

Adds first
changes next
deletes last

Deletes first
adds next
changes last

Deletes first
changes next
adds last

Part B: Update-type within date sequence

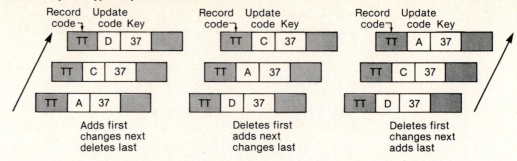

Part C: Time within date sequence

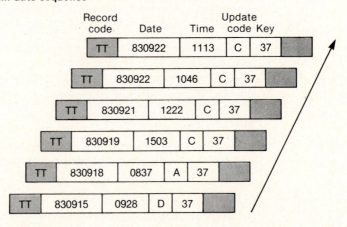

Figure 2C.6. Sequence alternatives for multiple transactions to be applied to the same master record.

The first sequence itemized above is frequently specified just because of the order of the alphabet. That is, add transactions are usually coded with an update code of "A," change transactions as "C," and delete transactions as "D." Therefore, when the update-code field is sorted in ascending sequence, any transactions for the same key value will fall into **a**dd-**c**hange-**d**elete order. The add transactions will be positioned first, change transactions next, and delete transactions last.

Actually, however, the second sequence listed above is better for most application situations, especially when master record key values are reused. For example, consider a telephone subscriber application. After one telephone subscriber disconnects his or her telephone, the number is eligible for reassignment to a new subscriber. Thus if one subscriber disconnects and a new subscriber is assigned to that same number within the same program-processing batch period, the "deletes-first" update-type sequence will properly process both transactions. When add transactions are processed first, the new subscriber would first be rejected (with an error message of "UNABLE TO ADD—MASTER RECORD ALREADY ON FILE") and then the old subscriber would be deleted. Such processing would necessitate the rejected add transaction to be reentered into the next processing batch.

In the second update-type sequence that is listed above, delete transactions can be coded as "1," add transactions as "2," and change transactions as "3." When the update-code field is sorted into ascending sequence, the delete transactions for a given key will be first, followed by the add transactions, and then finally by the change transactions.

The third sequence shown above is a minor variation of the second. It is often used because it can be conveniently implemented by sorting update-code values of "A," "C," and "D" in descending sequence.

Date Sequence

By sorting not only by update type but also by date, further update accuracy (as discussed earlier) can be achieved for multiple-change records. Date-update sequence requires that a transaction date field be included in the transaction record design and recorded when an update record is prepared.

Date and Time Sequence

Even further accuracy can be achieved by recording the time in addition to the date and sorting on both fields. Such **time-stamping** of transaction records is rarely specified for batch programs but is commonly done with on-line applications.

Change-Transaction Considerations

Three aspects of change transactions must be incorporated into master file maintenance program design: determination of modifiable fields, change-field formatting, and technique for changing fields to null values. Each of these subjects will be discussed.

Modifiable Fields

The programmer/analyst must determine just what fields are candidates for modification with changed values. Usually, all fields, except the following, should be candidates for modification:

1. the master record-code field
2. the key fields
3. special fields, such as delete-flag and date-last activity

It is obvious that the master record-code field should not be changed. Key fields cannot be modified by change transactions because, regardless of file-organization method, such changes would interfere with the logical integrity of the file. Through error or key-field value reassignments, however, it is sometimes necessary to reassign key values to master record data entities. Suppose that a record for part number AC2189 were incorrectly added to a master file with its key value transposed as AC2819. To rectify the error, it would be necessary to delete the AC2819 record and to add a corrected record with part number AC2189. Special fields, such as delete-flag and date-last-activity, that are filled by program control rather than data input should generally be changed by program operations rather than data input.

Positional field change record example:

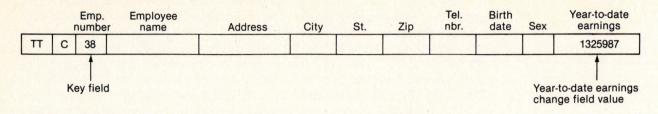

Keyword field change record example:

Field	Keyword
Employee name	EN
Address	AD
City	CI
State	ST
ZIP code	ZC
Telephone number	TN
Birth date	BD
Sex	SX
Year-to-date earnings	YE

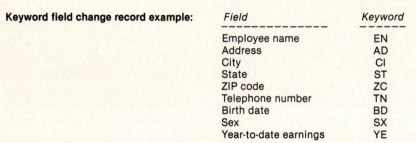

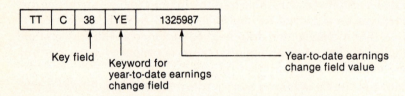

Figure 2C.7. Change-transaction record format methods.

Change-Record Formatting

There are two ways to format the fields of a change-transaction record: by position or by keyword. These change-transaction format methods are contrasted in Figure 2C.7. When a change transaction is formatted by **position**, the changed-field values are simply placed in a particular assigned location in the change-transaction record. The relative location for each field of the change-transaction record is usually, though not necessarily, the same as it is for the add-transaction record. With the **keyword** method, each modifiable field is assigned a code word or number and, to change a particular field, the keyword is entered and followed by the changed value.

Formatting by position results in less programming complexity; thus it is the predominant approach. However, the keyword method is appropriate for use when one or more of the following situations exist:

1. The master record contains so many fields or is of sufficient length that fixed-field positioning is either tedious or inaccurate.
2. The master record is formed from a composite of various transaction records.
3. The transaction records are variable-length records or contain variable-length fields.
4. The master records are variable-length records.

In certain instances, a change-transaction record will be designed with fixed-field positions for certain "core" fixed-length fields and keyword formatting for infrequently changed or variable-length fields.

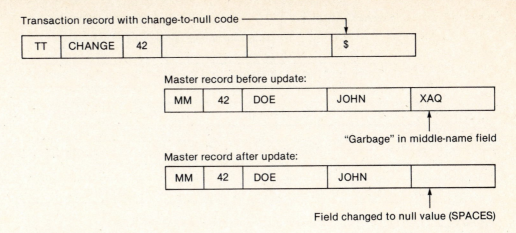

Transaction record with change-to-null code

TT	CHANGE	42			$

Master record before update:

MM	42	DOE	JOHN	XAQ

"Garbage" in middle-name field

Master record after update:

MM	42	DOE	JOHN	

Field changed to null value (SPACES)

Figure 2C.8. Change-to-null code example.

Changing a Field to Null Values

Sometimes it is necessary to change an existing field to a null value. A **null value** for an alphanumeric field is blank spaces; for a numeric field, it is zeros. The programmer/analyst must devise a method to deal with the situation in which a master record field that already contains data values must be changed to a null value.

Such a change will be required whenever one of two circumstances arises. One occurs when a value that was once present in the record no longer applies and there is no replacement value. Suppose that a customer record contains a street-address field and a separate apartment-number field. And say that a customer moves from Apartment #5 at 503 Park Drive to a single-family home at 123 Easy Street. This will require that the street-address field be changed from 503 Park Drive to 123 Easy Street and that the apartment-number field be changed from #5 to blank spaces. Another circumstance is when an optional field that should contain nothing has "junk" in it.

For example, as shown in Figure 2C.8, erroneous "garbage" has inadvertently been introduced into the middle-name field of the master record. Let us say that John Doe does not have a middle name, so we must prepare a change transaction (with fixed-field formatting) to transform the middle-name field of the master record to blank spaces. A problem arises, however, because a value of blank spaces in a change transaction implies that no change is to be made to the corresponding master record field.

Thus a way to trigger the change of a field to blank spaces must be provided. A common approach is to choose a character value that would not normally be encountered as a legitimate field value and use that value as a code to indicate that the field should be changed to the null value. As shown in the master record after the update in Figure 2C.8, a dollar sign ($) has been chosen as the **change-to-null code**. When the program detects a dollar sign in the first position of any field of a change transaction, the logic must provide for changing the corresponding master record field to the null value (spaces or zeros)— rather than to the value of the change-transaction field.

An alphanumeric field requires a change-to-null code to handle the change of a field to a null value; a numeric field may or may not. If numeric-change fields of the transaction record carry blank spaces when no change for that field is intended, a change-to-null code is not required. This is because the zeros will be recognized as an actual change value and thus trigger the change.

If, on the other hand, numeric-change fields of the transaction record carry zeros when no change is intended, a change-to-null code *will* be required.

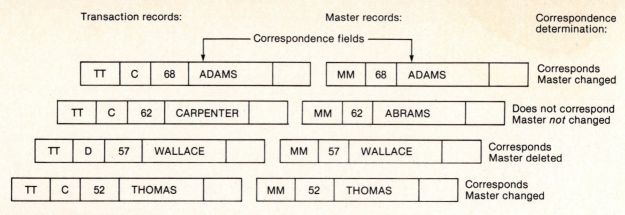

Transaction records: Master records: Correspondence
                                                   determination:

┌─── Correspondence fields ───┐

| TT | C | 68 | ADAMS | | MM | 68 | ADAMS | | Corresponds
Master changed |

| TT | C | 62 | CARPENTER | | MM | 62 | ABRAMS | | Does not correspond
Master *not* changed |

| TT | D | 57 | WALLACE | | MM | 57 | WALLACE | | Corresponds
Master deleted |

| TT | C | 52 | THOMAS | | MM | 52 | THOMAS | | Corresponds
Master changed |

Figure 2C.9. Change- and delete-transaction correspondence checking.

[Although usually a poorer design approach, zeros are sometimes used to indicate that no change is required when (1) the transaction record fields are specified with COMP or COMP-3 usage to minimize transaction record-length requirements and/or (2) for programming simplicity, spaces in numeric fields are always converted to zeros.] Because it is not consistent to place an alphanumeric change-to-null code such as a dollar sign in a numeric field, an unreasonable numeric value or sign configuration is sometimes used as the change-to-null code. Filling the field with the digit 9 is an example of an unreasonable numeric value that is sometimes used; a sign configuration of hexadecimal E is an example of an unreasonable EBCDIC sign configuration. Both of these are poor design approaches, however. All 9-digits could be an actual valid value; the use of a hexadecimal E contributes to hardware dependencies and its resulting maintenance difficulties.

Recognize that not all master record fields that can be changed are candidates for a change to null values. Required fields should not be changed to null values, whereas optional fields should allow such a change.

When selecting a change-to-null code, the programmer/analyst should ensure that it will never exist as an actual value. Further, each change field should be completely validated in the data-validation routine to guard against errors that might occur when recording or positioning the change-to-null code in the transaction record.

Change- and Delete-Transaction Correspondence Checking

Users, clerical personnel, and data-entry operators sometimes erroneously transcribe or transpose key-field values. When this happens with change or delete transactions, the wrong master record will be changed or deleted unless a safeguard is provided. For example, the Social Security Administration would incorrectly post up to 10% of its transaction records if it used the Social Security number key value alone. To counter this problem, a last-name field is included and its value is entered in the transaction record, as shown in Figure 2C.9. Then before posting data to a master record, the last-name field of the transaction record is matched against the last-name field of the master record before posting data to an account. Therefore, even though the key fields match, if the correspondence fields do not, the transaction record is rejected.

Such provision of a correspondence-checking field in each change- and delete-transaction record is a good practice. The only disadvantage is that it slightly increases data-entry requirements. An alternate approach is to use a **check digit** within a **self-checking number**.

Summary

Topic 2-A   File-Organization Concepts

There are three commonly used methods of data file organization: sequential, direct, and indexed-sequential.

Sequential organization—sometimes referred to as **physical sequential** or **standard sequential**—is the most straightforward approach. When records are arranged sequentially in accordance with the value of one or more **key fields**, it is a **key-sequenced** sequential file. If records are arranged chronologically or haphazardly, it can be considered to be an **entry-sequenced** sequential file. Sequential organization permits (1) effective utilization of disk and tape storage and (2) program and data portability. However, sequential access does not permit rapid retrieval of individual records. Sequential organization is thus limited to batch processing.

Direct organization permits rapid access to individual records within a file. To access a record directly, the **record address** or **relative record number** must be determined. Direct files can be either **directly addressed** or **indirectly addressed**. Directly addressed files require a record slot for each possible key value. Indirectly addressed files utilize a **randomizing** (or **hashing**) **algorithm** to convert each key value to a record-slot location. Randomizing algorithms inevitably produce **synonyms**, two records whose different key values convert to the same record location. A commonly used randomizing technique is the **division/remainder method**. The ANS COBOL method for handling direct files is by **relative record number** within a **relative file**. Although direct organization provides the fastest random-access capabilities, its use is limited and declining for commercial applications because (1) there are only a limited number of situations that are appropriate for directly addressed files, (2) programming complexities are involved with the randomizing and synonym handling tasks of indirectly addressed files, (3) increased disk hardware speeds and access software efficiency reduce direct organization's comparative advantage over indexed-sequential organization.

Indexed-sequential organization combines the sequential-access properties of sequential files with the rapid individual record-access capabilities of direct files. The sequential order of the data records is used to provide sequential access; **index records** are used for random retrieval of individual records. Indexed-sequential organization is currently a common choice for the organization of master files.

Topic 2-B   File and Record Design Concepts

Files can be classified according to their categories of use. A **master file** contains permanent and semipermanent information about the data entities that are contained within it. A collection of activity records that are used to update master records is called a **transaction file**. A **summary file** contains data that has been extracted and reduced from the records of another file. A collection of table-entry records is a **table file**. A **control file** contains a limited number of records that are used for program control or run statistics. A file that is maintained either to facilitate the reconstruction of a master file or to permit the retrieval of past transaction data is a **history file**. Certain history files are termed **backup** or **archive files**. A **journal file** is a special-purpose, chronologically sequenced history or audit file for on-line systems. A journal file that contains only transaction images is alternately termed a **log file**.

There are three fundamental file-processing characteristics: size, activity, and volatility. **File size** is determined by the number of records—or **population**—of the file in combination with the length of the records. For batch systems, **activity** refers to either the number of transaction records that are processed or the percentage of master records that are updated during a processing run. Activity for on-line systems is measured by the number of transactions that are processed during a time period, such as a minute. **Volatility** is the frequency with which records are added to or deleted from a file.

When the programmer/analyst is designing records, he or she must consider the **logical record length**, **record identification**, **field placement**, and **field length**. There are two specific fields that must be considered when one is designing master records: **date-last-activity** and **delete-flag**.

There are three typical update-transaction types: **add, change,** and **delete**. Occasionally, a **replace** transaction and other transaction types are specified.

Topic 2-C Master File Maintenance Program Design

When the programmer/analyst is designing a master file-maintenance program, he or she must determine whether **data validation** will be specified as a separate **front-end edit** or incorporated into the maintenance program. In addition to transaction-record data errors, certain interfile errors can occur: **add transaction with master record already on file, change transaction without matching master record**, and **delete transaction without matching master record**.

For batch master file-maintenance processing, the programmer/analyst must design an audit list and an error list or a combined audit/error list. For on-line processing, the journal file functions as an audit list and error messages are typically displayed on the video-display terminal that originated the transaction.

Error records can be handled by either the **error-rejection** or **error-abeyance approach**. With the former, errors are rejected from the validated file; with the latter, errors are maintained in an **abeyance file** until they can be corrected.

For a sequential file-maintenance program, the transaction file must be sorted in accordance with the master file sequence. Although sequencing of the transaction file is not usually necessary for indexed-sequential and direct master files, it is sometimes specified for processing efficiency, integrity of application, and/or clerical convenience.

There is always the possibility that multiple transactions may occur in the same run for one master record. To ensure proper processing, a sorted transaction file will require one or more minor sort keys: **update type, date**, and/or **time**.

For change-transaction processing, the following items must be considered: (1) which fields are **modifiable fields**, (2) whether change transactions shall be formatted by **position** or by **keyword**, and (3) which fields, if any, require a **change-to-null code**. For change and delete transactions, use of a correspondence-checking field could be considered.

CHAPTER 3

DESIGNING AND CODING A SEQUENTIAL FILE-MAINTENANCE PROGRAM

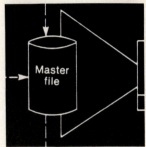

3

DESIGNING AND CODING A SEQUENTIAL FILE-MAINTENANCE PROGRAM

Sequential file-maintenance programs are the hub of most batch-application systems. They are commonly used to keep master files stored on tape and disk—payroll, inventory, general ledger, and so on—in a current status. Recently, the use of sequential master files has declined somewhat because of the general trend toward the use of data-base and on-line systems. Such systems require the use of a data-base management system or master file-organization method that provides random-access capabilities.

Nevertheless, sequential file-maintenance programs still play an important role within commercial data-processing installations. Tape files require the use of a sequential file-maintenance program to provide for their updating (unless, of course, they are updated on disk and then transferred to tape). A sequential master file maintenance program usually provides the most efficient batch processing for master files that possess high volatility together with high activity.

A sequential file-maintenance program processes at least four files: (1) the current, existing master file that is to be updated, sometimes referred to as the **old** or the **input master** file; (2) the transaction file that contains the add, change, and delete transactions that are to be applied to the master file; (3) the updated master file that the program creates, called the **new** or **output master file**; and (4) an audit/error list that identifies the update actions that are taken and reports any error conditions that are encountered during the update.

Figure 3.1 shows a system flowchart for a typical master file-maintenance program. Each sequential file-maintenance program run creates a new rendition, called a **generation**, of the master file. The new generation incorporates the old master file plus the effects of the transaction file processed against it. It then becomes the current generation of the file for the next processing cycle.

Cyclical creation of sequential master file generations can be compared to reproduction of offspring. With three generations of a master file, the oldest is considered the grandparent, the next generation the parent, and the current generation the child. Figure 3.2 diagrams generation processing.

A certain number of generations must be retained for a period of time to guard against master file contamination because of programming logic, data input, hardware, or media errors. For example, should an input master file tape break during processing, it could be reconstructed by rerunning the maintenance program and using its parent master and transaction files. In today's data-processing environment, however, such **reconstruction** (or **recovery**) **procedures** are more frequently initiated to correct programming or data-entry errors rather than hardware problems.

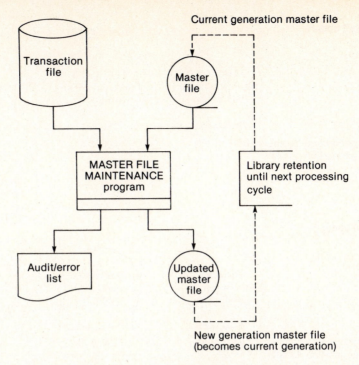

Figure 3.1. Typical system flowchart: sequential file-maintenance program.

A programmer/analyst (or operations analyst) must determine appropriate **retention** requirements for a sequential master file. Retention requirements are expressed in either time periods, the number of generations, or a combination of both. Retention that is based on time is expressed as either (1) a **retention period**, or number of days, that each generation of the file should be kept, or (2) an **expiration date** until which the file should be retained. Using a retention period is usually more satisfactory because the operating system can then calculate the actual expiration date. This eliminates date-computation errors and the possibility of neglecting to update the date.

When retention is based upon the number of generations, a number is chosen and when the volume of generations that are being saved exceeds this number, the older ones are released. Retention that is based upon the number of generations is usually more satisfactory than specific date-oriented periods.

The length of the retention period or number of generations should be based upon a number of factors: system stability, application sensitivity and critical aspects, data volumes, run frequency, existence of programming modifications, and so forth. Retention that provides at least three generations is the minimum, a number closer to seven generations is common, and more will be specified in certain instances.

Files retained for recovery purposes are often called **backup files**. When generation retention is specified, the file is termed a **generation data set**. The collection of generations for the file is a **generation data group**. An available, but seldom used, feature of certain operating systems allows the programmer to assign a **version number** for multiple editions of the same **generation number**.

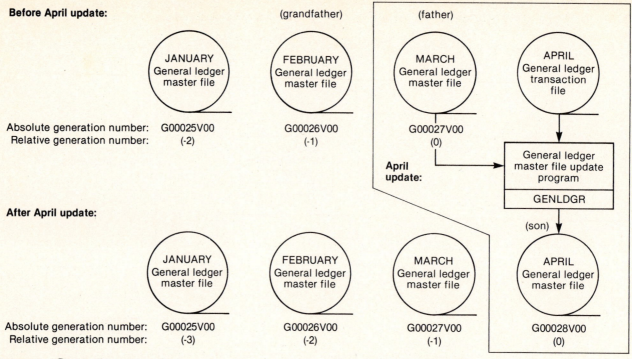

Before April update:

(grandfather)   (father)

JANUARY General ledger master file

FEBRUARY General ledger master file

MARCH General ledger master file

APRIL General ledger transaction file

Absolute generation number: G00025V00   G00026V00   G00027V00
Relative generation number: (-2)   (-1)   (0)

April update:

General ledger master file update program

GENLDGR

(son)

After April update:

JANUARY General ledger master file

FEBRUARY General ledger master file

MARCH General ledger master file

APRIL General ledger master file

Absolute generation number: G00025V00   G00026V00   G00027V00   G00028V00
Relative generation number: (-3)   (-2)   (-1)   (0)

Figure 3.2. Generation processing.

Before the actual sequential file update can take place, the transaction records must be sorted into the same sequence as the **control key** of the master records. This sort could occur in the previous program or by specifying the proper SORT logic in the sequential file-maintenance program.

After the transaction file has been sorted into the proper sequence, the general logic of a sequential master file-maintenance program is to read a record from the transaction file and locate its proper position in the master file by reading old input master records and writing new output master records until a matching or the first higher-control key value has been located. At that point, the update is applied to the master file, if possible; if not, an error condition is identified. Then the program proceeds to read the next sequential transaction record.

Although the narrative of the preceding paragraph may not reveal it, sequential file-maintenance program logic can be very difficult for a programmer who is not trained in its design and coding. Common errors that are encountered with sequential file-maintenance programs are (1) failure to consider all design aspects, (2) logic that does not allow all transactions to be applied to a particular master record when there are multiple transactions in the same run, and (3) erroneous end-of-file processing that causes the program to enter an endless loop or results in the creation of a new master file that is out of sequence.

In this chapter, we will cover the design and coding of a typical sequential file-maintenance program that will be called SEQMAINT (for **Se**quential File **Maint**enance). Topic 3-A presents and discusses aspects of the programming specifications. Program design considerations are covered in Topic 3-B. In Topic 3-C, the actual program coding is presented. Finally, in Topic 3-D, a few approaches to creating the initial sequential master file are briefly mentioned.

Sequential File-Maintenance Programming Specifications

Handling for Items That Apply to All File-Maintenance Programs

  Transaction Data Validation
  Audit/Error List Treatment
  Error Record Handling
  Transaction File Sorting
  Multiple Transactions for the Same Master Record
    Update-type sequence
  Change Transaction Considerations
    Modifiable fields
    Change-field formatting
    Changing a field to null values
  Change- and Delete-Transaction Correspondence Checking

Handling for Items That Apply Specifically to Sequential File-Maintenance Programs

  Sequence Checking of the Master File
  Sequence Checking of the Transaction File
  Record Counts

The programming specifications for this SEQMAINT program are presented in Figure 3A.1. With this program, a sequential master file of employee records is to be maintained. Recognize that the number of fields that are specified for the employee master record has been limited to emphasize the main program logic; additional fields would be required for an actual record.

The control key for this program has three fields: The major field is plant code, the intermediate field is department number, and the minor field is employee number. These fields have been specified to provide an example of a control key with multiple fields. Many employee master files are organized with the employee number as the only key field.

When the programmer/analyst is preparing the specifications for a file-maintenance program, he or she must make certain program design choices. Those design topics that apply to all file-maintenance programs, regardless of the type of organization method, were introduced in Chapter 2. In addition, there are a few design aspects that apply specifically to sequential file-maintenance programs. We will review how the SEQMAINT program specifications call for these various design alternatives to be handled.

Handling for Items That Apply to All File-Maintenance Programs

Transaction Data Validation

To allow concentration on the sequential file-maintenance logic, the program specifications state that another program has previously validated all transaction records. Hence no data validation will be done in this program.

Audit/Error List Treatment

The specifications for handling the audit/error list are relatively standard. However, it is generally preferable to display the master record prior to updating whenever a change or delete transaction occurs. To minimize the program's logic requirements, such treatment is not specified in this program.

System flowchart:

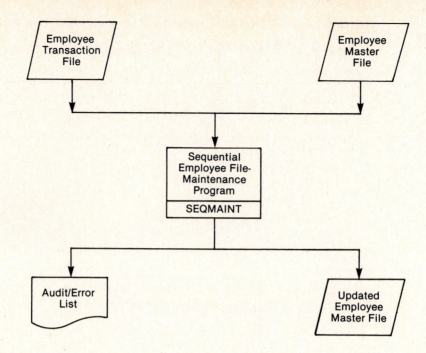

Record layouts:

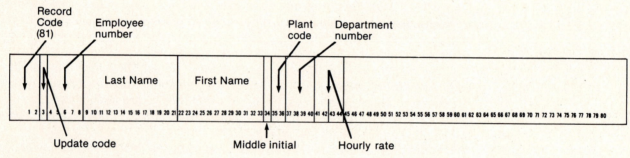

Employee-transaction record

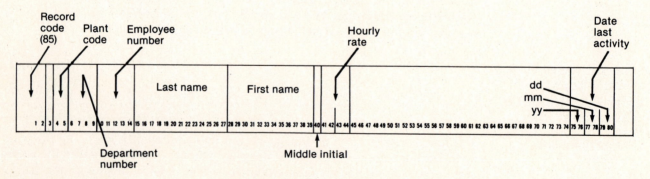

Employee master record

Figure 3A.1. Programming specifications: SEQMAINT program.

Print chart:

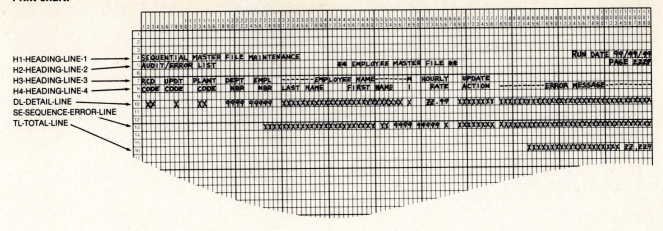

- H1-HEADING-LINE-1
- H2-HEADING-LINE-2
- H3-HEADING-LINE-3
- H4-HEADING-LINE-4
- DL-DETAIL-LINE
- SE-SEQUENCE-ERROR-LINE
- TL-TOTAL-LINE

Printer output example:

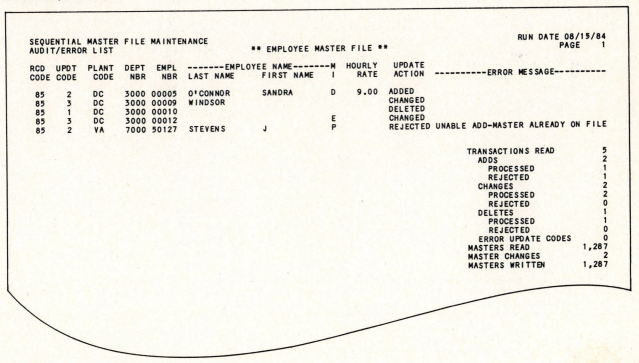

```
SEQUENTIAL MASTER FILE MAINTENANCE                                              RUN DATE 08/15/84
AUDIT/ERROR LIST                        ** EMPLOYEE MASTER FILE **                       PAGE    1

RCD  UPDT  PLANT  DEPT   EMPL  ------EMPLOYEE NAME-------M  HOURLY   UPDATE
CODE CODE  CODE   NBR    NBR   LAST NAME      FIRST NAME I   RATE    ACTION    ----------ERROR MESSAGE----------

85    2    DC    3000   00005  O'CONNOR       SANDRA     D   9.00   ADDED
85    3    DC    3000   00009  WINDSOR                             CHANGED
85    1    DC    3000   00010                                     DELETED
85    3    DC    3000   00012                            E        CHANGED
85    2    VA    7000   50127  STEVENS        J          P        REJECTED  UNABLE ADD-MASTER ALREADY ON FILE

                                                                  TRANSACTIONS READ          5
                                                                     ADDS                    2
                                                                        PROCESSED            1
                                                                        REJECTED             1
                                                                     CHANGES                 2
                                                                        PROCESSED            2
                                                                        REJECTED             0
                                                                     DELETES                 1
                                                                        PROCESSED            1
                                                                        REJECTED             0
                                                                     ERROR UPDATE CODES      0
                                                                  MASTERS READ           1,287
                                                                  MASTER CHANGES             2
                                                                  MASTERS WRITTEN        1,287
```

Figure 3A.1. (continued)

continued

Program name: Sequential Master File Maintenance   Program ID: SEQMAINT

Program description

The employee master file is to be updated by a transaction file containing add, change, and delete transactions. The transaction file has been validated and sorted in a prior program run. A new, updated employee master file is produced by the program together with an audit/error list documenting update actions taken. At the end of the audit/error list, record count totals are printed.

Input files

Employee update-transaction file
Organization = Sequential
Key fields   = Plant code   (major)
               Department number
               Employee number
               Update code   (minor)
Employee master file
Organization = Sequential
Key fields   = Plant code   (major)
               Department number
               Employee number   (minor)

Output files

(Updated) Employee master file
Employee master file—maintenance audit/error list

Program operations

A. Read each input employee update-transaction record.

1. Validate each transaction to ensure that it contains an update code of either "1" (delete transaction), "2" (add transaction), or "3" (change transaction).

   a. If the update-code field is not valid, print the contents of the transaction record on the audit/error list together with an update action of "REJECTED" and an error message of "UNABLE UPDATE—INVALID UPDATE CODE".

   Tally the record in the "ERROR UPDATE CODES" category.

   Do no further processing for the transaction record.

2. Check the sequence of each input employee update-transaction record to ensure that the key value of each record is not less than that of the preceding record.

   a. If a transaction record is encountered whose key value is less than that of the previous transaction, two error lines are to be printed on the audit/error list and the program run is to be terminated.

   The first error line is to contain the words "PREVIOUS TRANSACTION KEY", the previous transaction key value, an update action of "ABORTED" and an

error message of "TRANSACTION FILE OUT OF SEQUENCE".

The second error line is to contain the words "CURRENT TRANSACTION KEY" and the current transaction key value.

3. The program logic is to allow multiple transactions to be processed against the same master record. In accordance with the transaction key sequence and update-code values, delete transactions will be processed first, add transactions second, and change transactions last.

B. As input employee master records are being processed, check the sequence of each input employee master record to ensure that the key value of each record is greater than that of the preceding record.

1. If a master record is encountered whose key value is equal to or less than that of the previous master, two error lines are to be printed on the audit/error list and the program run is to be terminated.

   a. The first error line is to contain the words "PREVIOUS MASTER KEY", the previous master key value, an update action of "ABORTED" and an error message of "MASTER FILE OUT OF SEQUENCE".

   b. The second error line is to contain the words "CURRENT MASTER KEY" and the current master key value.

C. For each add transaction, do the following processing:

1. Read input master file records until a record with an equal or greater key value is located.

2. If a master record with an equal key value is located, it means that a corresponding master record is already on the file.

   a. If the master record is already on file, print the contents of the transaction record on the audit/error list together with an update action of "REJECTED" and an error message of "UNABLE ADD—MASTER ALREADY ON FILE".

   b. Tally the transaction record in the "ADDS REJECTED" category.

   c. Do no further processing for the transaction record.

3. If the master record is not already on file, create a master record from the transaction record as follows:

   a. Move each of the following fields from the input transaction record to the master record:
   —Plant code
   —Department number
   —Employee number

Figure 3A.1. (continued)

-Last name
-First name
-Middle initial
-Hourly rate

b. Set the record–code field of the master record to "85".

c. Set the date–last–activity field of the master record to the current run date.

d. Set all other positions of the master record to blank spaces.

e. Tally the transaction record in the "ADDS PROCESSED" category.

f. Print the contents of the transaction record on the audit/error list together with an update action of "ADDED".

g. Write the newly created master record to the output master file.

D. For each change transaction, do the following processing:

1. Read input master file records until a record with an equal key or greater value is located.

2. If a master record with an equal key value is not located, it means that the corresponding master record is not on the file.

a. If the master record is not on file, print the contents of the transaction record on the audit/error list together with an update action of "REJECTED" and an error message of "UNABLE CHANGE–MASTER NOT ON FILE".

b. Tally the transaction record in the "CHANGES REJECTED" category.

c. Do no further processing for the transaction record.

3. If the master record is on file, update the master record from the transaction record as follows:

a. Check each of the following fields of the transaction record to determine if it contains an entry:
-Last name
-First name
-Hourly rate
For each field that contains an entry, move it to the corresponding field of the master record.

b. Check the middle–initial field of the transaction record to determine if it contains an entry.
If the entry is a "$", move a blank space to the middle–initial field of the master record.
If it contains an entry other than a "$", move the contents of the middle–initial field of the transaction record to the master record.

c. If any of the above four fields of the master record are changed, set the date–last–activity field of the master record to the current run date.

d. Tally the transaction record in the "CHANGES PROCESSED" category.

e. Print the contents of the transaction record on the audit/error list together with an update action of "CHANGED".

f. Write the updated–master record to the updated master file in place of the old master record.

E. For each delete transaction, do the following processing:

1. Read input master file records until a record with an equal or greater key value is located.

2. If a master record with an equal key value is not located, it means that the corresponding master record is not on the file.

a. If the master record is not on file, print the contents of the transaction record on the audit/error list together with an update action of "REJECTED" and an error message of "UNABLE DELETE–MASTER NOT ON FILE".

b. Tally the transaction record in the "DELETES REJECTED" category.

c. Do no further processing for the transaction record.

3. If the corresponding master record is on file, delete the master record from the master file by not writing it to the output master file.

a. Print the contents of the transaction record on the audit/error list together with an update action of "DELETED".

b. Tally the transaction record in the "DELETES PROCESSED" category.

F. Tally master records as follows:

1. Tally each input master file record in the "MASTERS READ" category.

2. Tally each master record changed in the "MASTER CHANGES" category.

3. Tally each output master file record written in the "MASTERS WRITTEN" category.

G. Headings are to be printed on each page of the audit/error list. After 55 lines have been used on a report page and a new audit/error line is to be printed, the forms should be advanced to the next page and the report headings printed. Also, the report page is to be advanced and headings are to be printed immediately before printing the total lines.

1. The run date is to be obtained from the operating system and printed on the first heading line in accordance with the format shown on the print chart.

2. The page number is to be incremented each time the heading is printed and displayed on the second heading line in accordance with the format shown on the print chart.

H. Line spacing for the audit/error list is to be handled as follows:

1. The first detail or total line after the page headings is to be double–spaced from the last heading line.

Figure 3A.1. (continued)

continued

2. Second and successive detail lines are to be single-spaced from one another.
3. The report totals are to be printed on a new report page after the headings have been printed. Total lines are to be single-spaced from one another.

4. Should input—output error lines be required, the first one is to be triple-spaced from the last detail line. Successive input—output error lines should be single-spaced from one another.

Figure 3A.1. (continued)

Error Record Handling

Although the error-abeyance approach to handling erroneous transaction records is recommended for fail-safe processing of sensitive master files, the error-rejection method is more commonly implemented. Again, so that we can focus upon the main aspects of the sequential file-maintenance logic, error-rejection processing is specified for this program.

Transaction File Sorting

The specifications for this program state that a previous program has sorted the transaction records. Thus no sort logic will be coded in this program.

Multiple Transactions for the Same Master Record

The program specifications call for this program to handle any number and combination of transaction records for a given master record. Furthermore, the logic that will be developed for this program will handle transaction update codes presented in any sequence. Of course, different processing effects can occur with different transaction sequences, as was discussed in Chapter 2.

Update-type sequence

When there are multiple transaction records for the same master record, the transactions will be sequenced within control key by update type. The update-type sequence specified is the delete transactions first, followed next by the add transactions, and finally by the change transactions.

Change Transaction Considerations

Modifiable fields

As mentioned in the previous chapter, all fields of a master record are generally candidates for modification by a change transaction except for the record code, control key, and special fields such as the date-last-activity field.

Thus provisions for changing the following master record fields are to be incorporated into the maintenance program: last name, first name, middle initial, and hourly rate. The plant-code, department-number, and employee-number fields are key fields and thus cannot be changed. If it does become necessary to change one of these key values, the record with the "old" key value must be deleted and the record must be re-added to the file with the "new" key value.

Change-field formatting

Because only a few master record fields are specified, the positional method of formatting change-transaction fields is simpler and more straightforward than the keyword method. Hence the positional method is specified for this program.

Changing a field to null values

In order to demonstrate the technique for changing a field to null values, provisions have been specified for the middle-initial field. It is not specified for the other fields of the employee master record because they should not contain null values. That is, the last-name, first-name, plant-code, department-number, and hourly rate fields should always be present and should always contain actual— not null—values.

Change- and Delete-Transaction Correspondence Checking

No provisions to check the correspondence of another field for change and delete transactions have been listed in the programming specifications.

Handling for Items That Apply Specifically to Sequential File-Maintenance Programs

Sequence Checking of the Master File

With a sequential file-maintenance program, it is essential that the input master file be in correct control-key sequence. This can be assured by comparing the control key of each master record with the control key of the last master record that was previously processed. If the current master control key is greater than the previous one, correct sequence exists. An out-of-sequence condition exists when the current master control key is less than or equal to that of the previous master record.

Of course, when records have been sorted electronically on modern computer systems, the chance that an out-of-sequence condition will occur is slight. There are times, however, when the failure to process the files through all job steps will cause records to be out of the intended sequence. Also, in the testing phase of program development, programming bugs frequently cause master files to become arranged in an erroneous sequence.

Thus the programming specifications for this SEQMAINT program call for sequence checking of the records of the input master file. Some programmers alternately, or in addition to checking the input master, check the sequence of the records that are written to the output master file.

When an out-of-sequence master file has been detected, two lines are to be printed on the audit/error list. The first line identifies the control key of the master record immediately before the out-of-sequence condition occurred. The second line shows the control key of the master record that actually triggered the out-of-sequence detection. The control key on the second line is the one that caused a **step-down condition**, a master record whose control key is either equal to or less than the previous master record.

Recognize that it is important to print not only the step-down control key but also the immediately preceding key, as called for in the programming specifications. By displaying both keys, the actual location in the master file of the step-down record can be more easily determined.

Once a master file out-of-sequence condition is detected, there is no reason to continue with the program run, since the output master file will be contaminated by erroneous sequencing and/or updating. Hence after detection of a step-down condition, the program specifications call for the run to be terminated.

Sequence Checking of the Transaction File

Similarly, to ensure that update transactions are processed properly against the master file, the transaction file must be checked to make sure that it is in the proper sequence.

Proper sequence for the transaction file is the same control key as for the master file plus one additional field—the transaction update code. That is, once an update-code sequence is chosen, that sequence becomes the minor portion of the transaction control key for transaction sequence-checking purposes. This concept will be illustrated in Topic 3-C of this chapter.

Record Counts
The accumulation of detailed record counts can be an aid for assuring that a sequential file-maintenance program is correctly processing all records.

Observe that the programming specifications call for each transaction record to be counted in the "TRANSACTIONS READ" category. Then that transaction record will be tallied once in one of the following categories: "ADDS," "CHANGES," "DELETES," or "ERROR UPDATE CODES." (Actually, there should be no entries in the erroneous transaction update-code category because the specifications state that a prior program has validated the transaction

Part A: Example of record count totals with explanation of proof computations

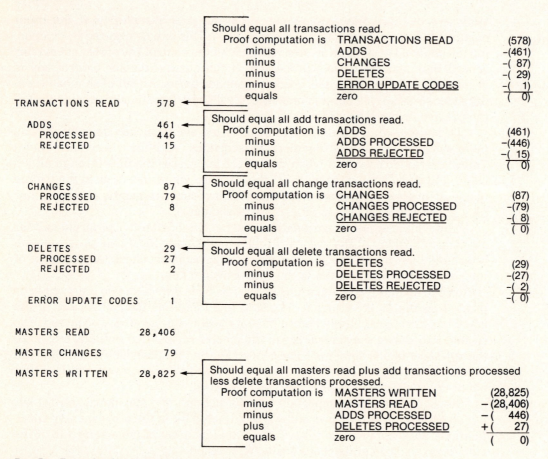

```
TRANSACTIONS READ      578 ◄─── Should equal all transactions read.
                                Proof computation is    TRANSACTIONS READ      (578)
                                   minus                ADDS                  -(461)
                                   minus                CHANGES               -( 87)
                                   minus                DELETES               -( 29)
                                   minus                ERROR UPDATE CODES    -(  1)
                                   equals               zero                  (  0)

ADDS                   461 ◄─── Should equal all add transactions read.
   PROCESSED           446          Proof computation is    ADDS                  (461)
   REJECTED             15             minus                ADDS PROCESSED       -(446)
                                       minus                ADDS REJECTED        -( 15)
                                       equals               zero                 (  0)

CHANGES                 87 ◄─── Should equal all change transactions read.
   PROCESSED            79          Proof computation is    CHANGES               (87)
   REJECTED              8             minus                CHANGES PROCESSED     -(79)
                                       minus                CHANGES REJECTED      -( 8)
                                       equals               zero                  ( 0)

DELETES                 29 ◄─── Should equal all delete transactions read.
   PROCESSED            27          Proof computation is    DELETES               (29)
   REJECTED              2             minus                DELETES PROCESSED     -(27)
                                       minus                DELETES REJECTED      -( 2)
ERROR UPDATE CODES       1             equals               zero                 -( 0)


MASTERS READ        28,406

MASTER CHANGES          79

MASTERS WRITTEN     28,825 ◄─── Should equal all masters read plus add transactions processed
                                less delete transactions processed.
                                   Proof computation is    MASTERS WRITTEN     (28,825)
                                      minus                MASTERS READ       - (28,406)
                                      minus                ADDS PROCESSED     - (   446)
                                      plus                 DELETES PROCESSED  + (    27)
                                      equals               zero                 (     0)
```

Part B: Example of out-of-balance record counts

```
TRANSACTIONS READ      578
   ADDS                461
      PROCESSED        446
      REJECTED          15
   CHANGES              87
      PROCESSED         79
      REJECTED           8
   DELETES              29
      PROCESSED         27
      REJECTED           2
   ERROR UPDATE CODES    1
MASTERS READ        28,406
MASTER CHANGES          79
MASTERS WRITTEN     28,824

** PROOF **            1-   RECORD COUNTS OUT OF BALANCE -
                           PLEASE NOTIFY APPLICATION PROGRAMMING DEPARTMENT
```

Figure 3A.2. Example of proof totals for record counts.

records. The category is provided, however, to maintain the integrity of the record counts in the event that an erroneous transaction code inadvertently enters the program run.) Then each transaction record that falls into one of the three update-type categories is classified as either "PROCESSED" or "REJECTED" within its classification.

Master records are to be counted in one or more of three categories: "MASTERS READ," "MASTER CHANGES," and/or "MASTERS WRITTEN."

Although the SEQMAINT program specifications do not call for it, at the end of the run—after the files have been closed and such record counts have been fully accumulated—the program logic can do a **proof total** of the counts to assure that incorrect processing did not occur. That is, the record counts should balance as shown in Figure 3A.2. If they do not, program logic within the maintenance program could print a message at the bottom of the report, such as "RECORD COUNTS OUT OF BALANCE—PLEASE NOTIFY APPLICATION PROGRAMMING DEPARTMENT."

■ TOPIC 3-B: ## Sequential File-Maintenance Program Design

Relationship of the Transaction Record Key to the Master Record Key

> Transaction Key Lower Than Master Key
> Transaction Key Equal to Master Key
> Transaction Key Higher Than Master Key

Storage Allocation for Input and Output Records

Processing Logic Design

> Acquiring a Transaction Record and a Master Record
> Adding a New Master Record
> > Add Step A: Creating a new master record
> > Add Step B: Writing out the new master record
> > Add Step C: Retrieving the unprocessed master record
> Passing a Master Record
> Changing a Master Record
> Deleting a Master Record

Relationship of the Transaction Record Key to the Master Record Key

When the transaction record control key is compared to the master record control key, three conditions can arise.

1. The transaction key is lower than the master key.
2. The transaction key is equal to the master key.
3. The transaction key is higher than the master key.

Based on which condition exists, one of six resulting action patterns is taken.

Transaction Key Lower Than Master Key

When a transaction key value is lower than the master key value, no matching master record exists for that transaction. For add transactions, this is a valid condition; for change and delete transactions, this situation reveals an interfile error. Thus, depending upon the transaction type, actions are to be taken as follows:

Add transaction:

1. This is a valid condition and means that the master record should be created (although not yet written out to the master file).

2. An audit line should be printed to document the addition.

3. The next transaction record should be read.

Change or delete transaction:

1. This is an invalid condition that means the record to be changed or deleted cannot be located, and so the transaction cannot be applied to the master file.

2. The error condition should be documented on the audit/error list.

3. The next transaction record should be read.

Transaction Key Equal to Master Key

If the transaction key value is equal to the master key value, it means that a matching master record has been located. A matching master record is sought for change and delete transactions. For an add transaction, however, a matching master record should *not* exist. The respective actions to be taken for each transaction type are as follows:

Change transaction:

1. The change should be applied to the master record.

2. An audit line should be printed to document the change.

3. The next transaction record should be read.

Delete transaction:

1. An audit line should be printed to document the deletion.

2. The next master record should be read to effect the deletion (by eradicating the data) of the corresponding master record.

3. The next transaction record should be read.

Add transaction:

1. An error condition exists because an add transaction should not be processed when it already exists on the master file (because duplicate master records would be introduced into the file).

2. An error should be identified on the audit/error list.

3. The next transaction record should be read.

Transaction Key Higher Than Master Key

Whenever the transaction key is higher than the master key, it means that the appropriate location in the master file for processing the transaction has not yet been reached. More input master records must be passed to the output master file before the transaction record can be processed. Thus regardless of the type of transaction, the following pair of actions must occur:

1. Write out the master record.

2. Read the next input master record.

This process must be repeated until the master key value "catches up" with the transaction key value, that is, until a master key of equal or higher value is encountered.

Storage Allocation for Input and Output Records

When designing the program, we must allocate areas in the FILE SECTION for the input transaction record, the input master record, and the output master record. It is a good practice to also define and process the input transaction record in the WORKING-STORAGE SECTION.

Furthermore, for straightforward processing, it is a good technique to provide one area in WORKING-STORAGE through which all master records pass and are processed. This area can be termed a **master work area**.

WORKING-STORAGE SECTION definition of input records provides two advantages: (1) it allows reference to fields of a record after end-of-file has been reached for that file, and (2) it makes it easier to determine the last input record of a file that was read when referring to a storage dump.

Definition of output records in the WORKING-STORAGE SECTION gives the following advantages: (1) it allows VALUE clauses to be specified for the initialization of fields within a record; (2) it eliminates double-buffering errors; (3) it allows reference to fields of a record that have already been written to an output device; and (4) it makes it easier to determine the current output record that is being processed when referring to a storage dump.

Although WORKING-STORAGE SECTION definition of input and output records may, in certain instances, consume more computer-storage space and cause more data movement, the advantages typically outweigh these possible disadvantages.

Processing Logic Design

The ensuing discussion and figures will describe the relationships among the various record areas and will demonstrate program design and processing for the various update functions. For ease of understanding, the control key is represented in the figures and discussion by a short 2-digit number rather than the full 3-field key of plant code, department number, and the 5-digit employee number. Also, the number of fields that are shown for the transaction and master record has been limited. Further, for clarity, the transaction record code is expressed as "TT" and the master record code as "MM."

Acquiring a Transaction Record and a Master Record

At point 1 of Figure 3B.1, a transaction record is read from the input transaction file and into the transaction record area of WORKING-STORAGE. As shown at point 2 of the figure, the master record is likewise obtained and placed in the master work area. Thus the figure depicts how storage will appear when a transaction record and a master record have each been acquired.

Notice that the transaction record is an add transaction and that the key of the transaction record (05) is less than the key of the master record (07). This means that a new master record for 05-O'CONNOR must be created.

Adding a New Master Record

Add Step A: Creating a new master record

To create a new master record, as depicted in Figure 3B.2, the transaction record fields are moved to the master work-area fields. Observe that this data movement will wipe out the master record that previously occupied the master work area (07-BRENNAN).

Add Step B: Writing out the new master record

When adding a new master record, the next step is to read another transaction record, as shown at point 1 of Figure 3B.3. The key of the transaction record that was just read (09) is higher than that of the master record (05). This means that there are no other transactions to be applied to the 05-O'CONNOR master record, so it should now be written to the output master file. This is accomplished by first moving the master work area to the output master record area and then writing the record to the output master file. This is shown at points 2 and 3 in the figure.

Add Step C: Retrieving the unprocessed master record

After a record is added to the master file, instead of obtaining the next master record from the input master file, the master that was eradicated from the master work area during the creation process must be retrieved because it has not yet been processed. Thus, as shown in Figure 3B.4, the 07-BRENNAN master record is moved once again from the input master record area to the master work area.

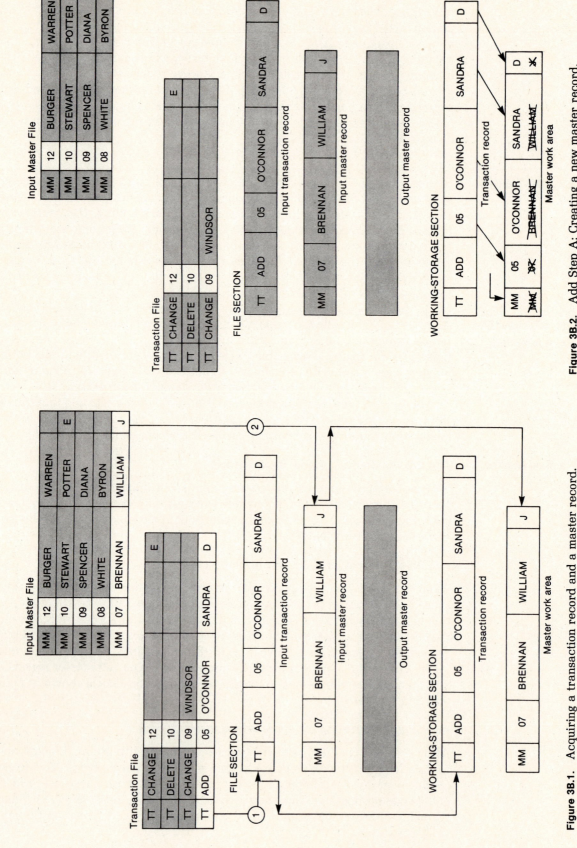

Figure 3B.1. Acquiring a transaction record and a master record.

Figure 3B.2. Add Step A: Creating a new master record.

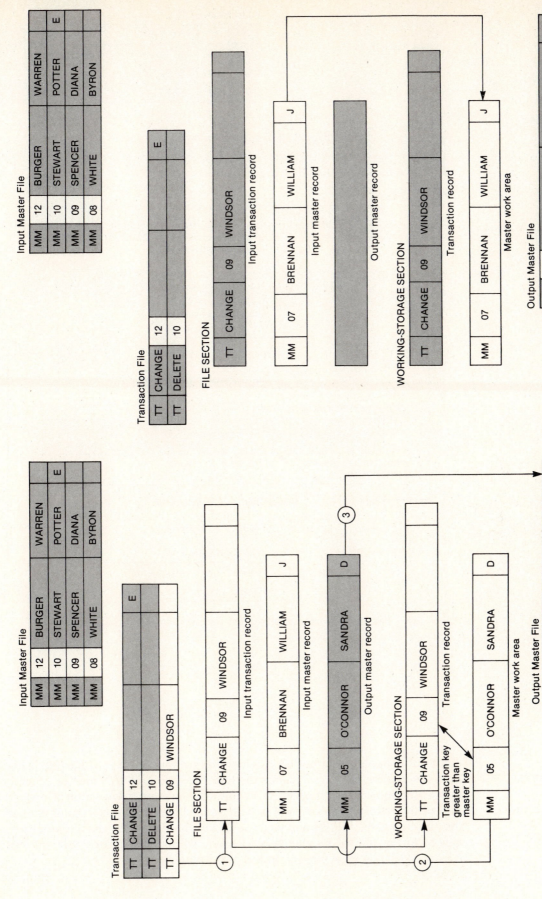

Figure 3B.4. Retrieving the unprocessed pending master record.

Figure 3B.3. Add Step B: Writing a new master record.

Input Master File

MM	12	BURGER	WARREN	
MM	10	STEWART	POTTER	E
MM	09	SPENCER	DIANA	
MM	08	WHITE	BYRON	

Transaction File

TT	CHANGE	12			E
TT	DELETE	10			

FILE SECTION

TT	CHANGE	09	WINDSOR		

Input transaction record

MM	07	BRENNAN	WILLIAM	J

Input master record

MM	07	BRENNAN	WILLIAM	J

Output master record

WORKING-STORAGE SECTION

TT	CHANGE	09	WINDSOR		

Transaction key greater than master key   Transaction record

MM	07	BRENNAN	WILLIAM	J

Master work area

Output Master File

MM	07	BRENNAN	WILLIAM	J
MM	05	O'CONNOR	SANDRA	D

Figure 3B.5. Passing a master record from the input to the output master file.

Passing a Master Record

Figure 3B.5 depicts a situation in which the transaction key value (09) is higher than the master key (07). This means that the 07-BRENNAN master record has no transactions to be applied to it. Whenever the master key value is lower than that of the transaction key, the master record is simply passed, unchanged, to the output master file. As shown at point 1 of the figure, the master work area is moved to the output master record area. Point 2 illustrates that the output master record is then written to the output master file.

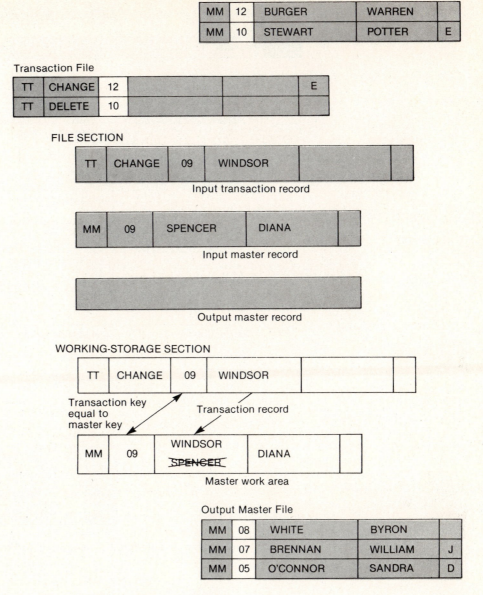

Figure 3B.6. Changing a master record.

Changing a Master Record

To process a change transaction, the transaction key must be equal to the master key, as shown in Figure 3B.6. The transaction record calls for the last-name field of the 09-SPENCER record to be changed to WINDSOR. So, the last-name field of the transaction record is moved to the last-name field of the master work area. Then, when the 09 record is written to the output master file, the new master record will carry the updated-data value of WINDSOR in the last-name field.

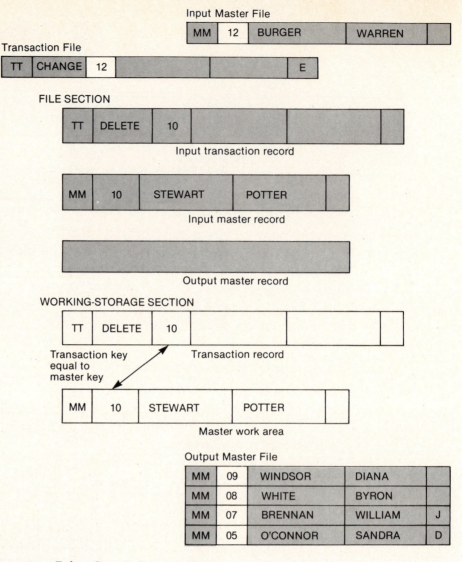

Input Master File

| MM | 12 | BURGER | WARREN | |

Transaction File

| TT | CHANGE | 12 | | | E |

FILE SECTION

| TT | DELETE | 10 | | | |

Input transaction record

| MM | 10 | STEWART | POTTER | |

Input master record

| |

Output master record

WORKING-STORAGE SECTION

| TT | DELETE | 10 | | | |

Transaction key
equal to
master key

Transaction record

| MM | 10 | STEWART | POTTER | |

Master work area

Output Master File

MM	09	WINDSOR	DIANA	
MM	08	WHITE	BYRON	
MM	07	BRENNAN	WILLIAM	J
MM	05	O'CONNOR	SANDRA	D

Figure 3B.7. Delete Step A: Locating the master record to be deleted.

**Deleting a
Master Record**

As illustrated in Figure 3B.7, the processing of a delete transaction also requires that the transaction key be equal to the master key.

Point 1 of Figure 3B.8 shows that, after the transaction key has been matched with the master key, a new transaction record will be read during the next processing cycle. What actually effects the deletion, as illustrated at point

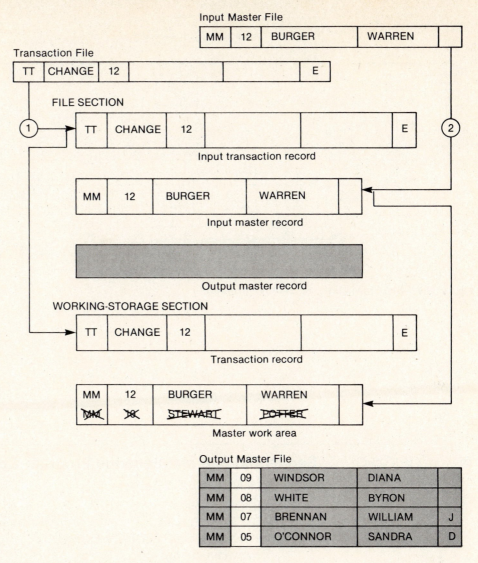

Figure 3B.8. Delete Step B: Deleting a master record.

2, is that another input master record is read into the master work area but the master record to be deleted is *not moved* to the output master record work area and is *not written* to the output master file. This wipes out the 10-STEWART master record and results in its deletion from the updated output master file.

A structure chart for the SEQMAINT program is shown in Figure 3B.9.

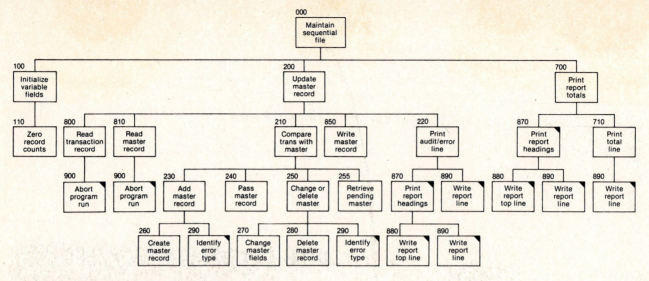

Figure 3B.9. Structure chart: SEQMAINT program.

```
270-CHANGE-MASTER-FIELDS
280-DELETE-MASTER-RECORD
290-IDENTIFY-ERROR-TYPE
700-PRINT-REPORT-TOTALS
710-PRINT-TOTAL-LINE
800-READ-TRANSACTION-RECORD
810-READ-MASTER-RECORD
850-WRITE-MASTER-RECORD
870-PRINT-REPORT-HEADINGS
880-WRITE-REPORT-TOP-LINE
890-WRITE-REPORT-LINE
900-ABORT-PROGRAM-RUN
```

The COBOL syntax for sequential file input-output processing is summarized in Figure 3C.1. The DATA and PROCEDURE DIVISION entries should be familiar to you. In the ENVIRONMENT DIVISION, observe that the ORGANIZATION and ACCESS clauses can be specified in the SELECT entry for a file. These optional entries are rarely coded, however, because SEQUENTIAL is the default ORGANIZATION method and ACCESS MODE.

The coding for the SEQMAINT program is shown in Figure 3C.2. Pertinent aspects of the program code will be covered in this topic.

ENVIRONMENT DIVISION Entries

Each of the four files that are used in this program is defined by a SELECT statement and assigned to an output device in the FILE-CONTROL paragraph. The four files are (1) the transaction file that contains updates to be processed (TRANSACTION-FILE), (2) the input sequential master file (OLD-MASTER-IN-FILE), (3) the output sequential master file (NEW-MASTER-OUT-FILE), and (4) the audit/error list (REPORT-FILE).

DATA DIVISION Entries

FILE SECTION Entries

In this program, as previously mentioned, rather than defining input and output record data-items in the FILE SECTION, they have been specified in the WORKING-STORAGE SECTION.

Thus, in the FILE SECTION, each of the four files contains a record-description entry composed of only a FILLER entry. The record-description entry for each of the four files is as follows:

1. Input   TRANSACTION-FILE: TRANSACTION-RECORD
2. Input   OLD-MASTER-IN-FILE: OLD-MASTER-IN-RECORD
3. Output   NEW-MASTER-OUT-FILE: NEW-MASTER-OUT-RECORD
4. Output   REPORT-FILE: REPORT-LINE

WORKING-STORAGE SECTION Entries

Eight major categories of field specifications are coded within the WORKING-STORAGE SECTION: (1) program switches, (2) sequence control fields, (3) report control fields, (4) a current date work area, (5) record count description and

```
        ENVIRONMENT DIVISION.
           .
           .
           .

        INPUT-OUTPUT SECTION.
        FILE-CONTROL.

                SELECT file-name
                    ASSIGN TO implementor-name
                    [ORGANIZATION IS SEQUENTIAL]
                    [ACCESS MODE IS SEQUENTIAL].


        DATA DIVISION.
        FILE SECTION.

        FD    file-name
                    [RECORD CONTAINS integer CHARACTERS]
                    [BLOCK CONTAINS integer RECORDS]
                    LABEL RECORDS ARE  { STANDARD  } .
                                       { OMITTED   }


        PROCEDURE DIVISION.

                OPEN  { INPUT file-name  }  ... .
                      { OUTPUT file-name }


                READ file-name RECORD
                    [INTO identifier]
                    AT END imperative-statement.


                WRITE record-name
                    [FROM identifier].


                CLOSE file-name  ... .
```

Figure 3C.1. COBOL sequential file-processing syntax summary.

```
001010 IDENTIFICATION DIVISION.
001020 PROGRAM-ID.    SEQMAINT.
001030*
001040*
001050*            SEQUENTIAL MASTER FILE MAINTENANCE
002010*
002020*
002030*
002040 ENVIRONMENT DIVISION.
002050*
002060*
002070 CONFIGURATION SECTION.
002080*
002090 SOURCE-COMPUTER.  IBM-370.
002100 OBJECT-COMPUTER.  IBM-370.
002110*
002120*
002130 INPUT-OUTPUT SECTION.
002140*
002150 FILE-CONTROL.
002160     SELECT TRANSACTION-FILE
002170         ASSIGN TO UT-S-TRNFILE.
002180     SELECT OLD-MASTER-IN-FILE
002190         ASSIGN TO UT-S-MINFILE.
002200     SELECT NEW-MASTER-OUT-FILE
002210         ASSIGN TO UT-S-MOUTFILE.
002220     SELECT REPORT-FILE
002230         ASSIGN TO UT-S-PRTFILE.
003010*
003020*
003030*
003040 DATA DIVISION.
003050*
003060*
003070 FILE SECTION.
003080*
003090*
003100 FD  TRANSACTION-FILE
003110         RECORD CONTAINS 80 CHARACTERS
003120         LABEL RECORDS ARE STANDARD.
003130*
003140 01  TRANSACTION-RECORD.
003150     05  FILLER                    PIC X(80).
004010*
004020*
004030 FD  OLD-MASTER-IN-FILE
004040         RECORD CONTAINS 80 CHARACTERS
004050         LABEL RECORDS ARE STANDARD.
004060*
004070 01  OLD-MASTER-IN-RECORD.
004080     05  FILLER                    PIC X(80).
005010*
005020*
005030 FD  NEW-MASTER-OUT-FILE
005040         RECORD CONTAINS 80 CHARACTERS
005050         LABEL RECORDS ARE STANDARD.
005060*
005070 01  NEW-MASTER-OUT-RECORD.
005080     05  FILLER                    PIC X(80).
006010*
006020*
006030 FD  REPORT-FILE
006040         RECORD CONTAINS 133 CHARACTERS
006050         LABEL RECORDS ARE OMITTED.
006060*
006070 01  REPORT-LINE.
006080     05  FILLER                    PIC X(133).
010010*
010020*
010030 WORKING-STORAGE SECTION.
010040*
010050*
010060 01  WS-SWITCHES.
010070*
010080     05  WS-TRANSACTION-END-OF-FILE-SW  PIC X(3).
010090         88  TRANSACTION-END-OF-FILE      VALUE 'YES'.
010100*
010110     05  WS-MASTER-END-OF-FILE-SW  PIC X(3).
010120         88  MASTER-END-OF-FILE           VALUE 'YES'.
010130*
010140     05  WS-TRANSACTION-REQUIRED-SW  PIC X(3).
010150         88  TRANSACTION-REQUIRED         VALUE 'YES'.
010160*
010170     05  WS-MASTER-REQUIRED-SW     PIC X(3).
010180         88  MASTER-REQUIRED              VALUE 'YES'.
010190*
010200     05  WS-MASTER-TO-BE-WRITTEN-SW  PIC X(3).
010210         88  MASTER-TO-BE-WRITTEN         VALUE 'YES'.
010220*
010230     05  WS-AUDIT-LINE-TO-BE-PRINTED-SW  PIC X(3).
010240         88  AUDIT-LINE-TO-BE-PRINTED     VALUE 'YES'.
010250*
010260     05  WS-MASTER-PENDING-SW      PIC X(3).
010270         88  MASTER-PENDING               VALUE 'YES'.
011010*
011020*
011030 01  WS-SEQUENCE-CONTROLS.
011040*
011050     05  WS-PREVIOUS-TRANS-SEQ-KEY.
011060         10  WS-PREVIOUS-TRANS-KEY.
011070             15  WS-PREVIOUS-TRANS-MAJOR-FIELD  PIC X(2).
011080             15  WS-PREVIOUS-TRANS-INTER-FIELD  PIC X(4).
011090             15  WS-PREVIOUS-TRANS-MINOR-FIELD  PIC X(5).
011100         10  WS-PREVIOUS-TRANS-UPDATE-CODE  PIC X(1).
011110*
011120     05  WS-CURRENT-TRANS-SEQ-KEY.
011130         10  WS-CURRENT-TRANS-KEY.
011140             15  WS-CURRENT-TRANS-MAJOR-FIELD  PIC X(2).
011150             15  WS-CURRENT-TRANS-INTER-FIELD  PIC X(4).
011160             15  WS-CURRENT-TRANS-MINOR-FIELD  PIC X(5).
011170         10  WS-CURRENT-TRANS-UPDATE-CODE  PIC X(1).
011180*
011190     05  WS-PREVIOUS-MASTER-KEY.
011200         10  WS-PREVIOUS-MASTER-MAJOR-FIELD  PIC X(2).
011210         10  WS-PREVIOUS-MASTER-INTER-FIELD  PIC X(4).
011220         10  WS-PREVIOUS-MASTER-MINOR-FIELD  PIC X(5).
011230*

011240     05  WS-CURRENT-MASTER-KEY.
011250         10  WS-CURRENT-MASTER-MAJOR-FIELD  PIC X(2).
011260         10  WS-CURRENT-MASTER-INTER-FIELD  PIC X(4).
011270         10  WS-CURRENT-MASTER-MINOR-FIELD  PIC X(5).
012010*
012020*
012030 01  WS-REPORT-CONTROLS.
012040     05  WS-PAGE-COUNT             PIC S9(4)       COMP-3.
012050     05  WS-LINES-PER-PAGE         PIC S9(2)  VALUE +55
012060                                             COMP SYNC.
012070     05  WS-LINES-USED             PIC S9(2)  COMP SYNC.
012080     05  WS-LINE-SPACING           PIC S9(2).
013010*
013020*
013030 01  WS-WORK-AREAS.
013040     05  WS-DATE-WORK              PIC 9(6).
013050     05  WS-DATE-REFORMAT REDEFINES WS-DATE-WORK.
013060         10  WS-YEAR               PIC 9(2).
013070         10  WS-MONTH              PIC 9(2).
013080         10  WS-DAY                PIC 9(2).
013090     05  WS-ERROR-MESSAGE-HOLD     PIC X(24).
013100     05  WS-SEQUENCE-KEY-HOLD      PIC X(12).
014010*
014020*
014030 01  TC-TABLE-CONTROLS.
014040     05  TC-SUBSCRIPT              PIC S9(4)       COMP SYNC.
014050     05  TC-NUMBER-OF-ENTRIES      PIC S9(4)  VALUE +14
014060                                             COMP SYNC.
015010*
015020 01  TC-COUNT-DESCRIPTION-DATA.
015030     05  FILLER    PIC X(20)  VALUE 'TRANSACTIONS READ   '.
015040     05  FILLER    PIC X(20)  VALUE '  ADDS              '.
015050     05  FILLER    PIC X(20)  VALUE '    PROCESSED       '.
015060     05  FILLER    PIC X(20)  VALUE '    REJECTED        '.
015070     05  FILLER    PIC X(20)  VALUE '  CHANGES           '.
015080     05  FILLER    PIC X(20)  VALUE '    PROCESSED       '.
015090     05  FILLER    PIC X(20)  VALUE '    REJECTED        '.
015100     05  FILLER    PIC X(20)  VALUE '  DELETES           '.
015110     05  FILLER    PIC X(20)  VALUE '    PROCESSED       '.
015120     05  FILLER    PIC X(20)  VALUE '    REJECTED        '.
015130     05  FILLER    PIC X(20)  VALUE '  ERROR UPDATE CODES'.
015140     05  FILLER    PIC X(20)  VALUE 'MASTERS READ        '.
015150     05  FILLER    PIC X(20)  VALUE 'MASTER CHANGES      '.
015160     05  FILLER    PIC X(20)  VALUE 'MASTERS WRITTEN     '.
015170 01  TC-COUNT-DESCRIPTION-TABLE
015180         REDEFINES TC-COUNT-DESCRIPTION-DATA.
015190     05  TC-COUNT-DESCRIPTION      OCCURS 14 TIMES
015200                                   PIC X(20).
016010*
016020 01  TC-RECORD-COUNT-ENTRIES                      COMP-3.
016030     05  TC-TOTAL-TRANS-READ       PIC S9(5).
016040     05  TC-TOTAL-ADD-TRANS-READ   PIC S9(5).
016050     05  TC-ADD-TRANS-PROCESSED    PIC S9(5).
016060     05  TC-ADD-TRANS-REJECTED     PIC S9(5).
016070     05  TC-TOTAL-CHANGE-TRANS-READ  PIC S9(5).
016080     05  TC-CHANGE-TRANS-PROCESSED  PIC S9(5).
016090     05  TC-CHANGE-TRANS-REJECTED  PIC S9(5).
016100     05  TC-TOTAL-DELETE-TRANS-READ  PIC S9(5).
016110     05  TC-DELETE-TRANS-PROCESSED  PIC S9(5).
016120     05  TC-DELETE-TRANS-REJECTED  PIC S9(5).
016130     05  TC-TOTAL-ERROR-UPDATE-CODES  PIC S9(5).
016140     05  TC-MASTERS-READ           PIC S9(5).
016150     05  TC-MASTER-CHANGES         PIC S9(5).
016160     05  TC-MASTERS-WRITTEN        PIC S9(5).
016170 01  TC-RECORD-COUNTS REDEFINES TC-RECORD-COUNT-ENTRIES.
016180     05  TC-RECORD-COUNT           OCCURS 14 TIMES
016190                                   PIC S9(5)       COMP-3.
020010*
020020*
020030 01  ET-EMPLOYEE-TRANSACTION-RECORD.
020040     05  ET-RECORD-CODE            PIC X(2).
020050     05  ET-UPDATE-CODE            PIC X(1).
020060         88  DELETE-TRANSACTION           VALUE '1'.
020070         88  ADD-TRANSACTION              VALUE '2'.
020080         88  CHANGE-TRANSACTION           VALUE '3'.
020090     05  ET-EMPLOYEE-NUMBER        PIC X(5).
020100     05  ET-LAST-NAME              PIC X(13).
020110     05  ET-FIRST-NAME             PIC X(12).
020120     05  ET-MIDDLE-INITIAL         PIC X(1).
020130     05  ET-PLANT-CODE             PIC X(2).
020140     05  ET-DEPARTMENT-NUMBER      PIC X(4).
020150     05  ET-HOURLY-RATE            PIC S9(2)V99.
020160     05  ET-HOURLY-RATE-X REDEFINES ET-HOURLY-RATE
020170                                   PIC X(4).
020180     05  FILLER                    PIC X(36).
025010*
025020*
025030 01  EM-EMPLOYEE-MASTER-WORK-AREA.
025040     05  EM-RECORD-CODE            PIC X(2).
025050     05  FILLER                    PIC X(1).
025060     05  EM-PLANT-CODE             PIC X(2).
025070     05  EM-DEPARTMENT-NUMBER      PIC X(4).
025080     05  EM-EMPLOYEE-NUMBER        PIC X(5).
025090     05  EM-LAST-NAME              PIC X(13).
025100     05  EM-FIRST-NAME             PIC X(12).
025110     05  EM-MIDDLE-INITIAL         PIC X(1).
025120     05  EM-HOURLY-RATE            PIC S9(2)V99.
025130     05  FILLER                    PIC X(30).
025140     05  EM-DATE-LAST-ACTIVITY     PIC 9(6).
030010*
030020*
030030 01  H1-HEADING-LINE-1.
030040     05  FILLER    PIC X(1).
030050     05  FILLER    PIC X(20)  VALUE 'SEQUENTIAL MASTER FI'.
030060     05  FILLER    PIC X(20)  VALUE 'LE MAINTENANCE      '.
030070     05  FILLER    PIC X(20)  VALUE '                    '.
030080     05  FILLER    PIC X(20)  VALUE '                    '.
030090     05  FILLER    PIC X(20)  VALUE '            RUN DAT'.
030100     05  FILLER    PIC X(2)   VALUE 'E '.
030110     05  H1-MONTH  PIC 9(2).
030120     05  FILLER    PIC X(1)   VALUE '/'.
030130     05  H1-DAY    PIC 9(2).
030140     05  FILLER    PIC X(1)   VALUE '/'.
030150     05  H1-YEAR   PIC 9(2).
030160     05  FILLER    PIC X(22)  VALUE SPACES.
031010*
031020*
```

Figure 3C.2. COBOL coding: SEQMAINT program.

continued

```
031030 01  H2-HEADING-LINE-2.
031040     05  FILLER            PIC X(1).
031050     05  FILLER            PIC X(20)    VALUE 'AUDIT/ERROR LIST   '.
031060     05  FILLER            PIC X(20)    VALUE '      ** EMPLOYEE MASTER'.
031070     05  FILLER            PIC X(20)    VALUE ' FILE **            '.
031080     05  FILLER            PIC X(20)    VALUE '                    '.
031090     05  FILLER            PIC X(6)     VALUE ' PAGE '.
031100     05  H2-PAGE-NBR       PIC ZZZ9.
031110     05  FILLER            PIC X(22)    VALUE SPACES.
031120
032010*
032020*
032030 01  H3-HEADING-LINE-3.
032040     05  FILLER            PIC X(1).
032050     05  FILLER            PIC X(20)    VALUE 'RCD UPDT PLANT DE'.
032060     05  FILLER            PIC X(20)    VALUE 'PT  EMPL ------EMP'.
032070     05  FILLER            PIC X(20)    VALUE 'LOYEE NAME------M'.
032080     05  FILLER            PIC X(20)    VALUE 'HOURLY    UPDATE '.
032090     05  FILLER            PIC X(20)    VALUE '                 '.
032100     05  FILLER            PIC X(20)    VALUE '                 '.
032110     05  FILLER            PIC X(12)    VALUE '            '.
033010*
033020*
033030 01  H4-HEADING-LINE-4.
033040     05  FILLER            PIC X(1).
033050     05  FILLER            PIC X(20)    VALUE 'CODE CODE    CODE    N'.
033060     05  FILLER            PIC X(20)    VALUE 'BR  NBR LAST NAME   '.
033070     05  FILLER            PIC X(20)    VALUE '    FIRST NAME  I '.
033080     05  FILLER            PIC X(20)    VALUE ' RATE   ACTION ---'.
033090     05  FILLER            PIC X(20)    VALUE '-------ERROR MESSAGE'.
033100     05  FILLER            PIC X(20)    VALUE '----------         '.
033110     05  FILLER            PIC X(12)    VALUE '            '.
034010*
034020*
034030 01  DL-DETAIL-LINE.
034040     05  FILLER                        PIC X(1).
034050     05  FILLER                        PIC X(1)     VALUE SPACES.
034060     05  DL-RECORD-CODE                PIC X(2).
034070     05  FILLER                        PIC X(4)     VALUE SPACES.
034080     05  DL-UPDATE-CODE                PIC X(1).
034090     05  FILLER                        PIC X(4)     VALUE SPACES.
034100     05  DL-PLANT-CODE                 PIC X(2).
034110     05  FILLER                        PIC X(4)     VALUE SPACES.
034120     05  DL-DEPARTMENT-NUMBER          PIC X(4).
034130     05  FILLER                        PIC X(1)     VALUE SPACES.
034140     05  DL-EMPLOYEE-NUMBER            PIC X(5).
034150     05  FILLER                        PIC X(2)     VALUE SPACES.
034160     05  DL-LAST-NAME                  PIC X(13).
034170     05  FILLER                        PIC X(1)     VALUE SPACES.
034180     05  DL-FIRST-NAME                 PIC X(12).
034190     05  FILLER                        PIC X(1)     VALUE SPACES.
034200     05  DL-MIDDLE-INITIAL             PIC X(1).
034210     05  FILLER                        PIC X(3)     VALUE SPACES.
034220     05  DL-HOURLY-RATE                PIC ZZ.99.
034230     05  DL-HOURLY-RATE-X REDEFINES DL-HOURLY-RATE
034240                                       PIC X(5).
034250     05  FILLER                        PIC X(2)     VALUE SPACES.
034260     05  DL-UPDATE-ACTION              PIC X(8).
034270     05  FILLER                        PIC X(1)     VALUE SPACES.
034280     05  DL-ERROR-MSG                  PIC X(33).
034290     05  FILLER                        PIC X(22)    VALUE SPACES.
035010*
035020*
035030 01  SE-SEQUENCE-ERROR-LINE REDEFINES DL-DETAIL-LINE.
035040     05  FILLER                        PIC X(1).
035050     05  FILLER                        PIC X(26).
035060     05  SE-ERROR-MESSAGE              PIC X(24).
035070     05  FILLER                        PIC X(1).
035080     05  SE-SEQUENCE-KEY               PIC XXBXXXXBXXXXXBX.
035090     05  FILLER                        PIC X(2).
036010*
036020*
036030 01  TL-TOTAL-LINE.
036040     05  FILLER                        PIC X(1).
036050     05  FILLER                        PIC X(83)    VALUE SPACES.
036060     05  TL-COUNT-DESCRIPTION          PIC X(20).
036070     05  FILLER                        PIC X(1)     VALUE SPACES.
036080     05  TL-RECORD-COUNT               PIC ZZ,ZZ9.
036090     05  FILLER                        PIC X(22)    VALUE SPACES.
050010*
050020*
050030*
050040 PROCEDURE DIVISION.
050050*
050060*
050070 000-MAINTAIN-SEQUENTIAL-FILE.
050080*
050090     OPEN INPUT  TRANSACTION-FILE
050100                 OLD-MASTER-IN-FILE
050110          OUTPUT NEW-MASTER-OUT-FILE
050120                 REPORT-FILE.
050130     PERFORM 100-INITIALIZE-VARIABLE-FIELDS.
050140     PERFORM 200-UPDATE-MASTER-RECORD
050150         UNTIL TRANSACTION-END-OF-FILE
050160           AND     MASTER-END-OF-FILE.
050170     PERFORM 700-PRINT-REPORT-TOTALS.
050180     CLOSE TRANSACTION-FILE
050190           OLD-MASTER-IN-FILE
050200           NEW-MASTER-OUT-FILE
050210           REPORT-FILE.
050220     STOP RUN.
100010*
100020*
100030 100-INITIALIZE-VARIABLE-FIELDS.
100040*
100050     MOVE 'NO ' TO WS-TRANSACTION-END-OF-FILE-SW
100060                    WS-MASTER-END-OF-FILE-SW
100070                    WS-MASTER-TO-BE-WRITTEN-SW
100080                    WS-AUDIT-LINE-TO-BE-PRINTED-SW
100090                    WS-MASTER-PENDING-SW.
100100     MOVE 'YES' TO WS-TRANSACTION-REQUIRED-SW
100110                    WS-MASTER-REQUIRED-SW.
100120     MOVE ZERO TO WS-PAGE-COUNT.

100130     ADD 1 WS-LINES-PER-PAGE GIVING WS-LINES-USED.
100140     ACCEPT WS-DATE-WORK FROM DATE.
100150     MOVE WS-MONTH TO H1-MONTH.
100160     MOVE WS-DAY TO H1-DAY.
100180     MOVE WS-YEAR TO H1-YEAR.
100180     MOVE LOW-VALUES TO WS-SEQUENCE-CONTROLS.
100190     MOVE SPACES TO DL-ERROR-MSG.
100200     PERFORM 110-ZERO-RECORD-COUNTS
100210         VARYING TC-SUBSCRIPT
100220         FROM 1
100230         BY 1
100240         UNTIL TC-SUBSCRIPT IS GREATER THAN TC-NUMBER-OF-ENTRIES.
110010*
110020*
110030 110-ZERO-RECORD-COUNTS.
110040*
110050     MOVE ZERO TO TC-RECORD-COUNT (TC-SUBSCRIPT).
200010*
200020*
200030 200-UPDATE-MASTER-RECORD.
200040*
200050     IF TRANSACTION-REQUIRED
200060         PERFORM 800-READ-TRANSACTION-RECORD.
200070*
200080     IF MASTER-REQUIRED
200090         IF MASTER-PENDING
200100             PERFORM 255-RETRIEVE-PENDING-MASTER
200110         ELSE
200120             PERFORM 810-READ-MASTER-RECORD
200130     ELSE
200140         NEXT SENTENCE.
200150*
200160     IF TRANSACTION-END-OF-FILE
200170     AND MASTER-END-OF-FILE
200180         NEXT SENTENCE
200190     ELSE
200200         PERFORM 210-COMPARE-TRANS-WITH-MASTER.
200210*
200220     IF MASTER-TO-BE-WRITTEN
200230     OR (TRANSACTION-END-OF-FILE
200240         AND MASTER-END-OF-FILE
200250         AND MASTER-PENDING)
200260             PERFORM 850-WRITE-MASTER-RECORD.
200270*
200280     IF AUDIT-LINE-TO-BE-PRINTED
200290         PERFORM 220-PRINT-AUDIT-ERROR-LINE.
210010*
210020*
210030 210-COMPARE-TRANS-WITH-MASTER.
210040*
210050     IF WS-CURRENT-TRANS-KEY IS LESS THAN WS-CURRENT-MASTER-KEY
210060         PERFORM 230-ADD-MASTER-RECORD
210070     ELSE IF WS-CURRENT-TRANS-KEY
210080              IS GREATER THAN WS-CURRENT-MASTER-KEY
210090         PERFORM 240-PASS-MASTER-RECORD
210100     ELSE
210110         PERFORM 250-CHANGE-OR-DELETE-MASTER.
220010*
220020*
220030 220-PRINT-AUDIT-ERROR-LINE.
220040*
220050     IF WS-LINES-USED IS NOT LESS THAN WS-LINES-PER-PAGE
220060         PERFORM 870-PRINT-REPORT-HEADINGS.
220070     MOVE ET-RECORD-CODE TO DL-RECORD-CODE.
220080     MOVE ET-UPDATE-CODE TO DL-UPDATE-CODE.
220090     MOVE ET-PLANT-CODE TO DL-PLANT-CODE.
220100     MOVE ET-DEPARTMENT-NUMBER TO DL-DEPARTMENT-NUMBER.
220110     MOVE ET-EMPLOYEE-NUMBER TO DL-EMPLOYEE-NUMBER.
220120     MOVE ET-LAST-NAME TO DL-LAST-NAME.
220130     MOVE ET-FIRST-NAME TO DL-FIRST-NAME.
220140     MOVE ET-MIDDLE-INITIAL TO DL-MIDDLE-INITIAL.
220150     IF ET-HOURLY-RATE IS NUMERIC
220160         MOVE ET-HOURLY-RATE TO DL-HOURLY-RATE
220170     ELSE
220180         MOVE ET-HOURLY-RATE-X TO DL-HOURLY-RATE-X.
220190     MOVE DL-DETAIL-LINE TO REPORT-LINE.
220200     MOVE 1 TO WS-LINE-SPACING.
220210     PERFORM 890-WRITE-REPORT-LINE.
220220     MOVE SPACES TO DL-DETAIL-LINE.
220230     MOVE 'NO ' TO WS-AUDIT-LINE-TO-BE-PRINTED-SW.
230010*
230020*
230030 230-ADD-MASTER-RECORD.
230040*
230050     IF ADD-TRANSACTION
230060         MOVE WS-CURRENT-TRANS-KEY TO WS-CURRENT-MASTER-KEY
230070         PERFORM 260-CREATE-MASTER-RECORD
230080         ADD 1 TO TC-TOTAL-ADD-TRANS-READ
230090         ADD 1 TO TC-ADD-TRANS-PROCESSED
230100         MOVE 'ADDED   ' TO DL-UPDATE-ACTION
230110         MOVE 'YES' TO WS-MASTER-PENDING-SW
230120     ELSE
230130         PERFORM 290-IDENTIFY-ERROR-TYPE.
230140     MOVE 'YES' TO WS-TRANSACTION-REQUIRED-SW
230150                    WS-AUDIT-LINE-TO-BE-PRINTED-SW.
240010*
240020*
240030 240-PASS-MASTER-RECORD.
240040*
240050     MOVE 'YES' TO WS-MASTER-TO-BE-WRITTEN-SW
240060                    WS-MASTER-REQUIRED-SW.
250010*
250020*
250030 250-CHANGE-OR-DELETE-MASTER.
250040*
250050     IF CHANGE-TRANSACTION
250060         PERFORM 270-CHANGE-MASTER-FIELDS
250070         ADD 1 TO TC-TOTAL-CHANGE-TRANS-READ
250080         ADD 1 TO TC-CHANGE-TRANS-PROCESSED
250090         ADD 1 TO TC-MASTER-CHANGES
250100         MOVE 'CHANGED ' TO DL-UPDATE-ACTION
250110     ELSE IF DELETE-TRANSACTION
250120         PERFORM 280-DELETE-MASTER-RECORD
```

Figure 3C.2. (continued)

```
250130          ADD 1 TO TC-TOTAL-DELETE-TRANS-READ
250140          ADD 1 TO TC-DELETE-TRANS-PROCESSED
250150          MOVE 'DELETED ' TO DL-UPDATE-ACTION
250160          MOVE 'YES' TO WS-MASTER-REQUIRED-SW
250170      ELSE
250180          PERFORM 290-IDENTIFY-ERROR-TYPE.
250190*
250200      MOVE 'YES' TO WS-TRANSACTION-REQUIRED-SW
250210                   WS-AUDIT-LINE-TO-BE-PRINTED-SW.
255010*
255020*
255030 255-RETRIEVE-PENDING-MASTER.
255040*
255050      MOVE OLD-MASTER-IN-RECORD TO EM-EMPLOYEE-MASTER-WORK-AREA.
255060      MOVE WS-CURRENT-MASTER-KEY TO WS-PREVIOUS-MASTER-KEY.
255070      MOVE EM-PLANT-CODE TO WS-CURRENT-MASTER-MAJOR-FIELD.
255080      MOVE EM-DEPARTMENT-NUMBER TO WS-CURRENT-MASTER-INTER-FIELD.
255090      MOVE EM-EMPLOYEE-NUMBER TO WS-CURRENT-MASTER-MINOR-FIELD.
255100      MOVE 'NO ' TO WS-MASTER-PENDING-SW
255110                   WS-MASTER-REQUIRED-SW.
260010*
260020*
260030 260-CREATE-MASTER-RECORD.
260040*
260050      MOVE SPACES TO EM-EMPLOYEE-MASTER-WORK-AREA.
260060      MOVE '85' TO EM-RECORD-CODE.
260070      MOVE ET-PLANT-CODE TO EM-PLANT-CODE.
260080      MOVE ET-DEPARTMENT-NUMBER TO EM-DEPARTMENT-NUMBER.
260090      MOVE ET-EMPLOYEE-NUMBER TO EM-EMPLOYEE-NUMBER.
260100      MOVE ET-LAST-NAME TO EM-LAST-NAME.
260110      MOVE ET-FIRST-NAME TO EM-FIRST-NAME.
260120      MOVE ET-MIDDLE-INITIAL TO EM-MIDDLE-INITIAL.
260130      MOVE ET-HOURLY-RATE TO EM-HOURLY-RATE.
260140      MOVE WS-DATE-WORK TO EM-DATE-LAST-ACTIVITY.
270010*
270020*
270030 270-CHANGE-MASTER-FIELDS.
270040*
270050      IF ET-LAST-NAME IS EQUAL TO SPACES
270060          NEXT SENTENCE
270070      ELSE
270080          MOVE ET-LAST-NAME TO EM-LAST-NAME.
270090*
270100      IF ET-FIRST-NAME IS EQUAL TO SPACES
270110          NEXT SENTENCE
270120      ELSE
270130          MOVE ET-FIRST-NAME TO EM-FIRST-NAME.
270140*
270150      IF ET-MIDDLE-INITIAL IS EQUAL TO SPACES
270160          NEXT SENTENCE
270170      ELSE IF ET-MIDDLE-INITIAL IS EQUAL TO '$'
270180          MOVE SPACES TO EM-MIDDLE-INITIAL
270190      ELSE
270200          MOVE ET-MIDDLE-INITIAL TO EM-MIDDLE-INITIAL.
270210*
270220      IF ET-HOURLY-RATE-X IS EQUAL TO SPACES
270230          NEXT SENTENCE
270240      ELSE
270250          MOVE ET-HOURLY-RATE TO EM-HOURLY-RATE.
270260*
270270      MOVE WS-DATE-WORK TO EM-DATE-LAST-ACTIVITY.
280010*
280020*
280030 280-DELETE-MASTER-RECORD.
280040*
280050      EXIT.
280060*                                  THIS IS A NULL MODULE
280070*                                  FOR THIS PROGRAM
290010*
290020*
290030 290-IDENTIFY-ERROR-TYPE.
290040*
290050      IF ADD-TRANSACTION
290060          ADD 1 TO TC-TOTAL-ADD-TRANS-READ
290070          ADD 1 TO TC-ADD-TRANS-REJECTED
290080          MOVE 'UNABLE ADD-MASTER ALREADY ON FILE' TO DL-ERROR-MSG
290090      ELSE IF CHANGE-TRANSACTION
290100          ADD 1 TO TC-TOTAL-CHANGE-TRANS-READ
290110          ADD 1 TO TC-CHANGE-TRANS-REJECTED
290120          MOVE 'UNABLE CHANGE-MASTER NOT ON FILE ' TO DL-ERROR-MSG
290130      ELSE IF DELETE-TRANSACTION
290140          ADD 1 TO TC-TOTAL-DELETE-TRANS-READ
290150          ADD 1 TO TC-DELETE-TRANS-REJECTED
290160          MOVE 'UNABLE DELETE-MASTER NOT ON FILE ' TO DL-ERROR-MSG
290170      ELSE
290180          ADD 1 TO TC-TOTAL-ERROR-UPDATE-CODES
290190          MOVE 'UNABLE UPDATE-INVALID UPDATE CODE' TO DL-ERROR-MSG.
290200*
290210      MOVE 'REJECTED' TO DL-UPDATE-ACTION.
700010*
700020*
700030 700-PRINT-REPORT-TOTALS.
700040*
700050      PERFORM 870-PRINT-REPORT-HEADINGS.
700060      PERFORM 710-PRINT-TOTAL-LINE
700070          VARYING TC-SUBSCRIPT
700080          FROM 1
700090          BY 1
700100          UNTIL TC-SUBSCRIPT IS GREATER THAN TC-NUMBER-OF-ENTRIES.
710010*
710020*
710030 710-PRINT-TOTAL-LINE.
710040*
710050      MOVE TC-COUNT-DESCRIPTION (TC-SUBSCRIPT)
710060          TO TL-COUNT-DESCRIPTION.
710070      MOVE TC-RECORD-COUNT (TC-SUBSCRIPT) TO TL-RECORD-COUNT.
710080      MOVE TL-TOTAL-LINE TO REPORT-LINE.
710090      MOVE 1 TO WS-LINE-SPACING.
710100      PERFORM 890-WRITE-REPORT-LINE.
800010*
800020*
800030 800-READ-TRANSACTION-RECORD.
```

```
800040*
800050      MOVE WS-CURRENT-TRANS-SEQ-KEY TO WS-PREVIOUS-TRANS-SEQ-KEY.
800060*
800070      READ TRANSACTION-FILE INTO ET-EMPLOYEE-TRANSACTION-RECORD
800080          AT END MOVE 'YES' TO WS-TRANSACTION-END-OF-FILE-SW
800090          MOVE HIGH-VALUES TO WS-CURRENT-TRANS-SEQ-KEY.
800100*
800110      IF NOT TRANSACTION-END-OF-FILE
800120          ADD 1 TO TC-TOTAL-TRANS-READ
800130          MOVE ET-PLANT-CODE TO WS-CURRENT-TRANS-MAJOR-FIELD
800140          MOVE ET-DEPARTMENT-NUMBER TO WS-CURRENT-TRANS-INTER-FIELD
800150          MOVE ET-EMPLOYEE-NUMBER TO WS-CURRENT-TRANS-MINOR-FIELD
800160          MOVE ET-UPDATE-CODE TO WS-CURRENT-TRANS-UPDATE-CODE.
800170*
800180      IF WS-CURRENT-TRANS-SEQ-KEY
800190          IS LESS THAN WS-PREVIOUS-TRANS-SEQ-KEY
800200          MOVE 'PREVIOUS TRANSACTION KEY' TO SE-ERROR-MESSAGE
800210          MOVE WS-PREVIOUS-TRANS-SEQ-KEY TO SE-SEQUENCE-KEY
800220          MOVE 'TRANSACTION FILE OUT OF SEQUENCE ' TO DL-ERROR-MSG
800230          MOVE ' CURRENT TRANSACTION KEY' TO SE-ERROR-MESSAGE-HOLD
800240          MOVE WS-CURRENT-TRANS-SEQ-KEY TO WS-SEQUENCE-KEY-HOLD
800250          PERFORM 900-ABORT-PROGRAM-RUN.
800260*
800270      MOVE 'NO ' TO WS-TRANSACTION-REQUIRED-SW.
810010*
810020*
810030 810-READ-MASTER-RECORD.
810040*
810050      MOVE WS-CURRENT-MASTER-KEY TO WS-PREVIOUS-MASTER-KEY.
810060*
810070      READ OLD-MASTER-IN-FILE
810080          AT END MOVE 'YES' TO WS-MASTER-END-OF-FILE-SW
810090          MOVE HIGH-VALUES TO WS-CURRENT-MASTER-KEY
810100                            OLD-MASTER-IN-RECORD.
810110*
810120      IF NOT MASTER-END-OF-FILE
810130          MOVE OLD-MASTER-IN-RECORD TO EM-EMPLOYEE-MASTER-WORK-AREA
810140          ADD 1 TO TC-MASTERS-READ
810150          MOVE EM-PLANT-CODE TO WS-CURRENT-MASTER-MAJOR-FIELD
810160          MOVE EM-DEPARTMENT-NUMBER
810170              TO WS-CURRENT-MASTER-INTER-FIELD
810180          MOVE EM-EMPLOYEE-NUMBER TO WS-CURRENT-MASTER-MINOR-FIELD.
810190*
810200      IF WS-CURRENT-MASTER-KEY
810210          IS NOT GREATER THAN WS-PREVIOUS-MASTER-KEY
810220          MOVE '      PREVIOUS MASTER KEY' TO SE-ERROR-MESSAGE
810230          MOVE WS-PREVIOUS-MASTER-KEY TO SE-SEQUENCE-KEY
810240          MOVE 'MASTER FILE OUT OF SEQUENCE     ' TO DL-ERROR-MSG
810250          MOVE '      CURRENT MASTER KEY' TO SE-ERROR-MESSAGE-HOLD
810260          MOVE WS-CURRENT-MASTER-KEY TO WS-SEQUENCE-KEY-HOLD
810270          PERFORM 900-ABORT-PROGRAM-RUN.
810280*
810290      MOVE 'NO ' TO WS-MASTER-REQUIRED-SW.
850010*
850020*
850030 850-WRITE-MASTER-RECORD.
850040*
850050      WRITE NEW-MASTER-OUT-RECORD
850060          FROM EM-EMPLOYEE-MASTER-WORK-AREA.
850070      ADD 1 TO TC-MASTERS-WRITTEN.
850080      MOVE 'NO ' TO WS-MASTER-TO-BE-WRITTEN-SW.
870010*
870020*
870030 870-PRINT-REPORT-HEADINGS.
870040*
870050      ADD 1 TO WS-PAGE-COUNT.
870060      MOVE WS-PAGE-COUNT TO H2-PAGE-NBR.
870070      MOVE H1-HEADING-LINE-1 TO REPORT-LINE.
870080      PERFORM 880-WRITE-REPORT-TOP-LINE.
870090      MOVE H2-HEADING-LINE-2 TO REPORT-LINE.
870100      MOVE 1 TO WS-LINE-SPACING.
870110      PERFORM 890-WRITE-REPORT-LINE.
870120      MOVE H3-HEADING-LINE-3 TO REPORT-LINE.
870130      MOVE 2 TO WS-LINE-SPACING.
870140      PERFORM 890-WRITE-REPORT-LINE.
870150      MOVE H4-HEADING-LINE-4 TO REPORT-LINE.
870160      MOVE 1 TO WS-LINE-SPACING.
870170      PERFORM 890-WRITE-REPORT-LINE.
870180      MOVE SPACES TO REPORT-LINE.
870190      PERFORM 890-WRITE-REPORT-LINE.
880010*
880020*
880030 880-WRITE-REPORT-TOP-LINE.
880040*
880050      WRITE REPORT-LINE
880060          AFTER ADVANCING PAGE.
880070      MOVE 1 TO WS-LINES-USED.
890010*
890020*
890030 890-WRITE-REPORT-LINE.
890040*
890050      WRITE REPORT-LINE
890060          AFTER ADVANCING WS-LINE-SPACING.
890070      ADD WS-LINE-SPACING TO WS-LINES-USED.
900010*
900020*
900030 900-ABORT-PROGRAM-RUN.
900040*
900050      MOVE 'ABORTED ' TO DL-UPDATE-ACTION.
900060      MOVE DL-DETAIL-LINE TO REPORT-LINE.
900070      MOVE 3 TO WS-LINE-SPACING.
900080      PERFORM 890-WRITE-REPORT-LINE.
900090      MOVE SPACES TO DL-DETAIL-LINE.
900100      MOVE WS-ERROR-MESSAGE-HOLD TO SE-ERROR-MESSAGE.
900110      MOVE WS-SEQUENCE-KEY-HOLD TO SE-SEQUENCE-KEY.
900120      MOVE DL-DETAIL-LINE TO REPORT-LINE.
900130      MOVE 1 TO WS-LINE-SPACING.
900140      PERFORM 890-WRITE-REPORT-LINE.
900150      MOVE 'YES' TO WS-TRANSACTION-END-OF-FILE-SW
900160                   WS-MASTER-END-OF-FILE-SW.
900170      MOVE 'NO ' TO WS-MASTER-REQUIRED-SW
900180                   WS-MASTER-PENDING-SW.
```

Figure 3C.2. (continued)

WORKING-STORAGE SECTION.

```
┌─────────────────────────────────────────────┐
│                                               │
│   01   WS-SWITCHES.                           │      Miscellaneous program switches
│                                               │
├─────────────────────────────────────────────┤
│                                               │      Transaction and master record
│   01   WS-SEQUENCE-CONTROLS.                  │      keys for sequence checking
│                                               │
├─────────────────────────────────────────────┤
│                                               │      Control fields for audit/error
│   01   WS-REPORT-CONTROLS.                    │      report printing
│                                               │
├─────────────────────────────────────────────┤
│                                               │      Current date work area
│   01   WS-WORK-AREAS.                         │      and temporary hold areas
│                                               │
├─────────────────────────────────────────────┤
│   01   TC-TABLE-CONTROLS.                     │      Record count description
│                                               │      and total tables
│   01   TC-COUNT-DESCRIPTION-DATA.             │
│                                               │
│   01   TC-COUNT-DESCRIPTION-TABLE             │
│            REDEFINES                           │
│              TC-COUNT-DESCRIPTION-DATA.       │
│                                               │
│   01   TC-RECORD-COUNT-ENTRIES.               │
│                                               │
│   01   TC-RECORD-COUNTS                       │
│            REDEFINES                           │
│              TC-RECORD-COUNT-ENTRIES.         │
│                                               │
├─────────────────────────────────────────────┤
│                                               │      Employee-transaction record
│   01   ET-EMPLOYEE-TRANSACTION-RECORD.        │      description
│                                               │
├─────────────────────────────────────────────┤
│                                               │      Employee master record
│   01   EM-EMPLOYEE-MASTER-WORK-AREA.          │      description and work area
│                                               │
├─────────────────────────────────────────────┤
│   01   H1-HEADING-LINE-1.                     │      Audit/error report heading lines
│                                               │
│   01   H2-HEADING-LINE-2.                     │
│                                               │
│   01   H3-HEADING-LINE-3.                     │
│                                               │
│   01   H4-HEADING-LINE-4.                     │
│                                               │
├─────────────────────────────────────────────┤
│                                               │      Audit/error line
│   01   DL-DETAIL-LINE.                        │
│                                               │
├─────────────────────────────────────────────┤
│                                               │      Error line printed when
│   01   SE-SEQUENCE-ERROR-LINE                 │      out-of-sequence condition detected
│            REDEFINES DL-DETAIL-LINE.          │
│                                               │
├─────────────────────────────────────────────┤
│                                               │      Record count total line
│   01   TL-TOTAL-LINE.                         │
│                                               │
└─────────────────────────────────────────────┘
```

Figure 3C.3. WORKING-STORAGE SECTION organization: SEQMAINT program.

total tables, (6) the input employee-transaction record description, (7) the master record work-area description, and (8) audit/error report line entries describing each report line field. The organization of these categories in the WORKING-STORAGE SECTION is depicted in Figure 3C.3.

The coding for each of these WORKING-STORAGE SECTION entry categories will be explained.

```
010040*
010050*
010060 01  WS-SWITCHES.
010070*
010080     05   WS-TRANSACTION-END-OF-FILE-SW    PIC X(3).
010090          88   TRANSACTION-END-OF-FILE                   VALUE 'YES'.
010100*
010110     05   WS-MASTER-END-OF-FILE-SW         PIC X(3).
010120          88   MASTER-END-OF-FILE                        VALUE 'YES'.
010130*
010140     05   WS-TRANSACTION-REQUIRED-SW       PIC X(3).
010150          88   TRANSACTION-REQUIRED                      VALUE 'YES'.
010160*
010170     05   WS-MASTER-REQUIRED-SW            PIC X(3).
010180          88   MASTER-REQUIRED                           VALUE 'YES'.
010190*
010200     05   WS-MASTER-TO-BE-WRITTEN-SW       PIC X(3).
010210          88   MASTER-TO-BE-WRITTEN                      VALUE 'YES'.
010220*
010230     05   WS-AUDIT-LINE-TO-BE-PRINTED-SW   PIC X(3).
010240          88   AUDIT-LINE-TO-BE-PRINTED                  VALUE 'YES'.
010250*
010260     05   WS-MASTER-PENDING-SW             PIC X(3).
010270          88   MASTER-PENDING                            VALUE 'YES'.
```

Figure 3C.4. Program switches: SEQMAINT program.

Program switches

The program switches are coded within the 01-level WS-SWITCHES entry. Seven switches are used to control the program flow. Each switch has two states—a value of "YES" or "NO." As shown in Figure 3C.4, each switch is prefixed by the initials WS (to indicate that it is a **W**ORKING-**S**TORAGE field) and suffixed by the initials SW (for **sw**itch). Each switch has an 88-level condition-name associated with it for the affirmative condition.

The first two switches, WS-TRANSACTION-END-OF-FILE-SW and WS-MASTER-END-OF-FILE-SW, are typical end-of-file switches. With many sequential file-processing programs, just one file controls the processing and hence only one end-of-file switch is required. However, with a sequential file-maintenance program, the run cannot be completed until both the transaction file and the master file have been completely processed. Depending upon the key values of the data records that are present in the run, either file may end first. Thus two end-of-file-switches—one for the transaction file and one for the master file—will initially be set to a value of "NO" and then set to a value of "YES" when their respective end-of-file has been detected.

The next four switches are used to control the reading of input records and the writing of output records. With many programs, there is a one-to-one relationship between program-processing iterations (the structured equivalent of a program loop) and I-O operations. That is, in a detail-printed report, one input record is read and one output line is printed during each detail-print cycle. However, in a sequential file-maintenance program, matches between the control keys of the transaction record and the master record must occur. Therefore, for a given match iteration, either (1) both a transaction record and a master record must be read, (2) only a transaction record should be read, or (3) only a master record should be read. Conditional processing is likewise required to control the writing of output master records and the printing of report lines.

The WS-TRANSACTION-REQUIRED-SW and WS-MASTER-REQUIRED-SW will be set to "YES" whenever the next transaction or master record, respectively, is to be read. Each will be set to "NO" immediately after the record has been read.

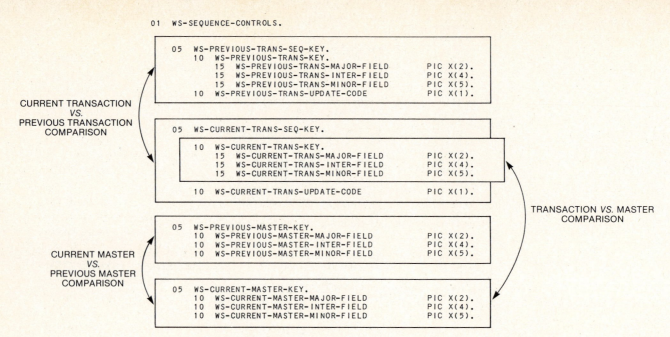

```
01  WS-SEQUENCE-CONTROLS.

     05   WS-PREVIOUS-TRANS-SEQ-KEY.
          10   WS-PREVIOUS-TRANS-KEY.
               15   WS-PREVIOUS-TRANS-MAJOR-FIELD        PIC X(2).
               15   WS-PREVIOUS-TRANS-INTER-FIELD        PIC X(4).
               15   WS-PREVIOUS-TRANS-MINOR-FIELD        PIC X(5).
          10   WS-PREVIOUS-TRANS-UPDATE-CODE             PIC X(1).


     05   WS-CURRENT-TRANS-SEQ-KEY.

          10   WS-CURRENT-TRANS-KEY.
               15   WS-CURRENT-TRANS-MAJOR-FIELD         PIC X(2).
               15   WS-CURRENT-TRANS-INTER-FIELD         PIC X(4).
               15   WS-CURRENT-TRANS-MINOR-FIELD         PIC X(5).

          10   WS-CURRENT-TRANS-UPDATE-CODE              PIC X(1).


     05   WS-PREVIOUS-MASTER-KEY.
          10   WS-PREVIOUS-MASTER-MAJOR-FIELD            PIC X(2).
          10   WS-PREVIOUS-MASTER-INTER-FIELD            PIC X(4).
          10   WS-PREVIOUS-MASTER-MINOR-FIELD            PIC X(5).


     05   WS-CURRENT-MASTER-KEY.
          10   WS-CURRENT-MASTER-MAJOR-FIELD             PIC X(2).
          10   WS-CURRENT-MASTER-INTER-FIELD             PIC X(4).
          10   WS-CURRENT-MASTER-MINOR-FIELD             PIC X(5).
```

CURRENT TRANSACTION
vs.
PREVIOUS TRANSACTION
COMPARISON

TRANSACTION *vs.* MASTER
COMPARISON

CURRENT MASTER
vs.
PREVIOUS MASTER
COMPARISON

Figure 3C.5. Sequence control fields: SEQMAINT program.

For output records, the WS-MASTER-TO-BE-WRITTEN-SW will be set to "YES" whenever a master record is to be written to the output master file and set to "NO" immediately after the record has been written. The WS-AUDIT-LINE-TO-BE-PRINTED-SW similarly controls the printing of output lines on the audit/error report.

The last switch specified, WS-MASTER-PENDING-SW, is used to identify the situation in which a transaction record has been used to create a master record. This means that a master record with a higher control-key value has already been read and placed in an abeyance or "pending" status until the newly created master record has been written to the output master file. This switch is tested to ensure that, after a new master is created from a transaction record, the pending master already read into storage is retrieved instead of acquiring another master record from the input master file. Reading another master record would eradicate the unprocessed pending master record. This would result in master records being "dropped" or lost during the program run. Therefore, the WS-MASTER-TO-BE-WRITTEN-SW is set to "YES" when a new master record is created from a transaction record and reset to "NO" immediately after the newly created master record is written to the output master file.

Sequence control fields

The WS-SEQUENCE-CONTROLS fields are used for two purposes: (1) to ensure that the transaction and master files are in the proper sequence, and (2) to match the transaction record control key with its corresponding location in the master file.

Notice in the diagram of Figure 3C.5 that, for sequence checking of the transaction file, the WS-CURRENT-TRANS-SEQ-KEY group entry is compared to

```
012010*
012020*
012030 01  WS-REPORT-CONTROLS.
012040     05  WS-PAGE-COUNT                   PIC S9(4)          COMP-3.
012050     05  WS-LINES-PER-PAGE               PIC S9(2)  VALUE +55
012060                                                        COMP SYNC.
012070     05  WS-LINES-USED                   PIC S9(2)      COMP SYNC.
012080     05  WS-LINE-SPACING                 PIC S9(2).
```

Figure 3C.6. Report control fields: SEQMAINT program.

the WS-PREVIOUS-TRANS-SEQ-KEY group entry. Both of these group entries contain not only the master file control key but also the transaction update code as the minor field.

To sequence check the input master file, the WS-CURRENT-MASTER-KEY is compared to the WS-PREVIOUS-MASTER-KEY field. These entries both contain the proper master control-key fields but do not contain a transaction update-code field. This is because there is no update-code field in the master records, of course.

Then, to compare the correspondence of the transaction file record key versus the master file record key for the updating process, the WS-CURRENT-TRANS-KEY and WS-CURRENT-MASTER-KEY entries are used. Notice that the WS-CURRENT-TRANS-UPDATE-CODE field is not included within the WS-CURRENT-TRANS-KEY group entry.

Report control fields

The WS-REPORT-CONTROLS fields, as displayed in Figure 3C.6, are used to control the typical report functions of sequential page numbering, page skipping over the continuous form perforations to the top of the next report page, and variable-line spacing.

The WS-PAGE-COUNT field is used to keep track of the page number of the report page that is to be printed. It will be incremented each time a page is headed. To make the incrementation arithmetic more efficient, a USAGE of COMP-3 has been specified. COMP-3 usage also provides efficient conversion to DISPLAY usage when the field is moved to the report heading line for printing.

To control the page span, the WS-LINES-PER-PAGE field is specified with a VALUE of + 55, as called for in the programming specifications.

The WS-LINES-USED field is coded to accumulate a running total of the number of lines that have been printed on each page. This WS-LINES-USED field accumulation will be compared with the WS-LINES-PER-PAGE limit value to determine when it is time to skip to a new report page and print the page headings.

Because the WS-LINES-USED field will be used for integer accumulation but not actually printed, it is specified with a USAGE of COMP to optimize the arithmetic operations. Since the WS-LINES-USED field must be compared with the WS-LINES-PER-PAGE field, the latter field has also been specified with COMP usage to make the comparison consistent and efficient.

The purpose of the WS-LINE-SPACING field is to hold the integer that is used to control the line spacing—single, double, triple, and so forth—on the report. This WS-LINE-SPACING field will be referenced in the ADVANCING phrase of the WRITE statement that prints the report lines.

Current date work area

The WS-DATE-WORK and WS-DATE-REFORMAT fields are used to obtain the run date from the operating system with the ACCEPT/FROM DATE statement

```
013010*
013020*
013030 01  WS-WORK-AREAS.
013040     05  WS-DATE-WORK                      PIC 9(6).
013050     05  WS-DATE-REFORMAT REDEFINES WS-DATE-WORK.
013060         10  WS-YEAR                       PIC 9(2).
013070         10  WS-MONTH                      PIC 9(2).
013080         10  WS-DAY                        PIC 9(2).
013090     05  WS-ERROR-MESSAGE-HOLD             PIC X(24).
013100     05  WS-SEQUENCE-KEY-HOLD              PIC X(12).
```

Figure 3C.7. Work areas: SEQMAINT program.

```
014010*
014020*
014030 01  TC-TABLE-CONTROLS.
014040     05  TC-SUBSCRIPT                      PIC S9(4)      COMP SYNC.
014050     05  TC-NUMBER-OF-ENTRIES              PIC S9(4)      VALUE +14
014060                                                          COMP SYNC.
015010*
015020 01  TC-COUNT-DESCRIPTION-DATA.
015030     05  FILLER        PIC X(20)   VALUE 'TRANSACTIONS READ   '.
015040     05  FILLER        PIC X(20)   VALUE '    ADDS            '.
015050     05  FILLER        PIC X(20)   VALUE '      PROCESSED     '.
015060     05  FILLER        PIC X(20)   VALUE '      REJECTED      '.
015070     05  FILLER        PIC X(20)   VALUE '    CHANGES         '.
015080     05  FILLER        PIC X(20)   VALUE '      PROCESSED     '.
015090     05  FILLER        PIC X(20)   VALUE '      REJECTED      '.
015100     05  FILLER        PIC X(20)   VALUE '    DELETES         '.
015110     05  FILLER        PIC X(20)   VALUE '      PROCESSED     '.
015120     05  FILLER        PIC X(20)   VALUE '      REJECTED      '.
015130     05  FILLER        PIC X(20)   VALUE '    ERROR UPDATE CODES'.
015140     05  FILLER        PIC X(20)   VALUE 'MASTERS READ        '.
015150     05  FILLER        PIC X(20)   VALUE 'MASTER CHANGES      '.
015160     05  FILLER        PIC X(20)   VALUE 'MASTERS WRITTEN     '.
015170 01  TC-COUNT-DESCRIPTION-TABLE
015180         REDEFINES TC-COUNT-DESCRIPTION-DATA.
015190     05  TC-COUNT-DESCRIPTION       OCCURS 14 TIMES
015200                                                PIC X(20).
016010*
016020 01  TC-RECORD-COUNT-ENTRIES                          COMP-3.
016030     05  TC-TOTAL-TRANS-READ            PIC S9(5).
016040     05  TC-TOTAL-ADD-TRANS-READ        PIC S9(5).
016050     05  TC-ADD-TRANS-PROCESSED         PIC S9(5).
016060     05  TC-ADD-TRANS-REJECTED          PIC S9(5).
016070     05  TC-TOTAL-CHANGE-TRANS-READ     PIC S9(5).
016080     05  TC-CHANGE-TRANS-PROCESSED      PIC S9(5).
016090     05  TC-CHANGE-TRANS-REJECTED       PIC S9(5).
016100     05  TC-TOTAL-DELETE-TRANS-READ     PIC S9(5).
016110     05  TC-DELETE-TRANS-PROCESSED      PIC S9(5).
016120     05  TC-DELETE-TRANS-REJECTED       PIC S9(5).
016130     05  TC-TOTAL-ERROR-UPDATE-CODES    PIC S9(5).
016140     05  TC-MASTERS-READ                PIC S9(5).
016150     05  TC-MASTER-CHANGES              PIC S9(5).
016160     05  TC-MASTERS-WRITTEN             PIC S9(5).
016170 01  TC-RECORD-COUNTS REDEFINES TC-RECORD-COUNT-ENTRIES.
016180     05  TC-RECORD-COUNT              OCCURS 14 TIMES
016190                                        PIC S9(5)        COMP-3.
```

Figure 3C.8. Record count description and total tables: SEQMAINT program.

and to reformat the date into *mmddyy* sequence for printing on the report heading. Figure 3C.7 shows these current date work-area fields and explains the reason for their redefinition.

Record count description and total tables

These tables are presented in Figure 3C.8. The TC-TABLE-CONTROLS fields control the printing of the record count totals. TC-SUBSCRIPT is the subscript that will be used to reference the table. For efficiency, it is assigned to a PICTURE clause of S9(4), a USAGE of COMP, and the SYNC clause. The TC-

```
020010*
020020*
020030 01  ET-EMPLOYEE-TRANSACTION-RECORD.
020040     05  ET-RECORD-CODE                    PIC X(2).
020050     05  ET-UPDATE-CODE                    PIC X(1).
020060         88   DELETE-TRANSACTION                          VALUE '1'.
020070         88   ADD-TRANSACTION                             VALUE '2'.
020080         88   CHANGE-TRANSACTION                          VALUE '3'.
020090     05  ET-EMPLOYEE-NUMBER                PIC X(5).
020100     05  ET-LAST-NAME                      PIC X(13).
020110     05  ET-FIRST-NAME                     PIC X(12).
020120     05  ET-MIDDLE-INITIAL                 PIC X(1).
020130     05  ET-PLANT-CODE                     PIC X(2).
020140     05  ET-DEPARTMENT-NUMBER              PIC X(4).
020150     05  ET-HOURLY-RATE                    PIC S9(2)V99.
020160     05  ET-HOURLY-RATE-X REDEFINES ET-HOURLY-RATE
020170                                           PIC X(4).
020180     05  FILLER                            PIC X(36).
```

Figure 3C.9. Input employee-transaction record description: SEQMAINT program.

NUMBER-OF-ENTRIES field is similarly specified for efficiency and is assigned a VALUE of +14 because there are 14 entries in the record count table.

The TC-COUNT-DESCRIPTION-DATA entries are used to establish the constant data for the record count descriptions. Then the TC-COUNT-DESCRIPTION-TABLE specifications REDEFINE the table data entries with an OCCURS clause so that they can be referenced with a subscript in the PROCEDURE DIVISION.

The TC-RECORD-COUNT-ENTRIES group item is specified with COMP-3 usage. This means that each of the elementary fields within the group has a USAGE of COMP-3. Then the TC-RECORD-COUNTS entry is coded to REDEFINE TC-RECORD-COUNT-ENTRIES so that the individual record count totals can be referenced with a subscript in the PROCEDURE DIVISION.

Actually, the TC-RECORD-COUNT-ENTRIES coding is not required; just the TC-RECORD-COUNTS entries (without the REDEFINES clause) would suffice. The former was included to assign an individual unique data-name to each record count field. This makes the PROCEDURE DIVISION program coding for incrementation of the count fields easier to understand. That is, the meaning of the statement ADD 1 TO TC-TOTAL-CHANGE-TRANS-READ is more readily apparent than ADD 1 TO TC-RECORD-COUNT (5).

Also, the TC-RECORD-COUNT entry could have been specified with an index (the INDEXED BY clause) rather than a subscript. A subscript is more effective in this instance, however, because these table entries are not used for lookups and because of the way they are referenced in conjunction with the TC-COUNT-DESCRIPTION entries.

Input employee-transaction record description

The input employee-transaction record has been specified as shown in Figure 3C.9. Each field has been assigned a prefix of ET for **Employee Transaction** record.

Notice that 88-level-condition-names of DELETE-TRANSACTION, ADD-TRANSACTION, and CHANGE-TRANSACTION have been assigned to the numeric update-code values of 1, 2, and 3, respectively.

Although the ET-EMPLOYEE-NUMBER and ET-DEPARTMENT-NUMBER fields are actually numeric fields, observe that they have been specified with an alphanumeric PICTURE clause. When there are numeric fields without decimal positions that are not involved in arithmetic operations, it is usually a good idea to define such fields as alphanumeric rather than numeric. Processing with numeric PICTURE clauses is generally less efficient because of the need for arithmetic sign handling. Also, on some computer systems, numeric fields introduce the possibility that data exceptions may occur and cause abnormal program termination.

Observe that the numeric ET-HOURLY-RATE field has been redefined as an alphanumeric field: ET-HOURLY-RATE-X. This alphanumeric redefinition is provided so that an alphanumeric relation condition IF statement can be used in the PROCEDURE DIVISION to test for the presence or absence of data within the field of a change transaction record.

Employee master record work-area description

The record definition for the area that is used to process the employee master records is exhibited in Figure 3C.10. Fields of the record have been prefixed with EM for **E**mployee **M**aster record.

```
025010*
025020*
025030 01   EM-EMPLOYEE-MASTER-WORK-AREA.
025040      05   EM-RECORD-CODE              PIC X(2).
025050      05   FILLER                      PIC X(1).
025060      05   EM-PLANT-CODE               PIC X(2).
025070      05   EM-DEPARTMENT-NUMBER        PIC X(4).
025080      05   EM-EMPLOYEE-NUMBER          PIC X(5).
025090      05   EM-LAST-NAME                PIC X(13).
025100      05   EM-FIRST-NAME               PIC X(12).
025110      05   EM-MIDDLE-INITIAL           PIC X(1).
025120      05   EM-HOURLY-RATE              PIC S9(2)V99.
025130      05   FILLER                      PIC X(30).
025140      05   EM-DATE-LAST-ACTIVITY       PIC 9(6).
```

Figure 3C.10. Employee master record work-area description: SEQMAINT program.

The record has been defined in accordance with its specifications (except for alphanumeric definition of the nonarithmetic numeric fields).

Audit/error report line entries

The formats of the four heading lines, one detail line, and one total line of the audit/error list conclude the WORKING-STORAGE SECTION entries for this SEQMAINT program. Each of the report lines is defined in accordance with its specifications.

Notice that the record image area of the DL-DETAIL-LINE is redefined to provide for the situation in which an out-of-sequence master or transaction file necessitates printing the SE-SEQUENCE-ERROR-LINE. This is depicted in Figure 3C.11.

Part A: Diagram of redefinition

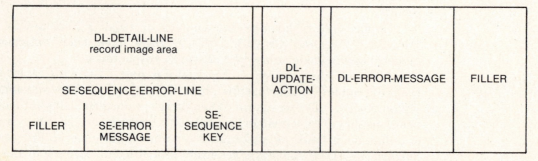

Figure 3C.11. Detail line with sequence error-line redefinition: SEQMAINT program.

```
034010*
034020*
034030 01  DL-DETAIL-LINE.
034040     05  FILLER                              PIC X(1).
034050     05  FILLER                              PIC X(1)     VALUE SPACES.
034060     05  DL-RECORD-CODE                      PIC X(2).
034070     05  FILLER                              PIC X(4)     VALUE SPACES.
034080     05  DL-UPDATE-CODE                      PIC X(1).
034090     05  FILLER                              PIC X(4)     VALUE SPACES.
034100     05  DL-PLANT-CODE                       PIC X(2).
034110     05  FILLER                              PIC X(4)     VALUE SPACES.
034120     05  DL-DEPARTMENT-NUMBER                PIC X(4).
034130     05  FILLER                              PIC X(1)     VALUE SPACES.
034140     05  DL-EMPLOYEE-NUMBER                  PIC X(5).
034150     05  FILLER                              PIC X(2)     VALUE SPACES.
034160     05  DL-LAST-NAME                        PIC X(13).
034170     05  FILLER                              PIC X(1)     VALUE SPACES.
034180     05  DL-FIRST-NAME                       PIC X(12).
034190     05  FILLER                              PIC X(1)     VALUE SPACES.
034200     05  DL-MIDDLE-INITIAL                   PIC X(1).
034210     05  FILLER                              PIC X(3)     VALUE SPACES.
034220     05  DL-HOURLY-RATE                      PIC ZZ.99.
034230     05  DL-HOURLY-RATE-X REDEFINES DL-HOURLY-RATE
034240                                             PIC X(5).
034250     05  FILLER                              PIC X(2)     VALUE SPACES.
034260     05  DL-UPDATE-ACTION                    PIC X(8).
034270     05  FILLER                              PIC X(1)     VALUE SPACES.
034280     05  DL-ERROR-MSG                        PIC X(33).
034290     05  FILLER                              PIC X(22)    VALUE SPACES.
035010*
035020*
035030 01  SE-SEQUENCE-ERROR-LINE REDEFINES DL-DETAIL-LINE.
035040     05  FILLER                              PIC X(1).
035050     05  FILLER                              PIC X(26).
035060     05  SE-ERROR-MESSAGE                    PIC X(24).
035070     05  FILLER                              PIC X(1).
035080     05  SE-SEQUENCE-KEY                     PIC XXBXXXXBXXXXXBX.
035090     05  FILLER                              PIC X(2).
```

Figure 3C.11. (continued)

PROCEDURE DIVISION Entries

The processing logic of each PROCEDURE DIVISION module for this SEQMAINT program will be explained.

000-MAINTAIN-SEQUENTIAL-FILE

This is the mainline module. First, the two input and two output files are opened. Then the 100-INITIALIZE-VARIABLE-FIELDS module is performed. This program uses the conditional-processing method of read statement handling, so no prim-

```
050050*
050060*
050070 000-MAINTAIN-SEQUENTIAL-FILE.
050080*
050090     OPEN INPUT  TRANSACTION-FILE
050100                 OLD-MASTER-IN-FILE
050110          OUTPUT NEW-MASTER-OUT-FILE
050120                 REPORT-FILE.
050130     PERFORM 100-INITIALIZE-VARIABLE-FIELDS.
050140     PERFORM 200-UPDATE-MASTER-RECORD
050150         UNTIL TRANSACTION-END-OF-FILE
050160         AND   MASTER-END-OF-FILE.
050170     PERFORM 700-PRINT-REPORT-TOTALS.
050180     CLOSE TRANSACTION-FILE
050190           OLD-MASTER-IN-FILE
050200           NEW-MASTER-OUT-FILE
050210           REPORT-FILE.
050220     STOP RUN.
```

ing read is present in this module. The record-processing module, 200-UPDATE-MASTER-RECORD, is performed until *both* the transaction file *and* the master file have reached end-of-file. After both files have been fully processed, the 700-PRINT-REPORT-TOTALS module is performed to print the record counts. Finally, the four files are closed and the run is stopped.

100-INITIALIZE-VARIABLE-FIELDS

```
100010*
100020*
100030 100-INITIALIZE-VARIABLE-FIELDS.
100040*
100050     MOVE 'NO ' TO WS-TRANSACTION-END-OF-FILE-SW
100060                   WS-MASTER-END-OF-FILE-SW
100070                   WS-MASTER-TO-BE-WRITTEN-SW
100080                   WS-AUDIT-LINE-TO-BE-PRINTED-SW
100090                   WS-MASTER-PENDING-SW.
100100     MOVE 'YES' TO WS-TRANSACTION-REQUIRED-SW
100110                   WS-MASTER-REQUIRED-SW.
100120     MOVE ZERO TO WS-PAGE-COUNT.
100130     ADD 1 WS-LINES-PER-PAGE GIVING WS-LINES-USED.
100140     ACCEPT WS-DATE-WORK FROM DATE.
100150     MOVE WS-MONTH TO H1-MONTH.
100160     MOVE WS-DAY TO H1-DAY.
100180     MOVE WS-YEAR TO H1-YEAR.
100180     MOVE LOW-VALUES TO WS-SEQUENCE-CONTROLS.
100190     MOVE SPACES TO DL-ERROR-MSG.
100200     PERFORM 110-ZERO-RECORD-COUNTS
100210        VARYING TC-SUBSCRIPT
100220        FROM 1
100230        BY 1
100240        UNTIL TC-SUBSCRIPT IS GREATER THAN TC-NUMBER-OF-ENTRIES.
110010*
110020*
110030 110-ZERO-RECORD-COUNTS.
110040*
110050     MOVE ZERO TO TC-RECORD-COUNT (TC-SUBSCRIPT).
```

In this initialization module, each of the seven switches is set to its appropriate initial value. Notice that the WS-TRANSACTION-REQUIRED-SW and the WS-MASTER-REQUIRED-SW are both set to "YES" (so that both a transaction and a master record will be read during the first iteration of the 200-UPDATE-MASTER-RECORD module).

After initializing the switches, the WS-REPORT-CONTROLS fields for the page count and the line span are set. The WS-PAGE-COUNT field is set to ZERO, and the WS-LINES-USED field is set to trigger the report heading lines for the first page of the audit/error list. (The heading lines for the first page will be printed during the first iteration of the 220-PRINT-AUDIT-ERROR-LINE module.)

Next, the run date is accepted into the WS-DATE-WORK field, and then the month, day, and year are individually moved to the corresponding fields of the first heading line. The WS-MONTH, WS-DAY, and WS-YEAR field must be moved individually because the run date is in *yymmdd* format (when obtained by the ACCEPT/FROM DATE statement), whereas the programming specifications call for the date to be expressed in *mmddyy* format on the heading line.

The WS-SEQUENCE-CONTROLS fields are set to LOW-VALUES to ensure that an out-of-sequence condition will not be erroneously signaled when sequence checking occurs for the first transaction record and first master record.

Finally, the record count fields are set to zero by the PERFORM/UNTIL statement that executes the 110-ZERO-RECORD-COUNTS module.

110-ZERO-RECORD-COUNTS

This module initializes each of the 14 TC-RECORD-COUNT fields to ZERO. It is important to recognize that, because these fields are in COMP-3 format, each elementary field must be individually set to zero. A statement that sets the group field to zero—MOVE ZERO TO TC-RECORD-COUNTS, for example—would result in erroneous initialization of the record count fields. This concept is illustrated in Figure 3C.12.

Part A: Correct initialization with COMP-3 ZEROS
(result of moving ZEROS to elementary fields)

TC-RECORD-COUNT

Occurrence 1	Occurrence 2	Occurrence 3	Occurrence 4	Occurrence 5	Occurrence 14
0 0 0 0 0 C	0 0 0 0 0 C	0 0 0 0 0 C	0 0 0 0 0 C	0 0 0 0 0 C	0 0 0 0 0 C

Part B: Incorrect initalization with DISPLAY ZEROS
(result of moving ZEROS to group field)

TC-RECORD-COUNT

Occurrence 1	Occurrence 2	Occurrence 3	Occurrence 4	Occurrence 5	Occurrence 14
F 0 F 0 F 0	F 0 F 0 F 0	F 0 F 0 F 0	F 0 F 0 F 0	F 0 F 0 F 0	F 0 F 0 F 0

Legend:
0 = Numeric ZERO
C = Valid COMP-3 arithmetic sign
F = Alphanumeric zone representation

Figure 3C.12. Initialization of COMP-3 fields to zero.

200-UPDATE-MASTER-RECORD

```
200010*
200020*
200030 200-UPDATE-MASTER-RECORD.
200040*
200050      IF TRANSACTION-REQUIRED
200060          PERFORM 800-READ-TRANSACTION-RECORD.
200070*
200080      IF MASTER-REQUIRED
200090          IF MASTER-PENDING
200100              PERFORM 255-RETRIEVE-PENDING-MASTER
200110          ELSE
200120              PERFORM 810-READ-MASTER-RECORD
200130      ELSE
200140          NEXT SENTENCE.
200150*
200160      IF TRANSACTION-END-OF-FILE
200170      AND MASTER-END-OF-FILE
200180          NEXT SENTENCE
200190      ELSE
200200          PERFORM 210-COMPARE-TRANS-WITH-MASTER.
200210*
200220      IF MASTER-TO-BE-WRITTEN
200230      OR (TRANSACTION-END-OF-FILE
200240          AND MASTER-END-OF-FILE
200250          AND MASTER-PENDING)
200260          PERFORM 850-WRITE-MASTER-RECORD.
200270*
200280      IF AUDIT-LINE-TO-BE-PRINTED
200290          PERFORM 220-PRINT-AUDIT-ERROR-LINE.
```

When the WS-TRANSACTION-REQUIRED-SW is set to "YES," it means a transaction record should be read so that the 800-READ-TRANSACTION-RECORD module is performed. Similarly, when the WS-MASTER-REQUIRED-SW is set to "YES," either the 810-READ-MASTER-RECORD or the 255-RETRIEVE-MASTER-RECORD module is performed to transfer a master record to the work area.

The next statement provides the conditional record-processing control by performing the 210-COMPARE-TRANS-WITH-MASTER paragraph on each iteration of this module except for the very last one when the TRANSACTION-END-OF-FILE and MASTER-END-OF-FILE conditions will both be true.

The 210-COMPARE-TRANS-WITH-MASTER module determines the proper processing actions to be taken, based upon the relationship between the transaction and master key values. As a result of the actions taken, the writing of a master record and/or the printing of a line on the audit/error list may be called for.

When it is necessary to write out a master record, the 850-WRITE-MASTER-RECORD module is performed. Two conditions will show the need to write an output master record. Usually, the requirement will be indicated by the WS-MASTER-TO-BE-WRITTEN-SW being set to "YES." The other condition will occur only once, if at all, during a program run. That is when the last transaction record is an add transaction and it has a control key value higher than the last record on the old master file. After the new master record has been constructed in the EM-EMPLOYEE-MASTER-WORK-AREA and after the end-of-file has been reached for both the transaction and master files, the newly created master record must be forced out of the work area and written to the output master file. This processing is handled by also performing the 850-WRITE-MASTER-RECORD module when the combined condition TRANSACTION-END-OF-FILE AND MASTER-END-OF-FILE AND MASTER-PENDING is true.

The last statement of this module causes the 220-PRINT-AUDIT-ERROR-LINE paragraph to be performed whenever the AUDIT-LINE-TO-BE-PRINTED-SW is set to "YES." This switch will be set whenever a transaction record is to be printed, either as an audit line or as an error line.

210-COMPARE-TRANS-WITH-MASTER

```
210010*
210020*
210030 210-COMPARE-TRANS-WITH-MASTER.
210040*
210050     IF WS-CURRENT-TRANS-KEY IS LESS THAN WS-CURRENT-MASTER-KEY
210060         PERFORM 230-ADD-MASTER-RECORD
210070     ELSE IF WS-CURRENT-TRANS-KEY
210080             IS GREATER THAN WS-CURRENT-MASTER-KEY
210090         PERFORM 240-PASS-MASTER-RECORD
210100     ELSE
210110         PERFORM 250-CHANGE-OR-DELETE-MASTER.
```

This module compares the WS-CURRENT-TRANS-KEY field with the WS-CURRENT-MASTER-KEY field. If the transaction key is lower, the 230-ADD-MASTER-RECORD paragraph is performed. If the transaction key is higher, the master record must be passed to the output master file, so the 240-PASS-MASTER-RECORD module is performed. If the transaction and master keys are equal, the 250-CHANGE-OR-DELETE-MASTER module will be performed.

220-PRINT-AUDIT-ERROR-LINE

```
220010*
220020*
220030 220-PRINT-AUDIT-ERROR-LINE.
220040*
220050     IF WS-LINES-USED IS NOT LESS THAN WS-LINES-PER-PAGE
220060         PERFORM 870-PRINT-REPORT-HEADINGS.
220070     MOVE ET-RECORD-CODE TO DL-RECORD-CODE.
220080     MOVE ET-UPDATE-CODE TO DL-UPDATE-CODE.
220090     MOVE ET-PLANT-CODE TO DL-PLANT-CODE.
220100     MOVE ET-DEPARTMENT-NUMBER TO DL-DEPARTMENT-NUMBER.
220110     MOVE ET-EMPLOYEE-NUMBER TO DL-EMPLOYEE-NUMBER.
220120     MOVE ET-LAST-NAME TO DL-LAST-NAME.
220130     MOVE ET-FIRST-NAME TO DL-FIRST-NAME.
220140     MOVE ET-MIDDLE-INITIAL TO DL-MIDDLE-INITIAL.
220150     IF ET-HOURLY-RATE IS NUMERIC
220160         MOVE ET-HOURLY-RATE TO DL-HOURLY-RATE
220170     ELSE
220180         MOVE ET-HOURLY-RATE-X TO DL-HOURLY-RATE-X.
220190     MOVE DL-DETAIL-LINE TO REPORT-LINE.
220200     MOVE 1 TO WS-LINE-SPACING.
220210     PERFORM 890-WRITE-REPORT-LINE.
220220     MOVE SPACES TO DL-DETAIL-LINE.
220230     MOVE 'NO ' TO WS-AUDIT-LINE-TO-BE-PRINTED-SW.
```

This module handles the printing of audit and error lines on the audit error report. Before the detail line is constructed, the WS-LINES-USED field is compared to the WS-LINES-PER-PAGE field. If the lines-used field is equal to or greater than the lines-per-page field, the 870-PRINT-REPORT-HEADINGS module will be performed to skip to a new report page and print the report headings. This will take place the first time through this module (to head the first report page) and whenever the current report page is full.

Then the detail audit/error line is constructed by moving each of the ET-EMPLOYEE-TRANSACTION-RECORD fields to the DL-DETAIL-LINE area of WORKING-STORAGE. The DL-DETAIL-LINE area is moved to the output REPORT-LINE area, the WS-LINE-SPACING field is set to single spacing in accordance with the programming specifications, and the 890-WRITE-REPORT-LINE module is performed.

Finally, the DL-DETAIL-LINE area is blanked out so that it will be ready for construction of the next report line. Because the audit line has now been printed, the WS-AUDIT-LINE-TO-BE-PRINTED-SW is reset to "NO."

Observe the conditional move of the ET-HOURLY-RATE field to the DL-HOURLY-RATE field. This is required because the ET-HOURLY-RATE field will be blank in delete-transaction records and in change transactions that do not change the hourly rate field.

If the ET-HOURLY-RATE field were moved unconditionally, problems would arise when processing transactions with a blank ET-HOURLY-RATE field. When the program is run on a computer that detects data exceptions, it would be canceled when the blank spaces were moved to the numeric-edited DL-HOURLY-RATE field. Even if the computer did not detect data exceptions, either erroneous data or a lone decimal point would appear on the audit/error line.

230-ADD-MASTER-RECORD

```
230010*
230020*
230030 230-ADD-MASTER-RECORD.
230040*
230050     IF ADD-TRANSACTION
230060         MOVE WS-CURRENT-TRANS-KEY TO WS-CURRENT-MASTER-KEY
230070         PERFORM 260-CREATE-MASTER-RECORD
230080         ADD 1 TO TC-TOTAL-ADD-TRANS-READ
230090         ADD 1 TO TC-ADD-TRANS-PROCESSED
230100         MOVE 'ADDED   ' TO DL-UPDATE-ACTION
230110         MOVE 'YES' TO WS-MASTER-PENDING-SW
230120     ELSE
230130         PERFORM 290-IDENTIFY-ERROR-TYPE.
230140     MOVE 'YES' TO WS-TRANSACTION-REQUIRED-SW
230150                   WS-AUDIT-LINE-TO-BE-PRINTED-SW.
```

This module is entered when the transaction key is lower than the master key. When this condition exists, only an add transaction can be correctly processed; a valid change or delete transaction would have already found a master key equal to the transaction key. Therefore, the update code of the transaction record is tested to ensure that an add transaction is being processed. If it is, the appropriate add master record processing can occur. If it is not, an error is identified on the audit/error list.

To add the master record, the following actions are taken:

1. The current transaction key is moved to the current master key field because the current transaction is now being converted into the current master record.

2. The 260-CREATE-MASTER-RECORD paragraph is performed to create the master record in the master work area.

3. The add-transaction record is tallied in the TC-TOTAL-ADD-TRANS-READ field.

4. The add-transaction record is also tallied in the TC-ADD-TRANS-PROCESSED field.
5. The update-action field of the audit/error list detail line is set to "ADDED."
6. The WS-MASTER-PENDING-SW is set to "YES" to indicate that the master record in the OLD-MASTER-IN-RECORD area of the FILE SECTION has not yet been processed.

If the transaction record does not contain an add update code, the 290-IDENTIFY-ERROR-TYPE paragraph is performed to identify the error on the audit/error line and to tally the error record counts.

Whether or not the transaction record is an add transaction, the WS-TRANSACTION-REQUIRED-SW and WS-AUDIT-LINE-TO-BE-PRINTED switches are set to "YES" because another transaction record is now required, and either an audit or an error line is to be printed.

240-PASS-MASTER-RECORD

```
240010*
240020*
240030 240-PASS-MASTER-RECORD.
240040*
240050     MOVE 'YES' TO WS-MASTER-TO-BE-WRITTEN-SW
240060                   WS-MASTER-REQUIRED-SW.
```

The 240-PASS-MASTER-RECORD module is entered whenever the transaction record key is greater than the master record key. This happens when the transaction record key value has not yet been reached in the master file, so a master record must be passed to the output master file.

This module simply sets the WS-MASTER-TO-BE-WRITTEN-SW and the WS-MASTER-REQUIRED-SW to "YES." Later in the processing cycle, this will cause the current master record that resides in the EM-EMPLOYEE-MASTER-WORK-AREA to be written and the next master record to be read.

250-CHANGE-OR-DELETE-MASTER

```
250010*
250020*
250030 250-CHANGE-OR-DELETE-MASTER.
250040*
250050     IF CHANGE-TRANSACTION
250060         PERFORM 270-CHANGE-MASTER-FIELDS
250070         ADD 1 TO TC-TOTAL-CHANGE-TRANS-READ
250080         ADD 1 TO TC-CHANGE-TRANS-PROCESSED
250090         ADD 1 TO TC-MASTER-CHANGES
250100         MOVE 'CHANGED ' TO DL-UPDATE-ACTION
250110     ELSE IF DELETE-TRANSACTION
250120         PERFORM 280-DELETE-MASTER-RECORD
250130         ADD 1 TO TC-TOTAL-DELETE-TRANS-READ
250140         ADD 1 TO TC-DELETE-TRANS-PROCESSED
250150         MOVE 'DELETED ' TO DL-UPDATE-ACTION
250160         MOVE 'YES' TO WS-MASTER-REQUIRED-SW
250170     ELSE
250180         PERFORM 290-IDENTIFY-ERROR-TYPE.
250190*
250200     MOVE 'YES' TO WS-TRANSACTION-REQUIRED-SW
250210                   WS-AUDIT-LINE-TO-BE-PRINTED-SW.
```

This module is entered if the transaction key is equal to the master key. When this occurs, the transaction type must be either a change or a delete. If the processing of an add transaction were permitted, a master record with a duplicate key value would be introduced into the master file. Therefore, the update code of the transaction record is tested to determine the type of transaction that is being processed. If it is a change or delete transaction, the appropriate processing occurs; if not, an error is identified on the audit/error list.

To change the master record, the following actions are taken:

1. The 270-CHANGE-MASTER-FIELDS paragraph is performed to change the master record in the master work area.
2. The change-transaction record is tallied in the TC-TOTAL-CHANGE-TRANS-READ field.
3. The change-transaction record is also tallied in the TC-CHANGE-TRANS-PROCESSED field.
4. The master record change is tallied in the TC-MASTER-CHANGES field.
5. The update-action field of the audit/error list detail line is set to "CHANGED."

To delete the master record, the following actions are taken:

1. The 280-DELETE-MASTER-RECORD paragraph is performed.
2. The delete-transaction record is tallied in the TC-TOTAL-DELETE-TRANS-READ field.
3. The delete-transaction record is also tallied in the TC-DELETE-TRANS-PROCESSED field.
4. The update-action field of the audit/error list detail line is set to "DELETED."
5. The WS-MASTER-REQUIRED-SW is set to "YES" so that the master to be deleted, now residing in the EM-EMPLOYEE-MASTER-WORK-AREA, will be eradicated by reading the next master record over it.

If the transaction record does not contain a change or delete update code, the 290-IDENTIFY-ERROR-TYPE paragraph is performed to identify the error on the audit/error line and to tally the error record counts.

Regardless of the type of transaction, the WS-TRANSACTION-REQUIRED-SW and WS-AUDIT-LINE-TO-BE-PRINTED switches are set to "YES" because another transaction record is now required and either an audit or an error line is to be printed.

255-RETRIEVE-PENDING-MASTER

```
255010*
255020*
255030 255-RETRIEVE-PENDING-MASTER.
255040*
255050     MOVE OLD-MASTER-IN-RECORD TO EM-EMPLOYEE-MASTER-WORK-AREA.
255060     MOVE WS-CURRENT-MASTER-KEY TO WS-PREVIOUS-MASTER-KEY.
255070     MOVE EM-PLANT-CODE TO WS-CURRENT-MASTER-MAJOR-FIELD.
255080     MOVE EM-DEPARTMENT-NUMBER TO WS-CURRENT-MASTER-INTER-FIELD.
255090     MOVE EM-EMPLOYEE-NUMBER TO WS-CURRENT-MASTER-MINOR-FIELD.
255100     MOVE 'NO ' TO WS-MASTER-PENDING-SW
255110                   WS-MASTER-REQUIRED-SW.
```

This module is entered from the 200-UPDATE-MASTER-RECORD module whenever the WS-MASTER-REQUIRED-SW and WS-MASTER-PENDING-SW are both on. The master-pending switch is set whenever a new master is created in the master work area. It signals that an unprocessed master record has been eradicated from the master work area. However, the unprocessed record still resides in the OLD-MASTER-IN-RECORD area in the FILE SECTION. This means that when a new master record is required—instead of reading a new record from the master file—the OLD-MASTER-IN-RECORD area should be transferred to the master work area.

In addition to handling this function, this module resets the master key fields. Then the master-pending and master-required switches are set off.

260-CREATE-
MASTER-RECORD

```
260010*
260020*
260030 260-CREATE-MASTER-RECORD.
260040*
260050     MOVE SPACES TO EM-EMPLOYEE-MASTER-WORK-AREA.
260060     MOVE '85' TO EM-RECORD-CODE.
260070     MOVE ET-PLANT-CODE TO EM-PLANT-CODE.
260080     MOVE ET-DEPARTMENT-NUMBER TO EM-DEPARTMENT-NUMBER.
260090     MOVE ET-EMPLOYEE-NUMBER TO EM-EMPLOYEE-NUMBER.
260100     MOVE ET-LAST-NAME TO EM-LAST-NAME.
260110     MOVE ET-FIRST-NAME TO EM-FIRST-NAME.
260120     MOVE ET-MIDDLE-INITIAL TO EM-MIDDLE-INITIAL.
260130     MOVE ET-HOURLY-RATE TO EM-HOURLY-RATE.
260140     MOVE WS-DATE-WORK TO EM-DATE-LAST-ACTIVITY.
```

This module builds the new master record in the master work area. It is entered from the 230-ADD-MASTER-RECORD paragraph whenever a valid add transaction is to be processed. First, SPACES are moved to the EM-EMPLOYEE-MASTER-WORK-AREA to blank out the master record that is currently present in the work area. Recognize that this master record that is being eradicated has not yet been written out to the new master file. However, it also resides in the OLD-MASTER-IN-RECORD area in the FILE SECTION from which it will be later reacquired.

Next, the master record is created by moving the record-code value of 85 and each of the ET-EMPLOYEE-TRANSACTION-RECORD fields to the individual EM-EMPLOYEE-MASTER-WORK-AREA fields.

At the end of the module, the EM-DATE-LAST-ACTIVITY field is set by moving the run date to it.

270-CHANGE-
MASTER-FIELDS

```
270010*
270020*
270030 270-CHANGE-MASTER-FIELDS.
270040*
270050     IF ET-LAST-NAME IS EQUAL TO SPACES
270060         NEXT SENTENCE
270070     ELSE
270080         MOVE ET-LAST-NAME TO TO EM-LAST-NAME.
270090*
270100     IF ET-FIRST-NAME IS EQUAL TO SPACES
270110         NEXT SENTENCE
270120     ELSE
270130         MOVE ET-FIRST-NAME TO EM-FIRST-NAME.
270140*
270150     IF ET-MIDDLE-INITIAL IS EQUAL TO SPACES
270160         NEXT SENTENCE
270170     ELSE IF ET-MIDDLE-INITIAL IS EQUAL TO '$'
270180         MOVE SPACES TO EM-MIDDLE-INITIAL
270190     ELSE
270200         MOVE ET-MIDDLE-INITIAL TO EM-MIDDLE-INITIAL.
270210*
270220     IF ET-HOURLY-RATE-X IS EQUAL TO SPACES
270230         NEXT SENTENCE
270240     ELSE
270250         MOVE ET-HOURLY-RATE TO EM-HOURLY-RATE.
270260*
270270     MOVE WS-DATE-WORK TO EM-DATE-LAST-ACTIVITY.
```

When a valid change transaction is to be processed, this module is entered from the 250-CHANGE-OR-DELETE-MASTER module. Each field of the transaction record for which a change is permitted is tested to see if change data is present. No action is taken if the field is blank; if it contains data, a change to the corresponding master record field is to be made.

Thus the ET-LAST-NAME, ET-FIRST-NAME, ET-MIDDLE-INITIAL, and ET-HOURLY-RATE-X fields are compared to SPACES. Remember that certain master record fields are not candidates for data value changes: the EM-

RECORD-CODE field is a constant value of 85; EM-PLANT-CODE, EM-DEPARTMENT-NUMBER, and EM-EMPLOYEE-NUMBER are control-key fields; and EM-DATE-LAST-ACTIVITY is updated not by transaction records but by the program.

Observe that the test for changing the middle-initial field contains additional logic to change the EM-MIDDLE-INITIAL field to a null value (a blank SPACE) when there is a "$" present in the ET-MIDDLE-INITIAL field.

At the end of the paragraph, the EM-DATE-LAST-ACTIVITY field is updated in the master record.

280-DELETE-MASTER-RECORD

For this SEQMAINT program, this is a null module because there are not any tasks to be performed here. If a correspondence test were to be applied before a delete transaction was made, this module could be coded with the appropriate logic.

290-IDENTIFY-ERROR-TYPE

```
290010*
290020*
290030 290-IDENTIFY-ERROR-TYPE.
290040*
290050     IF ADD-TRANSACTION
290060         ADD 1 TO TC-TOTAL-ADD-TRANS-READ
290070         ADD 1 TO TC-ADD-TRANS-REJECTED
290080         MOVE 'UNABLE ADD-MASTER ALREADY ON FILE' TO DL-ERROR-MSG
290090     ELSE IF CHANGE-TRANSACTION
290100         ADD 1 TO TC-TOTAL-CHANGE-TRANS-READ
290110         ADD 1 TO TC-CHANGE-TRANS-REJECTED
290120         MOVE 'UNABLE CHANGE-MASTER NOT ON FILE ' TO DL-ERROR-MSG
290130     ELSE IF DELETE-TRANSACTION
290140         ADD 1 TO TC-TOTAL-DELETE-TRANS-READ
290150         ADD 1 TO TC-DELETE-TRANS-REJECTED
290160         MOVE 'UNABLE DELETE-MASTER NOT ON FILE ' TO DL-ERROR-MSG
290170     ELSE
290180         ADD 1 TO TC-TOTAL-ERROR-UPDATE-CODES
290190         MOVE 'UNABLE UPDATE-INVALID UPDATE CODE' TO DL-ERROR-MSG.
290200*
290210     MOVE 'REJECTED' TO DL-UPDATE-ACTION.
```

This module is entered from either the 230-ADD-MASTER-RECORD or 250-CHANGE-OR-DELETE-MASTER routines whenever an interfile error condition is detected; that is, if the transaction is an add but a matching master key is already on file or if the corresponding master key was not found for a change or delete transaction.

The record is tallied into the proper transactions-read and transactions-rejected categories. Then the appropriate error message is moved to the DL-ERROR-MSG field of the audit/error detail line.

Notice that the last three statements of the module handle an invalid transaction update code. According to the programming specifications, this should not occur because the update code should have already been validated in a prior run. Nevertheless, the logic is provided to maintain the integrity of the record counts should an erroneous transaction code inadvertently enter the run.

700-PRINT-REPORT-TOTALS

```
700010*
700020*
700030 700-PRINT-REPORT-TOTALS.
700040*
700050     PERFORM 870-PRINT-REPORT-HEADINGS.
700060     PERFORM 710-PRINT-TOTAL-LINE
700070         VARYING TC-SUBSCRIPT
700080         FROM 1
700090         BY 1
700100         UNTIL TC-SUBSCRIPT IS GREATER THAN TC-NUMBER-OF-ENTRIES.
710010*
710020*
```

```
710030 710-PRINT-TOTAL-LINE.
710040*
710050     MOVE TC-COUNT-DESCRIPTION (TC-SUBSCRIPT)
710060         TO TL-COUNT-DESCRIPTION.
710070     MOVE TC-RECORD-COUNT (TC-SUBSCRIPT) TO TL-RECORD-COUNT.
710080     MOVE TL-TOTAL-LINE TO REPORT-LINE.
710090     MOVE 1 TO WS-LINE-SPACING.
710100     PERFORM 890-WRITE-REPORT-LINE.
```

The 700-PRINT-REPORT-TOTALS paragraph is entered from the mainline 000-MAINTAIN-SEQUENTIAL-FILE module after all of the transaction and master records have been processed. First, the 870-PRINT-REPORT-HEADINGS paragraph is performed to skip to a new page before printing the totals. Then, the 710-PRINT-TOTAL-LINE module is repeatedly performed to print each of the 14 total lines.

710-PRINT-TOTAL-LINE

Each time this module is performed, one of the 14 total lines is printed. The TC-SUBSCRIPT field is used to step through the description and record count table entries and move each to the TL-COUNT-DESCRIPTION and TL-RECORD-COUNT fields of the total line.

800-READ-TRANSACTION-RECORD

```
800010*
800020*
800030 800-READ-TRANSACTION-RECORD.
800040*
800050     MOVE WS-CURRENT-TRANS-SEQ-KEY TO WS-PREVIOUS-TRANS-SEQ-KEY.
800060*
800070     READ TRANSACTION-FILE INTO ET-EMPLOYEE-TRANSACTION-RECORD
800080         AT END MOVE 'YES' TO WS-TRANSACTION-END-OF-FILE-SW
800090         MOVE HIGH-VALUES TO WS-CURRENT-TRANS-SEQ-KEY.
800100*
800110     IF NOT TRANSACTION-END-OF-FILE
800120         ADD 1 TO TC-TOTAL-TRANS-READ
800130         MOVE ET-PLANT-CODE TO WS-CURRENT-TRANS-MAJOR-FIELD
800140         MOVE ET-DEPARTMENT-NUMBER TO WS-CURRENT-TRANS-INTER-FIELD
800150         MOVE ET-EMPLOYEE-NUMBER TO WS-CURRENT-TRANS-MINOR-FIELD
800160         MOVE ET-UPDATE-CODE TO WS-CURRENT-TRANS-UPDATE-CODE.
800170*
800180     IF WS-CURRENT-TRANS-SEQ-KEY
800190             IS LESS THAN WS-PREVIOUS-TRANS-SEQ-KEY
800200         MOVE 'PREVIOUS TRANSACTION KEY' TO SE-ERROR-MESSAGE
800210         MOVE WS-PREVIOUS-TRANS-SEQ-KEY TO SE-SEQUENCE-KEY
800220         MOVE 'TRANSACTION FILE OUT OF SEQUENCE ' TO DL-ERROR-MSG
800230         MOVE ' CURRENT TRANSACTION KEY' TO WS-ERROR-MESSAGE-HOLD
800240         MOVE WS-CURRENT-TRANS-SEQ-KEY TO WS-SEQUENCE-KEY-HOLD
800250         PERFORM 900-ABORT-PROGRAM-RUN.
800260*
800270     MOVE 'NO ' TO WS-TRANSACTION-REQUIRED-SW.
```

This is the read module for the transaction file. Before a record is read, the current transaction key is moved to the previous transaction key. Then the next transaction record is read from the input transaction file.

If there are no remaining transaction records, the WS-TRANSACTION-END-OF-FILE-SW is set to "YES" and HIGH-VALUES are moved to the current transaction key in WORKING-STORAGE.

After a record has been read into the transaction record area of WORKING-STORAGE, it is tallied as a transaction record read, and each of the transaction sequence key fields is moved from the input record to the current transaction key in WORKING-STORAGE.

Once these previous and current transaction keys have been set to reflect the existing relationship, the transaction sequence is tested. If the current transaction key is equal to or greater than the previous transaction key, the transaction records are in correct sequence.

Although it should not occur, if the current transaction key is less than that of the previous transaction, a transaction sequence error exists. When a transaction sequence error occurs, the program is to print two error lines. The first line displays the previous transaction key and the second shows the current transaction key. A transaction sequence error should not occur because the transaction records have been sorted in a previous run. However, should a transaction sequence error be revealed, data for the first error line is moved to the appropriate print line fields. Data for the second error line is moved to its respective hold area. Then the 900-ABORT-PROGRAM-RUN module is performed to print the lines and effect the orderly abnormal termination of the program run.

After the transaction sequence test, the WS-TRANSACTION-REQUIRED-SW is reset to "NO." Notice that this switch is reset unconditionally, regardless of end-of-file or sequence test results.

810-READ-
MASTER-RECORD

```
810010*
810020*
810030 810-READ-MASTER-RECORD.
810040*
810050     MOVE WS-CURRENT-MASTER-KEY TO WS-PREVIOUS-MASTER-KEY.
810060*
810070     READ OLD-MASTER-IN-FILE
810080        AT END MOVE 'YES' TO WS-MASTER-END-OF-FILE-SW
810090        MOVE HIGH-VALUES TO WS-CURRENT-MASTER-KEY
810100                          OLD-MASTER-IN-RECORD.
810110*
810120     IF NOT MASTER-END-OF-FILE
810130        MOVE OLD-MASTER-IN-RECORD TO EM-EMPLOYEE-MASTER-WORK-AREA
810140        ADD 1 TO TC-MASTERS-READ
810150        MOVE EM-PLANT-CODE TO WS-CURRENT-MASTER-MAJOR-FIELD
810160        MOVE EM-DEPARTMENT-NUMBER
810170            TO WS-CURRENT-MASTER-INTER-FIELD
810180        MOVE EM-EMPLOYEE-NUMBER TO WS-CURRENT-MASTER-MINOR-FIELD.
810190*
810200     IF WS-CURRENT-MASTER-KEY
810210            IS NOT GREATER THAN WS-PREVIOUS-MASTER-KEY
810220        MOVE '     PREVIOUS MASTER KEY' TO SE-ERROR-MESSAGE
810230        MOVE WS-PREVIOUS-MASTER-KEY TO SE-SEQUENCE-KEY
810240        MOVE 'MASTER FILE OUT OF SEQUENCE     ' TO DL-ERROR-MSG
810250        MOVE '      CURRENT MASTER KEY' TO WS-ERROR-MESSAGE-HOLD
810260        MOVE WS-CURRENT-MASTER-KEY TO WS-SEQUENCE-KEY-HOLD
810270        PERFORM 900-ABORT-PROGRAM-RUN.
810280*
810290     MOVE 'NO ' TO WS-MASTER-REQUIRED-SW.
```

The input master file is read in this module. Before a record is read, the current master key is moved to the previous master key. Then the next master record is read from the input master file.

If there are no remaining master records, the WS-MASTER-END-OF-FILE-SW is set to "YES" and HIGH-VALUES are moved to the current master key in WORKING-STORAGE. HIGH-VALUES are also moved to the OLD-MASTER-IN-RECORD in the FILE SECTION.

After a record has been read into the master work area, it is tallied as a master record read, and each of the key fields is moved from the input record to the current master key in WORKING-STORAGE.

Once these previous and current master keys have been set to reflect the existing relationship, the master sequence is tested. If the current master key is greater than the previous master key, the master records are in correct sequence.

Although it should not occur, if the current master key is equal to or less than that of the previous master, a master sequence error exists and the program is to print two error lines. The first line displays the previous master key and the second shows the current master key. A master sequence error should not occur because the master records should be maintained in correct sequence. However, should a master sequence error be revealed, data for the first error line is moved to the appropriate print line fields. Data for the second error line is moved to its respective hold area. Then the 900-ABORT-PROGRAM-RUN module is performed to print the lines and effect the orderly abnormal termination of the program run.

After the transaction sequence test, the WS-MASTER-REQUIRED-SW is reset to "NO." Notice that this switch is reset unconditionally, regardless of end-of-file or sequence test results.

850-WRITE-MASTER-RECORD

```
850010*
850020*
850030 850-WRITE-MASTER-RECORD.
850040*
850050     WRITE NEW-MASTER-OUT-RECORD
850060          FROM EM-EMPLOYEE-MASTER-WORK-AREA.
850070     ADD 1 TO TC-MASTERS-WRITTEN.
850080     MOVE 'NO ' TO WS-MASTER-TO-BE-WRITTEN-SW.
```

This module handles writing records to the new master file. A WRITE statement that contains the FROM phrase is used to transfer the master record from the work area to the output area before it is written.

After writing the record to the output master file, it is tallied as a master record written and the WS-MASTER-TO-BE-WRITTEN-SW is reset to "NO."

870-PRINT-REPORT-HEADINGS

```
870010*
870020*
870030 870-PRINT-REPORT-HEADINGS.
870040*
870050     ADD 1 TO WS-PAGE-COUNT.
870060     MOVE WS-PAGE-COUNT TO H2-PAGE-NBR.
870070     MOVE H1-HEADING-LINE-1 TO REPORT-LINE.
870080     PERFORM 880-WRITE-REPORT-TOP-LINE.
870090     MOVE H2-HEADING-LINE-2 TO REPORT-LINE.
870100     MOVE 1 TO WS-LINE-SPACING.
870110     PERFORM 890-WRITE-REPORT-LINE.
870120     MOVE H3-HEADING-LINE-3 TO REPORT-LINE.
870130     MOVE 2 TO WS-LINE-SPACING.
870140     PERFORM 890-WRITE-REPORT-LINE.
870150     MOVE H4-HEADING-LINE-4 TO REPORT-LINE.
870160     MOVE 1 TO WS-LINE-SPACING.
870170     PERFORM 890-WRITE-REPORT-LINE.
870180     MOVE SPACES TO REPORT-LINE.
870190     PERFORM 890-WRITE-REPORT-LINE.
880010*
880020*
880030 880-WRITE-REPORT-TOP-LINE.
880040*
880050     WRITE REPORT-LINE
880060          AFTER ADVANCING PAGE.
880070     MOVE 1 TO WS-LINES-USED.
890010*
890020*
890030 890-WRITE-REPORT-LINE.
890040*
890050     WRITE REPORT-LINE
890060          AFTER ADVANCING WS-LINE-SPACING.
890070     ADD WS-LINE-SPACING TO WS-LINES-USED.
```

The 870-PRINT-REPORT-HEADINGS module is a typical report heading routine. The page count is incremented and moved to the appropriate heading line. The first heading line to skip to the top of the page is printed by performing the 880-WRITE-REPORT-TOP-LINE module. For each successive line, the heading line is moved from WORKING-STORAGE to the output print area in the FILE SECTION, the line spacing is set, and the 890-WRITE-REPORT-LINE module is performed to print the line with variable-line spacing.

880-WRITE-REPORT-TOP-LINE

This module is used only for writing the first line of each page. The WRITE statement uses the PAGE option to handle skipping to the next report page. Then, since the first line has now been used, the WS-LINES-USED field is set to 1.

890-WRITE-REPORT-LINE

This module writes all lines except the top line of each page. The WRITE statement uses the identifier (WS-LINE-SPACING) option to control the number of lines to advance before printing the line. Then, since that number of lines has now been used, the WS-LINES-USED field is incremented by the current value of the WS-LINE-SPACING field.

900-ABORT-PROGRAM-RUN

```
900010*
900020*
900030 900-ABORT-PROGRAM-RUN.
900040*
900050     MOVE 'ABORTED ' TO DL-UPDATE-ACTION.
900060     MOVE DL-DETAIL-LINE TO REPORT-LINE.
900070     MOVE 3 TO WS-LINE-SPACING.
900080     PERFORM 890-WRITE-REPORT-LINE.
900090     MOVE SPACES TO DL-DETAIL-LINE.
900100     MOVE WS-ERROR-MESSAGE-HOLD TO SE-ERROR-MESSAGE.
900110     MOVE WS-SEQUENCE-KEY-HOLD TO SE-SEQUENCE-KEY.
900120     MOVE DL-DETAIL-LINE TO REPORT-LINE.
900130     MOVE 1 TO WS-LINE-SPACING.
900140     PERFORM 890-WRITE-REPORT-LINE.
900150     MOVE 'YES' TO WS-TRANSACTION-END-OF-FILE-SW
900160                   WS-MASTER-END-OF-FILE-SW.
900170     MOVE 'NO ' TO WS-MASTER-REQUIRED-SW
900180                   WS-MASTER-PENDING-SW.
```

This module is used only in the rare situation where the program run must be abnormally terminated because of a transaction or master file sequence error. It controls the printing of the two sequence error lines. Then it readies the program for abnormal termination by prematurely forcing the WS-TRANSACTION-END-OF-FILE-SW and WS-MASTER-END-OF-FILE-SW to reflect an end-of-file condition. Also, the WS-MASTER-REQUIRED-SW and WS-MASTER-PENDING-SW are reset to "NO" so that any pending but now unnecessary input-output operations are inhibited when control is returned to the 200-UPDATE-MASTER-RECORD module.

■ TOPIC 3-D: **Creating a Sequential Master File**

Utility Program Creation

Empty Input Master File

Dummy or Null Input Master File

OPTIONAL Phrase

To run a sequential master file-maintenance program, an input master file is required. However, for the very first processing cycle, provisions must be made to create the first-generation file. There are four ways that this can be done: by a utility creation program, an empty input master file, a dummy input master file, or the OPTIONAL phrase.

Utility Program Creation

An operating-system utility program can be used to create the first input sequential master file. This is an appropriate approach only when the first generation of validated master file records already exist. The records need not exist in exactly the same format or sequence, for utility and sort programs can reformat and resequence the records.

Empty Input Master File

If the master file is being created from add transactions during the first processing cycle, an empty input master file can be used. It would contain only the proper tape or disk-header labels, no data records, and an end-of-file marker. This will cause an end-of-file condition to be immediately detected for the input master file. A properly coded sequential file-maintenance program will then correctly process the add transactions to create the first actual master file as the output from the first processing cycle.

Dummy or Null Input Master File

Some operating systems allow specification of dummy or null files in the job control language. This has the same effect as an empty input master file in bringing the input master file to an immediate end-of-file. It is more convenient, however, because it does not require the actual creation and presence of an empty file.

OPTIONAL Phrase

The COBOL OPTIONAL phrase can be specified in the SELECT entry of the ENVIRONMENT DIVISION, as shown in Figure 3D.1. This allows the program to be run even though the OPTIONAL file is not present. This approach is similar to using a dummy job control language entry.

```
Format:

    SELECT [OPTIONAL] file-name
```

Example:

```
            SELECT OPTIONAL OLD-MASTER-IN-FILE
                ASSIGN TO UT-S-MINFILE.
```

Note: The OPTIONAL phrase can only be specified for input files.

Figure 3D.1. OPTIONAL phrase format and example.

However, the disadvantage to this approach is that the only time the input master file is not required is during the very first processing cycle. Thus the OPTIONAL phrase should be removed immediately after the first cycle to guard against operator errors. This would require that the program be recompiled after its first processing run.

Summary

Topic 3-A Sequential File-Maintenance Programming Specifications

When the programmer/analyst is specifying a file-maintenance program, he or she must choose appropriate handling for the following design alternatives: transaction data validation, audit/error list treatment, error-record handling, transaction file sorting, multiple transactions for the same master record, change-transaction modifiable fields, change-transaction formatting, change-to-null requirements, and transaction correspondence checking.

The following items that relate specifically to sequential file maintenance must also be considered: master file sequence checking, transaction file sequence checking, and record counts.

Topic 3-B Sequential File-Maintenance Program Design

For a sequential file-maintenance program, the transaction record key bears one of three relationships to the master record key: (1) the transaction key is lower than the master key, (2) the transaction key is equal to the master key, or (3) the transaction key is higher than the master key.

When the transaction key is lower than the master key, it means that no matching master record exists for that transaction. This condition is valid for add transactions and signifies an interfile error for change and delete transactions.

When the transaction key is equal to the master key, it means that a matching master record exists for that transaction. This condition is valid for change and delete transactions and signifies an interfile error for add transactions.

When the transaction key is higher than the master key, it means that the appropriate location in the master file for processing the transaction has not yet been reached. Additional input master records must be passed to the output master file before the transaction record can be processed.

When the programmer is designing the program, he or she must allocate FILE SECTION areas for the input transaction record, the input master record, and the output master record. A master work area through which all master records pass should be defined in the WORKING-STORAGE SECTION.

Topic 3-C Sequential File-Maintenance Program Coding

This section presents detailed program coding for the SEQMAINT program.

Topic 3-D Creating a Sequential Master File

The input master file for the first processing cycle can be created by (1) employing a utility program, (2) using an empty input master file, (3) specifying a dummy or null input master file, or (4) specifying the OPTIONAL phrase in the SELECT entry.

Programming Assignments

3-1: Sequential Part Master File Maintenance

Program description

An input sequential part master file is to be updated with input part transaction records. The input transaction file has been validated and sorted in a prior program step. An output updated-sequential part master file and an audit/error list are to be produced.

Input files

Part master file	Key field = Part number
Part transaction file	Key fields = Part number (major)
	Update code (minor)

Output files

Part master file (updated)
Audit/error list

Record formats

Part master record (Record code "PM")
Part transaction record (Record code "35")
Audit/error list

Part master record

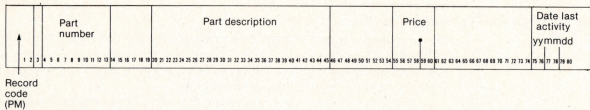

Record
code
(PM)

Part transaction record

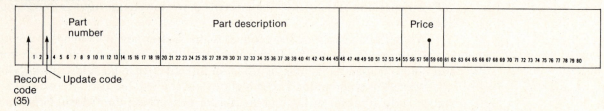

Record   Update code
code
(35)

Audit/error list

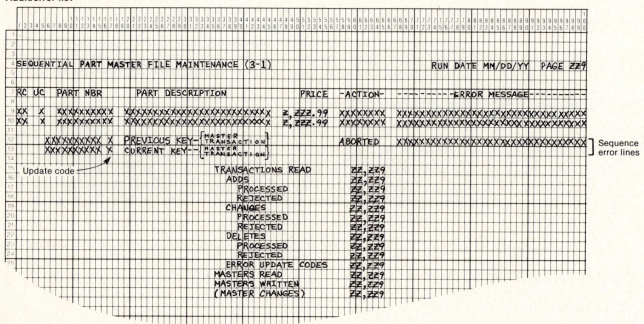

Program operations

A. Read each input part update-transaction record.
  1. Validate each transaction to ensure that it contains one of the following update codes:
     A (Add)
     C (Change)
     D (Delete)
  2. Sequence check the input transaction records.
B. Sequence check the input part master records.
C. Create a master record for each valid add transaction.

1. Store the run date as the date-last-activity in the master record.

D. If one or more of the following fields of a valid change transaction are not blank, change the master record fields accordingly.

    —Part description

    —Price

1. Store the run date as the date-last-activity in the master record.

E. Delete the master record for each valid delete transaction.

F. Tally master record counts as shown on the audit/error list print chart.

G. Print the audit/error list as shown on the audit/error list print chart.

1. Single-space each detail line (but double-space between the last heading line and the first detail line on each page).

2. Skip to a new page before printing the record-count totals.

3. Provide for a line span of 50 lines per page.

H. Identify the following error conditions.

Error condition	Error message
Add transaction but master already on file	UNABLE ADD-MASTER ALREADY ON FILE
Change transaction but master not on file	UNABLE CHANGE-MASTER NOT ON FILE
Delete transaction but master not on file	UNABLE DELETE-MASTER NOT ON FILE
Invalid update code	INVALID UPDATE CODE
Transaction file out of sequence	TRANSACTION FILE OUT OF SEQUENCE
Master file out of sequence	MASTER FILE OUT OF SEQUENCE

3-2: Sequential Vendor Master File Maintenance

Program description

An input sequential vendor master file is to be updated with input vendor-transaction records. The input transaction file has been validated and sorted in a prior program step. An output updated-sequential vendor master file and an audit/error list are to be produced.

Input files

    Vendor master file   Key fields = Vendor number (major)

                                                     Date due (minor)

    Vendor-transaction file   Key fields = Vendor number (major)

                                                     Date due (intermediate)

                                                         Update code (minor)

Output files

    Vendor master file (updated)

    Audit/error list

Record formats

    Vendor master record (Record code "VM")

    Vendor-transaction record (Record code "36")

    Audit/error list

Vendor master record

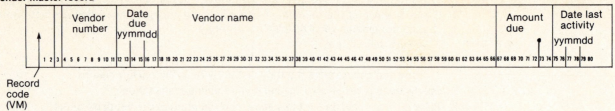

Record code (VM)

Vendor transaction record

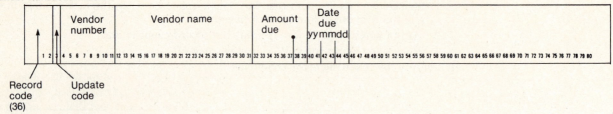

Record code (36) Update code

Audit/error list

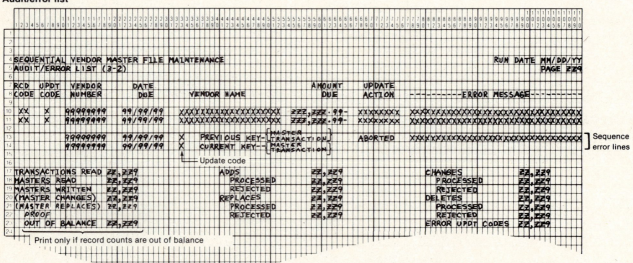

Program operations

A. Read each input vendor update-transaction record.
   1. Validate each transaction to ensure that it contains one of the following update codes:
      A (Add)
      C (Change)
      D (Delete)
      R (Replace)
   2. Sequence check the input transaction records.
B. Sequence check the input master records.
C. Create a master record for each valid add transaction.
   1. Store the run date as the date-last-activity in the master record.
D. If one or more of the following fields of a valid change transaction are not blank, change the master record fields accordingly.
   —Vendor name
   —Amount due (increment)
   1. Store the run date as the date-last-activity in the master record.
   2. Before printing the change-transaction record on the audit/error list, print a line that shows the master record contents before the change.

E. For a valid replacement transaction, replace the master record fields accordingly.
  —Vendor name
  —Amount due (replace)
  1. Store the run date as the date-last-activity in the master record.
  2. Before printing the replacement-transaction record on the audit/error list, print a line that shows the master record contents before the replacement.
F. Delete the master record for each valid delete transaction.
  1. Correspondence check the first six characters of the vendor name on the transaction record with the first six characters of the vendor name on the master record.
  2. Before printing the delete-transaction record on the audit/error list, print a line showing the master record contents before the deletion.
G. Tally master record counts as shown on the audit/error list print chart.
H. Print the audit/error list as shown on the audit/error list print chart.
  1. On the master-record contents line for change, delete, and replace transactions, print the word "MASTER" in the update-action field of the audit line.
  2. Single-space between master-record contents and transaction-record audit lines.
  3. Double-space between transactions.
  4. Provide for a line span of 50 lines per page (but do not break lines for a transaction or for the record-count totals between pages).
I. Identify the following error conditions.

Error condition	Error message
Add transaction but master already on file	UNABLE ADD-MASTER ALREADY ON FILE
Change transaction but master not on file	UNABLE CHANGE-MASTER NOT ON FILE
Replace transaction but master not on file	UNABLE REPLACE-MASTER NOT ON FILE
Delete transaction but master not on file	UNABLE DELETE-MASTER NOT ON FILE
Invalid update code	INVALID UPDATE CODE
Delete transaction but fails correspondence check	UNABLE DELETE-FAILS CORR CHECK
Transaction file out of sequence	TRANSACTION FILE OUT OF SEQUENCE
Master file out of sequence	MASTER FILE OUT OF SEQUENCE

3-3: Sequential Employee Master File Maintenance

Program description

An input sequential employee master file is to be updated with input employee-transaction records. The input transaction file has been sorted in a prior program step. An output updated-sequential employee master file and an audit/error list are to be produced.

Input files

Employee master file   Key fields = Plant code (major)
                                                         Department number (intermediate)
                                                          Employee number (minor)

Employee-transaction file   Key fields = Plant code (major)
                                                      Department number (intermediate-1)
                                                      Employee number (intermediate-2)
                                                       Update code (minor)

Output files

Employee master file (updated)

Audit/error list

Record formats

Employee master record (Record code "EM")

Employee-transaction record (Record code "37")

Audit/error list

Employee master record

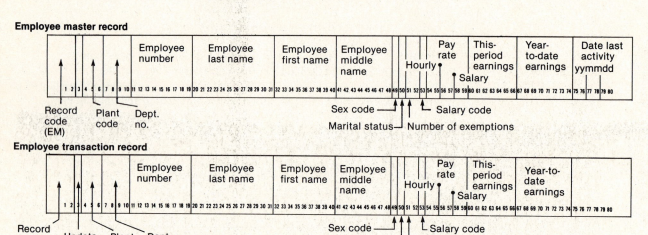

Employee transaction record

Audit/error list

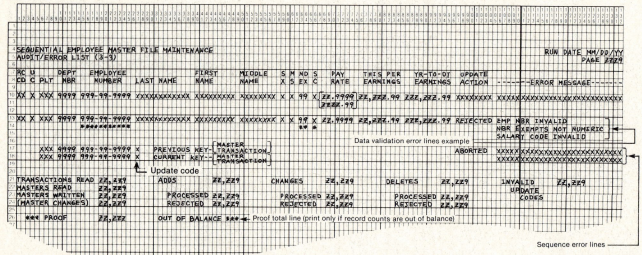

Program operations

A. Read each input employee-update transaction record.

   1. Validate each transaction record as discussed at item H, below.

   2. If a transaction contains one or more errors, identify each error and reject the entire transaction record.

   3. Sequence check the input transaction records.

B. Sequence check the input employee master records.

C. Create a master record for each valid add transaction.

   1. Store the run date as the date-last-activity in the master record.

D. If one or more of the following fields of a valid change transaction are not blank, change the master record fields accordingly.

—Employee last name
—Employee first name
—Employee middle name*
—Sex code
—Marital status
—Number of exemptions
—Salary code*
—Hourly rate
—Earnings this period

1. Store the run date as the date-last-activity in the master record.
2. Before printing the change-transaction record on the audit/error list, print a line showing the master record contents before the change.
3. If any one of the fields marked above by an asterisk contains an asterisk in the leftmost position of the field and the remainder (if any) of the positions are blank, change the corresponding field of the master record to spaces.

E. Delete the master record for each valid delete transaction.

1. Correspondence check the first six characters of the employee last name on the transaction record with the first six characters of the employee last name on the master record.
2. Before printing the delete-transaction record on the audit/error list, print a line that shows the master record contents before the deletion.

F. Tally master record counts as shown on the audit/error list print chart.

G. Print the audit/error list as shown on the audit/error list print chart.

1. On the master-record contents line for change and delete transactions, print the word "MASTER" in the update-action field of the audit line.
2. For each applicable transaction, single-space between master-record contents and transaction-record audit/error lines.
3. Double-space between transactions.
4. Provide for a line span of 50 lines per page (but do not break lines for a transaction or the record-count totals between pages).

H. Validate add and change transactions. When an error is detected, highlight the field in error on the audit/error list by underlining it with asterisks. Those fields marked below with an asterisk should be validated only for add transactions.

1. When a transaction record contains multiple errors:
   a. Print the first error message on the transaction audit/error line.
   b. Print the second error message on the asterisk-highlighted line.
   c. Print the third and following error messages, when applicable, on audit/error lines that are blank in the record-image area.

Field	Validation
Record code	Equal to "46"
Update code	Equal to "1" (Delete), "2" (Add), or "3" (Change)
Plant code*	Equal to "ATL" (Atlantic), "CTL" (Central), "MTN" (Mountain), or "PAC" (Pacific)
Department number*	Numeric
Employee number*	Numeric
Employee last name	Left justification. Presence for an add transaction
Employee first name	Left justification. Presence for an add transaction
Employee middle name	Left justification if present
Sex code	Equal to "M" (male) or "F" (female)

Field	Validation
Marital status	Equal to "M" (married), "S" (single), or "H" (head of household)
Number of exemptions	Numeric
Salary code	Equal to "H" (hourly) or blank space (salaried)
Pay rate	For hourly employees: equal to or greater than minimum wage and less than "20.0000"
	For salaried employees: equal to or greater than "1000.00"
This-period earnings	Numeric
Year-to-date earnings	Numeric

I. Identify the following error conditions.

Error condition	Error message
Add transaction but master already on file	UNABLE ADD-ALREADY ON FILE
Change transaction but master not on file	UNABLE CHANGE-NOT ON FILE
Replace transaction but master not on file	UNABLE REPLACE-NOT ON FILE
Delete transaction but master not on file	UNABLE DELETE-NOT ON FILE
Delete transaction but fails correspondence check	UNABLE DELETE-FAILS CORR CK
Transaction file out of sequence	TRANSACTION FILE OUT OF SEQ
Master file out of sequence	MASTER FILE OUT OF SEQUENCE
Invalid record code	RECORD CODE INVALID
Invalid update code	UPDATE CODE INVALID
Invalid plant code	PLANT CODE INVALID
Department number not numeric	DEPT NBR NOT NUMERIC
Employee number not numeric	EMP NBR NOT NUMERIC
Invalid Employee number	EMP NBR INVALID
Employee last name not present	EMP LAST NAME MISSING
Employee last name not left-justified	LAST NAME NOT LEFT JUST
Employee first name not present	EMP FIRST NAME MISSING
Employee first name not left-justified	FIRST NAME NOT LEFT JUST
Employee middle name not left-justified	MIDDLE NAME NOT LEFT JUST
Invalid sex code	SEX CODE INVALID
Invalid marital status	INVALID MARITAL STATUS
Number of exemptions not numeric	NBR EXEMPTS NOT NUMERIC
Invalid salary code	SALARY CODE INVALID
Invalid pay rate	PAY RATE INVALID
This-period earnings not numeric	THIS PER EARNINGS NOT NUMERIC
Year-to-date earnings not numeric	YTD EARNINGS NOT NUMERIC
Change transaction but no change fields present in record	CHANGE-NO CHANGE FIELDS
Change transaction contains a change-to-null code together with other data in the field	CHANGE-TO-NULL CODE ERROR

CHAPTER 4

DESIGNING AND CODING AN INDEXED FILE-MAINTENANCE PROGRAM

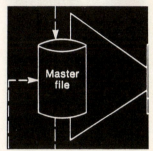

4 DESIGNING AND CODING AN INDEXED FILE-MAINTENANCE PROGRAM

Although the predominant file-organization method for large-batch master files has traditionally been sequential, the use of indexed organization has increased rapidly within the last few years and will probably soon nudge sequential organization from its customary position. The trend toward on-line systems coupled with recent improvements in disk hardware and indexed access-method software has contributed to this trend.

Indexed file organization is a favored method because it combines random record access and sequential-processing capabilities. However, whereas sequentially organized files can be updated on either tape or disk storage, indexed files are limited to direct-access storage devices.

An indexed file can be updated on either a sequential or a random-access basis. Looking back a few years, one would find that many indexed files were maintained by sequential update programs. This was because of slower disk-access speeds and limitations of the operating system's access-method software. Unless the volatility of a file were very low, randomly updated indexed files were often too time-consuming to process, especially when transactions were to be added to the file.

Today, however, most indexed files are updated randomly, thanks to advances in disk hardware and improvements in the efficiency of the access method software for indexed file processing.

An indexed file that is maintained randomly does not use separate input and output master files in the way that sequential updates do. Instead, the indexed file is updated **in-place**. Even though indexed updating may seem more complicated, an indexed file-maintenance program is usually easier for the application programmer to code than is a sequential one. The COBOL compiler, through the access method services of its operating system, handles all of the I-O access complexities, such as the maintenance of the index records.

The input transaction file is usually a sequential file and need not be, but sometimes is, sorted into control-key sequence before the actual update is made. The general logic of an indexed master file-maintenance program is to read a record from the transaction file and then try to locate the master record with a matching key on the indexed file. If the matching master record is found and the transaction record carries an update code of change or delete, the update is applied to the master file. If a matching master record is not found and the transaction record carries an update code of add, a new master is created and added to the file. Any other conditions cause an error condition to be identified.

Topics A through C of this chapter cover a typical random-access indexed file-maintenance program that we will call INDMAINT (for **Ind**exed File **Maint**enance). We will discuss aspects of the programming specifications, then cover the program design, and conclude with a study of the program coding.

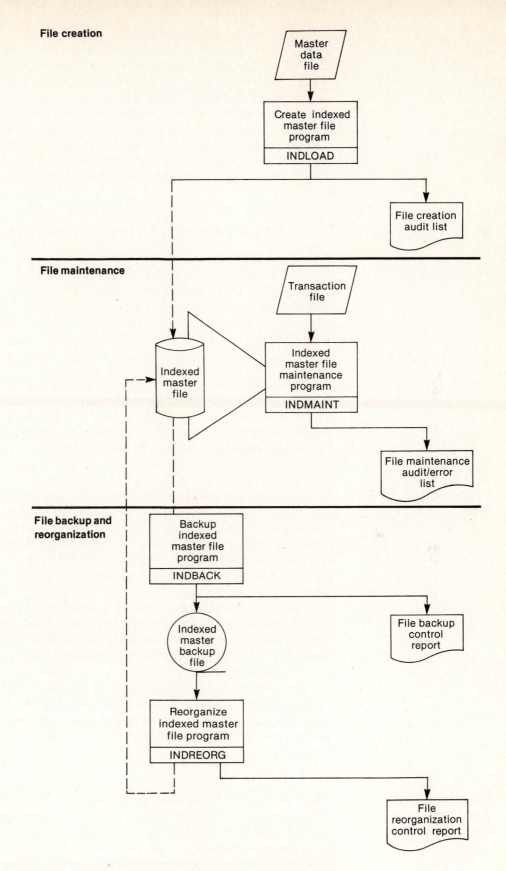

File creation

Master data file

Create indexed master file program

INDLOAD

File creation audit list

File maintenance

Transaction file

Indexed master file

Indexed master file maintenance program

INDMAINT

File maintenance audit/error list

File backup and reorganization

Backup indexed master file program

INDBACK

Indexed master backup file

File backup control report

Reorganize indexed master file program

INDREORG

File reorganization control report

Figure 4.1. Typical system flowchart: Indexed file maintenance.

As shown in the flowchart of a typical indexed file-maintenance system presented in Figure 4.1, additional indexed file-programming considerations must be addressed: file creation, backup, and reorganization. File creation is covered in Topic D; file backup and reorganization are discussed in Topic E.

Indexed file-coding syntax was introduced in the 1974 ANS COBOL standards. Many existing indexed file programs were written with 1968 ANS COBOL compilers. Even today, a number of indexed programs are written with these earlier standards. Therefore, Topic E presents the indexed file-maintenance program coded in accordance with the syntax of the most commonly used 1968 ANS COBOL compilers: those for IBM and IBM-compatible compilers.

■ TOPIC 4-A: **Indexed File-Maintenance Programming Specifications**

Transaction File Sequence
Master File Sequence Checking
Abnormal Program Termination
Record Counts

The programming specifications for the INDMAINT program are shown in Figure 4A.1. This program will perform application functions that are identical to those of the SEQMAINT program except that the master file records are stored in an indexed master file instead of a sequential one. Using an indexed master file causes a few minor changes to the programming specifications. Those differences will be discussed in this topic.

Transaction File Sequence

Although there is no need for the transaction records of a random indexed file update to be in sequence, sorted transaction files are often specified. When the transactions are sorted in accordance with the master key, all the updates for a particular master record will be grouped and, with appropriate program logic, maintenance program I-O processing can be minimized. A more common reason for using a sorted transaction file is simply to provide a sequenced audit/error list.

Also, if the transaction records contain a date or date/time field, sorting such fields can ensure that multiple updates will be applied in chronological sequence. However, such sequencing is not necessary in those situations where the transactions are captured in chronological order and immediately stored in an entry-sequenced file.

The programming specifications for the INDMAINT program do not require or preclude the use of a sequenced transaction file. Because an unsequenced transaction file is permitted, one function required for the sequential file-maintenance program—sequence checking of the transaction file—is eliminated.

Master File Sequence Checking

When an indexed file is updated in a random-access mode, only those master records with activity in the transaction file are retrieved; the program does not logically read the remaining master records. This precludes the ability to check the sequence of the master file records.

Thus an indexed file-maintenance program removes the need for another abnormal program termination routine: a master file out-of-sequence condition.

System flowchart:

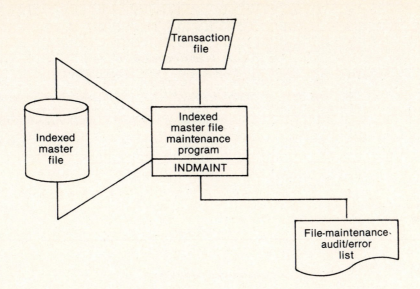

Record layouts:

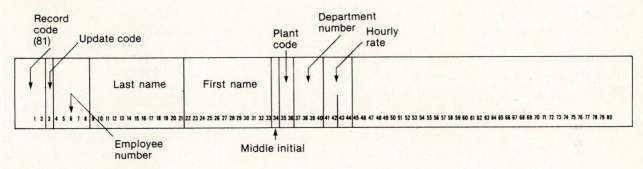

Employee-transaction record

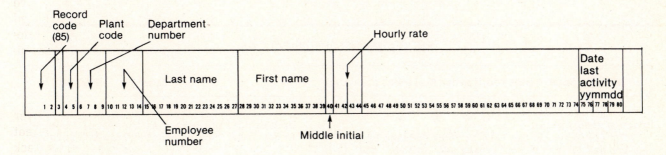

Employee master record

Figure 4A.1. Programming specifications: INDMAINT program.

continued

Print chart:

H1-HEADING-LINE-1
H2-HEADING-LINE-2
H3-HEADING-LINE-3
H4-HEADING-LINE-4
DL-DETAIL-LINE
IE-I-O-ERROR-LINE
TL-TOTAL-LINE

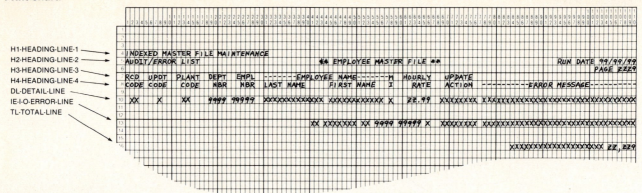

Printer output example:

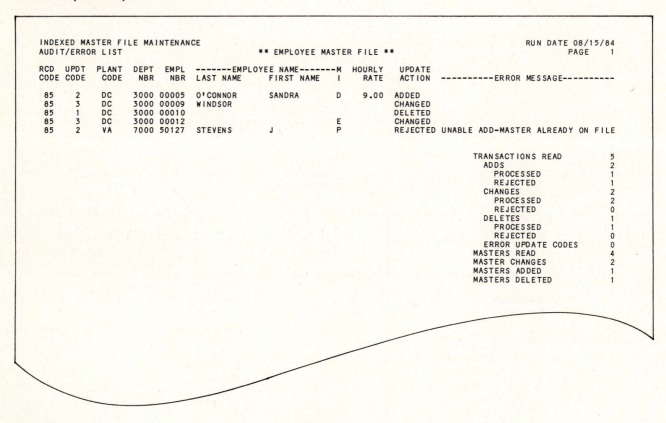

```
INDEXED MASTER FILE MAINTENANCE                                    RUN DATE 08/15/84
AUDIT/ERROR LIST                       ** EMPLOYEE MASTER FILE **          PAGE   1

RCD UPDT  PLANT  DEPT  EMPL  ------EMPLOYEE NAME-------M  HOURLY  UPDATE
CODE CODE  CODE  NBR   NBR   LAST NAME    FIRST NAME  I   RATE   ACTION  ----------ERROR MESSAGE----------

85    2    DC   3000  00005  O'CONNOR     SANDRA      D   9.00   ADDED
85    3    DC   3000  00009  WINDSOR                             CHANGED
85    1    DC   3000  00010                                      DELETED
85    3    DC   3000  00012                           E          CHANGED
85    2    VA   7000  50127  STEVENS      J           P          REJECTED UNABLE ADD-MASTER ALREADY ON FILE

                                                               TRANSACTIONS READ        5
                                                               ADDS                     2
                                                                   PROCESSED            1
                                                                   REJECTED             1
                                                               CHANGES                  2
                                                                   PROCESSED            2
                                                                   REJECTED             0
                                                               DELETES                  1
                                                                   PROCESSED            1
                                                                   REJECTED             0
                                                               ERROR UPDATE CODES       0
                                                               MASTERS READ             4
                                                               MASTER CHANGES           2
                                                               MASTERS ADDED            1
                                                               MASTERS DELETED          1
```

PROGRAMMING SPECIFICATIONS

Program name: Indexed Master File Maintenance   Program ID: INDMAINT

Program description

The employee master file is to be updated by a transaction file containing add, change, and delete transactions. The transaction file has been validated in a prior program run. An audit/error list is printed that documents update actions taken. At the end of the audit/error list, record count totals are printed.

Input file

Employee update-transaction file
Organization = Sequential

Figure 4A.1. (continued)

Input—output file
    Employee master file
        Organization = Indexed
        Record key   = Plant code   (major)
                   Department number
                   Employee number   (minor)

Output file
    Employee master file—maintenance audit/error
    list

Program operations

A. Read each input employee update—transaction record.

    1. Validate each transaction to ensure that it contains an update code of either "1" (delete transaction), "2" (add transaction), or "3" (change transaction).

        a. If the update—code field is not valid, print the contents of the transaction record on the audit/error list together with an update action of "REJECTED" and an error message of "UNABLE UPDATE—INVALID UPDATE CODE".

        b. Tally the record in the "ERROR UPDATE CODES" category.

        c. Do no further processing for the transaction record.

B. For each add transaction, do the following processing:

    1. Attempt to read a master record with an equal key value. (If the read operation causes a fatal I—0 error, print an I—0 error line on the audit/error list and terminate the program run as discussed in Point F, below.)

    2. If a master record with an equal key value is found, it means that a master record is already on the file.

        a. If the master record is already on file, print the contents of the transaction record on the audit/error list together with an update action of "REJECTED" and an error message of "UNABLE ADD—MASTER ALREADY ON FILE".

        b. Tally the transaction record in the "ADDS REJECTED" category.

        c. Do no further processing for the transaction record.

    3. If the master record is not already on file, create a master record from the transaction record as follows:

        a. Move each of the following fields from the input transaction record to the master record:

           —Plant code
           —Department number
           —Employee number
           —Last name
           —First name
           —Middle initial
           —Hourly rate

        b. Set the record—code field of the master record to "85".

        c. Set the date—last—activity field of the master record to the current run date.

        d. Set all other positions of the master record to blank spaces.

        e. Tally the transaction record in the "ADDS PROCESSED" category.

        f. Print the contents of the transaction record on the audit/error list together with an update action of "ADDED".

        g. Write the newly created master record to the employee master file.

        h. If the write operation is not successful, print an I—0 error line on the audit/error list and terminate the program run as discussed in Point F, below.

C. For each change transaction, do the following processing:

    1. Attempt to read a master record with an equal key value. (If the read operation causes a fatal I—0 error, print an I—0 error line on the audit/error list and terminate the program run as discussed in Point F, below.)

    2. If a master record with an equal key value is not located, it means that the corresponding master record is not on the file.

        a. If the master record is not on file, print the contents of the transaction record on the audit/error list together with an update action of "REJECTED" and an error message of "UNABLE CHANGE—MASTER NOT ON FILE".

        b. Tally the transaction record in the "CHANGES REJECTED" category.

        c. Do no further processing for the transaction record.

    3. If the master record is on file, update the master record from the transaction record as follows:

        a. Check each of the following fields of the transaction record to determine if it contains an entry:

           —Last name
           —First name
           —Hourly rate

           For each field that contains an entry, move it to the corresponding field of the master record.

        b. Check the middle—initial field of the transaction record to determine if it contains an entry.

           If the entry is a "$", move a blank space to the middle—initial field of the master record.

           If it contains an entry other than a "$", move the contents of the middle—initial field of the transaction record to the master record.

        c. If any of the above four fields of the master record are changed, set the date—last—activity field of the master record to the current run date.

Figure 4A.1. (continued)

continued

d. Tally the transaction record in the "CHANGES PROCESSED" category.

e. Print the contents of the transaction record on the audit/error list together with an update action of "CHANGED".

f. Rewrite the updated master record to the employee master file.

g. If the rewrite operation is not successful, print an I-0 error line on the audit/error list and terminate the program run as discussed in Point F, below.

D. For each delete transaction, do the following processing:

1. Attempt to read a master record with an equal key value. (If the read operation causes a fatal I-0 error, print an I-0 error line on the audit/error list and terminate the program run as discussed in Point F, below.)

2. If a master record with an equal key value is not located, it means that the corresponding master record is not on the file.

   a. If the master record is not on file, print the contents of the transaction record on the audit/error list together with an update action of "REJECTED" and an error message of "UNABLE DELETE—MASTER NOT ON FILE".

   b. Tally the transaction record in the "DELETES REJECTED" category.

   c. Do no further processing for the transaction record.

3. If the corresponding master record is on file, delete the master record from the employee master file.

   a. Print the contents of the transaction record on the audit/error list together with an update action of "DELETED".

   b. Tally the transaction record in the "DELETES PROCESSED" category.

   c. If the delete operation is not successful, print an I-0 error line on the audit/error list and terminate the program run as discussed in Point F, below.

E. Tally master records as follows:

1. Tally each master file record for which an attempted read was made in the "MASTERS READ" category.

2. Tally each master record added in the "MASTERS ADDED" category.

3. Tally each master record deleted in the "MASTERS DELETED" category.

F. If an I-0 error (a fatal I-0 error during a read, write, rewrite, or delete operation) occurs, print an error line on the audit/error list and terminate the program run. The error line should contain the following:

1. The file status code value.

2. A description of the I-0 operation ("READ", "WRITE", "REWRITE", or "DELETE").

3. The record key being accessed when the I-0 error occurred (plant code, department number, and employee number).

4. An update-action description of "ABORTED".

5. An error message of "I-0 ERROR OCCURRED".

G. Headings are to be printed on each page of the audit/error list. After 50 lines have been used on a report page and a new audit/error line is to be printed, the page should be advanced to the next page and the report headings printed. Also, the report page is to be advanced and headings are to be printed immediately before printing the total lines.

1. The run date is to be obtained from the operating system and printed on the first heading line in accordance with the format shown on the print chart.

2. The page number is to be incremented each time the heading is printed and displayed on the second heading line in accordance with the format shown on the print chart.

H. Line spacing for the audit/error list is to be handled as follows:

1. The first detail or total line after the page headings is to be double-spaced from the last heading line.

2. Second and successive detail lines are to be single-spaced from one another.

3. The report totals are to be printed on a new report page after the headings have been printed. Total lines are to be single-spaced from one another.

4. Should I-0 error lines be required, the first one is to be triple-spaced from the last detail line. Successive I-0 error lines should be single-spaced from one another.

Figure 4A.1. (continued)

Abnormal Program Termination

Although there is no need for abnormal program termination because out-of-sequence conditions are removed from a random indexed file-maintenance program, alternate program-termination causes are introduced in the INDMAINT specifications: input-output errors.

Because indexed organization requires more complicated record-access logic than sequential organization, additional types of I-O errors can occur. A

```
TRANSACTIONS READ        578

   ADDS                  461
      PROCESSED          446
      REJECTED            15

   CHANGES                87
      PROCESSED           79
      REJECTED             8

   DELETES                29
      PROCESSED           27
      REJECTED             2

   ERROR UPDATE CODES      1
```

MASTERS READ 121 Should equal change transactions processed plus delete transactions processed plus add transactions rejected.

	Proof computation is	CHANGES PROCESSED	(79)
	plus	DELETES PROCESSED	+(27)
	plus	ADDS REJECTED	+(15)
	minus	MASTERS READ	−(121)
	equals	zero	(0)

MASTER CHANGES 79 Should equal change transactions processed.

	Proof computation is	CHANGES PROCESSED	(79)
	minus	MASTER CHANGES	−(79)
	equals	zero	(0)

MASTERS ADDED 446 Should equal add transactions processed.

	Proof computation is	ADDS PROCESSED	(446)
	minus	MASTERS ADDED	−(446)
	equals	zero	(0)

MASTERS DELETED 27 Should equal delete transactions processed.

	Proof computation is	DELETES PROCESSED	(27)
	minus	MASTERS DELETED	−(27)
	equals	zero	(0)

Figure 4A.2. Example of proof totals for record counts.

thorough indexed file-maintenance program will trap certain serious I-O errors and bring about abnormal program termination upon their detection. (Programmers often call abnormal program termination an **abend**, which is pronounced **AB**-end.)

Thus the INDMAINT specifications call for abnormal program termination upon detection of unrecoverable I-O errors. This means that the error line on the audit/error list for abnormal program termination is of slightly different format, as shown on the print chart.

In addition to the key value of the record that is being accessed, the error line contains a file status code and a description of the type of I-O operation that is being performed at the time of the error. The file status code will be discussed in Topic B of this chapter; program logic for the I-O error detection will be explained in Topic C.

Record Counts

Because not every master record is read during each update run as it is with a sequential file-maintenance program, the master record count categories must be modified slightly for an indexed file-maintenance program.

Figure 4A.2 displays these master record count categories and explains the proof total logic for indexed file maintenance, which differs from that for sequential files.

Indexed File-Maintenance Program Design

Storage Allocation for Input and Output Records

The File Status Data-Item

Processing Logic Design

    Changing a Master Record

        Change Step A: Locating the master record

        Change Step B: Retrieving the master record

        Change Step C: Making the change and updating the master record

    Adding a New Master Record

        Add Step A: Checking to ensure that the master record is not already on file

        Add Step B: Creating and writing out the new master record

    Deleting a Master Record

Storage Allocation for Input and Output Records

When a programmer/analyst is designing an indexed file-maintenance program, he or she must allocate FILE SECTION storage areas for the input transaction record, the input-output master record, and the report line. (Observe that this INDMAINT program contains one less file than the SEQMAINT program because the input master and the output master are the same file.)

In accordance with our convention of defining records within WORKING-STORAGE, the transaction record and master work-area record descriptions are specified in the WORKING-STORAGE SECTION.

The File Status Data-Item

The 1974 ANS COBOL standards introduced a two-position field to be used for recording the status of input-output operations. It is called the **file status data-item** and, when it is used, the programmer codes it and the system updates it. After each I-O statement is executed, the system places a value in the file status field to indicate the status of the I-O operation. That is, the file status indicator tells the COBOL program whether or not the I-O function was completed successfully; if not, the reason is indicated by a 2-digit code. A complete list of the file status code values is presented in Figure 4B.1.

The file status data-item will be referred to briefly in the following discussion of transaction processing. Specifications for its coding are covered in Topic C of this chapter.

Processing Logic Design

To demonstrate logic design for an indexed file-maintenance program, the ensuing discussion and figures depict the processing steps that are to be taken for the various transaction types. As was done in Chapter 3 with the counterpart explanation for a sequential file-maintenance program, certain aspects are modified to aid comprehension. The control key is represented by a short 2-digit number, the fields of the records are limited, and the record codes are different from that called for in the programming specifications.

Changing a Master Record

Change Step A: Locating the master record

Point 1 of Figure 4B.2 shows a change-transaction record with a key value of 09 being read. The next step, illustrated at point 2, is to set the record key of the

File status code value	Status description
00	Successful completion —Input-output statement was successfully executed
02	Duplicate ALTERNATE RECORD KEY —READ statement issued to an INDEXED file and a duplicate ALTERNATE KEY exists —WRITE or REWRITE statement issued to an INDEXED file specified with an ALTERNATE KEY WITH DUPLICATES permitted that creates a duplicate alternate key
10	End-of-file —READ statement executed when ACCESS MODE IS SEQUENTIAL and the end-of-file has been reached —First READ statement executed for a file selected as OPTIONAL and the file was not available at OPEN time
21	Sequence error —WRITE statement issued to an INDEXED file opened as OUTPUT and current RECORD KEY is not greater than previous RECORD KEY value —REWRITE statement issued to an INDEXED file when ACCESS MODE IS SEQUENTIAL and the RECORD KEY value has changed since successful completion of the last READ statement
22	Duplicate key —WRITE statement issued to an INDEXED file that would create a duplicate RECORD KEY —WRITE statement issued to a RELATIVE file opened as I-O that would create a duplicate RELATIVE KEY —WRITE or REWRITE statement issued to an INDEXED file (specified with an ALTERNATE KEY but no WITH DUPLICATE phrase) that would create a duplicate ALTERNATE KEY
23	No record found —READ, REWRITE, DELETE, or START statement issued to an INDEXED or RELATIVE file record identified by key value and the record does not exist on the file
24	Boundary violation —WRITE statement issued to an INDEXED or RELATIVE file that is beyond the externally (JCL) defined boundaries of the file
30	Permanent error —Unsuccessful completion of an I-O statement because of an I-O error such as a data check, parity error, transmission error, etc.
34	Boundary violation —WRITE statement issued to a SEQUENTIAL file that is beyond the externally (JCL) defined boundaries of the file
9x	Implementor defined —May be specified by the compiler implementor to indicate a condition not provided for by the other file status codes

Figure 4B.1.   File status code values.

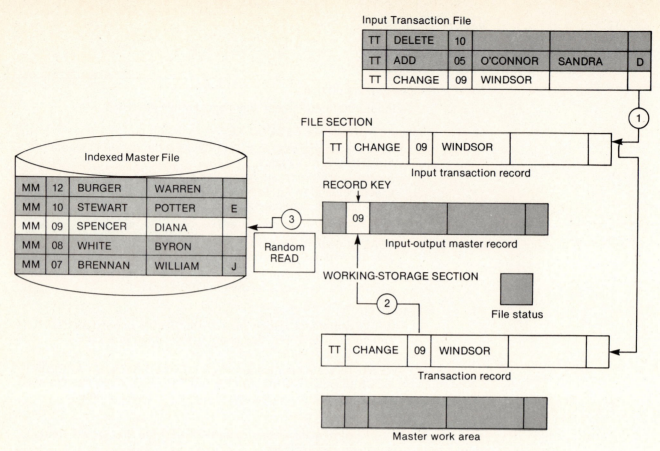

Figure 4B.2. Change Step A: Locating the master record.

input-output master record to the corresponding value (09). Then an attempt is made to locate the record by a random read operation, as depicted at point 3.

Change Step B: Retrieving the master record

Figure 4B.3 represents the situation in which the corresponding master record with a matching key value is located on the indexed file. The read operation retrieves the record from the file and brings it into storage, as shown at point 4. Point 5 of the figure shows that, because the read operation *was successful*, the system updates the file status field with a code (00), which indicates the successful completion of the I-O operation. If a matching key value were *not* found, another code value (23) would have been placed in the file status field.

Change Step C: Making the change and updating the master record

The next step is to apply the change to the master record, as shown at point 6 of Figure 4B.4. Then, as depicted at points 7 and 8, the record is updated by rewriting it on the indexed master file. Upon completion of the rewrite operation, the system resets the file status field to tell the status of the update. A successful completion is indicated at point 9 of the figure.

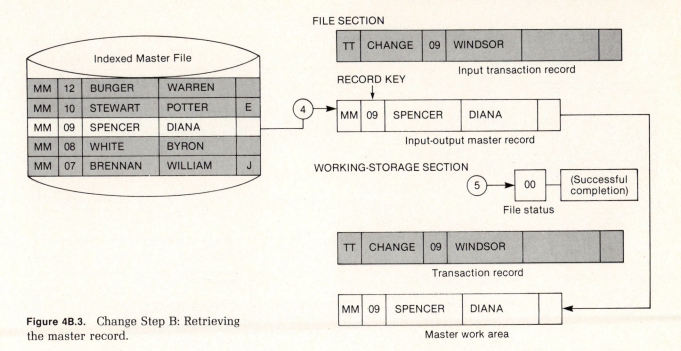

Figure 4B.3. Change Step B: Retrieving the master record.

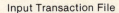

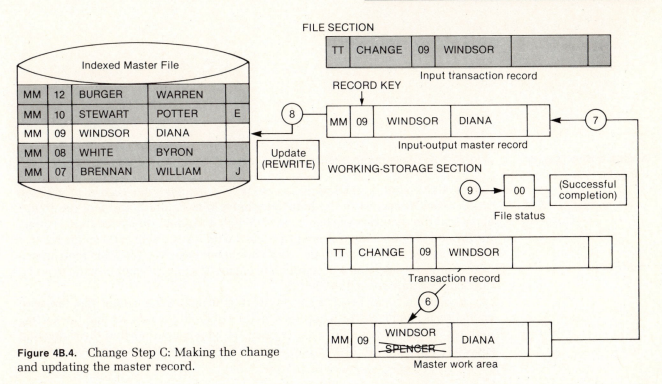

Figure 4B.4. Change Step C: Making the change and updating the master record.

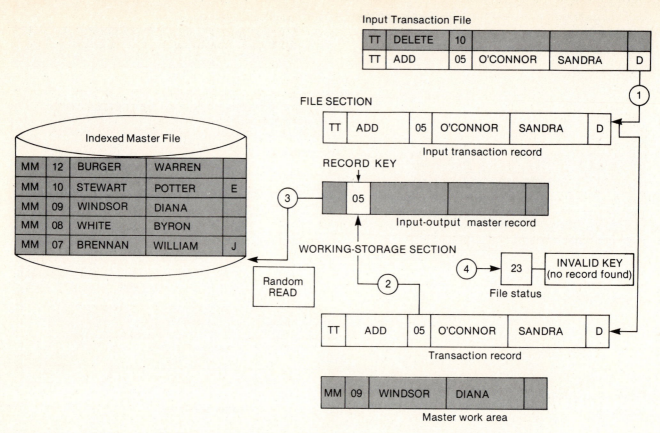

Figure 4B.5. Add Step A: Checking to ensure that the master record is not already on file.

Adding a New Master Record

Add Step A: Checking to ensure that the master record is not already on file

Figure 4B.5, point 1, depicts the reading of a transaction record to add the 05-O'CONNOR record to the indexed master file. Points 2 and 3 of the figure show that the record key is being set to 05 and a random read operation is being performed to determine if there is a record with a key value of 05 on the master file. Recognize that a matching record should *not* be on the file. This read operation is initiated solely as a precaution to ensure that no attempt is made to add a duplicate master record to the file.

Because a record with a key value of 05 is not on the master file, the read operation is unsuccessful. Therefore, point 4 of the figure shows that the system updates the file status field with a value (23), which signifies that the requested record was not found. Remember that, with this precautionary read operation

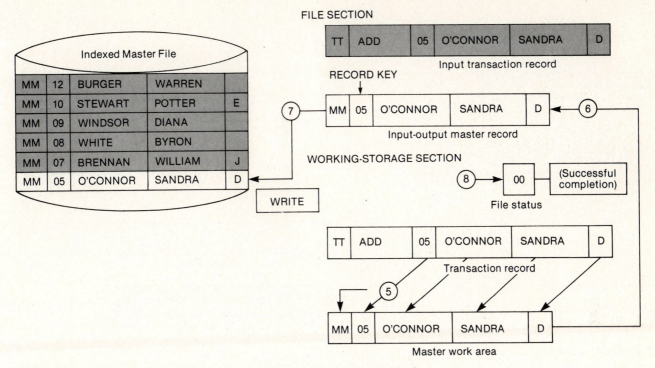

Figure 4B.6. Add Step B: Creating and writing out the new master record.

for an add transaction, the desired completion status is *no record found*. A successful completion would mean that an interfile-error situation had been detected.

Add Step B: Creating and writing out the new master record

Once the program logic has determined that the record to be added does *not* already exist on the master file, it takes the actions that are shown in Figure 4B.6. Point 5 depicts the creation of the master record from the transaction record. Then the newly created 05-O'CONNOR master record is written to the master file, as diagrammed at points 6 and 7. After the completion of the write operation, the system then updates the file status field. Point 8 of the figure indicates a successful completion.

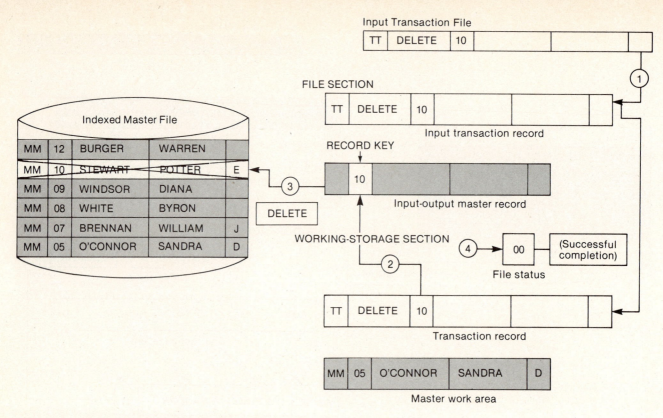

Figure 4B.7. Deleting a master record.

Deleting a Master Record

The reading of a delete transaction is shown at point 1 of Figure 4B.7. Point 2 shows that the record key is being set to the transaction key value of 10. Next, the delete operation is executed, as pictured at point 3. If the record to be deleted *is* located on the master file, the record is deleted and the system sets the file status field to indicate successful completion of the delete operation, as shown at point 4 of the figure. If the matching master record was *not* located on the indexed file, the system would have set the file status field with a no-record-found code value of 23.

A structure chart for the INDMAINT program is shown in Figure 4B.8.

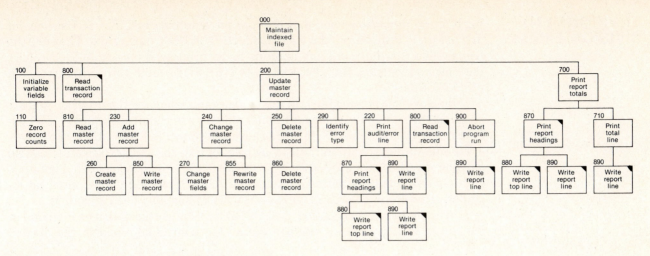

Figure 4B.8. Structure chart: INDMAINT program.

The COBOL syntax for indexed file processing is summarized in Figure 4C.1. The boxed entries are used for special retrieval purposes and will be discussed in Chapter 6.

The INDMAINT program coding appears in Figure 4C.2. Those aspects of COBOL syntax and application program coding that differ from what we already discussed for the SEQMAINT program in Chapter 3 will be explained in this topic.

ENVIRONMENT DIVISION Entries

Each of the three files used in this program is defined by a SELECT statement and assigned to an output device in the FILE-CONTROL paragraph. They are the transaction file that contains updates to be processed (TRANSACTION-FILE), the indexed master file (INDEXED-MASTER-FILE), and the audit/error list (REPORT-FILE).

Because this master file is of indexed organization and the program will access this file randomly, some additional clauses are required in the SELECT entry for the INDEXED-MASTER-FILE. These are shown in Figure 4C.3. Whenever a file has an organization other than sequential, the ORGANIZATION clause must be specified. Thus ORGANIZATION IS INDEXED has been coded. Similarly, if the access mode is not sequential, the ACCESS MODE clause must be included. Therefore, ACCESS MODE IS RANDOM has also been specified.

With indexed organization, a RECORD KEY clause must also be included in the SELECT entry. This is used to define the control-key field in the master

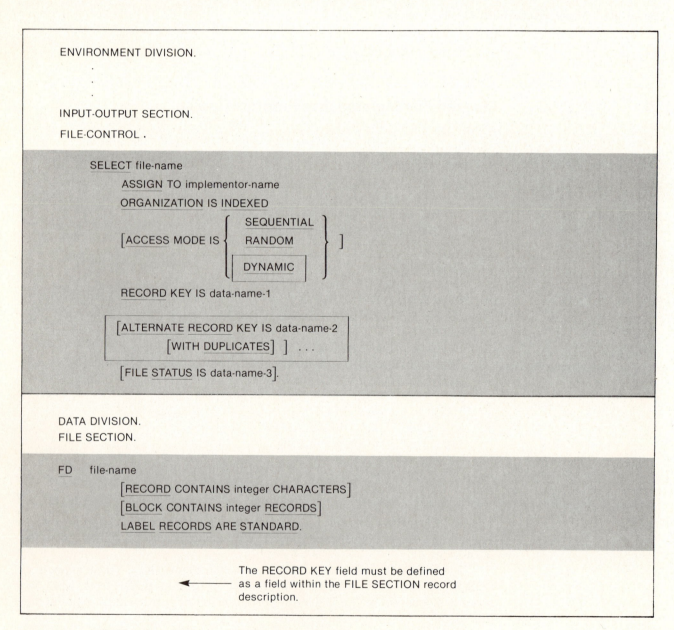

Figure 4C.1. COBOL indexed file-processing syntax summary.

PROCEDURE DIVISION.

OPEN $\left\{ \begin{array}{l} \underline{INPUT}\ file\text{-}name \\ \underline{I\text{-}O}\ file\text{-}name \\ \underline{OUTPUT}\ file\text{-}name \end{array} \right\}$ ... .

START file-name

$\left[\underline{KEY}\ IS \left\{ \begin{array}{l} \underline{EQUAL}\ TO \\ = \\ \underline{GREATER}\ THAN \\ > \\ \underline{NOT}\ \underline{LESS}\ THAN \\ \underline{NOT}\ < \end{array} \right\} data\text{-}name \right]$

[INVALID KEY imperative-statement].

Sequential retrieval:

READ file-name [NEXT] RECORD

[INTO identifier]

[AT END imperative-statement].

Random retrieval:

READ file-name RECORD

[INTO identifier]

[KEY IS data-name]

[INVALID KEY imperative-statement].

WRITE record-name

[FROM identifier]

[INVALID KEY imperative-statement].

REWRITE record-name

[FROM identifier]

[INVALID KEY imperative-statement].

DELETE file-name RECORD

[INVALID KEY imperative-statement].

CLOSE file name ... .

Figure 4C.1. (continued)

```
001010 IDENTIFICATION DIVISION.
001020 PROGRAM-ID.    INDMAINT.
001030*
001040*
001050*                       INDEXED MASTER FILE MAINTENANCE
002010*
002020*
002030*
002040 ENVIRONMENT DIVISION.
002050*
002060*
002070 CONFIGURATION SECTION.
002080*
002090 SOURCE-COMPUTER.  IBM-370.
002100 OBJECT-COMPUTER.  IBM-370.
002110*
002120*
002130 INPUT-OUTPUT SECTION.
002140*
002150 FILE-CONTROL.
002160     SELECT TRANSACTION-FILE
002170         ASSIGN TO UT-S-TRNFILE.
002180     SELECT INDEXED-MASTER-FILE
002190         ASSIGN TO INDFILE.
002194         ORGANIZATION IS INDEXED
002195         ACCESS MODE IS RANDOM
002196         RECORD KEY IS RK-INDEXED-KEY
002197         FILE STATUS IS WS-FILE-STATUS-FLAG.
002220     SELECT REPORT-FILE
002230         ASSIGN TO UT-S-PRTFILE.
003010*
003020*
003030*
003040 DATA DIVISION.
003050*
003060*
003070 FILE SECTION.
003080*
003090*
003100 FD  TRANSACTION-FILE
003110     RECORD CONTAINS 80 CHARACTERS
003120     LABEL RECORDS ARE STANDARD.
003130*
003140 01  TRANSACTION-RECORD.
003150     05  FILLER                       PIC X(80).
004010*
004020*
004030 FD  INDEXED-MASTER-FILE
004040     RECORD CONTAINS 80 CHARACTERS
004050     LABEL RECORDS ARE STANDARD.
004060*
004070 01  INDEXED-MASTER-RECORD.
004080     05  FILLER                       PIC X(3).
004090     05  RK-INDEXED-KEY.
004100         10  RK-PLANT-CODE            PIC X(2).
004110         10  RK-DEPARTMENT-NUMBER     PIC X(4).
004120         10  RK-EMPLOYEE-NUMBER       PIC X(5).
004130     05  FILLER                       PIC X(66).
006010*
006020*
006030 FD  REPORT-FILE
006040     RECORD CONTAINS 133 CHARACTERS
006050     LABEL RECORDS ARE OMITTED.
006060*
006070 01  REPORT-LINE.
006080     05  FILLER                       PIC X(133).
010010*
010020*
010030 WORKING-STORAGE SECTION.
010040*
010050*
010060 01  WS-SWITCHES.
010070*
010080     05  WS-TRANSACTION-END-OF-FILE-SW  PIC X(3).
010090         88  TRANSACTION-END-OF-FILE              VALUE 'YES'.
010300*
010310     05  WS-PROGRAM-ABEND-SW          PIC X(3).
010320         88  PROGRAM-ABEND                        VALUE 'YES'.
010330*
010340     05  WS-FILE-STATUS-FLAG          PIC X(2).
010350         88  SUCCESSFUL-COMPLETION              VALUE '00'.
010360         88  DUPLICATE-ALTERNATE-KEY            VALUE '02'.
010370         88  END-OF-FILE                        VALUE '10'.
010380         88  SEQUENCE-ERROR                     VALUE '21'.
010390         88  DUPLICATE-KEY                      VALUE '22'.
010400         88  NO-RECORD-FOUND                    VALUE '23'.
010410         88  BOUNDARY-VIOLATION-IND-REL         VALUE '24'.
010420         88  PERMANENT-I-O-DATA-ERROR           VALUE '30'.
010430         88  BOUNDARY-VIOLATION-SEQ             VALUE '34'.
010440         88  IMPLEMENTOR-DEFINED-ERROR          VALUE '9 '.
010450*
010460     05  WS-I-O-OPERATION-FLAG        PIC X(7).
012010*
012020*
012030 01  WS-REPORT-CONTROLS.
012040     05  WS-PAGE-COUNT                PIC S9(4)         COMP-3.
012050     05  WS-LINES-PER-PAGE            PIC S99 VALUE +55
012060                                                        COMP SYNC.
012070     05  WS-LINES-USED                PIC S9(2)         COMP SYNC.
012080     05  WS-LINE-SPACING              PIC S9(2).
013010*
013020*
013030 01  WS-WORK-AREAS.
013040     05  WS-DATE-WORK                 PIC 9(6).
013050     05  WS-DATE-REFORMAT REDEFINES WS-DATE-WORK.
013060         10  WS-YEAR                  PIC 9(2).
013070         10  WS-MONTH                 PIC 9(2).
013080         10  WS-DAY                   PIC 9(2).
014010*
014020*
014030 01  TC-TABLE-CONTROLS.
014040     05  TC-SUBSCRIPT                 PIC S9(4)         COMP SYNC.
014050     05  TC-NUMBER-OF-ENTRIES         PIC S9(4) VALUE +15
014060                                                        COMP SYNC.
015010*
015020 01  TC-COUNT-DESCRIPTION-DATA.
015030     05  FILLER        PIC X(20)   VALUE 'TRANSACTIONS READ   '.
015040     05  FILLER        PIC X(20)   VALUE '  ADDS              '.
015050     05  FILLER        PIC X(20)   VALUE '      PROCESSED     '.
015060     05  FILLER        PIC X(20)   VALUE '      REJECTED      '.
015070     05  FILLER        PIC X(20)   VALUE '  CHANGES           '.
015080     05  FILLER        PIC X(20)   VALUE '      PROCESSED     '.
015090     05  FILLER        PIC X(20)   VALUE '      REJECTED      '.
015100     05  FILLER        PIC X(20)   VALUE '  DELETES           '.
015110     05  FILLER        PIC X(20)   VALUE '      PROCESSED     '.
015120     05  FILLER        PIC X(20)   VALUE '      REJECTED      '.
015130     05  FILLER        PIC X(20)   VALUE ' ERROR UPDATE CODES'.
015140     05  FILLER        PIC X(20)   VALUE 'MASTERS READ        '.
015150     05  FILLER        PIC X(20)   VALUE 'MASTER CHANGES      '.
015160     05  FILLER        PIC X(20)   VALUE 'MASTERS ADDED       '.
015165     05  FILLER        PIC X(20)   VALUE 'MASTERS DELETED     '.
015170 01  TC-COUNT-DESCRIPTION-TABLE
015180     REDEFINES TC-COUNT-DESCRIPTION-DATA.
015190     05  TC-COUNT-DESCRIPTION         OCCURS 15 TIMES
015200                                      PIC X(20).
016010*
016020 01  TC-RECORD-COUNT-ENTRIES                        COMP-3.
016030     05  TC-TOTAL-TRANS-READ            PIC S9(5).
016040     05  TC-TOTAL-ADD-TRANS-READ        PIC S9(5).
016050     05  TC-ADD-TRANS-PROCESSED         PIC S9(5).
016060     05  TC-ADD-TRANS-REJECTED          PIC S9(5).
016070     05  TC-TOTAL-CHANGE-TRANS-READ     PIC S9(5).
016080     05  TC-CHANGE-TRANS-PROCESSED      PIC S9(5).
016090     05  TC-CHANGE-TRANS-REJECTED       PIC S9(5).
016100     05  TC-TOTAL-DELETE-TRANS-READ     PIC S9(5).
016110     05  TC-DELETE-TRANS-PROCESSED      PIC S9(5).
016120     05  TC-DELETE-TRANS-REJECTED       PIC S9(5).
016130     05  TC-TOTAL-ERROR-UPDATE-CODES    PIC S9(5).
016140     05  TC-MASTERS-READ                PIC S9(5).
016150     05  TC-MASTER-CHANGES              PIC S9(5).
016160     05  TC-MASTERS-ADDED               PIC S9(5).
016165     05  TC-MASTERS-DELETED             PIC S9(5).
016170 01  TC-RECORD-COUNTS REDEFINES TC-RECORD-COUNT-ENTRIES.
016180     05  TC-RECORD-COUNT                OCCURS 15 TIMES
016190                                        PIC S9(5)     COMP-3.
020010*
020020*
020030 01  ET-EMPLOYEE-TRANSACTION-RECORD.
020040     05  ET-RECORD-CODE             PIC X(2).
020050     05  ET-UPDATE-CODE             PIC X(1).
020060         88  DELETE-TRANSACTION                 VALUE '1'.
020070         88  ADD-TRANSACTION                    VALUE '2'.
020080         88  CHANGE-TRANSACTION                 VALUE '3'.
020084         88  VALID-UPDATE-CODE                  VALUE '1'.
020086                                                      '2'
020088                                                      '3'.
020090     05  ET-EMPLOYEE-NUMBER         PIC X(5).
020100     05  ET-LAST-NAME               PIC X(13).
020110     05  ET-FIRST-NAME              PIC X(12).
020120     05  ET-MIDDLE-INITIAL          PIC X(1).
020130     05  ET-PLANT-CODE              PIC X(2).
020140     05  ET-DEPARTMENT-NUMBER       PIC X(4).
020150     05  ET-HOURLY-RATE             PIC S9(2)V99.
020160     05  ET-HOURLY-RATE-X REDEFINES ET-HOURLY-RATE
020170                                    PIC X(4).
020180     05  FILLER                     PIC X(36).
025010*
025020*
025030 01  EM-EMPLOYEE-MASTER-WORK-AREA.
025040     05  EM-RECORD-CODE             PIC X(2).
025050     05  FILLER                     PIC X(1).
025060     05  EM-PLANT-CODE              PIC X(2).
025070     05  EM-DEPARTMENT-NUMBER       PIC X(4).
025080     05  EM-EMPLOYEE-NUMBER         PIC X(5).
025090     05  EM-LAST-NAME               PIC X(13).
025100     05  EM-FIRST-NAME              PIC X(12).
025110     05  EM-MIDDLE-INITIAL          PIC X(1).
025120     05  EM-HOURLY-RATE             PIC S9(2)V99.
025130     05  FILLER                     PIC X(30).
025140     05  EM-DATE-LAST-ACTIVITY      PIC 9(6).
030010*
030020*
030040 01  H1-HEADING-LINE-1.
030050     05  FILLER         PIC X(1).
030060     05  FILLER         PIC X(20)  VALUE 'INDEXED MASTER FILE '.
030070     05  FILLER         PIC X(20)  VALUE 'MAINTENANCE         '.
030080     05  FILLER         PIC X(20)  VALUE '                    '.
030090     05  FILLER         PIC X(20)  VALUE '                    '.
030100     05  FILLER         PIC X(20)  VALUE '            RUN DAT'.
030110     05  FILLER         PIC X(2)   VALUE 'E '.
030120     05  H1-MONTH       PIC 9(2).
030130     05  FILLER         PIC X(1)   VALUE '/'.
030140     05  H1-DAY         PIC 9(2).
030150     05  FILLER         PIC X(1)   VALUE '/'.
030160     05  H1-YEAR        PIC 9(2).
030170     05  FILLER         PIC X(22)  VALUE SPACES.
031010*
031020*
031030 01  H2-HEADING-LINE-2.
031040     05  FILLER         PIC X(1).
031050     05  FILLER         PIC X(20)  VALUE 'AUDIT/ERROR LIST    '.
031060     05  FILLER         PIC X(20)  VALUE '                    '.
031070     05  FILLER         PIC X(20)  VALUE '   ** EMPLOYEE MASTER'.
031080     05  FILLER         PIC X(20)  VALUE ' FILE **            '.
031090     05  FILLER         PIC X(20)  VALUE '                    '.
031100     05  FILLER         PIC X(6)   VALUE ' PAGE '.
031110     05  H2-PAGE-NBR    PIC ZZZ9.
031120     05  FILLER         PIC X(22)  VALUE SPACES.
032010*
032020*
032030 01  H3-HEADING-LINE-3.
032040     05  FILLER         PIC X(1).
032050     05  FILLER         PIC X(20)  VALUE 'RCD UPDT   PLANT  DE'.
032060     05  FILLER         PIC X(20)  VALUE 'PT EMPL ------EMP'.
032070     05  FILLER         PIC X(20)  VALUE 'LOYEE NAME------M '.
032080     05  FILLER         PIC X(20)  VALUE 'HOURLY   UPDATE     '.
032090     05  FILLER         PIC X(20)  VALUE '                    '.
032100     05  FILLER         PIC X(20)  VALUE '                    '.
032110     05  FILLER         PIC X(12)  VALUE '            '.
033010*
033020*
033030 01  H4-HEADING-LINE-4.
033040     05  FILLER         PIC X(1).
033050     05  FILLER         PIC X(20)  VALUE 'CODE CODE   CODE   N'.
033060     05  FILLER         PIC X(20)  VALUE 'BR  NBR  LAST NAME  '.
033070     05  FILLER         PIC X(20)  VALUE '  FIRST NAME   I '.
```

Figure 4C.2.   COBOL coding: INDMAINT program.

```
033080     05  FILLER         PIC X(20)    VALUE ' RATE   ACTION ---'.
033090     05  FILLER         PIC X(20)    VALUE '------ERROR MESSAGE'.
033100     05  FILLER         PIC X(20)    VALUE '---------      '.
033110     05  FILLER         PIC X(12)    VALUE '          '.
034010*
034020*
034030 01  DL-DETAIL-LINE.
034040     05  FILLER                      PIC X(1).
034050     05  FILLER                      PIC X(1).    VALUE SPACES.
034060     05  DL-RECORD-CODE              PIC X(2).
034070     05  FILLER                      PIC X(4).    VALUE SPACES.
034080     05  DL-UPDATE-CODE              PIC X(1).
034090     05  FILLER                      PIC X(4).    VALUE SPACES.
034100     05  DL-PLANT-CODE               PIC X(2).
034110     05  FILLER                      PIC X(4).    VALUE SPACES.
034120     05  DL-DEPARTMENT-NUMBER        PIC X(4).
034130     05  FILLER                      PIC X(1).    VALUE SPACES.
034140     05  DL-EMPLOYEE-NUMBER          PIC X(5).
034150     05  FILLER                      PIC X(2).    VALUE SPACES.
034160     05  DL-LAST-NAME                PIC X(13).
034170     05  FILLER                      PIC X(1).    VALUE SPACES.
034180     05  DL-FIRST-NAME               PIC X(12).
034190     05  FILLER                      PIC X(1).    VALUE SPACES.
034200     05  DL-MIDDLE-INITIAL           PIC X(1).
034210     05  FILLER                      PIC X(3).    VALUE SPACES.
034220     05  DL-HOURLY-RATE              PIC ZZ.99.
034230     05  DL-HOURLY-RATE-X REDEFINES DL-HOURLY-RATE
034240                                     PIC X(5).
034250     05  FILLER                      PIC X(2).    VALUE SPACES.
034260     05  DL-UPDATE-ACTION            PIC X(8).
034270     05  FILLER                      PIC X(1).    VALUE SPACES.
034280     05  DL-ERROR-MSG                PIC X(33).
034290     05  FILLER                      PIC X(22).   VALUE SPACES.
035010*
035020*
035030 01  IE-I-O-ERROR-LINE REDEFINES DL-DETAIL-LINE.
035040     05  FILLER                      PIC X(1).
035050     05  FILLER                      PIC X(40).
035062     05  IE-FILE-STATUS-FLAG         PIC X(2).
035064     05  FILLER                      PIC X(1).
035066     05  IE-I-O-OPERATION-FLAG       PIC X(7).
035070     05  FILLER                      PIC X(1).
035080     05  IE-ERROR-KEY                PIC XXBXXXXBXXXXX.
035090     05  FILLER                      PIC X(4).
036010*
036020*
036030 01  TL-TOTAL-LINE.
036040     05  FILLER                      PIC X(1).
036050     05  FILLER                      PIC X(83).   VALUE SPACES.
036060     05  TL-COUNT-DESCRIPTION        PIC X(20).
036070     05  FILLER                      PIC X(1).    VALUE SPACES.
036080     05  TL-RECORD-COUNT             PIC ZZ,ZZ9.
036090     05  FILLER                      PIC X(22).   VALUE SPACES.
050010*
050020*
050030*
050040 PROCEDURE DIVISION.
050050*
050060*
050070 000-MAINTAIN-INDEXED-FILE.
050080*
050090     OPEN INPUT TRANSACTION-FILE
050100          I-O INDEXED-MASTER-FILE
050120          OUTPUT REPORT-FILE.
050130     PERFORM 100-INITIALIZE-VARIABLE-FIELDS.
050135     PERFORM 800-READ-TRANSACTION-RECORD.
050140     PERFORM 200-UPDATE-MASTER-RECORD
050150         UNTIL TRANSACTION-END-OF-FILE.
050170     PERFORM 700-PRINT-REPORT-TOTALS.
050180     CLOSE TRANSACTION-FILE
050190           INDEXED-MASTER-FILE
050210           REPORT-FILE.
050220     STOP RUN.
100010*
100020*
100030 100-INITIALIZE-VARIABLE-FIELDS.
100040*
100050     MOVE 'NO ' TO WS-TRANSACTION-END-OF-FILE-SW
100055                   WS-PROGRAM-ABEND-SW.
100120     MOVE ZERO TO WS-PAGE-COUNT.
100130     ADD 1 WS-LINES-PER-PAGE GIVING WS-LINES-USED.
100140     ACCEPT WS-DATE-WORK FROM DATE.
100150     MOVE WS-MONTH TO H1-MONTH.
100160     MOVE WS-DAY TO H1-DAY.
100170     MOVE WS-YEAR TO H1-YEAR.
100190     MOVE SPACES TO DL-ERROR-MSG.
100200     PERFORM 110-ZERO-RECORD-COUNTS
100210         VARYING TC-SUBSCRIPT
100220             FROM 1
100230             BY 1
100240             UNTIL TC-SUBSCRIPT IS GREATER THAN TC-NUMBER-OF-ENTRIES.
110010*
110020*
110030 110-ZERO-RECORD-COUNTS.
110040*
110050     MOVE ZERO TO TC-RECORD-COUNT (TC-SUBSCRIPT).
200010*
200020*
200030 200-UPDATE-MASTER-RECORD.
200040*
200044     IF VALID-UPDATE-CODE
200046         PERFORM 810-READ-MASTER-RECORD.
200046*
200050     IF (ADD-TRANSACTION AND NO-RECORD-FOUND)
200060         PERFORM 230-ADD-MASTER-RECORD
200065*
200070     ELSE IF (CHANGE-TRANSACTION AND SUCCESSFUL-COMPLETION)
200080         PERFORM 240-CHANGE-MASTER-RECORD
200085*
200090     ELSE IF (DELETE-TRANSACTION AND SUCCESSFUL-COMPLETION)
200100         PERFORM 250-DELETE-MASTER-RECORD
200105*
200110     ELSE
200120         PERFORM 290-IDENTIFY-ERROR-TYPE.
200170*
200180     PERFORM 220-PRINT-AUDIT-ERROR-LINE.
200182*
200184     IF NOT PROGRAM-ABEND
200186         PERFORM 800-READ-TRANSACTION-RECORD
200188     ELSE
200190         PERFORM 900-ABORT-PROGRAM-RUN.
220010*
220020*
220030 220-PRINT-AUDIT-ERROR-LINE.
220040*
220050     IF WS-LINES-USED IS NOT LESS THAN WS-LINES-PER-PAGE
220060         PERFORM 870-PRINT-REPORT-HEADINGS.
220070     MOVE ET-RECORD-CODE TO DL-RECORD-CODE.
220080     MOVE ET-UPDATE-CODE TO DL-UPDATE-CODE.
220090     MOVE ET-PLANT-CODE TO DL-PLANT-CODE.
220100     MOVE ET-DEPARTMENT-NUMBER TO DL-DEPARTMENT-NUMBER.
220110     MOVE ET-EMPLOYEE-NUMBER TO DL-EMPLOYEE-NUMBER.
220120     MOVE ET-LAST-NAME TO DL-LAST-NAME.
220130     MOVE ET-FIRST-NAME TO DL-FIRST-NAME.
220140     MOVE ET-MIDDLE-INITIAL TO DL-MIDDLE-INITIAL.
220150     IF ET-HOURLY-RATE IS NUMERIC
220160         MOVE ET-HOURLY-RATE TO DL-HOURLY-RATE
220170     ELSE
220180         MOVE ET-HOURLY-RATE-X TO DL-HOURLY-RATE-X.
220190     MOVE DL-DETAIL-LINE TO REPORT-LINE.
220200     MOVE 1 TO WS-LINE-SPACING.
220210     PERFORM 890-WRITE-REPORT-LINE.
220220     MOVE SPACES TO DL-DETAIL-LINE.
230010*
230020*
230030 230-ADD-MASTER-RECORD.
230040*
230070     ADD 1 TO TC-TOTAL-ADD-TRANS-READ.
230080     PERFORM 260-CREATE-MASTER-RECORD.
230084     PERFORM 850-WRITE-MASTER-RECORD.
230088     IF NOT PROGRAM-ABEND
230090         ADD 1 TO TC-ADD-TRANS-PROCESSED
230100         MOVE 'ADDED   ' TO DL-UPDATE-ACTION.
240010*
240020*
240030 240-CHANGE-MASTER-RECORD.
240040*
240150     ADD 1 TO TC-TOTAL-CHANGE-TRANS-READ.
240160     PERFORM 270-CHANGE-MASTER-FIELDS.
240170     PERFORM 855-REWRITE-MASTER-RECORD.
240180     IF NOT PROGRAM-ABEND
240190         ADD 1 TO TC-CHANGE-TRANS-PROCESSED
240200         MOVE 'CHANGED ' TO DL-UPDATE-ACTION.
250010*
250020*
250030 250-DELETE-MASTER-RECORD.
250040*
250150     ADD 1 TO TC-TOTAL-DELETE-TRANS-READ.
250160     PERFORM 860-DELETE-MASTER-RECORD.
250170     IF NOT PROGRAM-ABEND
250180         ADD 1 TO TC-DELETE-TRANS-PROCESSED
250190         MOVE 'DELETED ' TO DL-UPDATE-ACTION.
260010*
260020*
260030 260-CREATE-MASTER-RECORD.
260040*
260050     MOVE SPACES TO EM-EMPLOYEE-MASTER-WORK-AREA.
260060     MOVE '85' TO EM-RECORD-CODE.
260070     MOVE ET-PLANT-CODE TO EM-PLANT-CODE.
260080     MOVE ET-DEPARTMENT-NUMBER TO EM-DEPARTMENT-NUMBER.
260090     MOVE ET-EMPLOYEE-NUMBER TO EM-EMPLOYEE-NUMBER.
260100     MOVE ET-LAST-NAME TO EM-LAST-NAME.
260110     MOVE ET-FIRST-NAME TO EM-FIRST-NAME.
260120     MOVE ET-MIDDLE-INITIAL TO EM-MIDDLE-INITIAL.
260130     MOVE ET-HOURLY-RATE TO EM-HOURLY-RATE.
260140     MOVE WS-DATE-WORK TO EM-DATE-LAST-ACTIVITY.
270010*
270020*
270030 270-CHANGE-MASTER-FIELDS.
270040*
270050     IF ET-LAST-NAME IS EQUAL TO SPACES
270060         NEXT SENTENCE
270070     ELSE
270080         MOVE ET-LAST-NAME TO TO EM-LAST-NAME.
270090*
270100     IF ET-FIRST-NAME IS EQUAL TO SPACES
270110         NEXT SENTENCE
270120     ELSE
270130         MOVE ET-FIRST-NAME TO EM-FIRST-NAME.
270140*
270150     IF ET-MIDDLE-INITIAL IS EQUAL TO SPACES
270160         NEXT SENTENCE
270170     ELSE IF ET-MIDDLE-INITIAL IS EQUAL TO '$'
270180         MOVE SPACES TO EM-MIDDLE-INITIAL
270190     ELSE
270200         MOVE ET-MIDDLE-INITIAL TO EM-MIDDLE-INITIAL.
270210*
270220     IF ET-HOURLY-RATE-X IS EQUAL TO SPACES
270230         NEXT SENTENCE
270240     ELSE
270250         MOVE ET-HOURLY-RATE TO EM-HOURLY-RATE.
270260*
270270     MOVE WS-DATE-WORK TO EM-DATE-LAST-ACTIVITY.
290010*
290020*
290030 290-IDENTIFY-ERROR-TYPE.
290040*
290050     IF ADD-TRANSACTION
290060         ADD 1 TO TC-TOTAL-ADD-TRANS-READ
290070         ADD 1 TO TC-ADD-TRANS-REJECTED
290080         MOVE 'UNABLE ADD-MASTER ALREADY ON FILE' TO DL-ERROR-MSG
290090     ELSE IF CHANGE-TRANSACTION
290100         ADD 1 TO TC-TOTAL-CHANGE-TRANS-READ
290110         ADD 1 TO TC-CHANGE-TRANS-REJECTED
290120         MOVE 'UNABLE CHANGE-MASTER NOT ON FILE ' TO DL-ERROR-MSG
290130     ELSE IF DELETE-TRANSACTION
290140         ADD 1 TO TC-TOTAL-DELETE-TRANS-READ
290150         ADD 1 TO TC-DELETE-TRANS-REJECTED
290160         MOVE 'UNABLE DELETE-MASTER NOT ON FILE ' TO DL-ERROR-MSG
290170     ELSE
290180         ADD 1 TO TC-TOTAL-ERROR-UPDATE-CODES
290190         MOVE 'UNABLE UPDATE-INVALID UPDATE CODE' TO DL-ERROR-MSG.
290200*
290210     MOVE 'REJECTED' TO DL-UPDATE-ACTION.
700010*
700020*
```

Figure 4C.2. (continued)

continued

```
700030 700-PRINT-REPORT-TOTALS.                        855080*
700040*                                                855090     IF SUCCESSFUL-COMPLETION
700050     PERFORM 870-PRINT-REPORT-HEADINGS.          855100         ADD 1 TO TC-MASTER-CHANGES
700060     PERFORM 710-PRINT-TOTAL-LINE                855110     ELSE
700070         VARYING TC-SUBSCRIPT                    855120         MOVE 'YES' TO WS-PROGRAM-ABEND-SW.
700080         FROM 1                                  860010*
700090         BY 1                                    860020*
700100         UNTIL TC-SUBSCRIPT IS GREATER THAN TC-NUMBER-OF-ENTRIES.   860030 860-DELETE-MASTER-RECORD.
710010*                                                860040*
710020*                                                860045     MOVE 'DELETE ' TO WS-I-O-OPERATION-FLAG.
710030 710-PRINT-TOTAL-LINE.                           860050     DELETE INDEXED-MASTER-FILE
710040*                                                860060         INVALID KEY MOVE 'YES' TO WS-PROGRAM-ABEND-SW.
710050     MOVE TC-COUNT-DESCRIPTION (TC-SUBSCRIPT)    860070*
710060         TO TL-COUNT-DESCRIPTION.                860080     IF SUCCESSFUL-COMPLETION
710070     MOVE TC-RECORD-COUNT (TC-SUBSCRIPT) TO TL-RECORD-COUNT.   860090         ADD 1 TO TC-MASTERS-DELETED
710080     MOVE TL-TOTAL-LINE TO REPORT-LINE.          860100     ELSE
710090     MOVE 1 TO WS-LINE-SPACING.                  860110         MOVE 'YES' TO WS-PROGRAM-ABEND-SW.
710100     PERFORM 890-WRITE-REPORT-LINE.              870010*
800010*                                                870020*
800020*                                                870030 870-PRINT-REPORT-HEADINGS.
800030 800-READ-TRANSACTION-RECORD.                    870040*
800040*                                                870050     ADD 1 TO WS-PAGE-COUNT.
800070     READ TRANSACTION-FILE INTO ET-EMPLOYEE-TRANSACTION-RECORD   870060     MOVE WS-PAGE-COUNT TO H2-PAGE-NBR.
800080         AT END MOVE 'YES' TO WS-TRANSACTION-END-OF-FILE-SW.   870070     MOVE H1-HEADING-LINE-1 TO REPORT-LINE.
800100*                                                870080     PERFORM 880-WRITE-REPORT-TOP-LINE.
800110     IF NOT TRANSACTION-END-OF-FILE              870090     MOVE H2-HEADING-LINE-2 TO REPORT-LINE.
800120         ADD 1 TO TC-TOTAL-TRANS-READ.           870100     MOVE 1 TO WS-LINE-SPACING.
810010*                                                870110     PERFORM 890-WRITE-REPORT-LINE.
810020*                                                870120     MOVE H3-HEADING-LINE-3 TO REPORT-LINE.
810030 810-READ-MASTER-RECORD.                         870130     MOVE 2 TO WS-LINE-SPACING.
810040*                                                870140     PERFORM 890-WRITE-REPORT-LINE.
810042     MOVE ET-PLANT-CODE TO RK-PLANT-CODE.        870150     MOVE H4-HEADING-LINE-4 TO REPORT-LINE.
810044     MOVE ET-DEPARTMENT-NUMBER TO RK-DEPARTMENT-NUMBER.   870160     MOVE 1 TO WS-LINE-SPACING.
810046     MOVE ET-EMPLOYEE-NUMBER TO RK-EMPLOYEE-NUMBER.   870170     PERFORM 890-WRITE-REPORT-LINE.
810065     MOVE 'READ   ' TO WS-I-O-OPERATION-FLAG.    870180     MOVE SPACES TO REPORT-LINE.
810070     READ INDEXED-MASTER-FILE                    870190     PERFORM 890-WRITE-REPORT-LINE.
810074         INTO EM-EMPLOYEE-MASTER-WORK-AREA.      880010*
810300*                                                880020*
810310     IF SUCCESSFUL-COMPLETION                    880030 880-WRITE-REPORT-TOP-LINE.
810320         ADD 1 TO TC-MASTERS-READ.               880040*
810330*                                                880050     WRITE REPORT-LINE
810340     IF PERMANENT-I-O-DATA-ERROR                 880060         AFTER ADVANCING PAGE.
810350         MOVE 'YES' TO WS-PROGRAM-ABEND-SW.      880070     MOVE 1 TO WS-LINES-USED.
850010*                                                890010*
850020*                                                890020*
850030 850-WRITE-MASTER-RECORD.                        890030 890-WRITE-REPORT-LINE.
850040*                                                890040*
850045     MOVE 'WRITE  ' TO WS-I-O-OPERATION-FLAG.    890050     WRITE REPORT-LINE
850050     WRITE INDEXED-MASTER-RECORD                 890060         AFTER ADVANCING WS-LINE-SPACING.
850060         FROM EM-EMPLOYEE-MASTER-WORK-AREA       890070     ADD WS-LINE-SPACING TO WS-LINES-USED.
850065         INVALID KEY MOVE 'YES' TO WS-PROGRAM-ABEND-SW.   900010*
850200*                                                900020*
850210     IF SUCCESSFUL-COMPLETION                    900030 900-ABORT-PROGRAM-RUN.
850220         ADD 1 TO TC-MASTERS-ADDED               900040*
850230     ELSE                                        900042     MOVE WS-FILE-STATUS-FLAG TO IE-FILE-STATUS-FLAG.
850240         MOVE 'YES' TO WS-PROGRAM-ABEND-SW.      900044     MOVE WS-I-O-OPERATION-FLAG TO IE-I-O-OPERATION-FLAG.
855010*                                                900046     MOVE RK-INDEXED-KEY TO IE-ERROR-KEY.
855020*                                                900050     MOVE 'ABORTED ' TO DL-UPDATE-ACTION.
855030 855-REWRITE-MASTER-RECORD.                      900055     MOVE 'I-O ERROR OCCURRED' TO DL-ERROR-MSG.
855040*                                                900060     MOVE DL-DETAIL-LINE TO REPORT-LINE.
855045     MOVE 'REWRITE' TO WS-I-O-OPERATION-FLAG.    900070     MOVE 3 TO WS-LINE-SPACING.
855050     REWRITE INDEXED-MASTER-RECORD               900080     PERFORM 890-WRITE-REPORT-LINE.
855060         FROM EM-EMPLOYEE-MASTER-WORK-AREA       900090     MOVE SPACES TO DL-DETAIL-LINE.
855070         INVALID KEY MOVE 'YES' TO WS-PROGRAM-ABEND-SW.   900150     MOVE 'YES' TO WS-TRANSACTION-END-OF-FILE-SW.
```

Figure 4C.2. (continued)

record. The RECORD KEY field *must be defined within the* FILE SECTION FD *for that file.* In this program we have specified RECORD KEY IS RK-INDEXED-KEY. In accordance with the programming specifications, RK-INDEXED-KEY will be defined in the DATA DIVISION as a group field that contains the three elementary control-key fields: plant code, department number, and employee number.

With 1974 ANS COBOL, the FILE STATUS clause can be optionally included to specify the two-character file status data-item in WORKING-STORAGE for the system to update with a completion code after each I-O operation. We have specified FILE STATUS IS WS-FILE-STATUS-FLAG. This file status field will be referred to in the PROCEDURE DIVISION.

DATA DIVISION
Entries

FILE SECTION
Entries

To gain the advantages of processing records in WORKING-STORAGE, the definition of input-output record data-items has been specified in the WORKING-STORAGE SECTION rather than in the FILE SECTION.

However, notice in Figure 4C.4 that, within the INDEXED-MASTER-RECORD, the group field RK-INDEXED-KEY together with its three elementary data-items has been defined. This is done because of the requirement that the

Format:

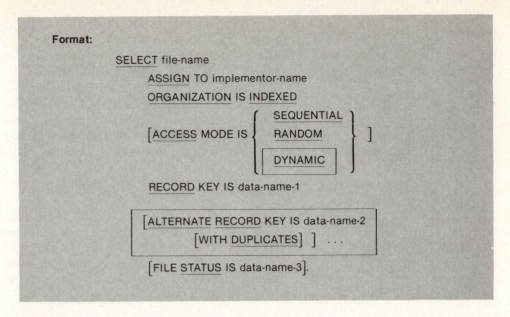

```
           SELECT file-name

                ASSIGN TO implementor-name

                ORGANIZATION IS INDEXED

                                  ⎧ SEQUENTIAL ⎫
                [ACCESS MODE IS   ⎨ RANDOM     ⎬ ]
                                  ⎩ DYNAMIC    ⎭

                RECORD KEY IS data-name-1

                ⎡ALTERNATE RECORD KEY IS data-name-2        ⎤
                ⎢       [WITH DUPLICATES]                   ⎥ ...
                └                                           ┘

                [FILE STATUS IS data-name-3].
```

Example:

```
        SELECT INDEXED-MASTER-FILE

            ASSIGN TO INDFILE

            ORGANIZATION IS INDEXED

            ACCESS MODE IS RANDOM

            RECORD KEY IS RK-INDEXED-KEY

            FILE STATUS IS WS-FILE-STATUS-FLAG.
```

Figure 4C.3.   SELECT statement format and example for an indexed file.

```
    DATA DIVISION.
    FILE SECTION.
    FD  INDEXED-MASTER-FILE
            RECORD CONTAINS 80 CHARACTERS
            LABEL RECORDS ARE STANDARD.
    01  INDEXED-MASTER-RECORD.
        05  FILLER                      PIC X(3).

        05  RK-INDEXED-KEY.
            10  RK-PLANT-CODE           PIC X(2).
            10  RK-DEPARTMENT-NUMBER    PIC X(4).
            10  RK-EMPLOYEE-NUMBER      PIC X(5).

        05  FILLER                      PIC X(66).
```

NOTE: The RECORD KEY field must be defined as a field within
        the FILE SECTION record description.

Figure 4C.4.   RECORD KEY definition example.

RECORD KEY be specified in the FILE SECTION within the FD record-description for that file.

It is not actually necessary to define the elementary fields (RK-PLANT-CODE, RK-DEPARTMENT-NUMBER, and RK-EMPLOYEE-NUMBER) here within the record-description; RK-INDEXED-KEY could have been specified as an elementary field with a PICTURE of X(11). Such detailed definition is coded only to clearly define the composition of the key field.

In any event, the RECORD KEY field must be an alphanumeric or group item (although certain compilers allow it to be coded as a numeric field of DISPLAY usage).

WORKING-STORAGE SECTION Entries

Seven major categories of field specifications are coded within the WORKING-STORAGE SECTION: program switches, report control fields, a current date work area, record count description and total tables, the input employee-transaction record description, the employee master record work-area description, and audit/error report line entries describing each report line field. (Because there is no sequence checking of the transaction or master file records, the sequence control fields of the SEQMAINT program are not coded in this program.) The organization of these categories in the WORKING-STORAGE SECTION is depicted in Figure 4C.5.

We will discuss those WORKING-STORAGE SECTION entries for this IND-MAINT program that differ from the SEQMAINT program.

Program switches

```
010040*
010050*
010060 01  WS-SWITCHES.
010070*
010080     05  WS-TRANSACTION-END-OF-FILE-SW   PIC X(3).
010090         88  TRANSACTION-END-OF-FILE                  VALUE 'YES'.
010300*
010310     05  WS-PROGRAM-ABEND-SW             PIC X(3).
010320         88  PROGRAM-ABEND                            VALUE 'YES'.
010330*
010340     05  WS-FILE-STATUS-FLAG             PIC X(2).
010350         88  SUCCESSFUL-COMPLETION                    VALUE '00'.
010360         88  DUPLICATE-ALTERNATE-KEY                  VALUE '02'.
010370         88  END-OF-FILE                              VALUE '10'.
010380         88  SEQUENCE-ERROR                           VALUE '21'.
010390         88  DUPLICATE-KEY                            VALUE '22'.
010400         88  NO-RECORD-FOUND                          VALUE '23'.
010410         88  BOUNDARY-VIOLATION-IND-REL               VALUE '24'.
010420         88  PERMANENT-I-O-DATA-ERROR                 VALUE '30'.
010430         88  BOUNDARY-VIOLATION-SEQ                   VALUE '34'.
010440*        88  IMPLEMENTOR-DEFINED-ERROR                VALUE '9 '.
010450*
010460     05  WS-I-O-OPERATION-FLAG           PIC X(7).
```

The program switches are coded within the 01-level WS-SWITCHES entry. Two switch fields and two flag fields are specified to control program operations.

The first switch, WS-TRANSACTION-END-OF-FILE-SW is a typical end-of-file switch. Unlike a sequential file-maintenance program in which end-of-run does not occur until both the transaction and master file have ended, end-of-run for a file-maintenance program in random-access mode is determined solely by the transaction file status. Thus, the transaction end-of-file switch will initially be set to a value of "NO" and then set to a value of "YES" after all of its records have been processed.

The second switch, WS-PROGRAM-ABEND-SW, is included to identify an error condition that will require abnormal program termination. It will initially be set to a value of "NO" and then be set to "YES" in the rare situation in which an I-O error occurs.

WORKING-STORAGE SECTION.

01 WS-SWITCHES.	Miscellaneous program switches
01 WS-REPORT-CONTROLS.	Control fields for audit/error report printing
01 WS-WORK-AREAS.	Current date work area

01   TC-TABLE-CONTROLS.
01   TC-COUNT-DESCRIPTION-DATA.
01   TC-COUNT-DESCRIPTION-TABLE
      REDEFINES
      TC-COUNT-DESCRIPTION-DATA.
01   TC-RECORD-COUNT-ENTRIES.
01   TC-RECORD-COUNTS
      REDEFINES
      TC-RECORD-COUNT-ENTRIES.
	Record count description and total tables

01 ET-EMPLOYEE-TRANSACTION-RECORD.	Employee-transaction record description
01 EM-EMPLOYEE-MASTER-WORK-AREA.	Employee master record description and work area
01 H1-HEADING-LINE-1. 01 H2-HEADING-LINE-2. 01 H3-HEADING-LINE-3. 01 H4-HEADING-LINE-4.	Audit/error report heading lines
01 DL-DETAIL-LINE.	Audit/error line
01 IE-I-O-ERROR-LINE REDEFINES DL-DETAIL-LINE.	Error line printed when fatal I-O error occurs
01 TL-TOTAL-LINE.	Record count total line

Figure 4C.5.   WORKING-STORAGE SECTION organization: INDMAINT program.

The last two fields of this WS-SWITCHES group item are suffixed by the word FLAG rather than SW. This is a fine distinction; a switch usually implies a two-state indicator, whereas a flag is a field that is used to indicate one of more than two conditions.

Recall that WS-FILE-STATUS-FLAG is the file status field that is defined in the FILE STATUS clause of the SELECT entry. The file status data-item must be specified as a two-character alphanumeric field in the WORKING-STORAGE SECTION.

The WS-I-O-OPERATION-FLAG is provided to temporarily hold a description of the I-O operation type (READ, WRITE, and so on) that is being performed so that an I-O error, should it occur, can be displayed on the error line.

Record count description and total tables

```
014010*
014020*
014030 01  TC-TABLE-CONTROLS.
014040     05  TC-SUBSCRIPT                     PIC S9(4)      COMP SYNC.
014050     05  TC-NUMBER-OF-ENTRIES             PIC S9(4)      VALUE +15
014060                                                         COMP SYNC.
015010*
015020 01  TC-COUNT-DESCRIPTION-DATA.
015030     05  FILLER           PIC X(20)   VALUE 'TRANSACTIONS READ   '.
015040     05  FILLER           PIC X(20)   VALUE '  ADDS              '.
015050     05  FILLER           PIC X(20)   VALUE '    PROCESSED       '.
015060     05  FILLER           PIC X(20)   VALUE '    REJECTED        '.
015070     05  FILLER           PIC X(20)   VALUE '  CHANGES           '.
015080     05  FILLER           PIC X(20)   VALUE '    PROCESSED       '.
015090     05  FILLER           PIC X(20)   VALUE '    REJECTED        '.
015100     05  FILLER           PIC X(20)   VALUE '  DELETES           '.
015110     05  FILLER           PIC X(20)   VALUE '    PROCESSED       '.
015120     05  FILLER           PIC X(20)   VALUE '    REJECTED        '.
015130     05  FILLER           PIC X(20)   VALUE '  ERROR UPDATE CODES'.
015140     05  FILLER           PIC X(20)   VALUE 'MASTERS READ        '.
015150     05  FILLER           PIC X(20)   VALUE 'MASTER CHANGES      '.
015160     05  FILLER           PIC X(20)   VALUE 'MASTERS ADDED       '.
015165     05  FILLER           PIC X(20)   VALUE 'MASTERS DELETED     '.
015170 01  TC-COUNT-DESCRIPTION-TABLE
015180         REDEFINES TC-COUNT-DESCRIPTION-DATA.
015190     05  TC-COUNT-DESCRIPTION             OCCURS 15 TIMES
015200                                          PIC X(20).
016010*
016020 01  TC-RECORD-COUNT-ENTRIES                          COMP-3.
016030     05  TC-TOTAL-TRANS-READ              PIC S9(5).
016040     05  TC-TOTAL-ADD-TRANS-READ          PIC S9(5).
016050     05  TC-ADD-TRANS-PROCESSED           PIC S9(5).
016060     05  TC-ADD-TRANS-REJECTED            PIC S9(5).
016070     05  TC-TOTAL-CHANGE-TRANS-READ       PIC S9(5).
016080     05  TC-CHANGE-TRANS-PROCESSED        PIC S9(5).
016090     05  TC-CHANGE-TRANS-REJECTED         PIC S9(5).
016100     05  TC-TOTAL-DELETE-TRANS-READ       PIC S9(5).
016110     05  TC-DELETE-TRANS-PROCESSED        PIC S9(5).
016120     05  TC-DELETE-TRANS-REJECTED         PIC S9(5).
016130     05  TC-TOTAL-ERROR-UPDATE-CODES      PIC S9(5).
016140     05  TC-MASTERS-READ                  PIC S9(5).
016150     05  TC-MASTER-CHANGES                PIC S9(5).
016160     05  TC-MASTERS-ADDED                 PIC S9(5).
016165     05  TC-MASTERS-DELETED               PIC S9(5).
016170 01  TC-RECORD-COUNTS REDEFINES TC-RECORD-COUNT-ENTRIES.
016180     05  TC-RECORD-COUNT                  OCCURS 15 TIMES
016190                                          PIC S9(5)      COMP-3.
```

As explained in Topic A of this chapter, master record counts for a randomly updated maintenance program differ slightly from that of a sequentially updated one. There is one additional master record count total field. This means that 15 table entries are required. Also, the master record count categories are named and described differently to properly define their function in this program.

Audit/error report line entries

```
034010*
034020*
034030 01  DL-DETAIL-LINE.
034040     05  FILLER                   PIC X(1).
034050     05  FILLER                   PIC X(1)    VALUE SPACES.
034060     05  DL-RECORD-CODE           PIC X(2).
034070     05  FILLER                   PIC X(4)    VALUE SPACES.
034080     05  DL-UPDATE-CODE           PIC X(1).
034090     05  FILLER                   PIC X(4)    VALUE SPACES.
034100     05  DL-PLANT-CODE            PIC X(2).
034110     05  FILLER                   PIC X(4)    VALUE SPACES.
034120     05  DL-DEPARTMENT-NUMBER     PIC X(4).
034130     05  FILLER                   PIC X(1)    VALUE SPACES.
```

```
034140      05  DL-EMPLOYEE-NUMBER                PIC X(5).
034150      05  FILLER                           PIC X(2)    VALUE SPACES.
034160      05  DL-LAST-NAME                     PIC X(13).
034170      05  FILLER                           PIC X(1)    VALUE SPACES.
034180      05  DL-FIRST-NAME                    PIC X(12).
034190      05  FILLER                           PIC X(1)    VALUE SPACES.
034200      05  DL-MIDDLE-INITIAL                PIC X(1).
034210      05  FILLER                           PIC X(3)    VALUE SPACES.
034220      05  DL-HOURLY-RATE                   PIC ZZ.99.
034230      05  DL-HOURLY-RATE-X REDEFINES DL-HOURLY-RATE
034240                                           PIC X(5).
034250      05  FILLER                           PIC X(2)    VALUE SPACES.
034260      05  DL-UPDATE-ACTION                 PIC X(8).
034270      05  FILLER                           PIC X(1)    VALUE SPACES.
034280      05  DL-ERROR-MSG                     PIC X(33).
034290      05  FILLER                           PIC X(22)   VALUE SPACES.
035010*
035020*
035030 01  IE-I-O-ERROR-LINE REDEFINES DL-DETAIL-LINE.
035040      05  FILLER                           PIC X(1).
035050      05  FILLER                           PIC X(40).
035062      05  IE-FILE-STATUS-FLAG              PIC X(2).
035064      05  FILLER                           PIC X(1).
035066      05  IE-I-O-OPERATION-FLAG            PIC X(7).
035070      05  FILLER                           PIC X(1).
035080      05  IE-ERROR-KEY                     PIC XXBXXXXBXXXXX.
035090      05  FILLER                           PIC X(4).
```

The abnormal program termination portion of the report line is named IE-I-O-ERROR-LINE to describe its function in identifying an I-O error. It contains three fields. IE-FILE-STATUS-FLAG is used to display the file status data-item value that causes the abnormal termination. The type of I-O operation that causes the termination will be indicated in the IE-I-O-OPERATION-FLAG field. The IE-ERROR-KEY field will display the RECORD KEY that the I-O operation is referencing.

PROCEDURE DIVISION Entries

The processing logic of each PROCEDURE DIVISION module for this INDMAINT program that differs from the SEQMAINT program is explained below.

000-MAINTAIN-INDEXED-FILE

```
050050*
050060*
050070 000-MAINTAIN-INDEXED-FILE.
050080*
050090      OPEN INPUT TRANSACTION-FILE
050100           I-O  INDEXED-MASTER-FILE
050120           OUTPUT REPORT-FILE.
050130      PERFORM 100-INITIALIZE-VARIABLE-FIELDS.
050135      PERFORM 800-READ-TRANSACTION-RECORD.
050140      PERFORM 200-UPDATE-MASTER-RECORD
050150           UNTIL TRANSACTION-END-OF-FILE.
050170      PERFORM 700-PRINT-REPORT-TOTALS.
050180      CLOSE TRANSACTION-FILE
050190            INDEXED-MASTER-FILE
050210            REPORT-FILE.
050220      STOP RUN.
```

This is a typical mainline module of the priming-read type. It differs from the SEQMAINT mainline in three ways.

First, the master file is opened as I-O. Whenever a file will be referenced with both input and output statements, it must be opened as I-O.

Second, as previously indicated, it uses a priming read, (PERFORM 800-READ-TRANSACTION-READ) prior to entering the main processing module (200-UPDATE-MASTER-RECORD) for the first iteration. (A priming read was not used in the SEQMAINT program because its logic requirements were better suited for conditional record processing.)

Third, conditional iteration of the 200-UPDATE-MASTER-RECORD module is based only upon the status of the transaction end-of-file switch. (In a sequential file-maintenance program, both the transaction file *and* the master file must end before the main processing iterations are suspended.)

100-INITIALIZE-VARIABLE-FIELDS

```
100010*
100020*
100030 100-INITIALIZE-VARIABLE-FIELDS.
100040*
100050     MOVE 'NO ' TO WS-TRANSACTION-END-OF-FILE-SW
100055                   WS-PROGRAM-ABEND-SW.
100120     MOVE ZERO TO WS-PAGE-COUNT.
100130     ADD 1 WS-LINES-PER-PAGE GIVING WS-LINES-USED.
100140     ACCEPT WS-DATE-WORK FROM DATE.
100150     MOVE WS-MONTH TO H1-MONTH.
100160     MOVE WS-DAY TO H1-DAY.
100170     MOVE WS-YEAR TO H1-YEAR.
100190     MOVE SPACES TO DL-ERROR-MSG.
100200     PERFORM 110-ZERO-RECORD-COUNTS
100210         VARYING TC-SUBSCRIPT
100220         FROM 1
100230         BY 1
100240         UNTIL TC-SUBSCRIPT IS GREATER THAN TC-NUMBER-OF-ENTRIES.
110010*
110020*
110030 110-ZERO-RECORD-COUNTS.
110040*
110050     MOVE ZERO TO TC-RECORD-COUNT (TC-SUBSCRIPT).
```

This initialization module is the same as that for the SEQMAINT program except for the switch settings. This INDMAINT program needs fewer switches. The two switches, WS-TRANSACTION-END-OF-FILE-SW and WS-PROGRAM-ABEND-SW, are initialized in this module.

The flags are not initialized here. The system automatically sets the WS-FILE-STATUS-FLAG at the completion of each input-output operation. The WS-I-O-OPERATION-FLAG is program-set prior to each I-O operation.

200-UPDATE-MASTER-RECORD

```
200010*
200020*
200030 200-UPDATE-MASTER-RECORD.
200040*
200044     IF VALID-UPDATE-CODE
200046         PERFORM 810-READ-MASTER-RECORD.
200046*
200050     IF (ADD-TRANSACTION AND NO-RECORD-FOUND)
200060         PERFORM 230-ADD-MASTER-RECORD
200065*
200070     ELSE IF (CHANGE-TRANSACTION AND SUCCESSFUL-COMPLETION)
200080         PERFORM 240-CHANGE-MASTER-RECORD
200085*
200090     ELSE IF (DELETE-TRANSACTION AND SUCCESSFUL-COMPLETION)
200100         PERFORM 250-DELETE-MASTER-RECORD
200105*
200110     ELSE
200120         PERFORM 290-IDENTIFY-ERROR-TYPE.
200170*
200180     PERFORM 220-PRINT-AUDIT-ERROR-LINE.
200182*
200184     IF NOT PROGRAM-ABEND
200186         PERFORM 800-READ-TRANSACTION-RECORD
200188     ELSE
200190         PERFORM 900-ABORT-PROGRAM-RUN.
```

This module is the main record-processing routine. Each time it is entered, the transaction record to be processed has already been read. (For the first time through, the priming read handles this. Every other time, the read is made at the end of this same paragraph during its immediately prior iteration.)

The first step is to determine the master file status of the transaction record key. If the transaction update code is valid, an attempt is made to locate a record with that key value by performing the 810-READ-MASTER-RECORD routine. If a record exists, the WS-FILE-STATUS-FLAG will be set to 00, which indicates SUCCESSFUL-COMPLETION of the input operation. On the other hand, if a record for that key value is *not* on the master file, the file status flag will be set to 23, which signifies NO-RECORD-FOUND. However, whether or not the transaction can actually be processed will depend on the relationship between the transaction update code and the file status setting.

Therefore, the next statement is a linear nested IF statement with combined conditions to direct the program flow to the proper processing module. If it is an ADD-TRANSACTION and there was NO-RECORD-FOUND, the 230-ADD-MASTER-RECORD module should be performed to allow addition of a new master record. If, however, it is a CHANGE-TRANSACTION, a SUCCESSFUL-COMPLETION status must be obtained in order to effect the change in the 240-CHANGE-MASTER-RECORD routine. Similarly, a DELETE-TRANSACTION requires a SUCCESSFUL-COMPLETION so that the 250-DELETE-MASTER module can process the delete transaction.

The 290-IDENTIFY-ERROR-TYPE module will be performed if the combination of the transaction update code and file status is any one of the following:

- ADD-TRANSACTION and SUCCESSFUL-COMPLETION
- CHANGE-TRANSACTION and NO-RECORD-FOUND
- DELETE-TRANSACTION and NO-RECORD-FOUND
- NOT ADD-TRANSACTION and NOT CHANGE-TRANSACTION and NOT DELETE-TRANSACTION

After the transaction record has been processed, the 220-PRINT-AUDIT-ERROR-LINE module is performed to print the audit or error line that describes the update action or error handling for the transaction record.

A PROGRAM-ABEND condition will exist only in the rare case in which a so-called **fatal I-O error** is detected during an I-O operation. A fatal error is one that the program logic cannot correct and, if the error is allowed to exist, it will harm the integrity of the indexed master file. In the normal situation in which the PROGRAM-ABEND condition does not exist, the 800-READ-TRANSACTION-RECORD module is performed to read the next transaction record. In the rare situation when a PROGRAM-ABEND condition exists, the 900-ABORT-PROGRAM-RUN module is performed to display the error condition on the audit/error list and to provide for orderly termination of the program run.

220-PRINT-AUDIT-ERROR-LINE

The 220-PRINT-AUDIT-ERROR-LINE module for this INDMAINT program is identical to its counterpart in the SEQMAINT program except that the last statement in the latter program—MOVE "NO" TO WS-AUDIT-LINE-TO-BE-PRINTED-SW— is omitted in this program. With a random update, a transaction record is processed during each processing iteration. Because an audit line must be printed during each iteration, no switch nor switch-setting is required.

230-ADD-MASTER-RECORD

```
230010*
230020*
230030 230-ADD-MASTER-RECORD.
230040*
230070     ADD 1 TO TC-TOTAL-ADD-TRANS-READ.
230080     PERFORM 260-CREATE-MASTER-RECORD.
230084     PERFORM 850-WRITE-MASTER-RECORD.
230088     IF NOT PROGRAM-ABEND
230090         ADD 1 TO TC-ADD-TRANS-PROCESSED
230100         MOVE 'ADDED   ' TO DL-UPDATE-ACTION.
```

This module is entered whenever the transaction record contains an add update code and that master key is not already present on the master file.

The add-transaction record is tallied in the TC-TOTAL-ADD-TRANS-READ field. To add a record to the master file, the 260-CREATE-MASTER-RECORD paragraph is performed to create the master record in the master work area. Then the record is written by the 850-WRITE-MASTER-RECORD module.

A PROGRAM-ABEND condition will exist if an I-O error occurred during the writing of the new master record. Normally, this will not happen, and thus the TC-ADD-TRANS-PROCESSED field is incremented. Finally, the word "ADDED" is moved to the update-action field of the audit/error line. If the program is "abending," the record is not added to the file. Thus these last two statements are made conditional upon a NOT PROGRAM-ABEND condition.

240-CHANGE-MASTER-RECORD

```
240010*
240020*
240030 240-CHANGE-MASTER-RECORD.
240040*
240150     ADD 1 TO TC-TOTAL-CHANGE-TRANS-READ.
240160     PERFORM 270-CHANGE-MASTER-FIELDS.
240170     PERFORM 855-REWRITE-MASTER-RECORD.
240180     IF NOT PROGRAM-ABEND
240190         ADD 1 TO TC-CHANGE-TRANS-PROCESSED
240200         MOVE 'CHANGED ' TO DL-UPDATE-ACTION.
```

When the transaction record contains a change update code and a matching key is found on the master file, this module is entered from the 200-UPDATE-MASTER-RECORD paragraph.

The change-transaction record is tallied in the TC-TOTAL-CHANGE-TRANS-READ field. To change the master record, the 270-CHANGE-MASTER-FIELDS module is performed. Once the master record has been changed in the master record work area, the 255-REWRITE-MASTER-RECORD module is performed to actually update the master record on the indexed master file. After the record is successfully updated, the TC-CHANGE-TRANS-PROCESSED field is incremented, and the word "CHANGED" is moved to the update-action field of the audit/error line.

250-DELETE-MASTER-RECORD

```
250010*
250020*
250030 250-DELETE-MASTER-RECORD.
250040*
250150     ADD 1 TO TC-TOTAL-DELETE-TRANS-READ.
250160     PERFORM 860-DELETE-MASTER-RECORD.
250170     IF NOT PROGRAM-ABEND
250180         ADD 1 TO TC-DELETE-TRANS-PROCESSED
250190         MOVE 'DELETED ' TO DL-UPDATE-ACTION.
```

This module is entered from the 200-UPDATE-MASTER-RECORD module whenever the transaction record contains a delete update code and the corresponding master record key is present on the master file.

The delete-transaction record is tallied in TC-TOTAL-DELETE-TRANS-READ field. To actually delete the record from the master file, the 860-DELETE-MASTER-RECORD module is performed. After the record has been successfully deleted, the TC-DELETE-TRANS-PROCESSED field is incremented and the word "DELETED" is moved to the update-action field of the audit/error line.

800-READ-TRANSACTION-RECORD

```
800010*
800020*
800030 800-READ-TRANSACTION-RECORD.
800040*
800070     READ TRANSACTION-FILE INTO ET-EMPLOYEE-TRANSACTION-RECORD
800080         AT END MOVE 'YES' TO WS-TRANSACTION-END-OF-FILE-SW.
800100*
800110     IF NOT TRANSACTION-END-OF-FILE
800120         ADD 1 TO TC-TOTAL-TRANS-READ.
```

This is the read module for the transaction file. A record is read sequentially from the transaction file. If there are no remaining transaction records, the WS-TRANSACTION-END-OF-FILE-SW is set to "YES." After a record has been read, it is tallied in the TC-TOTAL-TRANS-READ field.

810-READ-MASTER-RECORD

The format for a random READ statement is shown in Figure 4C.6. Before a random READ statement is executed, the RECORD KEY must be set with the key value of the record that is needed. If the record is not found, the system sets the file status field to 23 and, if specified, the INVALID KEY phrase is executed.

Example:

```
READ INDEXED-MASTER-FILE

    INTO EM-EMPLOYEE-MASTER-WORK-AREA

    INVALID KEY MOVE 'NO ' TO WS-MASTER-RECORD-FOUND-SW.
```

Figure 4C.6. Random READ statement format.


```
810010*
810020*
810030 810-READ-MASTER-RECORD.
810040*
810042     MOVE ET-PLANT-CODE TO RK-PLANT-CODE.
810044     MOVE ET-DEPARTMENT-NUMBER TO RK-DEPARTMENT-NUMBER.
810046     MOVE ET-EMPLOYEE-NUMBER TO RK-EMPLOYEE-NUMBER.
810065     MOVE 'READ  ' TO WS-I-O-OPERATION-FLAG.
810070     READ INDEXED-MASTER-FILE
810074          INTO EM-EMPLOYEE-MASTER-WORK-AREA.
810300*
810310     IF SUCCESSFUL-COMPLETION
810320          ADD 1 TO TC-MASTERS-READ.
810330*
810340     IF PERMANENT-I-O-DATA-ERROR
810350          MOVE 'YES' TO WS-PROGRAM-ABEND-SW.
```

The first step in this module, therefore, is to place the key value of the record that is to be read in the RECORD KEY area. This is done by moving the ET-PLANT-CODE, ET-DEPARTMENT-NUMBER, and ET-EMPLOYEE-NUMBER fields of the transaction record to the RK-PLANT-CODE, RK-DEPARTMENT-NUMBER, and RK-EMPLOYEE-NUMBER fields, respectively, of the RECORD KEY.

Then the WS-I-O-OPERATION-FLAG field is set to "READ." Should an input-output error occur, this flag will be printed in the 900-ABORT-PROGRAM-RUN module. When a program run must be aborted, it is generally helpful for the programmer to know the type of I-O operation that was in process at the time of termination.

Once the RECORD KEY and I-O-operation flag have been set, the READ statement is executed. It contains the INTO phrase to provide for moving the record, after it has been read, from the master area in the FILE SECTION to the master work area in WORKING-STORAGE.

If the record is *not* found on the master file, (1) the INVALID KEY phrase is executed if it is specified, and (2) the file status field, if specified, is set to 23 (a record not-found condition). The INVALID KEY phrase was not specified in this INDMAINT program because there are no additional actions to be taken; the file status setting can be used for proper program control. If a file status field were

Example:

```
WRITE INDEXED-MASTER-RECORD

    FROM EM-EMPLOYEE-MASTER-WORK-AREA

    INVALID KEY MOVE 'YES' TO WS-PROGRAM-ABEND-SW.
```

Figure 4C.7. Random WRITE statement format.

not used, a record-found switch would be required and should be set to "NO" in the INVALID KEY phrase, as was shown in Figure 4C.6. (It would also be necessary to initialize this switch to "YES" before the READ statement was executed.)

In the rare situation in which a permanent I-O data error occurs (data check, parity error, transmission error, and so on) during the READ operation, the WS-FILE-STATUS-FLAG will be set to a code value of 30. Should this happen, the program must be terminated so that the error can be diagnosed and corrected. Thus if the condition PERMANENT-I-O-DATA-ERROR is true, the WS-PROGRAM-ABEND-SW is set to "YES" so that the program can be aborted.

If the record *is* found on the master file, the system sets the file status field to 00. When this SUCCESSFUL-COMPLETION condition exists, the TC-MASTERS-READ field is incremented.

850-WRITE-MASTER-RECORD

```
850010*
850020*
850030 850-WRITE-MASTER-RECORD.
850040*
850045     MOVE 'WRITE ' TO WS-I-O-OPERATION-FLAG.
850050     WRITE INDEXED-MASTER-RECORD
850060         FROM EM-EMPLOYEE-MASTER-WORK-AREA
850065         INVALID KEY MOVE 'YES' TO WS-PROGRAM-ABEND-SW.
850200*
850210     IF SUCCESSFUL-COMPLETION
850220         ADD 1 TO TC-MASTERS-ADDED
850230     ELSE
850240         MOVE 'YES' TO WS-PROGRAM-ABEND-SW.
```

This module handles the writing of *new* records that are being added to the master file. The updating of existing master records is done in the 855-REWRITE-MASTER-RECORD module.

Figure 4C.7 shows the format of the random WRITE statement. Before the WRITE statement is executed, the RECORD KEY field must be set with the key

Example:

```
REWRITE INDEXED-MASTER-RECORD
    FROM EM-EMPLOYEE-MASTER-WORK-AREA
    INVALID KEY MOVE 'YES' TO WS-PROGRAM-ABEND-SW.
```

Figure 4C.8. REWRITE statement format.

value of the record that is to be written. If a record with a matching record key already exists on the file or if there is no room remaining within the file to write the record, the INVALID KEY phrase is executed.

The first statement of the module sets the WS-I-O-OPERATION-FLAG to "WRITE." Then the WRITE statement is specified with the FROM phrase. Observe that the record key value is not explicitly moved to the RECORD KEY field of the INDEXED-MASTER-RECORD within the FILE SECTION. Rather, it is handled by setting the key fields within the EM-EMPLOYEE-MASTER-WORK-AREA in the 260-CREATE-MASTER-RECORD module. By using the FROM phrase of the WRITE statement, the EM-EMPLOYEE-MASTER-WORK-AREA is implicitly moved to the INDEXED-MASTER-RECORD area immediately before the WRITE is executed, thereby setting the RECORD KEY.

Again, the WS-PROGRAM-ABEND-SW is set in the unusual situation when a permanent I-O data error occurs. Usually, a SUCCESSFUL-COMPLETION will be indicated, and so the TC-MASTERS-ADDED count will be incremented.

855-REWRITE-MASTER-RECORD

```
855010*
855020*
855030 855-REWRITE-MASTER-RECORD.
855040*
855045     MOVE 'REWRITE' TO WS-I-O-OPERATION-FLAG.
855050     REWRITE INDEXED-MASTER-RECORD
855060         FROM EM-EMPLOYEE-MASTER-WORK-AREA
855070         INVALID KEY MOVE 'YES' TO WS-PROGRAM-ABEND-SW.
855080*
855090     IF SUCCESSFUL-COMPLETION
855100         ADD 1 TO TC-MASTER-CHANGES
855110     ELSE
855120         MOVE 'YES' TO WS-PROGRAM-ABEND-SW.
```

The REWRITE verb is used to update an existing record when a file is opened as I-O. Its format is shown in Figure 4C.8. Before the REWRITE statement is executed, the RECORD KEY field must be set with the key value of the record that

Format:

> DELETE file-name RECORD
>   [INVALID KEY imperative-statement].

INVALID KEY conditions when ORGANIZATION IS INDEXED:

- ACCESS MODE IS RANDOM and record not found (with key value equal to RECORD KEY value)
  [File status code = 23]
- ACCESS MODE IS SEQUENTIAL and RECORD KEY value does not match that of the last record value.
  [File status code = 21]

Example:

```
DELETE INDEXED-MASTER-FILE

    INVALID KEY MOVE 'YES' TO WS-PROGRAM-ABEND-SW.
```

Figure 4C.9. DELETE statement format.

is to be updated. If a record with a matching key value is not on the file, an INVALID KEY condition exists.

The 855-REWRITE-MASTER-RECORD module is identical to the preceding 850-WRITE-MASTER-RECORD paragraph except that, instead of the WRITE verb, the REWRITE statement is coded. Again, the RECORD KEY value is implicitly set by the use of the FROM phrase. Observe that, although the INVALID KEY phrase has been specified, the condition should never occur because logic within the 200-UPDATE-MASTER-RECORD module ensures that the record has already been located on the master file.

860-DELETE-MASTER-RECORD

```
860010*
860020*
860030 860-DELETE-MASTER-RECORD.
860040*
860045     MOVE 'DELETE ' TO WS-I-O-OPERATION-FLAG.
860050     DELETE INDEXED-MASTER-FILE
860060         INVALID KEY MOVE 'YES' TO WS-PROGRAM-ABEND-SW.
860070*
860080     IF SUCCESSFUL-COMPLETION
860090         ADD 1 TO TC-MASTERS-DELETED
860100     ELSE
860110         MOVE 'YES' TO WS-PROGRAM-ABEND-SW.
```

The format of the DELETE statement is presented in Figure 4C.9. Before the DELETE statement is executed, the RECORD KEY must contain the key value of the master record that is to be deleted. If the record that is to be deleted is not located on the master file, the INVALID KEY statement(s) is executed.

Coding of this module is consistent with that of the other I-O paragraphs. The RECORD KEY is already present in the RECORD KEY field as a result of logic within the 200-UPDATE-MASTER-RECORD paragraph that caused the record to be read before it was deleted. Although not necessary for a DELETE operation, this preliminary read and its associated program logic ensures that an INVALID KEY condition should not occur within this module.

900-ABORT-PROGRAM-RUN

This module will be used only in those rare instances when an I-O error occurs during a READ, WRITE, REWRITE, or DELETE operation to the indexed master file. Should such an error occur, this module will print an error line on the audit/error list and then will cause the program to come to an orderly abnormal termination.

```
900010*
900020*
900030 900-ABORT-PROGRAM-RUN.
900040*
900042     MOVE WS-FILE-STATUS-FLAG TO IE-FILE-STATUS-FLAG.
900044     MOVE WS-I-O-OPERATION-FLAG TO IE-I-O-OPERATION-FLAG.
900046     MOVE RK-INDEXED-KEY TO IE-ERROR-KEY.
900050     MOVE 'ABORTED ' TO DL-UPDATE-ACTION.
900055     MOVE 'I-O ERROR OCCURRED' TO DL-ERROR-MSG.
900060     MOVE DL-DETAIL-LINE TO REPORT-LINE.
900070     MOVE 3 TO WS-LINE-SPACING.
900080     PERFORM 890-WRITE-REPORT-LINE.
900090     MOVE SPACES TO DL-DETAIL-LINE.
900150     MOVE 'YES' TO WS-TRANSACTION-END-OF-FILE-SW.
```

The WS-FILE-STATUS-FLAG, WS-I-O-OPERATION-FLAG, and RK-INDEXED-KEY fields are moved to the IE-I-O-ERROR-LINE together with the update action "ABORTED" and error message "I-O ERROR OCCURRED." Then the error line is printed. Finally, the WS-TRANSACTION-END-OF-FILE-SW is set so that iterations of the 200-UPDATE-MASTER-RECORD module will be prematurely suspended.

■ TOPIC 4-D: ## Creation of an Indexed File

Utility Program Creation

Custom-written COBOL Program Creation
  Program Design
  Program Coding
    SELECT statement for the indexed file
    OPEN statement for the indexed file
    Main processing logic
    WRITE statement for the indexed file

A separate program run is required to create or **load** an indexed file. This program run could use a utility program or a custom-written COBOL program.

Utility Program Creation

Most operating systems and many proprietary software packages have utility routines to create indexed files. Before the file can be created, the records must normally be sorted into key-field sequence and should have been validated by a data-validation program. The exact coding of parameters to handle the creation of the file differ, depending upon the specific operating system or software package requirements.

Custom-written COBOL Program Creation

If a utility program is not available or if it is otherwise deemed appropriate, a special COBOL program can be written to handle the creation of the indexed file.

When a COBOL program for loading an indexed file is written, there are two options to be considered: record sorting and data validation. That is, the creation program could use the COBOL SORT verb to sort the records, or they could be sorted in a prior program or utility sort step. Similarly, data validation could be handled within the creation program or as a prior separate program step.

In this topic, an example program to create an indexed file, called IND-LOAD, for **ind**exed file **load**, is presented.

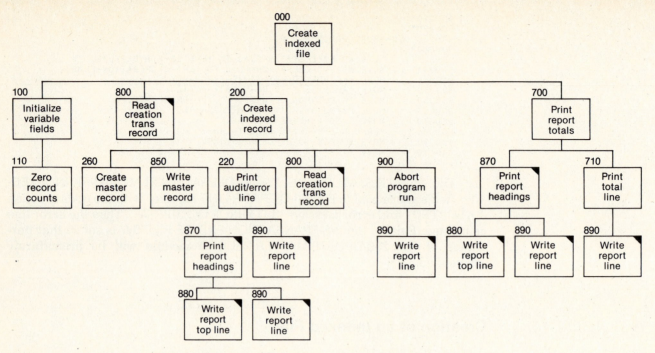

Figure 4D.1. Structure chart: INDLOAD program.

Program Design

File sorting and data-validation logic will not be included in this INDLOAD program. Consider that previous program steps have handled those two functions.

A structure chart for the INDLOAD program is presented in Figure 4D.1.

Program Coding

The coding of a program to load an indexed file is relatively straightforward and is not unlike the coding of a program to create a sequential file. The imput records must be on ascending RECORD KEY sequence and are written, one after another, to the output indexed file. The INDLOAD program is presented in Figure 4D.2. Pertinent aspects of the coding are shaded on the program listing and will be briefly discussed here.

SELECT statement for the indexed file

An indexed file is initially created as a sequential file. Thus its SELECT statement is coded with ACCESS MODE IS SEQUENTIAL. Otherwise, the statement is coded identically to the way that it appears in the INDMAINT program.

OPEN statement for the indexed file

When an indexed file is loaded, it must be opened as an output file. Thus, in the INDLOAD program, OPEN OUTPUT INDEXED-MASTER-FILE is coded in the mainline 000-CREATE-INDEXED-FILE module.

Main processing logic

In the 200-CREATE-INDEXED-RECORD module, after each input record is read, it is (1) reformatted into a master record in the 260-CREATE-MASTER-RECORD module, (2) written to the INDEXED-MASTER-FILE in the 850-WRITE-

```
001010 IDENTIFICATION DIVISION.                          015010*
001020 PROGRAM-ID.     INDLOAD.                           015020 01  TC-COUNT-DESCRIPTION-DATA.
001030*                                                   015030     05  FILLER          PIC X(20)   VALUE 'CREATION TRANS READ '.
001040*                                                   015160     05  FILLER          PIC X(20)   VALUE 'MASTERS WRITTEN     '.
001050*              INDEXED FILE LOAD                     015170 01  TC-COUNT-DESCRIPTION-TABLE
002010*                                                   015180         REDEFINES TC-COUNT-DESCRIPTION-DATA.
002020*                                                   015190     05  TC-COUNT-DESCRIPTION            OCCURS 2 TIMES
002030*                                                   015200                                        PIC X(20).
002040 ENVIRONMENT DIVISION.                              016010*
002050*                                                   016020 01  TC-RECORD-COUNT-ENTRIES                        COMP-3.
002060*                                                   016030     05  TC-TOTAL-TRANS-READ        PIC S9(5).
002070 CONFIGURATION SECTION.                             016160     05  TC-MASTERS-WRITTEN         PIC S9(5).
002080*                                                   016170 01  TC-RECORD-COUNTS REDEFINES TC-RECORD-COUNT-ENTRIES.
002090 SOURCE-COMPUTER.  IBM-370.                         016180     05  TC-RECORD-COUNT                OCCURS 2 TIMES
002100 OBJECT-COMPUTER.  IBM-370.                         016190                                        PIC S9(5)     COMP-3.
002110*                                                   020010*
002120*                                                   020020*
002130 INPUT-OUTPUT SECTION.                              020030 01  EC-EMPLOYEE-CREATION-RECORD.
002140*                                                   020040     05  EC-RECORD-CODE             PIC X(2).
002150 FILE-CONTROL.                                      020045     05  EC-UPDATE-CODE             PIC X(1).
002160     SELECT CREATION-TRANS-FILE                     020090     05  EC-EMPLOYEE-NUMBER         PIC X(5).
002170         ASSIGN TO UT-S-TRNFILE.                    020100     05  EC-LAST-NAME               PIC X(13).
002180     SELECT INDEXED-MASTER-FILE                     020110     05  EC-FIRST-NAME              PIC X(12).
002190         ASSIGN TO INDFILE                          020120     05  EC-MIDDLE-INITIAL          PIC X(1).
002194         ORGANIZATION IS INDEXED                    020130     05  EC-PLANT-CODE              PIC X(2).
002195         ACCESS MODE IS SEQUENTIAL                  020140     05  EC-DEPARTMENT-NUMBER       PIC X(4).
002196         RECORD KEY IS RK-INDEXED-KEY               020150     05  EC-HOURLY-RATE             PIC S9(2)V99.
002197         FILE STATUS IS WS-FILE-STATUS-FLAG.        020160     05  EC-HOURLY-RATE-X REDEFINES EC-HOURLY-RATE
002220     SELECT REPORT-FILE                             020170                                    PIC X(4).
002230         ASSIGN TO UT-S-PRTFILE.                    020180     05  FILLER                     PIC X(36).
003010*                                                   025010*
003020*                                                   025020*
003030*                                                   025030 01  EM-EMPLOYEE-MASTER-WORK-AREA.
003040 DATA DIVISION.                                     025040     05  EM-RECORD-CODE             PIC X(2).
003050*                                                   025050     05  FILLER                     PIC X(1).
003060*                                                   025060     05  EM-PLANT-CODE              PIC X(2).
003070 FILE SECTION.                                      025070     05  EM-DEPARTMENT-NUMBER       PIC X(4).
003080*                                                   025080     05  EM-EMPLOYEE-NUMBER         PIC X(5).
003090*                                                   025090     05  EM-LAST-NAME               PIC X(13).
003100 FD   CREATION-TRANS-FILE                           025100     05  EM-FIRST-NAME              PIC X(12).
003110      RECORD CONTAINS 80 CHARACTERS                 025110     05  EM-MIDDLE-INITIAL          PIC X(1).
003120      LABEL RECORDS ARE STANDARD.                   025120     05  EM-HOURLY-RATE             PIC S9(2)V99.
003130*                                                   025130     05  FILLER                     PIC X(30).
003140 01   CREATION-TRANS-RECORD.                        025140     05  EM-DATE-LAST-ACTIVITY      PIC 9(6).
003150      05  FILLER               PIC X(80).           030010*
004010*                                                   030020*
004020*                                                   030040 01  H1-HEADING-LINE-1.
004030 FD   INDEXED-MASTER-FILE                           030050     05  FILLER          PIC X(1).
004040      RECORD CONTAINS 80 CHARACTERS                 030060     05  FILLER          PIC X(20)   VALUE 'INDEXED MASTER FILE '.
004050      LABEL RECORDS ARE STANDARD.                   030070     05  FILLER          PIC X(20)   VALUE 'CREATION           '.
004060*                                                   030080     05  FILLER          PIC X(20)   VALUE '                   '.
004070 01   INDEXED-MASTER-RECORD.                        030090     05  FILLER          PIC X(20)   VALUE '                   '.
004080      05  FILLER               PIC X(3).            030100     05  FILLER          PIC X(20)   VALUE '           RUN DAT'.
004090      05  RK-INDEXED-KEY.                           030110     05  FILLER          PIC X(2)    VALUE 'E '.
004100          10  RK-PLANT-CODE        PIC X(2).        030120     05  H1-MONTH        PIC 9(2).
004110          10  RK-DEPARTMENT-NUMBER PIC X(4).        030130     05  FILLER          PIC X(1)    VALUE '/'.
004120          10  RK-EMPLOYEE-NUMBER   PIC X(5).        030140     05  H1-DAY          PIC 9(2).
004130      05  FILLER               PIC X(66).           030150     05  FILLER          PIC X(1)    VALUE '/'.
006010*                                                   030160     05  H1-YEAR         PIC 9(2).
006020*                                                   030170     05  FILLER          PIC X(22)   VALUE SPACES.
006030 FD   REPORT-FILE                                   031010*
006040      RECORD CONTAINS 133 CHARACTERS                031020*
006050      LABEL RECORDS ARE OMITTED.                    031030 01  H2-HEADING-LINE-2.
006060*                                                   031040     05  FILLER          PIC X(1).
006070 01   REPORT-LINE.                                  031050     05  FILLER          PIC X(20)   VALUE 'AUDIT/ERROR LIST    '.
006080      05  FILLER               PIC X(133).          031060     05  FILLER          PIC X(20)   VALUE '                   '.
010010*                                                   031070     05  FILLER          PIC X(20)   VALUE ' ** EMPLOYEE MASTER'.
010020*                                                   031080     05  FILLER          PIC X(20)   VALUE ' FILE **           '.
010030 WORKING-STORAGE SECTION.                           031090     05  FILLER          PIC X(20)   VALUE '                   '.
010040*                                                   031100     05  FILLER          PIC X(6)    VALUE ' PAGE '.
010050*                                                   031110     05  H2-PAGE-NBR     PIC ZZZ9.
010060 01   WS-SWITCHES.                                  031120     05  FILLER          PIC X(22)   VALUE SPACES.
010070*                                                   032010*
010080      05  WS-CREATION-END-OF-FILE-SW  PIC X(3).     032020*
010090          88  CREATION-END-OF-FILE         VALUE 'YES'. 032030 01  H3-HEADING-LINE-3.
010300*                                                   032040     05  FILLER          PIC X(1).
010310      05  WS-PROGRAM-ABEND-SW  PIC X(3).            032050     05  FILLER          PIC X(20)   VALUE 'RCD UPDT  PLANT  DE'.
010320          88  PROGRAM-ABEND                VALUE 'YES'. 032060     05  FILLER          PIC X(20)   VALUE 'PT  EMPL  -------EMP'.
010330*                                                   032070     05  FILLER          PIC X(20)   VALUE 'LOYEE NAME-------M'.
010340      05  WS-FILE-STATUS-FLAG  PIC X(2).            032080     05  FILLER          PIC X(20)   VALUE 'HOURLY   UPDATE    '.
010350          88  SUCCESSFUL-COMPLETION        VALUE '00'. 032090     05  FILLER          PIC X(20)   VALUE '                   '.
010360          88  DUPLICATE-ALTERNATE-KEY      VALUE '02'. 032100     05  FILLER          PIC X(20)   VALUE '                   '.
010370          88  END-OF-FILE                  VALUE '10'. 032110     05  FILLER          PIC X(12)   VALUE '            '.
010380          88  SEQUENCE-ERROR               VALUE '21'. 033010*
010390          88  DUPLICATE-KEY                VALUE '22'. 033020*
010400          88  NO-RECORD-FOUND              VALUE '23'. 033030 01  H4-HEADING-LINE-4.
010410          88  BOUNDARY-VIOLATION-IND-REL   VALUE '24'. 033040     05  FILLER          PIC X(1).
010420          88  PERMANENT-I-O-DATA-ERROR     VALUE '30'. 033050     05  FILLER          PIC X(20)   VALUE 'CODE CODE   CODE   N'.
010430          88  BOUNDARY-VIOLATION-SEQ       VALUE '34'. 033060     05  FILLER          PIC X(20)   VALUE 'BR   NBR  LAST NAME '.
010440*         88  IMPLEMENTOR-DEFINED-ERROR    VALUE '9 '. 033070     05  FILLER          PIC X(20)   VALUE '   FIRST NAME   I  '.
010450*                                                   033080     05  FILLER          PIC X(20)   VALUE ' RATE   ACTION ---'.
010460      05  WS-I-O-OPERATION-FLAG  PIC X(7).          033090     05  FILLER          PIC X(20)   VALUE '-------ERROR MESSAGE'.
012010*                                                   033100     05  FILLER          PIC X(20)   VALUE '                   '.
012020*                                                   033110     05  FILLER          PIC X(12)   VALUE '           '.
012030 01   WS-REPORT-CONTROLS.                           034010*
012040      05  WS-PAGE-COUNT        PIC S9(4)     COMP-3. 034020*
012050      05  WS-LINES-PER-PAGE    PIC S99 VALUE +55    034030 01  DL-DETAIL-LINE.
012060                                             COMP SYNC. 034040     05  FILLER               PIC X(1).
012070      05  WS-LINES-USED        PIC S9(2)    COMP SYNC. 034050     05  FILLER               PIC X(1)    VALUE SPACES.
012080      05  WS-LINE-SPACING      PIC S9(2).            034060     05  DL-RECORD-CODE       PIC X(2).
013010*                                                   034070     05  FILLER               PIC X(4)    VALUE SPACES.
013020*                                                   034080     05  DL-UPDATE-CODE       PIC X(1).
013030 01   WS-WORK-AREAS.                                034090     05  FILLER               PIC X(4)    VALUE SPACES.
013040      05  WS-DATE-WORK         PIC 9(6).            034100     05  DL-PLANT-CODE        PIC X(2).
013050      05  WS-DATE-REFORMAT REDEFINES WS-DATE-WORK.  034110     05  FILLER               PIC X(4)    VALUE SPACES.
013060          10  WS-YEAR          PIC 9(2).            034120     05  DL-DEPARTMENT-NUMBER PIC X(4).
013070          10  WS-MONTH         PIC 9(2).            034130     05  FILLER               PIC X(1)    VALUE SPACES.
013080          10  WS-DAY           PIC 9(2).            034140     05  DL-EMPLOYEE-NUMBER   PIC X(5).
014010*                                                   034150     05  FILLER               PIC X(2)    VALUE SPACES.
014020*                                                   034160     05  DL-LAST-NAME         PIC X(13).
014030 01   TC-TABLE-CONTROLS.                            034170     05  FILLER               PIC X(1)    VALUE SPACES.
014040      05  TC-SUBSCRIPT         PIC S9(4)    COMP SYNC. 034180     05  DL-FIRST-NAME        PIC X(12).
014050      05  TC-NUMBER-OF-ENTRIES PIC S9(4)   VALUE +2  034190     05  FILLER               PIC X(1)    VALUE SPACES.
014060                                             COMP SYNC. 034200     05  DL-MIDDLE-INITIAL    PIC X(1).
```

Figure 4D.2.   COBOL Coding: INDLOAD program.

continued

```
034210      05  FILLER                    PIC X(3)     VALUE SPACES.
034220      05  DL-HOURLY-RATE            PIC ZZ.99.
034230      05  DL-HOURLY-RATE-X REDEFINES DL-HOURLY-RATE
034240                                    PIC X(5).
034250      05  FILLER                    PIC X(2)     VALUE SPACES.
034260      05  DL-UPDATE-ACTION          PIC X(8).
034270      05  FILLER                    PIC X(1)     VALUE SPACES.
034280      05  DL-ERROR-MSG              PIC X(33).
034290      05  FILLER                    PIC X(22)    VALUE SPACES.
035010*
035020*
035030 01  IE-I-O-ERROR-LINE REDEFINES DL-DETAIL-LINE.
035040      05  FILLER                    PIC X(1).
035050      05  FILLER                    PIC X(40).
035062      05  IE-FILE-STATUS-FLAG       PIC X(2).
035064      05  FILLER                    PIC X(1).
035066      05  IE-I-O-OPERATION-FLAG     PIC X(7).
035070      05  FILLER                    PIC X(1).
035080      05  IE-ERROR-KEY              PIC XXBXXXXBXXXXX.
035090      05  FILLER                    PIC X(4).
036010*
036020*
036030 01  TL-TOTAL-LINE.
036040      05  FILLER                    PIC X(1).
036050      05  FILLER                    PIC X(83)    VALUE SPACES.
036060      05  TL-COUNT-DESCRIPTION      PIC X(20).
036070      05  FILLER                    PIC X(1)     VALUE SPACES.
036080      05  TL-RECORD-COUNT           PIC ZZ,ZZ9.
036090      05  FILLER                    PIC X(22)    VALUE SPACES.
050010*
050020*
050030*
050040 PROCEDURE DIVISION.
050050*
050060*
050070 000-CREATE-INDEXED-FILE.
050080*
050090      OPEN INPUT CREATION-TRANS-FILE
050100           OUTPUT INDEXED-MASTER-FILE
050120                  REPORT-FILE.
050130      PERFORM 100-INITIALIZE-VARIABLE-FIELDS.
050135      PERFORM 800-READ-CREATION-TRANS-RECORD.
050140      PERFORM 200-CREATE-INDEXED-RECORD
050150           UNTIL CREATION-END-OF-FILE.
050170      PERFORM 700-PRINT-REPORT-TOTALS.
050180      CLOSE CREATION-TRANS-FILE
050190            INDEXED-MASTER-FILE
050210            REPORT-FILE.
050220      STOP RUN.
100010*
100020*
100030 100-INITIALIZE-VARIABLE-FIELDS.
100040*
100050      MOVE 'NO ' TO WS-CREATION-END-OF-FILE-SW
100055                    WS-PROGRAM-ABEND-SW.
100120      MOVE ZERO TO WS-PAGE-COUNT.
100130      ADD 1 WS-LINES-PER-PAGE GIVING WS-LINES-USED.
100140      ACCEPT WS-DATE-WORK FROM DATE.
100150      MOVE WS-MONTH TO H1-MONTH.
100160      MOVE WS-DAY TO H1-DAY.
100170      MOVE WS-YEAR TO H1-YEAR.
100190      MOVE SPACES TO DL-ERROR-MSG.
100200      PERFORM 110-ZERO-RECORD-COUNTS
100210           VARYING TC-SUBSCRIPT
100220           FROM 1
100230           BY 1
100240           UNTIL TC-SUBSCRIPT IS GREATER THAN TC-NUMBER-OF-ENTRIES.
110010*
110020*
110030 110-ZERO-RECORD-COUNTS.
110040*
110050      MOVE ZERO TO TC-RECORD-COUNT (TC-SUBSCRIPT).
200010*
200020*
200030 200-CREATE-INDEXED-RECORD.
200040*
200172      PERFORM 260-CREATE-MASTER-RECORD.
200174      PERFORM 850-WRITE-MASTER-RECORD.
200180      PERFORM 220-PRINT-AUDIT-ERROR-LINE.
200182*
200184      IF NOT PROGRAM-ABEND
200186          PERFORM 800-READ-CREATION-TRANS-RECORD
200188      ELSE
200190          PERFORM 900-ABORT-PROGRAM-RUN.
220010*
220020*
220030 220-PRINT-AUDIT-ERROR-LINE.
220040*
220050      IF WS-LINES-USED IS NOT LESS THAN WS-LINES-PER-PAGE
220060          PERFORM 870-PRINT-REPORT-HEADINGS.
220070      MOVE EC-RECORD-CODE TO DL-RECORD-CODE.
220080      MOVE EC-UPDATE-CODE TO DL-UPDATE-CODE.
220090      MOVE EC-PLANT-CODE TO DL-PLANT-CODE.
220100      MOVE EC-DEPARTMENT-NUMBER TO DL-DEPARTMENT-NUMBER.
220110      MOVE EC-EMPLOYEE-NUMBER TO DL-EMPLOYEE-NUMBER.
220120      MOVE EC-LAST-NAME TO DL-LAST-NAME.
220130      MOVE EC-FIRST-NAME TO DL-FIRST-NAME.
220140      MOVE EC-MIDDLE-INITIAL TO DL-MIDDLE-INITIAL.
220150      IF EC-HOURLY-RATE IS NUMERIC
220160          MOVE EC-HOURLY-RATE TO DL-HOURLY-RATE
220170      ELSE
220180          MOVE EC-HOURLY-RATE-X TO DL-HOURLY-RATE-X.
220190      MOVE DL-DETAIL-LINE TO REPORT-LINE.
220200      MOVE 1 TO WS-LINE-SPACING.
220210      PERFORM 890-WRITE-REPORT-LINE.

220220      MOVE SPACES TO DL-DETAIL-LINE.
260010*
260020*
260030 260-CREATE-MASTER-RECORD.
260040*
260050      MOVE SPACES TO EM-EMPLOYEE-MASTER-WORK-AREA.
260060      MOVE '85' TO EM-RECORD-CODE.
260070      MOVE EC-PLANT-CODE TO EM-PLANT-CODE.
260080      MOVE EC-DEPARTMENT-NUMBER TO EM-DEPARTMENT-NUMBER.
260090      MOVE EC-EMPLOYEE-NUMBER TO EM-EMPLOYEE-NUMBER.
260100      MOVE EC-LAST-NAME TO EM-LAST-NAME.
260110      MOVE EC-FIRST-NAME TO EM-FIRST-NAME.
260120      MOVE EC-MIDDLE-INITIAL TO EM-MIDDLE-INITIAL.
260130      MOVE EC-HOURLY-RATE TO EM-HOURLY-RATE.
260140      MOVE WS-DATE-WORK TO EM-DATE-LAST-ACTIVITY.
700010*
700020*
700030 700-PRINT-REPORT-TOTALS.
700040*
700050      PERFORM 870-PRINT-REPORT-HEADINGS.
700060      PERFORM 710-PRINT-TOTAL-LINE
700070           VARYING TC-SUBSCRIPT
700080           FROM 1
700090           BY 1
700100           UNTIL TC-SUBSCRIPT IS GREATER THAN TC-NUMBER-OF-ENTRIES.
710010*
710020*
710030 710-PRINT-TOTAL-LINE.
710040*
710050      MOVE TC-COUNT-DESCRIPTION (TC-SUBSCRIPT)
710060           TO TL-COUNT-DESCRIPTION.
710070      MOVE TC-RECORD-COUNT (TC-SUBSCRIPT) TO TL-RECORD-COUNT.
710080      MOVE TL-TOTAL-LINE TO REPORT-LINE.
710090      MOVE 1 TO WS-LINE-SPACING.
710100      PERFORM 890-WRITE-REPORT-LINE.
800010*
800020*
800030 800-READ-CREATION-TRANS-RECORD.
800040*
800070      READ CREATION-TRANS-FILE INTO EC-EMPLOYEE-CREATION-RECORD
800080          AT END MOVE 'YES' TO WS-CREATION-END-OF-FILE-SW.
800100*
800110      IF NOT CREATION-END-OF-FILE
800120          ADD 1 TO TC-TOTAL-TRANS-READ.
850010*
850020*
850030 850-WRITE-MASTER-RECORD.
850040*
850045      MOVE 'WRITE ' TO WS-I-O-OPERATION-FLAG.
850050      WRITE INDEXED-MASTER-RECORD
850060           FROM EM-EMPLOYEE-MASTER-WORK-AREA
850064           INVALID KEY MOVE 'YES' TO WS-PROGRAM-ABEND-SW.
850200*
850210      IF SUCCESSFUL-COMPLETION
850220          ADD 1 TO TC-MASTERS-WRITTEN
850230      ELSE
850240          MOVE 'YES' TO WS-PROGRAM-ABEND-SW.
870010*
870020*
870030 870-PRINT-REPORT-HEADINGS.
870040*
870050      ADD 1 TO WS-PAGE-COUNT.
870060      MOVE WS-PAGE-COUNT TO H2-PAGE-NBR.
870070      MOVE H1-HEADING-LINE-1 TO REPORT-LINE.
870080      PERFORM 880-WRITE-REPORT-TOP-LINE.
870090      MOVE H2-HEADING-LINE-2 TO REPORT-LINE.
870100      MOVE 1 TO WS-LINE-SPACING.
870110      PERFORM 890-WRITE-REPORT-LINE.
870120      MOVE H3-HEADING-LINE-3 TO REPORT-LINE.
870130      MOVE 2 TO WS-LINE-SPACING.
870140      PERFORM 890-WRITE-REPORT-LINE.
870150      MOVE H4-HEADING-LINE-4 TO REPORT-LINE.
870160      MOVE 1 TO WS-LINE-SPACING.
870170      PERFORM 890-WRITE-REPORT-LINE.
870180      MOVE SPACES TO REPORT-LINE.
870190      PERFORM 890-WRITE-REPORT-LINE.
880010*
880020*
880030 880-WRITE-REPORT-TOP-LINE.
880040*
880050      WRITE REPORT-LINE
880060           AFTER ADVANCING PAGE.
880070      MOVE 1 TO WS-LINES-USED.
890010*
890020*
890030 890-WRITE-REPORT-LINE.
890040*
890050      WRITE REPORT-LINE
890060           AFTER ADVANCING WS-LINE-SPACING.
890070      ADD WS-LINE-SPACING TO WS-LINES-USED.
900010*
900020*
900030 900-ABORT-PROGRAM-RUN.
900040*
900041      MOVE SPACES TO IE-I-O-ERROR-LINE.
900042      MOVE WS-FILE-STATUS-FLAG TO IE-FILE-STATUS-FLAG.
900044      MOVE WS-I-O-OPERATION-FLAG TO IE-I-O-OPERATION-FLAG.
900046      MOVE RK-INDEXED-KEY TO IE-ERROR-KEY.
900050      MOVE 'ABORTED ' TO DL-UPDATE-ACTION.
900055      MOVE 'I-O ERROR OCCURRED' TO DL-ERROR-MSG.
900060      MOVE DL-DETAIL-LINE TO REPORT-LINE.
900070      MOVE 3 TO WS-LINE-SPACING.
900080      PERFORM 890-WRITE-REPORT-LINE.
900090      MOVE SPACES TO DL-DETAIL-LINE.
900130      MOVE 'YES' TO WS-CREATION-END-OF-FILE-SW.
```

Figure 4D.2. (continued)

MASTER-RECORD module, and (3) recorded on the audit/error list in the 220-PRINT-AUDIT-ERROR-LINE module. Then the next input record is read. This process is repeated until the end-of-file is reached.

WRITE statement for the indexed file

The sequential WRITE statement within the 850-WRITE-MASTER-RECORD module is coded the same as it is for a random WRITE operation. With both a sequential and a random WRITE, an INVALID KEY will occur with a boundary violation. With a sequential WRITE, an INVALID KEY will also happen if the RECORD KEY of the record key that is being written is not greater than that of the previously written record.

■ TOPIC 4-E: **Backup and Reorganization of an Indexed File**

Backup of an Indexed File
    Program Design
    Program Coding
        SELECT statement for the indexed file
        OPEN statement for the indexed file
        Main processing logic
        READ statement for the indexed file

Reorganization of an Indexed File

Backup of an Indexed File

Because it is updated in-place, an indexed file-maintenance run does not yield an old generation copy of the indexed file that can be kept for file-recovery use. Remember that, with a sequential file update, the input master file becomes an old generation that is retained for a period of time should it ever be needed for master file reconstruction. This means that a separate program run must be made to **back up**—or, in other words, **copy**—an indexed file for retention purposes.

Just as it is for the indexed file-creation function, an indexed-file backup program run could be made with either a utility program or a custom-written COBOL Program. Normally the backup run is made immediately after the file-maintenance run has been completed. Alternately, it could be run just before the file-maintenance processing.

In this topic, an example program to back up an indexed file, called IND-BACK, for **ind**exed file **back**up, is presented.

Program Design

An indexed-file backup program simply reads the indexed file sequentially and writes each record to a sequential file. The sequential file is usually stored on tape.

A structure chart for the INDBACK program is presented in Figure 4E.1.

Program Coding

The INDBACK program is shown in Figure 4E.2. Pertinent aspects of the coding are shaded on the program listing and will be briefly discussed here.

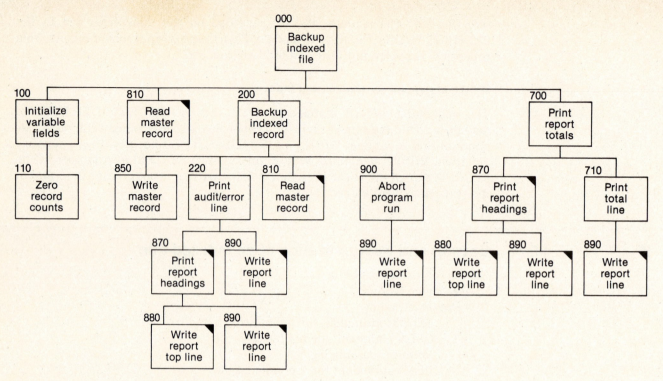

Figure 4E.1. Structure chart: INDBACK program.

SELECT statement for the indexed file

The indexed file to be backed up is accessed as a sequential file. Therefore, its SELECT statement is coded with ACCESS MODE IS SEQUENTIAL.

OPEN statement for the indexed file

When an indexed file is backed up, it is an input file to the program run. Thus, in the INDBACK program, OPEN INPUT INDEXED-MASTER-FILE is coded in the mainline 000-BACKUP-INDEXED-FILE module.

Main processing logic

In the 200-BACKUP-INDEXED-RECORD module, after each input indexed file record is read it is transferred to the BACKUP-FILE in the 850-WRITE-BACKUP-RECORD module. Although an audit list is not always specified for an indexed file-backup program, in this INDBACK program, the record that is backed up is then printed on the audit list in the 220-PRINT-AUDIT-ERROR-LINE module. Then the next input record is read. This process is repeated until the end of the indexed file is reached.

READ statement for the indexed file

Because the indexed file is being read sequentially, there is no INVALID KEY phrase specified in the READ statement within the 810-READ-MASTER-RECORD module.

```
001010 IDENTIFICATION DIVISION.
001020 PROGRAM-ID.    INDBACK.
001030*
001040*
001050*               INDEXED FILE BACKUP
002010*
002020*
002030*
002040 ENVIRONMENT DIVISION.
002050*
002060*
002070 CONFIGURATION SECTION.
002080*
002090 SOURCE-COMPUTER.   IBM-370.
002100 OBJECT-COMPUTER.   IBM-370.
002110*
002120*
002130 INPUT-OUTPUT SECTION.
002140*
002150 FILE-CONTROL.
002180     SELECT INDEXED-MASTER-FILE
002190         ASSIGN TO INDFILE
002194         ORGANIZATION IS INDEXED
002195         ACCESS MODE IS SEQUENTIAL
002196         RECORD KEY IS RK-INDEXED-KEY
002197         FILE STATUS IS WS-FILE-STATUS-FLAG.
002200     SELECT BACKUP-FILE
002210         ASSIGN TO UT-S-BKUFILE.
002220     SELECT REPORT-FILE
002230         ASSIGN TO UT-S-PRTFILE.
003010*
003020*
003030*
003040 DATA DIVISION.
003050*
003060*
003070 FILE SECTION.
004010*
004020*
004030 FD  INDEXED-MASTER-FILE
004040     RECORD CONTAINS 80 CHARACTERS
004050     LABEL RECORDS ARE STANDARD.
004060*
004070 01  INDEXED-MASTER-RECORD.
004080     05  FILLER                     PIC X(3).
004090     05  RK-INDEXED-KEY.
004100         10  RK-PLANT-CODE          PIC X(2).
004110         10  RK-DEPARTMENT-NUMBER   PIC X(4).
004120         10  RK-EMPLOYEE-NUMBER     PIC X(5).
004130     05  FILLER                     PIC X(66).
005010*
005020*
005030 FD  BACKUP-FILE
005040     RECORD CONTAINS 80 CHARACTERS
005050     LABEL RECORDS ARE STANDARD.
005060*
005070 01  BACKUP-RECORD.
005080     05  FILLER                     PIC X(80).
006010*
006020*
006030 FD  REPORT-FILE
006040     RECORD CONTAINS 133 CHARACTERS
006050     LABEL RECORDS ARE OMITTED.
006060*
006070 01  REPORT-LINE.
006080     05  FILLER                     PIC X(133).
010010*
010020*
010030 WORKING-STORAGE SECTION.
010040*
010050*
010060 01  WS-SWITCHES.
010070*
010110     05  WS-MASTER-END-OF-FILE-SW   PIC X(3).
010120         88  MASTER-END-OF-FILE              VALUE 'YES'.
010300*
010310     05  WS-PROGRAM-ABEND-SW        PIC X(3).
010320         88  PROGRAM-ABEND                   VALUE 'YES'.
010330*
010340     05  WS-FILE-STATUS-FLAG        PIC X(2).
010350         88  SUCCESSFUL-COMPLETION           VALUE '00'.
010360         88  DUPLICATE-ALTERNATE-KEY         VALUE '02'.
010370         88  END-OF-FILE                     VALUE '10'.
010380         88  SEQUENCE-ERROR                  VALUE '21'.
010390         88  DUPLICATE-KEY                   VALUE '22'.
010400         88  NO-RECORD-FOUND                 VALUE '23'.
010410         88  BOUNDARY-VIOLATION-IND-REL      VALUE '24'.
010420         88  PERMANENT-I-O-DATA-ERROR        VALUE '30'.
010430         88  BOUNDARY-VIOLATION-SEQ          VALUE '34'.
010440         88  IMPLEMENTOR-DEFINED-ERROR       VALUE '9 '.
010450*
010460     05  WS-I-O-OPERATION-FLAG      PIC X(7).
012010*
012020*
012030 01  WS-REPORT-CONTROLS.
012040     05  WS-PAGE-COUNT              PIC S9(4)      COMP-3.
012050     05  WS-LINES-PER-PAGE          PIC S99 VALUE +55
012060                                                   COMP SYNC.
012070     05  WS-LINES-USED              PIC S9(2)      COMP SYNC.
012080     05  WS-LINE-SPACING            PIC S9(2).
013010*
013020*
013030 01  WS-WORK-AREAS.
013040     05  WS-DATE-WORK               PIC 9(6).
013050     05  WS-DATE-REFORMAT REDEFINES WS-DATE-WORK.
013060         10  WS-YEAR                PIC 9(2).
013070         10  WS-MONTH               PIC 9(2).
013080         10  WS-DAY                 PIC 9(2).
014010*
014020*
014030 01  TC-COUNT-DESCRIPTION-DATA.
014040     05  FILLER          PIC X(20)  VALUE 'MASTERS READ        '.
014170     05  FILLER          PIC X(20)  VALUE 'BACKUP RCDS WRITTEN '.
014180 01  TC-COUNT-DESCRIPTION-TABLE
014190     REDEFINES TC-COUNT-DESCRIPTION-DATA.
014200     05  TC-COUNT-DESCRIPTION       OCCURS 2 TIMES
014210                                    PIC X(20).
015010*
```

```
015020*
015030 01  TC-TABLE-CONTROLS.
015040     05  TC-SUBSCRIPT               PIC S9(4)      COMP SYNC.
015050     05  TC-NUMBER-OF-ENTRIES       PIC S9(4)      VALUE +2
015060                                                   COMP SYNC.
016010*
016020 01  TC-RECORD-COUNT-ENTRIES                       COMP-3.
016030     05  TC-MASTERS-READ            PIC S9(5).
016160     05  TC-BACKUP-RCDS-WRITTEN     PIC S9(5).
016170*
016180 01  TC-RECORD-COUNTS REDEFINES TC-RECORD-COUNT-ENTRIES.
016190     05  TC-RECORD-COUNT            OCCURS 2 TIMES
016200                                    PIC S9(5)      COMP-3.
025010*
025020*
025030 01  EM-EMPLOYEE-MASTER-WORK-AREA.
025040     05  EM-RECORD-CODE             PIC X(2).
025050     05  EM-UPDATE-CODE             PIC X(1).
025060     05  EM-PLANT-CODE              PIC X(2).
025070     05  EM-DEPARTMENT-NUMBER       PIC X(4).
025080     05  EM-EMPLOYEE-NUMBER         PIC X(5).
025090     05  EM-LAST-NAME               PIC X(13).
025100     05  EM-FIRST-NAME              PIC X(12).
025110     05  EM-MIDDLE-INITIAL          PIC X(1).
025120     05  EM-HOURLY-RATE             PIC S9(2)V99.
025130     05  FILLER                     PIC X(30).
025140     05  EM-DATE-LAST-ACTIVITY      PIC 9(6).
030010*
030020*
030040 01  H1-HEADING-LINE-1.
030050     05  FILLER       PIC X(1).
030060     05  FILLER       PIC X(20)  VALUE 'INDEXED MASTER FILE '.
030070     05  FILLER       PIC X(20)  VALUE 'BACKUP              '.
030080     05  FILLER       PIC X(20)  VALUE '                    '.
030090     05  FILLER       PIC X(20)  VALUE '                    '.
030100     05  FILLER       PIC X(20)  VALUE '           RUN DAT'.
030110     05  FILLER       PIC X(2)   VALUE 'E '.
030120     05  H1-MONTH     PIC 9(2).
030130     05  FILLER       PIC X(1)   VALUE '/'.
030140     05  H1-DAY       PIC 9(2).
030150     05  FILLER       PIC X(1)   VALUE '/'.
030160     05  H1-YEAR      PIC 9(2).
030170     05  FILLER       PIC X(22)  VALUE SPACES.
031010*
031020*
031030 01  H2-HEADING-LINE-2.
031040     05  FILLER       PIC X(1).
031050     05  FILLER       PIC X(20)  VALUE 'AUDIT/ERROR LIST    '.
031060     05  FILLER       PIC X(20)  VALUE '                    '.
031070     05  FILLER       PIC X(20)  VALUE '  ** EMPLOYEE MASTER'.
031080     05  FILLER       PIC X(20)  VALUE ' FILE **            '.
031090     05  FILLER       PIC X(20)  VALUE '                    '.
031100     05  FILLER       PIC X(6)   VALUE ' PAGE '.
031110     05  H2-PAGE-NBR  PIC ZZZ9.
031120     05  FILLER       PIC X(22)  VALUE SPACES.
032010*
032020*
032030 01  H3-HEADING-LINE-3.
032040     05  FILLER       PIC X(1).
032050     05  FILLER       PIC X(20)  VALUE 'RCD UPDT PLANT  DE'.
032060     05  FILLER       PIC X(20)  VALUE 'PT  EMPL -------EMP'.
032070     05  FILLER       PIC X(20)  VALUE 'LOYEE NAME-------M '.
032080     05  FILLER       PIC X(20)  VALUE 'HOURLY   UPDATE    '.
032090     05  FILLER       PIC X(20)  VALUE '                   '.
032100     05  FILLER       PIC X(20)  VALUE '                   '.
032110     05  FILLER       PIC X(12)  VALUE '            '.
033010*
033020*
033030 01  H4-HEADING-LINE-4.
033040     05  FILLER       PIC X(1).
033050     05  FILLER       PIC X(20)  VALUE 'CODE CODE    CODE  N'.
033060     05  FILLER       PIC X(20)  VALUE 'BR   NBR  LAST NAME '.
033070     05  FILLER       PIC X(20)  VALUE '    FIRST NAME   I  '.
033080     05  FILLER       PIC X(20)  VALUE ' RATE   ACTION  ---'.
033090     05  FILLER       PIC X(20)  VALUE '------ERROR MESSAGE'.
033100     05  FILLER       PIC X(20)  VALUE '----------         '.
033110     05  FILLER       PIC X(12)  VALUE '            '.
034010*
034020*
034030 01  DL-DETAIL-LINE.
034040     05  FILLER                      PIC X(1).
034050     05  FILLER                      PIC X(1)   VALUE SPACES.
034060     05  DL-RECORD-CODE              PIC X(2).
034070     05  FILLER                      PIC X(4)   VALUE SPACES.
034080     05  DL-UPDATE-CODE              PIC X(1).
034090     05  FILLER                      PIC X(4)   VALUE SPACES.
034100     05  DL-PLANT-CODE               PIC X(2).
034110     05  FILLER                      PIC X(4)   VALUE SPACES.
034120     05  DL-DEPARTMENT-NUMBER        PIC X(4).
034130     05  FILLER                      PIC X(1)   VALUE SPACES.
034140     05  DL-EMPLOYEE-NUMBER          PIC X(5).
034150     05  FILLER                      PIC X(2)   VALUE SPACES.
034160     05  DL-LAST-NAME                PIC X(13).
034170     05  FILLER                      PIC X(1)   VALUE SPACES.
034180     05  DL-FIRST-NAME               PIC X(12).
034190     05  FILLER                      PIC X(1)   VALUE SPACES.
034200     05  DL-MIDDLE-INITIAL           PIC X(1).
034210     05  FILLER                      PIC X(3)   VALUE SPACES.
034220     05  DL-HOURLY-RATE              PIC ZZ.99.
034230     05  DL-HOURLY-RATE-X REDEFINES DL-HOURLY-RATE
034240                                     PIC X(5).
034250     05  FILLER                      PIC X(2)   VALUE SPACES.
034260     05  DL-UPDATE-ACTION            PIC X(8).
034270     05  FILLER                      PIC X(1)   VALUE SPACES.
034280     05  DL-ERROR-MSG                PIC X(33).
034290     05  FILLER                      PIC X(22)  VALUE SPACES.
035010*
035020*
035030 01  IE-I-O-ERROR-LINE REDEFINES DL-DETAIL-LINE.
035040     05  FILLER                      PIC X(1).
035050     05  FILLER                      PIC X(40).
035062     05  IE-FILE-STATUS-FLAG         PIC X(2).
035064     05  FILLER                      PIC X(1).
035066     05  IE-I-O-OPERATION-FLAG       PIC X(7).
035070     05  FILLER                      PIC X(1).
035080     05  IE-ERROR-KEY                PIC XXBXXXXBXXXXX.
035090     05  FILLER                      PIC X(4).
036010*
```

Figure 4E.2.   COBOL Coding: INDBACK program.

continued*continued*

TOPIC 4-E: BACKUP AND REORGANIZATION OF AN INDEXED FILE **185**

```
036020*
036030 01  TL-TOTAL-LINE.
036040     05  FILLER                        PIC X(1).
036050     05  FILLER                        PIC X(83)    VALUE SPACES.
036060     05  TL-COUNT-DESCRIPTION          PIC X(20).
036070     05  FILLER                        PIC X(1)     VALUE SPACES.
036080     05  TL-RECORD-COUNT               PIC ZZ,ZZ9.
036090     05  FILLER                        PIC X(22)    VALUE SPACES.
050010*
050020*
050030*
050040 PROCEDURE DIVISION.
050050*
050060*
050070 000-BACKUP-INDEXED-FILE.
050080*
050090     OPEN INPUT INDEXED-MASTER-FILE
050100          OUTPUT BACKUP-FILE
050120                 REPORT-FILE.
050130     PERFORM 100-INITIALIZE-VARIABLE-FIELDS.
050135     PERFORM 810-READ-MASTER-RECORD.
050140     PERFORM 200-BACKUP-INDEXED-RECORD
050150         UNTIL MASTER-END-OF-FILE.
050170     PERFORM 700-PRINT-REPORT-TOTALS.
050180     CLOSE INDEXED-MASTER-FILE
050190           BACKUP-FILE
050210           REPORT-FILE.
050220     STOP RUN.
100010*
100020*
100030 100-INITIALIZE-VARIABLE-FIELDS.
100040*
100050     MOVE 'NO ' TO WS-MASTER-END-OF-FILE-SW
100055                   WS-PROGRAM-ABEND-SW.
100120     MOVE ZERO TO WS-PAGE-COUNT.
100130     ADD 1 WS-LINES-PER-PAGE GIVING WS-LINES-USED.
100140     ACCEPT WS-DATE-WORK FROM DATE.
100150     MOVE WS-MONTH TO H1-MONTH.
100160     MOVE WS-DAY TO H1-DAY.
100170     MOVE WS-YEAR TO H1-YEAR.
100190     MOVE SPACES TO DL-ERROR-MSG.
100200     PERFORM 110-ZERO-RECORD-COUNTS
100210         VARYING TC-SUBSCRIPT
100220         FROM 1
100230         BY 1
100240         UNTIL TC-SUBSCRIPT IS GREATER THAN TC-NUMBER-OF-ENTRIES.
110010*
110020*
110030 110-ZERO-RECORD-COUNTS.
110040*
110050     MOVE ZERO TO TC-RECORD-COUNT (TC-SUBSCRIPT).
200010*
200020*
200030 200-BACKUP-INDEXED-RECORD.
200040*
200174     PERFORM 850-WRITE-BACKUP-RECORD.
200180     PERFORM 220-PRINT-AUDIT-ERROR-LINE.
200182*
200184     IF NOT PROGRAM-ABEND
200186         PERFORM 810-READ-MASTER-RECORD
200188     ELSE
200190         PERFORM 900-ABORT-PROGRAM-RUN.
220010*
220020*
220030 220-PRINT-AUDIT-ERROR-LINE.
220040*
220050     IF WS-LINES-USED IS NOT LESS THAN WS-LINES-PER-PAGE
220060         PERFORM 870-PRINT-REPORT-HEADINGS.
220070     MOVE EM-RECORD-CODE TO DL-RECORD-CODE.
220080     MOVE EM-UPDATE-CODE TO DL-UPDATE-CODE.
220090     MOVE EM-PLANT-CODE TO DL-PLANT-CODE.
220100     MOVE EM-DEPARTMENT-NUMBER TO DL-DEPARTMENT-NUMBER.
220110     MOVE EM-EMPLOYEE-NUMBER TO DL-EMPLOYEE-NUMBER.
220120     MOVE EM-LAST-NAME TO DL-LAST-NAME.
220130     MOVE EM-FIRST-NAME TO DL-FIRST-NAME.
220140     MOVE EM-MIDDLE-INITIAL TO DL-MIDDLE-INITIAL.
220160     MOVE EM-HOURLY-RATE TO DL-HOURLY-RATE.
220190     MOVE DL-DETAIL-LINE TO REPORT-LINE.
220200     MOVE 1 TO WS-LINE-SPACING.
220210     PERFORM 890-WRITE-REPORT-LINE.
220220     MOVE SPACES TO DL-DETAIL-LINE.
700010*
700020*
700030 700-PRINT-REPORT-TOTALS.
```

```
700040*
700050     PERFORM 870-PRINT-REPORT-HEADINGS.
700060     PERFORM 710-PRINT-TOTAL-LINE
700070         VARYING TC-SUBSCRIPT
700080         FROM 1
700090         BY 1
700100         UNTIL TC-SUBSCRIPT IS GREATER THAN TC-NUMBER-OF-ENTRIES.
710010*
710020*
710030 710-PRINT-TOTAL-LINE.
710040*
710050     MOVE TC-COUNT-DESCRIPTION (TC-SUBSCRIPT)
710060         TO TL-COUNT-DESCRIPTION.
710070     MOVE TC-RECORD-COUNT (TC-SUBSCRIPT) TO TL-RECORD-COUNT.
710080     MOVE TL-TOTAL-LINE TO REPORT-LINE.
710090     MOVE 1 TO WS-LINE-SPACING.
710100     PERFORM 890-WRITE-REPORT-LINE.
810010*
810020*
810030 810-READ-MASTER-RECORD.
810040*
810065     MOVE 'READ   ' TO WS-I-O-OPERATION-FLAG.
810070     READ INDEXED-MASTER-FILE INTO EM-EMPLOYEE-MASTER-WORK-AREA
810080         AT END MOVE 'YES' TO WS-MASTER-END-OF-FILE-SW.
810300*
810310     IF SUCCESSFUL-COMPLETION
810320         ADD 1 TO TC-MASTERS-READ
810325     ELSE
810350         MOVE 'YES' TO WS-PROGRAM-ABEND-SW.
850010*
850020*
850030 850-WRITE-BACKUP-RECORD.
850040*
850050     WRITE BACKUP-RECORD
850060         FROM EM-EMPLOYEE-MASTER-WORK-AREA.
850070     ADD 1 TO TC-BACKUP-RCDS-WRITTEN.
870010*
870020*
870030 870-PRINT-REPORT-HEADINGS.
870040*
870050     ADD 1 TO WS-PAGE-COUNT.
870060     MOVE WS-PAGE-COUNT TO H2-PAGE-NBR.
870070     MOVE H1-HEADING-LINE-1 TO REPORT-LINE.
870080     PERFORM 880-WRITE-REPORT-TOP-LINE.
870090     MOVE H2-HEADING-LINE-2 TO REPORT-LINE.
870100     MOVE 1 TO WS-LINE-SPACING.
870110     PERFORM 890-WRITE-REPORT-LINE.
870120     MOVE H3-HEADING-LINE-3 TO REPORT-LINE.
870130     MOVE 2 TO WS-LINE-SPACING.
870140     PERFORM 890-WRITE-REPORT-LINE.
870150     MOVE H4-HEADING-LINE-4 TO REPORT-LINE.
870160     MOVE 1 TO WS-LINE-SPACING.
870170     PERFORM 890-WRITE-REPORT-LINE.
870180     MOVE SPACES TO REPORT-LINE.
870190     PERFORM 890-WRITE-REPORT-LINE.
880010*
880020*
880030 880-WRITE-REPORT-TOP-LINE.
880040*
880050     WRITE REPORT-LINE
880060         AFTER ADVANCING PAGE.
880070     MOVE 1 TO WS-LINES-USED.
890010*
890020*
890030 890-WRITE-REPORT-LINE.
890040*
890050     WRITE REPORT-LINE
890060         AFTER ADVANCING WS-LINE-SPACING.
890070     ADD WS-LINE-SPACING TO WS-LINES-USED.
900010*
900020*
900030 900-ABORT-PROGRAM-RUN.
900040*
900042     MOVE WS-FILE-STATUS-FLAG TO IE-FILE-STATUS-FLAG.
900044     MOVE WS-I-O-OPERATION-FLAG TO IE-I-O-OPERATION-FLAG.
900046     MOVE RK-INDEXED-KEY TO IE-ERROR-KEY.
900050     MOVE 'ABORTED ' TO DL-UPDATE-ACTION.
900055     MOVE 'I-O ERROR OCCURRED' TO DL-ERROR-MSG.
900060     MOVE DL-DETAIL-LINE TO REPORT-LINE.
900070     MOVE 3 TO WS-LINE-SPACING.
900080     PERFORM 890-WRITE-REPORT-LINE.
900155     MOVE 'YES' TO WS-MASTER-END-OF-FILE-SW.
```

Figure 4E.2. (continued)

Reorganization of an Indexed File

Another program function that is associated with indexed file maintenance is **reorganization** of the indexed file. As new records are added to the file and existing records are deleted from the file, overflow record chains are created and unused record slots occur in the indexed file. This deterioration of the file's original organization causes the time that is required for the processing of the file to increase. To restore the file to optimum organization, an indexed file must be reorganized from time to time. The duration of the time between reorganization runs will vary, depending upon the file's volatility.

As shown at the beginning of this chapter in Figure 4.1, a reorganization run consists of the backup step plus a reload step, named INDREORG, for **ind**exed file **reorg**anization.

The general logic for a reorganization program is identical to that of an indexed load program. In fact, under certain circumstances, the same program can be used for both the initial load and for reorganization.

Slightly different program coding will be called for when (1) the format of the initial creation record is not exactly the same as that of the indexed master record, (2) the initial load program contains a SORT statement to sequence the input creation records, or (3) data validation is contained within the initial load program.

If the initial creation record does not match the indexed master record, then the coding of the 260-CREATE-MASTER-RECORD module must be modified for the reorganization program. Sorting or data validation is not necessary for records that are being reorganized, so it is more efficient to omit these functions from a reorganization program.

TOPIC 4-F: Indexed File Coding with 1968 COBOL Compilers

1968 COBOL Indexed File-Processing Syntax

Design Differences for the IN8MAINT Program
     Delete-Flag Method of Deleting Master Records
     Simulation of the File Status Data-Item

Coding Differences for the IN8MAINT Program
     SELECT Statement for the Indexed File
     Employee Master Work-Area Record Definition
     810-READ-MASTER-RECORD
     850-WRITE-MASTER-RECORD
     855-REWRITE-MASTER-RECORD
     860-DELETE-MASTER-RECORD

ANS COBOL statements for indexed files were not introduced until the 1974 version of the standards. Even so, most 1968 compilers contain extensions to handle indexed file-processing methods that are similar, though not identical, to the 1974 standard. In this topic, the 1968 indexed file syntax that is most commonly used is presented. The INDMAINT program has been recoded in accordance with these standards and given a PROGRAM-ID of IN8MAINT, for **in**dexed file (**1968** compiler) **maint**enance.

1968 COBOL Indexed File-Processing Syntax

The 1968 COBOL indexed file-processing syntax for IBM-compatible compilers is shown in Figure 4F.1. There are five primary coding differences from 1974 ANS COBOL:

1. The ORGANIZATION IS INDEXED clause is not specified in the SELECT entry. Instead, the indexed organization is specified through the choice of the ASSIGN clause implementor-name. (The syntax and coding of this clause will vary depending upon the particular compiler that is being used.)
2. The NOMINAL KEY data-item, instead of the RECORD KEY, is set with the key value when the READ, WRITE, REWRITE, and START statements are used to access the file. The NOMINAL KEY clause is specified in the SELECT entry and must be described in the WORKING-STORAGE SECTION.
3. The FILE STATUS data-item is not available.
4. The DELETE statement is not available.
5. The START statement has fewer relational operators.

```
        ENVIRONMENT DIVISION.
            .
            .
            .

        INPUT-OUTPUT SECTION.
        FILE-CONTROL.

            SELECT file-name
                ASSIGN TO implementor-name
                [ACCESS MODE IS RANDOM]
                RECORD KEY IS data-name-1
                NOMINAL KEY IS data-name-2.


        DATA DIVISION.
        FILE SECTION.

        FD    file-name
                [RECORD CONTAINS integer CHARACTERS]
                [BLOCK CONTAINS integer RECORDS]
                LABEL RECORDS ARE STANDARD.
```

The RECORD KEY field must be defined
as a field within the FILE SECTION record
description.

        WORKING-STORAGE SECTION.

The NOMINAL KEY field must be defined
as a field within the WORKING-STORAGE
SECTION. It must be set with the key
value before a READ, WRITE, REWRITE, or
START statement is executed.

Figure 4F.1. COBOL indexed file-processing syntax for IBM-compatible 1968 ANS COBOL compilers.

Design Differences for the IN8MAINT Program

The 1968 syntax necessitates two general areas in which program design of the IN8MAINT program differs from that of the INDMAINT program: master record deletion and file status simulation.

Delete-Flag Method of Deleting Master Records

Because there is no DELETE statement, deletion of master records is accomplished by specifying a delete-flag field as the first position of the master record. The delete-flag is initialized to SPACE when the master record is created and set to HIGH-VALUE to signify that the record has been deleted.

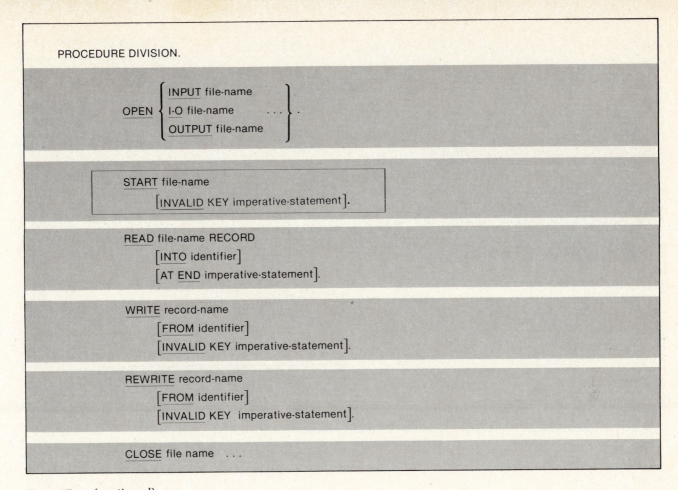

```
PROCEDURE DIVISION.

         ┌ INPUT file-name   ┐
OPEN   ┤ I-O file-name    ... ├  .
         └ OUTPUT file-name ┘


    START file-name
        [INVALID KEY imperative-statement].

    READ file-name RECORD
        [INTO identifier]
        [AT END imperative-statement].

    WRITE record-name
        [FROM identifier]
        [INVALID KEY imperative-statement].

    REWRITE record-name
        [FROM identifier]
        [INVALID KEY  imperative-statement].

    CLOSE file name  . . .
```

Figure 4F.1. (continued)

As shown in Figures 4F.2 and 4F.3, the master record to be deleted is first retrieved by a random read. Then, as illustrated in Figure 4F.4, the delete-flag field is set to HIGH-VALUE (hexadecimal value "FF"), and the record is replaced on the master file with a REWRITE statement. Although not physically deleted, the operating system considers a record that is residing on the master file with its first position set to HIGH-VALUE to be functionally deleted. A functionally deleted record is actually physically deleted from the file during the next reorganization run.

Simulation of the File Status Data-Item

Although such coding would not be expected to be present in existing programs that are written with 1968 system, the IN8MAINT program is designed to contain a simulated file status data-item that the program manually sets rather than have the system automatically update it. This design approach has been taken so that the program coding for this IN8MAINT program is as compatible as possible with the INDMAINT program. Also, it allows a person who is using a 1968 compiler to become acquainted with the 1974 standard file status concept.

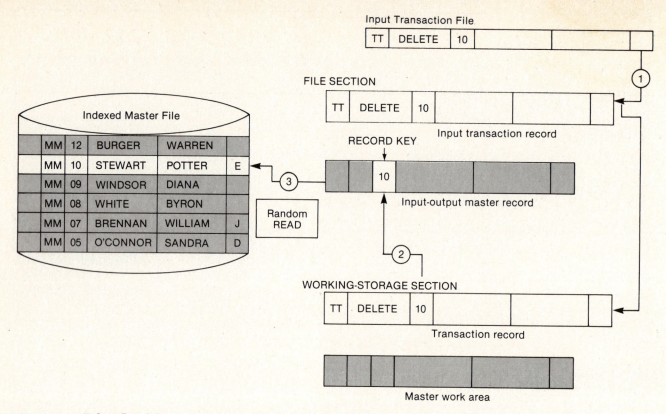

Figure 4F.2. Delete-flag deletion Step A: Locating the master record.

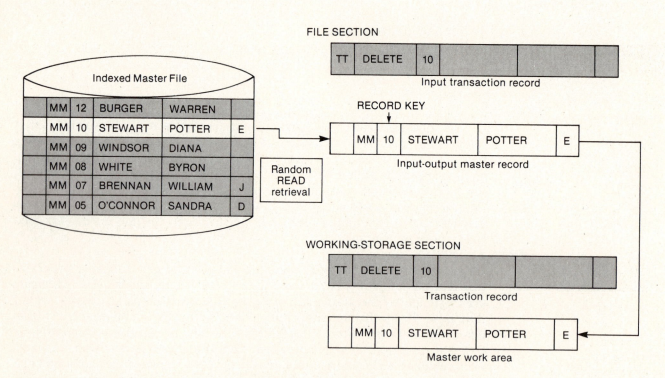

Figure 4F.3. Delete-flag deletion Step B: Retrieving the master record.

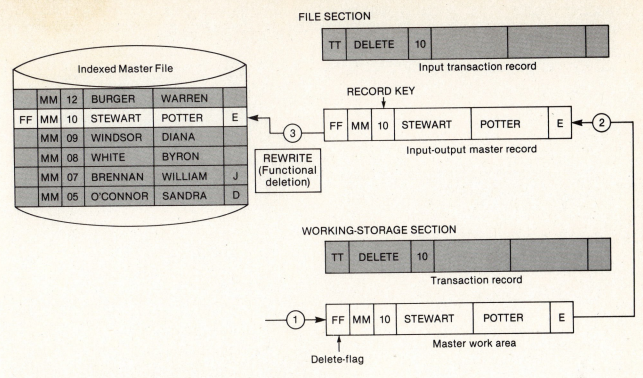

Figure 4F.4. Delete-flag deletion Step C: Setting the delete flag.

Coding Differences for the IN8MAINT Program

COBOL coding for the IN8MAINT program is shown in Figure 4F.5. Coding differences are shaded on the program listing and will be mentioned here.

SELECT Statement for the Indexed File

The SELECT statement must be coded without the ORGANIZATION IS INDEXED and FILE STATUS clauses.

Employee Master Work-Area Record Definition

The delete-flag must be specified as the first character of the indexed master record. Thus the EM-DELETE-FLAG field is specified as the first position of the EM-EMPLOYEE-MASTER-WORK-AREA record in WORKING-STORAGE.

810-READ-MASTER-RECORD

Because the file status data-item is being program-set, it is reset to successful completion before each I-O statement. Thus the first statement of the 810-READ-MASTER-RECORD module sets the WS-FILE-STATUS-FLAG to ZEROS.

If an INVALID KEY condition occurs on the random READ of the indexed file, it means that the master record that is requested does not exist. Therefore, the INVALID KEY phrase is coded to set the WS-FILE-STATUS-FLAG to "23"— the 1974 standard code for a no-record-found condition.

Even if the random READ has located the record, its delete-flag may be set on the record to signify that it has been functionally deleted. When a record has been found, the next IF statement is necessary to ensure that the delete-flag has not been set. If it has, the WS-FILE-STATUS-FLAG is set to "23."

850-WRITE-MASTER-RECORD

There are two conditions that could cause an INVALID KEY condition to occur with a random WRITE: (1) the key of the record that is being written already exists on the master file, or (2) there is no remaining file space in which to write the

```
001010  IDENTIFICATION DIVISION.
001020  PROGRAM-ID.   IN8MAINT.
001030*
001040*
001050*                     INDEXED MASTER FILE MAINTENANCE
001060*                         (FOR 1968 COMPILER)
002010*
002020*
002030*
002040  ENVIRONMENT DIVISION.
002050*
002060*
002070  CONFIGURATION SECTION.
002080*
002090  SOURCE-COMPUTER.  IBM-370.
002100  OBJECT-COMPUTER.  IBM-370.
002110*
002120*
002130  INPUT-OUTPUT SECTION.
002140*
002150  FILE-CONTROL.
002160      SELECT TRANSACTION-FILE
002170          ASSIGN TO UT-S-TRNFILE.
002180      SELECT INDEXED-MASTER-FILE
002190          ASSIGN TO DA-I-INDFILE
002195          ACCESS MODE IS RANDOM
002196          RECORD KEY IS RK-INDEXED-KEY
002198          NOMINAL KEY IS NK-INDEXED-KEY.
002220      SELECT REPORT-FILE
002230          ASSIGN TO UT-S-PRTFILE.
003010*
003020*
003030*
003040  DATA DIVISION.
003050*
003060*
003070  FILE SECTION.
003080*
003090*
003100  FD  TRANSACTION-FILE
003110          RECORD CONTAINS 80 CHARACTERS
003120          LABEL RECORDS ARE STANDARD.
003130*
003140  01  TRANSACTION-RECORD.
003150      05  FILLER                   PIC X(80).
004010*
004020*
004030  FD  INDEXED-MASTER-FILE
004040          RECORD CONTAINS 80 CHARACTERS
004050          LABEL RECORDS ARE STANDARD.
004060*
004070  01  INDEXED-MASTER-RECORD.
004080      05  FILLER                   PIC X(3).
004090      05  RK-INDEXED-KEY.
004100          10  RK-PLANT-CODE        PIC X(2).
004110          10  RK-DEPARTMENT-NUMBER PIC X(4).
004120          10  RK-EMPLOYEE-NUMBER   PIC X(5).
004130      05  FILLER                   PIC X(66).
006010*
006020*
006030  FD  REPORT-FILE
006040          RECORD CONTAINS 133 CHARACTERS
006050          LABEL RECORDS ARE OMITTED.
006060*
006070  01  REPORT-LINE.
006080      05  FILLER                   PIC X(133).
010010*
010020*
010030  WORKING-STORAGE SECTION.
010040*
010050*
010060  01  WS-SWITCHES.
010070*
010080      05  WS-TRANSACTION-END-OF-FILE-SW PIC X(3).
010090          88  TRANSACTION-END-OF-FILE       VALUE 'YES'.
010300*
010310      05  WS-PROGRAM-ABEND-SW      PIC X(3).
010320          88  PROGRAM-ABEND                 VALUE 'YES'.
010330*
010340      05  WS-FILE-STATUS-FLAG      PIC X(2).
010350          88  SUCCESSFUL-COMPLETION         VALUE '00'.
010360          88  DUPLICATE-ALTERNATE-KEY       VALUE '02'.
010370          88  END-OF-FILE                   VALUE '10'.
010380          88  SEQUENCE-ERROR                VALUE '21'.
010390          88  DUPLICATE-KEY                 VALUE '22'.
010400          88  NO-RECORD-FOUND               VALUE '23'.
010410          88  BOUNDARY-VIOLATION-IND-REL    VALUE '24'.
010420          88  PERMANENT-I-O-DATA-ERROR      VALUE '30'.
010430          88  BOUNDARY-VIOLATION-SEQ        VALUE '34'.
010440*         88  IMPLEMENTOR-DEFINED-ERROR     VALUE '9 '.
010450*
010460      05  WS-I-O-OPERATION-FLAG    PIC X(7).
010510*
010520*
010530  01  NK-INDEXED-KEY.
010540      05  NK-PLANT-CODE            PIC X(2).
010550      05  NK-DEPARTMENT-NUMBER     PIC X(4).
010560      05  NK-EMPLOYEE-NUMBER       PIC X(5).
012010*
012020*
012030  01  WS-REPORT-CONTROLS.
012040      05  WS-PAGE-COUNT            PIC S9(4)      COMP-3.
012050      05  WS-LINES-PER-PAGE        PIC S99 VALUE +55
012060                                                  COMP SYNC.
012070      05  WS-LINES-USED            PIC S9(2)      COMP SYNC.
012080      05  WS-LINE-SPACING          PIC S9(2).
013010*
013020*
013030  01  WS-WORK-AREAS.
013040      05  WS-DATE-WORK             PIC 9(6).
013050      05  WS-DATE-REFORMAT REDEFINES WS-DATE-WORK.
013060          10  WS-YEAR              PIC 9(2).
013070          10  WS-MONTH             PIC 9(2).
013080          10  WS-DAY               PIC 9(2).
014010*
014020*
014030  01  TC-TABLE-CONTROLS.
014040      05  TC-SUBSCRIPT             PIC S9(4)      COMP SYNC.
```

```
014050      05  TC-NUMBER-OF-ENTRIES         PIC S9(4)    VALUE +15
014060                                                    COMP SYNC.
015010*
015020  01  TC-COUNT-DESCRIPTION-DATA.
015030      05  FILLER          PIC X(20)  VALUE 'TRANSACTIONS READ  '.
015040      05  FILLER          PIC X(20)  VALUE '  ADDS             '.
015050      05  FILLER          PIC X(20)  VALUE '    PROCESSED      '.
015060      05  FILLER          PIC X(20)  VALUE '    REJECTED       '.
015070      05  FILLER          PIC X(20)  VALUE '  CHANGES          '.
015080      05  FILLER          PIC X(20)  VALUE '    PROCESSED      '.
015090      05  FILLER          PIC X(20)  VALUE '    REJECTED       '.
015100      05  FILLER          PIC X(20)  VALUE '  DELETES          '.
015110      05  FILLER          PIC X(20)  VALUE '    PROCESSED      '.
015120      05  FILLER          PIC X(20)  VALUE '    REJECTED       '.
015130      05  FILLER          PIC X(20)  VALUE '  ERROR UPDATE CODES'.
015140      05  FILLER          PIC X(20)  VALUE 'MASTERS READ       '.
015150      05  FILLER          PIC X(20)  VALUE 'MASTER CHANGES     '.
015160      05  FILLER          PIC X(20)  VALUE 'MASTERS ADDED      '.
015165      05  FILLER          PIC X(20)  VALUE 'MASTERS DELETED    '.
015170  01  TC-COUNT-DESCRIPTION-TABLE
015180          REDEFINES TC-COUNT-DESCRIPTION-DATA.
015190      05  TC-COUNT-DESCRIPTION         OCCURS 15 TIMES
015200                                                 PIC X(20).
016010*
016020  01  TC-RECORD-COUNT-ENTRIES                    COMP-3.
016030      05  TC-TOTAL-TRANS-READ          PIC S9(5).
016040      05  TC-TOTAL-ADD-TRANS-READ      PIC S9(5).
016050      05  TC-ADD-TRANS-PROCESSED       PIC S9(5).
016060      05  TC-ADD-TRANS-REJECTED        PIC S9(5).
016070      05  TC-TOTAL-CHANGE-TRANS-READ   PIC S9(5).
016080      05  TC-CHANGE-TRANS-PROCESSED    PIC S9(5).
016090      05  TC-CHANGE-TRANS-REJECTED     PIC S9(5).
016100      05  TC-TOTAL-DELETE-TRANS-READ   PIC S9(5).
016110      05  TC-DELETE-TRANS-PROCESSED    PIC S9(5).
016120      05  TC-DELETE-TRANS-REJECTED     PIC S9(5).
016130      05  TC-TOTAL-ERROR-UPDATE-CODES  PIC S9(5).
016140      05  TC-MASTERS-READ              PIC S9(5).
016150      05  TC-MASTER-CHANGES            PIC S9(5).
016160      05  TC-MASTERS-ADDED             PIC S9(5).
016165      05  TC-MASTERS-DELETED           PIC S9(5).
016170  01  TC-RECORD-COUNTS REDEFINES TC-RECORD-COUNT-ENTRIES.
016180      05  TC-RECORD-COUNT              OCCURS 15 TIMES
016190                                                 PIC S9(5)   COMP-3.
020010*
020020*
020030  01  ET-EMPLOYEE-TRANSACTION-RECORD.
020040      05  ET-RECORD-CODE           PIC X(2).
020050      05  ET-UPDATE-CODE           PIC X(1).
020060          88  DELETE-TRANSACTION                VALUE '1'.
020070          88  ADD-TRANSACTION                   VALUE '2'.
020080          88  CHANGE-TRANSACTION                VALUE '3'.
020084          88  VALID-UPDATE-CODE                 VALUE '1'
020086                                                      '2'
020088                                                      '3'.
020090      05  ET-EMPLOYEE-NUMBER       PIC X(5).
020100      05  ET-LAST-NAME             PIC X(13).
020110      05  ET-FIRST-NAME            PIC X(12).
020120      05  ET-MIDDLE-INITIAL        PIC X(1).
020130      05  ET-PLANT-CODE            PIC X(2).
020140      05  ET-DEPARTMENT-NUMBER     PIC X(4).
020150      05  ET-HOURLY-RATE           PIC S9(2)V99.
020160      05  ET-HOURLY-RATE-X REDEFINES ET-HOURLY-RATE
020170                                   PIC X(4).
020180      05  FILLER                   PIC X(36).
025010*
025020*
025030  01  EM-EMPLOYEE-MASTER-WORK-AREA.
025034      05  EM-DELETE-FLAG           PIC X(1).
025036          88  MASTER-DELETED                    VALUE HIGH-VALUES.
025040      05  EM-RECORD-CODE           PIC X(2).
025060      05  EM-PLANT-CODE            PIC X(2).
025070      05  EM-DEPARTMENT-NUMBER     PIC X(4).
025080      05  EM-EMPLOYEE-NUMBER       PIC X(5).
025090      05  EM-LAST-NAME             PIC X(13).
025100      05  EM-FIRST-NAME            PIC X(12).
025110      05  EM-MIDDLE-INITIAL        PIC X(1).
025120      05  EM-HOURLY-RATE           PIC S9(2)V99.
025130      05  FILLER                   PIC X(30).
025140      05  EM-DATE-LAST-ACTIVITY    PIC 9(6).
030010*
030020*
030040  01  H1-HEADING-LINE-1.
030050      05  FILLER          PIC X(1).
030060      05  FILLER          PIC X(20)  VALUE 'INDEXED MASTER FILE '.
030070      05  FILLER          PIC X(20)  VALUE 'MAINTENANCE         '.
030080      05  FILLER          PIC X(20)  VALUE '                    '.
030090      05  FILLER          PIC X(20)  VALUE '                    '.
030100      05  FILLER          PIC X(20)  VALUE '            RUN DAT'.
030110      05  FILLER          PIC X(2)   VALUE 'E '.
030120      05  H1-MONTH        PIC 9(2).
030130      05  FILLER          PIC X(1)   VALUE '/'.
030140      05  H1-DAY          PIC 9(2).
030150      05  FILLER          PIC X(1)   VALUE '/'.
030160      05  H1-YEAR         PIC 9(2).
030170      05  FILLER          PIC X(22)  VALUE SPACES.
031010*
031020*
031030  01  H2-HEADING-LINE-2.
031040      05  FILLER          PIC X(1).
031050      05  FILLER          PIC X(20)  VALUE 'AUDIT/ERROR LIST    '.
031060      05  FILLER          PIC X(20)  VALUE '                    '.
031070      05  FILLER          PIC X(20)  VALUE '  ** EMPLOYEE MASTER'.
031080      05  FILLER          PIC X(20)  VALUE ' FILE **            '.
031090      05  FILLER          PIC X(20)  VALUE '                    '.
031100      05  FILLER          PIC X(6)   VALUE ' PAGE '.
031110      05  H2-PAGE-NBR     PIC ZZZ9.
031120      05  FILLER          PIC X(22)  VALUE SPACES.
032010*
032020*
032030  01  H3-HEADING-LINE-3.
032040      05  FILLER          PIC X(1).
032050      05  FILLER          PIC X(20)  VALUE 'RCD  UPDT   PLANT DE'.
032060      05  FILLER          PIC X(20)  VALUE 'PT  EMPL  ------EMP'.
032070      05  FILLER          PIC X(20)  VALUE 'LOYEE NAME------M'.
032080      05  FILLER          PIC X(20)  VALUE 'HOURLY    UPDATE'.
032090      05  FILLER          PIC X(20)  VALUE '                    '.
032100      05  FILLER          PIC X(20)  VALUE '                    '.
032110      05  FILLER          PIC X(12)  VALUE '            '.
```

Figure 4F.5. COBOL Coding: IN8MAINT program.

```
033010*
033020 01  H4-HEADING-LINE-4.
033030 01  H4-HEADING-LINE-4.
033040     05  FILLER                 PIC X(1).
033050     05  FILLER                 PIC X(20)   VALUE 'CODE CODE    CODE    N'.
033060     05  FILLER                 PIC X(20)   VALUE 'BR  NBR  LAST NAME  '.
033070     05  FILLER                 PIC X(20)   VALUE '     FIRST NAME  I '.
033080     05  FILLER                 PIC X(20)   VALUE ' RATE  ACTION ---'.
033090     05  FILLER                 PIC X(20)   VALUE '------ERROR MESSAGE'.
033100     05  FILLER                 PIC X(20)   VALUE '---------- '.
033110     05  FILLER                 PIC X(12)   VALUE '          '.
034010*
034020*
034030 01  DL-DETAIL-LINE.
034040     05  FILLER                 PIC X(1).
034050     05  FILLER                 PIC X(1)    VALUE SPACES.
034060     05  DL-RECORD-CODE         PIC X(2).
034070     05  FILLER                 PIC X(4)    VALUE SPACES.
034080     05  DL-UPDATE-CODE         PIC X(1).
034090     05  FILLER                 PIC X(4)    VALUE SPACES.
034100     05  DL-PLANT-CODE          PIC X(2).
034110     05  FILLER                 PIC X(4)    VALUE SPACES.
034120     05  DL-DEPARTMENT-NUMBER   PIC X(4).
034130     05  FILLER                 PIC X(1)    VALUE SPACES.
034140     05  DL-EMPLOYEE-NUMBER     PIC X(5).
034150     05  FILLER                 PIC X(2)    VALUE SPACES.
034160     05  DL-LAST-NAME           PIC X(13).
034170     05  FILLER                 PIC X(1)    VALUE SPACES.
034180     05  DL-FIRST-NAME          PIC X(12).
034190     05  FILLER                 PIC X(1)    VALUE SPACES.
034200     05  DL-MIDDLE-INITIAL      PIC X(1).
034210     05  FILLER                 PIC X(3)    VALUE SPACES.
034220     05  DL-HOURLY-RATE         PIC ZZ.99.
034230     05  DL-HOURLY-RATE-X REDEFINES DL-HOURLY-RATE
034240                                PIC X(5).
034250     05  FILLER                 PIC X(2)    VALUE SPACES.
034260     05  DL-UPDATE-ACTION       PIC X(8).
034270     05  FILLER                 PIC X(2)    VALUE SPACES.
034280     05  DL-ERROR-MSG           PIC X(33).
034290     05  FILLER                 PIC X(22)   VALUE SPACES.
035010*
035020*
035030 01  IE-I-O-ERROR-LINE REDEFINES DL-DETAIL-LINE.
035040     05  FILLER                 PIC X(1).
035050     05  FILLER                 PIC X(40).
035062     05  IE-FILE-STATUS-FLAG    PIC X(2).
035064     05  FILLER                 PIC X(1).
035066     05  IE-I-O-OPERATION-FLAG  PIC X(7).
035070     05  FILLER                 PIC X(1).
035080     05  IE-ERROR-KEY           PIC XXBXXXXBXXXXX.
035090     05  FILLER                 PIC X(4).
036010*
036020*
036030 01  TL-TOTAL-LINE.
036040     05  FILLER                 PIC X(1).
036050     05  FILLER                 PIC X(83)   VALUE SPACES.
036060     05  TL-COUNT-DESCRIPTION   PIC X(20).
036070     05  FILLER                 PIC X(1)    VALUE SPACES.
036080     05  TL-RECORD-COUNT        PIC ZZ,ZZ9.
036090     05  FILLER                 PIC X(22)   VALUE SPACES.
050010*
050020*
050030*
050040 PROCEDURE DIVISION.
050050*
050060*
050070 000-MAINTAIN-INDEXED-FILE.
050080*
050090     OPEN INPUT TRANSACTION-FILE
050100          I-O  INDEXED-MASTER-FILE
050120          OUTPUT REPORT-FILE.
050130     PERFORM 100-INITIALIZE-VARIABLE-FIELDS.
050135     PERFORM 800-READ-TRANSACTION-RECORD.
050140     PERFORM 200-UPDATE-MASTER-RECORD
050150         UNTIL TRANSACTION-END-OF-FILE.
050170     PERFORM 700-PRINT-REPORT-TOTALS.
050180     CLOSE TRANSACTION-FILE
050190           INDEXED-MASTER-FILE
050210           REPORT-FILE.
050220     STOP RUN.
100010*
100020*
100030 100-INITIALIZE-VARIABLE-FIELDS.
100040*
100050     MOVE 'NO ' TO WS-TRANSACTION-END-OF-FILE-SW
100055                   WS-PROGRAM-ABEND-SW.
100120     MOVE ZERO TO WS-PAGE-COUNT.
100130     ADD 1 WS-LINES-PER-PAGE GIVING WS-LINES-USED.
100140     ACCEPT WS-DATE-WORK FROM DATE.
100150     MOVE WS-MONTH TO H1-MONTH.
100160     MOVE WS-DAY TO H1-DAY.
100170     MOVE WS-YEAR TO H1-YEAR.
100190     MOVE SPACES TO DL-ERROR-MSG.
100200     PERFORM 110-ZERO-RECORD-COUNTS
100210         VARYING TC-SUBSCRIPT
100220         FROM 1
100230         BY 1
100240         UNTIL TC-SUBSCRIPT IS GREATER THAN TC-NUMBER-OF-ENTRIES.
110010*
110020*
110030 110-ZERO-RECORD-COUNTS.
110040*
110050     MOVE ZERO TO TC-RECORD-COUNT (TC-SUBSCRIPT).
200010*
200020*
200030 200-UPDATE-MASTER-RECORD.
200040*
200044     IF VALID-UPDATE-CODE
200046         PERFORM 810-READ-MASTER-RECORD.
200046*
200050     IF (ADD-TRANSACTION AND NO-RECORD-FOUND)
200060         PERFORM 230-ADD-MASTER-RECORD
200065*
200070     ELSE IF (CHANGE-TRANSACTION AND SUCCESSFUL-COMPLETION)
200080         PERFORM 240-CHANGE-MASTER-RECORD
200085*
200090     ELSE IF (DELETE-TRANSACTION AND SUCCESSFUL-COMPLETION)
200100         PERFORM 250-DELETE-MASTER-RECORD
200105*
200110     ELSE
200120         PERFORM 290-IDENTIFY-ERROR-TYPE.
200170*
200180     PERFORM 220-PRINT-AUDIT-ERROR-LINE.
200182*
200184     IF PROGRAM-ABEND
200186         PERFORM 900-ABORT-PROGRAM-RUN
200188     ELSE
200190         PERFORM 800-READ-TRANSACTION-RECORD.
220010*
220020*
220030 220-PRINT-AUDIT-ERROR-LINE.
220040*
220050     IF WS-LINES-USED IS NOT LESS THAN WS-LINES-PER-PAGE
220060         PERFORM 870-PRINT-REPORT-HEADINGS.
220070     MOVE ET-RECORD-CODE TO DL-RECORD-CODE.
220080     MOVE ET-UPDATE-CODE TO DL-UPDATE-CODE.
220090     MOVE ET-PLANT-CODE TO DL-PLANT-CODE.
220100     MOVE ET-DEPARTMENT-NUMBER TO DL-DEPARTMENT-NUMBER.
220110     MOVE ET-EMPLOYEE-NUMBER TO DL-EMPLOYEE-NUMBER.
220120     MOVE ET-LAST-NAME TO DL-LAST-NAME.
220130     MOVE ET-FIRST-NAME TO DL-FIRST-NAME.
220140     MOVE ET-MIDDLE-INITIAL TO DL-MIDDLE-INITIAL.
220150     IF ET-HOURLY-RATE IS NUMERIC
220160         MOVE ET-HOURLY-RATE TO DL-HOURLY-RATE
220170     ELSE
220180         MOVE ET-HOURLY-RATE-X TO DL-HOURLY-RATE-X.
220190     MOVE DL-DETAIL-LINE TO REPORT-LINE.
220200     MOVE 1 TO WS-LINE-SPACING.
220210     PERFORM 890-WRITE-REPORT-LINE.
220220     MOVE SPACES TO DL-DETAIL-LINE.
230010*
230020*
230030 230-ADD-MASTER-RECORD.
230040*
230070     ADD 1 TO TC-TOTAL-ADD-TRANS-READ.
230080     PERFORM 260-CREATE-MASTER-RECORD.
230084     PERFORM 850-WRITE-MASTER-RECORD.
230088     IF NOT PROGRAM-ABEND
230090         ADD 1 TO TC-ADD-TRANS-PROCESSED
230100         MOVE 'ADDED   ' TO DL-UPDATE-ACTION.
240010*
240020*
240030 240-CHANGE-MASTER-RECORD.
240040*
240150     ADD 1 TO TC-TOTAL-CHANGE-TRANS-READ.
240160     PERFORM 270-CHANGE-MASTER-FIELDS.
240170     PERFORM 855-REWRITE-MASTER-RECORD.
240180     IF NOT PROGRAM-ABEND
240190         ADD 1 TO TC-CHANGE-TRANS-PROCESSED
240200         MOVE 'CHANGED ' TO DL-UPDATE-ACTION.
250010*
250020*
250030 250-DELETE-MASTER-RECORD.
250040*
250150     ADD 1 TO TC-TOTAL-DELETE-TRANS-READ.
250160     PERFORM 860-DELETE-MASTER-RECORD.
250170     IF NOT PROGRAM-ABEND
250180         ADD 1 TO TC-DELETE-TRANS-PROCESSED
250190         MOVE 'DELETED ' TO DL-UPDATE-ACTION.
260010*
260020*
260030 260-CREATE-MASTER-RECORD.
260040*
260050     MOVE SPACES TO EM-EMPLOYEE-MASTER-WORK-AREA.
260060     MOVE '85' TO EM-RECORD-CODE.
260070     MOVE ET-PLANT-CODE TO EM-PLANT-CODE.
260080     MOVE ET-DEPARTMENT-NUMBER TO EM-DEPARTMENT-NUMBER.
260090     MOVE ET-EMPLOYEE-NUMBER TO EM-EMPLOYEE-NUMBER.
260100     MOVE ET-LAST-NAME TO EM-LAST-NAME.
260110     MOVE ET-FIRST-NAME TO EM-FIRST-NAME.
260120     MOVE ET-MIDDLE-INITIAL TO EM-MIDDLE-INITIAL.
260130     MOVE ET-HOURLY-RATE TO EM-HOURLY-RATE.
260140     MOVE WS-DATE-WORK TO EM-DATE-LAST-ACTIVITY.
270010*
270020*
270030 270-CHANGE-MASTER-FIELDS.
270040*
270050     IF ET-LAST-NAME IS EQUAL TO SPACES
270060         NEXT SENTENCE
270070     ELSE
270080         MOVE ET-LAST-NAME TO TO EM-LAST-NAME.
270090*
270100     IF ET-FIRST-NAME IS EQUAL TO SPACES
270110         NEXT SENTENCE
270120     ELSE
270130         MOVE ET-FIRST-NAME TO EM-FIRST-NAME.
270140*
270150     IF ET-MIDDLE-INITIAL IS EQUAL TO SPACES
270160         NEXT SENTENCE
270170     ELSE IF ET-MIDDLE-INITIAL IS EQUAL TO '$'
270180         MOVE SPACES TO EM-MIDDLE-INITIAL
270190     ELSE
270200         MOVE ET-MIDDLE-INITIAL TO EM-MIDDLE-INITIAL.
270210*
270220     IF ET-HOURLY-RATE-X IS EQUAL TO SPACES
270230         NEXT SENTENCE
270240     ELSE
270250         MOVE ET-HOURLY-RATE TO EM-HOURLY-RATE.
270260*
270270     MOVE WS-DATE-WORK TO EM-DATE-LAST-ACTIVITY.
290010*
290020*
290030 290-IDENTIFY-ERROR-TYPE.
290040*
290050     IF ADD-TRANSACTION
290060         ADD 1 TO TC-TOTAL-ADD-TRANS-READ
290070         ADD 1 TO TC-ADD-TRANS-REJECTED
290080         MOVE 'UNABLE ADD-MASTER ALREADY ON FILE' TO DL-ERROR-MSG
290090     ELSE IF CHANGE-TRANSACTION
290100         ADD 1 TO TC-TOTAL-CHANGE-TRANS-READ
290110         ADD 1 TO TC-CHANGE-TRANS-REJECTED
290120         MOVE 'UNABLE CHANGE-MASTER NOT ON FILE ' TO DL-ERROR-MSG
290130     ELSE IF DELETE-TRANSACTION
290140         ADD 1 TO TC-TOTAL-DELETE-TRANS-READ
290150         ADD 1 TO TC-DELETE-TRANS-REJECTED
290160         MOVE 'UNABLE DELETE-MASTER NOT ON FILE ' TO DL-ERROR-MSG
```

Figure 4F.5. (continued)

continued

```
290170        ELSE
290180            ADD 1 TO TC-TOTAL-ERROR-UPDATE-CODES
290190            MOVE 'UNABLE UPDATE-INVALID UPDATE CODE' TO DL-ERROR-MSG.
290200*
290210        MOVE 'REJECTED' TO DL-UPDATE-ACTION.
700010*
700020*
700030 700-PRINT-REPORT-TOTALS.
700040*
700050        PERFORM 870-PRINT-REPORT-HEADINGS.
700060        PERFORM 710-PRINT-TOTAL-LINE
700070            VARYING TC-SUBSCRIPT
700080            FROM 1
700090            BY 1
700100            UNTIL TC-SUBSCRIPT IS GREATER THAN TC-NUMBER-OF-ENTRIES.
710010*
710020*
710030 710-PRINT-TOTAL-LINE.
710040*
710050        MOVE TC-COUNT-DESCRIPTION (TC-SUBSCRIPT)
710060            TO TL-COUNT-DESCRIPTION.
710070        MOVE TC-RECORD-COUNT (TC-SUBSCRIPT) TO TL-RECORD-COUNT.
710080        MOVE TL-TOTAL-LINE TO REPORT-LINE.
710090        MOVE 1 TO WS-LINE-SPACING.
710100        PERFORM 890-WRITE-REPORT-LINE.
800010*
800020*
800030 800-READ-TRANSACTION-RECORD.
800040*
800070        READ TRANSACTION-FILE INTO ET-EMPLOYEE-TRANSACTION-RECORD
800080            AT END MOVE 'YES' TO WS-TRANSACTION-END-OF-FILE-SW.
800100*
800110        IF NOT TRANSACTION-END-OF-FILE
800120            ADD 1 TO TC-TOTAL-TRANS-READ.
810010*
810020*
810030 810-READ-MASTER-RECORD.
810040*
810041        MOVE ZEROS TO WS-FILE-STATUS-FLAG.
810042        MOVE ET-PLANT-CODE TO NK-PLANT-CODE.
810044        MOVE ET-DEPARTMENT-NUMBER TO NK-DEPARTMENT-NUMBER.
810046        MOVE ET-EMPLOYEE-NUMBER TO NK-EMPLOYEE-NUMBER.
810065        MOVE 'READ ' TO WS-I-O-OPERATION-FLAG.
810070        READ INDEXED-MASTER-FILE
810074            INTO EM-EMPLOYEE-MASTER-WORK-AREA
810076            INVALID KEY MOVE '23' TO WS-FILE-STATUS-FLAG.
810300*
810310        IF SUCCESSFUL-COMPLETION
810312            IF MASTER-DELETED
810314                MOVE '23' TO WS-FILE-STATUS-FLAG
810316            ELSE
810320                ADD 1 TO TC-MASTERS-READ
810320        ELSE
810330            NEXT SENTENCE.
850010*
850020*
850030 850-WRITE-MASTER-RECORD.
850040*
850041        MOVE ZEROS TO WS-FILE-STATUS-FLAG.
850045        MOVE 'WRITE ' TO WS-I-O-OPERATION-FLAG.
850050        WRITE INDEXED-MASTER-RECORD
850060            FROM EM-EMPLOYEE-MASTER-WORK-AREA
850065            INVALID KEY MOVE '24' TO WS-FILE-STATUS-FLAG.
850200*
850210        IF SUCCESSFUL-COMPLETION
850220            ADD 1 TO TC-MASTERS-ADDED
850230        ELSE
850240            MOVE 'YES' TO WS-PROGRAM-ABEND-SW.
855010*
855020*
855030 855-REWRITE-MASTER-RECORD.
855040*
```

```
855041        MOVE ZEROS TO WS-FILE-STATUS-FLAG.
855045        MOVE 'REWRITE' TO WS-I-O-OPERATION-FLAG.
855050        REWRITE INDEXED-MASTER-RECORD
855060            FROM EM-EMPLOYEE-MASTER-WORK-AREA
855070            INVALID KEY MOVE '23' TO WS-FILE-STATUS-FLAG.
855080*
855090        IF SUCCESSFUL-COMPLETION
855100            ADD 1 TO TC-MASTER-CHANGES
855110        ELSE
855120            MOVE 'YES' TO WS-PROGRAM-ABEND-SW.
860010*
860020*
860030 860-DELETE-MASTER-RECORD.
860040*
860041        MOVE ZEROS TO WS-FILE-STATUS-FLAG.
860045        MOVE 'REWRITE' TO WS-I-O-OPERATION-FLAG.
860048        MOVE HIGH-VALUE TO EM-DELETE-FLAG.
860050        REWRITE INDEXED-MASTER-RECORD
860055            FROM EM-EMPLOYEE-MASTER-WORK-AREA
860060            INVALID KEY MOVE '23' TO WS-FILE-STATUS-FLAG.
860070*
860080        IF SUCCESSFUL-COMPLETION
860090            ADD 1 TO TC-MASTERS-DELETED
860100        ELSE
860110            MOVE 'YES' TO WS-PROGRAM-ABEND-SW.
870010*
870020*
870030 870-PRINT-REPORT-HEADINGS.
870040*
870050        ADD 1 TO WS-PAGE-COUNT.
870060        MOVE WS-PAGE-COUNT TO H2-PAGE-NBR.
870070        MOVE H1-HEADING-LINE-1 TO REPORT-LINE.
870080        PERFORM 880-WRITE-REPORT-TOP-LINE.
870090        MOVE H2-HEADING-LINE-2 TO REPORT-LINE.
870100        MOVE 1 TO WS-LINE-SPACING.
870110        PERFORM 890-WRITE-REPORT-LINE.
870120        MOVE H3-HEADING-LINE-3 TO REPORT-LINE.
870130        MOVE 2 TO WS-LINE-SPACING.
870140        PERFORM 890-WRITE-REPORT-LINE.
870150        MOVE H4-HEADING-LINE-4 TO REPORT-LINE.
870160        MOVE 1 TO WS-LINE-SPACING.
870170        PERFORM 890-WRITE-REPORT-LINE.
870180        MOVE SPACES TO REPORT-LINE.
870190        PERFORM 890-WRITE-REPORT-LINE.
880010*
880020*
880030 880-WRITE-REPORT-TOP-LINE.
880040*
880050        WRITE REPORT-LINE
880060            AFTER ADVANCING PAGE.
880070        MOVE 1 TO WS-LINES-USED.
890010*
890020*
890030 890-WRITE-REPORT-LINE.
890040*
890050        WRITE REPORT-LINE
890060            AFTER ADVANCING WS-LINE-SPACING.
890070        ADD WS-LINE-SPACING TO WS-LINES-USED.
900010*
900020*
900030 900-ABORT-PROGRAM-RUN.
900040*
900042        MOVE WS-FILE-STATUS-FLAG TO IE-FILE-STATUS-FLAG.
900044        MOVE WS-I-O-OPERATION-FLAG TO IE-I-O-OPERATION-FLAG.
900046        MOVE NK-INDEXED-KEY TO IE-ERROR-KEY.
900050        MOVE 'ABORTED ' TO DL-UPDATE-ACTION.
900055        MOVE 'I-O ERROR OCCURRED' TO DL-ERROR-MSG.
900060        MOVE DL-DETAIL-LINE TO REPORT-LINE.
900070        MOVE 3 TO WS-LINE-SPACING.
900080        PERFORM 890-WRITE-REPORT-LINE.
900090        MOVE SPACES TO DL-DETAIL-LINE.
900130        MOVE 'YES' TO WS-TRANSACTION-END-OF-FILE-SW.
```

Figure 4F.5. (continued)

record. However, in this program the first condition—record-already-exists—should not happen because the logic of the 200-UPDATE-MASTER-RECORD module does not allow this module to be entered if the record already exists. Only the second condition—boundary violation—should possibly occur.

Therefore, the INVALID KEY phrase sets the WS-FILE-STATUS-FLAG to the code (24) for boundary violation of an indexed file.

855-REWRITE-MASTER-RECORD

When the ACCESS MODE IS RANDOM and a REWRITE statement is issued, the INVALID KEY condition is caused when the record that is being rewritten does not already exist on the indexed file. If this occurs in this module, the WS-FILE-STATUS-FLAG is set to the respective file status code value (23). (Actually this condition should never occur in this program, however, because of the preliminary checking that was done in the 200-UPDATE-MASTER-RECORD module.)

860-DELETE-MASTER-RECORD

Because the DELETE statement is not available, record deletion is accomplished by rewriting the record after its delete-flag has been set to HIGH-VALUE.

Summary

Topic 4-A Indexed File-Maintenance Programming Specifications

An indexed master file can be updated by either sequential or random access. Random access typically provides the most efficient processing.

When the programmer/analyst is specifying a file-maintenance program, he or she must choose appropriate handling for the following design alternatives: transaction data validation, audit/error list treatment, error-record handling, transaction file sorting, multiple transactions for the same master record, change-transaction modifiable fields, change-transaction formatting, change-to-null requirements, and transaction correspondence checking.

The following items that relate specifically to indexed file maintenance must also be considered: access mode (*random* or *sequential*), transaction file sequencing, abnormal program termination due to an unrecoverable I-O error, and record counts.

Topic 4-B Indexed File-Maintenance Program Design

The **file status data-item** is used for recording the status of input-output operations. It is updated by the system after each I-O operation. When the programmer is updating an indexed master file on a random basis, the general processing logic is to (1) locate the status of the record key on the master file (already on file or not on file) and (2) make the appropriate update, unless an interfile error condition has been detected. An interfile error condition would be either (a) an add transaction with the corresponding master record already on file or (b) a change or delete transaction with the corresponding master record not on file.

When the programmer is designing the program, he or she must allocate FILE SECTION areas for the input transaction record and the I-O master record. A master work area in which master records are processed should be defined in the WORKING-STORAGE SECTION.

Topic 4-C Indexed File-Maintenance Program Coding

This topic presents detailed program coding for the INDMAINT program.

Topic 4-D Creation of an Indexed File

A separate program run is required to **create**, or **load**, the indexed file. This run can be handled by either a utility or a custom-written COBOL program.

Topic 4-E Backup and Reorganization of an Indexed File

Because an indexed file does not yield a separate prior-generation copy for file-backup purposes, a separate program processing step to **backup** the master file must be provided. This backup step, coupled with a re-creation step, will handle indexed file **reorganization**.

Programming Assignments

4-1: Indexed General Ledger Master File Maintenance

Program description

An indexed general ledger master file is to be randomly updated with input general ledger transaction records. The input transaction file has been validated in a prior program step. An audit/error list is to be produced.

Input file

    General ledger transaction file

Input-output file

    General ledger master file   Key field = General ledger account number

Output file

    Audit/error list

Record formats

    General ledger master record (Record code "LM")
    General ledger transaction record (Record code "45")
    Audit/error list

General ledger master record

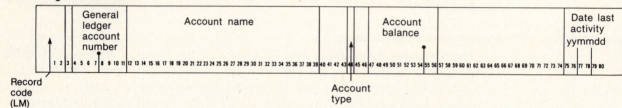

General ledger transaction record

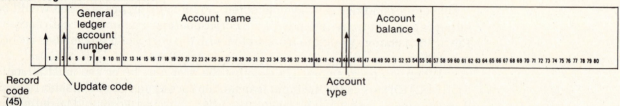

Audit/error list

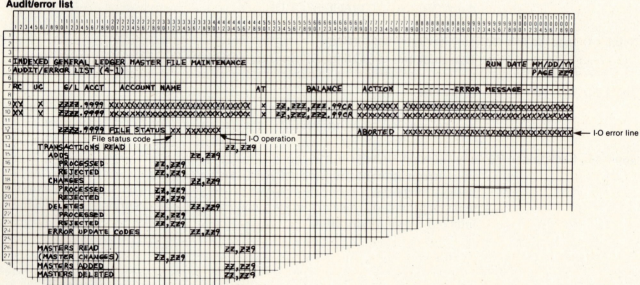

Program operations

A. Read each input general ledger update-transaction record.

   1. Validate each transaction to ensure that it contains one of the following update codes:

      A (Add)

        C (Change)

        D (Delete)

B. Create a master record for each valid add transaction.

  1. Store the run date as the date-last-activity in the master record.

C. If one or more of the following fields of a valid change transaction are not blank, change the master record fields accordingly.

  —Account name

  —Account type

  —Account balance

  1. Store the run date as the date-last-activity in the master record.

D. Delete the master record for each valid delete transaction.

E. Tally master record counts as shown on the audit/error list print chart.

F. Print the audit/error list as shown on the audit/error list print chart.

  1. Single-space each detail line (but double-space between the last heading and the first detail line on each page).

  2. Skip to a new page before printing the record-count totals.

  3. Provide for a line span of 50 lines per page.

G. Identify the following error conditions.

Error condition	Error message
Add transaction but master already on file	UNABLE ADD-MASTER ALREADY ON FILE
Change transaction but master not on file	UNABLE CHANGE-MASTER NOT ON FILE
Delete transaction but master not on file	UNABLE DELETE-MASTER NOT ON FILE
Invalid update code	INVALID UPDATE CODE
Input-output error	FATAL I-O ERROR HAS OCCURRED

Assignment 4-1   Option 1

  Write a program to create the indexed general ledger master file.

Assignment 4-1   Option 2

  Write a program to back up the indexed general ledger master file.

4-2: Indexed Vendor Master File Maintenance

Program description

  An indexed vendor master file is to be randomly updated with input vendor-transaction records. The input transaction file has been validated and sorted in a prior program step. An audit/error list is to be produced.

Input file

  Vendor-transaction file   Key fields = Vendor number (major)

                                 Date due (intermediate)

                                 Update code (minor)

Input-output file

  Vendor master file   Key fields = Vendor number (major)

                                 Date due (minor)

Output file

  Audit/error list

Record formats

  Vendor master record (Record code "VM")

  Vendor-transaction record (Record code "36")

  Audit/error list

Vendor master record

Record code (VM)

Vendor transaction record

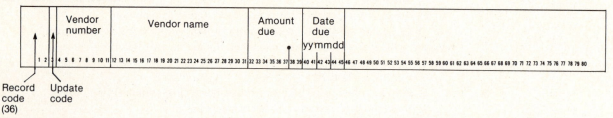

Record code (36) Update code

Audit/error list

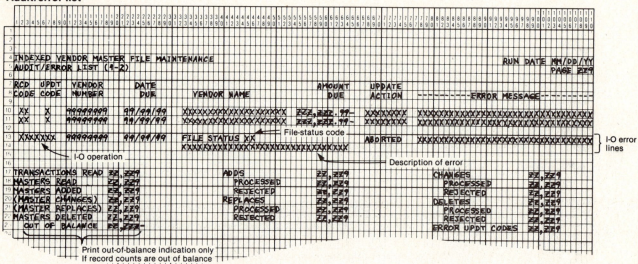

Print out-of-balance indication only if record counts are out of balance

Program operations

A. Read each input vendor update-transaction record.

  1. Validate each transaction to ensure that it contains one of the following update codes:

    A (Add)

    C (Change)

    D (Delete)

    R (Replace)

  2. **Do not write or rewrite the vendor master record until all transaction records for that record have been processed.**

B. Create a master record for each valid add transaction.

  1. Store the run date as the date-last-activity in the master record.

C. If one or more of the following fields of a valid change transaction are not blank, change the master record fields accordingly.

  —Vendor name

  —Amount due (increment)

  1. Store the run date as the date-last-activity in the master record.

  2. Before printing the change-transaction record on the audit/error list, print a line that shows the master record contents before the change.

D. For a replacement transaction, replace the master record fields accordingly.
   —Vendor name
   —Amount due (replace)
   1. Store the run date as the date-last-activity in the master record.
   2. Before printing the replacement transaction record on the audit/error list, print a line that shows the master record contents before the replacement.
E. Delete the master record for each valid delete transaction.
   1. Correspondence check the first six characters of the vendor name on the transaction record with the first six characters of the vendor name on the master record.
   2. Before printing the delete transaction record on the audit/error list, print a line that shows the master record contents before the deletion.
F. Tally master record counts as shown on the audit/error list print chart.
G. Print the audit/error list as shown on the audit/error list print chart.
   1. On the master-record contents line for change, delete, and replace transactions, print the word "MASTER" in the update-action field of the audit line.
   2. Single-space between master-record contents and transaction-record audit lines.
   3. Double-space between transactions.
   4. Provide for a line span of 50 lines per page (but do not break lines for a transaction or the record-count totals between pages).
H. Identify the following error conditions.

Error condition	Error message
Add transaction but master already on file	UNABLE ADD-MASTER ALREADY ON FILE
Change transaction but master not on file	UNABLE CHANGE-MASTER NOT ON FILE
Replace transaction but master not on file	UNABLE REPLACE-MASTER NOT ON FILE
Delete transaction but master not on file	UNABLE DELETE-MASTER NOT ON FILE
Invalid update code	INVALID UPDATE CODE
Delete transaction but fails correspondence check	UNABLE DELETE-FAILS CORR CHECK
Transaction file out of sequence	TRANSACTION FILE OUT OF SEQUENCE
Input-output error	FATAL I-O ERROR HAS OCCURRED

Assignment 4-2   Option 1
   Write a program to create the indexed-vendor master file.
Assignment 4-2   Option 2
   Write a program to back up the indexed-vendor master file.

4-3: Indexed Customer Master File Maintenance

Program description

An indexed customer master file is to be randomly updated with input customer-transaction records. The input transaction file has been sorted in a prior program step. An audit/error list is to be produced.

Input file

> Customer-transaction file   Key field = Region code (major)
> Territory number
> Customer account number
> Update code
> Record code (minor)

Input-output file

> Customer master file   Key fields = Region code (major)
> Territory number (intermediate)
> Customer account number (minor)

Output files

> Customer master file (updated)
> Audit/error list

Record formats

> Customer master record (Record code "CM")
> Customer add-transaction record (Record code "47" and "48")
> Customer change/delete-transaction record (Record code "49")
> Audit/error list

Customer master record

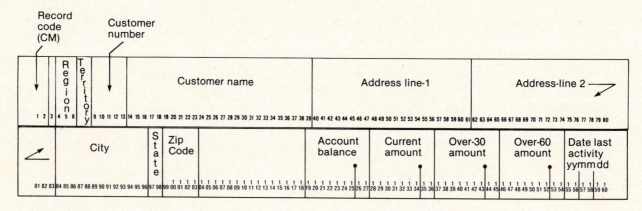

Customer add transaction record (record code 47)

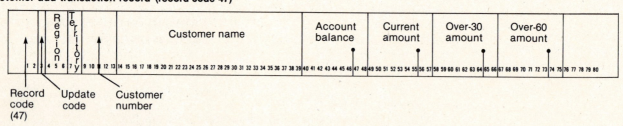

Customer add transaction record (record code 48)

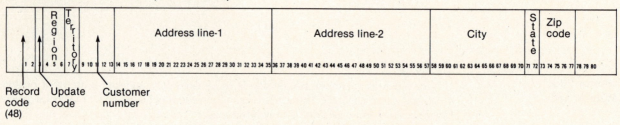

Customer change/delete transaction record (record code 49)

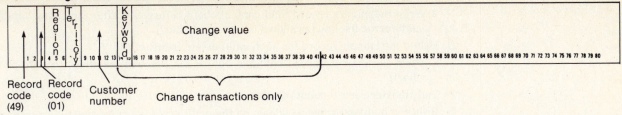

Audit/error list

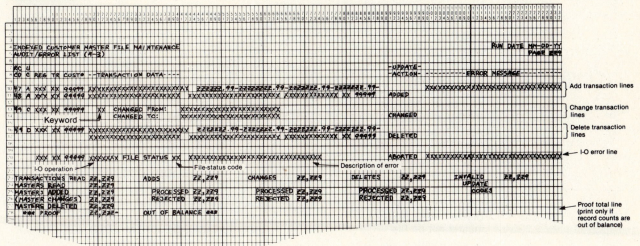

Program operations

A. Read each input customer update-transaction record.

  1. Validate each transaction to ensure that it contains one of the following update codes:

     1 (Delete)

     2 (Add)

     3 (Change)

  2. **Do not write or rewrite the customer master record until all transaction records for that record have been processed.**

B. Create a master record for each valid add transaction.

  1. Validate to ensure that both a code "47" and a code "48" record are present for each add transaction. If one is absent, do not add the master record.

  2. Store the run date as the date-last-activity in the master record.

C. Each change transaction will contain a keyword in the keyword field. The change value **of the proper length** to which the corresponding master field is to be changed will be **left-justified** in the change-to area.

Keyword	Field to be changed
CN	Customer name
A1	Address line-1
A2	Address line-2
CT	City
ST	State
ZP	Zip code
BL	Account balance
CU	Current amount
30	Over-30 amount
60	Over-60 amount

1. Store the run date as the date-last-activity in the master record.
2. Print the master-record field contents both before and after the change on the audit/error list line (as shown on the print chart).

D. Delete the master record for each valid delete transaction.
1. Print the master record contents before the deletion (as shown on the print chart).

E. Tally master record counts as shown on the audit/error list print chart.

F. Print the audit/error list as shown on the audit/error list print chart.
1. Provide for a line span of 50 lines per page (but do not break lines for a transaction or the record-count totals between pages).

G. Identify the following error conditions.

Error condition	Error message
Add transaction but master already on file	UNABLE ADD-MASTER ALREADY ON FILE
Add transaction but record code "47" missing	UNABLE ADD-CODE 47 MISSING
Add transaction but record code "48" missing	UNABLE ADD-CODE 48 MISSING
Change transaction but master not on file	UNABLE CHANGE-MASTER NOT ON FILE
Delete transaction but master not on file	UNABLE DELETE-MASTER NOT ON FILE
Invalid update code	INVALID UPDATE CODE
Change transaction with invalid keyword	UNABLE CHANGE-INVALID KEYWORD
Transaction file out of sequence	TRANSACTION FILE OUT OF SEQUENCE
Input-output error	FATAL I-O ERROR HAS OCCURRED

Assignment 4-3   Option 1
Write a program to create the indexed customer master file.

Assignment 4-3   Option 2
Write a program to back up the indexed customer master file.

CHAPTER 5

DESIGNING AND CODING A
RELATIVE FILE-MAINTENANCE PROGRAM

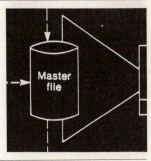

DESIGNING AND CODING A RELATIVE FILE-MAINTENANCE PROGRAM

In comparison to sequential and indexed master files, relative files are seldom used. There are two main reasons for this.

First, actual record key values are frequently not directly suitable for organization by relative record number. A relative file consists of a serial string of areas, each of which is capable of holding a logical record and each of which is identified by a relative record number. If the key values are not consecutive, there will be unoccupied—hence wasted—record area slots within the file. As an example, values of multiple-field keys tend to have a "stair-step" rather than consecutive distribution. Such interrupted distributions of key values usually produce enough wasted slots to prohibit a directly addressed relative organization. Relative organization is also not directly compatible to key-field values that contain alphabetic or other nonnumeric characters.

Second, by the time relative file syntax was introduced into the 1968 COBOL standards, direct file-processing language extensions had already been incorporated into many COBOL compilers. Because the extensions could be designed specifically for the architecture of each vendor's own disk hardware, it was usually more efficient for programmers to use the direct file extensions rather than the ANS relative file standards.

As disk-access speeds have improved, the attractiveness of relative file I-O processing efficiency tends to be outweighed by the inflexibility of the key value requirements. Currently, therefore, indexed organization is generally selected in preference to both relative and compiler-dependent direct files.

Nevertheless, relative file organization is a good choice for a single-field numeric key that does not contain large or frequent gaps in assigned key values. It will provide faster random processing because there is no index lookup and slightly more efficient sequential access since there are no overflow records. On the one hand, space utilization on the direct-access device will be improved because no index records are required. On the other hand, every unused key value will cause wasted space.

When discussing relative and direct files, it is important to distinguish between directly addressed and indirectly addressed files. When record key values contain large gaps or alphanumeric characters but the processing-speed advantages of a relative or direct file are still desired, a randomizing algorithm must be employed to maintain an indirectly addressed file.

Although indirectly addressed direct files were sometimes used for certain applications in the past, it is rare to see one coded today with COBOL relative file-processing syntax.

Indirectly addressed files raise complexities in the choice of a suitable randomizing algorithm and in the placement and location of records with synonym

File creation (formatting)

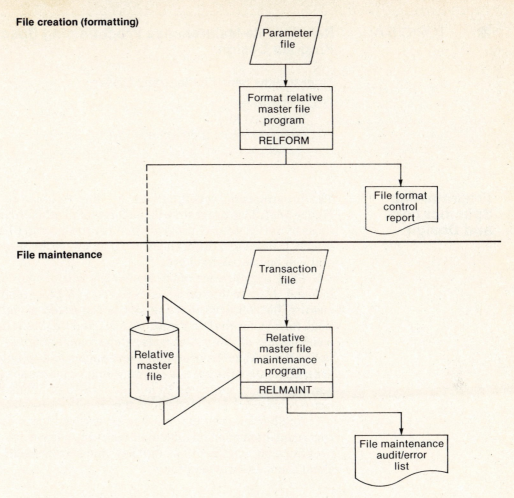

File maintenance

Figure 5.1. Typical system flowchart: Relative file maintenance.

key values. Moreover, sequential-processing requirements for reports and other outputs will necessitate sorting of the records.

The general logic for a directly addressed relative master file-maintenance program can be almost identical to that of an indexed file. A system flowchart for relative master file maintenance is shown in Figure 5.1. The only difference between this flowchart and its indexed file counterpart, which is presented in Chapter 4, is that a reorganization step is not required for a directly organized relative file. This is because a dedicated record slot is allocated for each key value.

Topics 5-A and 5-B of this chapter cover the programming of a directly addressed relative file-maintenance program, which we will call RELMAINT, for **rel**ative master file **maint**enance. The employee master file application that is used with the sequential and indexed file-maintenance program models will again be coded. File creation for a relative file requires special planning and is covered in Topic 5-C. Topic 5-D presents indirectly addressed file concepts.

Programming Specifications and Design

Program Design
    Embedded Key
    Deleted-Record Indication

Programming Specifications and Design

The programming specifications for this RELMAINT program are shown in Figure 5A.1. This program will perform application functions that are similar to those of the INDMAINT program that is presented in Chapter 4. Those few areas in which there are differences are shaded on the programming specifications and will be contrasted here.

First, organization of the master file will, of course, be relative rather than indexed. Also, so that this master file may be processed as a directly addressed relative file, observe that the key is composed of only the employee-number field. Remember that, in the SEQMAINT and INDMAINT programs, the key was a combination of the plant-code, department-number, and employee-number fields. It would not be practical to use such a multiple-field key for a directly addressed relative file because there would be too many gaps between plant codes and department numbers. In addition, the alphanumeric plant code would require conversion to a numeric value.

Another concern that applies to relative files is the range of key values. A record location must be allocated for every permissible key value. Notice in the programming specifications that key values from 00001 to 20000 (20,000 record slots) are to be provided for.

Program Design

With relative files, there are two particular design aspects that should be carefully considered: (1) whether or not to embed the key field in the record, and (2) the method of record deletion.

Embedded Key

With sequential and indexed organization, the key *must* be embedded as a data-item within the logical record. With relative files, however, it is not necessary for the key field to be contained within the record. The key value can be implicitly determined by its relative location within the file.

However, even though not required, it is usually a good idea to define the key field within the record. Therefore, an embedded key has been specified for the RELMAINT program. The amount of space that the key field consumes is usually trivial although it is often helpful for debugging and recovery purposes to have the key value present within the logical record. Recognize, however, that if the relative file is indirectly addressed (as will be discussed in Topic D of this chapter), it *is* necessary for the record to have a key field that is embedded in the record.

Deleted-Record Indication

Delete-flag methods of indicating record deletion are often used because most early COBOL compilers did not permit actual physical deletion of indexed or relative records. With 1974 ANS COBOL, records *can* be physically deleted so it is not necessary to use a delete-flag.

Even so, because of certain compiler-dependent file-creation requirements, delete-flags are still commonly specified for records of a relative file. As

System flowchart:

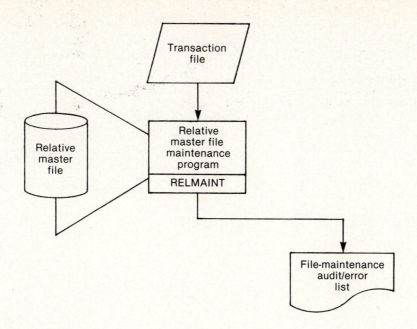

Record layouts:

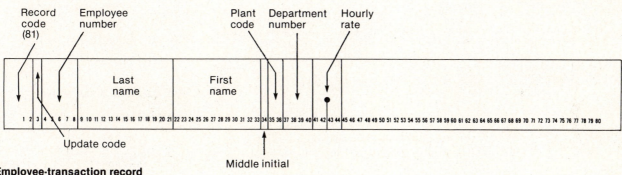

Employee-transaction record

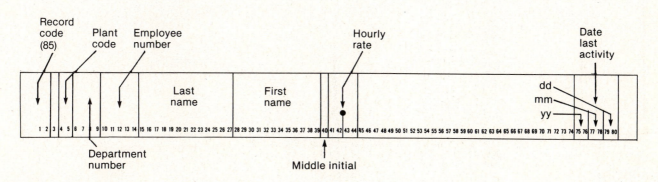

Employee master record

continued

Figure 5A.1. Programming specifications: RELMAINT program.

Print chart:

H1-HEADING-LINE-1 →
H2-HEADING-LINE-2 →
H3-HEADING-LINE-3 →
H4-HEADING-LINE-4 →
DL-DETAIL-LINE →
IE-I-O-ERROR-LINE →
TL-TOTAL-LINE →

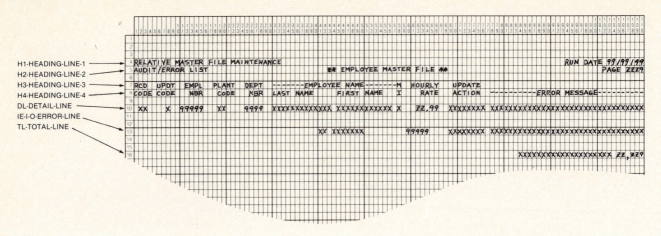

Printer output example:

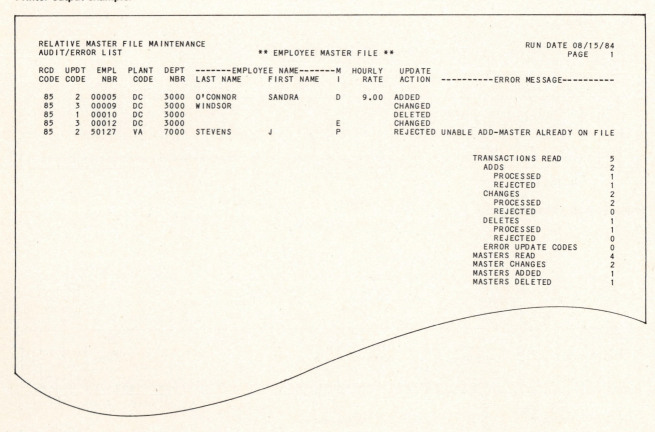

```
RELATIVE MASTER FILE MAINTENANCE                                        RUN DATE 08/15/84
AUDIT/ERROR LIST                      ** EMPLOYEE MASTER FILE **             PAGE    1

RCD  UPDT  EMPL  PLANT  DEPT  -------EMPLOYEE NAME-------M  HOURLY  UPDATE
CODE CODE   NBR  CODE   NBR   LAST NAME     FIRST NAME   I   RATE   ACTION   ----------ERROR MESSAGE----------

 85   2   00005   DC    3000  O'CONNOR      SANDRA       D   9.00   ADDED
 85   3   00009   DC    3000  WINDSOR                                CHANGED
 85   1   00010   DC    3000                                         DELETED
 85   3   00012   DC    3000                             E           CHANGED
 85   2   50127   VA    7000  STEVENS       J            P           REJECTED UNABLE ADD-MASTER ALREADY ON FILE

                                                              TRANSACTIONS READ        5
                                                                 ADDS                  2
                                                                    PROCESSED          1
                                                                    REJECTED           1
                                                                 CHANGES               2
                                                                    PROCESSED          2
                                                                    REJECTED           0
                                                                 DELETES               1
                                                                    PROCESSED          1
                                                                    REJECTED           0
                                                                 ERROR UPDATE CODES    0
                                                              MASTERS READ             4
                                                              MASTER CHANGES           2
                                                              MASTERS ADDED            1
                                                              MASTERS DELETED          1
```

Figure 5A.1. (continued)

Program name:	Relative Master File Maintenance	Program ID:	RELMAINT

Program description

The employee master file is to be updated by a transaction file containing add, change, and delete transactions. The transaction file has been validated in a prior program run. An audit/error list is printed that documents update actions taken. At the end of the audit/error list, record count totals are printed.

Input file

Employee update–transaction file
    Organization = Sequential

Input–output file

Employee master file
    Organization = Relative
    Relative key = Employee number
                   (values from 00001 to 20000)

Output file

Employee master file–maintenance audit/error list

Program operations

A. Read each input employee update–transaction record.
    1. Validate each transaction to ensure that it contains an update code of either "1" (delete transaction), "2" (add transaction), or "3" (change transaction).
        a. If the update–code field is not valid, print the contents of the transaction record on the audit/error list together with an update action of "REJECTED" and an error message of "UNABLE UPDATE–INVALID UPDATE CODE".
        b. Tally the record in the "ERROR UPDATE CODES" category.
        c. Do no further processing for the transaction record.
B. For each add transaction, do the following processing:
    1. Attempt to read an active master record with an equal key value. (If the read operation causes a fatal I–O error, print an I–O error line on the audit/error list and terminate the program run as discussed in Point F, below.)
    2. If an active master record with an equal key value is found, it means that a master record is already on the file.
        a. If the master record is already on file, print the contents of the transaction record on the audit/error

list together with an update action of "REJECTED" and an error message of "UNABLE ADD–MASTER ALREADY ON FILE".
        b. Tally the transaction record in the "ADDS REJECTED" category.
        c. Do no further processing for the transaction record.
    3. If an active master record is not already on file, create a master record from the transaction record as follows:
        a. Move each of the following fields from the input transaction record to the master record:
        –Plant code
        –Department number
        –Employee number
        –Last name
        –First name
        –Middle initial
        –Hourly rate
        b. Set the record–code field of the master record to "85".
        c. Set the date–last–activity field of the master record to the current run date.
        d. Set all other positions of the master record to blank spaces.
        e. Tally the transaction record in the "ADDS PROCESSED" category.
        f. Print the contents of the transaction record on the audit/error list together with an update action of "ADDED".
        g. Write the newly created master record to the employee master file.
        h. If the write operation is not successful, print an I–0 error line on the audit/error list and terminate the program run as discussed in Point F, below.
C. For each change transaction, do the following processing:
    1. Attempt to read an active master record with an equal key value. (If the read operation causes a fatal I–0 error, print an I–0 error line on the audit/error list and terminate the program run as discussed in Point F, below.)
    2. If an active master record with an equal key value is not located, it means that the corresponding master record is not on the file.
        a. If the master record is not on file, print the contents of the transaction record on the audit/error list

Figure 5A.1. (continued)

continued

together with an update action of
"REJECTED" and an error message of
"UNABLE CHANGE—MASTER NOT ON FILE."

  b. Tally the transaction record in the
"CHANGES REJECTED" category.

  c. Do no further processing for the
transaction record.

3. If an active master record is on file,
update the master record from the
transaction record as follows:

  a. Check each of the following fields of
the transaction record to determine
if it contains an entry:
—Plant code
—Department number
—Last name
—First name
—Hourly rate
For each field that contains an entry,
move it to the corresponding field of
the master record.

  b. Check the middle—initial field of the
transaction record to determine if it
contains an entry.
If the entry is a "$", move a blank
space to the middle—initial field of
the master record.
If it contains an entry other than a
"$", move the contents of the middle-
initial field of the transaction
record to the master record.

  c. If any of the above seven fields of the
master record are changed, set the
date—last—activity field of the
master record to the current run date.

  d. Tally the transaction record in the
"CHANGES PROCESSED" category.

  e. Print the contents of the transaction
record on the audit/error list
together with an update action of
"CHANGED"

  f. Rewrite the updated master record to
the employee master file.

  g. If the rewrite operation is not
successful, print an I—0 error line on
the audit/error list and terminate
the program run as discussed in Point
F, below.

D. For each delete transaction, do the following
processing:

  1. Attempt to read an active master record
with an equal key value. (If the read
operation causes a fatal I—0 error, print
an I—0 error line on the audit/error list
and terminate the program run as
discussed in Point F, below.)

  2. If an active master record with an equal
key value is not located, it means that
the corresponding master record is not on
the file.

    a. If the master record is not on file,
print the contents of the transaction
record on the audit/error list
together with an update action of
"REJECTED" and an error message of
"UNABLE DELETE—MASTER NOT ON FILE".

    b. Tally the transaction record in the
"DELETES REJECTED" category.

    c. Do no further processing for the
transaction record.

3. If an active corresponding master record
is on file, delete the master record from
the employee master file.

  a. Set the Employee number field to
zeros. Set the remainder of the record
to spaces. Rewrite this "dummy"
record to delete the master record.

  b. Print the contents of the transaction
record on the audit/error list
together with an update action of
"DELETED".

  c. Tally the transaction record in the
"DELETES PROCESSED" category.

  d. If the rewrite operation is not
successful, print an I—0 error line on
the audit/error list and terminate
the program run as discussed in Point
F, below.

E. Tally master records as follows:

  1. Tally each master file record for which
an attempted read was made in the
"MASTERS READ" category.

  2. Tally each master record added in the
"MASTERS ADDED" category.

  3. Tally each master record deleted in the
"MASTERS DELETED" category.

F. If an I—0 error (a fatal I—0 error during a
read or rewrite operation) occurs, print an
error line on the audit/error list and
terminate the program run. The error line
should contain the following:

  1. The file status code value.

  2. A description of the I—0 operation
("READ" or "REWRITE").

  3. The record key being accessed when
the I—0 error occurred (employee
number).

  4. An update action description of
"ABORTED".

  5. An error message of "I—0 ERROR OCCURRED".

G. Headings are to be printed on each page of the
audit/error list. After 50 lines have been
used on a report page and a new audit/error
line is to be printed, the forms should be
advanced to the next page and the report
headings printed. Also, the report page is to
be advanced and headings are to be printed
immediately before printing the total lines.

  1. The run date is to be obtained from the
operating system and printed on the first
heading line in accordance with the
format shown on the print chart.

  2. The page number is to be incremented each
time the heading is printed and displayed
on the second heading line in accordance
with the format shown on the print chart.

H. Line spacing for the audit/error list is to be
handled as follows:

  1. The first detail or total line after the
page headings is to be double—spaced from
the last heading line.

Figure 5A.1. (continued)

2. Second and successive detail lines are to be single-spaced from one another.
3. The report totals are to be printed on a new report page after the headings have been printed. Total lines are to be single-spaced from one another.

4. Should I-0 error lines be required, the first one is to be triple-spaced from the last detail line. Successive input/output error lines should be single-spaced from one another.

Figure 5A.1. (continued)

was discussed in Topic F of Chapter 4, a dedicated delete-flag field can be established. Another technique is to use the key field as the delete-flag. Since a key field is not actually required in a relative record, it need not contain the actual record slot value. Hence an approach that is sometimes used to denote functional record deletion is to set the key field to a value of zero, as will be done in this RELMAINT program.

A structure chart for the RELMAINT program appears in Figure 5A.2.

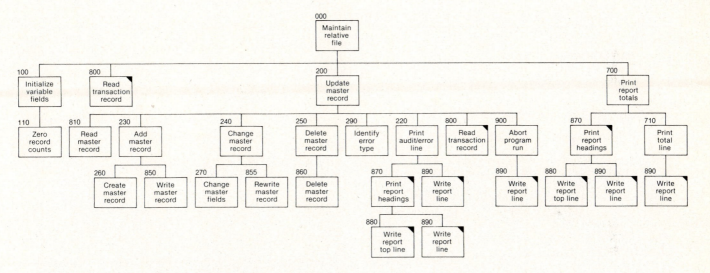

Figure 5A.2. Structure chart: RELMAINT program.

■ TOPIC 5-B: **Relative File-Maintenance Program Coding**

ENVIRONMENT DIVISION Entries

DATA DIVISION Entries
    FILE SECTION Entries
    WORKING-STORAGE SECTION Entries
        Program switches
        RELATIVE KEY field
        EM-EMPLOYEE-MASTER-WORK-AREA definition
        Audit/error report line entries

PROCEDURE DIVISION Entries
    000-MAINTAIN-RELATIVE-FILE
    200-UPDATE-MASTER-RECORD
    250-DELETE-MASTER-RECORD
    810-READ-MASTER-RECORD

850-WRITE-MASTER-RECORD
855-REWRITE-MASTER-RECORD
860-DELETE-MASTER-RECORD

The COBOL syntax for relative file processing is summarized in Figure 5B.1. The boxed entries are used for special retrieval purposes and are covered in Chapter 6.

The RELMAINT program coding appears in Figure 5B.2. Except for those aspects that differ because of the file organization and record deletion logic, the coding is almost the same as the coding for the INDMAINT program. The coding that differs is shaded on the program listing and will be reviewed here.

ENVIRONMENT DIVISION Entries

The file configuration for this program is the same as for the INDMAINT program except that the master file has been named RELATIVE-MASTER-FILE to describe its organization method.

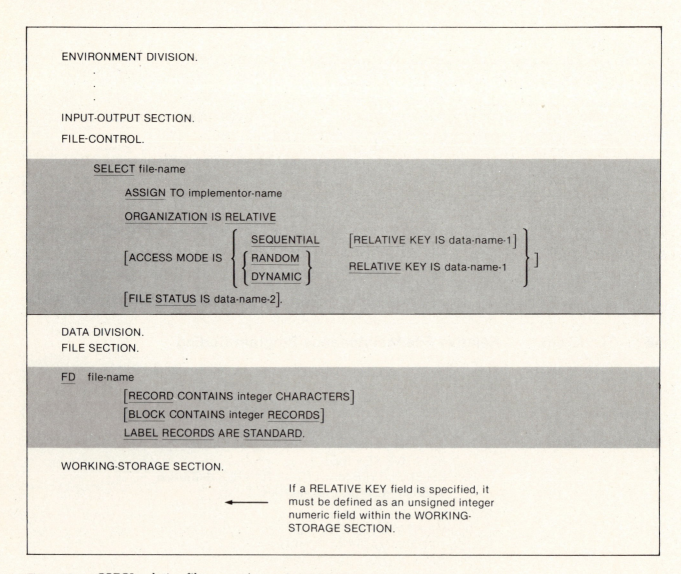

Figure 5B.1. COBOL relative file-processing syntax summary.

```
PROCEDURE DIVISION.

     OPEN ⎧ INPUT file-name  ⎫
          ⎨ I-O file-name   ...⎬ .
          ⎩ OUTPUT file-name ⎭

     START file-name

            ⎡          ⎧ EQUAL TO      ⎫          ⎤
            ⎢          ⎪ =             ⎪          ⎥
            ⎢          ⎪ GREATER THAN  ⎪          ⎥
            ⎢ KEY IS   ⎨ >             ⎬ data-name⎥
            ⎢          ⎪ NOT LESS THAN ⎪          ⎥
            ⎣          ⎩ NOT <         ⎭          ⎦

            [ INVALID KEY imperative-statement ] .
```

Sequential retrieval:
```
READ file-name [ NEXT ] RECORD
     [ INTO identifier ]
     [ AT END imperative-statement ] .
```

Random retrieval:
```
READ file-name RECORD
     [ INTO identifier ]
     [ INVALID KEY imperative-statement ] .

WRITE record-name
     [ FROM identifier ]
     [ INVALID KEY imperative-statement ] .

REWRITE record-name
     [ FROM identifier ]
     [ INVALID KEY imperative-statement ] .

DELETE file-name RECORD
     [ INVALID KEY imperative-statement ] .

CLOSE file-name  ... .
```

Figure 5B.1.   (continued)

The SELECT statement format for a relative file is shown in Figure 5B.3. In the SELECT entry for the RELATIVE-MASTER-FILE, the organization clause is specified as ORGANIZATION IS RELATIVE. With relative organization and random access, the RELATIVE KEY clause must be specified. This is the name of a numeric data-item in the WORKING-STORAGE SECTION that will be used to locate and keep track of the relative record number of the record to be processed.

```
001010 IDENTIFICATION DIVISION.
001020 PROGRAM-ID.    RELMAINT.
001030*
001040*
001050*             RELATIVE FILE MAINTENANCE
002010*
002020*
002030*
002040 ENVIRONMENT DIVISION.
002050*
002060*
002070 CONFIGURATION SECTION.
002080*
002090 SOURCE-COMPUTER.  IBM-370.
002100 OBJECT-COMPUTER.  IBM-370.
002110*
002120*
002130 INPUT-OUTPUT SECTION.
002140*
002150 FILE-CONTROL.
002160     SELECT TRANSACTION-FILE
002170         ASSIGN TO UT-S-TRNFILE.
002180     SELECT RELATIVE-MASTER-FILE
002190         ASSIGN TO RELFILE
002194         ORGANIZATION IS RELATIVE
002195         ACCESS MODE IS RANDOM
002196         RELATIVE KEY IS RK-RELATIVE-KEY
002197         FILE STATUS IS WS-FILE-STATUS-FLAG.
002220     SELECT REPORT-FILE
002230         ASSIGN TO UT-S-PRTFILE.
003010*
003020*
003030*
003040 DATA DIVISION.
003050*
003060*
003070 FILE SECTION.
003080*
003090*
003100 FD  TRANSACTION-FILE
003110     RECORD CONTAINS 80 CHARACTERS
003120     LABEL RECORDS ARE STANDARD.
003130*
003140 01  TRANSACTION-RECORD.
003150     05  FILLER                  PIC X(80).
004010*
004020*
004030 FD  RELATIVE-MASTER-FILE
004040     RECORD CONTAINS 80 CHARACTERS
004050     LABEL RECORDS ARE STANDARD.
004060*
004070 01  RELATIVE-MASTER-RECORD.
004080     05  FILLER                  PIC X(80).
006010*
006020*
006030 FD  REPORT-FILE
006040     RECORD CONTAINS 133 CHARACTERS
006050     LABEL RECORDS ARE OMITTED.
006060*
006070 01  REPORT-LINE.
006080     05  FILLER                  PIC X(133).
010010*
010020*
010030 WORKING-STORAGE SECTION.
010040*
010050*
010060 01  WS-SWITCHES.
010070*
010080     05  WS-TRANSACTION-END-OF-FILE-SW  PIC X(3).
010090         88  TRANSACTION-END-OF-FILE        VALUE 'YES'.
010270*
010280     05  WS-ACTIVE-RECORD-SW     PIC X(3).
010290         88  ACTIVE-RECORD           VALUE 'YES'.
010300*
010310     05  WS-PROGRAM-ABEND-SW     PIC X(3).
010320         88  PROGRAM-ABEND           VALUE 'YES'.
010330*
010340     05  WS-FILE-STATUS-FLAG     PIC X(2).
010350         88  SUCCESSFUL-COMPLETION       VALUE '00'.
010360         88  DUPLICATE-ALTERNATE-KEY     VALUE '02'.
010370         88  END-OF-FILE                 VALUE '10'.
010380         88  SEQUENCE-ERROR              VALUE '21'.
010390         88  DUPLICATE-KEY               VALUE '22'.
010400         88  NO-RECORD-FOUND             VALUE '23'.
010410         88  BOUNDARY-VIOLATION-IND-REL  VALUE '24'.
010420         88  PERMANENT-I-O-DATA-ERROR    VALUE '30'.
010430         88  BOUNDARY-VIOLATION-SEQ      VALUE '34'.
010440         88  IMPLEMENTOR-DEFINED-ERROR   VALUE '9 '.
010450*
010460     05  WS-I-O-OPERATION-FLAG   PIC X(7).
010510*
010520 01  WS-RELATIVE-KEY.
010530     05  RK-RELATIVE-KEY         PIC 9(5).
012010*
012020*
012030 01  WS-REPORT-CONTROLS.
012040     05  WS-PAGE-COUNT'          PIC S9(4)       COMP-3.
012050     05  WS-LINES-PER-PAGE       PIC S99 VALUE +55
012060                                     COMP SYNC.
012070     05  WS-LINES-USED           PIC S9(2)   COMP SYNC.
012080     05  WS-LINE-SPACING         PIC S9(2).
013010*
013020*
013030 01  WS-WORK-AREAS.
013040     05  WS-DATE-WORK            PIC 9(6).
013050     05  WS-DATE-REFORMAT REDEFINES WS-DATE-WORK.
013060         10  WS-YEAR             PIC 9(2).
013070         10  WS-MONTH            PIC 9(2).
013080         10  WS-DAY              PIC 9(2).
014010*
014020*
014030 01  TC-TABLE-CONTROLS.
014040     05  TC-SUBSCRIPT            PIC S9(4)   COMP SYNC.
014050     05  TC-NUMBER-OF-ENTRIES    PIC S9(4)  VALUE +15
014060                                     COMP SYNC.

015010*
015020 01  TC-COUNT-DESCRIPTION-DATA.
015030     05  FILLER       PIC X(20)  VALUE 'TRANSACTIONS READ   '.
015040     05  FILLER       PIC X(20)  VALUE '  ADDS              '.
015050     05  FILLER       PIC X(20)  VALUE '    PROCESSED       '.
015060     05  FILLER       PIC X(20)  VALUE '    REJECTED        '.
015070     05  FILLER       PIC X(20)  VALUE '  CHANGES           '.
015080     05  FILLER       PIC X(20)  VALUE '    PROCESSED       '.
015090     05  FILLER       PIC X(20)  VALUE '    REJECTED        '.
015100     05  FILLER       PIC X(20)  VALUE '  DELETES           '.
015110     05  FILLER       PIC X(20)  VALUE '    PROCESSED       '.
015120     05  FILLER       PIC X(20)  VALUE '    REJECTED        '.
015130     05  FILLER       PIC X(20)  VALUE '  ERROR UPDATE CODES'.
015140     05  FILLER       PIC X(20)  VALUE 'MASTERS READ        '.
015150     05  FILLER       PIC X(20)  VALUE 'MASTER CHANGES      '.
015160     05  FILLER       PIC X(20)  VALUE 'MASTERS ADDED       '.
015165     05  FILLER       PIC X(20)  VALUE 'MASTERS DELETED     '.
015170 01  TC-COUNT-DESCRIPTION-TABLE
015180         REDEFINES TC-COUNT-DESCRIPTION-DATA.
015190     05  TC-COUNT-DESCRIPTION            OCCURS 15 TIMES
015200                                         PIC X(20).
016010*
016020 01  TC-RECORD-COUNT-ENTRIES                    COMP-3.
016030     05  TC-TOTAL-TRANS-READ         PIC S9(5).
016040     05  TC-TOTAL-ADD-TRANS-READ     PIC S9(5).
016050     05  TC-ADD-TRANS-PROCESSED      PIC S9(5).
016060     05  TC-ADD-TRANS-REJECTED       PIC S9(5).
016070     05  TC-TOTAL-CHANGE-TRANS-READ  PIC S9(5).
016080     05  TC-CHANGE-TRANS-PROCESSED   PIC S9(5).
016090     05  TC-CHANGE-TRANS-REJECTED    PIC S9(5).
016100     05  TC-TOTAL-DELETE-TRANS-READ  PIC S9(5).
016110     05  TC-DELETE-TRANS-PROCESSED   PIC S9(5).
016120     05  TC-DELETE-TRANS-REJECTED    PIC S9(5).
016130     05  TC-TOTAL-ERROR-UPDATE-CODES PIC S9(5).
016140     05  TC-MASTERS-READ             PIC S9(5).
016150     05  TC-MASTER-CHANGES           PIC S9(5).
016160     05  TC-MASTERS-ADDED            PIC S9(5).
016165     05  TC-MASTERS-DELETED          PIC S9(5).
016170 01  TC-RECORD-COUNTS REDEFINES TC-RECORD-COUNT-ENTRIES.
016180     05  TC-RECORD-COUNT             OCCURS 15 TIMES
016190                                     PIC S9(5)       COMP-3.
020010*
020020*
020030 01  ET-EMPLOYEE-TRANSACTION-RECORD.
020040     05  ET-RECORD-CODE              PIC X(2).
020050     05  ET-UPDATE-CODE              PIC X(1).
020060         88  DELETE-TRANSACTION              VALUE '1'.
020070         88  ADD-TRANSACTION                 VALUE '2'.
020080         88  CHANGE-TRANSACTION              VALUE '3'.
020084         88  VALID-UPDATE-CODE               VALUE '1'
020086                                                   '2'
020088                                                   '3'.
020090     05  ET-EMPLOYEE-NUMBER          PIC X(5).
020100     05  ET-LAST-NAME                PIC X(13).
020110     05  ET-FIRST-NAME               PIC X(12).
020120     05  ET-MIDDLE-INITIAL           PIC X(1).
020130     05  ET-PLANT-CODE               PIC X(2).
020140     05  ET-DEPARTMENT-NUMBER        PIC X(4).
020150     05  ET-HOURLY-RATE              PIC S9(2)V99.
020160     05  ET-HOURLY-RATE-X REDEFINES ET-HOURLY-RATE
020170                                     PIC X(4).
020180     05  FILLER                      PIC X(36).
025010*
025020*
025030 01  EM-EMPLOYEE-MASTER-WORK-AREA.
025040     05  EM-RECORD-CODE              PIC X(2).
025050     05  FILLER                      PIC X(1).
025060     05  EM-PLANT-CODE               PIC X(2).
025070     05  EM-DEPARTMENT-NUMBER        PIC X(4).
025080     05  EM-EMPLOYEE-NUMBER          PIC X(5).
025085         88  MASTER-INACTIVE             VALUE ZEROS.
025090     05  EM-LAST-NAME                PIC X(13).
025100     05  EM-FIRST-NAME               PIC X(12).
025110     05  EM-MIDDLE-INITIAL           PIC X(1).
025120     05  EM-HOURLY-RATE              PIC S9(2)V99.
025130     05  FILLER                      PIC X(30).
025140     05  EM-DATE-LAST-ACTIVITY       PIC 9(6).
030010*
030020*
030040 01  H1-HEADING-LINE-1.
030050     05  FILLER          PIC X(1).
030060     05  FILLER          PIC X(20)  VALUE 'RELATIVE MASTER FILE'.
030070     05  FILLER          PIC X(20)  VALUE ' MAINTENANCE        '.
030080     05  FILLER          PIC X(20)  VALUE '                    '.
030090     05  FILLER          PIC X(20)  VALUE '                    '.
030100     05  FILLER          PIC X(20)  VALUE '           RUN DAT'.
030110     05  FILLER          PIC X(2)   VALUE 'E '.
030120     05  H1-MONTH        PIC 9(2).
030130     05  FILLER          PIC X(1)   VALUE '/'.
030140     05  H1-DAY          PIC 9(2).
030150     05  FILLER          PIC X(1)   VALUE '/'.
030160     05  H1-YEAR         PIC 9(2).
030170     05  FILLER          PIC X(22)  VALUE SPACES.
031010*
031020*
031030 01  H2-HEADING-LINE-2.
031040     05  FILLER          PIC X(1).
031050     05  FILLER          PIC X(20)  VALUE 'AUDIT/ERROR LIST    '.
031060     05  FILLER          PIC X(20)  VALUE '                    '.
031070     05  FILLER          PIC X(20)  VALUE '  ** EMPLOYEE MASTER'.
031080     05  FILLER          PIC X(20)  VALUE ' FILE **            '.
031090     05  FILLER          PIC X(6)   VALUE ' PAGE '.
031100     05  H2-PAGE-NBR     PIC ZZZ9.
031120     05  FILLER          PIC X(22)  VALUE SPACES.
032010*
032020*
032030 01  H3-HEADING-LINE-3.
032040     05  FILLER          PIC X(1).
032050     05  FILLER          PIC X(20)  VALUE 'RCD  UPDT  EMPL  PLA'.
032060     05  FILLER          PIC X(20)  VALUE 'NT  DEPT  ------EMP'.
032070     05  FILLER          PIC X(20)  VALUE 'LOYEE NAME------M'.
032080     05  FILLER          PIC X(20)  VALUE 'HOURLY   UPDATE     '.
032090     05  FILLER          PIC X(20)  VALUE '                    '.
032100     05  FILLER          PIC X(20)  VALUE '                    '.
032110     05  FILLER          PIC X(12)  VALUE '            '.
033010*
```

Figure 5B.2. COBOL coding: RELMAINT program.

```
033020*
033030 01  H4-HEADING-LINE-4.
033040     05  FILLER          PIC X(1).
033050     05  FILLER          PIC X(20)  VALUE 'CODE CODE    NBR  CO'.
033060     05  FILLER          PIC X(20)  VALUE 'DE    NBR  LAST NAME '.
033070     05  FILLER          PIC X(20)  VALUE '    FIRST NAME   I  '.
033080     05  FILLER          PIC X(20)  VALUE ' RATE   ACTION ---'.
033090     05  FILLER          PIC X(20)  VALUE '------ERROR MESSAGE'.
033100     05  FILLER          PIC X(20)  VALUE '----------          '.
033110     05  FILLER          PIC X(12)  VALUE '           '.
034010*
034020*
034030 01  DL-DETAIL-LINE.
034040     05  FILLER                       PIC X(1).
034050     05  FILLER                       PIC X(1)   VALUE SPACES.
034060     05  DL-RECORD-CODE               PIC X(2).
034070     05  FILLER                       PIC X(1)   VALUE SPACES.
034080     05  DL-UPDATE-CODE               PIC X(1).
034090     05  FILLER                       PIC X(2)   VALUE SPACES.
034140     05  DL-EMPLOYEE-NUMBER           PIC X(5).
034150     05  FILLER                       PIC X(3)   VALUE SPACES.
034152     05  DL-PLANT-CODE                PIC X(2).
034154     05  FILLER                       PIC X(4)   VALUE SPACES.
034156     05  DL-DEPARTMENT-NUMBER         PIC X(4).
034158     05  FILLER                       PIC X(2)   VALUE SPACES.
034160     05  DL-LAST-NAME                 PIC X(13).
034170     05  FILLER                       PIC X(1)   VALUE SPACES.
034180     05  DL-FIRST-NAME                PIC X(12).
034190     05  FILLER                       PIC X(1)   VALUE SPACES.
034200     05  DL-MIDDLE-INITIAL            PIC X(1).
034210     05  FILLER                       PIC X(3)   VALUE SPACES.
034220     05  DL-HOURLY-RATE               PIC ZZ.99.
034230     05  DL-HOURLY-RATE-X REDEFINES DL-HOURLY-RATE
034240                                      PIC X(5).
034250     05  FILLER                       PIC X(2)   VALUE SPACES.
034260     05  DL-UPDATE-ACTION             PIC X(8).
034270     05  FILLER                       PIC X(1)   VALUE SPACES.
034280     05  DL-ERROR-MSG                 PIC X(33).
034290     05  FILLER                       PIC X(22)  VALUE SPACES.
035010*
035020*
035030 01  IE-I-O-ERROR-LINE REDEFINES DL-DETAIL-LINE.
035040     05  FILLER                       PIC X(1).
035050     05  FILLER                       PIC X(40).
035062     05  IE-FILE-STATUS-FLAG          PIC X(2).
035064     05  FILLER                       PIC X(1).
035066     05  IE-I-O-OPERATION-FLAG        PIC X(7).
035100     05  FILLER                       PIC X(9).
035110     05  IE-ERROR-KEY                 PIC X(5).
035120     05  FILLER                       PIC X(4).
036010*
036020*
036030 01  TL-TOTAL-LINE.
036040     05  FILLER                       PIC X(1).
036050     05  FILLER                       PIC X(83)  VALUE SPACES.
036060     05  TL-COUNT-DESCRIPTION         PIC X(20).
036070     05  FILLER                       PIC X(1)   VALUE SPACES.
036080     05  TL-RECORD-COUNT              PIC ZZ,ZZ9.
036090     05  FILLER                       PIC X(22)  VALUE SPACES.
050010*
050020*
050030*
050040 PROCEDURE DIVISION.
050050*
050060*
050070 000-MAINTAIN-RELATIVE-FILE.
050080*
050090     OPEN INPUT TRANSACTION-FILE
050100          I-O RELATIVE-MASTER-FILE
050120          OUTPUT REPORT-FILE.
050130     PERFORM 100-INITIALIZE-VARIABLE-FIELDS.
050135     PERFORM 800-READ-TRANSACTION-RECORD.
050140     PERFORM 200-UPDATE-MASTER-RECORD
050150          UNTIL TRANSACTION-END-OF-FILE.
050170     PERFORM 700-PRINT-REPORT-TOTALS.
050180     CLOSE TRANSACTION-FILE
050190          RELATIVE-MASTER-FILE
050210          REPORT-FILE.
050220     STOP RUN.
100010*
100020*
100030 100-INITIALIZE-VARIABLE-FIELDS.
100040*
100050     MOVE 'NO ' TO WS-TRANSACTION-END-OF-FILE-SW
100055                   WS-PROGRAM-ABEND-SW.
100120     MOVE ZERO TO WS-PAGE-COUNT.
100130     ADD 1 WS-LINES-PER-PAGE GIVING WS-LINES-USED.
100140     ACCEPT WS-DATE-WORK FROM DATE.
100150     MOVE WS-MONTH TO H1-MONTH.
100160     MOVE WS-DAY TO H1-DAY.
100170     MOVE WS-YEAR TO H1-YEAR.
100190     MOVE SPACES TO DL-ERROR-MSG.
100200     PERFORM 110-ZERO-RECORD-COUNTS
100210          VARYING TC-SUBSCRIPT
100220          FROM 1
100230          BY 1
100240          UNTIL TC-SUBSCRIPT IS GREATER THAN TC-NUMBER-OF-ENTRIES.
110010*
110020*
110030 110-ZERO-RECORD-COUNTS.
110040*
110050     MOVE ZERO TO TC-RECORD-COUNT (TC-SUBSCRIPT).
200010*
200020*
200030 200-UPDATE-MASTER-RECORD.
200040*
200044     IF VALID-UPDATE-CODE
200046          PERFORM 810-READ-MASTER-RECORD.
200046*
200050     IF (ADD-TRANSACTION AND NOT ACTIVE-RECORD)
200060          PERFORM 230-ADD-MASTER-RECORD
200065*
200070     ELSE IF (CHANGE-TRANSACTION AND ACTIVE-RECORD)
200080          PERFORM 240-CHANGE-MASTER-RECORD
200085*
200090     ELSE IF (DELETE-TRANSACTION AND ACTIVE-RECORD)
200100          PERFORM 250-DELETE-MASTER-RECORD
```

```
200105*
200110     ELSE
200120          PERFORM 290-IDENTIFY-ERROR-TYPE.
200170     PERFORM 220-PRINT-AUDIT-ERROR-LINE.
200180*
200182     IF NOT PROGRAM-ABEND
200184          PERFORM 800-READ-TRANSACTION-RECORD
200186     ELSE
200188          PERFORM 900-ABORT-PROGRAM-RUN.
200190
220010*
220020*
220030 220-PRINT-AUDIT-ERROR-LINE.
220040*
220050     IF WS-LINES-USED IS NOT LESS THAN WS-LINES-PER-PAGE
220060          PERFORM 870-PRINT-REPORT-HEADINGS.
220070     MOVE ET-RECORD-CODE TO DL-RECORD-CODE.
220080     MOVE ET-UPDATE-CODE TO DL-UPDATE-CODE.
220090     MOVE ET-PLANT-CODE TO DL-PLANT-CODE.
220100     MOVE ET-DEPARTMENT-NUMBER TO DL-DEPARTMENT-NUMBER.
220110     MOVE ET-EMPLOYEE-NUMBER TO DL-EMPLOYEE-NUMBER.
220120     MOVE ET-LAST-NAME TO DL-LAST-NAME.
220130     MOVE ET-FIRST-NAME TO DL-FIRST-NAME.
220140     MOVE ET-MIDDLE-INITIAL TO DL-MIDDLE-INITIAL.
220150     IF ET-HOURLY-RATE IS NUMERIC
220160          MOVE ET-HOURLY-RATE TO DL-HOURLY-RATE
220170     ELSE
220180          MOVE ET-HOURLY-RATE-X TO DL-HOURLY-RATE-X.
220190     MOVE DL-DETAIL-LINE TO REPORT-LINE.
220200     MOVE 1 TO WS-LINE-SPACING.
220210     PERFORM 890-WRITE-REPORT-LINE.
220220     MOVE SPACES TO DL-DETAIL-LINE.
230010*
230020*
230030 230-ADD-MASTER-RECORD.
230040*
230070     ADD 1 TO TC-TOTAL-ADD-TRANS-READ.
230080     PERFORM 260-CREATE-MASTER-RECORD.
230084     PERFORM 850-WRITE-MASTER-RECORD.
230088     IF NOT PROGRAM-ABEND
230090          ADD 1 TO TC-ADD-TRANS-PROCESSED
230100          MOVE 'ADDED   ' TO DL-UPDATE-ACTION.
240010*
240020*
240030 240-CHANGE-MASTER-RECORD.
240040*
240150     ADD 1 TO TC-CHANGE-TRANS-PROCESSED.
240160     PERFORM 270-CHANGE-MASTER-FIELDS.
240170     PERFORM 855-REWRITE-MASTER-RECORD.
240180     IF NOT PROGRAM-ABEND
240190          ADD 1 TO TC-CHANGE-TRANS-PROCESSED
240200          MOVE 'CHANGED ' TO DL-UPDATE-ACTION.
250010*
250020*
250030 250-DELETE-MASTER-RECORD.
250040*
250150     ADD 1 TO TC-TOTAL-DELETE-TRANS-READ.
250154     MOVE SPACES TO EM-EMPLOYEE-MASTER-WORK-AREA.
250158     MOVE ZEROS TO EM-EMPLOYEE-NUMBER.
250160     PERFORM 860-DELETE-MASTER-RECORD.
250170     IF NOT PROGRAM-ABEND
250180          ADD 1 TO TC-DELETE-TRANS-PROCESSED
250190          MOVE 'DELETED ' TO DL-UPDATE-ACTION.
260010*
260020*
260030 260-CREATE-MASTER-RECORD.
260040*
260050     MOVE SPACES TO EM-EMPLOYEE-MASTER-WORK-AREA.
260060     MOVE '85' TO EM-RECORD-CODE.
260070     MOVE ET-PLANT-CODE TO EM-PLANT-CODE.
260080     MOVE ET-DEPARTMENT-NUMBER TO EM-DEPARTMENT-NUMBER.
260090     MOVE ET-EMPLOYEE-NUMBER TO EM-EMPLOYEE-NUMBER.
260100     MOVE ET-LAST-NAME TO EM-LAST-NAME.
260110     MOVE ET-FIRST-NAME TO EM-FIRST-NAME.
260120     MOVE ET-MIDDLE-INITIAL TO EM-MIDDLE-INITIAL.
260130     MOVE ET-HOURLY-RATE TO EM-HOURLY-RATE.
260140     MOVE WS-DATE-WORK TO EM-DATE-LAST-ACTIVITY.
270010*
270020*
270030 270-CHANGE-MASTER-FIELDS.
270040*
270050     IF ET-LAST-NAME IS EQUAL TO SPACES
270060          NEXT SENTENCE
270070     ELSE
270080          MOVE ET-LAST-NAME TO TO EM-LAST-NAME.
270090*
270100     IF ET-FIRST-NAME IS EQUAL TO SPACES
270110          NEXT SENTENCE
270120     ELSE
270130          MOVE ET-FIRST-NAME TO EM-FIRST-NAME.
270140*
270150     IF ET-MIDDLE-INITIAL IS EQUAL TO SPACES
270160          NEXT SENTENCE
270170     ELSE IF ET-MIDDLE-INITIAL IS EQUAL TO '$'
270180          MOVE SPACES TO EM-MIDDLE-INITIAL
270190     ELSE
270200          MOVE ET-MIDDLE-INITIAL TO EM-MIDDLE-INITIAL.
270210*
270220     IF ET-HOURLY-RATE-X IS EQUAL TO SPACES
270230          NEXT SENTENCE
270240     ELSE
270250          MOVE ET-HOURLY-RATE TO EM-HOURLY-RATE.
270260*
270270     MOVE WS-DATE-WORK TO EM-DATE-LAST-ACTIVITY.
290010*
290020*
290030 290-IDENTIFY-ERROR-TYPE.
290040*
290050     IF ADD-TRANSACTION
290060          ADD 1 TO TC-TOTAL-ADD-TRANS-READ
290070          ADD 1 TO TC-ADD-TRANS-REJECTED
290080          MOVE 'UNABLE ADD-MASTER ALREADY ON FILE' TO DL-ERROR-MSG
290090     ELSE IF CHANGE-TRANSACTION
290100          ADD 1 TO TC-TOTAL-CHANGE-TRANS-READ
290110          ADD 1 TO TC-CHANGE-TRANS-REJECTED
290120          MOVE 'UNABLE CHANGE-MASTER NOT ON FILE ' TO DL-ERROR-MSG
```

Figure 5B.2. (continued)

```
290130          ELSE IF DELETE-TRANSACTION
290140              ADD 1 TO TC-TOTAL-DELETE-TRANS-READ
290150              ADD 1 TO TC-DELETE-TRANS-REJECTED
290160              MOVE 'UNABLE DELETE-MASTER NOT ON FILE ' TO DL-ERROR-MSG
290170          ELSE
290180              ADD 1 TO TC-TOTAL-ERROR-UPDATE-CODES
290190              MOVE 'UNABLE UPDATE-INVALID UPDATE CODE' TO DL-ERROR-MSG.
290200*
290210          MOVE 'REJECTED' TO DL-UPDATE-ACTION.
700010*
700020*
700030 700-PRINT-REPORT-TOTALS.
700040*
700050      PERFORM 870-PRINT-REPORT-HEADINGS.
700060      PERFORM 710-PRINT-TOTAL-LINE
700070          VARYING TC-SUBSCRIPT
700080          FROM 1
700090          BY 1
700100          UNTIL TC-SUBSCRIPT IS GREATER THAN TC-NUMBER-OF-ENTRIES.
710010*
710020*
710030 710-PRINT-TOTAL-LINE.
710040*
710050      MOVE TC-COUNT-DESCRIPTION (TC-SUBSCRIPT)
710060          TO TL-COUNT-DESCRIPTION.
710070      MOVE TC-RECORD-COUNT (TC-SUBSCRIPT) TO TL-RECORD-COUNT.
710080      MOVE TL-TOTAL-LINE TO REPORT-LINE.
710090      MOVE 1 TO WS-LINE-SPACING.
710100      PERFORM 890-WRITE-REPORT-LINE.
800010*
800020*
800030 800-READ-TRANSACTION-RECORD.
800040*
800070      READ TRANSACTION-FILE INTO ET-EMPLOYEE-TRANSACTION-RECORD
800080          AT END MOVE 'YES' TO WS-TRANSACTION-END-OF-FILE-SW.
800100*
800110      IF NOT TRANSACTION-END-OF-FILE
800120          ADD 1 TO TC-TOTAL-TRANS-READ.
810010*
810020*
810030 810-READ-MASTER-RECORD.
810040*
810042      MOVE ET-EMPLOYEE-NUMBER TO RK-RELATIVE-KEY.
810065      MOVE 'READ   ' TO WS-I-O-OPERATION-FLAG.
810070      READ RELATIVE-MASTER-FILE
810075          INTO EM-EMPLOYEE-MASTER-WORK-AREA.
810300*
810310      IF SUCCESSFUL-COMPLETION
810314      AND NOT MASTER-INACTIVE
810316          MOVE 'YES' TO WS-ACTIVE-RECORD-SW
810320          ADD 1 TO TC-MASTERS-READ
810324      ELSE
810328          MOVE 'NO ' TO WS-ACTIVE-RECORD-SW.
850010*
850020*
850030 850-WRITE-MASTER-RECORD.
850040*
850045      MOVE 'REWRITE' TO WS-I-O-OPERATION-FLAG.
850050      REWRITE RELATIVE-MASTER-RECORD
850060          FROM EM-EMPLOYEE-MASTER-WORK-AREA
850064          INVALID KEY MOVE 'YES' TO WS-PROGRAM-ABEND-SW.
850200*
850210      IF SUCCESSFUL-COMPLETION
850220          ADD 1 TO TC-MASTERS-ADDED
850230      ELSE
850240          MOVE 'YES' TO WS-PROGRAM-ABEND-SW.
855010*
855020*
855030 855-REWRITE-MASTER-RECORD.
855040*
```

```
855045      MOVE 'REWRITE' TO WS-I-O-OPERATION-FLAG.
855050      REWRITE RELATIVE-MASTER-RECORD
855060          FROM EM-EMPLOYEE-MASTER-WORK-AREA
855070          INVALID KEY MOVE 'YES' TO WS-PROGRAM-ABEND-SW.
855080*
855090      IF SUCCESSFUL-COMPLETION
855100          ADD 1 TO TC-MASTER-CHANGES
855110      ELSE
855120          MOVE 'YES' TO WS-PROGRAM-ABEND-SW.
860010*
860020*
860030 860-DELETE-MASTER-RECORD.
860040*
860045      MOVE 'REWRITE' TO WS-I-O-OPERATION-FLAG.
860050      REWRITE RELATIVE-MASTER-RECORD
860060          INVALID KEY MOVE 'YES' TO WS-PROGRAM-ABEND-SW.
860070*
860080      IF SUCCESSFUL-COMPLETION
860090          ADD 1 TO TC-MASTERS-DELETED
860100      ELSE
860110          MOVE 'YES' TO WS-PROGRAM-ABEND-SW.
870010*
870020*
870030 870-PRINT-REPORT-HEADINGS.
870040*
870050      ADD 1 TO WS-PAGE-COUNT.
870060      MOVE WS-PAGE-COUNT TO H2-PAGE-NBR.
870070      MOVE H1-HEADING-LINE-1 TO REPORT-LINE.
870080      PERFORM 880-WRITE-REPORT-TOP-LINE.
870090      MOVE H2-HEADING-LINE-2 TO REPORT-LINE.
870100      MOVE 1 TO WS-LINE-SPACING.
870110      PERFORM 890-WRITE-REPORT-LINE.
870120      MOVE H3-HEADING-LINE-3 TO REPORT-LINE.
870130      MOVE 2 TO WS-LINE-SPACING.
870140      PERFORM 890-WRITE-REPORT-LINE.
870150      MOVE H4-HEADING-LINE-4 TO REPORT-LINE.
870160      MOVE 1 TO WS-LINE-SPACING.
870170      PERFORM 890-WRITE-REPORT-LINE.
870180      MOVE SPACES TO REPORT-LINE.
870190      PERFORM 890-WRITE-REPORT-LINE.
880010*
880020*
880030 880-WRITE-REPORT-TOP-LINE.
880040*
880050      WRITE REPORT-LINE
880060          AFTER ADVANCING PAGE.
880070      MOVE 1 TO WS-LINES-USED.
890010*
890020*
890030 890-WRITE-REPORT-LINE.
890040*
890050      WRITE REPORT-LINE
890060          AFTER ADVANCING WS-LINE-SPACING.
890070      ADD WS-LINE-SPACING TO WS-LINES-USED.
900010*
900020*
900030 900-ABORT-PROGRAM-RUN.
900040*
900041      MOVE SPACES TO IE-I-O-ERROR-LINE.
900042      MOVE WS-FILE-STATUS-FLAG TO IE-FILE-STATUS-FLAG.
900044      MOVE WS-I-O-OPERATION-FLAG TO IE-I-O-OPERATION-FLAG.
900046      MOVE RK-RELATIVE-KEY TO IE-ERROR-KEY.
900048      MOVE ET-UPDATE-CODE TO DL-UPDATE-CODE.
900050      MOVE 'ABORTED ' TO DL-UPDATE-ACTION.
900055      MOVE 'I-O ERROR OCCURRED' TO DL-ERROR-MSG.
900060      MOVE DL-DETAIL-LINE TO REPORT-LINE.
900070      MOVE 3 TO WS-LINE-SPACING.
900080      PERFORM 890-WRITE-REPORT-LINE.
900090      MOVE SPACES TO DL-DETAIL-LINE.
900150      MOVE 'YES' TO WS-TRANSACTION-END-OF-FILE-SW.
```

Figure 5B.2. (continued)

Contrast this RELATIVE KEY field for a relative file with the RECORD KEY field of an indexed file. Remember that the RECORD KEY field must be defined within the FD in the FILE SECTION; the RELATIVE KEY is specified in the WORKING-STORAGE SECTION. The RECORD KEY field is an alphanumeric item whereas the RELATIVE KEY field must be numeric.

DATA DIVISION
Entries

FILE SECTION Entries

The RELATIVE-MASTER-RECORD is defined within the RELATIVE-MASTER-FILE in the FILE SECTION. Notice that the record contains only a FILLER field because record definition is handled in WORKING-STORAGE.

WORKING-STORAGE SECTION Entries

There are only a few WORKING-STORAGE SECTION coding differences for this RELMAINT program. Each will be discussed.

Program switches

An additional switch, WS-ACTIVE-RECORD-SW, is used. Because the relative file is formatted with a dummy record in each record slot, a record-found condi-

Format:

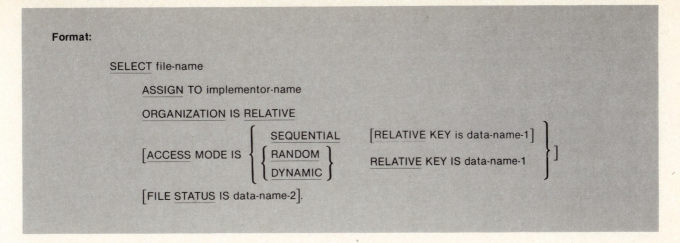

SELECT file-name

ASSIGN TO implementor-name

ORGANIZATION IS RELATIVE

[ACCESS MODE IS { SEQUENTIAL / RANDOM / DYNAMIC } { [RELATIVE KEY is data-name-1] / RELATIVE KEY IS data-name-1 }]

[FILE STATUS IS data-name-2].

Example:

```
SELECT RELATIVE-MASTER-FILE
    ASSIGN TO RELFILE
    ORGANIZATION IS RELATIVE
    ACCESS MODE IS RANDOM
    RELATIVE KEY IS RK-RELATIVE-KEY
    FILE STATUS IS WS-FILE-STATUS-FLAG.
```

Figure 5B.3. SELECT statement format and example for a relative file.

tion will always occur with valid keys regardless of whether or not an actual data record exists. Hence this switch is used to denote whether or not an actual active data record exists on the file. After a record has been read, the EM-EMPLOYEE-NUMBER field will be tested. If it contains a value other than ZEROS, the switch will be set to "YES" to indicate an ACTIVE-RECORD. The switch will be set to "NO" when a **dummy record** with the value of ZEROS is found.

RELATIVE KEY field

As shown in Figure 5B.4, the RELATIVE KEY field has been defined as RK-RELATIVE-KEY and specified with a PICTURE of 9(5). The RELATIVE KEY field must be specified as an unsigned numeric data-item and must be defined in the WORKING-STORAGE SECTION. The size of the item must be at least long enough to accommodate the total number of record slots that are allocated to the file.

EM-EMPLOYEE-MASTER-WORK-AREA definition

When the EM-EMPLOYEE-NUMBER field contains ZEROS, a MASTER-INACTIVE condition exists. This will occur when the record slot has not yet been used or after a record has been deleted. Both situations mean that the record slot is available for use by an actual data record. For coding uniformity, both dummy record cases are considered a MASTER-INACTIVE condition.

Audit/error report line entries

The description "RELATIVE MASTER FILE MAINTENANCE" has been specified as a constant value within H1-HEADING-LINE-1.

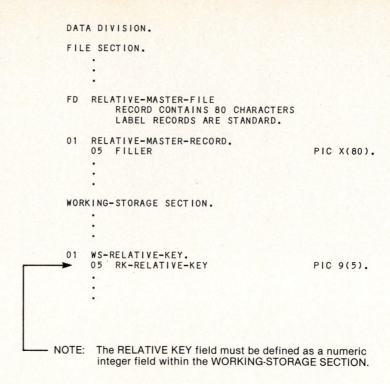

```
DATA DIVISION.

FILE SECTION.
           .
           .
           .

FD   RELATIVE-MASTER-FILE
           RECORD CONTAINS 80 CHARACTERS
           LABEL RECORDS ARE STANDARD.

01   RELATIVE-MASTER-RECORD.
     05   FILLER                            PIC X(80).
           .
           .
           .

WORKING-STORAGE SECTION.
           .
           .
           .

01   WS-RELATIVE-KEY.
     05   RK-RELATIVE-KEY                    PIC 9(5).
           .
           .
           .
```

NOTE: The RELATIVE KEY field must be defined as a numeric
        integer field within the WORKING-STORAGE SECTION.

Figure 5B.4   RELATIVE KEY definition example.

The arrangement of fields on DL-DETAIL-LINE of the audit/error list has been modified slightly so that the employee-number field is to the left of the plant-code and department-number fields. Although such an arrangement is not required, for ease of reference, it is logical to have the key field near the left side of the audit list.

The IE-ERROR-KEY field has been shortened because, in this program, the key field does not include the plant code and department number. To compensate, the FILLER entry that follows it has been lengthened.

PROCEDURE DIVISION Entries

The processing logic of each PROCEDURE DIVISION module for this RELMAINT program that differs from the INDMAINT program is explained below.

000-MAINTAIN-RELATIVE-FILE

This is a typical priming-read mainline module. The module name and master file names have been modified to appropriately describe the master file as being of relative organization.

200-UPDATE-MASTER-RECORD

Instead of SUCCESSFUL-COMPLETION, the condition ACTIVE-RECORD is used in this module to test whether or not the master record already exists on file. Remember that the system automatically sets the file status condition SUCCESSFUL-COMPLETION when a requested record has been located. With this program, however, a SUCCESSFUL-COMPLETION should always occur for a valid RELATIVE KEY value. This is because a record exists in each record slot, even though it may be only a dummy record.

Therefore, the WS-ACTIVE-RECORD-SW in WORKING-STORAGE is set to the ACTIVE-RECORD condition when an actual "live" data record is found in a record slot. If the record that is located is merely a dummy record, the NOT

Example:

```
READ RELATIVE-MASTER-FILE
    INTO EM-EMPLOYEE-MASTER-WORK-AREA
    INVALID KEY MOVE 'NO ' TO WS-MASTER-FOUND-SW.
```

Figure 5B.5. Random READ statement format.

ACTIVE-RECORD condition will be true. Otherwise, the logic of this module is the same as its counterpart in the INDMAINT program.

250-DELETE-MASTER-RECORD

To delete a record, the record area is first set to SPACES to eradicate the data of the deleted record. Next the EM-EMPLOYEE-NUMBER field is set to ZEROS to signify a dummy record and the record is then rewritten to the master file.

810-READ-MASTER-RECORD

The first statement within this module sets the RK-RELATIVE-KEY field in accordance with the ET-EMPLOYEE-NUMBER field of the transaction record. Figure 5B.5 shows the format of a random READ statement for a relative file.

After a record has been read, the last statement of this module tests to see whether or not an active data record exists. If the delete-flag is *not* set—a NOT MASTER-INACTIVE condition—the record is considered active. If the delete-flag is set, the record slot is logically vacant because it contains a dummy record.

If an active record exists, the WS-ACTIVE-RECORD-SW is set to "YES" and the TC-MASTERS-READ count is incremented. If a dummy record exists, the WS-ACTIVE-RECORD-SW is set to "NO."

850-WRITE-MASTER-RECORD

Although this paragraph is titled as a WRITE module to be consistent with other programs, it does not actually contain a WRITE statement. For this relative file application, a REWRITE statement must be used to add a new master record to the file. Because a dummy record exists even when a record is being initially placed on the file, a new record is added by updating the existing dummy record.

Even though a random WRITE statement to the relative file is not used here, its format is shown in Figure 5B.6 for reference. The format of a REWRITE statement for a relative file is shown in Figure 5B.7.

Example:

```
WRITE RELATIVE-MASTER-RECORD
    FROM EM-EMPLOYEE-MASTER-WORK-AREA
    INVALID KEY MOVE 'YES' TO WS-PROGRAM-ABEND-SW.
```

Figure 5B.6. Random WRITE statement format.

Example:

```
REWRITE RELATIVE-MASTER-RECORD
    FROM EM-EMPLOYEE-MASTER-WORK-AREA
    INVALID KEY MOVE 'YES' TO WS-PROGRAM-ABEND-SW.
```

Figure 5B.7. REWRITE statement format.

855-REWRITE-MASTER-RECORD Other than referring to a different record name, the REWRITE module for this RELMAINT program is the same as its counterpart in the INDMAINT program.

860-DELETE-MASTER-RECORD A REWRITE statement is again specified in this module. Before a record is deleted, remember that the EM-EMPLOYEE-NUMBER field has been set to

Format:

```
DELETE file-name RECORD
    [INVALID KEY imperative-statement].
```

INVALID KEY condition when ORGANIZATION IS RELATIVE:
■ Record not found (with key value equal to RELATIVE KEY value) [File status code = 23]

Example:

```
DELETE RELATIVE-MASTER-FILE
    INVALID KEY MOVE 'YES' TO WS-PROGRAM-ABEND-SW.
```

Figure 5B.8. DELETE statement format.

ZEROS. This has the effect of functionally deleting the record from the relative master file.

As an alternative, a DELETE statement, as shown in Figure 5B.8, could be specified. The REWRITE statement was chosen here so that, for consistency, an unused record area and a deleted record have the same representation on the master file.

■ TOPIC 5-C: **Creation of a Relative File**

Programming Specifications and Program Design

Program Coding
 ENVIRONMENT DIVISION Entries
 DATA DIVISION Entries
  FORMAT-PARAMETER-FILE
  Record count totals
  Audit/error report lines
 PROCEDURE DIVISION Entries
  000-FORMAT-RELATIVE-FILE
  100-INITIALIZE-VARIABLE-FIELDS
  130-PROCESS-PARAMETER-RECORD
  200-FORMAT-RELATIVE-RECORD
  850-WRITE-MASTER-RECORD
  900-ABORT-PROGRAM-RUN

Because a relative file contains a predefined number of record slot locations, it is a usual practice to erase, or otherwise **format**, each record area before adding any data records to the file. This makes the initial file-creation step for a relative file somewhat different in concept from that for other file-organization methods.

Remember that the initial population of data records for an indexed file is loaded during the creation step. Typically with a relative file, however, no actual data records are placed in the file during the load process. Instead, the record areas are merely formatted with dummy records. Then, during the first run of the maintenance program, the initial batch of data records is added to the file.

Before a relative file area is formatted, it is termed an **unformatted** or **unloaded** file. A relative file-maintenance program such as RELMAINT cannot process the file until it has been **formatted** or **loaded**. A formatted or loaded file that contains only dummy records is called an **empty** loaded file.

Formatting of a relative file is usually accomplished by setting the record area to HIGH-VALUES or SPACES. The exact format may depend upon the compiler or the operating system that is being used. The method of indicating deleted records will probably also be reflected in the formatting process.

Although the formatting requirements for a relative file may vary, a typical example of a program to format an empty relative file is presented here in this topic. The program is called RELFORM, for **rel**ative file **form**at.

Programming Specifications and Program Design

A relative file-formatting program is straightforward in logic. The program must simply step through the record slots, formatting each one. In this program, formatting will consist of setting all 80 characters of the master record to SPACES and then setting the 5 digits of the employee-number field to ZEROS. This will produce an empty file of dummy records.

Programming specifications for the RELFORM program are shown in Figure 5C.1. To provide for possible changes in record capacity requirements, the specifications call for an input parameter record that specifies the number of record slot locations to be formatted.

Because no actual data is being placed in the record areas, the printing of audit lines on the audit/error list would serve little purpose. Also, record count total requirements are reduced to a proof between the number of records that are specified in the parameter record and the number of record slot locations that the program actually formats.

Figure 5C.2 presents a structure chart for the RELFORM program.

Program Coding

COBOL coding for the RELFORM program is shown in Figure 5C.3. The logic that differs from previous programs is shaded on the program listing and will be discussed here.

ENVIRONMENT DIVISION Entries

When a relative file is accessed sequentially, the RELATIVE KEY clause of the SELECT statement is an optional entry. It is required only if the START statement is used in the program to reference the relative file. Thus the RELATIVE KEY clause has been omitted from this program.

DATA DIVISION Entries

FORMAT-PARAMETER-FILE

The input file should contain just one FORMAT-PARAMETER-RCD. Its record description in the WORKING-STORAGE SECTION is named FP-FORMAT-PARAMETER-RECORD. The record contains a record-code field plus a parameter field called FP-SLOTS-TO-BE-FORMATTED that is used to hold the number of relative record areas that are allocated to the file.

System flowchart:

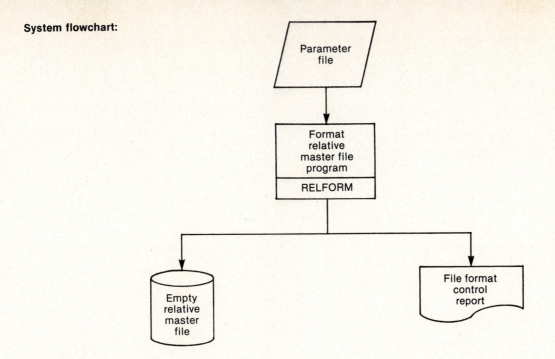

Record layouts:

Format parameter record

"Dummy" employee master record

Figure 5C.1. Programming specifications: RELFORM program.　　　　　　　　　*continued*

Record count totals

The first of the TC-RECORD-COUNT-ENTRIES fields, TC-SLOTS-TO-BE-FOR-MATTED, is not actually a record count. It is used to save the original value of the input FP-SLOTS-TO-BE-FORMATTED field so that, for audit and control purposes, it can later be printed on the audit list.

The second count field, TC-SLOTS-FORMATTED, is used to keep track of the number of record areas that are actually formatted. Both of these control figures will be printed in the total area of the audit/error list.

Print chart:

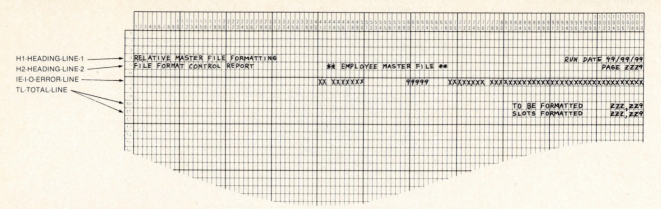

H1-HEADING-LINE-1 →
H2-HEADING-LINE-2 →
IE-I-O-ERROR-LINE →
TL-TOTAL-LINE →

```
RELATIVE MASTER FILE FORMATTING                                    RUN DATE 99/99/99
FILE FORMAT CONTROL REPORT              ** EMPLOYEE MASTER FILE **              PAGE ZZZ9

                                 XX XXXXXXX        99999  XXXXXXXX XXXXXXXXXXXXXXXXXXXXXXXXXXXXXX

                                                              TO BE FORMATTED        ZZZ,ZZ9
                                                              SLOTS FORMATTED        ZZZ,ZZ9
```

Output example:

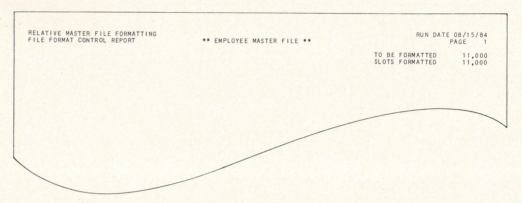

```
RELATIVE MASTER FILE FORMATTING                                    RUN DATE 08/15/84
FILE FORMAT CONTROL REPORT              ** EMPLOYEE MASTER FILE **              PAGE    1

                                                              TO BE FORMATTED        11,000
                                                              SLOTS FORMATTED        11,000
```

PROGRAMMING SPECIFICATIONS

Program name: Format Relative Master File   Program ID: RELFORM

Program description

The employee master file of relative organization is to be formatted with dummy records before it is loaded with data records. This program sequentially steps through the record slots and sets the data area to blank spaces except for the key field, employee number, which is set to zeros to signify a dummy, rather than a "live" active record. At the beginning of the run, an input parameter record is read that contains a field specifying the number of record slots to be formatted. At the end of the run, record counts specifying the number of slots to be formatted and tallying the number of slots actually formatted are printed.

Input file

Format parameter file
Organization = Sequential

Output files

Employee master file
Organization = Relative
Relative key = Employee number
File format control report

Program operations

A. Read the input format parameter record.

1. Check to ensure that an input record is present in the format parameter file.

a. If the format parameter file is empty, print an error line on the control report with the error message "PARAMETER RECORD MISSING". Also print the action "ABORTED" and abort the program run.

2. Validate the record code to ensure that it is equal to "08".

Figure 5C.1.   (continued)

a. If the update–code field is not valid, print an error line on the control report with the error message "INVALID PARAMETER RECORD CODE". Also print the action "ABORTED" and abort the program run.

3. Validate the slots–to–be–formatted field to ensure that it is numeric.

   a. If the slots–to–be–formatted field is not numeric, print an error line on the control report with the error message "INVALID PARAMETER FIELD". Also print the action "ABORTED" and abort the program run.

4. Check to ensure that there is only one format parameter record in the input format parameter file.

   a. If there is more than one format parameter record, print an error line on the control report with the error message "TOO MANY PARAMETER RECORDS". Also print the action "ABORTED" and abort the program run.

B. If the input format parameter record is valid, format the number of record slots specified by the slots–to–be–formatted field.

   1. Set the entire data record to a value of blank spaces except for the employee–number field which is to be set to zeros.

   2. If a fatal I–O error occurs while formatting the file, print an error line on the control report and abort the program run. The error line should contain the following information:

      a. The file status code value.
      b. A description of the I–O operation ("WRITE").
      c. The count of slots formatted when the I–O error occurred.
      d. The action "ABORTED".
      e. The error message "I–O ERROR OCCURRED".

C. At the end of the program run, print the number of slots to be formatted, as specified in the format parameter record, together with the number of slots actually formatted during the run.

Figure 5C.1. (continued)

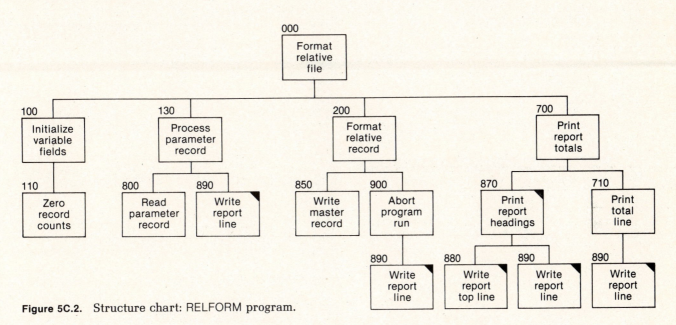

Figure 5C.2. Structure chart: RELFORM program.

Audit/error report lines

Because no audit/error lines are required for this program, no column heading or detail line record-descriptions have been specified. Four print line record-descriptions are thus coded: H1-HEADING-LINE-1, H2-HEADING-LINE-2, IE-I-O-ERROR-LINE, and TL-TOTAL-LINE. Observe that since the IE-I-O-ERROR-LINE does not redefine the detail line area in this program, this record description encompasses the full width of the print line. Also, VALUE SPACES clauses are specified for the FILLER areas.

```
001010 IDENTIFICATION DIVISION.
001020 PROGRAM-ID.    RELFORM.
001030*
001040*
001050*                RELATIVE FILE FORMAT
002010*
002020*
002030*
002040 ENVIRONMENT DIVISION.
002050*
002060*
002070 CONFIGURATION SECTION.
002080*
002090 SOURCE-COMPUTER.   IBM-370.
002100 OBJECT-COMPUTER.   IBM-370.
002110*
002120*
002130 INPUT-OUTPUT SECTION.
002140*
002150 FILE-CONTROL.
002160     SELECT FORMAT-PARAMETER-FILE
002170         ASSIGN TO UT-S-TRNFILE.
002180     SELECT RELATIVE-MASTER-FILE
002190         ASSIGN TO RELFILE
002194         ORGANIZATION IS RELATIVE
002195         ACCESS MODE IS SEQUENTIAL
002197         FILE STATUS IS WS-FILE-STATUS-FLAG.
002220     SELECT REPORT-FILE
002230         ASSIGN TO UT-S-PRTFILE.
003010*
003020*
003030*
003040 DATA DIVISION.
003050*
003060*
003070 FILE SECTION.
003080*
003090*
003100 FD  FORMAT-PARAMETER-FILE
003110         RECORD CONTAINS 80 CHARACTERS
003120         LABEL RECORDS ARE STANDARD.
003130*
003140 01  FORMAT-PARAMETER-RCD.
003150     05  FILLER                    PIC X(80).
004010*
004020*
004030 FD  RELATIVE-MASTER-FILE
004040         RECORD CONTAINS 80 CHARACTERS
004050         LABEL RECORDS ARE STANDARD.
004060*
004070 01  RELATIVE-MASTER-RECORD.
004080     05  FILLER                    PIC X(80).
006010*
006020*
006030 FD  REPORT-FILE
006040         RECORD CONTAINS 133 CHARACTERS
006050         LABEL RECORDS ARE OMITTED.
006060*
006070 01  REPORT-LINE.
006080     05  FILLER                    PIC X(133).
010010*
010020*
010030 WORKING-STORAGE SECTION.
010040*
010050*
010060 01  WS-SWITCHES.
010070*
010080     05  WS-PARAMETER-END-OF-FILE-SW  PIC X(3).
010090         88  PARAMETER-END-OF-FILE              VALUE 'YES'.
010300*
010310     05  WS-PROGRAM-ABEND-SW       PIC X(3).
010320         88  PROGRAM-ABEND                      VALUE 'YES'.
010330*
010340     05  WS-FILE-STATUS-FLAG       PIC X(2).
010350         88  SUCCESSFUL-COMPLETION              VALUE '00'.
010360         88  DUPLICATE-ALTERNATE-KEY            VALUE '02'.
010370         88  END-OF-FILE                        VALUE '10'.
010380         88  SEQUENCE-ERROR                     VALUE '21'.
010390         88  DUPLICATE-KEY                      VALUE '22'.
010400         88  NO-RECORD-FOUND                    VALUE '23'.
010410         88  BOUNDARY-VIOLATION-IND-REL         VALUE '24'.
010420         88  PERMANENT-I-O-DATA-ERROR           VALUE '30'.
010430         88  BOUNDARY-VIOLATION-SEQ             VALUE '34'.
010440         88  IMPLEMENTOR-DEFINED-ERROR          VALUE '9 '.
010450*
010460     05  WS-I-O-OPERATION-FLAG     PIC X(7).
012010*
012020*
012030 01  WS-REPORT-CONTROLS.
012040     05  WS-PAGE-COUNT             PIC S9(4)      COMP-3.
012050     05  WS-LINES-PER-PAGE         PIC S99 VALUE +55
012060                                                  COMP SYNC.
012070     05  WS-LINES-USED             PIC S9(2)      COMP SYNC.
012080     05  WS-LINE-SPACING           PIC S9(2).
013010*
013020*
013030 01  WS-WORK-AREAS.
013040     05  WS-DATE-WORK              PIC 9(6).
013050     05  WS-DATE-REFORMAT REDEFINES WS-DATE-WORK.
013060         10  WS-YEAR               PIC 9(2).
013070         10  WS-MONTH              PIC 9(2).
013080         10  WS-DAY                PIC 9(2).
014010*
014020*
014030 01  TC-TABLE-CONTROLS.
014040     05  TC-SUBSCRIPT              PIC S9(4)      COMP SYNC.
014050     05  TC-NUMBER-OF-ENTRIES      PIC S9(4) VALUE +2
014060                                                  COMP SYNC.
015010*
015020 01  TC-COUNT-DESCRIPTION-DATA.
015030     05  FILLER   PIC X(20)  VALUE 'TO BE FORMATTED    '.
015160     05  FILLER   PIC X(20)  VALUE 'SLOTS FORMATTED     '.
015170 01  TC-COUNT-DESCRIPTION-TABLE
015180         REDEFINES TD-COUNT-DESCRIPTION-DATA.
015190     05  TD-COUNT-DESCRIPTION      OCCURS 2 TIMES
015200                                   PIC X(20).
```

```
016010*
016020 01  TC-RECORD-COUNT-ENTRIES                     COMP-3.
016030     05  TC-SLOTS-TO-BE-FORMATTED  PIC S9(6).
016160     05  TC-SLOTS-FORMATTED        PIC S9(6).
016170 01  TC-RECORD-COUNTS REDEFINES TC-RECORD-COUNT-ENTRIES.
016180     05  TC-RECORD-COUNT           OCCURS 2 TIMES
016190                                   PIC S9(6)      COMP-3.
020010*
020020*
020030 01  FP-FORMAT-PARAMETER-RECORD.
020040     05  FP-RECORD-CODE            PIC X(2).
030044         88  FORMAT-PARAMETER-RECORD           VALUE '08'.
020045     05  FP-SLOTS-TO-BE-FORMATTED  PIC 9(6).
020180     05  FILLER                    PIC X(72).
025010*
025020*
025030 01  EM-EMPLOYEE-MASTER-WORK-AREA.
025040     05  EM-RECORD-CODE            PIC X(2).
025050     05  FILLER                    PIC X(1).
025060     05  EM-PLANT-CODE             PIC X(2).
025070     05  EM-DEPARTMENT-NUMBER      PIC X(4).
025080     05  EM-EMPLOYEE-NUMBER        PIC X(5).
025090     05  EM-LAST-NAME              PIC X(13).
025100     05  EM-FIRST-NAME             PIC X(12).
025110     05  EM-MIDDLE-INITIAL         PIC X(1).
025120     05  EM-HOURLY-RATE            PIC S9(2)V99.
025130     05  FILLER                    PIC X(30).
025140     05  EM-DATE-LAST-ACTIVITY     PIC 9(6).
030010*
030020*
030040 01  H1-HEADING-LINE-1.
030050     05  FILLER       PIC X(1).
030060     05  FILLER       PIC X(20)  VALUE 'RELATIVE MASTER FILE'.
030070     05  FILLER       PIC X(20)  VALUE ' FORMATTING         '.
030080     05  FILLER       PIC X(20)  VALUE '                    '.
030090     05  FILLER       PIC X(20)  VALUE '                    '.
030100     05  FILLER       PIC X(20)  VALUE '           RUN DAT'.
030110     05  FILLER       PIC X(2)   VALUE 'E '.
030120     05  H1-MONTH     PIC 9(2).
030130     05  FILLER       PIC X(1)   VALUE '/'.
030140     05  H1-DAY       PIC 9(2).
030150     05  FILLER       PIC X(1)   VALUE '/'.
030160     05  H1-YEAR      PIC 9(2).
030170     05  FILLER       PIC X(22)  VALUE SPACES.
031010*
031020*
031030 01  H2-HEADING-LINE-2.
031040     05  FILLER       PIC X(1).
031050     05  FILLER       PIC X(20)  VALUE 'FILE FORMAT CONTROL '.
031060     05  FILLER       PIC X(20)  VALUE 'REPORT             '.
031070     05  FILLER       PIC X(20)  VALUE ' ** EMPLOYEE MASTER'.
031080     05  FILLER       PIC X(20)  VALUE ' FILE **            '.
031090     05  FILLER       PIC X(20)  VALUE '                   '.
031100     05  FILLER       PIC X(6)   VALUE ' PAGE '.
031110     05  H2-PAGE-NBR  PIC ZZZ9.
031120     05  FILLER       PIC X(22)  VALUE SPACES.
035010*
035020*
035030 01  IE-I-O-ERROR-LINE.
035040     05  FILLER                   PIC X(1).
035050     05  FILLER                   PIC X(40)  VALUE SPACES.
035062     05  IE-FILE-STATUS-FLAG      PIC X(2).
035064     05  FILLER                   PIC X(1)   VALUE SPACES.
035066     05  IE-I-O-OPERATION-FLAG    PIC X(7).
035070     05  FILLER                   PIC X(9)   VALUE SPACES.
035080     05  IE-ERROR-KEY             PIC X(5).
035090     05  FILLER                   PIC X(3)   VALUE SPACES.
035260     05  IE-UPDATE-ACTION         PIC X(8).
035270     05  FILLER                   PIC X(1)   VALUE SPACES.
035280     05  IE-ERROR-MSG             PIC X(33).
035290     05  FILLER                   PIC X(23)  VALUE SPACES.
036010*
036020*
036040 01  TL-TOTAL-LINE.
036040     05  FILLER                   PIC X(1).
036050     05  FILLER                   PIC X(82)  VALUE SPACES.
036060     05  TL-COUNT-DESCRIPTION     PIC X(20).
036070     05  FILLER                   PIC X(1)   VALUE SPACES.
036080     05  TL-RECORD-COUNT          PIC ZZZ,ZZ9.
036090     05  FILLER                   PIC X(22)  VALUE SPACES.
050010*
050020*
050030*
050040 PROCEDURE DIVISION.
050050*
050060*
050070 000-FORMAT-RELATIVE-FILE.
050080*
050090     OPEN INPUT  FORMAT-PARAMETER-FILE
050100          OUTPUT RELATIVE-MASTER-FILE
050120                 REPORT-FILE.
050130     PERFORM 100-INITIALIZE-VARIABLE-FIELDS.
050134     PERFORM 870-PRINT-REPORT-HEADINGS.
050136     PERFORM 130-PROCESS-PARAMETER-RECORD.
050140     PERFORM 200-FORMAT-RELATIVE-RECORD
050150         UNTIL TC-SLOTS-FORMATTED
050155             IS NOT LESS THAN TC-SLOTS-TO-BE-FORMATTED.
050170     PERFORM 700-PRINT-REPORT-TOTALS.
050180     CLOSE FORMAT-PARAMETER-FILE
050190           RELATIVE-MASTER-FILE
050210           REPORT-FILE.
050220     STOP RUN.
100010*
100020*
100030 100-INITIALIZE-VARIABLE-FIELDS.
100040*
100050     MOVE 'NO ' TO WS-PARAMETER-END-OF-FILE-SW
100055                   WS-PROGRAM-ABEND-SW.
100120     MOVE ZERO TO WS-PAGE-COUNT.
100130     ADD 1 WS-LINES-PER-PAGE GIVING WS-LINES-USED.
100140     ACCEPT WS-DATE-WORK FROM DATE.
100150     MOVE WS-MONTH TO H1-MONTH.
100160     MOVE WS-DAY TO H1-DAY.
100170     MOVE WS-YEAR TO H1-YEAR.
100190     PERFORM 110-ZERO-RECORD-COUNTS
```

Figure 5C.3. COBOL coding: RELFORM program.

```
100200              VARYING TC-SUBSCRIPT
100210                  FROM 1
100220                  BY 1
100230                  UNTIL TC-SUBSCRIPT IS GREATER THAN TC-NUMBER-OF-ENTRIES.
100240          MOVE SPACES TO IE-I-O-ERROR-LINE.
100250          MOVE SPACES TO EM-EMPLOYEE-MASTER-WORK-AREA.
100260          MOVE ZEROS TO EM-EMPLOYEE-NUMBER.
110010*
110020*
110030  110-ZERO-RECORD-COUNTS.
110040*
110050          MOVE ZERO TO TC-RECORD-COUNT (TC-SUBSCRIPT).
120010*
120020*
120030  130-PROCESS-PARAMETER-RECORD.
120040*
120050          PERFORM 800-READ-PARAMETER-RECORD.
120060*
120070          IF NOT PARAMETER-END-OF-FILE
120080              IF FORMAT-PARAMETER-RECORD
120090                  IF FP-SLOTS-TO-BE-FORMATTED IS NUMERIC
120100                      MOVE FP-SLOTS-TO-BE-FORMATTED
120110                          TO TC-SLOTS-TO-BE-FORMATTED
120120                      PERFORM 800-READ-PARAMETER-RECORD
120130                  ELSE
120140                      MOVE 'INVALID PARAMETER FIELD' TO IE-ERROR-MSG
120150                      MOVE 'YES' TO WS-PROGRAM-ABEND-SW
120160              ELSE
120170                  MOVE 'INVALID PARAMETER RECORD CODE' TO IE-ERROR-MSG
120180                  MOVE 'YES' TO WS-PROGRAM-ABEND-SW
120190          ELSE
120200              MOVE 'PARAMETER RECORD MISSING' TO IE-ERROR-MSG
120210              MOVE 'YES' TO WS-PROGRAM-ABEND-SW.
120220*
120230          IF NOT PROGRAM-ABEND
120240          AND NOT PARAMETER-END-OF-FILE
120250              MOVE 'TOO MANY PARAMETER RECORDS' TO IE-ERROR-MSG
120260              MOVE 'YES' TO WS-PROGRAM-ABEND-SW.
120270*
120280          IF PROGRAM-ABEND
120290              MOVE 'ABORTED ' TO IE-UPDATE-ACTION
120300              MOVE IE-I-O-ERROR-LINE TO REPORT-LINE
120310              MOVE 3 TO WS-LINE-SPACING
120320              PERFORM 890-WRITE-REPORT-LINE
120330              MOVE ZEROS TO TC-SLOTS-TO-BE-FORMATTED.
200010*
200020*
200030  200-FORMAT-RELATIVE-RECORD.
200040*
200174          PERFORM 850-WRITE-MASTER-RECORD.
200182*
200184          IF PROGRAM-ABEND
200190              PERFORM 900-ABORT-PROGRAM-RUN.
700010*
700020*
700030  700-PRINT-REPORT-TOTALS.
700040*
700060          PERFORM 710-PRINT-TOTAL-LINE
700070              VARYING TC-SUBSCRIPT
700080                  FROM 1
700090                  BY 1
700100                  UNTIL TC-SUBSCRIPT IS GREATER THAN TC-NUMBER-OF-ENTRIES.
710010*
710020*
710030  710-PRINT-TOTAL-LINE.
```

```
710040*
710050          MOVE TC-COUNT-DESCRIPTION (TC-SUBSCRIPT)
710060              TO TL-COUNT-DESCRIPTION.
710070          MOVE TC-RECORD-COUNT (TC-SUBSCRIPT) TO TL-RECORD-COUNT.
710080          MOVE TL-TOTAL-LINE TO REPORT-LINE.
710090          MOVE 1 TO WS-LINE-SPACING.
710100          PERFORM 890-WRITE-REPORT-LINE.
800010*
800020*
800030  800-READ-PARAMETER-RECORD.
800040*
800070          READ FORMAT-PARAMETER-FILE INTO FP-FORMAT-PARAMETER-RECORD
800080              AT END MOVE 'YES' TO WS-PARAMETER-END-OF-FILE-SW.
850010*
850020*
850030  850-WRITE-MASTER-RECORD.
850040*
850045          MOVE 'WRITE ' TO WS-I-O-OPERATION-FLAG.
850050          WRITE RELATIVE-MASTER-RECORD
850060              FROM EM-EMPLOYEE-MASTER-WORK-AREA
850064              INVALID KEY MOVE 'YES' TO WS-PROGRAM-ABEND-SW.
850200*
850210          IF SUCCESSFUL-COMPLETION
850220              ADD 1 TO TC-SLOTS-FORMATTED
850230          ELSE
850240              MOVE 'YES' TO WS-PROGRAM-ABEND-SW.
870010*
870020*
870030  870-PRINT-REPORT-HEADINGS.
870040*
870050          ADD 1 TO WS-PAGE-COUNT.
870060          MOVE WS-PAGE-COUNT TO H2-PAGE-NBR.
870070          MOVE H1-HEADING-LINE-1 TO REPORT-LINE.
870080          PERFORM 880-WRITE-REPORT-TOP-LINE.
870090          MOVE H2-HEADING-LINE-2 TO REPORT-LINE.
870100          MOVE 1 TO WS-LINE-SPACING.
870110          PERFORM 890-WRITE-REPORT-LINE.
870180          MOVE SPACES TO REPORT-LINE.
870190          PERFORM 890-WRITE-REPORT-LINE.
880010*
880020*
880030  880-WRITE-REPORT-TOP-LINE.
880040*
880050          WRITE REPORT-LINE
880060              AFTER ADVANCING PAGE.
880070          MOVE 1 TO WS-LINES-USED.
890010*
890020*
890030  890-WRITE-REPORT-LINE.
890040*
890050          WRITE REPORT-LINE
890060              AFTER ADVANCING WS-LINE-SPACING.
890070          ADD WS-LINE-SPACING TO WS-LINES-USED.
900010*
900020*
900030  900-ABORT-PROGRAM-RUN.
900040*
900042          MOVE WS-FILE-STATUS-FLAG TO IE-FILE-STATUS-FLAG.
900044          MOVE WS-I-O-OPERATION-FLAG TO IE-I-O-OPERATION-FLAG.
900046          MOVE TC-SLOTS-FORMATTED TO IE-ERROR-KEY.
900050          MOVE 'ABORTED ' TO IE-UPDATE-ACTION.
900055          MOVE 'I-O ERROR OCCURRED' TO IE-ERROR-MSG.
900060          MOVE IE-I-O-ERROR-LINE TO REPORT-LINE.
900070          MOVE 3 TO WS-LINE-SPACING.
900080          PERFORM 890-WRITE-REPORT-LINE.
900160          MOVE ZEROS TO TC-SLOTS-FORMATTED.
```

Figure 5C.3. (continued)

PROCEDURE DIVISION Entries

000-FORMAT-RELATIVE-FILE

This is a typical mainline module except for two aspects. First, there is not a priming read because this program is not driven by input transaction occurrences. Instead, the 130-PROCESS-PARAMETER-RECORD module is performed to process the parameter record.

Also, because this program is driven by a parameter field rather than by input record occurrences, the condition that terminates iterations of the 200-FORMAT-RELATIVE-RECORD module is not an end-of-file switch. Instead, iterations should stop after all of the record slots have been formatted, as called for by the parameter field value. Thus the PERFORM/UNTIL statement is coded as PERFORM 200-FORMAT-RELATIVE-RECORD UNTIL TC-SLOTS-FORMATTED IS NOT LESS THAN TC-SLOTS-TO-BE-FORMATTED.

100-INITIALIZE-VARIABLE-FIELDS

This is a conventional initialization module. Notice that the last two statements of the module initialize the output record area in WORKING-STORAGE. The record area is first blanked by the statement MOVE SPACES TO EM-EMPLOYEE-MASTER-WORK-AREA. This is done to provide a "clean" dummy record. (Sometimes dummy records are formatted with HIGH-VALUES instead of SPACES.) Then the key field, EM-EMPLOYEE-NUMBER, is set to zeros so that, when the record is written, it will be a dummy record.

130-PROCESS-PARAMETER-RECORD

This module processes and validates the parameter file. First, the 800-READ-PARAMETER-RECORD paragraph is performed to read the first parameter record.

A nested IF statement is used to validate that (1) a record is present in the parameter file, (2) the FP-RECORD-CODE field contains the correct record-code value of 08, and (3) the FP-SLOTS-TO-BE-FORMATTED field contains a numeric value. The first of the above validations that are not satisfied is identified as an error by setting the IE-ERROR-MSG field with the appropriate error message and then setting the WS-PROGRAM-ABEND-SW to "YES" to reflect a PROGRAM-ABEND condition.

If a valid parameter record has been read, the FP-SLOTS-TO-BE-FOR-MATTED field is first moved to the total count table area so that it can be later printed. Then the 800-READ-PARAMETER-RECORD module is again performed as a check to ensure that no stray records are present in the parameter file.

The second IF statement in this paragraph makes the test for stray records. If it is not a PROGRAM-ABEND condition and not a PARAMETER-END-OF-FILE condition, it means that another record was encountered in the parameter file. If this occurs, an error message is moved to the IE-ERROR-MSG field and the WS-PROGRAM-ABEND-SW is set.

In the third IF statement of this module, the PROGRAM-ABEND condition is tested. If a PROGRAM-ABEND condition was identified in one of the two previous IF statements, the IE-UPDATE-ACTION field is set to "ABORTED," and the error line is moved to the output area and printed on the audit/error list.

200-FORMAT-RELATIVE-RECORD

This module simply writes the dummy record from the EM-EMPLOYEE-MASTER-WORK-AREA by performing the 850-WRITE-MASTER-RECORD module. In the unlikely event that a PROGRAM-ABEND condition occurs during a WRITE operation, the program will be brought to an orderly termination by performing the 900-ABORT-PROGRAM-RUN module.

850-WRITE-MASTER-RECORD

This module writes each dummy record. After the expected SUCCESSFUL-COMPLETION has been identified, the TC-SLOTS-FORMATTED field is incremented.

900-ABORT-PROGRAM-RUN

Minor changes from previous programs have been made in this module to reflect the data-name changes that are required because there is no DL-DETAIL-LINE specified for this program.

When the distribution of key values for a file's records are not consecutive or nearly consecutive, a directly addressed relative file could consume enough unused space to prohibit the use of relative organization. If the key values are not consecutive but the random record-processing speed advantages of direct organization are required, an indirectly addressed file could be used. As discussed in Chapter 2 (page 54), indirectly addressed files require the use of a **randomizing algorithm** to determine the record slot for each key value.

In this topic, two general approaches to handling indirectly addressed files will be covered. However, before we discuss them, a few words of explanation are in order.

First, there can be a certain amount of confusion in terminology. Both **directly addressed** and **indirectly addressed files** are considered and called **direct files**.

Second, indirectly addressed files are rarely coded with COBOL relative file-processing syntax. ANS COBOL provides for the processing of directly addressed relative files. If a randomizing routine is coded into the program, the COBOL relative file syntax could be used to handle an indirectly addressed relative file. However, indirectly addressed files are usually coded using the nonstandard direct file COBOL language extensions provided with the COBOL compilers of various computer hardware vendors. There are two main reasons for this: (1) direct file-processing extensions were usually available before COBOL relative file-processing syntax was standardized, and (2) such extensions are usually tailored to the specific disk hardware that the vendor manufactures and hence may offer advantages in processing speed and programming convenience.

Third, indirectly addressed direct file organization is rarely chosen today. Although it was more frequently specified in the past when indexed organization was either not available or inefficient, files of indexed organization have three major advantages over indirectly addressed files: (1) they are more flexible with regard to key-field changes or key-field value distributions; (2) they are simpler to code because no randomizing routine or synonym record-handling logic need be provided; and (3) not only random but also sequential record retrieval is permitted. Indexed organization became a part of ANS COBOL effective with the 1974 standard. Over the years, indexed-access software efficiency has generally been enhanced from that which earlier compilers provided. At the same time, disk-processing speeds have increased. As a result, indexed organization now may offer quicker access to individual records than do indirectly addressed files, especially when the synonym volume of the indirectly addressed file is high.

In this chapter, indirectly addressed file logic will be discussed within the COBOL relative file framework. Because indirectly addressed files are seldom coded with the COBOL relative file syntax, no actual program coding will be referenced. Instead, general indirectly addressed file logic is presented as an aid to understanding programs that may be coded in various ways, depending upon the particular architecture of the disk hardware and the specific syntax of the compiler that is being used.

Indirectly addressed files can be classified as being either a **chained overflow** or **progressive overflow** type. General logic for each will be presented.

Chained Overflow

An employee master file will again be used as an application example. However, for the indirectly addressed file, we will specify Social Security number as the key field.

With chained overflow, there are two record areas: a **prime area** and an **overflow area**. Each record must contain a **chain field** that is used as a **pointer** to an overflow record when a synonym record is present in the file.

Space for 10,000 employee records is allocated in the prime area. Thus each 9-digit Social Security number must be randomized to a 4-digit (0000 through 9999) relative, or **actual** address. (However, because a COBOL relative address begins with actual address 1, rather than zero, the actual addresses will range from 0001 to 10000.) Space for 1,000 overflow records is allocated at relative addresses 10001 through 11000.

As explained in Chapter 2, although a digit-extraction randomizing algorithm is usually not as effective as one that uses prime number division, it will be employed in the examples of this topic because it is easier to explain in the diagrams and discussion.

Locating a Record

When attempting to locate a record in the employee file, the program must first access the prime area actual address to which the Social Security number randomizes. If that Social Security number key value is not present in the prime areas and a chain pointer exists, the overflow area must be searched.

Prime area location example

Figure 5D.1 illustrates the logic that is required to locate a particular record within an indirectly addressed file. Step A shows that the first step is to obtain the key-field value of the record that is being searched for.

Then the randomizing algorithm must process the key value to obtain the actual relative address, as shown in step B. A digit-extraction algorithm is used where the 9th, 7th, 5th, and 2nd digit are selected, in that order, to become the 4-digit address. Thus the Social Security number of 536-72-5807 randomizes to an actual relative address of 7823.

As diagrammed at step C, after the address is accessed, the search key value is compared with the record key value stored at that address.

If, as exhibited at step D, the search key value is equal to the record key value, the desired record has been found.

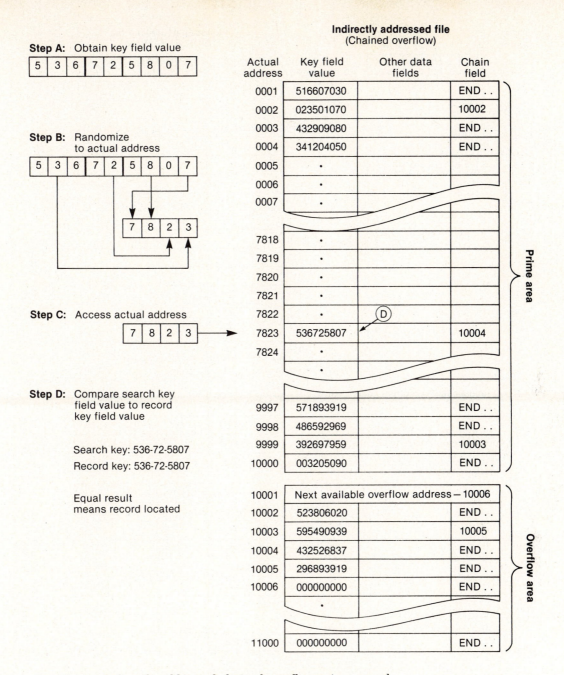

Step A: Obtain key field value

5	3	6	7	2	5	8	0	7

Step B: Randomize to actual address

5	3	6	7	2	5	8	0	7

7	8	2	3

Step C: Access actual address

7	8	2	3

Step D: Compare search key field value to record key field value

Search key: 536-72-5807

Record key: 536-72-5807

Equal result means record located

Indirectly addressed file
(Chained overflow)

Actual address	Key field value	Other data fields	Chain field	
0001	516607030		END ..	⎫
0002	023501070		10002	
0003	432909080		END ..	
0004	341204050		END ..	
0005	•			
0006	•			
0007				
7818	•			
7819	•			
7820	•			
7821	•			
7822	•	Ⓓ		Prime area
7823	536725807		10004	
7824	•			
	•			
9997	571893919		END ..	
9998	486592969		END ..	
9999	392697959		10003	
10000	003205090		END ..	⎭
10001	Next available overflow address — 10006			⎫
10002	523806020		END ..	
10003	595490939		10005	
10004	432526837		END ..	Overflow area
10005	296893919		END ..	
10006	000000000		END ..	
	•			
11000	000000000		END ..	⎭

Figure 5D.1. Locating an indirectly addressed chained-overflow prime record.

Overflow area location example

Figure 5D.2 provides an example of the logic that is required to locate a synonym record with a Social Security number of 432-52-6837, which is stored in the overflow area. Steps A through C are the same as in Figure 5D.1. However, at step D, notice that the search key value of 432-52-6837 is not equal to the prime area record key value of 536-72-5807.

As shown at step E, this means that the chain field that points to the overflow area must be tested to see if a synonym record is present in the overflow area.

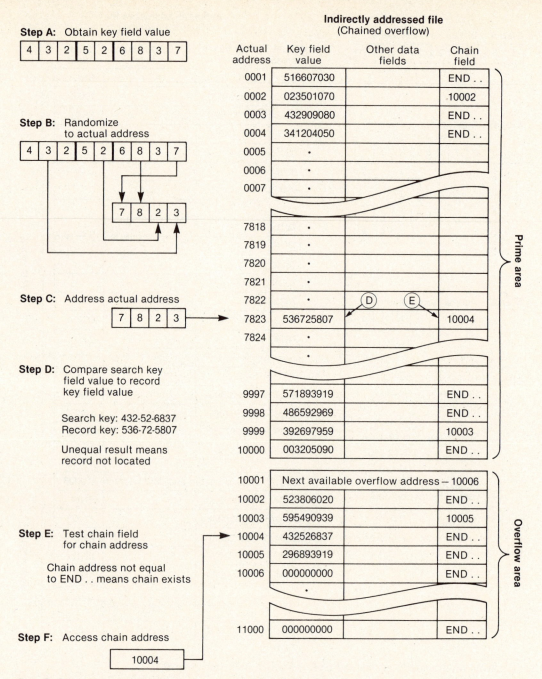

Step A: Obtain key field value

| 4 | 3 | 2 | 5 | 2 | 6 | 8 | 3 | 7 |

Step B: Randomize to actual address

| 4 | 3 | 2 | 5 | 2 | 6 | 8 | 3 | 7 |

| 7 | 8 | 2 | 3 |

Step C: Address actual address

| 7 | 8 | 2 | 3 |

Step D: Compare search key field value to record key field value

Search key: 432-52-6837
Record key: 536-72-5807

Unequal result means record not located

Step E: Test chain field for chain address

Chain address not equal to END . . means chain exists

Step F: Access chain address

| 10004 |

Step G: Compare search key field value to record key field value

Search key: 432-52-6837
Record key: 432-52-6837

Equal result means synonym record located

Indirectly addressed file
(Chained overflow)

Actual address	Key field value	Other data fields	Chain field	
0001	516607030		END . .	Prime area
0002	023501070		10002	
0003	432909080		END . .	
0004	341204050		END . .	
0005	.			
0006	.			
0007	.			
7818	.			
7819	.			
7820	.			
7821	.			
7822	.	Ⓓ Ⓔ		
7823	536725807		10004	
7824				
	.			
9997	571893919		END . .	
9998	486592969		END . .	
9999	392697959		10003	
10000	003205090		END . .	
10001	Next available overflow address — 10006			Overflow area
10002	523806020		END . .	
10003	595490939		10005	
10004	432526837		END . .	
10005	296893919		END . .	
10006	000000000		END . .	
	.			
11000	000000000		END . .	

Figure 5D.2. Locating an indirectly addressed chained-overflow synonym record.

A value of "END.." in the chain field signifies that it is the end of the chain—no additional synonym records are present in the file. (Although the specific value that is used to indicate end of chain is an arbitrary choice, zeros or a variation of the word "END" are probably most frequently used.) When a synonym record exists, the actual address of the chained synonym record is stored in the chain field.

At step F, therefore, the address that is contained in the chain field, 10004, is accessed. As shown at step G, the key-field values match. This means that the desired synonym record has been located. If there were more than one synonym record, steps E through G could be repeated until the matching key-field value was located or the end of the chain was reached. Observe that the actual address 9999 has a synonym chain of two records (at addresses 10003 and 10005) in the overflow area.

Notice in the figure that address 10001 contains an overflow control record rather than an employee master record. This overflow control record is used to keep track of the next available overflow record slot available for the addition of a new synonym record to the file. Although this example stores the overflow control record at the first overflow record address, it could be specified at alternative locations within the file or as a separate control file.

File-Maintenance Logic

As with all file-maintenance programs, a record cannot be added, changed, or deleted until it has been determined whether or not that key value already exists on the file. General logic for the file-maintenance requirements of locating, adding, changing, and deleting records of an indirectly addressed file with chained overflow will be presented in program flowchart form.

Locating a record

An overview of the procedure for locating a record within an indirectly addressed file was presented in Figures 5D.1 and 5D.2. Figure 5D.3 presents more detailed logic in flowchart form.

Observe that one work-area field and one switch field are referenced in the flowchart. The work-area field, Seek-address, is used to store the record slot address that is to be accessed. The Record-found switch is set to "YES" when a record match is made and set to "NO" when a matching record cannot be located.

The add, change, and delete record modules will use both fields. Hence this Locate-record module must be performed prior to each update function.

Adding a record

Logic for adding a new master record to the file is shown in the flowchart of Figure 5D.4. Recognize that three separate record areas must be provided in WORKING-STORAGE: one for creating new master records, one for saving records that the Locate-record module reads from the files, and one for the overflow control record.

Step A. Test Record-found switch.

The status of the Record-found switch, as set in the Locate-record module, is tested. If the Record-found switch is set to "YES," it means that a matching record is already present on the file, and so a new record should not be added. In this situation, an error routine is performed to identify the error, and then an exit is taken from this module.

If the Record-found switch is set to "NO," the record can be added to the file and the steps that follow are executed.

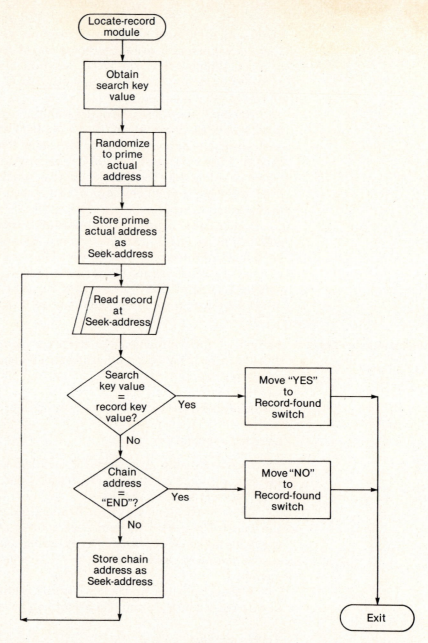

Figure 5D.3. Indirectly addressed chained-overflow logic for locating a record.

Step B. Create master record.

The master record is created in the master creation work area. This module would be similar to that coded in the RELMAINT program. In addition, a statement to set the chain field to the end-of-chain value must be provided.

Step C. Test Location of last record read.

If the Seek-address of the last record read in the Locate-record module was in the prime area, it means there was no record present in the prime area slot. Hence the record can simply be written at its appropriate prime area address, and then an exit may be taken from this module.

On the other hand, if the last record read was in the overflow area, additional steps must be taken to update synonym chains and the overflow control record.

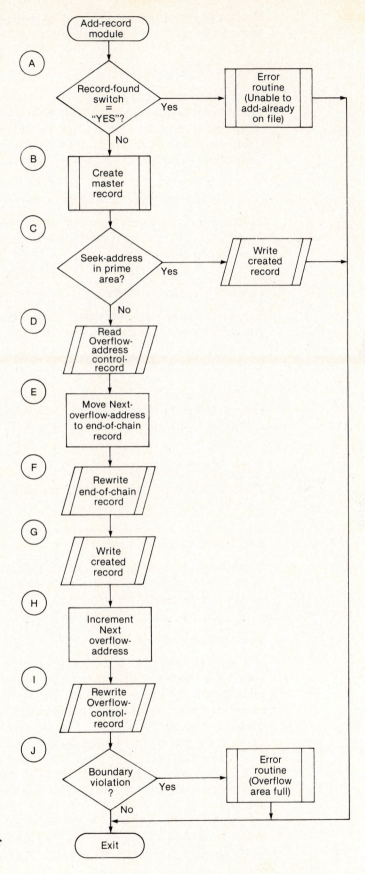

Figure 5D.4. Indirectly addressed chained-overflow logic for adding a record.

Step D. Read overflow control record.

The overflow control record must be read so that the location of the next unused record slot within the overflow area can be determined.

Step E. Link the chain field.

The last record read in the Locate-record module was at the previous end of the chain, so it contained an end-of-chain indication in the chain field. The new record that is being added must be added to this chain. Therefore, the next overflow address location that is obtained during step D must be moved to the chain field of the previous end-of-chain record.

Step F. Rewrite previous end-of-chain record.

The previous end-of-chain record must be rewritten with its chain field changed from "END.." to the actual address of the next overflow record slot where the new record will be added.

Step G. Write created record.

The new master record created at step B is now written at the next overflow record address. It is the new end-of-chain record for that synonym chain.

Step H. Increment next overflow address.

A record slot has just been consumed, so the next overflow address that is contained within the overflow control record must be incremented by 1 so that it will point to the next unused address.

Step I. Rewrite overflow control record.

The overflow control record, which now reflects the new next unused address, must be rewritten to the file.

Step J. Test boundary violation.

If the end of the overflow area has been reached, no additional add records can be processed in the overflow area. Hence an error message that identifies a full overflow area should be issued.

Other considerations.

If this program were a batch program that operated with exclusive control of the master file, it would be more efficient, in terms of I-O operations, not to read the overflow control record (step D) and to rewrite the overflow control record (step I) for each iteration of this module. Instead, the overflow control record could be read at the beginning of the run and saved in WORKING-STORAGE. Then, at the end of the run, the updated record control record could be written.

Also, to minimize "lock-out" time during an on-line run, it would be more efficient to move steps H and I to take place immediately after step D. (The flowchart sequence was chosen for ease of comprehension and use of terminology.)

Although the term "write" is used for the two I-O operations of the flowchart, it should be recognized that the actual coding would probably show a rewrite operation because of the usual file-formatting requirements.

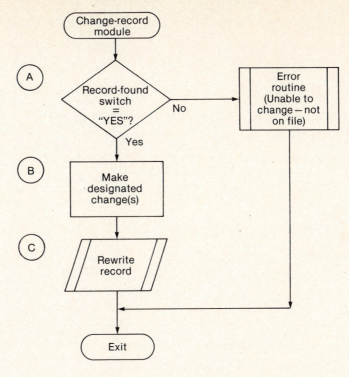

Figure 5D.5. Indirectly addressed chained-overflow logic for changing a record.

Changing a record

The logic for changing a record is not unlike that coded for the RELMAINT program. It is shown in the flowchart of Figure 5D.5.

Step A. Test Record-found switch.

If the record was not found in the Locate-record module, it cannot, of course, be changed. Instead, an error message must be issued and an exit made from the module.

Step B. Make change(s).

Any changes that are specified within the transaction record must be made to the master record.

Step C. Rewrite changed record.

To complete the change process, the changed record must be rewritten to the file.

Deleting a record

The logic for deleting a record is also similar to that coded for the RELMAINT program. Figure 5D.6 presents it in flowchart form.

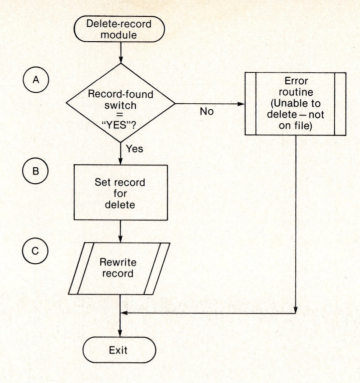

Figure 5D.6. Indirectly addressed chained-overflow logic for deleting a record.

Step A. Test Record-found switch.

If the record was not located in the Locate-record module, the record, of course, cannot be deleted. Instead, an error message must be issued and an exit made from the module.

Step B. Set record for delete.

Whatever method of deleted-record indication that is being used must be set in the master record.

Step C. Delete record.

To complete the delete process, the record that is being deleted must be rewritten to the file that carries the deleted-record indication.

Other considerations.

The logic of this module handles functional but not actual deletion of records. This means that deleted records will exist in the overflow chain; the space for deleted records is not reclaimed. With such processing, it is necessary to develop and periodically run a reorganization program to physically remove the deleted records, reposition the overflow records, and reset the overflow control record address.

Progressive Overflow

With the progressive overflow method of handling synonym records, there is no chain address field within each record or a separate overflow record area for the file. Instead, a synonym record is stored as close as possible, within a

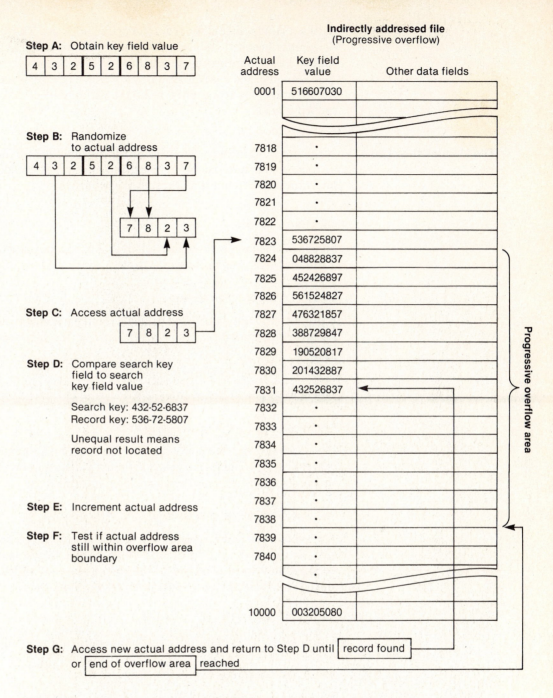

Step A: Obtain key field value

4	3	2	5	2	6	8	3	7

Step B: Randomize to actual address

4	3	2	5	2	6	8	3	7

7	8	2	3

Step C: Access actual address

7	8	2	3

Step D: Compare search key field to search key field value

Search key: 432-52-6837
Record key: 536-72-5807

Unequal result means record not located

Step E: Increment actual address

Step F: Test if actual address still within overflow area boundary

Indirectly addressed file
(Progressive overflow)

Actual address	Key field value	Other data fields
0001	516607030	
7818	•	
7819	•	
7820	•	
7821	•	
7822	•	
7823	536725807	
7824	048828837	
7825	452426897	
7826	561524827	
7827	476321857	
7828	388729847	
7829	190520817	
7830	201432887	
7831	432526837	
7832	•	
7833	•	
7834	•	
7835	•	
7836	•	
7837	•	
7838	•	
7839	•	
7840	•	
	•	
10000	003205080	

Progressive overflow area

Step G: Access new actual address and return to Step D until | record found |
or | end of overflow area | reached

Figure 5D.7. Locating an indirectly addressed progressive overflow synonym record.

chosen limit, to its prime actual address. The links in the chain of the progressive overflow method are simply adjacent record slots.

The logic for locating a record that is stored at its prime actual address is the same as that for the chained-overflow method (refer to Figure 5D.1).

Figure 5D.7 depicts records of a file in which synonym records are stored by the progressive overflow method. Observe that at steps A through D an attempt was made to locate a record with a Social Security number key value of 432-52-6837. However, a record with a different key is located at its prime address of 7823. In this example, it was decided that an overflow record be stored within a range of 15 slots from the prime address. Therefore, in steps E through G, adjacent record slots are searched until an equal key value is located or the search limit boundary is reached.

Although the search limit area of this example is expressed as a number of record slots, it is frequently defined as a number of disk tracks, disk sectors, or record blocks.

File-Maintenance Logic

Although similar logic can be used for the change and delete functions, modules to locate and add records to an indirectly addressed file with progressive overflow differ from that for chained overflow.

Locating a record

Figure 5D.8 shows a flowchart of logic that can be used to locate a record within a file that has progressive overflow.

Step A. Zero Closest-empty-slot field.

The Closest-empty-slot field is used to store the address of the closest empty record slot. It must be initialized to zero at the beginning of this module.

Step B. Obtain search key value.

The search key value of the record that is to be located must be obtained.

Step C. Randomize to Prime-relative-address.

The randomizing routine, whereby the search key value is converted to an actual address, is performed at this point. The actual address that is computed is stored in a field named Prime-relative-address.

Step D. Compute search boundary.

The record (or track, sector, block, and so on) limit within which the synonym may be located is stored in a field called Search-span-limit. This Search-address-limit field is added to the Prime-relative-address field, and the sum is stored in a field termed Search-limit-boundary.

Step E. Set Seek-address.

The Seek-address is initially set to the value of the Prime-relative-address field.

Step F. Read record at Seek-address.

A record is read from the Seek-address location.

Step G. Test matching key value.

The search key value is compared to the key value of the record just read from the file. If the keys are equal, the Record-found switch is set to "YES" and an exit is made from the module.

If, however, the key values are not equal, the following logic is executed.

Step H. Test if closest empty slot found yet.

The Closest-empty-slot field is compared to zero. If it is not zero, it means that the field already has been set with the address of the closest empty slot. In this case, the logic can continue to step I.

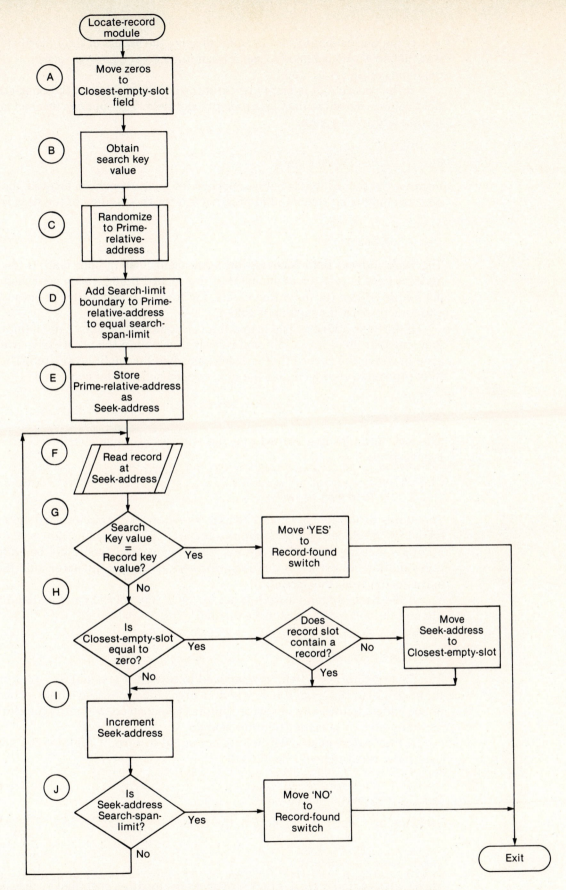

Figure 5D.8. Indirectly addressed progressive overflow logic for locating a record.

If the Closest-empty-slot is equal to zero, the status of the record slot that was just accessed is tested to see if it contains an active data record. If it does, the logic continues to step I.

If the record slot is empty or contains a deleted record, the Seek-address field value is moved to the Closest-empty-slot field. This slot can be used to store a valid add transaction.

Step I. Increment Seek-address.

Because the record that is being searched for has not yet been located, the Seek-address field is incremented in preparation for the reading of the next record.

Step J. Test Search-limit.

The Seek-address field is compared to the Search-span-limit field. If the Seek-address-field is greater, it means that the record that is being searched for is not on file. When this situation exists, the Record-found switch is set to "NO" and an exit from the module is taken.

If the Seek-address field is less than or equal to the Search-span-limit field, it means that there are additional record slots within the progressive overflow area in which the record that is being searched for might be located. The logic thus returns to step F so that the next record slot can be inspected.

Adding a record

The logic for adding a record to a file with progressive overflow is shown in Figure 5D.9.

Step A. Test Record-found switch.

The status of the Record-found switch, as set in the Locate-record module, is tested. If the Record-found switch is set to "YES," it means that a matching record is already present on the file, so a new record should not be added. In this situation, an error routine is performed to identify the error, and then an exit is taken from this module.

If the Record-found switch is set to "NO," the record can be added to the file and the following steps are executed.

Step B. Test if slot available.

The Closest-empty-slot field is compared to zero. If it is equal to zero, it means that there is no slot available in which to place the record, so a new record cannot be added. In this case, an error routine is performed to identify the situation, and then an exit is made from the module.

If the Closest-empty-slot field is not equal to zero, it contains the address where the record should be placed.

Step C. Create master record.

Because the record can be added, the record is created.

Step D. Write created record.

The newly created record is now written at the location specified by the Closest-empty-slot field. After the record is written, an exit is taken from this module.

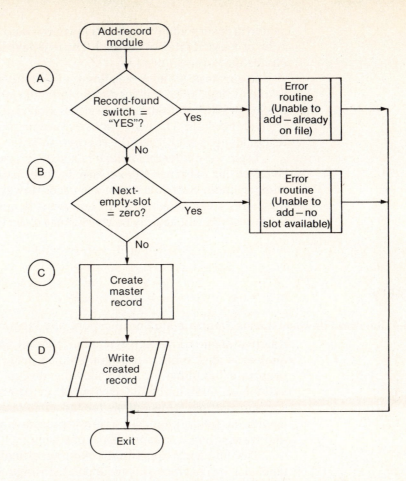

Figure 5D.9. Indirectly addressed progressive overflow logic for adding a record.

Discussion of Chained and Progressive Overflow Considerations

The chained overflow example discussed above used one separate **general overflow area**. Often with chained overflow, a portion of each cylinder is reserved as a **cylinder overflow area** and is used for synonym records whose prime record address is on that cylinder. This approach can reduce access time because the disk-access arm need not move to locate overflow records. When cylinder overflow areas are used, a general overflow area is often additionally specified to contain synonym records in the event that a cylinder overflow area is full.

Chained overflow is sometimes specified with no dedicated overflow area. Instead, as with the progressive overflow method, an adjacent, unused prime record area location is used to store synonym records.

Another chained overflow variation is that, rather than having a chain field within each record, one chain record is written on each disk track and is used to point to the next track where synonym records are located.

The way that an indirectly addressed file is loaded can affect record-retrieval speed. If a chained overflow technique is used with nondedicated overflow areas, a **two-pass load** will provide better retrieval results. During the first pass, only prime records are loaded. In the second pass, the synonym records are loaded and the chains are updated. If a one-pass load were used, a synonym record might be placed in what would be a prime location for a record to be processed later in the load. The two-pass load will minimize the number of chains that are required.

Regardless of how overflows are handled, **activity loading** can reduce retrieval time. With this load technique, the most frequently accessed records are loaded first so that they are either stored at their prime location or near the front of the chain. The use of activity loading requires the maintenance of statistics to identify each record's relative activity.

Logic for chained overflow is somewhat more complex than that which is required for progressive overflow but will usually result in shorter searches when cylinder overflow areas are used. However, the use of progressive overflow with a low-packing factor can provide equally good results because synonym records will usually be stored very close to their prime address locations.

Summary

Topic 5-A Relative File-Maintenance Programming Specifications and Program Design

Relative master files are typically updated randomly. When a programmer/analyst is specifying a file-maintenance program, he or she must choose appropriate handling for the following design alternatives: transaction data validation, audit/error list treatment, error-record handling, transaction file sorting, multiple transactions for the same master record, change-transaction modifiable fields, change-transaction formatting, change-to-null requirements, and transaction correspondence checking.

The following items that relate specifically to relative file maintenance must also be considered: key-field value range, whether or not to embed the key value in the record, deleted-record indication, transaction file sequencing, abnormal program termination due to an unrecoverable I-O error, and record counts.

Topic 5-B Relative File-Maintenance Program Coding

This topic presents detailed program coding for the RELMAINT program.

Topic 5-C Creation of a Relative File

Before a relative file area is formatted, it is termed an **unformatted** or **unloaded file**. A relative file is typically **formatted** or **loaded** by a program that initializes each record area with a dummy record in accordance with the application requirements. A file that contains only dummy records is called an **empty loaded file**.

Topic 5-D Indirectly Addressed File Logic

When the distribution of key values for a file's records are not consecutive or nearly consecutive, an indirectly addressed file that uses a **randomizing algorithm** can be specified. Indirectly addressed files can be classified as either the chained overflow or the progressive overflow type. With **chained overflow**, most records are stored in a **prime area**; however, synonym overflow records are stored in a separate **overflow area**. A **chain field** is used to link the synonyms. With the **progressive overflow** method, a separate overflow area is not provided. Instead, the synonym record is stored as close as possible, within a chosen limit, to its prime location.

Programming Assignments

5-1: Relative Commission Master File Maintenance

Program description

A relative commission master file is to be randomly updated with input commission-transaction records. The input transaction file has been validated in a prior program step. An audit/error list is to be produced.

Input file

Commission-transaction file

Input-output file

Commission master file   Key field = Salesperson number

Output file

Audit/error list

Record formats

Commission master record (Record code "SM")

Commission-transaction record (Record code "55")

Audit/error list

Commission master record

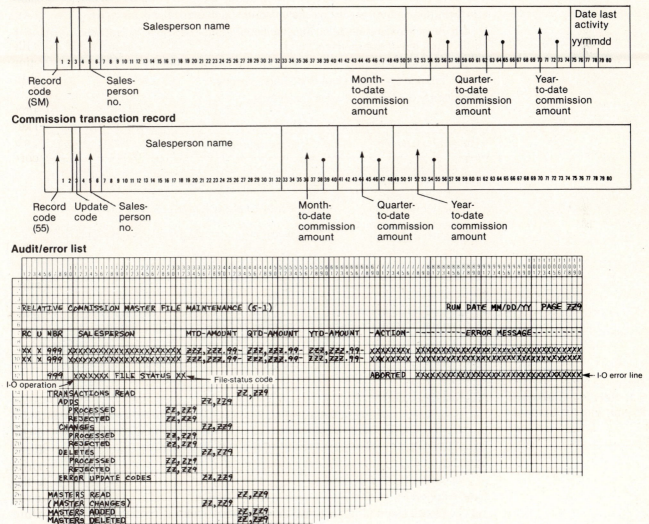

Commission transaction record

Audit/error list

Program operations

A. Read each input commission update-transaction record.

    1. Validate each transaction to ensure that it contains one of the following update codes:

        A (Add)

        C (Change)

        D (Delete)

B. Create a master record for each valid add transaction. **An inactive record (empty record slot) will either (1) contain zeros in the salesperson number field or (2) be a deleted record.**

    1. Store the run date as the date-last-activity in the master record.

C. If one or more of the following fields of a valid change transaction are not blank, change the master record fields accordingly.

    —Salesperson name

    —Month-to-date commission amount

    —Quarter-to-date commission amount

    —Year-to-date commission amount

    1. Store the run date as the date-last-activity in the master record.

D. Delete the master record for each valid delete transaction.

E. Tally master record counts as shown on the audit/error list print chart.

F. Print the audit/error list as shown on the audit/error list print chart.

    1. Single-space each detail line (but double-space between the last heading line and first detail line on each page).

    2. Skip to a new page before printing the record-count totals.

    3. Provide for a line span of 50 lines per page.

G. Identify the following error conditions.

Error condition	Error message
Add transaction but master already on file	UNABLE ADD-MASTER ALREADY ON FILE
Change transaction but master not on file	UNABLE CHANGE-MASTER NOT ON FILE
Delete transaction but master not on file	UNABLE DELETE-MASTER NOT ON FILE
Invalid update code	INVALID UPDATE CODE
Input-output error	FATAL I-O ERROR HAS OCCURRED

Assignment 5-1   Option 1

    Write a program to format the relative commission master file.

5-2: Relative Employee Master File Maintenance

Program description

    An indirectly addressed relative employee master file is to be randomly updated with input employee-transaction records. The input transaction file has been validated in a prior program step. An audit/error list is to be produced.

Input file

    Employee-transaction file

Input-output file

    Employee master file   Key field = Employee number (randomized)

Output file

    Audit/error list

Record formats

Employee master record (Record code "EM")
Employee-transaction record (Record code "37")
Audit/error list

Employee master record

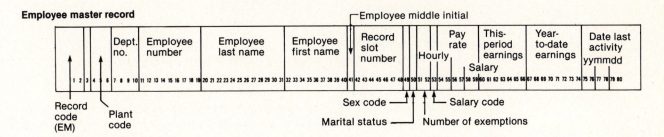

Employee transaction record

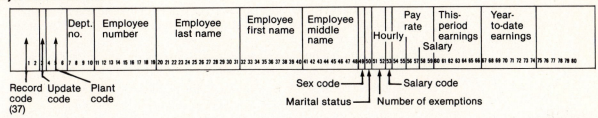

Audit/error list

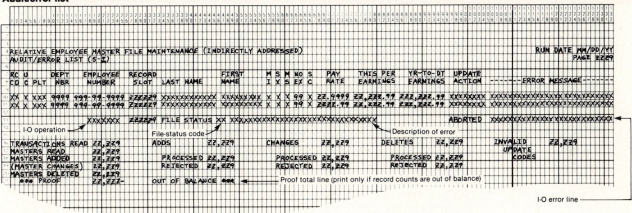

Program operations

A. **The relative file is to be indirectly addressed. 100 record slots are to be allocated. Use prime number division as a randomizing algorithm.**

B. Read each input employee update-transaction record.

1. Validate each transaction to ensure that it contains one of the following update codes:

    1 (Delete)

    2 (Add)

    3 (Change)

C. Create a master record for each valid add transaction.

1. Store the run date as the date-last-activity in the master record.

2. Store the relative record number in the master record.

D. If one or more of the following fields of a valid change transaction are not blank, change the master record fields accordingly.

—Employee last name

—Employee first name
—Employee middle initial*
—Sex code
—Marital status
—Number of exemptions
—Salary code*
—Hourly rate
—Earnings this period

1. Store the run date as the date-last-activity in the master record.

2. Before printing the change-transaction record on the audit/error list, print a line that shows the master record contents before the change.

3. If any one of the fields marked above by an asterisk contains an asterisk in the leftmost portion of the field and the remainder (if any) of the position are blank, change the corresponding field of the master record to spaces.

E. Delete the master record for each valid delete transaction.

1. Correspondence check the first six characters of the employee last name on the transaction record with the first six characters of the employee last name on the master record.

2. Before printing the delete-transaction record on the audit/error list, print a line that shows the master record contents before the deletion.

F. Tally master record counts as shown on the audit/error list print chart.

G. Print the audit/error list as shown on the audit/error list print chart.

1. On the master-record contents line for change and delete transactions, print the word "MASTER" in the update-action field of the audit line.

2. For each applicable transaction, single-space between master-record contents and transaction-record audit/error lines.

3. Double-space between transactions.

4. Provide for a line span of 50 lines per page (but do not break a transaction or the record-count totals between pages).

H. Identify the following error conditions.

Error condition	Error message
Add transaction but master already on file	UNABLE ADD-ALREADY ON FILE
Change transaction but master not on file	UNABLE CHANGE-NOT ON FILE
Delete transaction but master not on file	UNABLE DELETE-NOT ON FILE
Delete transaction but fails correspondence check	UNABLE DELETE-FAILS CORR CK
Invalid update code	UPDATE CODE INVALID
Synonym key value	UNABLE PROCESS-SYNONYM KEY
Input-output error	FATAL I-O ERROR OCCURRED

Assignment 5-2   Option 1
Write a program to format the relative employee master file.

Assignment 5-2   Option 2
Provide an extended search for storage and retrieval of synonyms within a span of 10 slots from the prime slot.

CHAPTER 6

CODING FOR RETRIEVAL PROGRAMS

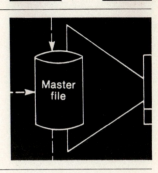

Topic 6-A: Record-Access Modes
Topic 6-B: Alternate Record Keys

6
CODING FOR RETRIEVAL PROGRAMS

COBOL provides three modes for accessing records within a file: SEQUENTIAL, RANDOM, and DYNAMIC. SEQUENTIAL and RANDOM access have been introduced in previous chapters. In Topic 6-A, a number of additional SEQUENTIAL access retrieval methods will be covered and the DYNAMIC access mode will be discussed.

Some COBOL compilers allow the specification of one or more **alternate record keys** (which are sometimes called **alternate indexes**) with files of INDEXED organization. Alternate keys are covered in Topic 6-B.

■ TOPIC 6-A: **Record-Access Modes**

The Current Record Pointer

SEQUENTIAL Access
    The Sequential READ Statement
    The START Statement
        START statement with KEY phrase EQUAL TO operator
        START statement with KEY phrase GREATER THAN operator
        START statement with KEY phrase NOT LESS THAN operator
        START statement with no KEY phrase
        START statement for generic processing
    Skip-Sequential Retrieval
    Generic Retrieval
    Limits Retrieval

RANDOM Access

DYNAMIC Access

The Current Record Pointer

Current record pointer is a term that is used to facilitate the description of the *next* record that is to be processed within a file. Recognize that the current record pointer is only a conceptual entity—not an actual field.

The current record pointer concept applies only to files that are opened as INPUT or I-O whose ACCESS MODE IS SEQUENTIAL or DYNAMIC (dynamic access will be covered later in this topic); it has no meaning for a file that is opened as OUTPUT or whose ACCESS MODE IS RANDOM. The setting of the current record pointer is affected only by the OPEN, READ, and START statements. Applicable OPEN statements set the current record pointer to the first logical record within the file (unless the REVERSED phrase is used, in which case the current record pointer is set to the last logical record of the file).

From time to time within this chapter, the current record pointer will be used to identify record-processing sequences.

Example:

```
READ INDEXED-MASTER-FILE

    INTO EM-EMPLOYEE-MASTER-WORK-AREA

    AT END MOVE 'YES' TO WS-MASTER-END-OF-FILE-SW.
```

Figure 6A.1. Sequential READ statement format.

SEQUENTIAL Access

SEQUENTIAL is the most commonly used ACCESS MODE for retrieval programs. It is used for all files whose ORGANIZATION IS SEQUENTIAL and for most report programs, regardless of the organization method.

The Sequential READ Statement

Figure 6A.1 shows the sequential READ statement format. It should be familiar, for this is the format that is used in the SEQMAINT program of Chapter 3 to read from sequential files. It was also used in the INDBACK program of Chapter 4 to read sequentially from an indexed file. Although an example is not provided in this text, the READ statement format could also be used to read sequentially from a relative file.

In the format, notice the entry NEXT. When ACCESS MODE IS SEQUENTIAL, use of the word NEXT is optional. However, when ACCESS MODE IS DYNAMIC, the reserved word NEXT *must* be specified.

The sequential READ statement always reads the record to which the current record pointer points and, after successful completion of the read operation, updates the current record pointer to point to the next logical record within the file.

Figure 6A.2 shows an example of a sequential employee roster report retrieved from the indexed employee master file that was introduced in Chapter 4. For example purposes, the number of records that are present in the file has been limited to seven.

An example of coding for a program to produce this type of report is presented in Figure 6A.3. It is called SEQRET, for **sequential retrieval**. The program begins the retrieval with the first record of the file and prints each record until end-of-file has been reached. This program presents no new programming

```
          EMPLOYEE ROSTER                    SEQUENTIAL RETRIEVAL
                                                PRIME RECORD KEY


          PLANT    DEPT    EMP     LAST       DATE 05/17/84
          CODE     NBR     NBR     NAME            PAGE    1

           NY      7777    50000   ERNST
           NY      7777    70000   KOCH
           NY      7777    80000   ERNST
           SF      1000    11111   STEELE
           SF      1000    44444   BASHFORD
           SF      1000    55555   FEINSTEIN
           SF      2000    22222   CAEN
```

Figure 6A.2. Sequential retrieval example.

```
001010 IDENTIFICATION DIVISION.
001020 PROGRAM-ID.     SEQRET.
001030*
001040*
001050*          EMPLOYEE ROSTER REPORT
001060*          INDEXED ORGANIZATION FILE
001070*          SEQUENTIAL RETRIEVAL - PRIME RECORD KEY
001080*
001090*
002010*
002020*
002030*
002040 ENVIRONMENT DIVISION.
002050*
002060*
002070 CONFIGURATION SECTION.
002080*
002090 SOURCE-COMPUTER.  IBM-370.
002100 OBJECT-COMPUTER.  IBM-370.
002110*
002120*
002130 INPUT-OUTPUT SECTION.
002140*
002150 FILE-CONTROL.
002180      SELECT INDEXED-MASTER-FILE
002190          ASSIGN TO INDFILE
002194          ORGANIZATION IS INDEXED
002195          ACCESS MODE IS SEQUENTIAL
002196          RECORD KEY IS RK-INDEXED-KEY
002199          FILE STATUS IS WS-FILE-STATUS-FLAG.
002220      SELECT REPORT-FILE
002230          ASSIGN TO UT-S-PRTFILE.
003010*
003020*
003030*
003040 DATA DIVISION.
003050*
003060*
003070 FILE SECTION.
003080*
003090*
004010*
004020*
004030 FD  INDEXED-MASTER-FILE
004040      RECORD CONTAINS 80 CHARACTERS
004050      LABEL RECORDS ARE STANDARD.
004060*
004070 01  INDEXED-MASTER-RECORD.
004080     05  FILLER                    PIC X(3).
004090     05  RK-INDEXED-KEY.
004100         10  RK-PLANT-CODE          PIC X(2).
004110         10  RK-DEPARTMENT-NUMBER   PIC X(4).
004120         10  RK-EMPLOYEE-NUMBER     PIC X(5).
004130     05  FILLER                    PIC X(66).
006010*
006020*
006030 FD  REPORT-FILE
006040      RECORD CONTAINS 133 CHARACTERS
006050      LABEL RECORDS ARE OMITTED.
006060*
006070 01  REPORT-LINE.
006080     05  FILLER                    PIC X(133).
010010*
010020*
010030 WORKING-STORAGE SECTION.
010040*
010050*
010060 01  WS-SWITCHES.
010070*
010100     05  WS-MASTER-END-OF-FILE-SW  PIC X(3).
010110         88  MASTER-END-OF-FILE                VALUE 'YES'.
010300     05  WS-PROGRAM-ABEND-SW        PIC X(3).
010310         88  PROGRAM-ABEND                     VALUE 'YES'.
010320     05  WS-FILE-STATUS-FLAG        PIC X(2).
```

```
010330         88  SUCCESSFUL-COMPLETION              VALUE '00'.
010340         88  DUPLICATE-ALTERNATE-KEY            VALUE '02'.
010350         88  END-OF-FILE                        VALUE '10'.
010360         88  SEQUENCE-ERROR                     VALUE '21'.
010370         88  DUPLICATE-KEY                      VALUE '22'.
010380         88  NO-RECORD-FOUND                    VALUE '23'.
010390         88  BOUNDARY-VIOLATION-IND-REL         VALUE '24'.
010400         88  PERMANENT-I-O-DATA-ERROR           VALUE '30'.
010410         88  BOUNDARY-VIOLATION-SEQ             VALUE '34'.
010420*        88  IMPLEMENTOR-DEFINED-ERROR          VALUE '9'.
010430     05  WS-I-O-OPERATION-FLAG      PIC X(7).
012010*
012020*
012030 01  WS-REPORT-CONTROLS.
012040     05  WS-PAGE-COUNT             PIC S9(4)        COMP-3.
012050     05  WS-LINES-PER-PAGE         PIC S99 VALUE +60
012060                                                   COMP SYNC.
012070     05  WS-LINES-USED             PIC S9(2)        COMP SYNC.
012080     05  WS-LINE-SPACING           PIC S9(2).
013010*
013020*
013030 01  WS-WORK-AREAS.
013040     05  WS-DATE-WORK              PIC 9(6).
013050     05  WS-DATE-REFORMAT REDEFINES WS-DATE-WORK.
013060         10  WS-YEAR               PIC 9(2).
013070         10  WS-MONTH              PIC 9(2).
013080         10  WS-DAY                PIC 9(2).
019010*
019020*
019030 01  FS-FILE-STATUS-TABLE-CONTROLS.
019040     05  FS-NUMBER-OF-ENTRIES      PIC S9(4)     VALUE +11
019050                                                   COMP SYNC.
019110*
019130 01  FS-FILE-STATUS-TABLE-DATA.
019140     05  FILLER PIC X(28) VALUE '00SUCCESSFUL COMPLETION       '.
019150     05  FILLER PIC X(28) VALUE '02DUPLICATE ALTERNATE KEY     '.
019160     05  FILLER PIC X(28) VALUE '10END OF FILE                 '.
019170     05  FILLER PIC X(28) VALUE '21SEQUENCE ERROR              '.
019180     05  FILLER PIC X(28) VALUE '22DUPLICATE KEY               '.
019190     05  FILLER PIC X(28) VALUE '23NO RECORD FOUND             '.
019200     05  FILLER PIC X(28) VALUE '24BOUNDARY VIOLATION-IND/REL'.
019210     05  FILLER PIC X(28) VALUE '30PERMANENT-I-O-DATA-ERROR    '.
019220     05  FILLER PIC X(28) VALUE '34BOUNDARY VIOLATION-SEQ      '.
019230     05  FILLER PIC X(28) VALUE '9 IMPLEMENTOR DEFINED ERROR '.
019240     05  FILLER PIC X(28) VALUE '  DESCRIPTION NOT AVAILABLE '.
019310*
019330 01  FS-FILE-STATUS-TABLE REDEFINES FS-FILE-STATUS-TABLE-DATA.
019340     05  FS-FILE-STATUS-ENTRY      OCCURS 11 TIMES
019350                                   INDEXED BY FS-INDEX.
019360         10  FS-FILE-STATUS-CODE         PIC X(2).
019370         10  FS-FILE-STATUS-DESCRIPTION PIC X(26).
025010*
025020*
025030 01  EM-EMPLOYEE-MASTER-WORK-AREA.
025040     05  EM-RECORD-CODE            PIC X(2).
025050     05  FILLER                    PIC X(1).
025060     05  EM-PLANT-CODE             PIC X(2).
025070     05  EM-DEPARTMENT-NUMBER      PIC X(4).
025080     05  EM-EMPLOYEE-NUMBER        PIC X(5).
025090     05  EM-LAST-NAME              PIC X(13).
025100     05  EM-FIRST-NAME             PIC X(12).
025110     05  EM-MIDDLE-INITIAL         PIC X(1).
025120     05  EM-HOURLY-RATE            PIC S9(2)V99.
025130     05  FILLER                    PIC X(30).
025140     05  EM-DATE-LAST-ACTIVITY     PIC 9(6).
030010*
030020*
030030 01  H1-HEADING-LINE-1.
030040     05  FILLER  PIC X(1).
030050     05  FILLER  PIC X(20)  VALUE '   EMPLOYEE ROSTER '.
030060     05  FILLER  PIC X(20)  VALUE '           SEQUENTIA'.
030070     05  FILLER  PIC X(20)  VALUE 'L RETRIEVAL        '.
030080     05  FILLER  PIC X(72)  VALUE SPACES.
031010*
```

Figure 6A.3. COBOL coding: SEQRET program.

```
031020*
031030 01  H2-HEADING-LINE-2.
031040     05  FILLER                   PIC X(1).
031050     05  FILLER                   PIC X(20)  VALUE '                    '.
031060     05  FILLER                   PIC X(20)  VALUE '            PRIME   '.
031070     05  FILLER                   PIC X(20)  VALUE ' RECORD KEY         '.
031080     05  FILLER                   PIC X(72)  VALUE SPACES.
032010*
032020*
032030 01  H3-HEADING-LINE-3.
032040     05  FILLER                   PIC X(1).
032050     05  FILLER                   PIC X(20)  VALUE '       PLANT    DEPT '.
032060     05  FILLER                   PIC X(20)  VALUE 'EMP     LAST     DA'.
032070     05  FILLER                   PIC X(03)  VALUE 'TE '.
032080     05  H1-MONTH                 PIC 9(2).
032090     05  FILLER                   PIC X(1)   VALUE '/'.
032100     05  H1-DAY                   PIC 9(2).
032110     05  FILLER                   PIC X(1)   VALUE '/'.
032120     05  H1-YEAR                  PIC 9(2).
032130     05  FILLER                   PIC X(81)  VALUE SPACES.
033010*
033020*
033030 01  H4-HEADING-LINE-4.
033040     05  FILLER                   PIC X(1).
033050     05  FILLER                   PIC X(20)  VALUE '       CODE    NBR  '.
033060     05  FILLER                   PIC X(20)  VALUE 'NBR     NAME        '.
033070     05  FILLER                   PIC X(07)  VALUE ' PAGE '.
033080     05  H2-PAGE-NBR              PIC ZZZ9.
033090     05  FILLER                   PIC X(83)  VALUE SPACES.
034010*
034020*
034030 01  DL-DETAIL-LINE.
034040     05  FILLER                   PIC X(1).
034050     05  FILLER                   PIC X(5)   VALUE SPACES.
034060     05  DL-PLANT-CODE            PIC X(2).
034070     05  FILLER                   PIC X(5)   VALUE SPACES.
034080     05  DL-DEPARTMENT-NUMBER     PIC X(4).
034090     05  FILLER                   PIC X(3)   VALUE SPACES.
034100     05  DL-EMPLOYEE-NUMBER       PIC X(5).
034110     05  FILLER                   PIC X(3)   VALUE SPACES.
034120     05  DL-LAST-NAME             PIC X(13).
034130     05  FILLER                   PIC X(92)  VALUE SPACES.
035010*
035020*
035030 01  IE-I-O-ERROR-LINE.
035040     05  FILLER                   PIC X(1).
035050     05  IE-ERROR-KEY             PIC X(9)   VALUE '    KEY '.
035060     05  FILLER                   PIC XXBXXXXBXXXXX.
035070     05  FILLER                   PIC X(7)   VALUE ' OPRN '.
035080     05  IE-I-O-OPERATION-FLAG    PIC X(7).
035090     05  FILLER                   PIC X(14)  VALUE ' FILE STATUS '.
035100     05  IE-FILE-STATUS-FLAG      PIC X(2).
035110     05  FILLER                   PIC X(2)   VALUE SPACES.
035120     05  IE-FILE-STATUS-DESCR     PIC X(26).
035130     05  FILLER                   PIC X(13)  VALUE ' RUN ABORTED'.
035140     05  FILLER                   PIC X(39)  VALUE SPACES.
050010*
050020*
050030*
050040 PROCEDURE DIVISION.
050050*
050060*
050070 000-PRINT-EMPLOYEE-ROSTER.
050080*
050090     OPEN INPUT  INDEXED-MASTER-FILE
050100          OUTPUT REPORT-FILE.
050110     PERFORM 100-INITIALIZE-VARIABLE-FIELDS.
050120     PERFORM 810-READ-INDEXED-RECORD.
050130     PERFORM 200-PROCESS-INDEXED-RECORD
050140         UNTIL MASTER-END-OF-FILE.
050150     CLOSE INDEXED-MASTER-FILE
050160           REPORT-FILE.
050170     STOP RUN.
100010*
100020*
100030 100-INITIALIZE-VARIABLE-FIELDS.
100040*
100050     MOVE 'NO ' TO WS-MASTER-END-OF-FILE-SW.
100060     MOVE ZERO TO WS-PAGE-COUNT.
100070     ADD 1 WS-LINES-PER-PAGE GIVING WS-LINES-USED.
100080     ACCEPT WS-DATE-WORK FROM DATE.
100090     MOVE WS-MONTH TO H1-MONTH.
100100     MOVE WS-DAY TO H1-DAY.
100110     MOVE WS-YEAR TO H1-YEAR.

200010*
200020*
200030 200-PROCESS-INDEXED-RECORD.
200040*
200050     IF WS-LINES-USED IS NOT LESS THAN WS-LINES-PER-PAGE
200060         PERFORM 870-PRINT-REPORT-HEADINGS.
200070     MOVE EM-PLANT-CODE TO DL-PLANT-CODE.
200080     MOVE EM-DEPARTMENT-NUMBER TO DL-DEPARTMENT-NUMBER.
200090     MOVE EM-EMPLOYEE-NUMBER TO DL-EMPLOYEE-NUMBER.
200100     MOVE EM-LAST-NAME TO DL-LAST-NAME.
200110     MOVE DL-DETAIL-LINE TO REPORT-LINE.
200120     MOVE 1 TO WS-LINE-SPACING.
200130     PERFORM 890-WRITE-REPORT-LINE.
200140     PERFORM 810-READ-INDEXED-RECORD.
810010*
810020*
810030 810-READ-INDEXED-RECORD.
810040*
810050     MOVE 'READ  ' TO WS-I-O-OPERATION-FLAG.
810060     READ INDEXED-MASTER-FILE
810070          INTO EM-EMPLOYEE-MASTER-WORK-AREA
810080          AT END MOVE 'YES' TO WS-MASTER-END-OF-FILE-SW.
810090     IF NOT SUCCESSFUL-COMPLETION
810100     AND NOT MASTER-END-OF-FILE
810110         MOVE 'YES' TO WS-PROGRAM-ABEND-SW
810120         PERFORM 900-ABORT-PROGRAM-RUN.
870010*
870020*
870030 870-PRINT-REPORT-HEADINGS.
870040*
870050     ADD 1 TO WS-PAGE-COUNT.
870060     MOVE WS-PAGE-COUNT TO H1-PAGE-NBR.
870070     MOVE H1-HEADING-LINE-1 TO REPORT-LINE.
870080     PERFORM 880-WRITE-REPORT-TOP-LINE.
870090     MOVE H2-HEADING-LINE-2 TO REPORT-LINE.
870100     MOVE 1 TO WS-LINE-SPACING.
870110     PERFORM 890-WRITE-REPORT-LINE.
870120     MOVE H3-HEADING-LINE-3 TO REPORT-LINE.
870130     MOVE 3 TO WS-LINE-SPACING.
870140     PERFORM 890-WRITE-REPORT-LINE.
870150     MOVE H4-HEADING-LINE-4 TO REPORT-LINE.
870160     MOVE 1 TO WS-LINE-SPACING.
870170     PERFORM 890-WRITE-REPORT-LINE.
870180     MOVE SPACES TO REPORT-LINE.
870190     PERFORM 890-WRITE-REPORT-LINE.
880010*
880020*
880030 880-WRITE-REPORT-TOP-LINE.
880040*
880050     WRITE REPORT-LINE
880060         AFTER ADVANCING PAGE.
880070     MOVE 1 TO WS-LINES-USED.
890010*
890020*
890030 890-WRITE-REPORT-LINE.
890040*
890050     WRITE REPORT-LINE
890060         AFTER ADVANCING WS-LINE-SPACING.
890070     ADD WS-LINE-SPACING TO WS-LINES-USED.
900010*
900020*
900030 900-ABORT-PROGRAM-RUN.
900040*
900050     MOVE RK-INDEXED-KEY TO IE-ERROR-KEY.
900060     MOVE WS-I-O-OPERATION-FLAG TO IE-I-O-OPERATION-FLAG.
900070     MOVE WS-FILE-STATUS-FLAG TO IE-FILE-STATUS-FLAG.
900080     PERFORM 910-LOOKUP-FILE-STATUS-DESCR.
900090     MOVE FS-FILE-STATUS-DESCRIPTION (FS-INDEX)
900100         TO IE-FILE-STATUS-DESCR.
900110     MOVE IE-I-O-ERROR-LINE TO REPORT-LINE.
900120     MOVE 2 TO WS-LINE-SPACING.
900130     PERFORM 890-WRITE-REPORT-LINE.
900140     MOVE 'YES' TO WS-MASTER-END-OF-FILE-SW.
910010*
910020*
910030 910-LOOKUP-FILE-STATUS-DESCR.
910040*
910050     SET FS-INDEX TO 1.
910060     SEARCH FS-FILE-STATUS-ENTRY
910070         AT END SET FS-INDEX TO FS-NUMBER-OF-ENTRIES
910080         WHEN FS-FILE-STATUS-CODE (FS-INDEX)
910090             IS EQUAL TO WS-FILE-STATUS-FLAG
910100             NEXT SENTENCE.
```

Figure 6A.3. (continued)

concepts from those that were presented in Chapter 4. It will be used as a base to introduce programming considerations that are associated with other types of retrieval programs.

The START Statement

The START statement provides the capability to start sequential processing for a file whose ORGANIZATION IS INDEXED or RELATIVE at a location other than at its first record. Figure 6A.4 shows the START statement format. The START statement can only be used when the ACCESS MODE IS SEQUENTIAL or DYNAMIC. Its use is also restricted to files that are opened as INPUT or I-O.

Observe that one of three optional relation operators can be specified in the KEY phrase of a START statement: EQUAL TO (or =), GREATER THAN (or >), or NOT LESS THAN (or NOT <). In addition, the START statement can be

Format:

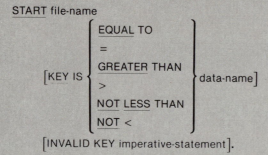

INVALID KEY conditions:

- Record not found (with key value that satisfies KEY phrase condition) [File status code = 23]

Notes:

- When ORGANIZATION IS INDEXED, data-name must be
  - the RECORD KEY, or
  - any ALTERNATE RECORD KEY field, or
  - a field subordinate to a group RECORD KEY field whose leftmost character position corresponds to the leftmost character position of the RECORD KEY field
- When ORGANIZATION IS RELATIVE, data-name must be the RELATIVE KEY field
- The START statement can be used only with files of INDEXED or RELATIVE organization
- The START statement can be used only with files opened as INPUT or I-O

Figure 6A.4. START statement format.

specified without a KEY phrase or for generic processing. Each of these five START statement variations will be discussed.

START statement with KEY phrase EQUAL TO operator

When the KEY phrase is specified and ORGANIZATION IS INDEXED, the data-name referenced must be one of the following: (1) the RECORD KEY field, (2) a field subordinate to a group RECORD KEY field whose leftmost character position is the same as the leftmost character position of the RECORD KEY field (such specification is used for generic processing and will be discussed later in this topic), or (3) an ALTERNATE RECORD KEY field (alternate keys are discussed in Topic 6-B). If ORGANIZATION IS RELATIVE, the data-name must be the RELATIVE KEY field. Before the START statement is executed, the desired starting value must be present in the data-name field.

Figure 6A.5 shows an example of a START statement with the EQUAL TO operator of the KEY phrase. Observe that the value of "NY777770000" is moved to the RECORD KEY field before the START statement is encountered. Since there is a record on file with an equal key, the current record pointer points to that record after the START statement has been executed. This is shown at point B in the figure. Because a record which fulfills the KEY phrase relationship is present on the file, the file status indicator is set to represent a successful completion. Point C in the figure illustrates an update of the file status indicator.

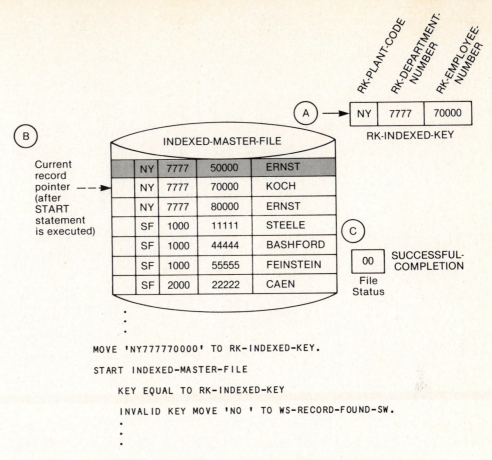

Figure 6A.5. START statement example with KEY phrase EQUAL TO operator.

If a record with an equal key were not on file, the file status indicator would have been set to signify a no-record-found condition, the current record pointer setting would be undefined, and an INVALID KEY condition would exist.

START statement with KEY phrase GREATER THAN operator

An example of the START statement with the GREATER THAN operator of the KEY phrase is shown in Figure 6A.6. For variety, the RECORD KEY field is set by moving values to each of the elementary fields rather than the group field. As shown at point B, the current record pointer is set to the first record with a key greater than the value that is placed in the RECORD KEY field. Because a record fulfilling the KEY phrase relationship is present on the file, the file status indicator is set to represent a successful completion. Point C in the figure illustrates an update of the file status indicator.

If the requested key value were higher than the last record on the file, the file status indicator would have been set to signify a no-record-found condition, the current record pointer setting would be undefined, and an INVALID KEY condition would exist.

START statement with KEY phrase NOT LESS THAN operator

Figure 6A.7 shows an example of the START statement with the NOT LESS THAN operator of the KEY phrase. This is the relation operator most frequently

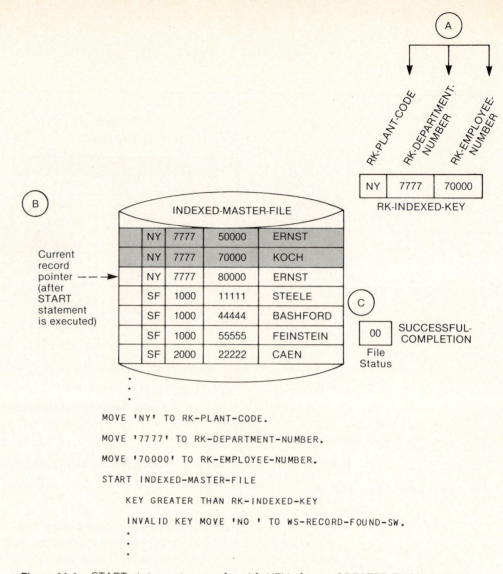

MOVE 'NY' TO RK-PLANT-CODE.

MOVE '7777' TO RK-DEPARTMENT-NUMBER.

MOVE '70000' TO RK-EMPLOYEE-NUMBER.

START INDEXED-MASTER-FILE

    KEY GREATER THAN RK-INDEXED-KEY

    INVALID KEY MOVE 'NO ' TO WS-RECORD-FOUND-SW.

Figure 6A.6. START statement example with KEY phrase GREATER THAN operator.

used because program requirements typically call for processing to begin with a given starting key value, if present, or else the next higher key value. In this example, the RECORD KEY value is set by moving a value to it from an input field. In the two previous examples, the value was set by hard-coded literals. Setting the value from an input parameter field is usually a better approach because it allows greater flexibility with regard to starting points than does a hard-coded value.

As shown at point B in the figure, the current record pointer is set to the first record with a key equal to or greater than the value placed in the RECORD KEY field. Because the requested KEY phrase relation was located on the file, the file status indicator, when specified, is set to represent a successful completion, as shown at point C in the figure.

If the requested key value were higher than the last record on the file, the file status indicator would have been set to signify a no-record-found condition, the current record pointer setting would be undefined, and an INVALID KEY condition would exist.

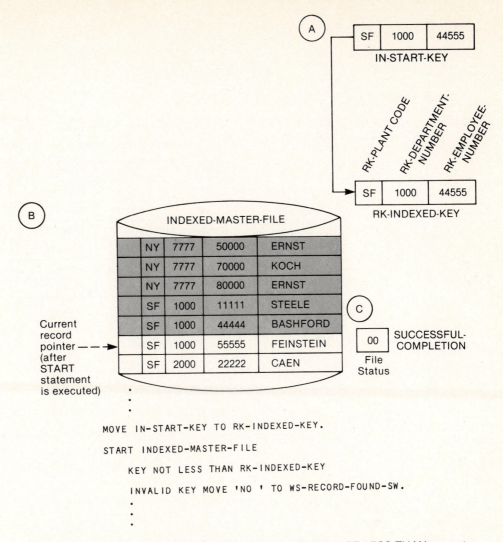

Figure 6A.7. START statement example with KEY phrase NOT LESS THAN operator.

START statement with no KEY phrase

By default, when the KEY phrase is omitted, the relation operator becomes EQUAL TO and the data-name is the prime record key (the RECORD KEY for an indexed file or the RELATIVE KEY for a relative file.).

Therefore, the START statement without a KEY phrase, shown in Figure 6A.8, is identical in processing to that shown with the EQUAL TO operator (Figure 6A.5).

START statement for generic processing

When a group of records with a common high-order portion of a key field are to be retrieved, it is termed **generic processing**. For example, as shown in Figure 6A.9, suppose a report on all of the employees in a certain plant were desired. Observe that only a portion of the RECORD KEY field is referenced. A generic key must begin in the same position as the leftmost position of the RECORD KEY.

Although any of the three relation operators can be specified for generic

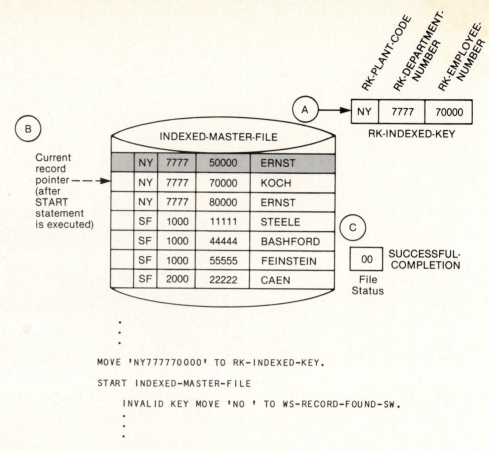

```
MOVE 'NY777770000' TO RK-INDEXED-KEY.

START INDEXED-MASTER-FILE

    INVALID KEY MOVE 'NO ' TO WS-RECORD-FOUND-SW.
```

Figure 6A.8. START statement example with no KEY phrase.

processing, the EQUAL TO option is usually most appropriate. Regardless of relation operator, when the comparison is made, the rightmost characters of the RECORD KEY field in excess of the length of the generic field (as specified in the START statement) are truncated.

A generic key may be used with indexed files but not with relative files.

Skip-Sequential Retrieval

When the START statement is used to begin record processing at a location other than at the beginning of the file, the resulting report or display is sometimes called a **skip-sequential** retrieval. Figure 6A.10 shows an example of an employee roster report where record processing starts with the key of "NY777780000." Notice that the first two records of the file were skipped.

Figure 6A.11 shows the COBOL-coding changes to the SEQRET program that will allow such skip-sequential processing. The new program has been named SKIPRET to indicate a **skip**-sequential **ret**rieval.

Observe that an input transaction file has been defined in the SKIPRET program. It should contain one SK-START-KEY-PARAMETER-RECORD that carries the starting key value for the retrieval.

In the mainline module, after the 100-INITIALIZE-VARIABLE-FIELDS paragraph has been completed, the 130-PROCESS-PARAMETER-RECORD module is performed. This routine handles processing of the input SK-START-KEY-PARAMETER-RECORD. If the input parameter record is erroneously absent or if a record with an incorrect record code is in the file, the starting key

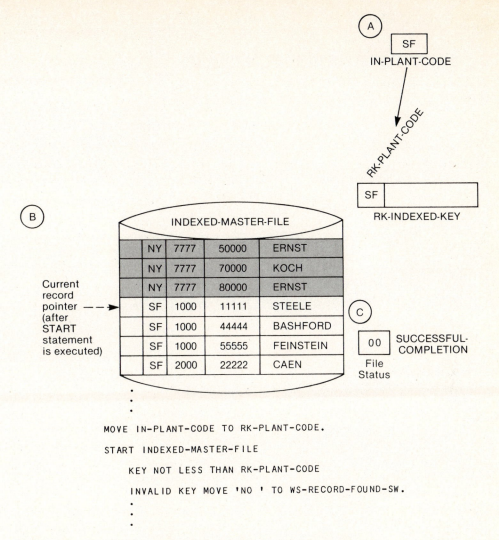

MOVE IN-PLANT-CODE TO RK-PLANT-CODE.

START INDEXED-MASTER-FILE

    KEY NOT LESS THAN RK-PLANT-CODE

    INVALID KEY MOVE 'NO ' TO WS-RECORD-FOUND-SW.

Figure 6A.9. START statement example for generic processing.

```
EMPLOYEE ROSTER           SKIP-SEQUENTIAL RETRIEVAL
                                  PRIME RECORD KEY


PLANT     DEPT     EMP     LAST          DATE 05/17/84
CODE      NBR      NBR     NAME              PAGE    1

 NY       7777    80000    ERNST
 SF       1000    11111    STEELE
 SF       1000    44444    BASHFORD
 SF       1000    55555    FEINSTEIN
 SF       2000    22222    CAEN
```

Figure 6A.10. Skip-sequential retrieval example.

```
001010 IDENTIFICATION DIVISION.                          050140          UNTIL MASTER-END-OF-FILE.
001020 PROGRAM-ID.  SKIPRET.                              050150      CLOSE INDEXED-MASTER-FILE
001030*                                                  050155            TRANSACTION-FILE
001040*                                                  050160            REPORT-FILE.
001050*                EMPLOYEE ROSTER REPORT            050170      STOP RUN.
001060*                INDEXED ORGANIZATION FILE         100010*
001070*          SEQUENTIAL RETRIEVAL WITH START STATEMENT  100020*
001075*                 - PRIME RECORD KEY               100030 100-INITIALIZE-VARIABLE-FIELDS.
001080*                                                  100040*
001090*                                                  100045      MOVE 'NO ' TO WS-TRANSACTION-END-OF-FILE-SW.
002040 ENVIRONMENT DIVISION.
002050*                                                  130010*
002060*                                                  130020*
          .                                              130030 130-PROCESS-PARAMETER-RECORD.
          .                                              130040*
          .                                              130050      PERFORM 800-READ-TRANSACTION-RECORD.
002110*                                                  130060      IF NOT START-KEY-PARAMETER-RECORD
002120*                                                  130070      OR TRANSACTION-END-OF-FILE
002130 INPUT-OUTPUT SECTION.                             130080          MOVE LOW-VALUES TO SK-START-KEY.
002140*                                                  130090      PERFORM 805-START-INDEXED-FILE.
002150 FILE-CONTROL.                                     130100      IF NOT PROGRAM-ABEND
002160      SELECT TRANSACTION-FILE                      130110          PERFORM 810-READ-INDEXED-RECORD.
002170          ASSIGN TO UT-S-TRNFILE.                  200010*
          .                                              200020*
          .                                              200030 200-PROCESS-INDEXED-RECORD.
          .                                              200040*
003010*
003020*                                                           .
003030*                                                           .
003040 DATA DIVISION.                                             .
003050*                                                  800010*
003060*                                                  800020*
003070 FILE SECTION.                                     800030 800-READ-TRANSACTION-RECORD.
003080*                                                  800040*
003090*                                                  800050      READ TRANSACTION-FILE INTO SK-START-KEY-PARAMETER-RECORD
003100 FD  TRANSACTION-FILE                              800060          AT END MOVE 'YES' TO WS-TRANSACTION-END-OF-FILE-SW.
003110      RECORD CONTAINS 80 CHARACTERS                805010*
003120      LABEL RECORDS ARE STANDARD.                  805020*
003130*                                                  805030 805-START-INDEXED-FILE.
003140 01  TRANSACTION-RECORD.                           805040*
003150      05  FILLER            PIC X(80).             805050      MOVE SK-START-KEY TO RK-INDEXED-KEY.
          .                                              805060      MOVE 'START ' TO WS-I-O-OPERATION-FLAG.
          .                                              805070      START INDEXED-MASTER-FILE
010010*                                                  805080          KEY NOT LESS THAN RK-INDEXED-KEY
010020*                                                  805090          INVALID KEY NEXT SENTENCE.
010030 WORKING-STORAGE SECTION.                          805100      IF NOT SUCCESSFUL-COMPLETION
010040*                                                  805110          MOVE 'YES' TO WS-PROGRAM-ABEND-SW
010050*                                                  805120          PERFORM 900-ABORT-PROGRAM-RUN.
010060 01  WS-SWITCHES.                                  810010*
010070*                                                  810020*
010080      05  WS-TRANSACTION-END-OF-FILE-SW PIC X(3).  810030 810-READ-INDEXED-RECORD.
010090          88  TRANSACTION-END-OF-FILE    VALUE 'YES'.  810040*
          .                                                       .
          .                                                       .
020010*                                                  870010*
020020*                                                  870020*
020030 01  SK-START-KEY-PARAMETER-RECORD.                870030 870-PRINT-REPORT-HEADINGS.
020040      05  SK-RECORD-CODE          PIC X(2).        870040*
020050          88  START-KEY-PARAMETER-RECORD  VALUE '09'.       .
020060      05  FILLER                  PIC X(1).                 .
020070      05  SK-START-KEY.                            880010*
020080          10  SK-PLANT-CODE       PIC X(2).        880020*
020090          10  SK-DEPARTMENT-NUMBER PIC X(4).       880030 880-WRITE-REPORT-TOP-LINE.
020100          10  SK-EMPLOYEE-NUMBER  PIC X(5).        880040*
020110      05  FILLER                  PIC X(66).                .
          .                                                       .
030010*                                                  890010*
030020*                                                  890020*
030030 01  H1-HEADING-LINE-1.                            890030 890-WRITE-REPORT-LINE.
030040      05  FILLER       PIC X(1).                   890040*
030050      05  FILLER       PIC X(20)  VALUE '   EMPLOYEE ROSTER '.   .
030060      05  FILLER       PIC X(20)  VALUE '     SKIP-SEQUENTIA'.   .
030070      05  FILLER       PIC X(20)  VALUE 'L RETRIEVAL        '.  900010*
030080      05  FILLER       PIC X(72)  VALUE SPACES.    900020*
          .                                              900030 900-ABORT-PROGRAM-RUN.
050010*                                                  900040*
050020*                                                           .
050030*                                                           .
050040 PROCEDURE DIVISION.                               900150      MOVE 'YES' TO WS-TRANSACTION-END-OF-FILE-SW.
050050*                                                  910010*
050060*                                                  910020*
050070 000-PRINT-EMPLOYEE-ROSTER.                        910030 910-LOOKUP-FILE-STATUS-DESCR.
050080*                                                  910040*
050090      OPEN INPUT INDEXED-MASTER-FILE                       .
050095                 TRANSACTION-FILE                          .
050100           OUTPUT REPORT-FILE.
050110      PERFORM 100-INITIALIZE-VARIABLE-FIELDS.
050115      PERFORM 130-PROCESS-PARAMETER-RECORD.
050130      PERFORM 200-PROCESS-INDEXED-RECORD
```

Figure 6A.11. COBOL coding: SKIPRET program.

value is set to a default value of LOW-VALUES so that the entire file will be processed. Otherwise, whatever key value is present in the parameter record will be used as the starting key value.

The 805-START-INDEXED-FILE module is then performed to set the current record pointer to the first record equal to or greater than the starting key value. Like the OPEN verb, execution of the START statement does not actually cause an input record to be read; it merely sets the current record pointer for the next READ operation.

```
┌──────────────────────────────────────────────────────────────┐
│                                                                │
│      EMPLOYEE ROSTER                    GENERIC RETRIEVAL      │
│                                         PRIME RECORD KEY       │
│                                                                │
│                                                                │
│        PLANT    DEPT    EMP     LAST      DATE 05/17/84        │
│        CODE     NBR     NBR     NAME          PAGE    1       │
│                                                                │
│         SF      1000    11111   STEELE                        │
│         SF      1000    44444   BASHFORD                      │
│         SF      1000    55555   FEINSTEIN                     │
│         SF      2000    22222   CAEN                          │
│                                                                │
│                                                                │
│                                                                │
└──────────────────────────────────────────────────────────────┘
```

Figure 6A.12. Generic retrieval example.

Hence, if the START statement is successfully completed, the last statement of the 130-PROCESS-PARAMETER-RECORD handles the priming-read from the indexed file.

Generic Retrieval

The employee roster report with a generic retrieval for plant-code "SF" is shown in Figure 6A.12. Figure 6A.13 presents coding changes to the SKIPSEQ program that will provide generic processing. The new program has been named GENRET to signify **gen**eric **ret**rieval.

Generic-retrieval programs are usually designed to accommodate multiple groups of generic output. Hence, whereas the SKIPRET program processed only one input parameter record, it is advisable to design a generic-retrieval program to handle any number of generic-retrieval requests. Although not necessary, the plant-code fields have been given higher-level data-names of GK-GENERIC-KEY and RK-GENERIC-KEY in the parameter record and indexed master record, respectively. This has been done merely to allow the coding of data-names that are not application-specific.

So long as there are input generic parameter request records in the transaction file, the 200-PROCESS-GENERIC-GROUP module is performed. So that each group of generic output is printed on a fresh page, the first step of this module is to perform the 870-PRINT-REPORT-HEADINGS routine.

Then, the 805-START-INDEXED-FILE module is performed. If the START operation is successfully completed, the priming-read for the generic group is handled by performing the 810-READ-INDEXED-FILE module. If there are no records within the file for the requested generic group, an error line is printed on the report.

Once the priming-read has been completed, the 210-PROCESS-INDEXED-RECORD module is performed until there are no more records for the requested generic key.

At that point, the next input generic parameter request record is read and the process is repeated until the end of the input transaction file is reached.

Limits Retrieval

A limits retrieval is similar to a generic retrieval except that, whereas the generic retrieval typically gathers a group of records with a common high-order value, a **limits retrieval** collects a group of records within a specified range of limits. This range may be either only a portion of a generic group or multiple-generic groups, depending upon the range values.

```
001010 IDENTIFICATION DIVISION.
001020 PROGRAM-ID.    GENRET.
001030*
001040*
001050*              EMPLOYEE ROSTER REPORT
001060*              INDEXED ORGANIZATION FILE
001070*              GENERIC RETRIEVAL - PRIME RECORD KEY
001080*
001090*
           .
           .
           .
003010*
003020*
003030*
003040 DATA DIVISION.
003050*
003060*
003070 FILE SECTION.
003080*
003090*
004010*
004020*
004030 FD  INDEXED-MASTER-FILE
004040         RECORD CONTAINS 80 CHARACTERS
004050         LABEL RECORDS ARE STANDARD.
004060*
004070 01  INDEXED-MASTER-RECORD.
004080     05  FILLER                    PIC X(3).
004090     05  RK-INDEXED-KEY.
004095         10  RK-GENERIC-KEY.
004100             15  RK-PLANT-CODE     PIC X(2).
004110         10  RK-DEPARTMENT-NUMBER  PIC X(4).
004120         10  RK-EMPLOYEE-NUMBER    PIC X(5).
004130     05  FILLER                    PIC X(66).
           .
           .
           .
020010*
020020*
020030 01  GK-GEN-KEY-PARAMETER-RECORD.
020040     05  GK-RECORD-CODE            PIC X(2).
020050         88  GENERIC-KEY-PARAMETER-RECORD      VALUE '10'.
020060     05  FILLER                    PIC X(1).
020070     05  GK-START-KEY.
020075         10  GK-GENERIC-KEY.
020080             15  GK-PLANT-CODE     PIC X(2).
020090         10  GK-DEPARTMENT-NUMBER  PIC X(4).
020100         10  GK-EMPLOYEE-NUMBER    PIC X(5).
020110     05  FILLER                    PIC X(66).
           .
           .
           .
030010*
030020*
030030 01  H1-HEADING-LINE-1.
030040     05  FILLER       PIC X(1).
030050     05  FILLER       PIC X(20)   VALUE '    EMPLOYEE ROSTER '.
030060     05  FILLER       PIC X(20)   VALUE '             GENERI'.
030070     05  FILLER       PIC X(20)   VALUE 'C RETRIEVAL        '.
030080     05  FILLER       PIC X(72)   VALUE SPACES.
           .
           .
           .
050010*
050020*
050030*
050040 PROCEDURE DIVISION.
050050*
050060*
050070 000-PRINT-EMPLOYEE-ROSTER.
050080*
050090     OPEN INPUT INDEXED-MASTER-FILE
050095                TRANSACTION-FILE
050100          OUTPUT REPORT-FILE.
050110     PERFORM 100-INITIALIZE-VARIABLE-FIELDS.
050120     PERFORM 800-READ-TRANSACTION-RECORD.
050130     PERFORM 200-PROCESS-GENERIC-GROUP
050140         UNTIL TRANSACTION-END-OF-FILE.
050150     CLOSE INDEXED-MASTER-FILE
050155           TRANSACTION-FILE
050160           REPORT-FILE.
050170     STOP RUN.
100010*
100020*
100030 100-INITIALIZE-VARIABLE-FIELDS.
100040*
           .
           .
           .
200010*
200020*
200030 200-PROCESS-GENERIC-GROUP.
```

```
200040*
200050     PERFORM 870-PRINT-REPORT-HEADINGS.
200060     PERFORM 805-START-INDEXED-FILE.
200070     PERFORM 210-PROCESS-INDEXED-RECORD
200080         UNTIL RK-GENERIC-KEY IS NOT EQUAL TO GK-GENERIC-KEY.
200090     PERFORM 800-READ-TRANSACTION-RECORD.
210010*
210020*
210030 210-PROCESS-INDEXED-RECORD.
210040*
210050     IF WS-LINES-USED IS NOT LESS THAN WS-LINES-PER-PAGE
210060         PERFORM 870-PRINT-REPORT-HEADINGS.
210070     MOVE EM-PLANT-CODE TO DL-PLANT-CODE.
210080     MOVE EM-DEPARTMENT-NUMBER TO DL-DEPARTMENT-NUMBER.
210090     MOVE EM-EMPLOYEE-NUMBER TO DL-EMPLOYEE-NUMBER.
210100     MOVE EM-LAST-NAME TO DL-LAST-NAME.
210110     MOVE DL-DETAIL-LINE TO REPORT-LINE.
210120     MOVE 1 TO WS-LINE-SPACING.
210130     PERFORM 890-WRITE-REPORT-LINE.
210140     PERFORM 810-READ-INDEXED-RECORD.
800010*
800020*
800030 800-READ-TRANSACTION-RECORD.
800040*
800050     READ TRANSACTION-FILE INTO GK-GEN-KEY-PARAMETER-RECORD
800060         AT END MOVE 'YES' TO WS-TRANSACTION-END-OF-FILE-SW.
805010*
805020*
805030 805-START-INDEXED-FILE.
805040*
805050     MOVE GK-GENERIC-KEY TO RK-GENERIC-KEY.
805060     MOVE 'START ' TO WS-I-O-OPERATION-FLAG.
805070     START INDEXED-MASTER-FILE
805080         KEY EQUAL TO RK-GENERIC-KEY
805090         INVALID KEY MOVE HIGH-VALUES TO RK-GENERIC-KEY.
805100     IF SUCCESSFUL-COMPLETION
805105         PERFORM 810-READ-INDEXED-RECORD
805130     ELSE
805140         MOVE SPACES TO DL-DETAIL-LINE
805150         MOVE GK-PLANT-CODE TO DL-PLANT-CODE
805160         MOVE 'NO SUCH PLANT' TO DL-LAST-NAME
805170         MOVE DL-DETAIL-LINE TO REPORT-LINE
805180         MOVE 1 TO WS-LINE-SPACING
805190         PERFORM 890-WRITE-REPORT-LINE.
810010*
810020*
810030 810-READ-INDEXED-RECORD.
810040*
810050     MOVE 'READ  ' TO WS-I-O-OPERATION-FLAG.
810060     READ INDEXED-MASTER-FILE
810070         INTO EM-EMPLOYEE-MASTER-WORK-AREA
810080         AT END MOVE HIGH-VALUES TO RK-GENERIC-KEY.
810090     IF NOT SUCCESSFUL-COMPLETION
810100     AND NOT MASTER-END-OF-FILE
810110         MOVE 'YES' TO WS-PROGRAM-ABEND-SW
810120         PERFORM 900-ABORT-PROGRAM-RUN.
870010*
870020*
870030 870-PRINT-REPORT-HEADINGS.
870040*
           .
           .
           .
880010*
880020*
880030 880-WRITE-REPORT-TOP-LINE.
880040*
           .
           .
           .
890010*
890020*
890030 890-WRITE-REPORT-LINE.
890040*
           .
           .
           .
900010*
900020*
900030 900-ABORT-PROGRAM-RUN.
900040*
           .
           .
           .
900160     MOVE HIGH-VALUES TO RK-GENERIC-KEY.
910010*
910020*
910030 910-LOOKUP-FILE-STATUS-DESCR.
910040*
           .
           .
           .
```

Figure 6A.13. COBOL coding: GENRET program.

Figure 6A.14 shows an example of a limits-retrieval employee roster report. The limits that were used were arbitrarily chosen as "NY777750000" and "SF999999999."

Coding changes to the GENRET program that will provide limits processing are shown in Figure 6A.15. The program has been named LIMRET to indicate **lim**its **ret**rieval.

Like generic-retrieval programs, limits-retrieval programs are typically designed to handle multiple-limit groups. The input parameter request record

```
┌─────────────────────────────────────────────────────┐
│                                                       │
│   EMPLOYEE ROSTER                    LIMITS RETRIEVAL │
│                                      PRIME RECORD KEY │
│                                                       │
│                                                       │
│   PLANT    DEPT    EMP     LAST      DATE 05/17/84    │
│   CODE     NBR     NBR     NAME         PAGE    1     │
│                                                       │
│    NY      7777    50000   ERNST                      │
│    NY      7777    70000   KOCH                       │
│    NY      7777    80000   ERNST                      │
│    SF      2000    22222   CAEN                       │
│                                                       │
│                                                       │
│                                                       │
└─────────────────────────────────────────────────────┘
```

Figure 6A.14. Limits retrieval example.

must contain not only the starting limit key but also the ending limit key as shown in the program coding. Otherwise, the logic for a limits-retrieval program closely parallels that of a generic retrieval.

RANDOM Access

The format for a random READ statement from an indexed file was presented in Chapter 4; a random READ from a relative file was introduced in Chapter 5. The INDMAINT and RELMAINT programs of those chapters are typical examples of RANDOM access processing. Hence, no additional coverage of random retrievals will be presented in this chapter.

DYNAMIC Access

When ACCESS MODE IS DYNAMIC records can, within the scope of the same OPEN statement, be (1) obtained from or placed into a mass-storage file on a random basis, and (2) read from the file in either a sequential or random manner. In other words, the functions of the INDMAINT program of Chapter 4 could be combined with the functions of the GENRET program to form one program that contains random retrievals, random updates, and sequential retrievals.

However, there are only limited practical applications for DYNAMIC access within batch programs. Suppose that the INDMAINT and GENRET program functions were combined into one DYNAMIC access program. Two different output reports would still be required because, as is usually the case, the output of the update function is entirely different from that of the retrieval function.

Thus superior program design quality and maintenance ease is generally facilitated by coding two separate programs as was done in the text. That is, the maintenance function is handled by the INDMAINT program with RANDOM access; the retrieval function by the GENRET with SEQUENTIAL access and use of the START statement.

DYNAMIC access capabilities are frequently required for on-line programs. For example, suppose a data-entry clerk has a change to make to a customer account record and knows the name of the account but not the account number that is needed to update the record. If this were a common situation, it would be appropriate to allow the clerk to key in the account name, and for the program to locate and sequentially display the account name and number of perhaps the 10 accounts that alphabetically precede the closest account name located and the 10 accounts alphabetically following that account. Then the clerk could choose the correct account number from the list and randomly update the record.

```
001010 IDENTIFICATION DIVISION.                                          .
001020 PROGRAM-ID.    LIMRET.                                            .
001030*                                                        800010*
001040*                                                        800020*
001050*            EMPLOYEE ROSTER REPORT                      800030 800-READ-TRANSACTION-RECORD.
001060*            INDEXED ORGANIZATION FILE                   800040*
001070*            LIMITS RETRIEVAL - PRIME RECORD KEY         800050    READ TRANSACTION-FILE INTO LK-LIMIT-KEY-PARAMETER-RECORD
001080*                                                        800060        AT END MOVE 'YES' TO WS-TRANSACTION-END-OF-FILE-SW.
001090*                                                        805010*
         .                                                     805020*
         .                                                     805030 805-START-INDEXED-FILE.
         .                                                     805040*
003010*                                                        805050    MOVE LK-START-KEY TO RK-INDEXED-KEY.
003020*                                                        805060    MOVE 'START ' TO WS-I-O-OPERATION-FLAG.
003030*                                                        805070    START INDEXED-MASTER-FILE
003040 DATA DIVISION.                                          805080        KEY NOT LESS THAN RK-INDEXED-KEY
         .                                                     805090        INVALID KEY MOVE HIGH-VALUES TO RK-INDEXED-KEY.
         .                                                     805100    IF SUCCESSFUL-COMPLETION
         .                                                     805105        PERFORM 810-READ-INDEXED-RECORD.
020010*                                                        805210    IF RK-INDEXED-KEY IS GREATER THAN LK-END-KEY
020020*                                                        805220        MOVE SPACES TO DL-DETAIL-LINE
020030 01  LK-LIMIT-KEY-PARAMETER-RECORD.                      805230        MOVE LK-PLANT-CODE TO DL-PLANT-CODE
020040     05  LK-RECORD-CODE              PIC X(2).           805240        MOVE LK-DEPARTMENT-NUMBER TO DL-DEPARTMENT-NUMBER
020050         88  LIMIT-KEY-PARAMETER-RECORD        VALUE '11'. 805255       MOVE LK-EMPLOYEE-NUMBER TO DL-EMPLOYEE-NUMBER
020060     05  FILLER                      PIC X(1).           805260        MOVE 'NO EMPS    ' TO DL-LAST-NAME
020070     05  LK-START-KEY.                                   805270        MOVE DL-DETAIL-LINE TO REPORT-LINE
020075         10  LK-GENERIC-KEY.                             805280        MOVE 1 TO WS-LINE-SPACING
020080             15  LK-PLANT-CODE       PIC X(2).           805290        PERFORM 890-WRITE-REPORT-LINE
020090         10  LK-DEPARTMENT-NUMBER    PIC X(4).           805300        MOVE LK-END-PLANT-CODE TO DL-PLANT-CODE
020100         10  LK-EMPLOYEE-NUMBER      PIC X(5).           805310        MOVE LK-END-DEPARTMENT-NUMBER TO DL-DEPARTMENT-NUMBER
020110     05  LK-END-KEY.                                     805320        MOVE LK-END-EMPLOYEE-NUMBER TO DL-EMPLOYEE-NUMBER
020120         10  LK-END-PLANT-CODE       PIC X(2).           805330        MOVE 'WITHIN LIMITS' TO DL-LAST-NAME
020130         10  LK-END-DEPARTMENT-NUMBER PIC X(4).          805340        MOVE DL-DETAIL-LINE TO REPORT-LINE
020140         10  LK-END-EMPLOYEE-NUMBER  PIC X(5).           805350        MOVE 1 TO WS-LINE-SPACING
020150     05  FILLER                      PIC X(55).          805360        PERFORM 890-WRITE-REPORT-LINE.
         .                                                     810010*
         .                                                     810020*
         .                                                     810030 810-READ-INDEXED-RECORD.
030010*                                                        810040*
030020*                                                        810050    MOVE 'READ   ' TO WS-I-O-OPERATION-FLAG.
030030 01  H1-HEADING-LINE-1.                                  810060    READ INDEXED-MASTER-FILE
030040     05  FILLER       PIC X(1).                          810070        INTO EM-EMPLOYEE-MASTER-WORK-AREA
030050     05  FILLER       PIC X(20)  VALUE '  EMPLOYEE ROSTER '. 810080    AT END MOVE HIGH-VALUES TO RK-INDEXED-KEY.
030060     05  FILLER       PIC X(20)  VALUE '          LIMIT'.  810090    IF NOT SUCCESSFUL-COMPLETION
030070     05  FILLER       PIC X(20)  VALUE 'S RETRIEVAL      '. 810100    AND NOT MASTER-END-OF-FILE
030080     05  FILLER       PIC X(72)  VALUE SPACES.            810110        MOVE 'YES' TO WS-PROGRAM-ABEND-SW
050010*                                                        810120        PERFORM 900-ABORT-PROGRAM-RUN.
050020*                                                        870010*
050030*                                                        870020*
050040 PROCEDURE DIVISION.                                     870030 870-PRINT-REPORT-HEADINGS.
050050*                                                        870040*
050060*                                                                 .
050070 000-PRINT-EMPLOYEE-ROSTER.                                       .
050080*                                                                 .
050090    OPEN INPUT  INDEXED-MASTER-FILE                      880010*
050095               TRANSACTION-FILE                          880020*
050100         OUTPUT REPORT-FILE.                             880030 880-WRITE-REPORT-TOP-LINE.
050110    PERFORM 100-INITIALIZE-VARIABLE-FIELDS.              880040*
050120    PERFORM 800-READ-TRANSACTION-RECORD.                          .
050130    PERFORM 200-PROCESS-LIMITS-GROUP                              .
050140        UNTIL TRANSACTION-END-OF-FILE.                            .
050150    CLOSE INDEXED-MASTER-FILE                            890010*
050155          TRANSACTION-FILE                               890020*
050160          REPORT-FILE.                                   890030 890-WRITE-REPORT-LINE.
050170    STOP RUN.                                            890040*
100010*                                                                 .
100020*                                                                 .
100030 100-INITIALIZE-VARIABLE-FIELDS.                                  .
100040*                                                        900010*
         .                                                     900020*
         .                                                     900030 900-ABORT-PROGRAM-RUN.
         .                                                     900040*
200010*                                                                 .
200020*                                                                 .
200030 200-PROCESS-LIMITS-GROUP.                                        .
200040*                                                        900150        MOVE HIGH-VALUES TO RK-INDEXED-KEY.
200050    PERFORM 870-PRINT-REPORT-HEADINGS.                   910010*
200060    PERFORM 805-START-INDEXED-FILE.                      910020*
200070    PERFORM 210-PROCESS-INDEXED-RECORD                   910030 910-LOOKUP-FILE-STATUS-DESCR.
200080        UNTIL RK-INDEXED-KEY IS GREATER THAN LK-END-KEY. 910040*
200090    IF NOT PROGRAM-ABEND                                          .
200100        PERFORM 800-READ-TRANSACTION-RECORD.                      .
210010*                                                                 .
210020*
210030 210-PROCESS-INDEXED-RECORD.
210040*
```

Figure 6A.15. COBOL coding: LIMRET program.

Although this is a common application for dynamic processing, specification of ACCESS MODE IS DYNAMIC is not usually employed to accomplish it. This is because COBOL does not yet have standard facilities for on-line processing. Hence, with most on-line COBOL programs, FILE-CONTROL entries are specified through specifications to a communications monitor program rather than through the COBOL SELECT statement.

Should an application for DYNAMIC access occur, it can be coded with the input-output statement syntax already presented in this text. The following points are presented as reminders for proper DYNAMIC access coding.

1. The SELECT statement for the file must contain the ACCESS MODE IS DYNAMIC phrase.

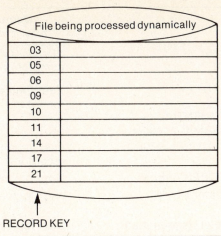

File being processed dynamically

| 03 |
| 05 |
| 06 |
| 09 |
| 10 |
| 11 |
| 14 |
| 17 |
| 21 |

RECORD KEY

RECORD KEY setting	Input-output operation	Completion status	Record processed	Current record pointer (CRP) [after I-O operation]
–	OPEN I-O	Successful	–	03
09	READ (random)	Successful	09	10
–	READ NEXT	Successful	10	11
–	READ NEXT	Successful	11	14
01	WRITE	Successful	01	14
–	READ NEXT	Successful	14	15
07	START (equal key)	Unsuccessful	–	Undefined (no CRP)
–	READ NEXT	Unsuccessful (because no CRP)	–	Undefined (no CRP)
21	READ (random)	Successful	21	AT END
–	READ NEXT	AT END	–	AT END

Figure 6A.16. DYNAMIC access record-processing example.

2. Before a READ NEXT operation is executed, the current record pointer setting must be established by a previous OPEN, START, or random READ operation.

3. Current record settings are affected only by OPEN, START, READ, and READ NEXT operations; WRITE, REWRITE, and DELETE operations do not change the current record pointer.

4. If an unsuccessful OPEN, START, READ, or READ NEXT operation occurs, the current record pointer setting becomes undefined and must be re-established before the next READ NEXT operation is executed.

Figure 6A.16 illustrates dynamic record-processing operations. A summary of current record pointer handling for all access modes is shown in Figure 6A.17.

| COBOL input-output statement | Current record pointer (CRP) setting after execution of input-output operation | |
	Successful completion	Unsuccessful completion
OPEN INPUT or OPEN I-O (SEQUENTIAL or DYNAMIC access)	First logical record in file	Undefined (No CRP)
OPEN INPUT REVERSED	Last logical record in file	Undefined (No CRP)
All other OPEN options	Not applicable	Not applicable
READ (random)	Next logical record	Undefined (No CRP)
READ [NEXT] (sequential)	Next logical record	Undefined (No CRP)
START	First logical record satisfying KEY phrase condition	Undefined (No CRP)
WRITE	No effect	No effect
REWRITE	No effect	No effect
DELETE	No effect	No effect

Figure 6A.17. Summary of current record pointer handling.

■ TOPIC 6-B: **Alternate Record Keys**

The ALTERNATE RECORD KEY Phrase
The WITH DUPLICATES Phrase
Alternate Record Key Indexes
Coding for Alternate Record Key Processing
    The SELECT Statement
    The START Statement
    The Sequential READ Statement
    The Random READ Statement
    The WRITE, REWRITE, and DELETE Statements

With indexed files, an ALTERNATE RECORD KEY may be established to permit retrieval of records in sequences other than the RECORD KEY sequence. For example, given the indexed employee master file, suppose we wanted to also retrieve records (1) in employee-number sequence (without regard to plant code or department number), and (2) in alphabetical sequence according to employee name.

The ALTERNATE RECORD KEY Phrase

This can be accomplished by specifying the ALTERNATE RECORD KEY phrase in the SELECT statement. Figure 6B.1 shows its format and provides an example. Observe that AK-EMPLOYEE-NUMBER has been specified as an alternate

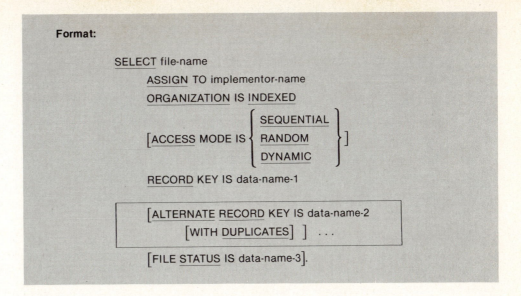

Format:

```
SELECT file-name
    ASSIGN TO implementor-name
    ORGANIZATION IS INDEXED
                        ┌ SEQUENTIAL ┐
    [ACCESS MODE IS ┤ RANDOM      ├ ]
                        └ DYNAMIC    ┘
    RECORD KEY IS data-name-1

        [ALTERNATE RECORD KEY IS data-name-2
          [WITH DUPLICATES] ] ...
        [FILE STATUS IS data-name-3].
```

Example:

```
SELECT INDEXED-MASTER-FILE
    ASSIGN TO INDFILE
    ORGANIZATION IS INDEXED
    ACCESS MODE IS SEQUENTIAL
    RECORD KEY IS RK-INDEXED-KEY
    ALTERNATE RECORD KEY IS AK-EMPLOYEE-NUMBER
    ALTERNATE RECORD KEY IS AK-LAST-NAME WITH DUPLICATES
    FILE STATUS IS WS-FILE-STATUS-FLAG.
```

Figure 6B.1. ALTERNATE RECORD KEY phrase format.

record key to provide the ability to retrieve records by employee number without regard to plant code or department number. Also, the AK-LAST-NAME field has been specified as an alternate record key to permit record retrieval by employee name. (Actually, it would be more appropriate to specify the complete employee name—last-, first-, and middle-name fields—rather than only the last name. However, for simplicity of discussion and presentation, just the last-name field is used in the examples.)

An ALTERNATE RECORD KEY field must be defined in the FILE SECTION within the FD entry for the indexed file. It can be any alphanumeric field within the indexed record except that it can not be a field whose leftmost character is the same as the leftmost character of the RECORD KEY field. (This restriction is of little concern because such an alternate record key would have the same sequence as the prime record key. It could be accessed as a generic key.)

The WITH DUPLICATES Phrase

Notice that the WITH DUPLICATES phrase has been specified for the AK-LAST-NAME alternate record key entry and omitted from the AK-EMPLOYEE-NUMBER entry. This optional phrase must be specified if records with equal alternate record key values are permitted to reside in the file.

When employee numbers are assigned, let us say that each employee is given a unique employee number. Employee numbers should not be duplicated,

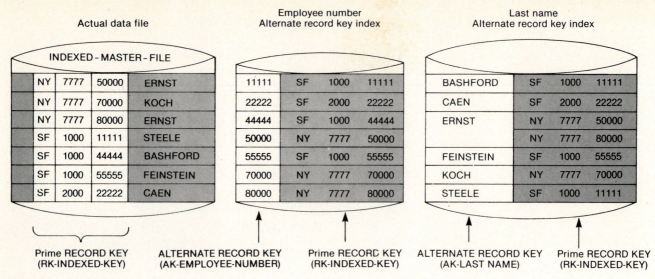

Employee number
Alternate record key index

Last name
Alternate record key index

	INDEXED – MASTER – FILE			
	NY	7777	50000	ERNST
	NY	7777	70000	KOCH
	NY	7777	80000	ERNST
	SF	1000	11111	STEELE
	SF	1000	44444	BASHFORD
	SF	1000	55555	FEINSTEIN
	SF	2000	22222	CAEN

11111	SF	1000	11111
22222	SF	2000	22222
44444	SF	1000	44444
50000	NY	7777	50000
55555	SF	1000	55555
70000	NY	7777	70000
80000	NY	7777	80000

BASHFORD	SF	1000	11111
CAEN	SF	2000	22222
ERNST	NY	7777	50000
	NY	7777	80000
FEINSTEIN	SF	1000	55555
KOCH	NY	7777	70000
STEELE	SF	1000	11111

Prime RECORD KEY (RK-INDEXED-KEY)   ALTERNATE RECORD KEY (AK-EMPLOYEE-NUMBER)   Prime RECORD KEY (RK-INDEXED-KEY)   ALTERNATE RECORD KEY (AK-LAST NAME)   Prime RECORD KEY (RK-INDEXED-KEY)

Figure 6B.2. Alternate record key example.

regardless of plant-code or department number. Hence the AK-EMPLOYEE-NUMBER alternate record key entry should not contain the WITH DUPLICATES phrase.

It is quite possible, however, that two or more employees within a large company could have the same names. Therefore, the AK-LAST-NAME alternate record key entry contains the WITH DUPLICATES phrase.

Alternate Record Key Indexes

A representation of the employee master file with alternate record keys is shown in Figure 6B.2. The actual data file, INDEXED-MASTER-FILE, exists just the same as if it has no alternate record keys. However, additional index files are built and maintained when the ALTERNATE RECORD KEY phrase is specified. The indexes are sequenced according to the alternate record key-field value and contain the prime RECORD KEY value as a pointer to the actual data record.

Notice the last-name alternate record key index entry for "ERNST." Because there are two data records for employees named "ERNST" in the employee master file, there are two prime record keys associated with the "ERNST" alternate record key index entry.

In the example, the prime record keys are shown in ascending sequence for the duplicate entries. That is, the lower RECORD KEY value "NY 7777 50000" precedes the higher key "NY 7777 80000" in the alternate index. Such ascending sequence of duplicate alternate key values will not always occur, however. Records with duplicate alternate key values are always stored in the file on a first in, first out, basis. That is, records will be stored and retrieved from the file in accordance with their chronological loading sequence.

During the file-creation process, ascending prime record key sequence of duplicate alternate key values can be accomplished by sorting the input creation file not only by the prime record key but also by the alternate record key value. With the example, the input file to create the INDEXED-MASTER-FILE would be sorted by plant code (major), department number, employee number, and last name (minor). However, when records with duplicate alternate key values are added to an existing file, they will be stored in accordance with their sequence of loading, not their prime record key value.

```
001010 IDENTIFICATION DIVISION.
001020 PROGRAM-ID.    ALTKEY.
001030*
001040*
001050*                 EMPLOYEE ROSTER REPORT
001060*                 INDEXED ORGANIZATION FILE
001070*           SEQUENTIAL RETRIEVAL WITH START STATEMENT
001075*                 - PRIME RECORD KEY
001078*                 AND TWO ALTERNATE RECORD KEYS
001080*
001090*
002010*
002020*
002030*
002040 ENVIRONMENT DIVISION.
002050*
002060*
002070 CONFIGURATION SECTION.
002080*
002090 SOURCE-COMPUTER.  IBM-370.
002100 OBJECT-COMPUTER.  IBM-370.
002110*
002120*
002130 INPUT-OUTPUT SECTION.
002140*
002150 FILE-CONTROL.
                    .
                    .
                    .
002180      SELECT INDEXED-MASTER-FILE
002190          ASSIGN TO INDFILE
002194          ORGANIZATION IS INDEXED
002195          ACCESS MODE IS SEQUENTIAL
002196          RECORD KEY IS RK-INDEXED-KEY
002197          ALTERNATE RECORD KEY IS AK-EMPLOYEE-NUMBER
002198          ALTERNATE RECORD KEY IS AK-LAST-NAME WITH DUPLICATES
002199          FILE STATUS IS WS-FILE-STATUS-FLAG.

003010*
003020*
003030*
003040 DATA DIVISION.
003050*
003060*
003070 FILE SECTION.
003080*
003090*
                    .
                    .
                    .
004010*
004020*
004030 FD  INDEXED-MASTER-FILE
004040      RECORD CONTAINS 80 CHARACTERS
004050      LABEL RECORDS ARE STANDARD.
004060*
004070 01  INDEXED-MASTER-RECORD.
004080     05  FILLER                      PIC X(3).
004090     05  RK-INDEXED-KEY.
004100         10  RK-PLANT-CODE            PIC X(2).
004110         10  RK-DEPARTMENT-NUMBER     PIC X(4).
004120         10  AK-EMPLOYEE-NUMBER       PIC X(5).
004125     05  AK-LAST-NAME                 PIC X(13).
004130     05  FILLER                       PIC X(53).

010010*
010020*
010030 WORKING-STORAGE SECTION.
010040*
010050*
                    .
                    .
                    .
020010*
020020*
020030 01  AP-ALT-KEY-PARAMETER-RECORD.
020040     05  AP-RECORD-CODE              PIC X(2).
020050         88  ALT-KEY-PARAMETER-RECORD         VALUE '12'.
020060     05  AP-RETRIEVAL-CODE           PIC X(1).
020062         88  PRIME-KEY-RETRIEVAL              VALUE 'P'.
020064         88  ALT-KEY-RETRIEVAL-EMP-NO         VALUE 'E'.
020064         88  ALT-KEY-RETRIEVAL-NAME           VALUE 'N'.
020070     05  AP-START-KEY.
020080         10  AP-PLANT-CODE           PIC X(2).
020090         10  AP-DEPARTMENT-NUMBER    PIC X(4).
020100         10  AP-EMPLOYEE-NUMBER      PIC X(5).
020105     05  AP-LAST-NAME                PIC X(13).
020110     05  FILLER                      PIC X(53).
                    .
                    .
                    .
030010*
030020*
030030 01  H1-HEADING-LINE-1.
030040     05  FILLER          PIC X(1).
030050     05  FILLER          PIC X(20)  VALUE '   EMPLOYEE ROSTER '.
030060     05  FILLER          PIC X(20)  VALUE '         ALTERNATE KE'.
030070     05  FILLER          PIC X(20)  VALUE 'Y RETRIEVAL         '.
030080     05  FILLER          PIC X(72)  VALUE SPACES.
031010*
031020*
031030 01  H2-HEADING-LINE-2.
031040     05  FILLER          PIC X(1).
031050     05  FILLER          PIC X(20)  VALUE '                    '.
031060     05  FILLER          PIC X(5)   VALUE '     '.
031065     05  H2-KEY-DESCR    PIC X(15)  JUSTIFIED RIGHT.
031070     05  FILLER          PIC X(20)  VALUE ' RECORD KEY         '.
031080     05  FILLER          PIC X(72)  VALUE SPACES.
                    .
                    .
                    .
```

```
050010*
050020*
050030*
050040 PROCEDURE DIVISION.
050050*
050060*
050070 000-PRINT-EMPLOYEE-ROSTER.
050080*
050090      OPEN INPUT INDEXED-MASTER-FILE
050095                 TRANSACTION-FILE
050100           OUTPUT REPORT-FILE.
050110      PERFORM 100-INITIALIZE-VARIABLE-FIELDS.
050115      PERFORM 130-PROCESS-PARAMETER-RECORD.
050130      PERFORM 200-PROCESS-INDEXED-RECORD
050140           UNTIL MASTER-END-OF-FILE.
050150      CLOSE INDEXED-MASTER-FILE
050155            TRANSACTION-FILE
050160            REPORT-FILE.
050170      STOP RUN.
100010*
100020*
100030 100-INITIALIZE-VARIABLE-FIELDS.
100040*
                    .
                    .
                    .
130010*
130020*
130030 130-PROCESS-PARAMETER-RECORD.
130040*
130050      PERFORM 800-READ-TRANSACTION-RECORD.
130060      IF NOT ALT-KEY-PARAMETER-RECORD
130070      OR TRANSACTION-END-OF-FILE
130080          MOVE LOW-VALUES TO AP-START-KEY.
130081      IF ALT-KEY-PARAMETER-RECORD
130082      AND ALT-KEY-RETRIEVAL-EMP-NO
130083          PERFORM 805-START-INDEXED-FILE-EMP-NO
130084      ELSE IF ALT-KEY-PARAMETER-RECORD
130085      AND ALT-KEY-RETRIEVAL-NAME
130086          PERFORM 807-START-INDEXED-FILE-NAME
130087      ELSE
130088          PERFORM 805-START-INDEXED-FILE-PRIME.
130100      IF NOT PROGRAM-ABEND
130110          PERFORM 810-READ-INDEXED-RECORD.
200010*
200020*
200030 200-PROCESS-INDEXED-RECORD.
200040*
                    .
                    .
                    .
800010*
800020*
800030 800-READ-TRANSACTION-RECORD.
800040*
800050      READ TRANSACTION-FILE INTO AP-ALT-KEY-PARAMETER-RECORD
800060          AT END MOVE 'YES' TO WS-TRANSACTION-END-OF-FILE-SW.
805010*
805020*
805030 805-START-INDEXED-FILE-PRIME.
805040*
805050      MOVE AP-START-KEY TO RK-INDEXED-KEY.
805060      MOVE 'START ' TO WS-I-O-OPERATION-FLAG.
805070      START INDEXED-MASTER-FILE
805080          KEY NOT LESS THAN RK-INDEXED-KEY
805090          INVALID KEY NEXT SENTENCE.
805100      IF NOT SUCCESSFUL-COMPLETION
805110          MOVE 'YES' TO WS-PROGRAM-ABEND-SW
805120          PERFORM 900-ABORT-PROGRAM-RUN.
806010*
806020*
806030 806-START-INDEXED-FILE-EMP-NO.
806040*
806050      MOVE AP-EMPLOYEE-NUMBER TO AK-EMPLOYEE-NUMBER.
806060      MOVE 'START  ' TO WS-I-O-OPERATION-FLAG.
806070      START INDEXED-MASTER-FILE
806080          KEY NOT LESS THAN AK-EMPLOYEE-NUMBER
806090          INVALID KEY NEXT SENTENCE.
806100      IF NOT SUCCESSFUL-COMPLETION
806110          MOVE 'YES' TO WS-PROGRAM-ABEND-SW
806120          PERFORM 900-ABORT-PROGRAM-RUN.
807010*
807020*
807030 807-START-INDEXED-FILE-NAME.
807040*
807050      MOVE AP-LAST-NAME TO AK-LAST-NAME.
807060      MOVE 'START ' TO WS-I-O-OPERATION-FLAG.
807070      START INDEXED-MASTER-FILE
807080          KEY NOT LESS THAN AK-LAST-NAME
807090          INVALID KEY NEXT SENTENCE.
807100      IF NOT SUCCESSFUL-COMPLETION
807110          MOVE 'YES' TO WS-PROGRAM-ABEND-SW
807120          PERFORM 900-ABORT-PROGRAM-RUN.
810010*
810020*
810030 810-READ-INDEXED-RECORD.
810040*
810050      MOVE 'READ   ' TO WS-I-O-OPERATION-FLAG.
810070      READ INDEXED-MASTER-FILE
810070          INTO EM-EMPLOYEE-MASTER-WORK-AREA
810080          AT END MOVE 'YES' TO WS-MASTER-END-OF-FILE-SW.
810090      IF NOT SUCCESSFUL-COMPLETION
810100      AND NOT MASTER-END-OF-FILE
810110          MOVE 'YES' TO WS-PROGRAM-ABEND-SW
810120          PERFORM 900-ABORT-PROGRAM-RUN.
870010*
870020*
870030 870-PRINT-REPORT-HEADINGS.
870040*
870050      ADD 1 TO WS-PAGE-COUNT.
870060      MOVE WS-PAGE-COUNT TO H1-PAGE-NBR.
870062      IF ALT-KEY-RETRIEVAL-EMP-NO
870063          MOVE 'EMPLOYEE NUMBER' TO H2-KEY-DESCR
870064      ELSE IF ALT-KEY-RETRIEVAL-NAME
870065          MOVE ' EMPLOYEE-NAME' TO H2-KEY-DESCR
```

continued

Figure 6B.3.   COBOL coding: ALTKEY program.

```
870066      ELSE
870067          MOVE '        PRIME' TO H2-KEY-DESCR.
870070      MOVE H1-HEADING-LINE-1 TO REPORT-LINE.
870080      PERFORM 880-WRITE-REPORT-TOP-LINE.
870090      MOVE H2-HEADING-LINE-2 TO REPORT-LINE.
870100      MOVE 1 TO WS-LINE-SPACING.
870110      PERFORM 890-WRITE-REPORT-LINE.
870120      MOVE H3-HEADING-LINE-3 TO REPORT-LINE.
870130      MOVE 3 TO WS-LINE-SPACING.
870140      PERFORM 890-WRITE-REPORT-LINE.
870150      MOVE H4-HEADING-LINE-4 TO REPORT-LINE.
870160      MOVE 1 TO WS-LINE-SPACING.
870170      PERFORM 890-WRITE-REPORT-LINE.
870180      MOVE SPACES TO REPORT-LINE.
870190      PERFORM 890-WRITE-REPORT-LINE.
                       .
                       .
                       .
880010*
880020*
880030 880-WRITE-REPORT-TOP-LINE.
880040*


890010*
890020*
890030 890-WRITE-REPORT-LINE.
890040*
                       .
                       .
                       .
900010*
900020*
900030 900-ABORT-PROGRAM-RUN.
900040*
                       .
                       .
                       .
910010*
910020*
910030 910-LOOKUP-FILE-STATUS-DESCR.
910040*
                       .
                       .
                       .
```

Figure 6B.3. (continued)

Coding for Alternate Record Key Processing

Figure 6B.3 shows the coding changes to the SKIPRET program to permit printing of the employee roster report in either prime record key sequence, employee number sequence, or name sequence. The program has been named ALTKEY for **alt**ernate record **key** retrieval.

Notice that the start key parameter record contains a field, AP-RETRIEVAL-CODE, to indicate the type of retrieval that should be printed. If the field contains a "P," retrieval by prime key should be made. An "E" in the field signifies an employee number sequence retrieval; an "N" designates name sequence.

The SELECT Statement

When alternate record keys exist for an indexed file, the applicable ALTERNATE RECORD KEY phrase or phrases should be included in the SELECT statement of each program that is using the file. (Some compilers do not require this but, even if not required, it serves as good documentation.)

The START Statement

To process a file in alternate record key sequence, the alternate record key must be established as the key of reference and the desired alternate record key starting value must be placed in the ALTERNATE RECORD KEY field. To establish the alternate record key as the key of reference when ACCESS MODE IS SEQUENTIAL, a START statement that references the ALTERNATE RECORD KEY field is used.

A generic key may be specified for an alternate record key.

The Sequential READ Statement

After the alternate record key is established as the key of reference, each successive sequential READ statement will use the alternate key until the key of reference is changed. When ACCESS MODE IS SEQUENTIAL, the key of reference is changed by issuing a START referencing another key field. An example of sequential retrieval by an alternate record key is shown in the 810-READ-INDEXED-RECORD module.

The Random READ Statement

To randomly retrieve a record by its alternate record key when ACCESS MODE IS RANDOM or ACCESS MODE IS DYNAMIC, the KEY phrase of the random READ statement must be specified referencing the alternate record key field. An example is shown in Figure 6B.4. If ACCESS MODE IS DYNAMIC, this statement will also establish the alternate record key as the key of reference for any following sequential READ operations.

Format:

READ file-name RECORD

[INTO identifier]

(KEY data name)

[INVALID imperative-statement]

INVALID KEY condition when ORGANIZATION IS INDEXED:

■ Record not found (with key value equal to RECORD KEY value)
[File status code = 23]

Example:

```
READ INDEXED-MASTER-FILE

    INTO EM-EMPLOYEE-MASTER-WORK-AREA

    KEY IS AK-EMPLOYEE NUMBER

    INVALID KEY MOVE 'NO ' TO WS-MASTER-RECORD-FOUND-SW.
```

Figure 6B.4. Random READ statement format for an ALTERNATE KEY.

If the KEY phrase is omitted from a random READ statement, the prime record key is considered the key of reference by default.

The WRITE, REWRITE, and DELETE Statements

The WRITE, REWRITE, and DELETE statements always use the prime record key as the key of reference. When records are added to the file, alternate key values are changed on the file, or records are deleted from the file, the system automatically handles all required changes to the alternate indexes.

If a record is written or rewritten to an indexed file that is specified with an ALTERNATE RECORD KEY but without the WITH DUPLICATES phrase, an INVALID KEY condition (file status code 22) will occur if an alternate record key value duplicates one already on file.

Summary

Topic 6-A Record-Access Modes

Current record pointer is a conceptual entity that is used to facilitate the description of the *next* record that is to be processed in a file opened as INPUT or I-O and whose ACCESS MODE IS SEQUENTIAL or DYNAMIC.

SEQUENTIAL is the most commonly used ACCESS MODE for retrieval programs. It is used for all files whose ORGANIZATION IS SEQUENTIAL and for most report programs, regardless of the organization method. The sequential READ statement is used to retrieve records from a file that is being accessed sequentially. The START statement is used to begin sequential processing for a file whose ORGANIZATION IS INDEXED or RELATIVE at a location other than at its first record. The START statement can only be used when the ACCESS MODE IS SEQUENTIAL or DYNAMIC and the file is opened as INPUT or I-O. The START statement can be used to provide **skip-sequential**, **generic**, or **limits retrieval processing.**

RANDOM access retrievals can be handled through use of the random

READ statement, as was used in the INDMAINT program that was presented in Chapter 4 and the RELMAINT program that was discussed in Chapter 5.

DYNAMIC access permits records—within the scope of the same OPEN statement—to be (1) obtained from or placed into a mass-storage file on a random basis and (2) read from the file in either a sequential or random manner.

Topic 6-B Alternate Record Keys

With INDEXED files, an ALTERNATE RECORD KEY may be established to permit retrieval of records in sequences other than the RECORD KEY sequence. To do this, the ALTERNATE RECORD KEY phrase must be specified in the SELECT statement for the file. If records with duplicate alternate key values are permitted to reside in the file, the WITH DUPLICATES phrase must also be specified.

Programming Assignments

6-1: Account Balance List Retrieval

Program description

Account balance data is to be retrieved from an indexed general ledger master file. The type of retrieval and the records that are to be retrieved are specified by input account parameter records. Account balance lists are to be prepared.

Input files

General ledger master file   Key field = General ledger account number

Account-retrieval parameter file

Output file

Account balance list

Record formats

General ledger master record (Record code "LM")

Account-retrieval parameter record (Record code "65")

Account balance list

General ledger master record

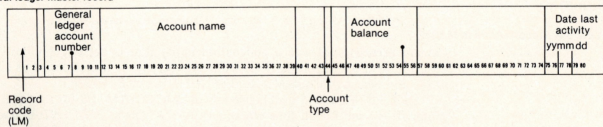

Account retrieval parameter record

Account balance list

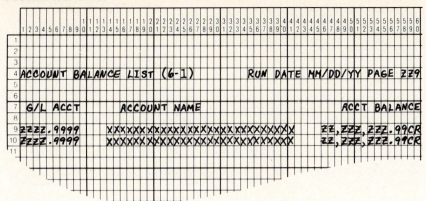

ACCOUNT BALANCE LIST (6-1)   RUN DATE MM/DD/YY PAGE ZZ9

G/L ACCT   ACCOUNT NAME   ACCT BALANCE
ZZZZ.9999   XXXXXXXXXXXXXXXXXXXXXXXXXXXX   ZZ,ZZZ,ZZZ.99CR
ZZZZ.9999   XXXXXXXXXXXXXXXXXXXXXXXXXXXX   ZZ,ZZZ,ZZZ.99CR

Program operations

A. Read each input account-retrieval parameter record.

  1. Validate each parameter record to ensure that it contains one of the following retrieval codes:

    1 (print accounts whose leftmost digit matches the value of the account-mask digit)

    2 (print accounts whose leftmost two digits match the value of the two account-mask digits)

    3 (print accounts whose leftmost three digits match value of the three account-mask digits)

    4 (print accounts whose leftmost four digits match the value of the four account-mask digits)

  2. The parameter record account-mask digits are left justified in the account-mask field.

B. Print each master record that satisfies the parameter record conditions above.

  1. If there are no accounts to be printed for an account-retrieval parameter record, print the exception message "NO G/L ACCOUNTS" together with the account-mask field value.

  2. If the retrieval code is invalid, print the exception message "INVALID RETRIEVAL CODE" together with the retrieval code value.

C. Print the account balance list as shown on the print chart.

  1. Skip to a new page for each account-retrieval parameter record.

  2. Single-space each detail line.

  3. Provide for a maximum line span of 57 lines per page.

6-2: Vendor-Payable List Retrieval

Program description

Vendor-payable data is to be retrieved from an indexed-vendor master file. The type of retrieval and records that are to be retrieved are specified by input vendor parameter records. Vendor-payable lists are to be prepared.

Input files

Vendor master file   Key fields = Vendor number (major)
                                   Date due (minor)

Vendor-retrieval parameter file

Output file

Vendor-payable list

Record formats

Vendor master record (Record code "VM")

Vendor-retrieval parameter record (Record code "66")

Vendor-payable list

Vendor master record

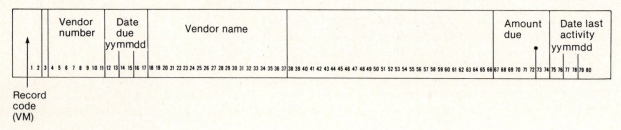

Record
code
(VM)

Vendor retrieval parameter record

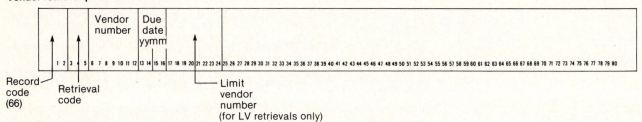

Record
code
(66)

Retrieval
code

Limit
vendor
number
(for LV retrievals only)

Vendor payable list

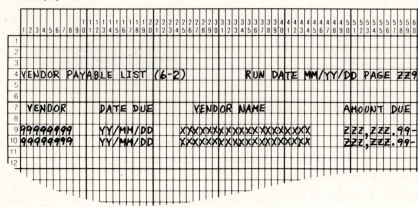

Program operations

A. Read each input vendor-retrieval parameter record.

1. Validate each parameter record to ensure that it contains one of the following retrieval codes:

   SV (Skip to vendor number and print remainder of file)

   GV (Generic retrieval by vendor number)

   GM (Generic retrieval by vendor number for month value)

   LV (Limits retrieval by vendor number)

2. If the retrieval code is "SV", start at the first record in the master file that has a vendor number equal to or greater than the vendor number of the retrieval parameter record.

a. Print each master record until end-of-file is reached.

b. If there are no master records for that vendor number, print the exception message "VENDOR NUMBER NOT ON FILE" together with the vendor number.

3. If the retrieval code is "GV", start at the first record in the master file that has a vendor number equal to the vendor number of the retrieval parameter record.

   a. Print each master record with that same vendor number.

   b. If there are no master records for that vendor number, print the exception message "VENDOR NUMBER NOT ON FILE" together with the vendor number.

4. If the retrieval code is "GM", start at the first master record in the file that has (a) a vendor number equal to the vendor number of the retrieval parameter record and (b) a due-date year and month equal to the due date of the retrieval parameter record.

   a. Print each master record with that same vendor number and due-date year and month.

   b. If there are no master records for that vendor number, print the exception message "VENDOR NUMBER NOT ON FILE" together with the vendor number.

   c. If there are no master records for that vendor number due that year and month, print the exception message "VENDOR/MONTH NOT ON FILE " together with the vendor number, year, and month.

5. If the retrieval code is "LV", start at the first master record in the file that has a vendor number equal to or greater than the vendor number of the retrieval parameter record.

   a. Print each master record until a vendor number that is higher than the vendor number of the retrieval parameter record is reached.

   b. If there are no master records within the limits span, print the exception message "NO VENDORS TO REPORT" together with the vendor-number limits.

6. If the retrieval code is invalid, print the exception message "INVALID PARAMETER RECORD" together with the contents of the retrieval parameter record.

B. Print the vendor payable list as shown on the print chart.

1. Skip to a new page for each vendor-retrieval parameter record.

2. Single-space each detail line.

3. Provide for a maximum line span of 57 lines per page.

6-3: Employee-Roster Retrieval

Program description

Employee rosters are to be retrieved from an indexed employee master file. The type of retrieval and records to be retrieved are specified by input roster parameter records. Employee-roster lists are to be prepared.

Input files

Employee master file

Key fields =	Plant code (major)
	Department number (intermediate)
	Employee number (minor)
Alternate key =	Employee number
Alternate key =	Employee name (with duplicates)

Roster-retrieval parameter file

Output file

    Employee-roster list

Record formats

    Employee master record (Record code "EM")

    Roster-retrieval parameter record (Record code "67")

    Employee-roster list

Employee master record

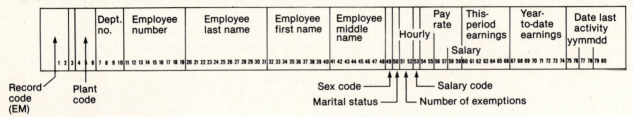

Employee retrieval parameter record

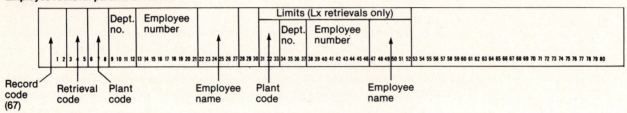

Employee roster

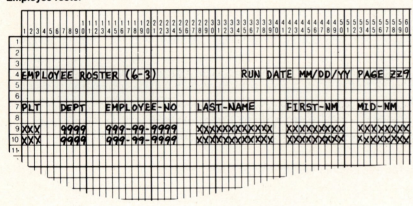

Program operations

    A. Read each input roster-retrieval parameter record.

        1. Validate each parameter record to ensure that it contains one of the following retrieval codes:

            SP (Skip to prime record key and print remainder of file)

            SE (Skip to employee number alternate key and print remainder of file)

            SN (Skip to name alternate key and print remainder of file)

            GP (Generic retrieval by plant prime key)

            GD (Generic retrieval by plant/department prime key)

            GN (Generic retrieval by name alternate key)

            LP (Limits retrieval by prime key)

            LE (Limits retrieval by employee number alternate key)

            LN (Limits retrieval by name alternate key)

        2. If the retrieval code is "SP", start at the first record in the master file that has a

prime record key equal to or greater than the prime record key (plant/department/employee number) of the retrieval parameter record.

   a. Print each master record until end-of-file is reached.

3. If the retrieval code is "SE", start at the first record in the master file that has an alternate employee number key equal to or greater than the employee number of the retrieval parameter record.

   a. Print each master record until end-of-file is reached.

4. If the retrieval code is "SN", start at the first record in the master file that has an alternate name key equal to or greater than the name field of the retrieval parameter record.

   a. Print each master record until end-of-file is reached.

5. If the retrieval code is "GP", start at the first record in the master file that has a plant code equal to the plant code of the retrieval parameter record.

   a. Print each master record with that same plant code.

   b. If there are no master records for that plant code and number, print the exception message "PLANT CODE NOT ON FILE" together with the plant code on the report line.

6. If the retrieval code is "GD", start at the first record in the master file that has a plant code and department number that are equal to the plant code and department number of the retrieval parameter record.

   a. Print each master record with that same plant code and department number.

   b. If there are no master records for that plant code and department number, print the exception message "PLANT/DEPT NOT ON FILE" together with the plant code and department number.

7. If the retrival code is "GN", start at the first record in the master file that has a name field in which the first six characters are equal to the name field of the retrieval parameter record.

   a. Print each master record with the same first six positions of the employee name.

   b. If there are no master records that have a name field with the same first six characters, print the exception message "NAME NOT ON FILE" together with the first six characters of the name.

8. If the retrieval code is "LP", start at the first master record in the file that has a prime key equal to or greater than the prime key (plant code/department number/employee number) of the retrieval parameter record.

   a. Print each master record until a prime key that is higher than the limit prime key of the retrieval parameter record is reached.

   b. If there are no master records within the limits span, print the exception message "NO EMPLOYEES TO REPORT" together with the prime key limits.

9. If the retrieval code is "LE", start at the first master record in the file that has an alternate employee number key equal to or greater than the employee number of the retrieval parameter record.

   a. Print each master record until an employee number that is higher than the limit employee number of the retrieval parameter record is reached.

   b. If there are no master records within the limits span, print the exception message "NO EMPLOYEES TO REPORT" together with the employee number limits.

10. If the retrieval code is "LN", start at the first master record in the file that has an alternate name key equal to or greater than the name of the retrieval parameter record.

   a. Print each master record until a name whose first six characters are alphabetically higher than the limit name of the retrieval parameter record is reached.

   b. If there are no master records within the limits span, print the exception message "NO EMPLOYEES TO REPORT" together with the name limits.

11. If the retrieval code is invalid, print the exception message "INVALID PARAMETER RECORD" together with the retrieval parameter record contents on the report line.

B. Print the employee roster as shown on the print chart.

1. Skip to a new page for each roster-retrieval parameter record.

2. Single-space each detail line.

3. Provide for a maximum line span of 57 lines per page.

COMPUTER PRINTERS AND REPORT DESIGN

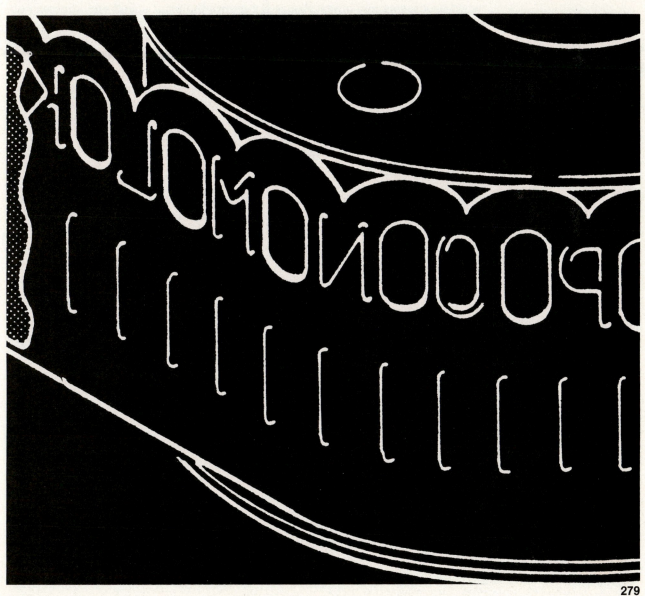

B
COMPUTER PRINTERS AND REPORT DESIGN

Computer Printers

Computer printers can be categorized as being of page, line, or serial orientation. **Page printers** are high-speed units that are used in large data-processing centers. **Line printers** are medium-speed devices that are used in practically all but the smallest data-processing installations. **Serial printers** are low-speed devices that are usually attached to computer terminals, microcomputers, and word-processing machines. Figure B.1 shows the print speed and approximate price ranges for the three categories of printers.

Computer printers can also be classified as either impact or nonimpact printers. **Impact printers** are the traditional type that form the printed character image by striking the print character against the ribbon onto the paper. **Nonimpact** printers use lasers, heat, ink jets, or other means to create images.

Impact printers have one significant advantage over nonimpact printers: they can produce multiple copies when carbon or sensitized paper is used. Quiet operation is an advantage of nonimpact printers. Certain nonimpact technologies also provide high-speed operation, character range, and/or character quality advantages.

Page Printers

Page printers are nonimpact, high-speed printers that use electrophotographic techniques to print on one-part computer paper. They were developed to print faster and provide more features than traditional impact line printers and, at the same time, to retain program compatibility. Page printers are popularly termed **laser printers** because they use a laser beam of light to create latent dot images on the surface of a photographic drum or belt. Figure B.2 shows a commonly used page printer: the IBM 3800 Printing Subsystem.

Line Printers

Most line printers that are currently being marketed are impact printers and have speeds ranging from approximately 100 to 3000 lines per minute. There are five types of line-printer mechanisms that are commonly used: train, chain, drum, band, and impact matrix. Figure B.3 shows characteristics of these impact mechanisms. In addition, a few nonimpact line printers are currently offered or are under development.

Train and chain

Train and **chain** mechanisms contain the characters on a train or chain that rotates in front of the printing positions at a uniform high rate of speed. Behind each print position is a small metal hammer. At the exact instant when the proper character is in front of the print position, the hammer strikes from behind the paper as the chain or train "flies" by. This causes the paper to come in contact with the ribbon and the character face, and thus forms the image on the paper.

Printer category	Approximate print speed range	Approximate price range
Page	12,000–20,000 lpm	$300,000–$400,000
Line	100–3,000 lpm	3,500–100,000
Serial	20–2,000 cps	175–10,000

Legend: lpm = lines per minute
              cps = characters per second

Figure B.1.   Categories of computer printers.

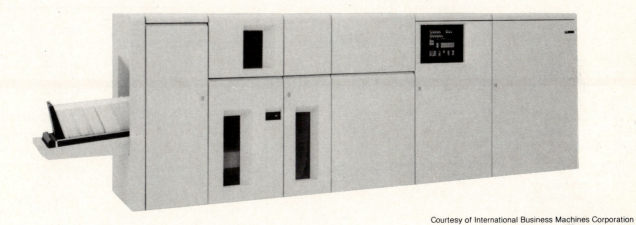

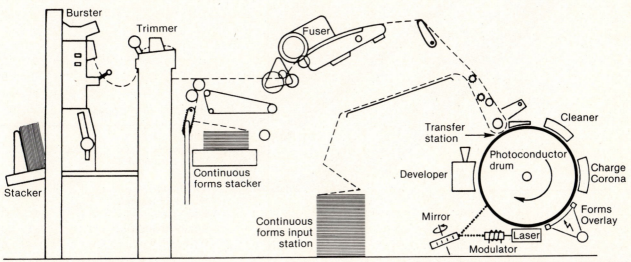

Adapted from IBM publication GC26-3859-0, p. 3, by courtesy of International Business Machines Corporation.

Figure B.2.   An example of a page printer.

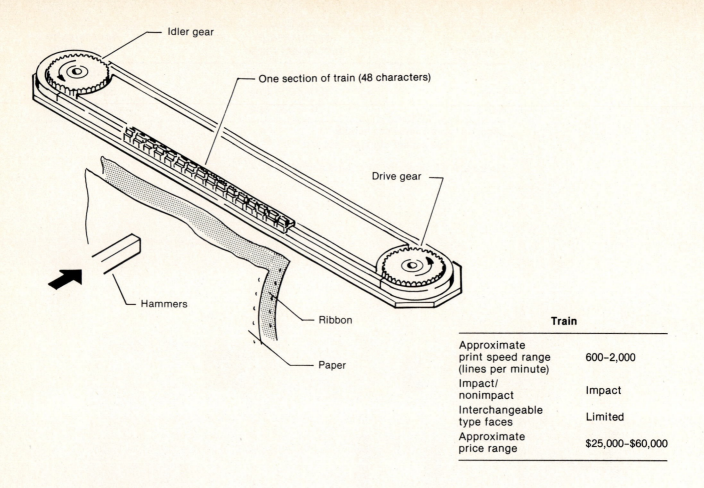

Train	
Approximate print speed range (lines per minute)	600–2,000
Impact/ nonimpact	Impact
Interchangeable type faces	Limited
Approximate price range	$25,000–$60,000

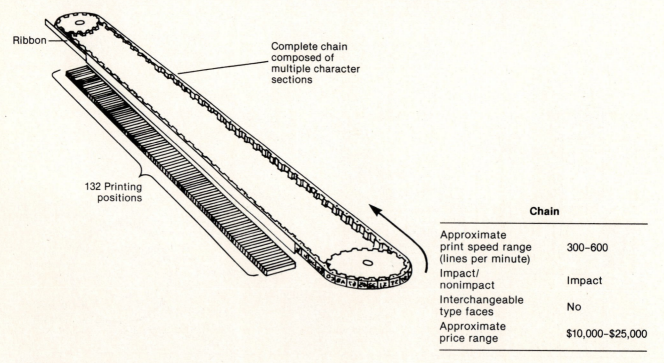

Chain	
Approximate print speed range (lines per minute)	300–600
Impact/ nonimpact	Impact
Interchangeable type faces	No
Approximate price range	$10,000–$25,000

Figure B.3. Line-printer mechanisms.
Courtesy of Dataproducts Corporation

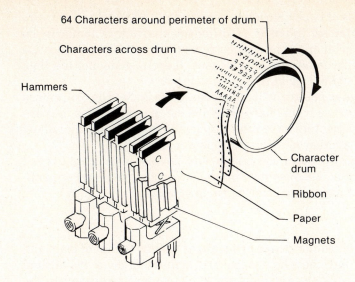

64 Characters around perimeter of drum

Characters across drum

Hammers

Character drum

Ribbon

Paper

Magnets

Drum	
Approximate print speed range (lines per minute)	300–1,250
Impact/ nonimpact	Impact
Interchangeable type faces	No
Approximate price range	$8,000–$25,000

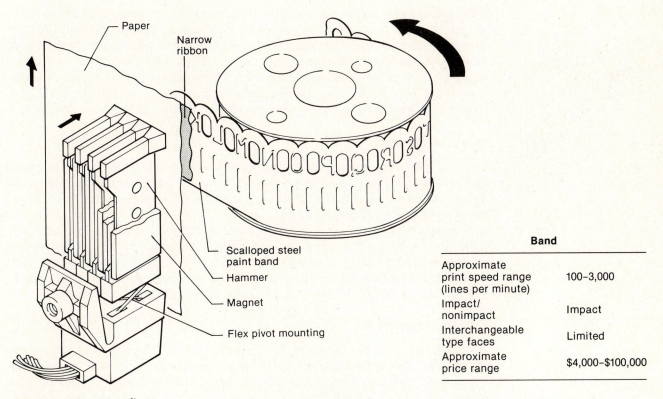

Paper

Narrow ribbon

Scalloped steel paint band

Hammer

Magnet

Flex pivot mounting

Band	
Approximate print speed range (lines per minute)	100–3,000
Impact/ nonimpact	Impact
Interchangeable type faces	Limited
Approximate price range	$4,000–$100,000

Figure B.3. (continued)

Multiple occurrences of each character are typically on the chain or train. The smaller the **character set** (number of different characters that can be printed), the higher the print speed at a given revolution rate. This is because more occurrences of each character are present, thereby reducing the time that is required to set a character in front of a column.

The difference between chain and train mechanisms is that the characters of a chain are linked whereas train characters are independent slugs that are rotating in a track. Train printers have interchangeable print trains that allow the printing of a limited number of different typefaces.

Most train and chain printers are heavy-duty devices with good overall reliability. They are popular because they produce a crisp image and are suitable for high-volume and multicopy printing requirements.

Drum

Drum printers form the character image in a manner similar to that of train and chain printers except that the characters are contained on a cylindrical rotating steel drum. There is one complete set of characters embossed on the drum for each print position. The hammer for each print position is activated as the proper character for that print position rotates in front of the print line.

Drum printers have been popular because of their general reliability and suitability for use with multicopy forms. However, because of their design, they often produce wavy lines when their timing and adjustments stray from specifications. Drum printers do not offer interchangeable fonts. Because of these maintenance requirements and typeface limitations, it appears that other print-mechanism technologies will gradually replace drum printers in the marketplace.

Band

Band printer mechanisms are similar to those of chain printers. The major difference is that the characters are embossed on a lighter-weight band rather than a chain. In terms of the units that are currently being manufactured, band printers are predominant among line printers. They offer good quality output at relatively high print speeds and multicopy forms capabilities. They are usually lower-cost, less heavy-duty devices than chain, train, or drum printers. The bands are interchangeable to provide a limited degree of typeface flexibility.

Impact matrix

Even though most **impact matrix** printers are of the serial type, there are a few line printers that use a matrix-printing technique. Characters are formed as a pattern of dots. Usually one horizontal line of dots is printed at a time as the paper is advanced one vertical dot row.

Impact matrix printers tend to be more electronically based and mechanically simpler than other impact line printers. This results in a generally lower-cost, quieter, and more reliable device. Although they do not produce print speeds as high as the faster, fully formed-character line printers, matrix printers can offer graphic, bar code, and expanded character-size features.

Nonimpact line printers

Although the multipart forms needs of most business applications limit their attractiveness, nonimpact line printers that use **electrostatic, thermal, ink-jet, ion deposition**, and **magnetographic** technologies are currently offered or are under development. Such devices have yet to gain a significant share of the

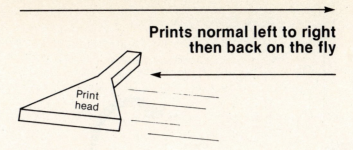

Prints normal left to right then back on the fly

Figure B.4. Bidirectional serial printing.

printer market but they do provide quiet operation and certain advantages for specialized applications. Given the current state-of-the-art, most nonimpact line printers suffer from a lack of "track record" with regard to manufacturing, application, and maintenance viability.

Serial Printers

Serial printers print in a manner similar to typewriters: one character after another across the page. For this reason, they are sometimes termed **character printers.** Some serial printers offer **bidirectional print** capabilities, as depicted in Figure B.4, where they print not only from left to right across the page but also from right to left on the return, thereby permitting a faster print rate. Figure B.5 presents a summary of the common characteristics of serial printers.

The speed and output quality of a serial printer is determined by the **print head** that is used to form its characters. Matrix and daisywheel print heads are the most commonly used, but thermal matrix, electrostatic, and ink-jet devices capture a portion of the market.

Those serial print heads, such as the daisywheel, that have fully formed characters are sometimes termed **solid-font** printers to distinguish them from the matrix devices that form each character as a dot pattern.

Impact matrix

Impact matrix print heads form each character as a pattern of small dots, often in a 5 × 7 or 9 × 7 dot matrix as shown in Figure B.6. As the print head moves across the page, the proper hammers are triggered from the matrix to form each character.

Matrix printers offer high-serial print speeds together with reliable operation and reasonable cost. In the past, the use of matrix printers was limited by the reduced legibility and print quality of its characters. Current improvements have centered on improving print quality with higher-density matrices so that certain matrix printers now print at or near the so-called **letter-quality** of the solid-font serial mechanisms. Unlike most solid-font serial printers, however, impact matrix serial printers usually have little or no flexibility in regard to typeface selection.

Daisywheel

Daisywheel printers use a plastic wheel with one character embossed at the end of each spoke. The wheel rotates in both directions to bring the proper character to hammer position for printing. As shown in Figure B.7, a **thimble** print-

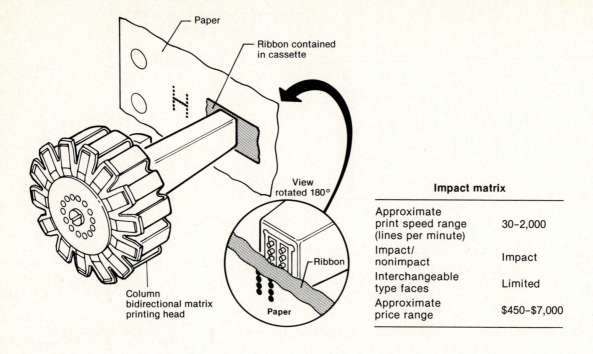

Impact matrix	
Approximate print speed range (lines per minute)	30–2,000
Impact/ nonimpact	Impact
Interchangeable type faces	Limited
Approximate price range	$450–$7,000

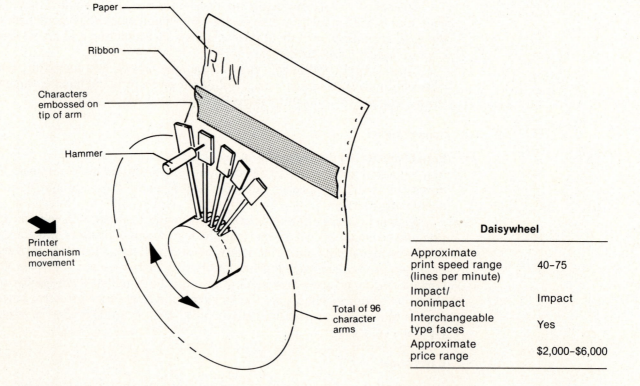

Daisywheel	
Approximate print speed range (lines per minute)	40–75
Impact/ nonimpact	Impact
Interchangeable type faces	Yes
Approximate price range	$2,000–$6,000

Figure B.5. Serial printer mechanisms.
Courtesy of Dataproducts Corporation

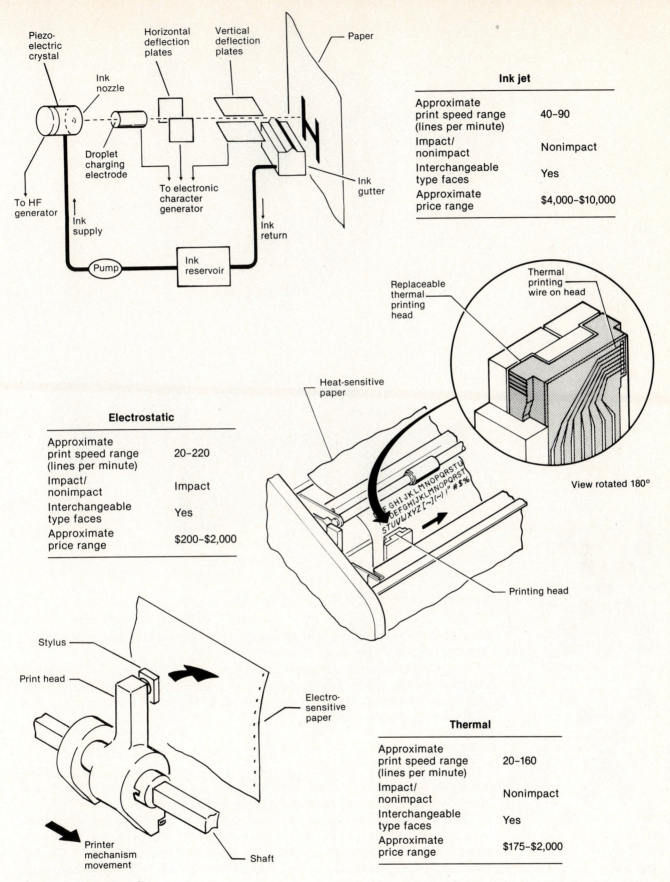

Ink jet	
Approximate print speed range (lines per minute)	40–90
Impact/ nonimpact	Nonimpact
Interchangeable type faces	Yes
Approximate price range	$4,000–$10,000

Electrostatic	
Approximate print speed range (lines per minute)	20–220
Impact/ nonimpact	Impact
Interchangeable type faces	Yes
Approximate price range	$200–$2,000

Thermal	
Approximate print speed range (lines per minute)	20–160
Impact/ nonimpact	Nonimpact
Interchangeable type faces	Yes
Approximate price range	$175–$2,000

Figure B.5. (continued)

Figure B.7. Daisywheel and thimble printwheels.

wheel is similar to a daisywheel except that the characters are contained on a cupped wheel that resembles a large thimble.

Daisywheel printers are popular because they offer high print quality at adequate speeds, together with a variety of interchangeable typefaces. Their print-speed and maintenance price/performance ratio does not match that of impact matrix devices, however.

Ink jet

Ink-jet printers employ electrostatic deflection plates to control a spray of electrically charged ink. Up to 500 dots comprise the ink-jet matrix, providing a print quality that appears to have been formed by a solid font.

As a nonimpact device, ink-jet printers offer a practically silent operation, together with high-resolution and high-speed printing capabilities. However, ink-jet printers are currently expensive and have suffered problems of reliability in the past. As such, only a limited number of ink-jet printers are presently being marketed and used.

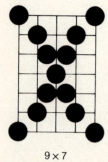

5 × 7

9 × 7

Figure B.6.
Matrix comparison.

10 characters per inch

```
THIS IS NORMAL.
THIS IS NORMAL,ITALICS.
THIS IS NORMAL,DOUBLESTRIKE.
THIS IS NORMAL,DOUBLESTRIKE,ITALICS.
THIS IS NORMAL,EMPHASIZED,DOUBLESTRIKE.
THIS IS NORMAL,EMPHASIZED,DOUBLESTRIKE,ITALICS.
THIS IS SUPERSCRIPT.
THIS IS SUPERSCRIPT,ITALICS.
```

5 characters per inch

```
THIS IS DOUBLEWIDTH.
THIS IS DOUBLEWIDTH,ITALICS.
THIS IS DOUBLEWIDTH,EMPHASIZED.
THIS IS DOUBLEWIDTH,EMPHASIZED,
   ITALICS.
THIS IS DOUBLEWIDTH,EMPHASIZED,
   DOUBLESTRIKE.
THIS IS DOUBLEWIDTH,EMPHASIZED,
   DOUBLESTRIKE,ITALICS.
```

8.58 characters per inch

```
THIS IS CONDENSED,DOUBLEWIDTH.
THIS IS CONDENSED,DOUBLEWIDTH,ITALICS.
THIS IS CONDENSED,DOUBLEWIDTH,DOUBLESTRIKE.
THIS IS CONDENSED,DOUBLEWIDTH,DOUBLESTRIKE,ITALICS.
```

17.16 characters per inch

```
THIS IS CONDENSED.
THIS IS CONDENSED,ITALICS.
THIS IS CONDENSED,DOUBLESTRIKE.
THIS IS CONDENSED,DOUBLESTRIKE,ITALICS.
THIS IS CONDENSED,SUPERSCRIPT.
THIS IS CONDENSED,SUPERSCRIPT,ITALICS.
```

Figure B.8. Serial matrix printer output examples.

Thermal and electrostatic

Thermal printers use heat to form dot-matrix character images on special heat-sensitive paper. **Electrostatic** printers use electricity, together with electrosensitive paper.

As nonimpact devices that are based more on electronics than mechanics, both thermal and electrostatic printers provide quiet operation and high reliability, together with ribbon-free operation. Their disadvantages are that they use expensive, special paper, provide only low-resolution print quality, and are limited to single-copy output.

Printer Specifications

Most computer printers provide 132 print positions for each horizontal report line. However, printers that are used with personal computers and microcomputers sometimes have print lines limited to 20, 40, or 80 characters. Also, some large-scale printers can span up to 150 print positions.

Characters are usually printed on the line at 10 characters per inch. Hence, a 132-character line spans 13.2 inches. Many serial printers that are used for word-processing applications also permit printing at 12 characters per inch. Certain serial matrix printers provide print variations such as those shown in Figure B.8. Page printers commonly offer 10-, 12-, or 15-pitch options.

Practically all printers print 6 lines to the vertical inch. Most line printers and word-processing printers also allow printing at 8 lines to the inch. Some page printers permit printing of up to 12 lines per inch.

Report Design

Reports are usually designed and documented on a gridlike form called a **print chart**. An example is shown in Figure B.9. The preprinted numbers that run

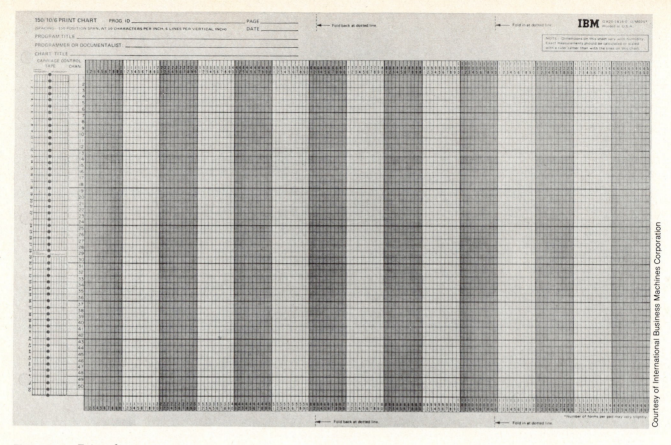

Figure B.9. Print chart.

across the top of the print chart identify the horizontal print positions; the numbers that run down the side of the chart represent the vertical line numbers.

Report Areas

The programmer/analyst has three general data areas to consider in designing a report: the heading area, the body area, and the grand-total area. Figure B.10 identifies each of these areas.

Heading area

The **heading area** of a report should contain data that will identify the report. Common examples of such data are report title, organization name, report date, and page number. Larger organizations also usually print a report-code number on reports to uniquely identify each report and facilitate identification of which computer program printed the report. When dates are printed on reports, it is often appropriate to print two dates: (1) the date (or period-ending date) to which the report applies, and (2) the date when the computer actually printed (or processed) the report. For example, consider an income statement for the month of October 1983. The period-ending date of 10/31/83 should, of course, be printed at the top of each page of the report. But this income statement will

Heading area ——→

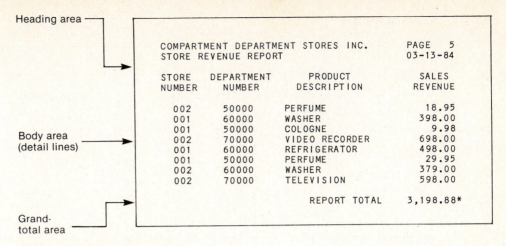

```
        COMPARTMENT DEPARTMENT STORES INC.        PAGE   5
        STORE REVENUE REPORT                      03-13-84

        STORE       DEPARTMENT      PRODUCT          SALES
        NUMBER        NUMBER      DESCRIPTION       REVENUE

         002         50000       PERFUME             18.95
         001         60000       WASHER             398.00
         001         50000       COLOGNE              9.98
         002         70000       VIDEO RECORDER     698.00
         001         60000       REFRIGERATOR       498.00
         001         50000       PERFUME             29.95
         002         60000       WASHER             379.00
         002         70000       TELEVISION         598.00

                                 REPORT TOTAL     3,198.88*
```

Body area
(detail lines) ——→

Grand-
total area ——→

Figure B.10. Report areas.

probably not be processed until sometime in early November. Providing the run date on the report in addition to the period-ending date is very helpful in case the report is modified, corrected, or revised at a later date.

The bottom part of the heading area usually contains column headings for the detail line fields printed below.

Report headings are usually repeated on each page of a report. Sometimes the headings are condensed or abbreviated for report pages after the first.

Body area

The **body area** of a report contains detail lines, summary lines, and/or subtotal lines. A **detail line** is a line that is logically related to an input record, usually on a one-to-one basis. If one or more body lines are printed for each input record, such lines are considered detail lines. A **summary line** is one in which multiple input records are accumulated or otherwise summarized and printed as one line. A **subtotal line** presents an accumulation of previously printed detail or summary lines. Subtotal lines are often termed **control break** lines.

Grand-total area

The **grand-total area** is usually at the end of the report. Commonly printed in this area are items such as record counts, grand totals for columns, and the results of calculations (such as averages, percentages, and so forth) that must be made after all applicable input records have been processed. Descriptive words to identify the total figures are also commonly provided. Report lines that contain such data are called **total lines**.

When page totals or other data is printed at the bottom of each page of the report, the area in which it is printed is termed the **page-footing** area.

Report Design Guidelines

There are certain guidelines for report design that should be considered when a programmer/analyst designs a report. A number of them will be discussed.

Identify the report

Every output report should have a title or some other identifier. If the output is destined to be read or used by someone outside the company or division, the name of the issuing organization should appear on the report. The run date of the report should be specified; the period-ending date of the report should also

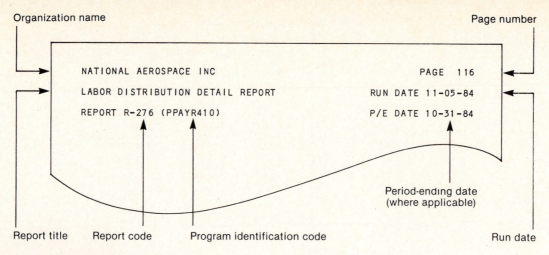

Organization name
Page number

```
NATIONAL AEROSPACE INC                          PAGE   116

LABOR DISTRIBUTION DETAIL REPORT             RUN DATE 11-05-84

REPORT R-276 (PPAYR410)                      P/E DATE 10-31-84
```

Report title   Report code   Program identification code

Period-ending date
(where applicable)

Run date

Figure B.11.   Report identification example.

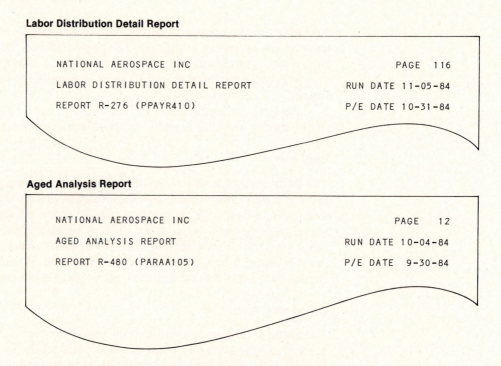

Labor Distribution Detail Report

```
NATIONAL AEROSPACE INC                          PAGE   116

LABOR DISTRIBUTION DETAIL REPORT             RUN DATE 11-05-84

REPORT R-276 (PPAYR410)                      P/E DATE 10-31-84
```

Aged Analysis Report

```
NATIONAL AEROSPACE INC                          PAGE    12

AGED ANALYSIS REPORT                         RUN DATE 10-04-84

REPORT R-480 (PARAA105)                      P/E DATE  9-30-84
```

Figure B.12.   Standardized-heading identification area example.

appear, when applicable. A report or program number that will uniquely identify the report should be assigned and noted on the output. For multipage reports, a page number should be provided. Figure B.11 provides an example of appropriate report identification.

Standardize-the-heading identification area

Having the report identification items in standard locations from one report to the next within an organization is helpful to the users and also presents a uniform appearance. That is, try not to have the report title in the upper left-hand corner of one report and in the lower right-hand space of the heading area on another. Figure B.12 shows an example of a standardized-heading identification area that is applied to two different reports.

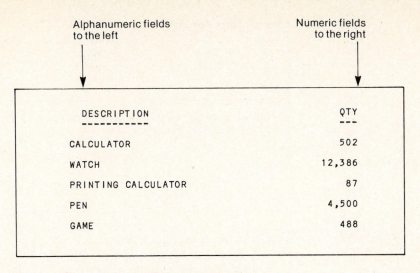

Alphanumeric fields to the left | Numeric fields to the right

```
DESCRIPTION                               QTY
-----------                               ---

CALCULATOR                                502

WATCH                                  12,386

PRINTING CALCULATOR                        87

PEN                                     4,500

GAME                                      488
```

Figure B.13. Column-heading positioning example.

Label all output fields

Data fields should not be displayed on a report without a descriptive text that explains what each field is. Such descriptions will usually take the form of column headings for detail line fields. For the total line and for other fields not contained in the regular lines, adjacent descriptive words on the same line may be required. Even though the programmer/analyst and the user may be very familiar with the report as it is being developed, data that is printed on reports without identification soon becomes confusing.

Position column headings properly

If a data field beneath a column heading contains a uniform number of characters to be printed on each line, it is probably most attractive to center the column heading. Usually, however, numeric fields will have blank positions to the left of the number (because of zero suppression) and alphanumeric fields will have blank positions to the right of the printed characters (because the length of the field is usually longer than the entry in the field).

Therefore, as depicted in Figure B.13, column headings for numeric fields are more pleasing visually when they are offset or justified to the right boundary of the data column; column headings for alphanumeric fields are best positioned at or near the left limit of the data column.

Determine report width and length

The maximum width of a printed report is usually 132 print positions, printed at 10 characters per inch. If the report can be accommodated easily in 85 print positions or less, it is a good idea to keep within that number; this allows the user to copy and file the report with 8½-inch-wide paper.

Some page printers provide for printing at 15 characters per horizontal inch. This allows 132 characters to be printed on 11-inch-wide forms.

A report page is typically 8½ or 11 inches in length. An 11-inch length is usually used with 14⅞-inch-wide forms printed at 6 lines per inch. When a report is printed at 8 lines per inch, 8½-inch-long forms are normally used.

Figure B.14 illustrates report width and length considerations. Figure B.15 presents a table of common stock form sizes and printing specifications.

Common Stock Form Widths

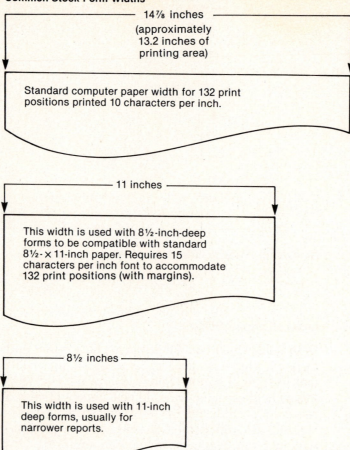

14 ⅞ inches
(approximately
13.2 inches of
printing area)

Standard computer paper width for 132 print positions printed 10 characters per inch.

11 inches

This width is used with 8½-inch-deep forms to be compatible with standard 8½- × 11-inch paper. Requires 15 characters per inch font to accommodate 132 print positions (with margins).

8½ inches

This width is used with 11-inch deep forms, usually for narrower reports.

Common Stock Form Lengths

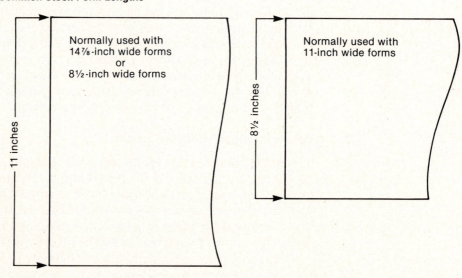

Normally used with
14 ⅞-inch wide forms
or
8½-inch wide forms

11 inches

Normally used with
11-inch wide forms

8½ inches

Figure B.14. Report width and length considerations.

Forms size in inches		Vertical lines per inch	Vertical lines per page	Horizontal characters per inch	Typical printer type
Length	Width				
11 × 14⅞		6	66	10	impact
8½ × 14⅞		8	68	10	impact
8½ × 11		8	68	15	nonimpact

Figure B.15. Common stock form sizes and printing specifications.

Consider top- and bottom-margin requirements

If the report is to be bound on the horizontal edges—as many nylon-post binders do—a generous top and bottom margin must be provided. Otherwise, some of the report page will be obscured after it is bound.

For example, if a report is to be kept in a standard three-ring binder, a left-margin area must be provided for the binder holes. The programmer/analyst should check to see if there are any special binding or filing requirements that will dictate any other report widths.

Make the report visually attractive

Do not cram the data together in a bunch; space the fields across the chosen report width. Provide extra blank lines before and after subtotal and total lines; this "white space" will make them easier to locate and read. Figure B.16 illustrates typical placement of blank lines.

Consider placement of filing code and identification number

As shown in Figure B.17, the upper right-hand corner of the page is usually the best place to print identification codes. For example, invoice numbers are usually printed at that location on an invoice form. If reports are to be filed in drawers other than standard file drawers, however, another location may be preferable.

Allow sufficient space for numeric results

For numeric amounts that are the result of an arithmetic operation, provide room for the largest possible amount that can occur. When just two values are involved in a calculation, the maximum size can be determined by formulas, as shown in Figure B.18.

In many situations, however, the total amount will be the result of successive arithmetic operations. For example, the maximum size of a field that is used to accumulate the grand total of account balances will depend upon the number of input records that are being processed. When this is the case, the space that is required for the maximum value cannot be determined by a formula but must instead be chosen by the programmer/analyst.

Consider intercolumn space requirements

When determining the number of horizontal print positions that are needed for numeric fields that contain column totals, it is the length of the *total* that must be provided for rather than the field length of the detail amounts. An alternate

After heading

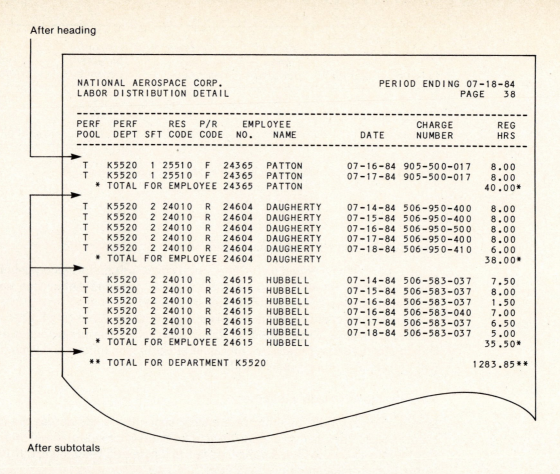

```
          NATIONAL AEROSPACE CORP.                      PERIOD ENDING 07-18-84
          LABOR DISTRIBUTION DETAIL                                PAGE    38

          ----------------------------------------------------------------------------
          PERF   PERF      RES  P/R   EMPLOYEE                      CHARGE          REG
          POOL   DEPT  SFT CODE CODE  NO.    NAME        DATE       NUMBER          HRS
          ----------------------------------------------------------------------------

            T    K5520  1  25510  F   24365  PATTON      07-16-84  905-500-017     8.00
            T    K5520  1  25510  F   24365  PATTON      07-17-84  905-500-017     8.00
               * TOTAL FOR EMPLOYEE 24365  PATTON                                 40.00*

            T    K5520  2  24010   R  24604  DAUGHERTY   07-14-84  506-950-400     8.00
            T    K5520  2  24010   R  24604  DAUGHERTY   07-15-84  506-950-400     8.00
            T    K5520  2  24010   R  24604  DAUGHERTY   07-16-84  506-950-500     8.00
            T    K5520  2  24010   R  24604  DAUGHERTY   07-17-84  506-950-400     8.00
            T    K5520  2  24010   R  24604  DAUGHERTY   07-18-84  506-950-410     6.00
               * TOTAL FOR EMPLOYEE 24604  DAUGHERTY                              38.00*

            T    K5520  2  24010   R  24615  HUBBELL     07-14-84  506-583-037     7.50
            T    K5520  2  24010   R  24615  HUBBELL     07-15-84  506-583-037     8.00
            T    K5520  2  24010   R  24615  HUBBELL     07-16-84  506-583-037     1.50
            T    K5520  2  24010   R  24615  HUBBELL     07-16-84  506-583-040     7.00
            T    K5520  2  24010   R  24615  HUBBELL     07-17-84  506-583-037     6.50
            T    K5520  2  24010   R  24615  HUBBELL     07-18-84  506-583-037     5.00
               * TOTAL FOR EMPLOYEE 24615  HUBBELL                               35.50*

              ** TOTAL FOR DEPARTMENT K5520                                    1283.85**
```

After subtotals

Figure B.16. Example of "white space" use.

Upper right-hand corner is usually best location for filing code and/or identification number

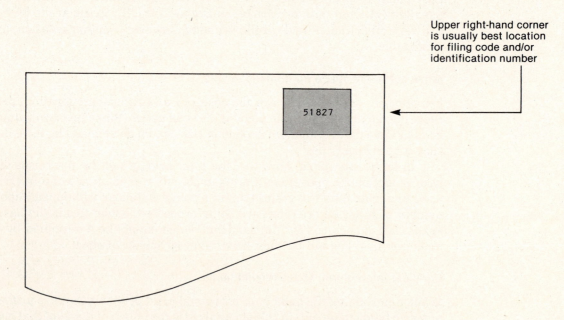

51 827

Figure B.17. Example of the placement of the filing code and identification number.

Arithmetic operation	Formula	Worked example	
ADDITION	Longest addend field length + 1	999999 + 99999 1099998	[6 + 1 = 7]
SUBTRACTION	Longest field (minuend or subtrahend) length + 1	99999- − 1 100000-	[5 + 1 = 6]
MULTIPLICATION	Sum of multiplier- and multiplicand-field lengths	9999 × 999 9989001	[4 + 3 = 7]
DIVISION Quotient	Dividend-field length	9999 1⌐9999	[5]
Remainder	Divisor-field length	6 remainder 400 500⌐3400	[3]

Note: The result-field size should be adjusted for the number of decimal positions (precision) required.

Figure B.18. Result-field digit requirements for two-factor arithmetic.

method, which conserves horizontal space on the detail line, is to stagger the totals.

Also, space for negative number indication should be considered and provided for. Figure B.19 depicts these considerations for intercolumn space requirements.

Choose suitable negative number indication

Most numeric amount fields should provide for negative representations so that negative adjustments can be handled. It is usually adequate to use a minus sign to indicate negative amounts on internal reports. The minus sign is convenient to use because it occupies only one character position. However, it is generally preferable to use the CR symbol for formal accounting and other external reports. When showing a credit balance on a customer's account, it is a good idea to print even further explanation—such as CREDIT BALANCE—DO NOT PAY—to ensure that the status of the account is understood. Figure B.20 shows examples of negative number indications.

Use appropriate editing

Suppress nonsignificant zeros of numeric amount fields, but numeric code numbers—such as Social Security or other account numbers—are usually easier to work with when their leftmost zeros are *not* suppressed. Insert decimal points when decimal positions are to be printed for a number value. Providing there is sufficient space on the line, insert commas into amount fields with over three or four integers. Place slashes or hyphens in 6-digit dates. Do not print dollar signs except on formal financial reports and checks; the column

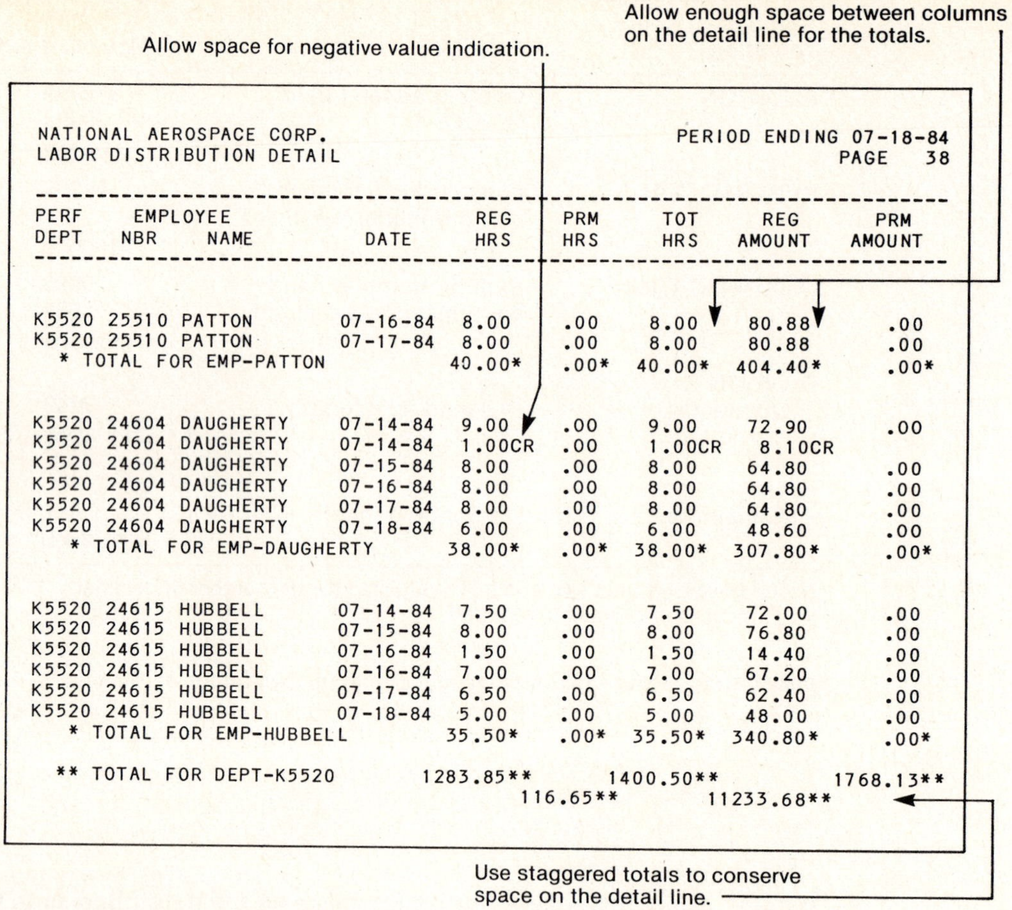

Allow space for negative value indication.

Allow enough space between columns on the detail line.

```
NATIONAL AEROSPACE CORP.                              PERIOD ENDING 07-18-84
LABOR DISTRIBUTION DETAIL                                         PAGE    38

-----------------------------------------------------------------------------
PERF    EMPLOYEE                        REG     PRM     TOT     REG      PRM
DEPT    NBR     NAME        DATE        HRS     HRS     HRS    AMOUNT   AMOUNT
-----------------------------------------------------------------------------

K5520  25510  PATTON      07-16-84    8.00    .00    8.00    80.88     .00
K5520  25510  PATTON      07-17-84    8.00    .00    8.00    80.88     .00
   * TOTAL FOR EMP-PATTON             40.00*  .00*  40.00*  404.40*   .00*

K5520  24604  DAUGHERTY   07-14-84    9.00    .00    9.00    72.90     .00
K5520  24604  DAUGHERTY   07-14-84    1.00CR  .00    1.00CR   8.10CR
K5520  24604  DAUGHERTY   07-15-84    8.00    .00    8.00    64.80     .00
K5520  24604  DAUGHERTY   07-16-84    8.00    .00    8.00    64.80     .00
K5520  24604  DAUGHERTY   07-17-84    8.00    .00    8.00    64.80     .00
K5520  24604  DAUGHERTY   07-18-84    6.00    .00    6.00    48.60     .00
   * TOTAL FOR EMP-DAUGHERTY          38.00*  .00*  38.00*  307.80*   .00*

K5520  24615  HUBBELL     07-14-84    7.50    .00    7.50    72.00     .00
K5520  24615  HUBBELL     07-15-84    8.00    .00    8.00    76.80     .00
K5520  24615  HUBBELL     07-16-84    1.50    .00    1.50    14.40     .00
K5520  24615  HUBBELL     07-16-84    7.00    .00    7.00    67.20     .00
K5520  24615  HUBBELL     07-17-84    6.50    .00    6.50    62.40     .00
K5520  24615  HUBBELL     07-18-84    5.00    .00    5.00    48.00     .00
   * TOTAL FOR EMP-HUBBELL            35.50*  .00*  35.50*  340.80*   .00*

  ** TOTAL FOR DEPT-K5520   1283.85**        1400.50**       1768.13**
                             116.65**        11233.68**
```

Use staggered totals to conserve space on the detail line.

Figure B.19. Intercolumn space requirements.

heading (plus the typical dollar-and-cents placement of the decimal point) should make it clear that it is a money figure. Figure B.21 shows editing examples.

Use underlining sparingly

Underlining fields is usually time- and space-consuming. Hence, most programmer/analysts try to avoid it. Sometimes, however, underlining will be required—as it normally is for formal accounting reports. Since most impact line printers do not contain an underscore character, the best way to handle a single underline is to print a separate line (single-spaced from the previous one) with hyphens in the area to be underlined. For double-underlining, an equals sign (=) is normally used.

Consider page totals for certain reports

For reports that require manual reconciliation and/or modifications to numeric column amounts, consider providing page totals. When manual changes must be made to amounts on reports, a column total of the amounts on that page will make it easier for clerks to recompute correct report totals after changes have been made to detail amounts. Figure B.22 provides an example.

SATISFACTORY
(and appropriate for internal reports):

```
                                    1.00-
```

BETTER
(for formal reports and customer statements, invoices, etc.):

```
                                    1.00 CR
```

BEST
(for customer statements):

```
                          1.00 CR  ** CREDIT BALANCE - DO NOT PAY **
```

Figure B.20. Alternatives for negative number indication.

Zero suppression for readability	`bbb15.03`
Commas for readability of longer numbers	`1,250,506`
Slashes for dates	`11/15/81`
# *Hyphens* for readability of longer strings of characters	`566-50-9224`
underlining (avoid or use sparingly)	`400.27`
Blank spaces for readability (in lieu of hyphens)	`566 50 9224`
Negative (or reverse) number indication	
—rightmost fixed-minus sign (commonly used)	`500.00-`
—floating minus sign	`-500.00`
—credit symbol	`500.00CR` `500.00 CR`
—debit symbol	`500.00DB` `500.00 DB`
—leftmost fixed-minus sign (rarely used because it is difficult to read)	`-    500.00`
Asterisk protection for dollar amounts on checks	`$***94.50`

Fixed-dollar sign on formal accounting reports
  $ first entry on page for each column, subtotal and total
  $ first entry after each subtotal and total
	`$   94.50`

Floating dollar sign	`$94.50`
# *Equals sign* for double underlining (avoid or use sparingly)	`$  1,026,782.64` `===============`

Not a COBOL editing symbol.

Figure B.21. Editing guidelines.

```
     ACCOUNTS  RECEIVABLE  REPORT                     PERIOD ENDING 05-31-84
                                                                PAGE    15

                                                   BALANCE          OVERDUE

     4038  PERCY AND WHITE                        1,289.45           210.58

     4039  CORCORAN, MAUREEN                         28.50              .00

     4041  SARATOGA SCHOOL DISTRICT              12,288.10              .00

     4042  ASSOCIATED STUDENT BODY                  33.60              .00

     4043  FENTON, JONES AND PARKER               805.88              .00

     4044  A & W DRAFTING                          112.13           112.13

     4045  E-Z DATA PROCESSING                   2,048.00         2,048.00

     4047  CALIFORNIA PRESS                      5,507.28              .00

     4048  TODD WALLACE                             15.48              .00

     4049  ABLE ELECTRONICS                      7,250.44         3,047.37

     4050  YOUNG AND BARSTOW                       506.73              .00

     4051  ALLIED ARTS                            980.41              .00

     4052  WINSTON AND ASSOCIATES                1,877.08              .00


           PAGE TOTAL                          32,743.08*         5,418.08*
```

Figure B.22. Example of a page total.

Use asterisks to identify total levels

Asterisks, or another legend, can be used to distinguish totals and subtotals from detail amounts. They also serve to indicate the "make-up" or level of the total amount, as shown in Figure B.23. Accountants sometimes refer to these as "one-star," "two-star," and so forth, totals.

Provide check protection for check amounts

The maximum amount of space that is allocated for check amounts on pre-printed check forms is usually larger than that required to handle the value of most checks. The unused space to the left could be altered fraudulently unless some protection method is employed.

One simple method of providing protection is to fill the amount with non-significant zeros. For example, if spaces were provided for six dollar digits (plus punctuation commas), a value of $1,234.56 could be printed as $001,234.56. However, such zero-filled amounts are difficult to read. A better approach is to use asterisk protection. With this method, asterisks replace the nonsignificant zeros. Our example would then appear as the more readable $**1,234.56.

An alternative method is to use a floating dollar sign, in which the dollar sign is printed immediately to the left of the leftmost significant digit. A further safeguard is to have a light background screen preprinted in the amount area. Any erasures or alterations will be more easily noticed, for they will be highlighted by disruption of the screen pattern. The various check-protection methods are shown in Figure B.24.

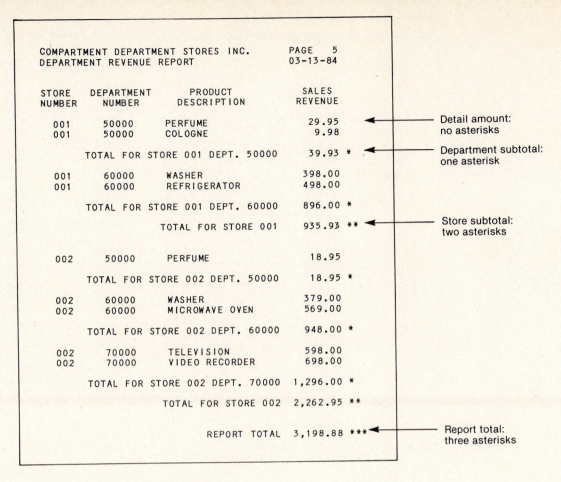

```
         COMPARTMENT DEPARTMENT STORES INC.      PAGE   5
         DEPARTMENT REVENUE REPORT               03-13-84

         STORE    DEPARTMENT      PRODUCT           SALES
         NUMBER     NUMBER      DESCRIPTION         REVENUE
          001       50000       PERFUME              29.95      ◄──────── Detail amount:
          001       50000       COLOGNE               9.98                no asterisks

                  TOTAL FOR STORE 001 DEPT. 50000    39.93 *    ◄──────── Department subtotal:
                                                                          one asterisk
          001       60000       WASHER              398.00
          001       60000       REFRIGERATOR        498.00

              TOTAL FOR STORE 001 DEPT. 60000      896.00 *

                      TOTAL FOR STORE 001          935.93 **    ◄──────── Store subtotal:
                                                                          two asterisks

          002       50000       PERFUME              18.95

                  TOTAL FOR STORE 002 DEPT. 50000    18.95 *

          002       60000       WASHER              379.00
          002       60000       MICROWAVE OVEN      569.00

              TOTAL FOR STORE 002 DEPT. 60000      948.00 *

          002       70000       TELEVISION          598.00
          002       70000       VIDEO RECORDER      698.00

              TOTAL FOR STORE 002 DEPT. 70000    1,296.00 *

                      TOTAL FOR STORE 002        2,262.95 **

                             REPORT TOTAL        3,198.88 ***   ◄──────── Report total:
                                                                          three asterisks
```

Figure B.23. Asterisk identification of total levels.

$001,234.56	Zero-filled (not normally used or recommended)
$**1,234.56	Asterisk protection
$1,234.56	Floating dollar sign
$**1,234.56	Screening (with asterisk protection)

Figure B.24. Check-protection alternatives.

Use group indication for control fields with repeating values

The data values within control fields for detail lines of a report with control-break or summary totals are often repeated from one line to the next. Part A of Figure B.25 shows a report with plant-code and department-number control fields. The report is easier to read, however, when the repeating control fields are not printed, except on the first line of the group. This technique is called **group indication** and is shown in part B of the figure.

If a group extends over a page break, the repeating fields should be printed again. Otherwise, the report becomes difficult to read because of the need to flip back the page to find the original entry.

Part A: Report without group indication

```
DEPARTMENTAL EARNINGS REPORT      PERIOD ENDING DATE 03/15/84    PAGE  1

PLANT    DEPT    SOCIAL SEC.                        EARNINGS    YEAR-TO-DATE
CODE     NBR      NUMBER      EMPLOYEE NAME          THIS PER.    EARNINGS

 100     1200    044-61-8275  ANDERSON, ANDY           110.25     1,870.30
 100     1200    174-85-7618  BACH, SUSANNE             53.60       964.00
 100     1200    333-91-9234  KNIGHT, JERRY            286.00     2,286.00
 100     1200    337-46-5869  JEFFERSON, JANICE        286.00       998.05
 100     1200    523-11-8123  THOMPSON, THOMAS         400.00     1,400.75
 100     1200                 DEPARTMENT TOTAL       1,135.85*    7,519.10*

 100     1300    299-19-2737  VICTOR, VERONICA         784.00     4,223.44
 100     1300    388-37-4655  UNDERWOOD, JAMES         196.00       988.75
 100     1300    512-91-6253  TUCKER, BRENT            371.80     2,244.12
 100     1300                 DEPARTMENT TOTAL       1,351.80*    7,456.31*
 100                          PLANT TOTAL            2,487.65**  14,975.41**

 102     1100    183-27-6586  BOULTON, ROBERT          208.00     1,055.34
 102     1100    342-84-7012  BUTTERFIELD, CATHY       784.00     1,435.56
 102     1100    372-84-7619  BENEDICT, BARBARA        232.95       988.54
 102     1100    534-10-0330  ZABRINSKI, LELAND        210.00     2,266.54
 102     1100    561-99-2736  WALLACE, TODD            250.00     1,987.45
 102     1100                 DEPARTMENT TOTAL       1,684.95*    7,733.43*

 102     1400    345-84-5015  BURKHART, RAE            309.44     1,887.69
 102     1400    512-78-3726  ABBOTT, MARILYN          330.00     1,755.48
 102     1400                 DEPARTMENT TOTAL         639.44*    3,643.17*
```

Part B: Report with group indication
of plant-code and department-number fields

```
DEPARTMENTAL EARNINGS REPORT        PERIOD ENDING DATE 03/15/84    PAGE  1

PLANT    DEPT    SOCIAL SEC.                        EARNINGS    YEAR-TO-DATE
CODE     NBR      NUMBER      EMPLOYEE NAME          THIS PER.    EARNINGS

 100     1200    044-61-8275  ANDERSON, ANDY           110.25     1,870.30
                 174-85-7618  BACH, SUSANNE             53.60       964.00
                 333-91-9234  KNIGHT, JERRY            286.00     2,286.00
                 337-46-5869  JEFFERSON, JANICE        286.00       998.05
                 523-11-8123  THOMPSON, THOMAS         400.00     1,400.75
                              DEPARTMENT TOTAL       1,135.85*    7,519.10*

         1300    299-19-2737  VICTOR, VERONICA         784.00     4,223.44
                 388-37-4655  UNDERWOOD, JAMES         196.00       988.75
                 512-91-6253  TUCKER, BRENT            371.80     2,244.12
                              DEPARTMENT TOTAL       1,351.80*    7,456.31*
                              PLANT TOTAL            2,487.65**  14,975.41**

 102     1100    183-27-6586  BOULTON, ROBERT          208.00     1,055.34
                 342-84-7012  BUTTERFIELD, CATHY       784.00     1,435.56
                 372-84-7619  BENEDICT, BARBARA        232.95       988.54
                 534-10-0330  ZABRINSKI, LELAND        210.00     2,266.54
                 561-99-2736  WALLACE, TODD            250.00     1,987.45
                              DEPARTMENT TOTAL       1,684.95*    7,733.43*

         1400    345-84-5015  BURKHART, RAE            309.44     1,887.69
                 512-78-3726  ABBOTT, MARILYN          330.00     1,755.48
                              DEPARTMENT TOTAL         639.44*    3,643.17*
```

Figure B.25. Group indication examples.

Part A: Example of unacceptable page break (control heading printed on last line of a page)

Part B: Example of appropriate page break (control heading not printed on a page unless room for following detail)

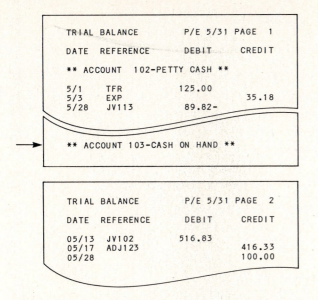

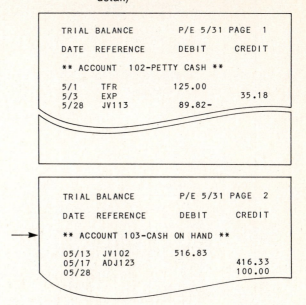

Figure B.26. Page-break convention example.

Determine page-break conventions

Even after the page-length span has been determined, there are a few other page-break considerations that the programmer/analyst should consider.

Special page-control breaks can facilitate the distribution of a report. Suppose that a retail chain produces a store revenue report that lists the sales for each of its stores. A special page-control break should be specified at a change in store number. This facilitates the distribution of the relevant portion of one copy of the report to each store manager. At the same time, a complete copy of the report is in a convenient format for the sales manager of the entire chain.

Another common place for a special page break is immediately before the printing of report totals, This is especially true when the totals consume many print lines. If they were begun on a page that is partially used for the report body, the total lines might be broken between two pages. This would not only make them more difficult to comprehend and refer to but would also cause confusion or omissions should the totals be copied and distributed. When special page-control breaks of the type discussed in the previous paragraph are used, a page break should be taken before the totals. Otherwise, the recipient of the last control portion of the report will also receive the grand totals—information which he or she may not be authorized to receive.

When typing a composition or thesis, one would not start typing a new paragraph on the last line of a page. Similarly, it is not good form to dangle control headings by themselves at the end of a report page. Figure B.26 shows how a page break can be used to improve a report's appearance.

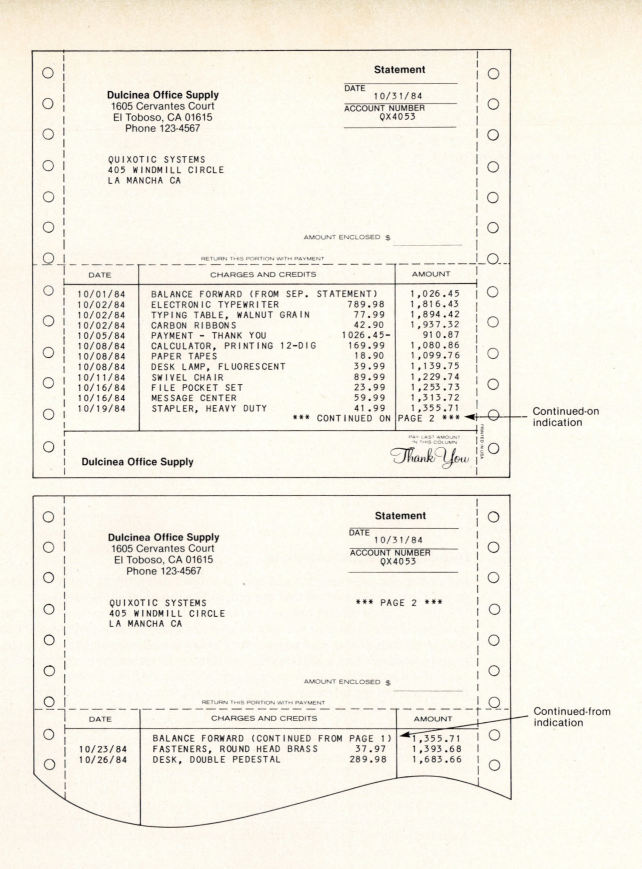

Figure B.27. Page-continuation indication example.

Consider page-continuation indication

Although page continuation is standard for most computer-generated reports and hence is not normally indicated, there are a couple of situations in which page continuation is helpful to the reader.

So-called unit documents, such as invoices, statements, packing lists, and so forth, are typically designed to accommodate all entries on one page, unless the entry volume is exceptionally large. For such exceptions, it is a good idea to print a message such as "CONTINUED ON PAGE 2" at the bottom of the page that is being continued, together with a notation on the continuation page, such as "CONTINUED FROM PAGE 1." This alerts the reader that there is more than one page of what is usually a single-page document. Figure B.27 provides an example of such page-continuation indication.

Another situation in which continuation indication might be specified is for a control-break report with control headings. If such a report also has control totals and a group spans a page break, the "continued on" indication is of questionable value; the absence of the control totals signifies the continuation. However, because the control heading is repeated on the next page, a casual glance at the continued page could mislead the reader into thinking that this was the beginning of the group. The "continued-from" indication "(CONTINUED)" on the continuation page clearly identifies that there is additional data for the group on a previous page.

Consider list-ups

When detail lines contain a relatively small number of characters to be printed in relation to the report width, it may be appropriate to print two or more input detail records on a single line. Such listings are usually termed **list-up** (or **two-up**, **three-up**, and so forth) reports. List-ups offer savings in printing time, paper, and report-storage space.

One problem with list-ups is that straightforward programming will cause the detail data to be sequenced from left to right, top to bottom. However, most users prefer to read reports that are sequenced from top to bottom, left to right. To obtain the latter sequence, a list-up program must contain a table. For example, to program a two-up report that contains 50 lines on each page, a 50-entry table would be required. The first 50 records of the file would be read into the table. Then, as the second 50 records were read in, the first page of the report could be printed. This process would be repeated for each page. Additional logic is required when end-of-file is reached so that the program will properly process the last page. Figure B.28 illustrates list-up report considerations.

Identify the end of the report

As shown in Figure B.29, it is usually a good idea to print ***END OF REPORT*** or some similar notation at the end of a report. Such an indication can be used to identify when pages are missing from the end of a report. Page numbers can be used to identify missing pages *within* a report but this trailer technique is required to allow the identification of pages that are missing at the *end* of a report.

A related consideration is to identify the situation in which there is no detail data to be reported during a particular program run period. Figure B.30 shows an example of such null report indication.

LEFT-TO RIGHT, TOP-TO-BOTTOM SEQUENCE
(normally easier programming but more difficult for the eye to follow)

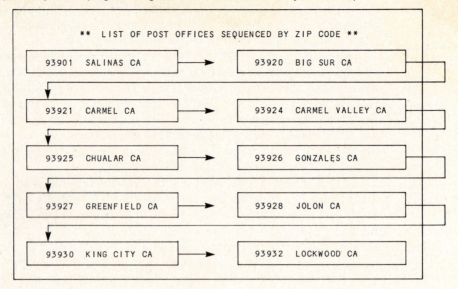

TOP-TO-BOTTOM, LEFT-TO-RIGHT SEQUENCE
(usually more difficult to program but easier to read)

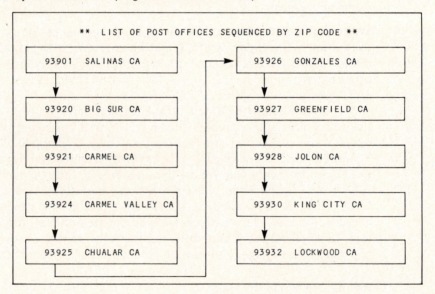

Figure B.28. List-up sequences.

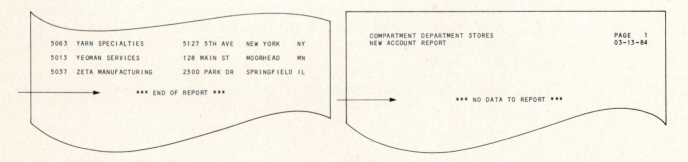

Figure B.29. End-of-report indication.   **Figure B.30.** Null report indication.

CHAPTER 7

REPORT PROGRAM LOGIC

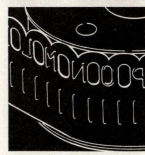

7 REPORT PROGRAM LOGIC

Most report programs fall into one of three basic listing categories: detail, exception, or summary. Within each of these three types of listings, there are two classifications of report accumulations: end-of-report and control-break totals. In addition, there are certain features that can be introduced into a report to enhance its readability and usefulness.

In this chapter, approaches to coding report programs are presented in a combined COBOL/pseudocode format that can be termed a program or coding **prototype**. These prototypes are organized into a "building-block" approach. Topic 7-A presents program prototypes for each of the three listing categories. In Topic 7-B, the additional coding that is required to produce totals is shown. Coding prototypes for common report features are given in Topic 7-C.

After the coding of a prototype module is discussed, the prototype coding for that module is not repeated for subsequent prototypes. Instead, the module is represented by a block that contains only the module name.

In this chapter, a number of report-programming guidelines are also presented. These are introduced at appropriate locations during the prototype discussions.

■ TOPIC 7-A: **Report Listings**

Detail List
    Report control entries
    Triggering of headings for the first report page
    Placement of the end-of-page test
    Blanking print lines before building
    Setting of the line-spacing indicator
    Page-skip handling
    Handling report lines with variable line spacing

Exception List
    Definition of the exception line
    Mainline module
    Process-record module
    Print module

Summary List
    First-record switch
    Summary control fields
    Summary total fields
    Definition of the summary line
    Mainline module

Initialization module
Process-record module
Print module
Read module

Reports can be categoried as being either a detail, exception, or summary type of listing. A **detail list** generally contains a **detail line** for each imput record that is to be read. Input records for a detail list are typically sorted or otherwise arranged in order according to one or more key fields. Figure 7A.1, part A, shows a detailed list for hardware product sales sequenced by store number within item code within produce class (major field = product class, intermediate field = item code, and minor field = store number).

An **exception list** is a report in which a detail line is printed only when an input record represents a special condition or an exception. For example, Figure 7A.1, part B, shows an exception list that reports only those hardware product sales records that represent power tools (indicated by the letter "P" as the rightmost character of the item number). Other examples of exception lists are: overdrawn bank-depositor reports, a list of employees with over 10 years of seniority, or a report that lists inventory items whose on-hand balance has fallen below the reorder point.

A **summary list** is a report in which—instead of listing each detail record—a **summary line** is printed for each group of input records that contain the same key value. Figure 7A.1, part C, shows an example in which a summary line is printed for each group of records with the same product class and item code. Notice that in the detail list (shown in Figure 7A.1, part A), there were six lines printed for the "CLAW HAMMER" product. In the summary list, only one line is printed for all six input records. The one extended amount figure printed is an accumulation of the six detail amounts. Summary lists, sometimes termed **group-printed** reports, are frequently used to reduce the length of a report when the number of input records is large and an itemization of the data for individual records is not required.

Detail List

Figure 7A.2 shows a structure chart for a typical program for a detail list report. The program prototype is presented in Figure 7A.3. This detail list program prototype is relatively straightforward in logic. Observe that it follows the structured coding conventions covered in Chapter 1; namely, WORKING-STORAGE definition of input and output record descriptions, data-item naming, module forming, module naming, initialization of variable fields, and independent input-output modules. It uses the priming-read method of READ statement handling.

Report control entries (Point A of Figure 7A.3)

Report-programming guideline 1: Always establish a report-controls group item in WORKING-STORAGE.

This group item should typically contain, as a minimum, the following fields: (1) a page-counter for printing and keeping track of the report page number; (2) a constant for specifying the last line number at which a detail, exception, or summary line should be printed on each report page; (3) a lines-used field to keep track of the last line number that has been printed on the current page; and (4) a line-spacing indicator to control line spacing within the WRITE module.

Part A: Detail list

```
HIGH-VALUE HARDWARE STORES                              03/15/84
DETAIL SALES REPORT                                     PAGE   1

PRODUCT   ITEM    STORE      ITEM                QTY                EXTENDED
CLASS     CODE    NBR     DESCRIPTION            SOLD     PRICE      AMOUNT

  HMR     3836-H   101    CLAW HAMMER              1      12.99       12.99
  HMR     3836-H   101    CLAW HAMMER              3      12.99       38.97
  HMR     3836-H   102    CLAW HAMMER              1      12.99       12.99
  HMR     3836-H   102    CLAW HAMMER              1      12.99       12.99
  HMR     3836-H   102    CLAW HAMMER              1      12.99       12.99
  HMR     3836-H   102    CLAW HAMMER             10      12.99      129.90
  HMR     3847-H   101    BALL PEEN HAMMER         1      13.99       13.99
  HMR     3847-H   101    BALL PEEN HAMMER         2      13.99       27.98
  HMR     3847-H   102    BALL PEEN HAMMER         1      13.99       13.99
  HMR     3852-H   102    TACK HAMMER              1       4.99        4.99
  HMR     3861-P   101    POWER HAMMER             1      29.99       29.99
  SAW     1977-P   102    RADIAL ARM SAW           1     529.99      529.99
  SAW     1977-P   102    RADIAL ARM SAW           1     529.99      529.99
  SAW     2425-P   101    TABLE SAW                1     569.99      569.99
  SAW     3619-H   102    WOOD SAW                 1      18.99       18.99
  SAW     3715-H   101    HACK SAW                 1       9.99        9.99
  SAW     3715-H   101    HACK SAW                 1       9.99        9.99
  SAW     3715-H   101    HACK SAW                 1       9.99        9.99
  SAW     3715-H   102    HACK SAW                 1       9.99        9.99
  SDR     2158-H   101    SLOTTED SCREWDRIVER      1       2.79        2.79
  SDR     2158-H   101    SLOTTED SCREWDRIVER      1       2.79        2.79
  SDR     2158-H   101    SLOTTED SCREWDRIVER      1       2.79        2.79
  SDR     2158-H   101    SLOTTED SCREWDRIVER      1       2.79        2.79
  SDR     2158-H   101    SLOTTED SCREWDRIVER      6       2.79       16.74
  SDR     2158-H   102    SLOTTED SCREWDRIVER      1       2.79        2.79
  SDR     2158-H   102    SLOTTED SCREWDRIVER      1       2.79        2.79
  SDR     2160-H   101    PHILLIPS SCREWDRIVER     2       2.99        5.98
  SDR     2160-H   101    PHILLIPS SCREWDRIVER     1       2.99        2.99
  SDR     2160-H   101    PHILLIPS SCREWDRIVER     1       2.99        2.99
  SDR     2160-H   101    PHILLIPS SCREWDRIVER     2       2.99        5.98
  SDR     2160-H   102    PHILLIPS SCREWDRIVER     1       2.99        2.99
  SDR     2160-H   102    PHILLIPS SCREWDRIVER     1       2.99        2.99
```

Part B: Exception list

```
HIGH-VALUE HARDWARE STORES                              03/15/84
EXCEPTION SALES REPORT                                  PAGE   1

PRODUCT   ITEM    STORE      ITEM                QTY                EXTENDED
CLASS     CODE    NBR     DESCRIPTION            SOLD     PRICE      AMOUNT

  HMR     3861-P   101    POWER HAMMER             1      29.99       29.99
  SAW     1977-P   102    RADIAL ARM SAW           1     529.99      529.99
  SAW     1977-P   102    RADIAL ARM SAW           1     529.99      529.99
  SAW     2425-P   101    TABLE SAW                1     569.99      569.99
```

Part C: Summary list

```
HIGH-VALUE HARDWARE STORES                              03/15/84
SUMMARY SALES REPORT                                    PAGE   1

PRODUCT   ITEM         ITEM                QTY                EXTENDED
CLASS     CODE      DESCRIPTION            SOLD     PRICE      AMOUNT

  HMR     3836-H   CLAW HAMMER             17      12.99      220.83
  HMR     3847-H   BALL PEEN HAMMER         4      13.99       55.96
  HMR     3852-H   TACK HAMMER              1       4.99        4.99
  HMR     3861-P   POWER HAMMER             1      29.99       29.99
  SAW     1977-P   RADIAL ARM SAW           2     529.99     1059.98
  SAW     2425-P   TABLE SAW                1     569.99      569.99
  SAW     3619-H   WOOD SAW                 1      18.99       18.99
  SAW     3715-H   HACK SAW                 4       9.99       39.96
  SDR     2158-H   SLOTTED SCREWDRIVER     12       2.79       33.48
  SDR     2160-H   PHILLIPS SCREWDRIVER     8       2.99       23.92
```

Figure 7A.1. Listing examples.

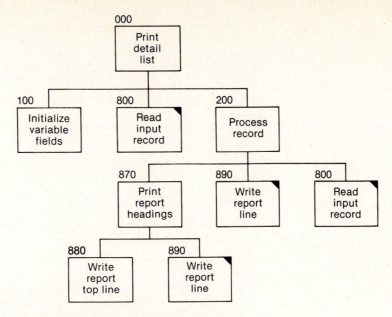

Figure 7A.2. Structure chart: Detail list program.

```
DATA DIVISION.
FILE SECTION.

FD  Input-file
        RECORD CONTAINS nnn CHARACTERS
        BLOCK CONTAINS nn RECORDS
        LABEL RECORDS ARE STANDARD/OMITTED.
01  Input-record.
    05  FILLER                          PIC X(nnn).


FD  REPORT-FILE
        RECORD CONTAINS nnn CHARACTERS
        LABEL RECORDS ARE OMITTED.
01  REPORT-LINE.
    05  FILLER                          PIC X(nnn).


WORKING-STORAGE SECTION.

01  WS-SWITCHES.
    05  WS-END-OF-FILE-SW               PIC X(3).
        88  END-OF-FILE                                VALUE 'YES'.
```

(A)
```
01  WS-REPORT-CONTROLS.
    05  WS-PAGE-COUNT                   PIC S9(5)      COMP-3.
    05  WS-LINES-PER-PAGE               PIC S9(2)      VALUE +nn
                                                       COMP SYNC.
    05  WS-LINES-USED                   PIC S9(2)      COMP SYNC.
    05  WS-LINE-SPACING                 PIC S9(2).
```

```
01  Input-record-description.
```

```
01  H1-HEADING-LINE-1.
```

```
01  Hn-HEADING-LINE-n.
                        (additional heading lines as required)
```

```
01  DL-DETAIL-LINE.
```

Figure 7A.3. Program prototype: Detail list program.   *continued*

```
PROCEDURE DIVISION.

000-mainline.

    OPEN files.
    PERFORM 100-INITIALIZE-VARIABLE-FIELDS.
    PERFORM 800-READ-input-record.                    [priming read]
    PERFORM 200-process-record
        UNTIL END-OF-FILE.
    CLOSE files.
    STOP RUN.
```

```
100-INITIALIZE-VARIABLE-FIELDS.

    MOVE 'NO ' TO WS-END-OF-FILE-SW.
    MOVE ZEROS TO WS-PAGE-COUNT.
    ADD 1 WS-LINES-PER-PAGE GIVING WS-LINES-USED.
```
(B)

```
200-process-record.

    IF WS-LINES-USED IS NOT LESS THAN WS-LINES-PER-PAGE
        PERFORM 870-PRINT-REPORT-HEADINGS.
    (Blank the detail-line.)                           [optional]
    Do detail-line calculations [if any] and
    Build detail-line.
    MOVE DL-DETAIL-LINE TO REPORT-LINE.
    PERFORM 890-WRITE-REPORT-LINE.
    Set WS-LINE-SPACING for next detail-line.
    PERFORM 800-READ-input-record.                    [read next record]
```
(C) (D) (E)

```
800-READ-input-record.

    READ INPUT-FILE INTO input-record-area
        AT END MOVE 'YES' TO WS-END-OF-FILE-SW.
```

```
870-PRINT-REPORT-HEADINGS.

    ADD 1 TO WS-PAGE-COUNT.
    MOVE WS-PAGE-COUNT TO Hn-page-number.
    MOVE H1-HEADING-LINE TO REPORT-LINE.
    PERFORM 880-WRITE-REPORT-TOP-LINE.

    MOVE Hn-HEADING-LINE TO REPORT-LINE.<   [If second heading line
    Set WS-LINE-SPACING.                 <---   (and repeat for each
    PERFORM 890-WRITE-REPORT-LINE.       < additional heading line)]

    Set WS-LINE-SPACING for next detail-line. <--- [To space after
                                                   column headings and
                                                         before the first
                                                   detail-line on each page]
```
(F)

```
880-WRITE-REPORT-TOP-LINE.
    WRITE REPORT-LINE
        AFTER ADVANCING PAGE.
    MOVE 1 TO WS-LINES-USED.
```
(G)

```
890-WRITE-REPORT-LINE.
    WRITE REPORT-LINE
        AFTER ADVANCING WS-LINE-SPACING.
    ADD WS-LINE-SPACING TO WS-LINES-USED.
```
(H)

Figure 7A.3. (continued)

In the prototype, the page-counter is called WS-PAGE-COUNT. A 4-digit page-counter will accommodate up to 9,999 pages, and is generally adequate. Notice in the prototype that the WS-PAGE-COUNT field is specified with PIC S9(5) and USAGE COMP-3. COMP-3, if available with the compiler that is being used, is the most efficient usage. (Refer to Appendix B for further coverage of USAGE clause considerations.) Because COMP-3 usage always provides an odd number of digits, the length has been increased to the next odd number higher than 4. It is defined as a signed field for arithmetic efficiency.

The page line span is named WS-LINES-PER-PAGE. A 2-digit field will usually suffice because few report pages span over 99 lines. A VALUE clause is specified with a numeric literal (actual value) that denotes the last line number on the page at which a detail, exception, or summary line should be printed. COMP usage is generally most efficient for this field because the number is an integer and will not, except in rare circumstances, be printed. SYNC has been specified for boundary-alignment efficiency but is not required with certain compilers. (SYNCHRONIZED clause considerations are also covered in Appendix B.)

Since the two fields will be compared, the WS-LINES-USED field has been defined to be consistent with the WS-LINES-PER-PAGE field. It is specified as a signed COMP field for arithmetic efficiency.

The line-spacing indicator is named WS-LINES-PER-PAGE. Most compilers require that this field be of DISPLAY usage, and it is implicitly specified as such. Although a 1-digit field length is generally adequate (because report lines are commonly single-, double-, or triple-spaced from one another), definition of a 2-digit length will accommodate longer-spacing spans for special purposes. It may be appropriate to specify the length of this field in accordance with the maximum line-spacing span that can be handled with the compiler that you are using.

Triggering of headings for the first report page (Point B of Figure 7A.3)

Report-programming guideline 2: Trigger the printing of report headings for the first page by initially setting the lines-used indicator higher than the line span.

Notice that the lines-used indicator is set higher than the line span by adding **1** to the WS-LINES-PER-PAGE field, then placing the sum in the WS-LINES-USED field. Some programmers provide for triggering headings by merely initializing the WS-LINES-USED field to an arbitrarily high value, such as 99. The method that is used in the prototype has the advantage of working with line spans of any length; even if the line span is increased, the logic remains correct.

Placement of the end-of-page test (Point C of Figure 7A.3)

Report-programming guideline 3: Always test for end-of-page and perform the report headings routine from the module that prints the body lines of the report.

More significant than how the lines-used indicator is initialized for the first-page headings, however, is the point in the program that is chosen to test for end-of-page. Observe that the need for headings is tested before the detail line is formatted and printed. As alternative approaches, some programmers produce the first-page headings by unconditionally performing the heading routine from the mainline module (immediately after the files have been opened) or from an initialization module. However, the method that is shown in the prototype is preferable because it will allow correct processing of headings when data from the input record is required in the headings. This concept will be covered in Topic C of this chapter.

Notice that the IF statement condition has been phrased IF WS-LINES-USED IS NOT LESS THAN WS-LINES-PER-PAGE. This test will trigger headings whenever the page line span has either been met or after the first time it is exceeded. An equivalent test can be expressed as IF WS-LINES-PER-PAGE IS NOT GREATER THAN WS-LINES-USED.

Actually, a more precise method of testing to ensure that the line span is never exceeded would consider the line spacing for the current detail line in the test. For example, given double-spacing of the detail line, the condition could be expressed as IF WS-LINES-PER-PAGE — WS-LINES-USED — 2 IS NEGATIVE. The number 2 in the statement represents the double-spacing for the line to be printed during the current iteration.

The end-of-page test that is specified in the prototypes has been chosen for general straightforwardness. However, unless single-spacing is used, the last line on a page will possibly be on a line number in excess of the line span. For example, given a WS-LINES-PER-PAGE value of 60 and double-spacing for the detail line, if the print module is entered with WS-LINES-USED containing a count of 59, the last detail line will be printed on line 61.

Blanking print lines before building (Point D of Figure 7A.3)

Report-programming guideline 4: Consider the method to be used for blanking print lines.

When a print line must be blanked, it should generally be done immediately before building the detail line. However, when the print lines are defined in the WORKING-STORAGE SECTION and when a line has only one format, it is more efficient to initialize the FILLER areas just once. This can be done by specifying VALUE SPACES in the data-item description or by moving SPACES to the entire line in the 100-INITIALIZE-VARIABLE-FIELDS module.

Therefore, in the programming prototypes, the need to blank lines is shown in parentheses before each line is built. This is to serve as a reminder that this action may be required if (1) conditional printing of individual fields on a line is called for, (2) redefinition of the print lines is specified, or (3) processing of records is done in the FILE SECTION instead of WORKING-STORAGE. Otherwise, one-time initial blanking by means of a VALUE clause or initialization statement will produce more efficient execution.

Setting of the line-spacing indicator (Points E and F of Figure 7A.3)

Report-programming guideline 5: Set the line-spacing indicator at the proper locations.

The best method of handling the line-spacing indicator is to set it for the normal body line spacing in the detail, exception, or summary print routine *after*—not before—the body line has been printed. This is shown at point E of the figure. With this approach, the line spacing between the last heading line and the first body line can be set at the end of the report headings module. This is shown at point F of the figure.

Suppose, as is commonly done, a detail report is specified with single-spacing for the body lines except that the first detail line on each page is to be single-spaced after the last heading line. With regard to the program prototype, the statement MOVE 2 TO WS-LINE-SPACING would be specified at point F of the figure. Then, when the program returns to the 200-PROCESS-RECORD module to print the first detail line on the page, the double-space setting that was made during the heading routine will be in effect. The statement MOVE 1 TO WS-LINE-SPACING would be specified at point E in the prototype. Then, after the first line on the page is printed, the line-spacing indicator will be set to single-spacing for all subsequent detail lines for that page.

This technique becomes even more helpful when programming more complicated control-break reports that call for varying numbers of blank lines after control-break lines. Such requirements are discussed in Topic B of this chapter.

Page-skip handling (Point G of Figure 7A.3)

Report-programming guideline 6: Establish an independent module to skip to the top line of each report page.

In accordance with ANS COBOL requirements, a separate WRITE statement must be specified to skip to a new page. To handle printing of the first line on each report page, therefore, it is appropriate to establish an independent WRITE module with the AFTER ADVANCING PAGE phrase. After the WRITE statement is executed, the printer is logically positioned at the first line, so the WS-LINES-USED indicator should be set to 1, as shown in the 880-WRITE-REPORT-TOP-LINE module.

Handling report lines with variable line spacing (Point H of Figure 7A.3)

Report-programming guideline 7: Establish an independent module to print all lines with variable spacing.

By specifying the identifier form of the ADVANCING phrase of the WRITE statement, one WRITE module can be used for all other print lines with variable line spacing. This is shown in the 890-WRITE-REPORT-LINE module. Then, the identifier (WS-LINE-SPACING in the prototype) can be used to conveniently increment the lines-used indicator (WS-LINES-USED).

A note of caution: Many programmers put the end-of-page test in this WRITE module, either at the end or the beginning. For example, a statement such as IF WS-LINES-USED IS NOT GREATER THAN WS-LINES-PER-PAGE, PERFORM 870-PRINT-REPORT-HEADINGS might be specified as the last statement of this module. If one attempts to depict this structure in a structure chart, the tangle of logic is quickly revealed. The practical disadvantage to this approach is that it does not offer as much flexibility with regard to where a page is ended. This will be mentioned in Topic B of this chapter with reference to control-break reports.

Exception List

A structure chart for an exception list program appears in Figure 7A.4. Figure 7 A.5 is the program prototype. This program is modeled in accordance with the basic framework of the detail list program. Differences will be discussed.

Definition of the exception line (Point A of Figure 7A.5)

The body line of the report has been named EL-EXCEPTION-LINE to accurately reflect its function. (The counterpart line in the detail list program is called DL-DETAIL-LINE.)

Mainline module (Point B of Figure 7A.5)

The mainline module for this exception list program is exactly the same as that for the detail list program except for the paragraph name that is referenced in the PERFORM/UNTIL statement. In this exception list program, the record-processing paragraph has been named 200-SELECT-EXCEPTION-RECORD to describe its role.

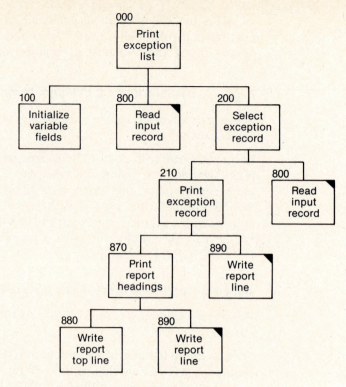

Figure 7A.4. Structure chart: Exception list program.

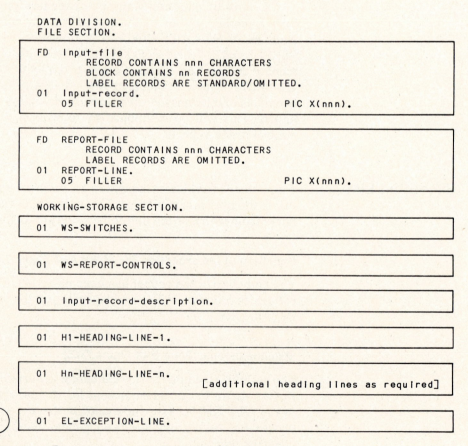

Figure 7A.5. Program prototype: Exception list program.

```
PROCEDURE DIVISION.
```

```
B    000-mainline.

         OPEN files.
         PERFORM 100-INITIALIZE-VARIABLE-FIELDS.
         PERFORM 800-READ-input-record.                    [priming read]
         PERFORM 200-select-exception-record
             UNTIL END-OF-FILE.
         CLOSE files.
         STOP RUN.
```

```
     100-INITIALIZE-VARIABLE-FIELDS.
```

```
C    200-select-exception-record.

         IF input-record is an exception
             PERFORM 210-print-exception-record.
         PERFORM 800-READ-input-record.                    [read next record]
```

```
D    210-print-exception-record.

         IF WS-LINES-USED IS NOT LESS THAN WS-LINES-PER-PAGE
             PERFORM 870-PRINT-REPORT-HEADINGS.
         (Blank the exception-line)
         Do exception-line calculations [if any] and
         Build EL-EXCEPTION-LINE.
         MOVE EL-EXCEPTION-LINE TO REPORT-LINE.
         PERFORM 890-WRITE-REPORT-LINE.
         Set WS-LINE-SPACING for the next exception-line.
```

```
     800-READ-input-record.
```

```
     870-PRINT-REPORT-HEADINGS.
```

```
     880-WRITE-REPORT-TOP-LINE.
```

```
     890-WRITE-REPORT-LINE.
```

Figure 7A.5.   (continued)

Process-record module (Point C of Figure 7A.5)

The first step in this record-processing module, 200-SELECT-EXCEPTION-RECORD, tests the input record just read to see if it reflects an exception condition. In the exception list example shown (Figure 7A.1, part B), the test would take the form of checking the rightmost character of the item code field to determine if it contained a value of "P."

If the record *is* an exception condition, the print module is performed to generate an exception line on the report. If it is *not* an exception, no further processing of that record is required.

In accordance with the priming-read method of READ statement handling, the read module is performed at the end of this paragraph to obtain the next input record.

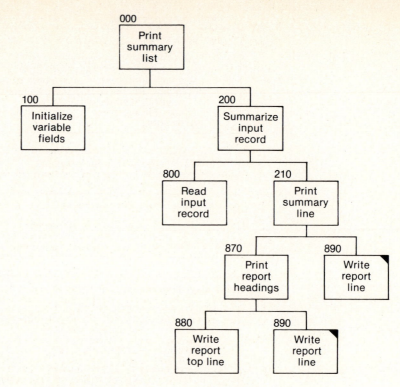

Figure 7A.6. Structure chart: Summary list program.

Print module (Point D of Figure 7A.5)

The essential difference between a detail list and an exception list is that, in the exception list, the print module is performed conditionally. It is thus placed one level below the record-selection paragraph. Otherwise, the print logic is identical.

Summary List

Figure 7A.6 presents a structure chart for a typical summary list program. The program prototype is shown in Figure 7A.7. Although modeled along the lines of the two preceding report programs, the summary list program introduces a number of additional considerations and will be discussed here.

First-record switch (Point A of Figure 7A.7)

Report-programming guideline 8: For summary list (and, as will be discussed in Topic B, control-break report) programs, specify a first-record switch.

With a summary list, it is necessary to know when the first record is being processed. Otherwise, a superfluous summary total would probably be printed before the first summary line. The first-record switch, named WS-FIRST-RECORD-SW, is defined in WORKING-STORAGE.

Summary control fields (Point B of Figure 7A.7)

Report-programming guideline 9: For summary lists, specify a group item for the summary control fields in the WORKING-STORAGE SECTION. Define two sets of control fields: one for the previous control key and one for the current control key. If the control key contains multiple fields, list the fields in major to minor order.

Unlike processing a simple detail or exception list, when printing a summary list, it is necessary to know the relationship between the current and the previous input records. Thus, a WS-SUMMARY-CONTROLS group item is established. Two control fields are required—one for the key of the current record and one for the key of the immediately preceding record.

When detail records are being summarized, the program specifications may call for the summarization to be based upon one or more fields from the input records. For example, the summary sales report example that is illustrated (Figure 7A.1, part C) contains two control fields: product class and item code. If the control key contains only one field, then both the WS-PREVIOUS-SUMMARY-CONTROL and WS-CURRENT-SUMMARY-CONTROL fields can be elementary items. However, if the control key contains more than one field, the WS-CURRENT-SUMMARY-CONTROL field must be a group item so that the individual fields of the control key can be defined as elementary fields within the group. The group WS-CURRENT-SUMMARY-CONTROL field is used for comparison with the WS-PREVIOUS-SUMMARY-CONTROL field; the elementary fields are defined to receive each of the individual control fields from the input record.

When the WS-CURRENT-SUMMARY-CONTROL field is a group item, it is logical to list the elementary fields in major to minor order, as shown in the prototype. For efficiency of comparisons and to minimize data exceptions (for computers that recognize such), it is generally advisable to specify numeric summary control fields as alphanumeric (PICTURE X) rather than as numeric (PICTURE 9).

Summary total fields (Point C of Figure 7A.7)

A group item called WS-SUMMARY-TOTAL-ACCUMULATORS has been established for the definition of the elementary fields that are to be used for accumulation of the summary totals. One or more elementary fields will be defined within this item. In the summary sales report example (Figure 7A.1, part C) there are two summary fields: quantity sold and extended amount. Depending upon the programming specifications, one or more summary totals will be required. Thus, one elementary field should be defined within the WS-SUMMARY-TOTAL-ACCUMULATORS group item for each summary total.

If the compiler that you are using supports COMP-3 usage, its specification for the summary totals will provide greater processing efficiency than DISPLAY usage. For report programs such as this one, COMP-3 usage is usually also more efficient than COMP usage.

Definition of the summary line (Point D of Figure 7A.7)

The summary line that is to be printed in the body of the report is named SL-SUMMARY-LINE to accurately describe its function.

Mainline module (Point E of Figure 7A.7)

Report-programming guideline 10: For summary list (and control-break report) programs, use the conditional-processing method of READ statement placement.

Summary list programs are appropriate candidates for the conditional-processing method rather than the priming-read method of READ statement handling. Therefore, the mainline module does not contain a priming-read state-

```
DATA DIVISION.
FILE SECTION.

FD   Input-file
         RECORD CONTAINS nnn CHARACTERS
         BLOCK CONTAINS nn RECORDS
         LABEL RECORDS ARE STANDARD/OMITTED.
01   Input-record.
     05   FILLER                          PIC X(nnn).


FD   REPORT-FILE
         RECORD CONTAINS nnn CHARACTERS
         LABEL RECORDS ARE OMITTED.
01   REPORT-LINE.
     05   FILLER                          PIC X(nnn).


WORKING-STORAGE SECTION.

01   WS-SWITCHES.
         .
         .
         .
     05   WS-FIRST-RECORD-SW              PIC X(3).
         88   FIRST-RECORD                             VALUE 'YES'.


01   WS-REPORT-CONTROLS.


01   WS-SUMMARY-CONTROLS.
     05   WS-PREVIOUS-SUMMARY-CONTROL              PIC X(nn).
     05   WS-CURRENT-SUMMARY-CONTROL.
          10   WS-CURRENT-major-SUMMARY-CONTROL    PIC X(nn).
          10   WS-CURRENT-inter-SUMMARY-CONTROL    PIC X(nn).  <------
          10   WS-CURRENT-minor-SUMMARY-CONTROL    PIC X(nn).  <-----|
                                                                     |
                                       [as required for the application]


01   WS-SUMMARY-TOTAL-ACCUMULATORS.
     05   summary-total-accumulator    PIC S9(n)      COMP-3.
          [additional total fields as required for summarization]


01   Input-record-description.


01   H1-HEADING-LINE-1.


01   Hn-HEADING-LINE-n.
                             [additional heading lines as required]


01   SL-SUMMARY-LINE.


PROCEDURE DIVISION.

000-mainline.

     OPEN files.
     PERFORM 100-INITIALIZE-VARIABLE-FIELDS.
                                               [no priming read]
     PERFORM 200-summarize-input-record
         UNTIL END-OF-FILE.
     CLOSE files.
     STOP RUN.
```

A
B
C
D
E

Figure 7A.7. Program prototype: Summary list program.

```
100-INITIALIZE-VARIABLE-FIELDS.

        .
        .
        .
F       MOVE 'YES' TO WS-FIRST-RECORD-SW.
        MOVE ZEROS
            TO each elementary WS-SUMMARY-TOTAL-ACCUMULATORS field.
```

```
G   200-summarize-input-record.

        PERFORM 800-READ-input-record.
        MOVE each summary-control-field from the input-record-area
            TO its respective WS-CURRENT-SUMMARY-CONTROL field.
        IF FIRST-RECORD
            MOVE WS-CURRENT-SUMMARY-CONTROL TO
                WS-PREVIOUS-SUMMARY-CONTROL
            MOVE 'NO ' TO WS-FIRST-RECORD-SW.
        IF WS-CURRENT-SUMMARY-CONTROL
                IS NOT EQUAL TO WS-PREVIOUS-SUMMARY-CONTROL
            PERFORM 210-PRINT-SUMMARY-LINE.
        IF NOT END-OF-FILE
            ADD each field-being-summarized
                TO its respective WS-SUMMARY-TOTAL-ACCUMULATORs field.
```

```
H   210-PRINT-SUMMARY-LINE.

        IF WS-LINES-USED IS NOT LESS THAN WS-LINES-PER-PAGE
            PERFORM 870-PRINT-REPORT-HEADINGS.
        (Blank the summary-line.)
        Do summary-line calculations [if any] and
        Build SL-SUMMARY-LINE.
        MOVE SL-SUMMARY-LINE TO REPORT-LINE.
        PERFORM 890-WRITE-REPORT-LINE.
        Set WS-LINE-SPACING for next summary-line.
        MOVE ZEROS
            to each elementary WS-SUMMARY-TOTAL-ACCUMULATORS field.
        MOVE WS-CURRENT-SUMMARY-CONTROL
            TO WS-PREVIOUS-SUMMARY-CONTROL.
```

```
800-READ-input-record.

        READ INPUT-FILE INTO input-record-area
            AT END MOVE 'YES' TO WS-END-OF-FILE-SW
            MOVE HIGH-VALUES
I               TO each summary-control-field in the input-record-area.
```

```
870-PRINT-REPORT-HEADINGS.
```

```
880-WRITE-REPORT-TOP-LINE.
```

```
890-WRITE-REPORT-LINE.
```

Figure 7A.7.   (continued)

ment. Observe also that the record-processing paragraph that is referenced in the PERFORM/UNTIL statement has been named 200-SUMMARIZE-INPUT-RECORD to describe its function.

Initialization module (Point F of Figure 7A.7)

The initialization module for this summary list program is the same as that for the detail and exception lists. In addition, statements are required to (1) set the first-record switch to "YES" to indicate that the first record is to be processed, and (2) initialize each summary total accumulator field to ZEROS. Remember, as discussed in Topic C of Chapter 3, when fields of COMP-3 usage are specified, they must be zeroed at the *elementary*—not the group—level.

Process-record module (Point G of Figure 7A.7)

Because this program uses the conditional-processing approach to READ statement handling, the first statement of this paragraph performs the read module.

After the record has been read, the next step is to move each of the summary control fields from the input record to its respective WS-CURRENT-SUMMARY-CONTROL field.

Then, the first-record switch is tested. When the first record is being processed, it is necessary to move the WS-CURRENT-SUMMARY-CONTROL field to the WS-PREVIOUS-SUMMARY-CONTROL field and to turn off the switch. If this step were not taken, the current control field would not be equal to the previous control field, and the next prototype statement would cause a superfluous control total to be printed before the first summary line on the report.

The next statement checks to see if it is time to print a summary line. If the control field of the input record that has just been read is not equal to that of the previous record, it means that the 210-PRINT-SUMMARY-LINE module must be performed to print a summary line for the records of the previous control group.

The last statement of this module processes the input record by adding the value of each field that is being summarized to its respective summary total accumulator. Notice, however, that the ADD statement is made conditional to a NOT END-OF-FILE condition. This is because, with conditional-processing READ statement placement, the last iteration of this module will be executed after end-of-file has been detected; thus, there will be no input record to process.

Print module (Point H of Figure 7A.7)

The print module at point H of the figure, 210-PRINT-SUMMARY-LINE, follows the same general pattern as that for the detail and exception list programs. However, the last two statements of this summary list print module are additional actions that are required specifically for a summary list program.

After the summary totals have been printed, the next to the last statement zeros the summary total accumulators. This is necessary so that the accumulators will be ready to start afresh with a new summary total. Then, since the processing of the control group has been completed, WS-CURRENT-SUMMARY-CONTROL is moved to WS-PREVIOUS-SUMMARY-CONTROL.

Read module (Point I of Figure 7A.7)

Report-programming guideline 11: For summary list (and control-break report) programs, in addition to setting the end-of-file switch when end-of-file has been detected, set the control fields in the input record area to HIGH-VALUES.

As shown at point I of the figure, an additional statement is required when end-of-file is detected. In addition to setting the end-of-file switch, the summary control field (or fields) within the input area in WORKING-STORAGE must be set to HIGH-VALUES. This is required so that a summary line for the last control group will be forced out during the last iteration of the 200-SUMMARIZE-INPUT-RECORD module. When the program returns to that module after end-of-file has been encountered, the HIGH-VALUES within the input summary control fields will be moved to the WS-CURRENT-SUMMARY-CONTROL area. This will cause

WS-CURRENT-SUMMARY-CONTROL to be unequal to WS-PREVIOUS-SUMMARY-CONTROL and thus trigger the printing of the summary line for the last control group.

■ TOPIC 7-B: **Report Accumulations**

End-of-Report Totals
       Report total fields
       Definition of the total line
       Mainline module
       Initialization module
       Process-record module
       Report total module

Control-Break Totals
   Single-Level Control-Break Totals
   Multiple-Level Control-Break Totals
       Control-break fields
       Control total accumulators
       Control total lines
       Mainline module
       Process-record module
       Print detail line module
       Print minor control total line
       Print other control total lines
       End-of-file processing

There are two basic types of report accumulations: end-of-report totals and control-break totals.

End-of-Report Totals

Regardless of the type of listing, the great majority of reports contain **end-of-report totals**. Figure 7B.1 shows the detail sales list example with end-of-report totals. Although end-of-report totals are commonly incorporated into all three types of report listings, the basic detail list is used here as a base. Similar logic could be incorporated into the exception list and summary list program logic.

A structure chart for a detail list with end-of-report totals appears in Figure 7B.2. Those modules that are applicable to the end-of-report totals are shaded. Figure 7B.3 presents prototype coding for end-of-report totals.

Report total fields (Point A of Figure 7B.3)

A group item named WS-REPORT-TOTAL-ACCUMULATORS is established for definition of the elementary fields that are required for accumulation of the report totals.

As with summary total fields, specification of COMP-3 usage normally provides optimum processing efficiency.

Definition of the total line (Point B of Figure 7B.3)

The total line is defined in WORKING-STORAGE and has been named TL-TOTAL-LINE to describe its function.

```
HIGH-VALUE HARDWARE STORES                                          03/15/84
DETAIL SALES REPORT                                                 PAGE    1

PRODUCT   ITEM    STORE        ITEM                QTY                EXTENDED
CLASS     CODE    NBR      DESCRIPTION            SOLD      PRICE      AMOUNT

  HMR     3836-H   101    CLAW HAMMER              1        12.99       12.99
  HMR     3836-H   101    CLAW HAMMER              3        12.99       38.97
  HMR     3836-H   102    CLAW HAMMER              1        12.99       12.99
  HMR     3836-H   102    CLAW HAMMER              1        12.99       12.99
  HMR     3836-H   102    CLAW HAMMER              1        12.99       12.99
  HMR     3836-H   102    CLAW HAMMER             10        12.99      129.90
  HMR     3847-H   101    BALL PEEN HAMMER         1        13.99       13.99
  HMR     3847-H   101    BALL PEEN HAMMER         2        13.99       27.98
  HMR     3847-H   102    BALL PEEN HAMMER         1        13.99       13.99
  HMR     3852-H   102    TACK HAMMER              1         4.99        4.99
  HMR     3861-P   101    POWER HAMMER             1        29.99       29.99
  SAW     1977-P   102    RADIAL ARM SAW           1       529.99      529.99
  SAW     1977-P   102    RADIAL ARM SAW           1       529.99      529.99
  SAW     2425-P   101    TABLE SAW                1       569.99      569.99
  SAW     3619-H   102    WOOD SAW                 1        18.99       18.99
  SAW     3715-H   101    HACK SAW                 1         9.99        9.99
  SAW     3715-H   101    HACK SAW                 1         9.99        9.99
  SAW     3715-H   101    HACK SAW                 1         9.99        9.99
  SAW     3715-H   102    HACK SAW                 1         9.99        9.99
  SDR     2158-H   101    SLOTTED SCREWDRIVER      1         2.79        2.79
  SDR     2158-H   101    SLOTTED SCREWDRIVER      1         2.79        2.79
  SDR     2158-H   101    SLOTTED SCREWDRIVER      1         2.79        2.79
  SDR     2158-H   101    SLOTTED SCREWDRIVER      1         2.79        2.79
  SDR     2158-H   101    SLOTTED SCREWDRIVER      6         2.79       16.74
  SDR     2158-H   102    SLOTTED SCREWDRIVER      1         2.79        2.79
  SDR     2158-H   102    SLOTTED SCREWDRIVER      1         2.79        2.79
  SDR     2160-H   101    PHILLIPS SCREWDRIVER     2         2.99        5.98
  SDR     2160-H   101    PHILLIPS SCREWDRIVER     1         2.99        2.99
  SDR     2160-H   101    PHILLIPS SCREWDRIVER     1         2.99        2.99
  SDR     2160-H   101    PHILLIPS SCREWDRIVER     2         2.99        5.98
  SDR     2160-H   102    PHILLIPS SCREWDRIVER     1         2.99        2.99
  SDR     2160-H   102    PHILLIPS SCREWDRIVER     1         2.99        2.99

                         REPORT TOTAL                               2,058.09*
```

Figure 7B.1.   Detail list with end-of-report totals example.

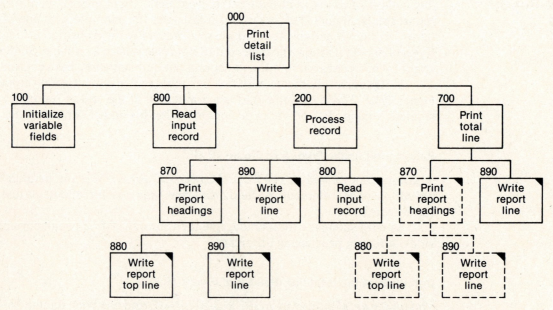

Figure 7B.2.   Structure chart: Detail list program with end-of-report totals.

```
                    DATA DIVISION.
                         .
                         .
                         .
                    WORKING-STORAGE SECTION.
   ┌───┐  ┌──────────────────────────────────────────────────────────────────────┐
   │ A │  │ 01   WS-REPORT-TOTAL-ACCUMULATORS.                                     │
   └───┘  │      05  report-total-accumulator          PIC S9(n)        COMP-3.    │
          │               [additional report total fields as required]            │
          └──────────────────────────────────────────────────────────────────────┘

   ┌───┐  ┌──────────────────────────────────────────────────────────────────────┐
   │ B │  │ 01   TL-TOTAL-LINE.                                                    │
   └───┘  └──────────────────────────────────────────────────────────────────────┘

                    PROCEDURE DIVISION.
          ┌──────────────────────────────────────────────────────────────────────┐
          │ 000-mainline.                                                          │
          │      .                                                                 │
          │      .                                                                 │
          │      .                                                                 │
   ┌───┐  │      PERFORM 700-PRINT-REPORT-TOTALS.                                  │
   │ C │  │      CLOSE files.                                                      │
   └───┘  │      STOP RUN.                                                         │
          └──────────────────────────────────────────────────────────────────────┘

          ┌──────────────────────────────────────────────────────────────────────┐
          │ 100-INITIALIZE-VARIABLE-FIELDS.                                        │
          │                                                                        │
          │      .                                                                 │
          │      .                                                                 │
   ┌───┐  │      MOVE ZEROS                                                        │
   │ D │  │          TO each elementary WS-REPORT-TOTAL-ACCUMULATORS field.        │
   └───┘  └──────────────────────────────────────────────────────────────────────┘

          ┌──────────────────────────────────────────────────────────────────────┐
          │ 200-process-record.                                                    │
          │                                                                        │
          │      .                                                                 │
          │      .                                                                 │
          │                                                                        │
   ┌───┐  │      PERFORM 890-WRITE-REPORT-LINE.                                    │
   │ E │  │      Accumulate each elementary WS-REPORT-TOTAL-ACCUMULATORS field.    │
   └───┘  │      .                                                                 │
          │      .                                                                 │
          │      .                                                                 │
          └──────────────────────────────────────────────────────────────────────┘

   ┌───┐  ┌──────────────────────────────────────────────────────────────────────┐
   │ F │  │ 700-PRINT-REPORT-TOTALS.                                               │
   └───┘  │      PERFORM 870-PRINT-REPORT-HEADINGS     <--- [If totals are to be   │
          │                                                 printed on a separate page]│
          │      (Blank the total-line.)                                          │
          │      Do total-line calculations [if any] and                          │
          │      Build TL-TOTAL-LINE.                                             │
          │      MOVE TL-TOTAL-LINE TO REPORT-LINE.                                │
          │      Set WS-LINE-SPACING for this total-line.                          │
          │      PERFORM 890-WRITE-REPORT-LINE.                                    │
          └──────────────────────────────────────────────────────────────────────┘
```

Figure 7B.3. Coding prototype: End-of-report totals.

Mainline module (Point C of Figure 7B.3)

After the body of the report has been printed and before the files are closed, the
700-PRINT-TOTAL-LINE module is performed from the mainline module.

Initialization module (Point D of Figure 7B.3)

In addition to other required initialization module functions, each elementary
field within the WS-REPORT-TOTAL-ACCUMULATORS group item must be initialized to ZERO.

Process-record module (Point E of Figure 7B.3)

At some point within the record-processing module, the elementary fields within the WS-REPORT-TOTAL-ACCUMULATORS group item must be accumulated. As has been done in the prototype, it is usually convenient to specify such coding after all detail processing has been completed for the record.

Report total module (Point F of Figure 7B.3)

This module prepares and prints the total line. If the totals are to be printed on a separate report page, the 870-PRINT-REPORT-HEADING module should be performed at the beginning of this paragraph, as shown in the prototype. The remainder of the module formats the report total line and performs the 890-WRITE-REPORT-LINE routine to actually print the total line.

Often, report totals will require more than one line of printing. In such situations, the second through the last line of this paragraph would be repeated, with different references as required, for each additional total line. Sometimes, table-processing iterations with subscripts or indexes will be appropriate, as was coded in Chapters 3 through 5 in the file-maintenance program examples.

Control-Break Totals

Control-break totals are subtotals for records that contain the same control key. They are sometimes called **summary totals** because they provide a summarized subtotal for a group of records. Control-break reports are usually detail lists but control totals are also often incorporated into exception and summary listings.

Reports with control-break totals can be categorized as being either **single-level** or **multiple-level**, depending upon whether there is one control field or more than one control field, respectively.

Single-Level Control-Break Totals

The detail sales list example with single-level control totals (plus end-of-report totals) is shown in Figure 7B.4. Observe that the control field is the item code. Whenever the item code changes, a total of the quantity sold and extended amount fields for the group of records that contain the previous item code control key is printed.

Figure 7B.5 shows a structure chart for a typical program with single-level control-break totals. The program prototype appears in Figure 7B.6.

The logic for a single-level control break report is similar in some respects to that of a summary list program and is closely akin to a multiple-level control-break report. Because of this, the single-level control-break program prototype will not be discussed here in the text. Any questions that may arise from a review of its logic can be resolved by referring to the discussion of the counterpart logic in the multiple-level control-break discussion that follows.

Multiple-Level Control-Break Totals

The detail sales list example is shown again in Figure 7B.7, this time with three control totals (plus end-of-report totals). Notice that there are three control fields: the major control field is product class, the intermediate field is item code, and the minor field is store number.

A structure chart for a detail list with multiple-level (in this example, three) control-break totals is shown in Figure 7B.8. Figure 7B.9 presents the program prototype.

Control-break fields (Point A of Figure 7B.9)

Report-programming guideline 12: For control-break reports, specify a group item for the control fields in the WORKING-STORAGE SECTION. Define two sets of control fields: one

```
HIGH-VALUE HARDWARE STORES                                    03/15/84
DETAIL SALES REPORT BY ITEM                                   PAGE   1

PRODUCT  ITEM    STORE       ITEM            QTY              EXTENDED
CLASS    CODE    NBR     DESCRIPTION         SOLD    PRICE     AMOUNT

 HMR    3836-H   101    CLAW HAMMER           1     12.99       12.99
 HMR    3836-H   101    CLAW HAMMER           3     12.99       38.97
 HMR    3836-H   102    CLAW HAMMER           1     12.99       12.99
 HMR    3836-H   102    CLAW HAMMER           1     12.99       12.99
 HMR    3836-H   102    CLAW HAMMER           1     12.99       12.99
 HMR    3836-H   102    CLAW HAMMER          10     12.99      129.90
 HMR    3836-H             ITEM TOTAL        17*               220.83*◄─┐

 HMR    3847-H   101    BALL PEEN HAMMER      1     13.99       13.99
 HMR    3847-H   101    BALL PEEN HAMMER      2     13.99       27.98
 HMR    3847-H   102    BALL PEEN HAMMER      1     13.99       13.99
 HMR    3847-H             ITEM TOTAL         4*                55.96*◄─┤

 HMR    3852-H   102    TACK HAMMER           1      4.99        4.99
 HMR    3852-H             ITEM TOTAL         1*                 4.99*◄─┤

 HMR    3861-P   101    POWER HAMMER          1     29.99       29.99
 HMR    3861-P             ITEM TOTAL         1*                29.99*◄─┤

 SAW    1977-P   102    RADIAL ARM SAW        1    529.99      529.99
 SAW    1977-P   102    RADIAL ARM SAW        1    529.99      529.99
 SAW    1977-P             ITEM TOTAL         2*             1,059.98*◄─┤

 SAW    2425-P   101    TABLE SAW             1    569.99      569.99
 SAW    2425-P             ITEM TOTAL         1*               569.99*◄─┤

 SAW    3619-H   102    WOOD SAW              1     18.99       18.99
 SAW    3619-H             ITEM TOTAL         1*                18.99*◄─┤

 SAW    3715-H   101    HACK SAW              1      9.99        9.99
 SAW    3715-H   101    HACK SAW              1      9.99        9.99
 SAW    3715-H   101    HACK SAW              1      9.99        9.99
 SAW    3715-H   102    HACK SAW              1      9.99        9.99
 SAW    3715-H             ITEM TOTAL         4*                39.96*◄─┤

 SDR    2158-H   101    SLOTTED SCREWDRIVER   1      2.79        2.79
 SDR    2158-H   101    SLOTTED SCREWDRIVER   1      2.79        2.79
 SDR    2158-H   101    SLOTTED SCREWDRIVER   1      2.79        2.79
```

```
HIGH-VALUE HARDWARE STORES                                    03/15/84
DETAIL SALES REPORT BY ITEM                                   PAGE   2

PRODUCT  ITEM    STORE       ITEM            QTY              EXTENDED
CLASS    CODE    NBR     DESCRIPTION         SOLD    PRICE     AMOUNT

 SDR    2158-H   101    SLOTTED SCREWDRIVER   1      2.79        2.79
 SDR    2158-H   101    SLOTTED SCREWDRIVER   6      2.79       16.74
 SDR    2158-H   102    SLOTTED SCREWDRIVER   1      2.79        2.79
 SDR    2158-H   102    SLOTTED SCREWDRIVER   1      2.79        2.79
 SDR    2158-H             ITEM TOTAL        12*                33.48*◄─┐

 SDR    2160-H   101    PHILLIPS SCREWDRIVER  2      2.99        5.98
 SDR    2160-H   101    PHILLIPS SCREWDRIVER  1      2.99        2.99
 SDR    2160-H   101    PHILLIPS SCREWDRIVER  1      2.99        2.99
 SDR    2160-H   101    PHILLIPS SCREWDRIVER  2      2.99        5.98
 SDR    2160-H   102    PHILLIPS SCREWDRIVER  1      2.99        2.99
 SDR    2160-H   102    PHILLIPS SCREWDRIVER  1      2.99        2.99
 SDR    2160-H             ITEM TOTAL         8*                23.92*◄─┘

                           REPORT TOTAL                     2,058.09**
```

Control-break totals

Figure 7B.4. Detail list with single-level control-break totals example.

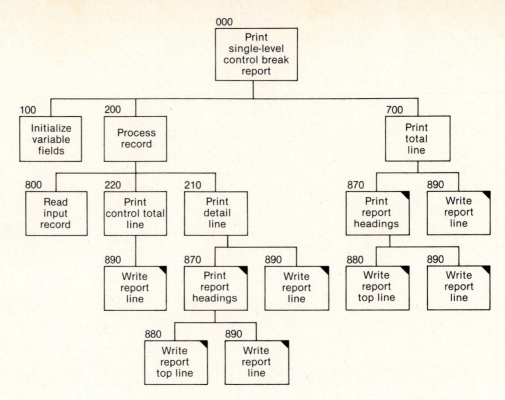

Figure 7B.5. Structure chart: Detail list program with single-level control-break totals.

for the previous control key and one for the current control key. If the control key contains multiple fields, list the fields in major to minor order.

Like a summary list, control-break logic requires knowledge of the relationship between the current record that is being processed and the previous record. Thus, a WS-BREAK-CONTROLS record-description is established in WORKING-STORAGE. Within its WS-PREVIOUS-BREAK-CONTROL and WS-CURRENT-BREAK-CONTROL group items, the control fields should be specified in major through minor order to ensure correct processing in the event that the group fields are compared.

For efficiency of comparisons and to minimize data exceptions (for computers that recognize such), it is generally advisable to specify numeric control fields as alphanumeric (PICTURE X) rather than numeric (PICTURE 9).

Control total accumulators (Point B of Figure 7B.9)

Report-programming guideline 13: For control-break reports, specify a group item for the control total accumulators. List each set of the elementary accumulator fields in minor through major sequence.

A group item called WS-CONTROL-TOTAL-ACCUMULATORS has been established for definition of the fields to be used for control total accumulations. Depending upon the programming specifications, one or more elementary fields will be required for each control level of the report. As with summary total and end-of-report total fields, specification of COMP-3 usage normally provides optimum processing efficiency.

Although it has no effect upon program processing, it is logical to list each set of control total accumulators in minor to major sequence, since that is the order in which the control totals will be printed on the report.

```
DATA DIVISION.
         .
         .
         .
WORKING-STORAGE SECTION.

┌─────────────────────────────────────────────────────────────────────────────┐
│ 01  WS-SWITCHES.                                                              │
│         .                                                                     │
│         .                                                                     │
│         .                                                                     │
│     05   WS-FIRST-RECORD-SW              PIC X(3).                            │
│          88   FIRST-RECORD                             VALUE 'YES'.           │
└─────────────────────────────────────────────────────────────────────────────┘

┌─────────────────────────────────────────────────────────────────────────────┐
│ 01  WS-REPORT-CONTROLS.                                                       │
└─────────────────────────────────────────────────────────────────────────────┘

┌─────────────────────────────────────────────────────────────────────────────┐
│ 01  WS-BREAK-CONTROLS.                                                        │
│     05   WS-PREVIOUS-BREAK-CONTROL        PIC X(nn).                          │
│     05   WS-CURRENT-BREAK-CONTROL         PIC X(nn).                          │
└─────────────────────────────────────────────────────────────────────────────┘

┌─────────────────────────────────────────────────────────────────────────────┐
│ 01  WS-CONTROL-TOTAL-ACCUMULATORS.                                            │
│     05   control-total-accumulator        PIC S9(n)        COMP-3.            │
│          [additional control total fields as required]                       │
└─────────────────────────────────────────────────────────────────────────────┘

┌─────────────────────────────────────────────────────────────────────────────┐
│ 01  WS-REPORT-TOTAL-ACCUMULATORS.                                             │
└─────────────────────────────────────────────────────────────────────────────┘

┌─────────────────────────────────────────────────────────────────────────────┐
│ 01  Input-record-description.                                                 │
└─────────────────────────────────────────────────────────────────────────────┘

┌─────────────────────────────────────────────────────────────────────────────┐
│ 01  H1-HEADING-LINE-1.                                                        │
└─────────────────────────────────────────────────────────────────────────────┘

┌─────────────────────────────────────────────────────────────────────────────┐
│ 01  Hn-HEADING-LINE-n.          [additional heading lines as required]        │
└─────────────────────────────────────────────────────────────────────────────┘

┌─────────────────────────────────────────────────────────────────────────────┐
│ 01  DL-DETAIL-LINE.                                                           │
└─────────────────────────────────────────────────────────────────────────────┘

┌─────────────────────────────────────────────────────────────────────────────┐
│ 01  CT-CONTROL-TOTAL-LINE.                                                    │
└─────────────────────────────────────────────────────────────────────────────┘

┌─────────────────────────────────────────────────────────────────────────────┐
│ 01  TL-TOTAL-LINE.                                                            │
└─────────────────────────────────────────────────────────────────────────────┘

PROCEDURE DIVISION.

┌─────────────────────────────────────────────────────────────────────────────┐
│ 000-mainline.                                                                 │
│                                                                               │
│     OPEN files.                                                               │
│     PERFORM 100-INITIALIZE-VARIABLE-FIELDS.                                   │
│                                                        [no priming read]      │
│     PERFORM 200-process-record                                                │
│         UNTIL END-OF-FILE.                                                    │
│     PERFORM 700-print-report-totals.                                          │
│     CLOSE files.                                                              │
│     STOP RUN.                                                                 │
└─────────────────────────────────────────────────────────────────────────────┘

┌─────────────────────────────────────────────────────────────────────────────┐
│ 100-INITIALIZE-VARIABLE-FIELDS.                                               │
│                                                                               │
│         .                                                                     │
│         .                                                                     │
│         .                                                                     │
│     MOVE 'YES' TO WS-FIRST-RECORD-SW.                                         │
│     MOVE ZEROS                                                                │
│         TO each elementary WS-CONTROL-TOTAL-ACCUMULATORS field                │
│            each elementary WS-REPORT-TOTAL-ACCUMULATORS field.                │
└─────────────────────────────────────────────────────────────────────────────┘
```

continued

Figure 7B.6.   Program prototype: Detail list with single-level control-break totals.

```
200-process-record.

    PERFORM 800-READ-input-record.
    MOVE each break-control-field from the input-record-area
         TO its respective WS-CURRENT-BREAK-CONTROL field.
    IF FIRST-RECORD
         MOVE WS-CURRENT-BREAK-CONTROL TO WS-PREVIOUS-BREAK-CONTROL
         MOVE 'NO ' TO WS-FIRST-RECORD-SW.
    IF WS-CURRENT-BREAK-CONTROL
            IS NOT EQUAL TO WS-PREVIOUS-BREAK-CONTROL
         PERFORM 220-PRINT-CONTROL-TOTAL-LINE.
    IF NOT END-OF-FILE
         PERFORM 210-PRINT-DETAIL-LINE.
```

```
210-PRINT-DETAIL-LINE.

    IF WS-LINES-USED IS NOT LESS THAN WS-LINES-PER-PAGE
         PERFORM 870-PRINT-REPORT-HEADINGS.
    (Blank the detail-line.)
    Do detail-line calculations [if any] and
    Build DL-DETAIL-LINE.
    MOVE DL-DETAIL-LINE TO REPORT-LINE.
    PERFORM 890-WRITE-REPORT-LINE.
    Set WS-LINE-SPACING for next detail-line.
    Accumulate WS-CONTROL-TOTAL-ACCUMULATORS field(s).
```

```
220-PRINT-CONTROL-TOTAL-LINE.

    (Blank the control-total-line.)
    MOVE WS-PREVIOUS-BREAK-CONTROL
         TO its CT-CONTROL-TOTAL-LINE field.          <---[If the
                                              control field is to be displayed
                                                 on the control-total line]
    MOVE each WS-CONTROL-TOTAL-ACCUMULATORS field
         TO its respective CT-CONTROL-TOTAL-LINE field.
    Build remainder of CT-CONTROL-TOTAL-LINE.
    MOVE CT-CONTROL-TOTAL-LINE TO REPORT-LINE.
    Set WS-LINE-SPACING for this control-total-line.
    PERFORM 890-WRITE-REPORT-LINE.
    ADD each WS-CONTROL-TOTAL-ACCUMULATORS field
         TO its respective WS-REPORT-TOTAL-ACCUMULATORS field.
    MOVE ZEROS
         TO each elementary WS-CONTROL-TOTAL-ACCUMULATORS field.
    MOVE WS-CURRENT-BREAK-CONTROL TO WS-PREVIOUS-BREAK-CONTROL.
    Set WS-LINE-SPACING for next detail-line.
```

```
700-PRINT-REPORT-TOTALS.
```

```
800-READ-input-record.
    READ INPUT-FILE INTO input-record-area
         AT END MOVE 'YES' TO WS-END-OF-FILE-SW
         MOVE HIGH-VALUES
              TO each break-control-field in the input-record-area.
```

```
870-PRINT-REPORT-HEADINGS.
```

```
880-WRITE-REPORT-TOP-LINE.
```

```
890-WRITE-REPORT-LINE.
```

Figure 7B.6. (continued)

Because end-of-report totals usually require one additional set of accumulators that could be considered to be the highest total level, it may be more convenient to merge the WS-REPORT-TOTAL-ACCUMULATORS into the WS-CONTROL-TOTAL-ACCUMULATORS group item instead of establishing a separate 01-level item as is shown in the prototype.

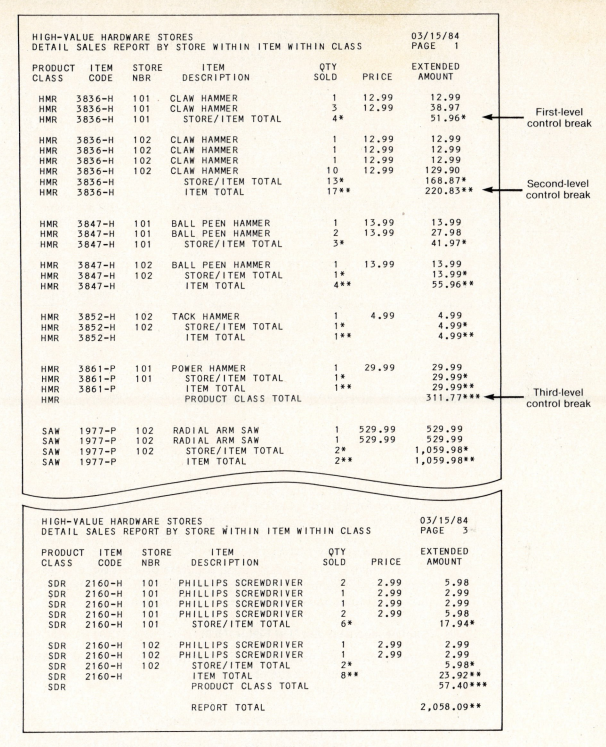

```
HIGH-VALUE HARDWARE STORES                          03/15/84
DETAIL SALES REPORT BY STORE WITHIN ITEM WITHIN CLASS   PAGE   1

PRODUCT   ITEM    STORE      ITEM             QTY                EXTENDED
CLASS     CODE    NBR        DESCRIPTION      SOLD    PRICE      AMOUNT

HMR       3836-H  101   CLAW HAMMER             1     12.99         12.99
HMR       3836-H  101   CLAW HAMMER             3     12.99         38.97      ◄──── First-level
HMR       3836-H  101        STORE/ITEM TOTAL   4*                  51.96*           control break

HMR       3836-H  102   CLAW HAMMER             1     12.99         12.99
HMR       3836-H  102   CLAW HAMMER             1     12.99         12.99
HMR       3836-H  102   CLAW HAMMER             1     12.99         12.99
HMR       3836-H  102   CLAW HAMMER            10     12.99        129.90
HMR       3836-H             STORE/ITEM TOTAL  13*                 168.87*     ◄──── Second-level
HMR       3836-H             ITEM TOTAL        17**                220.83**          control break

HMR       3847-H  101   BALL PEEN HAMMER        1     13.99         13.99
HMR       3847-H  101   BALL PEEN HAMMER        2     13.99         27.98
HMR       3847-H  101        STORE/ITEM TOTAL   3*                  41.97*

HMR       3847-H  102   BALL PEEN HAMMER        1     13.99         13.99
HMR       3847-H  102        STORE/ITEM TOTAL   1*                  13.99*
HMR       3847-H             ITEM TOTAL         4**                 55.96**

HMR       3852-H  102   TACK HAMMER             1      4.99          4.99
HMR       3852-H  102        STORE/ITEM TOTAL   1*                   4.99*
HMR       3852-H             ITEM TOTAL         1**                  4.99**

HMR       3861-P  101   POWER HAMMER            1     29.99         29.99
HMR       3861-P  101        STORE/ITEM TOTAL   1*                  29.99*
HMR       3861-P             ITEM TOTAL         1**                 29.99**
HMR                          PRODUCT CLASS TOTAL                   311.77***   ◄──── Third-level
                                                                                     control break

SAW       1977-P  102   RADIAL ARM SAW          1    529.99        529.99
SAW       1977-P  102   RADIAL ARM SAW          1    529.99        529.99
SAW       1977-P  102        STORE/ITEM TOTAL   2*                1,059.98*
SAW       1977-P             ITEM TOTAL         2**               1,059.98**
```

```
HIGH-VALUE HARDWARE STORES                          03/15/84
DETAIL SALES REPORT BY STORE WITHIN ITEM WITHIN CLASS   PAGE   3

PRODUCT   ITEM    STORE      ITEM             QTY                EXTENDED
CLASS     CODE    NBR        DESCRIPTION      SOLD    PRICE      AMOUNT

SDR       2160-H  101   PHILLIPS SCREWDRIVER    2      2.99          5.98
SDR       2160-H  101   PHILLIPS SCREWDRIVER    1      2.99          2.99
SDR       2160-H  101   PHILLIPS SCREWDRIVER    1      2.99          2.99
SDR       2160-H  101   PHILLIPS SCREWDRIVER    2      2.99          5.98
SDR       2160-H  101        STORE/ITEM TOTAL   6*                  17.94*

SDR       2160-H  102   PHILLIPS SCREWDRIVER    1      2.99          2.99
SDR       2160-H  102   PHILLIPS SCREWDRIVER    1      2.99          2.99
SDR       2160-H  102        STORE/ITEM TOTAL   2*                   5.98*
SDR       2160-H             ITEM TOTAL         8**                 23.92**
SDR                          PRODUCT CLASS TOTAL                    57.40***

                             REPORT TOTAL                        2,058.09**
```

Figure 7B.7. Detail list with multiple-level control-break totals example.

Control total lines (Point C of Figure 7B.9)

Report-programming guideline 14: Define control total lines in minor through major sequence.

Definition of one control total line for each report control level is generally required. An exception is when the control total lines closely resemble one

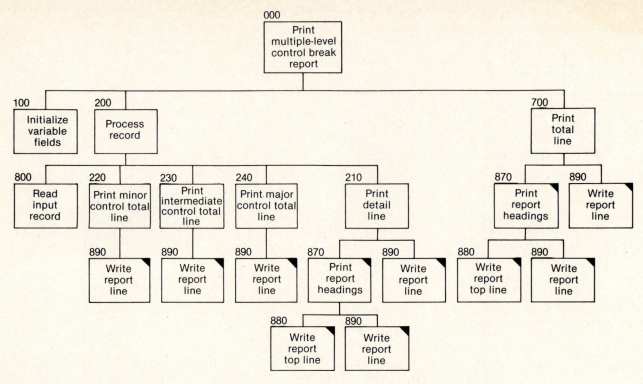

Figure 7B.8.   Structure chart: Detail list program with multiple-level control-break totals.

another in format. In that case, it may be possible to define one common control total line for use at all control-break levels. When this is done, it is usually necessary to define one or more fields to hold words that will identify each control level. Then, before the line is printed, a descriptive such as "STORE TOTAL" or "ITEM TOTAL" can be moved into the field.

Although it has no effect upon program processing, it is logical to list the control total lines in minor to major sequence, since that is the order in which the control total lines will be printed on the report.

Mainline module (Point D of Figure 7B.9)

A control-break program is usually best formed by using a conditional-processing method rather than the priming-read approach. Thus, the mainline module contains no priming-read.

Process-record module (Point E of Figure 7B.9)

Because this program uses the conditional-processing method of READ statement handling, the first step in this module is to perform the read routine. Then, each control field in the current input record is moved to its respective WS-CURRENT-BREAK-CONTROL field.

If this is the first input record, the WS-CURRENT-BREAK-CONTROL field is moved to the WS-PREVIOUS-BREAK-CONTROL field. By setting both the current and previous control fields to the same value, superfluous control totals at the beginning of the report are inhibited. Then the first-record switch is set to "NO," to inhibit this first-record action from occurring again.

```
                    DATA DIVISION.
                             .
                             .
                             .
                    WORKING-STORAGE SECTION.
```

```
        01  WS-SWITCHES.
                 .
                 .
                 .
            05  WS-FIRST-RECORD-SW          PIC X(3)
                88  FIRST-RECORD                        VALUE 'YES'.
```

```
        01  WS-REPORT-CONTROLS.
```

(A)
```
        01  WS-BREAK-CONTROLS.
            05  WS-PREVIOUS-BREAK-CONTROL.
                10   WS-PREVIOUS-major-BREAK-CONTROL    PIC X(nn).
                10   WS-PREVIOUS-inter-BREAK-CONTROL    PIC X(nn).
                10   WS-PREVIOUS-minor-BREAK-CONTROL    PIC X(nn).
            05  WS-CURRENT-BREAK-CONTROL.
                10   WS-CURRENT-major-BREAK-CONTROL     PIC X(nn).
                10   WS-CURRENT-inter-BREAK-CONTROL     PIC X(nn).
                10   WS-CURRENT-minor-BREAK-CONTROL     PIC X(nn).
```

(B)
```
        01  WS-CONTROL-TOTAL-ACCUMULATORS.

            05  minor-control-total-accumulator PIC S9(n)      COMP-3.
                [additional minor control total fields as required]

            05  inter-control-total-accumulator PIC S9(n)      COMP-3.
                [additional intermediate control total fields as required]

            05  major-control-total-accumulator PIC S9(n)      COMP-3.
                [additional major control total fields as required]
```

```
        01  WS-REPORT-TOTAL-ACCUMULATORS.
```

```
        01  Input-record-description.
```

```
        01  H1-HEADING-LINE-1.
```

```
        01  Hn-HEADING-LINE-n.
                              [additional heading lines as required]
```

```
        01  DL-DETAIL-LINE.
```

(C)
```
        01  C1-minor-CONTROL-TOTAL-LINE.
```

```
        01  C2-inter-CONTROL-TOTAL-LINE.
```

```
        01  C3-major-CONTROL-TOTAL-LINE.
```

```
        01  TL-TOTAL-LINE.
```

continued

Figure 7B.9. Program prototype: Detail list with multiple-level control-break totals.

```
PROCEDURE DIVISION.
```

Ⓓ
```
000-mainline.

    OPEN files.
    PERFORM 100-INITIALIZE-VARIABLE-FIELDS.
                                                    [no priming read]

    PERFORM 200-process-record
        UNTIL END-OF-FILE.
    PERFORM 700-PRINT-REPORT-TOTALS.
    CLOSE files.
    STOP RUN.
```

```
100-INITIALIZE-VARIABLE-FIELDS.

    .
    .
    .
    MOVE 'YES' TO WS-FIRST-RECORD-SW.
    MOVE ZEROS
        TO each elementary WS-CONTROL-TOTAL-ACCUMULATORS field
           each elementary WS-REPORT-TOTAL-ACCUMULATORS field.
```

Ⓔ
```
200-process-record.

    PERFORM 800-READ-input-record.
    MOVE each break-control-field from the input-record-area
        TO its respective WS-CURRENT-BREAK-CONTROL field.
    IF FIRST-RECORD
        MOVE WS-CURRENT-BREAK-CONTROL TO WS-PREVIOUS-BREAK-CONTROL
        MOVE 'NO ' TO WS-FIRST-RECORD-SW.
    IF WS-CURRENT-major-BREAK-CONTROL
            IS NOT EQUAL TO WS-PREVIOUS-major-BREAK-CONTROL
        PERFORM 220-PRINT-minor-CONTROL-TOTAL-LINE
        PERFORM 230-PRINT-inter-CONTROL-TOTAL-LINE
        PERFORM 240-PRINT-major-CONTROL-TOTAL-LINE
    ELSE IF WS-CURRENT-inter-BREAK-CONTROL
            IS NOT EQUAL TO WS-PREVIOUS-inter-BREAK-CONTROL
        PERFORM 220-PRINT-minor-CONTROL-TOTAL-LINE
        PERFORM 230-PRINT-inter-CONTROL-TOTAL-LINE
    ELSE IF WS-CURRENT-minor-BREAK-CONTROL
            IS NOT EQUAL TO WS-PREVIOUS-minor-CONTROL
        PERFORM 220-PRINT-minor-CONTROL-TOTAL-LINE
    ELSE
        NEXT SENTENCE.
    IF NOT END-OF-FILE
        PERFORM 210-PRINT-DETAIL-LINE.
```

```
210-PRINT-DETAIL-LINE.

    IF WS-LINES-USED IS NOT LESS THAN WS-LINES-PER-PAGE
        PERFORM 870-PRINT-REPORT-HEADINGS.
    (Blank the detail-line.)
    Do detail-line calculations [if any] and
    Build DL-DETAIL-LINE.
    MOVE DL-DETAIL-LINE TO REPORT-LINE.
    PERFORM 890-WRITE-REPORT-LINE.
```
Ⓕ
```
    Set WS-LINE-SPACING for next detail-line.
    Accumulate minor-control-total field(s).
```

Figure 7B.9. (continued)

Report-programming guideline 15: When checking for a control break, use a linear nested IF statement. Test control fields in major through minor sequence. Print the control-break lines starting with the minor control break and working upward to the level at which the control break was detected.

The test for a control break is the next step. After each input record has been read, it is necessary to determine if any of the control fields of the current record differ from those of the previous record. The important thing to remember when constructing a control-break test is to always test the major field first.

G

```
220-PRINT-minor-CONTROL-TOTAL-LINE.

    (Blank the minor-control-total-line.)
    MOVE WS-PREVIOUS-minor-BREAK-CONTROL
    (and WS-PREVIOUS-inter-BREAK-CONTROL
     and WS-PREVIOUS-major-BREAK-CONTROL
        TO its C1-minor-CONTROL-TOTAL-LINE field.       <---[If the
                                            control field is to be displayed
                                                   on the control-total line]
    MOVE each minor-control-total field
        TO its respective C1-minor-CONTROL-TOTAL-LINE field.
    Build remainder of C1-minor-CONTROL-TOTAL-LINE.
    MOVE C1-minor-CONTROL-TOTAL-LINE TO REPORT-LINE.
    Set WS-LINE-SPACING for this control-total-line.
    PERFORM 890-WRITE-REPORT-LINE.
    ADD each minor-control-total field
        TO its respective intermediate-control-total field.
    MOVE ZEROS
        TO each minor-control-total field.
    MOVE WS-CURRENT-minor-BREAK-CONTROL
        TO WS-PREVIOUS-inter-BREAK-CONTROL.
    Set WS-LINE-SPACING for next detail-line.
```

H

```
230-PRINT-inter-CONTROL-TOTAL-LINE.

    (Blank the inter-control-total-line.)
    MOVE WS-PREVIOUS-inter-CONTROL
    (and WS-PREVIOUS-major-CONTROL)
        TO its C2-inter-CONTROL-TOTAL-LINE field.       <---[If the
                                            control field is to be displayed
                                                   on the control-total line]
    MOVE each inter-control-total field
        TO its respective C2-inter-CONTROL-TOTAL-LINE field.
    Build remainder of C2-inter-CONTROL-TOTAL-LINE.
    MOVE C2-inter-CONTROL-TOTAL-LINE TO REPORT-LINE.
    Set WS-LINE-SPACING for this control-total-line.
    PERFORM 890-WRITE-REPORT-LINE.
    ADD each intermediate-control-total field
        TO its respective major-control-total field.
    MOVE ZEROS
        TO each inter-control-total field.
    MOVE WS-CURRENT-inter-BREAK-CONTROL
        TO WS-PREVIOUS-inter-BREAK-CONTROL.
    Set WS-LINE-SPACING for next detail-line.
```

```
240-PRINT-major-CONTROL-TOTAL-LINE.

    (Blank the major-control-total-line.)
    MOVE WS-PREVIOUS-major-BREAK-CONTROL
        TO its C3-major-CONTROL-TOTAL-LINE field.       <---[If the
                                            control field is to be displayed
                                                   on the control-total line]
    MOVE each major-control-total field
        TO its respective C3-major-CONTROL-TOTAL-LINE field.
    Build remainder of C3-major-CONTROL-TOTAL-LINE.
    MOVE C3-major-CONTROL-TOTAL-LINE TO REPORT-LINE.
    Set WS-LINE-SPACING for this control-total-line.
    PERFORM 890-WRITE-REPORT-LINE.
    ADD each major-control-total field
        TO its respective report-total field.
    MOVE ZEROS
        TO each major-control-total field.
    MOVE WS-CURRENT-major-BREAK-CONTROL
        TO WS-PREVIOUS-major-BREAK-CONTROL.
    Set WS-LINE-SPACING for next detail-line.
```

Figure 7B.9. (continued)   *continued*

After the major field has been checked, fields of lesser significance are tested until the minor field is reached. Then, as soon as a control break is detected, control-break lines should be printed starting with the minor control-break line and working back up to the level at which the control break was detected. This technique is shown in the linear nested IF control-break test shown in this module of the program prototype.

```
700-PRINT-REPORT-TOTALS.
```

```
800-READ-Input-record.
    READ INPUT-FILE INTO input-record-area
        AT END MOVE 'YES' TO WS-END-OF-FILE-SW
        MOVE HIGH-VALUES
            TO each break-control-field in the input-record-area.
```
(I)

```
870-PRINT-REPORT-HEADINGS.
```

```
880-WRITE-REPORT-TOP-LINE.
```

```
890-WRITE-REPORT-LINE.
```

Figure 7B.9. (continued)

Unless end-of-file has been reached, the last step in this module is to perform the print module to generate a detail line for the current record.

Print detail line module (Point F of Figure 7B.9)

Control-break programs are often specified with line spacing that will provide white space to enhance a report's readability and attractiveness. For example, in the multiple-level sales report (Figure 7B.7), notice that there is one blank space between a "STORE/ITEM TOTAL" line and the next detail line; two blank spaces between an "ITEM TOTAL" line and the next detail line; and three blank spaces between a "PRODUCT CLASS TOTAL" and the next detail line. The most convenient way to provide such line-spacing flexibility is by the approach shown in the prototype. That is, after the last line is printed in each module, set the line-spacing indicator for the next detail line.

The last step in this module is to add the control total fields from the input record into the minor-level control total accumulators.

Print minor control total line (Point G of Figure 7B.9)

The initial three statements of this module handle formatting of the print line. For identification purposes, applicable control fields are usually displayed on each control total line (as shown in the example of Figure 7B.7). It is important to remember that, when the control break occurs, the control fields for the control total line reside in the WS-PREVIOUS-BREAK-CONTROL fields—not in WS-CURRENT-BREAK-CONTROL or the input area. The current record, of course, is the one that caused the control break and thus has values that will be printed for the *next*, not the present, control break.

Another line-formatting requirement is to move the minor control total fields from the WS-CONTROL-TOTAL-ACCUMULATORS to their respective locations in the C1-MINOR-CONTROL-TOTAL-LINE. If there are additional fields to be printed, such as descriptions and the like, they should also be moved to the control total line at this time.

Once the line has been formatted, the C1-MINOR-CONTROL-TOTAL-LINE is moved to the REPORT-LINE. Then, the line-spacing indicator is set for the number of lines that are specified between the control total line and last detail

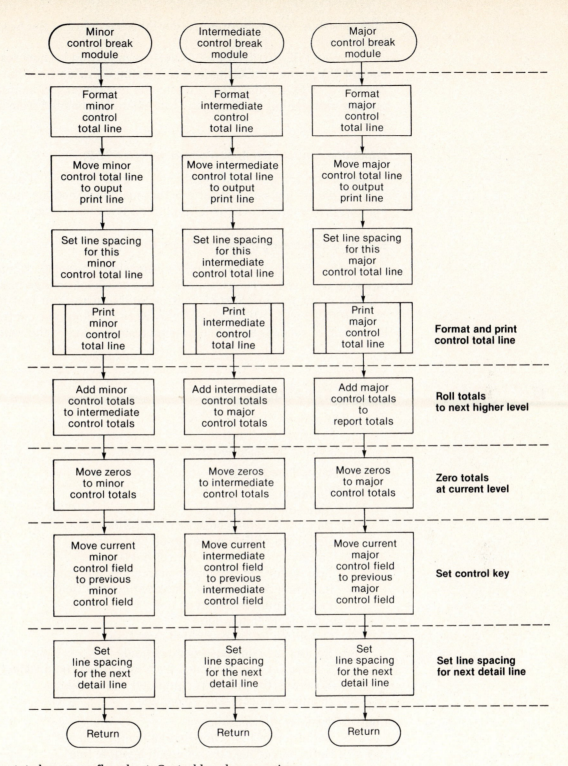

Figure 7B.10. Annotated-program flowchart: Control-break processing.

line of the control group. At that point, the 890-WRITE-REPORT-LINE module can be performed.

After the control total line has been printed, the minor control accumulation fields are added to the next higher level of totals. This step is termed **rolling totals** to their next higher level. Now that the minor control total fields have been printed and rolled, their function has been served for this control break.

They are thus zeroed in preparation for accumulating the next minor control break total.

The WS-PREVIOUS-BREAK-CONTROL minor field is now reset to reflect the control key of the current record by moving its value from the WS-CURRENT-BREAK-CONTROL group item. Finally, the line-spacing indicator is reset to the number of lines that the next detail line should be printed from the control total line.

Print other control total lines (Point H of Figure 7B.9)

Although occurring at a different control level, the logic of each control-break module follows the same pattern as that just described for the minor total line. Figure 7B.10 shows the logic in annotated flowchart form.

End-of-file processing (Point I of Figure 7B.9)

After end-of-file has been reached, it is necessary to set each control field in the input record area to HIGH-VALUES. This artificial change of key-field values will force out the last set of control totals during the last iteration of the 200-PROCESS-RECORD module. If this were not done, the control totals for the last group of records would be missing from the end of the report.

■   TOPIC 7-C: **Report Variations**

Group Indication
        Printing the detail line
        Setting the group-indication values

Control-Break Page Headings

Page-Continuation Indication
    Continued-on Indication
        Definition of the continued control fields
        Definition of the continued-on line
        Setting the continued control fields
        Testing for the continued-on indication requirement
        Resetting the previous continued control fields
        Printing the continued-on line
    Continued-from Indication
        Definition of the continued-from line
        Setting the continued control fields
        Testing for the continued-from indication requirement
        Resetting the previous continued control fields
        Printing the continued-from line

Control-Break Group Headings
        Definition of the group heading control fields
        Definition of the control group heading line
        Setting the group heading control fields
        Testing for the control group heading line requirement
        Printing the control group heading lines

Page Footings
        Definition of the page-total accumulators
        Definition of the page-footing line
        Triggering the page-footing line for the last report page
        Triggering the page-footing line for all other report pages

Regardless of listing or total type, there are certain features that can be incorporated into report programs when it is appropriate. Topic 7-C will present coding prototypes for a number of them.

Group Indication

Group indication is a technique that can improve the readability of sequenced listings. Group indication is called for when there are sequenced key fields in the body of a report, and the values that are printed are commonly repeated from one line to the next. With group indication, the key-field column or columns are printed only for the first detail line of the group and for the first line of each new page when a group spans more than one page.

Figure 7C.1 shows a report with group indication of the product class, item code, and store-number fields. Contrast this with the same report that is printed without group indication (in Figure 7B.4).

The coding prototype for additions to the multiple-level control-break program to produce group indication are shown in Figure 7C.2.

Report-programming guideline 16: Do not blank or set group-indication fields before building the print line but do blank group-indication fields immediately after printing the line. Set the appropriate group-indication fields in each control-break module and in the page-heading routine.

Printing the detail line (Points A through C of Figure 7C.2)

Observe at points A and B of the 210-PRINT-DETAIL-LINE module, that the group-indication fields in DL-DETAIL-LINE must not be blanked or set before the line is printed. Instead, other modules place the group-indication values in the line at the appropriate time. Then, after the line has been printed, each of the group-indication fields is blanked. Thus, immediately after the values are printed for the group-indication fields, they are eradicated from the line so that

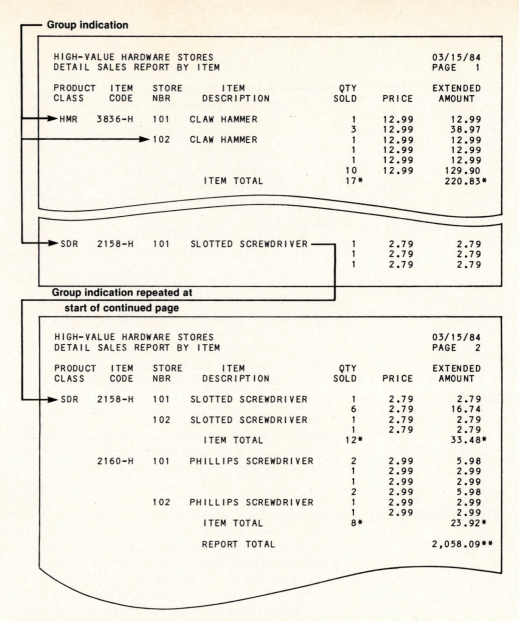

Group indication

```
                                                                        ┌── Group indication
                                                                        │
HIGH-VALUE HARDWARE STORES                                 03/15/84
DETAIL SALES REPORT BY ITEM                                PAGE    1

PRODUCT   ITEM    STORE       ITEM              QTY                 EXTENDED
CLASS     CODE    NBR     DESCRIPTION           SOLD     PRICE       AMOUNT

HMR      3836-H   101    CLAW HAMMER              1      12.99        12.99
                                                  3      12.99        38.97
                  102    CLAW HAMMER              1      12.99        12.99
                                                  1      12.99        12.99
                                                  1      12.99        12.99
                                                 10      12.99       129.90
                         ITEM TOTAL              17*                 220.83*


SDR      2158-H   101    SLOTTED SCREWDRIVER      1       2.79         2.79
                                                  1       2.79         2.79
                                                  1       2.79         2.79
```

**Group indication repeated at
start of continued page**

```
HIGH-VALUE HARDWARE STORES                                 03/15/84
DETAIL SALES REPORT BY ITEM                                PAGE    2

PRODUCT   ITEM    STORE       ITEM              QTY                 EXTENDED
CLASS     CODE    NBR     DESCRIPTION           SOLD     PRICE       AMOUNT

SDR      2158-H   101    SLOTTED SCREWDRIVER      1       2.79         2.79
                                                  6       2.79        16.74
                  102    SLOTTED SCREWDRIVER      1       2.79         2.79
                                                  1       2.79         2.79
                         ITEM TOTAL              12*                  33.48*

         2160-H   101    PHILLIPS SCREWDRIVER     2       2.99         5.98
                                                  1       2.99         2.99
                                                  1       2.99         2.99
                                                  2       2.99         5.98
                  102    PHILLIPS SCREWDRIVER     1       2.99         2.99
                                                  1       2.99         2.99
                         ITEM TOTAL               8*                  23.92*

                         REPORT TOTAL                              2,058.09**
```

Figure 7C.1. An example of group indication.

the fields will be properly initialized for the next print iteration, should it be for the same group. (An alternate but usually less efficient approach would be to blank the entire DL-DETAIL-LINE after printing.)

Setting the group-indication values (Points D through G of Figure 7C.2)

In each of the control-break modules (Points D, E, and F of the prototype) the group-indication field is moved from the appropriate WS-CURRENT-BREAK-CONTROL data-item to its respective field in DL-DETAIL-LINE. This produces the group indication for the first line of each control group during the next iteration of the 210-PRINT-DETAIL-LINE module.

Then, as shown at point G, all of the group-indication fields are moved to DL-DETAIL-LINE in the 870-PRINT-REPORT-HEADINGS module after the

```
PROCEDURE DIVISION.
                  .
                  .
                  .
```

```
    210-PRINT-DETAIL-LINE.

        IF WS-LINES-USED IS NOT LESS THAN WS-LINES-PER-PAGE
            PERFORM 870-PRINT-REPORT-HEADINGS.
        (Do not blank group-indication fields in DL-DETAIL-LINE)
        Do detail-line calculations [if any] and
        Build DL-DETAIL-LINE [except for group-indication fields].
        MOVE DL-DETAIL-LINE TO REPORT-LINE.
        PERFORM 890-WRITE-REPORT-LINE.
        MOVE SPACES TO group-indication fields in DL-DETAIL-LINE.
        Set WS-LINE-SPACING for next detail-line.
        Accumulate minor-control-total field(s).
```

(A) (B) (C)

```
    220-PRINT-minor-CONTROL-TOTAL-LINE.

                  .
                  .
                  .
        MOVE WS-CURRENT-minor-BREAK-CONTROL
            TO WS-PREVIOUS-minor-BREAK-CONTROL and
            ·the minor group-indication field in DL-DETAIL-LINE.
        Set WS-LINE-SPACING for next detail-line.
```

(D)

```
    230-PRINT-Inter-CONTROL-TOTAL-LINE.

                  .
                  .
                  .
        MOVE WS-CURRENT-Inter-BREAK-CONTROL
            TO WS-PREVIOUS-Inter-BREAK-CONTROL and
                the Intermediate group-indication field
                in DL-DETAIL-LINE.
        Set WS-LINE-SPACING for next detail-line.
```

(E)

```
    240-PRINT-major-CONTROL-TOTAL-LINE.

                  .
                  .
                  .
        MOVE WS-CURRENT-major-BREAK-CONTROL
            TO WS-PREVIOUS-major-BREAK-CONTROL and
                the major group-indication field in DL-DETAIL-LINE.
        Set WS-LINE-SPACING for next detail-line.
```

(F)

```
                  .
                  .
                  .
```

```
    870-PRINT-REPORT-HEADINGS.

        ADD 1 TO WS-PAGE-COUNT.
        MOVE WS-PAGE-COUNT TO Hn-page-number.
        MOVE H1-HEADING-LINE TO REPORT-LINE.
        PERFORM 880-WRITE-REPORT-TOP-LINE.

        MOVE Hn-HEADING-LINE TO REPORT-LINE.<   [If second heading line
        Set WS-LINE-SPACING.                 <--- (and repeat for each
        PERFORM 890-WRITE-REPORT-LINE.        < additional heading line)]

        Set WS-LINE-SPACING for next detail-line. <--- [To space after
                                                   column headings and
                                                   before the first
                                                   detail-line on each page]

        MOVE each group-indication field from WS-CURRENT-BREAK-CONTROL
            TO Its respective DL-DETAIL-LINE field.
```

(G)

```
                  .
                  .
                  .
```

Figure 7C.2. Coding prototype: Group indication.

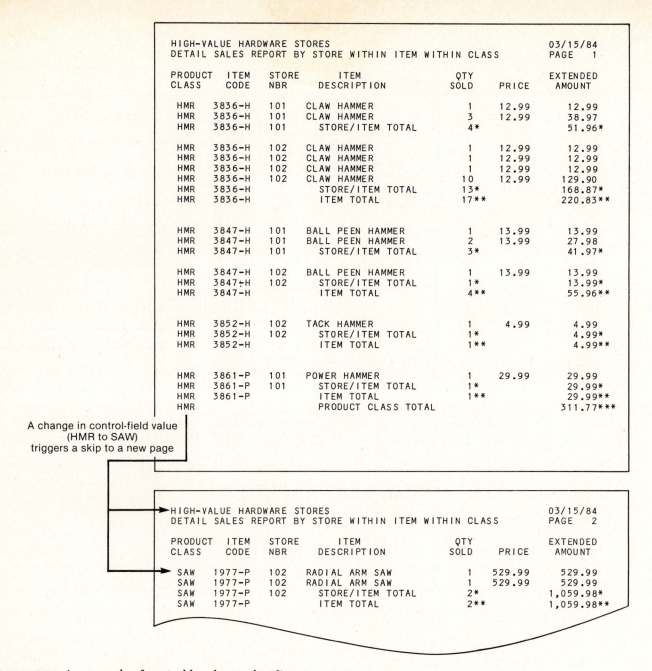

```
HIGH-VALUE HARDWARE STORES                                03/15/84
DETAIL SALES REPORT BY STORE WITHIN ITEM WITHIN CLASS     PAGE   1

PRODUCT  ITEM    STORE      ITEM              QTY                  EXTENDED
CLASS    CODE    NBR        DESCRIPTION       SOLD      PRICE      AMOUNT

HMR      3836-H  101     CLAW HAMMER             1      12.99        12.99
HMR      3836-H  101     CLAW HAMMER             3      12.99        38.97
HMR      3836-H  101        STORE/ITEM TOTAL     4*                  51.96*

HMR      3836-H  102     CLAW HAMMER             1      12.99        12.99
HMR      3836-H  102     CLAW HAMMER             1      12.99        12.99
HMR      3836-H  102     CLAW HAMMER             1      12.99        12.99
HMR      3836-H  102     CLAW HAMMER            10      12.99       129.90
HMR      3836-H             STORE/ITEM TOTAL    13*                 168.87*
HMR      3836-H             ITEM TOTAL          17**                220.83**

HMR      3847-H  101     BALL PEEN HAMMER        1      13.99        13.99
HMR      3847-H  101     BALL PEEN HAMMER        2      13.99        27.98
HMR      3847-H  101        STORE/ITEM TOTAL     3*                  41.97*

HMR      3847-H  102     BALL PEEN HAMMER        1      13.99        13.99
HMR      3847-H  102        STORE/ITEM TOTAL     1*                  13.99*
HMR      3847-H             ITEM TOTAL           4**                 55.96**

HMR      3852-H  102     TACK HAMMER             1       4.99         4.99
HMR      3852-H  102        STORE/ITEM TOTAL     1*                   4.99*
HMR      3852-H             ITEM TOTAL           1**                  4.99**

HMR      3861-P  101     POWER HAMMER            1      29.99        29.99
HMR      3861-P  101        STORE/ITEM TOTAL     1*                  29.99*
HMR      3861-P             ITEM TOTAL           1**                 29.99**
HMR                         PRODUCT CLASS TOTAL                     311.77***
```

A change in control-field value
(HMR to SAW)
triggers a skip to a new page

```
HIGH-VALUE HARDWARE STORES                                03/15/84
DETAIL SALES REPORT BY STORE WITHIN ITEM WITHIN CLASS     PAGE   2

PRODUCT  ITEM    STORE      ITEM              QTY                  EXTENDED
CLASS    CODE    NBR        DESCRIPTION       SOLD      PRICE      AMOUNT

SAW      1977-P  102     RADIAL ARM SAW          1     529.99       529.99
SAW      1977-P  102     RADIAL ARM SAW          1     529.99       529.99
SAW      1977-P  102        STORE/ITEM TOTAL     2*                1,059.98*
SAW      1977-P             ITEM TOTAL           2**               1,059.98**
```

Figure 7C.3. An example of control-break page headings.

headings have been printed. This will provide complete group indication for the first detail line on each page.

Control-Break Page Headings

Figure 7C.3 shows the sales report; it contains various product classes. Suppose that each product class were assigned to a different buyer. To facilitate the report's distribution, it would be convenient to skip to a new page whenever the product class changed. Notice in the figure that after the hammer (HMR) product class has been totaled, there is still space on the page. However, a page skip was programmed to cause each product class to begin on a new page.

```
PROCEDURE DIVISION.
       .
       .
       .

200-process-record.

    PERFORM 800-READ-Input-record.
    MOVE each break-control-field from the Input-record-area
        TO its respective WS-CURRENT-BREAK-CONTROL field.
    IF FIRST-RECORD
        MOVE WS-CURRENT-BREAK-CONTROL TO WS-PREVIOUS-BREAK-CONTROL
        MOVE 'NO ' TO WS-FIRST-RECORD-SW.
    IF WS-CURRENT-major-BREAK-CONTROL
            IS NOT EQUAL TO WS-PREVIOUS-major-BREAK-CONTROL
        PERFORM 220-PRINT-minor-CONTROL-TOTAL-LINE
        PERFORM 230-PRINT-Inter-CONTROL-TOTAL-LINE
        PERFORM 240-PRINT-major-CONTROL-TOTAL-LINE
        PERFORM 870-PRINT-REPORT-HEADINGS
    ELSE IF CURRENT-Inter-BREAK-CONTROL
            IS NOT EQUAL TO WS-PREVIOUS-Inter-BREAK-CONTROL
        PERFORM 220-PRINT-minor-CONTROL-TOTAL-LINE
        PERFORM 230-PRINT-Inter-CONTROL-TOTAL-LINE
    ELSE IF CURRENT-minor-BREAK-CONTROL
            IS NOT EQUAL TO WS-PREVIOUS-minor-BREAK-CONTROL
        PERFORM 220-PRINT-minor-CONTROL-TOTAL-LINE
    ELSE
        NEXT SENTENCE.
    IF NOT END-OF-FILE
        PERFORM 210-PRINT-DETAIL-LINE.
```

(A)

       .
       .
       .

Figure 7C.4. Coding prototype: Control-break headings.

The coding prototype appears in Figure 7C.4. The control-break page heading can be accomplished by merely coding an unconditional PERFORM 870-PRINT-REPORT-HEADINGS at the proper control level. This is shown at Point A of the figure.

Page-Continuation Indication

There are two types of page-continuation indication: **continued-on indication** and **continued-from indication**. Figure 7C.5 shows an example of each. Although certain reports may contain both continued-on and continued-from indication, most listings contain only one or the other.

Continued-on Indication

Figure 7C.6 presents the coding prototype for page continued-on indication.

Definition of the continued control fields (Point A of Figure 7C.6)

The WS-CONTINUED-CONTROLS group item has been specified at point A of the prototype. One or more elementary data-items to define both the WS-PREVIOUS-CONTINUED-CONTROL and the WS-CURRENT-CONTINUED-CONTROL must be coded.

Definition of the continued-on line (Point B of Figure 7C.6)

If the continued-on indication is to be printed on a separate line, the continued-on line should be defined in WORKING-STORAGE. In the prototype, this has been done and the line has been named CO-CONTINUED-ON-LINE to describe its function. An alternate approach is to print the continued-on indication within the detail line, provided there is sufficient room.

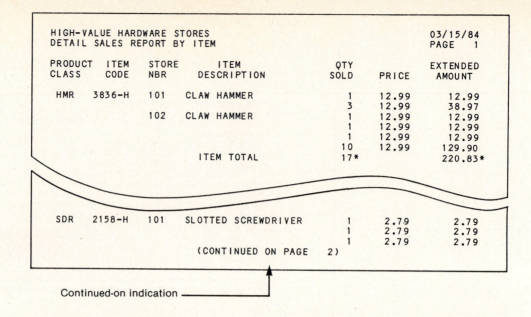

```
HIGH-VALUE HARDWARE STORES                               03/15/84
DETAIL SALES REPORT BY ITEM                              PAGE    1

PRODUCT   ITEM    STORE      ITEM                QTY            EXTENDED
CLASS     CODE    NBR        DESCRIPTION         SOLD   PRICE   AMOUNT

  HMR     3836-H  101    CLAW HAMMER              1     12.99    12.99
                                                 3     12.99    38.97
                  102    CLAW HAMMER              1     12.99    12.99
                                                 1     12.99    12.99
                                                 1     12.99    12.99
                                                10     12.99   129.90
                         ITEM TOTAL             17*             220.83*


  SDR     2158-H  101    SLOTTED SCREWDRIVER      1      2.79     2.79
                                                 1      2.79     2.79
                                                 1      2.79     2.79
                         (CONTINUED ON PAGE    2)
```

Continued-on indication

```
HIGH-VALUE HARDWARE STORES                               03/15/84
DETAIL SALES REPORT BY ITEM                              PAGE    2

PRODUCT   ITEM    STORE      ITEM                QTY            EXTENDED
CLASS     CODE    NBR        DESCRIPTION         SOLD   PRICE   AMOUNT

  SDR     2158-H  101    SLOTTED SCREWDRIVER  (CONTINUED FROM PAGE    1)
                                                 1      2.79     2.79
                                                 6      2.79    16.74
                  102    SLOTTED SCREWDRIVER      1      2.79     2.79
                                                 1      2.79     2.79
                         ITEM TOTAL             12*             33.48*

          2160-H  101    PHILLIPS SCREWDRIVER     2      2.99     5.98
                                                 1      2.99     2.99
                                                 1      2.99     2.99
                                                 2      2.99     5.98
                  102    PHILLIPS SCREWDRIVER     1      2.99     2.99
                                                 1      2.99     2.99
                         ITEM TOTAL              8*             23.92*

                         REPORT TOTAL                        2,058.09**
```

Continued-from indication

Figure 7C.5. Page-continued indication example.

Setting the continued control fields (Points C and D of Figure 7C.6)

After each input record that is to be printed has been read, each continued control field is moved from the input record area to the WS-CURRENT-CONTINUED-CONTROL field. This is shown at point C of the prototype. When the first record is read, as shown at point D, WS-PREVIOUS-CONTINUED-CONTROL is set to LOW-VALUES to ensure that a false continued-on indication will not be printed before the first page of the report.

Testing for the continued-on indication requirement (Point E of Figure 7C.6)

Whenever a new report page is required, the WS-CURRENT-CONTINUED-CONTROL is compared to WS-PREVIOUS-CONTINUED-CONTROL. If the control

```
                      DATA DIVISION.
                           •
                           •
                           •
                      WORKING-STORAGE SECTION.
                           •
                           •
                           •
    ┌───┐ ┌──────────────────────────────────────────────────────────────────────┐
    │ A │ │  01  WS-CONTINUED-CONTROLS.                                            │
    └───┘ │      05   WS-PREVIOUS-CONTINUED-CONTROL       PIC X(nn).               │
          │      05   WS-CURRENT-CONTINUED-CONTROL        PIC X(nn).               │
          └──────────────────────────────────────────────────────────────────────┘
                           •
                           •
                           •
    ┌───┐ ┌──────────────────────────────────────────────────────────────────────┐
    │ B │ │  01  CO-CONTINUED-ON-LINE.                                             │
    └───┘ │           •                                                            │
          │           •                                                            │
          │           •                                                            │
          │      05   CO-continued-on-indication          PIC X(nn).              │
          │      05   CO-continued-on-page-nbr            PIC ZZZ9.               │
          │           •                                                            │
          │           •                                                            │
          │           •                                                            │
          └──────────────────────────────────────────────────────────────────────┘
                           •
                           •
                           •
                      PROCEDURE DIVISION.
                           •
                           •
                           •
    ┌───┐ ┌──────────────────────────────────────────────────────────────────────┐
    │   │ │  200-process-record.                                                  │
    │   │ │                                                                        │
    │   │ │      PERFORM 800-READ-input-record.                                   │
    │   │ │      MOVE each break-control-field from the input-record-area         │
    │ C │ │           TO its respective WS-CURRENT-BREAK-CONTROL field.           │
    │   │ │      MOVE the continued-control-field from the input-record-area      │
    │   │ │           TO WS-CURRENT-CONTINUED-CONTROL.                            │
    │   │ │      IF FIRST-RECORD                                                   │
    │   │ │          MOVE each WS-CURRENT-BREAK-CONTROL field                      │
    │   │ │              TO its respective WS-PREVIOUS-BREAK-CONTROL field         │
    │ D │ │          MOVE LOW-VALUES TO WS-PREVIOUS-CONTINUED-CONTROL              │
    │   │ │          MOVE 'NO ' TO WS-FIRST-RECORD-SW.                            │
    │   │ │           •                                                            │
    │   │ │           •                                                            │
    │   │ │           •                                                            │
    └───┘ └──────────────────────────────────────────────────────────────────────┘

    ┌───┐ ┌──────────────────────────────────────────────────────────────────────┐
    │   │ │  210-PRINT-DETAIL-LINE.                                               │
    │   │ │                                                                        │
    │ E │ │      IF WS-LINES-USED IS NOT LESS THAN WS-LINES-PER-PAGE              │
    │   │ │          IF WS-CURRENT-CONTINUED-CONTROL                               │
    │   │ │                  IS EQUAL TO WS-PREVIOUS-CONTINUED-CONTROL            │
    │   │ │                  PERFORM 878-PRINT-CONTINUED-ON-LINE                  │
    │   │ │                  PERFORM 870-PRINT-REPORT-HEADINGS                    │
    │   │ │          ELSE                                                          │
    │   │ │                  PERFORM 870-PRINT-REPORT-HEADINGS                    │
    │   │ │      ELSE                                                              │
    │   │ │          NEXT SENTENCE.                                                │
    │   │ │      Do detail-line calculations [if any] and                         │
    │   │ │      Build remainder of DL-DETAIL-LINE.                                │
    │   │ │      MOVE DL-DETAIL-LINE TO REPORT-LINE.                               │
    │   │ │      PERFORM 890-WRITE-REPORT-LINE.                                    │
    │ F │ │      MOVE WS-CURRENT-CONTINUED-CONTROL                                 │
    │   │ │          TO WS-PREVIOUS-CONTINUED-CONTROL.                            │
    │   │ │      Set WS-LINE-SPACING for next detail-line.                         │
    │   │ │      Accumulate minor-control-total field(s).                         │
    └───┘ └──────────────────────────────────────────────────────────────────────┘
```

continued

Figure 7C.6. Coding prototype: Page continued-on indication.

⋮

```
  G    878-PRINT-CONTINUED-ON-LINE.

       (Blank the continued-on-line.)
       MOVE continued-on-indication to CO-continued-on-indication.
       ADD 1 WS-PAGE-COUNT GIVING CO-continued-on-page-nbr.
       Build remainder of CO-CONTINUED-ON-LINE [as applicable].
       MOVE CO-CONTINUED-ON-LINE TO REPORT-LINE.
       Set WS-LINE-SPACING for this continued-on-line.
       PERFORM 890-WRITE-REPORT-LINE.
```

⋮

Figure 7C.6.   (continued)

fields are equal, it means that the continued-on indication must be printed at the bottom of the current report page before report headings for the next page are printed. If the control fields are not equal, no continued-on indication is required. This logic is handled by the nested IF statement shown at the beginning of the 210-PRINT-DETAIL-LINE module.

Resetting the previous continued control fields (Point F of Figure 7C.6)

After each detail line has been printed, WS-CURRENT-CONTINUED-CONTROL should be moved to WS-PREVIOUS-CONTINUED-CONTROL.

Printing the continued-on line (Point G of Figure 7C.6)

This is a typical line-printing module. The continued-on line is formatted, the line-spacing indicator is set, and the line is written. Should printing of the continued-on page number be specified, it can be computed by incrementing the current WS-PAGE-COUNT by 1.

Continued-from Indication

The coding prototype for continued-from indication is shown in Figure 7C.7.

Definition of the continued-from line (Point A of Figure 7C.7)

If the continued-from indication is to be printed on a separate line, the continued-from line should be defined in WORKING-STORAGE. In the prototype, this has been done and the line has been named CO-CONTINUED-FROM-LINE to describe its function. An alternate approach is to print the continued-from indication within the detail line, provided there is sufficient room.

Setting the continued control fields (Points B and C of Figure 7C.7)

After each input record that is printed has been read, each continued control field is moved from the input record area to the WS-CURRENT-CONTINUED-CONTROL field. This is shown at point B of the prototype. When the first record is read, as shown at point C, WS-PREVIOUS-CONTINUED-CONTROL is set to LOW-VALUES to ensure that a false continued-from indication will not be printed on the first page of the report.

```
                DATA DIVISION.
                  •
                  •
                  •
                WORKING-STORAGE SECTION.
                  •
                  •
                  •
```

```
    01  WS-CONTINUED-CONTROLS.
        05  WS-PREVIOUS-CONTINUED-CONTROL     PIC X(nn).
        05  WS-CURRENT-CONTINUED-CONTROL      PIC X(nn).
```

```
                  •
                  •
                  •
```

(A)
```
    01  CF-CONTINUED-FROM-LINE.
          •
          •

        05  CF-continued-from-indication      PIC X(nn).
        05  CF-continued-from-page-nbr         PIC ZZZ9.
          •
          •
          •
```

```
                  •
                  •
                  •
                PROCEDURE DIVISION.
                  •
                  •
                  •
```

```
    200-process-record.

        PERFORM 800-READ-input-record.
        MOVE each break-control-field from the input-record-area
            TO its respective WS-CURRENT-BREAK-CONTROL field.
```
(B)
```
        MOVE the continued-control-field from the input-record-area
            TO WS-CURRENT-CONTINUED-CONTROL.
        IF FIRST-RECORD
            MOVE each WS-CURRENT-BREAK-CONTROL field
                TO its respective WS-PREVIOUS-BREAK-CONTROL field
```
(C)
```
            MOVE LOW-VALUES TO WS-PREVIOUS-CONTINUED-CONTROL
            MOVE 'NO ' TO WS-FIRST-RECORD-SW.
          •
          •
          •
```

(D)
```
    210-PRINT-DETAIL-LINE.

        IF WS-LINES-USED IS NOT LESS THAN WS-LINES-PER-PAGE
            IF WS-CURRENT-CONTINUED-CONTROL
                        IS EQUAL TO WS-PREVIOUS-CONTINUED-CONTROL
                    PERFORM 870-PRINT-REPORT-HEADINGS
                    PERFORM 872-PRINT-CONTINUED-FROM-LINE
            ELSE
                    PERFORM 870-PRINT-REPORT-HEADINGS
        ELSE
            NEXT SENTENCE.
        Do detail-line calculations [if any] and
        Build remainder of DL-DETAIL-LINE.
        MOVE DL-DETAIL-LINE TO REPORT-LINE.
        PERFORM 890-WRITE-REPORT-LINE.
```
(E)
```
        MOVE WS-CURRENT-CONTINUED-CONTROL
            TO WS-PREVIOUS-CONTINUED-CONTROL.
        Set WS-LINE-SPACING for next detail-line.
        Accumulate minor-control-total field(s).
```

Figure 7C.7. Coding prototype: Page continued-from indication.   *continued*

.
.
.

```
872-PRINT-CONTINUED-FROM-LINE.

     (Blank the continued-from-line.)
     MOVE continued-from-indication to CF-continued-from-indication.
     SUBTRACT 1 FROM WS-PAGE-COUNT
          GIVING CF-continued-from-page-nbr.
     Build remainder of CF-CONTINUED-FROM-LINE [as applicable].
     MOVE CF-CONTINUED-FROM-LINE TO REPORT-LINE.
     Set WS-LINE-SPACING for this continued-from-line.
     PERFORM 890-WRITE-REPORT-LINE.
     Set WS-LINE-SPACING for next detail-line. <--- [To space after
                                                     the continued-from
                                                     line and before the
                                              first detail-line on the page]
```

Figure 7C.7. (continued)

.
.
.

Testing for the continued-from indication requirement (Point D of Figure 7C.7)

Whenever a new report page is required, WS-CURRENT-CONTINUED-CON-TROL is compared to WS-PREVIOUS-CONTINUED-CONTROL. If the control fields are equal, it means that the continued-from indication must be printed immediately after the headings for the new page. If the control fields are not equal, no continued-from indication is required. This logic is handled by the nested IF statement shown at the beginning of the 210-PRINT-DETAIL-LINE module.

Resetting the previous continued control fields (Point E of Figure 7C.7)

After each detail line has been printed, WS-CURRENT-CONTINUED-CONTROL should be moved to WS-PREVIOUS-CONTINUED-CONTROL.

Printing the continued-from line (Point F of Figure 7C.6)

This is a typical line-printing module. The continued-on line is formatted, the line-spacing indicator is set, and the line is written. Should printing of the continued-from page number be specified, it can be computed by decrementing the current WS-PAGE-COUNT by 1.

After the continued-from line has been printed, the line-spacing indicator should be reset for the next detail line.

Control-Break Group Headings

Control-break group headings, or simply **control headings,** are an alternative to group indication. They are frequently used when report specifications call for printing fields that apply to a group of records but either (1) sufficient room is not available on the detail line to print them, or (2) such detail printing is not desired. Control headings are printed before the first detail or summary line for a control group and, when a control group spans more than one page, as the first body line of each new page. For the latter situation, continued-from indication is usually also provided within the control heading to clarify for the reader that it is being repeated.

Figure 7C.8 shows control-break group headings for the hardware sales report. Notice that whenever the product class changes, a description of the

```
HIGH-VALUE HARDWARE STORES                         03/15/84
DETAIL SALES REPORT BY ITEM                        PAGE   1

       ITEM    STORE      ITEM               QTY             EXTENDED
       CODE    NBR     DESCRIPTION           SOLD    PRICE    AMOUNT

   ** HAMMERS AND ACCESSORIES**

      3836-H   101   CLAW HAMMER              1     12.99      12.99
      3836-H   101   CLAW HAMMER              3     12.99      38.97
      3836-H   102   CLAW HAMMER              1     12.99      12.99
      3836-H   102   CLAW HAMMER              1     12.99      12.99
      3836-H   102   CLAW HAMMER              1     12.99      12.99
      3836-H   102   CLAW HAMMER             10     12.99     129.90
      3836-H            ITEM TOTAL           17*               220.83*

      3847-H   101   BALL PEEN HAMMER         1     13.99      13.99
      3847-H   101   BALL PEEN HAMMER         2     13.99      27.98
      3847-H   102   BALL PEEN HAMMER         1     13.99      13.99
      3847-H            ITEM TOTAL            4*                55.96*

      3852-H   102   TACK HAMMER              1      4.99       4.99
      3852-H            ITEM TOTAL            1*                 4.99*

      3861-P   101   POWER HAMMER             1     29.99      29.99
      3861-P            ITEM TOTAL            1*                29.99*

   ** SAWS, POWER AND HAND **

      1977-P   102   RADIAL ARM SAW           1    529.99     529.99
      1977-P   102   RADIAL ARM SAW           1    529.99     529.99
      1977-P            ITEM TOTAL            2*             1,059.98

      2425-P   101   TABLE SAW                1    569.99     569.99
      2425-P            ITEM TOTAL            1*               569.99*

      3619-H   102   WOOD SAW                 1     18.99      18.99
      3619-H            ITEM TOTAL            1*                18.99*

      3715-H   101   HACK SAW                 1      9.99       9.99
      3715-H   101   HACK SAW                 1      9.99       9.99
      3715-H   101   HACK SAW                 1      9.99       9.99
      3715-H   102   HACK SAW                 1      9.99       9.99
      3715-H            ITEM TOTAL            4*                39.96*

   ** SCREWDRIVERS AND ACCESSORIES **

      2158-H   101   SLOTTED SCREWDRIVER      1      2.79       2.79
      2158-H   101   SLOTTED SCREWDRIVER      1      2.79       2.79
      2158-H   101   SLOTTED SCREWDRIVER      1      2.79       2.79
```

```
HIGH-VALUE HARDWARE STORES                         03/15/84
DETAIL SALES REPORT BY ITEM                        PAGE   2

   PRODUCT  ITEM    STORE      ITEM           QTY             EXTENDED
   CLASS    CODE    NBR     DESCRIPTION       SOLD    PRICE    AMOUNT

   ** SCREWDRIVERS AND ACCESSORIES **   (CONTINUED)

      2158-H   101   SLOTTED SCREWDRIVER      1      2.79       2.79
      2158-H   101   SLOTTED SCREWDRIVER      6      2.79      16.74
      2158-H   102   SLOTTED SCREWDRIVER      1      2.79       2.79
      2158-H   102   SLOTTED SCREWDRIVER      1      2.79       2.79
      2158-H            ITEM TOTAL           12*                33.48*

      2160-H   101   PHILLIPS SCREWDRIVER     2      2.99       5.98
      2160-H   101   PHILLIPS SCREWDRIVER     1      2.99       2.99
      2160-H   101   PHILLIPS SCREWDRIVER     1      2.99       2.99
      2160-H   101   PHILLIPS SCREWDRIVER     2      2.99       5.98
      2160-H   102   PHILLIPS SCREWDRIVER     1      2.99       2.99
      2160-H   102   PHILLIPS SCREWDRIVER     1      2.99       2.99
      2160-H            ITEM TOTAL            8*                23.92*

                     REPORT TOTAL                          2,058.09**
```

Control-break group headings

Figure 7C.8. An example of control-break group headings.

product class is printed. In the example, the product class code (HMR for HAMMERS AND ACCESSORIES; SAW for SAWS; POWER AND HAND; and so forth) is not printed but could be if the programming specifications call for it.

The coding prototype for control-break group headings is shown in Figure 7C.9.

Definition of the group heading control fields (Point A of Figure 7C.9)

The WS-GROUP-HEADING-CONTROLS item is established in WORKING-STORAGE.

Definition of the control group heading line (Point B of Figure 7C.9)

A record description for the control-group heading line is defined in WORKING-STORAGE. It has been named CH-CONTROL-GROUP-HEADING-LINE.

Setting the group heading control fields (Points C and D of Figure 7C.9)

After each record is read, each group heading control field is moved from the input record area to its respective WS-CURRENT-GROUP-HDG-CONTROL field. After the first record has been read, the WS-PREVIOUS-GROUP-HDG-CONTROL field is set to LOW-VALUES to force a control-break group heading before the first detail line is printed.

Testing for the control group heading line requirement (Points E and F of Figure 7C.9)

The test for a new report page is made with the nested IF statement at point E of the coding prototype. If the current report page is full and WS-CURRENT-GROUP-HDG-CONTROL IS EQUAL TO WS-PREVIOUS-GROUP-HDG-CONTROL, the report heading and the control group heading modules are both performed. If the current report page is full and WS-CURRENT-GROUP-HDG-CONTROL is not equal to WS-PREVIOUS-GROUP-HDG-CONTROL, then only the report heading module is performed (the control group heading requirement will be picked up during the next test at point F). If the current report page is not full, no action is taken by this IF statement. Thus, the function of this statement is to (1) test for and cause report page headings to be printed when the current page is full, and (2) test for a continued control group heading and to print the "continued-from" control heading.

The test for a new control heading is made with the nested IF statement at point F of the coding prototype. If WS-CURRENT-GROUP-HDG-CONTROL is not equal to WS-PREVIOUS-GROUP-HDG-CONTROL, it means that a new control heading line is required. In the second condition test of the IF statement, the initials "nh" and "nd" represent the number of lines (counting preliminary blank lines) consumed by the control heading and the number of lines consumed up to and including the first (or second) detail line of the control group. The reason for this second test is to guard against printing a lone control heading on the bottom of a report page.

For example, suppose that (1) the WS-LINES-PER-PAGE span value is 60, (2) the WS-LINES-USED count is presently 57, (3) the control-heading line is triple-spaced from the previous control total, and (4) the detail line is double-spaced from the control-heading line. The arithmetic expression of the sign test is as follows (the values are shown in brackets): IF (WS-LINES-USED [57] + nh [3] + nd [2]) − (WS-LINES-PER-PAGE − 1) IS NOT NEGATIVE. The result [(57 + 3 + 2) − (60 − 1) = +1] is not negative. This means that so much of the current page has been used that the control heading plus one detail line will not fit within the page span. Hence, the report page-heading module is performed before the control group-heading routine so that the forms will be advanced to a new page.

```
                    DATA DIVISION.
                        .
                        .
                        .
                    WORKING-STORAGE SECTION.
                        .
                        .
                        .
```

```
      ┌──────────────────────────────────────────────────────────────────────┐
 (A)  │   01   WS-GROUP-HEADING-CONTROLS.                                       │
      │        05   WS-PREVIOUS-GROUP-HDG-CONTROL      PIC X(nn).               │
      │        05   WS-CURRENT-GROUP-HDG-CONTROL       PIC X(nn).               │
      └──────────────────────────────────────────────────────────────────────┘
                        .
                        .
                        .
      ┌──────────────────────────────────────────────────────────────────────┐
 (B)  │   01   CH-CONTROL-GROUP-HEADING-LINE.                                   │
      └──────────────────────────────────────────────────────────────────────┘
                        .
                        .
                        .
                    PROCEDURE DIVISION.
                        .
                        .
                        .
```

```
      ┌──────────────────────────────────────────────────────────────────────┐
      │   200-process-record.                                                  │
      │                                                                        │
      │       PERFORM 800-READ-input-record.                                   │
      │       MOVE each break-control-field from the input-record-area         │
      │            TO its respective WS-CURRENT-BREAK-CONTROL field.           │
      │       MOVE each group-heading-control-field                            │
 (C)  │               from the input-record-area                              │
      │            TO WS-CURRENT-GROUP-HDG-CONTROL.                            │
      │       IF FIRST-RECORD                                                   │
      │           MOVE WS-CURRENT-BREAK-CONTROL TO WS-PREVIOUS-BREAK-CONTROL    │
 (D)  │           MOVE LOW-VALUES TO WS-PREVIOUS-GROUP-HDG-CONTROL             │
      │           MOVE 'NO ' TO WS-FIRST-RECORD-SW.                            │
      │       IF WS-CURRENT-BREAK-CONTROL                                       │
      │               IS NOT EQUAL TO WS-PREVIOUS-BREAK-CONTROL                 │
      │           PERFORM 220-PRINT-CONTROL-TOTAL-LINE.                         │
      │       IF NOT END-OF-FILE                                                │
      │           PERFORM 210-PRINT-DETAIL-LINE.                                │
      └──────────────────────────────────────────────────────────────────────┘
```

```
      ┌──────────────────────────────────────────────────────────────────────┐
      │   210-PRINT-DETAIL-LINE.                                               │
      │                                                                        │
      │       IF WS-LINES-USED IS NOT LESS THAN WS-LINES-PER-PAGE              │
 (E)  │           IF WS-CURRENT-GROUP-HDG-CONTROL                              │
      │                   IS EQUAL TO WS-PREVIOUS-GROUP-HDG-CONTROL            │
      │               PERFORM 870-PRINT-REPORT-HEADINGS                        │
      │               PERFORM 876-PRINT-CONTROL-GROUP-HDGS                     │
      │           ELSE                                                          │
      │               PERFORM 870-PRINT-REPORT-HEADINGS                        │
      │       ELSE                                                              │
      │           NEXT SENTENCE.                                                │
 (F)  │       IF WS-CURRENT-GROUP-HDG-CONTROL                                  │
      │               IS NOT EQUAL TO WS-PREVIOUS-GROUP-HDG-CONTROL            │
      │           IF (WS-LINES-USED + nh + nd) - (WS-LINES-PER-PAGE - 1)        │
      │                   IS NOT NEGATIVE                                       │
      │               PERFORM 870-PRINT-REPORT-HEADINGS                        │
      │               PERFORM 876-PRINT-CONTROL-GROUP-HDGS                     │
      │           ELSE                                                          │
      │               PERFORM 876-PRINT-CONTROL-GROUP-HDGS                     │
      │       ELSE                                                              │
      │           NEXT SENTENCE.                                                │
      │                        .                                               │
      │                        .                                               │
      └──────────────────────────────────────────────────────────────────────┘
                        .
                        .
                        .
```

Figure 7C.9.   Coding protoype: Control-break group headings.   *continued*

```
876-PRINT-CONTROL-GROUP-HDGS.

    (Blank the control-group-heading-line.)
    Build CH-CONTROL-GROUP-HEADING-LINE
         [from WS-CURRENT-GROUP-HDG-CONTROL fields].
    IF WS-CURRENT-GROUP-HDG-CONTROL
       IS EQUAL TO WS-PREVIOUS-GROUP-HDG-CONTROL
           MOVE continued-from-indication        <-[If control-group
               TO CH-continued-from-indication  <  heading-line
           SUBTRACT 1 FROM WS-PAGE-COUNT          <  contains
               GIVING CH-continued-from-page-nbr.<continued-from
                                                      indication]
    MOVE CH-CONTROL-GROUP-HEADING-LINE TO REPORT-LINE.
    Set WS-LINE-SPACING for this control-group-heading-line.
    PERFORM 890-WRITE-REPORT-LINE.
    MOVE SPACES TO CH-continued-from-indication.<-[If control-group
    MOVE ZEROS TO CH-continued-from-page-nbr.     <  heading-line
                                                      contains
                                                      continued-from
                                                      indication]

    MOVE WS-CURRENT-GROUP-HDG-CONTROL
        TO WS-PREVIOUS-GROUP-HDG-CONTROL.

    Set WS-LINE-SPACING for next detail-line. <--- [To set spacing
                                                       for the first
                                                       detail-line
                                                of each control group]
```

Figure 7C.9. (continued)

Should the result of the expression be zero or negative, it means that the new control group can be started on the present page; hence, only the control group-heading module is performed. Thus, the function of this IF statement is to (1) test for and cause control headings to be printed when a new control group heading is required, and (2) test for proximity to end-of-page, so that a new control heading will not be printed unless it and at least one detail line can be printed within the line-span value.

Printing the control group heading lines (Point G of Figure 7C.9)

This module handles the actual printing of the control-break group-heading lines. The WS-CURRENT-GROUP-HDG-CONTROL fields contain the data that is applicable to the control heading line to be printed. If, as is usually the case, continued-from indication is to be shown within the control heading, a test for control-group continuation is made as shown in the IF statement of this module.

 After the control heading line is built, the line-spacing indicator is set, and the line is printed. If continued-from indication is being displayed, such fields should be blanked after printing so that they will not be erroneously printed on the first control heading line for a new group. Then, the line-spacing indicator is set for the next detail line.

Page Footings

Page footings are printed at the bottom of each report page. They typically contain descriptive information in regard to the report page, accumulative totals for certain columns printed on the page, or a combination of the two. A situation in which page totals are appropriate is when manual changes must be made to detail or summary lines of a report. A column total of the amounts on each individual report page can make it easier for clerks to recompute correct report totals after changes have been made to detail amounts. Figure 7C.10 provides

```
HIGH-VALUE HARDWARE STORES                              03/15/84
DETAIL SALES REPORT                                     PAGE    1

PRODUCT   ITEM    STORE        ITEM             QTY                 EXTENDED
CLASS     CODE    NBR       DESCRIPTION         SOLD     PRICE       AMOUNT

  HMR    3836-H   101    CLAW HAMMER              1      12.99        12.99
  HMR    3836-H   101    CLAW HAMMER              3      12.99        38.97
  HMR    3836-H   102    CLAW HAMMER              1      12.99        12.99
  HMR    3836-H   102    CLAW HAMMER              1      12.99        12.99
  HMR    3836-H   102    CLAW HAMMER              1      12.99        12.99
  HMR    3836-H   102    CLAW HAMMER             10      12.99       129.90
  HMR    3847-H   101    BALL PEEN HAMMER         1      13.99        13.99
  HMR    3847-H   101    BALL PEEN HAMMER         2      13.99        27.98
  HMR    3847-H   102    BALL PEEN HAMMER         1      13.99        13.99
  HMR    3852-H   102    TACK HAMMER              1       4.99         4.99
  HMR    3861-P   101    POWER HAMMER             1      29.99        29.99
  SAW    1977-P   102    RADIAL ARM SAW           1     529.99       529.99
  SAW    1977-P   102    RADIAL ARM SAW           1     529.99       529.99
  SAW    2425-P   101    TABLE SAW                1     569.99       569.99
  SAW    3619-H   102    WOOD SAW                 1      18.99        18.99
  SAW    3715-H   101    HACK SAW                 1       9.99         9.99
  SAW    3715-H   101    HACK SAW                 1       9.99         9.99
  SAW    3715-H   101    HACK SAW                 1       9.99         9.99
  SAW    3715-H   102    HACK SAW                 1       9.99         9.99
  SDR    2158-H   101    SLOTTED SCREWDRIVER      1       2.79         2.79
  SDR    2158-H   101    SLOTTED SCREWDRIVER      1       2.79         2.79
  SDR    2158-H   101    SLOTTED SCREWDRIVER      1       2.79         2.79

                         PAGE TOTAL                               2,009.06*
```

```
HIGH-VALUE HARDWARE STORES                              03/15/84
DETAIL SALES REPORT                                     PAGE    2

PRODUCT   ITEM    STORE        ITEM             QTY                 EXTENDED
CLASS     CODE    NBR       DESCRIPTION         SOLD     PRICE       AMOUNT

  SDR    2158-H   101    SLOTTED SCREWDRIVER      1       2.79         2.79
  SDR    2158-H   101    SLOTTED SCREWDRIVER      6       2.79        16.74
  SDR    2158-H   102    SLOTTED SCREWDRIVER      1       2.79         2.79
  SDR    2158-H   102    SLOTTED SCREWDRIVER      1       2.79         2.79
  SDR    2160-H   101    PHILLIPS SCREWDRIVER     2       2.99         5.98
  SDR    2160-H   101    PHILLIPS SCREWDRIVER     1       2.99         2.99
  SDR    2160-H   101    PHILLIPS SCREWDRIVER     1       2.99         2.99
  SDR    2160-H   101    PHILLIPS SCREWDRIVER     2       2.99         5.98
  SDR    2160-H   102    PHILLIPS SCREWDRIVER     1       2.99         2.99
  SDR    2160-H   102    PHILLIPS SCREWDRIVER     1       2.99         2.99

                         PAGE TOTAL                                  49.03*

                         REPORT TOTAL                            2,058.09**
```

Page footings

Figure 7C.10. Page-footings example.

an example of a report with page footings. The coding prototype for page footings with page totals is shown in Figure 7C.11.

Definition of the page-total accumulators (Point A of Figure 7C.11)

The page-total accumulators are specified within the WS-PAGE-TOTAL-ACCUMULATORS group item. One accumulator is required for each total on the page-footing line.

```
                    DATA DIVISION.
                        .
                        .
                        .

                    WORKING-STORAGE SECTION.
                        .
                        .
                        .
```

```
    ╭───╮  ┌─────────────────────────────────────────────────────────────────────────────┐
    │ A │  │  01   WS-PAGE-TOTAL-ACCUMULATORS.                                              │
    ╰───╯  │       05  page-total-accumulator              PIC 9(n)          COMP-3.        │
           │                 [additional page total fields as required]                    │
           └─────────────────────────────────────────────────────────────────────────────┘
```

```
                        .
                        .
                        .
```

```
    ╭───╮  ┌─────────────────────────────────────────────────────────────────────────────┐
    │ B │  │  01   PF-PAGE-FOOTING-LINE.                                                    │
    ╰───╯  └─────────────────────────────────────────────────────────────────────────────┘
```

```
                        .
                        .
                        .

                    PROCEDURE DIVISION.
                        .
                        .
                        .
```

```
    ╭───╮  ┌─────────────────────────────────────────────────────────────────────────────┐
    │   │  │  000-mainline.                                                                │
    │   │  │              .                                                                │
    │   │  │              .                                                                │
    │   │  │                                                                               │
    │   │  │      PERFORM 200-process-record                                               │
    │ C │  │          UNTIL END-OF-FILE.                                                    │
    │   │  │      PERFORM 878-PRINT-PAGE-FOOTING-LINE.                                      │
    │   │  │      PERFORM 700-PRINT-REPORT-TOTALS.                                          │
    │   │  │      CLOSE files.                                                             │
    ╰───╯  │      STOP RUN.                                                                │
           └─────────────────────────────────────────────────────────────────────────────┘
```

```
                        .
                        .
                        .
```

```
    ╭───╮  ┌─────────────────────────────────────────────────────────────────────────────┐
    │   │  │  200-process-record.                                                          │
    │ D │  │                                                                               │
    │   │  │      IF WS-LINES-USED IS NOT LESS THAN WS-LINES-PER-PAGE                       │
    │   │  │          IF WS-PAGE-COUNT IS NOT EQUAL TO ZERO                                 │
    │   │  │              PERFORM 878-PRINT-PAGE-FOOTING-LINE                               │
    │   │  │              PERFORM 870-PRINT-REPORT-HEADINGS                                 │
    │   │  │          ELSE                                                                 │
    │   │  │              PERFORM 870-PRINT-REPORT-HEADINGS                                 │
    │   │  │      ELSE                                                                     │
    │   │  │          NEXT SENTENCE.                                                        │
    │   │  │              .                                                                │
    │   │  │              .                                                                │
    │   │  │              .                                                                │
    ╭───╮  │                                                                               │
    │ E │  │      Accumulate each WS-PAGE-TOTAL-ACCUMULATORS field.                         │
    ╰───╯  └─────────────────────────────────────────────────────────────────────────────┘
```

```
                        .
                        .
                        .
```

```
    ╭───╮  ┌─────────────────────────────────────────────────────────────────────────────┐
    │ F │  │  878-PRINT-PAGE-FOOTING-LINE.                                                  │
    ╰───╯  │                                                                               │
           │      (Blank the page-footing-line.)                                           │
           │      Build PF-PAGE-FOOTING-LINE.                                              │
           │      MOVE PF-PAGE-FOOTING-LINE TO REPORT-LINE.                                 │
           │      Set WS-LINE-SPACING for this page-footing-line.                           │
           │      PERFORM 890-WRITE-REPORT-LINE.                                            │
           │      MOVE ZEROS to each page-total-accumulator field.                          │
           └─────────────────────────────────────────────────────────────────────────────┘
```

```
                        .
                        .
                        .
```

Figure 7C.11. Coding prototype: Page footings.

Definition of the page-footing line (Point B of Figure 7C.11)

The page-footing line is established in WORKING-STORAGE and has been named PF-PAGE-FOOTING-LINE.

Triggering the page-footing line for the last report page (Point C of Figure 7C.11)

In the mainline module, after end-of-file has been reached, the 878-PRINT-PAGE-FOOTING-LINE module must be performed to trigger the printing of a page-footing line on the last page of the report.

Triggering the page-footing line for all other report pages (Point D of Figure 7C.11)

The IF statement shown within the 200-PROCESS-RECORD module tests for the need to print page headings and footings. If a page heading is required and WS-PAGE-COUNT IS NOT EQUAL TO ZERO, it means that a page-footing line must be printed on the current page and a page heading must be printed on the next page. Hence, both the 878-PRINT-PAGE-FOOTING-LINE and 870-PRINT-REPORT-HEADINGS lines are performed.

However, no page footings should be printed when the page heading for the first page is printed. At this time the WS-PAGE-COUNT field will be equal to zero. Thus, only the 870-PRINT-REPORT-HEADINGS module is performed for the first report page.

Accumulating the page totals (Point E of Figure 7C.11)

In the record-processing module, after the detail operations have been completed for each line, the input fields that are reflected in the page totals are added to the page-total accumulators.

Printing the page-footing line (Point F of Figure 7C.11)

The 878-PRINT-PAGE-FOOTING-LINE handles the printing of each page-footing line. After the line is built in WORKING-STORAGE, it is moved to the output print area, the line-spacing indicator is set, and the 890-WRITE-REPORT-LINE module is performed. Once the line has been printed, each page-total accumulator must be reset to zero in preparation for totals of the new page.

Detail Data in Page Headings

Instead of printing control heading lines, the control heading data is sometimes printed in the page headings. This approach is usually used when portions of a report are distributed to various recipients. For example, suppose that seven stores should receive the hardware sales report, and the appropriate sales data for each store is to be forwarded to each store manager. To simplify distribution of the report, the programming specifications should call for a page break whenever lines for a different store are to be printed. With such indication processing, it would be appropriate to put the store number, store name, and so forth in the page headings. Figure 7C.12 shows the sales report with the store number in the page headings. (Recognize that, for this particular report, the detail record sequence has been changed so that store number is now the major field.)

It would not be uncommon to have a report that had both control data in the page headings and control headings. In such a case, more significant major control fields would be reflected in the page headings; less significant minor control fields would be represented in the WS-GROUP-HEADING-CONTROL fields.

Figure 7C.13 shows the coding prototype for a report with detail data in the page headings. Observe, at point A of the figure, that the WS-CURRENT-BREAK-

```
┌─────────────────────────────────────────────────────────────────┐
│                                                                   │
│   HIGH-VALUE HARDWARE STORES                        03/15/84      │
│   DETAIL SALES REPORT                               PAGE    1     │
│                         ** STORE 101 **  }◄──────────────────────┐│
│                                                                  ││
│   PRODUCT   ITEM        ITEM          QTY              EXTENDED   ││
│   CLASS   . CODE    DESCRIPTION       SOLD    PRICE     AMOUNT    ││
│                                                                  ││
│     HMR    3836-H   CLAW HAMMER         1      12.99     12.99    ││
│     HMR    3836-H   CLAW HAMMER         3      12.99     38.97    ││
│     HMR    3847-H   BALL PEEN HAMMER    1      13.99     13.99    ││
│     HMR    3847-H   BALL PEEN HAMMER    2      13.99     27.98    ││
│     HMR    3861-P   POWER HAMMER        1      29.99     29.99    ││
│     SAW    2425-P   TABLE SAW           1     569.99    569.99    ││
│     SAW    3715-H   HACK SAW            1       9.99      9.99    ││
│     SAW    3715-H   HACK SAW            1       9.99      9.99    ││
│     SAW    3715-H   HACK SAW            1       9.99      9.99    ││
│     SDR    2158-H   SLOTTED SCREWDRIVER 1       2.79      2.79    ││
│     SDR    2158-H   SLOTTED SCREWDRIVER 1       2.79      2.79    ││
│     SDR    2158-H   SLOTTED SCREWDRIVER 1       2.79      2.79    ││
│     SDR    2158-H   SLOTTED SCREWDRIVER 1       2.79      2.79    ││
│     SDR    2158-H   SLOTTED SCREWDRIVER 6       2.79     16.74    ││
│     SDR    2160-H   PHILLIPS SCREWDRIVER 2      2.99      5.98    ││
│     SDR    2160-H   PHILLIPS SCREWDRIVER 1      2.99      2.99    ││
│     SDR    2160-H   PHILLIPS SCREWDRIVER 1      2.99      2.99    ││
│     SDR    2160-H   PHILLIPS SCREWDRIVER 2      2.99      5.98    ││
│                                                                  ││
│             STORE TOTAL                                769.72*   ││
│                                                                  ││
└──────────────────────────────────────────────────────────────┐  ││
                                                                 │  ││
┌──────────────────────────────────────────────────────────────┼──┼┘
│                                                                │  │
│   HIGH-VALUE HARDWARE STORES                        03/15/84   │  │
│   DETAIL SALES REPORT                               PAGE    2   │  │
│                         ** STORE 102 **  }◄────────────────────┘  │
│                                                                   │
│   PRODUCT   ITEM        ITEM          QTY              EXTENDED    │
│   CLASS     CODE    DESCRIPTION       SOLD    PRICE     AMOUNT     │
│                                                                   │
│     HMR    3836-H   CLAW HAMMER         1      12.99     12.99     │
│     HMR    3836-H   CLAW HAMMER         1      12.99     12.99     │
│     HMR    3836-H   CLAW HAMMER         1      12.99     12.99     │
│     HMR    3836-H   CLAW HAMMER        10      12.99    129.90     │
│     HMR    3847-H   BALL PEEN HAMMER    1      13.99     13.99     │
│     HMR    3852-H   TACK HAMMER         1       4.99      4.99     │
│     SAW    1977-P   RADIAL ARM SAW      1     529.99    529.99     │
│     SAW    1977-P   RADIAL ARM SAW      1     529.99    529.99     │
│     SAW    3619-H   WOOD SAW            1      18.99     18.99     │
│     SAW    3715-H   HACK SAW            1       9.99      9.99     │
│     SDR    2158-H   SLOTTED SCREWDRIVER 1       2.79      2.79     │
│     SDR    2158-H   SLOTTED SCREWDRIVER 1       2.79      2.79     │
│     SDR    2160-H   PHILLIPS SCREWDRIVER 1      2.99      2.99     │
│     SDR    2160-H   PHILLIPS SCREWDRIVER 1      2.99      2.99     │
│                                                                   │
│             STORE TOTAL                               1288.37*    │
│                                                                   │
└───────────────────────────────────────────────────────────────┘
```

Data from
detail record
in
page heading

Figure 7C.12. Detail data in page-headings example.

CONTROL fields are simply moved to the appropriate heading line fields immediately before the headings are printed.

Period-Ending Date Indication

An example of **period-ending date indication** is shown in Figure 7C.14. Dedicated date records are typically used to provide the period-ending date. The date record can either be in a separate file or the first record of the input data file.

When a date record is required within a program, it is very important to ensure that it is actually present. For example, say that the date record was specified as the first record of the input data file. Suppose that, by oversight or

```
PROCEDURE DIVISION.
            .
            .
            .
```

```
      870-PRINT-REPORT-HEADINGS.

          ADD 1 TO WS-PAGE-COUNT.
          MOVE WS-PAGE-COUNT TO Hn-page-number.
          Obtain data from WS-CURRENT-BREAK-CONTROL
              and move to appropriate heading-line.
          MOVE H1-HEADING-LINE TO REPORT-LINE.
          PERFORM 880-WRITE-REPORT-TOP-LINE.
               .
               .
               .
```
(A)

```
          .
          .
          .
```

Figure 7C.13. Coding prototype: Detail data in page headings.

```
HIGH-VALUE HARDWARE STORES          PERIOD ENDING DATE: 03/15/84
DETAIL SALES REPORT                          RUN DATE: 03/16/84

PRODUCT   ITEM    STORE      ITEM          QTY              EXTENDED
CLASS     CODE    NBR    DESCRIPTION       SOLD    PRICE     AMOUNT

  HMR    3836-H    101   CLAW HAMMER         1     12.99      12.99
  HMR    3836-H    101   CLAW HAMMER         3     12.99      38.97
  HMR    3836-H    102   CLAW HAMMER         1     12.99      12.99
  HMR    3836-H    102   CLAW HAMMER         1     12.99      12.99
  HMR    3836-H    102   CLAW HAMMER         1     12.99      12.99
  HMR    3836-H    102   CLAW HAMMER        10     12.99     129.90
  HMR    3847-H    101   BALL PEEN HAMMER    1     13.99      13.99
```

Figure 7C.14. Period-ending date indication example.

error, the date record were omitted for a particular program run. If the program did not provide for such record checking, the first detail record would be processed as a date record. This would, of course, cause serious processing errors.

Figure 7C.15 shows the coding prototype for handling period-ending date indication. Variations are shown depending upon whether the date record is in the input data file or in a separate file.

Provision for abnormal program termination (Point A of Figure 7C.15)

Because the period-ending date record is required at the start of the program run so that it can be printed on each report page, it is common to abort the pro-

```
DATA DIVISION.
    .
    .
    .
WORKING-STORAGE SECTION.
    .
    .
    .
01  WS-SWITCHES.
        .
        .
        .
    05   WS-PROGRAM-ABEND-SW          PIC X(3).
         88   PROGRAM-ABEND                        VALUE 'YES'.
    .
    .
    .
01  Input-record-description.
01  DR-DATE-RECORD REDEFINES Input-record-description.
            [REDEFINES clause not applicable if the date record
                          is the only record in the input file]

    05   DR-RECORD-CODE               PIC X(n).
         88   DATE-RECORD                          VALUE 'xx'.
    05   DR-DATE                      PIC X(n).
         .
         .
         .
    .
    .
    .
01  Hn-HEADING-LINE-n.
        .
        .
        .
    05   Hn-DATE                      PIC 99/99/99.
        .
        .
        .
    .
    .
    .
01  ER-ERROR-LINE.
    .
    .
    .
PROCEDURE DIVISION.
    .
    .
    .
000-mainline.

    OPEN files.
    PERFORM 100-INITIALIZE-VARIABLE-FIELDS.
    PERFORM 120-PROCESS-DATE-RECORD.
    PERFORM 800-READ-input-record.      [If priming-read being used]
    PERFORM 200-process-record
         UNTIL END-OF-TRANS-FILE.
    CLOSE files.
    STOP RUN.
```

Ⓐ Ⓑ Ⓒ Ⓓ Ⓔ

Figure 7C.15. Coding prototype: Period-ending date indication.

．
．
．

                                 120-PROCESS-DATE-RECORD module if the date record
                                          is the first record in the input file;
                                               data records follow in the same file

```
F    120-PROCESS-DATE-RECORD.

         PERFORM 800-READ-input-record.
         (Blank the error-line.)
         IF END-OF-TRANS-FILE
             set date-record-missing error-message
             MOVE 'YES' TO WS-PROGRAM-ABEND-SW.
         IF NOT DATE-RECORD
             set date-record-missing error-message
             MOVE 'YES' TO WS-PROGRAM-ABEND-SW.
         IF date is not valid
             set invalid-date error-message
             MOVE 'YES' TO WS-PROGRAM-ABEND-SW.
         IF NOT PROGRAM-ABEND
             MOVE date from input-date-record-area TO Hn-DATE.
         IF PROGRAM-ABEND
             PERFORM 870-PRINT-REPORT-HEADINGS
             MOVE EL-ERROR-LINE TO REPORT-LINE
             PERFORM 890-WRITE-REPORT-LINE
             MOVE 'YES' TO WS-END-OF-TRANS-FILE-SW.
```

                                 120-PROCESS-DATE-RECORD module if the date record
                                          is the only record in the input file

```
G    120-PROCESS-DATE-RECORD.

         PERFORM 805-READ-date-record.
         (Blank the error-line.)
         IF END-OF-DATE-FILE
             set date-record-missing error-message
             MOVE 'YES' TO WS-PROGRAM-ABEND-SW.
         IF NOT DATE-RECORD
             set date-record-missing error-message
             MOVE 'YES' TO WS-PROGRAM-ABEND-SW.
         IF date is not valid
             set invalid-date error-message
             MOVE 'YES' TO WS-PROGRAM-ABEND-SW.
         IF NOT PROGRAM-ABEND
             MOVE date from date-record-area TO Hn-DATE
             PERFORM 805-READ-date-record.
         IF NOT END-OF-DATE-FILE
             set too-many-date-records error-message
             MOVE 'YES' TO WS-PROGRAM-ABEND-SW.
         IF PROGRAM-ABEND
             PERFORM 870-PRINT-REPORT-HEADINGS
             MOVE EL-ERROR-LINE TO REPORT-LINE
             PERFORM 890-WRITE-REPORT-LINE
             MOVE 'YES' TO WS-END-OF-TRANS-FILE-SW.
```

Figure 7C.15.   (continued)

gram run if the date record is missing. For such handling, an abnormal program
termination switch, such as WS-PROGRAM-ABEND-SW, is specified.

Definition of the date record (Point B of Figure 7C.15)

The date record is defined in WORKING-STORAGE. If the date record is the first
record of the input data file, it can be specified with a REDEFINES clause as
shown in the prototype. The redefinition simplifies processing and conserves
storage.

On the other hand, if the date record is in a separate file, specification of
the REDEFINES clause is not applicable to the DR-DATE-RECORD description.

Definition of the date field in a heading line (Point C of Figure 7C.15)

A field that is specified with a date editing picture character-string is specified in the appropriate heading-line record description.

Definition of an error line (Point D of Figure 7C.15)

If abnormal program termination is to occur should the date record be missing, a place to display the explanatory error message should be provided.

Triggering the date record processing (Point E of Figure 7C.15)

In the mainline module, the 120-PROCESS-DATE-RECORD module is performed after variable fields have been initialized and before normal input data records are processed.

Processing the date record (combined file) (Point F of Figure 7C.15)

An attempt to read the date record is made by performing the 800-READ-INPUT-RECORD module. If end-of-file is encountered, it means that the date record is missing from the file. Hence, a date-record-missing message is set in the error line and the program-abend switch is set. If the record code of the record that is read does not signify a date record, the date-record-missing message is also set in the error line and the program-abend switch is set. If the date is not valid, an invalid-date message is set in the error line and the program-abend switch is set.

If the program-abend switch has not been set, it means that a valid period-ending date has been obtained. Thus, the date is moved from the input date record area to the date field in the heading line.

On the other hand, if any of the above processing has set the program-abend switch, the following actions are taken: (1) report headings are printed (to identify the report that contains a date record error), (2) the error line is moved to the output print area, (3) the error line is printed, and (4) the end-of-file switch is set to inhibit further processing.

Processing the date record (separate file) (Point G of Figure 7C.15)

An attempt to read the date record is made by performing the 805-READ-DATE-RECORD module. If end-of-file is encountered, it means that the date record is missing from the file. Hence, a date-record-missing message is set in the error line and the program-abend switch is set. If the record code of the record read does not signify a date record, the date-record-missing message is also set in the error line and the program-abend switch is set. If the date is not valid, an invalid-date message is set in the error line and the program-abend switch is set.

If the program-abend switch has not been set, it means that a valid period-ending date has been obtained. Thus, the date is moved from the input date record area to the date field in the heading line. Then, assuming that the date record is to be the only record within the file, an attempt is made to read another record from the date file. If end-of-file is not detected, it means that extra records are in the date file. In this case, the too-many-date-records message is set in the error line and the program-abend switch is set.

If any of the above processing has set the program-abend switch, the following actions are taken: (1) report headings are printed (to identify the report that contains a date record error), (2) the error line is moved to the output print area, (3) the error line is printed, and (4) the end-of-file switch for the input data record transaction file is set to inhibit further processing.

Left-to-right/top-to-bottom example

```
HIGH-VALUE HARDWARE STORES                                    03/15/84
DETAIL SALES HISTORY                                          PAGE   1

PRODUCT   ITEM    STORE   QTY                PRODUCT   ITEM    STORE   QTY
CLASS     CODE    NBR     SOLD     PRICE     CLASS     CODE    NBR     SOLD     PRICE

HMR       3836-H  101     1        12.99     HMR       3836-H  101     3        12.99
HMR       3836-H  102     1        12.99     HMR       3836-H  102     1        12.99
HMR       3836-H  102     1        12.99     HMR       3836-H  102     10       12.99
HMR       3847-H  101     1        13.99     HMR       3847-H  101     2        13.99
HMR       3847-H  102     1        13.99     HMR       3852-H  102     1        4.99
HMR       3861-P  101     1        29.99     SAW       1977-P  102     1        529.99
SAW       1977-P  102     1        529.99    SAW       2425-P  101     1        569.99
SAW       3619-H  102     1        18.99     SAW       3715-H  101     1        9.99
SAW       3715-H  101     1        9.99      SAW       3715-H  101     1        9.99
SAW       3715-H  102     1        9.99      SDR       2158-H  101     1        2.79
SDR       2158-H  101     1        2.79      SDR       2158-H  101     1        2.79
SDR       2158-H  101     1        2.79      SDR       2158-H  101     6        2.79
SDR       2158-H  102     1        2.79      SDR       2158-H  102     1        2.79
SDR       2160-H  101     2        2.99      SDR       2160-H  101     1        2.99
SDR       2160-H  101     1        2.99      SDR       2160-H  101     2        2.99
SDR       2160-H  102     1        2.99      SDR       2160-H  102     1        2.99
```

Top-to-bottom/left-to-right example

```
HIGH-VALUE HARDWARE STORES                                    03/15/84
DETAIL SALES HISTORY                                          PAGE   1

PRODUCT   ITEM    STORE   QTY                PRODUCT   ITEM    STORE   QTY
CLASS     CODE    NBR     SOLD     PRICE     CLASS     CODE    NBR     SOLD     PRICE

HMR       3836-H  101     1        12.99     SAW       3715-H  101     1        9.99
HMR       3836-H  101     3        12.99     SAW       3715-H  101     1        9.99
HMR       3836-H  102     1        12.99     SAW       3715-H  102     1        9.99
HMR       3836-H  102     1        12.99     SDR       2158-H  101     1        2.79
HMR       3836-H  102     1        12.99     SDR       2158-H  101     1        2.79
HMR       3836-H  102     10       12.99     SDR       2158-H  101     1        2.79
HMR       3847-H  101     1        13.99     SDR       2158-H  101     1        2.79
HMR       3847-H  101     2        13.99     SDR       2158-H  101     6        2.79
HMR       3847-H  102     1        13.99     SDR       2158-H  102     1        2.79
HMR       3852-H  102     1        4.99      SDR       2158-H  102     1        2.79
HMR       3861-P  101     1        29.99     SDR       2160-H  101     2        2.99
SAW       1977-P  102     1        529.99    SDR       2160-H  101     1        2.99
SAW       1977-P  102     1        529.99    SDR       2160-H  101     1        2.99
SAW       2425-P  101     1        569.99    SDR       2160-H  101     2        2.99
SAW       3619-H  102     1        18.99     SDR       2160-H  102     1        2.99
SAW       3715-H  101     1        9.99      SDR       2160-H  102     1        2.99
```

Figure 7C.16. List-up examples.

List-ups

Figure 7C.16 shows a two-up list-up report in two different sequences: (1) left-to-right/top-to-bottom, and (2) top-to-bottom/left-to-right. The former sequence is easier to program but the latter arrangement generally provides greater readability.

**Left-to-right/
Top-to-bottom List-up**

The coding prototype for a left-to-right/top-to-bottom list-up is shown in Figure 7C.17.

Definition of the list-up control fields (Point A of Figure 7C.17)

Fields that are called WS-LIST-UP-COUNT and WS-LIST-UP-LIMIT are defined within the WS-LIST-UP-CONTROLS group entry in the WORKING-STORAGE SECTION.

```
                 DATA DIVISION.
                   .
                   .
                   .
                 WORKING-STORAGE SECTION.
                   .
                   .
                   .
```

```
   A      01   WS-LIST-UP-CONTROLS.
               05   WS-LIST-UP-COUNT                PIC S9(4)     COMP SYNC.
               05   WS-LIST-UP-LIMIT                PIC S9(4)     VALUE +n
                                                                  COMP SYNC.
```

```
                   .
                   .
                   .
```

```
   B      01   LU-LIST-UP-LINE.
               05   LU-list-up-entry                OCCURS n TIMES.
                    10   LU-list-up-field           PIC X(nn).  <------------

                    [additional fields as required for the application]
```

```
                   .
                   .
                   .
                 PROCEDURE DIVISION.
```

```
   C      000-mainline.

               OPEN files.
               PERFORM 100-INITIALIZE-VARIABLE-FIELDS.
               PERFORM 800-READ-input-record.                     [priming read]
               PERFORM 200-process-list-up-line
                   UNTIL END-OF-FILE.
               CLOSE files.
               STOP RUN.
```

```
                   .
                   .
                   .
```

```
   D      200-process-list-up-line.

               IF WS-LINES-USED IS NOT LESS THAN WS-LINES-PER-PAGE
                   PERFORM 870-PRINT-REPORT-HEADINGS.
               MOVE 1 TO WS-LIST-UP-COUNT.
               (Blank the list-up-line.)
               PERFORM 210-set-up-input-record
                   UNTIL WS-LIST-UP-COUNT IS GREATER THAN WS-LIST-UP-LIMIT.
               MOVE LU-LIST-UP-LINE TO REPORT-LINE.
               Set WS-LINE-SPACING for this list-up-line.
               PERFORM 890-WRITE-REPORT-LINE.
```

```
   E      210-set-up-input-record.

               MOVE each input field to be printed
                   TO its respective field within
                       LU-LIST-UP-LINE (WS-LIST-UP-COUNT).
               ADD 1 TO WS-LIST-UP-COUNT.
               PERFORM 800-READ-input-record.
```

```
   F      220-blank-list-up-area.

               MOVE SPACES TO each LU-list-up-entry field
                   subscripted by (WS-LIST-UP-COUNT).
               ADD 1 TO WS-LIST-UP-COUNT.
```

Figure 7C.17.   Coding prototype: Left-to-right/top-to-bottom list-up.

```
                  .
                  .
                  .
     ┌─────────────────────────────────────────────────────────┐
     │   800-READ-input-record.                                 │
     │                                                          │
     │       READ INPUT-FILE INTO input-record-area             │
 ╭───╮         AT END MOVE 'YES' TO WS-END-OF-FILE-SW           │
 │ G │         PERFORM 220-blank-list-up-area                   │
 ╰───╯             UNTIL WS-LIST-UP-COUNT                        │
     │                   IS GREATER THAN WS-LIST-UP-LIMIT.      │
     └─────────────────────────────────────────────────────────┘
                  .
                  .
                  .
```

Figure 7C.17. (continued)

The WS-LIST-UP-COUNT field is used to keep track of which list-up entry is being processed horizontally across the report line. The VALUE clause of the WS-LIST-UP-LIMIT field should be initialized with the number of list-up entries across a line. For example, a two-up report would be initialized with 2, a three-up report with 3, and so forth.

Definition of the list-up line (Point B of Figure 7C.17)

The LU-LIST-UP-LINE record description contains an LU-LIST-UP-ENTRY which occurs a number of times equal to the value of the WS-LIST-UP-LIMIT field. Within the LU-LIST-UP-ENTRY-FIELD, each of the fields to be printed is defined.

Processing the list-up line (Points C to E of Figure 7C.17)

The 200-PROCESS-LIST-UP-LINE module is performed from the mainline module until the end of the input file has been reached.

The first step within the module is to test to see if report headings are required. If they are, the 870-PRINT-REPORT-HEADINGS module is performed.

The next step is to initialize the WS-LIST-UP-COUNT field to a value of **1**. Then, the 210-SET-UP-INPUT-RECORD module is performed until the value of WS-LIST-UP-COUNT exceeds that of WS-LIST-UP-LIMIT. Such iterations of 210-SET-UP-INPUT-RECORD build the report line.

After the report line has been built, LU-LIST-UP-LINE is moved to the output print area, the line-spacing indicator is set, and the line is written.

End-of-file processing (Points E and F of Figure 7C.17)

When the end of the input file has been reached, in addition to setting the end-of-file switch, the 220-BLANK-LIST-UP-AREA module is performed to blank unused areas on the line. For example, given a three-up report, suppose the last record were printed in the first entry on the line. It would be necessary (assuming the line was not blanked prior to its formatting) to blank the second and third entries on the last line. If this were not done, those entries would be repeated from the next to last line.

Top-to-bottom/
Left-to-right List-up

The coding prototype for a top-to-bottom/left-to-right list-up is shown in Figure 7C.18.

```
                DATA DIVISION.
                    .
                    .
                    .
                WORKING-STORAGE SECTION.
                    .
                    .
                    .

       ┌──────────────────────────────────────────────────────────────────────────┐
       │  01   WS-LIST-UP-CONTROLS.                                                 │
       │       05   WS-LIST-UP-COUNT              PIC S9(4)       COMP SYNC.        │
       │       05   WS-LIST-UP-LIMIT              PIC S9(4)       VALUE +n          │
  (A)  │                                                         COMP SYNC.        │
       │       05   WS-LIST-UP-LINE-COUNT         PIC S9(4)       COMP SYNC.        │
       │       05   WS-LIST-UP-LINE-LIMIT         PIC S9(4)       VALUE +n          │
       │                                                         COMP SYNC.        │
       └──────────────────────────────────────────────────────────────────────────┘
                    .
                    .
                    .

       ┌──────────────────────────────────────────────────────────────────────────┐
  (B)  │  01   LU-LIST-UP-PAGE.                                                     │
       │       05   LU-LIST-UP-LINE               OCCURS nn TIMES.                  │
       │            10   LU-list-up-entry         OCCURS n TIMES.                   │
       │                 15   LU-list-up-field    PIC X(nn).  <------------         │
       │                                                                           │
       │                 [additional fields as required for the application]       │
       └──────────────────────────────────────────────────────────────────────────┘
                    .
                    .
                    .

                PROCEDURE DIVISION.

       ┌──────────────────────────────────────────────────────────────────────────┐
       │  000-mainline.                                                            │
       │                                                                           │
       │      OPEN files.                                                          │
       │      PERFORM 100-INITIALIZE-VARIABLE-FIELDS.                              │
  (C)  │      PERFORM 800-READ-input-record.                   [priming read]      │
       │      PERFORM 200-process-list-up-page                                     │
       │         UNTIL END-OF-FILE.                                                │
       │      CLOSE files.                                                         │
       │      STOP RUN.                                                            │
       └──────────────────────────────────────────────────────────────────────────┘
                    .
                    .
                    .

       ┌──────────────────────────────────────────────────────────────────────────┐
  (D)  │  200-process-list-up-page.                                                │
       │                                                                           │
       │      PERFORM 870-PRINT-REPORT-HEADINGS.                                   │
       │      MOVE 1 TO WS-LIST-UP-COUNT                                           │
       │                WS-LIST-UP-LINE-COUNT.                                     │
       │      PERFORM 210-set-up-input-record                                      │
       │         UNTIL WS-LIST-UP-COUNT IS EQUAL TO WS-LIST-UP-LIMIT.              │
       │      PERFORM 205-print-list-up-line                                       │
       │         UNTIL WS-LIST-UP-LINE-COUNT                                       │
       │               IS GREATER THAN WS-LIST-UP-LINE-LIMIT.                      │
       └──────────────────────────────────────────────────────────────────────────┘

       ┌──────────────────────────────────────────────────────────────────────────┐
  (E)  │  205-print-list-up-line.                                                  │
       │                                                                           │
       │      IF NOT END-OF-FILE                                                   │
       │          PERFORM 210-set-up-input-record                                  │
       │      ELSE                                                                 │
       │          PERFORM 220-blank-list-up-area.                                  │
       │      MOVE LU-LIST-UP-LINE (WS-LIST-UP-LINE-COUNT) TO REPORT-LINE.         │
       │      Set WS-LINE-SPACING for this list-up-line.                           │
       │      PERFORM 890-WRITE-REPORT-LINE.                                       │
       └──────────────────────────────────────────────────────────────────────────┘
```

Figure 7C.18.   Coding prototype: Top-to-bottom/left-to-right list-up.

(F)
```
210-set-up-input-record.

    MOVE each input field to be printed
        TO its respective field within
            LU-LIST-UP-LINE
                (WS-LIST-UP-LINE-COUNT WS-LIST-UP-COUNT).
    ADD 1 TO WS-LIST-UP-LINE-COUNT.
    IF WS-LIST-UP-LINE-COUNT
            IS GREATER THAN WS-LIST-UP-LINE-LIMIT
    AND WS-LIST-UP-COUNT IS NOT EQUAL TO WS-LIST-UP-LIMIT
        MOVE 1 TO WS-LIST-UP-LINE-COUNT
        ADD 1 TO WS-LIST-UP-COUNT.
    PERFORM 800-read-input-record.
```

(G)
```
220-blank-list-up-area.

    MOVE SPACES TO each LU-list-up-entry field
        subscripted by (WS-LIST-UP-LINE-COUNT WS-LIST-UP-COUNT).
    ADD 1 TO WS-LIST-UP-LINE-COUNT.
    IF WS-LIST-UP-LINE-COUNT
            IS GREATER THAN WS-LIST-UP-LINE-LIMIT
    AND WS-LIST-UP-COUNT IS NOT EQUAL TO WS-LIST-UP-LIMIT
        MOVE 1 TO WS-LIST-UP-LINE-COUNT
        ADD 1 TO WS-LIST-UP-COUNT.
```

.
.
.

(H)
```
800-READ-input-record.

    READ INPUT-FILE INTO input-record-area
        AT END MOVE 'YES' TO WS-END-OF-FILE-SW
        PERFORM 220-blank-list-up-area
            UNTIL WS-LIST-UP-LINE-COUNT
                IS EQUAL TO WS-LIST-UP-LINE-LIMIT.
```

.
.
.

Figure 7C.18. (continued)

Definition of the list-up control fields (Point A of Figure 7C.18)

In addition to the WS-LIST-UP-COUNT and WS-LIST-UP-LIMIT control fields for horizontal processing across the report line, fields named WS-LIST-UP-LINE-COUNT and WS-LIST-UP-LINE-LIMIT are defined to control vertical-line processing down the page.

Definition of the list-up page (Point B of Figure 7C.18)

In order to produce a top-to-bottom list-up, it is necessary to "table-up" the entries for a portion of the page. Hence, the LU-LIST-UP-PAGE entry is defined as a group entry in the WORKING-STORAGE SECTION.

Within the page entry, the LU-LIST-UP-LINE field is defined and given an OCCURS clause value that is equal to the number of list-up lines to be printed vertically on the page. For example, if the page will accommodate 50 list-up lines, the value would be set to 50.

Within the line entry, the LU-LIST-UP-ENTRY is given an OCCURS value that is equal to the number of entries to be printed across the list-up line.

Processing the list-up page (Points D through F of Figure 7C.18)

The 200-PROCESS-LIST-UP-PAGE module is performed from the mainline module until the end of the input file has been reached.

The first step within the module is to perform the 870-PRINT-REPORT-HEADINGS module to head the page. Then, the WS-LIST-UP-COUNT and WS-LIST-UP-LINE-COUNT fields are initialized to **1** to begin placing entries in the upper left-hand corner of the page.

At this point, the 210-SET-UP-INPUT-RECORD module is performed until the WS-LIST-UP-COUNT field is equal to the WS-LIST-UP-LIMIT field. Such iterations will have the effect of filling all but the rightmost column of the report page. For example, with a three-up report, the left and middle columns will be filled; with a two-up report, the left column will be filled.

Finally, the 205-PRINT-LIST-UP-LINE module is performed until the WS-LIST-UP-LINE-COUNT field is greater than the WS-LIST-UP-LINE-LIMIT field. Each iteration causes a line to be printed on the page. Observe that the 210-SET-UP-INPUT-RECORD module is also performed from this 205-PRINT-LIST-UP-LINE module. This causes the rightmost column of each list-up line to be filled immediately before it is printed.

End-of-file processing (Points E and F of Figure 7C.18)

When the end-of-the-file input has been reached, in addition to setting the end-of-file switch, the 220-BLANK-LIST-UP-AREA module is performed to blank unused areas on the lines.

Summary

Topic 7-A Report Listings

Reports can be categorized as being detail, exception, or summary types of listing. A **detail list** generally contains a **detail line** for each input record that is to be read. An **exception list** is a report in which a detail line is printed only when an input record represents a special condition or an exception. A **summary list** is a report in which—instead of listing each detail record—a **summary line** is printed for each group of input records that contain the same key value.

Topic 7-B Report Accumulations

There are two basic types of report accumulations: end-of-report totals and control-break totals. Regardless of the type of listing, the great majority of reports contain **end-of-report totals**. Subtotals for records that contain the same control key are known as **control-break totals**. They are sometimes called **summary totals** because they provide a summarized subtotal for a group of records. Reports with control-break totals can be categorized as being either **single-level** or **multiple-level**, depending upon whether there is one control field or more than one control field, respectively.

Topic 7-C Report Variations

Group indication is a technique that can improve the readability of sequenced listings. With group indication, the key-field column or columns are printed only for the first detail line of the group and for the first line of each new page when a group spans more than one page. **Control-break page headings** are used to facilitate the distribution of a report. **Page-continuation indication**—either **continued-on** or **continued-from** or both—is used to inform the user of material that it is continued from one page to the next. **Control-break group headings** or, simply, **control headings** are used as an alternative to group indication or to conserve space on the detail line. **Page footings** are lines that are printed at the bottom of each report page, which contain either descriptive information or page totals. Sometimes **detail data** will be printed **in page headings**. In addition to the run date, **period-ending date indication** is often provided on applicable reports. When **list-ups** are used, either of two different sequences may be specified: **left-to-right/top-to-bottom** and **top-to-bottom/left-to-right**.

Programming Assignments

7-1: Price List

Program description

A two-up price list is to be printed from a sequential part master file.

Input file

Part master file   Key field = Part number

Output file

Price list

Record formats

Part master record (Record code "PM")

Part master record

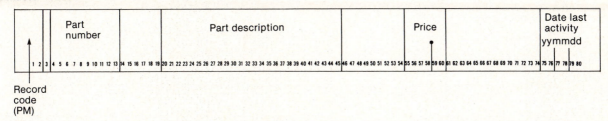

Record
code
(PM)

Price list

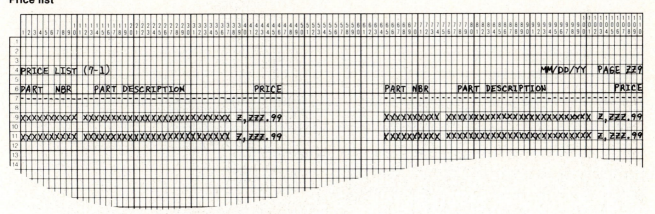

Program operations

A. Read each input part master record.

B. Print each part master record, two-up, in top-to-bottom, left-to-right sequence, as shown on the print chart.

  1. Double-space each detail line.

  2. Provide for a line span of 57 lines per page.

7-2: Trial Balance Report

Program description

A trial balance report is to be printed from a general ledger master file. Control headings, continued indication, control totals, and a report total are to be incorporated into the report.

Input files

General ledger master file   Key field = General ledger account number

Date-control file

Output file

Trial balance report

Record formats

General ledger master record (Record code "LM")

Date-control record (Record code "01")

Period-ending date record

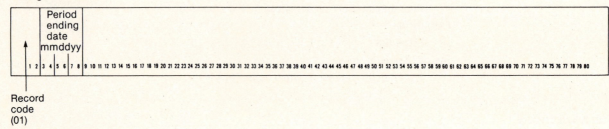

Record code (01)

General ledger master record

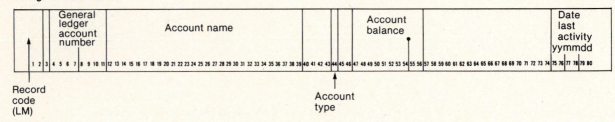

Record code (LM)

Account type

Trial balance

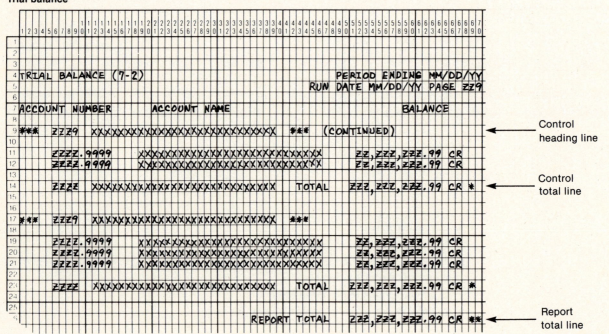

Program operations

A. Read the date-control file to obtain the period-ending date.
  1. Validate the period-ending date record as follows:
    a. Record code = "01".
    b. Month number numeric, greater than "00", and less than "13".
    c. Day number numeric, greater than "00", and less than "32".
    d. Year digits numeric.
  2. Check the date-control file to ensure that one period-ending date record is present and that multiple records are not present in the file.
  3. If any of the above error conditions occur, set the date to zeros and continue processing.
B. Read each input general ledger master record.
C. Print a trial balance report in accordance with the format shown on the print chart.
  1. When the first account number is encountered whose first four digits are equal to or greater than one of the account codes listed below, print a control heading line with the corresponding account-category description prior to printing the detail line.
  2. Print a control heading line with the continued indication whenever a control group is continued from the previous page.
  3. Print control totals whenever the first four digits of the account number change.
  4. Print report totals at the end of the report.
D. Handle line spacing as follows:
  1. Single-space each detail line.
  2. Do not print a control heading line on a page unless at least two detail lines can also be printed on the page.
  3. Triple-space before each control heading line (unless it is the first line after the page headings, in which case it is to be double-spaced from the headings).
  4. Double-space after each control heading line.
  5. Double-space before and after each control total line (except that a control total line immediately preceding a control heading line on the same page will be separated by a triple-space interval, as mentioned in point D.3, above).
  6. Provide for a line span of 55 lines per page, except for the following:
    a. As mentioned in point D.2 above.
    b. Always print a control total line on the same page as that of the last detail line for that group (never skip to a new page before printing a control total line).

Account code	Account-category description
1010	CURRENT ASSETS
2000	PROPERTY AND EQUIPMENT
2800	OTHER ASSETS
3010	CURRENT LIABILITIES
3700	OTHER LIABILITIES
3800	LONG-TERM DEBT
4000	DEFERRED INCOME
4100	STOCKHOLDERS' EQUITY
4200	RETAINED EARNINGS
4300	CAPITAL
5010	SALES
5500	COST OF SALES
5920	MANUFACTURING EXPENSE
7500	SELLING EXPENSE
8000	GENERAL AND ADMIN. EXPENSE
9000	OTHER INCOME
9400	OTHER EXPENSE

7-3: Aged Analysis Report

Program description

An aged analysis report is to be printed from a sequential customer master file. Detail data in the page headings, group indication, multiple-level control totals, and page totals are to be incorporated into the report. A period-ending date record is processed to obtain the period-ending date for the report.

Input files

Customer master file   Key fields = Region code (major)

                                                          Territory number (intermediate)

                                                           Customer account number (minor)

Date-control file

Output file

Aged analysis report

Record formats

Period-ending date record (Record code "01")

Customer master record (Record code "CM")

Aged analysis report

Program operations

A. Read the date-control file to obtain the period-ending date.
 1. Validate the period-ending date record as follows:
    a. Record code = "01".
    b. Month number numeric, greater than "00", and less than "13".
    c. Day number numeric, greater than "00", and less than "32".
    d. Year digits numeric.
 2. Check the date-control file to ensure that one period-ending date record is present and that multiple records are not present in the file.
 3. If any of the above error conditions occur, set the date to zeros and continue processing.
B. Read each input customer master record.
C. Print an aged analysis report in accordance with the format that is shown on the print chart.
 1. Given the following region codes, print the corresponding region name in the report heading.

Region code	Region name
ATL	ATLANTIC
CTL	CENTRAL
MTN	MOUNTAIN
PAC	PACIFIC

 2. When a region control break occurs, skip to a new page and restart page numbering at 1 prior to printing detail lines for that region.
 3. Use group indication for territory codes on the detail line.
 4. Print territory and region control totals.
 5. Print page totals for the detail amounts on each page.
D. Handle line spacing as follows:
 1. Double-space each detail line except for the following:
    a. Triple-space the first detail line of a territory from the territory control total when they are both printed on the same page.
 2. Provide for a line span of 50 lines per page, except for the following:
    a. Always print a control total line on the same page as that of the last detail line for that group (never skip to a new page before printing a control total line).
    b. Print the page total line on line 57 of each page.

Period-ending date record

Customer master record

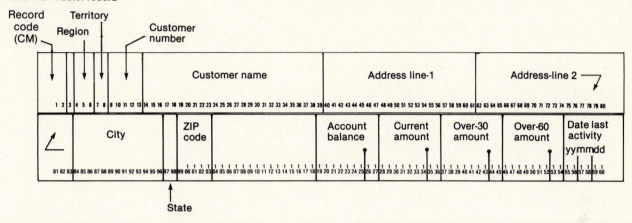

Aged analysis report

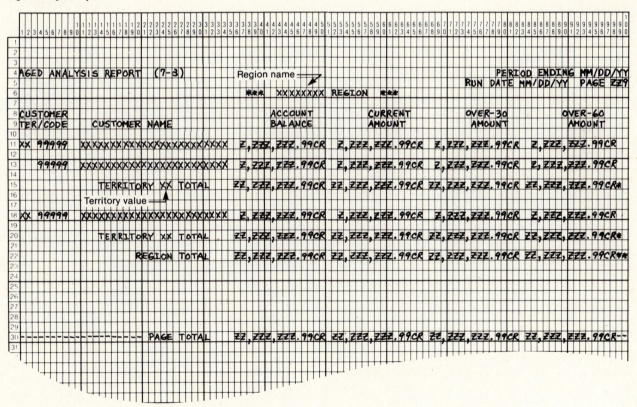

HARDWARE/SOFTWARE CONCEPTS
CHAPTER C

LOGIC FOR COMMONLY NEEDED APPLICATION ROUTINES

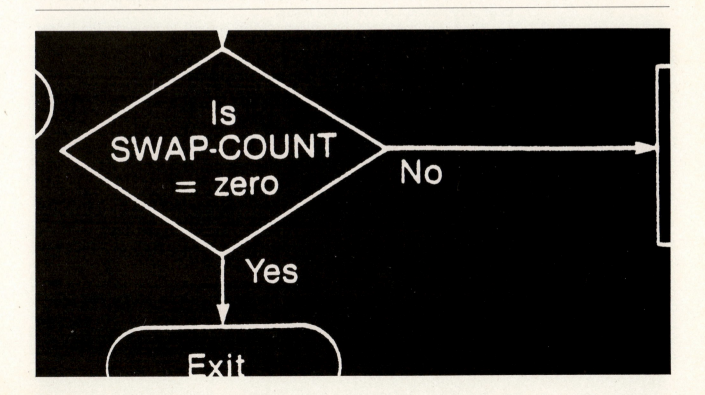

LOGIC FOR COMMONLY NEEDED APPLICATION ROUTINES

Certain routines are commonly called for within commercial application systems. This chapter presents a potpourri of background information, concepts, or logic for a number of these routines.

Calendar Routine Logic

When Rome emerged as a world power, the Roman calendar had 12 months: four months with 31 days, seven with 29 days, and February with 28 days, which resulted in a year of only 355 days. To bring the calendar into line with the seasons, the ruling priests added an extra month from time to time. As elected politicians, the priests tended to proclaim a long year when the other elected officials were of their own party and a short year when they were not.

By the time Julius Caesar came to power, the calendar was 80 days behind the sun. Caesar put an end to these calendar capers by imperial decree and made the solar year (365 days and 6 hours) the basis of the calendar in 46 B.C. Although it would have been ideal to form seven 30-day months and five 31-day months, Caesar made February shorter because the Romans thought it to be unlucky. This resulted in the current arrangement of month/day combinations. To handle the extra 6 hours, a leap year was declared for every fourth year. This system, named for Caesar, became known as the **Julian calendar**.

However, the actual length of the solar year is 11½ minutes shorter than the computation that Caesar used. Thus the Julian year is slightly too long; by the sixteenth century the calendar had slipped 10 days from the equinox. Pope Gregory XIII remedied this situation in 1582. After bringing the calendar year even with the solar system once again, he eliminated three out of four centesimal leap years. Thus 1600 was a leap year and 2000 will be a leap year, but 1700, 1800, and 1900 were not. This **Gregorian calendar** is accurate enough for most purposes and is still in use today.

Gregorian dates can be represented in several formats. In the United States, they are typically expressed in **mm/dd/yy** format (*mm* = month number from 01 to 12; *dd* = day number from 01 to 31; and *yy* = year number of the century from 00 to 99). In England and parts of Europe, dates are expressed in **dd/mm/yy** format. In the United States military, dates are commonly recorded as **dd mmm yyyy** (the month is represented as a three-letter month abbreviation, and all four digits of the year are usually recorded).

Within data-processing systems, ANS date representation calls for Gregorian dates to be recorded in either **yymmdd** or **yyyymmdd** format. This format is actually the most logical one because it conforms to normal number-representation conventions in which the most significant digit is positioned as the leftmost digit and the least significant as the rightmost. Because of this positional notation, the ANS format has the advantage of allowing the date to be used directly in calculations, such as finding the number of days between two dates. It also simplifies the process of comparing one date to another to determine which one is earlier or later.

Date computations are simplified even further by Julianizing the date. A **Julianized date** is one in which the year digits are represented on the left and a 3-digit sequential-day number (from 001 to 365, or 366 for a leap year) is recorded on the right. Thus, in accordance with the ANS standard, the date is stored in **yyddd** or **yyyyddd** format. The obvious advantage to a Julianized date is that date-span computations can be made without need for adjustments when dates are not within the same month.

Most programmers incorrectly call a Julianized date a "Julian" date. A **Julian** date is rarely encountered outside the science of astronomy. Because of the accuracy and compatibility problems inherent in other calendars, astronomers use a **Julian Day Calendar** in which days are numbered sequentially from an arbitrarily selected point in the year 4713 B.C. Thus July 4, 1776, has a Julian Day of 2,369,905.

Date Validation

Figure C.1 shows date-validation logic in an annotated pseudocode form. Checking a date for reasonableness, as shown in step A, is optional but recommended for most applications. Input transactions are typically dated near the processing date. The further a date is from the current date, the greater the likelihood that a date error has been made. Thus it is wise to establish a span of dates as a range check of reasonableness to identify distant entries. Although the choice of such a span may be somewhat arbitrary, it should be based upon the application requirements and processing schedule. Usually, the length of time permitted for past dates will be greater than that specified for future dates. For example, a sales transaction record dated for a prior month may be reasonable whereas one dated a week into the future may be suspect. Recognize that, whenever a check for reasonableness is made, provision must be made for a reentry override to allow valid exception conditions to be accepted back into the system.

Step B of the date-validation logic, in which 2-digit year numbers are converted to 4-digit year values, is not always done in practice but really should be done now that the beginning of a new century is near and adequate storage space is generally available. Countless programs have been written that test whether a 2-digit year is a leap year by dividing by 4 and, if the remainder is zero, consider the year to be a leap year. When the 2-digit year for the leap year 2000 (00) is encountered, the quotient of such a division will be zero and the remainder will be 4; hence the year will incorrectly be considered to be a common year rather than a leap year. Testing two dates for the earlier or later date is another commonly required date-handling routine that can fail when 2-digit year numbers are used and the dates are in different centuries.

Date-validation data fields:

```
DATE (mcyymmddddd)
    YEAR (mcyy)
        MILLENIUM-DIGIT (m)
        CENTURY-DIGIT (c)
        YEAR-DIGITS (yy)
    MONTH (mm)
    GREG-DAY (dd)
    JUL-DAY (ddd)

LEAP-YEAR-SW (yes/no)

VALID-MONTH-SW (yes/no)

VALID-DAY-SW (yes/no)

PRIOR-REASONABLE-DATE (mcyymmdd)

FUTURE-REASONABLE-DATE (mcyymmdd)

MAXIMUM-YEAR-DAYS (ddd)

DATE-EVALUATION-FLAG (valid/invalid/unreasonable)
```

Table of Maximum Days in Each Month

Month	MAXIMUM-DAYS
January	31
February	dd
March	31
April	30
May	31
June	30
July	31
August	31
September	30
October	31
November	*30
December	31

Figure C.1. Date-validation logic.

continued

Gregorian date-validation logic:

Step A. Establish reasonableness parameters in relation to current date.

    1. Establish or compute PRIOR-REASONABLE-DATE.

    2. Establish or compute FUTURE-REASONABLE-DATE.

Step B. If not recorded, establish century digits of date to be validated..

    1. If CENTURY-DIGIT not recorded (YEAR less than 0100),
        set CENTURY-DIGIT to correct value.

    2. If MILLENIUM-DIGIT not recorded (YEAR less than 1000),
        set MILLENIUM-DIGIT to correct value.

Step C. Determine if year to be validated is a leap year.

    1. If YEAR / 4 produces a remainder equal to 0
        set LEAP-YEAR-SW to "yes"
    else
        set LEAP-YEAR-SW to "no".

    2. If LEAP-YEAR-SW is equal to "yes"
    and YEAR-DIGITS are equal to zero
    and YEAR / 400 produces a remainder not equal to 0
        reset LEAP-YEAR-SW to "no".

Step D. Validate month.

    1. If MONTH is not numeric
    or MONTH is less than "01"
    or MONTH is greater than "12"
        set VALID-MONTH-SW to "no".

Step E. Validate day.

    1. If GREG-DAY is not numeric
    or GREG-DAY is less than "01"
        set VALID-DAY-SW to "no"
    else
        set VALID-DAY-SW to "yes".

    2. If LEAP-YEAR
        set MAXIMUM-DAYS (2) to "29"
    else
        set MAXIMUM-DAYS (2) to "28".

    3. If GREG-DAY is greater than MAXIMUM-DAYS (MONTH)
        reset VALID-MONTH-SW to "no".

Step F. Evaluate validity and reasonableness.

    1. If VALID-MONTH-SW is equal to "no"
    or VALID-DAY-SW is equal to "no"
        set DATE-EVALUATION-FLAG to "invalid"
    else
        set DATE-EVALUATION-FLAG to "valid".

    2. If DATE-EVALUATION-FLAG is equal to "valid"
    and DATE is less than PRIOR-REASONABLE-DATE
        set DATE-EVALUATION-FLAG to "unreasonable".

    3. If DATE-EVALUATION-FLAG is equal to "valid"
    and DATE is greater than FUTURE-REASONABLE-DATE
        set DATE-EVALUATION-FLAG to "unreasonable".

Julianized date-validation logic:

Step A. Establish reasonableness parameters in relation to current date. [Same as for Gregorian date validation.]

Step B. Establish century digits of date to be validated if not recorded. [Same as for Gregorian date validation.]

Figure C.1. (continued)

Step C. Determine if year to be validated is a leap year.
        [Same as for Gregorian date validation.]

Step D. Validate month. [Not applicable to Julianized date validation.]

Step E. Validate day.

        1. If JUL-DAY is not numeric
            or JUL-DAY is less than "001"
                set VALID-DAY-SW to "no"
            else
                set VALID-DAY-SW to "yes".

        2. If LEAP-YEAR
                move "366" to MAXIMUM-YEAR-DAYS
            else
                move "365" to MAXIMUM-YEAR-DAYS.

        3. If JUL-DAY is greater than MAXIMUM-YEAR-DAYS
                reset VALID-DAY-SW to "no".

Step F. Evaluate validity and reasonableness.
        [Same as for Gregorian date validation.]

Figure C.1. (continued)

Date-conversion data fields:

GREG-DATE (mcyymmdd)
    GREG-YEAR (mcyy)
        GREG-MILLENIUM-DIGIT (m)
        GREG-CENTURY-DIGIT (c)
        GREG-YEAR-DIGITS (yy)
    GREG-MONTH (mm)
    GREG-DAY (dd)

JUL-DATE (mcyyddd)
    JUL-YEAR (mcyy)
        JUL-MILLENIUM-DIGIT (m)
        JUL-CENTURY-DIGIT (c)
        JUL-YEAR-DIGITS (yy)
    JUL-DAY (ddd)

LEAP-YEAR-SW (yes/no)

Julianized Day Conversion Table

Month	MONTH-NBR	DAYS-BEFORE
January	01	000
February	02	031
March	03	059
April	04	090
May	05	120
June	06	151
July	07	181
August	08	212
September	09	243
October	10	273
November	11	304
December	12	334

Gregorian date to Julianized date conversion:

    1. Move GREG-YEAR to JUL-YEAR.

    2. Move DAYS-BEFORE (GREG-MONTH) to JUL-DAY.

    3. Add GREG-DAY to JUL-DAY.

    4. If LEAP-YEAR
        and GREG-MONTH is greater than "02"
            add 1 to JUL-DAY.

Julianized date to Gregorian date conversion:

    1. Move JUL-YEAR to GREG-YEAR.

    2. If LEAP-YEAR
        and JUL-DAY is greater than "060"
            subtract 1 from JUL-DAY.

    3. Find first DAYS-BEFORE value equal to or greater than JUL-DAY.

    4. Subtract 1 from corresponding MONTH-NBR giving GREG-MONTH.

    5. Subtract DAYS-BEFORE (GREG-MONTH) from JUL-DAY giving GREG-DAY.

Figure C.2. Date-conversion logic.

Date-span computation data fields:

```
JUL-EARLIER-DATE (mcyyddd)
    JUL-EARLIER-DATE-YEAR (mcyy)
    JUL-EARLIER-DATE-DAY (ddd)

JUL-LATER-DATE (mcyyddd)
    JUL-LATER-DATE-YEAR (mcyy)
    JUL-LATER-DATE-DAY (ddd)

GREG-EARLIER-DATE (mcyyddd)

GREG-LATER-DATE (mcyymmdd)

YEAR-SPAN (nnnn)

DAY-SPAN (nnn)

YEARS-LEFT (n)
```

Julianized date-span computation:

```
1.   Subtract JUL-EARLIER-YEAR from JUL-LATER-YEAR giving YEAR-SPAN.

2.   Subtract JUL-EARLIER-DATE-DAY from JUL-LATER-DATE-DAY
         giving DAY-SPAN.

3.   If YEAR-SPAN is not equal to zero
         compute DAY-SPAN = DAY-SPAN + (YEAR-SPAN * 365)
         divide YEAR-SPAN by 4
             add quotient to DAY-SPAN
             move remainder to YEARS-LEFT
         divide JUL-EARLIER-YEAR by 4
             subtract remainder from YEARS-LEFT
         if YEARS-LEFT is positive
             add 1 to DAY-SPAN.
```

Gregorian date-span computation:

```
1.   Convert GREG-EARLIER-DATE to JUL-EARLIER-DATE.

2.   Convert GREG-LATER-DATE to JUL-LATER-DATE.

3.   Use the Julianized date-span computation, above.
```

Figure C.3.   Date-span computation logic.

Date Conversion

The pseudocode to handle conversion from a Gregorian to a Julianized date and vice versa is presented in Figure C.2. Except for the adjustment that is required for leap years, such conversion is relatively straightforward.

Date-Span Computation

As specified in the pseudocode of Figure C.3, date spans are more easily computed in Julianized date format. Step 3 of the Julianized date-span computation provides the logic that is necessary to figure the date span when the two dates are in different years. Observe that it contains the logic to adjust each span for the appropriate number of extra leap year days.

Day-of-the-Week Computation

The name of the day of the week upon which a date falls can be computed arithmetically by the logic shown in Figure C.4. The principle behind this method is, for a given date, to begin with the century coefficient. This is a number one less than the day value of the first day of the century. Each common year starts one day later than the previous year; a leap year begins two days later. Thus one day is added for each year until the date that is being computed is reached. This, plus one day for each leap year, adjusts to the start of that year. The month coefficient, which adjusts to the start of the given month, is then added. Finally, the day number is added and the sum is divided by 7 to yield the day of the week.

Day-of-the-week computation data fields:

```
DATE (ccyymmddd)
    CENTURY-DIGITS (cc)
    YEAR-DIGITS (yy)
    MONTH (mm)
    DAY (ddd)

DAY-WORK (nnnn)

DAY-VALUE (n)
```

Century Coefficient Table		**Month Coefficient Table**		**Day Code Table**	
Century number	CENTURY-COEFFICIENT	Month	MONTH-COEFFICIENT	Day Code	DAY-NAME
0 (First century)	0	January	0	0	Sunday
100 (Second century)	1	February	3	1	Monday
200	2	March	3	2	Tuesday
300	3	April	6	3	Wednesday
400	4	May	1	4	Thursday
500	5	June	4	5	Friday
600	6	July	6	6	Saturday
700	7	August	2		
800	8	September	5		
900	9	October	0		
1000	8	November	3		
1100	7	December	5		
1200	6				
1300	5				
1400	4				
1500 (until 1582)	3				
1600	6				
1700	4				
1800	2				
1900	0				
2000	6				
2100	4				
2200	2				
2300	0				

Day-of-the-week computation from a Gregorian date:

1. Move CENTURY-COEFFICIENT (CENTURY-DIGITS + 1) to DAY-WORK.

2. Add YEAR-DIGITS to DAY-WORK.

3. Add quotient of (YEAR-DIGITS / 4) to DAY-WORK.

4. Add MONTH-COEFFICIENT (MONTH) to DAY-WORK.

5. Add DAY to DAY-WORK.

6. If leap-year and MONTH is less than 3 subtract 1 from DAY-WORK.

7. Divide DAY-WORK by 7 move remainder to DAY-VALUE.

8. Day-of-the-week = DAY-NAME (DAY-VALUE + 1).

Day-of-the-week computation from a Julianized date:

1. Move CENTURY-COEFFICIENT (CENTURY-DIGITS + 1) to DAY-WORK.

2. Add YEAR-DIGITS to DAY-WORK.

3. Add quotient of (YEAR-DIGITS / 4) to DAY-WORK.

4. Add DAY to DAY-WORK.

5. Divide DAY-WORK by 7 Move remainder to DAY-VALUE.

6. Day-of-the-week = DAY-NAME (DAY-VALUE).

Figure C.4. Day-of-the-week computation logic.

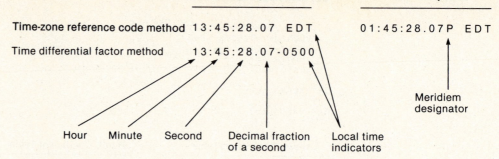

	24-hour system	12-hour system
Time-zone reference code method	13:45:28.07 EDT	01:45:28.07P EDT
Time differential factor method	13:45:28.07-0500	

Hour Minute Second Decimal fraction of a second Local time indicators Meridiem designator

Figure C.5. Time representation.

To simplify the logic, the value of 3 for the majority of the sixteenth century (until 1582) is shown in the century coefficient table. Because the calendar was reformed in October of 1582, a century coefficient of 3 should be used for dates before October 15, 1582; a century coefficient of 0 should actually be used for that and later dates in the sixteenth century.

Time Routine Logic

In everyday life, time is typically expressed in relation to a 12-hour clock. A 24-hour system is used instead in those pursuits—such as the military, astronomy, and aviation—that must frequently convert time from one geographical zone to another. Because of its pervasiveness in the armed forces, the 24-hour system is often called **military time**.

Regardless of 12- or 24-hour representation, time is generally measured in relation to **mean solar time**. Mean solar time is adjusted to **standard time** or **advanced (daylight-saving)** time. Otherwise, a clock on Long Island, for example, would be slightly ahead of one in Newark, New Jersey. The world is divided into 24 time zones, each 15 degrees longitude. There are also a few subzones, such as in Newfoundland, where the time differs from its neighboring zone by only half an hour. For geographical convenience, the time zones sometimes trace political or natural boundaries such as state lines, rivers, and the like.

By tradition, time zones are counted from the Greenwich Observatory in England, which is considered to be the zero meridian. The time zone where the observatory resides is called **Greenwich Mean Time (GMT)**, or **Universal Time (UTC)**. The date changes at the **International Date Line**, which is 12 hours or 180 degrees from Greenwich.

The North American continent spans nine time zones: Newfoundland, Atlantic (easternmost Canada, Puerto Rico, and the Virgin Islands), Eastern, Central, Mountain, Pacific, Yukon, Alaska-Hawaii, and Bering (westernmost Alaska). In accordance with the Uniform Time Act that the U.S. Congress passed in 1966, most of the United States observes daylight-saving time from 2 A.M. on the last Sunday in April until 2 A.M. on the last Sunday in October. During that period, clocks are set ahead one hour. Daylight-saving time is not observed in Arizona, Hawaii, most of Indiana, Puerto Rico, the Virgin Islands, or American Samoa.

As shown in Figure C.5, ANS time representations provide for either a 24- or 12-hour system. The 24-hour system is preferred because it is compatible with the International Standards Organization (ISO) provisions. In addition, it simplifies time conversion and time-span computation tasks.

24-hour system

The 24-hour time representation system uses an **hour value** from 00 through 23 and a **minute value** from 00 through 59. Additional optional time elements can also be included. The **second value** can range from 00 through 59. A **separator**— typically a colon (:)—may be included between the hour and minute and/or the minute and second fields. A **decimal fraction of a second field**, carried to as many positions as required, may be represented to the right of the second field. When a fractional second value is present, it must be separated from the second field by a decimal point.

Given a time expression that contains hours, minutes, and seconds with separators, midnight is represented as 00:00:00 (the start of the day). The local time reference can be supplied by either a **time-zone reference code** or a **time-differential factor**.

Time-zone reference code

The time-zone reference code is a three-character code (see Figure C.6), except that the single character "Z" can be used to represent Universal Time. When the time-zone reference code is present in the time expression, it must be separated from the low-order position of the time element by a space.

Time-differential factor

The time-differential factor (**TDF**) expresses the difference in hours and minutes between local time and Universal Time. It is represented by a 4-digit number and preceded by a plus (+) or a minus (–) sign. A plus sign indicates that the local time is ahead of Universal Time; a minus sign means that the local time is behind Universal Time.

The TDF values can range from – 1200 through – 0100 and from + 0000 through + 1300. The TDF for Universal Time is + 0000. When the TDF is used, it must be represented, without a separator, immediately to the right of the time expression.

12-hour system

The 12-hour system representation parallels that of the 24-hour system except that (1) the hour field values are limited to the range from 00 to 12, (2) a meridiem designator must be specified, and (3) only the time-zone reference code method can be used to represent local time; TDF values cannot be specified, and (4) the letter "Z" is not applicable as a time-zone reference code for universal time (GMT should be used).

The **meridiem designator** is specified immediately to the right of the time expression without a separator. The letter "A" is used to designate ante meridiem (A.M.); the letter "P" indicates post meridiem (P.M.). Given a time expression containing hours, minutes, and seconds with separators, midnight is represented by 12:00:00A; noon as 12:00:00P.

Time Validation, Conversion, and Span Computation

Annotated pseudocode for time validation is presented in Figure C.6. In Figure C.7, the logic to convert from the 12-hour to the 24-hour system, vice versa, and to Universal Time is shown. Time-span computation pseudocode is provided in Figure C.8.

Data-Validation Routine Logic

Certain data elements pose special data-validation requirements. Self-checking numbers, common code numbers, numeric amounts, and fields that should not contain embedded blank spaces will be covered here.

Time-validation data fields:

```
TIME (hhmmssddxxxsnnnn)
    HOUR (hh)
    MINUTE (mm)
    SECOND (ss)
    DECIMAL-FRACTION-OF-A-SECOND (dd)
    MERIDIEM-DESIGNATOR (x)
    TIME-ZONE-REFERENCE-CODE (xxx)
    TIME-DIFFERENTIAL-FACTOR (snnnn)
        TDF-SIGN (s)
        TDF-VALUE (nnnn)

VALID-HOUR-SW (yes/no)

VALID-MINUTE-SW (yes/no)

VALID-SECOND-SW (yes/no)

VALID-FRACTION-OF-A-SECOND-SW (yes/no)

VALID-MERIDIEM-SW (yes/no)

VALID-TIME-ZONE-SW (yes/no)

VALID-TDF-SW (yes/no)

VALID-TIME-SW (yes/no)
```

Table of Representative Time-Zone Reference Codes

Time zone reference code	Time zone	TDF
UTC or Z	Universal Time	+0000
GMT or Z	Greenwich Mean Time	+0000
NST	Newfoundland Standard Time	-0330
AST	Atlantic Standard Time	-0400
ADT	Atlantic Daylight Time	-0300
EST	Eastern Standard Time	-0500
EDT	Eastern Daylight Time	-0400
CST	Central Standard Time	-0600
CDT	Central Daylight Time	-0500
MST	Mountain Standard Time	-0700
MDT	Mountain Daylight Time	-0600
PST	Pacific Standard Time	-0800
PDT	Pacific Daylight Time	-0700
YST	Yukon Standard Time	-0900
YDT	Yukon Daylight Time	-0800
HST	Alaska-Hawaii Standard Time	-1000
HDT	Alaska-Hawaii Daylight Time	-0900
BST	Bering Standard Time	-1100
BDT	Bering Daylight Time	-1000

Time-validation logic:

```
Step A.  Validate hour.

         1.  If 12-hour system
                 If HOUR is less than "01" or greater than "12"
                     set VALID-HOUR-SW to "no"
                 else
                     set VALID-HOUR-SW to "yes"
             else if 24-hour-system
                 If HOUR is less than "00" or greater than "23"
                     set VALID-HOUR-SW to "no"
                 else
                     set VALID-HOUR-SW to "yes".


Step B.  Validate minute.

         1.  If MINUTE is less than "00" or greater than "59"
                 set VALID-MINUTE-SW to "no"
             else
                 set VALID-MINUTE-SW to "yes".
```

Figure C.6. Time-validation logic.

```
Step C.   Validate second.

          1.  If SECOND is less than "00" or greater than "59"
                    set VALID-SECOND-SW to "no"
              else
                    set VALID-SECOND-SW to "yes".


Step D.   Validate decimal-fraction-of-a-second.

          1.  If DECIMAL-FRACTION-OF-A-SECOND is not numeric
                    set VALID-FRACTION-OF-A-SECOND-SW to "no".
              else
                    set VALID-FRACTION-OF-A-SECOND-SW to "yes".


Step E.   Validate meridiem designator.

          1.  If 12-hour system
                  If MERIDIEM-DESIGNATOR is not equal to "A" or "P"
                        set VALID-MERIDIEM-SW to "no"
                  else
                        set VALID-MERIDIEM-SW to "yes"
              else if MERIDIEM-DESIGNATOR is equal to space
                        set VALID-MERIDIEM-SW to "yes"
                  else
                        set VALID-MERIDIEM-SW to "no".


Step F.   Validate time zone reference code.

          1.  Lookup TIME-ZONE-REFERENCE-CODE on a table of valid codes.

          2.  If found
                    set VALID-TIME-ZONE-SW to "yes"
              else
                    set VALID-TIME-ZONE-SW to "no".


Step G.   Validate time differential factor.

          1.  If TDF-SIGN is not equal to "+" or "-"
                    set VALID-TDF-SW to "no"
              else set VALID-TDF-SW to "yes".

          2.  If TDF-VALUE is not numeric
              or (TDF-SIGN is equal to "+"
                  and TDF-VALUE is greater than "1300")
              or (TDF-SIGN is equal to "-"
                  and TDF-VALUE is greater than "1200")
                        reset VALID-TDF-SW to "no".


Step H.   Evaluate validity.

          1.  If VALID-HOUR-SW is equal to "no"
              or VALID-MINUTE-SW is equal to "no"
              or VALID-SECOND-SW is equal to "no"
              or VALID-FRACTION-OF-A-SECOND-SW is equal to "no"
              or VALID-MERIDIEM-SW is equal to "no"
              or VALID-TIME-ZONE-SW is equal to "no"
              or VALID-TDF is equal to "no"
                    set VALID-TIME-SW to "no"
              else
                    set VALID-TIME-SW to "yes".
```

Figure C.6. (continued)

Self-Checking Numbers   **Self-checking numbers** are frequently used in banking, accounts receivable, and other application areas so that account code numbers can be validated without the need to carry a correspondence field in transaction records. A self-checking number is a code number with a calculated digit—called a **check digit**— appended to it so that clerical, data-entry, and data-transmission errors can be detected by recalculation. For example, suppose that 5-digit code

Time-conversion data fields:

```
TIME  (hhmmssddxxxsnnnn)
    HOUR (hh)
    MINUTE (mm)
    SECOND (ss)
    DECIMAL-FRACTION-OF-A-SECOND (dd)
    MERIDIEM-DESIGNATOR (x)
    TIME-ZONE-REFERENCE-CODE (xxx)
    TIME-DIFFERENTIAL-FACTOR (snnnn)
        TDF-SIGN (s)
        TDF-VALUE (nnnn)

TIME-SYSTEM-SW (12/24)

DAY-SWITCH (previous/next)
```

12-hour to 24-hour time conversion:

```
    1.  If MERIDIEM-DESIGNATOR is equal to "P"
            add 12 to HOUR.

    2.  If HOUR is equal to "24"
            move 00 to HOUR.

    3.  Move space to MERIDIEM-DESIGNATOR.
```

24-hour to 12-hour time conversion:

```
    1.  If HOUR is less than "12"
            move "A" to MERIDIEM-DESIGNATOR
        else
            subtract 12 from HOUR
            move "P" to MERIDIEM-DESIGNATOR.

    2.  If HOUR is equal to "00"
            move "12" to HOUR.
```

Local time to Universal Time conversion:

```
    1.  If 12-hour-system
            convert to 24-hour system.

    2.  If Time-zone-code used to identify local time
            lookup TIME-DIFFERENTIAL-FACTOR.

    3.  Add TIME-DIFFERENTIAL-FACTOR to HOUR-MINUTE.

    4.  Move +0000 to TIME-DIFFERENTIAL-FACTOR.

    5.  If HOUR is negative
            add 24 to HOUR
            set DAY-SW to "previous"
        else if HOUR is not less than 24
            subtract 2400 to HOUR-MINUTE
            set DAY-SW to "next".
```

Figure C.7. Time-conversion logic.

numbers are used to identify customer accounts within a charge account system. Whenever any charges, payments, returns, or adjustments are made to an account, it is, of course, necessary to identify the account code number to which each should be posted. Unless some control is exercised over the accuracy of the account codes that are entered into the system, it is probable that undetected errors will occur when recording the code numbers. The types of errors that will occur are

1. **Substitution error.** The wrong digit is written, such as 7 instead of 9.
2. **Simple transposition error.** The correct digits are written but their positional placement is reversed, as if code number 56789 were entered as 57689.
3. **Double transposition error.** The digits are transposed across a column, as if 56789 were recorded as 58769.

Time-span computation data fields:

```
EARLIER-CHRONOLOGICAL-TIME (hhmmssdd)
    EARLIER-CHRON-HOUR (hh)
    EARLIER-CHRON-MINUTE (mm)
    EARLIER-CHRON-SECOND (ss)
    EARLIER-CHRON-FRACTION-OF-A-SECOND (dd)
    EARLIER-CHRON-MERIDIEM (x)
    EARLIER-CHRON-TIME-ZONE-CODE
    EARLIER-CHRON-TDF

LATER-CHRONOLOGICAL-TIME (hhmmssdd)
    LATER-CHRON-HOUR (hh)
    LATER-CHRON-MINUTE (mm)
    LATER-CHRON-SECOND (ss)
    LATER-CHRON-FRACTION-OF-A-SECOND (dd)
    LATER-CHRON-MERIDIEM (x)
    LATER-CHRON-TIME-ZONE-CODE
    LATER-CHRON-TDF

TIME-SPAN (hhmmssdd)
    TIME-SPAN-HOURS (hh)
    TIME-SPAN-MINUTES (mm)
    TIME-SPAN-SECONDS (ss)
    TIME-SPAN-FRACTION-OF-A-SECONDS (dd)

TIME-SYSTEM-SW (12/24)

DAY-SPAN (ddd)
```

Time-span computation:

```
    1.  Compute DAY-SPAN.

    2.  If TIME-SYSTEM-SW is equal to "12"
            convert EARLIER-CHRONOLOGICAL-TIME to 24-hour-system
            convert LATER-CHRONOLOGICAL-TIME to 24-hour-system.

    3.  If EARLIER-CHRON-TIME-ZONE-CODE
            is not equal to LATER-CHRON-TIME-ZONE-CODE
        or EARLIER-CHRON-TDF is not equal to LATER-CHRON-TDF
            convert EARLIER-CHRONOLOGICAL-TIME to Universal Time
            convert LATER-CHRONOLOGICAL-TIME to Universal Time.

    4.  Subtract EARLIER-CHRONOLOGICAL-TIME
            from LATER-CHRONOLOGICAL-TIME giving TIME-SPAN.

    5.  If TIME-SPAN-HOURS is negative
            add 24 to TIME-SPAN-HOURS
            subtract 1 from DAY-SPAN.
```

Figure C.8. Time-span computation logic.

4. **Other transposition error.** The digits are transposed across two or more columns, as if 56789 were input as 59786.
5. **Omission error with right justification.** One or more of the digits is omitted and the resulting short number is justified to the right of the field, as if 56789 were entered as b5689 (b = blank space or other null value in the code position).
6. **Omission error with left justification.** One or more of the digits is omitted and the resulting short number is justified to the left of the field, as if 56789 were entered as 5689b.
7. **Right shift error.** All digits are correctly recorded on the input medium but the code value is shifted one or more positions to the right of the field boundary, as if 56789 were positioned within the field as b5678.
8. **Left shift error.** All digits are correctly recorded on the input medium but the code value is shifted one or more positions to the left of the field boundary, as if 56789 were positioned within the field as 6789b.
9. **Insertion error.** One or more extraneous digits are inserted into the code, as if 56789 were keyed as 567289.

Basic code number (without check digit)	5		0		8		1		7		3		2		9	

1. Assign checking factors: 1   2   1   2   1   2   1   2

2. Multiply each digit by its checking factor: 5   0   8   2   7   6   2   18

3. Crossfoot the products: 5 + 0 + 8 + 2 + 7 + 6 + 2 + 18 = 48

4. Divide the sum by 10:   48 / 10 = 4 with a remainder of 8

5. If remainder is not zero, subtract from 10:   10 − 8 = 2

6. Check digit is 2.

Full code number (with check digit)	5	0	8	1	7	3	2	9	2

Figure C.9. Modulus-10 check-digit computation example.

Recording errors may cause transaction records to be posted to the wrong account. Severe customer service problems occur when debits and credits are not correctly applied. To counter this situation, the programmer/analyst can specify that a check digit be incorporated into the basic code, typically as the terminal digit. A check digit could be formed by simply summing the individual digits of each account number. For account number 40212, for example, the check digit would be 9 (4 + 0 + 2 + 1 + 2 = 9). With this check digit suffixed to the original 5-digit code, the full self-checking account number is 402129. Should a clerk make a substitution error when he or she is transcribing or keying any of the digits (for example, 401129), the sum of the digits will not be equal to the check digit 9 (4 + 0 + 1 + 1 + 2 = 8). A check-digit validation routine can thus be employed to detect errors at data-entry time.

Check-digit system: Modulus-10

Although a simple sum-of-the-digits check-digit system can aid in detecting substitution errors as in the above example, it is not usually recommended or used because it fails to reveal transposition and certain other recording errors. To identify transposition errors, a self-checking system employing **weights** and a **modulus** must be used. The **modulus-10** method is an example of such a system. Although the weight values may vary, the check digit is usually computed as follows (see Figure C.9):

1. The units position and every second position of the basic code number is assigned a weight, or **checking factor**, of 2. The remaining digits are assigned a checking factor of 1.
2. Each digit of the basic code number is multiplied by its checking factor. (Because multiplication operations consume more processing time than addition, digit position values with a weight of 2 are, instead, sometimes added twice; those positions with a weight of 1 then use the code value directly. This check-digit system is hence often termed the **double-add-double method**.)
3. The products of the multiplication are summed.
4. The sum is divided by 10.
5. The remainder is subtracted from 10.
6. The difference becomes the check digit (unless the remainder at step 4, above, is zero, in which case the check digit is set to zero).

After the complete self-checking number (basic code number plus check digit) has been assigned to an account, the number can be checked by assigning

Basic code number (without check digit)	5	0	8	1	7	3	2	9	
1. Assign checking factors:	9	8	7	6	5	4	3	2	
2. Multiply each digit by its checking factor:	45	0	56	6	35	12	6	18	
3. Crossfoot the products:	45	+ 0	+ 56	+ 6	+ 35	+ 12	+ 6	+ 18	= 178
4. Divide the sum by 11:	178 / 11 = 16 with a remainder of 2								
5. If remainder is not zero, subtract from 11:	11 − 2 = 9								
6. Check digit is 9.									
Full code number (with check digit)	5	0	8	1	7	3	2	9	9

Figure C.10. Modulus-11 check-digit computation example.

a weight of 1 to the check-digit position and then performing steps 2, 3, and 4 above—this time including the check-digit value in the computation. If the remainder from the division at step 4 is zero, the number checks and is considered to be rendered correctly.

The modulus-10 method detects all substitution, most simple transposition, and certain other errors. It was often used in the past because its arithmetic operations were relatively simple and could thus be handled by punched-card equipment that contained limited computational power.

Check-digit system: Modulus-11

A check-digit system with superior error-detection capabilities is the **modulus-11** method. A modulus-11 check digit is computed as follows (see Figure C.10):

1. Starting with the units position, each digit of the basic code number is assigned a weight or checking factor in the range from 2 to 10. The checking factor is 2 for the units position, 3 for the tens position, 4 for the hundreds position, and so forth. Assignments continue until the full basic code number has been assigned. (Since there are nine checking factors, 2 through 10, a basic code number up to nine digits in length can be accommodated without repeating the weight value. Code numbers that contain more than nine digits are rare, but if a longer code is required, checking factors could be reassigned to any remaining digits by starting again with a checking factor of 2.)
2. Each digit of the basic code number is multiplied by its checking factor.
3. The products of the multiplication are summed.
4. The sum is divided by 11.
5. The remainder is subtracted from 11.
6. The difference becomes the check digit (unless the remainder at step 4, above, is zero, in which case the check digit is set to zero).

To check the number, the check digit is assigned a weight of 1, and steps 2, 3, and 4, above, are performed—this time including the check-digit value in the computation. If the remainder from the division at step 4 is zero, the number checks, and is considered to be rendered correctly.

When modulus-11 check digits are assigned to basic code numbers, certain codes produce a check digit of 10. This creates a problem because using this value would consume two check-digit positions. There are two alternative ways to handle check-digit value 10. One way is to simply discard those basic code numbers that result in a check digit of 10; that is, do not permit them to be

Error type	Typical error incidence percentage	Expected approximate percentage of errors that will be detected	
		Modulus-10 with weights 2 and 1	Modulus-11 with weights 2 through 10
Substitution	86%	100%	100%
Single transposition	8%	98%	100%
Double transposition	1%	0%	100%
Other	5%	69%	91%
Total all errors	100%	98.2%	99.5%

Figure C.11. Self-checking number error-detection rates.

assigned. The other approach is to choose another symbol, "X" for example, to indicate a value of 10 in one position. The former method wastes basic code numbers, which may be a problem if the code set is tightly packed; the latter introduces a nonnumeric character into a numeric code, which can cause some processing inconvenience.

Error-detection capabilities

The error-detection efficiency of the modulus-11 method is superior to modulus-10 because, although both systems are secure for substitution errors, the modulus-10 method does not detect (1) double transposition errors, (2) other transposition errors across an even number of columns, and (3) certain simple transposition errors (when digits 2 and 4 are transposed, for instance).

Figure C.11 gives an approximation of self-checking number error-detection capabilities. Observe that substitution, simple transposition, and double transposition errors taken together can be expected to account for about 95% of all errors. The error category of "Other" includes other transposition, omission, right shift, left shift, insertion errors, or any combination of two or more errors.

Given a processing volume of 100,000 transactions and an error rate of 1%, for example, about 18 erroneous transactions would escape detection by the modulus-10 system whereas about 5 would remain undetected with the modulus-11 method.

Looking at the negative side of self-checking numbers, use of a check digit—regardless of the computation method—increases the length of the code number. By doing so, the possibility of some sort of transcription error is increased slightly. Also, a precalculated index of valid code values, including the check digit, is required when the code number is initially assigned. Nevertheless, the code-validation power of a self-checking number usually outweighs these minor disadvantages.

Common self-checking code numbers

Most bank account and charge account code numbers are self-checking numbers. Although modulus-10 has traditionally been the prevalent system, there are a number of check-digit computation variations for such accounts because each issuing organization specifies its own method. More recently designed account code systems tend to use the modulus-11 method.

Universal Product Code

The familiar UPC symbol, found on grocery store items, uses an 11-digit basic code plus a modulus-10 check digit. Instead of using weights of 1 and 2, however, it employs checking factors of 1 and 3. You will not find the check digit printed among the ten digits; it is represented only in the machine-readable bar coding.

International Standard Book Number

An ISBN code is printed on the back, spine, and/or copyright page of most books. It is a 9-digit basic code plus a modulus-11 check digit. Weights 2 through 10 are used as described above. The letter "X" is used in lieu of check-digit value 10.

CUSIP Number

A CUSIP code number is assigned to financial security issues for uniform processing by banks, brokers, and other financial organizations. (The abbreviation CUSIP is drawn from the name of the Committee on Uniform Security Identification Procedures within the American Banking Association, which, together with the New York Clearing House Association, initiated development of the code.) The CUSIP code contains six numeric digits and two alphanumeric characters plus a modulus-10 check digit. When alphabetic characters are present in the code, the letter A is given a digit value of 10. The value for successive letters is that of the preceding letter incremented by one; the letter "Z" thus has a value of 35. However, letters "I" and "O" are excluded from assignment because of their similarity to the digits 1 and 0, respectively.

Data Universal Numbering System

D-U-N-S® is a service offered by the Dun & Bradstreet organization to facilitate identification of business establishments. The code number consists of an 8-digit basic code number plus a modulus-10 check digit. (D-U-N-S is a registered trademark and service mark of Dun & Bradstreet, Inc.)

Other Common Code Numbers

Certain commonly used codes are not self-checking but can be validated to a limited extent. Social Security numbers, telephone numbers, and ZIP code validations will be discussed.

Social Security numbers

A Social Security code number consists of nine digits. The first three digits are referred to as the **area indicator**, the next two are called the **group code**, and the last four digits are termed the **serial number**.

When the Social Security numbering system was originated, area-indicator codes were assigned to each state. The number of codes allocated was based on an estimate of the number of people covered by the original Social Security Act. Thus the first three digits of the Social Security number have geographical significance to the extent that they indicate the state in which an individual's Social Security card was applied for.

Currently, valid area indicators range from 001 through 595. In addition, area indicators from 700 through 728 were issued to railroad workers who were originally covered under a separate retirement system. All group codes and serial numbers are typically assigned. Because there is no check digit, the only Social Security number validation that can be done is to perform range checks on the area indicator as specified above. However, the programmer/

analyst should be aware that additional area indicators are assigned in sequence as new codes are required. The Social Security Administration expects that area indicators in the 600 range will begin to be assigned in the mid-1980s.

Telephone numbers

In the United States, telephone numbers are 10-digit codes. The first three digits are the **area code**, the next three specify the **prefix**, and the last three digits are called the **line number**.

The first digit of an area code number can be any number except zero or 1. (Zero is reserved for dialing the operator and a first digit of 1 is sometimes used to trigger an out-of-area call.) Conversely, the second digit of an area code is always zero or 1. The last digit of the area code can be any number.

Just as with the area code, the first digit of a prefix is never zero or 1. However, so that a prefix can be differentiated from an area code when only the former is dialed, the second digit of a prefix is also never zero or 1. The last digit of the prefix can be any number. However, the prefix value 555 is not valid for telephone subscribers. It is reserved for dialing directory assistance and to form fictitious numbers for use in motion pictures, novels, and the like. Line numbers can be any 4-digit value.

A limited validation of a telephone number could be performed by testing for numeric class and checking the first two digits of the area code and prefix in accordance with the parameters outlined above. A more effective validation would additionally use a table of valid area codes (there are approximately 105 within the United States) to do a code-existence check. An even better validation could be provided by making a consistency check between the area code and prefix. Where applicable, the validation could be made still "tighter" by doing a consistency check between geographical location (state abbreviation, perhaps) and area code value.

ZIP Codes

ZIP Codes are numerical codes that identify areas within the United States and its territories to facilitate the distribution of mail. A full ZIP Code, called **ZIP + 4**, contains nine digits. The first five digits form the basic code; the last four digits were added by the Budget Reconciliation Act of 1981 to permit mechanized sorting of mail to the firm, building, or carrier level. A hyphen separates the two groups of digits for output documents and displays; however, the hyphen is not usually stored internally.

The first digit of the basic 5-digit ZIP Code is a **national area code** that divides the country into 10 groups of states numbered from 0 in the Northeast to 9 in the Far West. Within these national areas, each state is divided into an average of 10 smaller geographical areas. These are identified by the second and third digits of the Code. The fourth and fifth digits identify a **local delivery area**.

The + 4 portion of the ZIP Code contains two subcodes. The first two digits signify a **sector**, which can be several blocks or groups of streets, large buildings, or a small geographical area. The last two digits subdivide the sectors into still smaller areas called **segments**. A segment can be one side of a city block or both sides of a particular street, one floor in a large building, a cluster of mailboxes, one post office box or group of boxes, or other similar limited delivery units.

Because most digit combinations are used, the only stand-alone data-validation check that can be made on a ZIP Code is to test the nine digits to ensure that they are of numeric class. A consistency check can be made between the state abbreviation and the first or the first three ZIP digits. Those data-processing installations that prepare significant mailing-address volumes typically acquire a copy of the ZIP Code Validation Tape from the Postal Service. This permits ZIP Code validation for each mailing address all the way to the house or building number level. Although the national tape contains approximately 3.5 million records, regional tapes are also available.

Numeric Amounts

When numeric-amount fields are entered into a system, they should be validated to ensure that they contain only valid numeric-field values.

Inputs to a batch-processing system are typically keyed by full-time data-entry operators and temporarily batched as collections of card, tape, or disk records. Because source documents are usually processed in batches, zero-filling and positioning of the numeric value can generally be handled by the limited logic capabilities of the data-entry device prior to the time that the records are input into the computer system. When the numeric value is already properly aligned on a decimal point within the field, there is no need to record a decimal point among the digits.

On the other hand, user personnel generally key inputs to on-line systems on an as-required basis. Instead of being collected on off-line storage media, the data is input directly into the computer system from a terminal. This means that the processing program must accept not only the numeric digits but also the decimal point and arithmetic sign representation when they are applicable. Then the program must strip out the decimal point and sign so that the zero-filled, properly signed, digit value is correctly positioned and represented in the field. This process is called **de-editing** a numeric field. A representative example of the logic that is required to de-edit a numeric field is as follows:

1. The maximum number of integer digit positions in the field is identified. Because the length of a COBOL data-item is limited to 18 digits, this will be within the range of zero through 18.
2. The maximum number of decimal fraction positions in the field is identified. This will be within a range of zero through 18 minus the maximum number of integer digit positions.
3. The allowable arithmetic sign representations are identified. This will typically be either (1) no sign, (2) a minus sign (–), or (3) a minus sign or a plus (+) sign.
4. The field is checked to ensure that no character values (including blank spaces), other than the following, are entered: (1) digits 0 through 9, (2) a decimal point, if decimal fraction digits are permitted, or (3) allowable arithmetic signs. Sometimes commas are also a permissible entry.
5. The number of decimal points entered is checked to ensure that not more than one has been entered.
6. The number of arithmetic signs entered is checked to ensure that not more than one has been entered. The sign placement could optionally be checked to ensure that it is the leftmost and/or the rightmost entry.
7. The number of integer position digits entered is checked to ensure that it is not greater than the maximum number allowed.
8. The number of decimal fraction digits entered is checked to ensure that it is not greater than the maximum number allowed.
9. If no error conditions have been detected, the following alignment operations are performed:
   a. The integer digit positions are right justified immediately to the right of the fixed assumed decimal point location. Excess leading integer positions are set to zero.

b. The decimal fraction digits are left justified immediately to the right of the fixed assumed decimal point location. Excess trailing decimal fraction positions are set to zero.

c. The arithmetic sign representation is set.

Embedded-Blank Check

Alphanumeric fields that contain certain code numbers and are used as key fields should generally be checked to ensure that blank positions have not been inadvertently entered among the code value characters. This is termed an **embedded-blank check**. An embedded blank is one that has nonblank characters represented within the field both to the left and the right of the blank position. Although embedded-blank spaces are permissible in many alphanumeric fields, they should be prohibited from certain ones. A part-number field, for example, is typically an alphanumeric field and often serves as a key field for inventory records and the like. If embedded-blank spaces were allowed within the field, different renderings of the part number could be expected to accidentally occur. This would cause confusion when entering and retrieving data. Each time an embedded blank was placed at a different location, it would be considered a different part number value.

Figure C.12 provides a flowchart of the logic that is required to detect embedded-blank spaces within a field. This logic will also detect leftmost, or leading, blank spaces, which are typically also prohibited whenever embedded blanks are. The steps are as follows:

1. A subscript or index is initialized with a value equal to the character length of the field that is being checked. In the flowchart, this subscript is called LOC-SUB, for **loc**ate **sub**script.

2. A field to count characters other than blank spaces, named CHAR-COUNT in the flowchart, is initialized to zero.

3. Starting with the rightmost character of the field, each position is checked to see if it contains a blank space. This is represented in the flowchart by checking to see if POSN (LOC-SUB) is equal to a space.

4. If the position being checked contains a space, the CHAR-COUNT is checked. If CHAR-COUNT is equal to zero, the blank space is not embedded but rather a permissible trailing blank. In this case, control advances to step 7, below.

5. An embedded blank has been detected when a blank space has been encountered and CHAR-COUNT is not equal to zero. Thus, an appropriate error-processing routine should be performed prior to exiting from the routine.

6. If POSN (LOC-SUB) does not contain a space, CHAR-COUNT is incremented by 1. (Instead of a counter, a simple two-state switch could be used for CHAR-COUNT. By using a counter, however, the length of the valid character-string will be available at the conclusion of the routine.)

7. LOC-SUB is decremented by 1 so that the next position will be checked on the next iteration.

8. The checking process continues by returning to step 3, above. When LOC-SUB is equal to zero, it means that all characters have been checked and an exit is made from the routine.

An alternate approach to checking for embedded blanks could be coded using the INSPECT statement, which is discussed in Chapter 9.

Editing Routine Logic

Most editing of output fields can be accomplished by either (1) specifying editing symbols within the PICTURE clause, (2) coding the BLANK WHEN ZERO clause, or (3) using the JUSTIFIED RIGHT clause. However, there are certain editing needs that require special logic. Three common ones will be discussed: left or

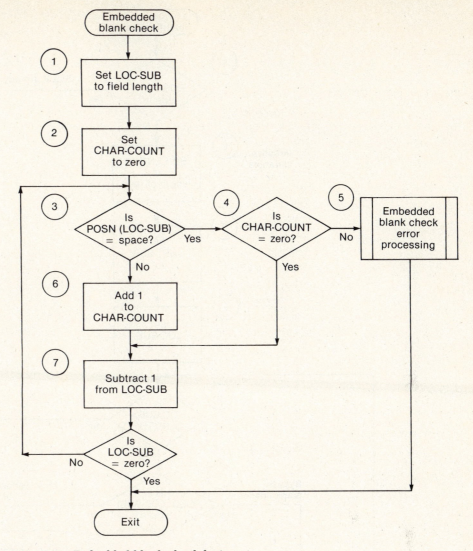

Figure C.12. Embedded blank check logic.

right justification of data within a field, elimination of excess blank spaces within a field, and trailing zero suppression.

Left or Right Justification of Data Within a Field

Although an entire field can be left or right justified into another simply by using the MOVE statement together with appropriate PICTURE clause and/or JUSTI-FIED RIGHT clause specifications, justification of significant characters *within* a field requires special coding. For example, consider an 8-digit numeric field with code numbers of various lengths justified to the right within the field. Suppose that, because of a change in specifications, it is now required that the code numbers be justified to the left.

Such justification requires that each nonblank character be located and moved to the first justified position or the next available one. Figure C.13 presents logic that can be used for left justification. The steps are as follows:

1. The leftmost character position of the field, POSN (1), is checked to determine if it contains a blank space. If it is not blank, the data is already left justified, so an exit is made from the routine.

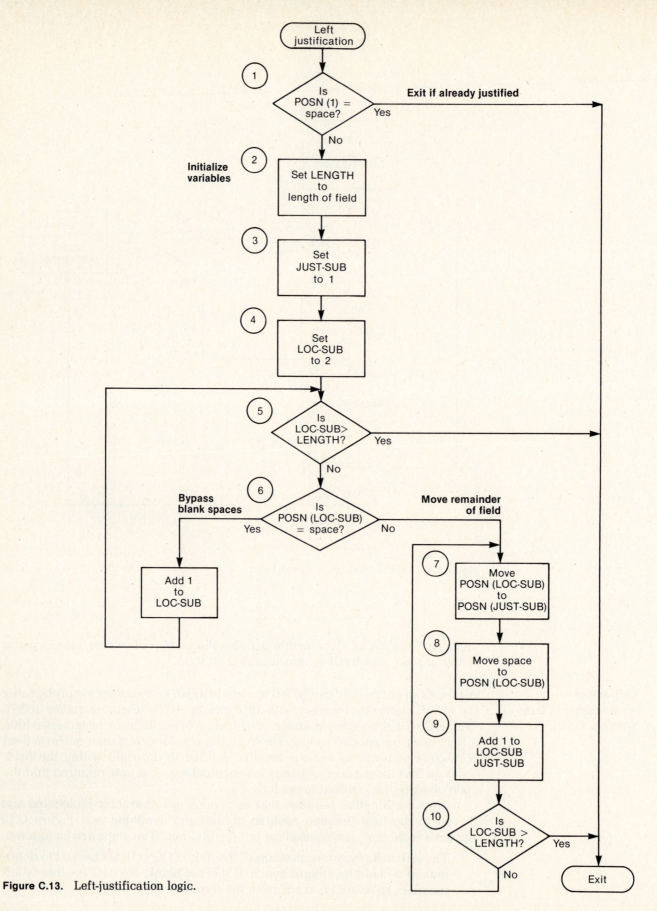

Figure C.13. Left-justification logic.

2. If a blank is present as the leftmost character, the field is either blank or not left justified. Hence a data-item to keep track of the field LENGTH is initialized with a value equal to the number of positions in the field that is being justified.
3. A subscript or index, called JUST-SUB for **just**ification **sub**script in the flowchart, is initialized to a value of 1. This subscript is used to keep track of the receiving, or justified, position within the field.
4. A subscript or index that is used to locate characters to be justified is initialized. Because the first position of the field to be justified has already been checked and is known to be a blank space (at step 1, above), LOC-SUB is set to a value of 2.
5. LOC-SUB is tested to see if it contains a value greater than the field LENGTH. This will, of course, not happen on the first iteration but if it does occur on a subsequent iteration, it means that the field is completely blank and an exit is thus made from the routine.
6. The next position of the field that is being justified, represented as POSN (LOC-SUB) in the flowchart, is checked to see if it contains a blank space. If it does, the blank space is a leading blank and must be bypassed. This bypass operation is handled by incrementing LOC-SUB and returning to test whether or not there are remaining positions of the field to check (step 5, above).
7. Once a nonblank value is encountered within the field, that value—which is in the POSN (LOC-SUB) position—is moved to the justified POSN (JUST-SUB) position.
8. The POSN (LOC-SUB) location is blanked to ensure that duplicate data will not remain in the rightmost positions of the field.
9. The LOC-SUB and JUST-SUB fields are incremented.
10. LOC-SUB is tested to determine if its value exceeds the field LENGTH value. Once it does, the justification has been completed and an exit is made from the routine. If there are remaining positions to be moved, the routine returns to that point (step 7, above). Observe that control is not returned to the point at which the blank space test is made (step 6, above). This is because alphanumeric fields may contain embedded blanks and, when they do, such blank spaces must be moved just as nonblank characters are.

Observe that the logic of this routine is designed to justify the data within the same field. Minor modifications could be made to cause the justification to occur in a separate receiving field. Similarly, minor modifications will permit the logic to be used for right justification.

Certain left-justification requirements could alternately be handled by the UNSTRING statement (which is discussed in Chapter 9).

Excess Blank Space Elimination

Excess blank spaces sometimes "creep" into alphanumeric fields. Someone's name field within a record, for example, may contain two blank spaces between the first and middle name when only a one space separator is intended. Although such excess blank spaces could be avoided, of course, by front-end data validation, such editing is often overlooked because the excess spaces usually cause few problems. Nevertheless, it is desirable to remove the excess spaces, even if only for cosmetic reasons.

Figure C.14 presents flowchart logic to eliminate excess blank spaces. The steps are as follows:

1. A LENGTH field is set to a value equal to the length of the field that is being processed.
2. A field, named BLANK-COUNT in the flowchart, is initialized to zero. This field will be used to tally blank spaces and to serve as a switch.
3. The subscript or index fields, LOC-SUB and JUST-SUB, are set to 1.

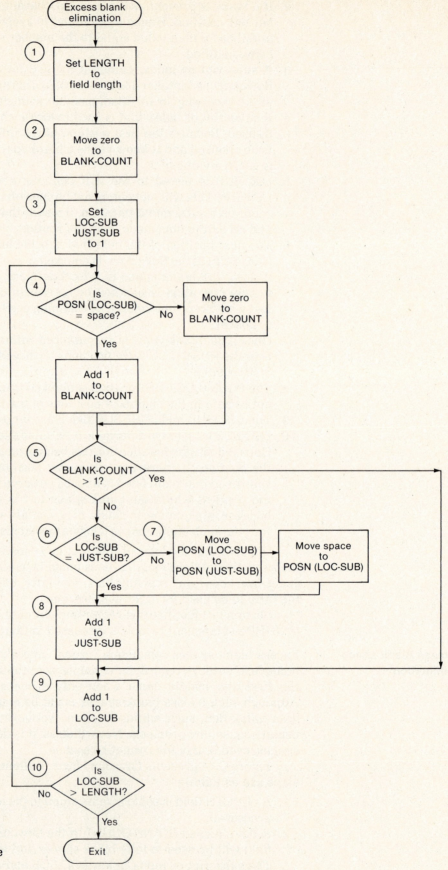

Figure C.14. Excess blank space
elimination logic.

4. The POSN (LOC-SUB) position is checked for a blank space. If it is blank, the BLANK-COUNT field is incremented; if not, the BLANK-COUNT field is reset to zero.

5. If the BLANK-COUNT field contains a value greater than 1, it means that an excess blank space has been detected. Because this excess blank is to be eliminated, control advances to step 9, below.

6. When the BLANK-COUNT field contains a value of zero, it means that a nonblank character has been encountered; a value of 1 indicates that a single (nonexcess) blank space has been detected. Both situations are treated similarly.

   The LOC-SUB field is compared to the JUST-SUB field. If they are equal, it means that an excess blank space has not yet been detected. Thus control advances to step 8, below.

7. If the LOC-SUB field is not equal to the JUST-SUB field, it reveals that one or more excess blank spaces were previously encountered. Hence all following positions must be moved to the left. This is handled by moving POSN (LOC-SUB) to POSN (JUST-SUB). Then the JUST-SUB and LOC-SUB fields are incremented.

8. JUST-SUB is incremented.

9. LOC-SUB is incremented.

10. LOC-SUB is compared with LENGTH to determine if the end of the field has been reached. If it has, an exit is made from the routine. Otherwise, control returns to that point in the logic where the next position is checked (step 4).

Certain excess blank or other delimiter elimination functions can alternately be handled by an UNSTRING statement with the DELIMITED BY ALL phrase.

Trailing Zero Suppression

Although the PICTURE symbol Z is provided for leading zero suppression, there is no counterpart editing symbol for trailing zero suppression of decimal fraction digits. Figure C.15 shows a flowchart for such trailing zero suppression. The logic is relatively straightforward. Starting at the rightmost position of the field, each digit position is compared to a zero until either a nonzero digit or the decimal point is located. Each zero digit is converted to a space. Depending upon the programming specifications, the routine could be modified to also blank the decimal point if there are no nonzero decimal fraction digits.

Recognize that the USAGE of the field that is being edited for trailing zero suppression must be of DISPLAY usage. Also, the routine must be performed *after* the decimal point has been edited into the field. Remember also that POSN must be specified as an alphanumeric field in order to compare each occurrence to a SPACE.

Arithmetic Routine Logic

There are a few arithmetically oriented routines that are appropriate for certain requirements. The following routines are covered: square root computation, changing the arithmetic sign of a field, balancing percentage totals, and check protection with words.

Square Root Computation

Although square root computations are not frequently needed in business-oriented programs, certain statistical applications require them. The calculation of economic order quantity within a materials management or requirements planning system is an example.

Even though COBOL does not contain an arithmetic operator or function for square root, it can be easily coded with a COMPUTE statement by the exponentiation of the value of a field to a power of .5 as shown in the following example:

COMPUTE SQUARE-ROOT = VALUE-TO-FIND-SQUARE-ROOT-OF ** .5

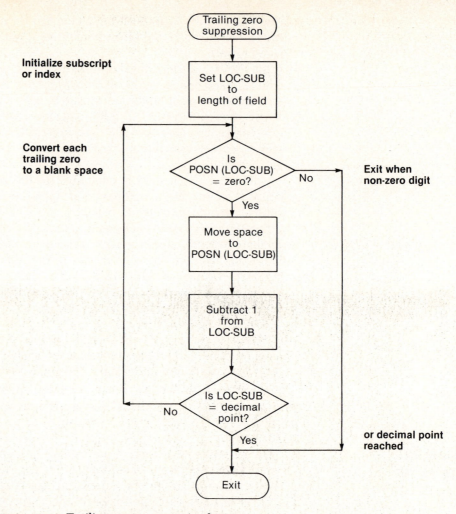

Initialize subscript or index

Convert each trailing zero to a blank space

Exit when non-zero digit

or decimal point reached

Figure C.15. Trailing zero suppression logic.

Changing the Arithmetic Sign of a Field

It is sometimes necessary to change a positive value to negative or vice versa. The simplest way to accomplish this is to multiply by a minus one (− 1). Remember that the product field must be defined with the symbol S in its PICTURE clause.

Balancing Percentage Totals

Figure C.16 presents a report showing the distribution of names according to the first letter of the last names. For example, of the 1,286,556 different last names that were in the Social Security Administration file at the time of the study, 61,336 surnames, or 4.7% started with the letter A.

Observe on the last report line that the total percentage of names sums to 99.99. This total should, of course, be 100.00%. Because of rounding errors, percentage totals such as this often sum to a figure that is either slightly higher or lower than the intended total.

If the programmer/analyst permits percentage totals that are slightly "out of whack" to be printed, he or she will be subjected to continuing questions from new users of the output who are not familiar with the problem. Then, too, for every user who asks about the situation, there are probably a few others who, although perhaps too timid or accepting to ask, nonetheless find the problem unsettling.

```
                    DISTRIBUTION OF NAMES
                 BY FIRST LETTER OF LAST NAME
      ----------------------------------------------
                      NUMBER          PERCENTAGE
      LETTER         OF NAMES          OF NAMES
      ------         --------         ----------

        A             61,336             4.77
        B             90,390             7.03
        C             70,687             5.49
        D             76,312             5.93
        E             32,667             2.54

        F             42,000             3.26
        G             66,960             5.20
        H             57,236             4.45
        I             15,790             1.23
        J             25,206             1.96

        K             82,589             6.42
        L             64,549             5.02
        M             83,284             6.47
        N             35,111             2.73
        O             33,351             2.59

        P             71,304             5.54
        Q              3,530              .27
        R             57,126             4.44
        S            126,057             9.80
        T             59,223             4.60

        U             12,069              .94
        V             34,122             2.65
        W             39,817             3.09
        X                721              .06
        Y             16,561             1.29
        Z             28,558             2.22
                   ----------           ------

      TOTAL        1,286,556*           99.99*  ◄────── Should be 100.00
```

Adapted from: "Report of Distribution of Surnames in the Social Security Number File, September 1, 1974," Department of Health and Human Services, Social Security Administration, Office of Operational Policy and Procedures, SSA Pub. No. 63-604, February 1981.

Figure C.16.   Example of the need to balance percentage totals.

Some programmer/analysts simply force the total to the desired amount. However, there is always a user who is going to manually recompute the totals for one reason or another. When totals are printed that are not a sum of the detail amounts, user confidence is *really* shattered. Therefore, this approach is not a good one.

One solution to the problem is, instead of rounding, to provide for balancing of the percentage totals. Before presenting this technique, let us review the way that COBOL compilers typically provide for rounding. Suppose that the result field of an arithmetic operation with the ROUNDED phrase is specified with a PICTURE of S9(3)V99. When the arithmetic computation is made, the COBOL compiler sets up a work field for itself which, in effect, has a PICTURE of S9(3)V999. Thus the arithmetic is carried out to one more decimal fraction position than that which is required for the answer. The compiler then adds 5 to the low-order position of the field. If that low-order position originally contained a 5 or greater, the addition of 5 will kick the remainder of the number up 1 to the next higher value. If the low-order position originally contained less than 5, the value is unchanged. Thus, after the compiler truncates the extra digit and

LETTER	NUMBER OF NAMES	Percentage carried to 5 decimal positions		Adjusting value		Adjusted percentage	PERCENTAGE OF NAMES
A	61,336	4.76745	+	.00500	=	4.77245	4.77
B	90,390	7.02573		.00245		7.02818	7.02 (−)
C	70,687	5.49428		.00818		5.50246	5.50 (+)
D	76,312	5.93149		.00246		5.93395	5.93
E	32,667	2.53910		.00395		2.54305	2.54
F	42,000	3.26452		.00305		3.26757	3.26
G	66,960	5.20459		.00757		5.21216	5.21 (+)
H	57,236	4.44877		.00216		4.45093	4.45
I	15,790	1.22730		.00093		1.22823	1.22 (−)
J	25,206	1.95918		.00823		1.96741	1.96
K	82,589	6.41938		.00741		6.42679	6.42
L	64,549	5.01719		.00679		5.02398	5.02
M	83,284	6.47340		.00398		6.47738	6.47
N	35,111	2.72906		.00738		2.73644	2.73
O	33,351	2.59226		.00644		2.59870	2.59
P	71,304	5.54223		.00870		5.55093	5.55 (+)
Q	3,530	.27437		.00093		.27530	.27
R	57,126	4.44022		.00530		4.44552	4.44
S	126,057	9.79801		.00552		9.80353	9.80
T	59,223	4.60321		.00353		4.60674	4.60
U	12,069	.93808		.00674		.94482	.94
V	34,122	2.65219		.00482		2.65701	2.65
W	39,817	3.09485		.00701		3.10186	3.10 (+)
X	721	.05604		.00186		.05790	.05 (−)
Y	16,561	1.28723		.00790		1.29513	1.29
Z	28,558	2.21972		.00513		2.22485	2.22
TOTAL	1,286,556*						100.00*

(+) = percentage .01 higher than obtained with conventional rounding.
(−) = percentage .01 lower than obtained with conventional rounding.

Figure C.17. Balanced percentage total example.

transfers the work area to the location that is specified in the program, the rounded value will be provided.

Figure C.17 shows the report again, this time with the computations that are necessary to balance the total to 100.00. The steps are as follows:

1. Choose the number of additional decimal positions to which the unadjusted answer can be carried. Three extra positions are generally sufficient to yield satisfactory results. Each percentage was thus computed to five decimal fraction positions (two to be printed plus the three additional ones). When this percentage is computed, it should *not* be rounded.
2. Establish a field to hold the adjusting value. This field must contain the same number of decimal fraction positions as chosen for the answer. The initial value of this adjusting value should contain all zeros except for a digit of 5 in the position that corresponds to the first position to the right of the rightmost digit that will be printed. This adjusting value is used in a manner similar to that used for rounding, as explained above. Thus, for the example, the adjusting value is initialized to .00500.
3. The adjusting value is added to the unrounded percentage.
4. The excess three digits are truncated to produce the adjusted percentage.
5. The truncated digits are stored as the adjusting value for the next computation.

This method will balance the detail values to the totals. However, as shown in Figure C.17, certain detail figures may be slightly different from the results produced with conventional rounding. Should this be disturbing, remember that all rounded values are approximations. In any event, when this balancing technique is used, it should be documented so that other users and programmer/analysts will recognize the technique and the reason for using it.

A related use for this balancing technique occurs when, as in cost accounting, a given total dollar (or other) value is distributed to two or more detail amounts that are based upon percentages. When the computed detail dollar amounts are summed, they may be similarly higher or lower than the original dollar amount.

Check Protection with Words

Protection of check dollar amounts is typically ensured by one or a combination of the following techniques: (1) asterisk-filling the numeric-check amount field, (2) printing the check amount field with a floating dollar sign, or (3) using check forms that have preprinted shaded areas for the numeric-check amount. Check protection with words is an even more effective method that adds a nice touch. This technique is commonly used for handwritten checks in which the dollar amount is written once with numeric digits, then represented again by spelling out with the English words for the amount. Although check protection with words is simple to handle manually, it requires relatively complex program logic.

To express a number in words requires the use of digit names, compound-number names, and position-value names. Digit names range from 1 to 9. Compound number names are used for 2-digit values from 10 to 99. Position-value names as high as quadrillion are used for a dollars and cents number of the maximum length that can be carried in a COBOL data-item (18 digits; 16 integer and 2 decimal fraction positions). Figure C.18 provides guidelines for the logic that is required to express numeric amounts in words. When computing the maximum field length required for the words, a value of all 7s should be used because it will require the most character positions.

Table Search and Sort Routine Logic

Routines that efficiently locate or rearrange items within a tabular list of entries can be rather complicated to code unless a sound approach is used. Two table search routines (linear selection and binary search), dynamic table building, and internal sorts are discussed here.

Selecting the Highest or Lowest Value from a List

There are many situations in which it is necessary to select the highest or lowest value from a list of table entries. For example, programming specifications could require that the lowest test score, the highest temperature, the least tax liability, or the closest flight time be chosen from a list of like entries. To accomplish such tasks, a table-processing technique known as **linear selection** is used.

Figure C.19 illustrates the processing that is required to select the lowest value from a list of entries. The list contains 11 ENTRY occurrences, each of which contains the 2-digit mile/hour speed, rounded to the nearest whole number, of an animal. In the example, the slowest animal is to be selected. An area, such as SELECTION, is established to hold the selected entry. A subscript or index field, such as SUB, is also specified. To begin the selection process, SELECTION is set to HIGH-VALUES and SUB is initialized, typically to the first entry. Whenever an ENTRY occurrence value lower than the SELECTION value is found, that value is moved to the SELECTION field. Depending upon the processing to be done, it may be desirable to store the subscript value of the selected entry rather than, or in addition to, the selected entry value.

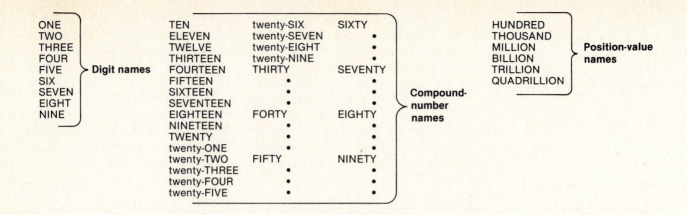

ONE	TEN	twenty-SIX	SIXTY
TWO	ELEVEN	twenty-SEVEN	•
THREE	TWELVE	twenty-EIGHT	•
FOUR	THIRTEEN	twenty-NINE	•
FIVE	FOURTEEN	THIRTY	SEVENTY
SIX	FIFTEEN	•	•
SEVEN	SIXTEEN	•	•
EIGHT	SEVENTEEN	•	•
NINE	EIGHTEEN	FORTY	EIGHTY

Digit names

Compound-number names

HUNDRED
THOUSAND
MILLION
BILLION
TRILLION
QUADRILLION

Position-value names

Position Wording Guidelines

Position	Number name		Position-value name
16	digit name		QUADRILLION
15	digit name	(rule 1)	HUNDRED (rule 1)
14	compound-number name	(rule 1)	
13	digit name	(rules 1, 2, & 3)	TRILLION (rule 4)
12	digit name	(rule 1)	HUNDRED (rule 1)
11	compound-number name	(rule 1)	
10	digit name	(rules 1, 2, & 3)	BILLION (rule 4)
9	digit name	(rule 1)	HUNDRED (rule 1)
8	compound-number name	(rule 1)	
7	digit name	(rules 1, 2, & 3)	MILLION (rule 4)
6	digit name	(rule 1)	HUNDRED (rule 1)
5	compound-number name	(rule 1)	
4	digit name	(rules 1, 2, & 3)	THOUSAND (rule 1)
3	digit name	(rule 1)	HUNDRED (rule 1)
2	compound-number name	(rule 1)	
1	digit name	(rules 1, 2, & 3)	

Rule 1: Null if digit in that position is zero.

Rule 2: Null if digit in position immediately to the left is 1.

Rule 3: Print preceding hyphen if not null and if digit value in position immediately to the left is from 2 through 9.

Rule 4: Null if digit value in two preceding positions to the left and that position are all equal to zero.

Example: The check amount of $43,506.87 should read:

FORTY-THREE THOUSAND FIVE HUNDRED SIX AND 87/100 DOLLARS

Figure C.18. Check protection with words logic.

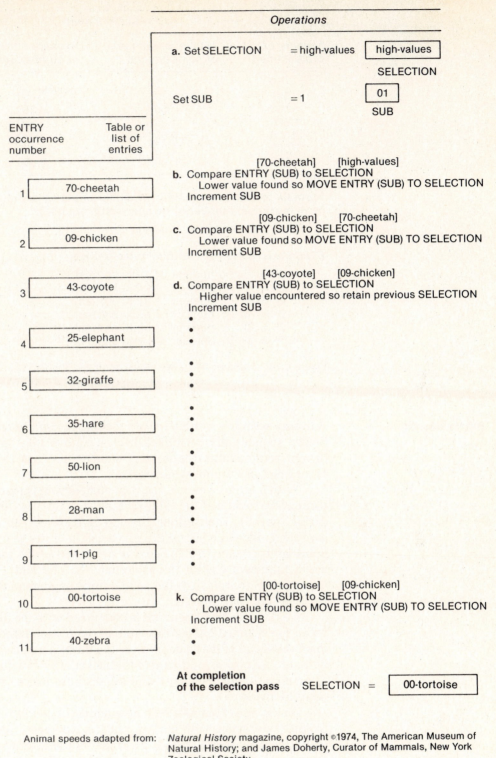

Figure C.19. Lowest value selection example.

| | Serial search | | Binary search |
Number of table entries	Maximum number of comparisons	Average number of comparisons	Maximum number of comparisons
50	50	25	6
100	100	50	7
500	500	250	9
1,000	1,000	500	10
2,000	2,000	1,000	11
5,000	5,000	2,500	13
10,000	10,000	5,000	14

Formula to compute maximum number of binary search comparisons (x = maximum number of comparisons required):

2^x > number of table entries

Example to solve for x with 50 table entries:

$2^1 = 2$ [< number of table entries]
$2^2 = 4$ [< number of table entries]
$2^3 = 8$ [< number of table entries]
$2^4 = 16$ [< number of table entries]
$2^5 = 32$ [< number of table entries]
⟶ $2^6 = 64$ [> number of table entries]

Figure C.20. Number of comparisons required for serial and binary searches.

Binary Search

A **binary search** is a table lookup technique used to reduce the search time for longer sequentially organized tables. Figure C.20 gives an indication of the drastic reduction in comparison volumes that can be realized by employing a binary rather than a serial search.

With a binary search, the first comparison is made against the table argument in the middle of the table (rather than the first argument as is done with a serial search). Then either the top half or the bottom half of the table is searched, depending upon the relationship of the search argument to that midpoint table argument. If the search argument is less than the middle table argument, the lower half of the table must be checked. Conversely, if the search argument is greater than the middle table argument, the upper half of the table becomes the search area.

Next the search argument is compared with the argument of the middle entry in the selected half of the table to determine their relationship. Depending upon the result of that comparison, the table is again split in half and the middle entry of that portion of the table is checked.This halving process is repeated until an equal table argument is found or there are no remaining portions of the table to divide.

Binary searches can be conveniently coded in COBOL through use of the SEARCH statement with the ALL phrase. However, this feature is not available on all compilers, so Figure C.21 presents the logic that can be coded in situations in which SEARCH/ALL is not available. The steps are as follows:

1. A field that is used to hold a lower table limit, called LO-LIM in the flowchart, is initialized to zero.
2. A field that is used to hold a higher table limit, called HI-LIM in the flowchart, is initialized to the occurrence number of the last table entry.
3. A field that will be used to hold the occurrence number of the table entry referenced during the immediately previous iteration, named LAST-MID in the flowchart, is initialized to zero.

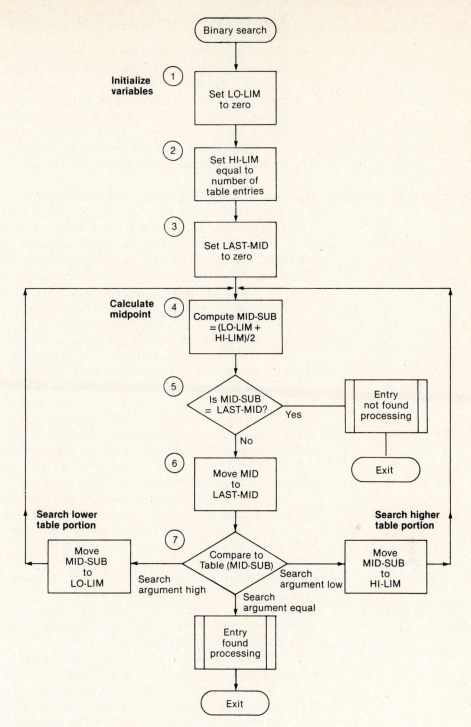

Figure C.21. Binary search logic.

4. The midpoint of the table is calculated by adding LO-LIM and HI-LIM, dividing the sum by two, and rounding to the nearest whole number. This midpoint is stored in a subscript field, called MID-SUB. (For this routine to operate correctly, it is imperative that this quotient be ROUNDED.)
5. MID-SUB is compared to LAST-MID. If they are equal, it means that the entry is not present in the table and thus the search has been completed.

Appropriate processing should be performed to handle such entry-not-found conditions.

6. The current MID-SUB value is stored in LAST-MID.
7. The search argument is compared to the table argument at the MID-SUB occurrence location. If the search argument is higher than the table argument, the MID-SUB value is moved to the LO-LIM value; if lower, MID-SUB is moved to HI-LIM. In both cases, control returns to the midpoint calculation, step 4, above.

When the search argument is equal to the table argument, the appropriate entry-found processing is performed.

Dynamic Table Building

Dynamic table building or **insertion sorting** as the process is sometimes called, is a technique for successively inserting additional entries into a growing list. It is an approach that is called for when either (1) the specific value of the table arguments is not known until the program is executing or (2) the value of possible table arguments is known beforehand but the volume of the total population of entries (as distinguished from the actual population to be processed) is greater than can be physically accommodated or efficiently processed in storage. Dynamic table building is a technique often employed in on-line systems because (1) transactions tend to be processed one by one and (2) minimal storage requirements are typically sought.

A concordance-type application can be used to illustrate dynamic table building. A **concordance** is an alphabetical index of the subjects, topics, or principal words of a written work. Suppose we wanted to alphabetize each word and count the number of times it occurs in a work. A table of all of the words in an unabridged dictionary could be used, but it would be not only an unnecessarily lengthy table, but also special technical words or variations that are not present in the table would probably be encountered from time to time.

Figure C.22 shows an example in which a concordance of the words of Abraham Lincoln's Gettysburg Address is to be prepared. A dynamic table area is allocated for table entries; an entry will contain a word and a count of the number of times the word is used in the Gettysburg Address.

A field named NBR-ENTRIES is initialized to zero. All words of the Address will be placed, one by one, in a field called NEXT-ENTRY; the NEXT-ENTRY field will be used as a search argument. During the table processing, NEXT-ENTRY is compared to each table-argument occurrence less than NBR-ENTRIES until a greater table-entry value is found.

When the first word—"Fourscore"—is processed, NBR-ENTRIES is equal to zero. "Fourscore" is thus inserted into the table as the first occurrence and NBR-ENTRIES is incremented by 1.

When the second word—"and"—is compared to the table entry, the table argument of "Fourscore" is higher. When a higher table argument is encountered, all higher entries in the table must be "pushed down." The search argument is then inserted at the previous location of the first higher entry.

The nineteenth word—"and"—has already been placed in the table. Thus the word count is incremented, and NBR-ENTRIES is not changed.

Internal Sorts

When the entries of a list or table residing in storage require sequencing, an **internal sort** may be used to order them. An internal sort is one in which the data is processed completely in primary storage. A frequently used internal sort algorithm is the **standard exchange method** or, as it is more commonly called, the **bubble sort**. The name depicts the effect of its logical process that "bubbles" the lesser key values to the top of the list.

The general method of a bubble sort is to pass through the list of entries as many times as is necessary to arrange them in sequence. The minimum number

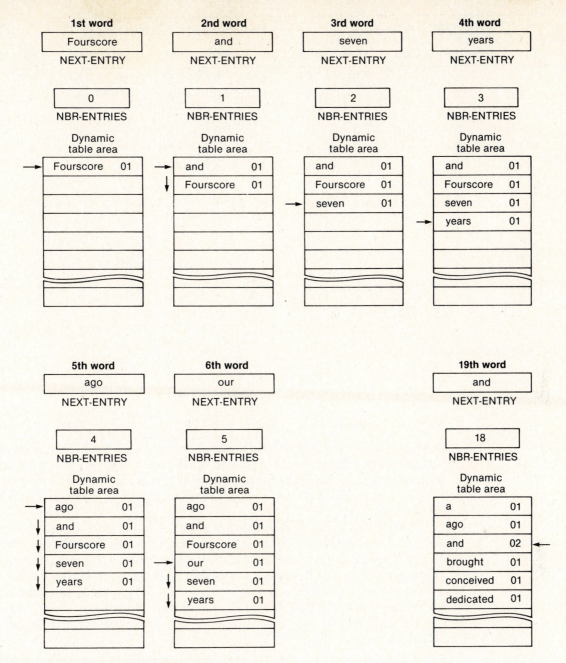

1st word	2nd word	3rd word	4th word
Fourscore	and	seven	years
NEXT-ENTRY	NEXT-ENTRY	NEXT-ENTRY	NEXT-ENTRY

0	1	2	3
NBR-ENTRIES	NBR-ENTRIES	NBR-ENTRIES	NBR-ENTRIES

Dynamic table area (×4)

Fourscore 01	and 01	and 01	and 01
	Fourscore 01	Fourscore 01	Fourscore 01
		seven 01	seven 01
			years 01

5th word	6th word	19th word
ago	our	and
NEXT-ENTRY	NEXT-ENTRY	NEXT-ENTRY

4	5	18
NBR-ENTRIES	NBR-ENTRIES	NBR-ENTRIES

Dynamic table area (×3)

ago 01	ago 01	a 01
and 01	and 01	ago 01
Fourscore 01	Fourscore 01	and 02
seven 01	our 01	brought 01
years 01	seven 01	conceived 01
	years 01	dedicated 01

Figure C.22. Dynamic table building example.

of passes that will be required is one (when the list happens to be already in sequence) whereas the maximum number of passes will be equal to a value of one less than the number of entries in the list.

The object of each pass is to place one entry in its final sorted position. Thus, as a minimum, the first pass positions the highest key value, the second pass sequences the next to the highest key value, and so forth. If descending sequence is required, lower key values rather than higher ones can be tested for.

During the first pass, the first entry in the list is compared to the second. As shown in Figure C.23, if the pair of entries is in sequence, the process continues to compare the second with its immediate successor. The second comparison of

Entry occurrence number	Initial table or list of entries	List after comparison of entries								
		1&2	2&3	3&4	4&5	5&6	6&7	7&8	8&9	9&10
1	5	5	5	5	5	5	5	5	5	5
2	12	12	8	8	8	8	8	8	8	8
3	8	8	12	3	3	3	3	3	3	3
4	3	3	3	12	9	9	9	9	9	9
5	9	9	9	9	12	4	4	4	4	4
6	4	4	4	4	4	12	12	12	12	12
7	13	13	13	13	13	13	13	1	1	1
8	1	1	1	1	1	1	1	13	11	11
9	11	11	11	11	11	11	11	11	13	7
10	7	7	7	7	7	7	7	7	7	13
Cumulative number of exchanges:		0	1	2	3	4	4	5	6	7

⟩ = exchange made

Figure C.23. Bubble sort example.

the figure shows that the entries are exchanged when a pair is not in sequence. Comparison and conditional exchange continues through the list; each entry is compared with its successor and exchanged if it is higher. The pass ends after the penultimate entry is compared with the last entry and the exchange is made, if called for.

Second and successive passes are identical to the first, except that ranked entries can be excluded from the processing. Thus one less entry is inspected during the second pass, two less during the third pass, and so on. A count of exchanges made during the pass is maintained. The sort is over when either (1) no exchanges are made during a pass or (2) the number of passes executed is equal to a value of one less than the number of entries in the list.

Detailed bubble-sort logic is presented in flowchart form in Figure C.24. The steps are as follows:

1. A field, named LIMIT in the flowchart, is initialized to the number of table or list entries that are to be sorted.
2. A counter or switch to keep track of whether an exchange occurs is initialized to zero. This field is called SWAP-COUNT in the flowchart.
3. A subscript or index, LO-SUB in the flowchart, is initialized to 1. This field is used to reference the lower entry of each comparison pair.
4. A subscript or index, HI-SUB in the flowchart, is initialized to 2. This field is used to reference the higher entry of each comparison pair.
5. The lower entry of each pair, ENTRY (LO-SUB), is compared to the higher, ENTRY (HI-SUB). If the lower entry is greater in value, it must be exchanged with the higher entry.
6. To accomplish the exchange, a temporary hold area is required. First, one of the entries, ENTRY (LO-SUB) is moved to the temporary hold area, ENTRY-HOLD. Next, the other entry, ENTRY (HI-SUB), is moved to the alternate entry, ENTRY (LO-SUB). To complete the exchange, ENTRY-HOLD is

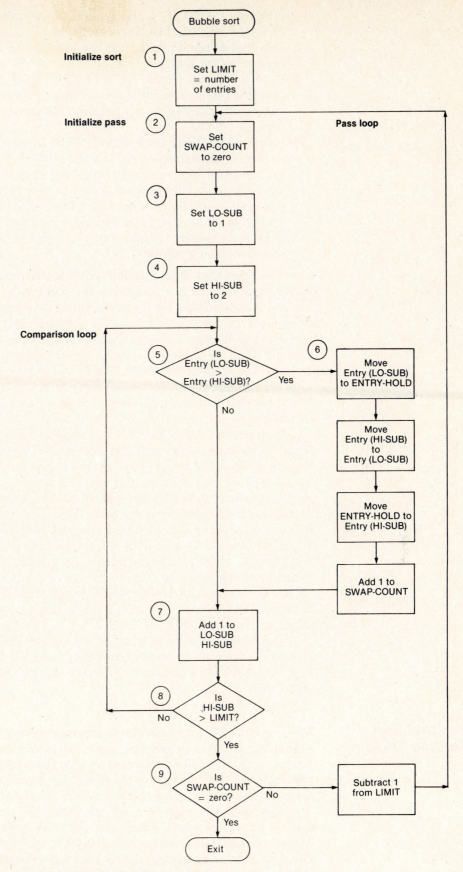

Figure C.24. Detailed bubble sort logic.

moved to ENTRY (HI-SUB). Finally, SWAP-COUNT is incremented to indicate that an exchange has been made.

7. Whether or not an exchange has been made, LO-SUB and HI-SUB are incremented for the next comparison.

8. HI-SUB is compared to LIMIT. If HI-SUB is not greater than LIMIT, it means that there are more pairs in the list to be processed during this pass. Hence control is returned to the beginning of the comparison iteration, step 5, above.

9. Should HI-SUB be greater than LIMIT, it means that all comparisons for that pass have been completed. Thus the SWAP-COUNT is tested to determine if an exchange has been made during the pass. If at least one swap was made, it means that at least one more pass is required. However, because one more entry has been placed in its final sorted location, that ranked entry can be eliminated from the comparisons of the next pass. Hence, LIMIT is decremented by 1. Then control is returned to the beginning of the pass iteration, step 2, above.

The flowchart logic handles entries that contain sort-entry keys. Only minor modifications are necessary to accommodate entries that contain both key and function fields. Just remember that the comparison involves only the key field; the exchange must process the complete entry.

The bubble sort is commonly used because its algorithm is relatively easy to understand and code. Although it performs adequately for short lists of up to 30 entries or so, the programmer/analyst should be aware that there are better internal sort algorithms for longer lists. Although it is beyond the scope of this text to provide detailed treatment of other sort methods, a few brief comments can be made.

A **sifting** or **shuttle sort** is a variation of the bubble sort that will provide faster processing under most circumstances. Whenever an exchange is made, the lower key is "shuttled" back up the list as far as it can go.

The **Shell sort** is named for its originator, D. L. Shell, and is sometimes referred to as a Shell-Metzner sort when an adaptation described by Marlene Metzner is used. Shell sorts are an extension of the sifting method and provide even quicker processing. Instead of comparing and exchanging adjacent entries, the Shell sort works with entries that are a longer, fixed distance apart. For example, entry 1 is compared to entry 6, entry 6 to 11, 11 to 16, and so forth. When an exchange occurs, the lower key is shuttled back through the previous entry comparisons as far as it will go. That is, if entries 11 and 16 are exchanged, the current value of entry 11 will be compared to entry 6, and if exchanged, then to entry 1.

Quicksort is a generic term for a sorting method first described by C.A.R. Hoare. Quicksorts are binary tree-based methods that can provide faster timings than Shell sorts unless the list is already sorted or very close to being in sequence.

External Sort Routine Logic

Most sorting within commercial application systems is by external sorts rather than internal ones. An **external sort** is one in which the entries to be sorted are processed as records on a secondary storage device such as disk or tape. This contrasts with an internal sort in which the items to be sorted are processed as table entries within primary storage.

External sorts must be used whenever the list of items to be sorted is too large to fit into the primary storage area. With COBOL programs, external sorts are invoked by specification of the COBOL SORT verb. Some COBOL installations instead handle their external sorts as a **stand-alone sort** step by specifying the sort parameters directly to the utility-sort program. Regardless of which ap-

Part A: Accounts Receivable System record formats

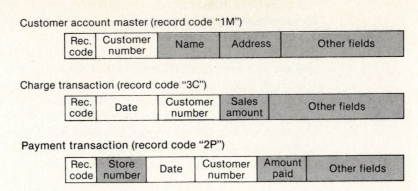

Customer account master (record code "1M")

Rec. code	Customer number	Name	Address	Other fields

Charge transaction (record code "3C")

Rec. code	Date	Customer number	Sales amount	Other fields

Payment transaction (record code "2P")

Rec. code	Store number	Date	Customer number	Amount paid	Other fields

Part B: Accounts Receivable System record formats with sort-key prefix

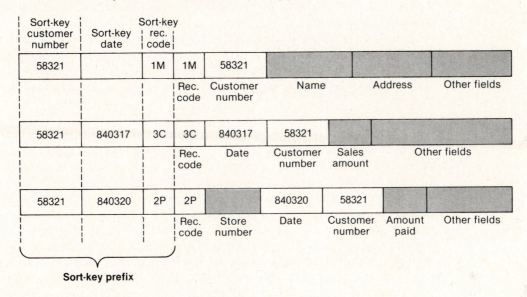

Sort-key customer number	Sort-key date	Sort-key rec. code						
58321		1M	1M	58321				
			Rec. code	Customer number	Name	Address	Other fields	

58321	840317	3C	3C	840317	58321			
			Rec. code	Date	Customer number	Sales amount	Other fields	

58321	840320	2P	2P		840320	58321		
			Rec. code	Store number	Date	Customer number	Amount paid	Other fields

Sort-key prefix

Figure C.25. Example of records with sort-key prefix.

proach is used, the same utility-sort program typically does the sorting. Utility-sort programs are designed so that when the list of items *will* fit in storage, the sort is processed internally.

A programmer/analyst who is familiar with the COBOL SORT statement or the utility-sort parameter syntax can handle most sorting requirements in a straightforward manner. However, there are two areas that require special sort design consideration: nonmatching record formats and alphabetical filing.

Nonmatching Record Formats

When designing records, it is a good practice to place the key fields for an application in the same relative location for all record types. Unfortunately, at the time a record is designed, it is sometimes not possible to define or foretell all of the future sorting requirements. When multiple record formats require sorting and the key fields are not in the same relative location within each record format, a **sort key prefix** must be appended to each record.

Figure C.25 shows an example of three record formats within an accounts receivable application: customer master, charge transaction, and payment transaction. To prepare monthly customer statements, suppose that the programming specifications call for the group of records for each account to be arranged with the customer master record first, then the charge and payment transactions in date sequence within the group. If, within the account group, a charge and payment transaction fall on the same date, the payment transaction is to precede the charge transaction.

Given these specifications, the major field of the sort key is the customer number. The intermediate field is the date, and the minor field is the record code. Part B of the figure shows the same record formats with the sort key prefix. (Actually, because the record-code field is in the same relative position in all records, it is not necessary to duplicate the field in the sort key prefix. Also, to ensure that the customer master record is positioned as the first record of an account group, its sort-key date field should be set to LOW-VALUES.)

When the COBOL SORT statement is used, the sort key prefix is typically constructed during the INPUT PROCEDURE processing. Within the OUTPUT PROCEDURE, the prefix will probably be stripped away if either (1) use of the original record descriptions within the program is desired or (2) the sorted records are to be stored as a file formatted in accordance with the original record description formats.

Another example of nonmatching record formats occurs when the record formats are of different lengths. If two or more fixed-length record formats must be sorted and the formats are not of uniform lengths, the shorter records must be padded—typically as a suffix with spaces—to equal the length of the longest record.

Alphabetical Filing

The alphabetizing of entries for files, lists, directories, library catalogs, and the like has traditionally posed problems for the creators and users of such information sources. The arrangement of items into alphabetical order may seem to be a straightforward task. To produce a useful information source, however, requires the establishment of rules and conventions to handle intricacies of the English language, numbers, and names. When alphabetical entries are sorted electronically, the problem is compounded because of the difficulty in identifying and rearranging those adjustments to strict alphabetical sequence that are generally handled, sometimes almost unconsciously, in manual systems.

Although the rules and conventions for alphabetical filing systems are many and sometimes conflict from one system to another, there are three basic conventions: letter-by-letter, word-by-word, and unit-by-unit. With the **letter-by-letter** approach, entries are arranged in alphabetical sequence, letter by letter, with blank spaces ignored. This method is seldom used. The **word-by-word** convention arranges entries word by word with each word filed letter by letter. This method is used by the Library of Congress for its Dictionary Catalogs. The **unit-by-unit** method is the one generally used in business filing systems, for it results in an arrangement that has been found to be easiest for clerks and other office personnel to use. Unless otherwise defined in a specific rule, each word, abbreviation, and initial is a separate filing unit. Entries are arranged unit by unit, and the units are arranged letter by letter. The listings in a telephone directory are filed in a variation of the unit-by-unit approach.

An unmodified computer sort will produce a letter-by-letter arrangement, except that blank spaces are considered in the sequencing. This results in a filing sequence that is similar to a word-by-word arrangement. Certain variations may occur based upon the computer collating sequence, capitalization, and special characters. To obtain a unit-by-unit arrangement, the specific unit-by-unit rules must be chosen (there are a number of variations commonly used) and programmed. Figure C.26 shows an example of a list arranged first by an unmodified COBOL sort and then sorted according to the unit-by-unit convention. Unit-by-unit filing requires a significant amount of logic to rearrange the units of each entry into an appropriate sort key prefix.

Computer collating sequence (EBCDIC)

Collating sequence rank

1	AARDVARK SOFTWARE, INC.
2	AARON BURR, ESQ.
3	ABC DATA INCORPORATED
4	GREEN, R. L.
5	GREENE, N. V.
6	GREENE, N. Z.
7	GREENING, JONATHAN
8	K AND O PROMOTIONS
9	K&O PRODUCTIONS
10	KJR INTERNATIONAL
11	KZAP RADIO
12	LIBBER-MCGEE, MOLLY
13	MAC DONALD, RONALD
14	MAC TRUCKING COMPANY
15	MAC'S CHOP SUEY
16	MACDONALD, DONALD
17	MCDONALD, HUEY
18	MR. GREENJEANS
19	MS. GLORIA LIBBER
20	SAMARITAN HOSPITAL
21	ST. CHRISTOPHER TRAVEL
22	THE GREENING OF AMERICA
23	RECKONWITH, AMANDA
24	ZODIAC SOLAR ENERGY CORP.
25	20TH CENTURY-GOOSE

Unit-by-unit alphabetical filing sequence

Computer sequence rank		Unit-1	Unit-2	Unit-3	Unit-4
3	ABC Data Incorporated	A	B	C	Data
1	Aardvark Software, Inc.	Aardvark	Software	Incorporated	
2	Aaron Burr, Esq.	Burr	Aaron	Esq	
4	Green, R. L.	Green	R	L	
5	Greene, N. V.	Greene	N	V	
6	Greene, N. Z.	Greene	N	Z	
22	The Greening of America	[The]Greening	[of]America		
7	Greening, Jonathan	Greening	Jonathan		
18	Mr. Greenjeans	Greenjeans	[Mr.]		
8	K and O Productions	K[and]	O	Productions	
9	K&O Promotions	K[&]	O	Promotions	
10	KJR International	K	J	R	International
11	KZAP Radio	K	Z	A	P
19	Ms. Gloria Libber	Libber	Gloria	[Ms.]	
12	Libber-Mcgee, Molly	Libber[-]Mcgee	Molly		
14	Mac Trucking Company	Mac	Trucking	Company	
16	MacDonald, Donald	MacDonald	Donald		
13	Mac Donald, Ronald	MacDonald	Ronald		
15	Mac's Chop Suey	Mac[']s	Chop	Suey	
17	McDonald, Huey	McDonald	Huey		
21	St. Christopher Travel	Saint	Christopher	Travel	
20	Samaritan Hospital	Samaritan	Hospital		
23	Reckonwith, Amanda	Reckonwith	Amanda		
25	20th Century-Goose	Twentieth	CenturyGoose		
24	Zodiac Solar Energy Corp.	Zodiac	Solar	Energy	Corporation

Figure C.26. Alphabetical filing examples.

Mailing Address Requirements

When the programmer/analyst is preparing output for mailing, he or she should be aware of the conventions and guidelines that the United States Postal Service developed so that the growing volume of mail would be processed efficiently. As the scheduled installation of optical character-recognition equipment occurs in major post offices, timely mail delivery will become increasingly dependent upon conformance with these requirements.

Address Formats

There are seven basic address formats, as shown in Figure C.27. A given address should conform to one of these formats and should be complete to the

1. Post Office Box address

```
MISS SALLY SMITH
PO BOX 34
DULUTH MN  55806-1234
```

2. Rural Route or Highway Contract Route address

```
H E BROWN                      B G LIGHT
RR 3 BOX 194-C                 HCR 2 BOX 293-A
CANTON OH  44730-1234          DULUTH MN  55811-1234
```

3. Business/personal name/building address

```
SOUTHERN CORP
ATTN SUE MOBLEY
LOUISIANA INDUSTRIAL PK
1725 E BEAUREGARD AVE
NEW ORLEANS LA  70124-1234
```

4. Standard street address (numeric street name)

```
MR JOHN DOE                    MISS K JONES
605 1ST ST APT 221             5765 E 53RD ST
DETROIT MI  48226-1234         CHICAGO IL  60615-1234
```

5. Standard street address (alphabetic street address)

```
MR JOHN DOE                    MR B BASS
605 FIRST ST APT 221           APT 306
DETROIT MI  48226-1234         1234 MASSACHUSETTS AVE N.W.
                               WASHINGTON DC  20005-1234
```

6. Community identity address

```
MR JOSEPH DEAL
HILLANDALE
28 ELTON RD
SILVER SPRING MD  20903-1234
```

7. Dual address

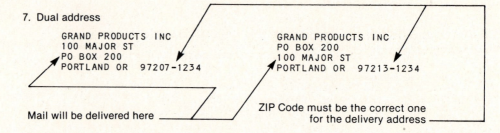

```
GRAND PRODUCTS INC             GRAND PRODUCTS INC
100 MAJOR ST                   PO BOX 200
PO BOX 200                     100 MAJOR ST
PORTLAND OR  97207-1234        PORTLAND OR  97213-1234
```

Mail will be delivered here _____

ZIP Code must be the correct one for the delivery address _____

Adapted from: "1982 National Five Digit ZIP Code and Post Office Directory," U.S. Postal Service, 1982.

Figure C.27. Postal address formats.

point of delivery, including suite, room, or apartment number for multioccupancy buildings. The following guidelines apply:

1. When an apartment, mail receptacle, office, or suite number appears in an address, it should be placed at the end of the delivery address line. If there is not enough space on this line, the unit identifier should then be put on the line immediately above the delivery address line.
2. For domestic addresses, the standard Postal Service two-letter state abbreviations should be used in preference to any other version of state abbreviation.

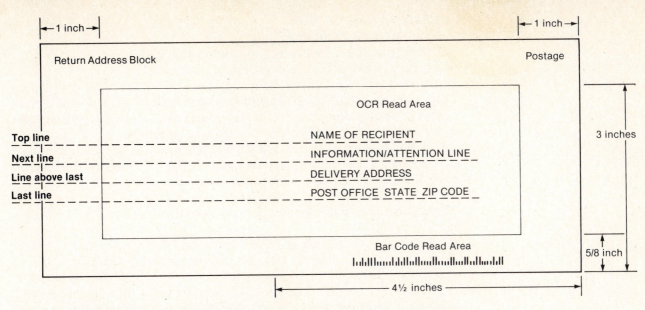

Source: "Addressing for Optical Character Recognition," U.S. Postal Service, Notice 165, June 1981.

Figure C.28. Postal addressing for optical character recognition.

3. The ZIP Code should be the last entry on the line that contains the post office and state. If, however, there is not enough space on this line, the ZIP Code may be placed at the left margin on a line immediately below the post office/state line.

4. For foreign addresses, the full name of the post office and country of destination should be represented in capital letters. The postal delivery zone number, if any, should be included. The name of the country must be the last entry on the line.

Address Abbreviations

The Postal Service has developed a number of standard abbreviations to be used in mail addresses. These abbreviations are printed in the National ZIP Code Directory, which is published annually.

There are two-letter state abbreviations for the 50 states, the District of Columbia, and the territories of Canal Zone, Guam, Puerto Rico, and the Virgin Islands.

In addition, there are standard abbreviations for street designators (the words "street," "avenue," "lane," etc.) and for other words (such as "university," "airport," "church," etc.) that appear frequently in post office place names. These abbreviations range from one to five characters in length.

So that all post office names can be represented within a fixed-field length of 13 characters, postal name abbreviations have been developed for those post offices whose names exceed 13 characters in length (after the standard abbreviations have been applied).

Addressing for Optical Character Recognition

The following specifications have been developed to permit mechanized mail processing by new Postal Service equipment with optical character recognition (OCR):

1. As shown in Figure C.28, the entire address should be located on the front of the piece of mail within an imaginary rectangle, called the **OCR read area**. The OCR read area rectangle is formed by the following boundaries:

—1 inch from the left edge
—1 inch from the right edge
—⅝ inch from the bottom edge (bottom of rectangle)
—3 inches from the bottom edge (top of rectangle)

2. Within the OCR read area, the entire space below the top line of the address block should be clear of printing other than the address itself. This includes information such as tic marks, underlines, boxes, advertising, computer hole punches, and similar nonaddress markings.

3. The bottom right-hand portion of the mailpiece, a 4½- by ⅝-inch rectangle, is reserved for the application of bar codes. This area, termed the **bar code read area**, should contain no printing or other markings.

4. The address block should have a uniform left margin.

5. To conserve character spaces, punctuation is not required in the address block.

6. When window envelopes are used, there must be a minimum of ¼-inch clearance between the window and both sides and the bottom of the address block throughout the insert's full movement inside the envelope.

7. Italic, artistic, Cyrillic, and scriptlike fonts cannot be read by the OCR equipment and thus should not be used. No font should be selected whose characters or numbers will overlap within a word or ZIP Code.

8. Preferred line spacing is 6 lines per inch. Uppercase characters are preferred. If 8 lines per inch spacing is used, use of uppercase characters is required.

9. The character pitch should be in the range of 7 to 12 characters per inch.

10. The character height must be within the range of .08 inch to .20 inch. All characters on the post office/state/ZIP line should be of the same height.

11. The character height to width ratio should be from 1.1:1 up to 1.7:1.

12. The space between words should be from 1 to 2 character spaces. However, the space between the last character of the state abbreviation and the first digit of the ZIP Code should be from 2 to 5 character spaces.

13. The space between address lines should be no less than .040 inch (1 millimeter). That vertical distance is measured from the bottommost point of either an uppercase or lowercase character to the highest point reached by the tallest character in the line below.

14. Maximum character and line skew of the address block relative to the bottom edge of the mailpiece is plus or minus 5 degrees.

15. Black ink on a white background is preferred, but color combinations may be used which provide a Print Reflectance Difference of at least 40% measured at a wavelength of 650 nanometers. Reverse color printing should not be used.

Data-Representation Conversion

As mentioned in Chapter A and delineated in Appendix I, two methods of data representation are commonly used within computer systems: EBCDIC and ASCII. EBCDIC representation is used by most IBM and IBM-compatible large- and medium-scale computers. ASCII representation is employed by most other vendors and is commonly used for data transmission over telecommunications lines.

Suppose that a data file were prepared on magnetic table data by an IBM computer in EBCDIC format, and we wanted to read the tape into an H-P computer that uses ASCII. Before the tape could be correctly processed by an application program on the H-P computer, it would be necessary to convert the EBCDIC characters to ASCII representation. There are two ways that this could be done: by operating system conversion or program conversion.

Operating System Conversion

Certain operating systems provide a job control language (JCL) or control statement option to provide output in the nonnative format. When this feature is available, it is convenient to use and will thus typically be employed to handle data-representation conversion tasks.

However, there is one situation in which this approach cannot be used—when the fields are not all in DISPLAY format, that is, when COMP or COMP-3 usage is used for one or more fields within the record format. If COMP or COMP-3 fields were processed through the conversion routine, each byte would erroneously be changed to its character equivalent.

Program Conversion

If the operating system conversion option is not available or if the records contain COMP or COMP-3 fields, a program must be written to handle the conversion. The general logic of the program would consist of processsing each DISPLAY format byte within the input record. Each byte that is not contained within a COMP or COMP-3 field would be individually selected, looked up on a table of corresponding values in the other representation, and replaced with the table value.

A table of 256 "to-format" (the representation being converted *to*) byte representations must be established in the program. These will be the table functions. It is not necessary to provide a table argument if the entries are positioned *according to the binary value of the "from-format"* (not the to-format) byte. The search argument will be the binary value of the from-format byte; the implicit table argument will be that table entry occurrence number. Hence, in the EBCDIC to ASCII conversion example described above, the search argument would be the EBCDIC byte within the input record; the table function would be its corresponding ASCII representation. Each table entry could thus be one byte long. However, to simplify definition of each VALUE clause, it may be more convenient to construct each table function with a length equal to the shortest binary field byte length that the particular computer permits (typically two bytes). However, only the low-order byte of the table function would actually be used.

File-Handling Logic

Most standard file-handling functions have been covered elsewhere in this or a prerequisite text. There are two additional ones that will be presented here: matching records from different files and file merging.

Matching Records from Different Files

The file-maintenance programs of Chapters 3-5 are applications in which records from different files are matched; the transaction record was matched to the master record for an update function. Another common—and simpler—matching function is one in which a transaction is matched to a master solely for the purpose of retrieving one or more fields of data. It is, in essence, an external table lookup. Figure C.29 presents a flowchart of such record-matching logic. (Remember that when records from different files are matched, all files to be matched must be in match key sequence.)

Merging Records from Two or More Files

The COBOL MERGE verb can be used to merge records from two or more files. However, not all compilers offer this facility. Also, because an INPUT PROCEDURE is not provided in the MERGE statement syntax, it is not possible to count the number of records that are processed from each input file. This is a serious limitation because it is a common requirement to make such counts for control purposes.

A flowchart of logic that will merge files without use of the MERGE statement is shown in Figure C.30. (Remember that when files are merged, each file must be in merge key sequence.)

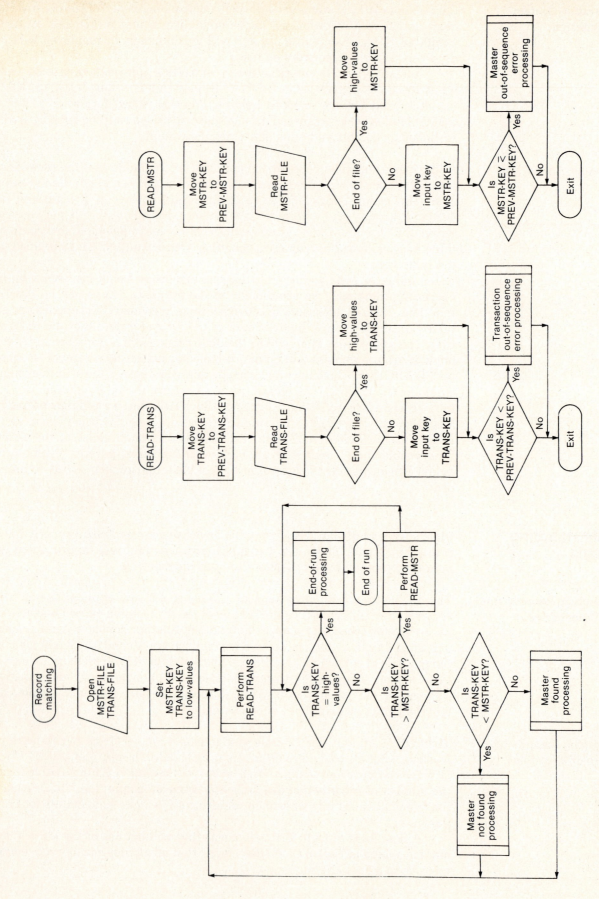

Figure C.29. Record-matching logic.

continued

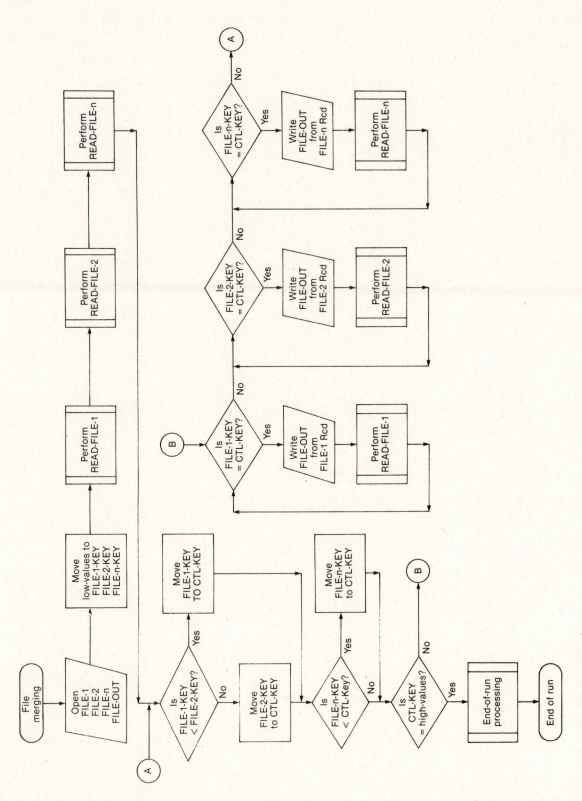

Figure C.30. File-merging logic.

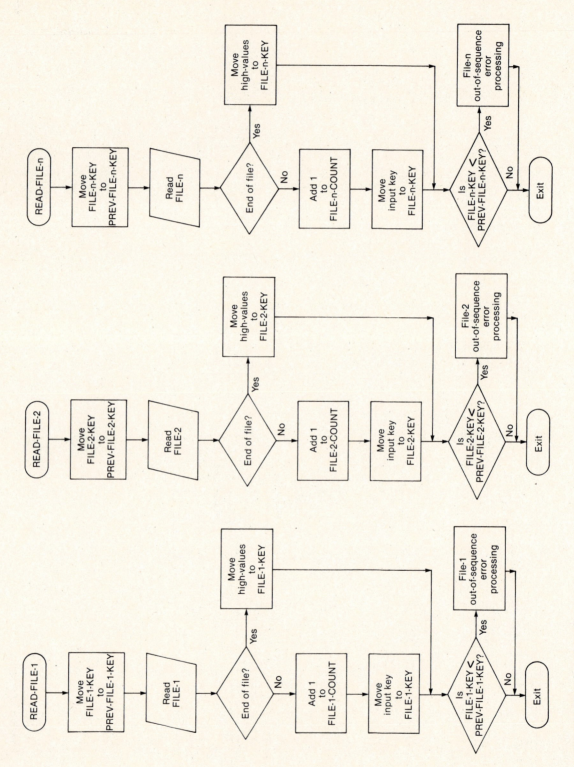

Figure C.30. (continued)

CHAPTER 8

PROCESSING VARIABLE-LENGTH RECORDS

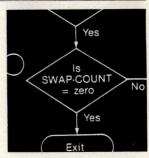

421

PROCESSING VARIABLE-LENGTH RECORDS

Logical records can be either fixed or variable in length. Fixed-length records are much more commonly used in COBOL because most applications lend themselves to the specification of uniform field lengths and uniform field population for all of the records of a file. The resulting fixed-length records also permit efficient processing and straightforward coding.

For certain applications, however, characteristics of the data to be stored do not efficiently conform to fixed-length record formats. Consider, for example, a college student-records system in which it is necessary to store one set of the following fields for each course that a student has completed: course number, date completed, units earned, and letter grade. Suppose it takes a segment of 15 characters to store such data for each course. A college senior may have completed 40 or more classes; an entering freshman will have completed none. If fixed-length records were used, space would be required in each record for as many course-completed segments as a graduating senior or graduate student might require. Perhaps seventy-five 15-character segments—1,125 character positions—would need to be allocated for a fixed-length record. However, of these positions, an entering freshman would actually use none of the area, a sophomore would consume about a quarter of the segments, and so forth. Clearly, file-storage space requirements will be minimized by forming a variable-length record that includes only as many course-completed segments for each student as required.

There are three types of variable-length records that can be designed, as shown in Figure 8.1. One type really uses fixed-length record specifications. The records are considered to be variable-length ones, however, because the resulting file contains records of various lengths. Another type is a record with a variable number of fixed-length segment occurrences. The student record that was mentioned in the previous paragraph is an example. The third type of variable-length record is one in which the length of one or more fields is variable. Consider a library catalog system in which it is necessary to store book titles and authors. The length of these fields, particularly the title, can vary considerably. Using the variable-length fields will eliminate superfluous blank positions and thereby permit more compact file storage.

Hence a record is considered to be a variable-length record if (1) the file in which it resides contains fixed-length records of various lengths, (2) it contains a variable number of fixed-length segment occurrences, or (3) it contains one or more fields of variable length. In COBOL, type (1) is specified by defining two or more record descriptions of different lengths within the file-description entry. Such processing is covered in Topic 8-A of this chapter. Types (2) and (3) are specified by coding the OCCURS/DEPENDING ON clause and are discussed in Topic 8-B. Sorting considerations for variable-length records are mentioned in Topic 8-C.

Fixed-length records of various lengths

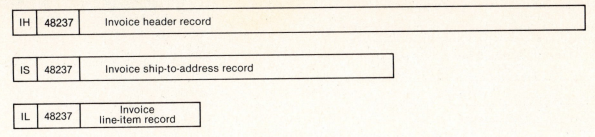

Variable number of fixed-length segments

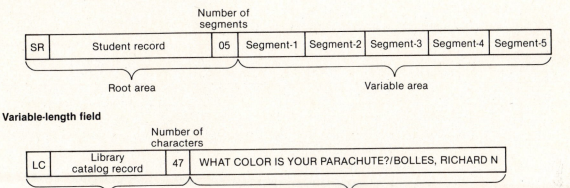

Figure 8.1. Variable-length record examples.

The main impetus for using variable-length records is to minimize disk- or tape-storage requirements. However, the programmer/analyst must beware of trivial applications. If either (1) the range between the minimum-length and maximum-length record is small or (2) the volume of records is low, fixed-length records are probably a better choice.

Variable-length records impose a record length "overhead" requirement. Space must be physically allocated in each record block and logical record to hold the block and record length, respectively. Figure 8.2 illustrates a commonly used method. The first four bytes of each record block are used for the block length; the first four bytes of each logical record are for the record length.

Before designing variable-length records, the programmer/analyst should be aware of the tradeoffs involved with their use. Variable-length records introduce disadvantages in the areas of processing speed, program portability, and coding complexity.

Variable-length records usually take a bit more time to process than fixed-length records do because the record length must be recomputed whenever the size of the record changes. However, a far more significant processing-speed disadvantage occurs when the records must be sorted. Sorts for variable-length records are much slower than those that process fixed-length records.

Unblocked variable-length record

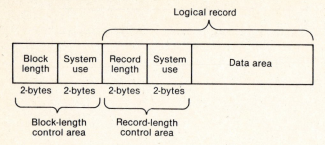

Blocked variable-length records

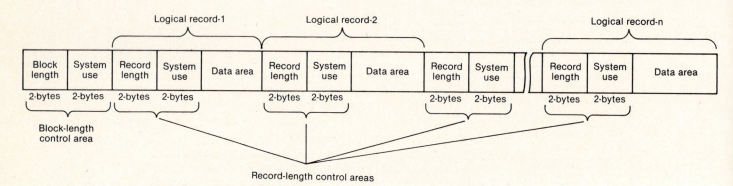

Figure 8.2. Example of block- and record-length areas for variable-length records.

Programs with variable-length records do not generally fare well with regard to program portability because the ANS COBOL variable-length record standards either (1) allow the implementor to define certain variable-length record-handling methods, or (2) the implementors interpret them in different ways. An example of the former point is the method for carrying the record-length indicator within the variable-length record. Each implementor can choose the method by which the record and block length are carried in the physical record. This can cause not only the programs but also the variable-length record data-files to be incompatible from one computer system to another. Examples of the latter point are typically limited to two areas. One area is the FD entry specifications for the RECORD CONTAINS and BLOCK CONTAINS clauses. The other area is the MOVE statement processing when the OCCURS/DEPENDING ON clause occurs in either the sending or receiving fields. Thus, although the intended or predominantly used syntax is presented for these three clauses in this chapter, the programmer should verify it in the COBOL reference manual for the specific compiler being used.

Programs that process variable-length records with a variable number of segments often introduce programming complexities. The complex processing requirements tend to center around routines that are necessary to handle segment deletions, segment sequencing, and segment overflow.

Hardware and software technology trends are contributing to a decreasing incidence of variable-length record usage in new applications. In the hardware area, decreasing cost and increasing capacity trends of disk and tape storage tend to minimize the advantages of variable-length records. With regard to software, increased prevalence of data-base management systems limits the need for variable-length records. Those very data characteristics that introduce variable-length record processing as a candidate are generally the same as those that data-base management systems are designed to handle.

TOPIC 8-A: Fixed-length Records of Various Lengths

The FD Entry for Variable-length Records
    RECORD CONTAINS Clause
    BLOCK CONTAINS Clause

Describing the Variable-length Records
    The Input INVOICE-FILE-IN File
    The Output INVOICE-FILE-OUT File
    WORKING-STORAGE SECTION Record Descriptions

Reading the Variable-length Records

Writing the Variable-length Records

An order entry system is an example of an application that may be suitable for the use of fixed-length records of various lengths. When an order is placed or shipped, the amount of record space that is required to store the data will vary widely depending upon the number of different items that are ordered. If a fixed-length record were used for each order, it would require an unreasonably long record length—much of which would often not be used.

Because there are distinct informational needs—some of which are applicable only to certain orders—variable-length records for an order entry system are usually better handled as fixed-length records of various lengths rather than by variable occurrences of fixed-length segments. Some orders, for example, will be shipped to a location other than the billing address. Certain orders will require lengthy shipping information or special instructions whereas most orders will not. By separation of each informational need into a separate functional record of appropriate length, storage requirements can be minimized.

In our discussion of fixed-length records of variable length, we will consider an invoicing file within an order entry system. There are three record formats within the file. Each invoice will be represented by an invoice-header record, 250 characters in length. If the ship-to address is different from the bill-to address contained within the invoice-header record, a ship-to-address record of 150 characters will be present. For each invoice line item, a 75-character line item record occurs.

Although, for our purposes here, details of the invoicing program specifications need not be covered, it should be understood that the program will read the input file of various length records and write that same file as output.

The FD Entry for Variable-length Records

Figure 8A.1 shows the FD-entry format for a file with variable-length records. Coding for the BLOCK CONTAINS and RECORD CONTAINS clauses must be carefully considered.

If the BLOCK CONTAINS clause is not specified, as in examples A and B (Figure 8A.1), it means that the records are unblocked—just as it also means for fixed-length records. However, there is a tricky aspect to specifying blocked records for a file with variable-length records. This aspect will be covered after the RECORD CONTAINS clause is discussed.

RECORD CONTAINS Clause

Remember that the RECORD CONTAINS clause is never required; it is always optional. However, use of the RECORD CONTAINS clause is recommended because it provides good documentation. Also, with variable-length records, its

Format:

```
FD file-name

    ┌                                               ┌ RECORDS    ┐ ┐
    │ BLOCK CONTAINS [integer-1 TO] integer-2      { CHARACTERS } │
    └                                               └            ┘ ┘

    ┌ RECORD CONTAINS [integer-3 TO] integer-4 CHARACTERS ┐
    └                                                     ┘

           ┌ RECORD IS   ┐ ┌ STANDARD ┐
    LABEL { RECORDS ARE  } { OMITTED  }
           └             ┘ └          ┘
```

Example A. BLOCK CONTAINS clause not specified (indicates that the records are un-blocked); RECORD CONTAINS clause not specified (to specify variable-length records, the record-description entry must then contain either (1) the OCCURS/DEPENDING ON clause or (2) two or more record descriptions of varying lengths):

```
FD   INVOICE-FILE

         LABEL RECORDS ARE STANDARD.
```

Example B. BLOCK CONTAINS clause not specified (indicates that the records are un-blocked); RECORD CONTAINS clause specified with the TO option (indicates that the RECORDS are variable in length):

```
FD   INVOICE-FILE

         RECORD CONTAINS 75 TO 250 CHARACTERS

         LABEL RECORDS ARE STANDARD.
```

Example C. BLOCK CONTAINS clause specified (indicates that the records are blocked); RECORD CONTAINS clause specified with the TO option (indicates that the RECORDS are variable in length):

```
FD   INVOICE-FILE

         BLOCK CONTAINS 10 RECORDS

         RECORD CONTAINS 75 TO 250 CHARACTERS

         LABEL RECORDS ARE STANDARD.
```

Figure 8A.1. FD-entry format and examples for files with variable-length records.

specification with the reserved word TO is one of the ways that the COBOL compiler can determine that variable-length records are to be processed.

When the TO option is used, integer-3 of the format specifies the size of the shortest record; integer-4 specifies the size of the longest record.

Examples B and C (Figure 8A.1) show an illustration of the RECORD CONTAINS clause with the TO option describing the variable-record length as a minimum of 75 characters up to a maximum of 250 characters. This character count *does not* include any record-length control bytes present in the record; they are not counted or described in the record description.

BLOCK CONTAINS Clause

The BLOCK CONTAINS clause is required within the file-description to describe blocked records. Example C (Figure 8A.1) provides an example of its specification with the RECORDS option. By specifying BLOCK CONTAINS 10 RECORDS,

Example A. BLOCK CONTAINS clause specified with RECORDS option (maximum block size is maximum record length times number of records specified *plus required block- and record-length control bytes*).

```
FD  INVOICE-FILE

    BLOCK CONTAINS 10 RECORDS

    RECORD CONTAINS 75 TO 250 CHARACTERS

    LABEL RECORDS ARE STANDARD.
```

Example B. BLOCK CONTAINS clause specified with CHARACTERS option (maximum block size is number of characters specified *including required block- and record-length control bytes*).

```
FD  INVOICE-FILE

    BLOCK CONTAINS 2544 CHARACTERS

    RECORD CONTAINS 75 TO 250 CHARACTERS

    LABEL RECORDS ARE STANDARD.
```

Figure 8A.2. Effect of BLOCK CONTAINS clause specifications upon maximum block size.

a maximum block length of 2,500 characters (10 times the maximum record length of 250 = 2,500) is established. Of course, if a block contains occurrences of only the 75-character invoice line item records, it would actually contain 33 records; a block length of 2,500 divided by a record length of 75 equals 33 (plus a remainder of 25).

The tricky aspect of specifying the BLOCK CONTAINS clause is shown in Figure 8A.2. As shown in example A (Figure 8A.2) when the RECORDS option is coded, the programmer ignores the block- and record-length control bytes; there is no reference to them. Also, when the RECORDS option is used, the TO option is meaningless; integer-1 of the format is ignored.

However, look at example B (Figure 8A.2). When the CHARACTERS option of the BLOCK CONTAINS clause is coded, the programmer *must include the block- and record-length control bytes in the character count*. Although the actual character count will vary depending upon the particular COBOL compiler or operating system that is being used, the block size that is used in the example is a result of the following calculation:

10 logical records	
times maximum 250 record length	2,500
4 record-length control bytes	
for each of the 10 records	40
4 block-length control bytes	
for the record block	+ 4
Block length	2,544

If this discrepancy between specifying CHARACTER lengths for the RECORD CONTAINS and BLOCK CONTAINS clauses seems confusing, the following guideline may be helpful: In the RECORD CONTAINS clause, the CHARACTERS in the logical record are coded; in the BLOCK CONTAINS clause, the CHARACTERS in the physical block are specified.

Observe in the BLOCK CONTAINS format that a block-length range may be specified by coding the reserved word TO. Unlike record lengths, with which the programmer is often concerned, documentation of the minimum length for a physical block is generally of little concern. However, if desired, a block length expressed with the CHARACTERS option could be coded as BLOCK CONTAINS 2291 TO 2544 CHARACTERS. When a range is coded, integer-3 of the format specifies the minimum block length and integer-4 identifies the maximum block length.

The RECORDS option of the BLOCK CONTAINS clause has an advantage of program portability because the size of the block- and record-length control areas are not represented in the coding. However, sometimes records are grouped, and this grouping will imply an incorrect block size. Suppose a block always contains 4 records: one 50-character record followed by three 100-character records. If BLOCK CONTAINS 4 RECORDS is specified, a maximum block size (not counting length-control bytes) of 400 is implied. In this case, it would be more appropriate to use the CHARACTERS option with the actual block length (350 plus the length-control bytes).

Describing the Variable-length Records

Figure 8A.3 shows the record descriptions for the variable-length records of our invoicing application. We will discuss first the input record descriptions, followed by those for the output file, and then the WORKING-STORAGE SECTION record descriptions.

The Input INVOICE-FILE-IN File

Notice that the input record, IR-INVOICE-RCD-IN, is defined with a length equal to the maximum-length record. Remember that the record-length control bytes are *not* specified within the record description.

Recognize that by *not* specifying two or more 01-level record descriptions with different lengths within the input file, the inclusion of the RECORD CONTAINS clause with the TO option is mandatory for the program to correctly process variable-length input records.

An alternative approach would be to describe each of the three different-length records (or just the maximum- and minimum-length records) as 01-level record-description entries. If this were done, it would not be necessary to specify the RECORD CONTAINS clause. The COBOL compiler would then determine that variable-length input records were to be processed because records with different lengths were defined for the file.

Remember that, within an FD entry, the 01-level record-description entries are implicitly redefined. This means that the longest record must be specified as the *first* 01-record. (A redefining entry cannot be longer than the area that it redefines.)

```
        DATA DIVISION.
*
*
*
        FILE SECTION.
            .
            .
            .
*
*
        FD  INVOICE-FILE-IN
                BLOCK CONTAINS 10 RECORDS
                RECORD CONTAINS 75 TO 250 CHARACTERS
                LABEL RECORDS ARE STANDARD.
*
        01  IR-INVOICE-RCD-IN.
            05  IR-RECORD-CODE-IN                    PIC X(2).
                88  INVOICE-HEADER-RECORD                        VALUE '50'.
                88  SHIP-TO-ADDRESS-RECORD                       VALUE '52'.
```

Figure 8A.3. Record-description examples for a file with records of various lengths.

```
                     88  INVOICE-LINE-RECORD            VALUE '55'.
                 05  FILLER                        PIC X(248).
                       .
                       .
                       .
 *
 *
 *
     FD  INVOICE-FILE-OUT
             BLOCK CONTAINS 10 RECORDS
             RECORD CONTAINS 75 TO 250 CHARACTERS
             LABEL RECORDS ARE STANDARD.
 *
     01  IR-INVOICE-HEADER-RCD-OUT.
         05  FILLER                        PIC X(250).
 *
     01  IR-SHIP-TO-ADDRESS-RCD-OUT.
         05  FILLER                        PIC X(150).
 *
     01  IR-INVOICE-LINE-RCD-OUT.
         05  FILLER                        PIC X(75).
                       .
                       .
                       .

     WORKING-STORAGE SECTION.
                       .
                       .
                       .
 *
 *
 *
     01  IH-INVOICE-HEADER-RCD.
         05  IH-RECORD-CODE                PIC X(2).
         05  IH-INVOICE-NUMBER             PIC X(5).
         05  IH-CUSTOMER-NUMBER            PIC X(5).
         05  IH-CUSTOMER-NAME              PIC X(30).
         05  IH-ADDRESS-LINE-1             PIC X(30).
         05  IH-ADDRESS-LINE-2             PIC X(30).
         05  IH-DESTINATION.
             10  IH-CITY                   PIC X(19).
             10  IH-STATE-ABBREV           PIC X(2).       250
             10  IH-ZIP-CODE               PIC X(9).     CHARACTERS
         05  IH-DATE-SHIPPED               PIC X(6).
         05  IH-TERMS-CODE                 PIC X(1).
         05  IH-CUSTOMER-PO-NUMBER         PIC X(15).
         05  IH-FOB-POINT                  PIC X(20).
         05  IH-SHIPPED-VIA                PIC X(20).
         05  IH-ROUTING                    PIC X(30).
         05  FILLER                        PIC X(26).
 *
     01  IS-SHIP-TO-ADDRESS-RCD.
         05  IS-RECORD-CODE                PIC X(2).
         05  IS-INVOICE-NUMBER             PIC X(5).
         05  IS-CUSTOMER-NUMBER            PIC X(5).
         05  IS-SHIP-TO-NAME               PIC X(30).
         05  IS-SHIP-TO-ADDRESS-LINE-1     PIC X(30).      150
         05  IS-SHIP-TO-ADDRESS-LINE-2     PIC X(30).    CHARACTERS
         05  IS-SHIP-TO-ADDRESS.
             10  IS-SHIP-TO-CITY           PIC X(19).
             10  IS-SHIP-TO-STATE-ABBREV   PIC X(2).
             10  IS-SHIP-TO-ZIP-CODE       PIC X(9).
         05  FILLER                        PIC X(18).
 *
     01  IL-INVOICE-LINE-RCD.
         05  IL-RECORD-CODE                PIC X(2).
         05  IL-INVOICE-NUMBER             PIC X(5).
         05  IL-CUSTOMER-NUMBER            PIC X(5).
         05  IL-LINE-NUMBER                PIC X(2).
         05  IL-LINE-TYPE-CODE             PIC X(2).
         05  IL-PRODUCT-CODE               PIC X(10).
         05  IL-PRODUCT-DESCRIPTION        PIC X(24).        75
         05  IL-QUANTITY-ORDERED           PIC S9(5)    COMP-3.  CHARACTERS
         05  IL-QUANTITY-SHIPPED           PIC S9(5)    COMP-3.
         05  IL-QUANTITY-BACKORDERED       PIC S9(5)    COMP-3.
         05  IL-PRICE                      PIC S9(7)V99 COMP-3.
         05  IL-TAX-RATE                   PIC S9(2)V99 COMP-3.
         05  FILLER                        PIC X(08).
                       .
                       .
                       .
```

Figure 8A.3. (continued)

The Output INVOICE-FILE-OUT File

Because the variable-length records for this invoicing application are not of the type that contain an OCCURS/DEPENDING ON clause within their record description, it is mandatory that a separate 01-level record description be specified for each different record length to be written to the output file.

Observe that three record descriptions of appropriate length have been coded: one each for the invoice-header records, ship-to-address records, and invoice line item records. Again, within an FD entry, it is necessary to specify the longest record description first.

WORKING-STORAGE SECTION Record Descriptions

In accordance with our general convention of processing records in the WORKING-STORAGE SECTION, each of the three records has been fully described here. Notice in the example (Figure 8A.3) that each record has been allocated a separate area within WORKING-STORAGE; no explicit redefinition is specified. This is the best approach when available storage resources are adequate and inter-record references must be made. When printing an invoice, for example, suppose that 10 line items can be printed on each page and the 11th line item has just been read. It will now be necessary to skip to a new page and reprint the customer heading information. By allocating an area for the header and ship-to-address records separate from the line item record area, the header and ship-to data is retained in storage and can be used to print the customer heading information for additional pages whenever required.

An alternative approach is to first specify the longest record description within WORKING-STORAGE and then code the REDEFINES clause on each subsequent record description within the file. If this were done for the example record descriptions, the 01-level entry for the IH-INVOICE-HEADER-RCD would remain the same; the 01-level entry for the ship-to-address record would read IS-SHIP-TO-ADDRESS-RCD REDEFINES IH-INVOICE-HEADER-RCD, and, for the line item record, the 01-level entry would be specified as IL-INVOICE-LINE-RCD REDEFINES IH-INVOICE-HEADER-RCD. Such redefinition reduces WORKING-STORAGE space requirements and is generally appropriate only when storage is limited or each record description is independent from the others.

Reading the Variable-length Records

Figure 8A.4 shows an example of a READ module for a file with records of various lengths. Observe that the READ statement syntax for reading variable-length records is identical to that for fixed-length records.

Because we have specified separate areas for each of the input record descriptions in WORKING-STORAGE, it is necessary to first determine the type of record that has been read and then transfer it to its particular record description. Therefore, after the record has been read, the IR-RECORD-CODE field is tested (by using the condition-names INVOICE-HEADER-RECORD, SHIP-TO-ADDRESS-RECORD, and INVOICE-LINE-RECORD). Depending upon the type of record that is detected, the input record is moved from the IR-INVOICE-RCD area of the FILE SECTION to the appropriate record-description in the WORKING-STORAGE SECTION.

If the input record-descriptions within WORKING-STORAGE all occupied the same area through use of the REDEFINES clause, such record-code testing would not be required in the READ module, of course. Instead, the READ statement could be specified with the INTO phrase or, as an alternative, a single MOVE statement could be used to transfer each input record from the FILE SECTION to WORKING-STORAGE.

```
     *
     *
      800-READ-INVOICE-RECORDS.
     *
          READ INVOICE-FILE-IN
              AT END MOVE 'YES' TO WS-END-OF-FILE-SW.
          IF END-OF-FILE
              NEXT SENTENCE
          ELSE IF INVOICE-HEADER-RECORD
              MOVE IR-INVOICE-RCD TO IH-INVOICE-HEADER-RCD
          ELSE IF SHIP-TO-ADDRESS-RECORD
              MOVE IR-INVOICE-RCD TO IS-SHIP-TO-ADDRESS-RCD
          ELSE IF INVOICE-LINE-RECORD
              MOVE IR-INVOICE-RCD TO IL-INVOICE-LINE-RCD
          ELSE
              MOVE 'YES' TO WS-INVALID-RECORD-SW.
```

Figure 8A.4. READ module example for a file with records of various lengths.

```
     *
     *
      850-WRITE-INVOICE-HEADER-RCD.
     *
          MOVE IH-INVOICE-HEADER-RCD TO IR-INVOICE-HEADER-RCD-OUT.
          WRITE IR-INVOICE-HEADER-RCD-OUT.
     *
     *
      852-WRITE-SHIP-TO-ADDRESS-RCD.
     *
          MOVE IS-SHIP-TO-ADDRESS-RCD TO IR-SHIP-TO-ADDRESS-RCD-OUT.
          WRITE IR-SHIP-TO-ADDRESS-RCD-OUT.
     *
     *
      854-WRITE-INVOICE-LINE-RCD.
     *
          WRITE IR-INVOICE-LINE-RCD-OUT
              FROM IL-INVOICE-LINE-RCD.
```

Figure 8A.5. WRITE module examples for a file with records of various lengths.

Writing the Variable-length Records

Whenever records are to be written to a file with records of various lengths and the OCCURS/DEPENDING ON clause is not specified within the variable-length record, a separate WRITE statement must be coded for each different record length. Figure 8A.5 shows WRITE module examples for the records of the invoicing application.

After each output record has been processed in the WORKING-STORAGE SECTION, it must first be moved to the appropriate output record area in the FILE SECTION and then written. Such processing can be specified either by (1) a MOVE statement that is followed by a WRITE statement, or (2) a WRITE statement that contains the FROM phrase. The former approach is shown in the 850-WRITE-INVOICE-HEADER-RCD and 852-WRITE-SHIP-TO-ADDRESS-RCD modules; the 854-WRITE-INVOICE-LINE-RCD module illustrates the latter method.

The program logic, of course, must ensure that the proper WRITE module is performed whenever a record is to be written.

Variable Occurrences of Fixed-length Segments

OCCURS Clause with the DEPENDING ON Option

Describing the Variable-length Records
       The Input STUDENT-FILE-IN File
       The Output STUDENT-FILE-OUT File
       WORKING-STORAGE SECTION Record Description

Reading the Variable-length Records

Writing the Variable-length Records

Maintaining the Variable-segment Occurrences

Processing Variable-length Fields

The OCCURS clause with the DEPENDING ON option must be specified whenever variable-length records that contain a variable number of fixed-length segment occurrences are to be processed. This type of record is most appropriate when either (1) each segment is relatively short, or (2) the maximum number of segments required is low.

In this topic we will consider a student-records application. There is one student record for each student. Each record contains a fixed-length portion, called the **root area**, and a **variable area** that contains from 1 to 75 course-completed **segment occurrences**.

OCCURS Clause with the DEPENDING ON Option

The format for the OCCURS clause with the DEPENDING ON option is shown in Figure 8B.1. Because it is rarely efficient or appropriate to use the KEY option with variable-length record applications, it is shown within the format enclosed by a box and will not be discussed in this chapter.

As shown in the example, the data-item that contains the OCCURS clause is termed the **subject of the OCCURS entry**. Any other data-description clauses that are specified with the subject (such as PICTURE, USAGE, and so forth) apply to each occurrence of the repeating item.

Except for two situations, the subject of the OCCURS entry must either be subscripted or indexed whenever it is referenced. The exceptions are when it is used as the object of (1) a SEARCH statement or (2) a REDEFINES clause.

The OCCURS clause cannot be specified for a subject that:

- has a level-number of 01, 66, 77, or 88.
- contains a VALUE clause.
- contains a REDEFINES clause. (However, an OCCURS clause may be specified subordinate to a group item that contains a REDEFINES clause.)
- contains a subordinate OCCURS clause with the DEPENDING ON option (that is, if the subject is a group item and it has an item within the group that contains an OCCURS/DEPENDING ON clause).

Integer-1 and integer-2 define the range of permissible segment occurrences. They must both be positive integers. The value of integer-1 must be greater than zero and the value of integer-2 must be greater than integer-1.

Data-name-1 in the format is called the **object of the DEPENDING ON entry**. The value that is stored within the object field represents the actual number of occurrences of the subject item. With regard to the example, if SR-COURSE-COUNT contains a value of 13, it means that there are 13 SR-COURSE-

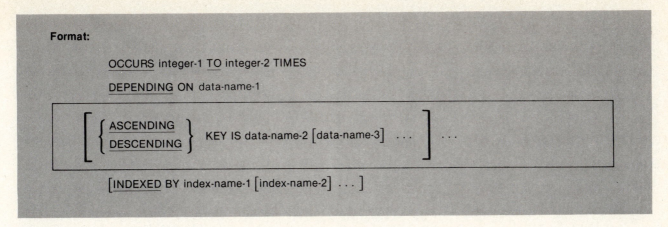

OCCURS integer-1 TO integer-2 TIMES

DEPENDING ON data-name-1

$$\left[\left\{ \begin{array}{l} \underline{\text{ASCENDING}} \\ \underline{\text{DESCENDING}} \end{array} \right\} \text{KEY IS data-name-2} \left[\text{data-name-3} \right] \ldots \right] \ldots$$

$$\left[\underline{\text{INDEXED}} \text{ BY index-name-1} \left[\text{index-name-2} \right] \ldots \right]$$

Example:

```
10   SR-COURSE-SEGMENT        OCCURS 1 TO 75 TIMES
                              DEPENDING ON SR-COURSE-COUNT
                                 PIC X(15).
```

Figure 8B.1. OCCURS/DEPENDING ON clause.

SEGMENT occurrences in the record. The field, such as SR-COURSE-COUNT, that is the object of the DEPENDING ON entry must:

- be described as a numeric data-item.
- not occupy any storage position within the range of the table. (That is, for a variable-length record, it must be defined in the root area of the record, not the variable portion.)
- contain, at execution time, a value within the range of integer-1 and integer-2.

Within any single 01-level record-description entry, a data-item that contains an OCCURS/DEPENDING ON entry can be followed only by items subordinate to it. In other words, the variable segments must be at the end of the record; all root area or fixed-occurrence fields must precede them.

Although OCCURS/DEPENDING ON *cannot* be specified for an item that is subordinate to an OCCURS clause, OCCURS *can* be specified for an item subordinate to an OCCURS/DEPENDING ON entry. Valid and invalid OCCURS clause relationships are shown in Figure 8B.2.

Describing the Variable-length Records

Figure 8B.3 shows an example of file and record descriptions for a variable-length record that contains the OCCURS/DEPENDING ON clause.

Those file-description considerations that were discussed in Topic 8-A for the BLOCK CONTAINS and RECORD CONTAINS clauses with records of various lengths apply also to variable-length records specified with the OCCURS/ DEPENDING ON clause. In this student-records application example, the RECORD CONTAINS clause has been specified with a range of 190 TO 1300 CHARACTERS. The minimum-length record—for a student who has completed no courses—is computed by adding the root area length (175 characters) plus one variable segment occurrence length (15 characters; 175 + 15 = 190). The maximum-length record—for a student who has completed 75 courses—is computed by adding the root area length (again 175 characters) plus 75 variable segment occurrence lengths (75 times 15 = 1,125 characters; 1,125 + 175 = 1,300).

Example A. Valid OCCURS/DEPENDING ON relationship:

```
    *
    01  SR-STUDENT-RECORD.
        05  SR-ROOT-AREA.
            10  FILLER                      PIC X(173).
            10  SR-COURSE-COUNT             PIC S9(4) COMP.
        05  SR-VARIABLE-AREA.
            10  SR-COURSE-SEGMENT
                                OCCURS 1 TO 75 TIMES
                                DEPENDING ON SR-COURSE-COUNT
                                     PIC X(15).
```

Example B. Invalid OCCURS/DEPENDING ON relationship
(Object of the DEPENDING ON entry must be a numeric data-item):

```
    *
    01  SR-STUDENT-RECORD.
        05  SR-ROOT-AREA.
            10  FILLER                      PIC X(173).
            10  SR-COURSE-COUNT             PIC X(2).    ◄——— Invalid
        05  SR-VARIABLE-AREA.
            10  SR-COURSE-SEGMENT

                                OCCURS 1 TO 75 TIMES
                                DEPENDING ON SR-COURSE-COUNT

                                     PIC X(15).
```

Example C. Invalid OCCURS/DEPENDING ON relationship
(Object of the DEPENDING ON entry must not be defined within the variable area):

```
    *
    01  SR-STUDENT-RECORD.
        05  SR-ROOT-AREA.
            10  FILLER                      PIC X(173).

        05  SR-VARIABLE-AREA.
            10  SR-COURSE-SEGMENT
                                OCCURS 1 TO 75 TIMES
                                DEPENDING ON SR-COURSE-COUNT
                                     PIC X(15).

            10  SR-COURSE-COUNT             PIC S9(4) COMP.   ◄——— Invalid
```

Example D. Invalid OCCURS/DEPENDING ON relationship
(OCCURS/DEPENDING ON clause must not be followed by an item not subordinate to it):

```
    *
    01  SR-STUDENT-RECORD.
        05  SR-ROOT-AREA.
            10  FILLER                      PIC X(173).
            10  SR-COURSE-COUNT             PIC S9(4) COMP.

        05  SR-VARIABLE-AREA.
            10  SR-COURSE-SEGMENT
                                OCCURS 1 TO 75 TIMES
                                DEPENDING ON SR-COURSE-COUNT
                                     PIC X(15).

        05  SR-COMMENCEMENT-DATE            PIC X(6).    ◄——— Invalid
```

Figure 8B.2. Valid and invalid OCCURS/DEPENDING ON clauses.

Example E. Valid OCCURS/DEPENDING ON relationship
(The OCCURS clause *can* be specified subordinate to an OCCURS/DEPENDING ON clause):

```
 *
  01   SR-STUDENT-RECORD.
       05   SR-ROOT-AREA.
            10   FILLER                     PIC X(173).
            10   SR-COURSE-COUNT            PIC S9(4) COMP.
       05   SR-VARIABLE-AREA.
            10   SR-COURSE-SEGMENT
                                    OCCURS 1 TO 75 TIMES
                                    DEPENDING ON SR-COURSE-COUNT.
                 15   SR-COURSE-NUMBER      PIC X(5).
                 15   SR-DATE-COMPLETED     PIC X(6).
                 15   SR-UNITS-EARNED       PIC S9V9 COMP-3.

                 15   SR-TEST-SCORES   OCCURS 5 TIMES
                                       PIC S9(3).

                 15   SR-LETTER-GRADE       PIC X(2).
```

Example F. Invalid OCCURS/DEPENDING ON relationship
(The OCCURS/DEPENDING ON clause must not be specified subordinate to an OCCURS/DEPENDING ON clause):

```
 *
  01   SR-STUDENT-RECORD.
       05   SR-ROOT-AREA.
            10   FILLER                     PIC X(171).
            10   SR-TEST-COUNT              PIC S9(4) COMP.
            10   SR-COURSE-COUNT            PIC S9(4) COMP.
       05   SR-VARIABLE-AREA.
            10   SR-COURSE-SEGMENT
                                    OCCURS 1 TO 75 TIMES
                                    DEPENDING ON SR-COURSE-COUNT.
                 15   SR-COURSE-NUMBER      PIC X(5).
                 15   SR-DATE-COMPLETED     PIC X(6).
                 15   SR-UNITS-EARNED       PIC S9V9 COMP-3.

                 15   SR-TEST-SCORES   OCCURS 1 TO 5 TIMES        ◄——— Invalid
                                       DEPENDING ON SR-TEST-COUNT
                                       PIC S9(3).

                 15   SR-LETTER-GRADE       PIC X(2).
```

Figure 8B.2. (continued)

The ANS COBOL requirement that the range of the OCCURS clause must start with a value of at least 1 is a complicating factor. As in the student record, application specifications often permit a record to contain no variable data. However, even though a beginning student should really have no course segments, the COBOL syntax makes it necessary to carry one dummy course segment for the minimum-length record.

The Input STUDENT-FILE-IN File

Notice that the SF-STUDENT-RECORD-IN record description within the input file has been defined as a maximum-length student record fixed in size, not with the OCCURS/DEPENDING ON clause. Even though OCCURS/DEPENDING ON has not been coded, the compiler will provide correct input processing for variable-length records because the RECORD CONTAINS clause has been specified with the TO option.

The SF-STUDENT-RECORD-IN record could alternately be described with its appropriate OCCURS/DEPENDING ON entry. If it were, specification of the RECORD CONTAINS clause would be optional. Remember that whenever a file that contains variable-length records is to be processed, it must be revealed to the compiler by one of the following entries: (1) inclusion of the RECORD CONTAINS clause with the reserved word TO together with a range of record lengths, (2) specification of the OCCURS/DEPENDING ON clause within an 01-level record description for the file, or (3) definition of two or more record descriptions of different lengths within a file description entry.

```
                    DATA DIVISION.
                *
                *
                *
                    FILE SECTION.
                        .
                        .
                        .
                *
                *
                    FD  STUDENT-FILE-IN
                            BLOCK CONTAINS 10 RECORDS
                            RECORD CONTAINS 190 TO 1300 CHARACTERS
                            LABEL RECORDS ARE STANDARD.
                *
                    01  SF-STUDENT-RECORD-IN.
                        05  FILLER                        PIC X(1300).
                        .
                        .
                        .


                *
                *
                    FD  STUDENT-FILE-OUT
                            BLOCK CONTAINS 10 RECORDS
                            RECORD CONTAINS 190 TO 1300 CHARACTERS
                            LABEL RECORDS ARE STANDARD.
                *
                    01  SF-STUDENT-RECORD-OUT.
                        05  SF-ROOT-AREA-OUT.
                            10  FILLER                    PIC X(173).
                            10  SF-COURSE-COUNT-OUT        PIC S9(4) COMP.
                        05  SF-VARIABLE-AREA-OUT.
                            10  SF-COURSE-SEGMENT-OUT
                                        OCCURS 1 TO 75 TIMES
                                        DEPENDING ON SF-COURSE-COUNT-OUT
                                        PIC X(15).
                        .
                        .
                        .
                    WORKING-STORAGE SECTION.
                        .
                        .
                        .
                *
                *
                    01  SR-STUDENT-RECORD.
                        05  SR-ROOT-AREA.
                            10  SR-RECORD-CODE            PIC X(2).
                            10  SR-STUDENT-NUMBER         PIC X(9).
                            10  SR-STUDENT-NAME           PIC X(30).
                            10  SR-STUDENT-ADDRESS        PIC X(30).
                            10  SR-STUDENT-CITY-STATE-ZIP PIC X(30).
                            10  SR-DATE-OF-BIRTH          PIC X(6).
                            10  SR-SEX-CODE               PIC X(1).
                            10  SR-DATE-ADMITTED          PIC X(6).
                            10  FILLER                    PIC X(59).
                            10  SR-COURSE-COUNT           PIC S9(4) COMP.
                        05  SR-VARIABLE-AREA.
                            10  SR-COURSE-SEGMENT  OCCURS 75 TIMES
                                                   INDEXED BY SR-INDEX.
                                15  SR-COURSE-NUMBER     PIC X(5).
                                15  SR-DATE-COMPLETED    PIC X(6).
                                15  SR-UNITS-EARNED      PIC S9V9 COMP-3.
                                15  SR-LETTER-GRADE      PIC X(2).
                        .
                        .
                        .
```

Figure 8B.3. Record-description examples for variable-length records specified with the OCCURS/DEPENDING ON clause.

The Output STUDENT-FILE-OUT File

In the output file, the OCCURS/DEPENDING ON clause *must* be included within the record description for SR-STUDENT-RECORD. It is mandatory that the exact length of a record that is to be written be established prior to the execution of the WRITE statement. The only way to establish the length of a variable-length record with variable-segment occurrences is by specification of the OCCURS/DEPENDING ON clause within the output 01-level record description.

Therefore, the course segment data-item, SF-COURSE-SEGMENT-OUT has been specified with the following clause: OCCURS 1 TO 75 TIMES DEPENDING ON SF-COURSE-COUNT-OUT. The object of the DEPENDING ON entry—SF-COURSE-COUNT-OUT—is defined in the root area of the record and, for efficiency, has been specified with COMP usage.

Whenever the OCCURS/DEPENDING ON clause is specified to describe the variable-segment area, it is necessary to define at least two other data-items within the output record description: the root area of the record and the object of the DEPENDING ON entry. Such definition is shown in the example (Figure 8B.3); the reason for it will be explained when the WRITE module is discussed later in this topic.

WORKING-STORAGE SECTION Record Description

In accordance with our general convention of defining and processing input and output records in the WORKING-STORAGE SECTION, the student record has been completely described in WORKING-STORAGE as SR-STUDENT-RECORD.

However, notice that the DEPENDING ON option has not been specified with the OCCURS clause, even though the record contains a variable number of course segments. Instead, SR-COURSE-SEGMENT has been assigned an OCCURS clause with a fixed length of 75 segments.

Although the DEPENDING ON entry could certainly be specified in this WORKING-STORAGE record description, it is not necessary, and its omission will usually provide more efficient processing. The inefficiency is caused because, whenever the field that is the object of the DEPENDING ON entry is changed—either by a MOVE statement or an arithmetical statement—the compiler must include time-consuming routines to recalculate the record length. Whereas the DEPENDING ON entry is mandatory within the output FILE SECTION record description so that a record of the correct size may be written, most WORKING-STORAGE SECTION processing can be handled just as effectively without it.

Reading the Variable-length Records

The READ module example shown in Figure 8B.4 introduces no new COBOL syntax. However, there is one aspect of this short routine that should be explained.

Observe that the READ statement has been specified with the INTO option to move the record from the FILE SECTION to the WORKING-STORAGE SECTION. The alternate method is to omit the INTO phrase from the READ statement and then code a separate MOVE statement to transfer SF-STUDENT-RECORD-IN to SR-STUDENT-RECORD.

The READ/INTO approach provides more straightforward and portable processing. When the record is read and transferred to WORKING-STORAGE by the INTO option, only the actual length of the input record is moved. As with MOVE statement processing, when the sending area is shorter, the excess rightmost positions in the receiving area are padded with spaces. On the other hand, the statement MOVE SF-STUDENT-RECORD-IN TO SR-STUDENT-RECORD will always move the maximum-record length (because the OCCURS/DEPENDING ON clause has not been specified within either the sending or receiving area).

The disadvantage of the MOVE statement approach is that, under certain circumstances, it will cause "garbage" data to be introduced into the SR-STUDENT-RECORD area. Suppose the previous record processed had 15 course-completion segments and that the current record has 10 course-completion segments. After the MOVE operation to transfer the current record to WORKING-STORAGE, the SR-STUDENT-RECORD area will contain not only

```
          *
          *
     800-READ-STUDENT-RECORD.
          *
          READ STUDENT-FILE-IN
              INTO SR-STUDENT-RECORD
              AT END MOVE 'YES' TO WS-END-OF-FILE-SW.
```

Figure 8B.4. READ module example for variable-length records specified with the OCCURS/DEPENDING ON clause.

10 segments for the current record but also the last 5 segments left from the previous record! Although such handling need not cause incorrect processing (as long as the object field of the DEPENDING ON entry is properly maintained), it will make storage dumps confusing and could wreak havoc to output data should certain bugs arise in the program.

Another way to achieve the same processing as that afforded by the READ/INTO approach is to code the OCCURS/DEPENDING ON clause together with its object field within the input FILE SECTION record description. Then the actual input record length will be used in the MOVE operation and any excess positions in the WORKING-STORAGE record area will be padded with spaces. The only disadvantage to this method is that it requires additional coding and introduces another area for program maintenance should field locations within the record ever change.

Writing the Variable-length Records

Figure 8B.5 shows an example of a WRITE module for a variable-length record that contains an OCCURS/DEPENDING ON clause. Observe that the first two statements individually move the root and variable areas of the record. Because the two moves cause the entire record to be transferred, one might question why a single MOVE SR-STUDENT-RECORD TO SF-STUDENT-RECORD-OUT statement were not instead coded.

The answer lies in the special processing that takes place when a group field that contains an OCCURS/DEPENDING ON clause is specified in a MOVE statement. The length of the group item that contains the clause is not necessarily the maximum length but rather the length based upon the current value within the field that is the object of the DEPENDING ON entry.

This special processing usually causes no special coding when the OCCURS/DEPENDING ON clause is present within the sending field; expected or intended processing normally occurs. That is, the object field value is used to determine the length of the sending field. If the receiving field is longer, it is padded with spaces. If the sending field is longer, it is truncated.

However, when the OCCURS/DEPENDING ON clause appears in the receiving field, unexpected processing can result unless the programmer is alert to the effect of its presence. As with a sending field, the object field value is used to determine the group item length. However, with a receiving field, this is rarely the desired processing.

Suppose, in the WRITE module, that we did code MOVE SR-STUDENT-RECORD TO SF-STUDENT-RECORD-OUT. Let us say that the last record in the SF-STUDENT-RECORD-OUT receiving area had 20 course segments; the current record in the SR-STUDENT-RECORD sending area has 30 course segments. When the MOVE statement is executed, the receiving field is shorter than the sending field. According to the MOVE statement processing rules, the last 10 course segments of the sending area will be truncated. Thus the full record will not be transferred to the output area; the last 10 segments will be lost.

```
      *
      *
      850-WRITE-STUDENT-RECORD.
      *
            MOVE SR-ROOT-AREA TO SF-ROOT-AREA-OUT.
            MOVE SR-VARIABLE-AREA TO SF-VARIABLE-AREA-OUT.
            WRITE SF-STUDENT-RECORD-OUT.
```

Figure 8B.5. WRITE module example for variable-length records specified with the OCCURS/DEPENDING ON clause.

To obtain the desired processing, SR-STUDENT-RECORD-IN in WORKING-STORAGE must be moved to the SF-STUDENT-RECORD-OUT output area as shown in the WRITE module. That is, first the root portion of the record must be moved to properly initialize the object field of the DEPENDING ON entry (SF-COURSE-COUNT-OUT) in the receiving area. Then the group entry for the variable portion of the record can be correctly moved.

Maintaining the Variable-segment Occurrences

Some variable-segment occurrence applications will introduce a need for segment maintenance. This requirement is similar in function—although not coding—to that for master file maintenance. It arises whenever programming specifications call for the addition, deletion, and/or modification of segments.

Figure 8B.6 shows an example of such maintenance. Notice that a number of WS-SEGMENT-CONTROLS fields are described in the WORKING-STORAGE SECTION. The WS-COMPRESSION-REQUIRED-SW is used to keep track of when a segment has been deleted from the record. When this occurs, the minimum-record length is achieved by compressing the segments and thus eliminating unused segment areas. This is done by shifting each segment to the left after the unused area so that the unused area is consumed.

WS-COURSE-LIMIT is a constant field that is used to determine when the last segment occurrence has been reached. Thus it contains a VALUE of 75 in accordance with the WS-STUDENT-RECORD description. WS-SHIFT-TO-SUB and WS-SHIFT-FROM-SUB are subscript fields that are used to shift segment occurrences when compressing the record. The former is used to represent the unused location that it is being shifted to; the latter identifies the segment that is being shifted. WS-SHIFT-TO-SUB-HOLD is used to keep track of the last used segment number.

In the PROCEDURE DIVISION, there are three main maintenance modules to handle the record addition, change, and deletion functions: 410-ADD-COURSE-SEGMENT, 420-CHANGE-COURSE-SEGMENT, and 430-DELETE-COURSE-SEGMENT. Before any of these routines is executed, the 400-LOCATE-COURSE-SEGMENT module must be performed to determine whether or not the corresponding segment is present in the record. If it is an add transaction, the corresponding segment must not already be present. If the transaction is to change or delete, the corresponding segment must be present and SR-INDEX must be set to its segment occurrence number.

The first statement within the 410-ADD-COURSE-SEGMENT module checks to ensure that the record is not full; that is, that there is space available to add a segment. If there is, the object of the DEPENDING ON entry—SR-COURSE-COUNT—is incremented. Then SR-INDEX is set, and each field from the input segment to be added is moved to unused segment, thus creating a new one.

Before a change can be made, the corresponding segment to which the change is to be applied must be located. Then, in the 420-CHANGE-COURSE-SEGMENT module, the modification is applied to the segment.

```
*
*
*
     WORKING-STORAGE SECTION.
*
*
        .
        .
        .
*
*
     01  WS-SEGMENT-CONTROLS.
         05  WS-ENTRY-FOUND-SW            PIC X(3).
             88  ENTRY-FOUND                        VALUE 'YES'.
         05  WS-COMPRESSION-REQUIRED-SW   PIC X(3).
             88  COMPRESSION-REQUIRED               VALUE 'YES'.
         05  WS-COURSE-LIMIT              PIC S9(4)    COMP SYNC
                                                   VALUE +75.
         05  WS-SHIFT-TO-SUB             PIC S9(4)    COMP SYNC.
         05  WS-SHIFT-FROM-SUB           PIC S9(4)    COMP SYNC.
         05  WS-SHIFT-TO-SUB-HOLD        PIC S9(4)    COMP SYNC.
*
     01  SR-STUDENT-RECORD.
         05  SR-ROOT-AREA.
             10  SR-RECORD-CODE          PIC X(2).
             10  SR-STUDENT-NUMBER       PIC X(9).
             10  SR-STUDENT-NAME         PIC X(30).
             10  SR-STUDENT-ADDRESS      PIC X(30).
             10  SR-STUDENT-CITY-STATE-ZIP  PIC X(30).
             10  SR-DATE-OF-BIRTH        PIC X(6).
             10  SR-SEX-CODE             PIC X(1).
             10  SR-DATE-ADMITTED        PIC X(6).
             10  FILLER                  PIC X(59).
             10  SR-COURSE-COUNT         PIC S9(4) COMP.
         05  SR-VARIABLE-AREA.
             10  SR-COURSE-SEGMENT       OCCURS 75 TIMES
                                         INDEXED BY SR-INDEX.
                 15  SR-COURSE-NUMBER    PIC X(5).
                 15  SR-DATE-COMPLETED   PIC X(6).
                 15  SR-UNITS-EARNED     PIC S9V9 COMP-3.
                 15  SR-LETTER-GRADE     PIC X(2).
        .
        .
        .


*
*
*
     PROCEDURE DIVISION.
*
*
        .
        .
        .

*
     400-LOCATE-COURSE-SEGMENT.
*
         MOVE 'NO ' TO WS-ENTRY-FOUND-SW.
         SET SR-INDEX TO ZERO.
         PERFORM 402-LOOKUP-COURSE-SEGMENT
             UNTIL ENTRY-FOUND
                 OR SR-INDEX IS NOT LESS THAN SR-COURSE-COUNT.
*
*
     402-LOOKUP-COURSE-SEGMENT.
*
         SET SR-INDEX UP BY 1.
         IF IN-COURSE-NUMBER
             IS EQUAL TO SR-COURSE-NUMBER (SR-INDEX)
                 MOVE 'YES' TO WS-ENTRY-FOUND-SW.
*
*
     410-ADD-COURSE-SEGMENT.
```

Figure 8B.6. Example of variable-length record processing with the OCCURS/DEPENDING ON clause.

```
          *
                IF WS-COURSE-LIMIT - SR-COURSE-COUNT - 1 IS NEGATIVE
                    PERFORM 999-IDENTIFY-FULL-RECORD
                ELSE
                    ADD 1 TO SR-COURSE-COUNT
                    SET SR-INDEX TO SR-COURSE-COUNT
                    MOVE IN-COURSE-NUMBER
                        TO SR-COURSE-NUMBER (SR-INDEX)
                    MOVE IN-DATE-COMPLETED
                        TO SR-DATE-COMPLETED (SR-INDEX)
                    MOVE IN-UNITS-EARNED
                        TO SR-UNITS-EARNED (SR-INDEX)
                    MOVE IN-LETTER-GRADE
                        TO SR-LETTER-GRADE (SR-INDEX).
      *
      *
       420-CHANGE-COURSE-SEGMENT.
      *
                IF IN-DATE-COMPLETED IS NOT EQUAL TO SPACES
                    MOVE IN-DATE-COMPLETED
                        TO SR-DATE-COMPLETED (SR-INDEX).
                IF IN-UNITS-EARNED IS NOT EQUAL TO SPACES
                    MOVE IN-UNITS-EARNED
                        TO SR-UNITS-EARNED (SR-INDEX).
                IF IN-LETTER-GRADE IS NOT EQUAL TO SPACES
                    MOVE IN-LETTER-GRADE
                        TO SR-LETTER-GRADE (SR-INDEX).
      *
      *
       430-DELETE-COURSE-SEGMENT.
      *
                MOVE SPACES TO SR-COURSE-SEGMENT (SR-INDEX).
                MOVE 'YES' TO WS-COMPRESSION-REQUIRED-SW.
      *
      *
       440-COMPRESS-COURSE-SEGMENTS.
      *
                MOVE 1 TO WS-SHIFT-TO-SUB.
                MOVE SR-COURSE-COUNT TO SR-SHIFT-TO-SUB-HOLD.
                PERFORM 442-SHIFT-COURSE-SEGMENT
                    UNTIL WS-SHIFT-TO-SUB IS EQUAL TO SR-COURSE-COUNT.
                MOVE WS-SHIFT-TO-SUB-HOLD TO SR-COURSE-COUNT.
      *
      *
       442-SHIFT-COURSE-SEGMENT.
      *
                PERFORM 444-FIND-BLANK-SEGMENT
                    UNTIL SR-COURSE-SEGMENT (WS-SHIFT-TO-SUB)
                            IS EQUAL TO SPACES
                        OR WS-SHIFT-TO-SUB IS EQUAL TO SR-COURSE-COUNT.
      *
                ADD 1 WS-SHIFT-TO-SUB GIVING WS-SHIFT-FROM-SUB.
      *
                PERFORM 446-FIND-OCCUPIED-SEGMENT
                    UNTIL SR-COURSE-SEGMENT (WS-SHIFT-FROM-SUB)
                            IS NOT EQUAL TO SPACES
                        OR WS-SHIFT-FROM-SUB
                            IS GREATER THAN SR-COURSE-COUNT.
      *
                IF WS-SHIFT-FROM-SUB
                        IS NOT GREATER THAN SR-COURSE-COUNT
                    MOVE SR-COURSE-SEGMENT (WS-SHIFT-FROM-SUB)
                        TO SR-COURSE-SEGMENT (WS-SHIFT-TO-SUB)
                    MOVE WS-SHIFT-TO-SUB TO WS-SHIFT-TO-SUB-HOLD
                    MOVE SPACES
                        TO SR-COURSE-SEGMENT (WS-SHIFT-FROM-SUB).
      *
      *
       444-FIND-BLANK-SEGMENT.
      *
                ADD 1 TO WS-SHIFT-TO-SUB.
      *
      *
       446-FIND-OCCUPIED-SEGMENT.
      *
                ADD 1 TO WS-SHIFT-FROM-SUB.
```

Figure 8B.6. (continued)

```
      *
      *
    01  LC-LIBRARY-CATALOG-RECORD.
        05  LC-ROOT-AREA.

            .
            .
            .

            10  LC-CHARACTER-COUNT           PIC S9(4) COMP.
        05  LC-VARIABLE-AREA.
            10  LC-TITLE-AUTHOR-CHARACTER
                                    OCCURS 1 TO 100 TIMES
                                    DEPENDING ON LC-CHARACTER-COUNT
                                    INDEXED BY LC-INDEX
                                    PIC X(1).
```

Figure 8B.7. Record-description example for variable-length field processing.

Again, before a delete is processed, the segment to be deleted must be located in the record. The deletion is accomplished in the 430-DELETE-COURSE-SEGMENT module by blanking the segment. Whenever a segment is deleted, the need for record compression arises. Record compression could be done after each segment deletion but the possibility of multiple deletions during the same program run usually exists. In such a case, more efficient processing occurs if compression is not performed until after all deletes have been processed. Thus the logic of the delete module shows that the WS-COMPRESSION-REQUIRED-SW is set to ''YES'' after a deletion is made. At some point in the program logic after all transactions for each record have been processed, the program logic must test the WS-COMPRESSION-REQUIRED-SW to determine whether compression is required. If it is, the 440-COMPRESS-COURSE-SEGMENTS module is performed. This module performs three subordinate modules: 442-SHIFT-COURSE-SEGMENT, 444-FIND-BLANK-SEGMENT, and 446-FIND-OCCUPIED-SEGMENT.

Recognize that more effective processing is achieved by making all deletions and performing the compression before any additions are processed. This allows segments to be added to a full record when deletions during the same run free the space.

There is one additional maintenance feature that is not provided for in the coding example, but which is appropriate in certain circumstances. This is to maintain the segment numbers in sequence. By keeping the segment numbers in sequence according to a key field, such as SR-COURSE-NUMBER, a binary search or early exit routine could be employed in any lookup routines. The only other change to the coding example would be that when a record is to be added, its proper sequential segment slot must be identified and a right-shift routine must be provided to open up room for the new segment when it must be added between existing segments.

**Processing
Variable-length
Fields**

When variable-length fields are required, they are specified in the same manner as segments. The only difference is that each character position is considered a variable segment. Figure 8B.7 shows a record-description example for variable-length field processing. A book title and author are stored in the LC-TITLE-AUTHOR-CHARACTER field that ranges in length from 1 to 100 characters.

Because of OCCURS/DEPENDING ON clause restrictions, it is not possible to have more than one variable-length field, such as one for the title and one for the author. In the example, the need for two fields has been circumvented by combining the two data elements into one field. This means that, within the LC-TITLE-AUTHOR-CHARACTER field, the title portion must be differentiated from the author portion. Such demarcation can be indicated by recording a special character, called a **delimiter**, between the title and the author. The actual value chosen for a delimiter must be one that cannot be present within the field value. In this example, a slash could perhaps be used.

Joining and extracting fields with delimiters is handled by the STRING and UNSTRING statements, which are discussed in Chapter 9.

■ TOPIC 8-C: **Sorting Variable-length Records**

Sorting Records of Various Lengths

Sorting Records with the OCCURS/DEPENDING ON Clause

When sorting variable-length records, the USING and GIVING options of the SORT statement should not be used because they will not always control the record lengths correctly. Instead, INPUT PROCEDURE and OUTPUT PROCEDURE should always be specified.

Sorting Records of Various Lengths

Figure 8C.1 shows coding for a program named SORTVARF that is an example of a program that **sorts** a file which contains records of **various** fixed lengths. The function of this program is to read the input INVOICE-FILE-IN and sort the records in ascending sequence in accordance with the contents of the following fields: invoice number (major), record code, line number, and line-type code (minor). The sorted records are written to the output INVOICE-FILE-OUT field.

With regard to the SD entry, remember that the BLOCK CONTAINS clause does not apply; the compiler's sort logic computes an appropriate block size. Observe that three record descriptions are specified after the SD entry. One must be provided for each record length that is to be sorted. Within the SD entry, as with FD entries for files with records of various lengths, the longest record description must be coded first.

Just as when sorting fixed-length records, any fields that are being sorted must be in the same relative location within all records. The record descriptions for the invoice records (presented in Figure 8A.3) show that the record-code and invoice-number fields are in the same relative location within all three record descriptions. Even though the line-number and line-type code fields appear only in the invoice line records, the sort will sequence the records properly because these two fields have been specified minor to the record-code field and major to no common fields. This, coupled with the fact that only one each of the invoice-header and ship-to-address records is permitted for an invoice, allows correct sequencing by line-number and line-type code. Because the invoice number and record code fields *are* in the same relative position within all records, they have been specified within the SF-INVOICE-HEADER-RCD record description and— for convenience but not necessity—omitted from the SF-SHIP-TO-ADDRESS-RCD and SF-INVOICE-LINE-RCD descriptions.

A separate RELEASE statement must be coded and used in the INPUT PROCEDURE for each different record length that is released to the sort work file. This is parallel to the requirement that records of various lengths must be written with individual WRITE statements. The RELEASE statements are shown in the 2850-RELEASE-INV-HEADER-RCD, 2852-RELEASE-SHIP-TO-ADS-RCD, and 2854-RELEASE-INVOICE-LINE-RCD modules.

When, as with the SORTVARF program, the sorted records are to be

```
001010 IDENTIFICATION DIVISION.                               050190            INPUT PROCEDURE IS 2000-IP-PROCESS-UNSORTED-RCDS
001020 PROGRAM-ID.     SORTVARF.                               050200            OUTPUT PROCEDURE IS 3000-OP-PROCESS-SORTED-RCDS.
001030*                                                        050210        CLOSE INVOICE-FILE-IN
001040*                                                        050220              INVOICE-FILE-OUT.
001050                 THIS PROGRAM SORTS RECORDS OF VARIOUS LENGTHS   050230        STOP RUN.
002010*                                                        200010*
002020*                                                        200020*
002030*                                                        200030 2000-IP-PROCESS-UNSORTED-RCDS SECTION.
002040 ENVIRONMENT DIVISION.                                   220010*
002050*                                                        220020*
002060*                                                        220030 2200-PROCESS-UNSORTED-RCDS.
002070 CONFIGURATION SECTION.                                  220040*
002080*                                                        220050        MOVE 'NO ' TO WS-END-OF-FILE-SW.
002090 SOURCE-COMPUTER.  IBM-370.                              220060        PERFORM 2210-PROCESS-UNSORTED-RCD
002100 OBJECT-COMPUTER.  IBM-370.                              220070              UNTIL END-OF-FILE.
002110*                                                        220080        GO TO 2999-IP-EXIT.
002120*                                                        221010*
002130 INPUT-OUTPUT SECTION.                                   221020*
002140*                                                        221030 2210-PROCESS-UNSORTED-RCD.
002150 FILE-CONTROL.                                           221040*
002160     SELECT INVOICE-FILE-IN                              221050        PERFORM 2800-READ-INVOICE-FILE.
002170        ASSIGN TO UT-S-INFILE.                           221060        IF END-OF-FILE
002180     SELECT INVOICE-FILE-OUT                             221070            NEXT SENTENCE
002190        ASSIGN TO UT-S-OUTFILE.                          221080        ELSE IF INVOICE-HEADER-RECORD
002200     SELECT SORT-FILE                                    221090            PERFORM 2850-RELEASE-INV-HEADER-RCD
002210        ASSIGN TO UT-S-SORTWORK.                         221100        ELSE IF SHIP-TO-ADDRESS-RECORD
003010*                                                        221110            PERFORM 2852-RELEASE-SHIP-TO-ADS-RCD
003020*                                                        221120        ELSE IF INVOICE-LINE-RECORD
003030*                                                        221130            PERFORM 2854-RELEASE-INVOICE-LINE-RCD.
003040 DATA DIVISION.                                          280010*
003050*                                                        280020*
003060*                                                        280030 2800-READ-INVOICE-FILE.
003070 FILE SECTION.                                           280040*
003080*                                                        280050        READ INVOICE-FILE-IN
003090*                                                        280060            INTO SF-INVOICE-HEADER-RCD
003100 FD  INVOICE-FILE-IN                                     280070            AT END MOVE 'YES' TO WS-END-OF-FILE-SW.
003110     BLOCK CONTAINS 10 RECORDS                           285010*
003120     RECORD CONTAINS 75 TO 250 CHARACTERS                285020*
003130     LABEL RECORDS ARE STANDARD.                         285030 2850-RELEASE-INV-HEADER-RCD.
003140*                                                        285040*
003150 01  IR-INVOICE-RCD-IN.                                  285050        RELEASE SF-INVOICE-HEADER-RCD.
003160     05  IR-RECORD-CODE-IN        PIC X(2).              285210*
003170     05  FILLER                   PIC X(248).            285220*
004010*                                                        285230 2852-RELEASE-SHIP-TO-ADS-RCD.
004020*                                                        285240*
004030 FD  INVOICE-FILE-OUT                                    285250        RELEASE SF-SHIP-TO-ADDRESS-RCD.
004040     BLOCK CONTAINS 10 RECORDS                           285410*
004050     RECORD CONTAINS 75 TO 250 CHARACTERS                285420*
004060     LABEL RECORDS ARE STANDARD.                         285430 2854-RELEASE-INVOICE-LINE-RCD.
004070*                                                        285440*
004080 01  IR-INVOICE-HEADER-RCD-OUT.                          285450        RELEASE SF-INVOICE-LINE-RCD.
004090     05  FILLER                   PIC X(250).            299910*
004100*                                                        299920*
004110 01  IR-SHIP-TO-ADDRESS-RCD-OUT.                         299930 2999-IP-EXIT.
004120     05  FILLER                   PIC X(150).            299940*
004130*                                                        299950        EXIT.
004140 01  IR-INVOICE-LINE-RCD-OUT.                            300010*
004150     05  FILLER                   PIC X(75).             300020*
005010*                                                        300030 3000-OP-PROCESS-SORTED-RCDS SECTION.
005020*                                                        320010*
005030 SD  SORT-FILE                                           320020*
005040     RECORD CONTAINS 75 TO 250 CHARACTERS.               320030 3200-PROCESS-SORTED-RCDS.
005050*                                                        320040*
005060 01  SF-INVOICE-HEADER-RCD.                              320050        MOVE 'NO ' TO WS-END-OF-FILE-SW.
005070     05  SF-RECORD-CODE           PIC X(2).              320060        PERFORM 3210-PROCESS-SORTED-RCD
005080         88  INVOICE-HEADER-RECORD        VALUE '50'.    320070              UNTIL END-OF-FILE.
005090         88  SHIP-TO-ADDRESS-RECORD       VALUE '52'.    320080        GO TO 3999-OP-EXIT.
005100         88  INVOICE-LINE-RECORD          VALUE '55'.    321010*
005110     05  SF-INVOICE-NUMBER        PIC X(5).              321020*
005120     05  FILLER                   PIC X(243).            321030 3210-PROCESS-SORTED-RCD.
005130*                                                        321040*
005140 01  SF-SHIP-TO-ADDRESS-RCD.                             321050        PERFORM 3800-RETURN-SORTED-RCD.
005150     05  FILLER                   PIC X(150).            321060        IF END-OF-FILE
005160*                                                        321070            NEXT SENTENCE
005170 01  SF-INVOICE-LINE-RCD.                                321080        ELSE IF INVOICE-HEADER-RECORD
005180     05  FILLER                   PIC X(12).             321090            PERFORM 3850-WRITE-INV-HEADER-RCD
005190     05  SF-LINE-NUMBER           PIC X(2).              321100        ELSE IF SHIP-TO-ADDRESS-RECORD
005200     05  SF-LINE-TYPE-CODE        PIC X(2).              321110            PERFORM 3852-WRITE-SHIP-TO-ADS-RCD
005210     05  FILLER                   PIC X(69).             321120        ELSE IF INVOICE-LINE-RECORD
010010*                                                        321130            PERFORM 3854-WRITE-INVOICE-LINE-RCD.
010020*                                                        380010*
010030 WORKING-STORAGE SECTION.                                380020*
010040*                                                        380030 3800-RETURN-SORTED-RCD.
010050*                                                        380040*
010060 01  WS-SWITCHES.                                        380050        RETURN SORT-FILE
010070     05  WS-END-OF-FILE-SW        PIC X(3).              380060            INTO IR-INVOICE-HEADER-RCD-OUT
010080         88  END-OF-FILE                  VALUE 'YES'.   380070            AT END MOVE 'YES' TO WS-END-OF-FILE-SW.
050010*                                                        385010*
050020*                                                        385020*
050030*                                                        385030 3850-WRITE-INV-HEADER-RCD.
050040 PROCEDURE DIVISION.                                     385040*
050050*                                                        385050        WRITE IR-INVOICE-HEADER-RCD-OUT.
050060*                                                        385210*
050070 0000-ML-SORT-INVOICE-RECORDS SECTION.                   385220*
050080*                                                        385230 3852-WRITE-SHIP-TO-ADS-RCD.
050090*                                                        385240*
050100 0000-SORT-INVOICE-RECORDS                               385250        WRITE IR-SHIP-TO-ADDRESS-RCD-OUT.
050110*                                                        385410*
050120     OPEN INPUT INVOICE-FILE-IN                          385420*
050130          OUTPUT INVOICE-FILE-OUT.                       385430 3854-WRITE-INVOICE-LINE-RCD.
050140     SORT SORT-FILE                                      385440*
050150         ASCENDING KEY SF-INVOICE-NUMBER                 385450        WRITE IR-INVOICE-LINE-RCD-OUT.
050160                       SF-RECORD-CODE                    399910*
050170                       SF-LINE-NUMBER                    399920*
050180                       SF-LINE-TYPE-CODE                 399930 3999-OP-EXIT.
                                                               399940*
                                                               399950        EXIT.
```

Figure 8C.1. Program coding: SORTVARF program.

written as variable-length records to an output file, it is similarly necessary to code separate WRITE statements in the OUTPUT PROCEDURE for each different record length that is written. This is shown in the 3850-WRITE-INV-HEADER-RCD, 3852-WRITE-SHIP-TO-ADS-RCD, and 3854-WRITE-INVOICE-LINE-RCD modules.

There are alternative methods by which (1) the unsorted records can be transferred from the input file to the sort work file and (2) the sorted records can be transferred from the sort work file to the output file. These are summarized in Figure 8C.2. For clarity, the coding presented in the figure is not separated into independently structured modules.

INPUT PROCEDURE. Transferring unsorted records of various lengths from an input file to the sort work file

Method A. READ, MOVE, and RELEASE

```
READ INVOICE-FILE-IN
    AT END imperative-statement.
MOVE IR-INVOICE-RCD-IN TO SF-INVOICE-HEADER-RCD.
IF END-OF-FILE
    NEXT SENTENCE
ELSE IF INVOICE-HEADER-RECORD (in input or sort record areas)
    RELEASE SF-INVOICE-HEADER-RCD
ELSE IF SHIP-TO-ADDRESS-RECORD (in input or sort record areas)
    RELEASE SF-SHIP-TO-ADDRESS-RCD
ELSE IF INVOICE-LINE-RECORD (in input or sort record areas)
    RELEASE SF-INVOICE-LINE-RCD.
```

Method B. READ/INTO and RELEASE

```
READ INVOICE-FILE-IN
    INTO SF-INVOICE-HEADER-RCD
    AT END imperative-statement.
IF END-OF-FILE
    NEXT SENTENCE
ELSE IF INVOICE-HEADER-RECORD (in input or sort record areas)
    RELEASE SF-INVOICE-HEADER-RCD
ELSE IF SHIP-TO-ADDRESS-RECORD (in input or sort record areas)
    RELEASE SF-SHIP-TO-ADDRESS-RCD
ELSE IF INVOICE-LINE-RECORD (in input or sort record areas)
    RELEASE SF-INVOICE-LINE-RCD.
```

Method C. READ and RELEASE/FROM

```
READ INVOICE-FILE-IN
    AT END imperative-statement.
IF END-OF-FILE
    NEXT SENTENCE
ELSE IF INVOICE-HEADER-RECORD (in input record area)
    RELEASE SF-INVOICE-HEADER-RCD
        FROM IR-INVOICE-RCD-IN
ELSE IF SHIP-TO-ADDRESS-RECORD (in input record area)
    RELEASE SF-SHIP-TO-ADDRESS-RCD
        FROM IR-INVOICE-RCD-IN
ELSE IF INVOICE-LINE-RECORD (in input record area)
    RELEASE SF-INVOICE-LINE-RCD
        FROM IR-INVOICE-RCD-IN.
```

continued

Figure 8C.2. SORT I-O processing for records of various lengths.

OUTPUT PROCEDURE. Transferring sorted records of various lengths from the sort work file to an output file

Method A. RETURN, MOVE, and WRITE

```
RETURN SORT-FILE
    AT END Imperative-statement.
MOVE SF-INVOICE-HEADER-RCD TO IR-INVOICE-HEADER-RCD-OUT.
IF END-OF-FILE
    NEXT SENTENCE
ELSE IF INVOICE-HEADER-RECORD (In sort or output record areas)
    WRITE IR-INVOICE-HEADER-RCD-OUT
ELSE IF SHIP-TO-ADDRESS-RECORD (In sort or output record areas)
    WRITE IR-SHIP-TO-ADDRESS-RCD-OUT
ELSE IF INVOICE-LINE-RECORD (In sort or output record areas)
    WRITE IR-INVOICE-LINE-RCD-OUT.
```

Method B. RETURN/INTO and WRITE

```
RETURN SORT-FILE
    INTO IR-INVOICE-HEADER-RCD-OUT
    AT END Imperative-statement.
IF END-OF-FILE
    NEXT SENTENCE
ELSE IF INVOICE-HEADER-RECORD (In sort or output record areas)
    WRITE IR-INVOICE-HEADER-RCD-OUT
ELSE IF SHIP-TO-ADDRESS-RECORD (In sort or output record areas)
    WRITE IR-SHIP-TO-ADDRESS-RCD-OUT
ELSE IF INVOICE-LINE-RECORD (In sort or output record areas)
    WRITE IR-INVOICE-LINE-RCD-OUT.
```

Method C. RETURN and WRITE/FROM

```
RETURN SORT-FILE
    AT END Imperative-statement.
IF END-OF-FILE
    NEXT SENTENCE
ELSE IF INVOICE-HEADER-RECORD (In sort record area)
    WRITE IR-INVOICE-HEADER-RCD-OUT
        FROM SF-INVOICE-HEADER-RCD
ELSE IF SHIP-TO-ADDRESS-RECORD (In sort record area)
    WRITE IR-SHIP-TO-ADDRESS-RCD-OUT
        FROM SF-INVOICE-HEADER-RCD
ELSE IF INVOICE-LINE-RECORD (In sort record area)
    WRITE IR-INVOICE-LINE-RCD-OUT
        FROM SF-INVOICE-HEADER-RCD.
```

Figure 8C.2. (continued)

Sorting Records with the OCCURS/ DEPENDING ON Clause

Figure 8C.3 shows coding for a program named SORTVARD that is an example of a program that **sort**s a file of **vari**able-length records that are specified with the OCCURS/DEPENDING ON clause. The function of this program is to read the input STUDENT-FILE-IN and sort the records in ascending sequence in accordance with the student-number field.

Unlike the coding presented in Topic 8-B in which the OCCURS/DEPENDING ON clause was coded only in the output area, notice that the OCCURS/DEPENDING ON phrase has been specified at three locations: (1) within the input STUDENT-FILE-IN area, (2) within the SORT-FILE sort work area, and (3) within the output STUDENT-FILE-OUT area.

There is only one method by which the unsorted records can be transferred from the input file to the sort work file. Similarly, there is only one method to transfer the sorted records from the sort work file to the output file. These are summarized in Figure 8C.4.

```
001010 IDENTIFICATION DIVISION.
001020 PROGRAM-ID.    SORTVARD.
001030*
001040*
001050*              THIS PROGRAM SORTS VARIABLE-LENGTH RECORDS
001060*              THAT CONTAIN THE OCCURS/DEPENDING ON CLAUSE
002010*
002020*
002030*
002040 ENVIRONMENT DIVISION.
002050*
002060*
002070 CONFIGURATION SECTION.
002080*
002090 SOURCE-COMPUTER.   IBM-370.
002100 OBJECT-COMPUTER.   IBM-370.
002110*
002120*
002130 INPUT-OUTPUT SECTION.
002140*
002150 FILE-CONTROL.
002160     SELECT STUDENT-FILE-IN
002170         ASSIGN TO UT-S-INFILE.
002180     SELECT STUDENT-FILE-OUT
002190         ASSIGN TO UT-S-OUTFILE.
002200     SELECT SORT-FILE
002210         ASSIGN TO UT-S-SORTWORK.
003010*
003020*
003040*
003050 DATA DIVISION.
003060*
003070*
003080 FILE SECTION.
003090*
003100*
003110 FD  STUDENT-FILE-IN
003120     BLOCK CONTAINS 10 RECORDS
003130     RECORD CONTAINS 190 TO 1300 CHARACTERS
003140     LABEL RECORDS ARE STANDARD.
003150*
003160 01  SF-STUDENT-RECORD-IN.
003170     05  SF-ROOT-AREA-IN.
003180         10  FILLER              PIC X(173).
003190         10  SF-COURSE-COUNT-IN  PIC S9(4) COMP.
003200     05  SF-VARIABLE-AREA-IN.
003210         10  SF-COURSE-SEGMENT-IN
003220                 OCCURS 1 TO 75 TIMES
003230                 DEPENDING ON SF-COURSE-COUNT-IN
003240                 PIC X(15).
004010*
004020*
004030 FD  STUDENT-FILE-OUT
004050     BLOCK CONTAINS 10 RECORDS
004060     RECORD CONTAINS 190 TO 1300 CHARACTERS
004070     LABEL RECORDS ARE STANDARD.
004080*
004090 01  SF-STUDENT-RECORD-OUT.
004100     05  SF-ROOT-AREA-OUT.
004110         10  FILLER              PIC X(173).
004120         10  SF-COURSE-COUNT-OUT PIC S9(4) COMP.
004130     05  SF-VARIABLE-AREA-OUT.
004140         10  SF-COURSE-SEGMENT-OUT
004150                 OCCURS 1 TO 75 TIMES
004160                 DEPENDING ON SF-COURSE-COUNT-OUT
004170                 PIC X(15).
005010*
005020*
005030 SD  SORT-FILE
005040     RECORD CONTAINS 190 TO 1300 CHARACTERS.
005050*
005060 01  SX-STUDENT-RECORD.
005070     05  SX-ROOT-AREA.
005080         10  FILLER              PIC X(2).
005090         10  SX-STUDENT-NUMBER   PIC X(9).
005100         10  FILLER              PIC X(162).
005110         10  SX-COURSE-COUNT     PIC S9(4) COMP.
005120     05  SX-VARIABLE-AREA.
005130         10  SX-COURSE-SEGMENT
005140                 OCCURS 1 TO 75 TIMES
005150                 DEPENDING ON SX-COURSE-COUNT
005160                 PIC X(15).
010010*
010020*
010030 WORKING-STORAGE SECTION.
010040*
010050*
010060 01  WS-SWITCHES.
010070     05  WS-END-OF-FILE-SW       PIC X(3).
010080         88  END-OF-FILE                     VALUE 'YES'.
```

```
050010*
050020*
050030*
050040 PROCEDURE DIVISION.
050050*
050060*
050070 0000-ML-SORT-STUDENT-RECORDS SECTION.
050080*
050090*
050100 0000-SORT-STUDENT-RECORDS.
050110*
050120     OPEN INPUT STUDENT-FILE-IN
050130          OUTPUT STUDENT-FILE-OUT.
050140     SORT SORT-FILE
050150         ASCENDING KEY SX-STUDENT-NUMBER
050160             INPUT PROCEDURE IS 2000-IP-PROCESS-UNSORTED-RCDS
050170             OUTPUT PROCEDURE IS 3000-OP-PROCESS-SORTED-RCDS.
050180     CLOSE STUDENT-FILE-IN
050190           STUDENT-FILE-OUT.
050200     STOP RUN.
200010*
200020*
200030 2000-IP-PROCESS-UNSORTED-RCDS SECTION.
220010*
220020*
220030 2200-PROCESS-UNSORTED-RCDS.
220040*
220050     MOVE 'NO ' TO WS-END-OF-FILE-SW.
220060     PERFORM 2210-PROCESS-UNSORTED-RCD
220070         UNTIL END-OF-FILE.
220080     GO TO 2999-IP-EXIT.
221010*
221020*
221030 2210-PROCESS-UNSORTED-RCD.
221040*
221050     PERFORM 2800-READ-STUDENT-FILE.
221060     IF NOT END-OF-FILE
221070         MOVE SF-ROOT-AREA-IN TO SX-ROOT-AREA
221080         MOVE SF-VARIABLE-AREA-IN TO SX-VARIABLE-AREA
221090         PERFORM 2850-RELEASE-STUDENT-RECORD.
280010*
280020*
280030 2800-READ-STUDENT-FILE.
280040*
280050     READ STUDENT-FILE-IN
280060         AT END MOVE 'YES' TO WS-END-OF-FILE-SW.
285010*
285020*
285030 2850-RELEASE-INV-HEADER-RCD.
285040*
285050     RELEASE SX-STUDENT-RECORD.
299910*
299920*
299930 2999-IP-EXIT.
299940*
299950     EXIT.
300010*
300020*
300030 3000-OP-PROCESS-SORTED-RCDS SECTION.
320010*
320020*
320030 3200-PROCESS-SORTED-RCDS.
320040*
320050     MOVE 'NO ' TO WS-END-OF-FILE-SW.
320060     PERFORM 3210-PROCESS-SORTED-RCD
320070         UNTIL END-OF-FILE.
320080     GO TO 3999-OP-EXIT.
321010*
321020*
321030 3210-PROCESS-SORTED-RCD.
321040*
321050     PERFORM 3800-RETURN-SORTED-RCD.
321060     IF NOT END-OF-FILE
321070         MOVE SX-ROOT-AREA TO SF-ROOT-AREA-OUT
321080         MOVE SX-VARIABLE-AREA TO SF-VARIABLE-AREA-OUT
321090         PERFORM 3850-WRITE-STUDENT-RCD.
380010*
380020*
380030 3800-RETURN-SORTED-RCD.
380040*
380050     RETURN SORT-FILE
380060         AT END MOVE 'YES' TO WS-END-OF-FILE-SW.
385010*
385020*
385030 3850-WRITE-STUDENT-RCD.
385040*
385050     WRITE SF-STUDENT-RECORD-OUT.
399910*
399920*
399930 3999-OP-EXIT.
399940*
399950     EXIT.
```

Figure 8C.3. Program coding: SORTVARD program.

When transferring records to and from the sort work area, observe that the record is moved in two portions. First the root area is moved; then the variable area. As discussed in Topic 8-B, such handling is always required when both the sending and receiving record areas contain the OCCURS/DEPENDING ON clause. Otherwise, the object of the OCCURS/DEPENDING ON entry will not contain the correct value and the receiving area length will not be interpreted correctly.

INPUT PROCEDURE.   **Transferring unsorted records of various lengths from an input file to the sort work file**

Method A.   READ, MOVE, and RELEASE

```
READ STUDENT-FILE-IN
    AT END imperative-statement.
IF NOT END-OF-FILE
    MOVE SF-ROOT-AREA-IN TO SX-ROOT-AREA
    MOVE SF-VARIABLE-AREA-IN TO SX-VARIABLE-AREA
    RELEASE SX-STUDENT-RECORD.
```

OUTPUT PROCEDURE.   **Transferring sorted records of various lengths from the sort work file to an output file**

Method A.   RETURN, MOVE, and WRITE

```
RETURN SORT-FILE
    AT END imperative-statement.
IF NOT END-OF-FILE
    MOVE SX-ROOT-AREA TO SF-ROOT-AREA-OUT
    MOVE SX-VARIABLE-AREA TO SF-VARIABLE-AREA-OUT
    WRITE SF-STUDENT-RECORD-OUT.
```

Figure 8C.4.   SORT I-O processing for records with the OCCURS/DEPENDING ON clause.

Summary

There are three types of variable-length record situations: (1) a file that contains fixed-length records of various lengths, (2) a file with records that contain a variable number of fixed-length segment occurrences, and (3) a file with records that contain one or more fields of variable length. In COBOL, type 1 is specified by defining two or more record-descriptions of different lengths within the file-description entry. Types 2 and 3 are specified by coding the OCCURS/DEPENDING ON clause.

Programming Assignments

8-1: Grade Report

Program description
    A grade report is to be printed from a file of variable-length student records.
Input file
    Student file
Output file
    Grade report
Record formats
    Student record (Record code "SR")

Student record

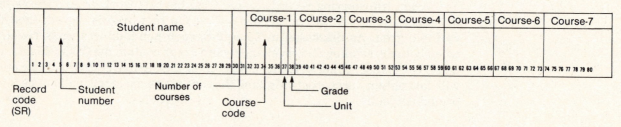

Grade report

GRADE REPORT (8-1)				MM/DD/YY PAGE ZZ9		
STUDENT NUMBER	STUDENT NAME	NBR COURSES	COURSE CODE	UNITS	GRADE	GRADE POINTS
99999	XXXXXXXXXXXXXXXXXXXXX	99	XXXXX	9	X	Z9
			XXXXX	9	X	Z9
			XXXXX	9	X	Z9
			XXXXX	9	X	Z9
			XXXXX	9	X	Z9
			XXXXX	9	X	Z9
				29*		ZZ9* GPA 9.99
99999	XXXXXXXXXXXXXXXXXXXXX	99	XXXXX	9	X	Z9

Program operations

A. Read each input student record.
   1. There will be from 1 to 7 course segments, depending upon the value of the number-of-courses field.
B. Print each student record on the grade report, as shown on the print chart.
   1. Print one line for each course segment.
   2. Assign grade points to grades as follows:
      A = 4
      B = 3
      C = 2
      D = 1
   3. After all course segments have been printed, print a student total line that contains the total units and grade-point average (total grade points divided by total units).
   4. Handle line spacing as follows:
      a. Single-space each course segment line for the same student.
      b. Double-space between student records.
      c. Provide for a line span of at least 50 lines per page. However, skip pages only between student records (do not break a student record between two pages).

Assignment 8-A   Option 1
   Perform a bubble sort on the course segments so that they are arranged on the grade report in ascending course code sequence. (Bubble sorts are covered in Chapter C under the topic "*Table Search and Sort Routine Logic: Internal Sorts.*")

8-2: Invoice Register

Program description

An invoice register is to be printed from an invoice file that contains records of various lengths. An output invoice file is to be updated with extended invoice line-item amounts and invoice-trailer records.

Input file

Invoice file   Key fields = Invoice number (major)
                               Record code (intermediate)
                               Line number (minor)

Output files
     Invoice file (updated)
     Invoice register
Record formats
     Invoice-header record (Record code "85")
     Ship-to-address record (Record code "86")
     Line-item record (Record code "87")
     Invoice-trailer record (Record code "88")

Invoice header record

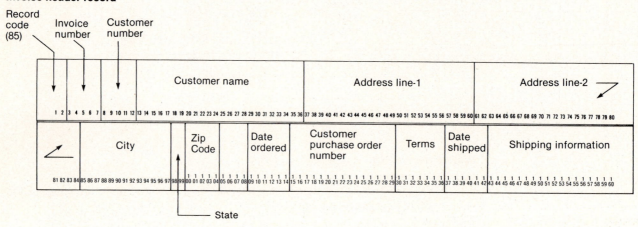

Ship-to-address record

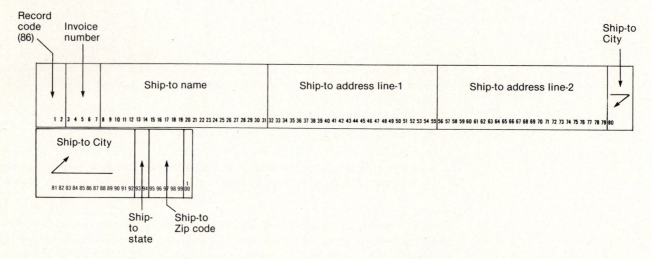

Line-item record

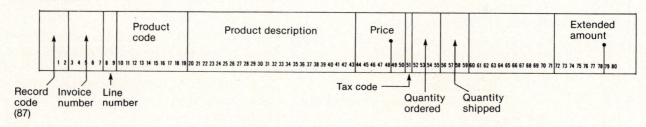

Invoice trailer record

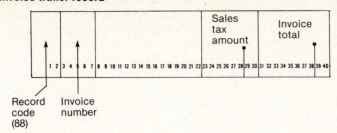

Record code (88)   Invoice number   Sales tax amount   Invoice total

Invoice register

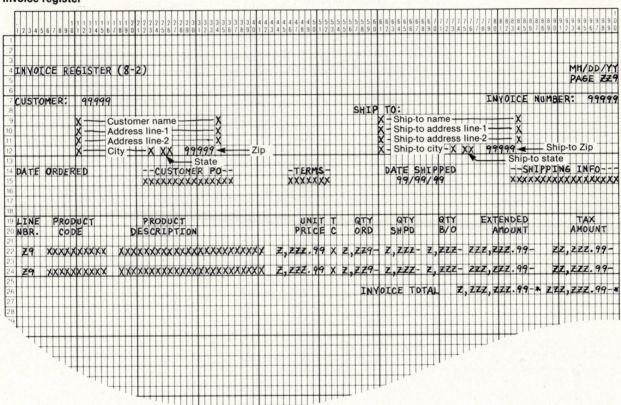

Program operations

A. Read each invoice file record.

1. The file will contain the following records:

Record type		Length
Invoice header record	(1 per invoice)	160
Ship-to-address record	(0 or 1 per invoice)	100
Line-item record	(1 to 99 per invoice)	80

2. For each line-item record, process the following:

a. Compute the extended amount (quantity shipped times price).

b. Accumulate the extended amounts.

c. Accumulate the sales tax amount. The sales tax is to be computed for any line-item record whose tax-code field contains a value of "T". (The field will contain a blank space for nontaxable items.)

d. The sales tax rate will be applied in accordance with the tax for the state to which the products are shipped. Thus, if a ship-to-address record is present in the set of invoice records, the ship-to-state code is to be used to look up the sales tax rate. If a ship-to-address record is not present, it means that the ship-to-address is the same as the bill-to-address of the invoice-header record and the state code of the invoice-header record should thus be used to look up the sales tax rate. Tax rates for each state code are shown in the accompanying table.

C. Print a set of invoice register lines for each invoice number in accordance with the format shown on the print chart.

   1. Skip to a new page for each invoice.

D. Write out an updated-invoice file with the following records:

   1. The invoice-header record (unchanged).

   2. The ship-to-address record (if present).

   3. All line-item records (with the extended-amount field computed).

   4. An invoice-trailer record (record length = 40) with the total accumulated sales tax for all applicable line items and the invoice total amount (accumulated extended amounts for each line item plus the sales tax amount).

State code	Percent tax rate	State code	Percent tax rate	State code	Percent tax rate	State code	Percent tax rate
AL	4.0	IN	4.0	NE	3.0	SD	4.0
AZ	4.0	IA	3.0	NV	5.75	TN	4.5
AR	3.0	KS	3.0	NJ	5.0	TX	4.0
CA	4.75	KY	5.0	NM	3.5	UT	4.0
CO	3.0	LA	3.0	NY	4.0	VT	3.0
CT	7.5	ME	5.0	NC	3.0	VA	3.0
DC	6.0	MD	5.0	ND	3.0	WA	4.5
FL	4.0	MA	5.0	OH	4.0	WV	5.0
GA	3.0	MI	4.0	OK	2.0	WI	4.0
HI	4.0	MN	4.0	PA	6.0	WY	3.0
ID	3.0	MS	5.0	RI	6.0		
IL	4.0	MO	3.125	SC	4.0		

8-3: Check Register

Program description

A check register is to be printed from variable-length check master file records.

Input files

Check master file — Key field = Account number

Check transaction file — Key fields = Account number (major)
Update code (minor)

Output files

Check master file (updated)

Check register

Record formats

Check master record (Record code "CR")

Check register line

Check master record

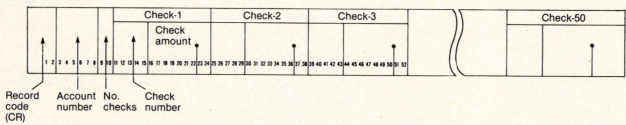

Record code (CR) Account number No. checks Check number

Check transaction record

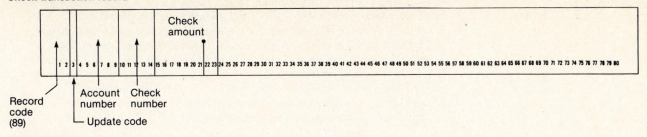

Record code (89)

Account number

Update code

Check number

Check amount

Check register

CHECK REGISTER (8-3)			MM/DD/YY PAGE ZZ9		
ACCOUNT NUMBER	CHECKS BEFORE	CHECK NUMBER	CHECK AMOUNT		CHECKS AFTER
999999	99	ZZZZ9	Z,ZZZ,ZZZ.99		
		ZZZZ9	Z,ZZZ,ZZZ.99		
		ZZZZ9	Z,ZZZ,ZZZ.99	D	
		ZZZZ9	Z,ZZZ,ZZZ.99		
		ZZZZ9	Z,ZZZ,ZZZ.99	A	
		ZZZZ9	Z,ZZZ,ZZZ.99	A	
		ZZZZ9	Z,ZZZ,ZZZ.99		
		ZZZZ9	Z,ZZZ,ZZZ.99	A	
			ZZ,ZZZ,ZZZ.99*		99
999999	99	ZZZZ9	Z,ZZZ,ZZZ.99		

Program operations

A. Read each input check transaction record.
   1. Each transaction record will contain one of the following update codes:
     A (Add)
     D (Delete)

B. Locate the check master record with a matching account number. A check master record can contain from 1 to 50 check segments, depending upon the value of the number-of-checks fields.
   1. If there is no matching check master record, create one from the transaction data.
   2. For an add transaction, add the check segment (in check number sequence) to the check master record. (To provide space for the segment, it will be necessary to shift to the right all segments with a higher check number.)
     a. Multiple check master records for a given account number may reside in the file. If the check master record already contains 50 check segments, create or use another check master record for the highest key value.
   3. For a delete transaction, remove the check master record from the check master record. (To reclaim the segment space, it will be necessary to shift to the left all segments with a higher check number.)
   4. Update the number of checks field in accordance with the master record processing.

C. Print each master record for which there are transactions, as shown on the print chart.
   1. Print one line for each check segment.
   2. On the first check segment line for each master record line, print the value of the number-of-checks field before the master is updated.

3. Group indicate the account number field.
4. Print the update code to the right of the updated check segment.
5. After the last check segment line for each master record, print the following:
    a. The total of the master check amounts (do not include deleted checks).
    b. The value of the number-of-checks field after the master record is updated.
6. Handle line spacing as follows:
    a. Single-space each check segment line for the same master record.
    b. Double-space between master records.
    c. Provide for a line-span of 57 lines per page.

CHAPTER 9

CHARACTER MANIPULATION STATEMENTS

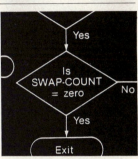

9

CHARACTER MANIPULATION STATEMENTS

The COBOL character-manipulation statements—INSPECT, STRING, and UNSTRING—operate on individual characters within a field. There are three major uses for the character-manipulation statements: data validation, character translation, and text editing.

Data validation means checking a field to ensure that it contains valid data. For example, numeric fields should not contain blank spaces. Similarly, certain characters may be restricted from a particular alphanumeric field. The INSPECT statement can be used to identify situations in which, for instance, blank spaces occur in a numeric field or unwanted commas exist in a name field.

Character translation refers to the conversion of individual characters within a field from one value to another value. Unkeyed characters of a numeric field are often translated from blank spaces to zeros. Code conversion is another example. For example, the code for a blank-space symbol is represented as a hexadecimal value of "40" on some computer systems and as "20" on others. The INSPECT statement can also be used to facilitate such character-translation requirements.

Text-editing applications handle the manipulation of words or strings of words within fields or strings of data. Extraction of a surname from a full-name field is one example. Another example is to take a name field in which the surname is positioned first, and to rearrange the names so that the first name can be printed in front of the surname. To satisfy minor editing needs, such as the inclusion of hyphens in a Social Security number, the INSPECT statement can be used. However, most text-editing requirements call for use of the STRING and UNSTRING statements.

Topic 9-A covers the INSPECT statement. The STRING and UNSTRING statements are covered in Topics 9-B and 9-C, respectively. All three of these statements were introduced in the 1974 COBOL Standard. Therefore, if you are using a 1968-standard compiler, these statements are not available. The EXAMINE statement, however, was a predecessor to and was superseded by the INSPECT statement. Hence it operates similarly and can be used for many of the same functions. Syntax for the EXAMINE statement is summarized in Appendix B.

■ TOPIC 9-A: **The INSPECT Statement**

INSPECT with the REPLACING Phrase
    REPLACING ALL Option
    REPLACING LEADING Option
    REPLACING FIRST Option
    REPLACING CHARACTERS BY Option
    INSPECT/REPLACING Syntactical Rules

INSPECT with the TALLYING Phrase
    TALLYING/ALL Option
    TALLYING/LEADING Option
    TALLYING/CHARACTERS Option
    INSPECT/TALLYING Syntactical Rules

INSPECT with Both the TALLYING and REPLACING Phrases

The INSPECT statement handles character replacement, character counting, and combined character-replacement and character-counting operations. Such functions are provided by specification of the REPLACING, TALLYING, and both the REPLACING and the TALLYING phrases, respectively.

INSPECT with the REPLACING Phrase

The INSPECT statement with the REPLACING phrase is typically used for character-translation and field-editing applications. Its format is shown in Figure 9A.1. To clarify and simplify the ensuing discussion of the INSPECT statement, identifiers and literals within the format have been assigned names that describe their function. The field that is being inspected (identifier-1) is called the **inspected field**. The value that is being looked for (identifier-5 or literal-3) is referred to as the **search field value**. The value that is to be replaced (identifier-6 or literal-4) is termed the **replacement field value**. The field that is used to terminate BEFORE INITIAL operations or to begin AFTER INITIAL operations (identifier-7 or literal-5) is called the **delimiter field value**. When BEFORE INITIAL or AFTER INITIAL is specified, the entire inspected field may or may not participate in the inspection. Hence the term **inspected area** is used to signify the entire inspected field when the INITIAL phrase is absent from the statement or the portion that is actually inspected when the INITIAL phrase is present.

REPLACING ALL Option

The INSPECT statement with the REPLACING ALL option causes all search field values in the inspected area to be converted to the replacement field value. Its typical use is for character-translation applications.

A common programming need is to insert hyphens into certain fields, such as dates, Social Security numbers, and 9-digit zip codes. The hyphen, however, is not a COBOL editing symbol.

As shown in example A (Figure 9A.1), the INSPECT statement with the REPLACING ALL option is one way to accomplish editing with characters that are not COBOL editing symbols. Suppose we have a Social Security number in 9-digit format (without hyphens) in an alphanumeric field called IN-SOCIAL-SECURITY-NUMBER. On a report, however, the Social Security number is to be displayed with the hyphens. To do this, we could define the report output field, OUT-SOCIAL-SECURITY-NUMBER, with a picture clause of PIC XXXBXXBXXXX. Then, to edit the field, the 9-character IN-SOCIAL-SECURITY-NUMBER field is moved to the 11-character OUT-SOCIAL-SECURITY-NUMBER field. During this MOVE operation, blank spaces are inserted at the hyphen locations. Then the statement INSPECT OUT-SOCIAL-SECURITY-NUMBER REPLACING ALL SPACES BY '-' will produce the desired editing by replacing each of the two blank spaces with a hyphen.

Although it is convenient to use the INSPECT statement for this type of editing requirement, the programmer should be aware that it is usually more efficient instead to use MOVE statements for such fixed-location insertion editing. That is, to optimize run timings, it would be preferable to define each of the three numeric segments of the IN-SOCIAL-SECURITY-NUMBER and OUT-SOCIAL-SECURITY-NUMBER fields separately. In the OUT-SOCIAL-SECURITY-

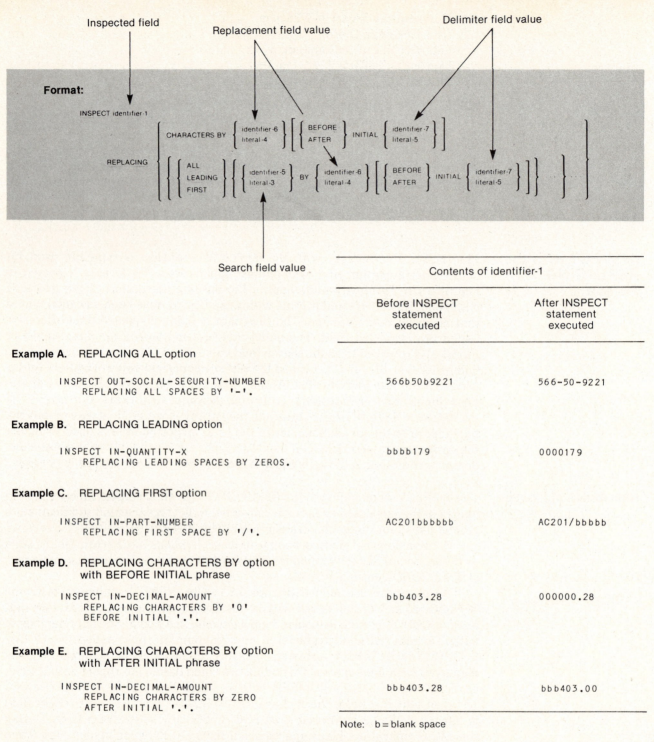

Format:

INSPECT identifier-1

```
           ┌ CHARACTERS BY { identifier-6 } [ { BEFORE } INITIAL { identifier-7 } ]                                              ┐
           │                { literal-4   }   { AFTER  }         { literal-5   }                                                 │
 REPLACING │     ┌ { ALL     }   { identifier-5 }      { identifier-6 } [ { BEFORE } INITIAL { identifier-7 } ] ┐                 │ ...
           │     │ { LEADING }   { literal-3    }  BY  { literal-4    }   { AFTER  }         { literal-5   }   │                 │
           └     │ { FIRST   }                                                                                │                 ┘
```

	Contents of identifier-1	
	Before INSPECT statement executed	After INSPECT statement executed

Example A. REPLACING ALL option

```
INSPECT OUT-SOCIAL-SECURITY-NUMBER
    REPLACING ALL SPACES BY '-'.
```
566b50b9221 → 566-50-9221

Example B. REPLACING LEADING option

```
INSPECT IN-QUANTITY-X
    REPLACING LEADING SPACES BY ZEROS.
```
bbbb179 → 0000179

Example C. REPLACING FIRST option

```
INSPECT IN-PART-NUMBER
    REPLACING FIRST SPACE BY '/'.
```
AC201bbbbbb → AC201/bbbbb

Example D. REPLACING CHARACTERS BY option with BEFORE INITIAL phrase

```
INSPECT IN-DECIMAL-AMOUNT
    REPLACING CHARACTERS BY '0'
    BEFORE INITIAL '.'.
```
bbb403.28 → 000000.28

Example E. REPLACING CHARACTERS BY option with AFTER INITIAL phrase

```
INSPECT IN-DECIMAL-AMOUNT
    REPLACING CHARACTERS BY ZERO
    AFTER INITIAL '.'.
```
bbb403.28 → bbb403.00

Note: b = blank space

Figure 9A.1. INSPECT statement examples with the REPLACING phrase.

NUMBER field, the two 1-character hyphen fields would also be specified at the proper locations. Then five MOVE statements (three for the numeric segments and two for the hyphens) could be coded to produce the properly rendered Social Security number.

Thus, as a general rule, use of the INSPECT statement for fixed-location replacement can minimize programmer-coding chores but it will probably reduce program efficiency. When used sparingly, timing differences will probably be trivial. If optimum performance is required, however, the alternate approach with MOVE statements should be used.

On the other hand, the INSPECT statement is invaluable and efficient for character translation when the replacement is to be made at variable locations rather than fixed ones in the inspected area.

REPLACING LEADING Option

With the REPLACING LEADING option of the INSPECT statement, only leftmost occurrences of the search field value are converted to the replacement field value. If the search field value is present in the high-order position of the inspected area, replacement is made and continues with following positions until any other value is encountered. If the search field value is not present in the high-order position of the inspected area, no replacement is made.

The REPLACING LEADING option is typically used to force unused positions of a numeric field to zero. When numeric fields are initially entered into a system, unused positions will sometimes contain blank spaces. To use the field for arithmetic operations or numeric editing, however, there should be no blank spaces within the field. As shown in example B (Figure 9A.1), an INSPECT statement with the REPLACING LEADING option can be used to ensure that valid numeric fields will contain no blank spaces.

Some programmers instead use the REPLACING ALL option to force zeros into a numeric field. However, the REPLACING LEADING option is preferable. Suppose the numeric data within a field is misaligned and contains a blank space, either embedded within the actual correct digits or to the right of the value. In this situation, REPLACING ALL SPACES BY ZEROS will cause the numeric value of the field to be erroneously represented. For example, if the value 1856 is misaligned one position to the left within a 5-digit field, the value will be converted to 18560. Because the results of the INSPECT statement execution mask the error, the field erroneously passes a numeric class test during a later data-validation routine.

However, if REPLACING LEADING were instead specified, the original miskeyed value would retain its rightmost blank space. During a subsequent data-validation routine, a numeric class test would still correctly detect the error.

REPLACING FIRST Option

With the REPLACING FIRST option of the INSPECT statement, the first occurrence of the search field value is converted to the replacement field value. When there are multiple occurrences of the search field value, only the leftmost occurrence is changed. If the search field value is not present in the inspected area, no replacement is made.

The REPLACING FIRST option has fewer uses than the two options previously discussed. One typical application, however, is to insert a delimiter into a field.

Suppose an 11-character field called IN-PART-NUMBER contains a left-justified part number, with no embedded blanks, that ranges from 1 to 10 characters in length. The programming specifications call for a slash delimiter character to be inserted immediately after the part number so that it can be formatted as a variable-length field. As shown in example C (Figure 9A.1), the REPLACING FIRST option can be used to convert the first, and only the first, blank space to a slash.

For the type of task just described, it should be recognized that the inspected field should be validated in a prior program step or run to ensure that correct processing will occur. With regard to the example, the IN-PART-NUMBER field should be validated to ensure that the part number is actually left-justified and that it contains no embedded blank spaces or slashes.

REPLACING CHARACTERS BY Option

The REPLACING CHARACTERS BY option of the INSPECT statement is another lesser-used feature. No search field value is specified with this option. All characters, regardless of value, are converted to the replacement field value. Hence, if the INITIAL phrase is omitted, an INSPECT statement with the REPLACING CHARACTERS BY option is equivalent to a MOVE statement with the ALL phrase.

When this option is used, the INITIAL phrase is usually specified. This provides the ability to isolate leftmost or rightmost segments of a field. If BEFORE INITIAL is specified, only that portion of the inspected field to the left of the first occurrence of the delimiter field value is operated upon. If AFTER INITIAL is specified, only that portion of the inspected field to the right of the first occurrence of the delimiter field value is operated upon.

Consider an amount field with an actual decimal point value keyed into the field. As shown in example D (Figure 9A.1), the REPLACING CHARACTERS BY option with the BEFORE INITIAL phrase can be used to isolate the decimal fraction portion of the value. When the BEFORE INITIAL phrase is specified, *all* characters, regardless of value, are converted to the replacement field value until the INITIAL search field value is encountered. If the INITIAL search field value is not present in the inspected field, all characters are replaced.

As shown in example E (Figure 9A.1), the integer portion of the field can be isolated by using the AFTER INITIAL phrase. When the AFTER INITIAL phrase is specified, no characters are replaced until after the INITIAL search field value is encountered. Once this value is found, all of the following characters are replaced. If such a value is not present, no replacement occurs.

Recognize that use of the BEFORE INITIAL and AFTER INITIAL phrases is not limited to the REPLACING CHARACTERS BY option. They can also be used with the other three REPLACING options that were previously discussed.

INSPECT/REPLACING Syntactical Rules

The following syntactical rules apply to the **inspected field** (identifier-1):

- It must be of DISPLAY usage.
- It can be either an elementary or a group item.

The following syntactical rules apply to the **search field** (identifier-5 or literal-3) and to the **replacement field** (identifier-6 or literal-4):

- Each must be an elementary field, a literal, or a figurative constant.
- There are no restrictions upon data class. However, if either one is not an alphanumeric (or alphabetic) item, the following treatment is accorded:
  - **Alphanumeric-edited, numeric-edited, or unsigned numeric item:** It is treated as if the field were redefined as alphanumeric, and the INSPECT statement applies to the alphanumeric item.
  - **Signed numeric item:** It is treated as though it were moved to an unsigned numeric item of the same length and then redefined as alphanumeric. The INSPECT statement applies to the alphanumeric item.
- The search field and the replacement field must be the same length.
- If the search field is a figurative constant, it is considered to be one character in length.
- If the replacement field is a figurative constant, it is considered to be the same length as the search field.
- If the search field value is more than one character in length, the entire search field value must be matched in the inspected area on a character-by-character basis. Otherwise, no replacement is made.

The following syntactical rules apply to the **delimiter field** (identifier-7 or literal-5):

- It must be an elementary field, a literal, or a figurative constant.
- There is no restriction upon data class. However, if it is not an alphanumeric (or alphabetic) item, the following treatment is accorded.
  - **Alphanumeric-edited, numeric-edited, or unsigned numeric item:** It is treated as if the field were redefined as alphanumeric, and the INSPECT statement applies to the alphanumeric item.
  - **Signed numeric item:** It is treated as though it were moved to an unsigned numeric item of the same length and then redefined as the alphanumeric. The INSPECT statement applies to the alphanumeric item.
- If the delimiter field is a figurative constant, it is considered to be one character in length.

When the programmer is using INSPECT/REPLACING methods, he or she must remember to maintain data-class compatibility among the inspected, search, and replacement fields. A common source of diagnostic errors is to define the inspected field with a numeric field and to then request that all SPACES be replaced by ZEROS. Such coding is not consistent because SPACES is an alphanumeric value and hence theoretically should not be present in a numeric field. The simplest way to handle the frequently encountered situation in which the blank spaces within a numeric field are to be forced to zeros is to redefine the inspected field with an alphanumeric PICTURE.

INSPECT with the TALLYING Phrase

The INSPECT statement with the REPLACING phrase is typically used for character-counting applications. Its format is shown in Figure 9A.2. In the discussion, the field that is being inspected (identifier-1) is called the **inspected field**. The field in which the character count is tallied (identifier-2) is referred to as the **tallying field**. The value being looked for (identifier-3 or literal-1) is called the **search field value**. The field used to terminate BEFORE INITIAL operations or to begin AFTER INITIAL operations (identifier-4 or literal-2) is called the **delimiter field value**. When BEFORE INITIAL or AFTER INITIAL is specified, the entire inspected field may or may not participate in the inspection. Hence the term **inspected area** is used to signify the entire inspected field when the INITIAL phrase is absent from the statement or that portion actually inspected when the INITIAL phrase is present.

The tallying field must be defined as an elementary numeric field. Specification of COMP usage will provide most efficient processing. Whenever the tallying field is used, it is the programmer's responsibility to initialize the tallying field before the INSPECT statement is executed. Hence, immediately before the INSPECT statement, the tallying field is typically initialized with a statement such as, for example, MOVE ZERO TO WS-TALLY.

TALLYING/ALL Option

The INSPECT statement with the TALLYING/ALL option counts occurrences of a character or a string of characters within the inspected area. When validating numeric input fields that are permitted to contain a decimal point, it is necessary to ensure that not more than one decimal point has been keyed. Example A of Figure 9A.2 provides an example of the INSPECT statement to handle this task.

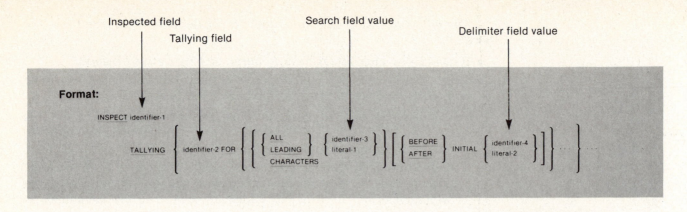

Format:

Inspected field → INSPECT identifier-1

Tallying field → TALLYING { identifier-2 FOR { { { ALL / LEADING / CHARACTERS } { identifier-3 / literal-1 } } [{ BEFORE / AFTER } INITIAL { identifier-4 / literal-2 }] } ... } ...

Search field value

Delimiter field value

	Contents of identifier-1	Contents of WS-TALLY after INSPECT statement executed (Initial value = 0)
Example A. TALLYING/ALL option		
INSPECT IN-NUMERIC-AMOUNT-X TALLYING WS-TALLY FOR ALL '.'.	5216.98	1
Example B. TALLYING/LEADING option		
INSPECT IN-QUANTITY TALLYING WS-TALLY FOR LEADING ZEROS.	0000008	6
Example C. TALLYING/CHARACTERS option with BEFORE INITIAL phrase		

INSPECT IN-SIGNED-AMOUNT-X
    TALLYING WS-TALLY
    FOR CHARACTERS BEFORE INITIAL '-'.
	-23712.38	0

Example D. TALLYING/CHARACTERS option with AFTER INITIAL phrase		

INSPECT IN-SIGNED-AMOUNT-X
    TALLYING WS-TALLY
    FOR CHARACTERS AFTER INITIAL '-'.
	23712.3-8	1

Note: b = blank space

Figure 9A.2. INSPECT statement examples with the TALLYING phrase.

TALLYING/LEADING Option

With the TALLYING/LEADING option of the INSPECT statement, only leftmost occurrences of the search field value are counted. If the search value is present in the high-order position of the inspected area, a tally is made and continues with following positions until any other value is encountered. If the search value is not present in the high-order position of the inspected area, no tally occurs.

Example B (Figure 9A.2) shows an example of how the TALLYING/LEADING option can be used to determine the end of the nonsignificant zeros and thus the beginning of the significant digits within the IN-QUANTITY field. The resulting count in the WS-TALLY field could then be used, for example, as a subscript or index (after incrementation by 1) to access the first significant digit within the field.

| TALLYING/ | The TALLYING/CHARACTERS option can be used to count occurrences before |
| CHARACTERS Option | or after a delimiter is encountered. Examples C and D (Figure 9A.2) show |

TALLYING/ CHARACTERS Option

The TALLYING/CHARACTERS option can be used to count occurrences before or after a delimiter is encountered. Examples C and D (Figure 9A.2) show methods that might be used to ensure that a minus sign, if entered in a numeric field, has been entered as either the leftmost or rightmost digit.

INSPECT/TALLYING Syntactical Rules

The following syntactical rules apply to the **inspected field** (identifier-1):

- It must be of DISPLAY usage.
- It can be either an elementary or a group item.

The following syntactical rules apply to the **tallying field** (identifier-2):

- It must be defined as an elementary integer field and must not contain any decimal scaling positions (PICTURE symbol P).
- It is the programmer's responsibility to initialize the field before the INSPECT statement is executed.

The following syntactical rules apply to the **search field** (identifier-3 or literal-1):

- It must be an elementary field, a literal, or a figurative constant.
- There are no restrictions upon data class. However, if it is not an alphanumeric (or alphabetic) item, the following treatment is accorded.

  - **Alphanumeric-edited, numeric-edited, or unsigned numeric item:** It is treated as if the field were redefined as alphanumeric, and the INSPECT statement applies to the alphanumeric item.
  - **Signed numeric item:** It is treated as though it were moved to an unsigned numeric item of the same length and then redefined as alphanumeric. The INSPECT statement applies to the alphanumeric item.

- If the search field is a figurative constant, it is considered to be one character in length.
- If the search field value is more than one character in length, the entire search field value must be matched in the inspected area on a character-by-character basis. Otherwise, no tally is made.

The following syntactical rules apply to the **delimiter field** (identifier-4 or literal-2):

- It must be an elementary field, a literal, or a figurative constant.
- There is no restriction upon data class. However, if it is not an alphanumeric (or alphabetic) item, the following treatment is accorded.

  - **Alphanumeric-edited, numeric-edited, or unsigned numeric item:** It is treated as if the field were redefined as alphanumeric, and the INSPECT statement applies to the alphanumeric item.
  - **Signed numeric item:** It is treated as though it were moved to an unsigned numeric item of the same length and then redefined as alphanumeric. The INSPECT statement applies to the alphanumeric item.

- If the delimiter field is a figurative constant, it is considered to be one character in length.

When using INSPECT/TALLYING, the programmer must remember to maintain data-class compatibility between the inspected field and the search field. A common source of diagnostic errors is to request a tally of alphanumeric characters within a numeric field. Such coding is not consistent because alphanumeric values theoretically should not be present in a numeric field. The simplest way to accomplish this requirement is to redefine the inspected field with an alphanumeric PICTURE.

Format:

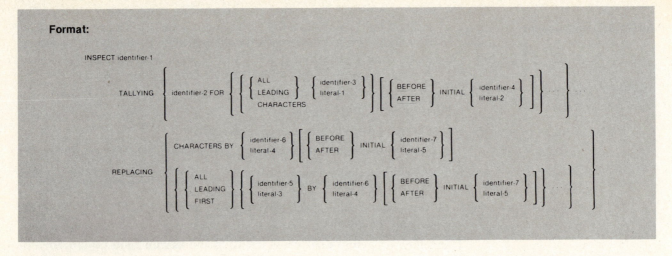

Example:

```
INSPECT IN-QUANTITY
    TALLYING WS-TALLY FOR LEADING SPACES
    REPLACING LEADING SPACES BY ZEROS.
```

Figure 9A.3. INSPECT statement example with the REPLACING and TALLYING phrases.

INSPECT with Both the TALLYING and REPLACING Phrases

As shown in Figure 9A.3, an INSPECT statement can be coded with both the TALLYING and REPLACING phrases. The statement is executed as if it were an INSPECT/TALLYING statement immediately followed by an INSPECT/REPLACING statement. Syntactical considerations for this hybrid form are the same as those presented above for the individual phrases.

■ TOPIC 9-B: **The STRING Statement**

Basic STRING Statement Example

STRING Statement Options
   The POINTER Option
   The ON OVERFLOW Option

STRING Statement Syntactical Rules

The STRING statement is used to join the partial or complete contents of two or more fields within another single field. Its format is shown in Figure 9B.1.

The fields being joined (identifier-1, identifier-2, identifier-4, and identifier-5, or their corresponding literals) are the **sending fields**. The area in which they are joined (identifier-7) is the **receiving field**.

Delimiters (identifier-3 and identifier-6, or their corresponding literals) are character-strings within the sending fields that terminate data transfer from its respective field to the receiving field. The delimiters themselves are not transferred. When the entire sending field is to be transferred, the reserved word SIZE is specified as the delimiter.

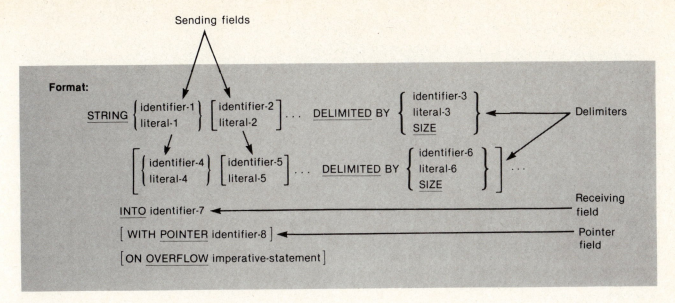

Format:

Sending fields

STRING $\left\{ \begin{matrix} \text{identifier-1} \\ \text{literal-1} \end{matrix} \right\}$ $\left[\begin{matrix} \text{identifier-2} \\ \text{literal-2} \end{matrix} \right]$ ... DELIMITED BY $\left\{ \begin{matrix} \text{identifier-3} \\ \text{literal-3} \\ \underline{\text{SIZE}} \end{matrix} \right\}$ ⟵ Delimiters

$\left[\left\{ \begin{matrix} \text{identifier-4} \\ \text{literal-4} \end{matrix} \right\} \left[\begin{matrix} \text{identifier-5} \\ \text{literal-5} \end{matrix} \right] ... \underline{\text{DELIMITED BY}} \left\{ \begin{matrix} \text{identifier-6} \\ \text{literal-6} \\ \underline{\text{SIZE}} \end{matrix} \right\} \right]$ ...

INTO identifier-7 ⟵ Receiving field

[WITH POINTER identifier-8] ⟵ Pointer field

[ON OVERFLOW imperative-statement]

Example:

```
STRING IN-CITY DELIMITED BY ','
       ' ' DELIMITED BY SIZE
       IN-STATE DELIMITED BY SIZE
       ' ' DELIMITED BY SIZE
       IN-ZIP DELIMITED BY SIZE
INTO OUT-DESTINATION.
```

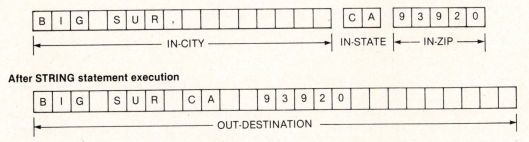

| B | I | G | | S | U | R | , | | | | | | | | C | A | | 9 | 3 | 9 | 2 | 0 |

←————————————— IN-CITY —————————————→ ← IN-STATE → ←— IN-ZIP —→

After STRING statement execution

| B | I | G | | S | U | R | | C | A | | | 9 | 3 | 9 | 2 | 0 | | | | | | | |

←————————————————— OUT-DESTINATION —————————————————→

Figure 9B.1. STRING statement example.

Basic STRING Statement Example

As an example of STRING statement use, consider a record with three separate fields for the mailing destination: IN-CITY, IN-STATE, and IN-ZIP. If each of these fields were simply moved to the output destination line of a mailing label, there would be a varying number of blank spaces between the city name and the state abbreviation; the shorter the city name, the more blank spaces. Let us say that we want to uniformly provide one blank space between the city name and the state abbreviation. In accordance with the U.S. Postal Service regulations, two blank spaces are to appear between the state abbreviation and the zip code. The STRING statement example shown in Figure 9B.2 will accomplish such formatting.

When the programmer is using the STRING statement, he or she should recognize that, unlike a MOVE statement, unfilled positions of the receiving field are *not* padded with blank spaces. Therefore, if unused receiving field position values are not to be carried forward from what they were before the STRING statement was executed, the receiving field should be initialized to SPACES prior to each STRING statement execution.

```
MOVE SPACES TO OUT-NAME-ADDRESS.
MOVE 1 TO WS-POINTER.
STRING   IN-NAME DELIMITED BY ' '
         '/' DELIMITED BY SIZE
         IN-ADDRESS DELIMITED BY ' '
         '/' DELIMITED BY SIZE
         IN-DESTINATION DELIMITED BY ' '
     INTO OUT-NAME-ADDRESS
         WITH POINTER WS-POINTER
         ON OVERFLOW PERFORM 999-IDENTIFY-STRING-OVERFLOW.
```

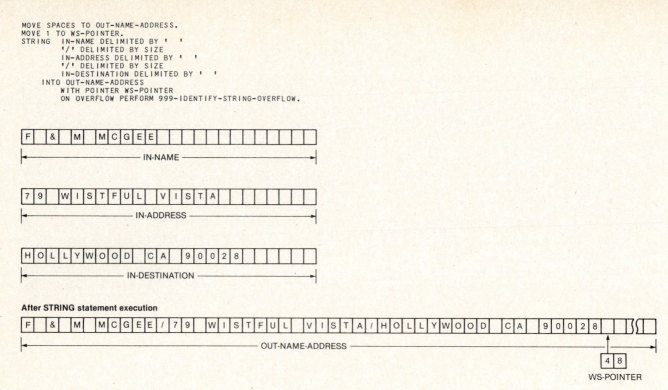

Figure 9B.2. STRING statement example using the WITH POINTER and ON OVERFLOW phrases.

STRING Statement Options

For certain STRING applications, use of the POINTER and/or OVERFLOW options is appropriate. Figure 9B.2 illustrates use of these options for an application that assembles a variable-length name-and-address record from a series of fixed-length fields.

The POINTER Option

The POINTER phrase permits specification of a data-item that allows the programmer to control positioning of data within the receiving field. The programmer can also use the POINTER field to determine how much of a receiving field the STRING operation has filled.

The POINTER field (identifier-8 in the STRING statement format) must be defined as an elementary integer data-item in the DATA DIVISION. It must be long enough to accommodate a value equal to the character length of the receiving field plus 1. Its USAGE can be either DISPLAY, COMP, or COMP-3 (if available). Specification of COMP usage will provide most efficient processing.

If POINTER is specified, it is the programmer's responsibility to initialize the field to a value not less than 1 and not greater than the character length of the receiving field. Such initialization should generally be specified to occur before each execution of the STRING statement.

When the STRING statement is executed, the character position of the receiving field that is indicated by the POINTER field value is the first position to which data is transferred. Beginning with that character, data is positioned character-by-character from left to right. After each character is positioned in the receiving field, the pointer is automatically incremented by a value of 1. Thus, after completion of STRING statement execution, the POINTER field contains a value equal to the character position of the last character that is placed in the receiving field plus 1.

A pointer specified by the POINTER phrase is considered to be an explicit pointer. If the POINTER phrase is not specified, the compiler establishes an implicit pointer. The compiler always sets the implicit pointer to an initial value of 1. Its contents are not available to the programmer.

The ON OVERFLOW Option

The ON OVERFLOW phrase can be specified to detect situations in which the receiving field is not large enough to accommodate all of the data that is sent to it. If either the explicit or implicit pointer field value exceeds the length of the receiving field and there is still data to be transferred from a sending field, data transfer is terminated and the ON OVERFLOW imperative statement is executed.

When the ON OVERFLOW phrase is not specified and an overflow condition occurs, STRING statement execution is terminated and control passes to the next program statement.

STRING Statement Syntactical Rules

The following syntactical rules apply to the **sending fields** (identifier-1, identifier-2, identifier-4, and identifier-5, or their corresponding literals):

- Each field must be of DISPLAY usage.
- Any number of sending fields may be specified.
- There are no restrictions on data class. However, if any field is specified as a numeric data-item, it must be an integer field and its PICTURE clause must not contain any decimal scaling positions (PICTURE symbol P).
- If a literal is specified, it must be a nonnumeric literal.
- If a figurative constant is specified, it is considered to be a one-character nonnumeric literal.

The following syntactical rules apply to the **receiving field** (identifier-7):

- The receiving field must be an elementary alphanumeric field.
- Its PICTURE clause must not contain any editing symbols.
- Its data-item description must not contain the JUSTIFIED clause.

The following syntactical rules apply to the **delimiter fields** (identifier-3, identifier-6, and their corresponding literals):

- Each field must be of DISPLAY usage.
- There are no restrictions on data class. However, if any field is specified as a numeric data-item, it must be an integer field and its PICTURE clause must not contain any decimal scaling positions.
- If a literal is specified, it must be a nonnumeric literal.
- If a figurative constant is specified, it is considered to be a one-character nonnumeric literal.

The following syntactical rules apply to the **pointer field** (identifier-8):

- It must be an elementary numeric integer data-item.
- Its PICTURE clause must not contain any decimal scaling positions.
- It must be large enough to accommodate a value equal to the character length of the receiving field plus 1.
- When the WITH POINTER option is specified, it is the programmer's responsibility to initialize the field before the STRING statement is executed.

The UNSTRING Statement

Basic UNSTRING Statement Example

ALL Option of the DELIMITED BY Phrase

UNSTRING Statement Options
  DELIMITER IN Option
  COUNT IN Option
  WITH POINTER Option
  TALLYING IN Option
  ON OVERFLOW Option

UNSTRING Statement Syntactical Rules

The UNSTRING statement permits the contents of a field to be separated and dispersed to one or more receiving fields. Its format is shown in Figure 9C.1.

The field to be separated, identifier-1 within the format, is called the **sending field**. It must be specified as an alphanumeric data-item.

The **receiving fields** are represented in the format as identifier-4 and identifier-7. Any number of receiving fields may be specified as part of the INTO phrase.

The **delimiters** within the sending field that identify the separation and thus control the data transfer are specified in the DELIMITED BY phrase. They can be expressed as either a data-name or a literal and are represented in the format as identifier-2 and identifier-3, or their corresponding literals (literal-1 and literal-2). The delimiters are not transferred to the receiving fields. One or more delimiters may be specified; the maximum number varies depending upon the particular compiler that is being used. When multiple delimiters are used, they must be joined by the reserved word OR.

Basic UNSTRING Statement Example

Extraction of the first, middle, and/or last name from a full-name field is an example of a situation in which the UNSTRING statement is commonly used. Suppose an employee's full name is stored, last name first, in an input field called IN-FULL-NAME. Programming specifications call for the name to be separated into three individual fields: OUT-LAST-NAME, OUT-FIRST-NAME, and OUT-MIDDLE-NAME. The example (Figure 9C.1) shows the UNSTRING coding that will fulfill this requirement.

When the programmer uses the UNSTRING statement, he or she should recognize that, unlike a MOVE statement, unfilled positions of the receiving fields are *not* padded with blank spaces. Therefore, if unused receiving field-position values are not to be carried forward from what they were before the UNSTRING statement was executed, the receiving fields should be initialized to SPACES prior to each UNSTRING statement execution.

ALL Option of the DELIMITED BY Phrase

When DELIMITED BY ALL is specified, multiple contiguous occurrences of the delimiter are treated as if they were only one delimiter occurrence. If, instead, just DELIMITED BY is specified, each contiguous delimiter is processed as a separate entity.

Format:

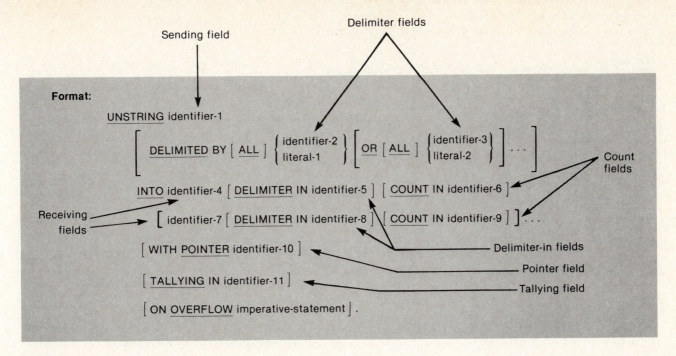

Example:

```
UNSTRING IN-FULL-NAME DELIMITED BY ', '
                        OR ALL ' '
     INTO OUT-LAST-NAME
          OUT-FIRST-NAME
          OUT-MIDDLE-NAME.
```

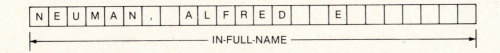

After UNSTRING statement execution

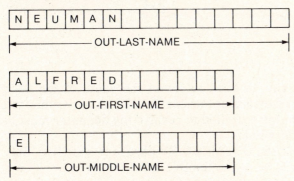

Figure 9C.1. UNSTRING statement example.

UNSTRING Statement Options

There are five additional options that can be included within an UNSTRING statement: DELIMITER IN, COUNT IN, WITH POINTER, TALLYING IN, and ON OVERFLOW. Figure 9C.2 shows an example with these options specified.

```
MOVE SPACES TO OUT-NAME
              OUT-ADS-1
              OUT-ADS-2
              OUT-ADS-3.
MOVE 3 TO WS-POINTER.
MOVE ZERO TO WS-TALLY.
UNSTRING IN-NAME-AND-ADDRESS
    DELIMITED BY ALL '/'
            OR '#'
    INTO OUT-NAME
         DELIMITER IN WS-NAME-DELIM
         COUNT IN WS-NAME-COUNT
         OUT-ADS-1
         DELIMITER IN WS-ADS-1-DELIM
         COUNT IN WS-ADS-1-COUNT
         OUT-ADS-2
         DELIMITER IN WS-ADS-2-DELIM
         COUNT IN WS-ADS-2-COUNT
         OUT-ADS-3
         DELIMITER IN WS-ADS-3-DELIM
         COUNT IN WS-ADS-3-COUNT
    WITH POINTER WS-POINTER
    TALLYING IN WS-TALLY
    ON OVERFLOW PERFORM 999-IDENTIFY-UNSTRING-OVERFLOW.
```

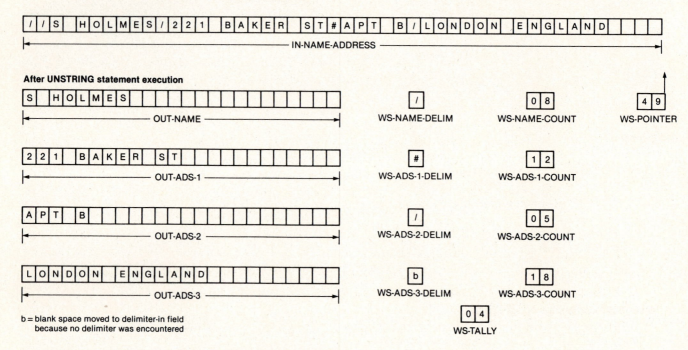

Figure 9C.2. UNSTRING statement with optional phrases.

DELIMITER IN Option

The DELIMITER IN option can be used to retain the value of the delimiter detected in the sending field that causes termination of data positioning into the receiving field. The field that is specified to receive the delimiter must be defined as an alphanumeric data-item.

When the ALL option of the DELIMITED BY phrase is specified, only one occurrence of the delimiter is moved to the DELIMITER IN field.

The DELIMITER IN field is filled according to the rules for an alphanumeric to alphanumeric move. That is, the delimiter is left-justified in the receiving DELIMITER IN field; if the receiving field is longer than the delimiter that is sent, padding with SPACES occurs. When the delimiting condition is not a delimiter but rather the end of the sending field, the DELIMITER IN field is filled with SPACES.

If the DELIMITED BY phrase is not specified, the DELIMITER IN option cannot be used.

COUNT IN Option

The COUNT IN option can be specified to record the number of characters that are transferred to a receiving field. The character count does not include delimiter characters. The field that is specified to receive the count must be defined as a numeric data-item. The data-item must be of a length that will accommodate a value equal to the number of character positions in the receiving field with which it is associated.

If the DELIMITED BY phrase is not specified, the COUNT IN option cannot be used.

WITH POINTER Option

The WITH POINTER phrase permits specification of a data-item that allows the programmer to control initial positioning within the sending field. The programmer can also use it to determine the amount of a sending field that the UNSTRING operation has processed.

The POINTER field must be defined as an elementary integer data-item in the DATA DIVISION. The data-item must be long enough to accommodate a value equal to the character length of the sending field plus 1. Its USAGE can be either DISPLAY, COMP, or COMP-3 (if available). Specification of COMP usage will provide most efficient processing.

If the POINTER phrase is specified, it is the programmer's responsibility to initialize the field to a value not less than 1 and not greater than the character length of the sending field.

When the UNSTRING statement is executed, the relative character position of the sending field that is indicated by the POINTER field value is the first position examined. After each sending field character is processed, the POINTER is automatically incremented by a value of 1. Thus, after completion of STRING statement execution, the POINTER field contains a value equal to the character position of the last character examined in the sending field plus 1.

A pointer that is specified by the POINTER phrase is considered to be an explicit pointer. If the POINTER phrase is not specified, the compiler establishes an implicit pointer. The compiler always sets the implicit pointer to an initial value of 1. The contents of an implicit pointer are not available to the programmer.

TALLYING IN Option

The TALLYING IN phrase allows specification of a data-item to count the number of receiving fields that the UNSTRING statement acts upon. The count includes null fields (that is, those fields that were skipped because the delimiter was encountered before any characters were transferred).

The TALLYING field must be defined as an elementary integer data-item in the DATA DIVISION. It must not contain any decimal scaling positions. It must be long enough to accommodate a value equal to the number of receiving fields plus the initial value. Its USAGE can be either DISPLAY, COMP, or COMP-3 (if available). Specification of COMP usage will provide most efficient processing.

If the TALLYING phrase is specified, it is the programmer's responsibility to initialize the field prior to execution of the UNSTRING statement. Usually, the field should be initialized to zero before each execution of the UNSTRING statement.

ON OVERFLOW Option

The ON OVERFLOW phrase can be specified to detect and act upon situations in which all receiving fields have been processed but there are still unexamined characters in the sending field. An ON OVERFLOW condition also exists when the UNSTRING statement execution is initiated and the value of an explicit pointer field is less than 1 or greater than the length of the sending field.

When the ON OVERFLOW phrase is not specified and an overflow condition occurs, the UNSTRING statement execution is terminated, and program control passes to the next statement to be executed.

UNSTRING Statement Syntactical Rules

The following syntactical rule applies to the **sending field** (identifier-1):

- It must be an alphanumeric data-item.

The following syntactical rules apply to the **delimiter fields** (identifier-2 and identifier-3, or their corresponding literals—literal-1 and literal-2):

- Each delimiter must be an alphanumeric data-item.
- If a literal is specified, it must be a non-numeric literal.
- If a figurative constant is specified, it is considered to be a one-character nonnumeric literal.

The following syntactical rules apply to the **receiving fields** (identifier-4 and identifier-7):

- They must be of DISPLAY usage.
- There are no restrictions on data class. However, if any field is specified as a numeric data-item, it must be an integer field, and its PICTURE clause must not contain any decimal scaling positions (PICTURE symbol P).

The following syntactical rules apply to the DELIMITER IN field (identifier-5, identifier-8, and so forth):

- It must be an alphanumeric field.
- It cannot be specified unless the DELIMITED BY option is specified.

The following syntactical rules apply to the COUNT IN field (identifier-6, identifier-9, and so forth):

- It must be a numeric integer field, and its PICTURE clause must not contain any decimal scaling positions.
- It cannot be specified unless the DELIMITED BY option is specified.

The following syntactical rules apply to the POINTER field (identifier-10):

- It must be a numeric integer field, and its PICTURE clause must not contain any decimal scaling positions.
- It must be large enough to accommodate a value equal to the character length of the sending field plus 1.
- When the WITH POINTER option is specified, it is the programmer's responsibility to initialize the field before the UNSTRING statement is executed.

The following syntactical rules apply to the TALLYING IN field (identifier-9):

- It must be a numeric integer field, and its PICTURE clause must not contain any decimal scaling positions.
- It must be large enough to accommodate a value equal to the number of receiving fields plus its initial value.
- When the TALLYING IN option is specified, it is the programmer's responsibility to initialize the field before the UNSTRING statement is executed.

Summary

Topic 9-A The INSPECT Statement

The INSPECT statement with the REPLACING phrase is typically used for character-translation and field-editing applications. The REPLACING ALL option causes all search field values in the inspected area to be converted to the replacement field value. With the REPLACING LEADING option, only leftmost occurrences of the search field value are converted to the replacement field value. The REPLACING FIRST option causes the first occurrence of the search field value to be converted to the replacement field value. With the REPLACING CHARACTERS BY option, no search field is specified. This option is typically specified together with either a BEFORE INITIAL or AFTER INITIAL phrase so that all characters before or after a certain delimiter are replaced.

The INSPECT statement with the TALLYING phrase is typically used for character-counting applications. The TALLYING ALL option counts occurrences of a character or a string of characters within the inspected area. With the TALLYING LEADING option, only leftmost occurrences of the search field value are counted. The TALLYING CHARACTERS option is used to count occurrences before or after a delimiter is encountered.

An INSPECT statement can be coded with both the TALLYING and REPLACING phrases.

Topic 9-B The STRING Statement

The STRING statement is used to join the partial or complete contents of two or more fields within another single field. The POINTER option can be used to control the positioning of data within the receiving field. The ON OVERFLOW phrase is specified to detect situations in which the receiving field is not large enough to accommodate all of the data that is sent to it.

Topic 9-C The UNSTRING Statement

The UNSTRING statement permits the contents of a field to be separated and dispersed to one or more receiving fields. When the ALL option of the DELIMITED BY phrase is specified, multiple contiguous occurrences of the delimiter are treated as if they all were only one delimiter occurrence. The DELIMITER IN option can be used to retain the value of the delimiter that is detected in the sending field. When the COUNT IN option is used, the characters that are transferred to the receiving field are counted. The WITH POINTER phrase provides control of initial positioning within the sending field. By specifying the TALLYING IN option, the number of receiving fields that are acted upon are counted. The ON OVERFLOW option can be specified to detect situations in which all data-receiving fields have been processed but there are still unexamined characters in the sending field.

Programming Assignments

9-1: Address Register

Program description

Fixed-length address records that contain address fields of varying lengths are to be formatted on an address register list.

Input file

Address file

Output file

Address register

Record formats

Address record (Record code "95")

Address register line

Name/address record

Record
code
(95)

Address register

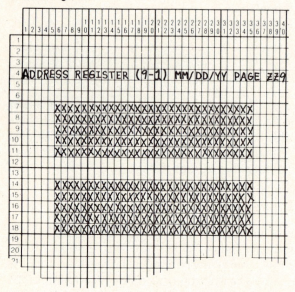

ADDRESS REGISTER (9-1) MM/DD/YY PAGE ZZ9

Program operations

A. Read each input address record.

   1. Each address record contains at least three address fields: recipient name, address, and destination.

      a. The recipient-name field is always first.

      b. The address field is preceded by a double slash (//).

      c. The destination field is always last and is also preceded by a double slash.

   2. The address record may optionally contain a company-name field, a building-name field, and/or a room-number field.

      a. The company-name and building-name fields are preceded by a slash and an asterisk (/*).

      b. The room number field is preceded by a slash and a comma (/,).

B. For each input address record, print up to five address register lines in accordance with the formats presented in Chapter C: Figure C.27. Also provide for the following specifications.

   1. If there are fewer than five lines to be printed for a record, bottom-justify the lines. That is, for a three-line address, leave two blank lines before the first line is printed.

   2. If any field extends beyond the 30 characters that are provided for each line, truncate the field and identify the situation by printing 5 asterisks to the left (print positions 1 to 5) of the line.

   3. If there are more than six fields for an input record, attempt to join them on one line so that they will not extend beyond the 30-character maximum.

   4. Triple-space between each five-line block.

   5. Print the heading plus eight address blocks on each page.

9-2: Numeric-Amount Validation and Formatting

Program description

Transaction records that contain an amount field with a variable-entry format are to be validated and the amount field is to be formatted into a fixed-length numeric field. Each transaction is to be printed on a numeric-amount formatting list.

Input file

Amount transaction file

Output file

Numeric-amount formatting list

Record formats

Amount transaction record (Record code "96")

Numeric-amount line

Amount transaction record

Numeric amount formatting list

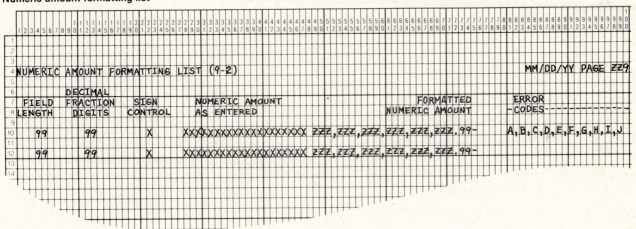

Program operations

A. Read each input amount transaction record.

   1. Validate the following fields in accordance with the guidelines presented in Chapter C within the subject "*Data-Validation Routine Logic: Numeric Amounts.*"

      a. Field length (*Note:* This field contains the number of digits that are permitted in the numeric field, *not* the number of characters that are entered in the numeric-amount field.)

      b. Number of decimal fraction digits.

   2. Validate the sign control field to ensure that it contains a plus sign (+), a minus sign (–), or a blank space.

   3. The amount value will usually, but not necessarily, be left-justified within the numeric-amount field. If a decimal point is not entered in the field, all digits are integers. Validate the amount field in accordance with the guidelines that are presented in Chapter C. Also incorporate the following specifications:

a. If the sign control field contains a plus sign, either a plus sign or a minus sign is valid within the amount field.

b. If the sign control field contains a minus sign, a minus sign is valid within the amount field but a plus sign is invalid.

c. If the sign control field contains a blank space, both a plus and a minus sign are invalid within the amount field.

d. No commas are permitted in the input amount field.

B. Print each input amount transaction record.

1. If the input numeric-amount field is valid, format the numeric amount so that it is aligned by decimal points and the proper arithmetic sign is set. Print a report line as shown on the print chart.

2. If any of the input fields are invalid, print the input record contents, together with the error codes (left-justified and separated by commas), in the error code field of the report line. Error codes are as follows:

A = Value of field-length field less than 1 or greater than 18

B = Value of decimal-fraction-digits field greater than field-length field value

C = Invalid character entered in sign control field

D = Invalid characters entered in numeric-amount field

E = More than one decimal point entered in numeric-amount field

F = More than one arithmetic sign entered in numeric-amount field

G = Arithmetic sign not leftmost or rightmost entry in numeric-amount field

H = Excessive number of integer digits entered in numeric-amount field

I = Excessive number of decimal fraction digits entered in numeric amount field

J = Embedded-blank space entered in numeric amount field

3. Double-space each detail line.

4. Provide for a line span of 56 lines per page.

9-3: Check Protection with Words

Program description

Check-transaction records that contain numeric dollars-and-cents check amounts are to be read. The check amount is to be expressed in words on a check register.

Input file

Check-transaction file

Output file

Check register

Record formats

Check-transaction record (Record code "97")

Check-register line

Check record

Record code (97)

Check number

Check register

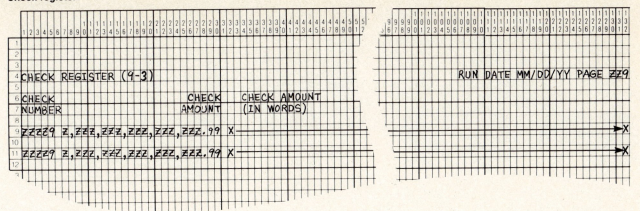

```
          1 1 1 1 1 1 1 1 1 1 2 2 2 2 2 2 2 2 2 2 3 3 3 3 3 3 3 3 3 3 4 4 4 4 4 4 4 4 4 4 5 5 5          9 9 9 9 0 0 0 0 0 0 0 0 0 0 1 1 1 1 1 1 1 1 1 1 2 2 2 2 2 2 2 2 2 2 3 3 3
1 2 3 4 5 6 7 8 9 0 1 2 3 4 5 6 7 8 9 0 1 2 3 4 5 6 7 8 9 0 1 2 3 4 5 6 7 8 9 0 1 2 3 4 5 6 7 8 9 0 1 2          6 7 8 9 0 1 2 3 4 5 6 7 8 9 0 1 2 3 4 5 6 7 8 9 0 1 2 3 4 5 6 7 8 9 0 1 2
 1
 2
 3
 4  CHECK REGISTER (9-3)                                                                                                   RUN DATE MM/DD/YY PAGE ZZ9
 5
 6  CHECK                              CHECK      CHECK AMOUNT
 7  NUMBER                             AMOUNT     (IN WORDS)
 8
 9  ZZZZ9  Z,ZZZ,ZZZ,ZZZ,ZZZ,ZZZ.99  X─────────────────────────────────────────────────►X
10
11  ZZZZ9  Z,ZZZ,ZZZ,ZZZ,ZZZ,ZZZ.99  X─────────────────────────────────────────────────►X
12
 3
```

Program operations

    A. Read each input check-transaction record.

    B. Convert the numeric-check amount so that it is expressed in words in accordance with the logic that is presented in Chapter C within the subject "*Arithmetic Routine Logic: Check Protection with Words.*"

    C. Print a check-register line for each check-transaction record.

        1. If, for a particular check amount, the words will not fit within the allocated field length (101 positions), fill the area with asterisks.

        2. Double-space each detail line.

        3. Provide for a line span of 57 lines per page.

CHAPTER 10

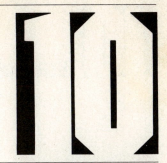

USING AND CODING SUBPROGRAMS

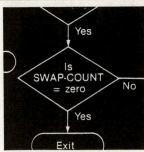

479

10 USING AND CODING SUBPROGRAMS

Within a data-processing installation or application system, there are usually certain programming routines that a number of programs require. Many of the routines that are discussed in Chapter C—date conversion, testing for embedded blank spaces, check-digit computation, and the like—are examples. There are three general ways that common routines can be incorporated into programs.

One way is by what can be termed the **"reinvent the wheel"** approach. That is, have each programmer code the routine from scratch every time that it is needed. Then the routine must be tested each time that it is coded to ensure that it has been specified correctly. This method wastes programmer time and can be a source of program bugs.

Storage of source program code in a **COPY library** is another way to handle common routines. Then when the routine is needed within a program, the programmer uses the COPY statement to include it in the source program. This approach has the obvious advantage of eliminating the recoding and rekeying of common routines. It also reduces the amount of retesting that is required.

However, the COPY library method has drawbacks in the area of program maintenance. Whenever a change must be made to the common routine, each source program that uses the routine must be identified and recompiled so that the modification will be reflected in the object program.

A third approach is through the use of **subprograms**, which is the subject of this chapter. With this method, the common routine is coded as a separate program, which is called a **subprogram**. The subprogram is independently compiled and becomes a separate object module. When a programmer requires the common routine, he or she codes a CALL statement in the source COBOL program that specifies the subprogram name together with data-names of fields for data that will be passed to the subprogram. At link-edit or program execution time, the subprogram is combined with the programmer's main program.

The subprogram method is the best way to handle common routines. Use of subprograms eliminates needless recoding and testing of common program logic. It also eliminates the need to recompile the main program when the logic of the subprogram is changed. Subprogram usage, in addition to providing benefits when it is used for the logic of common routines, can also offer division of labor, flexibility of programming language, and advantages in program structure.

When program logic is organized into subprograms, more programmers can usually work on the same project at the same time. Such assignment of multiple programmers can be of benefit in two situations. First, when the schedule is tight in relation to the calendar days that are available, having a number of programmers who contribute to the task may help to ensure on-time program completion. Second, when the project team possesses a range of programming skill levels, assignments can be made in accordance with proficiency. The complex tasks can be assigned to the more competent programmers and simpler coding to less experienced personnel.

Most operating systems permit subprograms to be coded in a language other than COBOL. Some routines—such as character translation, character validation, and text editing—can be coded easier and executed more efficiently in assembler language than COBOL. Therefore, if desired, the main program could be written in COBOL and a character translation routine could be coded as an assembler language subprogram. However, multiple-language usage should generally be avoided unless particular execution speed or storage-reduction results are required. Within most data-processing installations, as the execution speed and storage size of computers improve, the number of programmers who are proficient in languages other than COBOL decreases. Thus maintenance difficulties that are imposed by multiple language use tend to quickly outweigh any processing efficiencies that are provided.

Organization of application code into subprograms fits well within the precepts and conventions of structured programming. Subprogram usage can improve program cohesion and significantly reduce coupling.

General subprogram terminology and calling program syntax will be presented in Topic 10-A of this chapter. Topic 10-B will cover the called subprograms. Subprogram linkage is discussed in Topic 10-C.

■ TOPIC 10-A: **Calling Programs**

General Subprogram Terminology

Calling Programs
   The CALL Statement

On a structure chart, a subprogram—like other program modules—is usually expressed as a rectangle. To indicate that it is a subprogram rather than an internal program module, however, a common convention is to draw a line across the bottom or top of the rectangle. The subprogram name is placed within the resulting **stripe** that is formed.

General Subprogram Terminology

Suppose that we have a payroll calculation program, named PAYCALC, whose function is to process input time-card records to produce calculated output records that will later be input into programs to prepare payroll checks, check registers, and so forth. Let us say that the program uses one subprogram named DATEVAL to validate the date-worked and another subprogram named GROSS-PAY to calculate the dollars of gross pay. Figure 10A.1 presents a structure chart skeleton for the PAYCALC program that depicts the subprogram modules.

A program that uses one or more subprograms, as PAYCALC does, is termed a **calling program**. A subprogram, as DATEVAL and GROSSPAY are, is referred to as a **called program**. Observe in the PAYCALC structure chart that the GROSSPAY subprogram also uses a subprogram called MFGCAL, which stands for **m**anufacturing day **cal**endar lookup. The function of MFGCAL is to identify company holidays that must, when worked, be paid at double-time.

Figure 10A.2 shows that, with this subprogram structure, GROSSPAY is both a called program (by PAYCALC) and a calling program (of MFGCAL). Because PAYCALC is a calling program but not a called program, it is termed

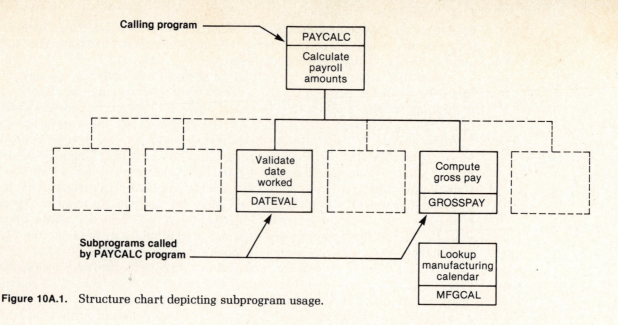

Figure 10A.1. Structure chart depicting subprogram usage.

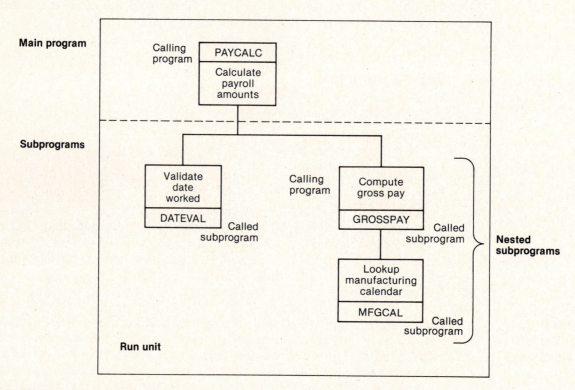

Figure 10A.2. Subprogram relationships.

the **main program**. When a subprogram calls one or more additional subprograms, as GROSSPAY does, the resulting structure is sometimes referred to as **nested subprograms**. The set of programs that function together as a unit at execution time to provide the programming solution—PAYCALC, DATEVAL, GROSS-PAY, and MFGCAL in the example—es called a **run unit**.

A summary of COBOL syntax for calling programs and called subprograms is presented in Figure 10A.3.

Calling program syntax

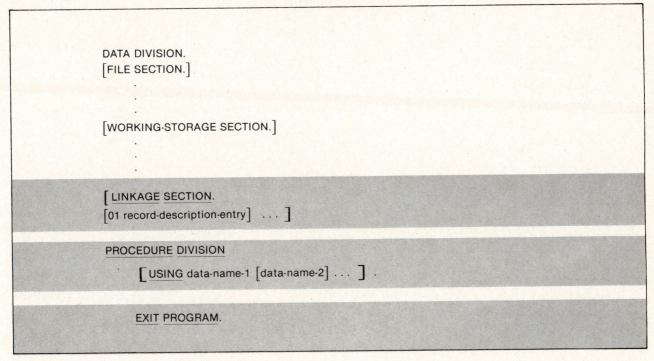

PROCEDURE DIVISION.

CALL $\left\{ \begin{array}{l} \text{identifier-1} \\ \text{literal-1} \end{array} \right\}$ [<u>USING</u> data-name-1 [data-name-2] ...]

[ON <u>OVERFLOW</u> imperative-statement].

CANCEL $\left\{ \begin{array}{l} \text{identifier-1} \\ \text{literal-1} \end{array} \right\}$ $\left\{ \begin{array}{l} \text{identifier-2} \\ \text{literal-2} \end{array} \right\}$ ... .

Called subprogram syntax

DATA DIVISION.
[FILE SECTION.]
.
.
.
[WORKING-STORAGE SECTION.]
.
.
.
[<u>LINKAGE</u> SECTION.
[01 record-description-entry] ...]

PROCEDURE DIVISION
[<u>USING</u> data-name-1 [data-name-2] ...] .

<u>EXIT</u> PROGRAM.

Figure 10A.3. Subprogram syntax summary.

Calling Programs

One of the tasks encompassed within the PAYCALC program is to validate an input date field. To do the date validation, the PAYCALC program calls the DATEVAL subprogram.

The CALL Statement

Calling programs contain one or more CALL statements in the PROCEDURE DIVISION. The CALL statement format is shown in Figure 10A.4. Observe that, according to the format, the program-name of the called subprogram is

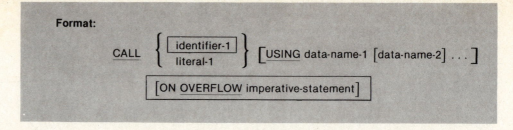

Format:

$$\text{CALL} \left\{ \begin{array}{l} \text{identifier-1} \\ \text{literal-1} \end{array} \right\} \left[\underline{\text{USING}} \text{ data-name-1} \left[\text{data-name-2} \right] \ldots \right]$$

$$\left[\text{ON } \underline{\text{OVERFLOW}} \text{ imperative-statement} \right]$$

Example:

```
CALL 'DATEVAL' USING WS-DATE-FIELDS.
```

Figure 10A.4. CALL statement example.

Example A. Valid USING phrase relationship:

```
01  WS-DATE-FIELDS.
    05  WS-DATE.
        10  WS-MONTH                PIC X(2).
        10  WS-DAY                  PIC X(2).
        10  WS-YEAR                 PIC X(2).
        .
        .
        .
    CALL 'DATEVAL' USING WS-DATE-FIELDS.
```

Example B. Invalid USING phrase relationship (data-names must be 01-level):

```
01  WS-DATE-FIELDS.
    05  WS-DATE.
        10  WS-MONTH                PIC X(2).
        10  WS-DAY                  PIC X(2).
        10  WS-YEAR                 PIC X(2).
        .
        .
        .
    CALL 'DATEVAL' USING WS-MONTH
                         WS-DAY
                         WS-YEAR.
```

Example C. Valid USING phrase relationship:

```
01  WS-YEAR                         PIC X(2).
01  WS-MONTH                        PIC X(2).
01  WS-DAY                          PIC X(2).
        .
        .
        .
    CALL 'DATEVAL' USING WS-MONTH
                         WS-DAY
                         WS-YEAR.
```

Figure 10A.5. Valid and invalid CALL statement USING phrase relationships.

specified either by an identifier or as a literal. However, not all COBOL compilers permit specification of the subprogram name with the identifier option. Its use indicates that the subprogram is dynamically—rather than statically—linked to the calling program. The ON OVERFLOW phrase applies only to dynamically linked subprograms. Hence these two features—the identifier option and the ON OVERFLOW option—are boxed in the format. They will be discussed in Topic-10C, which covers subprogram linkage.

```
      IDENTIFICATION DIVISION.
      PROGRAM-ID.     PAYCALC.
      *
      *                THIS MAIN PROGRAM CALLS
      *                THE DATEVAL SUBPROGRAM
      *
                      .
                      .
                      .

      ENVIRONMENT DIVISION.
                      .
                      .
                      .

      DATA DIVISION.
                      .
                      .
                      .

      WORKING-STORAGE SECTION.
                      .
                      .
                      .

      01   WS-DATE-FIELDS.
           05   WS-DATE.
                10   WS-MONTH              PIC X(2).
                10   WS-DAY                PIC X(2).
                10   WS-YEAR               PIC X(2).
           05   WS-VALID-DATE-SW           PIC X(3).
                88   VALID-DATE                       VALUE 'YES'.
                88   INVALID-DATE                     VALUE 'NO '.
                      .
                      .
                      .

      PROCEDURE DIVISION.
                      .
                      .
                      .

      200-PROCESS-TIMECARD-RECORD.
                      .
                      .
                      .

           CALL 'DATEVAL' USING WS-DATE-FIELDS.
           IF VALID-DATE
                PERFORM 999-COMPUTE-TIMECARD-AMOUNTS
           ELSE
                PERFORM 999-IDENTIFY-DATE-ERROR.
                      .
                      .
                      .
```

Figure 10A.6. Calling program skeleton: PAYCALC program.

When a literal is used to specify the program-name, it must be a non-numeric literal. After the name of the subprogram is specified, the reserved word USING is written, followed by the names of any of the fields of the calling program that are to be made available to the called subprogram. The data-names that are listed must be 01-level items. They may be either group or elementary items. Figure 10A.5 provides examples of valid and invalid relationships between data-item descriptions and their specifications in the USING phrase of the CALL statement.

As an example of the coding that is required for a calling program, the applicable code for the PAYCALC program is shown in Figure 10A.6.

The LINKAGE SECTION

The USING Phrase of the PROCEDURE DIVISION Header

The EXIT PROGRAM Statement

Subprogram Example

Subprograms differ from other COBOL programs in a number of ways. Subprograms often do not contain an INPUT-OUTPUT SECTION within the ENVIRONMENT DIVISION or a FILE SECTION within the DATA DIVISION. The reason for this is because input-output processing is usually done in the main program. However, sometimes certain I-O operations are coded as individual subprograms or a subprogram will handle exception reporting. Whenever I-O processing is done in the subprogram, INPUT-OUTPUT SECTION and FILE SECTION specifications are required.

Most subprograms contain a DATA DIVISION section that is not applicable to most other programs: the LINKAGE SECTION. It is specified in the subprogram to define fields that are passed from the calling program to the called subprogram and vice versa.

In the PROCEDURE DIVISION of the called subprogram, fields from the calling program that are to be made available to the subprogram are specified with a USING phrase within the PROCEDURE DIVISION header. The data-names that are coded as the object of the USING phrase are typically identical to those that are coded in the USING phrase of the CALL statement within the calling program.

In a regular or main COBOL program, the STOP RUN statement is, of course, used to specify the end of program execution. To specify termination of subprogram execution, the EXIT PROGRAM statement is used. When this statement is encountered in a called subprogram, control is returned to the calling program.

The detailed syntax of these three subprogram entries—the LINKAGE SECTION, the USING phrase of the PROCEDURE DIVISION header, and the EXIT PROGRAM statement—will be covered in this topic.

The LINKAGE SECTION

The LINKAGE SECTION is used to describe data in the called subprogram that is referred to by both itself and the calling program. Its format is shown in Figure 10B.1. LINKAGE SECTION structure is identical to that of the WORKING-STORAGE SECTION. Except in the case of index-names, no actual storage space is allocated to LINKAGE SECTION fields in the subprogram. Instead, the location of the corresponding field in the calling program is referred to. Because of this, VALUE clauses cannot be specified to initialize LINKAGE SECTION data-items. However, it is permissible to specify 88-level condition-name VALUE clauses within the LINKAGE SECTION.

Within the DATA DIVISION of a subprogram, the sections should be specified in the following order: FILE SECTION first (if present), WORKING-STORAGE SECTION next (if present), and LINKAGE SECTION last (if present).

Format:

```
[ LINKAGE SECTION.

  [01  record-description-entry] ... ]
```

Example:

```
*
*
  LINKAGE SECTION.
*
*
  01  LS-DATE-FIELDS.
      05  LS-DATE.
          10  LS-MONTH             PIC X(2).
          10  LS-DAY               PIC X(2).
          10  LS-YEAR              PIC X(2).
      05  LS-VALID-DATE-SW         PIC X(3).
```

Figure 10B.1. LINKAGE SECTION example.

Format:

```
PROCEDURE DIVISION

    [ USING data-name-1 [data-name-2] ... ] .
```

Example:

```
*
*
*
  PROCEDURE DIVISION USING LS-DATE-FIELDS.
*
*
```

Figure 10B.2. PROCEDURE DIVISION header example with the USING phrase.

The USING Phrase of the PROCEDURE DIVISION Header

The USING phrase of a called program is specified as part of the PROCEDURE DIVISION header. The format is shown in Figure 10B.2. As with the USING phrase of the CALL statement, the data-names that are specified must be 01-level items, either group or elementary. Each data-item that is listed must be defined within the LINKAGE SECTION of the subprogram.

An equal number of data-items must be specified in the subprogram USING phrase as were listed in the CALL statement USING phrase within the calling program. When more than one data-name is specified, each one must be specified in the *exact same sequence*. This is because the COBOL compiler links the called program data-name to the calling program field by relative placement with the USING phrases, not by data-name or location with the LINKAGE SECTION. Thus even though it is not necessary that the same data-names be

Example A.   Valid USING phrase relationship:

Calling program:

```
CALL 'DATEVAL' USING WS-DATE-FIELDS.
```

Called subprogram:

```
PROCEDURE DIVISION USING WS-DATE-FIELDS.
```

Example B.   Valid USING phrase relationship:

Calling program:

```
CALL 'DATEVAL' USING WS-DATE-FIELDS.
```

Called subprogram:

```
PROCEDURE DIVISION USING LS-DATE-FIELDS.
```

Example C.   Valid USING phrase relationship:

Calling program:

```
CALL 'DATEVAL' USING WS-MONTH
                     WS-DAY
                     WS-YEAR.
```

Called subprogram:

```
PROCEDURE DIVISION USING LS-MONTH
                         LS-DAY
                         LS-YEAR.
```

Example D.   Invalid USING phrase relationship (data-names must be matched by position — not name):

Calling program:

```
CALL 'DATEVAL' USING WS-MONTH
                     WS-DAY
                     WS-YEAR.
```

Called subprogram:

```
PROCEDURE DIVISION USING WS-YEAR
                         WS-MONTH
                         WS-DAY.
```

Example E.   Invalid USING phrase relationship (number of data-names must be the same):

Calling program:

```
CALL 'DATEVAL' USING WS-YEAR
                     WS-MONTH
                     WS-DAY.
```

Called subprogram:

```
PROCEDURE DIVISION USING LS-YEAR
                         LS-MONTH.
```

Example F: Invalid USING phrase relationship (phrase must be present in both calling and called program or omitted from both):

Calling program:

```
CALL 'DATEVAL'.
```

Called subprogram:

```
PROCEDURE DIVISION USING LS-DATE-FIELDS.
```

Figure 10B.3.   Valid and invalid USING phrase relationships.

Format:

```
       EXIT PROGRAM.
```

Example:

```
 *
        EXIT PROGRAM.
```

Figure 10B.4. EXIT PROGRAM statement example.

used for the corresponding calling and called program data-items, it is logical and consistent to do so. (For clarity, within the coding examples in the text, subprogram LINKAGE SECTION data-names are prefixed by LS- but are otherwise identical to their calling program names.)

Examples of valid and invalid USING phrase relationships between calling and called programs are shown in Figure 10B.3.

The EXIT PROGRAM Statement

To mark the exit point of a called program, the EXIT PROGRAM statement is used. Its format is shown in Figure 10B.4. The EXIT PROGRAM statement must be the only statement of the paragraph in which it resides. It must be terminated by a period. Execution of the EXIT PROGRAM statement in a called subprogram causes control to be returned to the calling program. Program execution in the calling program resumes at the next executable statement following the CALL statement.

When an EXIT PROGRAM statement is encountered in a program that is not operating as a called subprogram, it behaves as an EXIT statement. That is, it is either a return from a PERFORM statement or a null statement (if not terminating a PERFORM statement).

As discussed in Chapter 1, structured coding conventions often recommend self-contained single-paragraph modules that are independently performed; logic that "falls through" multiple paragraphs creates multiple entry and exit points. The syntax requirement that the EXIT PROGRAM statement appear only within its own paragraph imposes an exception to such conventions.

Subprogram Example

Subprogram coding for the DATEVAL program is shown in Figure 10B.5. Figure 10B.6 shows the relationship between the USING phrase fields of the calling PAYCALC program and the called DATEVAL subprogram. Observe that the LINKAGE SECTION fields are not actually contained with the DATEVAL subprogram but instead point to the PAYCALC program fields.

It is important to recognize that a static subprogram is in its initial state only the first time that it is called within a run unit. On all successive entries into the called subprogram, the state of the static subprogram is as it was the last time that it was exited. This includes the status of files, the positioning of files, and WORKING-STORAGE data fields.

```
                    IDENTIFICATION DIVISION.
                    PROGRAM-ID.     DATEVAL.
                    *
                    *
                    *                   THIS CALLED SUBPROGRAM IS PASSED
                    *                   A GREGORIAN DATE IN MMDDYY FORMAT.
                    *                   IT VALIDATES THE DATE AND SETS
                    *                   A SWITCH TO INDICATE VALID OR INVALID.
                    *
                    *
                    ENVIRONMENT DIVISION.
                    *
                    *
                    CONFIGURATION SECTION.
                    *
                    SOURCE-COMPUTER.  IBM-370.
                    OBJECT-COMPUTER.  IBM-370.
                    *
                    *
                    DATA DIVISION.
                    *
                    *
                    WORKING-STORAGE SECTION.
                    *
                    *
                    01  DT-MONTH-TABLE-DATA.
                        05   DT-JANUARY      PIC X(2)    VALUE '31'.
                        05   DT-FEBRUARY     PIC X(2)    VALUE '29'.
                        05   DT-MARCH        PIC X(2)    VALUE '31'.
                        05   DT-APRIL        PIC X(2)    VALUE '30'.
                        05   DT-MAY          PIC X(2)    VALUE '31'.
                        05   DT-JUNE         PIC X(2)    VALUE '30'.
                        05   DT-JULY         PIC X(2)    VALUE '31'.
                        05   DT-AUGUST       PIC X(2)    VALUE '31'.
                        05   DT-SEPTEMBER    PIC X(2)    VALUE '30'.
                        05   DT-OCTOBER      PIC X(2)    VALUE '31'.
                        05   DT-NOVEMBER     PIC X(2)    VALUE '30'.
                        05   DT-DECEMBER     PIC X(2)    VALUE '31'.
                    *
                    01  DT-MONTH-TABLE REDEFINES DT-MONTH-TABLE-DATA.
                        05   DT-MONTH-ENTRY  OCCURS 12 TIMES.
                            10  DT-MAX-DAYS-IN-MONTH      PIC X(2).
                    *
                    *
                    LINKAGE SECTION.
                    *
                    *
                    01  LS-DATE-FIELDS.
                        05   LS-DATE.
                            10   LS-MONTH                 PIC X(2).
                            10   LS-DAY                   PIC X(2).
                            10   LS-YEAR                  PIC X(2).
                        05   LS-VALID-DATE-SW             PIC X(3).
                    *
                    *
                    *
                    PROCEDURE DIVISION USING LS-DATE-FIELDS.
                    *
                    *
                    000-MAINLINE-CONVERT-DATE.
                    *
                        PERFORM 200-VALIDATE-DATE.
                    
                    000-EXIT-PROGRAM.
                    *
                        EXIT PROGRAM.
                    *
                    *
                    200-VALIDATE-DATE.
                    *
                        IF LS-DATE IS NUMERIC
                        AND LS-MONTH IS GREATER THAN ZERO
                        AND LS-MONTH IS LESS THAN '13'
                        AND LS-DAY IS GREATER THAN ZERO
                        AND LS-DAY
                                IS NOT GREATER THAN DT-MAX-DAYS-IN-MONTH (LS-MONTH)
                            MOVE 'YES' TO LS-VALID-DATE-SW
                        ELSE
                            MOVE 'NO ' TO LS-VALID-DATE-SW.
```

Figure 10B.5. Called subprogram coding: DATEVAL program.

```
PROGRAM-ID.     PAYCALC.

  DATA DIVISION.
  FILE SECTION.
          .
          .
          .

  WORKING-STORAGE SECTION.
          .
          .
          .

  01   WS-DATE-FIELDS.
       05   WS-DATE.
            10   WS-MONTH              PIC X(2).
            10   WS-DAY                PIC X(2).
            10   WS-YEAR               PIC X(3).
       05   WS-VALID-DATE-SW
            88   VALID-DATE                       VALUE 'YES'.
            88   INVALID-DATE                     VALUE 'NO '.

  PROCEDURE DIVISION.
          .
          .
          .

       CALL 'DATEVAL' USING WS-DATE-FIELDS.
          .
          .
          .
```

```
          LINKAGE SECTION.
          01   LS-DATE-FIELDS.
               05   LS-DATE.
                    10   LS-MONTH              PIC X(2).
                    10   LS-DAY                PIC X(2).
                    10   LS-YEAR               PIC X(2).
               05   LS-VALID-DATE-SW           PIC X(3).
```

```
PROGRAM-ID.   DATEVAL.

  DATA DIVISION.
  WORKING-STORAGE SECTION.
          .
          .
          .

  PROCEDURE DIVISION USING LS-DATE-FIELDS.
          .
          .
          .

  000-EXIT-PROGRAM.
       EXIT PROGRAM.
          .
          .
          .
```

Figure 10B.6.   Relationship between calling PAYCALC program and called DATEVAL subprogram.

As a result, subprograms should typically be coded as **re-entrant** modules. That is, initialization of necessary fields and I-O requirements should be coded into the PROCEDURE DIVISION logic in a manner so that the program will yield equivalent results whether it is being entered for the first iteration or a successive one.

A subprogram may contain CALL statements; a nested subprogram structure is the result. However, a called subprogram must not contain a CALL statement that directly or indirectly calls a calling program.

■ **TOPIC 10-C:** **Subprogram Linkage**

Dynamic CALL Option
  ON OVERFLOW Phrase

CANCEL Statement

A subprogram is either statically or dynamically linked to the calling program. Not all COBOL compilers provide the ability to dynamically link subprograms. With **static subprogram linkage**, the calling program and the called subprogram are compiled separately but **link-edited** together to form one **load module**. With **dynamic subprogram linkage**, the subprogram is not link-edited with the main program. This means that the subprogram is not only compiled as a separate program but also link-edited as a separate program and stored as a separate load module. Figure 10C.1 depicts these concepts of subprogram linkage.

During run time, a run unit in storage contains the main program, all statically linked subprograms, and those dynamically linked subprograms that have been called for.

There are two chief advantages to dynamic subprogram linkage: (1) it eases program-maintenance tasks, and (2) it can reduce run-unit storage requirements.

Whenever the source code of a statically linked subprogram is modified, it is necessary to re-link the subprogram with the calling program. Although the re-linking itself is not a particularly time-consuming task, it can be a considerable chore to (1) keep track of which calling programs use each subprogram and (2) coordinate, schedule, and implement the changeover to the new version. Dynamically linked subprograms reduce effectivity-date problems and help to ensure that the latest subprogram version is being used.

Dynamic subprogram linkage can reduce run-unit storage requirements in certain circumstances. For example, when a seldomly executed subprogram is dynamically linked, it will occupy run-unit storage only during those runs in which its CALL is executed. Another example is a calling program that, during a particular program run, selects only one or some of two or multiple subprograms. When dynamically linked, only the chosen programs will occupy run-unit storage. One more example is a subprogram that is used for only a short period of time. It can be dynamically called at the time that it is needed and released immediately after its execution has been completed.

A feature of dynamic subprogram linkage that might be considered an advantage in limited situations is that it allows a subprogram to be **refreshed** within the run unit. If, for some reason, a subprogram was not coded to be re-entrant, a fresh copy can be acquired by canceling the current copy and calling for it again.

The only disadvantage of dynamic linkage is that the process of loading the subprogram into the run unit expends a little time and thus causes some execution time overhead.

As a rule of thumb, therefore, dynamic subprogram linkage may be advantageous when (1) the subprogram requires frequent modifications, (2) the subprogram is not executed during each calling program run, (3) run-unit storage requirements are to be minimized, (4) a subprogram is used for only a brief period of total run time, or (5) subprogram refreshability is required. If run-time requirements are to be optimized, static subprogram linkage should be considered. However, because program-maintenance requirements usually over-

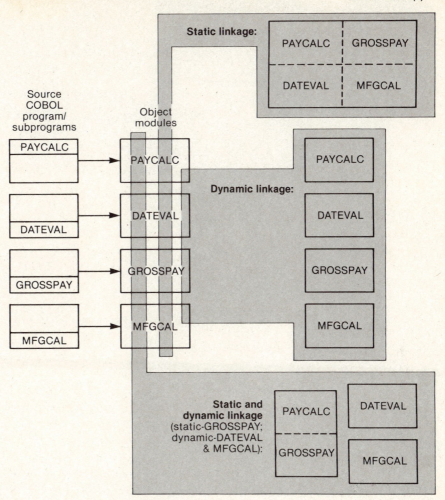

Figure 10C.1. Subprogram linkage.

shadow slight timing degradations, the programming conventions of many organizations specify that dynamic subprogram linkage should be used on a standard basis.

Dynamic CALL Option

The ANS COBOL standards for the CALL statement syntax do not explicitly differentiate dynamic calls from static calls. Thus specification of subprogram linkage is generally handled through the job control language of the operating system that is being used. However, if the identifier option of the CALL statement is used, the compiler does not know the name of the subprogram that is being called for. Thus the syntax of certain common compilers use the convention that, for static linkage, the program-name must be specified with a literal. With dynamic linkage, the program-name can be expressed as either a literal or an identifier. Figure 10C.2 illustrates this convention.

When the program-name is specified with an identifier, the field that the identifier indicates must be a nonnumeric data-item and consistent with the rules of the operating system for forming a program-name. For example, if the operating system uses eight-character program-names, the identifier field

Figure 10C.2. Typical dynamic versus static CALL statement formats.

```
DATA DIVISION.
WORKING-STORAGE SECTION.
    .
    .
    .

    05  WS-SUBPROGRAM                    PIC X(8).
    .
    .
    .
01  WS-DATE-FIELDS.
    .
    .
    .
PROCEDURE DIVISION.
    .
    .
    .
    IF GREGORIAN-DATE
        MOVE 'GREGVAL ' TO WS-SUBPROGRAM
    ELSE
        MOVE 'JULVAL  ' TO WS-SUBPROGRAM.

    CALL WS-SUBPROGRAM USING WS-DATE-FIELDS.
    .
    .
    .
```

Figure 10C.3. Coding example for dynamic CALL.

should be defined as PIC X(8). When the CALL statement is executed, the contents of the identifier field must conform to the operating system rules for the formation of a program-name.

Figure 10C.3 provides an example of a dynamic CALL statement within a calling program. When a dynamic CALL is executed, the operating system must check to see if the subprogram is already present in the run unit. If it is, the existing subprogram copy is used. If it is not, the load module is obtained from the program library and added to the run unit.

ON OVERFLOW Phrase   The ON OVERFLOW option permits specification of actions to be taken when, at run time, there is not sufficient storage available to accommodate the called subprogram. When this situation occurs, the imperative statement of the ON OVERFLOW phrase is executed; otherwise it is skipped.

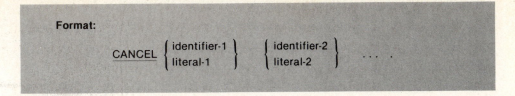

Example:

```
CANCEL WS-SUBPROGRAM.
```

Figure 10C.4. CANCEL statement example.

If the ON OVERFLOW phrase is omitted and the subprogram will not fit in storage, the specific handling is defined by the particular implementor of the compiler. The ON OVERFLOW phrase is not applicable to a static call.

CANCEL Statement

The CANCEL statement format is shown in Figure 10C.4. It causes the storage that is occupied by a dynamically linked subprogram to be released. Rules in regard to specification of literals and identifiers are the same as those for the CALL statement.

After the CANCEL statement is executed, the subprogram that is canceled is logically removed from the run unit. A subsequently executed CALL statement to the canceled subprogram will cause a fresh copy of the subprogram in its initial state to be introduced into the run unit.

If a CANCEL statement references a program that is not present in the run unit or already in a canceled state, no action is taken.

A called subprogram may contain CANCEL statements but must not directly or indirectly cancel a calling program or any other program higher in the calling hierarchy than itself.

Summary

Topic 10-A Calling Programs

A program that uses one or more subprograms is termed a **calling program**. A **subprogram** is referred to as a **called program**. A subprogram can be both a calling and a called program. A program that is only a calling program is termed a **main program**. When a subprogram calls one or more additional subprograms, the resulting structures are sometimes referred to as **nested subprograms**. The set of programs that function together at run time to provide the programming solution is called a **run unit**.

The CALL statement is used to transfer control to a subprogram. Fields of the calling program that are to be made available to the called program are specified in the USING phrase. Each field must be a 01-level item.

Topic 10-B Called Subprograms

The LINKAGE SECTION is used to describe data in the called subprogram that is referred to by both itself and the calling program. Fields that are to be received from the calling program must be defined in the LINKAGE SECTION and specified in the USING phrase of the PROCEDURE DIVISION header. In the header, they must be specified in the exact same sequence as they were in the CALL statement of the calling program. To return control from the called program to the calling program, the EXIT PROGRAM statement is specified.

With **static subprogram linkage**, the calling program and the called subprogram are compiled separately but **link-edited** together to form one **load module**. With **dynamic subprogram linkage**, the subprogram is compiled and link-edited as a separate program.

The ON OVERFLOW phrase of a dynamic CALL statement permits specification of actions to be taken when, at run time, there is not sufficient storage available to accommodate the called subprogram. The CANCEL statement causes the storage that is occupied by a dynamically linked subprogram to be released.

Programming Assignments

10-1: Check-Digit Validation Subprogram

Program description

Seven-digit self-checking code numbers (six basic code digits plus one check digit) are to be validated. A main program is to read code-transaction records and print a check-digit validation list that identifies whether or not the code number is valid. Check-digit computation and validation is to be done in a subprogram named "CHKDIG".

Input file

Code-transaction file

Output file

Code-validation list

Record formats

Code-transaction record (Record code "A5")

Check-digit validation list

Code transaction record

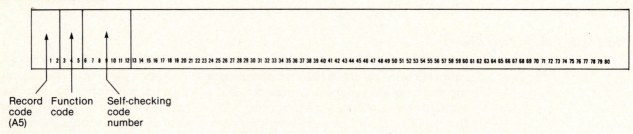

Record code (A5)   Function code   Self-checking code number

Code validation list

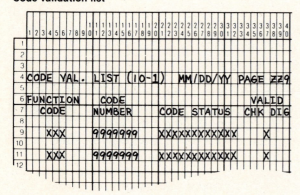

Program operations

A. Read each input code-transaction record.

    1. Validate each code-transaction record to ensure that it contains one of the following function codes:

        V10 (Validate code number: Modulus 10)

        V11 (Validate code number: Modulus 11)

    2. If the function code is equal to "V10" or "V11", pass the following field values to a subprogram named CHKDIG:

        a. Function code

        b. Self-checking code number

    3. If the function code is not equal to "V10" or "V11", print the error message "INVALID FUNCTION CODE" together with the transaction record contents.

B. The "CHKDIG" subprogram should perform the following operations:

    1. If the function code passed is "V10", the code number is to be validated in accordance with the modulus-10 check-digit formula that is presented in Chapter C, Figure C.9.

        a. Weights 2 and 1 should be used.

    2. If the function code passed is "V11", the code number is to be validated in accordance with the modulus-11 check-digit formula that is presented in Chapter C, Figure C.10.

        a. Weights 2 through 7 should be used.

        b. Code numbers with a check digit of 10 were not assigned.

    3. Pass back to the main program the following field values:

        a. Valid/invalid code ("V" = valid code number;
                  "I" = invalid code number)

        b. Correct digit (if the code is invalid; for a valid code, set this field to a blank space)

    4. The subprogram should not modify the function code or code-number field values passed by the main program.

C. After control has been returned to the main program, a report line should be printed as shown on the print chart.

    1. Each detail line is to be double-spaced and will contain the function code and 7-digit (including check digit) code number.

    2. If the check digit is valid, "VALID CODE" should be printed in the code status field.

    3. If the check digit is invalid, "INVALID CODE" should be printed in the code status field, together with the correct check digit in the valid check-digit field.

    4. Provide for a line span of 57 lines per page.

Assignment 10-1   Option 1
Print Master Check Digit List

If a function code of "L10" or "L11" is present in the input code-transaction record, pass control to a subprogram named "CHKLST" and print a master check-digit list in accordance with the following:

1. The code-transaction record will contain a starting basic code number (without the check digit) in positions 6 through 11 and an ending basic code number in positions 13 through 18.

2. Control is to be passed to a subprogram named "CHKLST" together with the following field values:

    a. Function code

    b. Starting basic code number

    c. Ending basic code number

3. The "CHKLST" subprogram is to skip to a new report page and print a master check-digit list.

    a. The check digit is to be computed for each consecutive value within the code number range.

    b. Each 7-digit code (basic code plus check digit) is to be printed on a separate line.

    c. Detail lines are to be single-spaced.

    d. Provide for a line span of 57 lines per page.

4. After the ending code value has been printed, control is to be returned to the main program.

10-2: Date-Processing Subprogram

Program description

Various date-validation, conversion, and span-computational functions are to be performed. A main program will read date-transaction records and print a date-processing report that fulfills the date-processing function requirements. The date processing is to be done in a subprogram named "DATES".

Input file

    Date-transaction file

Output file

    Date-processing list

Record formats

    Date-transaction record (Record code "A6")

    Date-processing line

Date transaction record

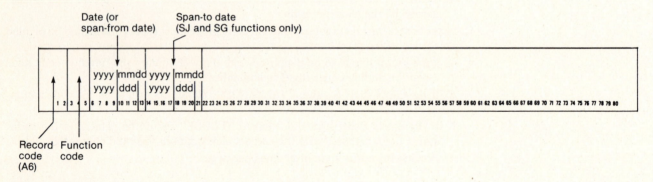

Date processing list

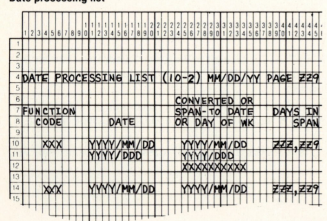

Program operations

A. Read each input date-transaction record.

    1. Validate each date-transaction record to ensure that it contains one of the following function codes:

        VJ   (Validate Julianized date)

        VG (Validate Gregorian date)

        CJG (Convert Julianized date to a Gregorian date)

        CGJ (Convert Gregorian date to a Julianized date)

        SJ   (Compute span from a Julianized date)

        SG (Compute span from a Gregorian date)

        DJ   (Compute day-of-the-week from a Julianized date)

        DG (Compute day-of-the-week from a Gregorian date)

    2. If the function code is equal to "VJ", "VG", "CJG", "CGJ", "DJ", or "DG", pass the following field values to a subprogram named "DATES":

      a. Function code

      b. Date

    3. If the function code is equal to "SJ" or "SG", pass the following field values to the "DATES" subprogram:

      a. Function code

      b. Span-from date

      c. Span-to date

    4. If the function code is not equal to one of the valid function codes that are listed above, print the transaction record contents, together with an asterisk, in the print position immediately to the left of the function code (print position 3).

B. The "DATES" subprogram should perform the following operations:

    1. If the function code is "VJ" or "VG", validate the date in accordance with the applicable logic that is presented in Chapter C, Figure C.1. Return the following field to the main program:

      a. Valid/invalid date ("V" = valid date;

                      "I" = invalid date)

    2. If the function code is "CJG", convert the date in accordance with the applicable logic that is presented in Chapter C, Figure C.2. Return the following field to the main program:

      a. Converted Gregorian date

    3. If the function code is "CGJ", convert the date in accordance with the applicable logic that is presented in Chapter C, Figure C.2. Return the following field to the main program:

      a. Converted Julian date

    4. If the function code is "SJ" or "SG", compute the date span in accordance with the applicable logic that is presented in Chapter C, Figure C.3. Return the following field to the main program:

      a. Days in span

    5. If the function code is "DJ" or "DG", compute the day of the week in accordance with the applicable logic that is presented in Chapter C, Figure C.4. Return the following field to the main program:

      a. Day of the week

    6. The subprogram should not modify the function code or date values passed by the main program.

C. After control has been returned to the main program, a report line should be printed as shown on the print chart.

    1. Detail lines are to be double-spaced.

    2. If (for a "VJ" or "VG" function) the date is invalid, print an asterisk in print position 10.

    3. Provide for a line span of 56 lines per page.

10-3: Field-Editing Subprogram

Program description

Various field-editing functions are to be performed. A main program will read unedited-transaction records and, after editing by a subprogram, print an editing list showing the editing that has been performed. The editing is to be done in three subprograms, "JUSTIFY", "ELIMXBL", and "TRZSUPP".

Input file

Unedited-transaction file

Output file

Editing list

Record formats

Unedited-transaction record (Record code "A7")

Editing list line

Unedited transaction record

Data to be edited

Field length

Record code (A7)

Function code

Editing list

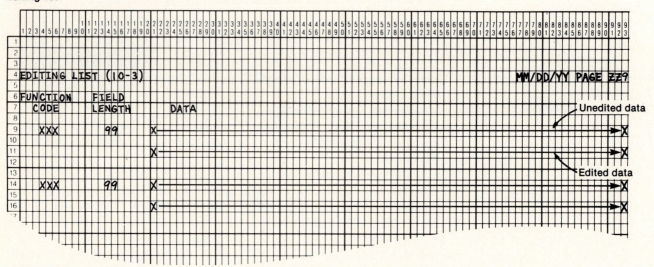

Program operations

A. Read each input unedited-transaction record.

    1. Validate each date-transaction record to ensure that it contains one of the following function codes:

       LJ   (Left justification)

       RJ   (Right justification)

       LJB (Left justification with excess blank space elimination)

RJB (Right justification with excess blank space elimination)

BE   (Excess blank space elimination)

TZS (Trailing zero suppression)

2. If the function code is equal to "LJ" or "RJ", pass the following field values to the "JUSTIFY" subprogram:

   a. Function code
   b. Field length
   c. Data to be edited

3. If the function code is equal to "LJB", "RJB", or "BE", pass the following field values to the "ELIMXBL" subprogram:

   a. Function code
   b. Field length
   c. Data to be edited

4. If the function code is equal to "TZS", pass the following field values to the "ELIMXBL" subprogram:

   a. Field length
   b. Data to be edited

5. If the function code is not equal to one of the valid function codes that are listed above, print the transaction record contents (as shown on the print chart), together with an asterisk, in the print position immediately to the left of the function code (print position 3).

6. If the field-length value is less than "02" or greater than "73", print the transaction record contents (as shown on the print chart), together with an asterisk, in the print position immediately to the left of the field length (print position 13).

B. Each subprogram should perform the specified editing functions and return an edited field to the main program. The field values that are passed by the main program should not be modified.

C. After control has been returned to the main program, two report lines should be printed for each transaction, as shown on the print chart.

1. The first line contains data that is entered on the unedited-transaction record. Each of these lines (except the first on each page) is to be triple-spaced from the previous line.

2. The second line contains the edited data. It is to be double-spaced from the previous line.

3. Provide for a line span of 56 lines per page.

VIDEO DISPLAY TERMINAL HARDWARE

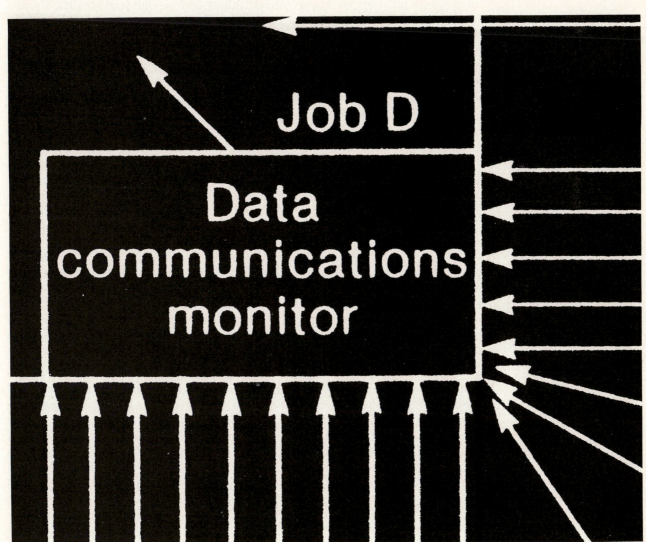

VIDEO DISPLAY TERMINAL HARDWARE

The **video-display terminal (VDT)** is the hardware device by which most programmers and users interact and communicate with a computer system. Many refer to a video-display terminal as a CRT, which is an acronym for **cathode-ray tube**, the name for the type of screen that is most commonly used. However, the term *video-display terminal* is preferable because not all VDTs use cathode-ray tube technology. Further, a VDT usually contains not only a screen but also a keyboard. A VDT is also sometimes called a **workstation**, **screen**, **tube**, or simply a **terminal**.

VDTs are generally classified as either dumb, smart, or intelligent. A **dumb terminal** is the least expensive type and represents the more mature technology. These bare-bones units were originally introduced in the late 1960s to allow computer users to interact with computers without the clatter, paper consumption, and maintenance problems of teleprinters. Indeed, VDTs were sometimes called "glass Teletypes" in reference to their physical characteristics and the teleprinters that they so often replaced. (Teletype is a registered trademark and service mark of Teletype Corporation.)

Smart terminals, with a limited amount of local buffer storage, were developed to provide professional programmers and data-entry operators with the ability to work with a full screen of data rather than on the line-by-line basis of the dumb terminals. More expensive than dumb terminals, the smart terminals use their limited intelligence to provide additional functions such as screen formatting, field protection, data compression, and tabbing. Smart terminals are the most prevalent in use today; roughly two-thirds of installed terminals are currently in this category.

Intelligent terminals serve dual roles as small, stand-alone computers and as a communications device to larger computer systems. As the microcomputer industry progresses, the distinction between intelligent terminals and micros is blurring.

Ergonomic Features

The science of **ergonomics** is concerned with the relationship between person and machine. ("Erg" is the Greek word for "work.") Sometimes alternatively referred to as **biotechnology** or **human factors engineering**, ergonomics is playing a significant role in the physical design of modern VDT devices. A VDT that employs so-called ergonomic features is shown in Figure D.1. We will discuss a number of general VDT features that can be considered within this category.

Detached Keyboard

Most early VDTs had their keyboards attached to the display screen. **Detached keyboard** models better accommodate restrictions of the desk area, space requirements for source documents, and needs for physical comfort.

A detached keyboard is connected to the body of the hardware unit by a cable that is similar to the one used to attach a telephone receiver to a telephone set. The flexible cord permits the operator to easily adjust the keyboard for comfortable keying after the screen has been positioned for optimum visual presentation.

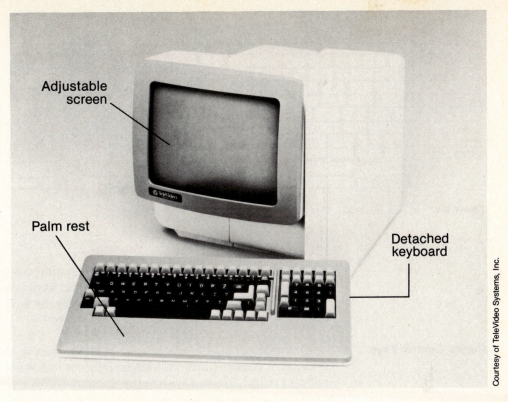

Adjustable
screen

Palm rest

Detached
keyboard

Courtesy of TeleVideo Systems, Inc.

Figure D.1. Ergonomically designed terminal.

Adjustable Screen

Certain VDT models have not only a detached keyboard but also an adjustable screen. That is, the display screen is mounted so that it will easily tilt and/or swivel to a convenient viewing position for the operator. Adjustable screens typically provide for tilt from 5 degrees forward to 15 degrees backward.

Glare Protection

Antireflective properties can be built into a VDT screen to offset glare, minimize flicker, and improve character quality. Such glare protection is usually provided by coatings, plastic panels, or etching of the screen faceplate. Some units also include an overhang above the display to minimize glare.

Palm Rest

To allow the operator a place on which to rest his or her hands, a front-edge keyboard housing extension is provided on some VDT models.

Brightness Control

Most display terminals have an adjustable **brightness control** that is similar to the one found on a television set. It enables the operator to adjust the screen brightness to a comfortable level in relation to the working environment.

Keyboard Features

Figure D.2 shows an example of a full-stroke VDT keyboard with cursor control keys, a numeric keypad, and function keys. These features plus numeric lock and key-click control will be discussed.

Keyboard Type

There are three general types of keyboards: full-stroke, calculator, and monopanel. A full-stroke keyboard with sculptured keytops is the type found on high-quality electric typewriters and is considered to be ideal for professional use.

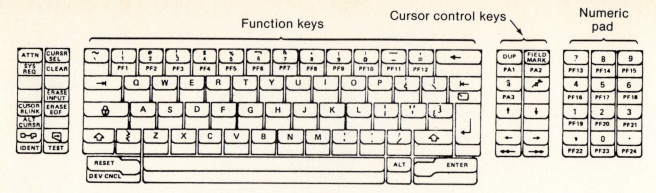

Figure D.2. VDT keyboard.

Calculator-type keyboards are of medium quality and are used on a few less expensive devices. Monopanels have no actual keys—the keyboard is a flat panel with touch-sensitive areas. These flat-membrane keyboards are typically found only on inexpensive home computer keyboards.

Cursor Control Keys

The special symbol displayed on the VDT screen to identify data-entry location is called a **cursor.** Most VDT keyboards contain a set of four keys dedicated to cursor control. These keys are the up arrow, down arrow, left arrow, and right arrow.

Numeric Keypad

A numeric keypad is a set of numeric keys that are grouped as they are on a calculator. This feature permits rapid entry of numeric data by limiting the operator hand movement that is required. In addition to the 10 number keys, numeric keypads typically contain a decimal-point key, a minus-sign key, and sometimes a plus-sign key.

Function Keys

Many keyboards contain a set of function keys. These keys, also termed **program function, programmable function,** or **program attention** keys, can be used—under program control—to enlist special program functions. The application programmer can code the program to detect the depression of one of these function keys. The program flow can then be directed in accordance with the function key that is selected.

The number of function keys, when present on a keyboard, will vary. On IBM 3270 Display Stations for example, there are 3 program-attention keys, 12 standard program-function keys, and 12 additional program-function keys available as an optional feature.

Numeric Lock

When an operator is entering data into a numeric field, he or she should enter only numeric digits. The **numeric lock** feature ensures such data entry. When the cursor is positioned in a field that is defined in the program as numeric, this feature electronically locks out all keys other than the digits 0 through 9, the decimal point, and the arithmetic sign.

Key-Click Control

A few VDT models offer a **key-click control** feature that permits the operator to adjust the intensity of sound level made by the depression of the keys. This feature was particularly important for terminal users who were previously keypunch operators and hence accustomed to the noise of the card-punch keyboard. Such operators tended to use the noise as their reinforcement that a key was properly depressed.

Number of lines

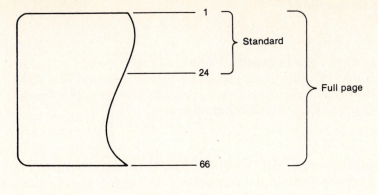

Characters per line

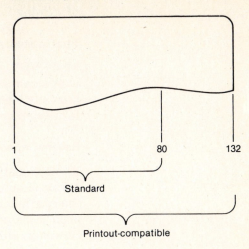

Figure D.3. Screen dimension examples.

Screen Features

VDT screens are typically classified as either alphanumeric or graphic. An **alphanumeric screen** is the type that is typically used for business applications. This screen provides for the display of alphanumeric characters just as computer printers do. A **graphics screen** additionally permits pictorial displays. It is used for applications such as engineering design and others in which such capabilities can be employed.

Alphanumeric-screen character quality is measured by the character-formation matrix that is used. The more dense the matrix, the better the character quality. Typical dot densities for alphanumeric screen characters range from 5×7 to 14×10. The number of different character symbols that can be represented on an alphanumeric screen—the **character set**—is typically 96 or 128.

Graphic screen capabilities are measured by the density of the addressable dots for the entire screen. Each dot is considered a picture element and is termed a **pixel**. Typical resolution rates range from 256×640 to 1024×1280 pixels.

Screen Dimensions

Just as with television, the physical size of a VDT screen is usually expressed according to its diagonal measurement. The most commonly used size is 12 inches, but sizes from 5 to 19 inches are available with certain models.

More important than physical size to most alphanumeric screen users is the number of characters and lines that can be displayed on the screen. Some examples of screen dimension are shown in Figure D.3. The standard arrangement is 24 lines of 80 characters. To be compatible with the familiar 132-character wide printout, screens displaying 132 characters across the line are also available. For word-processing applications, it is often convenient to view a standard 11-inch long page as a whole. Thus line capacities up to 66 lines are available from some vendors.

Home- and special-purpose systems occasionally use screens with less than a 24-line by 80-character display. Certain 24-line displays provide a **25th-line** for status identification and related uses.

Operator Attention Aids

To command the operator's attention or to otherwise aid the operator, a number of viewing features are available.

Dual intensity

Many VDT screens offer a **dual-intensity** feature whereby screen areas or words can be highlighted by being displayed at a brighter intensity. This dual-intensity feature is useful for indicating errors during data-entry operations or for deemphasizing constant data within a data display.

Reverse video

Another method of highlighting is with **reverse video**. This feature causes the background area around and within the character to be lighted, thus causing the character image to be formed from the dark screen. Using reverse video is even more effective than dual intensity for commanding operator attention. However, although distinctive, it is more difficult to read when large areas are reversed.

Reverse video is convenient to use for "fill-in-the-blank" data-entry situations. The highlighted block is immediately apparent to the operator, and the maximum length of the field is also exhibited. Reverse video can also be used in editing applications to indicate added characters or material that is to be deleted.

As a strong attention-getting device, reverse video is commonly used for displaying error, exception, and warning messages.

Blinking characters

An even stronger attention-getter than reverse video, **blinking characters** are also used for error messages. However, excessive use of blinking characters can be not only distracting but downright irritating to the operator. Thus it is a device that should be used sparingly and restricted to more serious problems in which the operator's immediate attention is required.

Audible alarm

Either a bell, beeper, or buzzer, the **audible alarm** is a good device to summon the operator when he or she is frequently away from the terminal. Like blinking characters, however, the audible alarm can be irritating; therefore, its use should be limited. Generally, it should *not* be used to indicate an erroneous entry. Such an audible signal can be plainly heard by others within the work area. Thus the audible alarm is intimidating to operators—especially to novices.

Column separators

Available on only a few VDT devices, **column separators** are narrow hairline indications between character positions on a line. It is an excellent way to indicate the location and maximum length of fields to be entered. For this use, it is similar in function to reverse video, but column separators are less distracting and hence easier on the eyes.

Dark intensity

When passwords and other sensitive or security-restricted data must be entered into the terminal, **dark intensity** should be used. With dark intensity, data keyed on the terminal is transmitted but not displayed on the screen.

Scrolling

Scrolling, a software-dependent feature, refers to the upward or downward movement of text on the display screen. With **line scrolling**, the first line in the direction of movement disappears from the screen, the remaining lines move in that direction, and a new line appears at the opposite end of the screen. **Page scrolling** is the same function except that, instead of line movement, all or most of the total screen—the page—is moved.

Depending on the hardware characteristics, the line movement of scrolling can produce jerking, flickering images. When the screen hardware is designed to eliminate this effect, it is called **smooth scrolling**.

Split-screen displays

The **split-screen** hardware feature allows two different displays, called **windows**, to be simultaneously shown on the screen. A common application for this feature is to use half of the screen for data entry and thus permit the other half of the screen to be available for the display of source or reference data.

Auxiliary port

An auxiliary port is somewhat like a speaker jack on a stereo. It permits another device—typically a printer—to be connected to the VDT. A printer could be used to simply reproduce the screen image on paper or to receive data to be printed from a central computer via the terminal.

CHAPTER 11

ON-LINE PROCESSING CONCEPTS

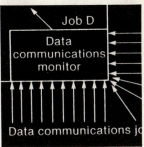

11 ON-LINE PROCESSING CONCEPTS

With **on-line processing**, a computer maintains continual control of the application system. This permits user input data to be entered directly into the system at the time that a transaction occurs. Certain outputs can then be immediately prepared and quickly returned to the user on a VDT and/or printer. On-line processing can be contrasted with **batch processing**, in which input transactions are collected into a batch and then submitted as a group to the computer system. The batch system processes the input and prepares all of the outputs during a scheduled processing period. Upon completion, the outputs—typically printed reports—are distributed to the users.

Computers, operating systems, communications software, data transmission, and remote terminals are among the technical considerations that must be addressed when planning and developing an on-line system. This combination of ingredients—coupled with the fact that ANS COBOL does not presently contain features for VDT screen handling—has caused most on-line systems to be dependent on a particular vendor's hardware and software products. Although hardware standards are being set in place and the CODASYL COBOL committee has a Screen Management Task Group (SMTG) that is working on screen-handling functions, an on-line system must still be developed in accordance with the standards, methods, and procedures of particular hardware and/or software vendors.

Thus, although most commercial on-line systems are written in the COBOL language, the on-line programs contain vendor-dependent syntax for screen-handling and certain communications functions. This situation precludes the presentation of specific on-line syntax in a standard text such as this.

In this chapter, therefore, certain concepts and terminology that apply to on-line processing in general will be presented. Topic 11-A discusses general on-line processing characteristics. An overview of certain on-line application design considerations is presented in Topic 11-B.

■ TOPIC 11-A: **Characteristics of On-Line Systems**

Differences Between On-Line and Batch Systems
Data-Communications Monitors
 Data-Communications Monitor Functions
  Terminal management

Task management
Storage management
Program management
File management
Multitasking and Multithreading
Program Design for CICS
Page-Fault Minimization
Locality of reference
Size of the working set
Validity of reference
Execution Time-Span Minimization

It is estimated that at the beginning of the 1980s approximately 65 percent of medium- and large-scale data-processing installations had on-line applications. By the mid-1980s, that figure is expected to reach 95 percent. As shown in Figure 11A.1, there are a number of on-line system categories. For the COBOL programmer/analyst, however, the transaction processing type is the focal point.

On-line system type	Typical response time requirement	Typical relative message lengths		Typical auxiliary on-line file processing requirements	Application example
		Input	Output		
Transaction processing	1–10 seconds	medium	medium	medium-high	Airline reservations
Conversational	2–5 seconds	short	short	low-medium	Computer-assisted instruction
Data collection	2–20 seconds	varies	short	low/medium	Accounting data entry
Remote job entry	minutes/hours	long	long	low	Order processing
Message switching	seconds/minutes	varies	varies	low	Telex system
Process control (sensor-based)	varies	varies	varies	varies	Environment control

Figure 11A.1. On-line system categories.

Differences Between On-Line and Batch Systems

With batch processing, users submit source documents or recorded data to a central location at a specific time, in accordance with a prearranged schedule. After submission, the responsibility for computer processing shifts from the user to the data-center staff. Hence the data-processing department serves as a buffer between the user and the application system. When there is a hardware or software problem or malfunction, the user is generally insulated from it.

On the other hand, users submit data at various times when they are working with an on-line system. Thus processing requirements are not prescheduled (except that sometimes certain blocks of time are reserved for system maintenance or another use and hence are unavailable). Because the users interface directly with the system, immediate response is required. With no buffer be-

With batch processing . . .	With on-line processing . . .
▪ Users submit input documents/data to a central location	▪ Users submit input data from their own work station
▪ Data is submitted in accordance with a prearranged schedule	▪ Data is submitted at various unscheduled times
▪ Data center staff assumes responsibility for processing the data	▪ Users interface directly with the system
▪ User is insulated from hardware or software malfunctions	▪ Users become intolerant of hardware and software malfunctions
▪ Security is controlled by traditional means	▪ Security facilities must be built into the system
▪ Lapse of time occurs between submission of input and receipt of output	▪ Immediate response is generally required
▪ Predefined job stream with rigid job step execution sequence	▪ User controls execution sequence
▪ Program may consume a considerable amount of real storage	▪ Limited amount of real storage is allocated to each program
▪ Program may process various input record types	▪ Programs typically process only one transaction type
▪ Program may have lengthy execution time	▪ Programs tend to be short
▪ Program calls for input records	▪ Input transactions call for the program
▪ Concurrent sharing of data files is limited	▪ Concurrent sharing of data files is common
▪ Predominant form of display output is a printed report	▪ Predominant form of display output is a VDT screen format

Figure 11A.2. Differences between batch and on-line processing.

tween them and the system, hardware or software malfunctions are readily apparent. Users become intolerant when breakdowns occur frequently.

A lapse of time exists between input submission and output receipt for a batch-processing system whereas on-line systems must typically provide immediate response. Providing an acceptable response time on a continuing basis is a prime concern of most on-line system designers and programmers.

The run processing for a batch application has a rigid job step execution sequence as specified in the job control language of a predefined job stream. A batch program may consume a considerable amount of storage and have a lengthy execution time. The program will frequently handle various types of input records. The program requests each data record when it is ready for it. The sharing of files by different programs is limited.

The submission of an on-line transaction initiates program execution. Thus, although batch programs call for transactions, on-line transactions call for programs. Because a number of users will be concurrently interacting with the system, only a limited amount of real storage can be allocated to each. This means that, to minimize virtual storage paging, each program should be short and contain straight-line logic. To keep programs short, each program typically processes only one type of transaction. With various transactions being processed concurrently, the sharing of files among users by different—and the same—programs is common.

Differences between batch and on-line systems are summarized in Figure 11A.2.

Data-Communications Monitors

Just as an operating system provides support for batch systems, a **data-communications monitor** provides support for on-line systems. However, a data-communications monitor does not replace the operating system. Instead, it runs as a job under control of the operating system to handle the on-line applications that the computer must process. Data-communications monitors are sometimes referred to as a **teleprocessing** or a **telecommunications monitor**. The abbreviations **DC** and **TP** are frequently used in place of their respective words.

In order to understand the relationship of a data-communications monitor to the operating system, it is helpful to trace the development of operating systems and on-line applications.

During the first and second computer generations, storage sizes and execution speeds did not permit the running of more than one program at a time. As the third generation of computers evolved, storage sizes and execution speeds had increased to a point at which throughput could be increased by concurrently executing a limited number of batch programs to make use of input-output interruption times. As shown in phase 1 of Figure 11A.3, this **multiprogramming** concept was conceived during the early 1960s and provided in many operating systems that were released in the mid-1960s.

By the mid-1960s, as shown in phase 2 of Figure 11A.3, on-line applications started to appear. These early systems typically used teletypewriters for I-O devices and served only a limited number of functions and terminals. The operating system—designed primarily for batch applications—typically treated on-line jobs in the same manner as batch jobs.

By the late 1960s (see phase 3 of Figure 11A.3), the number of on-line applications had increased—both in number and complexity. Instead of handling just one application, some systems handled two or more. To handle additional volumes and functions, more terminals were hooked into the system. Video-display terminals started to become cost effective. Various terminal hardware types and features were introduced into the I-O environment. As a result of these factors, the operating system started to bog down because it was originally designed for a limited number of batch jobs. Further, the programming time that was required to provide for the environment component of the on-line system was beginning to impact unfavorably the amount of time spent on the actual application components.

The solution to these problems (depicted in phase 4 of Figure 11A.3) was to use a data-communications monitor. This DC monitor could run as a job within a single storage region or partition to handle all the on-line transactions.

As shown in Figure 11A.4, the most widely used data-communications monitor is IBM's Customer Information Control System (CICS). (Its current name is Customer Information Control System/Virtual Storage, or CICS/VS, but the shorter generic abbreviation will be used in this text.)

Data-Communications Monitor Functions

The DC monitor serves as an interface between on-line transactions and the operating system. As does CICS, DC monitors typically provide terminal, task, storage, program, and file-management facilities.

Terminal management

Data must be accepted as soon as it is ready to be transmitted. Thus terminals must be polled to see if they have data to be transmitted. Before data is to be transmitted, the terminal must be addressed to determine if it is in a ready mode for acceptance.

When data-communications errors occur, they should be detected and logged for control purposes.

Phase 1 (early 1960s): Multiprogramming concept conceived and implemented

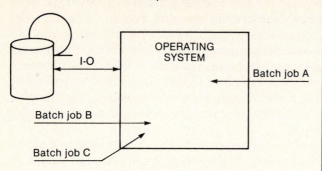

- Operating system is designed for a limited number of jobs

Phase 2 (mid-1960s): On-line systems originated to serve a limited number of functions and terminals

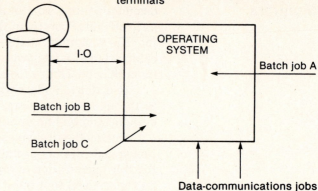

- Operating system treats on-line jobs same as batch jobs

Phase 3 (later 1960s): Number of on-line system applications and terminals increases

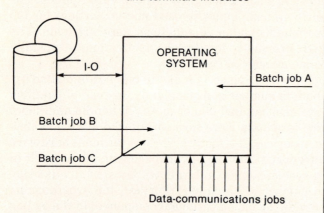

- Operating system bogs down because it was not designed for high-volume on-line processing

Phase 4 (late 1960s): Data communication monitors are introduced to provide an interface for on-line processing

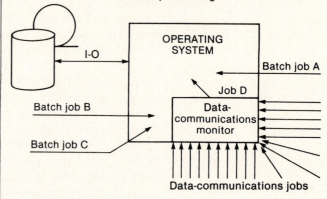

- Operating system can once again deal with a limited number of jobs

Figure 11A.3. Evolution of data-communications monitors.

Task management

Data that is entered from a terminal creates a **task** for processing. Different tasks may have different priorities, depending on the terminal being used, the operator initiating the task, or the type of transaction. A DC monitor provides the facility to handle the allocation of priorities, calculation of total priority, and scheduling in accordance with the calculated priority.

Once scheduled, the DC monitor must keep track of each terminal's use of application programs.

Storage management

Each task will create a need for storage. The DC monitor must acquire storage areas for both new tasks and for executing tasks that request additional storage. When storage areas are no longer needed, the DC monitor releases the storage.

Data-communications monitor	Vendor	Operating system	Approximate number of users*	Year introduced
CICS/VS	IBM	IBM OS DOS	3500†	1967
Shadow II	Altergo Products	IBM OS DOS	900	1970
ENVIRON/1	Cincom Systems	IBM OS DOS	600	1970
TASK/MASTER	TSI International	IBM OS DOS	400	1970
MPGSWIFT, ATLAS	Mathematica Products Group	IBM DOS	300	1973 1982
DATACOM/DC	Applied Data Research	IBM OS DOS	300	1973
COM-PLETE	Software AG	IBM OS DOS	300	1976
IDMS/DC	Cullinane	IBM OS DOS	300	1979

*Number of users provided by vendor 1/83 rounded to next hundred
†Vendor does not provide user information. Figure based upon best available estimate.

Figure 11A.4. Representative data-communications monitors.

Program management

The program management function keeps track of which application programs are in use and where they are located in storage. If a program is not a resident in storage, it is acquired from the program library and loaded.

Should a program check occur, the DC monitor must intercept it so that the other tasks executing within the partition or region are not abnormally terminated.

File management

As records are read into or written from I-O areas, the file management function must ensure that the I-O operation has been successfully completed.

Multitasking and Multithreading

When an operator keys a transaction from a terminal, a task is created. Just as an operating system is typically designed to permit the computer to run multiple programs at the same time (multiprogramming), high-performance DC monitors are designed to handle processing requirements for multiple terminals simultaneously. This concurrent execution of two or more tasks is called **multitasking**, which is diagrammed in Figure 11A.5.

With multitasking, an operator at one terminal could be checking a customer's account balance, another could be posting an inventory receipt, and a

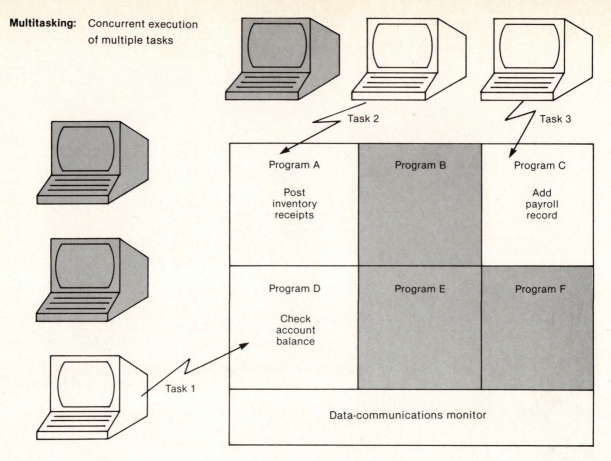

Multitasking: Concurrent execution of multiple tasks

Task 2

Task 3

Program A Post inventory receipts	Program B	Program C Add payroll record
Program D Check account balance	Program E	Program F

Data-communications monitor

Task 1

Figure 11A.5. Multitasking.

third could be adding an employee to the payroll master file. If one operator wanted to check another customer's balance at the same time that the first operator did, they would simultaneously need the services of not only the same computer system but also the same program. Such concurrent execution of a single program is termed **multithreading**, as shown in Figure 11A.6. When a DC monitor provides this capability, it is said to be **multithreaded**; otherwise, it is a **single-threaded** monitor.

Program Design for CICS

On-line programs must be designed differently from batch programs because of the demands that are imposed by multitasking and multithreading. That is, (1) many tasks are executing concurrently and thus vying for real storage space and (2) multiple tasks will be using the same program concurrently. As a result, unlike batch programs, on-line programs tend to be short and handle only one or a limited number of functions for a particular transaction type.

Specific program design concepts in this topic will be discussed in relation to CICS. Two program-design considerations are essential to writing programs that will provide efficient system utilization: page-fault minimization and execution time-span minimization.

Page-Fault Minimization

With virtual storage paging, a certain number of **page** areas are allocated in real storage for program execution. When the program consumes more virtual

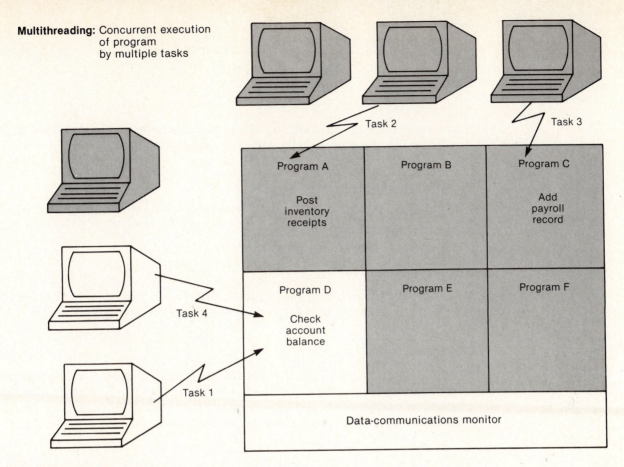

Multithreading: Concurrent execution of program by multiple tasks

Task 2

Task 3

Program A

Post inventory receipts

Program B

Program C

Add payroll record

Task 4

Program D

Check account balance

Program E

Program F

Task 1

Data-communications monitor

Figure 11A.6. Multithreading.

pages than are allocated in real storage and the program must reference instructions or data not currently in real storage, a **page fault** occurs. When this happens, an I-O operation must be performed to bring the virtual page into real storage. As paging increases, system performance, of course, decreases. Three program-design considerations should be considered to minimize page faults: locality of reference, size of the working set, and validity of reference.

Locality of reference

Page faults are minimized by referring to the same or a limited number of pages (in relation to the total number of pages) for longer periods of time. A number of programming techniques can be used to achieve such locality of reference. Observe that some of these techniques run counter to certain structured-programming principles and conventions.

Sequential logic flow.

Straight-line logic flow is the objective. That is, PERFORM and GO TO branches should be kept to a minimum. When control is transferred, the module should be placed as close as possible to its branching PERFORM or GO TO statement.

To minimize transfers of control, short modules that are invoked only once or twice could be replicated in-line. Because GO TO statements need not always return, it is sometimes more efficient to use them than PERFORM statements.

Initialization proximity.

Switches, flags, and other fields should be initialized as close to their first use as possible.

Table organization.

Place table functions adjacent to the table argument for each entry. That is, do not define the arguments and functions in separate tables.

Avoid COBOL statements that require subroutines.

The EXAMINE statement and a variable-length MOVE statement (one in which one of the fields is associated with an OCCURS/DEPENDING ON clause) falls into this category.

Size of the working set

By minimizing the length of the program, the span of storage referred to is, of course, reduced. Techniques to reduce the size of the working set follow.

Design modular programs.

When it is appropriate, functions should be separated into modular programs with regard to frequency and expected time of reference. However, since the tradeoff to modularity is the time required for transfer of control, programs should not be modularized for reasons of size alone.

Use literals in the PROCEDURE DIVISION rather than constant fields in WORKING-STORAGE.

To comprehend the reason for this, one must understand a bit about how CICS handles the program. To provide multitasking capabilities, a program must be **reentrant**. CICS achieves this by taking one **serially reusable** PROCEDURE DIVISION, replicating a copy of the DATA DIVISION for each task. Thus, if three tasks are using a program concurrently, all three tasks use one copy of the PROCEDURE DIVISION whereas there are three copies—one for each task—of the DATA DIVISION. The literal pool is stored with the PROCEDURE DIVISION and hence not replicated, thus conserving storage.

Validity of reference

Validity of reference means direct addressing of the correct page rather than paging through nonapplicable data. It can be compared to using an index to locate a subject rather than paging through a text to find it. This calls for the use of positionally organized tables that can be directly addressed, when possible, in preference to lengthy searches.

Execution Time-Span Minimization

During an on-line processing session, lengthy calculation or lookup processing should, of course, be avoided, if possible. If not, the routine should either be redesigned to better distribute the processing time or utilize a suspend command to permit other transaction processing to proceed.

A particularly severe source of long execution time spans could arise from the conversational nature of on-line operations. While the transaction is taking place, the terminal operator is communicating with the computer system in what is referred to as a conversational mode; an exchange of data is occurring between operator and computer.

However, most operators would feel little compunction about leaving in mid-transaction to get a cup of coffee or answer the telephone. To make the system wait for these delays would seriously degrade performance. Hence applications are normally programmed in what is called a **pseudo-conversational** manner.

Pseudo-conversational programs give the appearance of operating in a conversational mode although they actually are not. After a message or screen is transmitted to the terminal, the task is terminated. This frees the system resources so that the computer system need not be "waiting for" the operator. Once the operator completes the keying of the transaction and depresses an enter key, a task is again initiated. The program processes the data, returns the next message or screen to the operator, and terminates the task. Thus the system is being used only for those short intervals between the transmission of entered data and regeneration of the screen display.

■ TOPIC 11-B: **On-Line Application Design Considerations**

System/Operator Dialogue
    Presentation/Collection Dialogue
        Fill-in-the-blanks format
        Free-form panel
        Code-selection format
    Question and Answer Dialogue
Screen Panel Design Guidelines
    General
    Menu Design
    Text Presentation
    Data Presentation
    Messages and Replies
Response Time
Data Validation
Concurrency
    Concurrent Update Problems
        Lost updates
        Voided entries
        Phantom processing
    Lockout

A VDT with a display screen and keyboard is the link by which most users communicate with an on-line system. Well-formed system/operator dialogue, together with display screen panels of good design, not only contributes to the acceptance of and satisfaction with a system but also can produce processing efficiencies—both for the user and for the computer system. This topic will discuss system/operator dialogue, screen panel design, and related on-line application design subjects.

System/Operator Dialogue

With regard to on-line systems, a dialogue is the exchange of information between the computer system and a terminal operator. Two basic types of dialogue are (1) presentation/collection and (2) question and answer (prompting).

Presentation/Collection Dialogue

The bulk of on-line transaction processing system dialogue is of the **presentation/collection** type. Information is presented to the operator so that data can be collected from the operator response. The information that is presented can be classified as either text or data. **Text presentation** is the display of constant data such as titles, captions, and explanations. **Data presentation** is the display of variable fields from one or more of the logical records for the application. Data entry into the system is considered **data collection**.

There are three general categories of application functions for on-line transaction processing systems: inquiry, file maintenance/update, and data collection.

An **inquiry** function is one in which the operator requests data from the system, such as the display of a passenger list for a flight from an airline reservation system. Inquiries result mainly in data presentation, some text presentation, and only an incidental amount of data entry.

For a **file maintenance/update** function, the operator is adding, changing, or deleting a record or specific data elements within the on-line files. Adding a flight to the airline schedule or reserving a seat on a flight are examples. Updates contain a mix of text presentation, data presentation, and data collection aspects.

A pure **data collection** function is much like data entry for a batch application. It is sometimes used to prepare inputs for batch processing or to fulfill high-volume data-entry requirements for an on-line system. Creating files, converting files, or making large-scale data additions are examples. Data-collection applications have some text presentation and limited data-presentation requirements.

In addition to application function, dialogue design will be affected by the type of operator. There are two general types of operators that will use a system: dedicated or casual.

A **dedicated operator** is typically found within the data-processing department or another high processing-volume group. A data-entry operator who spends the full shift at the terminal is an example. With the trend toward distributed data processing, dedicated operators for a particular application are now frequently found closer to the source of the input—in the plant, at a branch sales office, or at a remote warehouse, for example. Operating personnel who have been trained in and are frequent users of the system can also be considered dedicated operators, even though they may perform other job functions.

A **casual operator** is someone who has received minimal, if any, formal training on the system and uses it only infrequently or for a limited range of functions. This type of operator will, of course, require more explicit instructions and help functions than the dedicated operator. Recognize that the dedicated operator for one application may be a casual operator for another.

There are three general formats for presentation/collection dialogue: fill-in-the-blanks, free form, and code selection.

Fill-in-the-blanks format

Also called **fixed-form, fill-in-the-blanks** format is the most common choice for most inquiry and file update applications. It permits the screen image to resemble a source document. Part A of Figure 11B.1 shows an example. A fill-in-the-blanks format is a particularly good choice for casual operators because it is readily understandable to most users.

A variation to the fill-in-the-blanks form is the **check-or-change option**. This approach can speed data entry when the data to be entered is relatively uniform in value or when the program can determine the probable value. With this option, the expected response value is displayed on the screen. The operator

Part A: Fill-in-the-blanks format

```
┌──────────────────────────────────────────────────────────────────────────┐
│   ┌────────────────────────────────────────────────────────────────────┐  │
│   │                                                                      │  │
│   │  04/17/84                  EMPLOYEE NEW-HIRE               EMP001    │  │
│   │                                                                      │  │
│   │               SS NBR: _____   DEPT NBR: _____                  │  │
│   │                                                                      │  │
│   │     EMP NAME (LAST/FIRST/MID): _____               │  │
│   │                                                                      │  │
│   │                    ADDRESS: _____          │  │
│   │                                                                      │  │
│   │                       CITY: _____  ST: __  ZIP: _____   │  │
│   │                                                                      │  │
│   │                  TELEPHONE: _____                              │  │
│   │                                                                      │  │
│   │  DATE OF BIRTH: _____   SEX: _   MAR STAT: _   NBR. EXEMPTIONS: __ │  │
│   │                                                                      │  │
│   │  PAY CODE: _   RATE: _____   DATE OF HIRE: _____   EXT: _____│  │
│   │                                                                      │  │
│   │                                                                      │  │
│   │                                          PF4 TO RETURN TO MAIN MENU  │  │
│   │                                          PF5 TO REFRESH SCREEN       │  │
│   │                                                                      │  │
│   └────────────────────────────────────────────────────────────────────┘  │
└──────────────────────────────────────────────────────────────────────────┘
```

Part B: Free-form panel

```
┌──────────────────────────────────────────────────────────────────────────┐
│   ┌────────────────────────────────────────────────────────────────────┐  │
│   │                                                                      │  │
│   │  04/17/84                SALES LEAD MEMORANDUM            SLS212     │  │
│   │                                                                      │  │
│   │                                                                      │  │
│   │  FORMAT=CONTACT PERSON; CO-NAME; TEL-NBR; DT NXT CONTACT (MMDDYY); COMMENTS │
│   │                                                                      │  │
│   │  JOAN PARSONS;MARQUIS PRODUCTS;4085552525;100184;ADVISE STATUS OF #225 │ │
│   │                                                                      │  │
│   │  STEVE BROWNE;UNITED MACHINE AND FOUNDRY;4155558798;011085;DETERMINE IF BUDGET │
│   │  APPROVED FOR 8 #8106                                                 │  │
│   │                                                                      │  │
│   │  DAVID GARIBALDI;TEMPO;;051184;BE SURE TO GET BACK TO HIM WITH INSTRUCTIONS ON │
│   │  HOW TO HANDLE 8105/8117 INTERFACE                                   │  │
│   │                                                                      │  │
│   └────────────────────────────────────────────────────────────────────┘  │
└──────────────────────────────────────────────────────────────────────────┘
```

Part C: Code-selection format

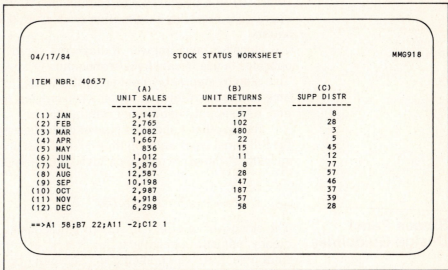

```
   04/17/84                STOCK STATUS WORKSHEET            MMG918

   ITEM NBR: 40637
                         (A)              (B)              (C)
                      UNIT SALES      UNIT RETURNS      SUPP DISTR
                      ------------    ------------      ------------
       (1)  JAN          3,147             57                8
       (2)  FEB          2,765            102               28
       (3)  MAR          2,082            480                3
       (4)  APR          1,667             22                5
       (5)  MAY            836             15               45
       (6)  JUN          1,012             11               12
       (7)  JUL          5,876              8               77
       (8)  AUG         12,587             28               57
       (9)  SEP         10,198             47               46
      (10)  OCT          2,987            187               37
      (11)  NOV          4,918             57               39
      (12)  DEC          6,298             58               28

   ==>A1 58;B7 22;A11 -2;C12 1
```

Figure 11B.1.   Screen panel formats.

can either check and accept it or change it by keying in an override value. The disadvantage to this method is that, unless the operator conscientiously checks each default entry, some erroneous entries will probably enter the system.

Free-form panel

Data fields of a **free-form** panel are separated by delimiters, as shown in Part B of Figure 11B.1. A free-form panel is appropriate for data-collection applications because it minimizes cursor positioning requirements and typically permits multiple transactions to be entered on one panel.

The free-form panel is considerably more difficult for a casual operator to use than the fixed-form panel. However, for a high-volume situation with a dedicated operator—as many data-collection applications are—an experienced operator usually prefers free-form input because it allows more rapid, less interrupted keying.

Code-selection format

Code-selection is a modified free-form approach that employs the use of codes or keywords. Its applications are limited, but this form of panel is sometimes used when a variable number of differing fields of the same general type must be entered. An example is shown in Part C of Figure 11B.1.

Use of a code-selection panel should typically be restricted to dedicated operators.

Question and Answer Dialogue

Question and answer dialogue is appropriate for interactive communication requirements. Instead of the full panel orientation of presentation/collection dialogues, it is characterized by line-by-line transmission. The system transmits a question, usually called a **prompt**, to the operator. The operator responds to the prompt, and it is transmitted back to the system. Based upon the response, the system presents another prompt and the process is repeated until the transaction has been consummated. If the system detects any erroneous input, the operator is notified immediately.

This type of dialogue is typically used when many diverse paths could be taken to the completion of the transaction. That is, a situation exists in which each specific step to be taken is based upon the previous response. Thus question and answer dialogue is not frequently used when the operator is making reference to a prepared source document, but it could be employed when an operator is receiving information piecemeal, such as from a telephone conversation.

Question and answer dialogue is typically the easiest for the casual operator to use because the transaction is broken into short, separate entries. This step-by-step entry minimizes the feeling of being overwhelmed, provides time for the operator to think between entries, permits convenient error correction, and supplies continuing reinforcement.

On the other hand, this type of dialogue requires more transmissions than the full panel types and will thus be slow and probably annoying to experienced operators who are working on high-volume applications.

Screen Panel Design Guidelines

The objectives of effective screen panel design are to maximize operator efficiency, minimize operator input errors, and provide operator satisfaction. A final objective, which should not normally be considered until after the preceding ones, is to optimize computer processing and communications line transmission time. This section will present some panel design guidelines.

General

Identify the panel

Just as it is necessary to identify a printed report, each panel should contain identifying fields. Generally, every panel should have a title and be identified with a panel number or code. The panel number is the logical equivalent of a report or form number. If the panel data can extend beyond the screen boundaries and thus require multiple page images, a page number should be provided. Often the current date is displayed on the report for convenience. If the effective date of the data is earlier than the current date, it is important to display the applicable date.

Standardize panel identification, error, and instructional message areas

Having the panel identification items in standard locations from one panel to the next within the application is helpful to users and presents a uniform appearance. It is usually a good practice to center the panel title and to place the panel number at either the left- or right-hand boundary of the screen. Uniform top line locations for dates and page numbers should also be selected.

Error messages should be displayed in a consistent location; the lower left-hand corner is a good spot. Standard instructional messages, such as how to proceed to the next screen or how to back up, should also be placed in a consistent location such as the lower right-hand corner.

Standardize key functions

A number of standard screen and transaction functions are required for on-line systems. Examples are scrolling forward, scrolling backward, returning to the previous screen, advancing to the next screen (in a sequence of screens), and refreshing the screen (that is, erasing all information just entered on the panel). Standard program function keys should be used for a given function. That is, do not use PF8 (program function key 8) to scroll forward at certain times and PF9 at other times.

Position the cursor properly

For data-collection panels, always position the cursor at the location of the first entry. When a panel is rejected to display an erroneous entry, position the cursor at the location of the error (or first error, when there are multiple ones).

Use appropriate attention-getting features

In accordance with available VDT features, use operator attention-getting devices such as dual intensity, underlining, reverse video, blinking characters, audible alarm, and column separators, as discussed in Chapter D. Attention-getting devices should be used on a consistent basis, so that their meaning is immediately associated. However, the programmer/analyst should guard against excessive use of them, for not only will their value be diminished but they will also become distracting.

Consider color and visual aids

If the VDTs that are being used support color and/or graphics, such features can be introduced on a limited basis when it is appropriate. Use of color and graphics is an entire field of its own. One suggestion for the programmer/analyst in regard to the use of color is to choose colors with regard to their meaning within the workplace or with a generally accepted use. For example, green indicates go or normal, yellow means caution, and red means stop, danger, or error.

Provide help-screens

A **help-screen** is one or more panels dedicated to the display of operating instructions and examples. It is typically selected by depression of a program function key. Help-screens permit normal screen explanations to be brief for the experienced operator; they also make available more detailed explanations for the inexperienced or casual operator.

Menu Design

A **menu** is a panel that presents a list of application function choices from which the operator can select a choice. Figure 11B.2 shows examples. When menu panels are used extensively, the system is sometimes termed a **menu-driven** system.

Format the panel properly

Each function choice should be described clearly and concisely, listed as a left-justified column, and positioned in the center of the screen.

Organize the choices logically

For menus with a smaller number of options (perhaps seven or fewer), the choices should be ordered by sequence of occurrence, if applicable. Otherwise, the choices should be listed by frequency of occurrence, with the more frequently used functions listed first.

Functions for menus that have no sequence or usage patterns or that contain a larger number of options should be listed in alphabetical order.

Use hierarchical menus for large choice lists

When the number of choices is great or the application requirements suggest it, hierarchical menus should be designed. With hierarchical menus, the top-level menu that displays the primary functions or choices is displayed on what is called the **main menu.** Lower-level menus nested beneath it are termed **subordinate** or **subsystem menus.**

When the menus are nested more than two levels, a "menu-skip" option should be provided so that experienced users can proceed more directly to the panel they desire.

Both inexperienced and experienced users generally require a "menu-backtrack" capability so that, should the user make an erroneous choice, he or she can return to the point at which the error occurred. It is a nice touch to highlight the selection that was previously made as the backtrack is in process.

Limit the choices to available options

If certain functions are restricted by password or terminal identification and are thus not available to a particular user, such options should be omitted from the displayed list. In other words, make password and security restrictions "transparent" to the operator.

Consider the menu response method

There are two approaches to handling menu responses: adjacent multiple-selection fields and single-selection field. With **adjacent multiple-selection fields**, a response field is positioned to the left of each alternative. The **single-selection field** approach uses a single field—positioned at the top or bottom of the list—for entry of the menu selection.

The single-selection field is usually preferable, especially for longer menu lists. The advantage is that cursor movement is minimized with a single field.

Hierarchical menus

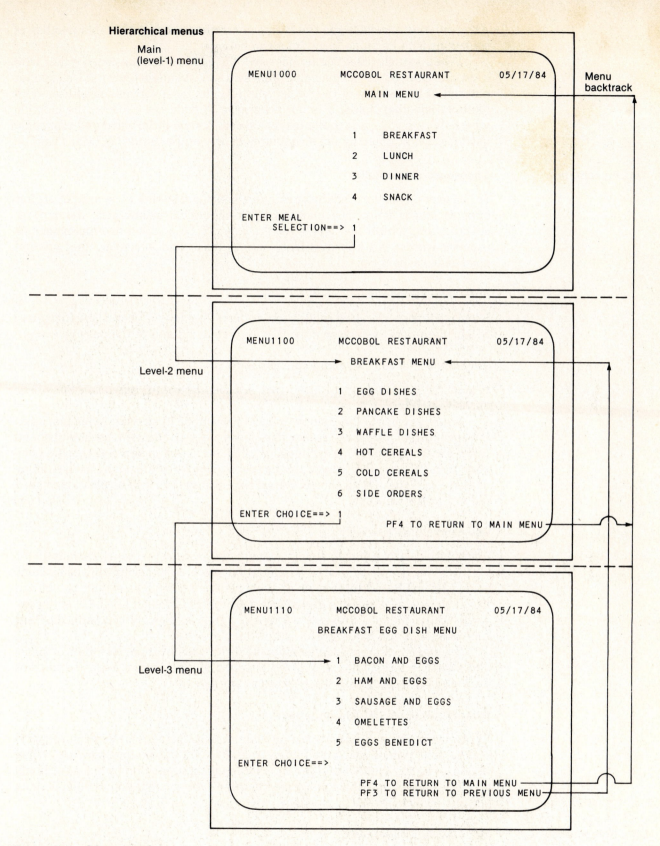

Main
(level-1) menu

Menu
backtrack

```
MENU1000          MCCOBOL RESTAURANT          05/17/84

                        MAIN MENU


              1      BREAKFAST

              2      LUNCH

              3      DINNER

              4      SNACK

   ENTER MEAL
      SELECTION==> 1
```

Level-2 menu

```
MENU1100          MCCOBOL RESTAURANT          05/17/84

                      BREAKFAST MENU


              1   EGG DISHES

              2   PANCAKE DISHES

              3   WAFFLE DISHES

              4   HOT CEREALS

              5   COLD CEREALS

              6   SIDE ORDERS

   ENTER CHOICE==> 1

                      PF4 TO RETURN TO MAIN MENU
```

Level-3 menu

```
MENU1110          MCCOBOL RESTAURANT          05/17/84

                   BREAKFAST EGG DISH MENU


              1   BACON AND EGGS

              2   HAM AND EGGS

              3   SAUSAGE AND EGGS

              4   OMELETTES

              5   EGGS BENEDICT

   ENTER CHOICE==>

                  PF4 TO RETURN TO MAIN MENU
                  PF3 TO RETURN TO PREVIOUS MENU
```

Figure 11B.2. Menu panels.

Adjacent multiple-selection fields are convenient when a variable number of selections is to be made from the menu list.

When a single-selection field is used, the options must be coded either with a choice number or a mnemonic abbreviation. A single-digit choice number entered at the bottom of the list is generally the most convenient to use. With multiple-selection fields, it is not necessary to code the choices; the location where the entry is made indicates the choice. A straightforward and commonly used method of entering the selection is by keying the letter "Y" (for **yes**).

Text Presentation

Choose words carefully

For ease of inspection and interpretation, short words should be used in preference to longer ones. The chosen words should be meaningful, descriptive, specific, and within the user's vocabularly. To be avoided are ambiguous or esoteric words and abbreviations, contractions, and acronyms that are not commonly recognized.

Form brief sentences

Short sentences are more readily understood than longer ones. Use affirmative rather than negative statements. Use the active instead of the passive voice.

Structure sentences and paragraphs properly

If a sentence or paragraph describes a series of events, sequence the words chronologically.

Studies indicate that people tend to remember longer the items placed at the beginning of a message rather than those placed at the end. Items embedded in the middle of a message are the most difficult to remember. Hence more complex items or those that require longer recall should be placed at the beginning of messages. Those with shorter recall requirements should be positioned near the end of the message.

Use punctuation sparingly

Place periods at the end of complete sentences and elsewhere where helpful for clarification. However, other punctuation such as commas and semicolons should be minimized by the use of short sentences. Periods should be omitted from common contractions and acronyms such as *CPA* and *LIFO*. Do not break words at the end of a line with a hyphen. If the word will not fit on the current line, move it to the next line.

Special characters such as the symbols for greater than, less than, at signs, and crosshatches should be avoided because they are less standard and more difficult to interpret than the equivalent words.

Provide "white space" appropriately

Paragraphs should be separated by a blank line. On a normal 80-column-wide screen, text collections should span from 50 to 65 characters per line. When text is arranged in columns, the columns should be separated by at least 3 blank spaces if the column has a uniformly justified right margin and at least 5 blank spaces for a ragged right margin.

Data Presentation

Limit the data displayed

Don't overload the operator with data. When too much information is displayed, it not only consumes additional operator time to find the sought-for data but also is a source for error. Display only the information required by the operator to perform the task, make related decisions, and answer typical inquiries. If auxiliary data is required for exception conditions, consider a hierarchical panel display option in which the operator can request an auxiliary screen with the exception data.

Position data properly

Position the data that is most frequently requested or referred to in or near the upper left-hand corner of the screen. When displays span multiple panels, ensure that frequently referred to information is on the first or earlier panels.

A top-to-bottom, left-to-right, columnar presentation generally provides the best organization for single-panel displays. For multiple-page displays, top-to-bottom orientation should be used for those entries that will take a variable number of lines. Left-to-right, top-to-bottom formatting can be used for short, sequenced entries to minimize the page span.

Present data in a directly usable form

Don't make the operator look up the meaning of codes, add up columns, or make other calculations. Design the panel and the system so that the program handles those functions.

Standardize the presentation of like fields

Operators locate the field they are looking for by scanning the screen to find a recognizable format. Therefore, fields such as dates, times, codes, and names should always be presented in the same format. For example, in the United States, a date should typically be presented in mm/dd/yy format and separated by slashes. Don't display it sometimes with the year first or at times separated by hyphens and at some other times separated by blank spaces.

Always try to present data in its familiar, everyday format. A name and address, for example, should be displayed in the sequence and format that people are familiar with, not in a jumbled presentation.

Caption fields consistently

Field captions should be expressed in clear, concise language on a uniform basis. For example, always refer to a customer account code number by the same terminology. Do not call it a customer code on one panel and an account number on another.

Differentiate captions from data

Differentiation of captions from data should be made by position, separating character, and/or other visual features. Suggested guidelines follow:

Single-occurrence fields or fields with multiple occurrences on the same horizontal line (row format). Position the caption to the left of the data. Separate the caption from the data by a colon and a blank space. As an alternative separator, two equal signs and a greater than sign (= = >) is sometimes used.

Multiple-occurrence fields in column format. Position the caption above the data column. Either center the caption or justify it in accordance with the data justification. That is, for left-justified alphanumeric data, justify the caption toward the left above the data column; for right-justified numeric data, justify the caption to the right.

Captions should typically be presented in upper-case and at normal intensity.

Messages and Replies

Keep the operator informed

If a record retrieval, table lookup, or other processing operation is going to take longer than the normal response time, it is a good idea to display a message that informs the operator that the task is in process. It is discomforting to an operator if, after making an entry, either the screen goes blank or nothing happens for an extended period of time.

Consider message level

Novice operators need complete error messages; experienced operators usually prefer concise error indications. Some systems handle this situation by providing two message levels—sometimes called **verbose** and **terse**—for the operator to select from.

Avoid humor and punishment

Although a little humor is sometimes fun the first time a message is encountered, it does not wear well and will soon become annoying to an operator. On the other hand, disciplinary messages are not only threatening to the rookie operator but are also unnecessary. Helpful messages will quickly produce the desired results.

Response Time

With on-line processing, **response time** is the interval between (1) the time the operator enters a command and (2) the time the computer responds. As was shown in Figure 11A.1, acceptable response times vary depending upon the system type.

Although provision and maintenance of acceptable response times are largely dependent upon hardware planning and systems programming groups, the programmer/analyst should be aware of the following general guidelines.

1. Operators will generally accept longer response times for requests perceived to be more complicated.
2. Operators will generally accept longer response times for those commands placed at a recognizable end or closure point of a series of entries.
3. Studies have indicated that the variability of response times is typically more discomforting to users than is the length of the response time. In other words, operators will become accustomed to the usual response time. Intervals longer than normal are the frustrating ones.

    This consideration can cause a problem as new on-line applications are added to the workload of the hardware. The first application to go on-line will typically provide rapid response rates. As new applications are added, the system will bog down under the increased workload, and the longer response times will be unfavorably received. To counter this situation, many installations artificially delay response times during the early, unloaded application period.

Data Validation

Considerations regarding data validation at initial input for on-line processing are essentially the same as those for batch processing. However, there are a couple of variations that the programmer/analyst must sometimes provide for.

First, numeric fields are typically left-justified rather than decimal point aligned or right-justified during initial input. Although such alignment and justification are handled automatically by certain compilers and software aids, the programmer is often responsible for such data positioning within the field

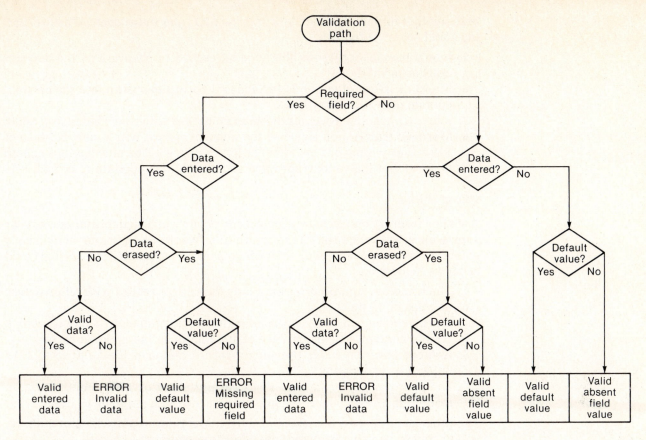

Figure 11B.3. Data validation logic for on-line data entry.

(as is the case with CICS). Applicable logic for validating and justifying numeric amount fields is presented in Chapter C.

Second, an erased field may be presented differently than a null, or non-entered, field. For example, with CICS systems, an erased field contains a hexa-decimal value of '80' whereas a null field is represented with binary zeros.

This is an important consideration because default values for non-entered and erased fields are commonly used with on-line processing rather than the field duplication or filling during data entry technique often used for batch processing. Figure 11B.3 provides a data-validation flowchart that incorporates such default-processing logic.

Concurrency

Concurrency considerations are usually minimal for batch processing because only one program is typically updating a file at any particular time. However, with multitasking and multithreading on-line systems, the sharing of records and files between two or more tasks can cause inconsistent results to occur.

Concurrent Update Problems

There are three major sources of errors caused by concurrent updates: lost updates, voided entries, and phantom processing.

Lost updates

Suppose John and Marcia have a joint checking account with a $500 balance. During his lunch-hour, John deposits $100 in the account through the automatic teller machine. By coincidence, across town at the exact same instant, Marcia uses another automatic teller to withdraw $20 from the account. The processing could occur as follows:

1. John's transaction reads the account record to ensure that the account number is valid.
2. Marcia's transaction reads the account record to ensure that the account contains the necessary funds.
3. John's transaction rewrites the account record with a new balance of $600.
4. Marcia's transaction rewrites the account record with a new balance of $480, thus wiping out the effect of John's deposit. The new balance should be $580, but the concurrent updates caused John's update to be lost.

Voided entries

A similar form of concurrency problem can occur when an operator corrects or aborts an erroneous entry. Take a situation where an operator erroneously enters an inventory receipt of 1000 widgets and then voids it. Processing could occur as follows:

1. The inventory update program reads the widget record with an inventory balance of 17 units.
2. The inventory update program adds the receipt value of 1000 units, which results in an erroneous balance of 1017 units on the updated record.
3. Another program reads the widget record and uses the balance of 1017 units in its processing.
4. The operator voids the erroneous receipt entry of 1000 units and, as a result, the widget record balance is returned to a value of 17 units.

The program that read the widget record in the interim period, point 3 above, will of course be using incorrect data for its processing.

Phantom processing

Let us say that Sam is registered at Silicon Valley State and decides to drop DP64 and to add ZOO101. At the time his drop-and-add is being processed, course rosters are being printed. The processing could occur as follows:

1. The roster program prints the DP64 roster with Sam as a member of the class.
2. The drop-and-add program drops Sam from DP64.
3. The drop-and-add program adds Sam to ZOO101.
4. The roster program prints the ZOO101 roster with Sam as a member of the class.

Thus, Sam will appear as a "phantom record" on the DP64 roster.

Another form of phantom processing could occur if Sam's sister Samantha transferred $100 from her checking account number 11-1111 to Sam's account number 88-8888 while, at the same time, the bank was preparing an account balance list. The processing could occur as follows:

1. The account balance list program reads Samantha's account 11-1111 and lists a balance of $300.
2. The account update program deducts $100 from Samantha's account, so that the updated record has a balance of $200.
3. The account update program reads Sam's account 88-8888 with a balance of $25 and adds the deposit of $100, so that the updated record has a balance of $125.
4. The account balance list program reads Sam's account 88-8888 and lists a balance of $125.

Clearly, the account balance list will show a total that is $100 greater than it actually should because of the phantom processing.

Lockout

The solution to concurrent update problems is to restrict one record file from other tasks while the record or file is being used by another task. Such handling is called **lockout**, or **locking**. There are two types of locking: shared locks and exclusive locks.

A **shared lock** is typically used when a task is reading but not updating records. This permits other concurrent tasks to also read the record, but it prevents them from updating the record. An **exclusive lock** is granted to a task that is updating a record. This type of lock prevents any other task from either reading or writing data from or to the record and/or file.

An exclusive record lock on a single record will counter the lost update and voided entry problems. To solve phantom processing problems, an exclusive lock against additions and modifications to the entire file is required.

When one task locks two or more sets of data and another task simultaneously competes for an exclusive lock on two of the same sets, **deadlock** may occur. An example is as follows:

1. Task 1 places an exclusive lock on data resource A.
2. Task 2 places an exclusive lock on data resource B.
3. Task 1 attempts to place an exclusive lock on data resource B. Because data resource B is currently locked, Task 1 must wait.
4. Task 2 attempts to place an exclusive lock on data resource A. Because data resource A is currently locked, Task 2 must wait.

As a result of the above events, Task 1 is waiting for Task 2 to release B. However, Task 2 cannot release B because it is waiting for Task 1 to release A. This deadlock, more colorfully referred to as a **deadly embrace**, causes the system to hang up because of the resulting circular wait chain.

Lockout provisions are provided by most data-communications monitors. However, the programmer/analyst must typically select the proper options and design the system in a manner that will ensure that data integrity and system performance are maintained.

Summary

Topic 11-A Characteristics of On-Line Systems

There are a number of differences between **on-line** and **batch** systems.

A **data-communications monitor** (also referred to as a **teleprocessing** or a **telecommunications monitor**) runs as a job under control of the operating system to handle the on-line applications that the computer must process. DC monitors typically provide terminal, task, storage, program, and file-management facilities.

Concurrent execution of two or more tasks is called **multitasking**. Concurrent execution of a single program by two or more tasks is termed **multithreading**.

When designing on-line programs operating under CICS, the programmer should seek to minimize page-faults and execution time. Page-fault minimization can be achieved by locality of reference, reduction of the working set size, and validity of reference. Execution time can be minimized by effective program design and programming in a **pseudo-conversational** manner.

Topic 11-B On-Line Application Design Considerations

With regard to on-line systems, **dialogue** is the exchange of information between the computer system and a terminal operator. Two basic types of dialogue are (1) presentation/collection and (2) question and answer.

The bulk of on-line transaction processing dialogue is of the **presentation/collection** type. **Text presentation** is the display of constant data. **Data presentation** is the display of variable fields. **Data collection** is data entry into the system.

Application functions for on-line transaction processing systems can be categorized as **inquiry, file maintenance/update**, or **data collection**.

General screen panel guidelines are as follows:

- Identify the panel.
- Standardize panel identification, error, and instructional message areas.
- Standardize key functions.
- Position the cursor properly.
- Use appropriate attention-getting features.
- Consider color and visual aids.
- Provide help-screens.

Menu design guidelines are as follows:

- Format the panel properly.
- Organize the choices logically.
- Use hierarchical menus for large choice lists.
- Limit the choices to available options.
- Consider the menu response method.

Text-presentation guidelines are as follows:

- Choose words carefully.
- Form brief sentences.
- Structure sentences and paragraphs properly.
- Use punctuation sparingly.
- Provide "white space" appropriately.

Data-presentation guidelines are as follows:

- Limit the data displayed.
- Position data properly.
- Present data in a directly usable form.
- Standardize the presentation of like fields.
- Caption fields consistently.
- Differentiate captions from data.

Messages and replies guidelines are as follows:

- Keep the operator informed.
- Consider message level.
- Avoid humor and punishment.

Response time is the interval between (1) the time the operator enters a command and (2) the time the computer responds.

Two data-validation considerations for on-line processing that do not normally apply to batch data validation are (1) alignment of numeric data within a field and (2) differentiation of an erased field from a blank or null value.

There are three major sources of errors caused by concurrent updates: lost updates, voided entries, and phantom processing.

The solution to concurrent update problems is to **lockout** records being updated. A **shared lock** is typically used when a task is reading but not updating a record. An **exclusive lock** is granted to a task that is updating a record.

When one task locks two or more sets of data and another task simultaneously competes for an exclusive lock, **deadlock** (often called a **deadly embrace**) may occur.

HARDWARE/SOFTWARE CONCEPTS
CHAPTER E

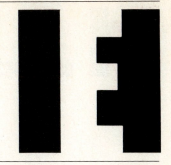

DATA-BASE MANAGEMENT SYSTEMS

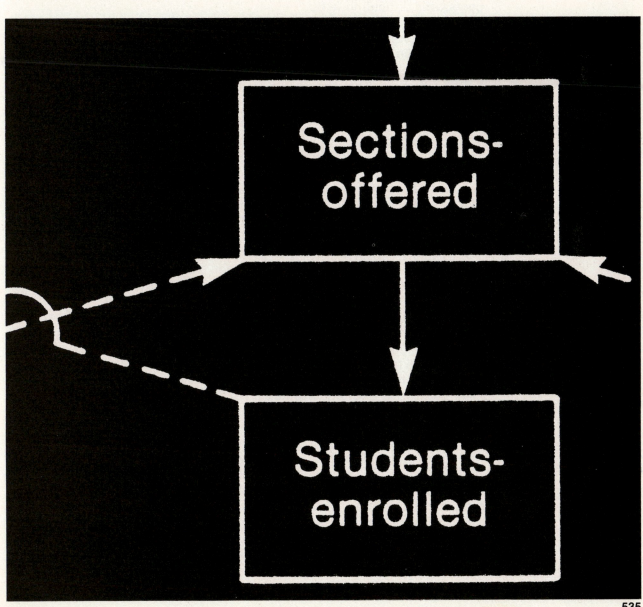

▐ DATA-BASE MANAGEMENT SYSTEMS

After the introduction of the commercial digital computer in the early 1950s, computer system applications for business organizations multiplied. Throughout the 1950s and especially the 1960s, many application systems were implemented and myriad programs were written.

Problems of File-Oriented Systems

As more and more of an organization's data-processing functions were assigned to the computer, the deficiencies of regular file-processing methods began to surface. As an increasing amount of data was collected and stored, it became more and more difficult to efficiently maintain the burgeoning inventory of computer programs. Further, requests for new outputs and applications were unnecessarily difficult to fulfill.

These problems arose because of certain traits of traditional file-oriented application systems. These systems tend to isolate data into individual files. Because of the isolation, redundant data must be introduced into files. All of the programs that access a particular file are dependent upon the data specifications for that file. These aspects of traditional systems of data isolation, data redundancy, and data dependency will be briefly discussed.

Data Isolation

To keep a data-processing project targeted within a manageable scope, files are typically created for each specific application need. Programs within each application area usually access only those files that are dedicated to that application. Consider, for example, the processing for a college or university. As shown in part A of Figure E.1, the payroll system contains an employee file, the class-scheduling system contains a class-offerings file, and the student-records system contains a student file.

To prepare payroll checks, the payroll system accesses the employee file. When class schedules are to be printed, the class-scheduling system uses the class-offerings file. The student-records system posts grades to the student file so that grade reports and transcripts can be prepared from it.

Each of these file-oriented systems may well be effective in preparing the specific output for which it was designed. That is, the payroll system may do an excellent job in getting correct payroll checks out on time. The class-scheduling system might produce factual, convenient class schedules. The student-records system may issue timely, accurate grade reports and transcripts. However, most businesses and organizations exist in a dynamic environment. As requirements change, new or modified outputs from data-processing systems are needed.

Because of the isolation of data into separate files and systems, requests for reports that require data from multiple file-oriented systems are difficult to fulfill. Suppose that an administrative official of the college wants to know the average hourly cost of the instruction that is offered to adults who are registered for night classes. This requires access to the files of the three separate systems. The programmer/analyst who must satisfy such an output request will probably be confronted with incompatibility and complexity problems. For example, the systems may use different computer equipment or the files may not

Part A: File-oriented systems

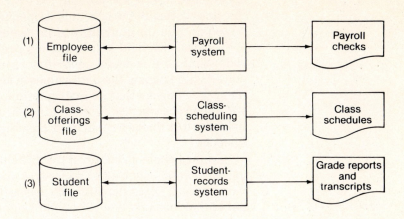

Part B: Data-base management system

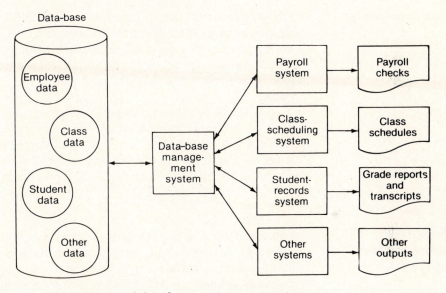

Figure E.1. File-oriented and data-base management systems.

be recorded in compatible formats. The records within one or more of the files will probably require formatting and sorting into an appropriate sequence for processing. Worse yet, the relationships between data entities or records from one file to the next may be ill-defined or not readily apparent. Because efforts to overcome these incompatibility and complexity problems can be time-consuming and complex, they are not only expensive but fraught with complications and unknowns.

Data Redundancy

Because file-oriented systems foster the propagation of isolated files for each application area, data fields must be duplicated from one file to the next.

In the college/university system example, it is, of course, necessary to carry an instructor's name in the employee record so that it can be printed on his or her paycheck. The name is also required in at least one record within the class-scheduling system so that the instructor's identity will appear adjacent to the class listing in the schedule. Depending upon the system design, it may also be required in the student-records system.

Even if the field is lengthy, the problem that is posed by such duplicate, redundant data is seldom one of storage space. Instead, it is the difficulty involved with keeping the data values synchronized from one field occurrence to the next. Suppose that an instructor marries. A name change may result. Control and processing requirements mushroom when changes occurring to data in fields such as this are replicated in multiple records and in different application systems.

Many people complain of the difficulties that they have experienced in trying to get data—such as an address or account balance—changed within a computer system. Often the difficulty arises not because the change was not applied but rather because not all of the required changes were correctly made. A related lament is the one heard when a person requests what he or she thinks is a minor change, and then is handed a motley bundle of transmittal forms to fill out. Once again, redundant data is the culprit.

Data Dependency

File-oriented programs access each data file independently. That is, the file descriptions, record descriptions, and field definitions for every data file that the program will access is hard-coded within each program. Then, when even small changes are made to any of these specifications, some or all of the programs that reference that file must be modified, recompiled, relink-edited, and tested.

Not only do these tasks consume programmer and computer time, they increase management and control requirements. Each time a change is made, it is necessary to coordinate, schedule, and implement the changeover to the new program versions. Simply keeping track of which programs are affected by a given data-specification change can be a challenge unto itself.

Data-Base Management Systems

These problems of data isolation, data redundancy, and data dependency tend to result in inefficient, unresponsive data-processing services. Data-base management systems were developed to counter this predicament.

A **data base** can be defined as a collection of data that is organized to fulfill the information requirements of a body of users on a timely basis. The **data-base management system (DBMS)** is a software product that is designed to manage the data base through its organization, access, control, security, and recovery facilities.

With data-base management systems, all applications share a single copy of the data. This means that the view of the data can be consistent across all applications. Data relationships across application boundaries are known and defined. Thus the problem of data isolation is checked.

Because all applications share the data base, there is no unplanned data redundancy. (A limited amount of data redundancy is sometimes specified for performance reasons.)

When a DBMS is used, data-definition tasks are separated from the program logic. As a result, little or no programming, recompilation, and retesting are required when data formats change (except, of course, for programs that use new fields added to the data base). Data independence is achieved.

The DBMS is an interface between the application program and the data base. It accepts program requests for data retrieval or update functions. Upon receipt of a request, the DBMS handles the specified security controls, locates the data or storage area and performs I-O error-checking operations. Appropriate data and/or control information is passed back to the application program. The DBMS automatically provides designated statistical, audit trail, and recovery capabilities.

As a result, use of a DBMS permits the programmer to concentrate on application-processing requirements. That is, the programmer can devote his or her attention to solving the business problem as a result of being freed from certain data definition, I-O error handling, security, recovery, and statistical responsibilities.

DBMS Development

The origins of data-base management systems can be traced to efforts to more effectively utilize direct-access storage devices to satisfy manufacturing application system requirements for bill-of-material and associated engineering data control (EDC) and manufacturing requirements planning (MRP) outputs.

Charles W. Bachman is recognized as one of the pioneers in this area. In the early 1960s, while employed by General Electric, he developed a software system to link, or **chain**, together different records of different types. The system was named Integrated Data Store. I-D-S, as it is commonly referred to, was released as a software aid for General Electric mainframe computers in 1964.

Software to fulfill somewhat similar requirements for bill-of-material data was designed in conjunction with the Apollo program at North American Rockwell Corporation in the mid-1960s. This system was called Data Language/1 (DL/1).

During the same period, others in the business, scientific, and academic community were concerned with the task of retrieving information easily from data files. Before the term *data base* was used, the function was generally referred to as "bill-of-material" or "list" processing. The term *list processing* arises from the way that the linked chain of records can be considered to be a list.

In 1963 a software firm headquartered in Southern California, System Development Corporation, sponsored a symposium titled "Development and Management of a Computer-Centered Data Base." In 1965 a second symposium on the subject was held. These meetings are credited with popularizing the term "data base" and generally considered to be the kernel from which the data-base management system discipline has emerged.

A List Processing Task Force was formed in 1965 within the CODASYL (**Con**ference on **Da**ta **Sy**stems **L**anguages) COBOL committee. In 1967 the name of this body was changed to the Data Base Task Group (DBTG). Charles Bachman was a member of this group and I-D-S played a prominent role in the work of the committee.

By 1968 IBM—who had participated in the DL/1 development effort—adopted DL/1 and offered it to its OS users under the name Information Management System (IMS). In 1969, the first DBMS from an independent software company—TOTAL—was released by Cincom Systems.

The initial DBTG report, entitled "COBOL Extensions to Handle Data Bases," was issued in 1968. This was followed in 1969 by the first set of language specifications. The final DBTG report was issued in 1971 and accepted later that year by its parent committee, then called the Programming Language Committee.

During these years, B. F. Goodrich—an I-D-S user—had switched from a GE to an IBM computer. Thus, for their own internal use, they converted the DBMS functions to an IBM-360 computer and named the system Integrated Database

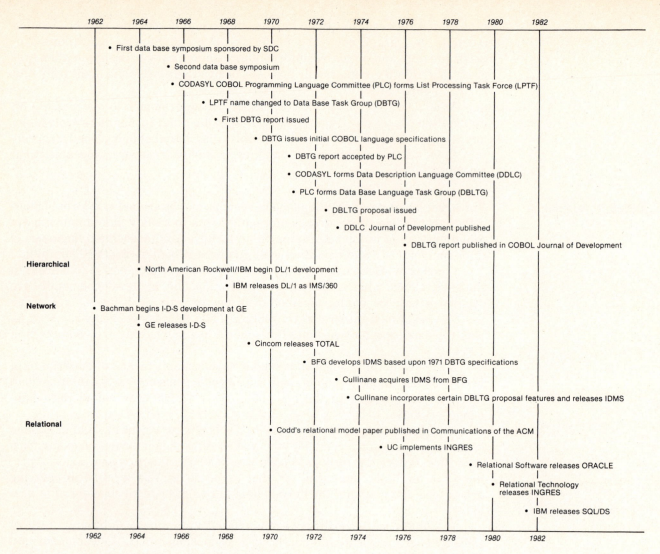

Figure E.2. DBMS development milestones.

Management System (IDMS). It was based on the DBTG specifications and was implemented in early 1972.

After the DBTG report was accepted, CODASYL separated responsibility for definition of the data-description specifications from those for the COBOL program processing. This resulted in formation of a separate CODASYL Data Description Language Committee (DDLC) for the former function and the Data Base Language Task Group (DBLTG)—a COBOL subcommittee—for the latter. DBLTG took the work of DBTG and prepared specifications in a form that could be integrated into the COBOL *Journal of Development*. The result of this effort was released in proposal form in 1973 and published in the CODASYL COBOL *Journal of Development* in 1976.

In the meantime, a software firm—Cullinane Database Systems—acquired IDMS from Goodrich. Certain features of the DBLTG proposal were incorporated into the system, and it was released as a program product for IBM-compatible mainframes in 1974.

Thus, although CODASYL data-base syntax has been published, it has not yet achieved the status of a standard issued through the American National Standards Institute.

One factor—but by no means the only one—that has retarded the CODASYL data-base standards effort is the advent of a data-structure model that is a departure from the network model of the CODASYL standards. This model, termed relational, was described by E. F. Codd in his 1970 article "A Relational Model of Data for Large Shared Data Banks" published in *Communications of the ACM*.

On the basis of that article, a relational DBMS was developed at the University of California, Berkeley. Called INGRES, it was implemented in 1975. The first commercial relational DBMS—ORACLE—was released in 1979 by Relational Software. In 1980, INGRES became a commercial product of Relational Technology. IBM did developmental work on their System R relational DBMS during the 1970s and released it in 1982 under the name SQL/DS.

DBMS development milestones are presented graphically in Figure E.2.

DBMS Characteristics

Although the objectives and functions of data-base management systems tend to converge, specific DBMS products achieve their results by different approaches. Three important DBMS characteristics will be discussed: data-structure models, storage-access methods, and programming languages.

Data-structure models

Data-base management systems are typically categorized as adhering to either a hierarchical, network, or relational data-structure model. As with many classifications, attempting to fit a particular DBMS into one category is sometimes an oversimplification. Nevertheless, a familiarity with the general data-structure models can aid one's comprehension of DBMS fundamentals. Figure E.3 contrasts these three models using the student-records portion of a data base as an example.

The **hierarchical model** is a descendant of the bill-of-material processors of the early 1960s. In the hierarchical model, relationships are expressed as **hierarchies** with **parent** and **child records**. Each child may have only one physical parent.

The hierarchical example in Figure E.3 shows three hierarchies. A solid line indicates a physical relationship. The arrowhead points to the child; the opposite end of the arrow is the parent. Hierarchical systems typically permit additional logical relationships to be expressed. These are indicated by broken lines.

As previously mentioned, the CODASYL specifications describe a **network model**. Relationships of a network model are generally expressed as **sets** of **owner-** and **member-**record types. In network structures, a member can have multiple owners. Hence a hierarchical structure can be considered to be a subset of the network model.

The network example shown in Figure E.3 used a method of graphic representation called—in reference to its originator—a **Bachman diagram**. Record types are identified within rectangles; set relationships are expressed with arrows. Arrows emanate from the owner-record type; the arrowhead points to the member. Names are affixed both to record types and sets.

The **relational model** is a significant departure from the hierarchical and network models. Relations are structured as tables containing columns and rows. The rows correspond to record occurrences; the columns represent fields within the records.

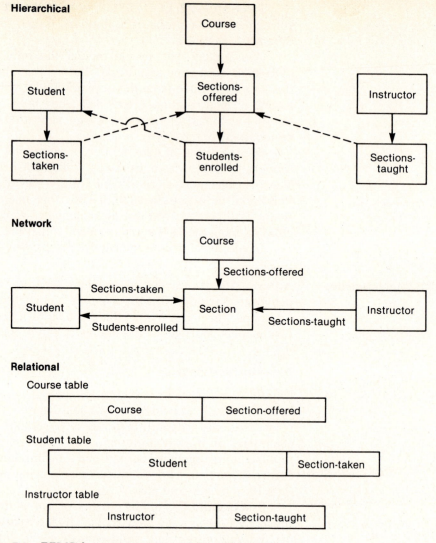

Figure E.3. DBMS data-structure model examples.

Hence the relational example of Figure E.3 shows three tables. Each record-type occurrence is an entry, or row, within the table; each field is considered a column. For example, an institution that offers 1,500 sections would thus have 1,500 rows in the course table. With formal relational terminology, rows are called **tuples**, columns are referred to as **domains**, and tables are named **relations**. New relations are formed by performing **selection**, **projection**, and **join operations** upon the tables.

The hierarchical and network models require the programmer to navigate through the data base to locate record-type occurrences or extract outputs. The relational model, on the other hand, uses **flat-file tables** and supports automatic navigation to the target data.

Storage-access methods

The logical relationships of DBMS data structures must be translated into physical structures for data access. Just as different data-structure models are employed by various data-base management systems, so it also is with storage-access methods.

Access method	Advantages	Disadvantages
Embedded link	Run-time processing efficiency capabilities for pre-defined relationships	Different access paths can require different coding techniques (programmer must navigate)
		Certain output needs will require sort processing prior to presentation
		Not flexible to data-structure requirement changes
Inverted list	Can accommodate changes to data-structure requirements	Processing overhead for add/delete updates and known retrieval requirements
	Minimizes sort requirements	
	Permits "ad hoc" searches and retrievals	
Relational	Easily accommodates changes to data-structure requirements	Risk of inefficient processing
	Nonprocedural data-manipulation language is easy to use	
	Appropriate for user queries	

Figure E.4. Advantages and disadvantages of DBMS access methods.

Hierarchical and network systems typically use either the embedded-link storage-access method or the inverted-list storage-access method. With the **embedded-link method**, the addresses of related records are physically stored in fields within the data records. The embedded-link method is also known by the terms **embedded pointer**, **physical link**, **path access**, and **navigational access**.

The **inverted-list technique** uses separate index records in which the addresses of related records are stored. An inverted list is typically used to process alternate record keys for traditional INDEXED organization files (see Figure 6B.2).

Pre-established relationships between different tables are absent from the relational model. Instead, relationships are determined at execution time. Hence, although index structures are typically used for run-time processing, the storage-access method is usually also termed **relational** to denote the difference in approach.

Figure E.4 summarizes advantages and disadvantages of the various access methods.

Programming languages

For the writing of application programs, most data-base management systems either utilize a **host language** or provide an **independent language**. With the host-language approach, an existing programming language, such as COBOL, is used as the framework within which the DBMS access commands are coded. Most data-base management systems employ host languages.

However, when discussing DBMS languages, one should distinguish between data-description and data-manipulation specifications. Remember that

DBMS	Vendor	Data-structure model	Data-management method	Computer hardware	Host language(s)	Year introduced	Approximate number of users[a]
I-D-S II	Honeywell	Network[b]	Embedded link	Honeywell	COBOL	1964	100
IMS/VS	IBM	Hierarchical	Embedded link	IBM	COBOL PL/1	1968	1,400[e]
TOTAL	Cincom Systems	Network	Embedded link	IBM Burroughs DEC Honeywell NCR Univac	COBOL FORTRAN PL/1 RPG II Assembler[d]	1969	5,500
ADABAS	Software AG	Network	Inverted list	IBM DEC	COBOL FORTRAN PL/1 Assembler[d]	1970	1,100
DMS	Sperry Univac	Network[b]	Embedded link	Univac	COBOL	1970	600
DL/1-DOS/VS	IBM	Hierarchical	Embedded link	DL1/DOS-VS	COBOL	1972	800[e]
SYSTEM 2000	Intel Systems	Hierarchical	Inverted list	IBM CDC Univac	COBOL FORTRAN PL/1 Assembler[d]	1972	600
DBMS-10	Digital Equipment	Network[b]	Embedded link	DEC	COBOL FORTRAN	1973	200
IDMS	Cullinane Data Base Systems	Network[b, c]	Embedded link	IBM	COBOL PL/1 Assembler[d]	1973	1200
DMS-II	Burroughs	Network	Embedded link	Burroughs	COBOL PL/1 ALGOL	1974	100
IMAGE	Hewlett-Packard	Network	Embedded link	H-P	COBOL BASIC FORTRAN RPG	1974	14,000[f]
INGRES	Relational Technology	Relational	Relational	DEC Micros	COBOL BASIC C FORTRAN Pascal	1975[g]	200
DMS-170	Control Data	Network[b, c]	Inverted list	CDC	COBOL	1977	100
DBMS	Prime Computer	Network[b]	Embedded link	Prime	COBOL FORTRAN	1977	200
MDBS	Micro Data Base Systems	Network[c]	Embedded link	Micros	COBOL	1979	3,000
ORACLE	Relational Software	Relational	Relational	IBM DEC	COBOL Assembler[d] BASIC C FORTRAN Pascal PL/1	1979	200
dBASE II	Ashton-Tate	Relational	Relational	Micros	Independent language	1980	12,000
SQL/DS	IBM	Relational	Relational	IBM	COBOL PL/1 Assembler[d]	1982	100[e]

[a] Number of users provided by vendor (9/82) rounded to next hundred.

[b] CODASYL-compliant.

[c] Relational capabilities.

[d] IBM 360/370/3xxx/43xx Assembler Language.

[e] Vendor does not provide user information. Figure based upon best available estimate.

[f] DBMS is distributed with operating system. Figure represents number of operating system users.

[g] Noncommercial installation.

Figure E.5. Characteristics of representative DBMS offerings.

data independence is achieved by separating the data-description function from the program code. Hence host languages are typically used for program logic coding whereas—because traditional programming languages do not include such provisions—the DBMS must provide its own method for specifying the data descriptions.

The CODASYL approach clearly differentiates the two types of language specifications. The Data Description Language (DDL) was designed so that it could be used with various Data Manipulation Languages (DML). The DDLC developed the DDL under the assumption that multiple DMLs—COBOL, PL/1, FORTRAN, for example—would be used for the writing of application programs.

Figure E.5 summarizes characteristics of representative commercially available data-base management systems. Network systems that are based upon the CODASYL specifications are generally referred to as CODASYL-compliant systems. Certain network systems have capabilities that are similar to a relational system's but do not qualify as such according to a strict definition of the term. A relational DBMS is one that has a data language that is equivalent to the relational algebra or relational calculus and contains no user-visible links between tables.

APPENDIXES AND INDEX

APPENDIX A

COBOL LANGUAGE ELEMENTS

This appendix presents definitions and specifications for the COBOL language elements.

Reserved Words

Reserved words have predefined meanings in the COBOL language. A complete list of reserved words is printed facing the inside back cover.

User-Defined Words

The programmer creates user-defined words in accordance with certain rules. A user-defined word must

- be composed only of alphabetic characters (A through Z), digits (0 through 9), and hyphens (-)
- contain at least one letter
- not exceed 30 characters
- not begin or end with a hyphen
- not contain any blank spaces (embedded blanks)
- not be the same as a reserved word

Comment-Entries

Comment-entries may be any combination of characters that are acceptable to the computer. They may be specified in certain IDENTIFICATION DIVISION paragraphs.

Comment-Lines

Comment-lines contain an asterisk (*) in position 7 and contain comments that are not COBOL language elements.

Page-Eject Lines

Page-eject lines contain a diagonal slash (/) in position 7 and are used to control page skipping within the COBOL program.

Literals

Literals may be used to introduce actual values into a program.

Numeric literals must

- be composed only of digits (0 through 9), an arithmetic sign (+ or −), and a decimal point.
- contain at least 1 digit but not more than 18 digits
- contain not more than one sign character (when present it must be the leftmost character of the literal)
- contain not more than one decimal point (a decimal point must *not* be the rightmost character of the literal)

Nonnumeric literals

- must be enclosed by quotation marks
- may contain any characters acceptable to the computer that is being used
- must not exceed 120 characters in length

Figurative Constants

Figurative constants are reserved words that have predefined values.

Figurative constant	Value that fills field
SPACE SPACES	Blank spaces
ZERO ZEROS ZEROES	Zeros
QUOTE QUOTES	Quotation marks
HIGH-VALUE HIGH-VALUES	Highest possible value
LOW-VALUE LOW-VALUES	Lowest possible value
ALL nonnumeric literal	Repeat the specified literal throughout the field

Level Indicators

Level indicators identify a specific type of file or a position in hierarchy.

Level indicator	Identification
FD	File-description entry
SD	Sort file-description entry
RD	Report file-description entry

Level Numbers

Level numbers indicate the position of a data-item in the hierarchical structure of a logical record or special properties of a data-description entry.

Level number	Indication
01	Record-description entry
02 through 49	Data-item description entry
66	Renaming entry
77	Independent data-item description entry
88	Condition-name entry

PICTURE Clauses

PICTURE clauses describe the following characteristics of elementary data-items:

- data class (numeric, alphabetic, alphanumeric, numeric-edited, or alphanumeric-edited)
- size (length)
- location of assumed decimal point (for numeric fields)
- arithmetic sign presence or absence (for numeric fields)
- editing to be performed on the field

PICTURE Character-Strings

Picture character-strings are formed from the following picture symbols:

Numeric symbols	Numeric-editing symbols		Alphabetic symbol	Alphanumeric symbol	Alphanumeric-editing symbols	
9 Digit	Z	Zero suppression with blank-space replacement	A Alphabetic character	X Alphanumeric character	B	Blank space
V Assumed decimal point	*	Zero suppression with asterisk replacement			/	Slash
S Arithmetic sign	,	Comma			0	Zero
P Decimal scaling position	/	Slash				
	B	Blank space				
	0	Zero				
	.	Decimal point				
	−	Minus sign				
	+	Plus sign				
	CR	Credit symbol				
	DB	Debit symbol				
	$	Dollar sign				

Punctuation Characters

Punctuation characters are used to comply with syntactical rules and to aid readability.

Punctuation character	Meaning
.	Period
" or '	Quotation mark
(	Left parenthesis
)	Right parenthesis
	Blank space
,	Comma
;	Semicolon

APPENDIX B

COBOL SYNTAX AND STYLE REFERENCE

This appendix contains a reference summary of syntax and style considerations presented in *Structured COBOL: Fundamentals and Style,* the prerequisite volume to this text. Certain statements and phrases were introduced in the first volume and discussed in greater detail in this text. In such cases, the items are omitted from this appendix; reference should instead be made to the textual portion of this volume.

General Coding

Style recommendations:

- Make user-defined words meaningful and descriptive.
- Use hyphens in user-defined words to separate multiple English words and abbreviations.
- Do not use commas or semicolons as punctuation.
- Provide vertical spacing between divisions, sections, and certain paragraphs by inserting blank comment lines.
- Write only one COBOL sentence, statement, clause, or phrase per coding line.
- When a sentence, statement, or clause extends over multiple coding lines, indent each line after the first.
- When indentation is called for, indent in four-space units. Exceptions are cases where vertical alignment of entries is desired or where four-space indentations consume too much space on the coding line.

IDENTIFICATION DIVISION

Format:

IDENTIFICATION DIVISION.

PROGRAM-ID. program-name.

[AUTHER. [comment-entry] . . .]

[INSTALLATION. [comment-entry] . . .]

[DATE-WRITTEN. [comment-entry] . . .]

[DATE-COMPILED. [comment-entry] . . .]

[SECURITY. [comment-entry] . . .]

Example:

```
IDENTIFICATION DIVISION.
PROGRAM-ID.      EMP-RPT.
AUTHOR.          WELBURN.
INSTALLATION.    SILICON VALLEY MANUFACTURING COMPANY.
DATE-WRITTEN.    DEC 8,1984.
DATE-COMPILED.   DEC 8,1984.
SECURITY.        NONE.
*
*
*                THIS PROGRAM READS NAME-AND-ADDRESS RECORDS
*                AND PRINTS AN EMPLOYEE REPORT.
*
```

Style recommendations:

- Limit the program-name to the maximum number of characters allowed by the operating system that is being used.

- Vertically align the program-name and comment-entries at position 23 (or where the compiler starts the DATE-COMPILED entry).

REMARKS paragraph (1968 ANS only)

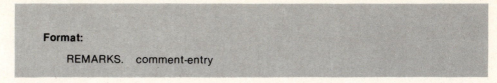

Format:

REMARKS.   comment-entry

Example:

```
REMARKS.   THE REMARKS PARAGRAPH WAS PROVIDED SO THAT
           OVERALL PROGRAM DOCUMENTATION COMMENTS
           COULD BE PROVIDED IN THE IDENTIFICATION DIVISION.
```

Style recommendation:

- Do not use the REMARKS entry. It has been dropped from the 1974 ANS COBOL standards. Comment lines (* in position 7) should instead be used.

ENVIRONMENT DIVISION

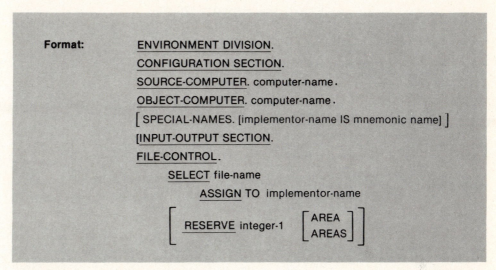

Format:

ENVIRONMENT DIVISION.

CONFIGURATION SECTION.

SOURCE-COMPUTER. computer-name.

OBJECT-COMPUTER. computer-name.

[SPECIAL-NAMES. [implementor-name IS mnemonic name]]

[INPUT-OUTPUT SECTION.

FILE-CONTROL.

SELECT file-name

ASSIGN TO implementor-name

$$\left[\underline{RESERVE} \text{ integer-1} \left[\begin{array}{c} AREA \\ AREAS \end{array} \right] \right]$$

Example:

```
*
*
*
  ENVIRONMENT DIVISION.
*
*
  CONFIGURATION SECTION.
*
  SOURCE-COMPUTER.   IBM-3081.
  OBJECT-COMPUTER.   IBM-3081.
*
  SPECIAL-NAMES.
       C01 IS TO-TOP-OF-PAGE.
*
*
  INPUT-OUTPUT SECTION.
*
  FILE-CONTROL.
       SELECT NAME-ADDRESS-FILE
            ASSIGN TO UT-S-INFILE
            RESERVE 2 AREAS.
```

SPECIAL-NAMES paragraph style recommendation:

- Instead of using the mnemonic-name option of the WRITE statement to provide for page-skipping to the top of the page, use the reserved word PAGE. This means that implementor-name definition of page-skipping functions will be required only in those few cases where skipping to other locations on the page is required. (However, the reserved word PAGE is not available on pre-1974 ANS compilers.)

SELECT and ASSIGN clause style recommendations:

- Write the SELECT sentence so that the ASSIGN clause begins on a separate line. Indent the ASSIGN clause four spaces (to position 16).
- Sequence the SELECT statements so that the input files are listed first and then the output files.
- Do not choose file-names that refer to specific input-output devices (such as CARD-FILE, TAPE-FILE, or DISK-FILE).

RESERVE clause style recommendation:

- Use the RESERVE clause only when it is necessary to change the number of input-output buffer areas from that normally provided by the compiler. By default, most mainframe compilers provide from two to five buffer areas; certain microcomputer compilers provide only one. Specification of multiple areas generally increases input-output processing efficiency; a single area conserves storage.

DATA DIVISION

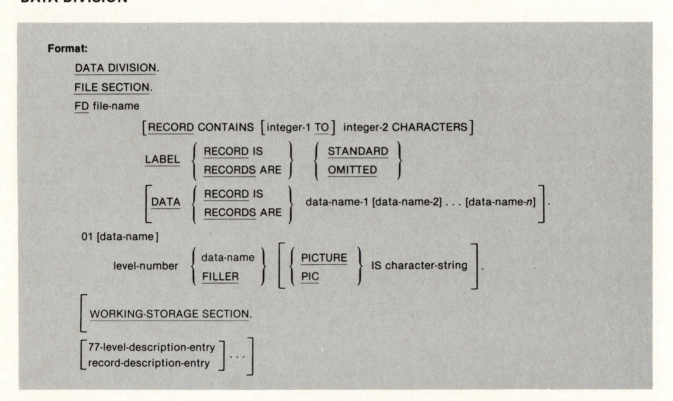

Format:

```
DATA DIVISION.
FILE SECTION.
FD file-name
        [RECORD CONTAINS [integer-1 TO] integer-2 CHARACTERS]
    LABEL  { RECORD IS  }  { STANDARD }
           { RECORDS ARE }  { OMITTED  }
    [ DATA { RECORD IS  }  data-name-1 [data-name-2] . . . [data-name-n] ].
           { RECORDS ARE }
    01 [data-name]
        level-number { data-name }  [ { PICTURE } IS character-string ].
                     { FILLER    }    { PIC     }
    [ WORKING-STORAGE SECTION.
    [ 77-level-description-entry ] . . . ]
    [ record-description-entry  ]
```

Example:

```
*
*
*
 DATA DIVISION.
*
*
  FILE SECTION.
*
```

```
FD  EMPLOYEE-FILE
        RECORD CONTAINS 80 CHARACTERS
        BLOCK CONTAINS 10 RECORDS
        LABEL RECORDS ARE STANDARD
        DATA RECORD IS NA-NAME-ADDRESS-RECORD.
*
01  NA-NAME-ADDRESS-RECORD.
    05  NA-RECORD-CODE                  PIC X(2).
    05  NA-EMPLOYEE-NAME                PIC X(20).
    05  NA-EMPLOYEE-ADDRESS             PIC X(24).
    05  NA-EMPLOYEE-CITY-STATE-ZIP      PIC X(24).
    05  NA-EMPLOYEE-HIRE-DATE.
        10  NA-EMPLOYEE-HIRE-MONTH      PIC 9(2).
        10  NA-EMPLOYEE-HIRE-DAY        PIC 9(2).
        10  NA-EMPLOYEE-HIRE-YEAR       PIC 9(2).
    05  FILLER                          PIC X(4).
    .
    .
    .

*
*
WORKING-STORAGE SECTION.
*
01  WS-PROGRAM-SWITCHES.
    05  WS-END-OF-FILE-SW               PIC X(3).
    .
    .
    .
```

FD entry style recommendations:

- Do not choose file-names that refer to specific input-output devices (such as CARD-FILE, TAPE-FILE, or DISK-FILE).

- Write each clause of the FD entry on a separate line. Indent each clause after the file-name to position 16.

- Use the optional RECORD CONTAINS clause of the FD.

- Omit the optional DATA RECORDS clause of the FD.

- Specify record-blocking factors by using the easier to comprehend RECORDS option of the BLOCK CONTAINS clause rather than the CHARACTERS option.

- When possible, it is generally advisable to provide record-blocking specifications through the computer operating system job control language rather than the COBOL BLOCK CONTAINS clause of the FD. This allows changes to the blocking factor without requiring recompilation of the COBOL program.

Data-item level number and indentation style recommendations:

- Use gap level-number assignment (01, 05, 10, 15, and so on).

- Indent each data-item subdivision four spaces (level-number 05 at position 12, level-number 10 at position 16, and so forth). If four-space indentations consume too much space on the coding line, use two-space indentations.

- Do not use 77-level data-items. Instead, organize WORKING-STORAGE independent data-items into collections of logically related fields, using level-numbers 01 through 49.

Data-name style recommendations:

- Choose meaningful, descriptive data-names.

- Prefix all data-names of a record with a two-, three-, or four-character abbreviation for that record. The prefix for each record of the program should be unique. As an alternative approach, suffixes can be used.

- Assign unique data-names so that qualification need not be used in the PROCEDURE DIVISION.

Numeric symbols	Numeric-editing symbols		Alphabetic symbol	Alphanumeric symbol	Alphanumeric-editing symbols	
9 Digit	Z	Zero suppression with blank-space replacement	A Alphabetic character	X Alphanumeric character	B	Blank space
V Assumed decimal point					/	Slash
	*	Zero suppression with asterisk replacement			0	Zero
S Arithmetic sign	,	Comma				
P Decimal scaling position	/	Slash				
	B	Blank space				
	0	Zero				
	.	Decimal point				
	−	Minus sign				
	+	Plus sign				
	CR	Credit symbol				
	DB	Debit symbol				
	$	Dollar sign				

PICTURE clause style recommendations:

- To conserve space on the coding line, use the abbreviation PIC rather than the word PICTURE.

- Do not use the optional word IS in the PICTURE clause. It consumes space on the coding line and does not significantly improve program documentation.

- Vertically align FILE SECTION PICTURE clauses at position 48.

- Do not use the alphabetic PICTURE symbol A. Instead use the symbol X for both alphabetic and alphanumeric fields.

- When an entire field is defined by the same symbol (or the same symbol plus an S), use the parentheses method to express the field length. For example, a seven-character alphanumeric field can be defined as PIC X(7); an eight-integer signed numeric field can be defined as PIC S9(8).

- When a field contains editing characters, specify each symbol so that the editing PICTURE is more easily readable. (That is, write PIC $ZZ,ZZZ.99− not PIC $Z(2),Z(3).9(2)−.)

- When a V appears in a numeric picture character-string, use the parentheses method before the V and the repetition method after it (e.g. PIC 9(8)V99).

- Define nonarithmetic integer numeric fields as alphanumeric rather than numeric. Numeric PICTURE clauses are usually less efficient because of the need for arithmetic sign handling. Also, on some computer systems, numeric fields introduce the possibility that data exceptions may occur and cause abnormal program termination.

- When describing records in the WORKING-STORAGE SECTION that contain primarily constant values, start the PICTURE clauses in position 32 and the VALUE clauses in position 44.

- When describing records in the WORKING-STORAGE SECTION that contain primarily variable fields with short constant literals or figurative constants, start the PICTURE clauses in position 48 and the VALUE clauses in position 60.

BLANK WHEN ZERO clause

Format:

BLANK WHEN ZERO

Examples:

```
05   XX-PRICE       PIC ZZ,ZZZ.99 BLANK WHEN ZERO.

05   XX-CODE-NBR    PIC 99999     BLANK WHEN ZERO.

05   XX-DATE        PIC 99/99/99  BLANK WHEN ZERO.
```

Style recommendation:

■ When possible, it is generally more convenient to use PICTURE symbols to provide BLANK WHEN ZERO indication. For example, PIC ZZ,ZZZ.ZZ is equivalent to PIC ZZ,ZZZ.99 BLANK WHEN ZERO.

JUSTIFIED RIGHT clause

Format:

$$\left\{ \begin{array}{c} \text{JUSTIFIED} \\ \text{JUST} \end{array} \right\} \text{RIGHT}$$

Example:

```
05   XX-DATE        PIC X(6).
05   XX-YEAR        PIC X(2) JUSTIFIED RIGHT.
     .
     .
     .
MOVE XX-DATE TO XX-YEAR.
```

Syntax consideration:

■ Remember that JUSTIFIED RIGHT processing occurs only when the receiving field (of the MOVE statement) contains the JUSTIFIED RIGHT clause. When the JUSTIFIED RIGHT clause is affixed to the sending field and the receiving field does not contain the JUSTIFIED RIGHT clause, right justification does not occur.

OCCURS clause

(See Appendix C: Table-Processing Reference.)

REDEFINES clause

Format:

level-number data-name-1 REDEFINES data-name-2

Example:

```
05   XX-PRICE                              PIC ZZ,ZZZ.99.
05   XX-NC-PRICE REDEFINES XX-PRICE   PIC X(9).
```

Syntax considerations:

- A data-item with a REDEFINES clause must immediately follow, *at that level number,* the object of the REDEFINES clause (the field that is being redefined).
- A data-item with a REDEFINES clause must be equal or shorter in length than the field that is being redefined.
- A data-item with a REDEFINES clause cannot contain a VALUE clause.
- A data-item with a REDEFINES clause cannot contain an editing PICTURE.
- A data-item may have multiple redefinitions.

RENAMES clause

Format:

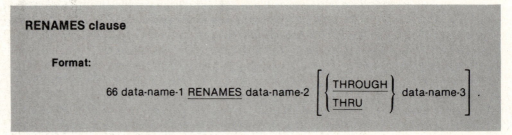

Example:

```
*
01   NA-NAME-AND-ADDRESS-RECORD.
     05   NA-FIRST-NAME    PIC X(10).
     05   NA-MID-INITIAL   PIC X(1).
     05   NA-LAST-NAME     PIC X(12).
     05   NA-ADDRESS       PIC X(24).
     05   NA-CITY          PIC X(13).
     05   NA-STATE         PIC X(2).
     05   NA-ZIP-CODE      PIC X(5).
*
     66   NA-FULL-NAME RENAMES NA-FIRST-NAME THRU NA-LAST-NAME.
     66   NA-STREET-ADDRESS RENAMES NA-ADDRESS.
     66   NA-DESTINATION RENAMES NA-CITY THRU NA-ZIP-CODE.
```

Syntax considerations:

- A data-item with a RENAMES clause must be a 66-level item.
- It must be specified immediately following the record-description to which it applies.
- Level number 01, 66, 77, and 88 items cannot be renamed.
- Neither data-name-2 nor data-name-3 may have an OCCURS clause in its data-description entry or be subordinate to an item that contains an OCCURS clause.
- Data-name-3 must physically follow data-name-2 in the record description and cannot be subordinate to data-name-2.

SD entry

(See Appendix D: SORT/MERGE Program Reference.)

SIGN clause

Format:

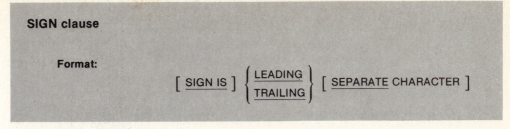

Examples:

```
05  XX-AMT-1 PIC S9(5) SIGN IS LEADING SEPARATE CHARACTER.
05  XX-AMT-2 PIC S9(5) SIGN IS TRAILING SEPARATE CHARACTER.
```

Syntax consideration:

■ The SIGN clause is seldom used except for those rare situations in which either (1) two or more sign representations are to be used within a program (embedded sign, separate left-most character or separate rightmost character) or (2) the sign representation is to be placed at a location different from the normal one for the compiler.

SYNCHRONIZED clause

Format:

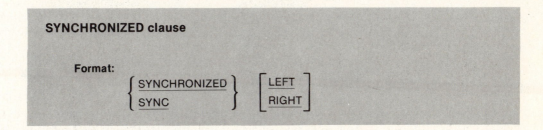

Example:

```
05  XX-BINARY-FIELD              PIC S9(8)     COMP SYNC.
```

Syntax consideration:

■ When specifying COMP usage for WORKING-STORAGE SECTION fields that are not part of an input or output record, include the SYNC clause to ensure proper internal alignment for optimum processing efficiency.

Style recommendation:

■ Use the abbreviation SYNC rather than the full word SYNCHRONIZED. It conserves space on the coding line and is equally understandable.

USAGE clause

Format:

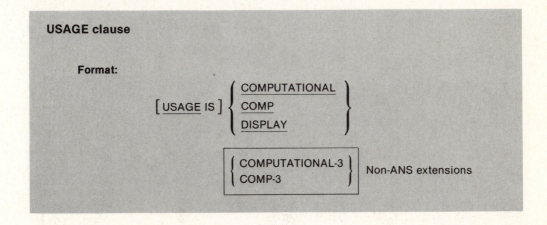

Examples:

```
05  XX-BINARY-FLD              PIC S9(8)    COMP SYNC.
05  XX-ALPHA-FLD               PIC X(24).
05  XX-DECIMAL-FLD             PIC S9(7)V99   COMP-3.
```

Specification guidelines:

- COMP usage is limited to numeric fields. COMP usage is often referred to as **binary** format.

- COMP-3 usage is not an ANS COBOL standard but a commonly used IBM-originated method of data representation for decimal arithmetic fields. COMP-3 usage is sometimes called **packed decimal** or **internal decimal** representation.

- DISPLAY usage is alternately called **character** format.

- Because arithmetic operations are typically executed by the computer in COMP or COMP-3 format, it is usually more efficient to specify such usage for WORKING-STORAGE fields involved in arithmetic calculations or numeric comparisons.

- Input data from punched cards or keyboard devices generally must be specified (implicitly or explicitly) as DISPLAY usage. The same is true for output data directed to a printer or VDT screen.

- Conversion from one usage to another takes place during execution of a MOVE statement or after an arithmetic result has been calculated. For example, conversion of data from COMP usage to DISPLAY usage occurs when a MOVE statement is specified that has a sending field with COMP usage and a receiving field with DISPLAY usage. Such conversion takes processing time and can thus degrade performance.

- Both COMP and COMP-3 usage will store longer numeric fields in less storage space.

- Although USAGE choice depends on many considerations and is affected by (1) the architecture of the particular computer system being used and (2) the logic of the compiler, the following general guidelines are suggested:

  —When tape- or disk-storage space is to be optimized, longer numeric fields should be stored in COMP or COMP-3 usage.

  a. If available, choose COMP-3 usage when the field has decimal fraction positions. Do this because COMP fields are usually stored in binary format. Fractional decimal values will usually require rounding to a binary equivalent. This may introduce minor rounding discrepancies.

  b. If the field has no decimal fraction positions, COMP usage may provide more efficient storage and processing than COMP-3.

  —When WORKING-STORAGE fields are involved in arithmetic or many numeric comparisons, specify COMP or COMP-3 usage to optimize arithmetic processing.

  a. Choose COMP (in preference to COMP-3) for integer fields that (1) will not be moved to fields with DISPLAY or COMP-3 usage, and/or (2) will not often be compared to DISPLAY or COMP-3 fields.

  b. Choose COMP-3 (in preference to COMP), if available, for fields that (1) will be moved to or from DISPLAY or COMP-3 fields, (2) will be compared to DISPLAY or COMP-3 fields, and/or (3) contain decimal-fraction digits.

Style recommendations:

- When specifying the USAGE clause for data-item descriptions, omit the optional words USAGE and IS. They consume valuable space on the coding line and impart little additional meaning.

- Rather than explicitly coding the USAGE clause for DISPLAY usage, omit the USAGE clause; implicit DISPLAY usage will be provided.

- Use of the abbreviations COMP for COMPUTATIONAL and COMP-3 for COMPUTATIONAL-3 conserves space on the coding line and is equally understandable.

- When specifying COMP usage for WORKING-STORAGE SECTION fields that are not part of an input or output record, include the SYNC clause to ensure proper internal alignment for optimum processing efficiency.

- A convenient position in which to start the USAGE clause words COMP (when SYNC is not specified) or COMP-3 is position 66. When COMP and SYNC are both specified, position 63 is an appropriate starting position.

- Choose field lengths of an odd number of digits when specifying COMP-3 fields. Also, assign the PICTURE symbol S.

- [IBM OS/DOS] Specify COMP fields as 4, 9, or 18 digits in length. Assign the PICTURE symbol S.

- When a subscript is used, processing efficiency will usually be enhanced by specifying COMP usage and the SYNC clause with a PICTURE of S9(4).

VALUE clause

Format:

VALUE IS literal

Examples:

```
05  WS-PI           PIC S9(1)V9999   VALUE +3.1416.

05  WS-CHRISTMAS    PIC 9(4)         VALUE '1225'.

05  WS-FIRST-RCD-SW PIC X(3)         VALUE 'YES'.

05  WS-DATE                          VALUE ZEROS.
    10  WS-MONTH    PIC 9(2).
    10  WS-DAY      PIC 9(2).
    10  WS-YEAR     PIC 9(2).
```

Syntax considerations:

- The literal that is specified must be consistent with the data class that is specified by the PICTURE clause. When the PICTURE is numeric, a numeric literal must be specified. When the PICTURE is alphanumeric, a nonnumeric literal must be specified.

- The literal cannot be longer than the field length defined by the PICTURE clause.

- A figurative constant of the appropriate data class can be used in place of a literal.

- If the VALUE clause is specified with a group data-item, the literal must be specified as either a nonnumeric literal or a figurative constant. The group area is initialized without regard to the data class or usage of individual elementary or group items within the group.

- Places where the initializing VALUE clause cannot be specified are as follows:

  —in the FILE SECTION
  —in the LINKAGE SECTION
  —with a data-item description entry that contains an editing PICTURE clause
  —with a data-item description entry that contains a REDEFINES clause
  —with a data-item description entry that contains an OCCURS clause
  —with a data-item description entry that is subordinate to an entry that contains the VALUE clause

Style recommendations:

- Do not use the optional word IS in the VALUE clause. It consumes space on the coding line and does not significantly improve program documentation.

- When describing records in the WORKING-STORAGE SECTION that contain primarily constant values, start the PICTURE clauses in position 32 and the VALUE clauses in position 44.

- In the WORKING-STORAGE SECTION, when describing longer records that contain primarily nonnumeric constant values, define such values in groups of 20 characters.
- In the WORKING-STORAGE SECTION, when describing records that contain primarily variable fields with short constant literals or figurative constants, start the PICTURE clause in position 48 and the VALUE clause in position 60.
- Initialize constant fields with VALUE clauses in the DATA DIVISION; initialize variable fields with PROCEDURE DIVISION statements. Doing so aids program documentation and tends to make modules reentrant.

WORKING-STORAGE SECTION definition of input and output records

Style recommendations:

- Define output records in the WORKING-STORAGE SECTION. Such definition provides the following advantages:
  - —It allows VALUE clauses to be used for the initialization of constant fields within the record.
  - —It eliminates double-buffering problems.
  - —It allows reference to fields of a record that have already been written to an output device.
  - —It makes it easier to determine the current output record being processed when referring to a storage dump.
- In most cases, define input records in the WORKING-STORAGE SECTION. The advantages of input record definition in WORKING-STORAGE are not as great as those for output record definition, but it does provide the following advantages:
  - —It allows reference to fields of a record after the next input record has been read into the FILE SECTION (or end-of-file has been reached).
  - —It makes it easier to determine the last input record that was read when referring to a storage dump.

WORKING-STORAGE SECTION field organization

Style recommendations:

- When specifying fields are used to hold the control fields of the previous record, it is logical to list them in major through minor sequence.
- When specifying control total accumulation fields, it is logical to list them in minor through major sequence.

66-level items

See RENAMES clause, above.

77-level items

Style recommendation:

- Do not use 77-level data-items. Instead, organize WORKING-STORAGE independent data-items into collections of logically related fields, using level-numbers 01 through 49.

88-level condition-name items

Format:

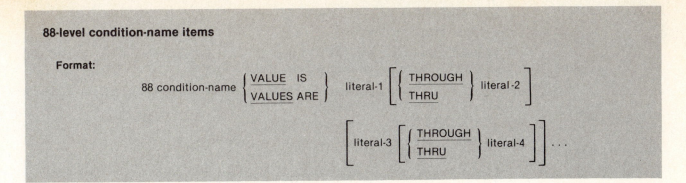

$$88 \; \text{condition-name} \; \begin{Bmatrix} \underline{\text{VALUE}} \; \text{IS} \\ \underline{\text{VALUES}} \; \text{ARE} \end{Bmatrix} \; \text{literal-1} \; \left[\begin{Bmatrix} \underline{\text{THROUGH}} \\ \underline{\text{THRU}} \end{Bmatrix} \text{literal-2} \right]$$

$$\left[\text{literal-3} \; \left[\begin{Bmatrix} \underline{\text{THROUGH}} \\ \underline{\text{THRU}} \end{Bmatrix} \text{literal-4} \right] \right] \dots$$

Examples:

```
05  XX-MARITAL-STATUS        PIC X(1).
    88  SINGLE                          VALUE 'S'.
    88  MARRIED                         VALUE 'M'.

05  XX-MONTH-ABBREV          PIC X(3).
    88  30-DAY-MONTH                    VALUE 'APR'
                                             'JUN'
                                             'SEP'
                                             'NOV'.
    88  31-DAY-MONTH                    VALUE 'JAN'
                                             'MAR'
                                             'MAY'
                                             'JUL'
                                             'AUG'
                                             'OCT'
                                             'DEC'.
    88  28-29-DAY-MONTH                 VALUE 'FEB'.
```

Syntax considerations:

■ The level-number 88 must be specified for condition-name entries.

■ Although many other syntactical considerations are the same, placement restrictions for the initializing VALUE clause do not apply to the condition-name VALUE clause. That is, a condition-name VALUE clause *may* be specified in the following situations:

—in the FILE SECTION
—in the LINKAGE SECTION
—with a data-item description entry that contains an editing PICTURE clause
—with a data-item description entry that contains a REDEFINES clause
—with a data-item desciption entry that contains an OCCURS clause
—with a data-item description entry that is subordinate to an entry that contains the VALUE clause

PROCEDURE DIVISION

Module Formation

Style recommendations:

■ Do not use sections unless they are required by the COBOL syntax.

■ Provide only a single-entry point and a single-exit point for each program module.

■ To ensure a single-entry and a single-exit point, try to form each program module as a single paragraph except where it is necessary to form a program module as a single section for

(1) the SORT/MERGE statement with an INPUT PROCEDURE or an OUTPUT PROCEDURE

(2) program segmentation

(3) declaratives

(4) the case structure

- Establish one READ and/or WRITE module for each file. Conditions in which more than one WRITE module will be required for a file are when

(1) a report file requires one WRITE module to skip to the top of the page and another to handle variable line spacing

(2) variable-length records are written

Module Naming and Numbering

Style recommendations:

- Generally name each program module with a one-word verb and a two-word object.

- Number each program module in accordance with a module-numbering system and arrange the program modules in order according to that number.

Arithmetic Statements

General arithmetic style recommendation:

- When an arithmetic statement will not fit on one coding line, break the statement at a phrase and continue it, indented, on the next coding line.

ADD statement

Format-1

ADD { identifier-1 / literal-1 } [identifier-2 / literal-2] ... TO identifier-*m* [ROUNDED]

[identifier-*n* [ROUNDED]] ... [ON SIZE ERROR imperative-statement]

Format-2

ADD { identifier-1 / literal-1 } { identifier-2 / literal-2 } [identifier-3 / literal-3] ...

GIVING identifier-*m* [ROUNDED] [identifier-*n* [ROUNDED]] ...

[ON SIZE ERROR imperative-statement]

Examples:

```
ADD CA-BALANCE-FORWARD TO WS-BALANCE-WORK.

ADD XX-TOTAL-PURCHASES XX-TAX-AMOUNT
    GIVING XX-TOTAL-SALES-AMOUNT.
```

Syntax consideration:

- Observe that the reserved word TO is required with format-1 but absent from format-2.

SUBTRACT statement

Format-1

SUBTRACT { identifier-1 / literal-1 } [identifier-2 / literal-2] ... FROM identifier-*m* [ROUNDED]

[identifier-*n* [ROUNDED]] ... [ON SIZE ERROR imperative-statement]

Format-2

$$\text{\underline{SUBTRACT}} \left\{ \begin{array}{l} \text{identifier-1} \\ \text{literal-1} \end{array} \right\} \left[\begin{array}{l} \text{identifier-2} \\ \text{literal-2} \end{array} \right] \dots \text{\underline{FROM}} \left\{ \begin{array}{l} \text{identifier-}m \\ \text{literal-}m \end{array} \right\}$$

$$\text{\underline{GIVING}} \text{ identifier-}n \; [\text{ \underline{ROUNDED} }] \; [\text{ identifier-}o \; [\text{ \underline{ROUNDED} }]] \dots$$

$$[\text{ ON \underline{SIZE ERROR} imperative-statement }]$$

Examples:

```
SUBTRACT CA-MONTH-PAYMENTS FROM WS-BALANCE-WORK.

SUBTRACT XX-DISCOUNT-AMOUNT FROM XX-SALES-AMOUNT
    GIVING XX-TOTAL-PURCHASE-AMOUNT.
```

Syntax consideration:

- Observe that the reserved word FROM is required with both format-1 and format-2.

MULTIPLY statement

Format-1

$$\text{\underline{MULTIPLY}} \left\{ \begin{array}{l} \text{identifier-1} \\ \text{literal-1} \end{array} \right\} \text{\underline{BY}} \text{ identifier-2 } [\text{ \underline{ROUNDED} }]$$

$$[\text{ identifier-3 } [\text{ \underline{ROUNDED} }]] \dots [\text{ ON \underline{SIZE ERROR} imperative-statement }]$$

Format-2

$$\text{\underline{MULTIPLY}} \left\{ \begin{array}{l} \text{identifier-1} \\ \text{literal-1} \end{array} \right\} \text{\underline{BY}} \left\{ \begin{array}{l} \text{identifier-2} \\ \text{literal-2} \end{array} \right\}$$

$$\text{\underline{GIVING}} \text{ identifier-3 } [\text{ \underline{ROUNDED} }] \; [\text{ identifier-4 } [\text{ \underline{ROUNDED} }]] \dots$$

$$[\text{ ON \underline{SIZE ERROR} imperative-statement }]$$

Examples:

```
MULTIPLY XX-TAX-RATE BY XX-TAX-WORK-AREA.

MULTIPLY CA-MONTH-PURCHASE-AMT BY .06
    GIVING WS-BALANCE-WORK.
```


DIVIDE statement

Format-1

$$\text{\underline{DIVIDE}} \left\{ \begin{array}{l} \text{identifier-1} \\ \text{literal-1} \end{array} \right\} \text{\underline{INTO}} \text{ identifier-2 } [\text{ \underline{ROUNDED} }]$$

$$[\text{ identifier-3 } [\text{ \underline{ROUNDED} }]] \dots [\text{ ON \underline{SIZE ERROR} imperative-statement }]$$

Format-2

```
DIVIDE { identifier-1 }  INTO { identifier-2 }
       { literal-1    }        { literal-2    }

    GIVING identifier-3 [ ROUNDED ] [ identifier-4 [ ROUNDED ] ] ...

    [ ON SIZE ERROR imperative-statement ]
```

Format-3

```
DIVIDE { identifier-1 }  BY { identifier-2 }
       { literal-1    }     { literal-2    }

    GIVING identifier-3 [ ROUNDED ] [ identifier-4 [ ROUNDED ] ] ...

    [ ON SIZE ERROR imperative-statement ]
```

Format-4

```
DIVIDE { identifier-1 }  INTO { identifier-2 }
       { literal-1    }       { literal-2    }

    GIVING identifier-3 [ ROUNDED ] REMAINDER identifier-4

    [ ON SIZE ERROR imperative-statement ]
```

Format-5

```
DIVIDE { identifier-1 }  BY { identifier-2 }
       { literal-1    }     { literal-2    }

    GIVING identifier-3 [ ROUNDED ] REMAINDER identifier-4

    [ ON SIZE ERROR imperative-statement ]
```

Examples:

```
DIVIDE XX-FIELD-A INTO XX-FIELD-B.

DIVIDE CA-NBR-PURCHASES INTO CA-MONTH-PURCHASE-AMT
    GIVING DL-AVG-PURCHASE-AMT.

DIVIDE CA-MONTH-PURCHASE-AMT BY CA-NBR-MONTH-PURCHASES
    GIVING DL-AVG-PURCHASE-AMT.

DIVIDE 60 INTO XX-TOTAL-MINUTES
    GIVING XX-HOURS REMAINDER XX-MINUTES.

DIVIDE XX-TOTAL-MINUTES BY 60
    GIVING XX-HOURS REMAINDER XX-MINUTES.
```

Syntax consideration:

■ Observe that when the BY operator is used, the GIVING phrase must be specified.

COMPUTE statement

Format:

```
COMPUTE identifier-1 [ ROUNDED ] [ identifier-2 [ ROUNDED ] ]  ...

    = arithmetic-expression [ ON SIZE ERROR imperative-statement ]
```

Examples:

```
COMPUTE XX-FLD-X = XX-FLD-A + XX-FLD-B - XX-FLD-C XX-FLD-D
    / XX-FLD-E ** XX-FLD-F.

COMPUTE X = (A + B) / C
```

Syntax considerations:

- Arithmetic operators are as follows:

  - \+   addition
  - −   subtraction
  - *   multiplication
  - /   division
  - ** exponentiation

- Hierarchy of operations is as follows, from left to right within the arithmetic expression:

  (1) exponentiation
  (2) multiplication and division
  (3) addition and subtraction

- Parentheses can be specified to control the hierarchy.

Style recommendations:

- Use parentheses within COMPUTE statement arithmetic expressions to control the sequence of arithmetic operations rather than relying upon the normal sequence of operations. Using parentheses not only ensures that the expression easier to read and understand, but also helps to ensure that the correct computation is made.

- Try to limit each COMPUTE statement to three or four factors in order to avoid overly complex expressions.

ROUNDED phrase

Style recommendation:

- Use when half-adjusting of the calculated result is desired.

ON SIZE ERROR phrase

Syntax considerations:

- When an arithmetic calculation generates a value that exceeds the size of the receiving field, a size error occurs. When a size error is detected and the ON SIZE ERROR phrase is *not* specified, the excess high-order positions are truncated; no indication of the erroneous value is provided.

- When the ON SIZE ERROR phrase is specified and a size error occurs, the value contained in the result field of the arithmetic operation is unpredictable and program control is transferred to the imperative statement following the ON SIZE ERROR phrase.

Style recommendation:

- Minimize use of the ON SIZE ERROR phrase. Instead, try to define fields large enough to ensure that a SIZE error does not occur. An alternate or supplemental approach is to prevalidate the values with a range check in a prior data-validation program.

Style recommendation:

- Do not use the CORRESPONDING phrase with the ADD or SUBTRACT statements. It is a "bug-breeder" option.

Compiler-Directing Statements

Syntax considerations:

(1968 ANS)

- The copy statement is limited to use in certain locations of the source program. Common locations are as follows:

    FD file-name COPY library-name.
    SD file-name COPY library-name.
    01 record-name COPY library-name.
    Section-name SECTION COPY library-name.
    Paragraph-name COPY library-name.

- When the COPY statement appears as a 01-level record description, the 01-level record-name coded by the programmer replaces the 01-level record-name from the library.

(1974 ANS)

- The COPY statement may be used at practically any location in the source program.

- The record-name preceding the word COPY is not substituted in the copied coding.

Examples:

1968 ANS Standard COPY Statement

Source statements in library entry named NARECORD:

```
01   NA-NAME-AND-ADDRESS-RECORD.
     05   NA-RECORD-CODE              PIC X(2).
     05   NA-NAME                     PIC X(20).
     05   NA-ADDRESS                  PIC X(24).
     05   NA-CITY                     PIC X(13).
     05   NA-STATE                    PIC X(2).
     05   NA-ZIP-CODE                 PIC X(9).
     05   NA-TELEPHONE-NUMBER         PIC X(10).
```

Programmer writes this statement on the source listing:

```
01   NA-CUSTOMER-RECORD COPY NARECORD.
```

The following code is included in the source program (note that the 01-level record-name has been replaced in the program with the name assigned by the programmer):

```
  01   NA-CUSTOMER-RECORD COPY NARECORD.
C 01   NA-CUSTOMER-RECORD.
C      05   NA-RECORD-CODE              PIC X(2).
C      05   NA-NAME                     PIC X(20).
C      05   NA-ADDRESS                  PIC X(24).
C      05   NA-CITY                     PIC X(13).
C      05   NA-STATE                    PIC X(2).
C      05   NA-ZIP-CODE                 PIC X(9).
C      05   NA-TELEPHONE-NUMBER         PIC X(10).
```

1974 Standard COPY Statement

Source statement in library entry named NARECORD (notice that the 01-level record-name has been specified in the library as a comment-entry):

```
*01  NA-NAME-AND-ADDRESS-RECORD.
     05   NA-RECORD-CODE              PIC X(2).
     05   NA-NAME                     PIC X(20).
     05   NA-ADDRESS                  PIC X(24).
     05   NA-CITY                     PIC X(13).
     05   NA-STATE                    PIC X(2).
     05   NA-ZIP-CODE                 PIC X(9).
     05   NA-TELEPHONE-NUMBER         PIC X(10).
```

Programmer writes this statement and the source listing (notice that the COPY statement is written as a separate sentence):

```
01   NA-CUSTOMER-RECORD.   COPY NARECORD.
```

The following code is included in the source program:

```
  01   NA-CUSTOMER-RECORD.   COPY NARECORD.
C *01 NA-NAME-AND-ADDRESS-RECORD.
C      05   NA-RECORD-CODE              PIC X(2).
C      05   NA-NAME                     PIC X(20).
C      05   NA-ADDRESS                  PIC X(24).
C      05   NA-CITY                     PIC X(13).
C      05   NA-STATE                    PIC X(2).
C      05   NA-ZIP-CODE                 PIC X(9).
C      05   NA-TELEPHONE-NUMBER         PIC X(10).
```

NOTE statement (1968 ANS only)

Format:

NOTE. comment-entry

Example:

```
NOTE.    THE NOTE STATEMENT WAS PROVIDED SO THAT EXPLANATORY
         PROGRAM DOCUMENTATION COMMENTS COULD BE PROVIDED
         IN THE PROCEDURE DIVISION.
```

Style recommendation:

- Do not use the NOTE statement. It has been dropped from the 1974 ANS COBOL standards. Comment lines (* in position 7) should instead be used.

IF statement

Format:

IF condition $\left\{\begin{array}{c}\text{statement-1}\\\underline{\text{NEXT SENTENCE}}\end{array}\right\}$ $\left\{\begin{array}{c}\underline{\text{ELSE}}\text{ statement-2}\\\underline{\text{ELSE NEXT SENTENCE}}\end{array}\right\}$

Simple IF statement examples:

```
IF XX-SEX-CODE IS EQUAL TO 'M'
    ADD 1 TO XX-TOTAL-MALES-ACCUM.


IF XX-SEX-CODE IS EQUAL TO 'M'
    ADD 1 TO XX-TOTAL-MALES-ACCUM
    MOVE 'MALE' TO XX-SEX.


IF XX-SEX-CODE IS EQUAL TO 'M'
    ADD 1 TO XX-TOTAL-MALES-ACCUM
ELSE
    ADD 1 TO XX-TOTAL-FEMALES-ACCUM.


IF XX-SEX-CODE IS EQUAL TO 'M'
    NEXT SENTENCE
ELSE
    ADD 1 TO XX-TOTAL-FEMALES-ACCUM.
```

Combined IF statement examples:

```
IF XX-UNITS-THIS-SEMESTER IS GREATER THAN 11.0
AND XX-GRADE-POINT-AVERAGE IS GREATER THAN 3.75
    PERFORM 999-PLACE-ON-DEANS-LIST.


IF CREDIT-CARD-LOST-OR-STOLEN
OR ACCOUNT-BALANCE IS GREATER THAN XX-CREDIT-LIMIT
    PERFORM 999-EXAMINE-ACCOUNT
ELSE
    PERFORM 999-POST-CHARGE-TO-ACCOUNT.


IF XX-DATE IS NUMERIC
AND XX-MONTH IS GREATER THAN ZERO
AND XX-MONTH IS LESS THAN 13
AND XX-DAY IS GREATER THAN ZERO
AND XX-DAY IS LESS THAN 32
AND VALID-YEAR
    PERFORM 999-PROCESS-DATE
ELSE
    PERFORM 999-IDENTIFY-DATE-ERROR.


IF XX-RECORD-CODE IS EQUAL TO '23'
OR XX-UPDATE-CODE IS EQUAL TO 'D'
AND XX-BALANCE IS ZERO
    PERFORM 999-DELETE-RECORD.


IF XX-RECORD-CODE IS EQUAL TO '23'
OR (XX-UPDATE-CODE IS EQUAL TO 'D'
        AND XX-BALANCE IS ZERO)
    PERFORM 999-DELETE-RECORD.


IF XX-MONTH IS GREATER THAN ZERO
            AND LESS THAN '13'
            AND NOT EQUAL TO '02'
    PERFORM 999-STANDARD-DAY-CHECK.
```

```
IF XX-BALANCE IS LESS THAN 1000.00
                            AND XX-CREDIT-LIMIT
    PERFORM 999-POST-PAYMENT.
```

Nested IF statement examples:

```
IF XX-TRANSACTION-TYPE IS EQUAL TO 'NA'
    PERFORM 999-PROCESS-NAME-ADDRESS
ELSE IF XX-TRANSACTION-TYPE IS EQUAL TO 'WE'
    PERFORM 999-PROCESS-WEEKLY-EARNINGS
ELSE IF XX-TRANSACTION-TYPE IS EQUAL TO 'YE'
    PERFORM 999-PROCESS-YEARLY-EARNINGS
ELSE IF XX-TRANSACTION-TYPE IS EQUAL TO 'PD'
    PERFORM 999-PROCESS-PERSONNEL-DATA
ELSE
    PERFORM 999-PROCESS-ERROR-TRANSACTION.


IF HOURLY-EMPLOYEE
    IF REGULAR-WORKDAY
        PERFORM 999-COMPUTE-NORMAL-PAY
    ELSE
        PERFORM 999-COMPUTE-SUNDAY-HOLIDAY-PAY
ELSE
    PERFORM 999-COMPUTE-SALARY-PAY.


IF HOURLY-EMPLOYEE
    MULTIPLY XX-RATE BY XX-HOURS GIVING XX-REG-PAY
    IF XX-HOURS IS GREATER THAN 40
        SUBTRACT 40 FROM XX-HOURS GIVING XX-OT-HOURS
        MULTIPLY XX-RATE BY .5 GIVING XX-OT-HOURS
        MULTIPLY XX-OT-RATE BY XX-OT-HOURS GIVING XX-OT-PAY
        IF XX-HOURS IS GREATER THAN 48
            SUBTRACT 48 FROM XX-HOURS GIVING XX-PREM-HOURS
            MULTIPLY XX-RATE BY XX-PREM-HOURS
                GIVING XX-PREM-PAY
            ADD XX-REG-PAY XX-OT-PAY XX-PREM-PAY
                GIVING XX-GROSS-PAY
        ELSE
            ADD XX-REG-PAY XX-OT-PAY GIVING XX-GROSS-PAY
    ELSE
        MOVE XX-REG-PAY TO XX-GROSS-PAY
ELSE
    MOVE XX-SALARY TO XX-GROSS-PAY.
```

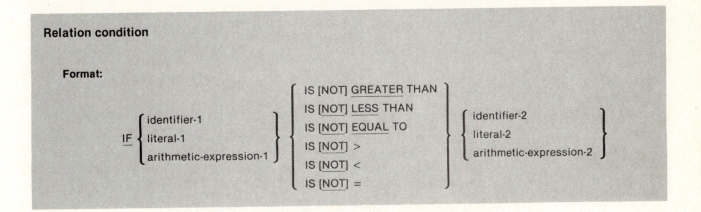

Relation condition

Format:

```
       ┌ identifier-1              ┐  ┌ IS [NOT] GREATER THAN ┐  ┌ identifier-2              ┐
IF     │ literal-1                 │  │ IS [NOT] LESS THAN    │  │ literal-2                 │
       │ arithmetic-expression-1   │  │ IS [NOT] EQUAL TO     │  │ arithmetic-expression-2   │
       └                           ┘  │ IS [NOT] >            │  └                           ┘
                                      │ IS [NOT] <            │
                                      └ IS [NOT] =            ┘
```

Syntax considerations:

- When the subject and the object of the comparison are both numeric items, comparison of the two values is made according to their algebraic value. The relative length of the fields does not matter. The location of the assumed decimal points does, of course, affect the comparison values.

- The result of alphanumeric comparisons depends upon the collating sequence of the computer system being used.

	Collating sequence		
	EBCDIC	*ASCII*	
Low	Blank space	Blank space	Low
	Special characters	Special characters	
	Letters (A-Z)	Numbers (0-9)	
High	Numbers (0-9)	Letters (A-Z)	High

- Given an alphanumeric comparison with different length subject and object fields, the shorter field is treated as if it were extended on the right with blank spaces to equal the length of the longer field. Then the comparison is made.

- Comparison processing for relation conditions is as follows:

	Object Field	
Subject field	*Numeric data-item or Numeric literal*	*Alphanumeric data-item or Non-numeric literal or Group item*
Numeric data-item or Numeric literal	Numeric (algebraic) comparison	Alphanumeric (character-by-character) comparison
Alphanumeric data-item or Non-numeric literal or Group item	Alphanumeric (character-by-character) comparison	Alphanumeric (character-by-character) comparison

Class condition

Format:

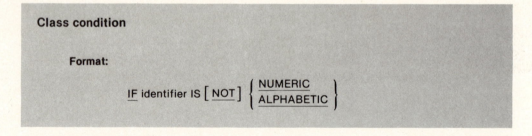

IF identifier IS [NOT] { NUMERIC / ALPHABETIC }

Syntax considerations:

- To be considered NUMERIC, a field must contain only values from 0 (zero) through 9.

  —If a numeric PICTURE character-string contains the symbol S, a signed numeric value will be considered NUMERIC.

  —If the PICTURE character-string does not contain the symbol S, a signed numeric value will be considered NOT NUMERIC.

- To be considered ALPHABETIC, a field must contain only alphabetic values from A through Z and blank spaces.

Sign condition

Format:

$$\text{IF arithmetic-expression IS } [\underline{\text{NOT}}] \left\{ \begin{array}{l} \underline{\text{POSITIVE}} \\ \underline{\text{NEGATIVE}} \\ \underline{\text{ZERO}} \end{array} \right\}$$

Syntax considerations:

- The arithmetic-expression may be a single numeric field.
- ZERO is considered a unique value that is neither positive nor negative.

Condition-name condition

Format:

$$\text{IF condition-name}$$

Syntax consideration:

- The condition-name must be defined as an 88-level item in the DATA DIVISION.

Combined condition

Format:

$$\text{IF condition } \left\{ \left\{ \begin{array}{l} \underline{\text{AND}} \\ \underline{\text{OR}} \end{array} \right\} \text{condition} \right\} \dots$$

Syntax considerations:

- When conditions are linked by the AND operator, **both** (or *all*) conditions must be true for the combined condition to be true. If one condition is false, the combined condition is considered false.
- When conditions are linked by the OR operator, **only one** condition must be true for the combined condition to be true. If both (or all) conditions are false, the combined condition is considered false.

IF statement style recommendations:

- For relation conditions, make the data class of the subject and the object consistent. That is, if the subject is alphanumeric, the object should also be alphanumeric.
- Use the relation condition words (EQUAL TO, LESS THAN, and GREATER THAN) in preference to the symbols (= , < , and >) because (1) certain older computer printers do not contain the greater-than and less-than symbols, (2) the internal data representation for symbols varies with different computer systems, and (3) most people understand the words more readily than the symbols.

- Compound conditions (the operators AND and OR used within the same IF statement) should be avoided because they are confusing. If used, parentheses should be inserted to make the condition understandable and to explicitly specify the evaluation sequence.

- Implied subjects and relation operations should not be used in an IF statement. They tend to cause confusion.

- Nested IF statements should be limited to three or four levels to prevent them from becoming overly complex.

- IF statement clarity is enhanced by providing appropriate indentation. Suggested indentation forms are shown below.

Simple IF statement:

```
IF condition
    true condition statement(s)
ELSE
    false condition statement(s).
```

Combined IF statement:

```
IF condition-1
AND/OR condition-2
    true condition statement(s)
ELSE
    false condition statement(s).
```

Linear nested IF statement:

```
IF condition-1
    true condition-1 statement(s)
ELSE IF condition-2
    true condition-2 statement(s)
ELSE IF condition-3
    true condition-3 statement(s)
ELSE IF condition-4
    true condition-4 statement(s)
ELSE
    all conditions false statement(s).
```

Non-linear nested IF statement
(all action statements after conditions):

```
IF condition-1
    IF condition-2
        IF condition-3
            all conditions true statement(s)
        ELSE
            false condition-3 statement(s)
    ELSE
        false condition-2 statement(s)
ELSE
    false condition-1 statement(s).
```

Non-linear nested IF statement
(interspersed conditions and action statements):

```
IF condition-1
    true condition-1 statement(s)
    IF condition-2
        true condition-2 statement(s)
        IF condition-3
            true condition-3 statement(s)
        ELSE
            false condition-3 statement(s)
    ELSE
        false condition-2 statement(s)
ELSE
    false condition-1 statement(s).
```

MOVE statement

Format:

$$\underline{\text{MOVE}} \left\{ \begin{array}{l} \text{identifier-1} \\ \text{literal} \end{array} \right\} \underline{\text{TO}} \text{ identifier-2 [identifier-3]} \ldots$$

Examples:

```
MOVE NA-EMPLOYEE-NAME TO ER-EMPLOYEE-NAME.

MOVE 'YES' TO WS-END-OF-FILE-SW.

MOVE SPACES TO ER-EMPLOYEE-LINE
              ER-TOTAL-LINE.
```

Syntax considerations:

- Depending upon the MOVE statement sending and receiving field types, justification, truncation, padding, and/or decimal-point alignment will occur as follows:

Group 1.

Alphanumeric sending to alphanumeric receiving, or **Numeric integer sending to alphanumeric receiving,** or **Group sending or group receiving**

—Left justification in receiving field.

—If receiving field is shorter, excess rightmost positions from the sending field are truncated.

—If receiving field is longer, excess rightmost positions in the receiving field are padded with spaces.

Group 2.

Alphanumeric sending to alphanumeric edited receiving

—Same as Group 1.

—Editing is performed for the receiving field in accordance with its PICTURE clause.

Group 3.

Numeric sending to numeric receiving

—Decimal-point alignment.

—If receiving field is shorter (on either side of the decimal point), excess sending field positions are truncated (leftmost integer positions; rightmost decimal fraction positions).

—If receiving field is longer (on either side of the decimal point), excess receiving field positions are padded with zeros (leading zeros for integer positions, trailing zeros for decimal fraction positions).

Group 4.

Numeric sending to numeric edited receiving

—Same as Group 3.

—Editing is performed for the receiving field in accordance with its PICTURE clause.

To provide for right justification of alphanumeric fields, the JUSTIFIED RIGHT clause should be specified for the receiving field.

A complete table of MOVE statement categories is as follows:

			Receiving field			
		Alphanumeric	Numeric	Alphanumeric edited	Numeric edited	Group
Sending field	Alphanumeric	Left justification Receiving field shorter: Truncation Receiving field longer: Padding with spaces	ILLEGAL	Same as AN/AN Editing is performed	ILLEGAL	Same as AN/AN
	Numeric *Integer*	Same as AN/AN	Decimal point alignment Receiving field shorter: Truncation	Same as AN/AN Editing is performed	Same as N/N Editing is performed	Same as AN/AN
	Noninteger	ILLEGAL	Receiving field longer: Padding with zeros	ILLEGAL		
	Alphanumeric edited	Same as AN/AN	ILLEGAL	Same as AN/AN Editing is performed	ILLEGAL	Same as AN/AN
	Numeric edited	Same as AN/AN	ILLEGAL	Same as AN/AN Editing is performed	ILLEGAL	Same as AN/AN
	Group	Same as AN/AN	ILLEGAL	Same as AN/AN (No editing is performed)	ILLEGAL	Same as AN/AN

Note: Unshaded areas indicate most common MOVE categories

AN/AN = Alphanumeric to alphanumeric
N/N = Numeric to numeric

Style recommendations:

■ When the MOVE statement will not fit on one coding line, write the reserved word TO and the receiving field on a separate line and indent them four spaces.

■ If a MOVE statement has multiple receiving fields, write each receiving field (after the first one) aligned vertically on a separate line.

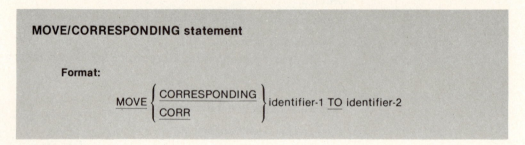

MOVE/CORRESPONDING statement

Format:

$$\text{MOVE} \left\{ \begin{array}{l} \underline{\text{CORRESPONDING}} \\ \underline{\text{CORR}} \end{array} \right\} \text{identifier-1 } \underline{\text{TO}} \text{ identifier-2}$$

Example:

```
*
 01   RECORD-A.
      05   FIELD-AA          PIC  X(2).
      05   FIELD-BB          PIC  S9(5).
      05   FIELD-CC          PIC  X(12).
      05   FIELD-DD          PIC  S9(5).
      05   FIELD-EE          PIC  X(2).
      05   FIELD-FF          PIC  9(6).
*
 01   RECORD-B.
      05   FIELD-AA          PIC  X(2).
      05   FIELD-CC          PIC  X(12).
      05   FIELD-DD          PIC  S9(5).
      05   FIELD-FF          PIC  9(6).
      05   FIELD-GG          PIC  X(25).
      .
      .
      .

      MOVE CORRESPONDING RECORD-A TO RECORD-B.
```

Style recommendation:

■ Do not use the CORRESPONDING phrase with the MOVE statement. It is a "bug-breeder" option.

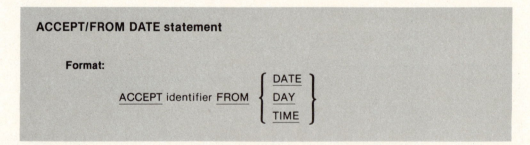

ACCEPT/FROM DATE statement

Format:

$$\underline{\text{ACCEPT}} \text{ identifier } \underline{\text{FROM}} \left\{ \begin{array}{l} \underline{\text{DATE}} \\ \underline{\text{DAY}} \\ \underline{\text{TIME}} \end{array} \right\}$$

Examples:

```
ACCEPT WS-DATE FROM DATE.

ACCEPT WS-DAY FROM DAY.

ACCEPT WS-TIME FROM TIME.
```

Syntax considerations:

■ When DATE is specified, the identifier must be a 6-digit unsigned integer field; the date will be returned in **yymmdd** format.

- When DAY is specified, the identifier must be a 5-digit unsigned integer field; the day will be returned in **yyddd** format.
- When TIME is specified, the identifier must be an 8-digit unsigned integer numeric field; the time will be returned in **hhmmsscc** format (**hh** = hour digits, **mm** = minute digits, **ss** = second digits, **cc** = hundredths of a second digits).

Style recommendation:

- Unless the compiler being used is a pre-1974 standard, use this COBOL standard ACCEPT/FROM DATE statement rather than implementor-defined methods to acquire the current date.

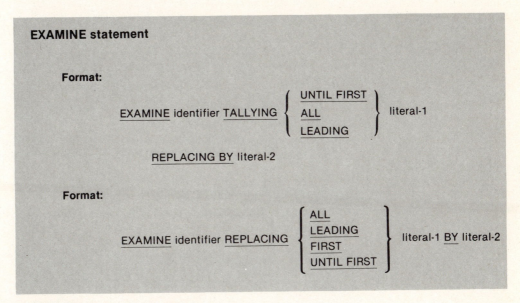

EXAMINE statement

Format:

EXAMINE identifier TALLYING { UNTIL FIRST / ALL / LEADING } literal-1

REPLACING BY literal-2

Format:

EXAMINE identifier REPLACING { ALL / LEADING / FIRST / UNTIL FIRST } literal-1 BY literal-2

Examples:

```
EXAMINE XX-DOLLAR-AMOUNT
    TALLYING ALL '.'.

EXAMINE XX-QUANTITY
    REPLACING LEADING SPACES BY ZEROS.

EXAMINE XX-DATE
    REPLACING ALL '/' BY '-'.
```

Syntax considerations:

- The literals must be a single-character alphanumeric literal or a figurative constant.
- If the identifier is a numeric field, the literal or figurative constant must be a numeric digit character.
- When TALLYING is specified, a field named TALLY is implicitly provided by the compiler with a PICTURE of S9(5). This field can be tested and moved by the programmer.
- TALLY is implicitly zeroed prior to execution of each EXAMINE statement.

Style recommendation:

- Unless the compiler being used is a pre-1974 standard, use the 1974-standard INSPECT statement that supersedes the EXAMINE statement. The INSPECT statement is presented in Chapter 9.

OPEN Statement

Format:

$$\text{OPEN} \left\{ \begin{array}{l} \underline{\text{INPUT}} \text{ file-name-1 [file-name-2] } \ldots \\ \underline{\text{OUTPUT}} \text{ file-name-3 [file-name-4] } \ldots \\ \text{I-O file-name-5 [file-name-6] } \ldots \end{array} \right\} \ldots$$

Examples:

```
OPEN INPUT  EMPLOYEE-FILE
            DEPARTMENTAL-FILE
     OUTPUT EMPLOYEE-REPORT
            DEPARTMENTAL-SUMMARY-FILE.

OPEN INPUT  EMPLOYEE-FILE.
OPEN INPUT  DEPARTMENTAL-FILE.
OPEN OUTPUT EMPLOYEE-REPORT.
OPEN OUTPUT DEPARTMENTAL-SUMMARY-FILE.
```

Syntax consideration:

- Each file used in a COBOL program must be "opened" before any other input/output operations (other than ACCEPT or DISPLAY) that involve the file can be executed.

Style recommendation:

- Write the OPEN statement with each file-name on a separate line and align it vertically.

READ Statement

Format:

$$\underline{\text{READ}} \text{ file-name RECORD } \left[\underline{\text{INTO}} \text{ identifier} \right]$$
$$\left[\text{at } \underline{\text{END}} \text{ imperative-statement} \right]$$

Examples:

```
READ PAYROLL-FILE
     AT END MOVE 'YES' TO WS-END-OF-FILE-SW.

READ PAYROLL-FILE
     INTO PR-PAYROLL-RECORD
     AT END MOVE 'YES' TO WS-END OF FILE-SW.
```

Syntax considerations:

- The READ statement causes a record to be transferred from the external storage medium to the record-description area within the FD for the file.
- Specification of the INTO phrase additionally causes the record to be transferred to the area named by the object of the INTO phrase. It is equivalent to a READ statement followed by a MOVE statement.

Style recommendation:

- Write the READ statement with the AT END (and INTO, if used) phrase on a separate line and indent it four spaces.

WRITE Statement

Format:

```
WRITE record-name [ FROM identifier-1 ]


  [  ⎧ BEFORE ⎫                ⎧ identifier-2  ⎫  ⎡ LINE  ⎤  ]
  [  ⎨        ⎬  ADVANCING  ⎧  ⎨ integer       ⎬  ⎢ LINES ⎥  ⎫ ]
  [  ⎩ AFTER  ⎭               ⎨ mnemonic-name ⎬  ⎣       ⎦  ⎬ ]
                             ⎩  PAGE           ⎭            ⎭
```

Examples:

```
WRITE ER-EMPLOYEE-LINE
    AFTER ADVANCING 2 LINES.

WRITE ER-EMPLOYEE-LINE
    AFTER ADVANCING WS-LINE-SPACING.

WRITE ER-EMPLOYEE-LINE
    AFTER ADVANCING TO-TOP-OF-PAGE.

WRITE ER-EMPLOYEE-LINE
    AFTER ADVANCING PAGE.
```

Syntax considerations:

- The WRITE statement causes a record to be transferred from the record-description area within the FD for the file to the external storage medium.

- Specification of the FROM phrase additionally causes the record to first be transferred from the area named by the object of the FROM phrase. It is equivalent to a MOVE statement followed by a WRITE statement.

- The ADVANCING phrase is used to specify the number of line spaces to be advanced in conjunction with the WRITE operation.

Style recommendations:

- Place the ADVANCING phrase (and the INTO phrase, if used) of the WRITE statement on a separate line and indent it four spaces.

- Unless the compiler being used is a pre-1974 standard version, use the COBOL standard PAGE option of the ADVANCING phrase rather than the mnemonic-name option to advance printer forms to the next page.

- Avoid use of the FROM phrase for multiple-record files because it is not consistent with the formation of independent modules, as discussed in Chapter 1 of the text.

CLOSE Statement

Format:

```
CLOSE file-name-1 [file-name-2] . . .
```

Examples:

```
CLOSE EMPLOYEE-FILE
      DEPARTMENTAL-FILE
      EMPLOYEE-REPORT
      DEPARTMENTAL-SUMMARY-FILE.
```

```
CLOSE  EMPLOYEE-FILE.
CLOSE  DEPARTMENTAL-FILE.
CLOSE  EMPLOYEE-REPORT.
CLOSE  DEPARTMENTAL-SUMMARY-FILE.
```

Syntax consideration:

■ After all input-output operations have been executed for a file and before program execution ends, each "opened" file must be "closed."

Style recommendation:

■ Write the CLOSE statement with each file-name on a separate line and align it vertically.

ACCEPT statement

Format:

ACCEPT identifier [FROM mnemonic-name]

Examples:

Part A: ACCEPT from input device

```
ACCEPT  WS-PERIOD-ENDING-DATE.
```

Part B: ACCEPT from console

ENVIRONMENT DIVISION

```
SPECIAL-NAMES.
    CONSOLE IS TYPEWRITER.
```

PROCEDURE DIVISION

```
ACCEPT  WS-PERIOD-ENDING-DATE FROM TYPEWRITER.
```

Syntax considerations:

■ The ACCEPT statement obtains low-volume input data from an input device or the computer operator console and transfers it to the identifier area.

■ The identifier may be either an elementary item of DISPLAY usage or a group item. (The maximum length of the transfer is typically 80 characters.)

Style recommendation:

■ Minimize use of the ACCEPT statement. Use the READ statement for normal record processing.

DISPLAY statement

Format:

$$\text{DISPLAY} \begin{Bmatrix} \text{identifier-1} \\ \text{literal-1} \end{Bmatrix} \begin{bmatrix} \text{identifier-2} \\ \text{literal-2} \end{bmatrix} \dots \begin{bmatrix} \underline{\text{UPON}} \ \text{mnemonic-name} \end{bmatrix}$$

Examples:

Part A: DISPLAY upon output device

```
DISPLAY 'RUN CANCELED DUE TO '  WS-ERROR-MESSAGE.
```

Part B: DISPLAY upon console
ENVIRONMENT DIVISION

```
SPECIAL-NAMES.
     CONSOLE IS TYPEWRITER.
```

PROCEDURE DIVISION

```
DISPLAY 'ENTER PERIOD ENDING DATE' UPON TYPEWRITER.
```

Syntax considerations:

- The DISPLAY statement transfers low-volume output data from the identifier area to an output device or the computer operator console.
- The identifier may be either an elementary item of DISPLAY usage, a group item or a literal. (The maximum length of the transfer is typically 120 characters.)

Style recommendation:

- Minimize use of the DISPLAY statement. Use the WRITE statement for normal record processing.

SORT/MERGE statements

(See Appendix D: SORT/MERGE Program Reference.)

Table-handling statements

(See Appendix C: Table-Processing Reference.)

Transfer of Control Statements

PERFORM statement

Format:

$$\underline{\text{PERFORM}} \ \text{procedure-name-1} \begin{bmatrix} \begin{Bmatrix} \underline{\text{THROUGH}} \\ \underline{\text{THRU}} \end{Bmatrix} \ \text{procedure-name-2} \end{bmatrix}$$

Example:

```
PERFORM 100-INITIALIZE-VARIABLE-FIELDS.
```

Syntax consideration:

■ The PERFORM statement causes program control to be transferred to the procedure specified. Control is returned when the end of procedure-name-1 (or, if the THRU phrase is specified, the end of procedure-name-2) is reached. Program execution continues with the next sequential executable instruction following the PERFORM statement.

Style recommendation:

■ Do not use the optional THRU phrase because it introduces multiple-entry and -exit points into the file.

PERFORM/UNTIL statement

Format:

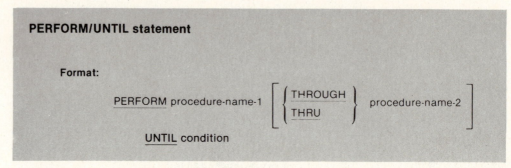

Example:

```
PERFORM 200-PROCESS-NAME-ADS-RECORD
    UNTIL WS-END-OF-FILE-SW IS EQUAL TO 'YES'.
```

Syntax considerations:

■ The PERFORM/UNTIL statement operates as the basic PERFORM does except for two differences:

  1. Control is transferred conditionally, depending upon the condition expressed following the reserved word UNTIL. If the condition is false, the named procedure is performed. If the condition is true, the procedure is not performed but program execution instead continues with the next sequential executable statement.
  2. Return from the performed procedure is made *not* to the next sequential executable statement but instead to test the condition. Additional iterations of the performed procedure are made until the condition is true.

Style recommendations:

■ Write the PERFORM/UNTIL statement with the UNTIL condition on a separate line and indented four spaces.

■ Do not use the optional THRU phrase because it introduces multiple-entry and -exit points into the file.

PERFORM/TIMES statement

Format:

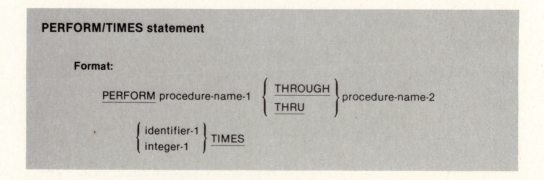

Examples:

```
        PERFORM 999-PRINT-OUTPUT-FORM 2 TIMES.

        PERFORM 999-PRINT-OUTPUT-FORM WS-COPIES-REQUIRED TIMES.
```

Syntax consideration:

- The specified procedure is repeatedly performed as specified by the value of the literal or identifier.

Style recommendation:

- Do not use the optional THRU phrase because it introduces multiple-entry and -exit points into the program.

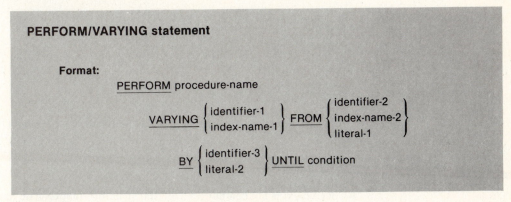

PERFORM/VARYING statement

Format:

PERFORM procedure-name

VARYING $\left\{ \begin{array}{c} \text{identifier-1} \\ \text{index-name-1} \end{array} \right\}$ FROM $\left\{ \begin{array}{c} \text{identifier-2} \\ \text{index-name-2} \\ \text{literal-1} \end{array} \right\}$

BY $\left\{ \begin{array}{c} \text{identifier-3} \\ \text{literal-2} \end{array} \right\}$ UNTIL condition

Example:

```
        PERFORM 999-LOOKUP-STATE-NAME
            VARYING ST-SUBSCRIPT
            FROM 1
            BY 1
                UNTIL ST-ENTRY-FOUND.
```

Syntax considerations:

- The identifier or index is initialized to the FROM value before the procedure is performed for the first time.
- The identifier or index is incremented with the BY value immediately after each iteration of the procedure.
- The UNTIL condition is tested immediately before each iteration of the procedure (which is after initialization or incrementation). This means that, for a table lookup, once the match between search and table arguments has been located, the subscript or index must typically be decremented so that it will reflect the table entry occurrence number at which the match was located.

Style recommendation:

- Do not use the optional THRU phrase because it introduces multiple-entry and -exit points into the program.

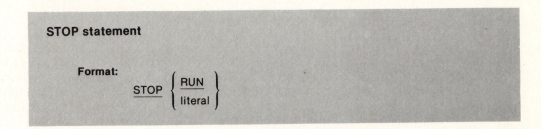

STOP statement

Format:

STOP $\left\{ \begin{array}{c} \text{RUN} \\ \text{literal} \end{array} \right\}$

Example:

```
                STOP RUN.
```

Syntax consideration:

- The STOP RUN statement stops execution of the program and causes control to be returned to the operating system.

GO TO statement

Format:

```
GO TO procedure-name
```

Example:

```
            GO TO 2999-SORT-PROCEDURE-EXIT.
```

Syntax consideration:

- The GO TO statement causes program control to be transferred to the specified procedure-name.

Style recommendation:

- Because it is not compatible with the structure theorem, do not use the GO TO statement except where required for

    1. the SORT/MERGE statements with an INPUT PROCEDURE or an OUTPUT PROCEDURE
    2. the case structure

GO TO/DEPENDING ON statement

Format:

```
GO TO procedure-name-1 [procedure-name-2] . . . , procedure-name-n

    DEPENDING ON identifier
```

Example:

```
            GO TO 999-PROCESS-RECORD-A
                  999-PROCESS-RECORD-B
                  999-PROCESS-RECORD-C
                  999-PROCESS-RECORD-D
                  999-PROCESS-RECORD-E
                     DEPENDING ON WS-RECORD-CODE-FLAG.
```

Syntax consideration:

- The GO TO/DEPENDING ON statement causes program control to be transferred to a relative procedure in accordance with the value of the identifier. That is, if the identifier contains a 1, program control is transferred to the first procedure named; if the identifier contains a 2, program control is transferred to the second procedure named, and so forth. If the identifier contains a value that is less than 1 or greater than the number of procedures specified, no transfer is made; program control flows to the next sequential executable statement.

Style recommendation:

■ Because it is easier to maintain and permits the use of PERFORM statements, use a linear nested IF statement with relation conditions to achieve the same effect as the GO TO/ DEPENDING ON statement.

EXIT statement

Format:

```
EXIT.
```

Example:

```
EXIT.
```

Syntax consideration:

■ EXIT is a dummy statement that provides a null entry point for a dummy paragraph. When EXIT is specified, it must be the only statement contained in the paragraph.

ALTER statement

Format:

ALTER procedure-name-1 TO [PROCEED TO] procedure-name-2

[procedure-name-3 TO [PROCEED TO] procedure-name-4] . . .

Example:

```
*
*
 999-CONTROL-PROCEDURE.
*
     GO TO 999-PROCESS-DETAIL-RECORD.
*
*
 999-NEXT-PROCEDURE.
*
                    .
                    .
                    .

                    .
                    .
                    .

     ALTER 999-CONTROL-PROCEDURE
         TO PROCEED TO 999-PROCESS-CONTROL-BREAK.
```

Syntax consideration:

■ Procedure-name-1 must be a paragraph that contains only a GO TO statement, as does 999-CONTROL-PROCEDURE, above. After the ALTER statement is executed, the GO TO statement will transfer control to the 999-PROCESS-CONTROL-BREAK procedure rather than the 999-PROCESS-DETAIL-RECORD procedure. (Typically there will be another ALTER statement elsewhere in the program to change control back to the 999-PROCESS-DETAIL-RECORD procedure when required.)

Style recommendation:

■ Do not use the ALTER statement. It is a "bug-breeder" statement and therefore scheduled to be removed from the next COBOL standard.

APPENDIX C

TABLE-PROCESSING REFERENCE

Table-Processing Concepts

Table-Handling Terminology

A **table** is a collection of **table entries**. A table entry may contain a **table argument** and/or one or more **table functions**. Typically a table contains one **table argument** and one or more **table functions**. When a table is organized positionally, it will normally contain only table functions. For code-existence checks, tables composed only of arguments are sometimes used.

Month number	Month name abbreviation	Maximum days in month	
01	JAN	31	
02	FEB	29	
03	MAR	31	
04	APR	30	
05	MAY	31	
06	JUN	30	
07	JUL	31	Table entries
08	AUG	31	
09	SEP	30	
10	OCT	31	
11	NOV	30	
12	DEC	31	
↑ Table argument	↑ Table function-1	↑ Table function-2	

Table Organization

Table organization can be **random, sequential**, by **usage-frequency**, or **positional**. Tables are rarely organized randomly, for such organization provides no advantages and is difficult to maintain. Sequential organization is the most commonly used organization method.

Random organization		Sequential organization	
Product code (Table argument)	Soft drink flavor (Table function)	Product code (Table argument)	Soft drink flavor (Table function)
110	ORANGE	100	LEMON-LIME
300	GINGER ALE	110	ORANGE
320	CREME SODA	120	CHERRY COLA
120	CHERRY COLA	130	STRAWBERRY
200	ROOT BEER	140	GRAPE
310	LIME RICKEY	150	FRUIT PUNCH
500	COLA	200	ROOT BEER
100	LEMON-LIME	300	GINGER ALE
150	FRUIT PUNCH	310	LIME RICKEY
140	GRAPE	320	CREME SODA
130	STRAWBERRY	500	COLA

Usage/frequency organization		Positional organization	
Product code (Table argument)	Soft drink flavor (Table function)	Month name abbreviation	Maximum days in month
500	COLA	JAN	31
100	LEMON-LIME	FEB	29
200	ROOT BEER	MAR	31
120	CHERRY COLA	APR	30
110	ORANGE	MAY	31
300	GINGER ALE	JUN	30
140	GRAPE	JUL	31
150	FRUIT PUNCH	AUG	31
130	STRAWBERRY	SEP	30
320	CREME SODA	OCT	31
310	LIME RICKEY	NOV	30
		DEC	31

If the table arguments are an unbroken sequence of numeric values, positional organization can be used. With positional organization, the relative table-entry slot number indicates the argument value so that the table argument values need not be stored in the table.

Table-Lookup Methods

Tables with random, sequential, or usage-frequency organization can be processed by a **serial lookup**. For sequential tables, it is usually more efficient to use a **serial lookup with early exit** or a **binary search lookup**. Positionally organized tables can take advantage of **positional addressing**.

Serial lookup:

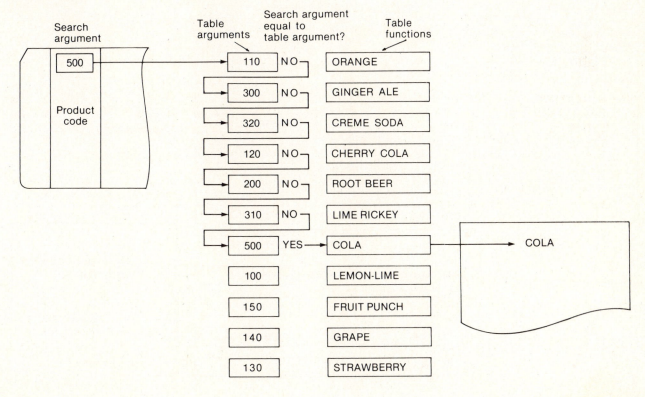

Serial lookup with early exit:

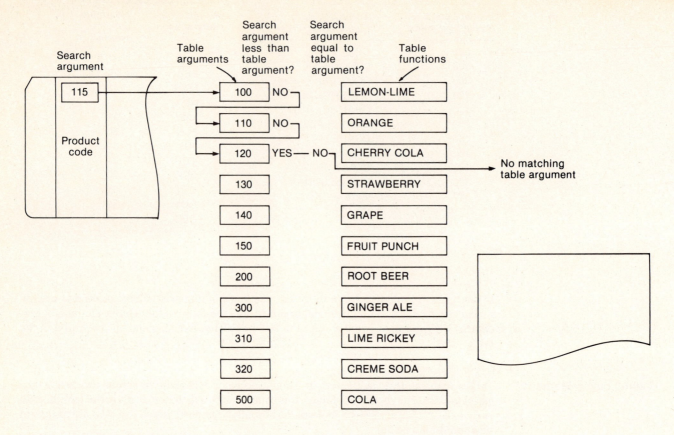

Binary search lookup:

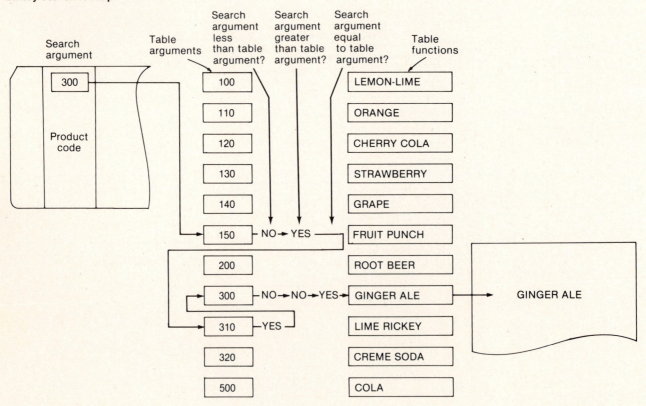

Positional addressing:

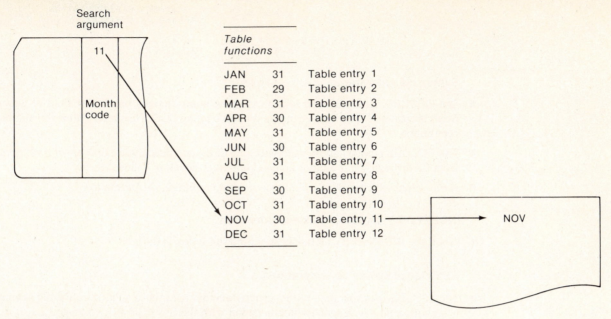

Summary of table organization and lookup methods

Table organization	Lookup method			
	Serial search	Serial search with early exit	Binary search	Positional addressing
Random	Same lookup efficiency as for sequential organization			
Sequential	Lookup may be slow if number of table entries is large	Improves serial search when many search arguments do not have matching table argument	Most efficient sequential lookup for longer tables (differential increases as table gets longer)	
Usage-frequency	Efficient lookup if great majority of search arguments are just a few table entries			
Positionally				Immediate lookup

DATA DIVISION
Table-Processing Entries

OCCURS Clause

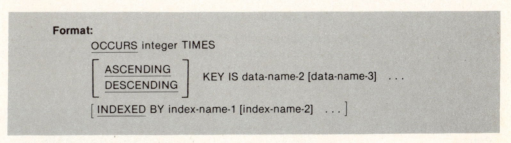

Examples:

```
05  MT-MONTH-ABBREVIATION     OCCURS 12 TIMES
                              PIC X(3).


05  MT-MONTH-ABBREVIATION     OCCURS 12 TIMES
                              INDEXED BY MT-INDEX
                              PIC X(3).
```

```
05   ST-STATE-ENTRY                    OCCURS 12 TIMES
                                        ASCENDING KEY
                                            ST-STATE-ABBREVIATION
                                        INDEXED BY ST-INDEX.

     10   ST-STATE-ABBREVIATION        PIC X(2).
     10   ST-STATE-NAME                PIC X(20).
```

Syntax considerations:

- The OCCURS clause is used to indicate how many times a particular field or group of fields is repeated. The integer that is specified in the OCCURS clause states the number of repetitions.

- The OCCURS clause can be used with any data-item description that has a level number from 02 through 49; it cannot be used with a 01-level or 77-level item.

- A data-item with an OCCURS clause cannot contain a VALUE clause.

INDEXED BY clause syntax consideration:

- When the INDEXED BY clause is specified, an index is defined.

KEY clause syntax considerations:

- The KEY clause is specified with a group item that contains a subordinate table argument used with a binary search (which is coded with the SEARCH ALL statement).

- ASCENDING or DESCENDING KEY can be coded. The programmer must ensure that the table arguments are actually in the sequence specified.

Subscript Data-Items

Example:

```
05   ST-SUBSCRIPT              PIC S9(4)          COMP SYNC.
```

Syntax considerations:

- A subscript is defined in the DATA DIVISION and used in the PROCEDURE DIVISION to reference a specific occurrence of a repeated field defined with the OCCURS clause. The subscript value indicates which occurrence of the field is referenced.

- A subscript must be defined as an elementary numeric integer data-item.

- The length of the subscript field must be sufficient to contain the number of occurrences specified in the OCCURS clause.

- When the subscript is used while the program is executing, its value should be greater than zero and not greater than the number of occurrences of the field being subscripted, as specified in its OCCURS clause.

Style considerations:

- Specification of the PICTURE symbol S and COMP SYNC usage typically results in most efficient processing. For IBM-compatible compilers, a PICTURE character-string of S9(4), or S9(8) is appropriate.

USAGE IS INDEX Clause

Format:

[USAGE IS] INDEX

Example:

```
05   XX-INDEX-ITEM                               USAGE IS INDEX.

05   XX-INDEX-ITEM                                          INDEX.
```

- The USAGE IS INDEX clause is specified to establish a data-item for the storage of index values for later use without conversion to occurrence numbers.

- PICTURE and VALUE clauses cannot be specified with an index data-item.

Establishing a Hard-Coded Table in the WORKING-STORAGE SECTION

To establish a hard-coded table, the programmer must first define the entries with VALUE clauses. After the table data has been established with VALUE clauses, the table must be redefined with an OCCURS clause.

Example:

```
*
 01  ST-STATE-DATA.                                                                    Table
     05  FILLER    PIC X(22) VALUE 'AKALASKA           '.   05  FILLER   PIC X(22) VALUE 'NDNORTH DAKOTA      '.
     05  FILLER    PIC X(22) VALUE 'ALALABAMA          '.   05  FILLER   PIC X(22) VALUE 'NENEBRASKA          '.
     05  FILLER    PIC X(22) VALUE 'ARARKANSAS         '.   05  FILLER   PIC X(22) VALUE 'NHNEW HAMPSHIRE     '.
     05  FILLER    PIC X(22) VALUE 'AZARIZONA          '.   05  FILLER   PIC X(22) VALUE 'NJNEW JERSEY        '.
     05  FILLER    PIC X(22) VALUE 'CACALIFORNIA       '.   05  FILLER   PIC X(22) VALUE 'NMNEW MEXICO        '.
     05  FILLER    PIC X(22) VALUE 'COCOLORADO         '.   05  FILLER   PIC X(22) VALUE 'NVNEVADA            '.
     05  FILLER    PIC X(22) VALUE 'CTCONNECTICUT      '.   05  FILLER   PIC X(22) VALUE 'NYNEW YORK          '.
     05  FILLER    PIC X(22) VALUE 'DCDISTRICT OF COLUMBIA'.   05  FILLER   PIC X(22) VALUE 'OHOHIO              '.
     05  FILLER    PIC X(22) VALUE 'DEDELAWARE         '.   05  FILLER   PIC X(22) VALUE 'OKOKLAHOMA          '.
     05  FILLER    PIC X(22) VALUE 'FLFLORIDA          '.   05  FILLER   PIC X(22) VALUE 'OROREGON            '.
     05  FILLER    PIC X(22) VALUE 'GAGEORGIA          '.   05  FILLER   PIC X(22) VALUE 'PAPENNSYLVANIA      '.
     05  FILLER    PIC X(22) VALUE 'HIHAWAII           '.   05  FILLER   PIC X(22) VALUE 'RIRHODE ISLAND      '.
     05  FILLER    PIC X(22) VALUE 'IAIOWA             '.   05  FILLER   PIC X(22) VALUE 'SCSOUTH CAROLINA    '.
     05  FILLER    PIC X(22) VALUE 'IDIDAHO            '.   05  FILLER   PIC X(22) VALUE 'SDSOUTH DAKOTA      '.
     05  FILLER    PIC X(22) VALUE 'ILILLINOIS         '.   05  FILLER   PIC X(22) VALUE 'TNTENNESSEE         '.
     05  FILLER    PIC X(22) VALUE 'ININDIANA          '.   05  FILLER   PIC X(22) VALUE 'TXTEXAS             '.
     05  FILLER    PIC X(22) VALUE 'KSKANSAS           '.   05  FILLER   PIC X(22) VALUE 'UTUTAH              '.
     05  FILLER    PIC X(22) VALUE 'KYKENTUCKY         '.   05  FILLER   PIC X(22) VALUE 'VAVIRGINIA          '.
     05  FILLER    PIC X(22) VALUE 'LALOUISIANA        '.   05  FILLER   PIC X(22) VALUE 'VTVERMONT           '.
     05  FILLER    PIC X(22) VALUE 'MAMASSACHUSETTS    '.   05  FILLER   PIC X(22) VALUE 'WAWASHINGTON        '.
     05  FILLER    PIC X(22) VALUE 'MDMARYLAND         '.   05  FILLER   PIC X(22) VALUE 'WIWISCONSIN         '.
     05  FILLER    PIC X(22) VALUE 'MEMAINE            '.   05  FILLER   PIC X(22) VALUE 'WVWEST VIRGINIA     '.
     05  FILLER    PIC X(22) VALUE 'MIMICHIGAN         '.   05  FILLER   PIC X(22) VALUE 'WYWYOMING           '.
     05  FILLER    PIC X(22) VALUE 'MNMINNESOTA        '. 01  ST-STATE-TABLE REDEFINES ST-STATE-DATA.
     05  FILLER    PIC X(22) VALUE 'MOMISSOURI         '.   05  ST-STATE-ENTRY          OCCURS 51 TIMES.
     05  FILLER    PIC X(22) VALUE 'MSMISSISSPI        '.      10  ST-STATE-ABBREVIATION  PIC X(2).
     05  FILLER    PIC X(22) VALUE 'MTMONTANA          '.      10  ST-STATE-NAME          PIC X(20).
     05  FILLER    PIC X(22) VALUE 'NCNORTH CAROLINA   '.
```

Establishing an Input-Loaded Table

To establish a table that is to be loaded from input, it is not necessary to define the entries with VALUE clauses or to use the REDEFINES clause because the table data will be supplied by the input data.

Example:

```
 01  ST-STATE-TABLE.
     05  ST-STATE-ENTRY          OCCURS 51 TIMES.
         10  ST-STATE-ABBREVIATION  PIC X(2).
         10  ST-STATE-NAME          PIC X(20).
```

Table Establishment Guidelines

- Determine the optimum table organization method for the table: random, sequential, usage-frequency, or positional.

- Arrange the table arguments adjacent to the table functions to ease programmer checking, debugging, and maintenance functions.

- When hard-coding the table data with VALUE clauses, try to specify a separate data-item for each table entry. This will also ease programmer checking and maintenance functions.

- When hard-coded table entries (1) are too long to fit on one coding line or (2) contain data-items with varying USAGE clauses, one table entry will require multiple data-items.

- More efficient processing is usually provided by use of indexes rather than subscripts. Therefore, the programmer should specify the INDEXED BY clause for most tables.

- If the table is organized sequentially and contains over 30 or so entries, consider sequential organization and specification of the ASCENDING KEY or DESCENDING KEY phrase so that a binary search lookup can be used.

- For ease of reference, establish required table control fields immediately before the table. Typical table control fields are as follows:

  —an entry-found switch
  —a subscript field (when an index is not used)
  —a number-of-table-entries field (when a dummy end-of-table entry and/or the SEARCH statement are not used)

PROCEDURE DIVISION Table-Processing Entries

SEARCH Statement

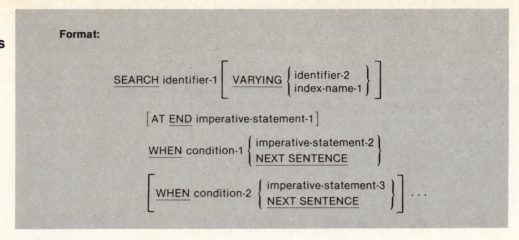

Format:

$$\underline{\text{SEARCH}} \text{ identifier-1} \left[\underline{\text{VARYING}} \begin{Bmatrix} \text{identifier-2} \\ \text{index-name-1} \end{Bmatrix} \right]$$

$$\left[\text{AT } \underline{\text{END}} \text{ imperative-statement-1} \right]$$

$$\underline{\text{WHEN}} \text{ condition-1} \begin{Bmatrix} \text{imperative-statement-2} \\ \underline{\text{NEXT SENTENCE}} \end{Bmatrix}$$

$$\left[\underline{\text{WHEN}} \text{ condition-2} \begin{Bmatrix} \text{imperative-statement-3} \\ \underline{\text{NEXT SENTENCE}} \end{Bmatrix} \right] \ldots$$

Example:

```
SEARCH ST-STATE-ENTRY
    AT END MOVE 'NO' TO ST-ENTRY-FOUND-SW
    WHEN ST-STATE-ABBREVIATION (ST-INDEX)
            IS EQUAL TO IN-STATE-ABBREVIATION
        MOVE 'YES' TO ST-ENTRY-FOUND-SW.
```

Syntax considerations:

- The SEARCH statement provides a serial search for a table defined with the INDEXED BY clause.

- The table specified is searched, entry by entry, until the condition expressed in the WHEN phrase is satisfied. SEARCH statement processing ends after the WHEN phrase statement actions have been executed.

- If end-of-table is reached before the WHEN condition is satisfied, the AT END phrase statement actions are executed.

- It is the programmer's responsibility to initialize the index by coding a SET statement, typically immediately before the SEARCH statement. Index incrementation is handled automatically by the SEARCH statement.

SEARCH/ALL Statement

Format:

$$\underline{\text{SEARCH ALL}} \text{ identifier-1} \left[\text{AT } \underline{\text{END}} \text{ imperative-statement-1} \right]$$

$$\underline{\text{WHEN}} \begin{Bmatrix} \text{data-name-1} \begin{Bmatrix} \text{IS } \underline{\text{EQUAL}} \text{ TO} \\ \text{IS } = \end{Bmatrix} \begin{Bmatrix} \text{identifier-3} \\ \text{literal-1} \\ \text{arithmetic-expression-1} \end{Bmatrix} \\ \text{condition-name-1} \end{Bmatrix}$$

$$\left[\underline{\text{AND}} \begin{Bmatrix} \text{data-name-2} \begin{Bmatrix} \text{IS } \underline{\text{EQUAL}} \text{ TO} \\ \text{IS } = \end{Bmatrix} \begin{Bmatrix} \text{identifier-4} \\ \text{literal-2} \\ \text{arithmetic-expression-2} \end{Bmatrix} \\ \text{condition-name-2} \end{Bmatrix} \right] \ldots$$

$$\begin{Bmatrix} \text{imperative-statement-2} \\ \underline{\text{NEXT SENTENCE}} \end{Bmatrix}$$

Example:

```
SEARCH ALL ST-STATE-ENTRY
    AT END MOVE 'NO' TO ST-ENTRY-FOUND-SW
    WHEN ST-STATE-ABBREVIATION (ST-INDEX)
         IS EQUAL TO IN-STATE-ABBREVIATION
    MOVE 'YES' TO ST-ENTRY-FOUND-SW.
```

Syntax considerations:

- The SEARCH/ALL statement provides a binary search for a table defined with the INDEXED BY and KEY clauses.

- A binary search is made until the condition expressed in the WHEN phrase is satisfied. Observe that a SEARCH statement with the ALL phrase is limited to an EQUAL relationship condition in the WHEN phrase. SEARCH statement processing ends after the WHEN phrase statement actions have been executed.

- If end-of-table is reached before the WHEN condition is satisfied, the AT END phrase statement actions are executed.

- Index initialization and incrementation are handled automatically by the SEARCH/ALL statement.

SET Statement

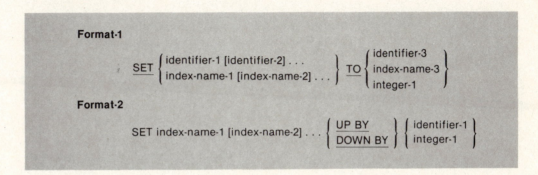

Format-1

$$\underline{SET} \left\{ \begin{array}{l} \text{identifier-1 [identifier-2]} \dots \\ \text{index-name-1 [index-name-2]} \dots \end{array} \right\} \underline{TO} \left\{ \begin{array}{l} \text{identifier-3} \\ \text{index-name-3} \\ \text{integer-1} \end{array} \right\}$$

Format-2

$$SET \text{ index-name-1 [index-name-2]} \dots \left\{ \begin{array}{l} \underline{UP \ BY} \\ \underline{DOWN \ BY} \end{array} \right\} \left\{ \begin{array}{l} \text{identifier-1} \\ \text{integer-1} \end{array} \right\}$$

Example:

```
SET ST-INDEX TO 1.

SET ST-INDEX UP BY 1.

SET ST-INDEX DOWN BY 1.
```

Syntax considerations:

- The SET statement is used to initialize, increment, or decrement index data-items. (Other statements, such as MOVE, ADD, SUBTRACT, and so forth, cannot be used to modify the value of an index data-item.) SET statement processing is summarized below:

Form: SET receiving-field TO sending field

	Sending-field		
Receiving field	Integer or numeric identifier	Index	Index data-item
Index	Index set to index value corresponding to occurrence number of sending-field	Index set to index value corresponding to occurrence number of sending-field's occurrence	Index data-item moved to index without conversion
Numeric identifier	Illegal	Numeric identifier set to occurrence number corresponding to index value	Illegal
Index data-item	Illegal	Index moved to index data-item without conversion	Index data-item moved to index data-item without conversion

Table Lookups

Table Lookups Using a SEARCH Statement Driver

This section presents table lookup examples.

The SEARCH statement typically provides most efficient table lookup processing and thus, if available, should be used for most table lookup tasks.

Serial search example

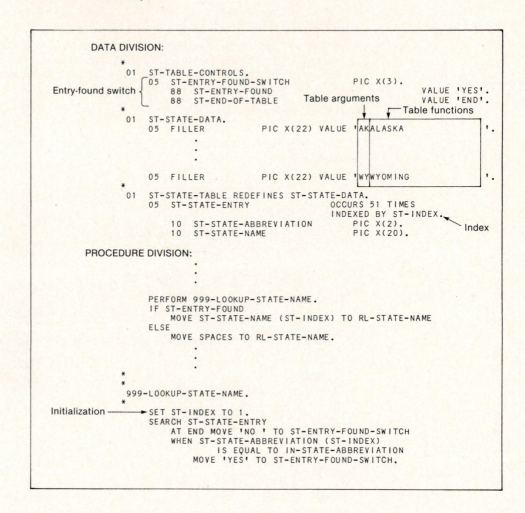

```
                    DATA DIVISION:
                    *
                    01   ST-TABLE-CONTROLS.
                         05   ST-ENTRY-FOUND-SWITCH              PIC X(3).
  Entry-found switch {       88   ST-ENTRY-FOUND                               VALUE 'YES'.
                             88   ST-END-OF-TABLE    Table arguments           VALUE 'END'.
                    *                                            Table functions
                    01   ST-STATE-DATA.
                         05   FILLER             PIC X(22) VALUE 'AK ALASKA               '.
                                    .
                                    .
                                    .
                         05   FILLER             PIC X(22) VALUE 'WY WYOMING              '.
                    *
                    01   ST-STATE-TABLE REDEFINES ST-STATE-DATA.
                         05   ST-STATE-ENTRY                OCCURS 51 TIMES
                                                            INDEXED BY ST-INDEX.
                              10   ST-STATE-ABBREVIATION     PIC X(2).          Index
                              10   ST-STATE-NAME             PIC X(20).

                    PROCEDURE DIVISION:
                                    .
                                    .
                                    .
                         PERFORM 999-LOOKUP-STATE-NAME.
                         IF ST-ENTRY-FOUND
                             MOVE ST-STATE-NAME (ST-INDEX) TO RL-STATE-NAME
                         ELSE
                             MOVE SPACES TO RL-STATE-NAME.
                                    .
                                    .
                                    .
                    *
                    *
                    999-LOOKUP-STATE-NAME.
                    *
  Initialization ──►  SET ST-INDEX TO 1.
                      SEARCH ST-STATE-ENTRY
                          AT END MOVE 'NO ' TO ST-ENTRY-FOUND-SWITCH
                          WHEN ST-STATE-ABBREVIATION (ST-INDEX)
                              IS EQUAL TO IN-STATE-ABBREVIATION
                          MOVE 'YES' TO ST-ENTRY-FOUND-SWITCH.
```

Binary search example

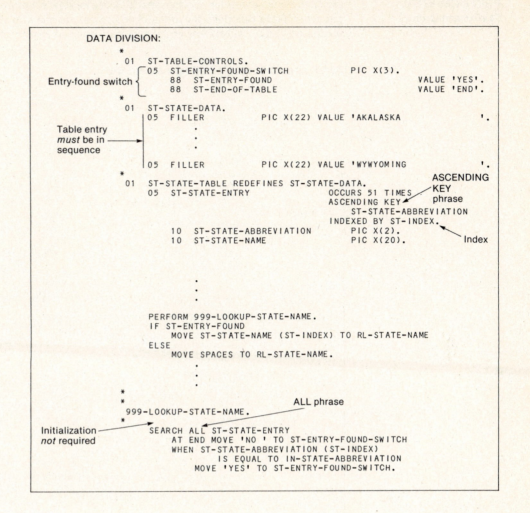

```
        DATA DIVISION:
        *
        01  ST-TABLE-CONTROLS.
                05   ST-ENTRY-FOUND-SWITCH          PIC X(3).
                     88   ST-ENTRY-FOUND                         VALUE 'YES'.
                     88   ST-END-OF-TABLE                        VALUE 'END'.
        *
        01  ST-STATE-DATA.
                05   FILLER          PIC X(22) VALUE 'AKALASKA                '.
                                .
                                .
                                .
                05   FILLER          PIC X(22) VALUE 'WYWYOMING               '.
        *
        01  ST-STATE-TABLE REDEFINES ST-STATE-DATA.
                05   ST-STATE-ENTRY                OCCURS 51 TIMES
                                                   ASCENDING KEY
                                                     ST-STATE-ABBREVIATION
                                                   INDEXED BY ST-INDEX.
                     10   ST-STATE-ABBREVIATION      PIC X(2).
                     10   ST-STATE-NAME              PIC X(20).


                                .
                                .
                                .

        PERFORM 999-LOOKUP-STATE-NAME.
        IF ST-ENTRY-FOUND
                MOVE ST-STATE-NAME (ST-INDEX) TO RL-STATE-NAME
        ELSE
                MOVE SPACES TO RL-STATE-NAME.
                                .
                                .
                                .
        *
        *
        999-LOOKUP-STATE-NAME.
        *
                SEARCH ALL ST-STATE-ENTRY
                     AT END MOVE 'NO ' TO ST-ENTRY-FOUND-SWITCH
                     WHEN ST-STATE-ABBREVIATION (ST-INDEX)
                             IS EQUAL TO IN-STATE-ABBREVIATION
                     MOVE 'YES' TO ST-ENTRY-FOUND-SWITCH.
```

Entry-found switch

Table entry *must* be in sequence

ASCENDING KEY phrase

Index

ALL phrase

Initialization *not* required

Table Lookups Using a PERFORM/UNTIL Statement Driver

The PERFORM/UNTIL statement can be used to drive the table lookup when the SEARCH statement is not available or when special table lookup techniques are required (for example, when table functions for unmatched arguments must be accumulated or otherwise processed). Either subscripts or indexes may be used to reference the table.

Serial search example (using a subscript)

```
                DATA DIVISION:

                *
                  01   ST-TABLE-CONTROLS.
Subscript ——————→ 05    ST-SUBSCRIPT                      PIC S9(4)      COMP SYNC.
Table limit ————→ 05    ST-NUMBER-OF-ENTRIES              PIC S9(4)    VALUE +51
                                                                        COMP SYNC.
                  05    ST-ENTRY-FOUND-SWITCH             PIC X(3).
Entry-found switch {    88   ST-ENTRY-FOUND                             VALUE 'YES'.
                        88   ST-END-OF-TABLE                            VALUE 'END'.
                *
                  01   ST-STATE-DATA.
                    05   FILLER          PIC X(22) VALUE 'AKALASKA            '.
                                  .
                                  .
                                  .
                    05   FILLER          PIC X(22) VALUE 'WYWYOMING            '.
                *
                  01   ST-STATE-TABLE REDEFINES ST-STATE-DATA.
                    05   ST-STATE-ENTRY              OCCURS 51 TIMES.
                      10   ST-STATE-ABBREVIATION        PIC X(2).
                      10   ST-STATE-NAME                PIC X(20).


                PROCEDURE DIVISION:
                                  .
                                  .
                                  .
Initialization { MOVE 'NO ' TO ST-ENTRY-FOUND-SWITCH.
               { MOVE ZERO TO ST-SUBSCRIPT.
                 PERFORM 999-LOOKUP-STATE-NAME
                     UNTIL ST-ENTRY-FOUND
                     OR ST-END-OF-TABLE.
                 IF ST-ENTRY-FOUND
                     MOVE ST-STATE-NAME (ST-SUBSCRIPT) TO RL-STATE-NAME
                 ELSE
                     MOVE SPACES TO RL-STATE-NAME.
                                  .
                                  .
                                  .
                *
                *
                  999-LOOKUP-STATE-NAME.
                *
Incrementation ——→ ADD 1 TO ST-SUBSCRIPT.
Test for         { IF IN-STATE-ABBREVIATION
correspondence   {     IS EQUAL TO ST-STATE-ABBREVIATION (ST-SUBSCRIPT)
                           MOVE 'YES' TO ST-ENTRY-FOUND-SWITCH
Test for         { ELSE IF ST-SUBSCRIPT IS NOT LESS THAN ST-NUMBER-OF-ENTRIES
end-of-table     {     MOVE 'END' TO ST-ENTRY-FOUND-SWITCH.
```

Serial search with early exit example (using a subscript)

```
           DATA DIVISION:
                *
                01  ST-TABLE-CONTROLS.
Subscript ————————→ 05  ST-SUBSCRIPT                     PIC S9(4)        COMP SYNC.
                    05  ST-ENTRY-FOUND-SWITCH            PIC X(3).
Entry-found switch {    88  ST-ENTRY-FOUND                                VALUE 'YES'.
                        88  ST-END-OF-TABLE                               VALUE 'END'.
                *
                01  ST-STATE-DATA.
                    05  FILLER          PIC X(22) VALUE 'AKALASKA            '.
                                              .
                                              .
                                              .
Dummy end-of-table  05  FILLER          PIC X(22) VALUE 'WYWYOMING            '.
entry ——————————→   05  FILLER          PIC X(22) VALUE HIGH-VALUES. ┐
                *                                                    │
                01  ST-STATE-TABLE REDEFINES ST-STATE-DATA. ←────────┘
                    05  ST-STATE-ENTRY              OCCURS 52 TIMES.
                        10  ST-STATE-ABBREVIATION   PIC X(2).
                        10  ST-STATE-NAME           PIC X(20).

           PROCEDURE DIVISION:
                          .
                          .
                          .
               MOVE 'NO ' TO ST-ENTRY-FOUND-SWITCH.
               MOVE ZERO TO ST-SUBSCRIPT.
               PERFORM 999-LOOKUP-STATE-NAME
                   UNTIL ST-ENTRY-FOUND
                   OR ST-END-OF-TABLE.
               IF ST-ENTRY-FOUND
                   MOVE ST-STATE-NAME (ST-SUBSCRIPT) TO RL-STATE-NAME
               ELSE
                   MOVE SPACES TO RL-STATE-NAME.
                          .
                          .
                          .
           *
           *
            999-LOOKUP-STATE-NAME.
           *
               ADD 1 TO ST-SUBSCRIPT.
               IF IN-STATE-ABBREVIATION
                   IS GREATER THAN ST-STATE-ABBREVIATION (ST-SUBSCRIPT)
                   NEXT SENTENCE
               ELSE IF IN-STATE-ABBREVIATION
                   IS EQUAL TO ST-STATE-ABBREVIATION (ST-SUBSCRIPT)
                   MOVE 'YES' TO ST-ENTRY-FOUND-SWITCH
               ELSE
                   MOVE 'END' TO ST-ENTRY-FOUND-SWITCH.
```

Table Lookups Using a PERFORM/VARYING Statement Driver

The PERFORM/VARYING statement can be used as an alternative to a PERFORM/UNTIL driver. Either a subscript or an index can be used to reference the table entry. However, use of an index will typically provide more efficient processing.

It is important to note that, once the match between search and table arguments has been made, the subscript or index must be decremented by 1 to cause it to reflect the proper table occurrence number. This is because of the PERFORM/VARYING statement processing, which causes the subscript to be incremented one time after the matching condition has been identified and prior to the test for entry-found.

Serial search with early exit example (using an index)

```
            DATA DIVISION:

        *
        01   ST-TABLE-CONTROLS.
             05   ST-ENTRY-FOUND-SWITCH          PIC X(3).
                  88   ST-ENTRY-FOUND                          VALUE 'YES'.
                  88   ST-END-OF-TABLE                         VALUE 'END'.
        *
        01   ST-STATE-DATA.
             05   FILLER           PIC X(22) VALUE 'AKALASKA              '.
                                    .
                                    .
                                    .
             05   FILLER           PIC X(22) VALUE 'WYWYOMING             '.
             05   FILLER           PIC X(22) VALUE HIGH-VALUES.
        *
        01   ST-STATE-TABLE REDEFINES ST-STATE-DATA.
             05   ST-STATE-ENTRY                 OCCURS 52 TIMES
                                                 INDEXED BY ST-INDEX.
                  10   ST-STATE-ABBREVIATION     PIC X(2).
                  10   ST-STATE-NAME             PIC X(20).


            PROCEDURE DIVISION:
                                    .
                                    .
                                    .
             MOVE 'NO ' TO ST-ENTRY-FOUND-SWITCH.
             PERFORM 999-LOOKUP-STATE-NAME
                  VARYING ST-INDEX
                      FROM 1
                      BY 1
                          UNTIL ST-ENTRY-FOUND
                          OR ST-TABLE-END.
             IF ST-ENTRY-FOUND
                  SET ST-INDEX DOWN BY 1
                  MOVE ST-STATE-NAME (ST-INDEX) TO RL-STATE-NAME
             ELSE
                  MOVE SPACES TO RL-STATE-NAME.
                                    .
                                    .
                                    .
        *
        *
        999-LOOKUP-STATE-NAME.
        *
             IF IN-STATE-ABBREVIATION
                    IS GREATER THAN ST-STATE-ABBREVIATION (ST-INDEX)
                NEXT SENTENCE
             ELSE IF IN-STATE-ABBREVIATION
                    IS EQUAL TO ST-STATE-ABBREVIATION (ST-INDEX)
                MOVE 'YES' TO ST-ENTRY-FOUND-SWITCH
             ELSE
                  MOVE 'END' TO ST-ENTRY-FOUND-SWITCH.
```

Initialization ────────────▶ FROM 1
Incrementation ────────────▶ BY 1
Test for end-of-table ─────▶ OR ST-TABLE-END.

Multiple-Level Tables

COBOL provides the capability to handle multiple-level tables of two or three dimensions.

Two-Level Table Example

Part A: Rate-of-pay table data

Job classification	Rate of pay		
	Shift 1 (days)	Shift 2 (swing)	Shift 3 (grave)
A1	9.64	10.60	11.09
A2	8.93	9.82	10.27
B1	7.12	7.83	8.19
C1	6.80	7.48	7.82
C2	6.07	6.68	6.98
C3	5.41	5.95	6.22
C4	4.39	4.83	5.04

Part B: Rate-of-pay table occurrences

Job classification	Rate of pay		
	Shift 1 (days)	Shift 2 (swing)	Shift 3 (grave)
A1	(1, 1)	(1, 2)	(1, 3)
A2	(2, 1)	(2, 2)	(2, 3)
B1	(3, 1)	(3, 2)	(3, 3)
C1	(4, 1)	(4, 2)	(4, 3)
C2	(5, 1)	(5, 2)	(5, 3)
C3	(6, 1)	(6, 2)	(6, 3)
C4	(7, 1)	(7, 2)	(7, 3)

Part C: Table definition:

```
*
 01  RT-RATE-DATA.
     05  FILLER              PIC X(14)    VALUE 'A1096410601109'.
     05  FILLER              PIC X(14)    VALUE 'A2089309821027'.
     05  FILLER              PIC X(14)    VALUE 'B1071207830819'.
     05  FILLER              PIC X(14)    VALUE 'C1068007480782'.
     05  FILLER              PIC X(14)    VALUE 'C2060706680698'.
     05  FILLER              PIC X(14)    VALUE 'C3054105950622'.
     05  FILLER              PIC X(14)    VALUE 'C4043904830504'.
 01  RT-RATE-TABLE REDEFINES RT-RATE-DATA.
     05  RT-JOB-ENTRY                     OCCURS 7 TIMES
                                          INDEXED BY RT-JOB-INDEX.
         10  RT-JOB-CLASSIFICATION        PIC X(2).
         10  RT-RATE-ENTRY                OCCURS 3 TIMES
                                          INDEXED BY RT-RATE-INDEX.
             15  RT-RATE-OF-PAY           PIC 99V99.
```

Part D: Reference to table entry:

```
RT-RATE-OF-PAY (RT-JOB-INDEX, RT-RATE-INDEX)
```

Three-Level Table Example

Part A: Quantity-ordered/Customer-type price table data

Product-code	Quantity-ordered							
	1		2-6		7-12		13-up	
	Customer-type-1	Customer-type-2	Customer-type-1	Customer-type-2	Customer-type-1	Customer-type-2	Customer-type-1	Customer-type-2
A1818	$110.00	$102.00	$100.00	$ 92.00	$ 95.00	$ 86.00	$ 90.00	$ 81.00
A2418	128.00	115.00	117.00	105.00	111.00	100.00	106.00	95.00
A3018	139.00	125.00	127.00	114.00	120.00	108.00	114.00	103.00
A2424	149.00	134.00	136.00	122.00	129.00	116.00	123.00	111.00
A3024	161.00	146.00	146.00	132.00	139.00	125.00	131.00	118.00
A3624	173.00	158.00	157.00	141.00	149.00	144.00	142.00	128.00
A4824	200.00	180.00	182.00	164.00	173.00	156.00	164.00	148.00

Part B: Quantity-ordered/Customer-type price table occurrences

| | Quantity-ordered | | | | | | | |
| | 1 | | 2-6 | | 7-12 | | 13-up | |
Product-code	Customer-type-1	Customer-type-2	Customer-type-1	Customer-type-2	Customer-type-1	Customer-type-2	Customer-type-1	Customer-type-2
A1818	(1, 1, 1)	(1, 1, 2)	(1, 2, 1)	(1, 2, 2)	(1, 3, 1)	(1, 3, 2)	(1, 4, 1)	(1, 4, 2)
A2418	(2, 1, 1)	(2, 1, 2)	(2, 2, 1)	(2, 2, 2)	(2, 3, 1)	(2, 3, 2)	(2, 4, 1)	(2, 4, 2)
A3018	(3, 1, 1)	(3, 1, 2)	(3, 2, 1)	(3, 2, 2)	(3, 3, 1)	(3, 3, 2)	(3, 4, 1)	(3, 4, 2)
A2424	(4, 1, 1)	(4, 1, 2)	(4, 2, 1)	(4, 2, 2)	(4, 3, 1)	(4, 3, 2)	(4, 4, 1)	(4, 4, 2)
A3024	(5, 1, 1)	(5, 1, 2)	(5, 2, 1)	(5, 2, 2)	(5, 3, 1)	(5, 3, 2)	(5, 4, 1)	(5, 4, 2)
A3624	(6, 1, 1)	(6, 1, 2)	(6, 2, 1)	(6, 2, 2)	(6, 3, 1)	(6, 3, 2)	(6, 4, 1)	(6, 4, 2)
A4824	(7, 1, 1)	(7, 1, 2)	(7, 2, 1)	(7, 2, 2)	(7, 3, 1)	(7, 3, 2)	(7, 4, 1)	(7, 4, 2)

Part C: Depiction of table definition

PP-PRODUCT-PRICE-ENTRY
occurrence 1

| | Quantity ordered | | | | | | | |
| | 1 | | 2-6 | | 7-12 | | 13-up | |
Product-code	Customer-type-1	Customer-type-2	Customer-type-1	Customer-type-2	Customer-type-1	Customer-type-2	Customer-type-1	Customer-type-2
A1818	$110.00	$102.00	$100.00	$ 92.00	$ 95.00	$ 86.00	$ 90.00	$ 81.00

PP-PRODUCT-CODE
occurrence 1

PP-QTY-ENTRY
occurrence 1

PP-QTY-ENTRY
occurrence 2

PP-QTY-ENTRY
occurrence 3

PP-QTY-ENTRY
occurrence 4

PP-CUST-ENTRY
occurrence 1

PP-CUST-ENTRY
occurrence 1

PP-CUST-ENTRY
occurrence 1

PP-CUST-ENTRY
occurrence 1

PP-CUST-ENTRY
occurrence 2

PP-CUST-ENTRY
occurrence 2

PP-CUST-ENTRY
occurrence 2

PP-CUST-ENTRY
occurrence 2

Part D: COBOL coding

DATA DIVISION:

```
*
01  PP-TABLE-CONTROLS.
    05  PP-ENTRY-FOUND-SWITCH       PIC X(3).
        88  PP-ENTRY-FOUND                      VALUE 'YES'.
*
01  PP-PRODUCT-PRICE-DATA.
    05  FILLER  PIC X(45)
        VALUE 'A18181100010200100000920009500086000900000 8100'.
    05  FILLER  PIC X(45)
        VALUE 'A2418128001150011700105001110010000106000 9500'.
    05  FILLER  PIC X(45)
        VALUE 'A3018139001250012700114001200010800114000 10300'.
    05  FILLER  PIC X(45)
        VALUE 'A2424149001340013600122001290011600123000 11100'.
    05  FILLER  PIC X(45)
        VALUE 'A3024161001460014600132001390012500131000 11800'.
    05  FILLER  PIC X(45)
        VALUE 'A36241730015800157001410014900144001420001 2800'.
    05  FILLER  PIC X(45)
        VALUE 'A4824200001800018200164001730015600164000 14800'.
01  PP-PRODUCT-PRICE-TABLE REDEFINES PP-PRODUCT-PRICE-DATA.
    05  PP-PRODUCT-PRICE-ENTRY       OCCURS 7 TIMES
                                     INDEXED BY PP-PRODUCT-INDEX.
        10  PP-PRODUCT-CODE          PIC X(5).
        10  PP-QTY-ENTRY             OCCURS 4 TIMES
                                     INDEXED BY PP-QTY-INDEX.
            15  PP-CUST-ENTRY        OCCURS 2 TIMES
                                     INDEXED BY PP-CUST-INDEX.
                20  PP-PRICE         PIC 9(3)V99.
```

PROCEDURE DIVISION:

```
        .
        .
        .
    PERFORM 999-LOOKUP-PRODUCT-PRICE.
    IF PP-ENTRY-FOUND
        MOVE PP-PRICE
            (PP-PRODUCT-INDEX, PP-QTY-INDEX, PP-CUST-INDEX)
            TO RL-PRICE.
        .
        .
        .
*
 999-LOOKUP-PRODUCT-PRICE.
*
    SET PP-PRODUCT-INDEX TO 1.
    SEARCH PRODUCT-PRICE-ENTRY
        AT END MOVE 'NO ' TO PP-ENTRY-FOUND-SWITCH
        WHEN PP-PRODUCT-CODE (PP-PRODUCT-INDEX)
                IS EQUAL TO IN-PRODUCT-CODE
            MOVE 'YES' TO PP-ENTRY-FOUND-SWITCH.
    IF IN-QTY-ORDERED IS LESS THAN 2
        SET PP-QTY-INDEX TO 1
    ELSE IF IN-QTY-ORDERED IS LESS THAN 7
        SET PP-QTY-INDEX TO 2
    ELSE IF IN-QTY-ORDERED IS LESS THAN 13
        SET PP-QTY-INDEX TO 3
    ELSE
        SET PP-QTY-INDEX TO 4.
    IF IN-CUST-TYPE IS LESS THAN 2
        SET PP-CUST-INDEX TO 1
    ELSE
        SET PP-CUST-INDEX TO 2.
```

SORT/MERGE PROGRAM REFERENCE

This appendix contains a reference summary of syntax considerations for programs using the SORT and MERGE statements.

SORT and MERGE Statement Formats

SORT Formats:

ENVIRONMENT DIVISION.

INPUT-OUTPUT SECTION.

FILE CONTROL.

    <u>SELECT</u> sort-file-name

        <u>ASSIGN</u> TO implementor-name.

DATA DIVISION.

FILE SECTION.

$$\left[\begin{array}{l} \text{SD sort-file-name} \\ \quad \left[\, \underline{\text{RECORD CONTAINS}} \; [\, \text{integer-1} \; \underline{\text{TO}} \,] \; \text{integer-2 CHARACTERS} \,\right] \\ \quad \left[\, \underline{\text{DATA}} \left\{ \begin{array}{l} \underline{\text{RECORD}} \text{ IS} \\ \underline{\text{RECORDS}} \text{ ARE} \end{array} \right\} \text{data-name-1 [data-name-2]} \ldots \right]. \\ \quad \left\{ \text{record-description-entry} \right\} \ldots \end{array}\right] \ldots$$

PROCEDURE DIVISION.

$$\underline{\text{SORT}} \; \text{sort-file-name ON} \left\{ \begin{array}{l} \underline{\text{ASCENDING}} \\ \underline{\text{DESCENDING}} \end{array} \right\} \text{KEY data-name-1 [data-name-2]} \ldots$$

$$\left[\text{ON} \left\{ \begin{array}{l} \underline{\text{ASCENDING}} \\ \underline{\text{DESCENDING}} \end{array} \right\} \text{KEY data-name-3 [data-name-4]} \ldots \right] \ldots$$

$$\left\{ \begin{array}{l} \underline{\text{INPUT PROCEDURE}} \text{ IS section-name-1} \\ \underline{\text{USING}} \text{ file-name-1 [file-name-3]} \ldots \end{array} \right\}$$

$$\left\{ \begin{array}{l} \underline{\text{OUTPUT PROCEDURE}} \text{ IS section-name-2} \\ \underline{\text{GIVING}} \text{ file-name-2} \end{array} \right\}$$

MERGE merge-file-name ON $\left\{\begin{array}{l}\text{ASCENDING}\\\text{DESCENDING}\end{array}\right\}$ KEY data-name-1 [data-name-2] ...

$\left[\text{ON} \left\{\begin{array}{l}\text{ASCENDING}\\\text{DESCENDING}\end{array}\right\} \text{KEY data-name-3 [data-name-4]} \ldots \right] \ldots$

USING file-name-1, file-name-2 [file-name-3] ...

$\left\{\begin{array}{l}\text{OUTPUT PROCEDURE IS section-name-1}\\\text{GIVING file-name-4}\end{array}\right\}$

RELEASE record-name   FROM identifier

RETURN file-name RECORD   INTO identifier

    AT END imperative-statement

ENVIRONMENT DIVISION SORT/MERGE Entries

SELECT and ASSIGN Clauses

Format:

SELECT sort-file-name

    ASSIGN TO implementor-name.

Example:

```
SELECT SORT-FILE
    ASSIGN TO UT-S-SORTWORK.
```

Syntax considerations:

- A SELECT entry must be provided for the sort-file named in each SORT statement (or merge-file named in each MERGE statement).
- With certain compilers, the implementor-name must conform to specific sort-file naming requirements.

DATA DIVISION SORT/MERGE Entries

SD Entry

Format:

$\left[\begin{array}{l}\text{SD sort-file-name}\\\quad \left[\text{RECORD CONTAINS [integer-1 } \underline{\text{TO}} \text{] integer-2 CHARACTERS }\right]\\\quad \left[\underline{\text{DATA}} \left\{\begin{array}{l}\underline{\text{RECORD}} \text{ IS}\\\underline{\text{RECORDS}} \text{ ARE}\end{array}\right\} \text{data-name-1 [data-name-2] } \ldots \right].\\\quad \{\text{record-description-entry}\} \ldots \end{array}\right] \ldots$

Example:

```
*
SD  SORT-FILE
        RECORD CONTAINS 80 CHARACTERS.
*
01  SR-SORT-RECORD.
    05  FILLER                    PIC X(2).
    05  SR-WAREHOUSE-CODE         PIC X(2).
    05  SR-PART-NUMBER            PIC X(15).
    05  FILLER                    PIC X(52).
    05  SR-INVENTORY-VALUE        PIC S9(7)V99.
```

Syntax considerations:

- An SD entry must be provided for each sort-file (or merge-file).

- An SD entry is similar to an FD entry except that the BLOCK CONTAINS and LABEL RECORDS clauses are not specified.

- Following the SD entry, a record-description entry describing the record to be sorted is specified. The record-description must contain the sort-key (or merge-key) fields named in the KEY phrase of the SORT (or MERGE) statement. The sort-key fields may appear at any place and in any order within the record.

- Multiple record-descriptions may be specified, but the sort-key (or merge-key) fields must be in the same relative position within each record.

PROCEDURE DIVISION SORT/ MERGE Entries

SORT Statement

Format:

$$\underline{\text{SORT}} \text{ sort-file-name ON} \left\{ \begin{array}{l} \underline{\text{ASCENDING}} \\ \underline{\text{DESCENDING}} \end{array} \right\} \text{KEY data-name-1 [data-name-2]} \ldots$$

$$\left[\text{ON} \left\{ \begin{array}{l} \underline{\text{ASCENDING}} \\ \underline{\text{DESCENDING}} \end{array} \right\} \text{KEY data-name-3 [data-name-4]} \ldots \right] \ldots$$

$$\left\{ \begin{array}{l} \underline{\text{INPUT PROCEDURE}} \text{ IS section-name-1} \\ \underline{\text{USING}} \text{ file-name-1 [file-name-3]} \ldots \end{array} \right\}$$

$$\left\{ \begin{array}{l} \underline{\text{OUTPUT PROCEDURE}} \text{ IS section-name-2} \\ \underline{\text{GIVING}} \text{ file-name-2} \end{array} \right\}$$

Examples:

```
SORT SORT-FILE
    ASCENDING KEY   SR-WAREHOUSE-CODE
    DESCENDING KEY  SR-INVENTORY-VALUE
    ASCENDING KEY   SR-PART-NUMBER
        USING   INVENTORY-FILE
        GIVING SORTED-INVENTORY-FILE.


SORT SORT-FILE
    ASCENDING KEY   XX-DEPARTMENT-NUMBER
                    XX-EMPLOYEE-NUMBER
        INPUT PROCEDURE IS 2000-IP-SELECT-INPUT-RECORDS
        GIVING SORTED-EMPLOYEE-FILE.


SORT SORT-FILE
    ASCENDING KEY   XX-DEPARTMENT-NUMBER
                    XX-EMPLOYEE-NUMBER
        INPUT PROCEDURE IS 2000-IP-SELECT-INPUT-RECORDS
        OUTPUT PROCEDURE IS 3000-OP-PROCESS-SORTED-RECORDS.


SORT SORT-FILE
    ASCENDING KEY   XX-DEPARTMENT-NUMBER
                    XX-EMPLOYEE-NUMBER
        USING EMPLOYEE-FILE
        OUTPUT PROCEDURE IS 3000-OP-PROCESS-SORTED-RECORDS.
```

SORT phrase syntax consideration:

- The SD file-name to be used as the sort work file must be named in the SORT phrase.

KEY phrase syntax considerations:

- ASCENDING KEY or DESCENDING KEY must be specified to indicate whether the field is to be sorted in ascending sequence or descending sequence, respectively. (ASCENDING KEY and DESCENDING KEY phrases may be mixed within the same SORT statement.)
- KEY fields are listed with the major field first. If there is more than one KEY field, additional fields are listed in order of decreasing significance (minor field last).
- If a KEY field contains numeric values with mixed sign representations (plus, minus, and/or unsigned), the field named must be defined within the sort file record-description entry as an elementary numeric item with the PICTURE symbol S and the correct USAGE specification. Otherwise, the records may not be ordered in correct algebraic sequence for that field.

USING phrase syntax considerations:

- The USING phrase is specified when all records of an input file (or files) are to be sorted.
- When USING is specified, the SORT statement will cause the USING file (or files) to be opened, transferred to the sort work file, and closed. Thus the programmer must not code OPEN or CLOSE statements for files named in a USING phrase.
- The 1974 ANS COBOL standards provide for the specification of multiple USING files. (However, some compilers do not support this feature.)

GIVING phrase syntax considerations:

- The GIVING phrase is specified when all sorted records are to be written to one output sorted file.
- When GIVING is specified, the SORT statement will cause the GIVING file to be opened, the sorted records from the sort work file will be transferred to it, and the GIVING file will be closed. Thus the programmer must not code OPEN or CLOSE statements for a file named in a GIVING phrase.

INPUT PROCEDURE and OUTPUT PROCEDURE syntax considerations:

- An INPUT PROCEDURE is specified to provide the ability to process input records before they are sorted (preprocessing of the input file).
- An OUTPUT PROCEDURE is specified to provide the ability to process output records after they are sorted and, if applicable, before they are written to a sorted output file (post-processing of the sorted file).
- The INPUT PROCEDURE and OUTPUT PROCEDURE procedure-names must be section-names.
- The INPUT PROCEDURE and OUTPUT PROCEDURE sections must not be referenced except by a SORT statement.
- From within an INPUT PROCEDURE or OUTPUT PROCEDURE, program control cannot be transferred to procedures outside it. (That is, a GO TO or PERFORM statement cannot reference a procedure-name that is not within that INPUT PROCEDURE or OUTPUT PROCEDURE.)
- An INPUT PROCEDURE or an OUTPUT PROCEDURE cannot contain a SORT (or MERGE) statement.

MERGE Statement

Format:

MERGE merge-file-name ON $\left\{\begin{array}{l}\underline{ASCENDING}\\\underline{DESCENDING}\end{array}\right\}$ KEY data-name-1 [data-name-2] . . .

$\left[\text{ON}\left\{\begin{array}{l}\underline{ASCENDING}\\\underline{DESCENDING}\end{array}\right\}\text{KEY data-name-3 [data-name-4] . . .}\right]$ . . .

<u>USING</u> file-name-1, file-name-2 [file-name-3] . . .

$\left\{\begin{array}{l}\underline{OUTPUT\ PROCEDURE}\ IS\ section\text{-}name\text{-}1\\\underline{GIVING}\ file\text{-}name\text{-}4\end{array}\right\}$

<u>RETURN</u> file-name RECORD [<u>INTO</u> identifier]

      AT <u>END</u> imperative-statement

Example:

```
MERGE MERGE-FILE
    ASCENDING KEY MR-CUSTOMER-CODE
    USING  CHARGE-ACCOUNT-TRANS-FILE
           CASH-RECEIPTS-TRANS-FILE
    GIVING MERGED-TRANS-FILE.
```

Syntax consideration:

■ MERGE statement syntax is parallel to SORT statement syntax except for the following:

    —At least two USING files are always specified.

    —An INPUT PROCEDURE cannot be specified (thus the RELEASE statement also cannot be used).

RELEASE Statement

Format:

RELEASE record-name [<u>FROM</u> identifier]

Examples:

```
RELEASE SR-SORT-RECORD.

RELEASE SR-SORT-RECORD
    FROM IR-INVENTORY-RECORD.
```

Syntax considerations:

■ The RELEASE statement is, in effect, a WRITE statement to a sort work file. If the FROM phrase is not specified, the record to be released must be physically present in the SD record-description area (that is, previously moved to the SD record-description area) prior to executing the RELEASE. If the FROM phrase is specified, the object of the FROM phrase will be moved prior to the RELEASE.

■ The RELEASE statement can only be specified within an INPUT PROCEDURE.

RETURN Statement

Examples:

```
RETURN SORT-FILE
    AT END MOVE 'YES' TO WS-END-OF-FILE-SW.


RETURN SORT-FILE
    INTO SI-INVENTORY-RECORD
    AT END MOVE 'YES' TO WS-END-OF-FILE-SW.
```

Syntax considerations:

- The RETURN statement is, in effect, a READ statement from the sort work file. The INTO and AT END phrase operate as they do for the READ statement.
- The RETURN statement can be specified only within an OUTPUT PROCEDURE.

SORT-only Program

A **sort-only** program sorts the records of an input file and creates a sorted output file but performs no other processing operations upon the files. Such a program is seldom coded because it provides no I-O efficiency advantages and it requires more coding than specification of the sort parameters directly to the utility sort program. A sort-only program is characterized by specification of the SORT statement USING and GIVING phrases.

Example:

```
001010 IDENTIFICATION DIVISION.
001020 PROGRAM-ID.    SRT-ONLY.
001080*
001090*
001100*            THIS IS A SORT-ONLY PROGRAM.
001110
001120*            THE FOLLOWING SORT STATEMENT PHRASES ARE SPECIFIED
001130*                    USING
001140*                    GIVING
002010*
002020*
002030*
002040 ENVIRONMENT DIVISION.
002050*
002060*
002070 CONFIGURATION SECTION.
002080*
002090 SOURCE-COMPUTER.  IBM-370.
002100 OBJECT-COMPUTER.  IBM-370.
002110*
002120*
002130 INPUT-OUTPUT SECTION.
002140*
002150 FILE-CONTROL.
002160     SELECT INVENTORY-FILE
002170         ASSIGN TO UT-S-INFILE.
002180     SELECT SORTED-INVENTORY-FILE
002190         ASSIGN TO UT-S-OUTFILE.
002220     SELECT SORT-FILE
002230         ASSIGN TO UT-S-SORTWORK.
003010*
003020*
003030*
003040 DATA DIVISION.
003050*
003060*
003070 FILE SECTION.
003080*
003090 FD  INVENTORY-FILE
```

```
003100          RECORD CONTAINS 80 CHARACTERS
003110          BLOCK CONTAINS 20 RECORDS
003120          LABEL RECORDS ARE STANDARD.
003130*
003140 01  IR-INVENTORY-RECORD.
003150     05  FILLER                     PIC X(80).
004010*
004020 FD  SORTED-INVENTORY-FILE
004030          RECORD CONTAINS 80 CHARACTERS
004040          BLOCK CONTAINS 20 RECORDS
004050          LABEL RECORDS ARE STANDARD.
004060*
004070 01  SI-INVENTORY-RECORD.
004080     05  FILLER                     PIC X(80).
007010*
007020 SD  SORT-FILE
007030          RECORD CONTAINS 80 CHARACTERS.
007040*
007050 01  SR-SORT-RECORD.
007060     05  FILLER                     PIC X(2).
007070     05  SR-WAREHOUSE-CODE          PIC X(2).
007080     05  SR-PART-NUMBER             PIC X(15).
007090     05  FILLER                     PIC X(52).
007100     05  SR-INVENTORY-VALUE         PIC S9(7)V99.
050010*
050020*
050030*
050040 PROCEDURE DIVISION.
050050*
050060*
050070 000-SORT-INVENTORY-RECORDS.
050080*
050160     SORT SORT-FILE
050170         ASCENDING KEY   SR-WAREHOUSE-CODE
050180         DESCENDING KEY  SR-INVENTORY-VALUE
050190         ASCENDING KEY   SR-PART-NUMBER
050200             USING  INVENTORY-FILE
050210             GIVING SORTED-INVENTORY-FILE.
050220     STOP RUN.
```

SORT Program with Preprocessing of the Input File to be Sorted

A **SORT program with preprocessing of the input file to be sorted** is called for when any of the following functions are required:

—to select certain records from the input file and to sort only those selected records

—to create additional records to augment the input file and to sort the augmented file

—to change the record (record length, field size, field values, field locations, build a sort key prefix, and so forth) prior to sorting

— to edit or validate the records prior to sorting

— to list the input records prior to sorting

— to count the records contained within the input file

Such a program is characterized by specification of the SORT statement INPUT PROCEDURE phrase.

Example:

```
001010 IDENTIFICATION DIVISION.
001020 PROGRAM-ID.     SRT-PRE.
001080*
001090*
001100*              THIS IS A SORT PROGRAM WITH PRE-PROCESSING
001110*                  OF THE INPUT FILE.
001120*
001130*              THE FOLLOWING SORT STATEMENT PHRASES ARE SPECIFIED
001140*                  INPUT PROCEDURE
001150*                  GIVING
002010*
002020*
002030*
002040 ENVIRONMENT DIVISION.
002050*
002060*
002070 CONFIGURATION SECTION.
002080*
002090 SOURCE-COMPUTER. IBM-370.
002100 OBJECT-COMPUTER. IBM-370.
002110*
002120*
002130 INPUT-OUTPUT SECTION.
002140*
002150 FILE-CONTROL.
002160     SELECT INVENTORY-FILE
002170         ASSIGN TO UT-S-INFILE.
002180     SELECT SORTED-INVENTORY-FILE
002190         ASSIGN TO UT-S-OUTFILE.
002200     SELECT SORT-FILE
002210         ASSIGN TO UT-S-SORTWORK.
003010*
003020*
003030*
003040 DATA DIVISION.
003050*
003060*
003070 FILE SECTION.
003080*
003090 FD  INVENTORY-FILE
003100     RECORD CONTAINS 80 CHARACTERS
003110     BLOCK CONTAINS 20 RECORDS
003120     LABEL RECORDS ARE STANDARD.
004010*
004020 01  IR-INVENTORY-RECORD.
004030     05  FILLER                    PIC X(19).
004040     05  IR-INVENTORY-CLASS-CODE    PIC X(1).
004050     05  FILLER                    PIC X(60).
006010*
006020 FD  SORTED-INVENTORY-FILE
006030     RECORD CONTAINS 80 CHARACTERS
006040     BLOCK CONTAINS 20 RECORDS
006050     LABEL RECORDS ARE STANDARD.
006060*
006070 01  SI-INVENTORY-RECORD.
006080     05  FILLER                    PIC X(80).
007010*
007020 SD  SORT-FILE
007030     RECORD CONTAINS 80 CHARACTERS.
007040*
007050 01  SR-SORT-RECORD.
007060     05  FILLER                    PIC X(2).
007070     05  SR-WAREHOUSE-CODE          PIC X(2).
007080     05  SR-PART-NUMBER             PIC X(15).
007090     05  FILLER                    PIC X(52).
007100     05  SR-INVENTORY-VALUE         PIC S9(7)V99.
```

```
020010*
020020*
020030 WORKING-STORAGE SECTION.
020040*
020050*
020060 01  WS-SWITCHES.
020070     05  WS-END-OF-FILE-SW          PIC X(3).
020080         88  END-OF-FILE                         VALUE 'YES'.
050010*
050020*
050030*
050040 PROCEDURE DIVISION.
050050*
050060*
050070 0000-ML-SORT-INV-RECORDS SECTION.
050080*
050090*
050100 0000-SORT-INV-RECORDS.
050110*
050120     OPEN INPUT INVENTORY-FILE.
050130     SORT SORT-FILE
050140         ASCENDING KEY  SR-WAREHOUSE-CODE
050150         DESCENDING KEY SR-INVENTORY-VALUE
050160         ASCENDING KEY  SR-PART-NUMBER                Before sort
050170         INPUT PROCEDURE IS  2000-IP-SELECT-INV-RECORDS
050180         GIVING SORTED-INVENTORY-FILE.
050190     CLOSE INVENTORY-FILE.
050100     STOP RUN.
200010*
200020*
200030 2000-IP-SELECT-INV-RECORDS SECTION.
220010*
220030 2200-SELECT-INVENTORY-RECORDS.
220040*
220050     MOVE 'NO ' TO WS-END-OF-FILE-SW.
220060     PERFORM 2800-READ-INVENTORY-RECORD.
220070     PERFORM 2210-SELECT-INVENTORY-RECORD
220080         UNTIL END-OF-FILE.                           After end-of-file
220090     GO TO 2999-EXIT.
221010*
221020*
221030 2210-SELECT-INVENTORY-RECORD.
221040*
221050     IF IR-INVENTORY-CLASS-CODE IS EQUAL TO 'A'
221060         MOVE IR-INVENTORY-RECORD TO SR-SORT-RECORD
221070         PERFORM 2830-RELEASE-INVENTORY-RECORD.
221080     PERFORM 2800-READ-INVENTORY-RECORD.
280010*
280020*
280030 2800-READ-INVENTORY-RECORD.
280040*
280050     READ INVENTORY-FILE
280060         AT END MOVE 'YES' TO WS-END-OF-FILE-SW.
283010*
283020*
283030 2830-RELEASE-INVENTORY-RECORD.
283040*
283050     RELEASE SR-SORT-RECORD.
299010*
299020*
299030 2999-EXIT.
299040*
299050     EXIT.
```

SORT Program with Postprocessing of the Sorted Output File

A **SORT program with postprocessing of the sorted output file** is called for when any of the following functions are required:

— to create more than one sorted output file for the same set of records

— to select or summarize records after sorting and before writing them to the sorted output file

— to create additional records to augment the sorted output file

— to change the record (record length, field size, field values, field locations, and so forth) after sorting

— to list the sorted records

— to count records contained within the sorted output file

Such a program is characterized by specification of the SORT statement OUTPUT PROCEDURE phrase.

Example:

```
001010 IDENTIFICATION DIVISION.                                    007050 01    SR-SORT-RECORD.
001020 PROGRAM-ID.    SRT-POST.                                    007060    05    FILLER                    PIC X(2).
001080*                                                            007070    05    SR-WAREHOUSE-CODE         PIC X(2).
001090*                                                            007080    05    SR-PART-NUMBER            PIC X(15).
001100*              THIS IS A SORT PROGRAM WITH POST-PROCESSING   007090    05    FILLER                    PIC X(52).
001110*                   OF THE SORTED OUTPUT FILE                007100    05    SR-INVENTORY-VALUE        PIC S9(7)V99.
001120*                                                            020010*
001130*              THE FOLLOWING SORT STATEMENT PHRASES ARE SPECIFIED  020020*
001140*                   USING                                    020030 WORKING-STORAGE SECTION.
001150*                   OUTPUT PROCEDURE                          020040*
002010*                                                            020050*
002020*                                                            020060 01    WS-SWITCHES.
002030*                                                            020070    05    WS-END-OF-FILE-SW         PIC X(3).
002040 ENVIRONMENT DIVISION.                                       020080       88    END-OF-FILE                            VALUE 'YES'.
002050*                                                            050010*
002060*                                                            050020*
002070 CONFIGURATION SECTION.                                      050030*
002080*                                                            050040 PROCEDURE DIVISION.
002090 SOURCE-COMPUTER.   IBM-370.                                 050050*
002100 OBJECT-COMPUTER.   IBM-370.                                 050060*
002110*                                                            050070 0000-ML-SORT-INV-RECORDS SECTION.
002120*                                                            050080*
002130 INPUT-OUTPUT SECTION.                                       050090*
002140*                                                            050100 0000-SORT-INV-RECORDS.
002150 FILE-CONTROL.                                               050110*
002160    SELECT INVENTORY-FILE                                    050120    OPEN OUTPUT INVENTORY-REPORT-FILE
002170       ASSIGN TO UT-S-INFILE.                                050130                 SORTED-INVENTORY-FILE.
002180    SELECT INVENTORY-REPORT-FILE                             050140    SORT SORT-FILE
002190       ASSIGN TO UT-S-PRTFILE.                               050150       ASCENDING KEY  SR-WAREHOUSE-CODE
002200    SELECT SORTED-INVENTORY-FILE                             050160       DESCENDING KEY SR-INVENTORY-VALUE
002210       ASSIGN TO UT-S-OUTFILE.                               050170       ASCENDING KEY  SR-PART-NUMBER
002220    SELECT SORT-FILE                                         050180          USING INVENTORY-FILE
002230       ASSIGN TO UT-S-SORTWORK.                              050190          OUTPUT PROCEDURE IS 3000-OP-PROCESS-SORTED-RECORDS.
003010*                                                            050200    CLOSE INVENTORY-REPORT-FILE
003020*                                                            050210          SORTED-INVENTORY-FILE.
003030*                                                            050220    STOP RUN.
003040 DATA DIVISION.                                              300010*
003050*                                                            300020*
003060*                                                            300030 3000-OP-PROCESS-SORTED-RECORDS SECTION.
003070 FILE SECTION.                                               320040*
003080*                                                            320050*
003090 FD   INVENTORY-FILE                                         320060 3200-PROCESS-SORTED-RECORDS.
003100       RECORD CONTAINS 80 CHARACTERS                         320070*
003110       BLOCK CONTAINS 20 RECORDS                             320080    MOVE 'NO ' TO WS-END-OF-FILE-SW.
003120       LABEL RECORDS ARE STANDARD.                           320090    PERFORM 3210-PROCESS-SORTED-INV-RECORD
004010*                                                            320100       UNTIL END-OF-FILE.
004020 01    IR-INVENTORY-RECORD.                                  320110    GO TO 3999-EXIT.
004030    05    FILLER                     PIC X(19).              321010*
004040    05    IR-INVENTORY-CLASS-CODE    PIC X(1).               321020*
004050    05    FILLER                     PIC X(60).              321030 3210-PROCESS-SORTED-INV-RECORD.
005010*                                                            321040*
005020 FD   INVENTORY-REPORT-FILE                                  321050    PERFORM 3800-RETURN-SORTED-INV-RECORD.
005030       RECORD CONTAINS 133 CHARACTERS                        321060    IF NOT END-OF-FILE
005040       LABEL RECORDS ARE OMITTED.                            321070       MOVE SPACES TO RL-REPORT-LINE
005050*                                                            321080       MOVE SI-WAREHOUSE-CODE TO RL-WAREHOUSE-CODE
005060 01    RL-REPORT-LINE.                                       321090       MOVE SI-PART-NUMBER TO RL-PART-NUMBER
005070    05    FILLER                     PIC X(1).               321100       MOVE SI-INVENTORY-CLASS-CODE TO RL-INVENTORY-CLASS-CODE
005080    05    RL-WAREHOUSE-CODE          PIC X(2).               321110       MOVE SI-INVENTORY-VALUE TO RL-INVENTORY-VALUE
005090    05    FILLER                     PIC X(2).               321120       ADD SI-INVENTORY-VALUE TO WS-INVENTORY-VALUE-ACCUM
005100    05    RL-PART-NUMBER             PIC X(15).              321130       PERFORM 3830-WRITE-SORTED-INV-RECORD
005110    05    FILLER                     PIC X(2).               321140       PERFORM 3890-WRITE-REPORT-LINE.
005120    05    RL-PART-DESCRIPTION        PIC X(25).              380010*
005130    05    FILLER                     PIC X(2).               380020*
005140    05    RL-INVENTORY-VALUE         PIC Z,ZZZ,ZZZ.99-.      380030 3800-RETURN-SORTED-INV-RECORD.
005150    05    FILLER                     PIC X(73).              380040*
006010*                                                            380050    RETURN SORT-FILE INTO SI-INVENTORY-RECORD
006020 FD   SORTED-INVENTORY-FILE                                  380060       AT END MOVE 'YES' TO WS-END-OF-FILE-SW.
006030       RECORD CONTAINS 80 CHARACTERS                         383010*
006040       BLOCK CONTAINS 20 RECORDS                             383020*
006050       LABEL RECORDS ARE STANDARD.                           383030 3830-WRITE-SORTED-INV-RECORD.
006060*                                                            383040*
006070 01    SI-INVENTORY-RECORD.                                  383050    WRITE SI-INVENTORY-RECORD.
006080    05    SI-RECORD-CODE             PIC X(2).               383060*
006090    05    SI-WAREHOUSE-CODE          PIC X(2).               383070*
006100    05    SI-PART-NUMBER             PIC X(15).              383080 3890-WRITE-REPORT-LINE.
006110    05    SI-INVENTORY-CLASS-CODE    PIC X(1).               383090*
006120    05    SI-DESCRIPTION             PIC X(25).              383100    WRITE RL-REPORT-LINE
006130    05    FILLER                     PIC X(26).              383110       AFTER ADVANCING 1 LINE.
006140    05    SI-INVENTORY-VALUE         PIC S9(7)V99.           399010*
007010*                                                            399020*
007020 SD   SORT-FILE                                              399030 3999-EXIT.
007030       RECORD CONTAINS 80 CHARACTERS.                        399040*
007040*                                                            399050    EXIT.
```

SORT Program with Preprocessing of the Input File and Postprocessing of the Sorted Output File

A **SORT program with preprocessing of the input file and postprocessing of the sorted output file** is characterized by specification of the SORT statement INPUT PROCEDURE and OUTPUT PROCEDURE phrases.

Example:

```
001010 IDENTIFICATION DIVISION.                           002020*
001020 PROGRAM-ID.    SRT-P-P.                             002030*
001080*                                                    002040 ENVIRONMENT DIVISION.
001090*                                                    002050*
001100*              THIS IS A SORT PROGRAM WITH PRE-PROCESSING   002060*
001110*                   OF THE INPUT FILE                 002070 CONFIGURATION SECTION.
001120*                   AND POST-PROCESSING OF THE SORTED OUTPUT FILE   002080*
001130*                                                    002090 SOURCE-COMPUTER.   IBM-370.
001140*              THE FOLLOWING SORT STATEMENT PHRASES ARE SPECIFIED   002100 OBJECT-COMPUTER.   IBM-370.
001150*                   INPUT PROCEDURE                   002110*
001160*                   OUTPUT PROCEDURE                  002120*
002010*                                                    002130 INPUT-OUTPUT SECTION.
```

```
002140*
002150 FILE-CONTROL.
002160     SELECT INVENTORY-FILE
002170         ASSIGN TO UT-S-INFILE.
002180     SELECT INVENTORY-REPORT-FILE
002190         ASSIGN TO UT-S-PRTFILE.
002200     SELECT SORTED-INVENTORY-FILE
002210         ASSIGN TO UT-S-OUTFILE.
002220     SELECT SORT-FILE
002230         ASSIGN TO UT-S-SORTWORK.
003010*
003020*
003030*
003040 DATA DIVISION.
003050*
003060*
003070 FILE SECTION.
003080*
003090 FD  INVENTORY-FILE
003100     RECORD CONTAINS 80 CHARACTERS
003110     BLOCK CONTAINS 20 RECORDS
003120     LABEL RECORDS ARE STANDARD.
004010*
004020 01  IR-INVENTORY-RECORD.
004030     05  FILLER                     PIC X(19).
004040     05  IR-INVENTORY-CLASS-CODE    PIC X(1).
004050     05  FILLER                     PIC X(60).
005010*
005020 FD  INVENTORY-REPORT-FILE
005030     RECORD CONTAINS 133 CHARACTERS
005040     LABEL RECORDS ARE OMITTED.
005050*
005060 01  RL-REPORT-LINE.
005070     05  FILLER                     PIC X(1).
005080     05  RL-WAREHOUSE-CODE          PIC X(2).
005090     05  FILLER                     PIC X(2).
005100     05  RL-PART-NUMBER             PIC X(15).
005110     05  FILLER                     PIC X(2).
005120     05  RL-PART-DESCRIPTION        PIC X(25).
005130     05  FILLER                     PIC X(2).
005140     05  RL-INVENTORY-VALUE         PIC Z,ZZZ,ZZZ.99-.
005150     05  FILLER                     PIC X(71).
006010*
006020 FD  SORTED-INVENTORY-FILE
006030     RECORD CONTAINS 80 CHARACTERS
006040     BLOCK CONTAINS 20 RECORDS
006050     LABEL RECORDS ARE STANDARD.
006060*
006070 01  SI-INVENTORY-RECORD.
006080     05  SI-RECORD-CODE             PIC X(2).
006090     05  SI-WAREHOUSE-CODE          PIC X(2).
006100     05  SI-PART-NUMBER             PIC X(15).
006110     05  SI-INVENTORY-CLASS-CODE    PIC X(1).
006120     05  SI-DESCRIPTION             PIC X(25).
006130     05  FILLER                     PIC X(26).
006140     05  SI-INVENTORY-VALUE         PIC S9(7)V99.
007010*
007020 SD  SORT-FILE
007030     RECORD CONTAINS 80 CHARACTERS.
007040*
007050 01  SR-SORT-RECORD.
007060     05  FILLER                     PIC X(2).
007070     05  SR-WAREHOUSE-CODE          PIC X(2).
007080     05  SR-PART-NUMBER             PIC X(15).
007090     05  FILLER                     PIC X(52).
007100     05  SR-INVENTORY-VALUE         PIC S9(7)V99.
020010*
020020*
020030 WORKING-STORAGE SECTION.
020040*
020050*
020060 01  WS-SWITCHES.
020070     05  WS-END-OF-FILE-SW          PIC X(3).
020080         88  END-OF-FILE                          VALUE 'YES'.
050010*
050020*
050030*
050040 PROCEDURE DIVISION.
050050*
050060*
050070 0000-ML-SORT-INV-RECORDS SECTION.
050080*
050090*
050100 0000-SORT-INV-RECORDS.
050110*
050120     OPEN INPUT INVENTORY-FILE
050130         OUTPUT INVENTORY-REPORT-FILE
050140                SORTED-INVENTORY-FILE.
050150     SORT SORT-FILE
050160         ASCENDING KEY  SR-WAREHOUSE-CODE
050170         DESCENDING KEY SR-INVENTORY-VALUE
050180         ASCENDING KEY  SR-PART-NUMBER
050190         INPUT PROCEDURE IS  2000-IP-SELECT-INV-RECORDS
050200         OUTPUT PROCEDURE IS 3000-OP-PROCESS-SORTED-RECORDS.
050210     CLOSE INVENTORY-FILE
050220         INVENTORY-REPORT-FILE
050230         SORTED-INVENTORY-FILE.
050240     STOP RUN.
200010*
200020*
200030 2000-IP-SELECT-INV-RECORDS SECTION.
220010*
220020*
220030 2200-SELECT-INVENTORY-RECORDS.
220040*
220050     MOVE 'NO ' TO WS-END-OF-FILE-SW.
220070     PERFORM 2210-SELECT-INVENTORY-RECORD
220080         UNTIL END-OF-FILE.
220090     GO TO 2999-EXIT.
221010*
221020*
221030 2210-SELECT-INVENTORY-RECORD.
221040*
221050     PERFORM 2800-READ-INVENTORY-RECORD.
221060     IF NOT END-OF-FILE
221070     AND IR-INVENTORY-CLASS-CODE IS EQUAL TO 'A'
221080         PERFORM 2830-RELEASE-INVENTORY-RECORD.
280010*
280020*
280030 2800-READ-INVENTORY-RECORD.
280040*
280050     READ INVENTORY-FILE
280060         AT END MOVE 'YES' TO WS-END-OF-FILE-SW.
283010*
283020*
283030 2830-RELEASE-INVENTORY-RECORD.
283040*
283050     RELEASE SR-SORT-RECORD FROM IR-INVENTORY-RECORD.
299020*
299030 2999-EXIT.
299040*
299050     EXIT.
300010*
300020*
300030 3000-OP-PROCESS-SORTED-RECORDS SECTION.
320040*
320050*
320060 3200-PROCESS-SORTED-RECORDS.
320070*
320080     MOVE 'NO ' TO WS-END-OF-FILE-SW.
320090     PERFORM 3800-RETURN-SORTED-INV-RECORD.
320100     PERFORM 3210-PROCESS-SORTED-INV-RECORD
320110         UNTIL END-OF-FILE.
320120     GO TO 3999-EXIT.
321010*
321020*
321030 3210-PROCESS-SORTED-INV-RECORD.
321040*
321050     MOVE SR-SORT-RECORD TO SI-INVENTORY-RECORD.
321060     MOVE SPACES TO RL-REPORT-LINE.
321070     MOVE SI-WAREHOUSE-CODE TO RL-WAREHOUSE-CODE.
321080     MOVE SI-PART-NUMBER TO RL-PART-NUMBER.
321090     MOVE SI-INVENTORY-CLASS-CODE TO RL-INVENTORY-CLASS-CODE.
321100     MOVE SI-INVENTORY-VALUE TO RL-INVENTORY-VALUE.
321110     PERFORM 3830-WRITE-SORTED-INV-RECORD.
321120     PERFORM 3890-WRITE-REPORT-LINE.
321130     PERFORM 3800-RETURN-SORTED-INV-RECORD.
380010*
380020*
380030 3800-RETURN-SORTED-INV-RECORD.
380040*
380050     RETURN SORT-FILE
380060         AT END MOVE 'YES' TO WS-END-OF-FILE-SW.
383010*
383020*
383030 3830-WRITE-SORTED-INV-RECORD.
383040*
383050     WRITE SI-INVENTORY-RECORD.
383060*
383070*
383080 3890-WRITE-REPORT-LINE.
383090*
383100     WRITE RL-REPORT-LINE
383110         AFTER ADVANCING 1 LINE.
399010*
399020*
399030 3999-EXIT.
399040*
399050     EXIT.
```

APPENDIX E

DATA-VALIDATION CHECKLIST

This appendix presents a checklist of validation considerations for data at the time of initial input.

Character Testing

The most basic form of data validation is the testing of individual character positions. There are two basic forms of **character tests**: class and sign.

Class test

A **class test** is used to determine whether data within a field is numeric, alphabetic, or alphanumeric. The **numeric** class is limited to the digits zero through 9 and a valid arithmetic sign. Letters A through Z and a blank-space value are valid characters for an **alphabetic** field. The **alphanumeric** class encompasses all character representations: digits, letters, and special characters.

As a general rule, all numeric fields should be validated to ensure that they are purely numeric. If alphabetic or special characters are present in a numeric field, the data is in error. Strictly alphabetic fields are rarely specified; therefore, alphabetic tests are seldom made. Because an alphanumeric field encompasses all data values, there is no test for alphabetic.

Sign test

A **sign test** is sometimes specified for numeric fields. Numeric fields can be categorized as containing either **absolute** or **algebraic** values. Most numeric codes—Social Security numbers, ZIP Codes, and the like—are examples of absolute values. Amount fields such as quantities and dollar values usually require handling as algebraic values.

There are three normal arithmetic sign configurations: **positive**, **negative**, and **unsigned**.

Field Checking

In addition to the basic character testing of input data fields, most data elements can be subjected to further, more rigorous checks. A list of various types of **field checks** follows.

Presence check

A **presence check** should be specified for all required, mandatory fields.

Absence check

An **absence check** is sometimes applied to unused portions of a record to ensure that data is properly aligned in the field areas.

Range check

A **range check** can be applied to certain code and other field values.

Limit check

A **limit check** is used to test certain numeric fields against maximum and/or minimum values.

Reasonableness check

A **reasonableness check** identifies abnormal data values. Because abnormal values may be valid, provisions must be included in the system to permit any valid exceptions that are rejected by the reasonableness check to be reentered into the system.

Consistency check

A **consistency check** (sometimes called a **relationship check** or **combination check**) is the consideration of two or more data elements in relation to one another.

Justification check	A **justification check** is used to assure proper alignment of data within a field.
Embedded-blank check	An **embedded-blank check** is used to check certain key alphanumeric fields and code fields to ensure that blank positions have not inadvertently been entered. An embedded blank is a blank that has data characters present within the field both to the left and to the right of the blank space.
Date check	A **date check** is used to ensure the validity of calendar dates.
Self-checking number	A **check-digit** computation can be performed on a **self-checking number** to determine whether it is valid.
Name-correspondence check	A **name-correspondence check** is a consistency check that is typically used to ensure the correct match of a transaction record to a master record. When matching key-field values are found, another field—usually a last name, company name, or the like—is also tested for correspondence.
Code-existence check	A **code-existence check** is used to assure that a particular code value is valid. A table-look-up routine is typically used.

Record Checking

Not only must the character positions and field values of fields be validated, but it is often necessary to check the completeness and status of record relationships.

Record set-relationship checks	As an example, in a student-registration system, specifications may call for one student name-and-address record and from one to seven class records (one for each course in which the student is enrolled). Set-relationship errors to be checked for would include (1) student name-and-address record present but no class record occurrences, (2) one or more class records present but name-and-address record absent, or (3) too many (over seven in this example) class records present.
Record sequence checks	A sequential file should be checked to ensure that it is in the proper sequence. A file is out of sequence when a **step-down condition** exists. The key-field value for each record read should typically be greater than the value of the previous record. A step-down condition occurs when the key of the current record is less than the key of the previous record. If—as is usually the case—duplicate key values are not permitted in the file, an out-of-sequence condition also exists when an **equal condition** occurs.

APPENDIX F

DISK-CAPACITY TABLES

This appendix presents disk capacity tables for selected IBM cylinder/track and for IBM fixed-block architecture (FBA) disk drives. Programmer/analysts typically use these tables to determine appropriate blocking factors and/or disk-space requirements for a file as follows:

1. Determine whether the disk-storage device is of the cylinder/track or fixed-block architecture type. Proceed to step 2 in the respective classification.

Cylinder/Track Device

2. Choose an approximate block size. This can be expressed either as a block length (4000 bytes, for example) or as a track-size fraction (quarter-track blocking, for example).

3. Find the columns for the DASD model that is being used (3330, for example) in Figure F.1, the track-capacity table.

4. Determine whether the records are (for existing records) or are to be (for new files) formatted with keys or without keys. The considerations in the accompanying table apply.

File organization	(Count-data format) Formatted without keys?	(Count-key-data format) Formatted with keys?
SEQUENTIAL	Yes, almost always	Rarely
INDEXED	No, cannot be	Yes, must be
RELATIVE	Yes, usually	

Find the appropriate min-max columns: either with keys or w/o (without) keys.

5. **If block size is being expressed as a block length:**

   a. If the records are formatted with keys, add the key length to the block length to obtain the approximate block length including key.

   b. Find the min-max line that encompasses the approximate block length obtained at step 5a.

   c. If the approximate block length is not close to the maximum figure, you may want to either (i) increase the blocking factor so that the block length is close to, but does not exceed the maximum length or (ii) reduce the blocking factor so that the block length is close to but does not exceed the maximum length for the next line down on the chart. This will provide most efficient disk-space utilization.

   d. The record blocks per track column for that line indicates the number of physical records (that is, record blocks) that can be contained on one track.

   If block size is being expressed as a track fraction:

   a. Find the denominator in the record blocks per track column. For example, with quarter-track (¼ track) blocking, find the line for four record blocks per track.

   b. Find the max figure for the appropriate model and keys column.

c. Divide the max figure by the record length to determine the blocking factor.

d. If the records are formatted with keys, and the key length is greater than the remainder, subtract one record from the blocking factor.

e. Multiply the record length by the blocking factor. If the records are formatted with keys, add the key length. The result is the block length.

6. To determine the number of logical records that can be stored on one track, multiply the number of physical records that can be contained on one track (the record blocks per track column) by the blocking factor.

7. To determine the number of logical records that can be stored on one cylinder, multiply the number of logical records per track (the product from step 6, above) by the tracks per cylinder value for the DASD model as shown in Figure A.10 of Chapter A.

8. To determine the number of tracks that are required for the file, divide the number of records present in (or allocated to) the file by the number of logical records that can be stored on one track.

9. To determine the number of cylinders that are required for the file, divide the number of logical records present in (or allocated to) the file by the number of records that can be stored on one cylinder.

Worked Example A

Given 3350 DASD; 80-character logical records; formatted without keys, 20,000 records in the file.

Step 1. The 3350 is of the cylinder/track device type.

Step 2. Desired approximate block size is 4,000.

Step 3. Locate 3350 columns in Figure F.1.

Step 4. Records are formatted without keys.

Step 5. a. Not applicable.

b. Min-max figures are 3666-4628.

c. Block length of either 3600 or 4560 would provide better utilization of the track. Block length of 4560 chosen.

d. 4 physical records (record blocks) will fit on each track.

e. The blocking factor is 57 (4560/80).

Step 6. 228 logical records will fit on one track (4×57).

Step 7. 6,840 logical records will fit on one cylinder (228×30).

Step 8. 88 tracks required (20,000/228).

Step 9. 3 cylinders required (20,000/6,840).

Worked Example B

Given 3330 DASD; 200 character logical records; formatted without keys, 15,000 records in the file.

Step 1. The 3330 is of the cylinder/track device type.

Step 2. One third-track blocking is desired.

Step 3. Locate 3330 columns in Figure F.1.

Step 4. Records are formatted without keys.

Step 5. a. 3 record-blocks-per-track line is located.

b. Max figure is 4253.

c. Blocking factor is 21 (4253/200).

d. Not applicable.

e. Block length is 4200 (200×21).

Step 6. 63 logical records will fit on one track (3×21).

Step 7. 1197 logical records will fit on one cylinder (63×19).

Step 8. 239 tracks required (15,000/63).

Step 9. 13 cylinders required (15,000/1197).

Worked Example C

Given 3350 DASD; 300-character logical records; formatted with keys, key length is 11, 10,000 records in the file.

Bytes per record block

Left portion (3330, 3340, 3350 DASD). For these devices the four sub‑columns are, in printed order: W/o keys min, W/o keys max, With keys min, With keys max.

Record blocks per track	3330 W/o min	3330 W/o max	3330 With keys min	3330 With keys max	3340 W/o min	3340 W/o max	3340 With keys min	3340 With keys max	3350 W/o min	3350 W/o max	3350 With keys min	3350 With keys max
1	6448	13030	6392	12974	4101	8368	4026	8293	9443	19069	9361	18978
2	4254	6447	4198	6391	2679	4100	2604	4025	6234	9442	6152	9360
3	3157	4253	3101	4197	1967	2678	1892	2603	4629	6233	4547	6151
4	2499	3156	2443	3100	1541	1966	1466	1891	3666	4628	3584	4546
5	2060	2498	2004	2442	1256	1540	1181	1465	3025	3665	2943	3583
6	1746	2059	1690	2003	1053	1255	978	1180	2566	3024	2484	2942
7	1511	1745	1455	1689	900	1052	825	977	2222	2565	2140	2483
8	1328	1510	1272	1454	782	899	707	824	1955	2221	1873	2139
9	1182	1327	1126	1271	687	781	612	706	1741	1954	1659	1872
10	1062	1181	1006	1125	609	686	534	611	1566	1740	1484	1658
11	963	1061	907	1005	545	608	470	533	1420	1565	1338	1483
12	878	962	822	906	490	544	415	469	1297	1419	1215	1337
13	806	877	750	821	443	489	368	414	1191	1296	1109	1214
14	743	805	687	749	403	442	328	367	1099	1190	1017	1108
15	688	742	632	686	367	402	292	327	1019	1098	937	1016
16	640	687	584	631	336	366	261	291	948	1018	866	936
17	597	639	541	583	308	335	233	260	885	947	803	865
18	558	596	502	540	283	307	208	232	829	884	747	802
19	524	557	468	501	260	282	185	207	778	828	696	746
20	492	523	436	467	240	259	165	184	732	777	650	695
21	464	491	408	435	225	239	146	164	691	731	609	649
22	438	463	382	407	205	220	130	145	653	690	571	608
23	414	437	358	381	189	204	114	129	618	652	536	570
24	392	413	336	357	175	188	100	113	586	617	504	535
25	372	391	316	335	162	174	87	99	556	585	474	503
26	353	371	297	315	150	161	75	86	529	555	447	473
27	336	352	280	296	138	149	63	74	503	528	421	446
28	319	335	263	279	128	137	53	62	479	502	397	420
29	304	318	248	262	118	127	43	52	457	478	375	396
30	290	303	234	247	109	117	34	42	437	456	355	374
31	277	289	221	233	100	108	25	33	417	436	335	354
32	264	276	208	220	92	99	17	24	399	416	317	334
33	253	263	197	207	85	91	10	16	382	398	300	316
34	242	252	186	196	77	84		9	366	381	284	299
35	231	241	175	185	71	76			350	365	268	283
36	221	230	165	174	64	70			336	349	254	267
37	212	220	156	164	58	63			322	335	240	253
38	203	211	147	155	52	57			309	321	227	239
39	195	202	139	146	47	51			297	308	215	226
40	187	194	131	138	42	46			285	296	203	214
41	179	186	123	130	37	41			274	284	192	202
42	172	178	116	123	32	36			263	273	181	191
43	165	171	109	115	27	31			253	262	171	180
44	158	164	102	108	23	26			243	252	161	170
45	152	157	96	101	19	22			234	242	152	160
46	146	151	90	95	15	18			225	233	143	151
47	140	145	84	89	11	14			217	224	135	142
48	134	139	78	83	8	10			208	216	126	134
49	129	133	73	77	4	7			201	207	119	125
50	124	128	68	72		3			193	200	111	118

Right portion (3375, 3380 DASD). For these devices the four sub‑columns are, in printed order: With keys max, With keys min, W/o keys max, W/o keys min.

3375 With keys max	3375 With keys min	3375 W/o max	3375 W/o min	3380 With keys max	3380 With keys min	3380 W/o max	3380 W/o min	Record blocks per track
35456*	17441	35616	17601	47420*	23241	47476	23477	1
17440	11457	17600	11617	23240	15241	23476	15477	2
11456	8449	11616	8609	15240	11241	15476	11477	3
8448	6657	8608	6817	11240	8841	11476	9077	4
6656	5441	6816	5601	8840	7241	9076	7477	5
5440	4577	5600	4737	7240	6121	7476	6357	6
4576	3937	4736	4097	6120	5257	6356	5493	7
3936	3457	4096	3617	5256	4585	5492	4821	8
3456	3041	3616	3201	4584	4041	4820	4277	9
3040	2721	3200	2881	4040	3625	4276	3861	10
2720	2433	2880	2593	3624	3241	3860	3477	11
2432	2209	2592	2369	3240	2953	3476	3189	12
2208	2017	2368	2177	2952	2697	3188	2933	13
2016	1857	2176	2017	2696	2441	2932	2677	14
1856	1697	2016	1857	2440	2249	2676	2485	15
1696	1569	1856	1729	2248	2089	2484	2343	16
1568	1441	1728	1601	2088	1929	2342	2165	17
1440	1345	1600	1505	1928	1769	2164	2005	18
1344	1249	1504	1409	1768	1641	2004	1877	19
1248	1153	1408	1313	1640	1545	1876	1781	20
1152	1089	1312	1249	1544	1449	1780	1685	21
1088	993	1248	1153	1448	1353	1684	1589	22
992	929	1152	1089	1352	1257	1588	1493	23
928	897	1088	1057	1256	1161	1492	1397	24
896	833	1056	993	1160	1097	1396	1333	25
832	769	992	897	1096	1033	1332	1269	26
768	737	928	833	1032	969	1268	1205	27
736	673	896	801	968	905	1204	1141	28
672	641	832	769	904	841	1140	1077	29
640	609	800	737	840	809	1076	1045	30
608	577	768	705	808	745	1044	981	31
576	545	736	673	744	713	980	949	32
544	513	704	641	712	681	948	917	33
512	481	672	609	680	617	916	853	34
480	449	640	577	616	585	852	821	35
448	417	608	545	584	553	820	789	36
416	385	576	513	552	521	788	757	37
384	353	544	481	520	489	756	725	38
352	321	512	449	488	457	724	693	39
320	289	480	417	456	425	692	661	40
288	257	448	385	424	393	660	629	41
256	225	416	353	392	361	628	597	42
224	193	384	321	360	329	596	565	43
192	161	352	289	328	297	564	533	44
				296	265	532	501	45
				264	233	500	469	46
				232	201	468	437	47
								48
								49
								50

Figure F.1. — Track-capacity table for selected IBM cylinder/track direct-access storage devices.

51	119	123	63	67	186	192	104	110	289	320	129	160	405	436	169	200	51
52	114	118	58	62	179	185	97	103	257	288	97	128	373	404	137	168	52
53	109	113	53	57	172	178	90	96					341	372	105	136	53
54	105	108	49	52	166	171	84	89									54
55	101	104	45	48	159	165	77	83									55
56	96	100	40	44	153	158	71	76	225	256	65	96	309	340	73	104	56
57	92	95	36	39	147	152	65	70									57
58	89	91	33	35	142	146	60	64	193	224			277	308	41	72	58
59	85	88	29	32	136	141	54	59				64					59
60	81	84	25	28	131	135	49	53									60
61	78	80	22	24	126	130	44	48	161	192			245	276		40	61
62	74	77	18	21	121	125	39	43									62
63	71	73	15	17	116	120	34	38									63
64	68	70	12	14	112	115	30	33					213	244			64
65	65	67	9	11	107	111	25	29									65
66	62	64	6	8	103	106	21	24	129	160							66
67	59	61	3	5	99	102	17	20					181	212			67
68	56	58		2	95	98	13	16									68
69	54	55			91	94	9	12	97	128							69
70	51	53			87	90	5	8									70
71	48	50			83	86		4					149	180			71
72	46	47			79	82											72
73	43	45			76	78							117	148			73
74	41	42			72	75			65	96							74
75	39	40			69	71											75
76	36	38			66	68											76
77	34	35			62	65							85	116			77
78	32	33			59	61											78
79	30	31			56	58			33	64							79
80	28	29			53	55											80
81	26	27			50	52											81
82	24	25			47	49							53	84			82
83	22	23			45	46											83
84	20	21			42	44											84
85	19	19			39	41											85
86	17	18			37	38				32							86
87	15	16			34	36											87
88	13	14			32	33							21	52			88
89	12	12			29	31											89
90	10	11			27	28											90
91	9	9			25	26											91
92	7	8			23	24											92
93	6	6			20	22								20			93
94	4	5			18	19											94
95	3	3			16	17											95
96					14	15											96
97	2	2			12	13											97
98					10	11											98
99					8	9											99
100					6	7											100
101					4	5											101
102					2	3											102
103					1	1											103

* The maximum block size supported by IBM-supplied access methods is 32,760 bytes

Figure F.1. Track-capacity table for selected IBM cylinder/track direct-access storage devices.

Step 1. The 3350 is of the cylinder/track device type.

Step 2. Desired approximate block size is 1200.

Step 3. Locate 3350 columns in Figure F.1.

Step 4. Records are formatted with keys.

Step 5. a. Block length including key is 1211 (11 + 1200).

       b. Min-max figures are 1109-1214.

       c. Not applicable.

       d. 13 physical records (record blocks) will fit on each track.

       e. The blocking factor is 4 (1200/300).

Step 6. 52 logical records will fit on one track (13 × 4).

Step 7. 988 logical records will fit on one cylinder (52 × 19).

Step 8. 193 tracks required (10,000/52).

Step 9. 11 cylinders required (10,000/988).

Fixed-Block Architecture Device

2. Choose the logical block size. For an existing file stored on a cylinder/track device, this will be the block length (physical record size). For a new file, the logical block size will typically be the same as the logical record length.

3. Find the column for the chosen logical block size in Figure F.2, the control interval size calculation table. If the exact logical block size does not appear in the table, locate the column with the smallest logical block size that is greater than the desired logical block size. (**Note: Figure F.2 contains only a few selected logical block sizes. It is valid only for those sizes listed.** The complete table contains approximately 50 times more entries than shown in the figure.) This column shows the number of logical blocks that will fit into a single FBA block of 512 bytes.

4. Choose the **control interval (CI)** size. With FBA devices, a control interval is the transfer unit between the DASD and main storage. A control interval contains logical record blocks plus certain control data. The CI size chosen must be greater than the logical block size and a multiple of 512 bytes. The minimum CI size is 512 bytes; the maximum is 32,768 bytes.

    When choosing a CI size, the programmer/analyst must consider I-O performance, disk utilization and main storage requirements. The highest value in the logical block size column will correspond to the CI size that most efficiently uses the FBA device. However, the programmer/analyst must ensure that this CI size is appropriate for I/O processing and also does not consume too much main storage.

5. To determine the number of FBA blocks per CI, divide the CI size by the standard FBA block length (512 bytes).

6. To determine the number of FBA blocks required for the file, divide the number of logical blocks in the file by the table value located at the intersection of the chosen CI size and logical block size.

7. Round the quotient to a CI boundary (the smallest number equal to or greater than the quotient that is a multiple of the number of FBA blocks per CI).

8. Add one additional CI for the software end-of-file (SEOF). The result is the total number of FBA blocks required for the file.

Worked Example

Given FBA DASD, 160-character logical records, blocking factor is 5, 10,000 records in the file.

Step 1. The DASD is of the FBA device type.

Step 2. Logical block size is 800 (160 × 5).

Step 3. Logical block size column headed 799-800 is located.

Step 4. CI size of 5632 bytes chosen.

Step 5. 11 FBA blocks per CI (5632/12)

Step 6. 3175 FBA blocks required for the file (2000/.63). [2000 logical blocks in the file (10,000 logical records divided by the blocking factor of 5).]

Step 7. Next CI boundary is 3179.

Step 8. A total of 3190 FBA blocks is required for the file (3179 + 11).

Number of logical blocks per FBA block

Logical block size

CI size	80	160	200	300	400	500	600-601	700	799-800	896-900	993-1014	1927-2038	2979-3062	3893-4086	4914-5110	5733-6134	6824-7158	7678-8182	8872-9211	9555-10230
512	6.00	3.00	2.00	1.00	1.00	1.00	—	—	—	—	—	—	—	—	—	—	—	—	—	—
1024	6.00	3.00	2.50	1.50	1.00	1.00	0.50	0.50	0.50	0.50	0.50	—	—	—	—	—	—	—	—	—
1536	6.33	3.00	2.33	1.66	1.00	1.00	0.66	0.66	0.33	0.33	0.33	—	—	—	—	—	—	—	—	—
2048	6.25	3.00	2.50	1.50	1.25	1.00	0.75	0.50	0.50	0.50	0.50	0.25	—	—	—	—	—	—	—	—
2560	6.20	3.00	2.40	1.60	1.20	1.00	0.80	0.60	0.60	0.40	0.40	0.20	—	—	—	—	—	—	—	—
3072	6.33	3.16	2.50	1.66	1.16	1.00	0.83	0.66	0.50	0.50	0.50	0.16	.166	—	—	—	—	—	—	—
3584	6.28	3.14	2.42	1.57	1.14	1.00	0.71	0.71	0.57	0.42	0.42	0.14	.142	—	—	—	—	—	—	—
4096	6.37	3.12	2.50	1.62	1.25	1.00	0.75	0.62	0.62	0.50	0.50	0.25	.125	.125	—	—	—	—	—	—
4608	6.33	3.11	2.44	1.66	1.22	1.00	0.77	0.66	0.55	0.55	0.44	0.22	.111	.111	—	—	—	—	—	—
5120	6.30	3.19	2.50	1.70	1.20	1.00	0.80	0.70	0.60	0.50	0.50	0.20	.100	.100	.100	—	—	—	—	—
5632	6.36	3.18	2.54	1.63	1.27	1.00	0.81	0.72	0.63	0.54	0.45	0.18	.090	.090	.090	—	—	—	—	—
6144	6.33	3.16	2.50	1.66	1.25	1.00	0.83	0.66	0.58	0.50	0.50	0.25	.166	.083	.083	.083	—	—	—	—
6656	6.38	3.15	2.53	1.69	1.23	1.00	0.84	0.69	0.61	0.53	0.46	0.23	.153	.076	.076	.076	—	—	—	—
7168	6.35	3.14	2.54	1.64	1.21	1.00	0.78	0.71	0.57	0.50	0.50	0.21	.142	.071	.071	.071	.071	—	—	—
7680	6.33	3.13	2.53	1.66	1.26	1.00	0.80	0.66	0.60	0.53	0.46	0.20	.133	.066	.066	.066	.066	—	—	—
8192	6.37	3.18	2.50	1.68	1.25	1.00	0.81	0.68	0.62	0.56	0.50	0.25	.125	.125	.062	.062	.062	.062	—	—
10240	6.35	3.15	2.55	1.70	1.25	1.00	0.85	0.70	0.60	0.55	0.50	0.25	.150	.100	.100	.050	.050	.050	.050	.050
12288	6.37	3.16	2.54	1.66	1.25	1.00	0.83	0.70	0.62	0.54	0.50	0.25	.166	.125	.083	.083	.041	.041	.041	.041
14336	6.33	3.17	2.53	1.67	1.25	1.00	0.82	0.71	0.60	0.53	0.50	0.25	.142	.107	.071	.071	.066	.035	.035	.035
16384	6.37	3.18	2.53	1.68	1.25	1.00	0.84	0.71	0.62	0.56	0.50	0.25	.156	.125	.093	.062	.062	.062	.031	.031
18432	6.38	3.19	2.55	1.69	1.27	1.00	0.83	0.72	0.63	0.55	0.50	0.25	.166	.111	.083	.083	.055	.055	.055	.027
20480	6.37	3.17	2.55	1.70	1.27	1.00	0.85	0.72	0.62	0.55	0.50	0.25	.150	.125	.100	.075	.050	.050	.050	.050
22528	6.38	3.18	2.54	1.70	1.27	1.02	0.84	0.72	0.63	0.56	0.50	0.25	.159	.113	.090	.068	.068	.045	.045	.045
24576	6.39	3.18	2.54	1.68	1.27	1.02	0.83	0.72	0.62	0.56	0.50	0.25	.166	.125	.083	.083	.062	.062	.041	.041
26624	6.38	3.19	2.55	1.69	1.26	1.01	0.84	0.73	0.63	0.55	0.50	0.25	.153	.115	.096	.076	.057	.057	.038	.038
28672	6.39	3.19	2.55	1.69	1.26	1.01	0.83	0.71	0.62	0.55	0.50	0.25	.160	.125	.089	.071	.071	.053	.053	.035
30720	6.38	3.18	2.55	1.70	1.26	1.01	0.85	0.71	0.63	0.56	0.50	0.25	.166	.116	.100	.083	.066	.050	.050	.050
32768	6.39	3.18	2.54	1.70	1.26	1.01	0.84	0.71	0.62	0.56	0.50	0.25	.156	.125	.093	.078	.062	.062	.046	.046

Figure F.2. Control interval size calculation table (abridged) for IBM fixed-block architecture direct-access storage devices.

Blocks per 2400-foot reel = inches-per-block / 28,440

Inches per block:

$$6250\ bpi = 0.3 + 1 / 6250 * (b + 82)$$
$$1600\ bpi = 0.6 + 1 / 1600 * (b + 82)$$
$$800\ bpi\ (9\text{-track}) = 0.6 + 1 / 800 * (b)$$
$$800\ bpi\ (7\text{-track}) = 0.75 + 1 / 800 * (b)$$
$$556\ bpi = 0.75 + 1 / 556 * (b)$$
$$200\ bpi = 0.75 + 1 / 200 * (b)$$

Legend:

bpi = bytes per inch
b = block length in bytes
28,440 = 2400 feet times 12 inches less a 15-foot leader and a 15-foot trailer

Blocks per 2400-foot reel for selected block lengths

bpi	Block length in bytes						
	80	250	500	1,000	2,500	5,000	10,000
6250	87,261	80,906	72,334	60,112	39,881	25,550	14,866
1600	40,556	35,220	29,510	22,284	12,847	7,531	4,121
800 (9-track)	40,629	31,167	23,216	15,373	7,635	4,151	2,171
800 (7-track)	33,459	29,767	20,684	14,220	7,339	4,092	2,162
556	31,816	23,707	17,224	11,159	5,421	2,939	1,524
200	24,730	14,220	8,751	4,946	2,146	1,104	560

APPENDIX H

LIST OF SELECTED PRIME NUMBERS

Number of records	Nearest smaller prime number	Number of records	Nearest smaller prime number	Number of records	Nearest smaller prime number
		30,000	29,989	70,000	69,997
100	97	31,000	30,983	71,000	70,999
200	199	32,000	31,991	72,000	71,999
300	293	33,000	32,999	73,000	72,997
400	397	34,000	33,997	74,000	73,999
500	499	35,000	34,981	75,000	74,959
600	599	36,000	35,999	76,000	75,997
700	691	37,000	36,997	77,000	76,991
800	797	38,000	37,997	78,000	77,999
900	887	39,000	38,993	79,000	78,989
		40,000	39,989	80,000	79,999
1,000	997	41,000	40,993	81,000	80,989
2,000	1,999	42,000	41,999	82,000	81,973
3,000	2,999	43,000	42,989	83,000	82,997
4,000	3,989	44,000	43,997	84,000	83,987
5,000	4,999	45,000	44,987	85,000	84,991
6,000	5,987	46,000	45,989	86,000	85,999
7,000	6,997	47,000	46,997	87,000	86,993
8,000	7,993	48,000	47,981	88,000	87,991
9,000	8,999	49,000	48,991	89,000	88,997
10,000	9,973	50,000	49,999	90,000	89,989
11,000	10,993	51,000	50,993	91,000	90,997
12,000	11,987	52,000	51,991	92,000	91,997
13,000	12,983	53,000	52,991	93,000	92,993
14,000	13,999	54,000	53,993	94,000	93,997
15,000	14,983	55,000	54,983	95,000	94,999
16,000	15,991	56,000	55,997	96,000	95,989
17,000	16,993	57,000	56,999	97,000	96,997
18,000	17,989	58,000	57,991	98,000	97,987
19,000	18,979	59,000	58,997	99,000	98,999
20,000	19,997	60,000	59,999	100,000	99,991
21,000	20,983	61,000	60,961		
22,000	21,997	62,000	61,991		
23,000	22,993	63,000	62,989		
24,000	23,993	64,000	63,997		
25,000	24,989	65,000	64,997		
26,000	25,999	66,000	65,993		
27,000	26,993	67,000	66,977		
28,000	27,997	68,000	67,993		
29,000	28,979	69,000	68,993		

APPENDIX I

EBCDIC AND ASCII DATA REPRESENTATION

Decimal value	Binary repre-sentation	Hexa-decimal notation	Graphics & Controls EBCDIC	Graphics & Controls ASCII	IBM punched card code
0	0000 0000	00	NUL	NUL	12-0-1-8-9
1	0000 0001	01	SOH	SOH	12-1-9
2	0000 0010	02	STX	STX	12-2-9
3	0000 0011	03	ETX	ETX	12-3-9
4	0000 0100	04	SEL	EOT	12-4-9
5	0000 0101	05	HT	ENQ	12-5-9
6	0000 0110	06	RNL	ACK	12-6-9
7	0000 0111	07	DEL	BEL	12-7-9
8	0000 1000	08	GE	BS	12-8-9
9	0000 1001	09	SPS	HT	12-1-8-9
10	0000 1010	0A	RPT	LF	12-2-8-9
11	0000 1011	0B	VT	VT	12-3-8-9
12	0000 1100	0C	FF	FF	12-4-8-9
13	0000 1101	0D	CR	CR	12-5-8-9
14	0000 1110	0E	SO	SO	12-6-8-9
15	0000 1111	0F	SI	SI	12-7-8-9
16	0001 0000	10	DLE	DLE	12-11-1-8-9
17	0001 0001	11	DC1	DC1	11-1-9
18	0001 0010	12	DC2	DC2	11-2-9
19	0001 0011	13	DC3	DC3	11-3-9
20	0001 0100	14	RES	DC4	11-4-9
21	0001 0101	15	NL	NAK	11-5-9
22	0001 0110	16	BS	SYN	11-6-9
23	0001 0111	17	POC	ETB	11-7-9
24	0001 1000	18	CAN	CAN	11-8-9
25	0001 1001	19	EM	EM	11-1-8-9
26	0001 1010	1A	UBS	SUB	11-2-8-9
27	0001 1011	1B	CU1	ESC	11-3-8-9
28	0001 1100	1C	IFS	FS	11-4-8-9
29	0001 1101	1D	IGS	GS	11-5-8-9
30	0001 1110	1E	IRS	RS	11-6-8-9
31	0001 1111	1F	ITB	US	11-7-8-9
32	0010 0000	20	DS	SP	11-0-1-8-9
33	0010 0001	21	SOS	!	0-1-9
34	0010 0010	22	FS	"	0-2-9
35	0010 0011	23	WUS	#	0-3-9
36	0010 0100	24	BYP	$	0-4-9
37	0010 0101	25	LF	%	0-5-9
38	0010 0110	26	ETB	&	0-6-9
39	0010 0111	27	ESC	'	0-7-9
40	0010 1000	28	SA	(	0-8-9
41	0010 1001	29	SFE	)	0-1-8-9
42	0010 1010	2A	SM	*	0-2-8-9
43	0010 1011	2B	CSP	+	0-3-8-9
44	0010 1100	2C	MFA	,	0-4-8-9
45	0010 1101	2D	ENQ	–	0-5-8-9

Decimal value	Binary representation	Hexa-decimal notation	Graphics & controls		IBM punched card code
			EBCDIC	ASCII	
46	0010 1110	2E	ACK	.	0-6-8-9
47	0010 1111	2F	BEL	/	0-7-8-9
48	0011 0000	30		0	12-11-0-1-8-9
49	0011 0001	31		1	1-9
50	0011 0010	32	SYN	2	2-9
51	0011 0011	33	IR	3	3-9
52	0011 0100	34	PP	4	4-9
53	0011 0101	35	TRN	5	5-9
54	0011 0110	36	NBS	6	6-9
55	0011 0111	37	EOT	7	7-9
56	0011 1000	38	SBS	8	8-9
57	0011 1001	39	IT	9	1-8-9
58	0011 1010	3A	RFF	:	2-8-9
59	0011 1011	3B	CU3	;	3-8-9
60	0011 1100	3C	DC4	<	4-8-9
61	0011 1101	3D	NAK	=	5-8-9
62	0011 1110	3E		>	6-8-9
63	0011 1111	3F	SUB	?	7-8-9
64	0100 0000	40	space	@	no punches
65	0100 0001	41		A	12-0-1-9
66	0100 0010	42		B	12-0-2-9
67	0100 0011	43		C	12-0-3-9
68	0100 0100	44		D	12-0-4-9
69	0100 0101	45		E	12-0-5-9
70	0100 0110	46		F	12-0-6-9
71	0100 0111	47		G	12-0-7-9
72	0100 1000	48		H	12-0-8-9
73	0100 1001	49		I	12-1-8
74	0100 1010	4A	¢	J	12-2-8
75	0100 1011	4B	.	K	12-3-8
76	0100 1100	4C	<	L	12-4-8
77	0100 1101	4D	(	M	12-5-8
78	0100 1110	4E	+	N	12-6-8
79	0100 1111	4F	I	O	12-7-8
80	0101 0000	50	&	P	12
81	0101 0001	51		Q	12-11-1-9
82	0101 0010	52		R	12-11-2-9
83	0101 0011	53		S	12-11-3-9
84	0101 0100	54		T	12-11-4-9
85	0101 0101	55		U	12-11-5-9
86	0101 0110	56		V	12-11-6-9
87	0101 0111	57		W	12-11-7-9
88	0101 1000	58		X	12-11-8-9
89	0101 1001	59		Y	11-1-8
90	0101 1010	5A	!	Z	11-2-8
91	0101 1011	5B	$	[	11-3-8
92	0101 1100	5C	*	/	11-4-8
93	0101 1101	5D	)	]	11-5-8
94	0101 1110	5E	;	¬	11-6-8
95	0101 1111	5F	¬	_	11-7-8
96	0110 0000	60	-	\	11
97	0110 0001	61	/	a	0-1
98	0110 0010	62		b	11-0-2-9
99	0110 0011	63		c	11-0-3-9
100	0110 0100	64		d	11-0-4-9
101	0110 0101	65		e	11-0-5-9
102	0110 0110	66		f	11-0-6-9
103	0110 0111	67		g	11-0-7-9
104	0110 1000	68		h	11-0-8-9
105	0110 1001	69		i	0-1-8

Decimal value	Binary representation	Hexa-decimal notation	Graphics & controls		IBM punched card code
			EBCDIC	ASCII	
106	0110 1010	6A	¦	j	12-11
107	0110 1011	6B	,	k	0-3-8
108	0110 1100	6C	%	l	0-4-8
109	0110 1101	6D	_	m	0-5-8
110	0110 1110	6E	>	n	0-6-8
111	0110 1111	6F	?	o	0-7-8
112	0111 0000	70		p	12-11-0
113	0111 0001	71		q	12-11-0-1-9
114	0111 0010	72		r	12-11-0-2-9
115	0111 0011	73		s	12-11-0-3-9
116	0111 0100	74		t	12-11-0-4-9
117	0111 0101	75		u	12-11-0-5-9
118	0111 0110	76		v	12-11-0-6-9
119	0111 0111	77		w	12-11-0-7-9
120	0111 1000	78		x	12-11-0-8-9
121	0111 1001	79	\	y	1-8
122	0111 1010	7A	:	z	2-8
123	0111 1011	7B	#	{	3-8
124	0111 1100	7C	@	¦	4-8
125	0111 1101	7D	'	}	5-8
126	0111 1110	7E	=	~	6-8
127	0111 1111	7F	"	DEL	7-8
128	1000 0000	80			12-0-1-8
129	1000 0001	81	a		12-0-1
130	1000 0010	82	b		12-0-2
131	1000 0011	83	c		12-0-3
132	1000 0100	84	d		12-0-4
133	1000 0101	85	e		12-0-5
134	1000 0110	86	f		12-0-6
135	1000 0111	87	g		12-0-7
136	1000 1000	88	h		12-0-8
137	1000 1001	89	i		12-0-9
138	1000 1010	8A			12-0-2-8
139	1000 1011	8B			12-0-3-8
140	1000 1100	8C			12-0-4-8
141	1000 1101	8D			12-0-5-8
142	1000 1110	8E			12-0-6-8
143	1000 1111	8F			12-0-7-8
144	1001 0000	90			12-11-1-8
145	1001 0001	91	j		12-11-1
146	1001 0010	92	k		12-11-2
147	1001 0011	93	l		12-11-3
148	1001 0100	94	m		12-11-4
149	1001 0101	95	n		12-11-5
150	1001 0110	96	o		12-11-6
151	1001 0111	97	p		12-11-7
152	1001 1000	98	q		12-11-8
153	1001 1001	99	r		12-11-9
154	1001 1010	9A			12-11-2-8
155	1001 1011	9B			12-11-3-8
156	1001 1100	9C			12-11-4-8
157	1001 1101	9D			12-11-5-8
158	1001 1110	9E			12-11-6-8
159	1001 1111	9F			12-11-7-8
160	1010 0000	A0			11-0-1-8
161	1010 0001	A1	~		11-0-1
162	1010 0010	A2	s		11-0-2
163	1010 0011	A3	t		11-0-3
164	1010 0100	A4	u		11-0-4
165	1010 0101	A5	v		11-0-5
166	1010 0110	A6	w		11-0-6
167	1010 0111	A7	x		11-0-7
168	1010 1000	A8	y		11-0-8

Decimal value	Binary repre- sentation	Hexa- decimal notation	Graphics & controls		IBM punched card code
			EBCDIC	ASCII	
169	1010 1001	A9	z		11-0-9
170	1010 1010	AA			11-0-2-8
171	1010 1011	AB			11-0-3-8
172	1010 1100	AC			11-0-4-8
173	1010 1101	AD			11-0-5-8
174	1010 1110	AE			11-0-6-8
175	1010 1111	AF			11-0-7-8
176	1011 0000	B0			12-11-0-1-8
177	1011 0001	B1			12-11-0-1
178	1011 0010	B2			12-11-0-2
179	1011 0011	B3			12-11-0-3
180	1011 0100	B4			12-11-0-4
181	1011 0101	B5			12-11-0-5
182	1011 0110	B6			12-11-0-6
183	1011 0111	B7			12-11-0-7
184	1011 1000	B8			12-11-0-8
185	1011 1001	B9			12-11-0-9
186	1011 1010	BA			12-11-0-2-8
187	1011 1011	BB			12-11-0-3-8
188	1011 1100	BC			12-11-0-4-8
189	1011 1101	BD			12-11-0-5-8
190	1011 1110	BE			12-11-0-6-8
191	1011 1111	BF			12-11-0-7-8
192	1100 0000	C0	{		12-0
193	1100 0001	C1	A		12-1
194	1100 0010	C2	B		12-2
195	1100 0011	C3	C		12-3
196	1100 0100	C4	D		12-4
197	1100 0101	C5	E		12-5
198	1100 0110	C6	F		12-6
199	1100 0111	C7	G		12-7
200	1100 1000	C8	H		12-8
201	1100 1001	C9	I		12-9
202	1100 1010	CA			12-0-2-8-9
203	1100 1011	CB			12-0-3-8-9
204	1100 1100	CC	⌠		12-0-4-8-9
205	1100 1101	CD			12-0-5-8-9
206	1100 1110	CE	Ψ		12-0-6-8-9
207	1100 1111	CF			12-0-7-8-9
208	1101 0000	D0	}		11-0
209	1101 0001	D1	J		11-1
210	1101 0010	D2	K		11-2
211	1101 0011	D3	L		11-3
212	1101 0100	D4	M		11-4
213	1101 0101	D5	N		11-5
214	1101 0110	D6	O		11-6
215	1101 0111	D7	P		11-7
216	1101 1000	D8	Q		11-8
217	1101 1001	D9	R		11-9
218	1101 1010	DA			12-11-2-8-9
219	1101 1011	DB			12-11-3-8-9
220	1101 1100	DC			12-11-4-8-9
221	1101 1101	DD			12-11-5-8-9
222	1101 1110	DE			12-11-6-8-9
223	1101 1111	DF			12-11-7-8-9
224	1110 0000	E0	\		0-2-8
225	1110 0001	E1			11-0-1-9
226	1110 0010	E2	S		0-2
227	1110 0011	E3	T		0-3
228	1110 0100	E4	U		0-4
229	1110 0101	E5	V		0-5
230	1110 0110	E6	W		0-6
231	1110 0111	E7	X		0-7

Decimal value	Binary representation	Hexadecimal notation	Graphics & controls EBCDIC	ASCII	IBM punched card code
232	1110 1000	E8	Y		0-8
233	1110 1001	E9	Z		0-9
234	1110 1010	EA			11-0-2-8-9
235	1110 1011	EB			11-0-3-8-9
236	1110 1100	EC			11-0-4-8-9
237	1110 1101	ED			11-0-5-8-9
238	1110 1110	EE			11-0-6-8-9
239	1110 1111	EF			11-0-7-8-9
240	1111 0000	F0	0		0
241	1111 0001	F1	1		1
242	1111 0010	F2	2		2
243	1111 0011	F3	3		3
244	1111 0100	F4	4		4
245	1111 0101	F5	5		5
246	1111 0110	F6	6		6
247	1111 0111	F7	7		7
248	1111 1000	F8	8		8
249	1111 1001	F9	9		9
250	1111 1010	FA	|		12-11-0-2-8-9
251	1111 1011	FB			12-11-0-3-8-9
252	1111 1100	FC			12-11-0-4-8-9
253	1111 1101	FD			12-11-0-5-8-9
254	1111 1110	FE			12-11-0-6-8-9
255	1111 1111	FF	EO		12-11-0-7-8-9

APPENDIX J

PROGRAM INTERRUPTIONS FOR IBM OS AND DOS SYSTEMS

With IBM medium- and large-scale computer systems (and PCMs), the computer system diagnoses each machine-language instruction and the results of certain arithmetic operations to ensure that incorrect processing does not occur. When an obviously incorrect instruction is provided for execution (such as one containing an invalid operation code or an address that is greater than the available storage for the computer), a program check occurs. A **program interruption** (formerly termed a **program check**) causes the system to terminate program processing and to cancel the program. Programmers usually refer to this as **abnormal termination** or an "**abend**."

There are 15 types of program checks as shown in Figure J.1. Most of them are encountered only rarely with COBOL programs. A few of the ones that occur more frequently with COBOL programs are discussed below.

Operation Exception (0C1)

COBOL programs that contain certain logic errors will trigger operation exceptions. Following are some typical causes.

- Attempting to READ or WRITE a file before it has been opened or after it has been closed.
- Failure to CLOSE files before the STOP RUN statement is executed.
- When the identifier field of the AFTER ADVANCING phrase of the WRITE statement contains a value outside the range of permissible values (should be 0 to 99).
- Missing JCL statement for a file.

Protection Exception (0C4)

Although this error does not normally occur with COBOL programs on account of boundary-protection errors, it may occur because of the following programming errors:

- Subscript or index not initialized prior to use.
- Incorrect ASSIGN clause system-name.
- Assign clause system-name does not match the JCL statement system-name.
- Missing JCL statement for a file.
- Attempting to READ an unopened input file.

Addressing and Specification Exceptions (0C5 and 0C6)

One of these exceptions may occur when one of the following programming errors is made:

- Incorrect value in a subscript or index.
- Improper exit from a performed procedure.
- Attempting to refer to a field of an input record that is defined within the FILE section after the AT END phrase of the READ statement has been executed.
- Attempting to refer to a field of an output record that is defined within the FILE section before the OPEN statement has been executed.

Exception	Completion code (OS)	Cause
Operation	0C1	The computer has attempted to execute an invalid operation code.
Privileged-operation	0C2	An application program has requested the computer to execute an operation code that only the operating system supervisor program is permitted to execute.
Execute	0C3	Will not normally occur with a COBOL program.
Protection	0C4	The program has attempted to access or move data to an area of storage that does not belong to the program.
Addressing	0C5	The program has attempted to reference an address beyond the limit of the computer's physical storage.
Specification	0C6	A machine-language instruction address is invalid.
Data	0C7	The program has requested that a decimal arithmetic operation be performed on data that is not numeric.
Fixed-point-overflow	0C8	A calculated binary value is too large to be contained within a register.
Fixed-point-divide	0C9	The program has attempted to divide a binary field by zero or the quotient exceeds the register size.
Decimal-overflow	0CA	A calculated, packed decimal value is too large to be contained within the result field.
Decimal-divide	0CB	The program has attempted to divide a packed decimal field by zero or the quotient exceeds the register size.
Exponent-overflow	0CC	Will not normally occur with a COBOL program.
Exponent-underflow	0CD	Will not normally occur with a COBOL program.
Significance	0CE	Will not normally occur with a COBOL program.
Floating-point	0CF	Will not normally occur with a COBOL program.

Figure J.1. Program interruptions.

Data Exception (0C7)

This is probably the most commonly encountered program check and one that generally haunts beginning programmers. Its cause is simple: attempting to operate numerically on nonnumeric data with decimal arithmetic instructions. Fields that are being processed by decimal arithmetic instructions must contain a valid digit (0 though 9) in each digit position of the field and a valid sign (plus, minus, unsigned assumed positive, or unsigned) in the sign position.

There are two general situations in which a data exception will occur.

The first situation is one in which a WORKING-STORAGE field is not initialized before it is used in the program. When the program begins, fields that are not properly initialized by VALUE clauses or PROCEDURE DIVISION statements contain either unpredictable values or, depending upon the operating system, binary zeros. (Binary zeros do not contain a valid decimal arithmetic sign.) Therefore, if the programmer neglects to initialize or improperly initializes a decimal arithmetic field, the field will probably contain data that is not valid for the decimal arithmetic instructions. Thus a data exception will occur.

A second situation is one in which input data is read into a program that does not contain decimal numeric data in a field that is specified with the picture symbol 9. For example, if a quantity field is input with blank spaces, a data exception will occur if the program attempts to ADD or otherwise operate numerically on those blank spaces with decimal arithmetic instructions.

The first situation described above is generally detected early in program testing. However, the second situation—because it is usually caused by input errors rather than programming errors—can happen long after a program has been tested and put into production unless proper validation of each input field is provided at some point in the program processing. This is the reason why data-validation programs are so important.

It should be noted that errors in field specifications can also cause the second type of data exception. That is, if a 5-digit quantity field is defined as S9(6), a data exception may well result.

The COBOL programmer should recognize that, since COBOL uses arithmetic instructions for certain other verbs, a data exception can occur with the following statements:

- Arithmetic statements (ADD, SUBTRACT, MULTIPLY, DIVIDE, and COMPUTE) that operate on DISPLAY or COMP-3 fields.
- IF statement relation and condition-name conditions in which both the subject and object fields are numeric (and both are not of COMP usage).
- IF statement sign conditions in which the subject field is of DISPLAY or COMP-3 usage.
- MOVE statements from a DISPLAY or COMP-3 field to a COMP-3 or COMP field.
- MOVE statements to a numeric-edited field.

Following is a checklist of common data-exception causes:

- A numeric field was not initialized before it was used.
- A numeric field was incorrectly initialized.
  a. Moving ZEROS to a group field will produce invalid data for COMP and COMP-3 fields within the group. (ZEROS must be moved to the elementary COMP and COMP-3 fields.)
  b. Moving SPACES to either a group or elementary numeric field will produce invalid data for numeric fields.
  c. Moving 0 (a literal of a single zero) to a group field will produce invalid data for COMP and COMP-3 fields within the group. (This causes one zero to be moved to the first position of the group field and the remainder of the positions are padded with blank spaces.)
  d. Moving LOW-VALUES or HIGH-VALUES to a DISPLAY or COMP-3 field will produce invalid numeric data.
- A subscript or index was not initialized.
- A subscript or index contains an incorrect value.
  a. zero
  b. a negative number
  c. a number greater than the number of table-entry occurrences.
- Invalid data was read into a numeric field.
  a. blank spaces
  b. certain nonnumeric characters
- Incorrect record-descriptions and/or data-item descriptions.
  a. wrong length specifications
  b. wrong usage specifications

Overflow Exceptions (0C8 and 0CA)

This exception may occur if the result of a calculation exceeds the size of a register or the result field (and the statement does not contain an ON SIZE ERROR phrase). However, COBOL will normally not cause this interruption to be triggered with DISPLAY or COMP-3 fields. Instead, a result that is too long to be contained in the answer field will be truncated. The overflow error will not be identified (unless the ON SIZE ERROR phrase is specified).

Divide Exception (0C9 and 0CB)

According to the rules of mathematics, it is impossible to divide by zero. Thus, if a divisor field contains zero and a DIVIDE operation (without an ON SIZE ERROR phrase) is executed, a divide exception occurs. Before each DIVIDE statement, it is a good practice to validate the divisor field to ensure that it does not contain a zero. If the divisor field does contain a zero, either the DIVIDE statement should not be executed or, depending upon desired handling, the divisor should be changed to a value of 1. Such processing will eliminate divide exceptions.

Other Exceptions

When errors in subscript or index handling cause program data to overlay program instructions in storage, practically any program interruption can occur. In such cases, the type of program interruption is probably not meaningful.

COMPLETE COBOL LANGUAGE FORMATS

K

This appendix contains the composite language formats skeleton of the American National Standard COBOL. It is intended to completely display all COBOL language formats.

General Format for IDENTIFICATION DIVISION

```
IDENTIFICATION DIVISION.

PROGRAM-ID. program-name.

[AUTHOR. [comment-entry] ... ]

[INSTALLATION. [comment-entry] ... ]

[DATE-WRITTEN. [comment-entry] ... ]

[DATE-COMPILED. [comment-entry] ... ]

[SECURITY. [comment-entry] ... ]
```

General Format for ENVIRONMENT DIVISION

```
ENVIRONMENT DIVISION.

CONFIGURATION SECTION.

SOURCE-COMPUTER. ; computer-name [WITH DEBUGGING MODE] .

OBJECT-COMPUTER. computer-name

    [, MEMORY SIZE integer {WORDS / CHARACTERS / MODULES}]

    [, PROGRAM COLLATING SEQUENCE IS alphabet-name]

    [, SEGMENT-LIMIT IS segment-number] .

[SPECIAL-NAMES. [, implementor-name

    { IS mnemonic-name [, ON STATUS IS condition-name-1 [, OFF STATUS IS condition-name-2]]
      IS mnemonic-name [, OFF STATUS IS condition-name-2 [, ON STATUS IS condition-name-1]]
      ON STATUS IS condition-name-1 [, OFF STATUS IS condition-name-2]
      OFF STATUS IS condition-name-2 [, ON STATUS IS condition-name-1] } ] ...

    [, alphabet-name IS { STANDARD-1
                          NATIVE
                          implementor-name
                          literal-1 [{THROUGH / THRU} literal-2
                                     ALSO literal-3 [, ALSO literal-4]...]
                                    [literal-5 [{THROUGH / THRU} literal-6
                                                ALSO literal-7 [, ALSO literal-8]...]]... } ] ...

    [, CURRENCY SIGN IS literal-9]

    [, DECIMAL-POINT IS COMMA] .
```

```
[INPUT-OUTPUT SECTION.

 FILE-CONTROL.

    {file-control-entry} ...

[I-O-CONTROL.

   [; RERUN [ON {file-name-1          }]
                {implementor-name}

                   { {[END OF] {REEL}}                  }
      EVERY        { {         {UNIT}} OF file-name-2    }  ...
                   { integer-1 RECORDS                  }
                   { integer-2 CLOCK-UNITS              }
                   { condition-name                     }

          [RECORD   ]
   [; SAME [SORT     ] AREA FOR file-name-3 {, file-name-4} ... ] ...
          [SORT-MERGE]

   [; MULTIPLE FILE TAPE CONTAINS file-name-5 [POSITION integer-3]

         [, file-name-6 [POSITION integer-4]] ... ] ...  .]]
```

General Format for FILE-CONTROL Entry

FORMAT 1:

SELECT [OPTIONAL] file-name

   ASSIGN TO implementor-name-1 [, implementor-name-2] ...

   [; RESERVE integer-1 [AREA]]
                        [AREAS]

   [; ORGANIZATION IS SEQUENTIAL]

   [; ACCESS MODE IS SEQUENTIAL]

   [; FILE STATUS IS data-name-1] .

FORMAT 2:

SELECT file-name

   ASSIGN TO implementor-name-1 [, implementor-name-2] ...

   [; RESERVE integer-1 [AREA]]
                        [AREAS]

   ; ORGANIZATION IS RELATIVE

   [{ SEQUENTIAL [, RELATIVE KEY IS data-name-1] }]
   [; ACCESS MODE IS   {   }]
   [{ {RANDOM }   }]
   [{ {DYNAMIC} , RELATIVE KEY IS data-name-1   }]

   [; FILE STATUS IS data-name-2] .

FORMAT 3:

SELECT file-name

   ASSIGN TO implementor-name-1 [, implementor-name-2] ...

   [; RESERVE integer-1 [AREA]]
                        [AREAS]

   ; ORGANIZATION IS INDEXED

   [{ SEQUENTIAL }]
   [; ACCESS MODE IS   { RANDOM   }]
   [{ DYNAMIC   }]

```
                    ; RECORD KEY IS data-name-1

                    [; ALTERNATE RECORD KEY IS data-name-2 [WITH DUPLICATES]] ...

                    [; FILE STATUS IS data-name-3] .


          FORMAT 4:

          SELECT file-name ASSIGN TO implementor-name-1 [, implementor-name-2] ...
```

General Format for DATA DIVISION

```
          DATA DIVISION.

          [FILE SECTION.

          [FD  file-name

                    [; BLOCK CONTAINS [integer-1 TO] integer-2 {RECORDS   }]
                                                               {CHARACTERS}

                    [; RECORD CONTAINS [integer-3 TO] integer-4 CHARACTERS]

                    ; LABEL {RECORD IS  } {STANDARD}
                            {RECORDS ARE} {OMITTED }

                    [; VALUE OF implementor-name-1 IS {data-name-1}
                                                      {literal-1  }

                         [, implementor-name-2 IS {data-name-2}] ...]
                                                  {literal-2  }

                    [; DATA {RECORD IS  } data-name-3 [, data-name-4] ...]
                            {RECORDS ARE}

                    [; LINAGE IS {data-name-5} LINES [, WITH FOOTING AT {data-name-6}]
                                 {integer-5  }                          {integer-6  }

                         [, LINES AT TOP {data-name-7}] [, LINES AT BOTTOM {data-name-8}]]
                                         {integer-7  }                     {integer-8  }

                    [; CODE-SET IS alphabet-name]

                    [; {REPORT IS   } report-name-1 [, report-name-2] ... ] .
                       {REPORTS ARE }

          [record-description-entry] ... ] ...


          [SD  file-name

                    [; RECORD CONTAINS [integer-1 TO] integer-2 CHARACTERS]

                    [; DATA {RECORD IS  } data-name-1 [, data-name-2] ...] .
                            {RECORDS ARE}

          {record-description-entry} ... ] ...]


          [WORKING-STORAGE SECTION.

          [77-level-description-entry] ...]
          [record-description-entry ]


          [LINKAGE SECTION.

          [77-level-description-entry] ...]
          [record-description-entry ]


          [COMMUNICATION SECTION.

          [communication-description-entry

          [record-description-entry] ... ] ...]
```

```
[REPORT SECTION.

[RD  report-name

    [; CODE literal-1]

    [; {CONTROL IS  }  {data-name-1 [, data-name-2] ...                    }]
       {CONTROLS ARE}  {FINAL [, data-name-1 [, data-name-2] ...]}

    [; PAGE [LIMIT IS  ] integer-1 [LINE ]  [, HEADING integer-2]
            [LIMITS ARE]           [LINES]

        [, FIRST DETAIL integer-3]  [, LAST DETAIL integer-4]

        [, FOOTING integer-5 ] ] .

  {report-group-description-entry } ... ] ...]
```

General Format for Data Description Entry

FORMAT 1:

```
level-number  {data-name-1}
              {FILLER     }

    [; REDEFINES data-name-2]

    [; {PICTURE}  IS character-string]
       {PIC    }

    [; [USAGE IS]  {COMPUTATIONAL}  ]
                   {COMP         }
                   {DISPLAY      }
                   {INDEX        }

    [; [SIGN IS]  {LEADING }  [SEPARATE CHARACTER]]
                  {TRAILING}

    [; OCCURS  {integer-1 TO integer-2 TIMES DEPENDING ON data-name-3}
               {integer-2 TIMES                                      }

        [{ASCENDING }  KEY IS data-name-4  [, data-name-5] ... ] ...
         {DESCENDING}

        [INDEXED BY index-name-1  [, index-name-2] ... ]]

    [; {SYNCHRONIZED}  [LEFT ]]
       {SYNC        }   [RIGHT]

    [; {JUSTIFIED}  RIGHT]
       {JUST     }

    [; BLANK WHEN ZERO]

    [; VALUE IS literal ]  .
```

FORMAT 2:

```
66  data-name-1; RENAMES data-name-2  [{THROUGH}  data-name-3 ] .
                                       {THRU   }
```

FORMAT 3:

```
88  condition-name; {VALUE IS  }  literal-1  [{THROUGH}  literal-2 ]
                    {VALUES ARE}              {THRU   }

    [, literal-3  [{THROUGH}  literal-4 ]] ...   .
                   {THRU   }
```

General Format for Communication Description Entry

FORMAT 1:

CD cd-name;

$$
\begin{array}{l}
\text{FOR } [\text{INITIAL}] \text{ INPUT}
\end{array}
\left[
\begin{array}{l}
[\text{; SYMBOLIC } \underline{\text{QUEUE}} \text{ IS data-name-1}] \\
\quad [\text{; SYMBOLIC } \underline{\text{SUB-QUEUE-1}} \text{ IS data-name-2}] \\
\quad [\text{; SYMBOLIC } \underline{\text{SUB-QUEUE-2}} \text{ IS data-name-3}] \\
\quad [\text{; SYMBOLIC } \underline{\text{SUB-QUEUE-3}} \text{ IS data-name-4}] \\
\quad [\text{; } \underline{\text{MESSAGE}} \ \underline{\text{DATE}} \text{ IS data-name-5}] \\
\quad [\text{; } \underline{\text{MESSAGE}} \ \underline{\text{TIME}} \text{ IS data-name-6}] \\
\quad [\text{; SYMBOLIC } \underline{\text{SOURCE}} \text{ IS data-name-7}] \\
\quad [\text{; } \underline{\text{TEXT}} \ \underline{\text{LENGTH}} \text{ IS data-name-8}] \\
\quad [\text{; } \underline{\text{END}} \ \underline{\text{KEY}} \text{ IS data-name-9}] \\
\quad [\text{; } \underline{\text{STATUS}} \ \underline{\text{KEY}} \text{ IS data-name-10}] \\
\quad [\text{; } \underline{\text{MESSAGE}} \ \underline{\text{COUNT}} \text{ IS data-name-11}] \\
[\text{data-name-1, data-name-2, ..., data-name-11}]
\end{array}
\right]
$$

FORMAT 2:

CD cd-name; FOR OUTPUT

[; DESTINATION COUNT IS data-name-1]

[; TEXT LENGTH IS data-name-2]

[; STATUS KEY IS data-name-3]

[; DESTINATION TABLE OCCURS integer-2 TIMES

    [; INDEXED BY index-name-1 [, index-name-2]...]]

[; ERROR KEY IS data-name-4]

[; SYMBOLIC DESTINATION IS data-name-5] .

General Format for Report Group Description Entry

FORMAT 1:

01 [data-name-1]

$$
\left[\text{; } \underline{\text{LINE}} \text{ NUMBER IS } \left\{ \begin{array}{l} \text{integer-1 } [\text{ON } \underline{\text{NEXT}} \ \underline{\text{PAGE}}] \\ \underline{\text{PLUS}} \text{ integer-2} \end{array} \right\} \right]
$$

$$
\left[\text{; } \underline{\text{NEXT}} \ \underline{\text{GROUP}} \text{ IS } \left\{ \begin{array}{l} \text{integer-3} \\ \underline{\text{PLUS}} \text{ integer-4} \\ \underline{\text{NEXT}} \ \underline{\text{PAGE}} \end{array} \right\} \right]
$$

$$
\text{; } \underline{\text{TYPE}} \text{ IS } \left\{ \begin{array}{ll} \left\{ \begin{array}{l} \underline{\text{REPORT}} \ \underline{\text{HEADING}} \\ \underline{\text{RH}} \end{array} \right\} & \\ \left\{ \begin{array}{l} \underline{\text{PAGE}} \ \underline{\text{HEADING}} \\ \underline{\text{PH}} \end{array} \right\} & \\ \left\{ \begin{array}{l} \underline{\text{CONTROL}} \ \underline{\text{HEADING}} \\ \underline{\text{CH}} \end{array} \right\} & \left\{ \begin{array}{l} \text{data-name-2} \\ \underline{\text{FINAL}} \end{array} \right\} \\ \left\{ \begin{array}{l} \underline{\text{DETAIL}} \\ \underline{\text{DE}} \end{array} \right\} & \\ \left\{ \begin{array}{l} \underline{\text{CONTROL}} \ \underline{\text{FOOTING}} \\ \underline{\text{CF}} \end{array} \right\} & \left\{ \begin{array}{l} \text{data-name-3} \\ \underline{\text{FINAL}} \end{array} \right\} \\ \left\{ \begin{array}{l} \underline{\text{PAGE}} \ \underline{\text{FOOTING}} \\ \underline{\text{PF}} \end{array} \right\} & \\ \left\{ \begin{array}{l} \underline{\text{REPORT}} \ \underline{\text{FOOTING}} \\ \underline{\text{RF}} \end{array} \right\} & \end{array} \right\}
$$

[; [USAGE IS] DISPLAY] .

<u>FORMAT 2</u>:

level-number [data-name-1]

  [; <u>LINE</u> NUMBER IS $\left\{\begin{array}{l}\text{integer-1 }[\text{ON }\underline{\text{NEXT PAGE}}]\\ \underline{\text{PLUS}}\text{ integer-2}\end{array}\right\}$]

  [; [<u>USAGE</u> IS] <u>DISPLAY</u>] .

<u>FORMAT 3</u>:

level-number [data-name-1]

  [; <u>BLANK</u> WHEN <u>ZERO</u>]

  [; <u>GROUP</u> INDICATE]

  [; $\left\{\begin{array}{l}\underline{\text{JUSTIFIED}}\\ \underline{\text{JUST}}\end{array}\right\}$ RIGHT]

  [; <u>LINE</u> NUMBER IS $\left\{\begin{array}{l}\text{integer-1 }[\text{ON }\underline{\text{NEXT PAGE}}]\\ \underline{\text{PLUS}}\text{ integer-2}\end{array}\right\}$]

  [; <u>COLUMN</u> NUMBER IS integer-3]

  ; $\left\{\begin{array}{l}\underline{\text{PICTURE}}\\ \underline{\text{PIC}}\end{array}\right\}$ IS character-string

$\left\{\begin{array}{l}\text{; }\underline{\text{SOURCE}}\text{ IS identifier-1}\\[4pt] \text{; }\underline{\text{VALUE}}\text{ IS literal}\\[4pt] \{\text{; }\underline{\text{SUM}}\text{ identifier-2 }[,\text{ identifier-3}]\ ...\\ \quad\quad[\underline{\text{UPON}}\text{ data-name-2 }[,\text{ data-name-3}]\ ...\ ]\}\ ...\\ \quad\quad[\underline{\text{RESET}}\text{ ON }\left\{\begin{array}{l}\text{data-name-4}\\ \underline{\text{FINAL}}\end{array}\right\}]\end{array}\right\}$

  [; [<u>USAGE</u> IS] <u>DISPLAY</u>] .

General Format for PROCEDURE DIVISION

<u>FORMAT 1</u>:

<u>PROCEDURE</u> <u>DIVISION</u> [<u>USING</u> data-name-1 [, data-name-2] ...] .

[<u>DECLARATIVES</u>.

{section-name <u>SECTION</u> [segment-number] . declarative-sentence

[paragraph-name. [sentence] ...] ... } ...

<u>END</u> <u>DECLARATIVES</u>.]

{section-name <u>SECTION</u> [segment-number] .

[paragraph-name. [sentence] ...] ... } ...

<u>FORMAT 2</u>:

<u>PROCEDURE</u> <u>DIVISION</u> [<u>USING</u> data-name-1 [, data-name-2] ...] .

{paragraph-name. [sentence] ... } ...

General Format for Verbs

ACCEPT identifier [FROM mnemonic-name]

ACCEPT identifier FROM $\left\{ \begin{array}{l} \underline{DATE} \\ \underline{DAY} \\ \underline{TIME} \end{array} \right\}$

ACCEPT cd-name MESSAGE COUNT

ADD $\left\{ \begin{array}{l} \text{identifier-1} \\ \text{literal-1} \end{array} \right\}$ [, identifier-2] ... TO identifier-m [ROUNDED]

    [, identifier-n [ROUNDED]] ... [; ON SIZE ERROR imperative-statement]

ADD $\left\{ \begin{array}{l} \text{identifier-1} \\ \text{literal-1} \end{array} \right\}$, $\left\{ \begin{array}{l} \text{identifier-2} \\ \text{literal-2} \end{array} \right\}$ [, identifier-3] ...

    GIVING identifier-m [ROUNDED] [, identifier-n [ROUNDED]] ...

    [; ON SIZE ERROR imperative-statement]

ADD $\left\{ \begin{array}{l} \underline{CORRESPONDING} \\ \underline{CORR} \end{array} \right\}$ identifier-1 TO identifier-2 [ROUNDED]

    [; ON SIZE ERROR imperative-statement]

ALTER procedure-name-1 TO [PROCEED TO] procedure-name-2

    [, procedure-name-3 TO [PROCEED TO] procedure-name-4] ...

CALL $\left\{ \begin{array}{l} \text{identifier-1} \\ \text{literal-1} \end{array} \right\}$ [USING data-name-1 [, data-name-2] ...]

    [; ON OVERFLOW imperative-statement]

CANCEL $\left\{ \begin{array}{l} \text{identifier-1} \\ \text{literal-1} \end{array} \right\}$ [, identifier-2] ...

CLOSE file-name-1 $\left[\begin{array}{l} \left\{ \begin{array}{l} \underline{REEL} \\ \underline{UNIT} \end{array} \right\} \left[\begin{array}{l} \text{WITH NO REWIND} \\ \text{FOR REMOVAL} \end{array} \right] \\ \text{WITH} \left\{ \begin{array}{l} \underline{NO~REWIND} \\ \underline{LOCK} \end{array} \right\} \end{array} \right]$

$\left[, \text{file-name-2} \left[\begin{array}{l} \left\{ \begin{array}{l} \underline{REEL} \\ \underline{UNIT} \end{array} \right\} \left[\begin{array}{l} \text{WITH NO REWIND} \\ \text{FOR REMOVAL} \end{array} \right] \\ \text{WITH} \left\{ \begin{array}{l} \underline{NO~REWIND} \\ \underline{LOCK} \end{array} \right\} \end{array} \right] \right]$ ...

CLOSE file-name-1 [WITH LOCK] [, file-name-2 [WITH LOCK]] ...

COMPUTE identifier-1 [ROUNDED] [, identifier-2 [ROUNDED]] ...

    = arithmetic-expression [; ON SIZE ERROR imperative-statement]

DELETE file-name RECORD [; INVALID KEY imperative-statement]

DISABLE $\left\{ \begin{array}{l} \underline{INPUT} \text{ [TERMINAL] } \\ \underline{OUTPUT} \end{array} \right\}$ cd-name WITH KEY $\left\{ \begin{array}{l} \text{identifier-1} \\ \text{literal-1} \end{array} \right\}$

DISPLAY $\left\{ \begin{array}{l} \text{identifier-1} \\ \text{literal-1} \end{array} \right\}$ [, identifier-2] ... [UPON mnemonic-name]

DIVIDE $\left\{ \begin{array}{l} \text{identifier-1} \\ \text{literal-1} \end{array} \right\}$ INTO identifier-2 [ROUNDED]

    [, identifier-3 [ROUNDED]] ... [; ON SIZE ERROR imperative-statement]

DIVIDE $\left\{ \begin{array}{l} \text{identifier-1} \\ \text{literal-1} \end{array} \right\}$ INTO $\left\{ \begin{array}{l} \text{identifier-2} \\ \text{literal-2} \end{array} \right\}$ GIVING identifier-3 [ROUNDED]

    [, identifier-4 [ROUNDED]] ... [; ON SIZE ERROR imperative-statement]

DIVIDE $\left\{ \begin{array}{l} \text{identifier-1} \\ \text{literal-1} \end{array} \right\}$ BY $\left\{ \begin{array}{l} \text{identifier-2} \\ \text{literal-2} \end{array} \right\}$ GIVING identifier-3 [ROUNDED]

    [, identifier-4 [ROUNDED]] ... [; ON SIZE ERROR imperative-statement]

DIVIDE $\begin{Bmatrix} \text{identifier-1} \\ \text{literal-1} \end{Bmatrix}$ <u>INTO</u> $\begin{Bmatrix} \text{identifier-2} \\ \text{literal-2} \end{Bmatrix}$ <u>GIVING</u> identifier-3 [<u>ROUNDED</u>]

    REMAINDER identifier-4 [; ON <u>SIZE</u> <u>ERROR</u> imperative-statement]

DIVIDE $\begin{Bmatrix} \text{identifier-1} \\ \text{literal-1} \end{Bmatrix}$ <u>BY</u> $\begin{Bmatrix} \text{identifier-2} \\ \text{literal-2} \end{Bmatrix}$ <u>GIVING</u> identifier-3 [<u>ROUNDED</u>]

    REMAINDER identifier-4 [; ON <u>SIZE</u> <u>ERROR</u> imperative-statement]

<u>ENABLE</u> $\left\{ \begin{array}{l} \underline{\text{INPUT}} \\ \underline{\text{OUTPUT}} \end{array} \left[\underline{\text{TERMINAL}}\right] \right\}$ cd-name WITH <u>KEY</u> $\begin{Bmatrix} \text{identifier-1} \\ \text{literal-1} \end{Bmatrix}$

<u>ENTER</u> language-name [routine-name] .

<u>EXIT</u> [<u>PROGRAM</u>] .

<u>GENERATE</u> $\begin{Bmatrix} \text{data-name} \\ \text{report-name} \end{Bmatrix}$

<u>GO</u> TO [procedure-name-1]

<u>GO</u> TO procedure-name-1 [, procedure-name-2] ...   , procedure-name-n

    <u>DEPENDING</u> ON identifier

<u>IF</u> condition; $\begin{Bmatrix} \text{statement-1} \\ \underline{\text{NEXT}}\ \underline{\text{SENTENCE}} \end{Bmatrix} \begin{Bmatrix} ;\ \underline{\text{ELSE}}\ \text{statement-2} \\ ;\ \underline{\text{ELSE}}\ \underline{\text{NEXT}}\ \underline{\text{SENTENCE}} \end{Bmatrix}$

<u>INITIATE</u> report-name-1 [, report-name-2] ...

<u>INSPECT</u> identifier-1 <u>TALLYING</u>

  $\left\{, \text{identifier-2}\ \underline{\text{FOR}}\ \left\{, \begin{Bmatrix} \underline{\text{ALL}} \\ \underline{\text{LEADING}} \\ \underline{\text{CHARACTERS}} \end{Bmatrix} \begin{Bmatrix} \text{identifier-3} \\ \text{literal-1} \end{Bmatrix} \left[\begin{Bmatrix} \underline{\text{BEFORE}} \\ \underline{\text{AFTER}} \end{Bmatrix} \text{INITIAL} \begin{Bmatrix} \text{identifier-4} \\ \text{literal-2} \end{Bmatrix}\right] \right\} \cdots \right\} \cdots$

<u>INSPECT</u> identifier-1 <u>REPLACING</u>

  $\left\{ \begin{array}{l} \underline{\text{CHARACTERS}}\ \underline{\text{BY}} \begin{Bmatrix} \text{identifier-6} \\ \text{literal-4} \end{Bmatrix} \left[\begin{Bmatrix} \underline{\text{BEFORE}} \\ \underline{\text{AFTER}} \end{Bmatrix} \text{INITIAL} \begin{Bmatrix} \text{identifier-7} \\ \text{literal-5} \end{Bmatrix}\right] \\ \left\{, \begin{Bmatrix} \underline{\text{ALL}} \\ \underline{\text{LEADING}} \\ \underline{\text{FIRST}} \end{Bmatrix} \right\} \left\{, \begin{Bmatrix} \text{identifier-5} \\ \text{literal-3} \end{Bmatrix} \underline{\text{BY}} \begin{Bmatrix} \text{identifier-6} \\ \text{literal-4} \end{Bmatrix} \left[\begin{Bmatrix} \underline{\text{BEFORE}} \\ \underline{\text{AFTER}} \end{Bmatrix} \text{INITIAL} \begin{Bmatrix} \text{identifier-7} \\ \text{literal-5} \end{Bmatrix}\right] \right\} \cdots \end{array} \right\} \cdots$

<u>INSPECT</u> identifier-1 <u>TALLYING</u>

  $\left\{, \text{identifier-2}\ \underline{\text{FOR}}\ \left\{, \begin{Bmatrix} \underline{\text{ALL}} \\ \underline{\text{LEADING}} \\ \underline{\text{CHARACTERS}} \end{Bmatrix} \begin{Bmatrix} \text{identifier-3} \\ \text{literal-1} \end{Bmatrix} \left[\begin{Bmatrix} \underline{\text{BEFORE}} \\ \underline{\text{AFTER}} \end{Bmatrix} \text{INITIAL} \begin{Bmatrix} \text{identifier-4} \\ \text{literal-2} \end{Bmatrix}\right] \right\} \cdots \right\} \cdots$

  <u>REPLACING</u>

  $\left\{ \begin{array}{l} \underline{\text{CHARACTERS}}\ \underline{\text{BY}} \begin{Bmatrix} \text{identifier-6} \\ \text{literal-4} \end{Bmatrix} \left[\begin{Bmatrix} \underline{\text{BEFORE}} \\ \underline{\text{AFTER}} \end{Bmatrix} \text{INITIAL} \begin{Bmatrix} \text{identifier-7} \\ \text{literal-5} \end{Bmatrix}\right] \\ \left\{, \begin{Bmatrix} \underline{\text{ALL}} \\ \underline{\text{LEADING}} \\ \underline{\text{FIRST}} \end{Bmatrix} \right\} \left\{, \begin{Bmatrix} \text{identifier-5} \\ \text{literal-3} \end{Bmatrix} \underline{\text{BY}} \begin{Bmatrix} \text{identifier-6} \\ \text{literal-4} \end{Bmatrix} \left[\begin{Bmatrix} \underline{\text{BEFORE}} \\ \underline{\text{AFTER}} \end{Bmatrix} \text{INITIAL} \begin{Bmatrix} \text{identifier-7} \\ \text{literal-5} \end{Bmatrix}\right] \right\} \cdots \end{array} \right\} \cdots$

<u>MERGE</u> file-name-1 ON $\begin{Bmatrix} \underline{\text{ASCENDING}} \\ \underline{\text{DESCENDING}} \end{Bmatrix}$ KEY data-name-1 [, data-name-2] ...

    $\left[\text{ON} \begin{Bmatrix} \underline{\text{ASCENDING}} \\ \underline{\text{DESCENDING}} \end{Bmatrix} \text{KEY data-name-3} \left[, \text{data-name-4}\right] \cdots \right]$ ...

  [COLLATING <u>SEQUENCE</u> IS alphabet-name]

    <u>USING</u> file-name-2, file-name-3 [, file-name-4] ...

  $\left\{ \begin{array}{l} \underline{\text{OUTPUT}}\ \underline{\text{PROCEDURE}}\ \text{IS section-name-1} \left[\begin{Bmatrix} \underline{\text{THROUGH}} \\ \underline{\text{THRU}} \end{Bmatrix} \text{section-name-2}\right] \\ \underline{\text{GIVING}}\ \text{file-name-5} \end{array} \right\}$

MOVE $\left\{\begin{array}{l}\text{identifier-1}\\ \text{literal}\end{array}\right\}$ TO identifier-2 [, identifier-3] ...

MOVE $\left\{\begin{array}{l}\underline{\text{CORRESPONDING}}\\ \underline{\text{CORR}}\end{array}\right\}$ identifier-1 TO identifier-2

MULTIPLY $\left\{\begin{array}{l}\text{identifier-1}\\ \text{literal-1}\end{array}\right\}$ BY identifier-2 [ROUNDED]

   [, identifier-3 [ROUNDED]] ... [; ON SIZE ERROR imperative-statement]

MULTIPLY $\left\{\begin{array}{l}\text{identifier-1}\\ \text{literal-1}\end{array}\right\}$ BY $\left\{\begin{array}{l}\text{identifier-2}\\ \text{literal-2}\end{array}\right\}$ GIVING identifier-3 [ROUNDED]

   [, identifier-4 [ROUNDED]] ... [; ON SIZE ERROR imperative-statement]

OPEN $\left\{\begin{array}{l}\underline{\text{INPUT}}\text{ file-name-1 }\left[\begin{array}{l}\underline{\text{REVERSED}}\\ \text{WITH }\underline{\text{NO REWIND}}\end{array}\right]\left[\text{, file-name-2 }\left[\begin{array}{l}\underline{\text{REVERSED}}\\ \text{WITH }\underline{\text{NO REWIND}}\end{array}\right]\right]\ ...\\ \underline{\text{OUTPUT}}\text{ file-name-3 }[\text{WITH }\underline{\text{NO REWIND}}]\ [\text{, file-name-4 }[\text{WITH }\underline{\text{NO REWIND}}]]\ ...\\ \underline{\text{I-O}}\text{ file-name-5 }[\text{, file-name-6}]\ ...\\ \underline{\text{EXTEND}}\text{ file-name-7 }[\text{, file-name-8}]\ ...\end{array}\right\}$ ...

OPEN $\left\{\begin{array}{l}\underline{\text{INPUT}}\text{ file-name-1 }[\text{, file-name-2}]\ ...\\ \underline{\text{OUTPUT}}\text{ file-name-3 }[\text{, file-name-4}]\ ...\\ \underline{\text{I-O}}\text{ file-name-5 }[\text{, file-name-6}]\ ...\end{array}\right\}$ ...

PERFORM procedure-name-1 $\left[\left\{\begin{array}{l}\underline{\text{THROUGH}}\\ \underline{\text{THRU}}\end{array}\right\}\text{ procedure-name-2}\right]$

PERFORM procedure-name-1 $\left[\left\{\begin{array}{l}\underline{\text{THROUGH}}\\ \underline{\text{THRU}}\end{array}\right\}\text{ procedure-name-2}\right]$ $\left\{\begin{array}{l}\text{identifier-1}\\ \text{integer-1}\end{array}\right\}$ TIMES

PERFORM procedure-name-1 $\left[\left\{\begin{array}{l}\underline{\text{THROUGH}}\\ \underline{\text{THRU}}\end{array}\right\}\text{ procedure-name-2}\right]$ UNTIL condition-1

PERFORM procedure-name-1 $\left[\left\{\begin{array}{l}\underline{\text{THROUGH}}\\ \underline{\text{THRU}}\end{array}\right\}\text{ procedure-name-2}\right]$

   VARYING $\left\{\begin{array}{l}\text{identifier-2}\\ \text{index-name-1}\end{array}\right\}$ FROM $\left\{\begin{array}{l}\text{identifier-3}\\ \text{index-name-2}\\ \text{literal-1}\end{array}\right\}$

    BY $\left\{\begin{array}{l}\text{identifier-4}\\ \text{literal-3}\end{array}\right\}$ UNTIL condition-1

   $\left[\underline{\text{AFTER}}\ \left\{\begin{array}{l}\text{identifier-5}\\ \text{index-name-3}\end{array}\right\}\ \underline{\text{FROM}}\ \left\{\begin{array}{l}\text{identifier-6}\\ \text{index-name-4}\\ \text{literal-3}\end{array}\right\}\right.$

    BY $\left\{\begin{array}{l}\text{identifier-7}\\ \text{literal-4}\end{array}\right\}$ UNTIL condition-2

   $\left[\underline{\text{AFTER}}\ \left\{\begin{array}{l}\text{identifier-8}\\ \text{index-name-5}\end{array}\right\}\ \underline{\text{FROM}}\ \left\{\begin{array}{l}\text{identifier-9}\\ \text{index-name-6}\\ \text{literal-5}\end{array}\right\}\right.$

    BY $\left\{\begin{array}{l}\text{identifier-10}\\ \text{literal-6}\end{array}\right\}$ UNTIL condition-3 $\Big]\Big]$

READ file-name RECORD [INTO identifier] [; AT END imperative-statement]

READ file-name [NEXT] RECORD [INTO identifier]

  [; AT END imperative-statement]

READ file-name RECORD [INTO identifier] [; INVALID KEY imperative-statement]

READ file-name RECORD [INTO identifier]

  [; KEY IS data-name]

  [; INVALID KEY imperative-statement]

RECEIVE cd-name $\left\{\begin{array}{l}\underline{\text{MESSAGE}}\\ \underline{\text{SEGMENT}}\end{array}\right\}$ INTO identifier-1 [; NO DATA imperative-statement]

RELEASE record-name [FROM identifier]

RETURN file-name RECORD [INTO identifier] ; AT END imperative-statement

REWRITE record-name [FROM identifier]

REWRITE record-name [FROM identifier] [; INVALID KEY imperative-statement]

SEARCH identifier-1 [VARYING {identifier-2 / index-name-1}] [; AT END imperative-statement-1]

  ; WHEN condition-1 {imperative-statement-2 / NEXT SENTENCE}

  [; WHEN condition-2 {imperative-statement-3 / NEXT SENTENCE}] ...

SEARCH ALL identifier-1 [; AT END imperative-statement-1]

  ; WHEN { data-name-1 {IS EQUAL TO / IS =} {identifier-3 / literal-1 / arithmetic-expression-1} / condition-name-1 }

    [AND { data-name-2 {IS EQUAL TO / IS =} {identifier-4 / literal-2 / arithmetic-expression-2} / condition-name-2 }] ...

    {imperative-statement-2 / NEXT SENTENCE}

SEND cd-name FROM identifier-1

SEND cd-name [FROM identifier-1] {WITH identifier-2 / WITH ESI / WITH EMI / WITH EGI}

  [{BEFORE / AFTER} ADVANCING { {identifier-3 / integer} [LINE / LINES] / mnemonic-name / PAGE }]

SET {identifier-1 [, identifier-2] ... / index-name-1 [, index-name-2] ...} TO {identifier-3 / index-name-3 / integer-1}

SET index-name-4 [, index-name-5] ... {UP BY / DOWN BY} {identifier-4 / integer-2}

SORT file-name-1 ON {ASCENDING / DESCENDING} KEY data-name-1 [, data-name-2] ...

  [ON {ASCENDING / DESCENDING} KEY data-name-3 [, data-name-4] ...] ...

  [COLLATING SEQUENCE IS alphabet-name]

  { INPUT PROCEDURE IS section-name-1 [{THROUGH / THRU} section-name-2] / USING file-name-2 [, file-name-3] ... }

  { OUTPUT PROCEDURE IS section-name-3 [{THROUGH / THRU} section-name-4] / GIVING file-name-4 }

START file-name [KEY {IS EQUAL TO / IS = / IS GREATER THAN / IS > / IS NOT LESS THAN / IS NOT <} data-name]

  [; INVALID KEY imperative-statement]

STOP $\left\{ \begin{array}{l} \underline{RUN} \\ literal \end{array} \right\}$

STRING $\left\{ \begin{array}{l} identifier-1 \\ literal-1 \end{array} \right\}$ $\left[\begin{array}{l} , identifier-2 \\ , literal-2 \end{array} \right]$ ... DELIMITED BY $\left\{ \begin{array}{l} identifier-3 \\ literal-3 \\ \underline{SIZE} \end{array} \right\}$

   $\left[, \left\{ \begin{array}{l} identifier-4 \\ literal-4 \end{array} \right\} \left[\begin{array}{l} , identifier-5 \\ , literal-5 \end{array} \right] ... \underline{DELIMITED} \text{ BY } \left\{ \begin{array}{l} identifier-6 \\ literal-6 \\ \underline{SIZE} \end{array} \right\} \right]$ ...

   INTO identifier-7 [WITH POINTER identifier-8]

   [; ON OVERFLOW imperative-statement]

SUBTRACT $\left\{ \begin{array}{l} identifier-1 \\ literal-1 \end{array} \right\}$ $\left[\begin{array}{l} , identifier-2 \\ , literal-2 \end{array} \right]$ ... FROM identifier-m [ROUNDED]

   [, identifier-n [ROUNDED]] ... [; ON SIZE ERROR imperative-statement]

SUBTRACT $\left\{ \begin{array}{l} identifier-1 \\ literal-1 \end{array} \right\}$ $\left[\begin{array}{l} , identifier-2 \\ , literal-2 \end{array} \right]$ ... FROM $\left\{ \begin{array}{l} identifier-m \\ literal-m \end{array} \right\}$

   GIVING identifier-n [ROUNDED] [, identifier-o [ROUNDED]] ...

   [; ON SIZE ERROR imperative-statement]

SUBTRACT $\left\{ \begin{array}{l} \underline{CORRESPONDING} \\ \underline{CORR} \end{array} \right\}$ identifier-1 FROM identifier-2 [ROUNDED]

   [; ON SIZE ERROR imperative-statement]

SUPPRESS PRINTING

TERMINATE report-name-1 [, report-name-2] ...

UNSTRING identifier-1

   $\left[\underline{DELIMITED} \text{ BY } [\underline{ALL}] \left\{ \begin{array}{l} identifier-2 \\ literal-1 \end{array} \right\} \left[, \underline{OR} \text{ } [\underline{ALL}] \left\{ \begin{array}{l} identifier-3 \\ literal-2 \end{array} \right\} \right] ... \right]$

   INTO identifier-4 [, DELIMITER IN identifier-5] [, COUNT IN identifier-6]

      [, identifier-7 [, DELIMITER IN identifier-8] [, COUNT IN identifier-9]] ...

   [WITH POINTER identifier-10] [TALLYING IN identifier-11]

   [; ON OVERFLOW imperative-statement]

USE AFTER STANDARD $\left\{ \begin{array}{l} \underline{EXCEPTION} \\ \underline{ERROR} \end{array} \right\}$ PROCEDURE ON $\left\{ \begin{array}{l} file-name-1 \text{ } [, file-name-2] ... \\ \underline{INPUT} \\ \underline{OUTPUT} \\ \underline{I-O} \\ \underline{EXTEND} \end{array} \right\}$.

USE AFTER STANDARD $\left\{ \begin{array}{l} \underline{EXCEPTION} \\ \underline{ERROR} \end{array} \right\}$ PROCEDURE ON $\left\{ \begin{array}{l} file-name-1 \text{ } [, file-name-2] ... \\ \underline{INPUT} \\ \underline{OUTPUT} \\ \underline{I-O} \end{array} \right\}$.

USE BEFORE REPORTING identifier.

USE FOR DEBUGGING ON $\left\{ \begin{array}{l} cd-name-1 \\ [\underline{ALL} \text{ REFERENCES OF}] \text{ identifier-1} \\ file-name-1 \\ procedure-name-1 \\ \underline{ALL} \text{ } \underline{PROCEDURES} \end{array} \right\}$

   $\left[, \begin{array}{l} cd-name-2 \\ [\underline{ALL} \text{ REFERENCES OF}] \text{ identifier-2} \\ file-name-2 \\ procedure-name-2 \\ \underline{ALL} \text{ } \underline{PROCEDURES} \end{array} \right]$ ... .

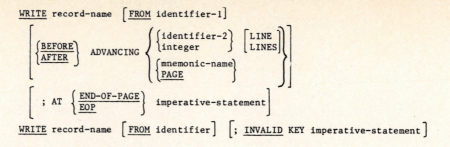

```
WRITE record-name [FROM identifier-1]

[ {BEFORE}  ADVANCING  { {identifier-2}  [LINE ] } ]
[ {AFTER }             { {integer    }   [LINES] } ]
[                      {                         } ]
[                      { {mnemonic-name}         } ]
[                      { PAGE          }          ]

[ ; AT {END-OF-PAGE}  imperative-statement ]
[      {EOP        }                       ]

WRITE record-name [FROM identifier]  [; INVALID KEY imperative-statement]
```

General Format for Conditions

RELATION CONDITION:

```
{identifier-1            }  { IS [NOT] GREATER THAN }  {identifier-2            }
{literal-1               }  { IS [NOT] LESS THAN    }  {literal-2               }
{arithmetic-expression-1 }  { IS [NOT] EQUAL TO     }  {arithmetic-expression-2 }
{index-name-1            }  { IS [NOT] >            }  {index-name-2            }
                            { IS [NOT] <            }
                            { IS [NOT] =            }
```

CLASS CONDITION:

```
identifier IS [NOT] {NUMERIC   }
                    {ALPHABETIC}
```

SIGN CONDITION:

```
                            {POSITIVE}
arithmetic-expression is [NOT] {NEGATIVE}
                            {ZERO    }
```

CONDITION-NAME CONDITION:

condition-name

SWITCH-STATUS CONDITION:

condition-name

NEGATED SIMPLE CONDITION:

NOT simple-condition

COMBINED CONDITION:

```
condition { {AND}  condition } ...
          { {OR }            }
```

ABBREVIATED COMBINED RELATION CONDITION:

```
relation-condition { {AND} [NOT] [relational-operator] object } ...
                   { {OR }                                    }
```

Miscellaneous Formats

QUALIFICATION:

```
{data-name-1    } [ {OF}  data-name-2 ] ...
{condition-name } [ {IN}              ]

paragraph-name  [ {OF}  section-name ]
                [ {IN}               ]

text-name  [ {OF}  library-name ]
           [ {IN}               ]
```

SUBSCRIPTING:

$$\left\{\begin{matrix} \text{data-name} \\ \text{condition-name} \end{matrix}\right\} \text{(subscript-1 [, subscript-2 [, subscript-3]])}$$

INDEXING:

$$\left\{\begin{matrix} \text{data-name} \\ \text{condition-name} \end{matrix}\right\} \quad \left(\begin{Bmatrix} \text{index-name-1} \; [\{\pm\} \; \text{literal-2}] \\ \text{literal-1} \end{Bmatrix}\right.$$

$$\left[, \begin{Bmatrix} \text{index-name-2} \; [\{\pm\} \; \text{literal-4}] \\ \text{literal-3} \end{Bmatrix} \left[, \begin{Bmatrix} \text{index-name-3} \; [\{\pm\} \; \text{literal-6}] \\ \text{literal-5} \end{Bmatrix} \right] \right] \right) ,$$

IDENTIFIER: FORMAT 1

$$\text{data-name-1} \quad \left[\begin{Bmatrix} \underline{OF} \\ \underline{IN} \end{Bmatrix} \text{data-name-2} \right] \dots \left[\text{(subscript-1 [, subscript-2} \right.$$

$$\left. \text{[, subscript-3]])} \right]$$

IDENTIFIER: FORMAT 2

$$\text{data-name-1} \quad \left[\begin{Bmatrix} \underline{OF} \\ \underline{IN} \end{Bmatrix} \text{data-name-2} \right] \dots \left(\begin{Bmatrix} \text{index-name-1} \; [\{\pm\} \; \text{literal-2}] \\ \text{literal-1} \end{Bmatrix}\right.$$

$$\left[, \begin{Bmatrix} \text{index-name-2} \; [\{\pm\} \; \text{literal-4}] \\ \text{literal-3} \end{Bmatrix} \left[, \begin{Bmatrix} \text{index-name-3} \; [\{\pm\} \; \text{literal-6}] \\ \text{literal-5} \end{Bmatrix} \right] \right] \right)$$

General Format for COPY Statement

$$\underline{COPY} \text{ text-name} \left[\begin{Bmatrix} \underline{OF} \\ \underline{IN} \end{Bmatrix} \text{library-name} \right]$$

$$\left[\underline{REPLACING} \left\{ , \begin{Bmatrix} \text{==pseudo-text-1==} \\ \text{identifier-1} \\ \text{literal-1} \\ \text{word-1} \end{Bmatrix} \underline{BY} \begin{Bmatrix} \text{==pseudo-text-2==} \\ \text{identifier-2} \\ \text{literal-2} \\ \text{word-2} \end{Bmatrix} \right\} \dots \right]$$

FILE-STATUS CHART

This appendix presents a chart of the possible file-status code settings that can occur, depending upon the file organization, input-output operation, access mode, and how the file was opened.

Input-output operation	Access mode	SEQUENTIAL				INDEXED			RELATIVE		
		File opened INPUT	File opened I-O	File opened OUTPUT	File opened EXTEND	File opened INPUT	File opened I-O	File opened OUTPUT	File opened INPUT	File opened I-O	File opened OUTPUT
READ	SEQUENTIAL	10–End of file	10–End of file			10–End of file	10–End of file		10–End of file	10–End of file	
	RANDOM or DYNAMIC					23–Key not found 10–End of file	23–Key not found 10–End of file		23–Relative key not found 10–End of file	23–Relative key not found 10–End of file	
WRITE	SEQUENTIAL		34–Boundary violation	34–Boundary violation	34–Boundary violation		22–Duplicate prime key or duplicate alternate key (without duplicates) 24–Boundary violation *02–Duplicate alternate key (with duplicates)	21–Sequence error (prime key not greater than last record written) 22–Duplicate prime key or duplicate alternate key (without duplicates) 24–Boundary violation *02–Duplicate alternate key (with duplicates)		24–Boundary violation	24–Boundary violation
	RANDOM or DYNAMIC						22–Duplicate prime key or duplicate alternate key (without duplicates) 24–Boundary violation *02–Duplicate alternate key (with duplicates)	22–Duplicate prime key or duplicate alternate key (without duplicates) 24–Boundary violation *02–Duplicate alternate key (with duplicates)		22–Duplicate relative key 24–Boundary violation	22–Duplicate relative key 24–Boundary violation

File organization

File-Status Chart (columns: Sequential organization, Indexed organization, Relative organization)

Operation	Access Mode	Sequential	Indexed	Relative
REWRITE	SEQUENTIAL	21-Sequence error (key not equal to last record read)	21-Sequence error (prime key not equal to last record read) / 22-Duplicate alternate key (without duplicates) / *02-Duplicate alternate key (with duplicates)	21-Sequence error relative key not equal to last record read)
REWRITE	RANDOM or DYNAMIC		23-Record key not found / 22-Duplicate alternate key (without duplicates) / *02-Duplicate alternate key (with duplicates)	23-Relative key not found
DELETE	SEQUENTIAL		21-Sequence error (prime key not equal to last record read)	21-Sequence error (key not equal to last record read)
DELETE	RANDOM or DYNAMIC		23-Record key not found	23-Relative key not found
START	SEQUENTIAL		23-Key not found	23-Relative key not found
START	RANDOM			23-Relative key not found
START	DYNAMIC		23-Key not found	23-Relative key not found
OPEN	SEQUENTIAL			
OPEN	RANDOM or DYNAMIC			
CLOSE	SEQUENTIAL			
CLOSE	RANDOM or DYNAMIC			

Legend:

Shaded-area intersection = Invalid ACCESS MODE/ORGANIZATION method/OPEN mode combination.

*Not an error condition.

Note: In addition to the file status codes shown, the following additional codes could occur as a result of any input-output operation:

00—Successful completion

30—Permanent I-O data error

INDEX

Data Manipulation Language, 545
Data module, 32
Data presentation, 522, 528–529
Data redundancy, 537–538
Data representation conversion, 416–417
Data-structure models, 541–542
Data transfer time, 37
Data Universal Numbering System, 389
Data validation
  checklist, 610
  dates, 375–377
  embedded blank check, 392, 393
  numeric amounts, 391–392
  on-line processing, 530, 531
  self-checking numbers, 383–389
  Social Security numbers, 389–390
  telephone numbers, 390
  time, 381, 382–383
  ZIP Codes, 390–391
Date check, 611
DATE-COMPILED paragraph, 552
Date conversion, 377–378
Date-last-activity field
  change transaction aspects, 83
  master file maintenance, 71–73
  sequential master-file maintenance, 98
Date period-ending indication, 356–360
Date-span computation, 378
Date validation, 375–377
DATE-WRITTEN paragraph, 552
Dates
  Gregorian, 374
  Julian, 375
  Julianized, 374
Day-of-the-week computation, 378–380
Daylight saving time, 380
DBMS, *See* Data-base management
  system
DBTG, 539
DBTLG, 540
DC monitor, 515–518
DDL, 545
DDLC, 540
Deadlock, 533
Deadly embrace, 533
Dedicated operator, 522
Delete-flag field
  master file maintenance, 73
  master record deletion, 188–191
  nonmodification aspect, 83
DELETE statement
  ALTERNATE KEY processing, 271
  indexed file processing, 163, 178
  relative file processing, 213, 221
Delete transaction
  correspondence checking, 86, 99
  interfile errors, 77
  record design, 74
Deleted-record indication
  indexed file, 188–191
  relative file, 206–211
DELIMITED BY phrase
  STRING statement, 464, 465
  UNSTRING statement, 468, 469, 470,
    471, 472

DELIMITER IN option of the UNSTRING
  statement, 469, 470, 472
Density
  cartridge tape, 46
  reel-to-reel tape, 42
DEPENDING ON option of the OCCURS
  clause, 432–443, 448
DESCENDING KEY clause
  MERGE statement, 605
  OCCURS clause, 589–590
  SORT statement, 603–604
Detached keyboard, 504
Detail line, 309
Detail list, 309–315
  example, 310
  program prototype, 311–312
  structure chart, 311
Detail list with end-of-report totals,
  323–326
  coding prototype, 325
  example, 324
Dialogue, 521–524
Digit extraction randomizing algorithm,
  58
Digit transformation randomizing algorithm, 58
Dijkstra, Edgar W., 3, 4
Direct-access storage device, 28–40
  access arm, 34–35
  access mechanism, 34–35
  cylinder concept, 34–35
  data module, 32
  data transfer time, 37
  disk cartridge, 32
  disk pack, 28–32
  diskette, 32–33
  fixed block architecture, 33
  fixed disk, 32
  fixed-head disk, 35
  fixed-sealed disk, 32
  file labels, 37–38
  labels, 37–38
  Phoenix disk cartridge, 32
  read/write heads, 34–35
  record access, 36–37
  record blocking, 38
  recording formats 33–35
  rotational delay, 37
  sector, 36
  timing, 36
  tracks, 33–34
  volume, 37–38
  volume table of contents, 38
  Winchester, 32, 39
Direct file organization, 52–59
Directly addressed file, 53–54
Directory of a PDS, 61, 63
Disk capacity tables, 612–617
Disk cartridge, 32
Disk drive. *See* Direct-access storage
  device
Disk labels, 37–38
Disk pack, 28–32
Diskette, 32
DISPLAY statement, 581

DISPLAY usage, 559–560
Divide exception, 628
DIVIDE statement, 565–566
DL/1, 539
DML, 545
Do-while structure, 4
Domain, 542
Double-add-double check digit, 386
Drum printer, 282–283, 284
Dual intensity VDT feature, 508
Dumb terminal, 504
Dun & Bradstreet, Inc., 389
DUNS, 389
DYNAMIC access, 62–63, 263–265
Dynamic CALL, 493–495
Dynamic subprogram linkage, 492,
  493–495
Dynamic table building, 406, 407

EBCDIC, 42, 416–417, 620, 624
Editing PICTURE clause, 561
Editing routine logic
  excess blank-space elimination,
    395–397
  justification, 392–393
  trailing zero suppression, 397, 398
Electrostatic printer, 284–285, 286–287,
  289
Embedded blank check, 392, 393, 611
Embedded key field, 206
Embedded link DBMS access, 543
Embedded pointer DBMS access, 543
End-of-report totals, 323–326
End-of-tape marker, 43
Entry-sequenced file, 51
ENVIRONMENT DIVISION
  indexed file maintenance, 162, 166
  relative file maintenance, 212–216
  sequential file maintenance, 111, 112
  syntax, 553–554
Ergonomics, 504
Error list. *See* Audit/error list; Update/
  error list
Error messages, 77–78
Error record handling, 79–80, 98
EXAMINE statement, 456, 520, 577
Exception list, 315–318
  example, 310
  program prototype, 316–317
  structure chart, 316
Excess blank-space elimination, 395–397
Exchange sort, 406–410
Exclusive lock, 533
Exit-GO TO module, 9
EXIT PROGRAM statement, 489, 490, 491
EXIT statement, 9, 585
Expiration date, 91
Extended Binary Coded Decimal Inter-
  change Code. *See* EBCDIC
External coupling, 22–23
External decimal representation, 560
External sorts, 411–413

FD entry
  level indicator, 550

COBOL reserved words

These words have preassigned meanings in COBOL and must not be used as user-defined words

---

ACCEPT	DATA	HEADING	OBJECT-COMPUTER	SAME	VALUE
ACCESS	DATE	HIGH-VALUE	OCCURS	SD	VALUES
ADD	DATE-COMPILED	HIGH-VALUES	OF	SEARCH	VARYING
ADVANCING	DATE-WRITTEN		OFF	SECTION	
AFTER	DAY	I-O	OMITTED	SECURITY	WHEN
ALL	DE	I-O-CONTROL	ON	SEGMENT	WITH
ALPHABETIC	DEBUG-CONTENTS	IDENTIFICATION	OPEN	SEGMENT-LIMIT	WORDS
ALSO	DEBUG-ITEM	IF	OPTIONAL	SELECT	WORKING-STORAGE
ALTER	DEBUG-LINE	IN	OR	SEND	WRITE
ALTERNATE	DEBUG-NAME	INDEX	ORGANIZATION	SENTENCE	
AND	DEBUG-SUB-1	INDEXED	OUTPUT	SEPARATE	ZERO
ARE	DEBUG-SUB-2	INDICATE	OVERFLOW	SEQUENCE	ZEROES
AREA	DEBUG-SUB-3	INITIAL		SEQUENTIAL	ZEROS
AREAS	DEBUGGING	INITIATE	PAGE	SET	
ASCENDING	DECIMAL-POINT	INPUT	PAGE-COUNTER	SIGN	+
ASSIGN	DECLARATIVES	INPUT-OUTPUT	PERFORM	SIZE	−
AT	DELETE	INSPECT	PF	SORT	.
AUTHOR	DELIMITED	INSTALLATION	PH	SORT-MERGE	/
	DELIMITER	INTO	PIC	SOURCE	..
BEFORE	DEPENDING	INVALID	PICTURE	SOURCE-COMPUTER	
BLANK	DESCENDING	IS	PLUS	SPACE	>
BLOCK	DESTINATION		POINTER	SPACES	<
BOTTOM	DETAIL	JUST	POSITION	SPECIAL-NAMES	=
BY	DISABLE	JUSTIFIED	POSITIVE	STANDARD	
	DISPLAY		PRINTING	STANDARD-1	
CALL	DIVIDE	KEY	PROCEDURE	START	
CANCEL	DIVISION		PROCEDURES	STATUS	
CD	DOWN	LABEL	PROCEED	STOP	
CF	DUPLICATES	LAST	PROGRAM	STRING	
CH	DYNAMIC	LEADING	PROGRAM-ID	SUB-QUEUE-1	
CHARACTER		LEFT		SUB-QUEUE-2	
CHARACTERS	EGI	LENGTH	QUEUE	SUB-QUEUE-3	
CLOCK-UNITS	ELSE	LESS	QUOTE	SUBTRACT	
CLOSE	EMI	LIMIT	QUOTES	SUM	
COBOL	ENABLE	LIMITS		SUPPRESS	
CODE	END	LINAGE	RANDOM	SYMBOLIC	
CODE-SET	END-OF-PAGE	LINAGE-COUNTER	RD	SYNC	
COLLATING	ENTER	LINE	READ	SYNCHRONIZED	
COLUMN	ENVIRONMENT	LINE-COUNTER	RECEIVE		
COMMA	EOP	LINES	RECORD	TABLE	
COMMUNICATION	EQUAL	LINKAGE	RECORDS	TALLYING	
COMP	ERROR	LOCK	REDEFINES	TAPE	
COMPUTATIONAL	ESI	LOW-VALUE	REEL	TERMINAL	
COMPUTE	EVERY	LOW-VALUES	REFERENCES	TERMINATE	
CONFIGURATION	EXCEPTION		RELATIVE	TEXT	
CONTAINS	EXIT	MEMORY	RELEASE	THAN	
CONTROL	EXTEND	MERGE	REMAINDER	THROUGH	
CONTROLS		MESSAGE	REMOVAL	THRU	
COPY	FD	MODE	RENAMES	TIME	
CORR	FILE	MODULES	REPLACING	TIMES	
CORRESPONDING	FILE-CONTROL	MOVE	REPORT	TO	
COUNT	FILLER	MULTIPLE	REPORTING	TOP	
CURRENCY	FINAL	MULTIPLY	REPORTS	TRAILING	
	FIRST		RERUN	TYPE	
	FOOTING	NATIVE	RESERVE		
	FOR	NEGATIVE	RESET	UNIT	
	FROM	NEXT	RETURN	UNSTRING	
		NO	REVERSED	UNTIL	
	GENERATE	NOT	REWIND	UP	
	GIVING	NUMBER	REWRITE	UPON	
	GO	NUMERIC	RF	USAGE	
	GREATER		RH	USE	
	GROUP		RIGHT	USING	
			ROUNDED		
			RUN		

CASPIAN SEA

Bosporus

CRIMEA

BLACK SEA

Tomis

Odessus

Bosporus

Byzantium/
Constantinople

ASIA

Pergamum

Smyrna

Ephesus

Aphrodisias

Halicarnassus

RHODES

TA

Gortyn

Hierapytna

MARE

Amastris

BITHYNIA

Nicomedia

GALATIA

Ancyra

CILICIA

Tarsus

CYPRUS

Paphos

Trapezus

PONTUS

Amaseia

CAPPADOCIA

Caesarea
(Mazaca)

Edessa

Antioch

Qal'at Sim'an

SYRIA

Raphaneae

Berytus

Sidon

Tyre

Caesarea

Jerusalem

Bethlehem

Gaza

Canopus

Alexandria

Nile

AEGYPTUS

Dendera

Coptos

THEBAIS

ARMENIA

Tigris

MESOPOTAMIA

Carrhae

OSROENE

Euphrates

Emesa

Palmyra

Damascus

Bostra

Qumran

Madaba

Dead
Sea

Petra

SINAI

RED SEA

P A R T H I A

Naqsh-I Rustam

Persepolis

Ctesiphon

Seleucia

PERSIAN
GULF

ARABIA

AXUM

F   G   H   J

Ancient World Mapping Center 2011